BLACK PANTHER

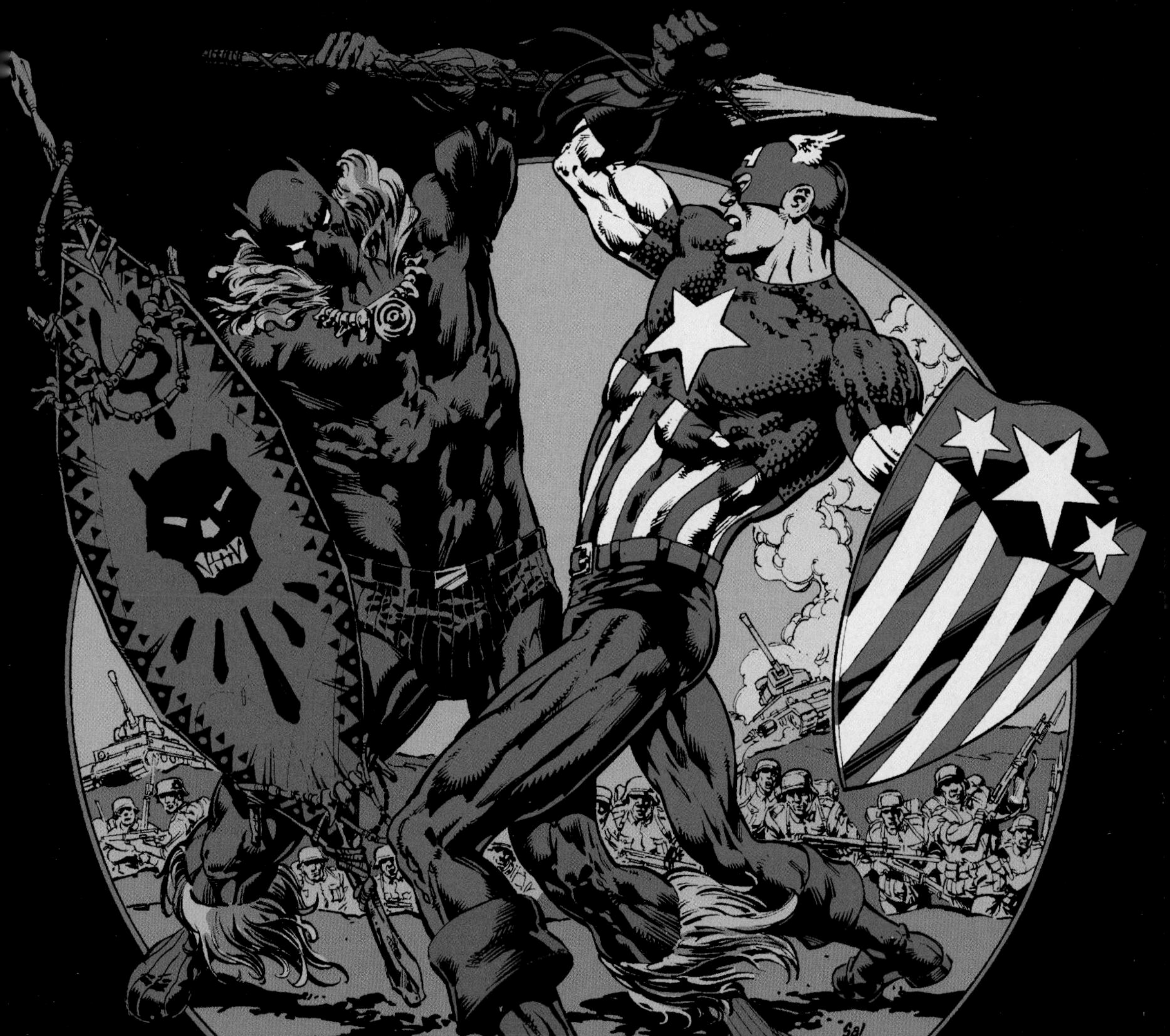
Sal Velluto MM

WRITER **CHRISTOPHER PRIEST**

PENCILERS **KYLE HOTZ, SAL VELLUTO, JIM CALAFIORE, MARK BRIGHT & NORM BREYFOGLE** WITH **TOMM COKER**

INKERS **ERIC POWELL, BOB ALMOND, JON HOLDREDGE, WALDEN WONG, NORM BREYFOGLE & LIVESAY** WITH **JIMMY PALMIOTTI, MARK McKENNA & WARREN MARTINECK**

COLORISTS **STEVE OLIFF, SHANNON BLANCHARD & VLM**

LETTERERS **CHRIS ELIOPOULOS** AND **SHARPEFONT & PAUL TUTRONE**

ASSISTANT EDITORS **FRANK DUNKERLEY, MIKE RAICHT & MARC SUMERAK**

EDITORS **TOM BREVOORT & MIKE MARTS**

BLACK PANTHER CREATED BY STAN LEE & JACK KIRBY

FRONT COVER ARTISTS: **SAL VELLUTO, BOB ALMOND & TOM CHU**
BACK COVER ARTISTS: **SAL VELLUTO, BOB ALMOND & TOM SMITH**

COLLECTION EDITOR **MARK D. BEAZLEY**
ASSISTANT EDITOR **CAITLIN O'CONNELL** ASSOCIATE MANAGING EDITOR **KATERI WOODY**
ASSOCIATE MANAGER, DIGITAL ASSETS **JOE HOCHSTEIN**
SENIOR EDITOR, SPECIAL PROJECTS **JENNIFER GRÜNWALD**
VP PRODUCTION & SPECIAL PROJECTS **JEFF YOUNGQUIST**
RESEARCH & LAYOUT **JEPH YORK** PRODUCTION **RYAN DEVALL** BOOK DESIGNER **JAY BOWEN**
SVP PRINT, SALES & MARKETING **DAVID GABRIEL**

EDITOR IN CHIEF **C.B. CEBULSKI** CHIEF CREATIVE OFFICER **JOE QUESADA**
PRESIDENT **DAN BUCKLEY** EXECUTIVE PRODUCER **ALAN FINE**

SPECIAL THANKS TO BOB ALMOND

BLACK PANTHER BY CHRISTOPHER PRIEST: THE COMPLETE COLLECTION VOL. 2. Contains material originally published in magazine form as BLACK PANTHER #18-35 and DEADPOOL #44. Second printing 20
ISBN 978-0-7851-9811-6. Published by MARVEL WORLDWIDE, INC., a subsidiary of MARVEL ENTERTAINMENT, LLC. OFFICE OF PUBLICATION: 135 West 50th Street, New York, NY 10020. Copyright © 2015 MAR
No similarity between any of the names, characters, persons, and/or institutions in this magazine with those of any living or dead person or institution is intended, and any such similarity which may exist is pu
coincidental. **Printed in the U.S.A.** DAN BUCKLEY, President, Marvel Entertainment; JOHN NEE, Publisher; JOE QUESADA, Chief Creative Officer; TOM BREVOORT, SVP of Publishing; DAVID BOGART, SVP of Busin
Affairs & Operations, Publishing & Partnership; DAVID GABRIEL, SVP of Sales & Marketing, Publishing; JEFF YOUNGQUIST, VP of Production & Special Projects; DAN CARR, Executive Director of Publishing Technolc
ALEX MORALES, Director of Publishing Operations; SUSAN CRESPI, Production Manager; STAN LEE, Chairman Emeritus. For information regarding advertising in Marvel Comics or on Marvel.com, please contact
DeBellis, Custom Solutions & Integrated Advertising Manager, at vdebellis@marvel.com. For Marvel subscription inquiries, please call 888-511-5480. **Manufactured between 3/21/2018 and 4/10/2018 by I
COMMUNICATIONS INC., KENDALLVILLE, IN, USA.**

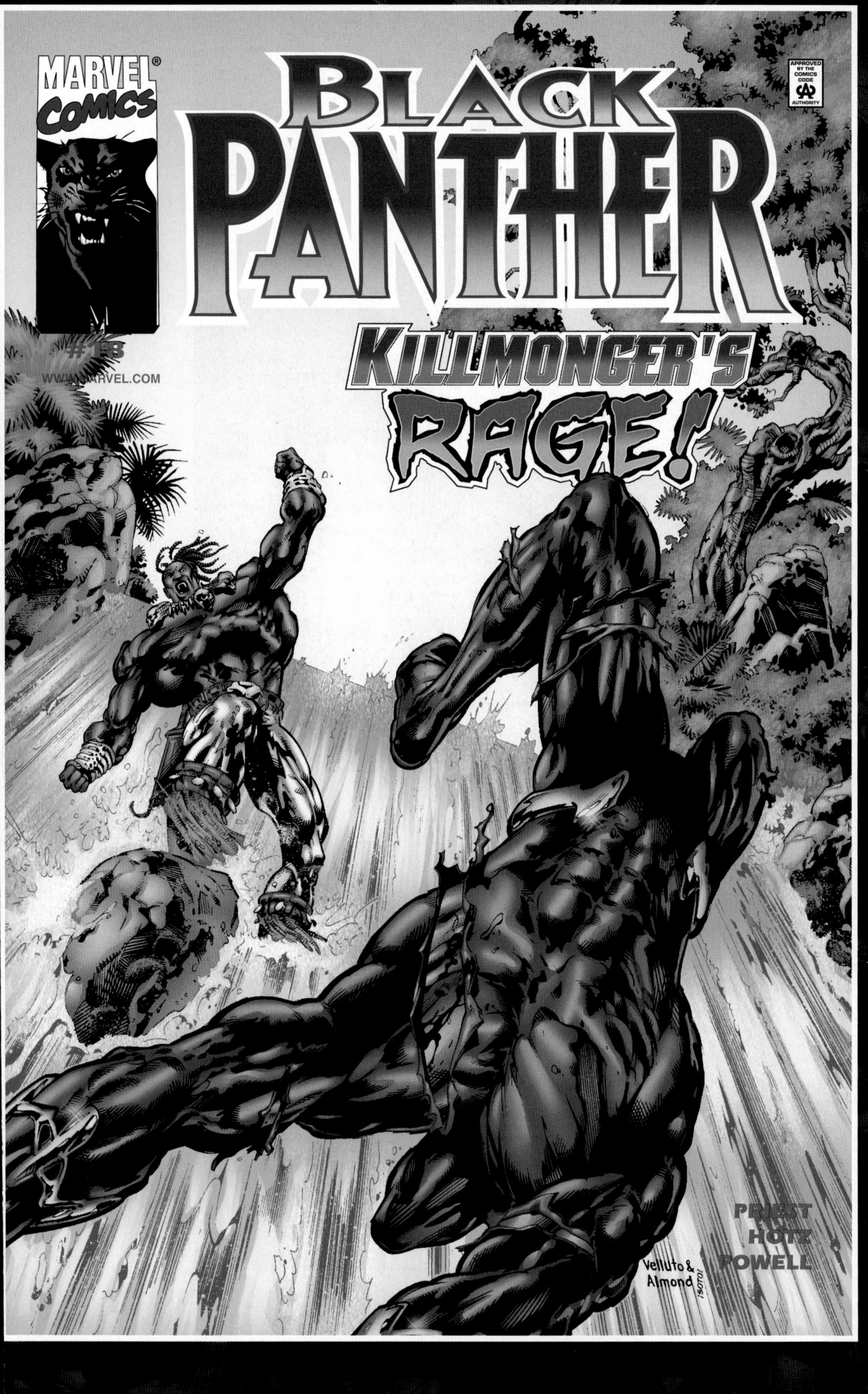

MARVEL COMICS
BLACK PANTHER
#18
WWW.MARVEL.COM
APPROVED BY THE COMICS CODE AUTHORITY
KILLMONGER'S RAGE!
PRIEST
HOTZ
POWELL
Velluto & Almond
SOTO

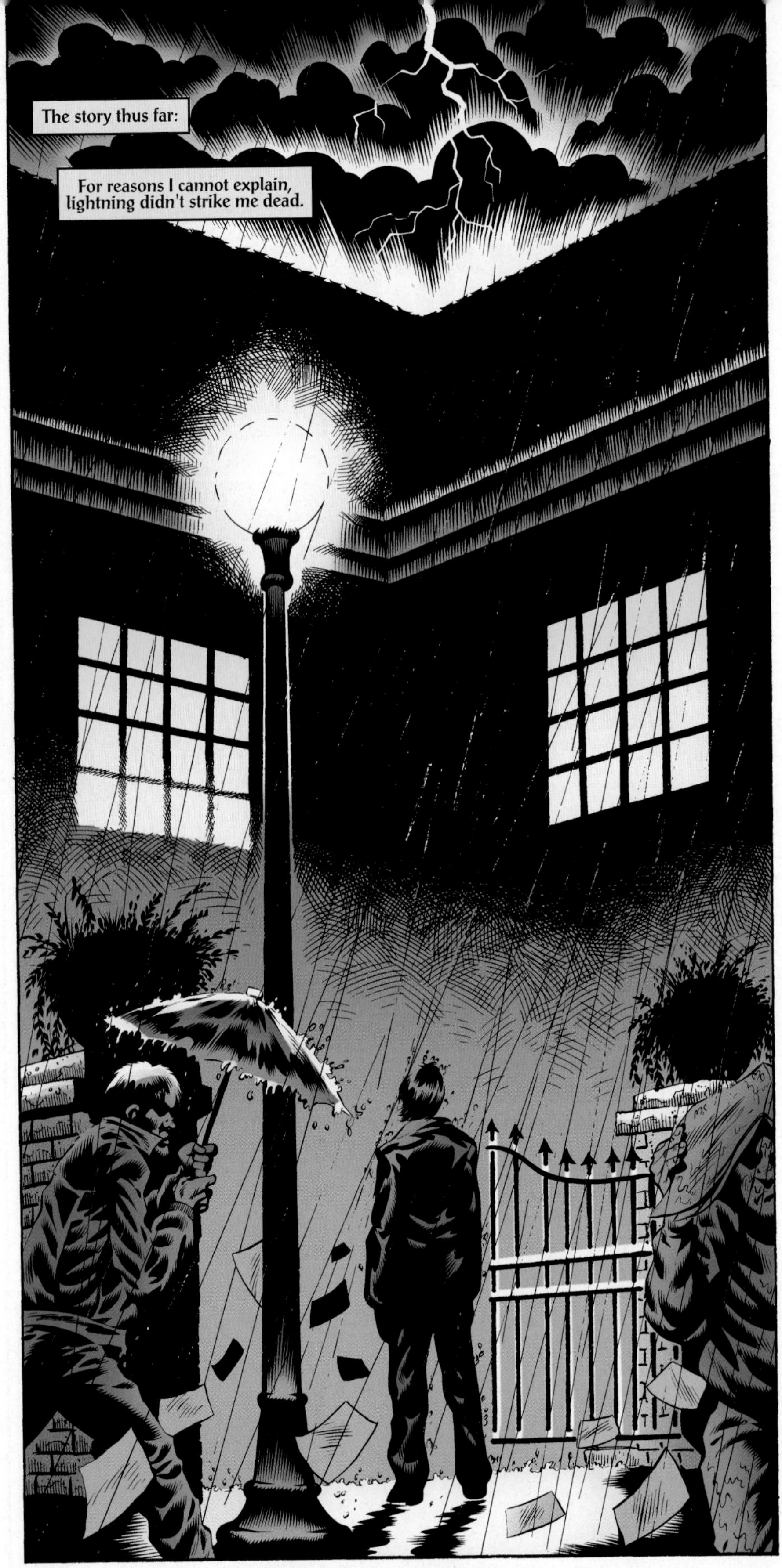
The story thus far:
For reasons I cannot explain, lightning didn't strike me dead.

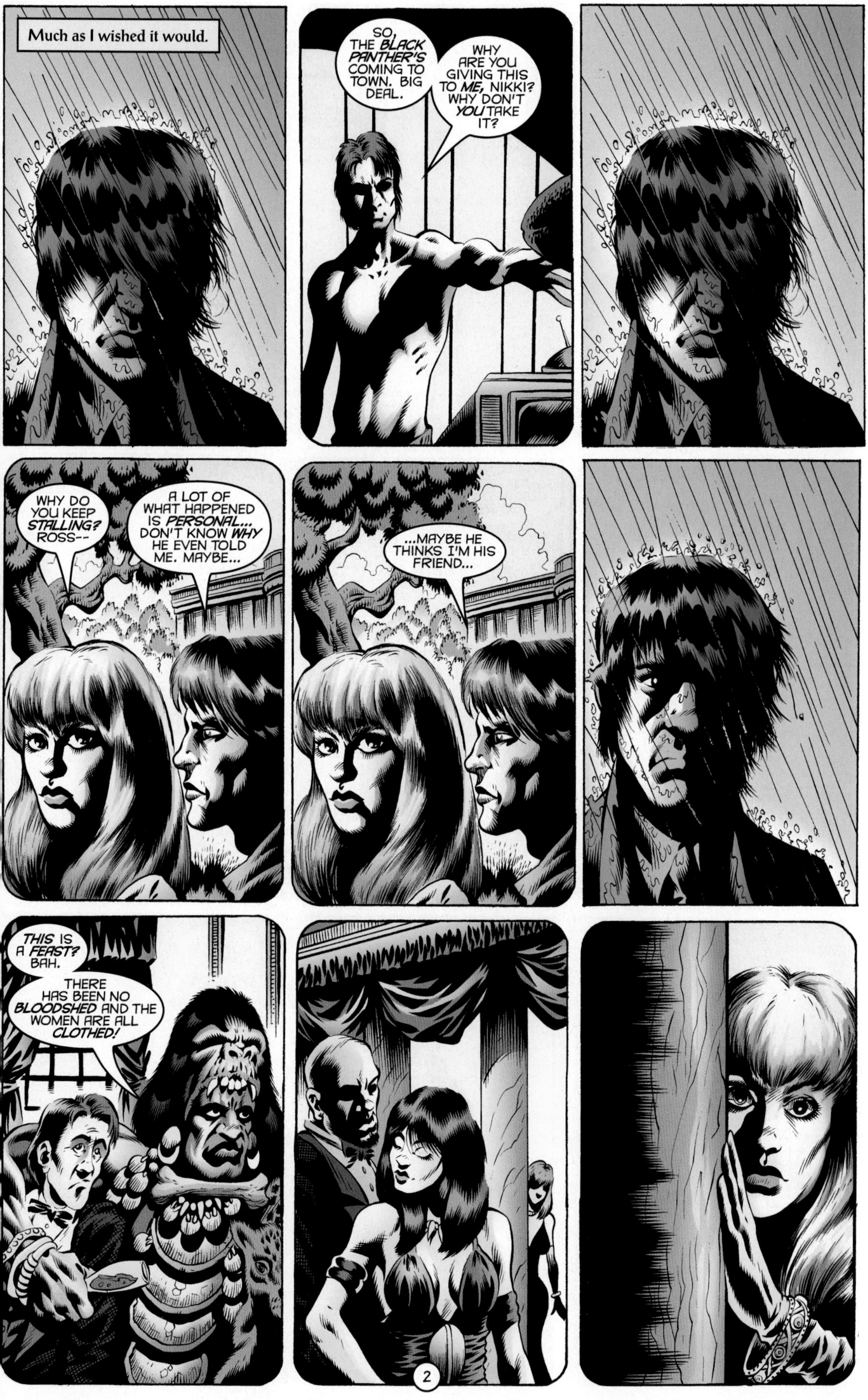

Much as I wished it would.
SO, THE BLACK PANTHER'S COMING TO TOWN. BIG DEAL.
WHY ARE YOU GIVING THIS TO ME, NIKKI? WHY DON'T YOU TAKE IT?
WHY DO YOU KEEP STALLING? ROSS--
A LOT OF WHAT HAPPENED IS PERSONAL... DON'T KNOW WHY HE EVEN TOLD ME. MAYBE...
...MAYBE HE THINKS I'M HIS FRIEND...
THIS IS A FEAST? BAH.
THERE HAS BEEN NO BLOODSHED AND THE WOMEN ARE ALL CLOTHED!

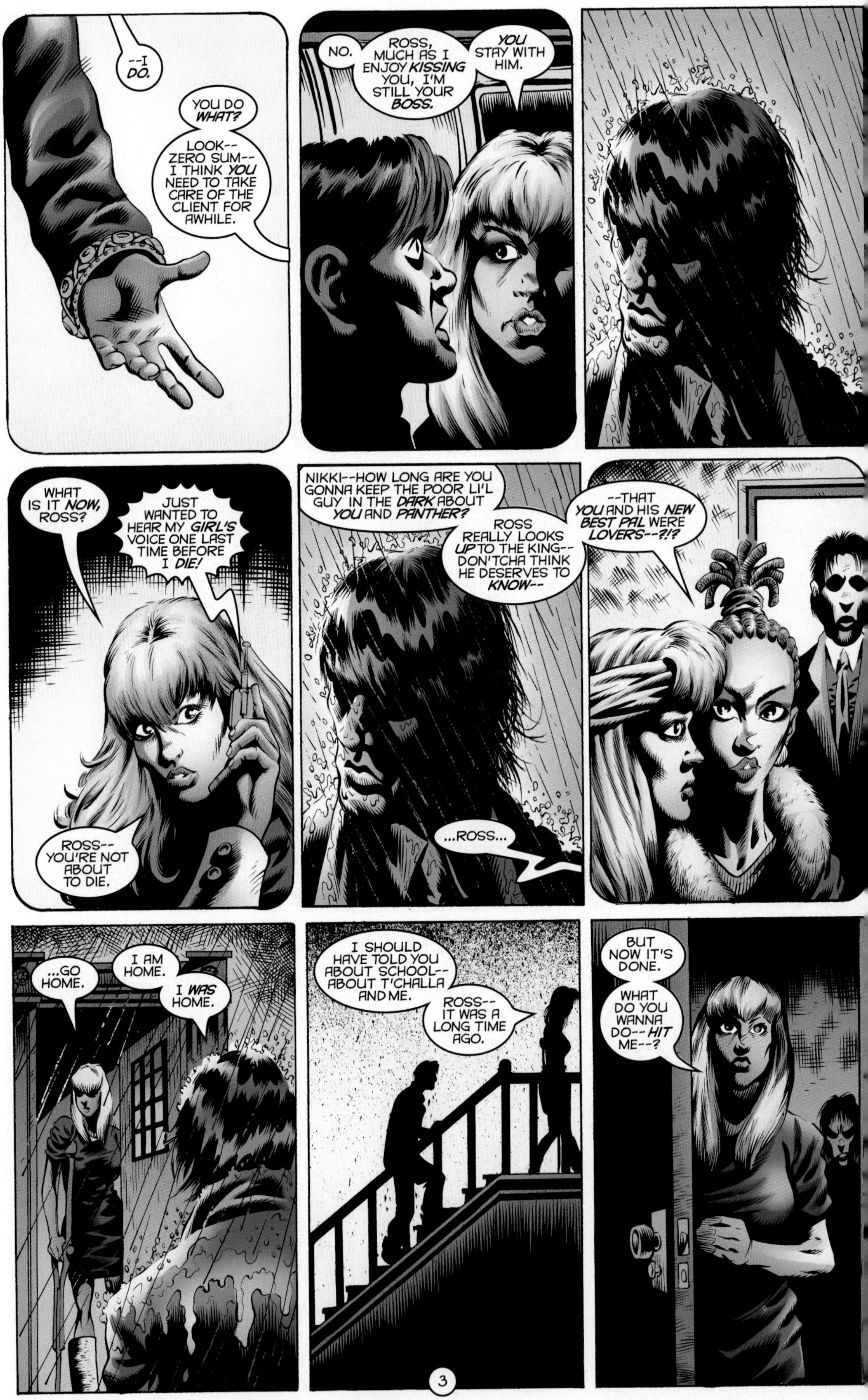
--I DO.
YOU DO WHAT?
LOOK-- ZERO SUM-- I THINK YOU NEED TO TAKE CARE OF THE CLIENT FOR AWHILE.
NO.
ROSS, MUCH AS I ENJOY KISSING YOU, I'M STILL YOUR BOSS.
YOU STAY WITH HIM.
WHAT IS IT NOW, ROSS?
JUST WANTED TO HEAR MY GIRL'S VOICE ONE LAST TIME BEFORE I DIE!
ROSS-- YOU'RE NOT ABOUT TO DIE.
NIKKI--HOW LONG ARE YOU GONNA KEEP THE POOR LI'L GUY IN THE DARK ABOUT YOU AND PANTHER?
ROSS REALLY LOOKS UP TO THE KING-- DON'TCHA THINK HE DESERVES TO KNOW--
...ROSS...
--THAT YOU AND HIS NEW BEST PAL WERE LOVERS--?!?
...GO HOME.
I AM HOME.
I WAS HOME.
I SHOULD HAVE TOLD YOU ABOUT SCHOOL-- ABOUT T'CHALLA AND ME.
ROSS-- IT WAS A LONG TIME AGO.
BUT NOW IT'S DONE.
WHAT DO YOU WANNA DO--HIT ME--?

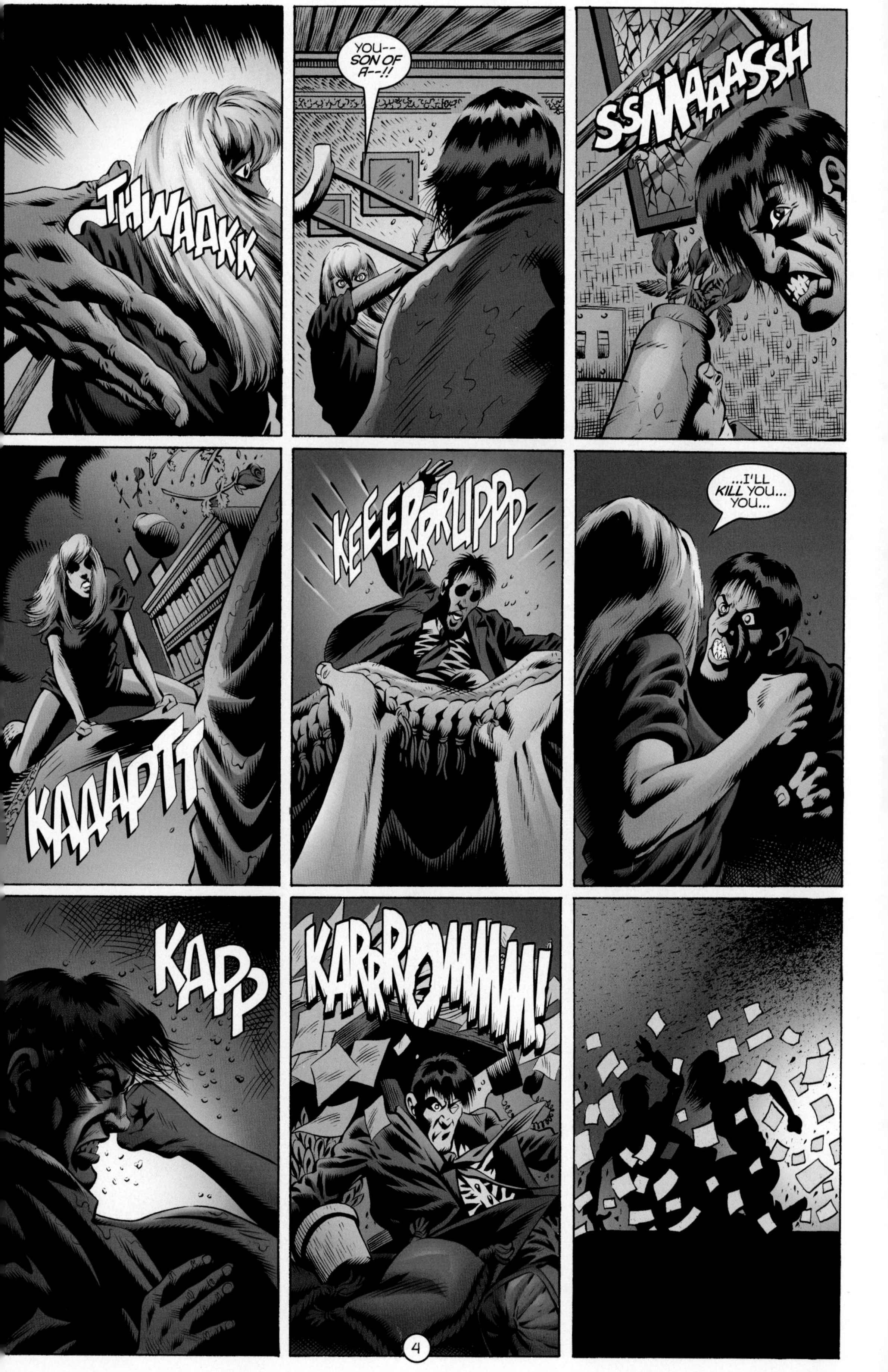
THWAAKK
YOU-- SON OF A--!!
SSMAAASSH
KAAAPTT
KEEERRRUPPP
...I'LL *KILL* YOU... YOU...
KAPP
KARRROMMMM!

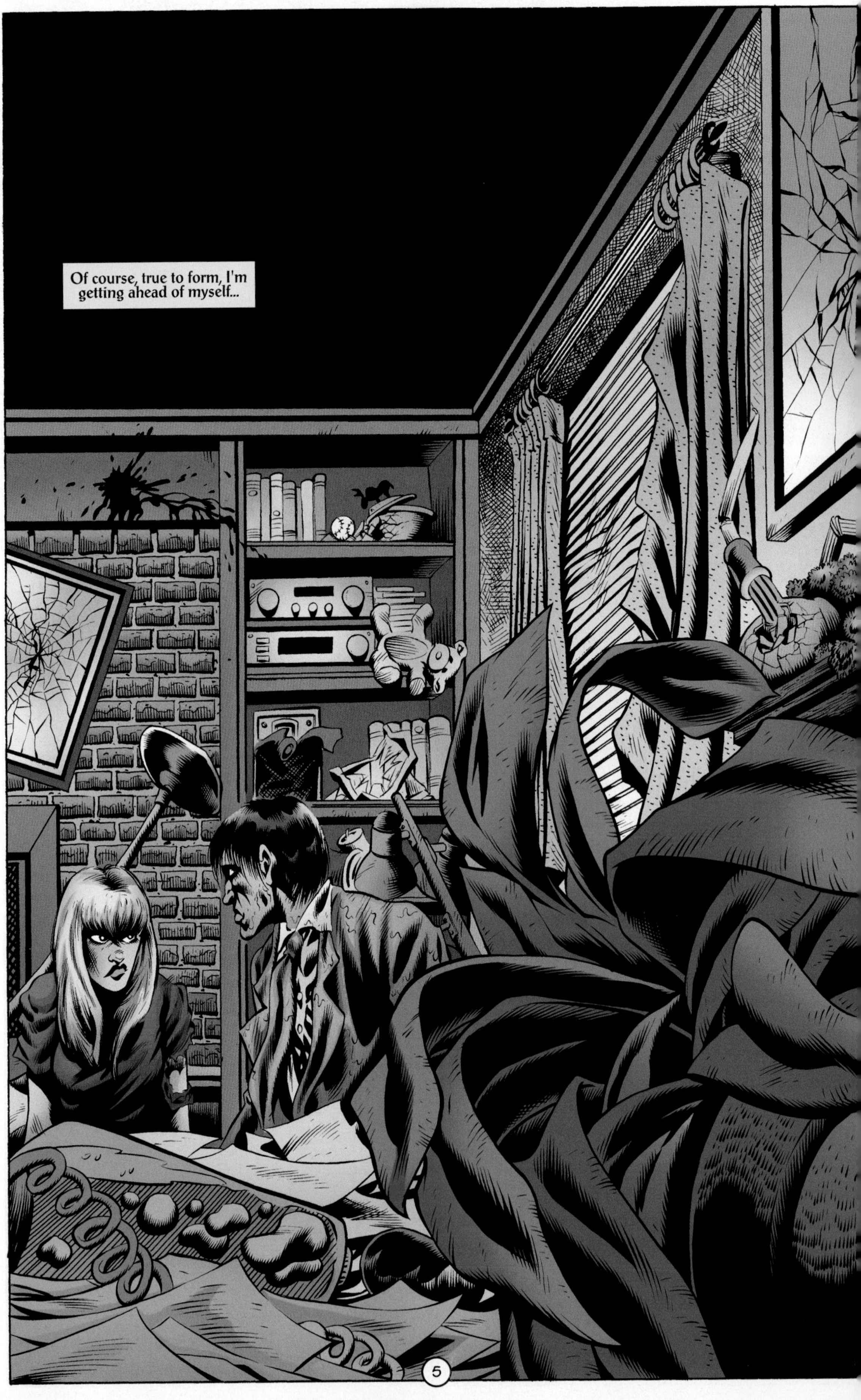
Of course, true to form, I'm getting ahead of myself...

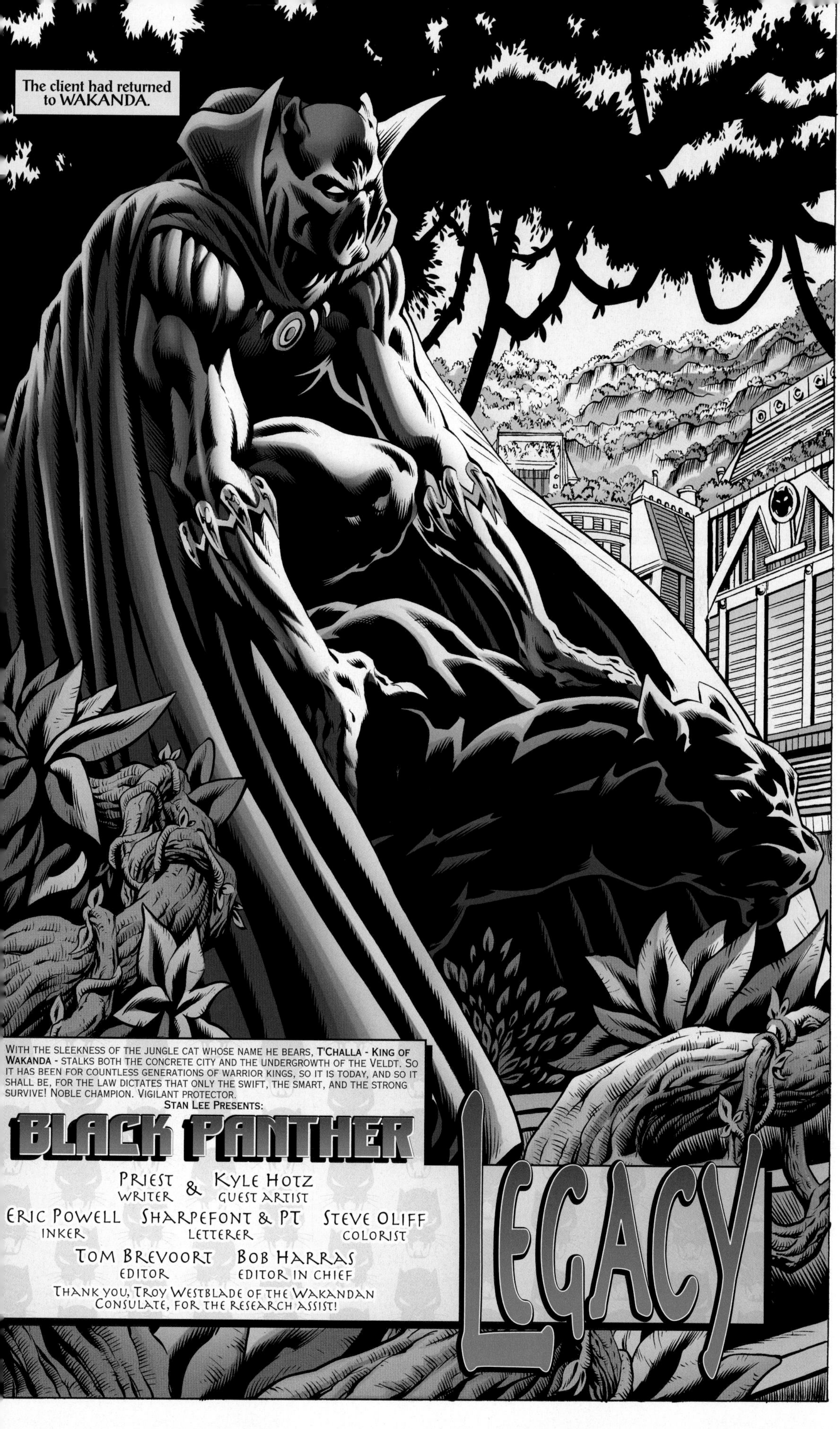

The client had returned to WAKANDA.
WITH THE SLEEKNESS OF THE JUNGLE CAT WHOSE NAME HE BEARS, T'CHALLA - KING OF WAKANDA - STALKS BOTH THE CONCRETE CITY AND THE UNDERGROWTH OF THE VELDT. SO IT HAS BEEN FOR COUNTLESS GENERATIONS OF WARRIOR KINGS, SO IT IS TODAY, AND SO IT SHALL BE, FOR THE LAW DICTATES THAT ONLY THE SWIFT, THE SMART, AND THE STRONG SURVIVE! NOBLE CHAMPION. VIGILANT PROTECTOR.
STAN LEE PRESENTS:
BLACK PANTHER
PRIEST WRITER & KYLE HOTZ GUEST ARTIST
ERIC POWELL INKER
SHARPEFONT & PT LETTERER
STEVE OLIFF COLORIST
TOM BREVOORT EDITOR
BOB HARRAS EDITOR IN CHIEF
THANK YOU, TROY WESTBLADE OF THE WAKANDAN CONSULATE, FOR THE RESEARCH ASSIST!
LEGACY

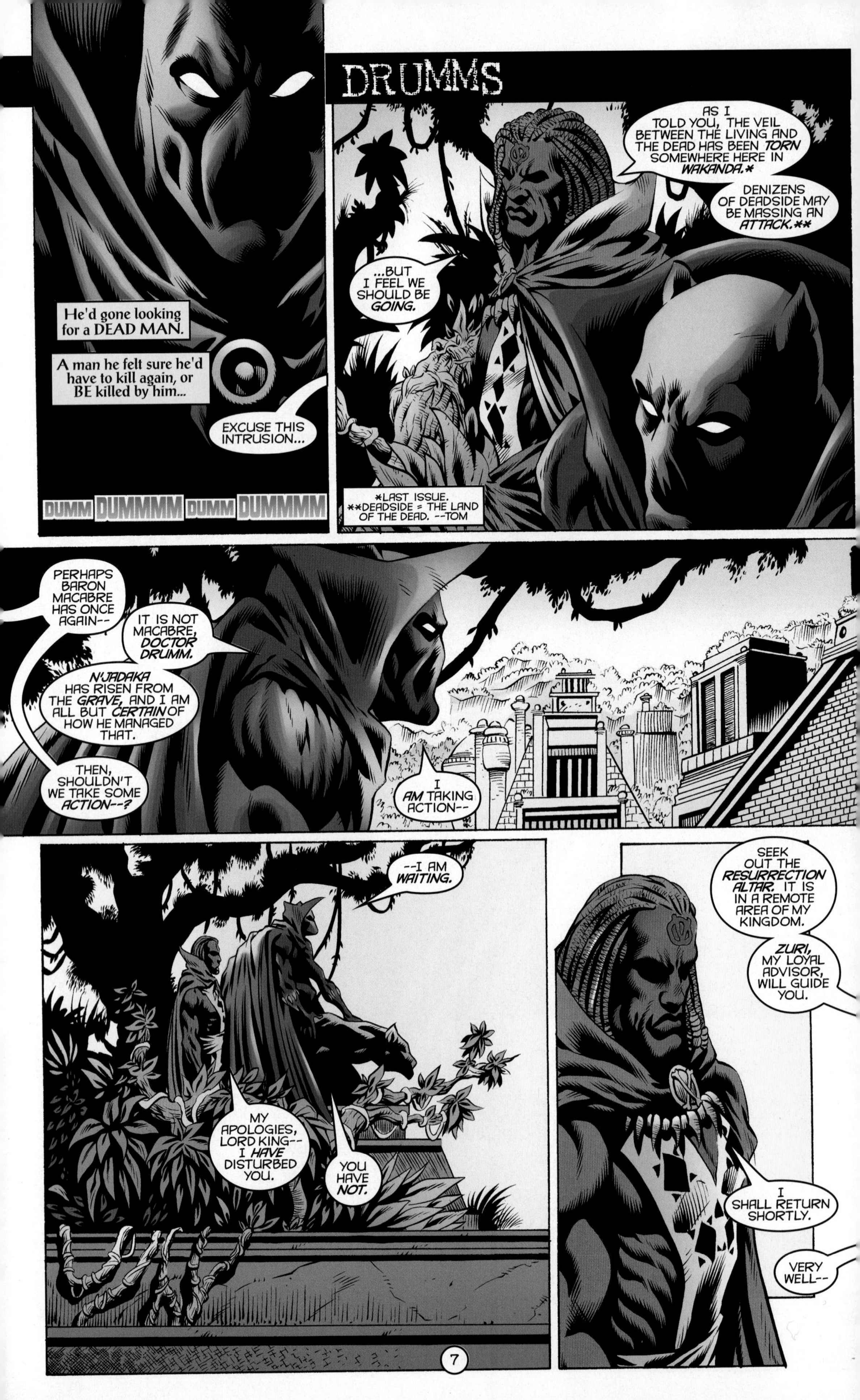
He'd gone looking for a DEAD MAN.
A man he felt sure he'd have to kill again, or BE killed by him...
EXCUSE THIS INTRUSION...
DUMM DUMMMM DUMM DUMMMM
DRUMMS
AS I TOLD YOU, THE VEIL BETWEEN THE LIVING AND THE DEAD HAS BEEN TORN SOMEWHERE HERE IN WAKANDA.*
DENIZENS OF DEADSIDE MAY BE MASSING AN ATTACK.**
...BUT I FEEL WE SHOULD BE GOING.
*LAST ISSUE. **DEADSIDE = THE LAND OF THE DEAD. --TOM
PERHAPS BARON MACABRE HAS ONCE AGAIN--
IT IS NOT MACABRE, DOCTOR DRUMM.
N'JADAKA HAS RISEN FROM THE GRAVE, AND I AM ALL BUT CERTAIN OF HOW HE MANAGED THAT.
THEN, SHOULDN'T WE TAKE SOME ACTION--?
I AM TAKING ACTION--
--I AM WAITING.
MY APOLOGIES, LORD KING-- I HAVE DISTURBED YOU.
YOU HAVE NOT.
SEEK OUT THE RESURRECTION ALTAR. IT IS IN A REMOTE AREA OF MY KINGDOM.
ZURI, MY LOYAL ADVISOR, WILL GUIDE YOU.
I SHALL RETURN SHORTLY.
VERY WELL--

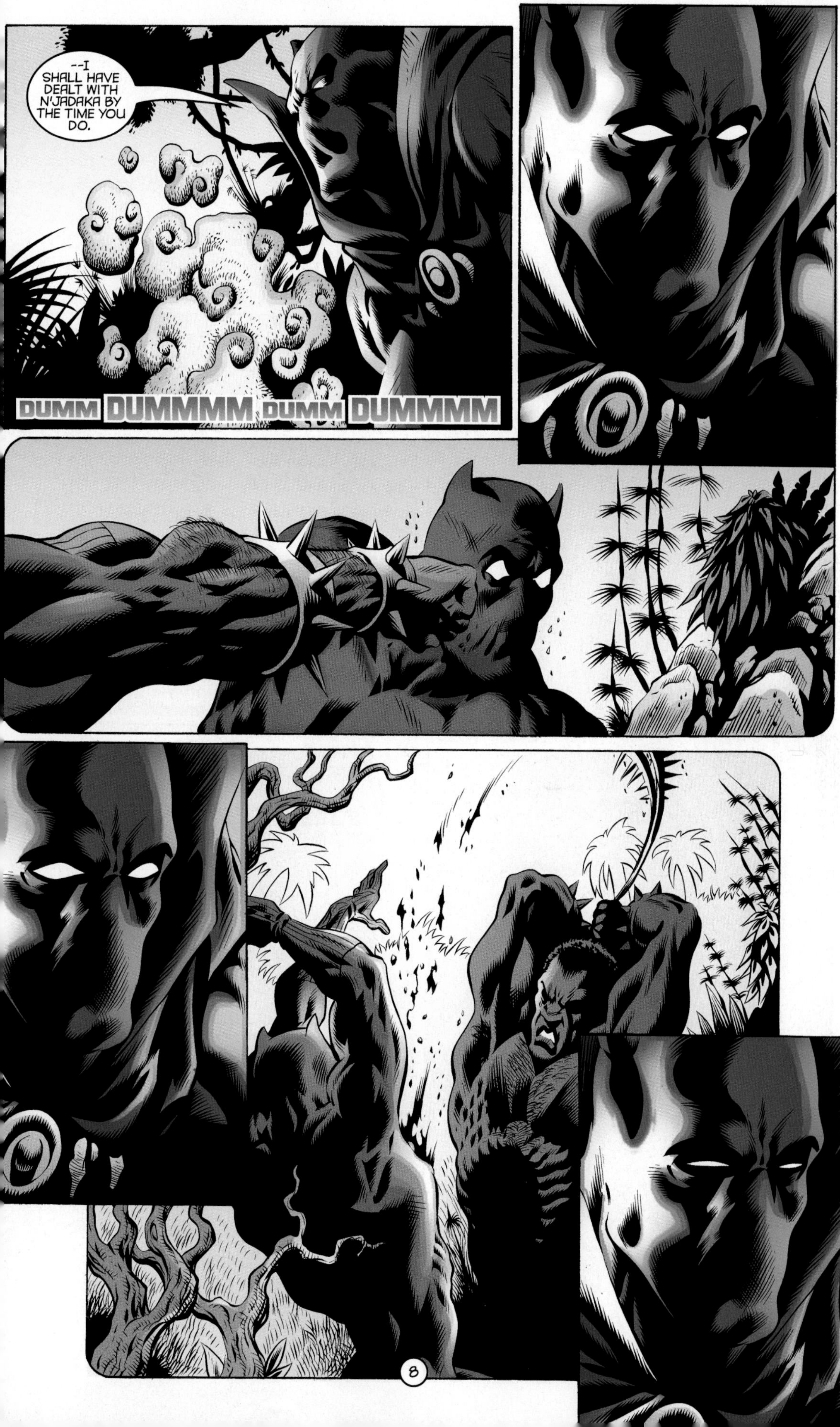
--I SHALL HAVE DEALT WITH N'JADAKA BY THE TIME YOU DO.
DUMM DUMMMM DUMM DUMMMM

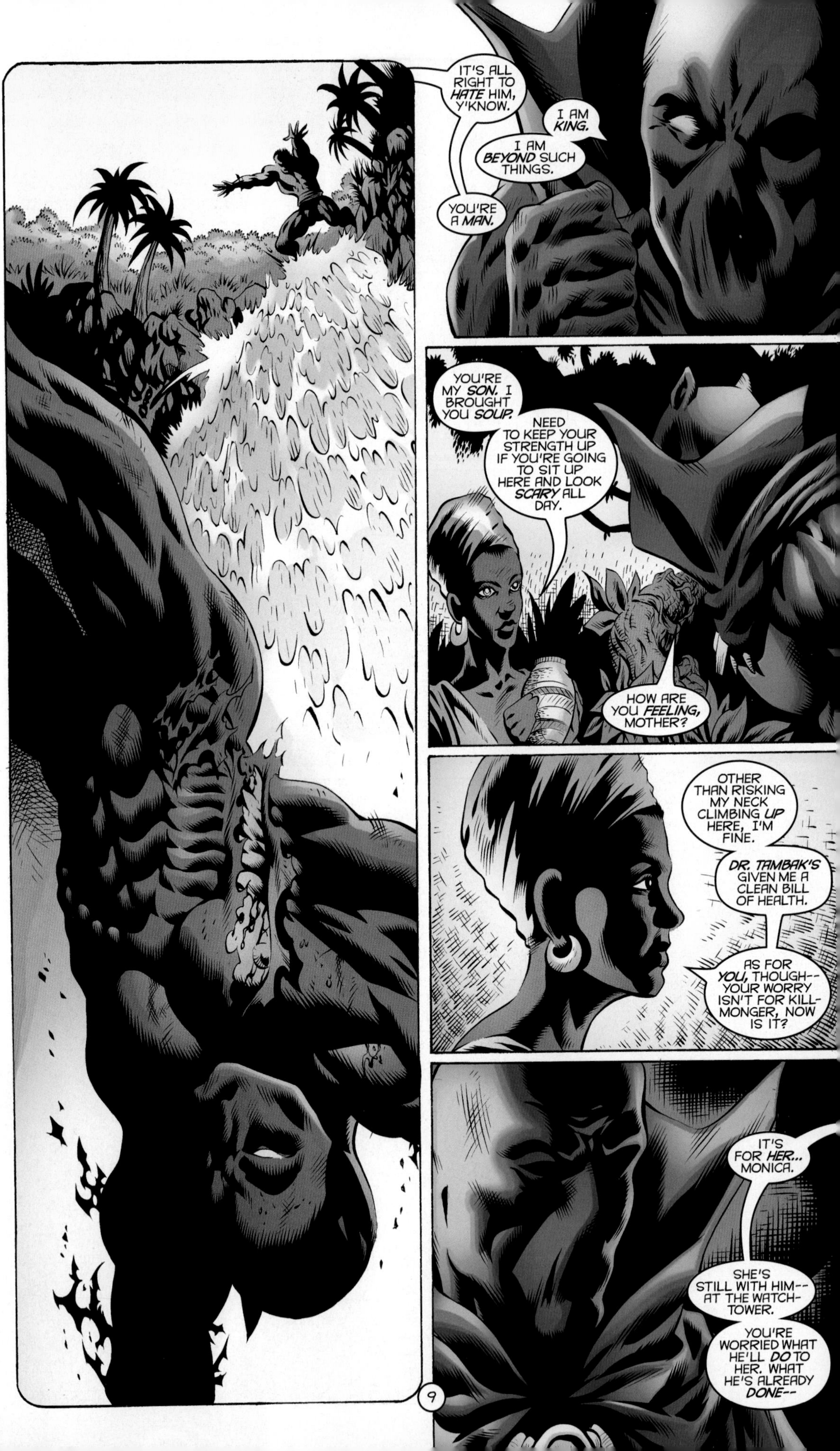

IT'S ALL RIGHT TO HATE HIM, Y'KNOW.
I AM KING.
I AM BEYOND SUCH THINGS.
YOU'RE A MAN.
YOU'RE MY SON. I BROUGHT YOU SOUP.
NEED TO KEEP YOUR STRENGTH UP IF YOU'RE GOING TO SIT UP HERE AND LOOK SCARY ALL DAY.
HOW ARE YOU FEELING, MOTHER?
OTHER THAN RISKING MY NECK CLIMBING UP HERE, I'M FINE.
DR. TAMBAK'S GIVEN ME A CLEAN BILL OF HEALTH.
AS FOR YOU, THOUGH-- YOUR WORRY ISN'T FOR KILL-MONGER, NOW IS IT?
IT'S FOR HER... MONICA.
SHE'S STILL WITH HIM-- AT THE WATCH-TOWER.
YOU'RE WORRIED WHAT HE'LL DO TO HER. WHAT HE'S ALREADY DONE--

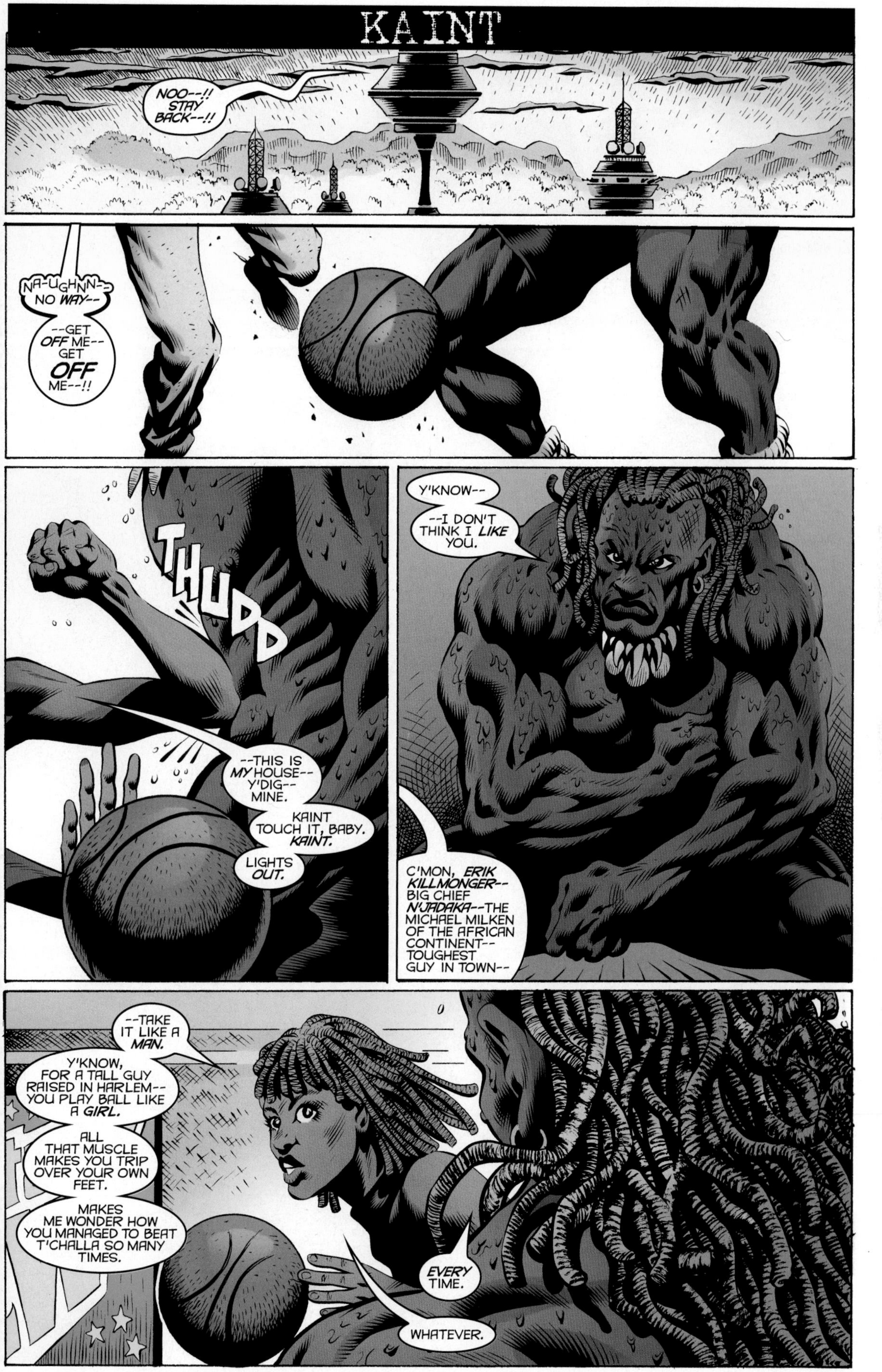
KAINT
NOO--!! STAY BACK--!!
NA-UGHNN-- NO WAY--
--GET OFF ME--GET OFF ME--!!
THUDD
--THIS IS MY HOUSE--Y'DIG--MINE.
KAINT TOUCH IT, BABY. KAINT.
LIGHTS OUT.
Y'KNOW--
--I DON'T THINK I LIKE YOU.
C'MON, ERIK KILLMONGER--BIG CHIEF N'JADAKA--THE MICHAEL MILKEN OF THE AFRICAN CONTINENT--TOUGHEST GUY IN TOWN--
--TAKE IT LIKE A MAN.
Y'KNOW, FOR A TALL GUY RAISED IN HARLEM--YOU PLAY BALL LIKE A GIRL.
ALL THAT MUSCLE MAKES YOU TRIP OVER YOUR OWN FEET.
MAKES ME WONDER HOW YOU MANAGED TO BEAT T'CHALLA SO MANY TIMES.
EVERY TIME.
WHATEVER.

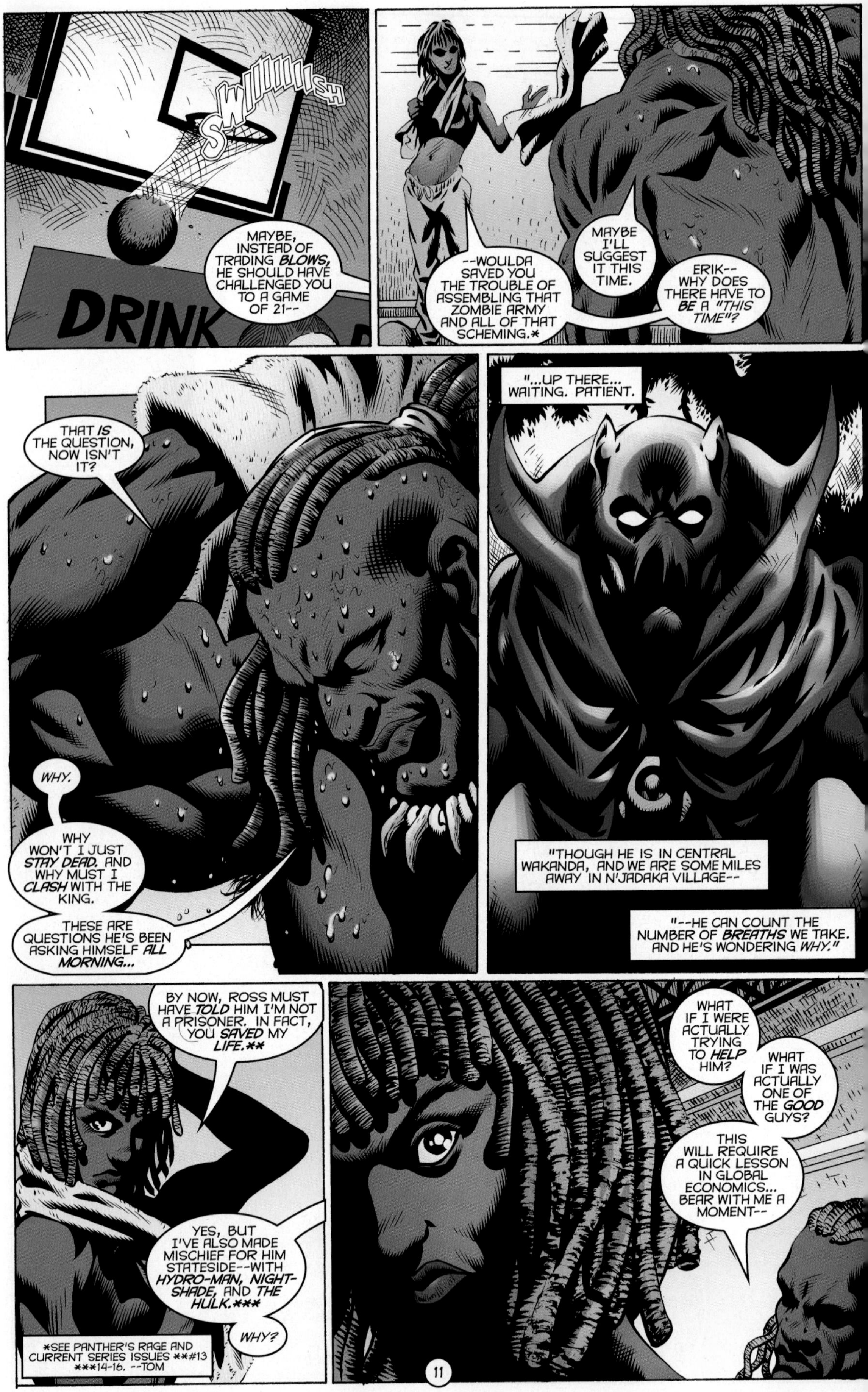

SWIIIIIISH
MAYBE, INSTEAD OF TRADING BLOWS, HE SHOULD HAVE CHALLENGED YOU TO A GAME OF 21--
DRINK
--WOULDA SAVED YOU THE TROUBLE OF ASSEMBLING THAT ZOMBIE ARMY AND ALL OF THAT SCHEMING.*
MAYBE I'LL SUGGEST IT THIS TIME.
ERIK-- WHY DOES THERE HAVE TO BE A "THIS TIME"?
THAT IS THE QUESTION, NOW ISN'T IT?
WHY.
WHY WON'T I JUST STAY DEAD. AND WHY MUST I CLASH WITH THE KING.
THESE ARE QUESTIONS HE'S BEEN ASKING HIMSELF ALL MORNING...
"...UP THERE... WAITING. PATIENT.
"THOUGH HE IS IN CENTRAL WAKANDA, AND WE ARE SOME MILES AWAY IN N'JADAKA VILLAGE--
"--HE CAN COUNT THE NUMBER OF BREATHS WE TAKE. AND HE'S WONDERING WHY."
BY NOW, ROSS MUST HAVE TOLD HIM I'M NOT A PRISONER. IN FACT, YOU SAVED MY LIFE.**
YES, BUT I'VE ALSO MADE MISCHIEF FOR HIM STATESIDE--WITH HYDRO-MAN, NIGHT-SHADE, AND THE HULK.***
WHY?
*SEE PANTHER'S RAGE AND CURRENT SERIES ISSUES **#13 ***14-16. --TOM
WHAT IF I WERE ACTUALLY TRYING TO HELP HIM?
WHAT IF I WAS ACTUALLY ONE OF THE GOOD GUYS?
THIS WILL REQUIRE A QUICK LESSON IN GLOBAL ECONOMICS... BEAR WITH ME A MOMENT--

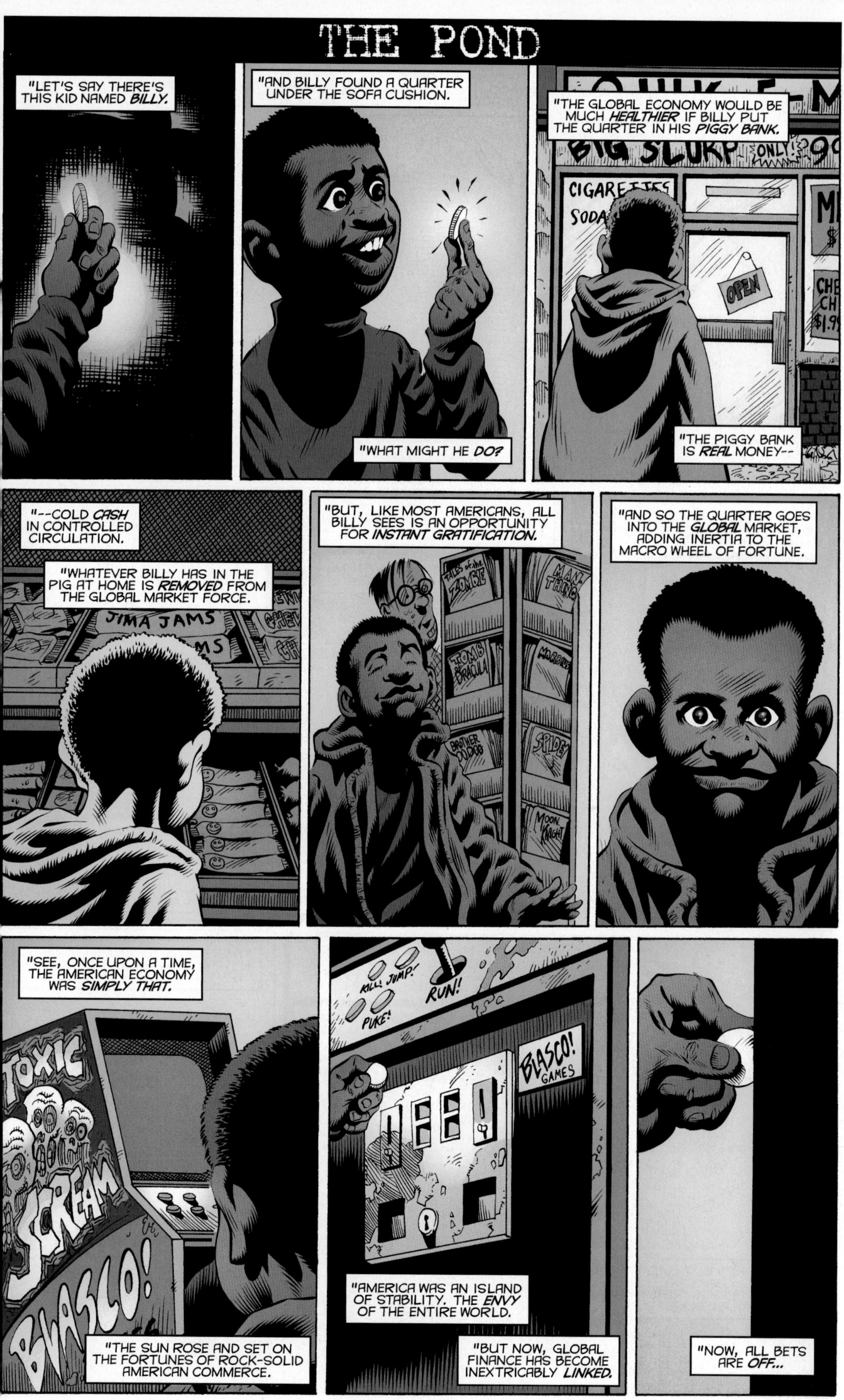
THE POND
"LET'S SAY THERE'S THIS KID NAMED BILLY.
"AND BILLY FOUND A QUARTER UNDER THE SOFA CUSHION.
"WHAT MIGHT HE DO?
"THE GLOBAL ECONOMY WOULD BE MUCH HEALTHIER IF BILLY PUT THE QUARTER IN HIS PIGGY BANK.
BIG SLURP ONLY!
CIGARETTES
SODA
OPEN
"THE PIGGY BANK IS REAL MONEY--
"--COLD CASH IN CONTROLLED CIRCULATION.
"WHATEVER BILLY HAS IN THE PIG AT HOME IS REMOVED FROM THE GLOBAL MARKET FORCE.
JIMA JAMS
"BUT, LIKE MOST AMERICANS, ALL BILLY SEES IS AN OPPORTUNITY FOR INSTANT GRATIFICATION.
TALES of the ZOMBIE
MAN THING
TOMB DRACULA
MORBIUS
BROTHER VOODOO
SPIDEY
MOON KNIGHT
"AND SO THE QUARTER GOES INTO THE GLOBAL MARKET, ADDING INERTIA TO THE MACRO WHEEL OF FORTUNE.
"SEE, ONCE UPON A TIME, THE AMERICAN ECONOMY WAS SIMPLY THAT.
TOXIC SCREAM
BLASCO!
"THE SUN ROSE AND SET ON THE FORTUNES OF ROCK-SOLID AMERICAN COMMERCE.
KILL! JUMP!
RUN!
PUKE!
BLASCO! GAMES
"AMERICA WAS AN ISLAND OF STABILITY. THE ENVY OF THE ENTIRE WORLD.
"BUT NOW, GLOBAL FINANCE HAS BECOME INEXTRICABLY LINKED.
"NOW, ALL BETS ARE OFF...

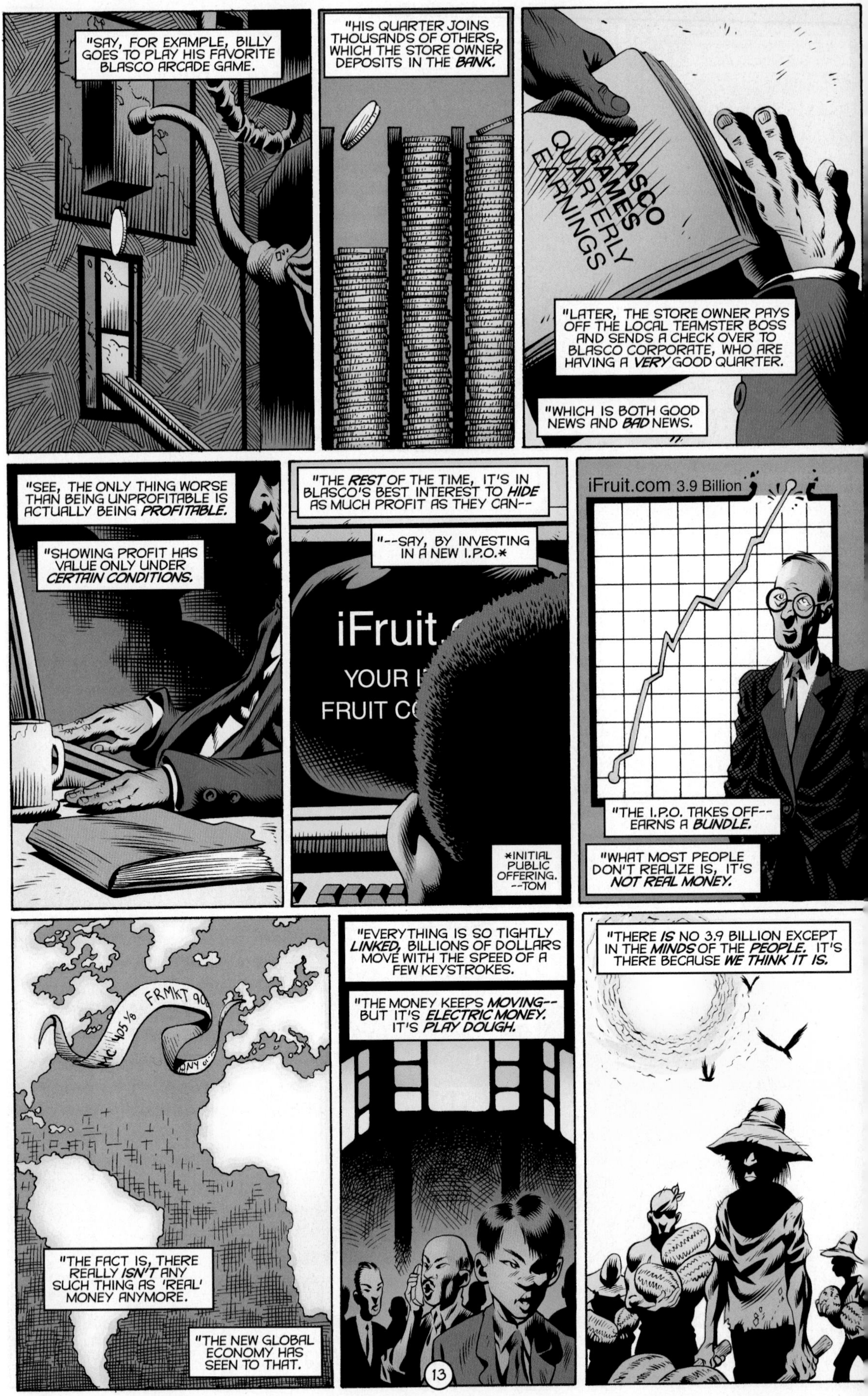
"SAY, FOR EXAMPLE, BILLY GOES TO PLAY HIS FAVORITE BLASCO ARCADE GAME.
"HIS QUARTER JOINS THOUSANDS OF OTHERS, WHICH THE STORE OWNER DEPOSITS IN THE *BANK.*
BLASCO GAMES QUARTERLY EARNINGS
"LATER, THE STORE OWNER PAYS OFF THE LOCAL TEAMSTER BOSS AND SENDS A CHECK OVER TO BLASCO CORPORATE, WHO ARE HAVING A *VERY* GOOD QUARTER.
"WHICH IS BOTH GOOD NEWS AND *BAD* NEWS.
"SEE, THE ONLY THING WORSE THAN BEING UNPROFITABLE IS ACTUALLY BEING *PROFITABLE.*
"SHOWING PROFIT HAS VALUE ONLY UNDER *CERTAIN CONDITIONS.*
"THE *REST* OF THE TIME, IT'S IN BLASCO'S BEST INTEREST TO *HIDE* AS MUCH PROFIT AS THEY CAN--
"--SAY, BY INVESTING IN A NEW I.P.O.*
iFruit.c
YOUR I
FRUIT C
*INITIAL PUBLIC OFFERING. --TOM
iFruit.com 3.9 Billion
"THE I.P.O. TAKES OFF-- EARNS A *BUNDLE.*
"WHAT MOST PEOPLE DON'T REALIZE IS, IT'S *NOT REAL MONEY.*
FRMKT 90
"THE FACT IS, THERE REALLY *ISN'T* ANY SUCH THING AS 'REAL' MONEY ANYMORE.
"THE NEW GLOBAL ECONOMY HAS SEEN TO THAT.
"EVERYTHING IS SO TIGHTLY *LINKED,* BILLIONS OF DOLLARS MOVE WITH THE SPEED OF A FEW KEYSTROKES.
"THE MONEY KEEPS *MOVING--* BUT IT'S *ELECTRIC MONEY.* IT'S *PLAY DOUGH.*
"THERE *IS* NO 3.9 BILLION EXCEPT IN THE *MINDS* OF THE *PEOPLE.* IT'S THERE BECAUSE *WE THINK IT IS.*

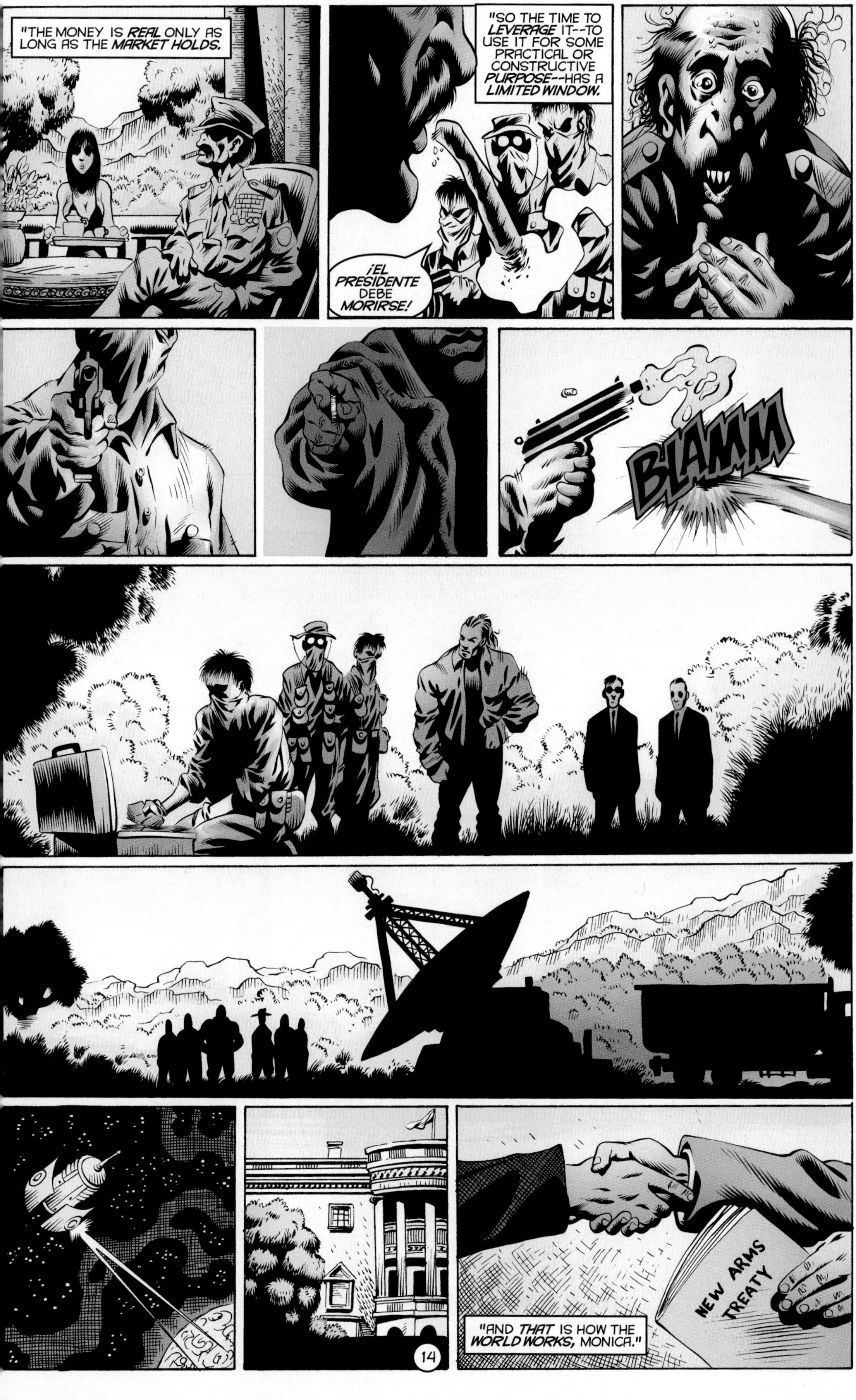
"THE MONEY IS REAL ONLY AS LONG AS THE MARKET HOLDS.
"SO THE TIME TO LEVERAGE IT--TO USE IT FOR SOME PRACTICAL OR CONSTRUCTIVE PURPOSE--HAS A LIMITED WINDOW.
¡EL PRESIDENTE DEBE MORIRSE!
BLAMM
NEW ARMS TREATY
"AND THAT IS HOW THE WORLD WORKS, MONICA."

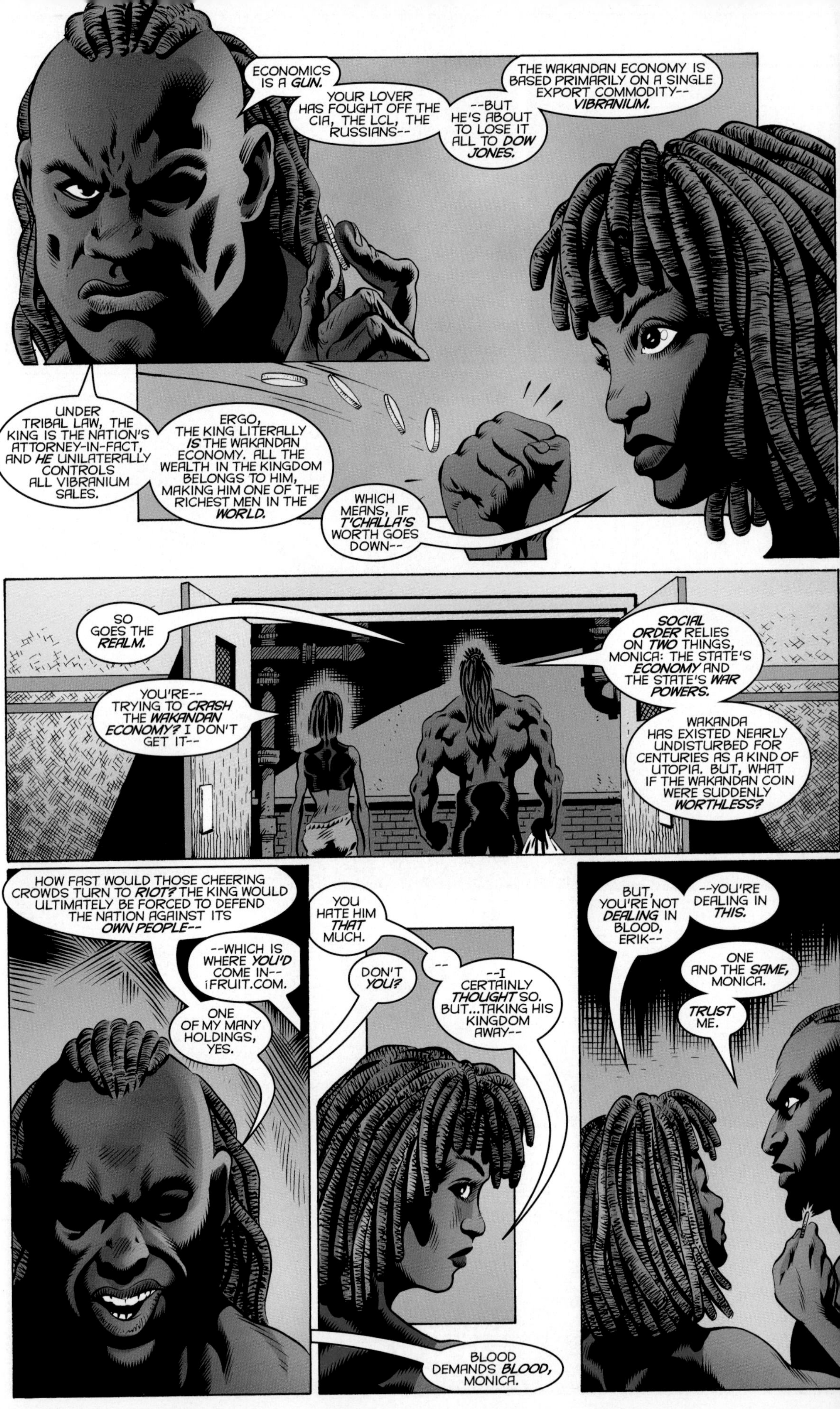
ECONOMICS IS A GUN.
YOUR LOVER HAS FOUGHT OFF THE CIA, THE LCL, THE RUSSIANS--
--BUT HE'S ABOUT TO LOSE IT ALL TO DOW JONES.
THE WAKANDAN ECONOMY IS BASED PRIMARILY ON A SINGLE EXPORT COMMODITY-- VIBRANIUM.
UNDER TRIBAL LAW, THE KING IS THE NATION'S ATTORNEY-IN-FACT, AND HE UNILATERALLY CONTROLS ALL VIBRANIUM SALES.
ERGO, THE KING LITERALLY IS THE WAKANDAN ECONOMY. ALL THE WEALTH IN THE KINGDOM BELONGS TO HIM, MAKING HIM ONE OF THE RICHEST MEN IN THE WORLD.
WHICH MEANS, IF T'CHALLA'S WORTH GOES DOWN--
SO GOES THE REALM.
YOU'RE-- TRYING TO CRASH THE WAKANDAN ECONOMY? I DON'T GET IT--
SOCIAL ORDER RELIES ON TWO THINGS, MONICA: THE STATE'S ECONOMY AND THE STATE'S WAR POWERS.
WAKANDA HAS EXISTED NEARLY UNDISTURBED FOR CENTURIES AS A KIND OF UTOPIA. BUT, WHAT IF THE WAKANDAN COIN WERE SUDDENLY WORTHLESS?
HOW FAST WOULD THOSE CHEERING CROWDS TURN TO RIOT? THE KING WOULD ULTIMATELY BE FORCED TO DEFEND THE NATION AGAINST ITS OWN PEOPLE--
--WHICH IS WHERE YOU'D COME IN-- iFRUIT.COM.
ONE OF MY MANY HOLDINGS, YES.
YOU HATE HIM THAT MUCH.
DON'T YOU?
--
--I CERTAINLY THOUGHT SO. BUT...TAKING HIS KINGDOM AWAY--
BLOOD DEMANDS BLOOD, MONICA.
BUT, YOU'RE NOT DEALING IN BLOOD, ERIK--
--YOU'RE DEALING IN THIS.
ONE AND THE SAME, MONICA.
TRUST ME.

CHANGES

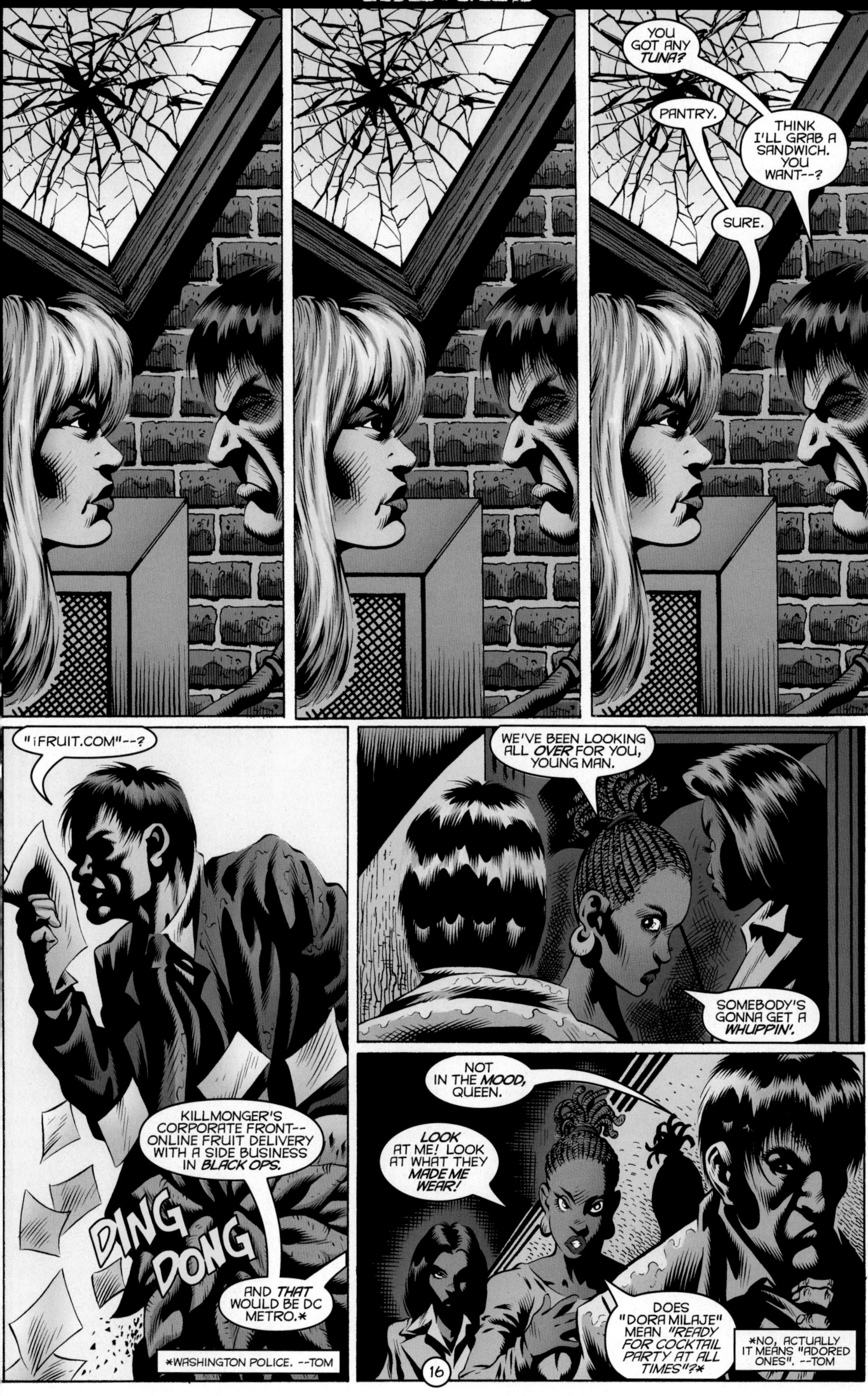
YOU GOT ANY TUNA?
PANTRY.
THINK I'LL GRAB A SANDWICH. YOU WANT--?
SURE.
"iFRUIT.COM"--?
KILLMONGER'S CORPORATE FRONT-- ONLINE FRUIT DELIVERY WITH A SIDE BUSINESS IN BLACK OPS.
DING DONG
AND THAT WOULD BE DC METRO.*
*WASHINGTON POLICE. --TOM
WE'VE BEEN LOOKING ALL OVER FOR YOU, YOUNG MAN.
SOMEBODY'S GONNA GET A WHUPPIN'.
NOT IN THE MOOD, QUEEN.
LOOK AT ME! LOOK AT WHAT THEY MADE ME WEAR!
DOES "DORA MILAJE" MEAN "READY FOR COCKTAIL PARTY AT ALL TIMES"?*
*NO, ACTUALLY IT MEANS "ADORED ONES". --TOM

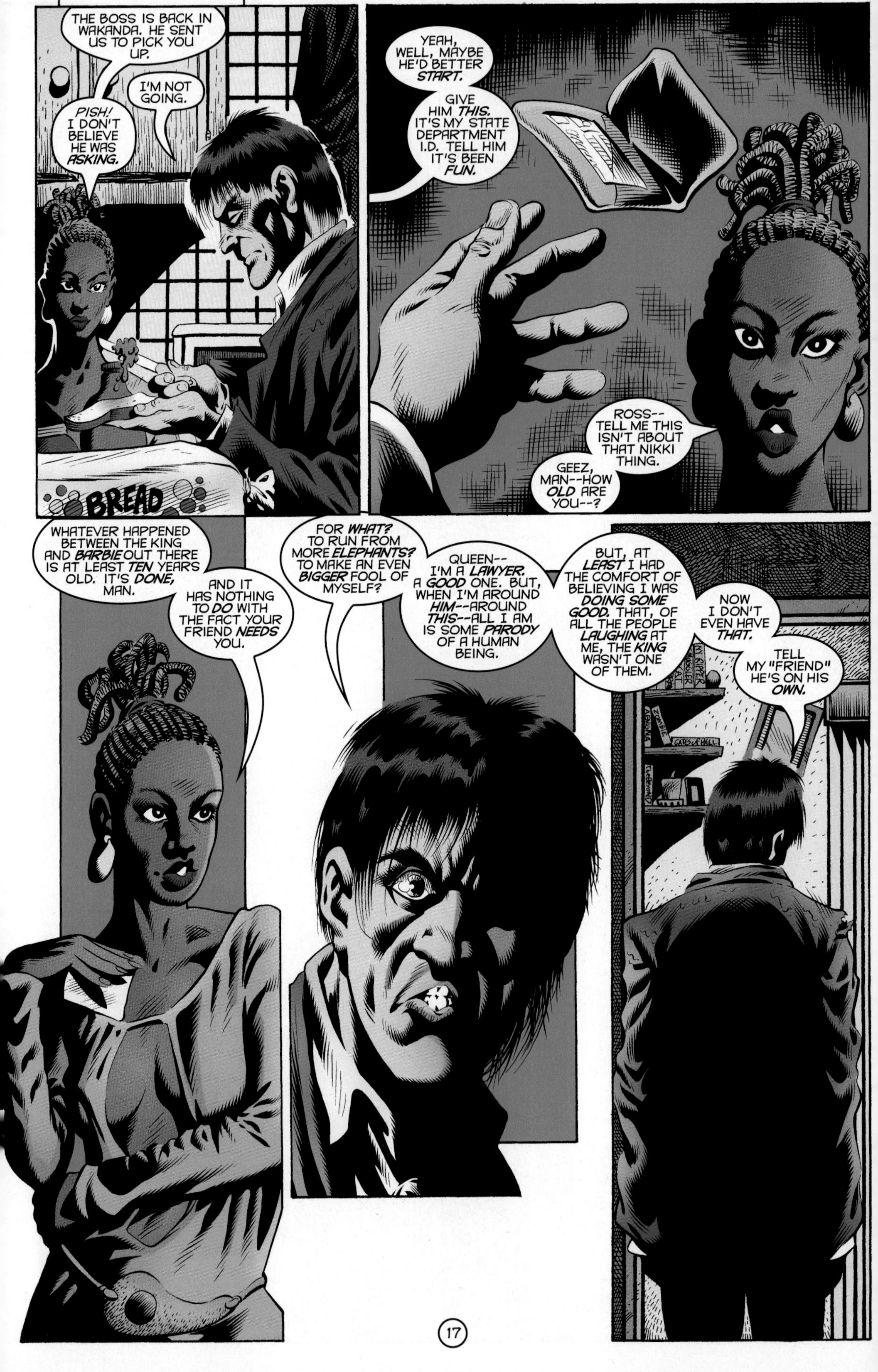
THE BOSS IS BACK IN WAKANDA. HE SENT US TO PICK YOU UP.
I'M NOT GOING.
PISH! I DON'T BELIEVE HE WAS ASKING.
BREAD
YEAH, WELL, MAYBE HE'D BETTER START.
GIVE HIM THIS. IT'S MY STATE DEPARTMENT I.D. TELL HIM IT'S BEEN FUN.
ROSS--TELL ME THIS ISN'T ABOUT THAT NIKKI THING.
GEEZ, MAN--HOW OLD ARE YOU--?
WHATEVER HAPPENED BETWEEN THE KING AND BARBIE OUT THERE IS AT LEAST TEN YEARS OLD. IT'S DONE, MAN.
AND IT HAS NOTHING TO DO WITH THE FACT YOUR FRIEND NEEDS YOU.
FOR WHAT? TO RUN FROM MORE ELEPHANTS? TO MAKE AN EVEN BIGGER FOOL OF MYSELF?
QUEEN--I'M A LAWYER. A GOOD ONE. BUT, WHEN I'M AROUND HIM--AROUND THIS--ALL I AM IS SOME PARODY OF A HUMAN BEING.
BUT, AT LEAST I HAD THE COMFORT OF BELIEVING I WAS DOING SOME GOOD. THAT, OF ALL THE PEOPLE LAUGHING AT ME, THE KING WASN'T ONE OF THEM.
NOW I DON'T EVEN HAVE THAT.
TELL MY "FRIEND" HE'S ON HIS OWN.
GATES OF HELL

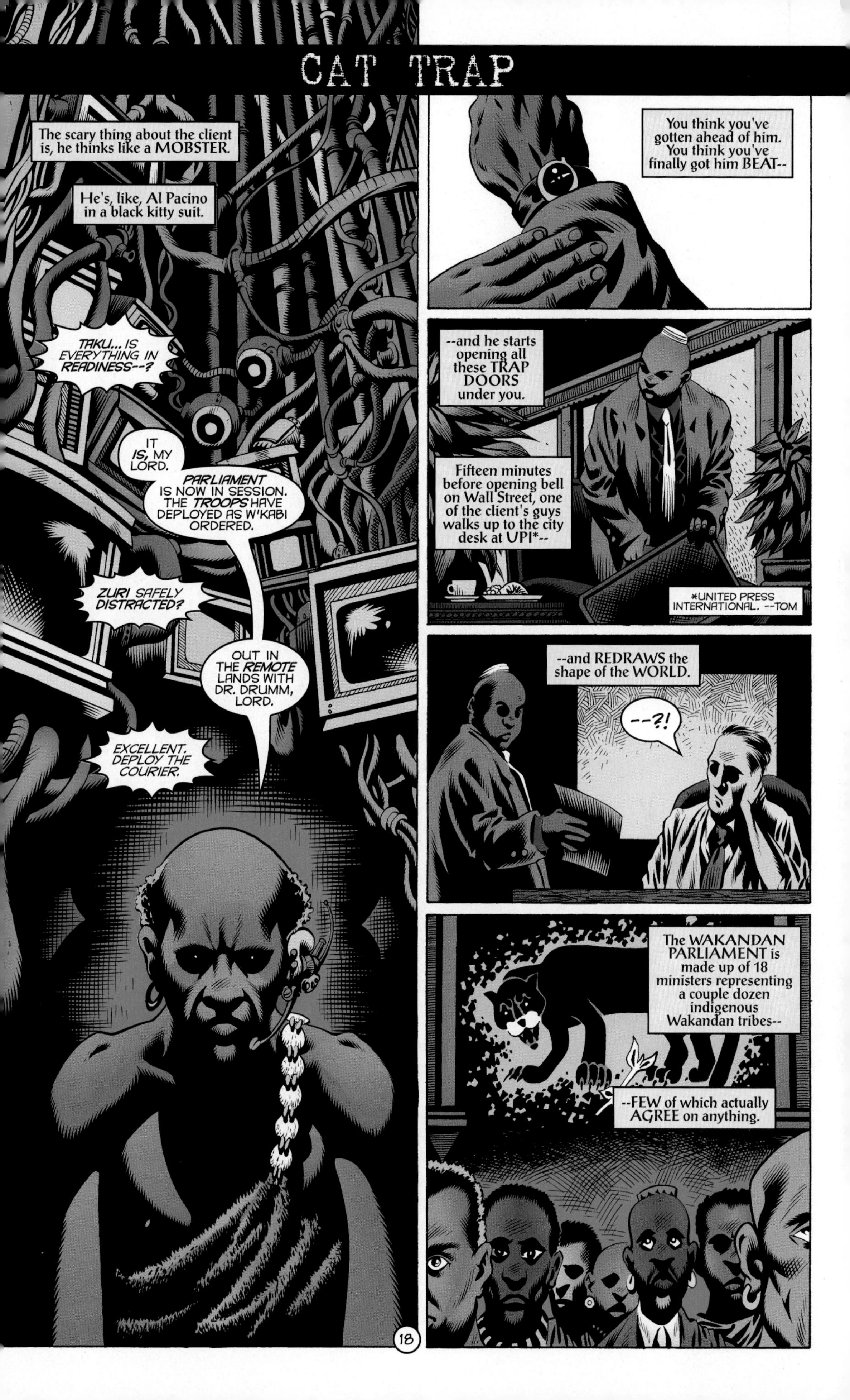
CAT TRAP
The scary thing about the client is, he thinks like a MOBSTER.
He's, like, Al Pacino in a black kitty suit.
TAKU... IS EVERYTHING IN READINESS--?
IT IS, MY LORD.
PARLIAMENT IS NOW IN SESSION. THE TROOPS HAVE DEPLOYED AS W'KABI ORDERED.
ZURI SAFELY DISTRACTED?
OUT IN THE REMOTE LANDS WITH DR. DRUMM, LORD.
EXCELLENT. DEPLOY THE COURIER.
You think you've gotten ahead of him. You think you've finally got him BEAT--
--and he starts opening all these TRAP DOORS under you.
Fifteen minutes before opening bell on Wall Street, one of the client's guys walks up to the city desk at UPI*--
*UNITED PRESS INTERNATIONAL. --TOM
--and REDRAWS the shape of the WORLD.
--?!
The WAKANDAN PARLIAMENT is made up of 18 ministers representing a couple dozen indigenous Wakandan tribes--
--FEW of which actually AGREE on anything.

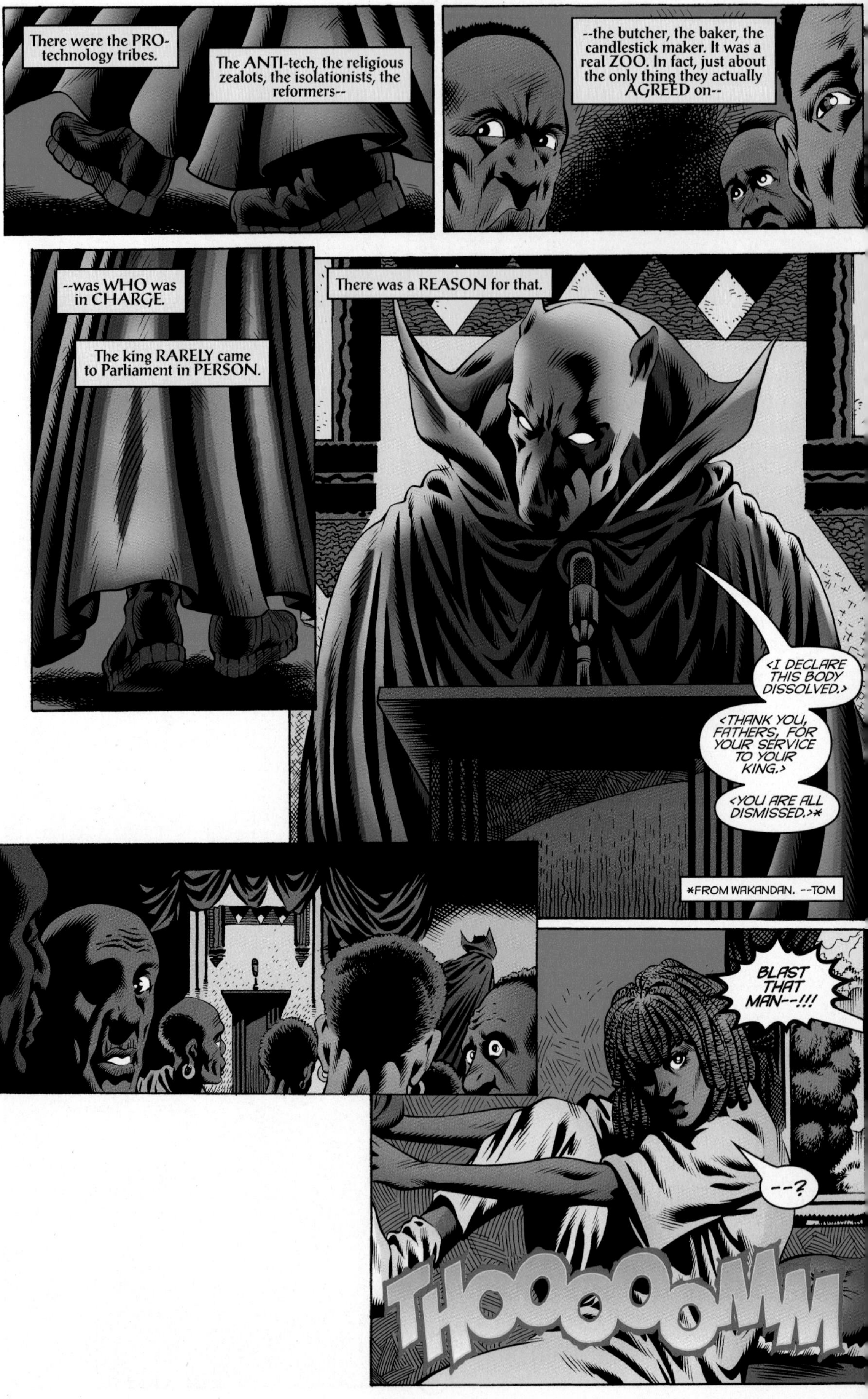
There were the PRO-technology tribes.
The ANTI-tech, the religious zealots, the isolationists, the reformers--
--the butcher, the baker, the candlestick maker. It was a real ZOO. In fact, just about the only thing they actually AGREED on--
--was WHO was in CHARGE.
The king RARELY came to Parliament in PERSON.
There was a REASON for that.
<I DECLARE THIS BODY DISSOLVED.>
<THANK YOU, FATHERS, FOR YOUR SERVICE TO YOUR KING.>
<YOU ARE ALL DISMISSED.>*
*FROM WAKANDAN. --TOM
BLAST THAT MAN--!!!
--?
THOOOOOMM

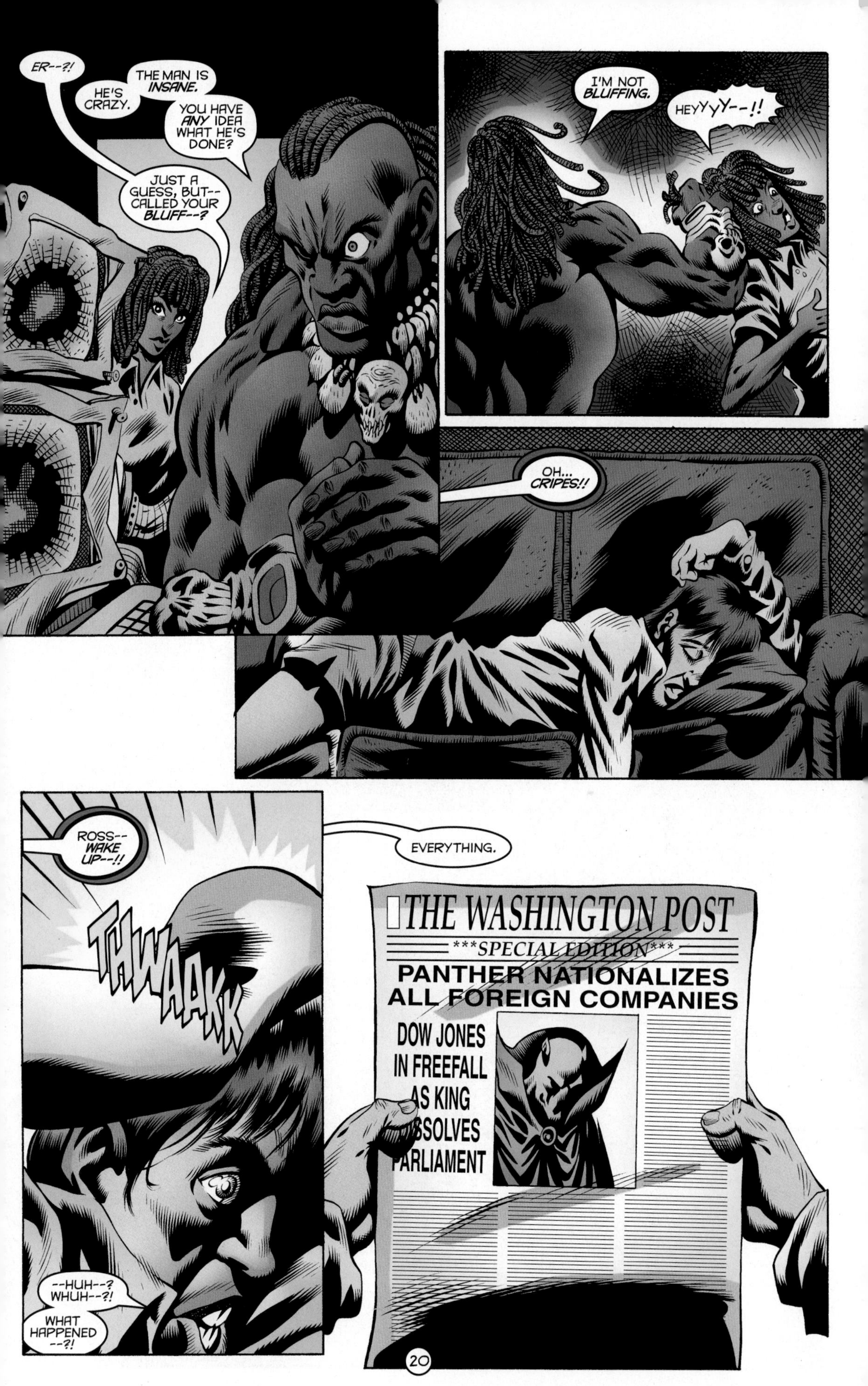
ER--?!
HE'S CRAZY.
THE MAN IS INSANE.
YOU HAVE ANY IDEA WHAT HE'S DONE?
JUST A GUESS, BUT-- CALLED YOUR BLUFF--?
I'M NOT BLUFFING.
HEYYYY--!!
OH... CRIPES!!
ROSS-- WAKE UP--!!
THWAAKK
--HUH--? WHUH--?!
WHAT HAPPENED --?!
EVERYTHING.
THE WASHINGTON POST
SPECIAL EDITION
PANTHER NATIONALIZES ALL FOREIGN COMPANIES
DOW JONES IN FREEFALL AS KING DISSOLVES PARLIAMENT

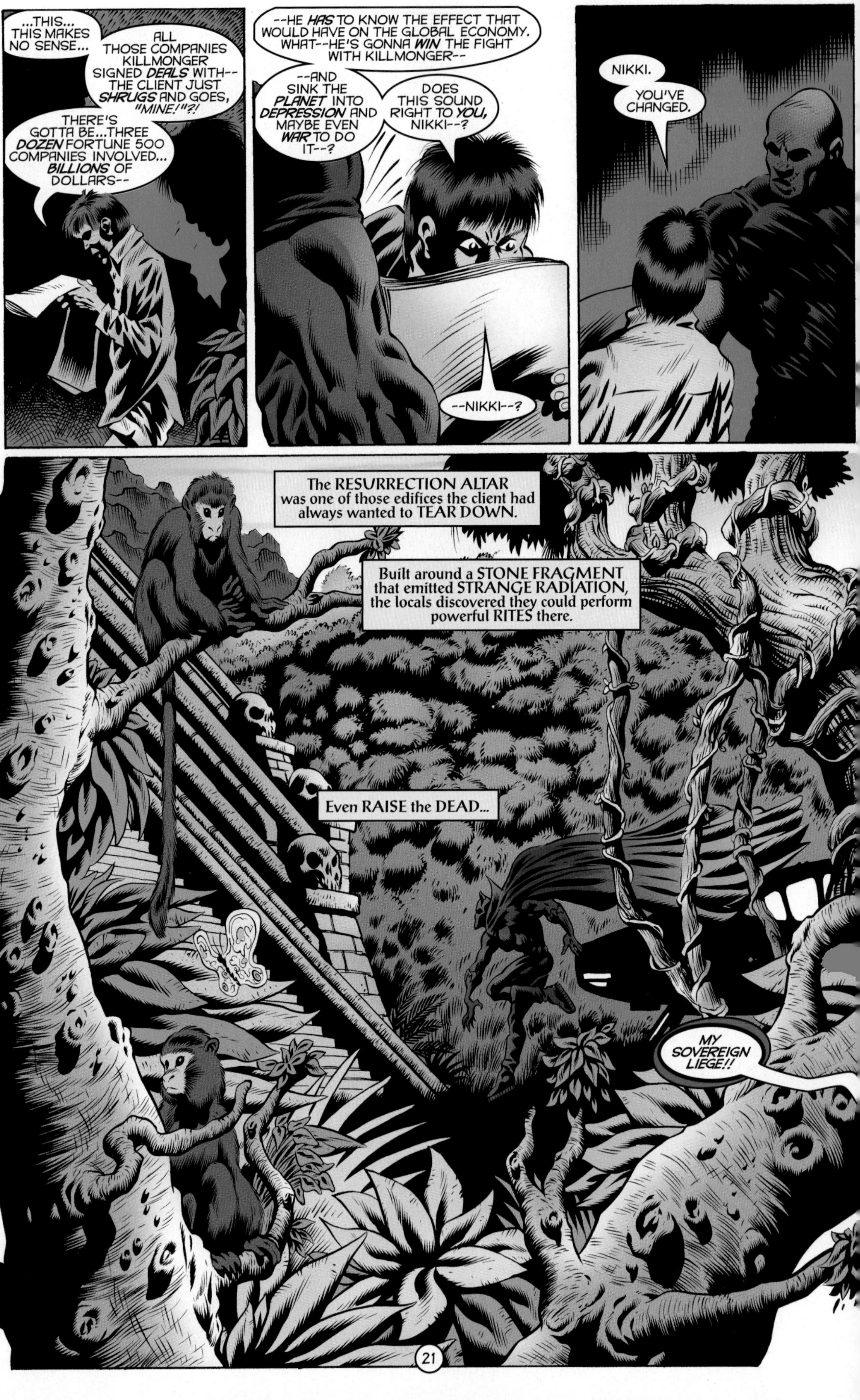
...THIS... THIS MAKES NO SENSE...
ALL THOSE COMPANIES KILLMONGER SIGNED DEALS WITH-- THE CLIENT JUST SHRUGS AND GOES, "MINE!"?!
THERE'S GOTTA BE...THREE DOZEN FORTUNE 500 COMPANIES INVOLVED... BILLIONS OF DOLLARS--
--HE HAS TO KNOW THE EFFECT THAT WOULD HAVE ON THE GLOBAL ECONOMY. WHAT--HE'S GONNA WIN THE FIGHT WITH KILLMONGER--
--AND SINK THE PLANET INTO DEPRESSION AND MAYBE EVEN WAR TO DO IT--?
DOES THIS SOUND RIGHT TO YOU, NIKKI--?
--NIKKI--?
NIKKI.
YOU'VE CHANGED.
The RESURRECTION ALTAR was one of those edifices the client had always wanted to TEAR DOWN.
Built around a STONE FRAGMENT that emitted STRANGE RADIATION, the locals discovered they could perform powerful RITES there.
Even RAISE the DEAD...
MY SOVEREIGN LIEGE!!

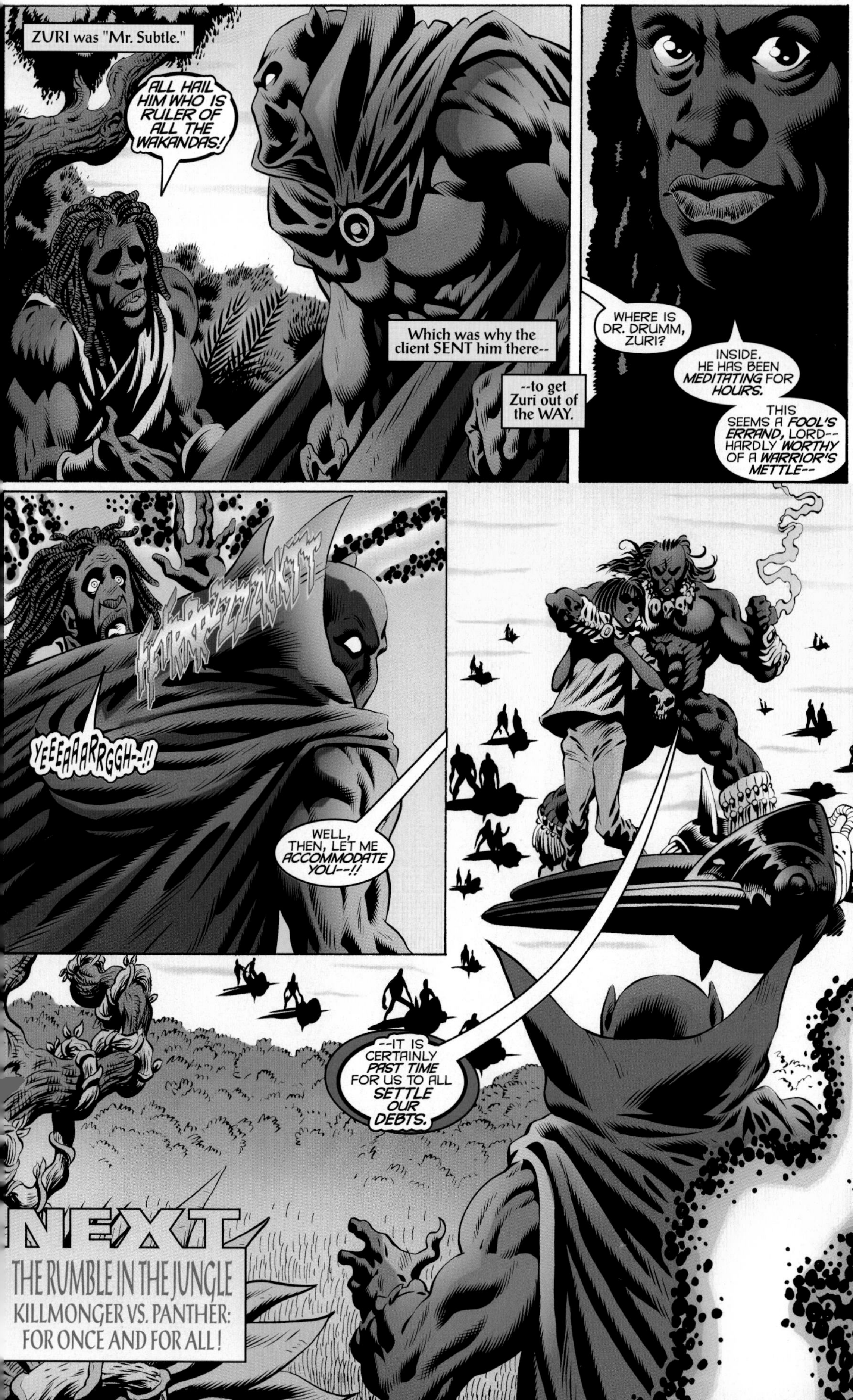

ZURI was "Mr. Subtle."
ALL HAIL HIM WHO IS RULER OF ALL THE WAKANDAS!
Which was why the client SENT him there--
--to get Zuri out of the WAY.
WHERE IS DR. DRUMM, ZURI?
INSIDE. HE HAS BEEN MEDITATING FOR HOURS.
THIS SEEMS A FOOL'S ERRAND, LORD--HARDLY WORTHY OF A WARRIOR'S METTLE--
YEEEAARRGGH--!!
WELL, THEN, LET ME ACCOMMODATE YOU--!!
--IT IS CERTAINLY PAST TIME FOR US TO ALL SETTLE OUR DEBTS.
NEXT
THE RUMBLE IN THE JUNGLE
KILLMONGER VS. PANTHER: FOR ONCE AND FOR ALL!

MARVEL KNIGHTS ANNUAL. IT TAKES PLACE BETWEEN BLACK PANTHER #5-6.

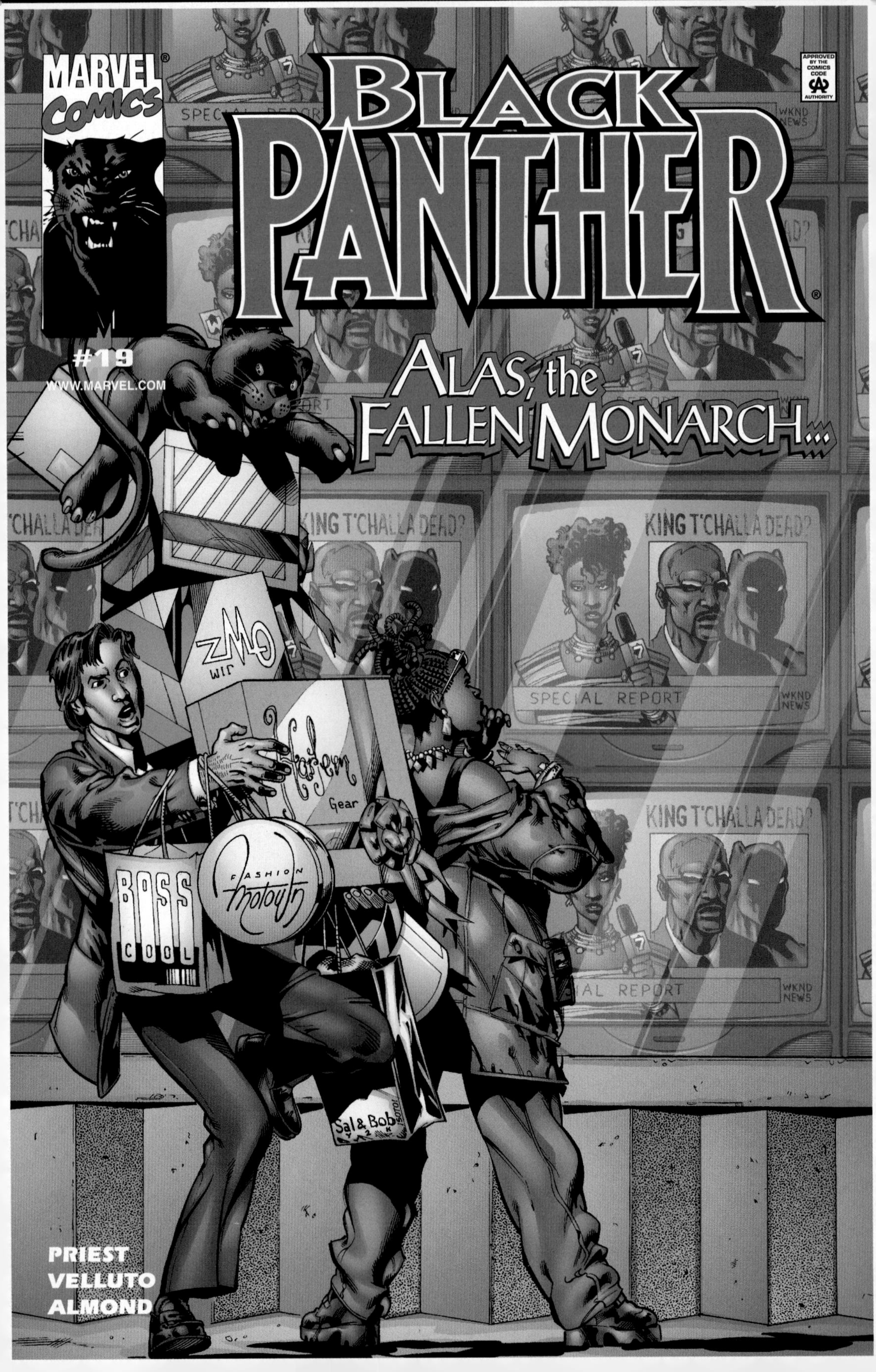

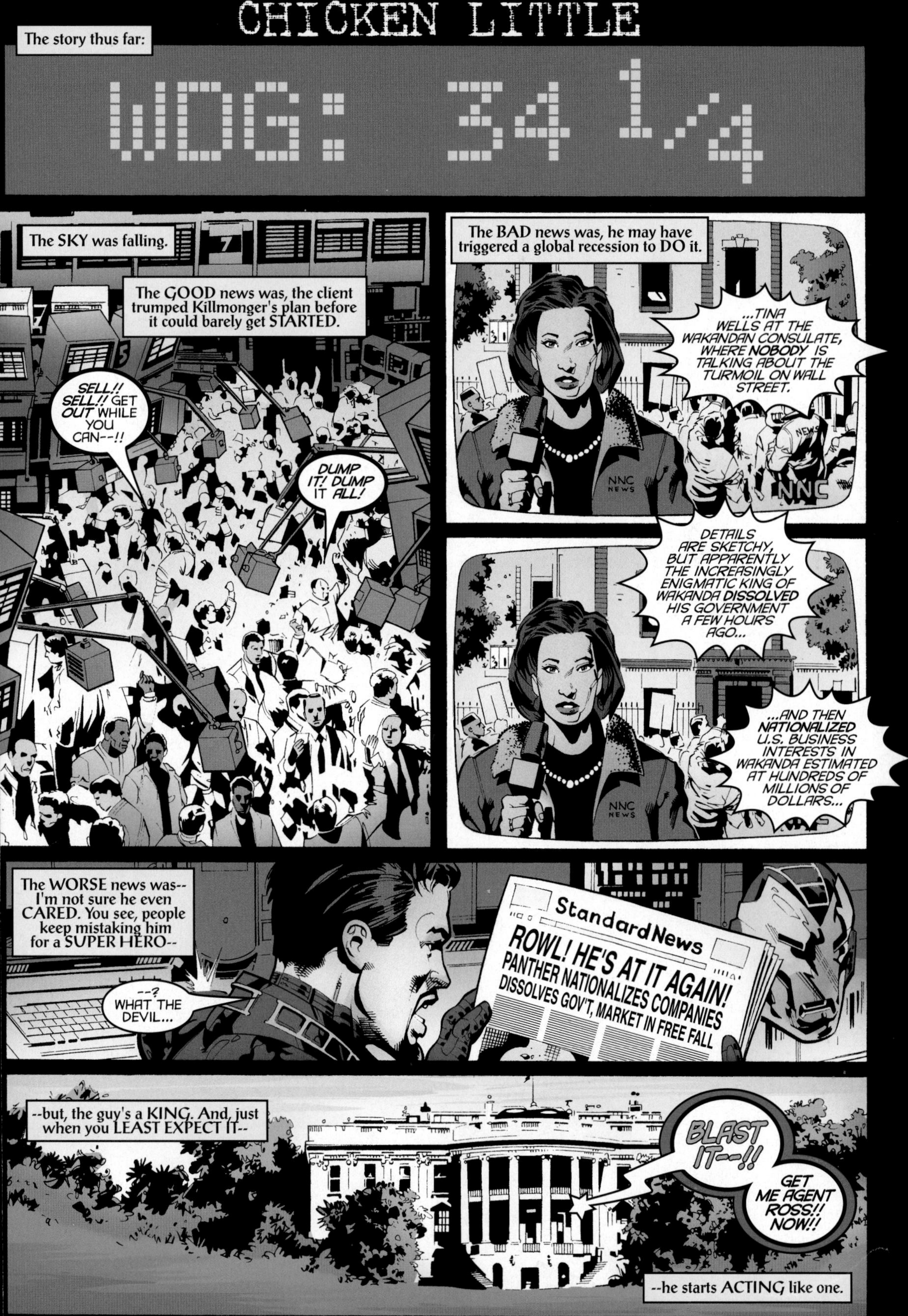
CHICKEN LITTLE
The story thus far:
WDG: 34 1/4
The SKY was falling.
The GOOD news was, the client trumped Killmonger's plan before it could barely get STARTED.
SELL!! SELL!! GET OUT WHILE YOU CAN--!!
DUMP IT! DUMP IT ALL!
The BAD news was, he may have triggered a global recession to DO it.
...TINA WELLS AT THE WAKANDAN CONSULATE, WHERE NOBODY IS TALKING ABOUT THE TURMOIL ON WALL STREET.
NNC NEWS
DETAILS ARE SKETCHY, BUT APPARENTLY THE INCREASINGLY ENIGMATIC KING OF WAKANDA DISSOLVED HIS GOVERNMENT A FEW HOURS AGO...
...AND THEN NATIONALIZED U.S. BUSINESS INTERESTS IN WAKANDA ESTIMATED AT HUNDREDS OF MILLIONS OF DOLLARS...
The WORSE news was-- I'm not sure he even CARED. You see, people keep mistaking him for a SUPER HERO--
--? WHAT THE DEVIL...
Standard News
ROWL! HE'S AT IT AGAIN! PANTHER NATIONALIZES COMPANIES DISSOLVES GOV'T, MARKET IN FREE FALL
--but, the guy's a KING. And, just when you LEAST EXPECT IT--
BLAST IT--!!
GET ME AGENT ROSS!! NOW!!
--he starts ACTING like one.

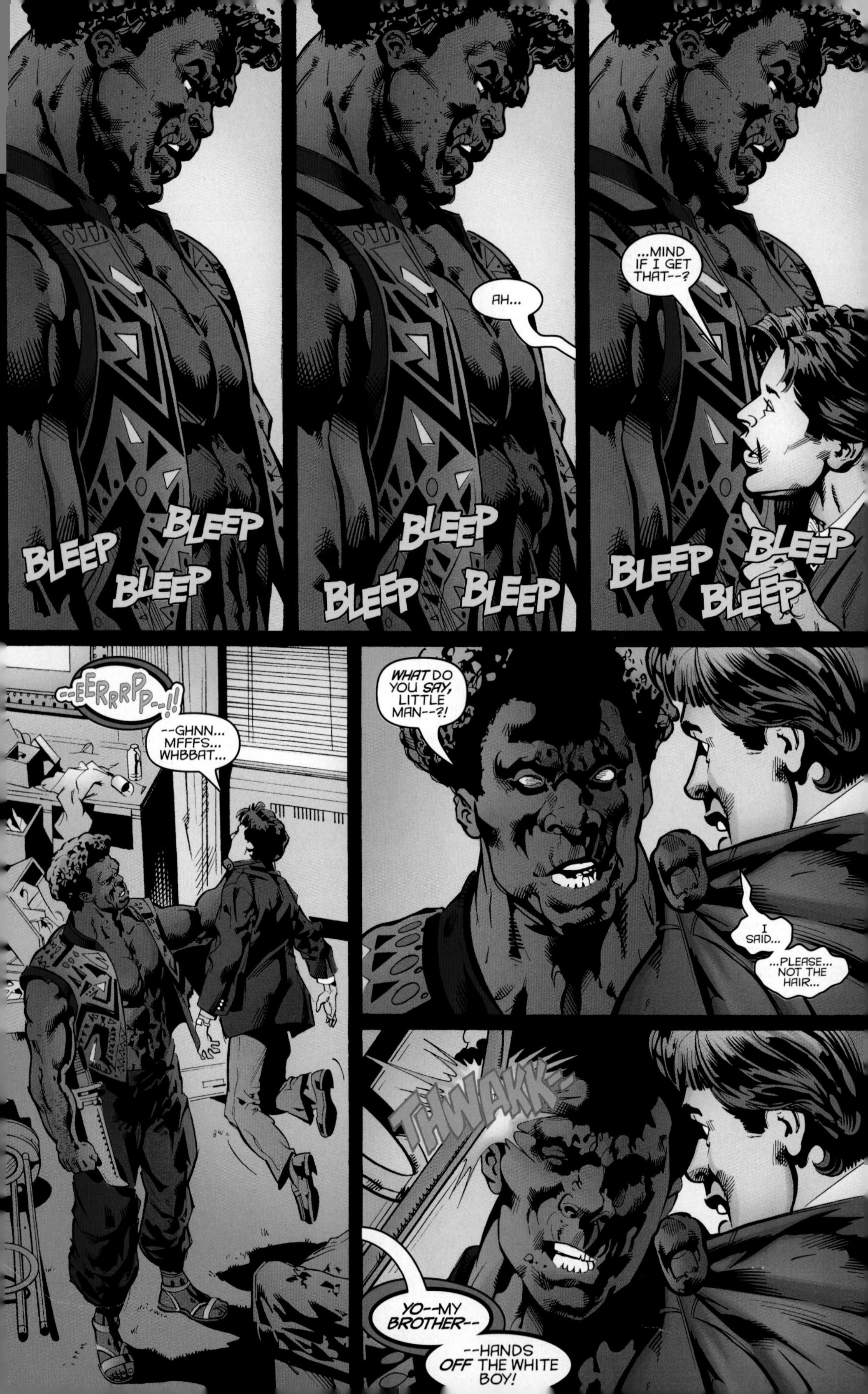
BLEEP
BLEEP
BLEEP
AH...
BLEEP
BLEEP
BLEEP
...MIND IF I GET THAT--?
BLEEP
BLEEP
BLEEP
--EERRRPP--!!
--GHNN... MFFFS... WHBBAT...
WHAT DO YOU SAY, LITTLE MAN--?!
I SAID...
...PLEASE... NOT THE HAIR...
THWAKK!
YO--MY BROTHER--
--HANDS OFF THE WHITE BOY!

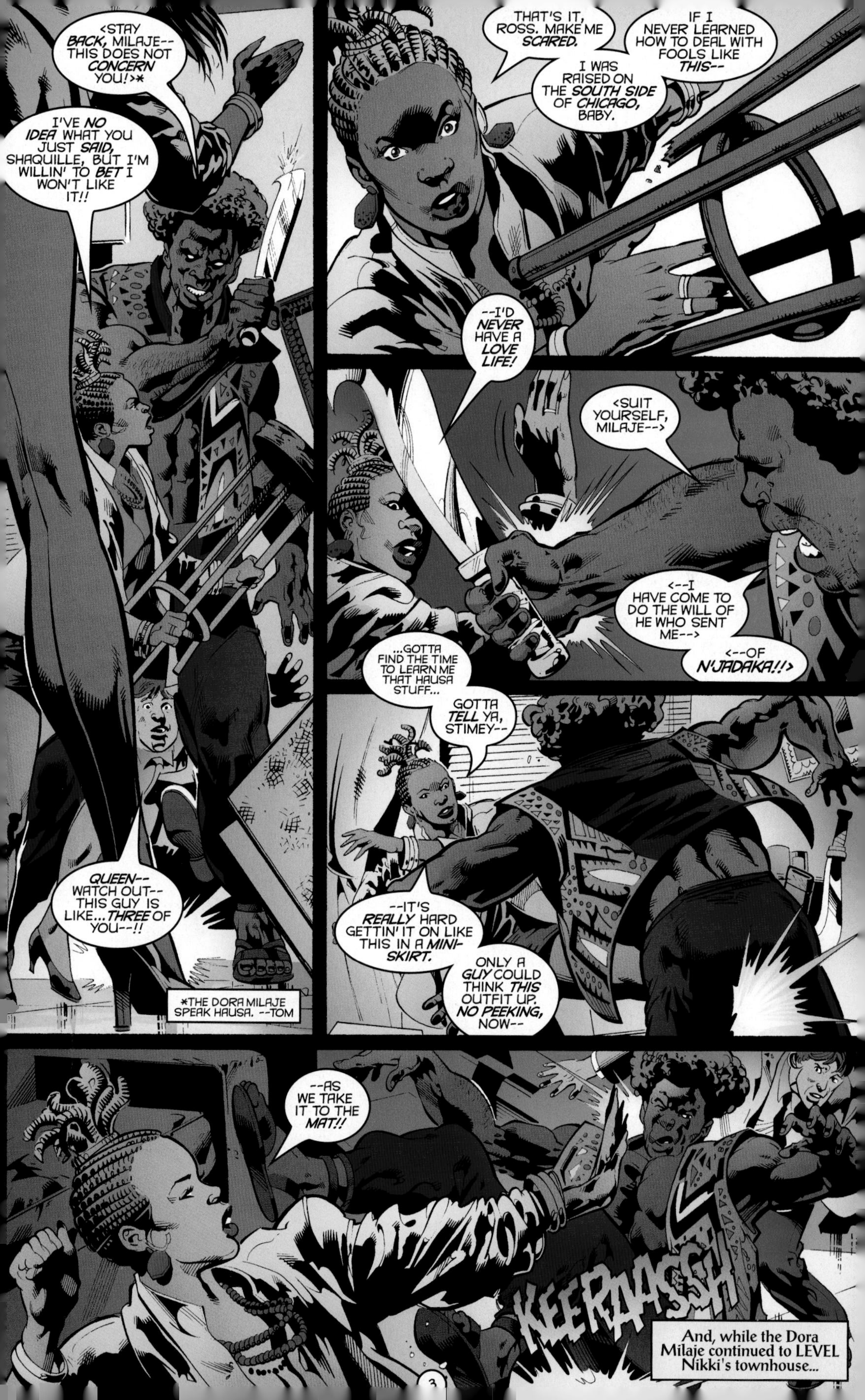

<STAY BACK, MILAJE-- THIS DOES NOT CONCERN YOU!>*
I'VE NO IDEA WHAT YOU JUST SAID, SHAQUILLE, BUT I'M WILLIN' TO BET I WON'T LIKE IT!!
QUEEN-- WATCH OUT-- THIS GUY IS LIKE...THREE OF YOU--!!
*THE DORA MILAJE SPEAK HAUSA. --TOM
THAT'S IT, ROSS. MAKE ME SCARED.
IF I NEVER LEARNED HOW TO DEAL WITH FOOLS LIKE THIS--
I WAS RAISED ON THE SOUTH SIDE OF CHICAGO, BABY.
--I'D NEVER HAVE A LOVE LIFE!
<SUIT YOURSELF, MILAJE-->
<--I HAVE COME TO DO THE WILL OF HE WHO SENT ME-->
<--OF N'JADAKA!!>
...GOTTA FIND THE TIME TO LEARN ME THAT HAUSA STUFF...
GOTTA TELL YA, STIMEY--
--IT'S REALLY HARD GETTIN' IT ON LIKE THIS IN A MINI-SKIRT.
ONLY A GUY COULD THINK THIS OUTFIT UP. NO PEEKING, NOW--
--AS WE TAKE IT TO THE MAT!!
KEERAASSH
And, while the Dora Milaje continued to LEVEL Nikki's townhouse...

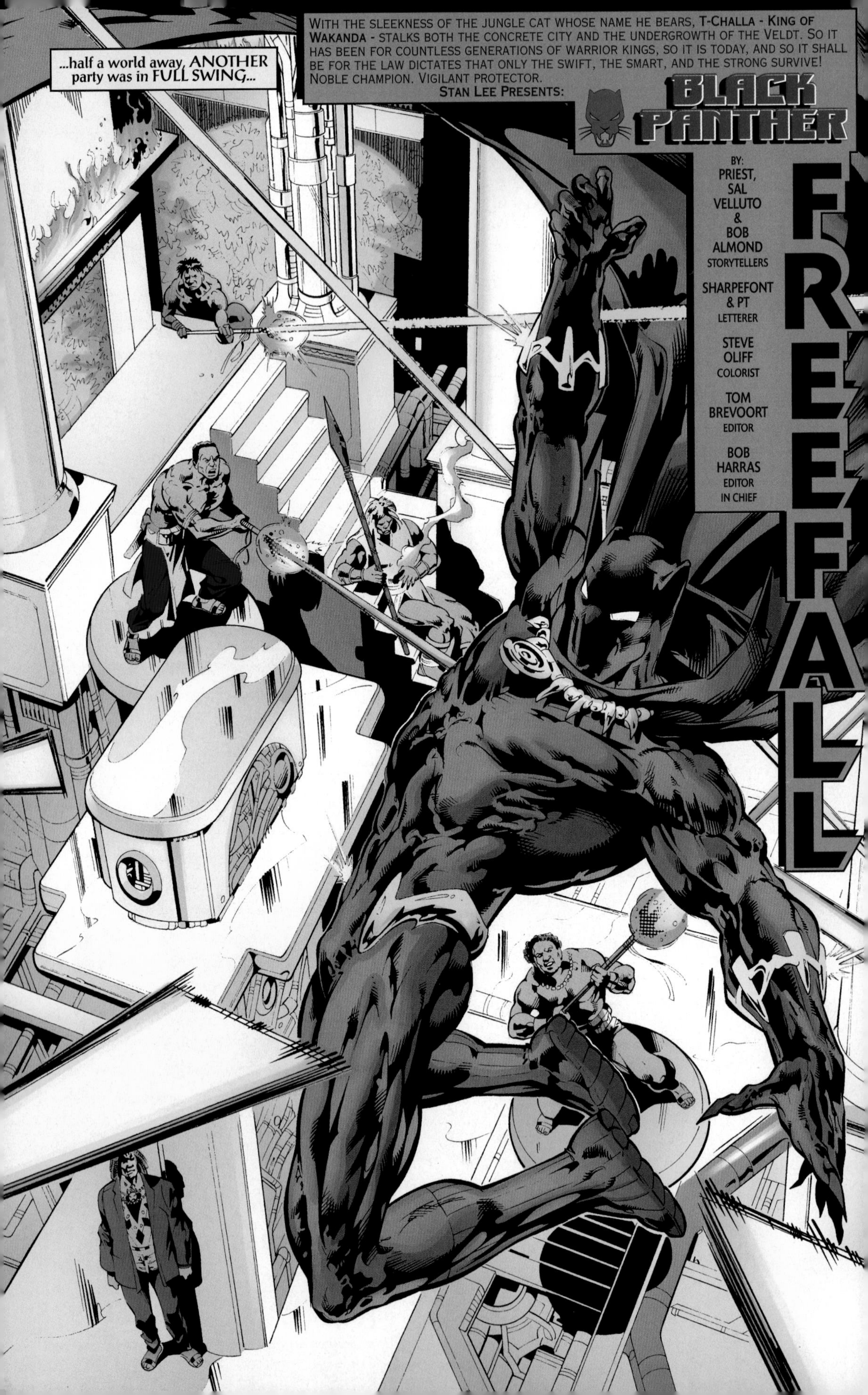
...half a world away, ANOTHER party was in FULL SWING...
WITH THE SLEEKNESS OF THE JUNGLE CAT WHOSE NAME HE BEARS, T-CHALLA - KING OF WAKANDA - STALKS BOTH THE CONCRETE CITY AND THE UNDERGROWTH OF THE VELDT. SO IT HAS BEEN FOR COUNTLESS GENERATIONS OF WARRIOR KINGS, SO IT IS TODAY, AND SO IT SHALL BE FOR THE LAW DICTATES THAT ONLY THE SWIFT, THE SMART, AND THE STRONG SURVIVE! NOBLE CHAMPION. VIGILANT PROTECTOR.
STAN LEE PRESENTS:
BLACK PANTHER
BY: PRIEST, SAL VELLUTO & BOB ALMOND STORYTELLERS
SHARPEFONT & PT LETTERER
STEVE OLIFF COLORIST
TOM BREVOORT EDITOR
BOB HARRAS EDITOR IN CHIEF
FREEFALL

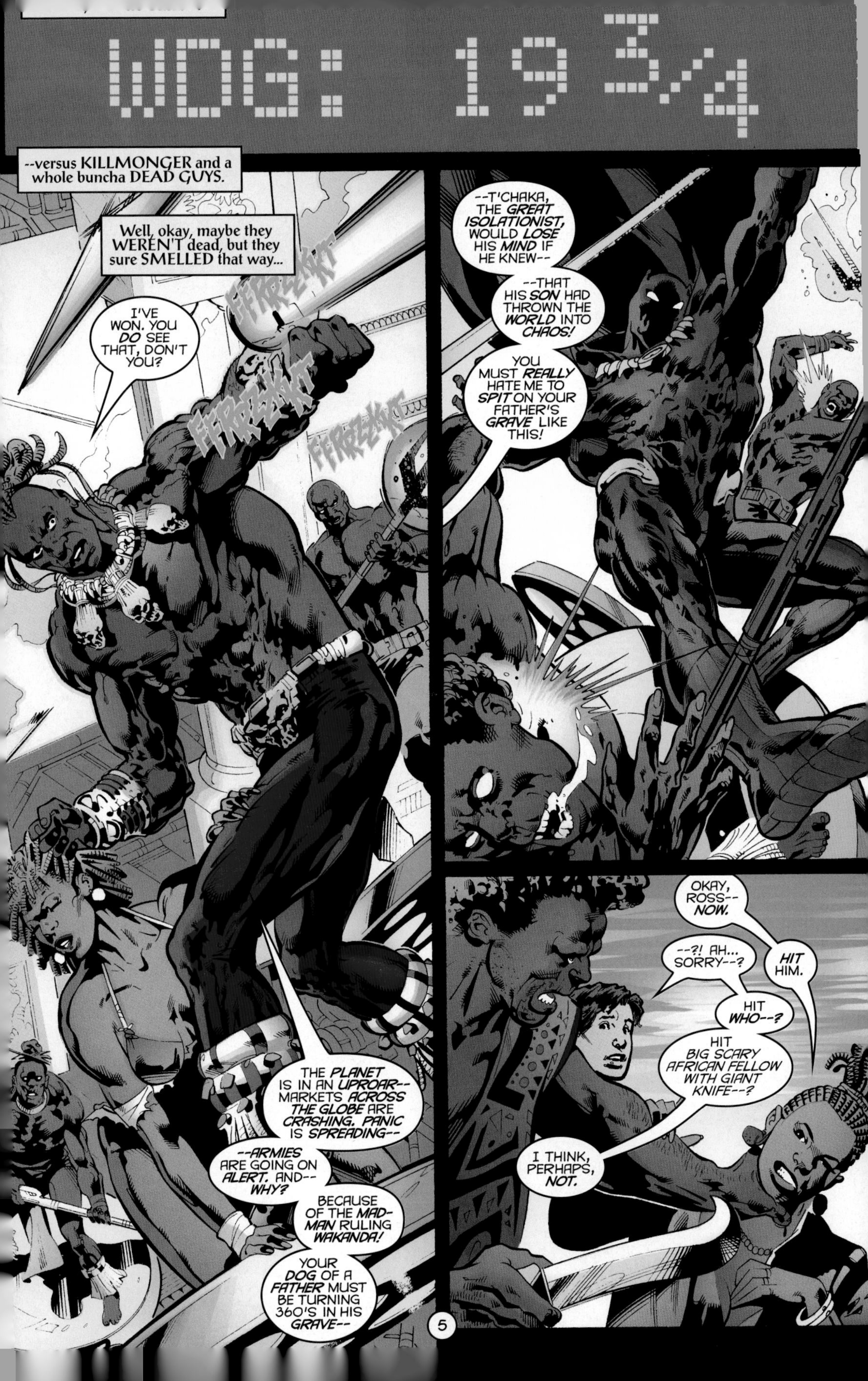

WDG: 19 3/4
--versus KILLMONGER and a whole buncha DEAD GUYS.
Well, okay, maybe they WEREN'T dead, but they sure SMELLED that way...
I'VE WON. YOU DO SEE THAT, DON'T YOU?
FFRRZZKKT
FFRRZZKKT
FFRRZZKKT
FFRRZZKKT
THE PLANET IS IN AN UPROAR-- MARKETS ACROSS THE GLOBE ARE CRASHING. PANIC IS SPREADING--
--ARMIES ARE GOING ON ALERT. AND-- WHY?
BECAUSE OF THE MADMAN RULING WAKANDA!
YOUR DOG OF A FATHER MUST BE TURNING 360'S IN HIS GRAVE--
--T'CHAKA, THE GREAT ISOLATIONIST, WOULD LOSE HIS MIND IF HE KNEW--
--THAT HIS SON HAD THROWN THE WORLD INTO CHAOS!
YOU MUST REALLY HATE ME TO SPIT ON YOUR FATHER'S GRAVE LIKE THIS!
OKAY, ROSS-- NOW.
HIT HIM.
--?! AH... SORRY--?
HIT WHO--?
HIT BIG SCARY AFRICAN FELLOW WITH GIANT KNIFE--?
I THINK, PERHAPS, NOT.

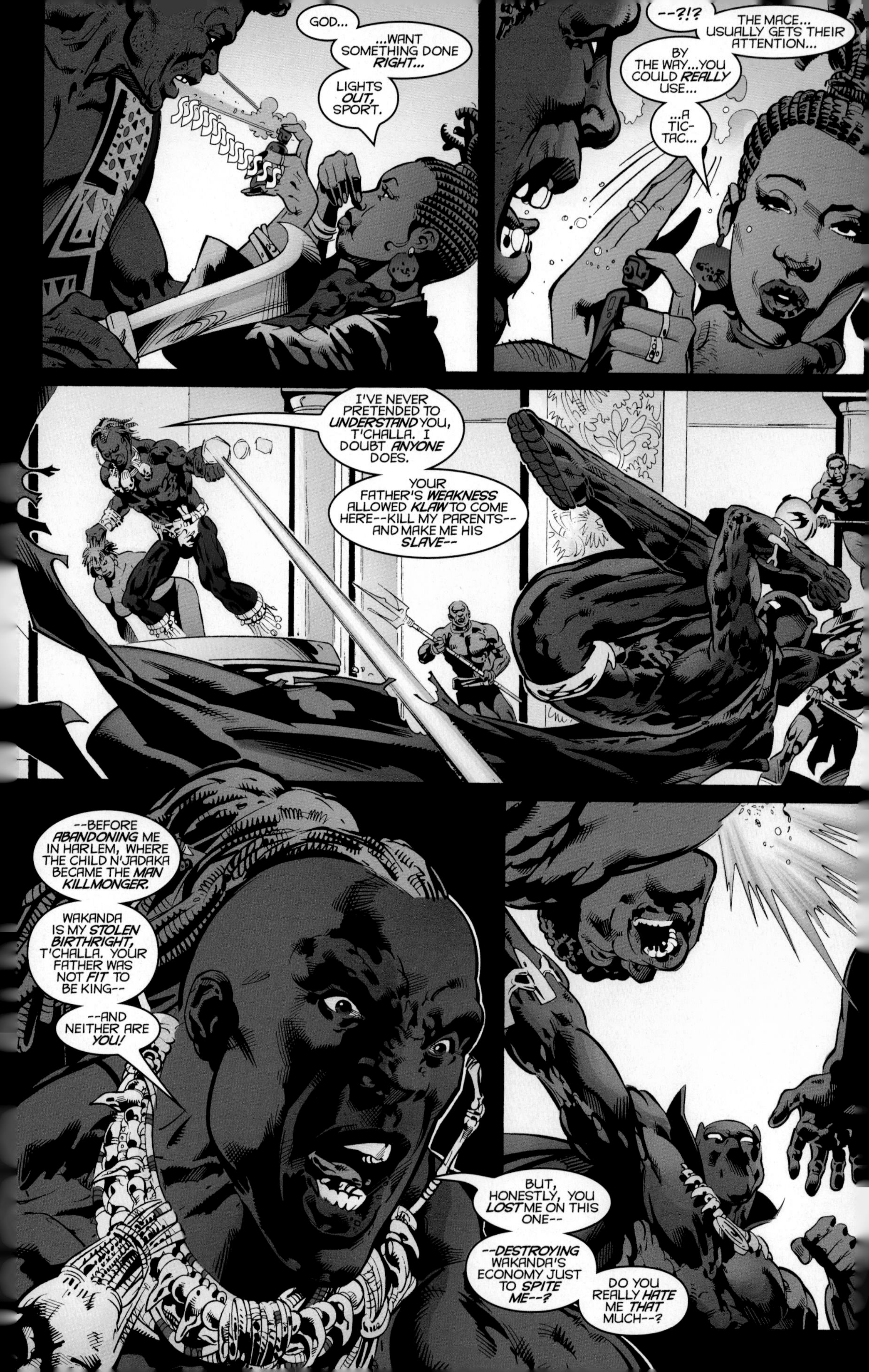
GOD...
...WANT SOMETHING DONE RIGHT...
LIGHTS OUT, SPORT.
SSSSSSSSSSSSSS
--?!?
THE MACE... USUALLY GETS THEIR ATTENTION...
BY THE WAY...YOU COULD REALLY USE...
...A TIC-TAC...
I'VE NEVER PRETENDED TO UNDERSTAND YOU, T'CHALLA. I DOUBT ANYONE DOES.
YOUR FATHER'S WEAKNESS ALLOWED KLAW TO COME HERE--KILL MY PARENTS--AND MAKE ME HIS SLAVE--
--BEFORE ABANDONING ME IN HARLEM, WHERE THE CHILD N'JADAKA BECAME THE MAN KILLMONGER.
WAKANDA IS MY STOLEN BIRTHRIGHT, T'CHALLA. YOUR FATHER WAS NOT FIT TO BE KING--
--AND NEITHER ARE YOU!
BUT, HONESTLY, YOU LOST ME ON THIS ONE--
--DESTROYING WAKANDA'S ECONOMY JUST TO SPITE ME--?
DO YOU REALLY HATE ME THAT MUCH--?

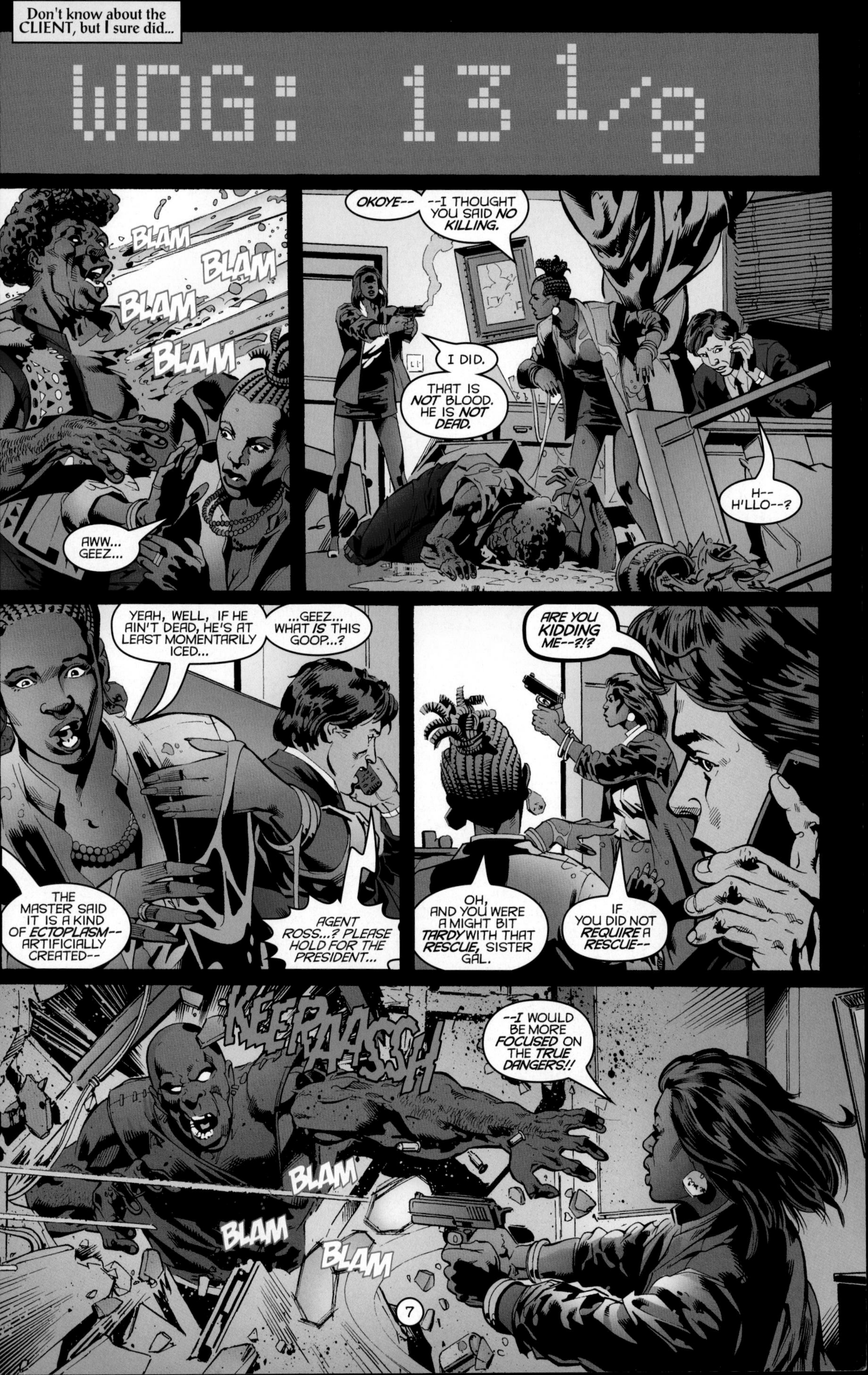

Don't know about the CLIENT, but I sure did...
WDG: 13 1/8
BLAM
BLAM
BLAM
BLAM
AWW... GEEZ...
OKOYE--
--I THOUGHT YOU SAID NO KILLING.
I DID.
THAT IS NOT BLOOD. HE IS NOT DEAD.
H-- H'LLO--?
YEAH, WELL, IF HE AIN'T DEAD, HE'S AT LEAST MOMENTARILY ICED...
...GEEZ... WHAT IS THIS GOOP...?
THE MASTER SAID IT IS A KIND OF ECTOPLASM-- ARTIFICIALLY CREATED--
AGENT ROSS...? PLEASE HOLD FOR THE PRESIDENT...
ARE YOU KIDDING ME--?!?
OH, AND YOU WERE A MIGHT BIT TARDY WITH THAT RESCUE, SISTER GAL.
IF YOU DID NOT REQUIRE A RESCUE--
KEERAASCH
--I WOULD BE MORE FOCUSED ON THE TRUE DANGERS!!
BLAM
BLAM
BLAM

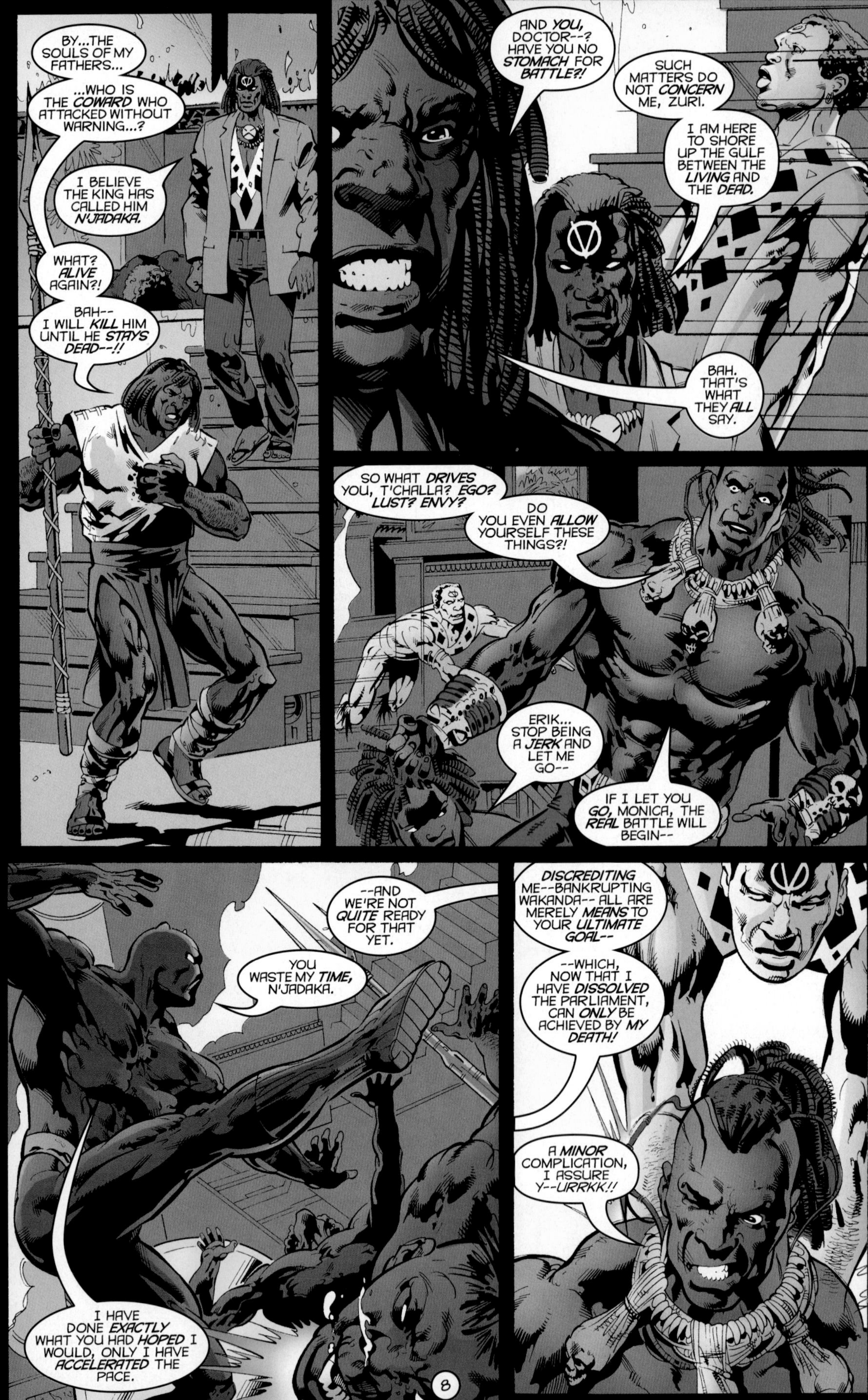
BY...THE SOULS OF MY FATHERS...
...WHO IS THE COWARD WHO ATTACKED WITHOUT WARNING...?
I BELIEVE THE KING HAS CALLED HIM N'JADAKA.
WHAT? ALIVE AGAIN?!
BAH-- I WILL KILL HIM UNTIL HE STAYS DEAD--!!
AND YOU, DOCTOR--? HAVE YOU NO STOMACH FOR BATTLE?!
SUCH MATTERS DO NOT CONCERN ME, ZURI.
I AM HERE TO SHORE UP THE GULF BETWEEN THE LIVING AND THE DEAD.
BAH. THAT'S WHAT THEY ALL SAY.
SO WHAT DRIVES YOU, T'CHALLA? EGO? LUST? ENVY?
DO YOU EVEN ALLOW YOURSELF THESE THINGS?!
ERIK... STOP BEING A JERK AND LET ME GO--
IF I LET YOU GO, MONICA, THE REAL BATTLE WILL BEGIN--
--AND WE'RE NOT QUITE READY FOR THAT YET.
YOU WASTE MY TIME, N'JADAKA.
I HAVE DONE EXACTLY WHAT YOU HAD HOPED I WOULD, ONLY I HAVE ACCELERATED THE PACE.
DISCREDITING ME--BANKRUPTING WAKANDA-- ALL ARE MERELY MEANS TO YOUR ULTIMATE GOAL--
--WHICH, NOW THAT I HAVE DISSOLVED THE PARLIAMENT, CAN ONLY BE ACHIEVED BY MY DEATH!
A MINOR COMPLICATION, I ASSURE Y--URRKK!!
8

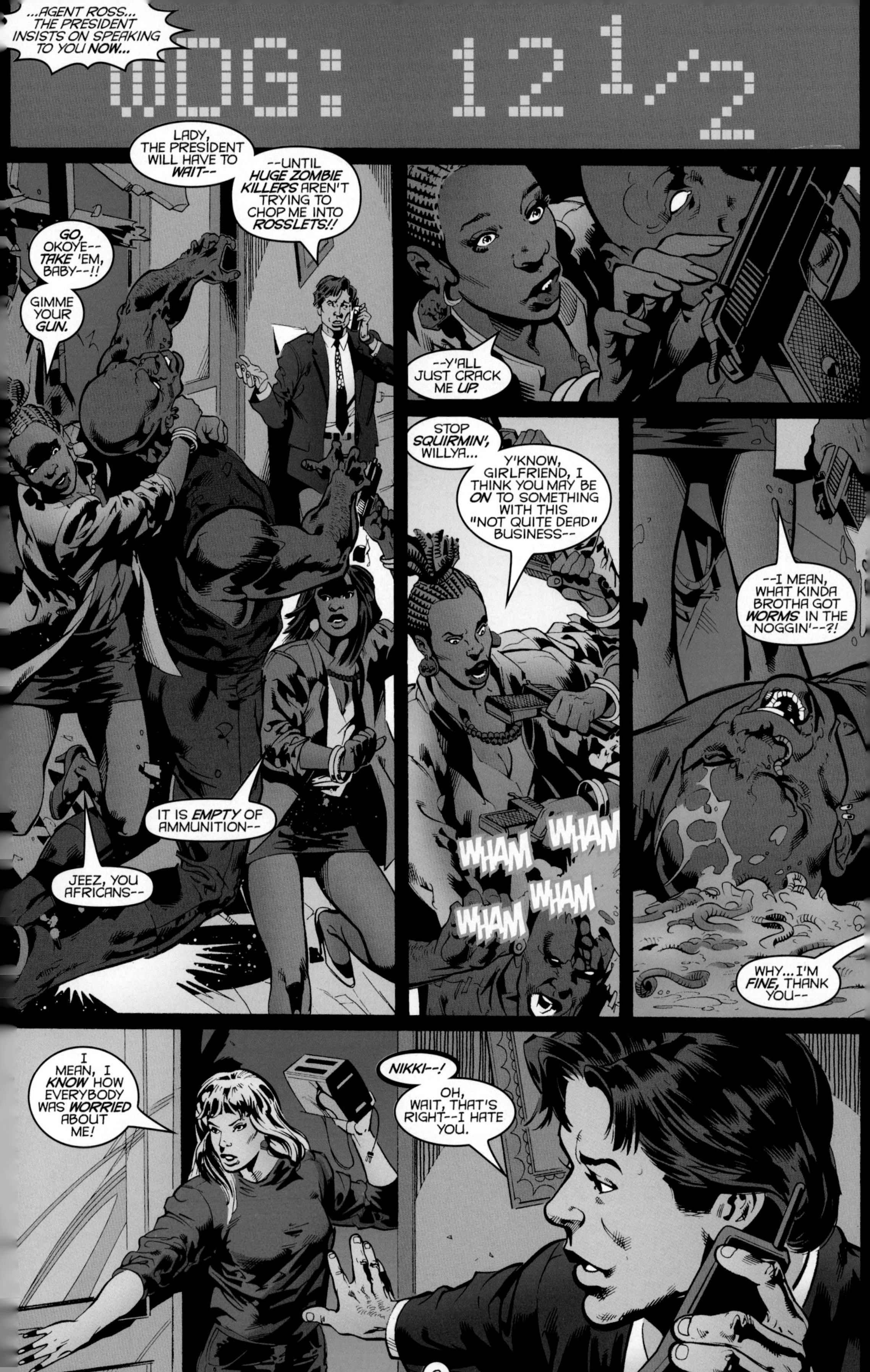
...AGENT ROSS... THE PRESIDENT INSISTS ON SPEAKING TO YOU NOW...
WDG: 12 1/2
LADY, THE PRESIDENT WILL HAVE TO WAIT--
--UNTIL HUGE ZOMBIE KILLERS AREN'T TRYING TO CHOP ME INTO ROSSLETS!!
GO, OKOYE-- TAKE 'EM, BABY--!!
GIMME YOUR GUN.
IT IS EMPTY OF AMMUNITION--
JEEZ, YOU AFRICANS--
--Y'ALL JUST CRACK ME UP.
STOP SQUIRMIN', WILLYA...
Y'KNOW, GIRLFRIEND, I THINK YOU MAY BE ON TO SOMETHING WITH THIS "NOT QUITE DEAD" BUSINESS--
WHAM WHAM WHAM WHAM
--I MEAN, WHAT KINDA BROTHA GOT WORMS IN THE NOGGIN'--?!
WHY...I'M FINE, THANK YOU--
I MEAN, I KNOW HOW EVERYBODY WAS WORRIED ABOUT ME!
NIKKI--!
OH, WAIT, THAT'S RIGHT--I HATE YOU.

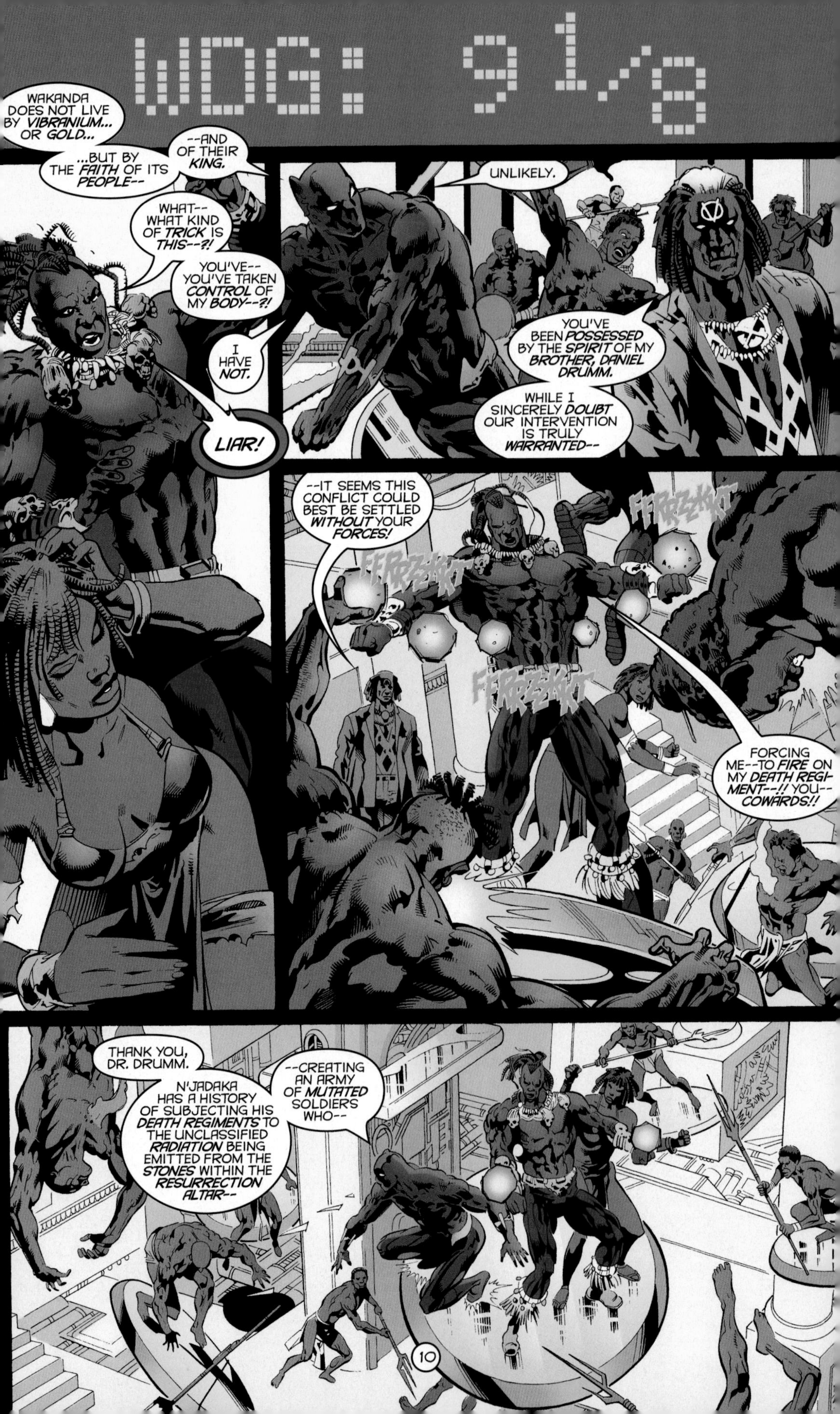
WDG: 9 1/8
WAKANDA DOES NOT LIVE BY VIBRANIUM... OR GOLD...
...BUT BY THE FAITH OF ITS PEOPLE--
--AND OF THEIR KING.
UNLIKELY.
WHAT-- WHAT KIND OF TRICK IS THIS--?!
YOU'VE-- YOU'VE TAKEN CONTROL OF MY BODY--?!
I HAVE NOT.
LIAR!
YOU'VE BEEN POSSESSED BY THE SPIRIT OF MY BROTHER, DANIEL DRUMM.
WHILE I SINCERELY DOUBT OUR INTERVENTION IS TRULY WARRANTED--
--IT SEEMS THIS CONFLICT COULD BEST BE SETTLED WITHOUT YOUR FORCES!
FFRRZZKKT
FFRRZZKKT
FFRRZZKKT
FORCING ME--TO FIRE ON MY DEATH REGIMENT--!! YOU-- COWARDS!!
THANK YOU, DR. DRUMM.
N'JADAKA HAS A HISTORY OF SUBJECTING HIS DEATH REGIMENTS TO THE UNCLASSIFIED RADIATION BEING EMITTED FROM THE STONES WITHIN THE RESURRECTION ALTAR--
--CREATING AN ARMY OF MUTATED SOLDIERS WHO--

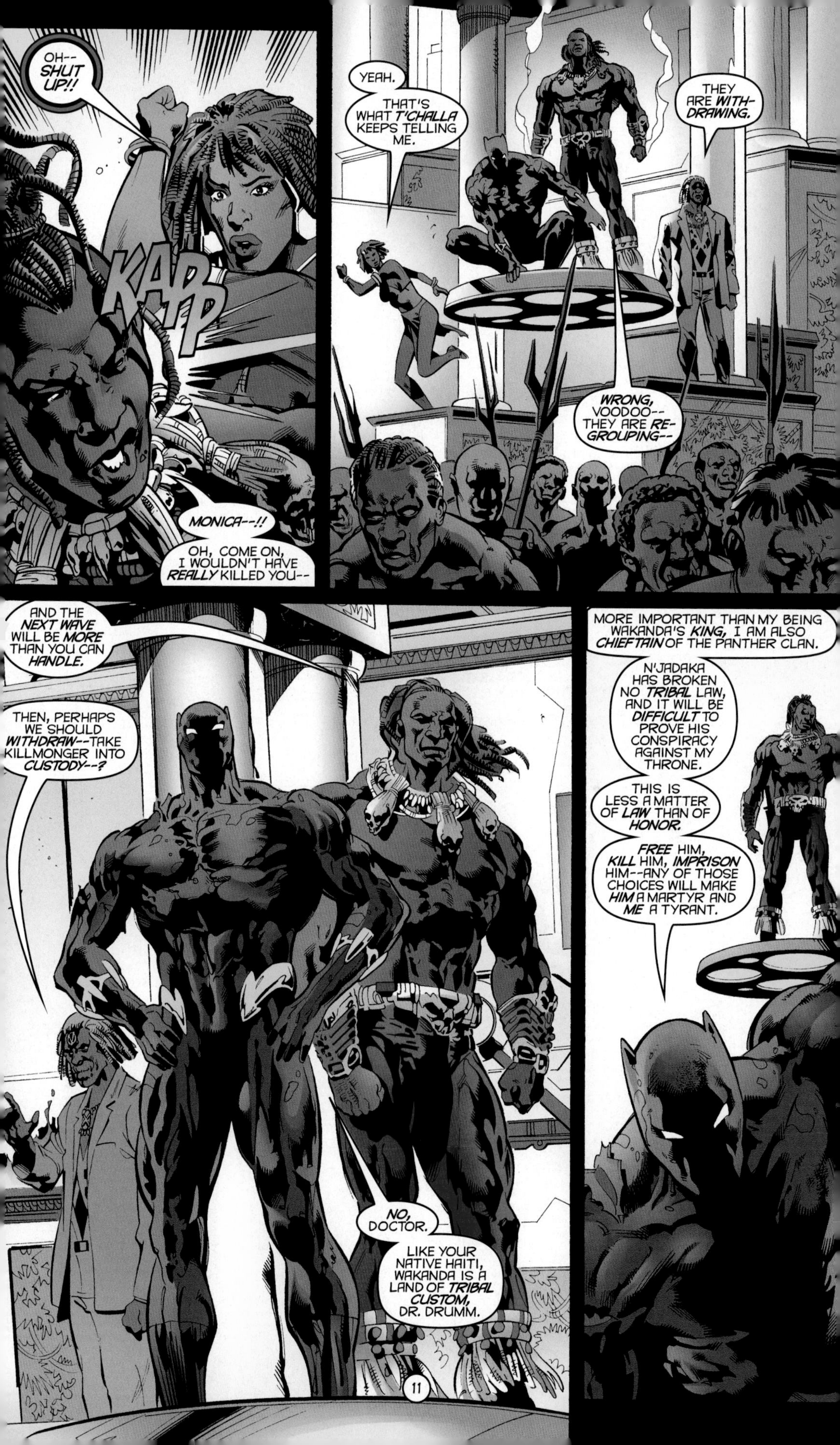

OH-- SHUT UP!!
KAP
MONICA--!!
OH, COME ON, I WOULDN'T HAVE REALLY KILLED YOU--
YEAH.
THAT'S WHAT T'CHALLA KEEPS TELLING ME.
THEY ARE WITH-DRAWING.
WRONG, VOODOO-- THEY ARE RE-GROUPING--
AND THE NEXT WAVE WILL BE MORE THAN YOU CAN HANDLE.
THEN, PERHAPS WE SHOULD WITHDRAW--TAKE KILLMONGER INTO CUSTODY--?
NO, DOCTOR.
LIKE YOUR NATIVE HAITI, WAKANDA IS A LAND OF TRIBAL CUSTOM, DR. DRUMM.
MORE IMPORTANT THAN MY BEING WAKANDA'S KING, I AM ALSO CHIEFTAIN OF THE PANTHER CLAN.
N'JADAKA HAS BROKEN NO TRIBAL LAW, AND IT WILL BE DIFFICULT TO PROVE HIS CONSPIRACY AGAINST MY THRONE.
THIS IS LESS A MATTER OF LAW THAN OF HONOR.
FREE HIM, KILL HIM, IMPRISON HIM--ANY OF THOSE CHOICES WILL MAKE HIM A MARTYR AND ME A TYRANT.

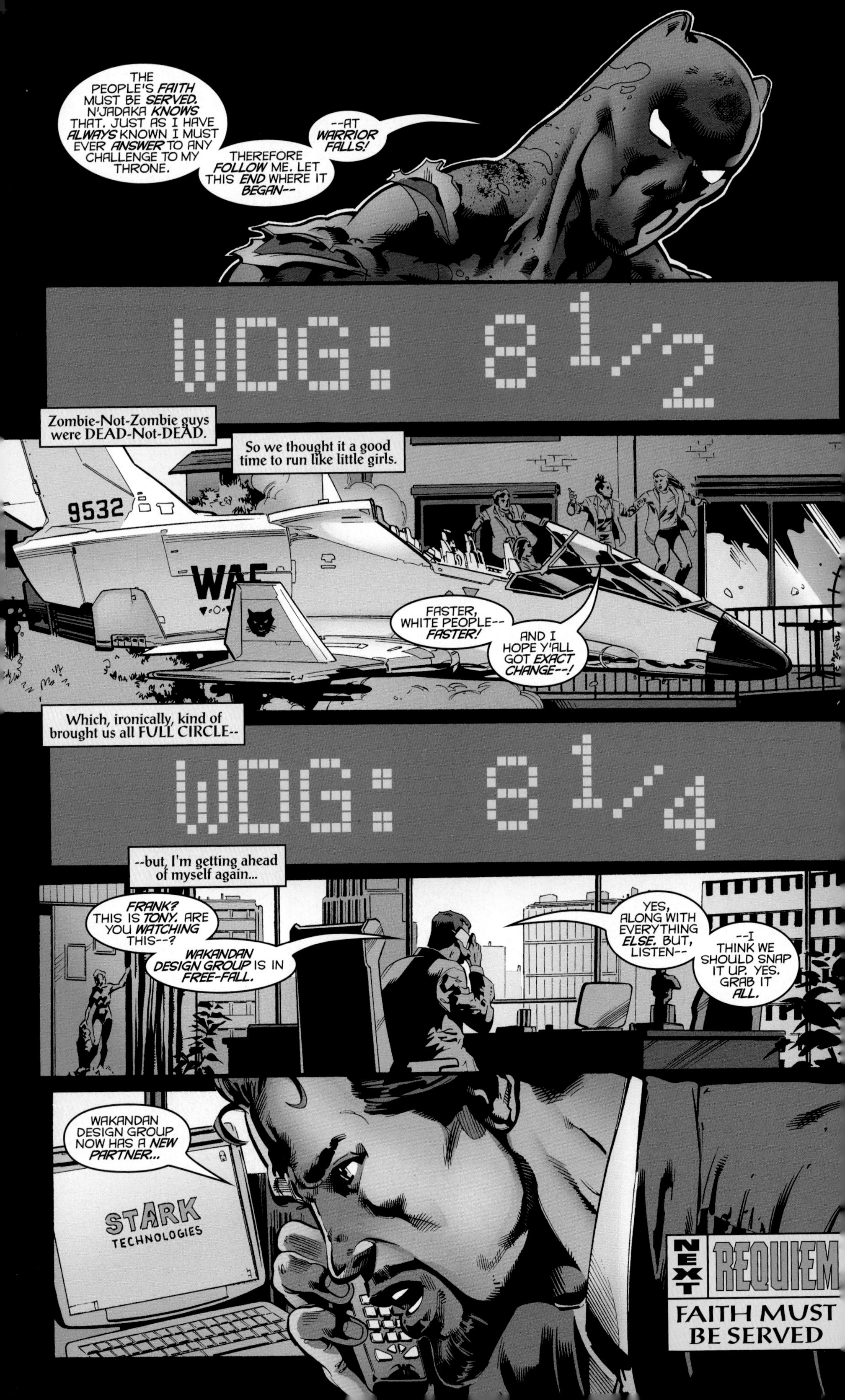

THE PEOPLE'S FAITH MUST BE SERVED. N'JADAKA KNOWS THAT. JUST AS I HAVE ALWAYS KNOWN I MUST EVER ANSWER TO ANY CHALLENGE TO MY THRONE.
THEREFORE FOLLOW ME. LET THIS END WHERE IT BEGAN--
--AT WARRIOR FALLS!
WDG: 8 1/2
Zombie-Not-Zombie guys were DEAD-Not-DEAD.
So we thought it a good time to run like little girls.
9532
WAF
FASTER, WHITE PEOPLE-- FASTER!
AND I HOPE Y'ALL GOT EXACT CHANGE--!
Which, ironically, kind of brought us all FULL CIRCLE--
WDG: 8 1/4
--but, I'm getting ahead of myself again...
FRANK? THIS IS TONY. ARE YOU WATCHING THIS--?
WAKANDAN DESIGN GROUP IS IN FREE-FALL.
YES, ALONG WITH EVERYTHING ELSE. BUT, LISTEN--
--I THINK WE SHOULD SNAP IT UP. YES. GRAB IT ALL.
WAKANDAN DESIGN GROUP NOW HAS A NEW PARTNER...
STARK TECHNOLOGIES
NEXT REQUIEM
FAITH MUST BE SERVED

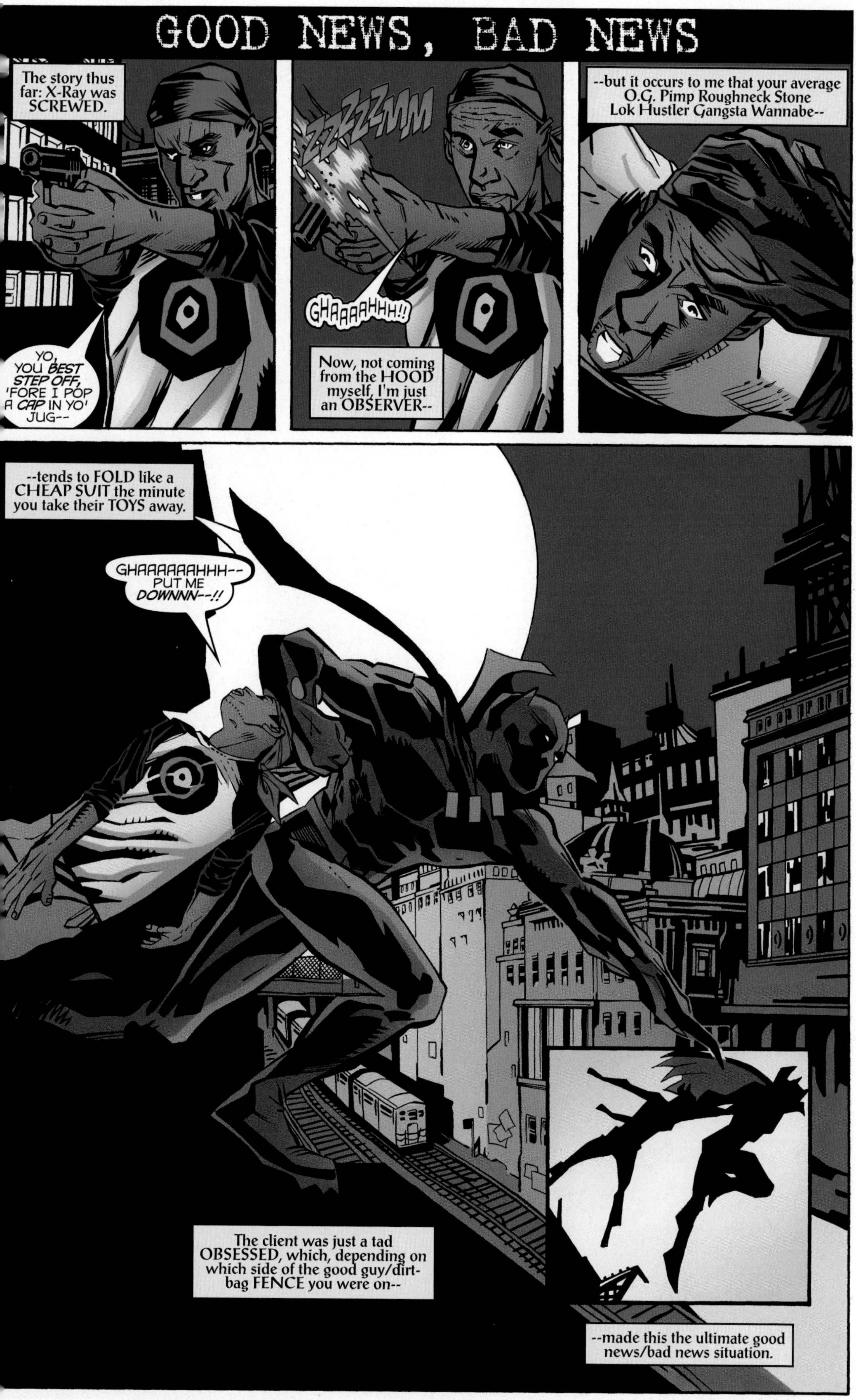
GOOD NEWS, BAD NEWS
The story thus far: X-Ray was SCREWED.
YO, YOU BEST STEP OFF, 'FORE I POP A CAP IN YO' JUG--
ZZZZZMM
GHAAAAHHH!!
Now, not coming from the HOOD myself, I'm just an OBSERVER--
--but it occurs to me that your average O.G. Pimp Roughneck Stone Lok Hustler Gangsta Wannabe--
--tends to FOLD like a CHEAP SUIT the minute you take their TOYS away.
GHAAAAAAHHH-- PUT ME DOWNNN--!!
The client was just a tad OBSESSED, which, depending on which side of the good guy/dirt-bag FENCE you were on--
--made this the ultimate good news/bad news situation.

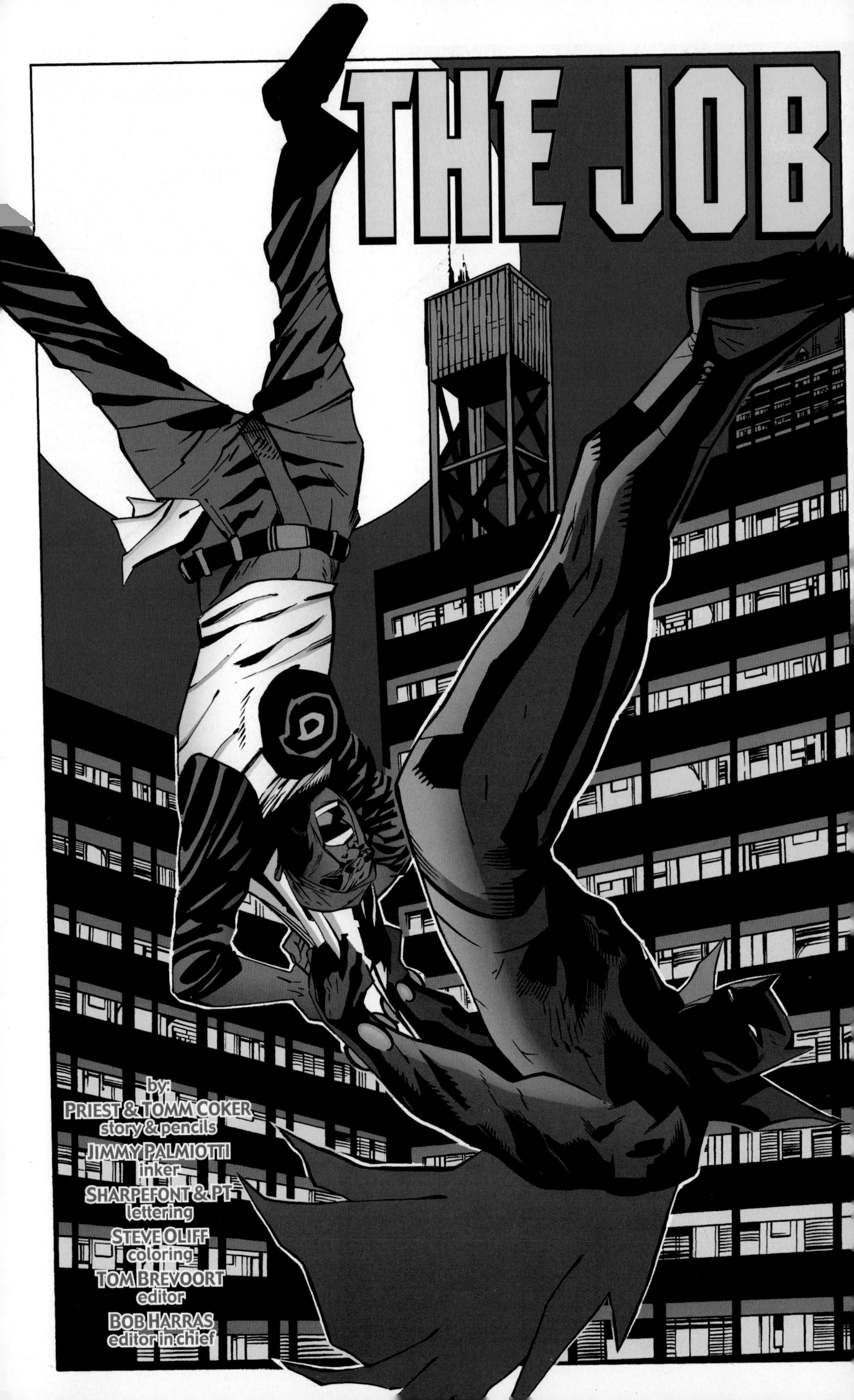
THE JOB
by:
PRIEST & TOMM COKER
story & pencils
JIMMY PALMIOTTI
inker
SHARPEFONT & PT
lettering
STEVE OLIFF
coloring
TOM BREVOORT
editor
BOB HARRAS
editor in chief

I wonder how that WORKS, exactly.

I mean, how do you stand in front of a mirror wearing spandex and think, "Yeah... I look goooood..."

< THEY NEED TO BE TAUGHT. >

WE ARE SURRENDERING THE VEHICLE.

JACK IS UP, WITCH!!

GETCHA JUG OUT THE CAR, FO' I PEEL 'LAT CAP.

YOU DEAF, WITCH--?!?

< MY LORD--? >

< DO NOT KILL THEM, BELOVED-- THEY ARE CHILDREN-- >

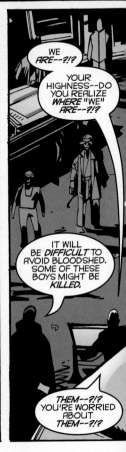

WE ARE--?!?

YOUR HIGHNESS--DO YOU REALIZE WHERE "WE" ARE--?!?

IT WILL BE DIFFICULT TO AVOID BLOODSHED. SOME OF THESE BOYS MIGHT BE KILLED.

THEM--?!? YOU'RE WORRIED ABOUT THEM--?!?

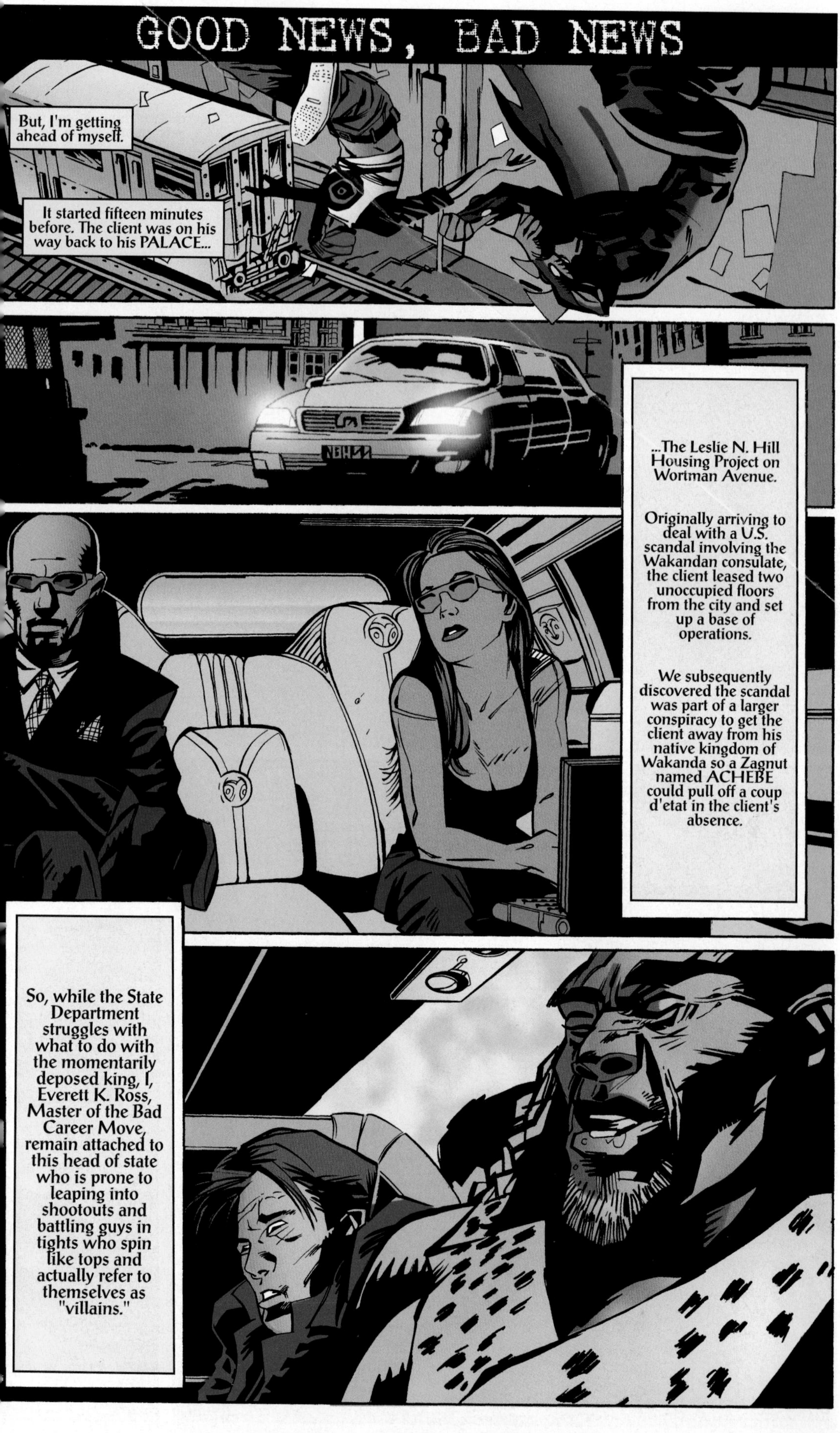
GOOD NEWS, BAD NEWS
But, I'm getting ahead of myself.
It started fifteen minutes before. The client was on his way back to his PALACE...
...The Leslie N. Hill Housing Project on Wortman Avenue.
Originally arriving to deal with a U.S. scandal involving the Wakandan consulate, the client leased two unoccupied floors from the city and set up a base of operations.
We subsequently discovered the scandal was part of a larger conspiracy to get the client away from his native kingdom of Wakanda so a Zagnut named ACHEBE could pull off a coup d'etat in the client's absence.
So, while the State Department struggles with what to do with the momentarily deposed king, I, Everett K. Ross, Master of the Bad Career Move, remain attached to this head of state who is prone to leaping into shootouts and battling guys in tights who spin like tops and actually refer to themselves as "villains."

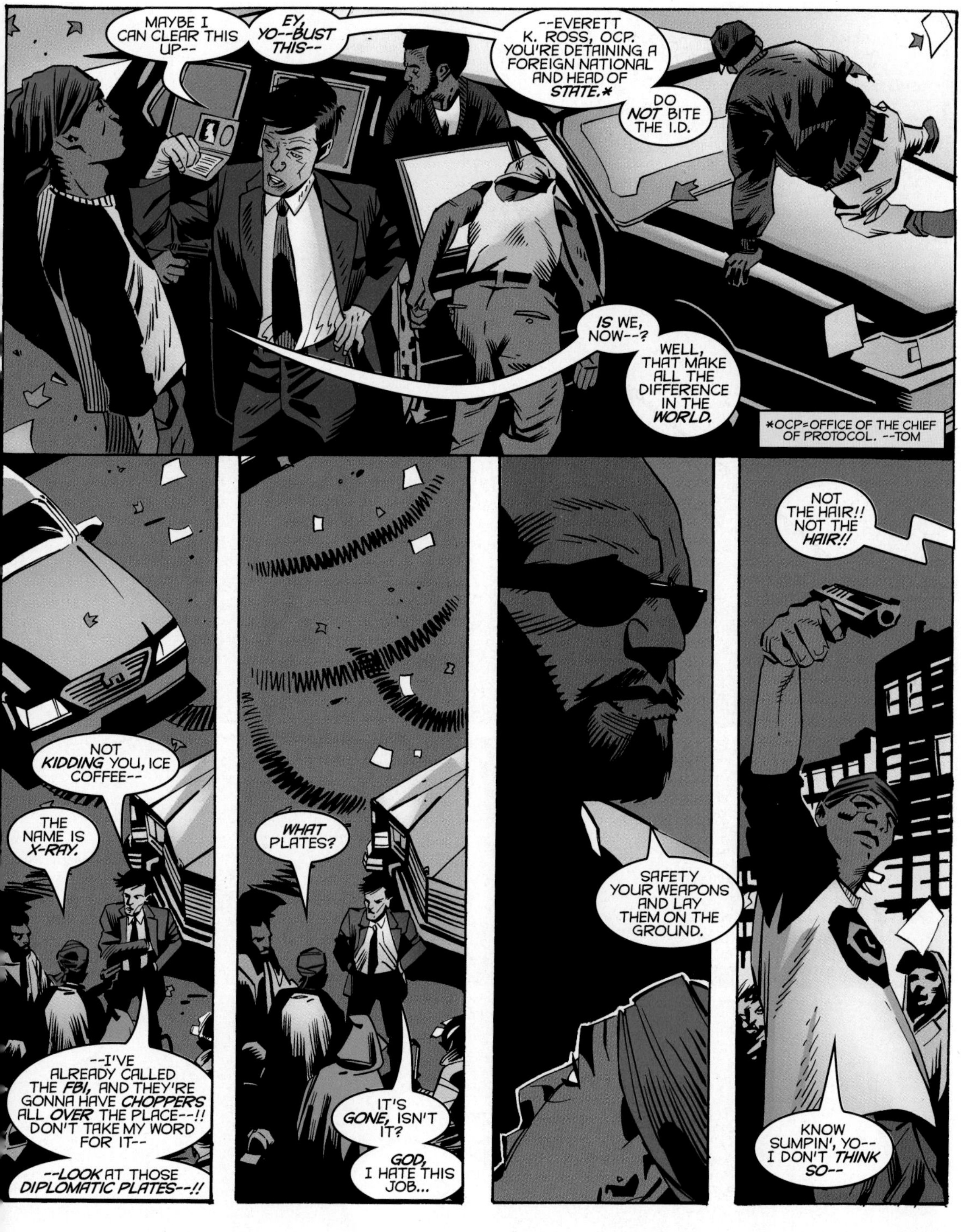

MAYBE I CAN CLEAR THIS UP--
EY, YO--BUST THIS--
--EVERETT K. ROSS, OCP. YOU'RE DETAINING A FOREIGN NATIONAL AND HEAD OF STATE.*
DO NOT BITE THE I.D.
IS WE, NOW--?
WELL, THAT MAKE ALL THE DIFFERENCE IN THE WORLD.
*OCP=OFFICE OF THE CHIEF OF PROTOCOL. --TOM
NOT KIDDING YOU, ICE COFFEE--
THE NAME IS X-RAY.
--I'VE ALREADY CALLED THE FBI, AND THEY'RE GONNA HAVE CHOPPERS ALL OVER THE PLACE--!! DON'T TAKE MY WORD FOR IT--
--LOOK AT THOSE DIPLOMATIC PLATES--!!
WHAT PLATES?
IT'S GONE, ISN'T IT?
GOD, I HATE THIS JOB...
SAFETY YOUR WEAPONS AND LAY THEM ON THE GROUND.
NOT THE HAIR!! NOT THE HAIR!!
KNOW SUMPIN', YO-- I DON'T THINK SO--

Suddenly, without making a sound, the biggest, brightest flashbulb I'd ever seen went off.

With my luck...I figured it was ALIENS...

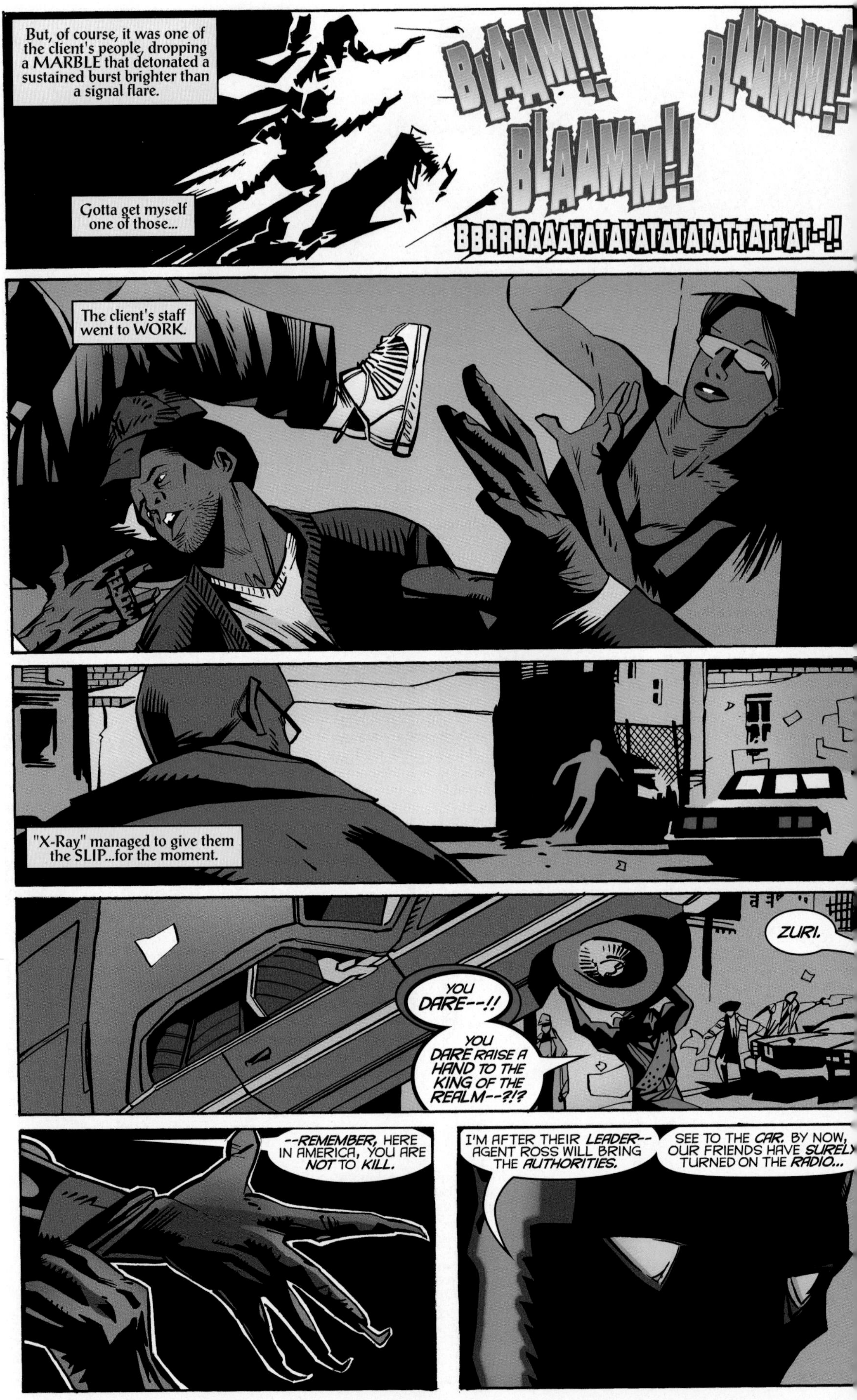
But, of course, it was one of the client's people, dropping a MARBLE that detonated a sustained burst brighter than a signal flare.
BLAAMM!!
BLAAMM!!
BLAAMM!!
Gotta get myself one of those...
BBRRRAAATATATATATATATTATTAT--!!
The client's staff went to WORK.
"X-Ray" managed to give them the SLIP...for the moment.
ZURI.
YOU DARE--!!
YOU DARE RAISE A HAND TO THE KING OF THE REALM--?!?
--REMEMBER, HERE IN AMERICA, YOU ARE NOT TO KILL.
I'M AFTER THEIR LEADER-- AGENT ROSS WILL BRING THE AUTHORITIES.
SEE TO THE CAR. BY NOW, OUR FRIENDS HAVE SURELY TURNED ON THE RADIO...

As it turned out, the client's car had one heck of an anti-theft system.

YO, MAN, KICK SOME *BEATS* UP IN THIS PIECE, MAN...

Think they call it "The Home Boybegone." What's so SAD is--

--I'M ALL *BORED* AND SPIT...

--it was SO OBVIOUS.

A neural stun blast put everybody on the floor--

SSSZZZAAACCKKK

GGGNNNNAAAAAAAAAAAHHHHH--!!

--and his DRIVER took charge of the car remotely.

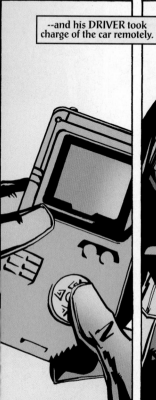

SCREEEEEE--

Which only left Mr. X-Ray, who'd managed to give us the SLIP--

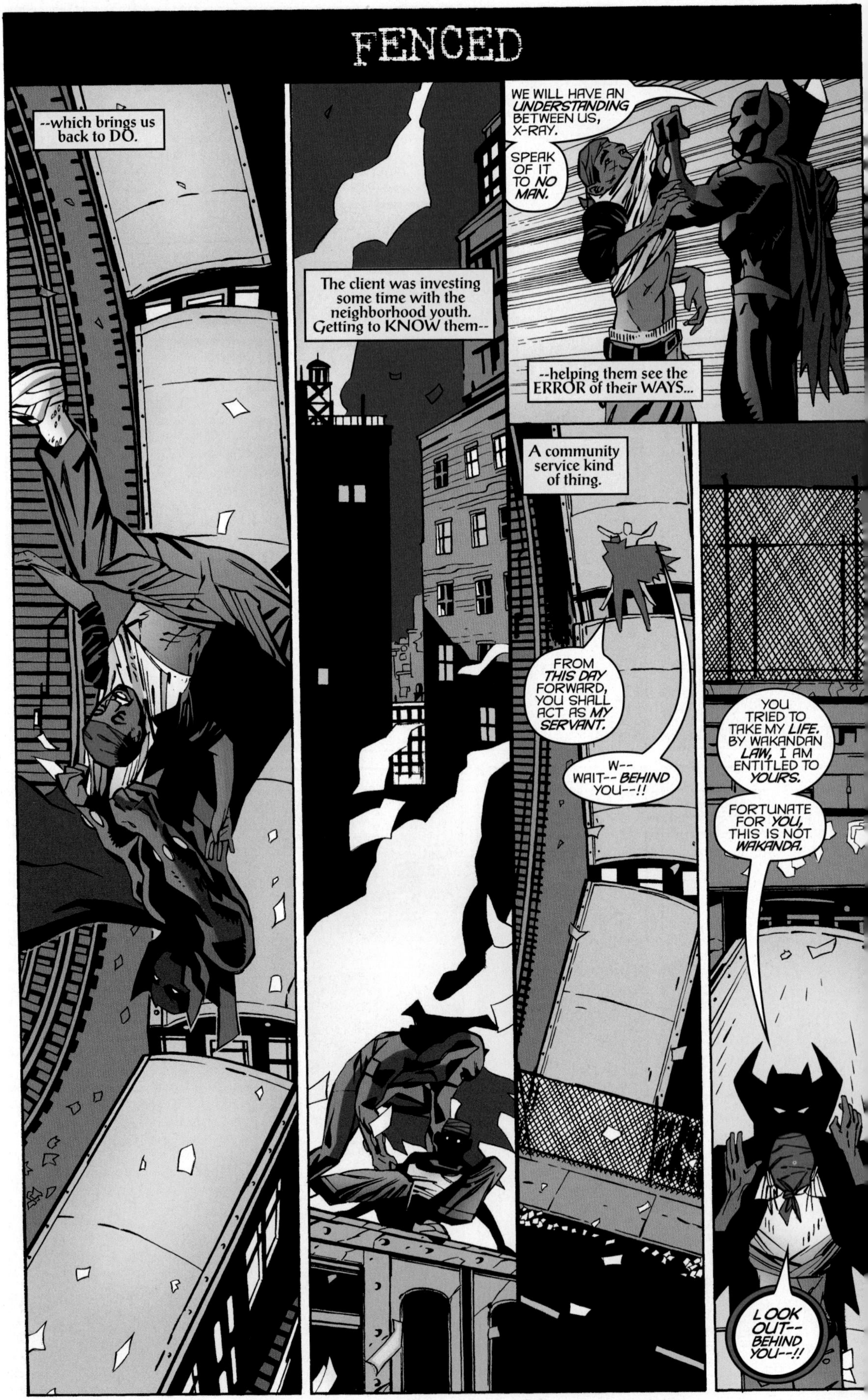
FENCED
--which brings us back to DO.
The client was investing some time with the neighborhood youth. Getting to KNOW them--
WE WILL HAVE AN UNDERSTANDING BETWEEN US, X-RAY.
SPEAK OF IT TO NO MAN.
--helping them see the ERROR of their WAYS...
A community service kind of thing.
FROM THIS DAY FORWARD, YOU SHALL ACT AS MY SERVANT.
W-- WAIT-- BEHIND YOU--!!
YOU TRIED TO TAKE MY LIFE. BY WAKANDAN LAW, I AM ENTITLED TO YOURS.
FORTUNATE FOR YOU, THIS IS NOT WAKANDA.
LOOK OUT-- BEHIND YOU--!!

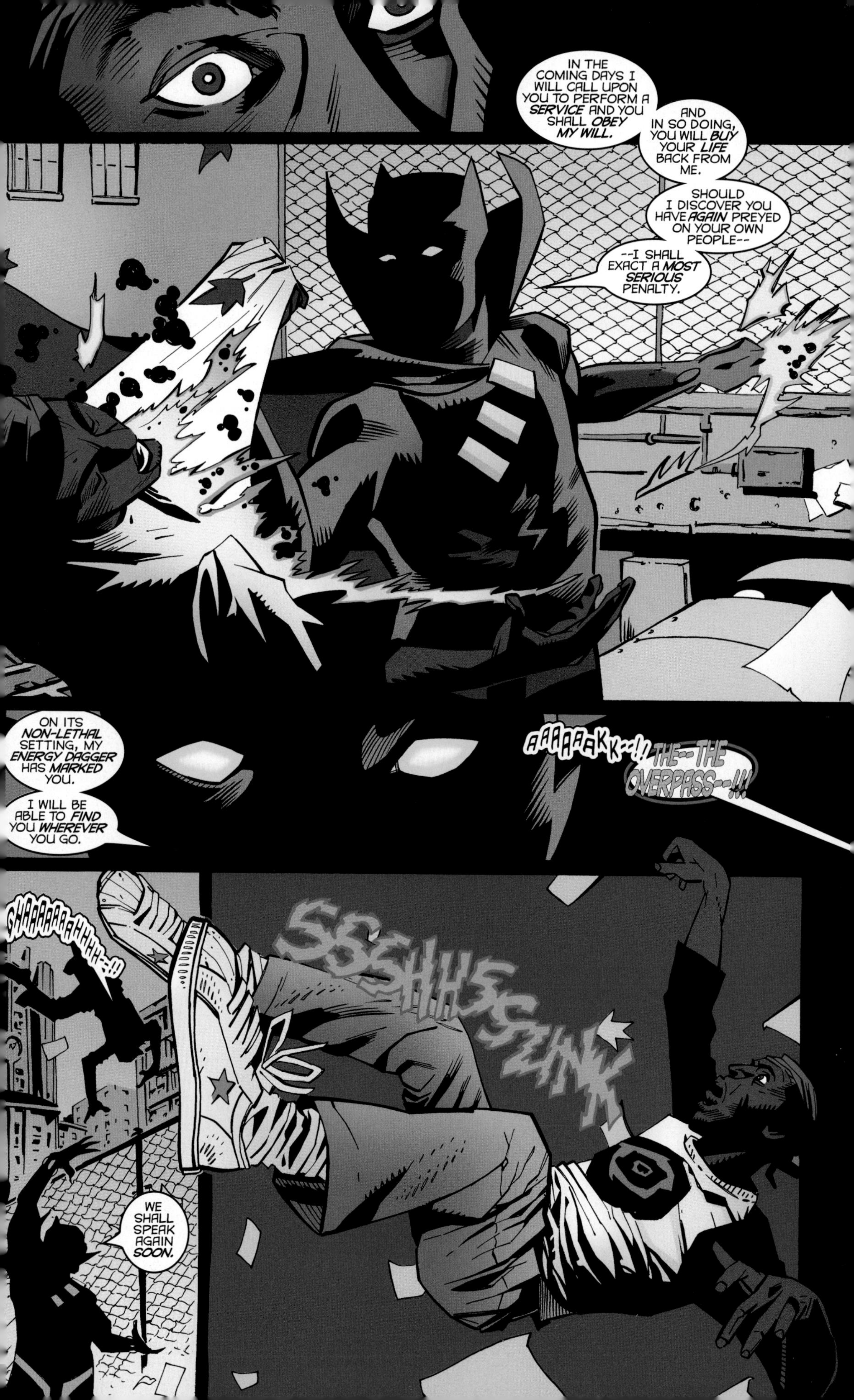

IN THE COMING DAYS I WILL CALL UPON YOU TO PERFORM A SERVICE AND YOU SHALL OBEY MY WILL.
AND IN SO DOING, YOU WILL BUY YOUR LIFE BACK FROM ME.
SHOULD I DISCOVER YOU HAVE AGAIN PREYED ON YOUR OWN PEOPLE--
--I SHALL EXACT A MOST SERIOUS PENALTY.
ON ITS NON-LETHAL SETTING, MY ENERGY DAGGER HAS MARKED YOU.
I WILL BE ABLE TO FIND YOU WHEREVER YOU GO.
AAAAAAKK--!! THE-- THE OVERPASS--!!!
SSSHHSSSINK
GHAAAAAAAHHH--!!
WE SHALL SPEAK AGAIN SOON.

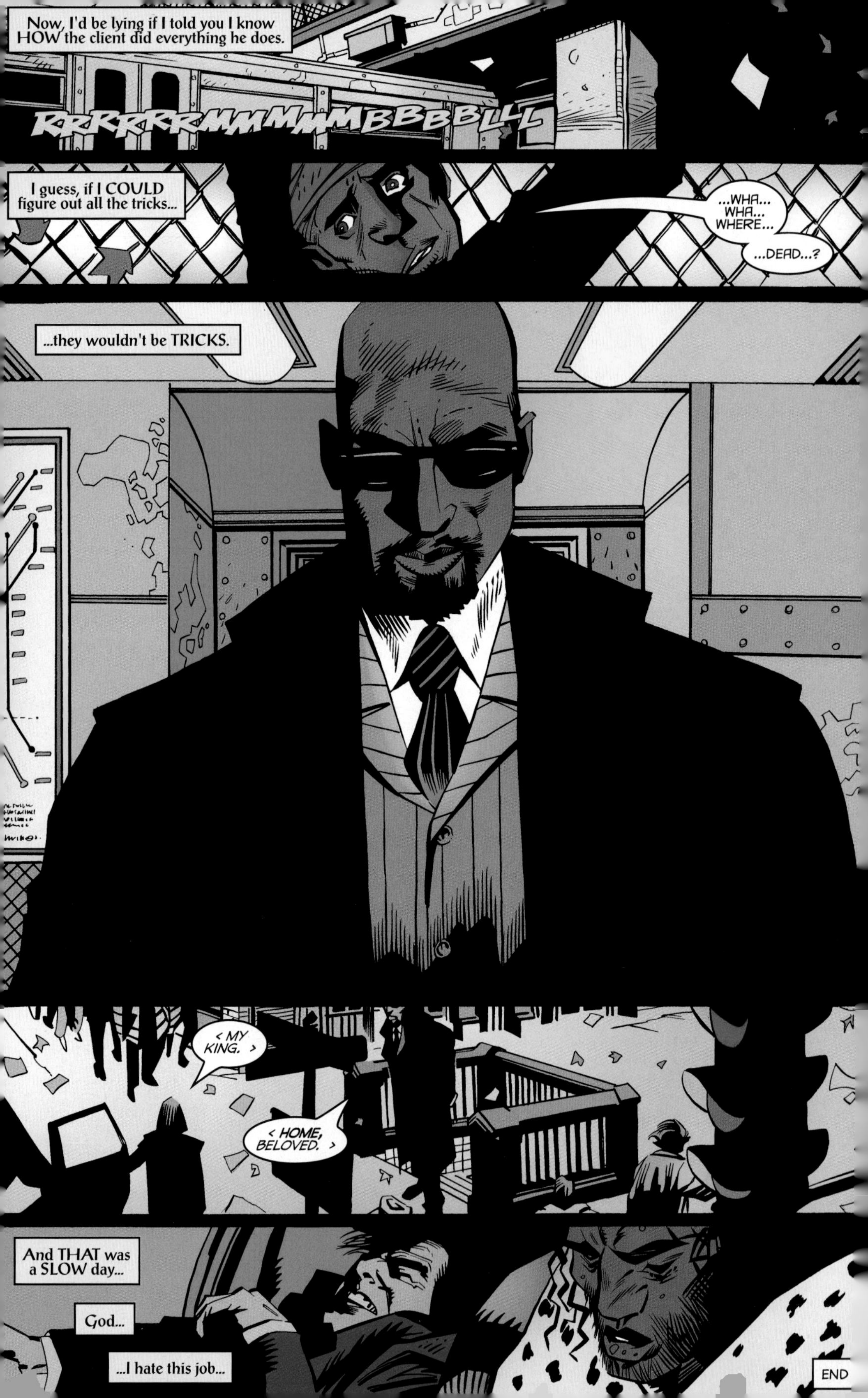
Now, I'd be lying if I told you I know HOW the client did everything he does.
RRRRRRRMMMMMMBBBBBLLL
I guess, if I COULD figure out all the tricks...
...WHA... WHA... WHERE...
...DEAD...?
...they wouldn't be TRICKS.
< MY KING. >
< HOME, BELOVED. >
And THAT was a SLOW day...
God...
...I hate this job...
END

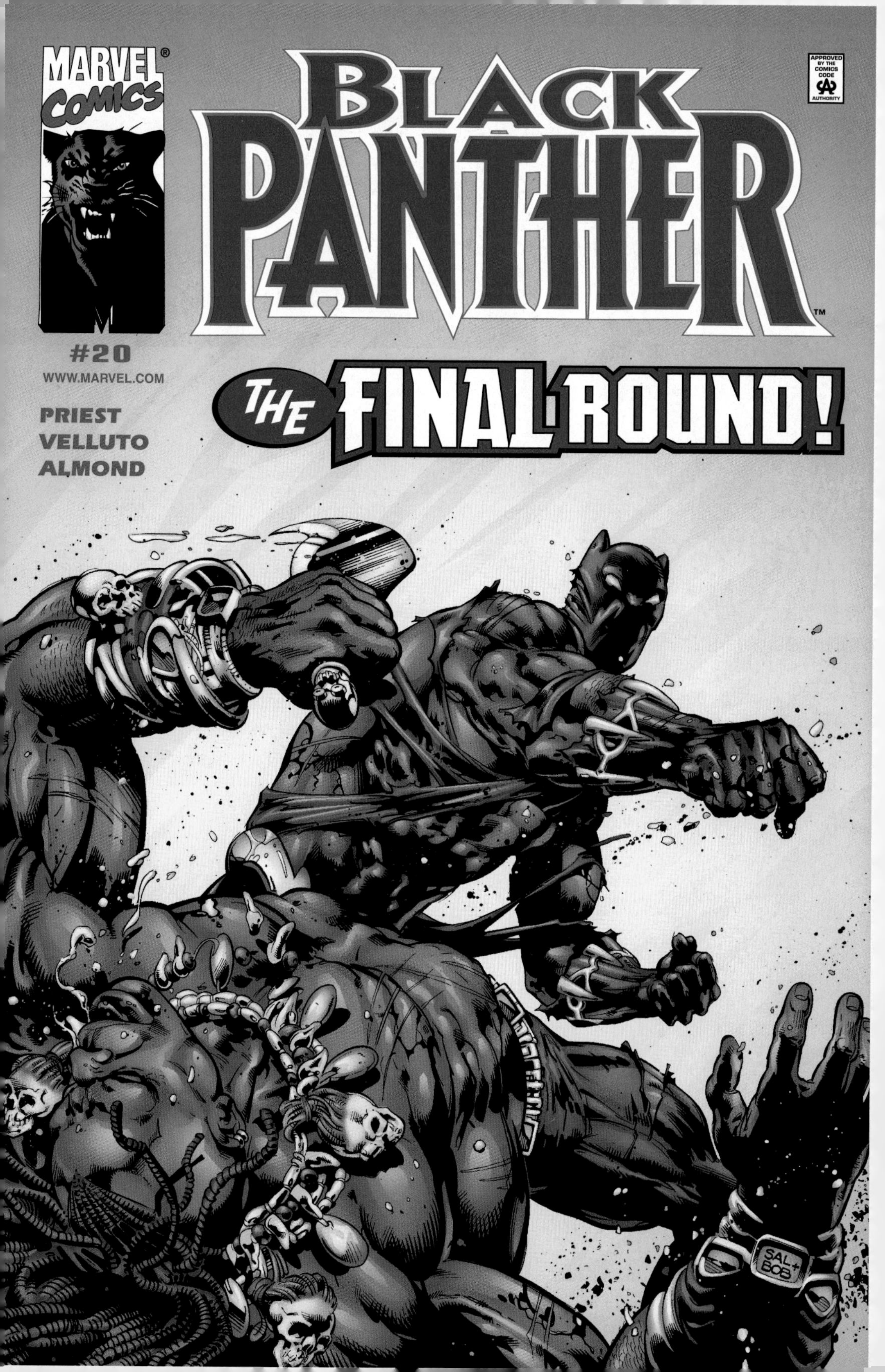
MARVEL COMICS
APPROVED BY THE COMICS CODE AUTHORITY
BLACK PANTHER™
#20
WWW.MARVEL.COM
PRIEST
VELLUTO
ALMOND
THE FINAL ROUND!
SAL + BOB

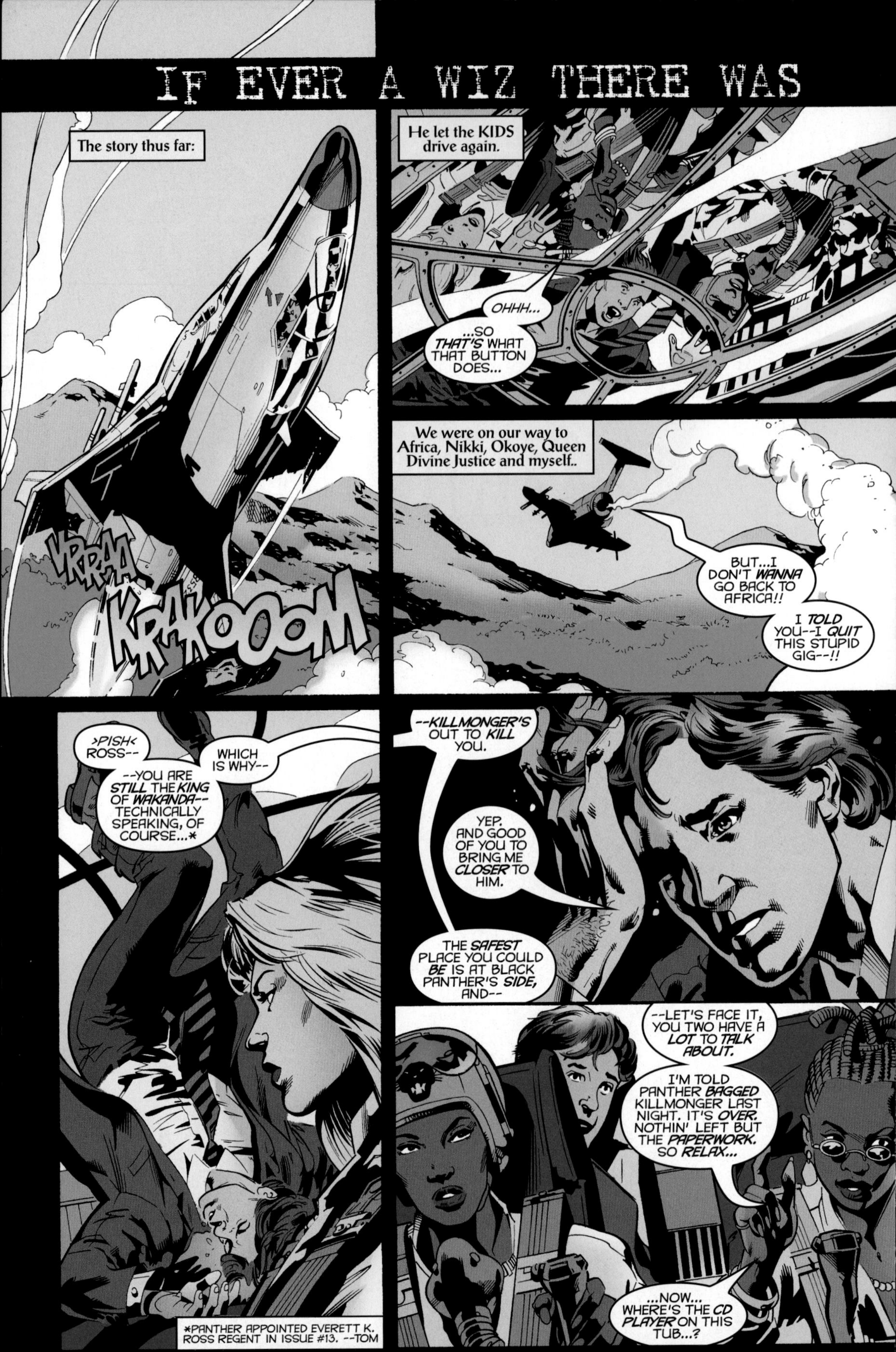

IF EVER A WIZ THERE WAS
The story thus far:
VRRAA
KRAKOOOM
He let the KIDS drive again.
OHHH...
...SO THAT'S WHAT THAT BUTTON DOES...
We were on our way to Africa, Nikki, Okoye, Queen Divine Justice and myself..
BUT...I DON'T WANNA GO BACK TO AFRICA!!
I TOLD YOU--I QUIT THIS STUPID GIG--!!
>PISH< ROSS--
WHICH IS WHY--
--YOU ARE STILL THE KING OF WAKANDA-- TECHNICALLY SPEAKING, OF COURSE...*
--KILLMONGER'S OUT TO KILL YOU.
YEP. AND GOOD OF YOU TO BRING ME CLOSER TO HIM.
THE SAFEST PLACE YOU COULD BE IS AT BLACK PANTHER'S SIDE, AND--
--LET'S FACE IT, YOU TWO HAVE A LOT TO TALK ABOUT.
I'M TOLD PANTHER BAGGED KILLMONGER LAST NIGHT. IT'S OVER. NOTHIN' LEFT BUT THE PAPERWORK. SO RELAX...
...NOW... WHERE'S THE CD PLAYER ON THIS TUB...?
*PANTHER APPOINTED EVERETT K. ROSS REGENT IN ISSUE #13. --TOM

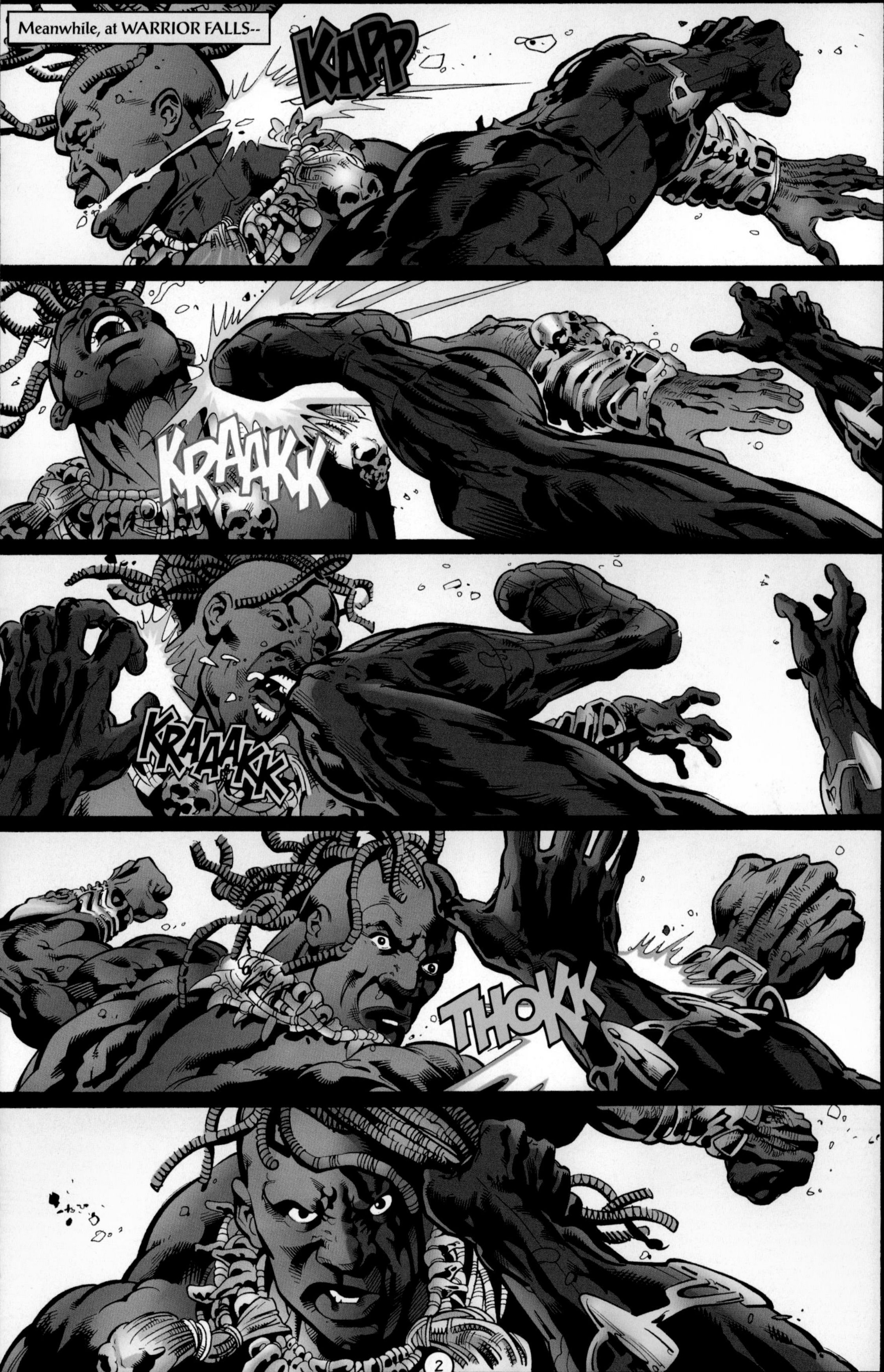
Meanwhile, at WARRIOR FALLS--
KAPP
KRAAKK
KRAAAKK
THOKK

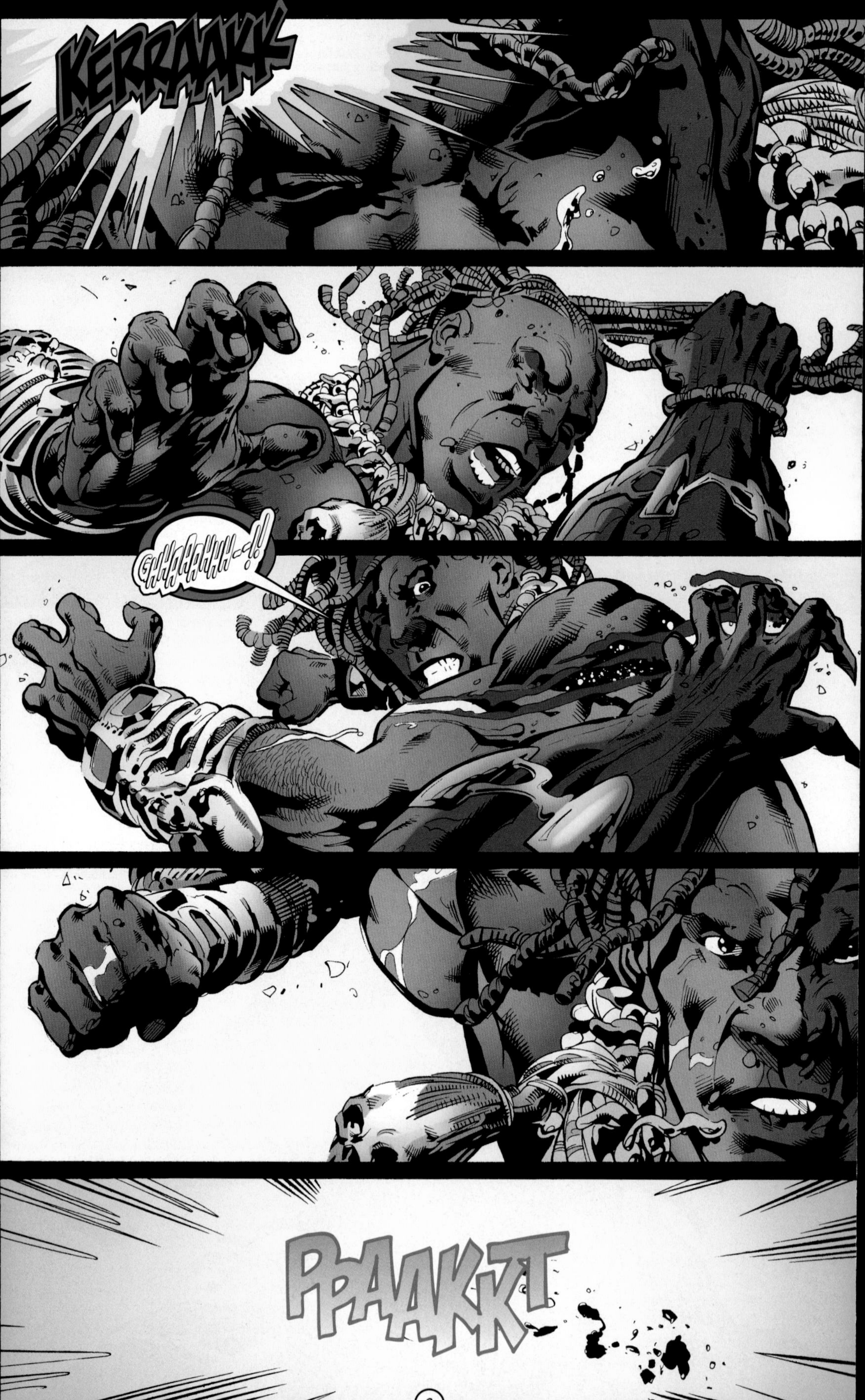
KERRAAKK
GHAAAHHH--!!
PRAAKKT

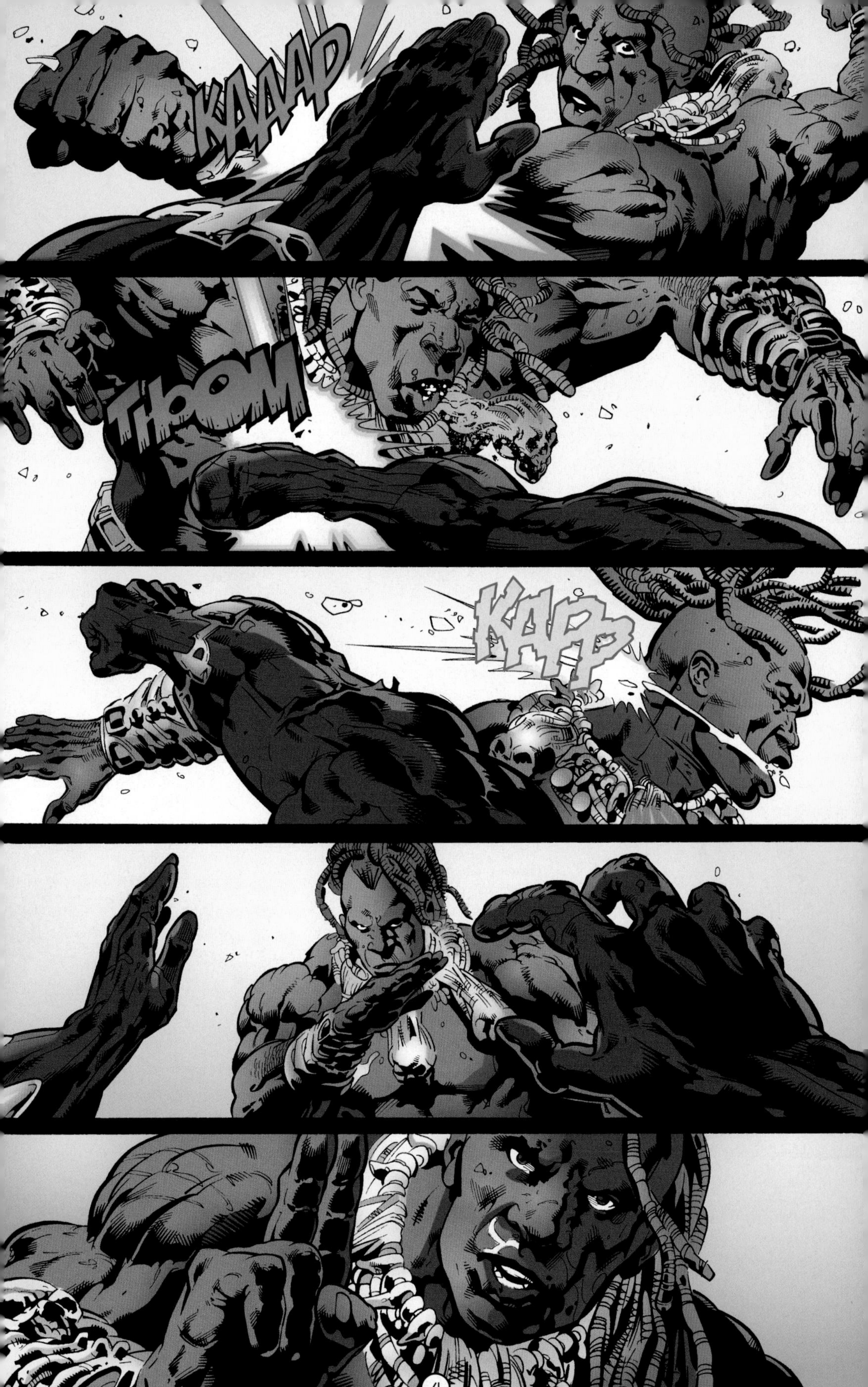
KAAAP
THOOM
KAP

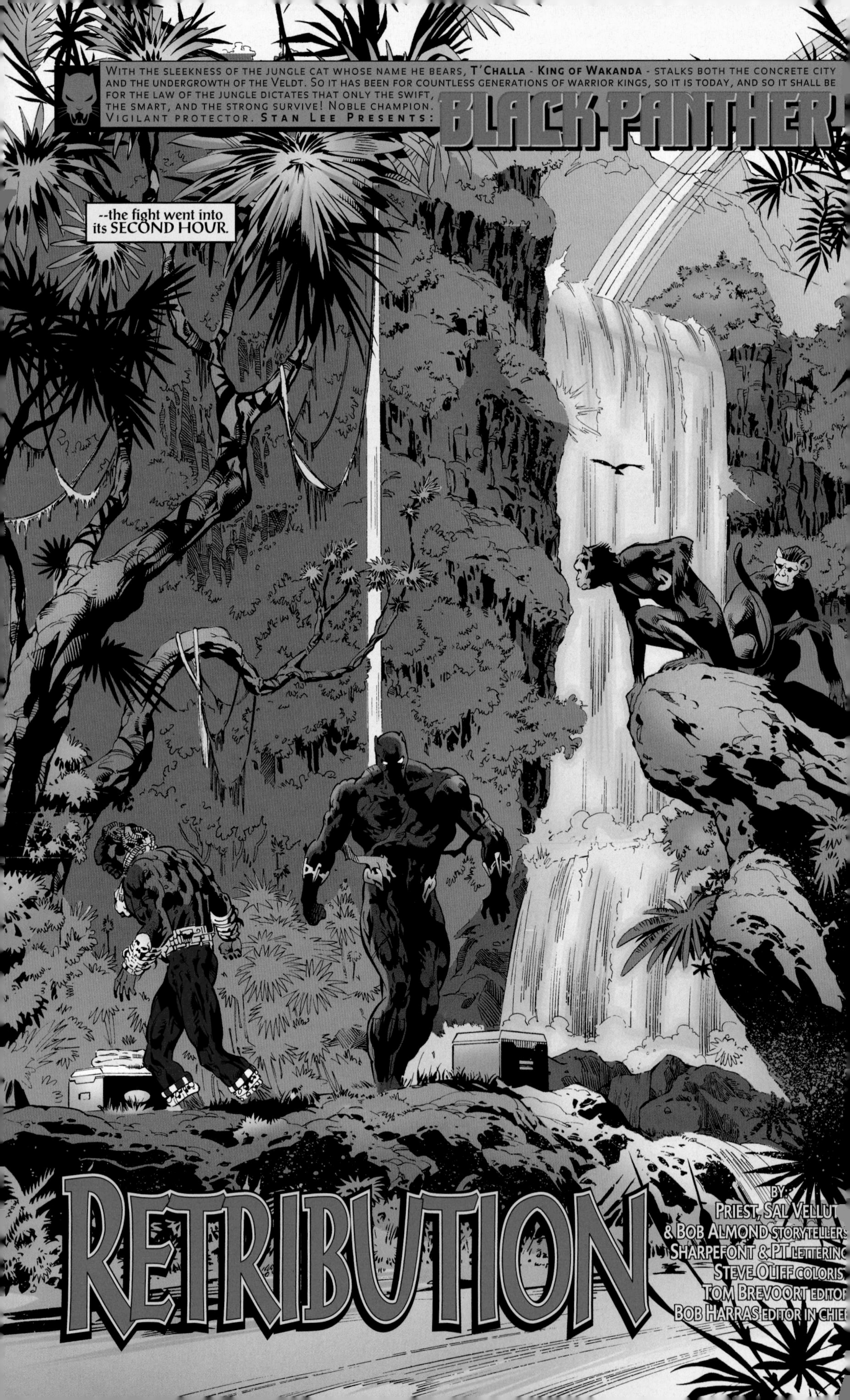
With the sleekness of the jungle cat whose name he bears, T'Challa - King of Wakanda - stalks both the concrete city and the undergrowth of the Veldt. So it has been for countless generations of warrior kings, so it is today, and so it shall be for the law of the jungle dictates that only the swift, the smart, and the strong survive! Noble champion. Vigilant protector. Stan Lee Presents:
BLACK PANTHER!
--the fight went into its SECOND HOUR.
RETRIBUTION
BY:
PRIEST, SAL VELLUT
& BOB ALMOND STORYTELLERS
SHARPEFONT & PT LETTERING
STEVE OLIFF COLORIST
TOM BREVOORT EDITOR
BOB HARRAS EDITOR IN CHIE

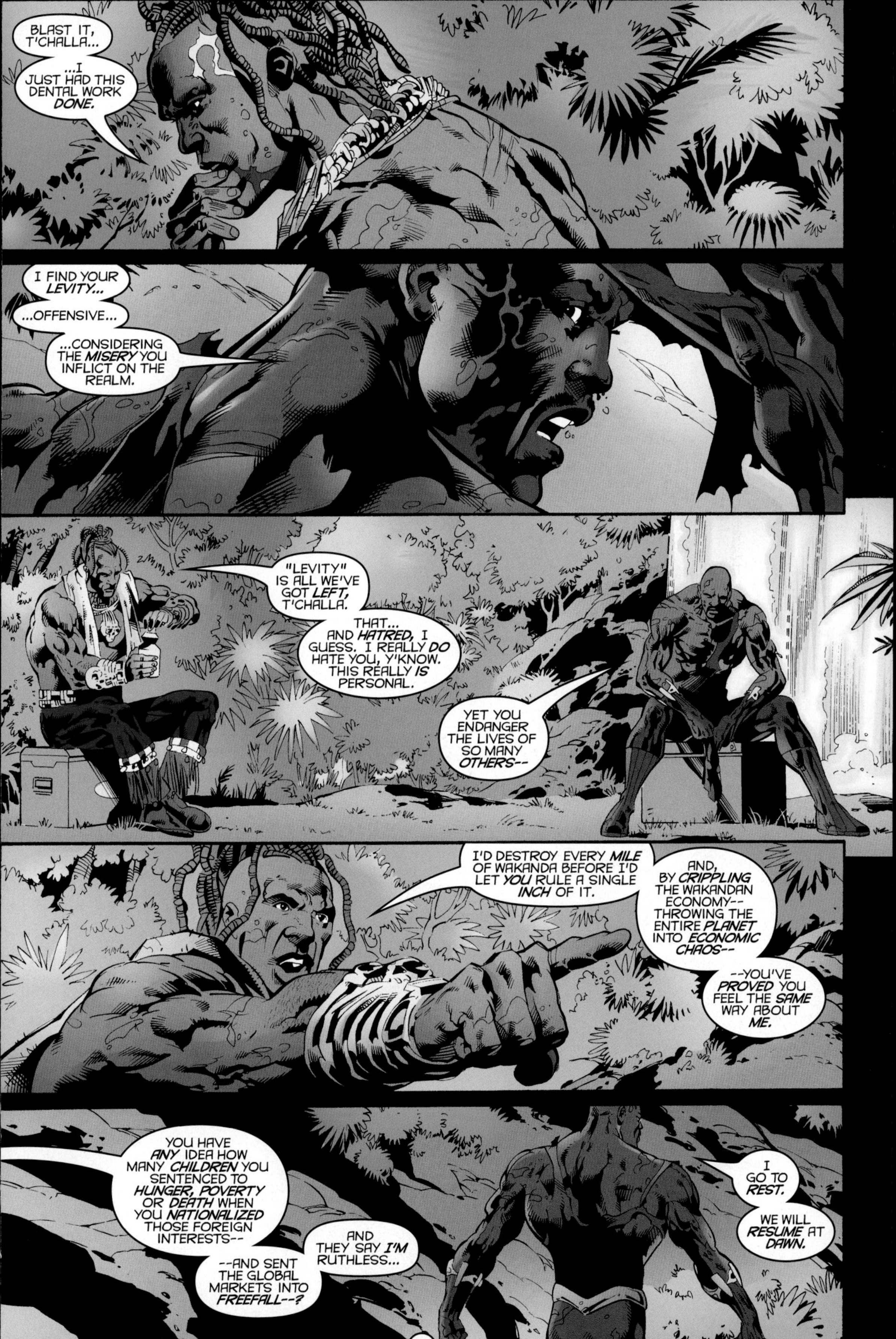
BLAST IT, T'CHALLA...
...I JUST HAD THIS DENTAL WORK DONE.
I FIND YOUR LEVITY...
...OFFENSIVE...
...CONSIDERING THE MISERY YOU INFLICT ON THE REALM.
"LEVITY" IS ALL WE'VE GOT LEFT, T'CHALLA.
THAT... AND HATRED, I GUESS. I REALLY DO HATE YOU, Y'KNOW. THIS REALLY IS PERSONAL.
YET YOU ENDANGER THE LIVES OF SO MANY OTHERS--
I'D DESTROY EVERY MILE OF WAKANDA BEFORE I'D LET YOU RULE A SINGLE INCH OF IT.
AND, BY CRIPPLING THE WAKANDAN ECONOMY-- THROWING THE ENTIRE PLANET INTO ECONOMIC CHAOS--
--YOU'VE PROVED YOU FEEL THE SAME WAY ABOUT ME.
YOU HAVE ANY IDEA HOW MANY CHILDREN YOU SENTENCED TO HUNGER, POVERTY OR DEATH WHEN YOU NATIONALIZED THOSE FOREIGN INTERESTS--
--AND SENT THE GLOBAL MARKETS INTO FREEFALL--?
AND THEY SAY I'M RUTHLESS...
I GO TO REST.
WE WILL RESUME AT DAWN.

THE WELCOME WAGON

By the time we arrived at N'JADAKA VILLAGE, it was MORNING--which, I guess, was about right.

The first thing I noticed was Killmonger's WATCHTOWER was still standing.

Which meant we really needed to get out of there.

IT'S NOT *OVER*. GET US *OUT* OF HERE.

WHAT?

THAT THING IS KILLMONGER'S *HOUSE*. TRUST ME--

--BEFORE THIS IS OVER, SOMEBODY WILL HAVE *BLOWN* THE TOWER *UP*!

THERE'S *NO OTHER REASON* FOR IT TO *BE* HERE!

ZZZAPP!

ZZZAPP!

SEE--?!! SEE--?!

TO THINK...I HAD MY *RUN* OF THE JOINT JUST A FEW *DAYS* AGO...

BUT-- THE BOSS THREW A *NET* OVER THIS KILLMONGER CHUMP YESTERDAY.* IT *SHOULD* BE *SAFE*--

ERIK'S *NOT* "BAGGED"! THERE *IS* NO *BAG*!!

*LAST ISSUE. --TOM

QUEEN-- IF YOU LEARN *NOTHING ELSE* ABOUT MY CLIENT, LEARN *THIS*:

WHATEVER YOU *THINK* HE'S DOING, HE'S DOING *SOMETHING ELSE*!

NOW, BURN *OUTTA* HERE BEFORE--

ZZAPP!

--GREAT. JUST GREAT.

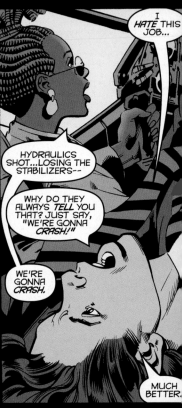

I *HATE* THIS JOB...

HYDRAULICS SHOT...LOSING THE STABILIZERS--

WHY DO THEY ALWAYS *TELL* YOU THAT? JUST SAY, "WE'RE GONNA *CRASH*!"

WE'RE GONNA *CRASH*.

MUCH BETTER.

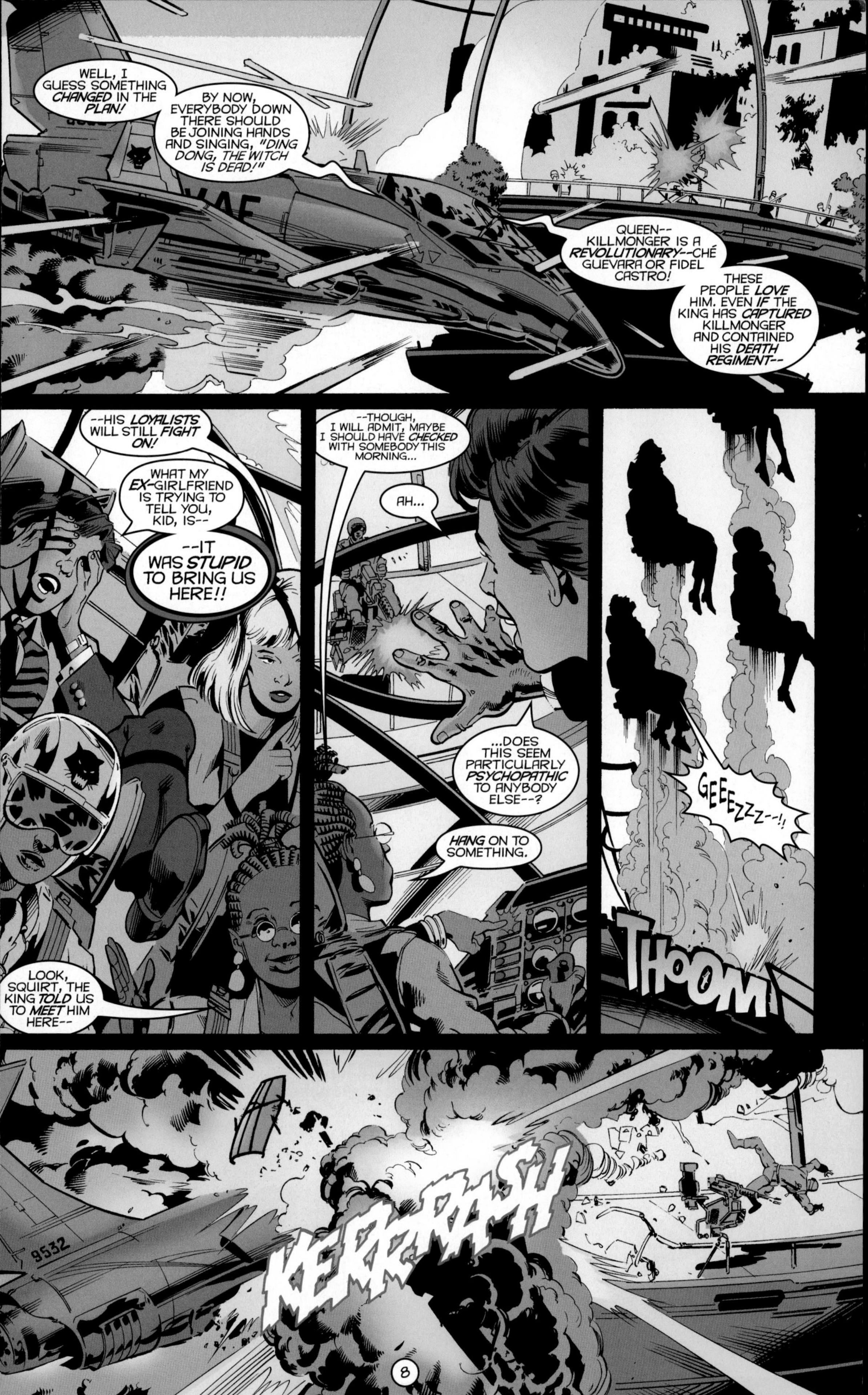
WELL, I GUESS SOMETHING CHANGED IN THE PLAN!
BY NOW, EVERYBODY DOWN THERE SHOULD BE JOINING HANDS AND SINGING, "DING DONG, THE WITCH IS DEAD!"
QUEEN-- KILLMONGER IS A REVOLUTIONARY--CHÉ GUEVARA OR FIDEL CASTRO!
THESE PEOPLE LOVE HIM. EVEN IF THE KING HAS CAPTURED KILLMONGER AND CONTAINED HIS DEATH REGIMENT--
--HIS LOYALISTS WILL STILL FIGHT ON!
WHAT MY EX-GIRLFRIEND IS TRYING TO TELL YOU, KID, IS--
--IT WAS STUPID TO BRING US HERE!!
LOOK, SQUIRT, THE KING TOLD US TO MEET HIM HERE--
--THOUGH, I WILL ADMIT, MAYBE I SHOULD HAVE CHECKED WITH SOMEBODY THIS MORNING...
AH...
...DOES THIS SEEM PARTICULARLY PSYCHOPATHIC TO ANYBODY ELSE--?
HANG ON TO SOMETHING.
GEEEZZZ--!!
THOOM
KERRASH

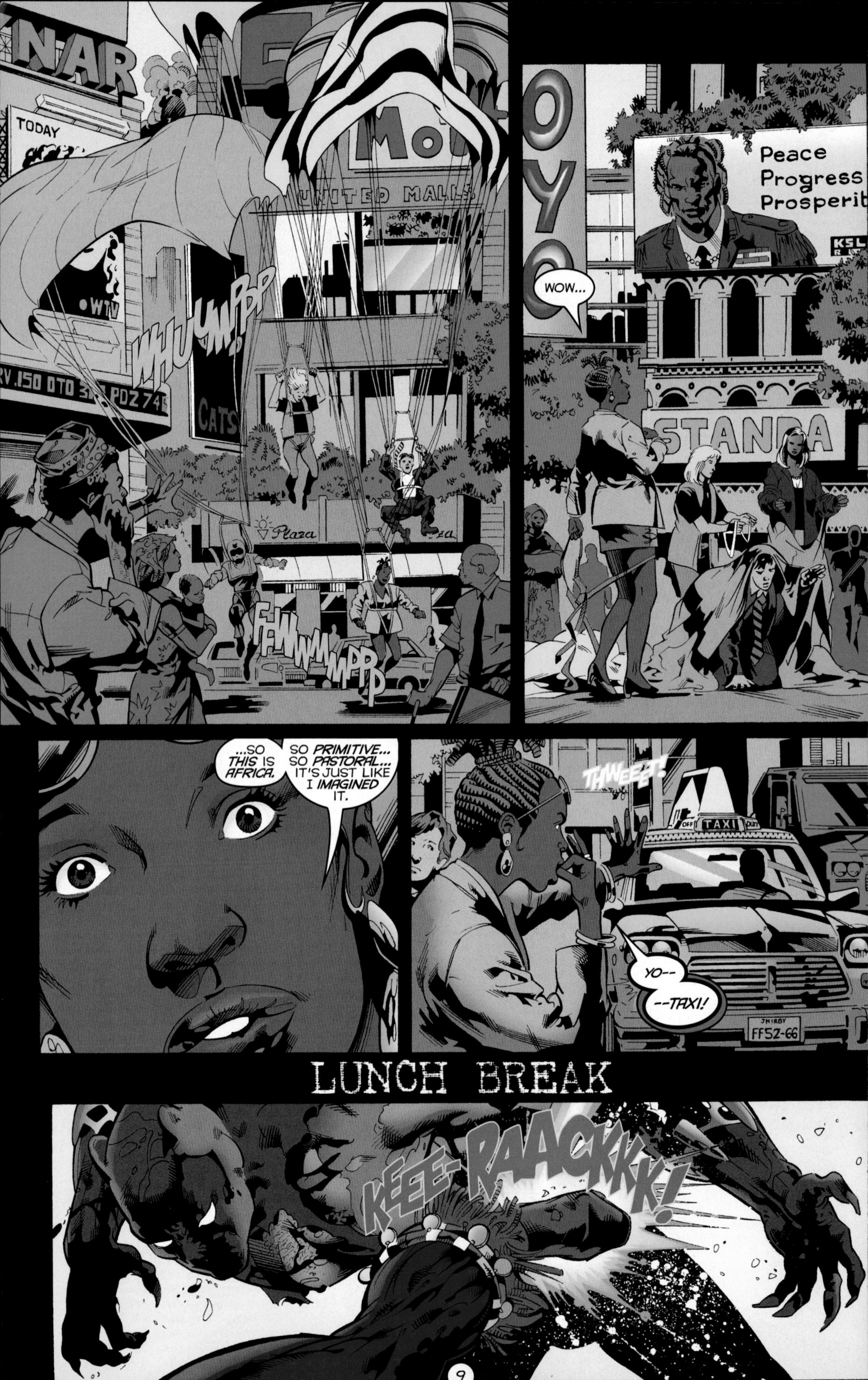
WHUUMPP
FFWWUMMPPP
Peace
Progress
Prosperit
WOW...
...SO THIS IS AFRICA.
SO PRIMITIVE... SO PASTORAL... IT'S JUST LIKE I IMAGINED IT.
THWEEET!
TAXI
YO--
--TAXI!
FF52-66
LUNCH BREAK
KEEE-RAACKKK!

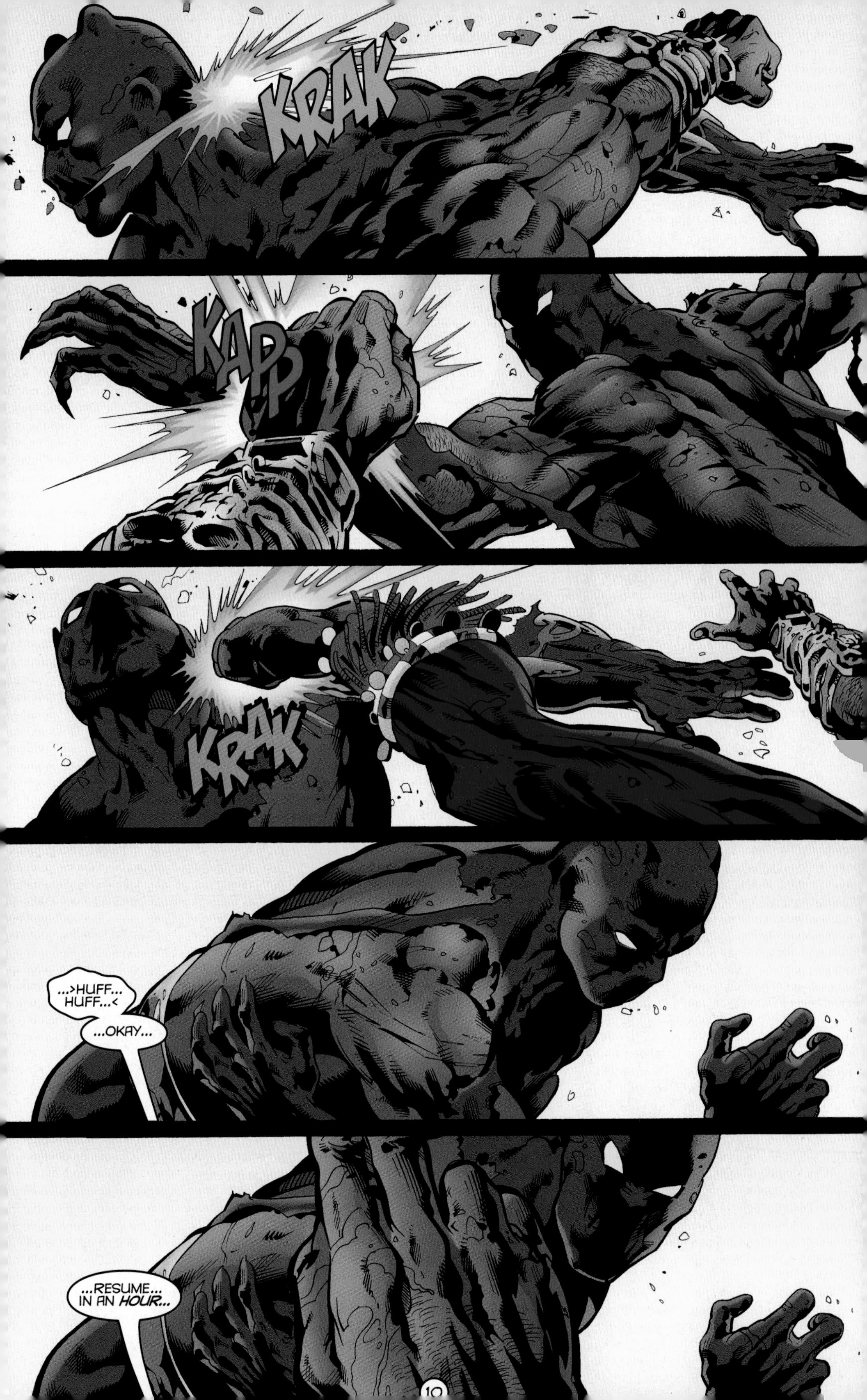
KRAK
KAPP
KRAK
...>HUFF...
HUFF...<
...OKAY...
...RESUME...
IN AN *HOUR*...

A STITCH IN TIME

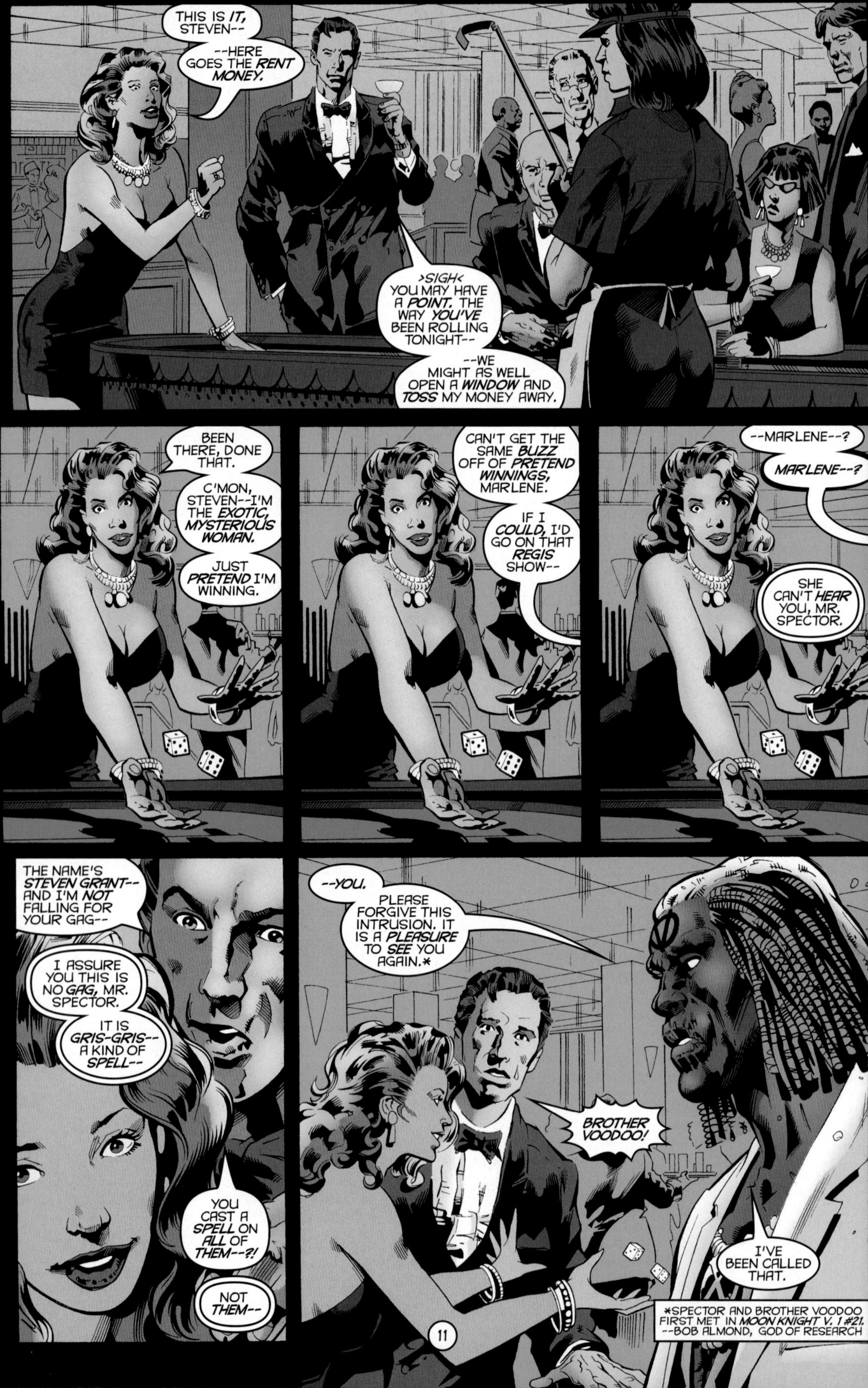

THIS IS *IT,* STEVEN--
--HERE GOES THE *RENT MONEY.*
>SIGH< YOU MAY HAVE A *POINT.* THE WAY *YOU'VE* BEEN ROLLING TONIGHT--
--WE MIGHT AS WELL OPEN A *WINDOW* AND *TOSS* MY MONEY AWAY.
BEEN THERE, DONE THAT.
C'MON, STEVEN--I'M THE *EXOTIC, MYSTERIOUS WOMAN.*
JUST *PRETEND* I'M WINNING.
CAN'T GET THE SAME *BUZZ* OFF OF *PRETEND WINNINGS,* MARLENE.
IF I *COULD,* I'D GO ON THAT *REGIS* SHOW--
--MARLENE--?
MARLENE--?
SHE CAN'T *HEAR* YOU, MR. SPECTOR.
THE NAME'S *STEVEN GRANT--* AND I'M *NOT* FALLING FOR YOUR GAG--
I ASSURE YOU THIS IS NO *GAG,* MR. SPECTOR.
IT IS *GRIS-GRIS--* A KIND OF *SPELL--*
YOU CAST A *SPELL* ON *ALL* OF *THEM--?!*
NOT THEM--
--YOU.
PLEASE FORGIVE THIS INTRUSION. IT IS A *PLEASURE* TO *SEE* YOU AGAIN.*
BROTHER VOODOO!
I'VE BEEN CALLED THAT.
*SPECTOR AND BROTHER VOODOO FIRST MET IN *MOON KNIGHT V. 1 #21.* --BOB ALMOND, GOD OF RESEARCH

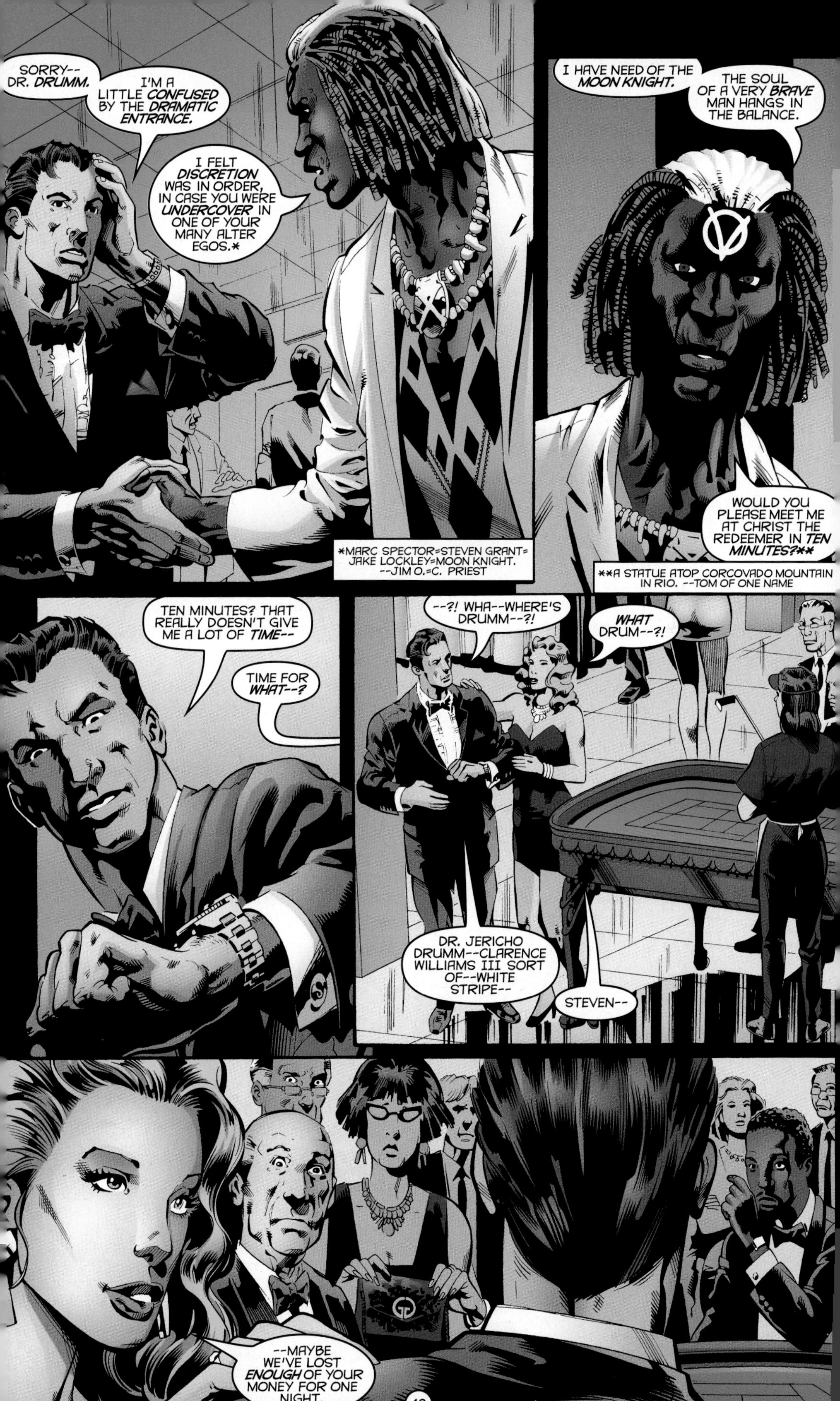

SORRY-- DR. DRUMM.
I'M A LITTLE CONFUSED BY THE DRAMATIC ENTRANCE.
I FELT DISCRETION WAS IN ORDER, IN CASE YOU WERE UNDERCOVER IN ONE OF YOUR MANY ALTER EGOS.*
*MARC SPECTOR=STEVEN GRANT= JAKE LOCKLEY=MOON KNIGHT. --JIM O.=C. PRIEST
I HAVE NEED OF THE MOON KNIGHT.
THE SOUL OF A VERY BRAVE MAN HANGS IN THE BALANCE.
WOULD YOU PLEASE MEET ME AT CHRIST THE REDEEMER IN TEN MINUTES?**
**A STATUE ATOP CORCOVADO MOUNTAIN IN RIO. --TOM OF ONE NAME
TEN MINUTES? THAT REALLY DOESN'T GIVE ME A LOT OF TIME--
TIME FOR WHAT--?
--?! WHA--WHERE'S DRUMM--?!
WHAT DRUM--?!
DR. JERICHO DRUMM--CLARENCE WILLIAMS III SORT OF--WHITE STRIPE--
STEVEN--
--MAYBE WE'VE LOST ENOUGH OF YOUR MONEY FOR ONE NIGHT.

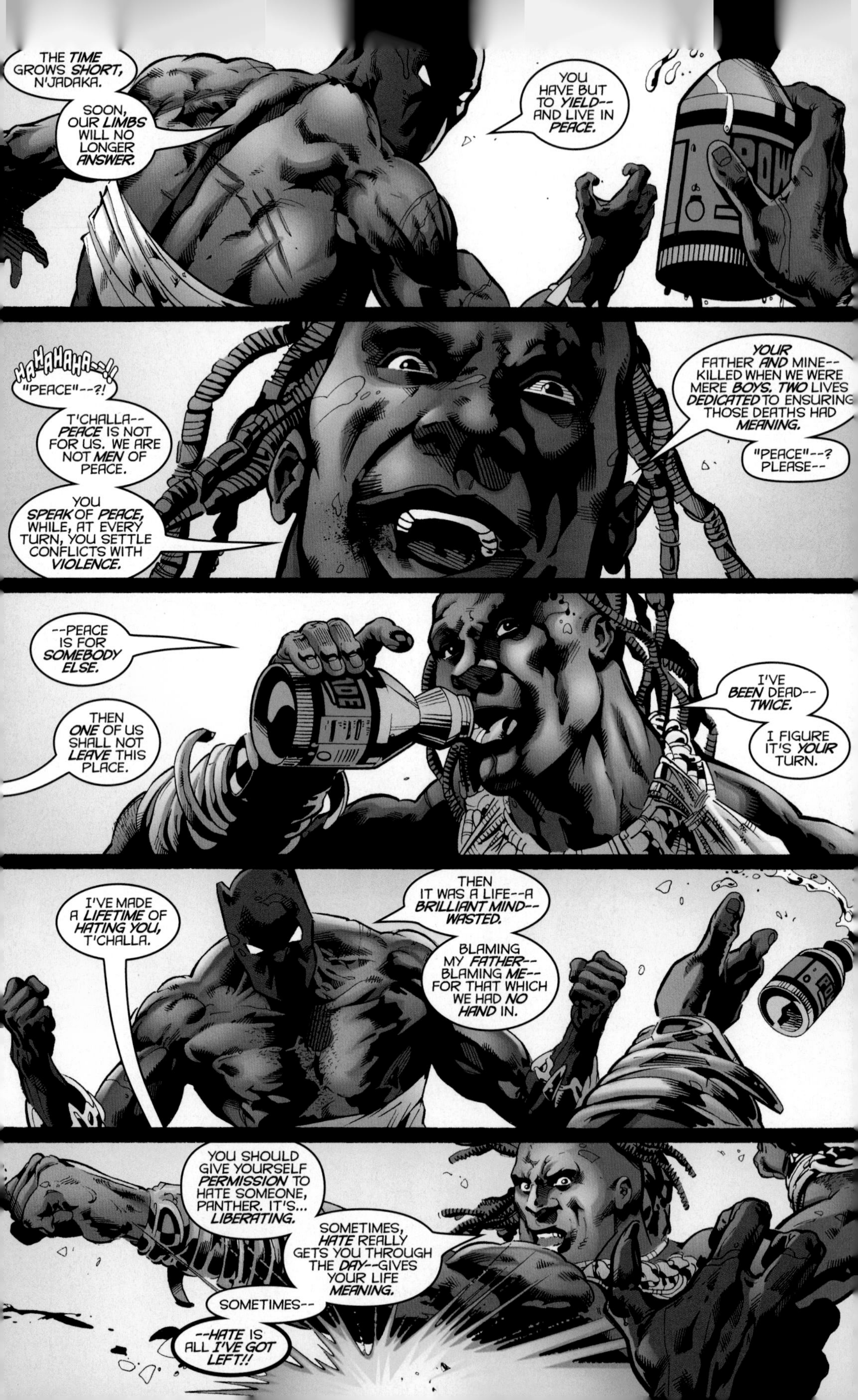
THE TIME GROWS SHORT, N'JADAKA.
SOON, OUR LIMBS WILL NO LONGER ANSWER.
YOU HAVE BUT TO YIELD-- AND LIVE IN PEACE.
HAHAHAHA--!!
"PEACE"--?!
T'CHALLA-- PEACE IS NOT FOR US. WE ARE NOT MEN OF PEACE.
YOU SPEAK OF PEACE, WHILE, AT EVERY TURN, YOU SETTLE CONFLICTS WITH VIOLENCE.
YOUR FATHER AND MINE-- KILLED WHEN WE WERE MERE BOYS. TWO LIVES DEDICATED TO ENSURING THOSE DEATHS HAD MEANING.
"PEACE"--? PLEASE--
--PEACE IS FOR SOMEBODY ELSE.
THEN ONE OF US SHALL NOT LEAVE THIS PLACE.
I'VE BEEN DEAD-- TWICE.
I FIGURE IT'S YOUR TURN.
I'VE MADE A LIFETIME OF HATING YOU, T'CHALLA.
THEN IT WAS A LIFE--A BRILLIANT MIND-- WASTED.
BLAMING MY FATHER-- BLAMING ME-- FOR THAT WHICH WE HAD NO HAND IN.
YOU SHOULD GIVE YOURSELF PERMISSION TO HATE SOMEONE, PANTHER. IT'S... LIBERATING.
SOMETIMES, HATE REALLY GETS YOU THROUGH THE DAY--GIVES YOUR LIFE MEANING.
SOMETIMES--
--HATE IS ALL I'VE GOT LEFT!!

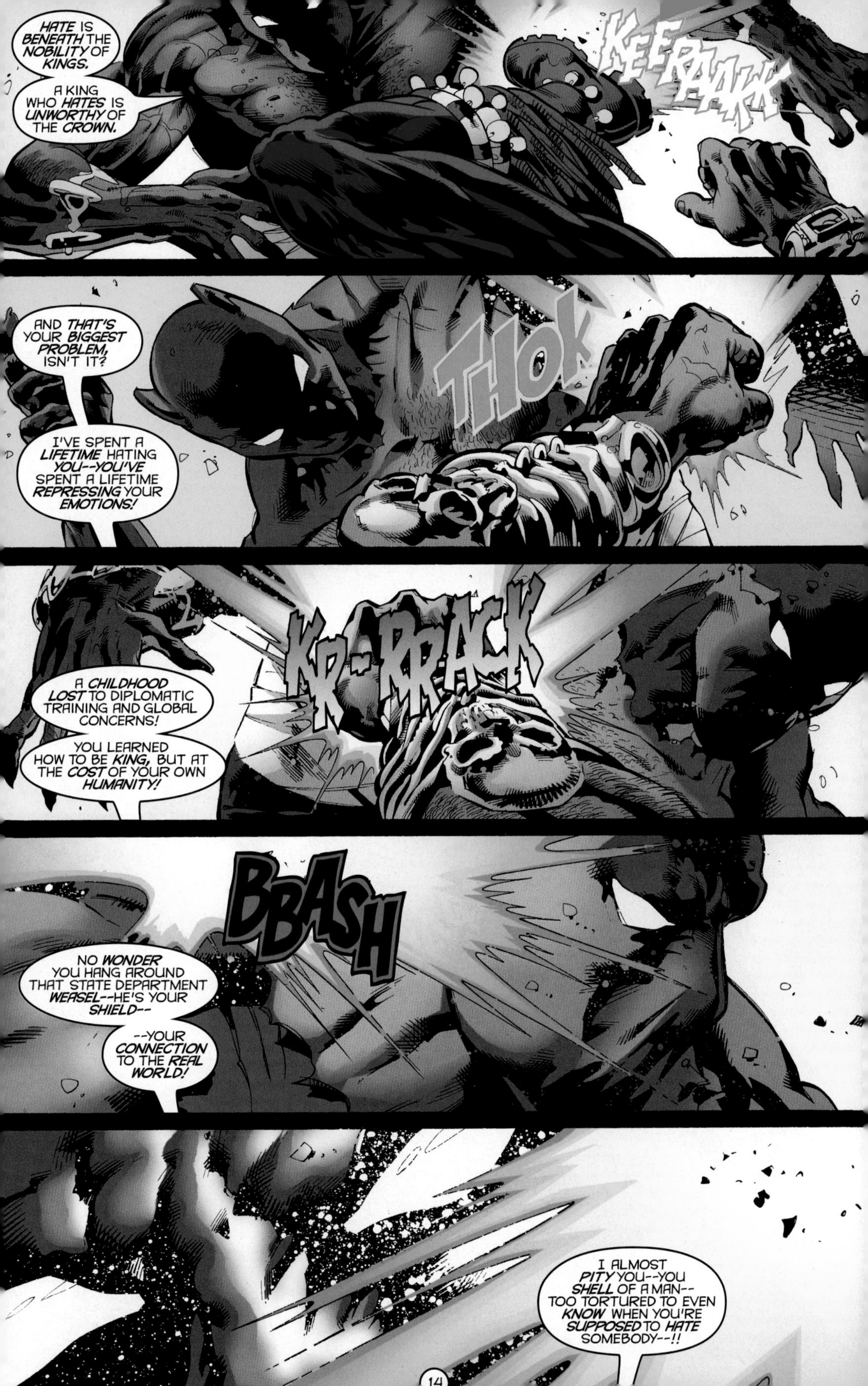
HATE IS BENEATH THE NOBILITY OF KINGS.
A KING WHO HATES IS UNWORTHY OF THE CROWN.
KEERAAKK
AND THAT'S YOUR BIGGEST PROBLEM, ISN'T IT?
THOK
I'VE SPENT A LIFETIME HATING YOU--YOU'VE SPENT A LIFETIME REPRESSING YOUR EMOTIONS!
KR-RRACK
A CHILDHOOD LOST TO DIPLOMATIC TRAINING AND GLOBAL CONCERNS!
YOU LEARNED HOW TO BE KING, BUT AT THE COST OF YOUR OWN HUMANITY!
BBASH
NO WONDER YOU HANG AROUND THAT STATE DEPARTMENT WEASEL--HE'S YOUR SHIELD--
--YOUR CONNECTION TO THE REAL WORLD!
I ALMOST PITY YOU--YOU SHELL OF A MAN--TOO TORTURED TO EVEN KNOW WHEN YOU'RE SUPPOSED TO HATE SOMEBODY--!!

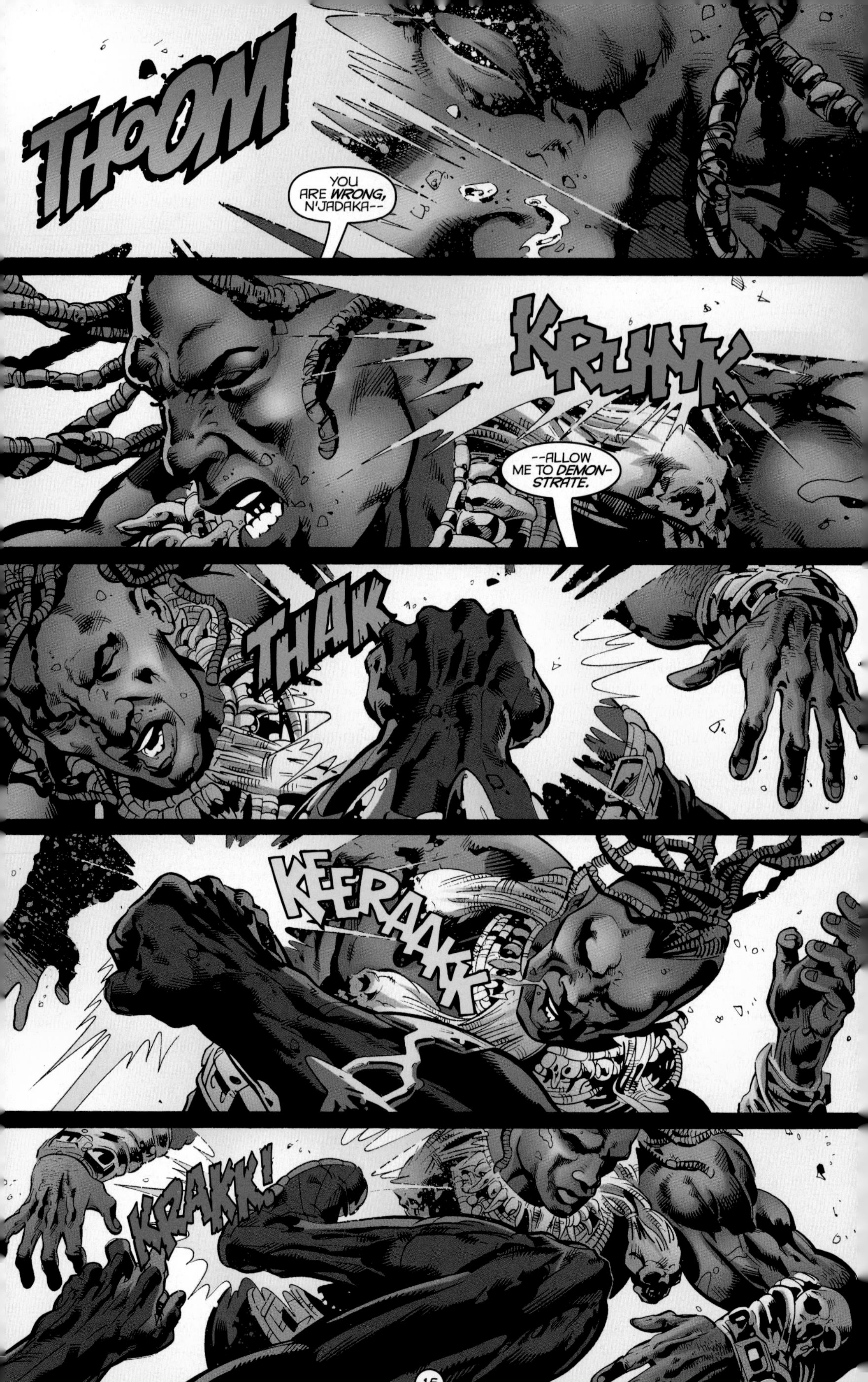
THOOM
YOU ARE *WRONG*, N'JADAKA--
KRUNK
--ALLOW ME TO *DEMON-STRATE.*
THAK
KEERAAKK
KRAKK!

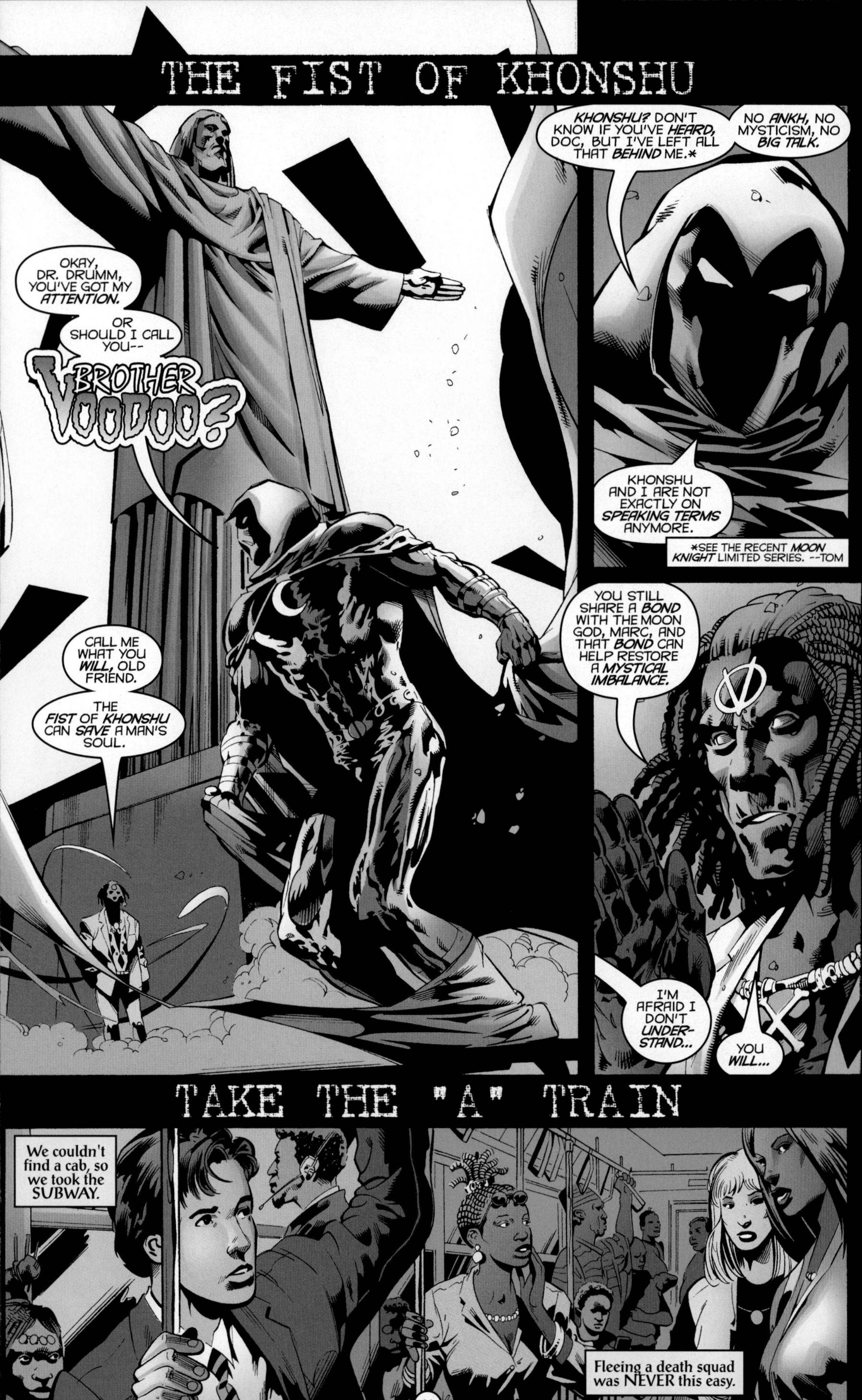
THE FIST OF KHONSHU
OKAY, DR. DRUMM, YOU'VE GOT MY ATTENTION.
OR SHOULD I CALL YOU--
BROTHER VOODOO?
KHONSHU? DON'T KNOW IF YOU'VE HEARD, DOC, BUT I'VE LEFT ALL THAT BEHIND ME.*
NO ANKH, NO MYSTICISM, NO BIG TALK.
KHONSHU AND I ARE NOT EXACTLY ON SPEAKING TERMS ANYMORE.
*SEE THE RECENT MOON KNIGHT LIMITED SERIES. --TOM
CALL ME WHAT YOU WILL, OLD FRIEND.
THE FIST OF KHONSHU CAN SAVE A MAN'S SOUL.
YOU STILL SHARE A BOND WITH THE MOON GOD, MARC, AND THAT BOND CAN HELP RESTORE A MYSTICAL IMBALANCE.
I'M AFRAID I DON'T UNDERSTAND...
YOU WILL...
TAKE THE "A" TRAIN
We couldn't find a cab, so we took the SUBWAY.
Fleeing a death squad was NEVER this easy.

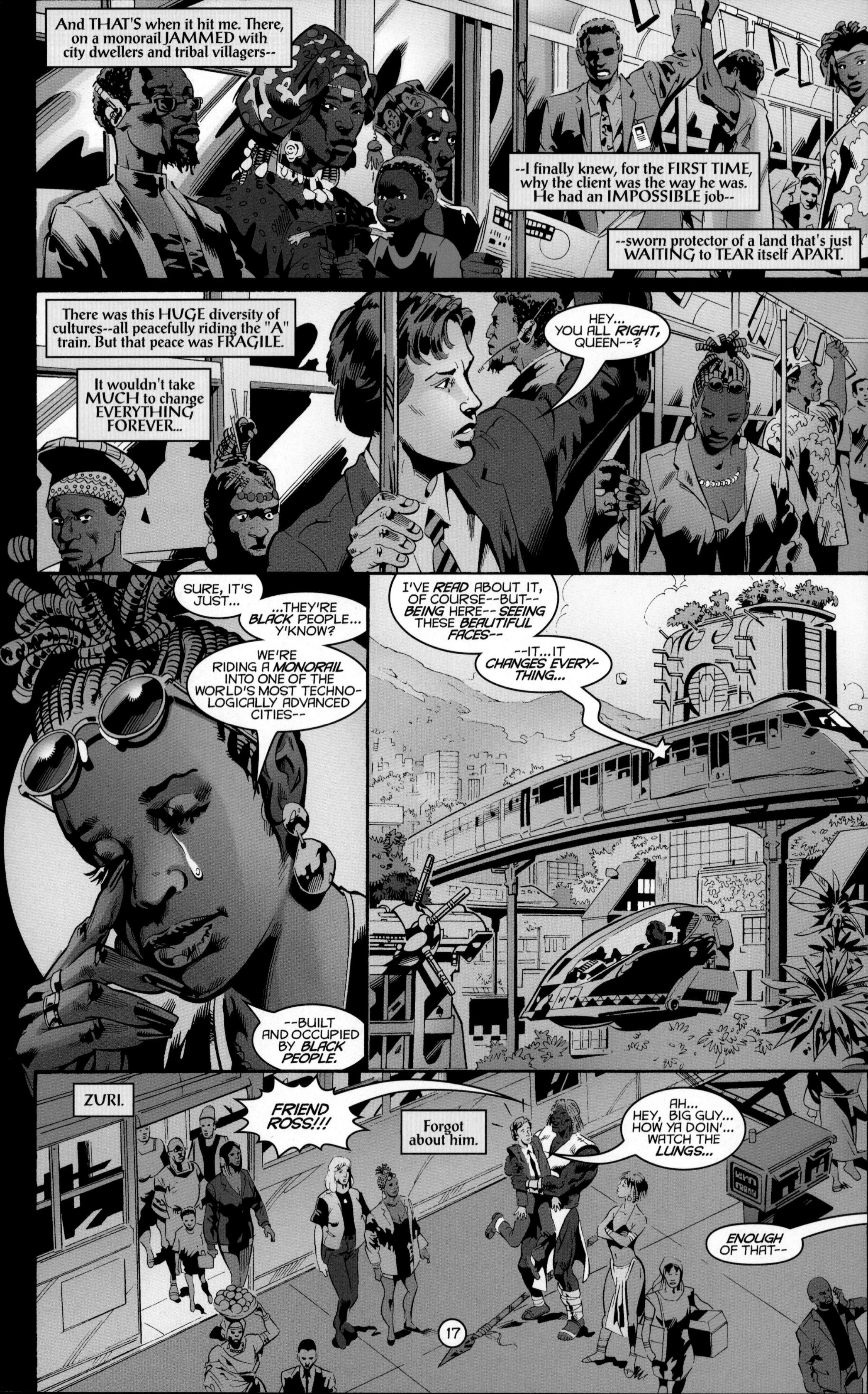
And THAT'S when it hit me. There, on a monorail JAMMED with city dwellers and tribal villagers--
--I finally knew, for the FIRST TIME, why the client was the way he was. He had an IMPOSSIBLE job--
--sworn protector of a land that's just WAITING to TEAR itself APART.
There was this HUGE diversity of cultures--all peacefully riding the "A" train. But that peace was FRAGILE.
It wouldn't take MUCH to change EVERYTHING FOREVER...
HEY... YOU ALL RIGHT, QUEEN--?
SURE, IT'S JUST...
...THEY'RE BLACK PEOPLE... Y'KNOW?
WE'RE RIDING A MONORAIL INTO ONE OF THE WORLD'S MOST TECHNOLOGICALLY ADVANCED CITIES--
--BUILT AND OCCUPIED BY BLACK PEOPLE.
I'VE READ ABOUT IT, OF COURSE--BUT--BEING HERE--SEEING THESE BEAUTIFUL FACES--
--IT...IT CHANGES EVERYTHING...
ZURI.
FRIEND ROSS!!!
Forgot about him.
AH... HEY, BIG GUY... HOW YA DOIN'... WATCH THE LUNGS...
ENOUGH OF THAT--

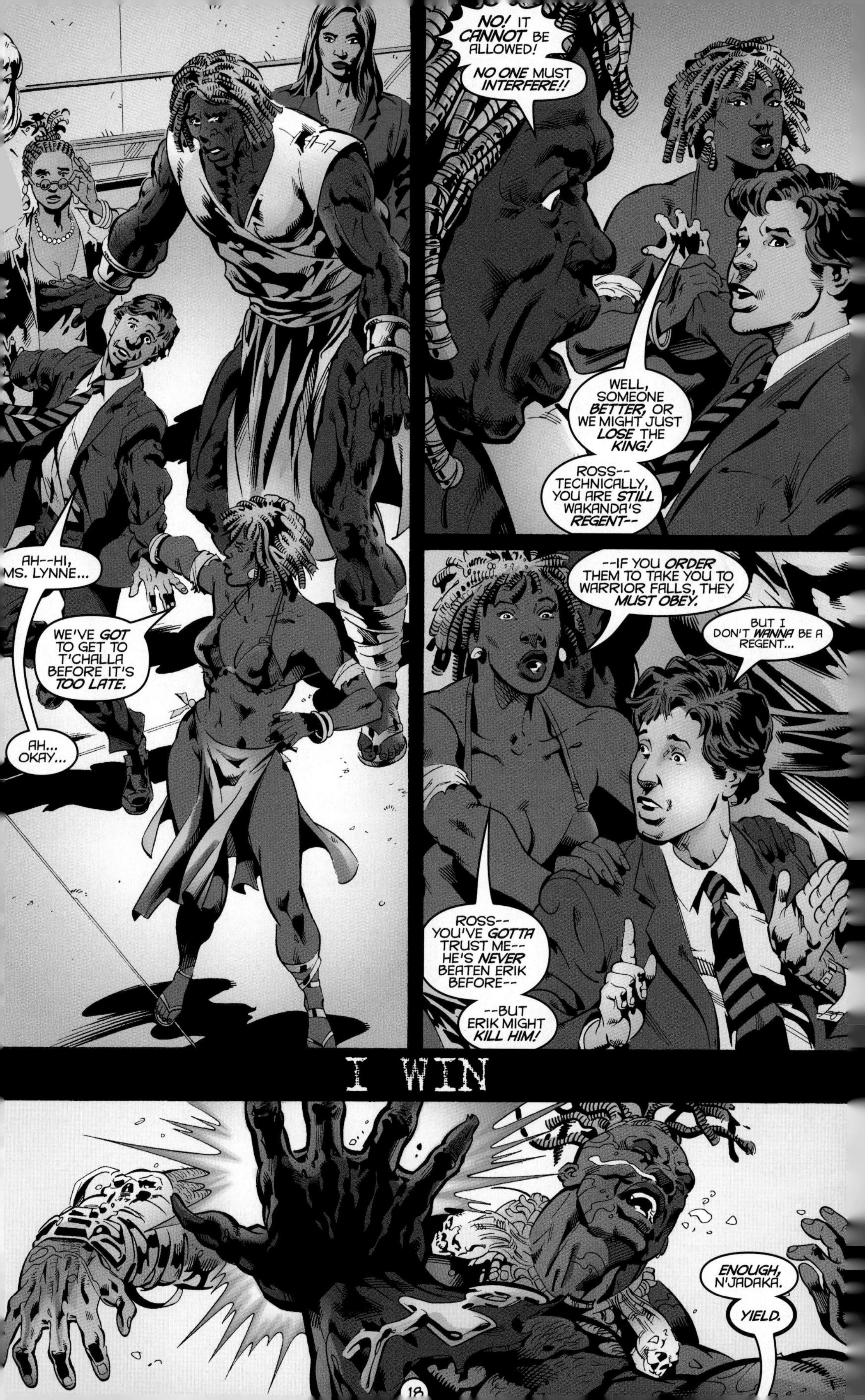

AH--HI, MS. LYNNE...
WE'VE GOT TO GET TO T'CHALLA BEFORE IT'S TOO LATE.
AH... OKAY...
NO! IT CANNOT BE ALLOWED!
NO ONE MUST INTERFERE!!
WELL, SOMEONE BETTER, OR WE MIGHT JUST LOSE THE KING!
ROSS-- TECHNICALLY, YOU ARE STILL WAKANDA'S REGENT--
--IF YOU ORDER THEM TO TAKE YOU TO WARRIOR FALLS, THEY MUST OBEY.
BUT I DON'T WANNA BE A REGENT...
ROSS-- YOU'VE GOTTA TRUST ME-- HE'S NEVER BEATEN ERIK BEFORE--
--BUT ERIK MIGHT KILL HIM!
I WIN
ENOUGH, N'JADAKA.
YIELD.

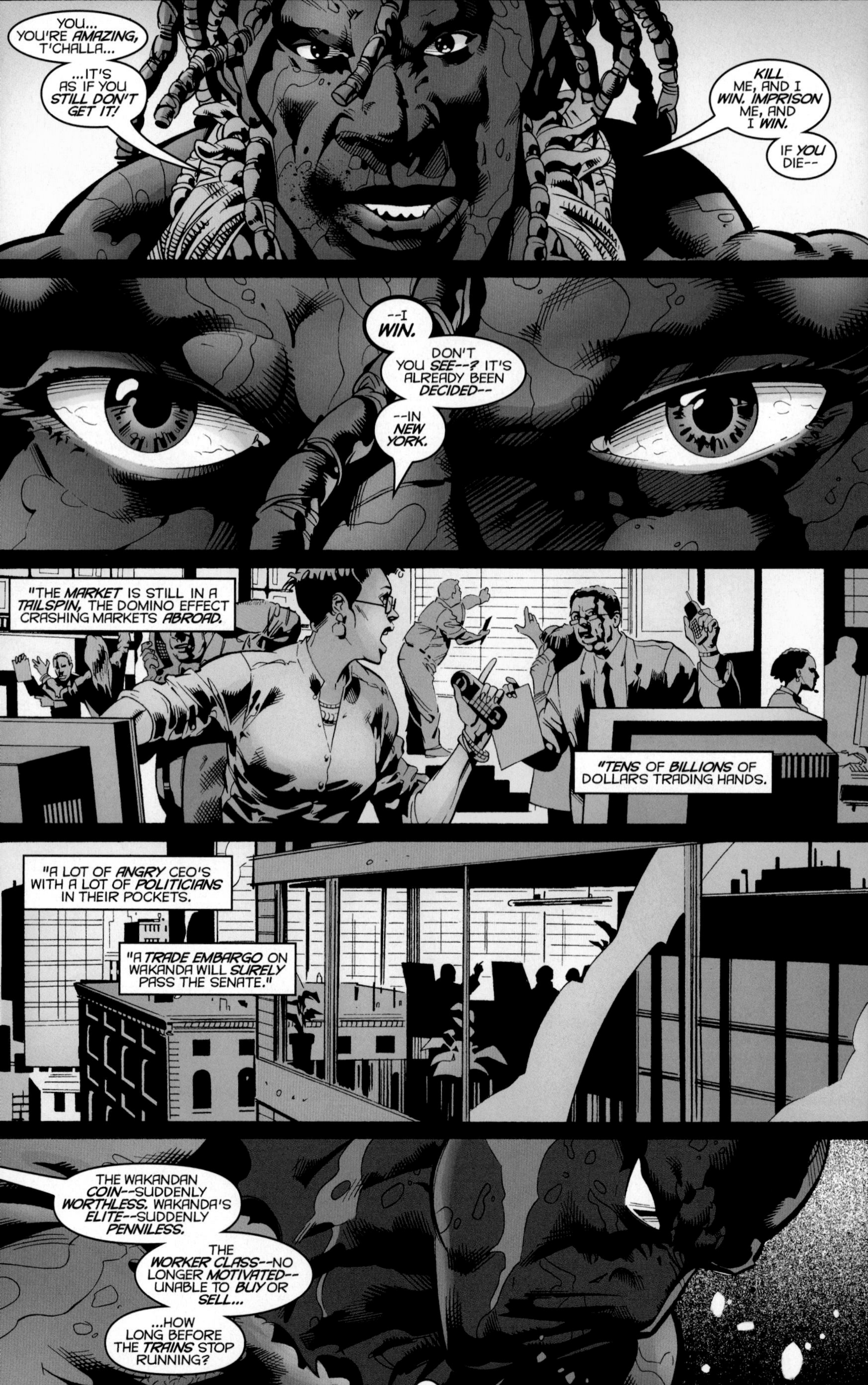
YOU... YOU'RE AMAZING, T'CHALLA...
...IT'S AS IF YOU STILL DON'T GET IT!
KILL ME, AND I WIN. IMPRISON ME, AND I WIN.
IF YOU DIE--
--I WIN.
DON'T YOU SEE--? IT'S ALREADY BEEN DECIDED--
--IN NEW YORK.
"THE MARKET IS STILL IN A TAILSPIN, THE DOMINO EFFECT CRASHING MARKETS ABROAD.
"TENS OF BILLIONS OF DOLLARS TRADING HANDS.
"A LOT OF ANGRY CEO'S WITH A LOT OF POLITICIANS IN THEIR POCKETS.
"A TRADE EMBARGO ON WAKANDA WILL SURELY PASS THE SENATE."
THE WAKANDAN COIN--SUDDENLY WORTHLESS. WAKANDA'S ELITE--SUDDENLY PENNILESS.
THE WORKER CLASS--NO LONGER MOTIVATED--UNABLE TO BUY OR SELL...
...HOW LONG BEFORE THE TRAINS STOP RUNNING?

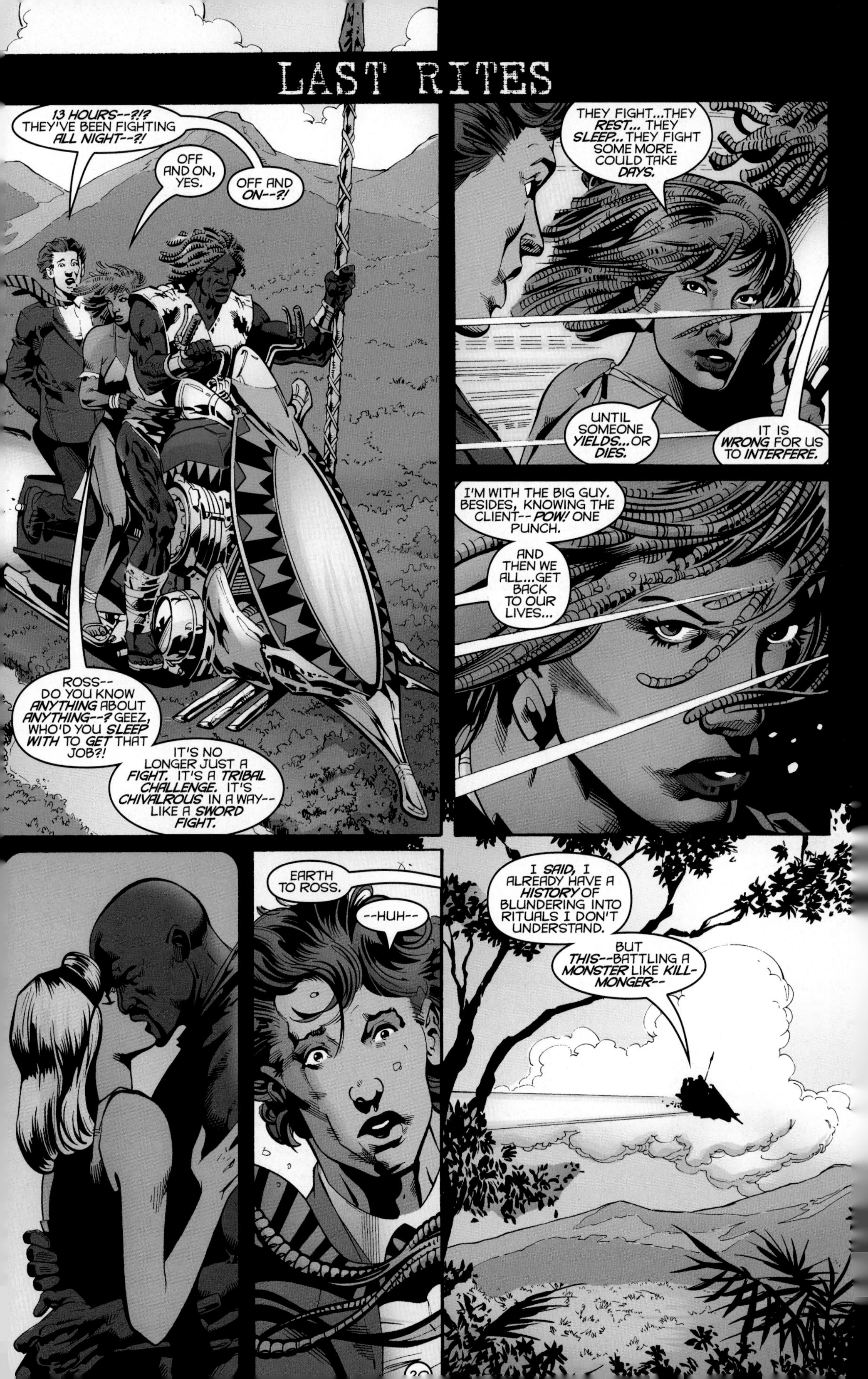
LAST RITES
13 HOURS--?!? THEY'VE BEEN FIGHTING ALL NIGHT--?!
OFF AND ON, YES.
OFF AND ON--?!
THEY FIGHT...THEY REST... THEY SLEEP... THEY FIGHT SOME MORE. COULD TAKE DAYS.
UNTIL SOMEONE YIELDS...OR DIES.
IT IS WRONG FOR US TO INTERFERE.
ROSS-- DO YOU KNOW ANYTHING ABOUT ANYTHING--? GEEZ, WHO'D YOU SLEEP WITH TO GET THAT JOB?!
IT'S NO LONGER JUST A FIGHT. IT'S A TRIBAL CHALLENGE. IT'S CHIVALROUS IN A WAY-- LIKE A SWORD FIGHT.
I'M WITH THE BIG GUY. BESIDES, KNOWING THE CLIENT-- POW! ONE PUNCH.
AND THEN WE ALL...GET BACK TO OUR LIVES...
EARTH TO ROSS.
--HUH--
I SAID, I ALREADY HAVE A HISTORY OF BLUNDERING INTO RITUALS I DON'T UNDERSTAND.
BUT THIS--BATTLING A MONSTER LIKE KILL-MONGER--

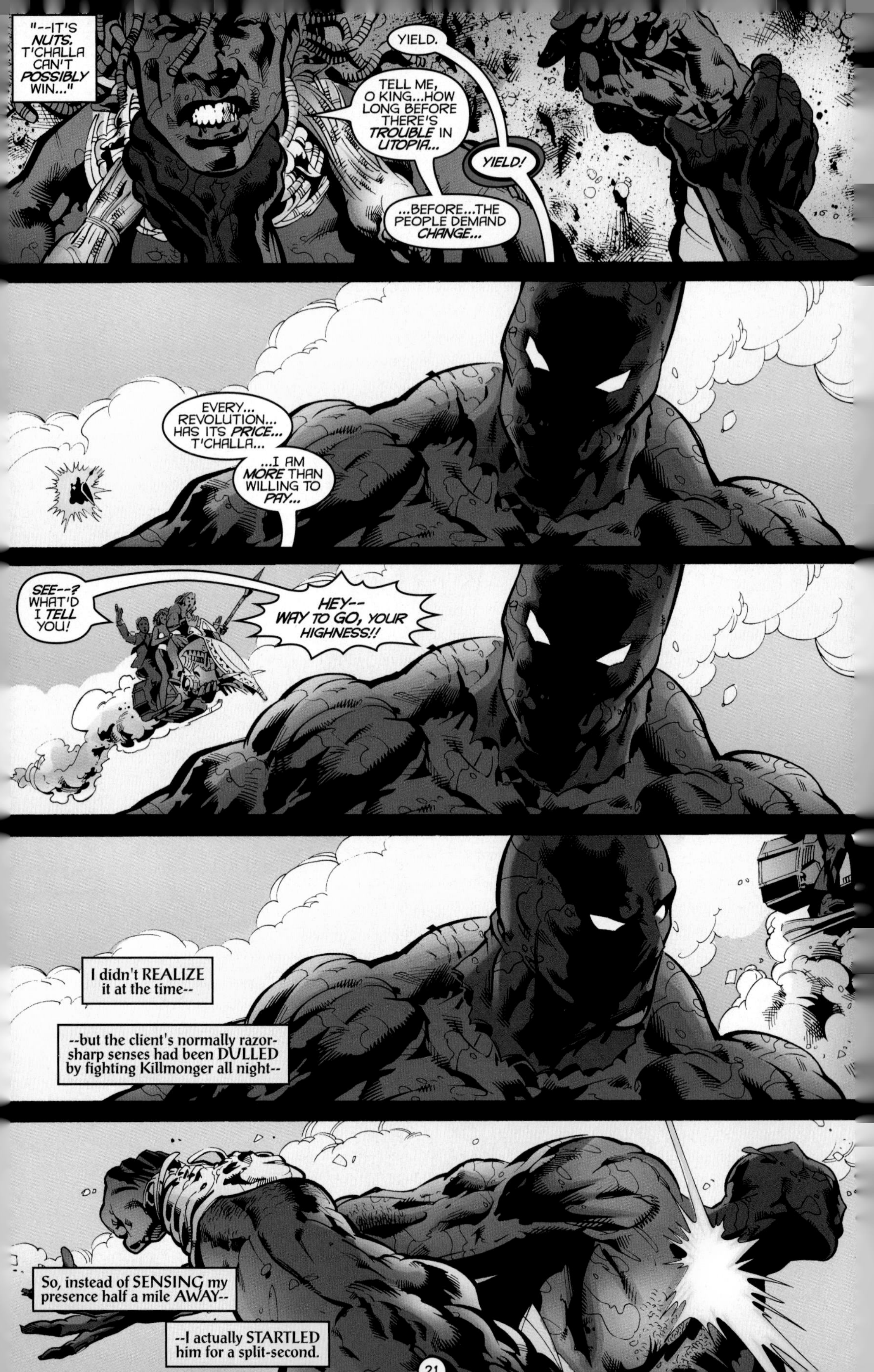
"--IT'S NUTS. T'CHALLA CAN'T POSSIBLY WIN..."
YIELD.
TELL ME, O KING...HOW LONG BEFORE THERE'S TROUBLE IN UTOPIA...
YIELD!
...BEFORE...THE PEOPLE DEMAND CHANGE...
EVERY... REVOLUTION... HAS ITS PRICE... T'CHALLA...
...I AM MORE THAN WILLING TO PAY...
SEE--? WHAT'D I TELL YOU!
HEY-- WAY TO GO, YOUR HIGHNESS!!
I didn't REALIZE it at the time--
--but the client's normally razor-sharp senses had been DULLED by fighting Killmonger all night--
So, instead of SENSING my presence half a mile AWAY--
--I actually STARTLED him for a split-second.

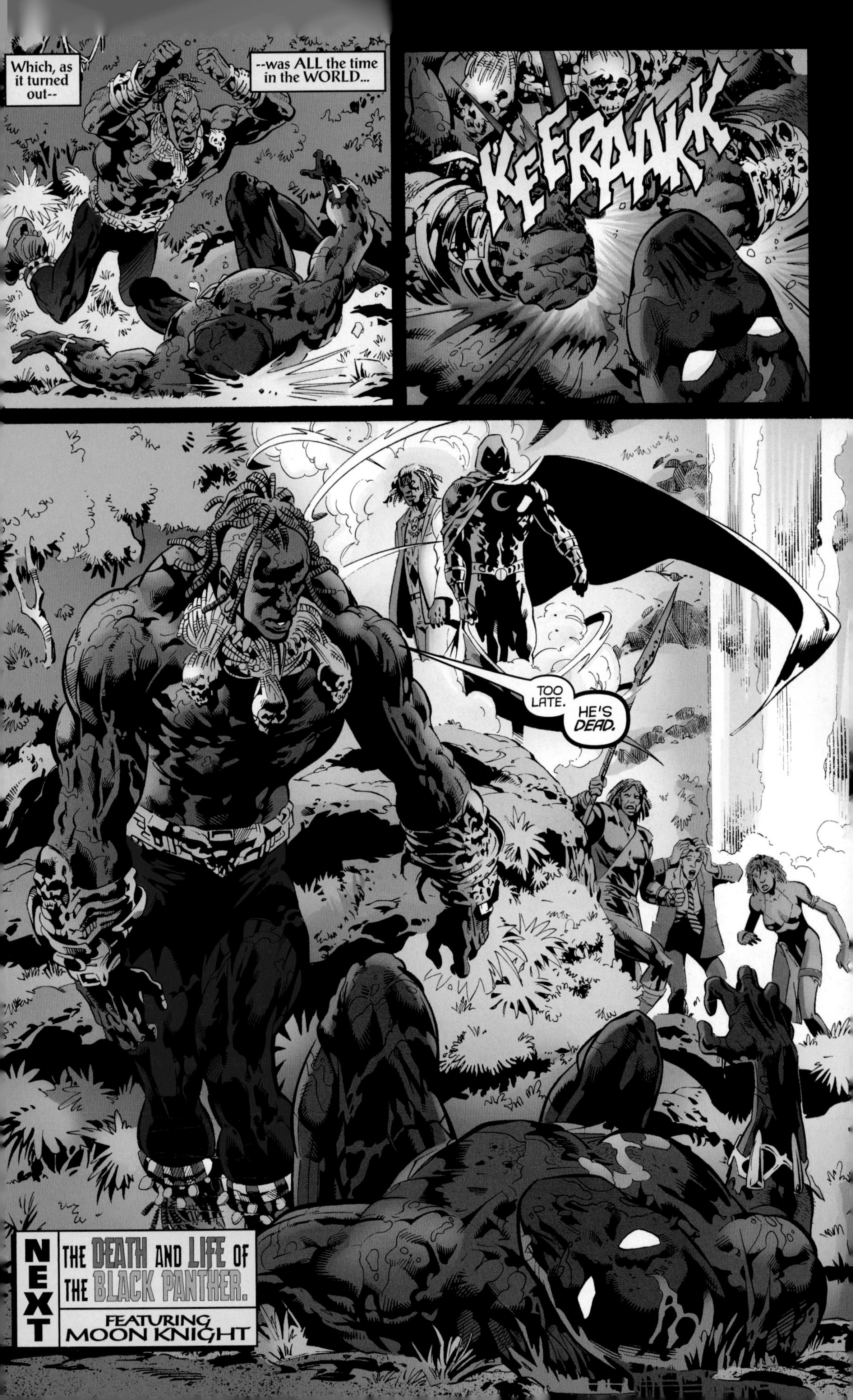
Which, as it turned out--
--was ALL the time in the WORLD...
KEFRAKK
TOO LATE.
HE'S DEAD.
NEXT
THE DEATH AND LIFE OF THE BLACK PANTHER.
FEATURING MOON KNIGHT

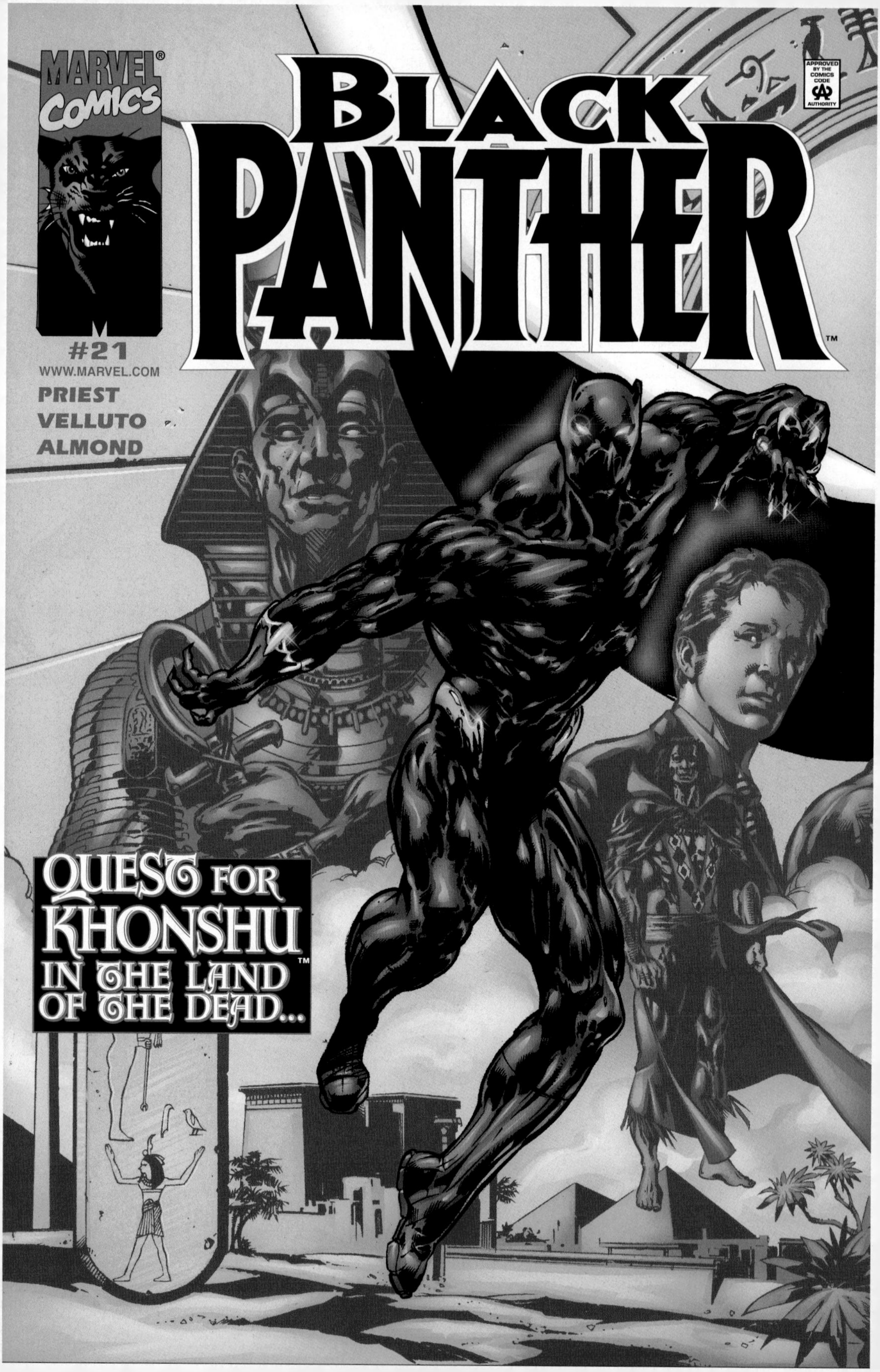

MARVEL COMICS
BLACK PANTHER
#21
WWW.MARVEL.COM
PRIEST
VELLUTO
ALMOND
APPROVED BY THE COMICS CODE AUTHORITY
QUEST FOR KHONSHU IN THE LAND OF THE DEAD...

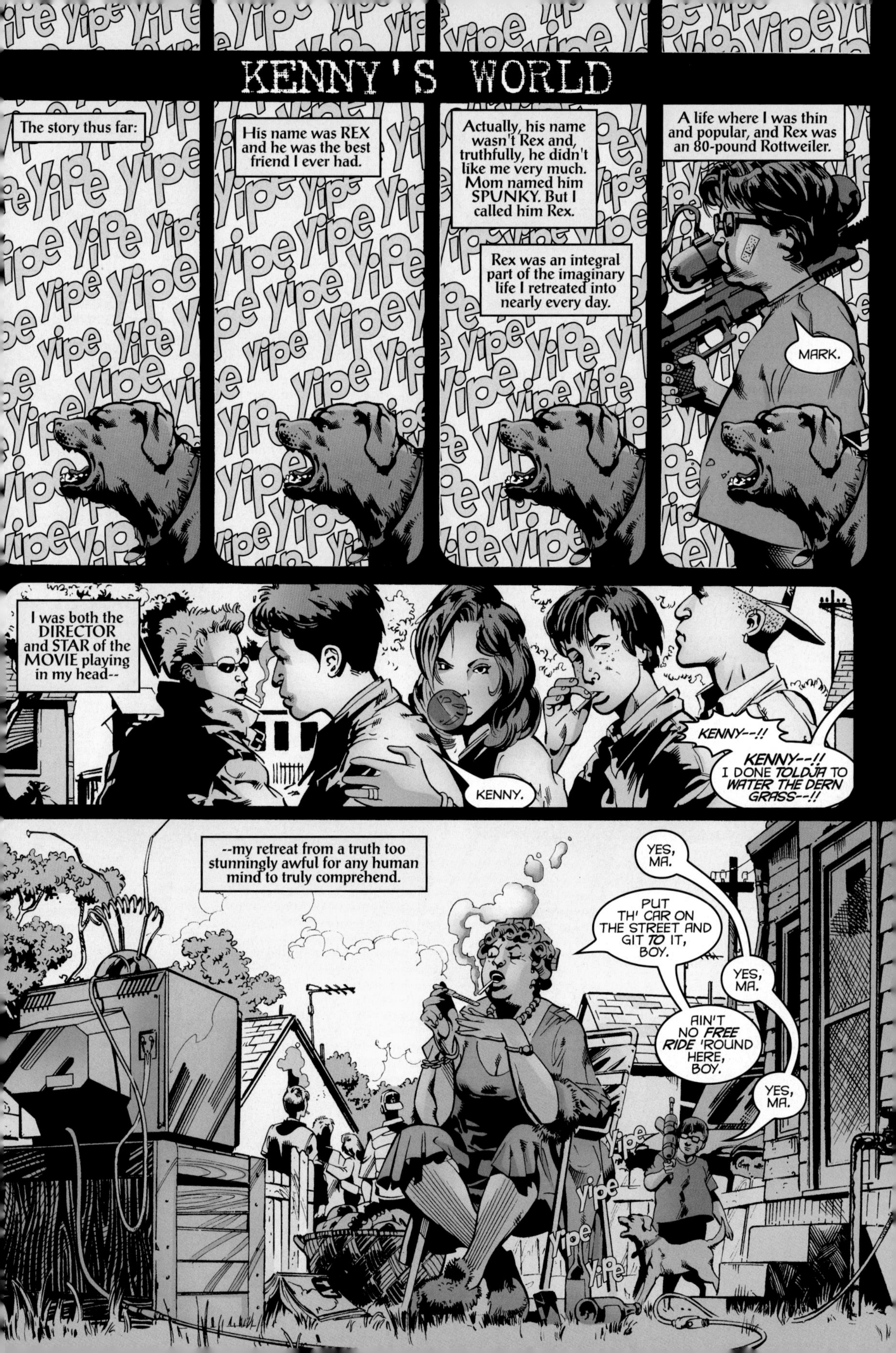
KENNY'S WORLD
The story thus far:
His name was REX and he was the best friend I ever had.
Actually, his name wasn't Rex and, truthfully, he didn't like me very much. Mom named him SPUNKY. But I called him Rex.
Rex was an integral part of the imaginary life I retreated into nearly every day.
A life where I was thin and popular, and Rex was an 80-pound Rottweiler.
MARK.
I was both the DIRECTOR and STAR of the MOVIE playing in my head--
KENNY.
KENNY--!!
KENNY--!! I DONE TOLDJA TO WATER THE DERN GRASS--!!
--my retreat from a truth too stunningly awful for any human mind to truly comprehend.
YES, MA.
PUT TH' CAR ON THE STREET AND GIT TO IT, BOY.
YES, MA.
AIN'T NO FREE RIDE 'ROUND HERE, BOY.
YES, MA.
yipe
yipe
yipe
yipe

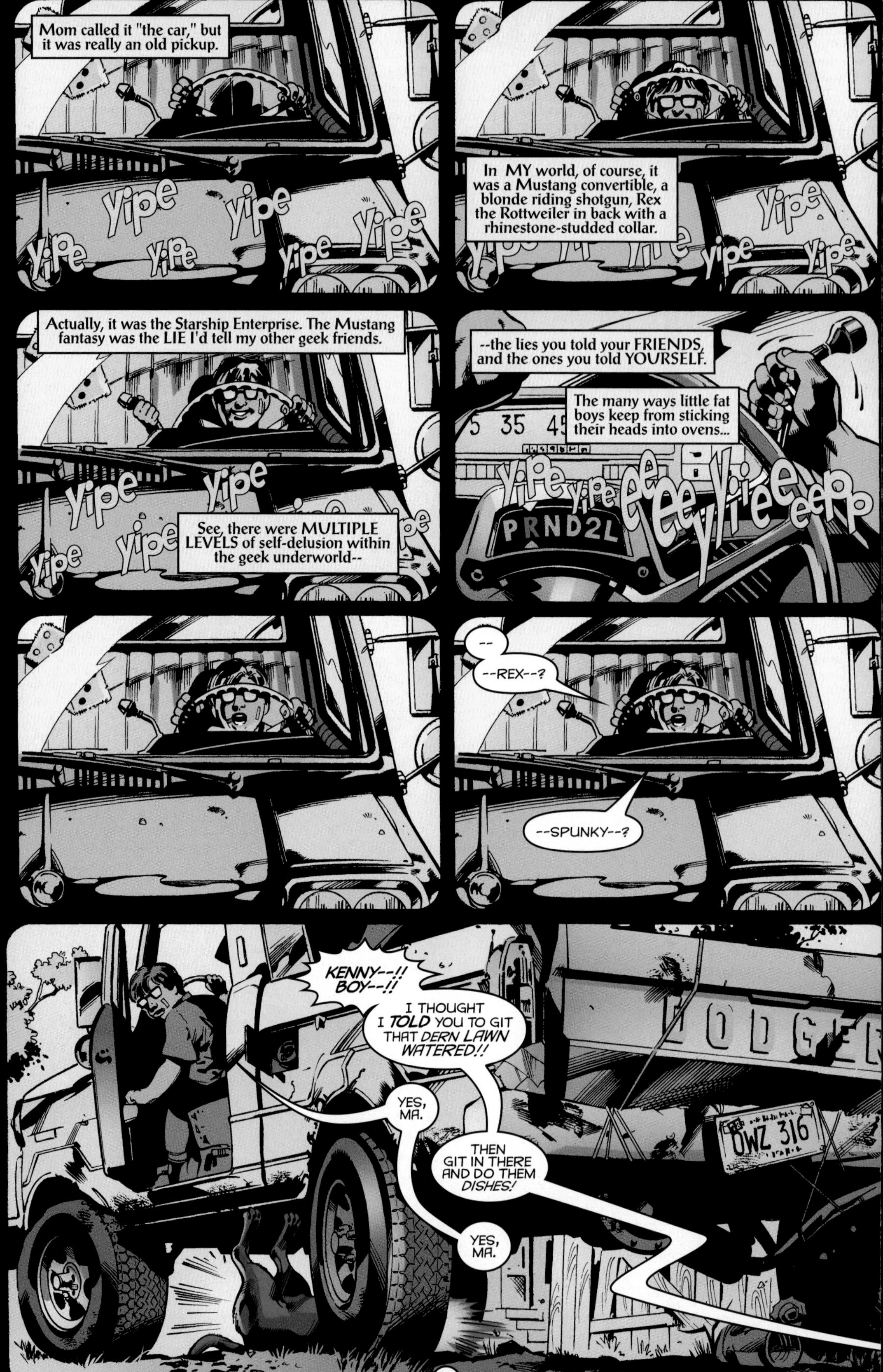

Mom called it "the car," but it was really an old pickup.
yipe yipe yipe yipe yipe yipe
In MY world, of course, it was a Mustang convertible, a blonde riding shotgun, Rex the Rottweiler in back with a rhinestone-studded collar.
yipe yipe
Actually, it was the Starship Enterprise. The Mustang fantasy was the LIE I'd tell my other geek friends.
yipe yipe yipe yipe
See, there were MULTIPLE LEVELS of self-delusion within the geek underworld--
--the lies you told your FRIENDS, and the ones you told YOURSELF.
The many ways little fat boys keep from sticking their heads into ovens...
PRND2L
yipe yipe eeeeyiieeeepp
--
--REX--?
--SPUNKY--?
KENNY--!! BOY--!!
I THOUGHT I TOLD YOU TO GIT THAT DERN LAWN WATERED!!
YES, MA.
THEN GIT IN THERE AND DO THEM DISHES!
YES, MA.
DODGE
OWZ 316

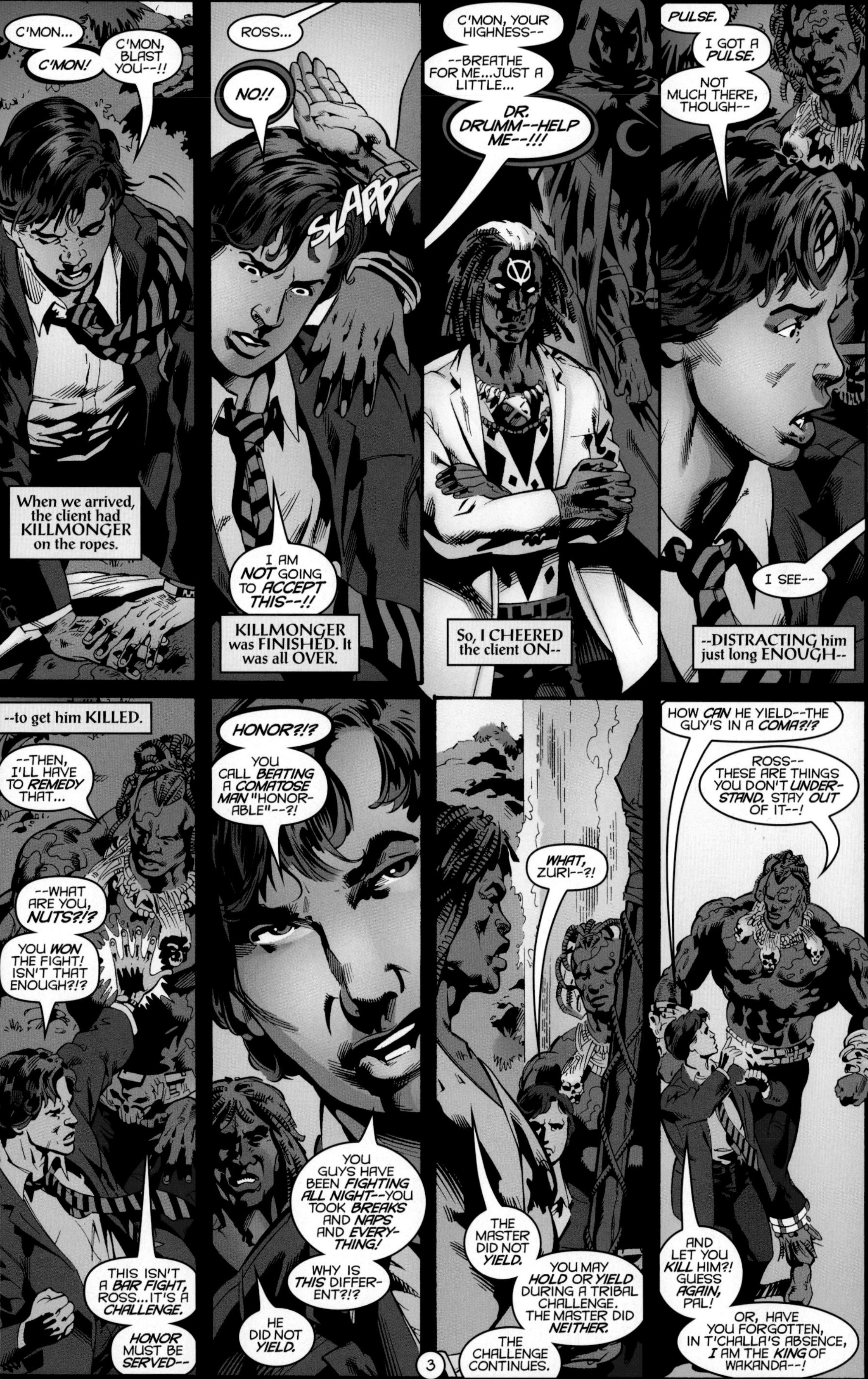
C'MON...
C'MON!
C'MON, BLAST YOU--!!
When we arrived, the client had KILLMONGER on the ropes.
ROSS...
NO!!
SLAPP
I AM NOT GOING TO ACCEPT THIS--!!
KILLMONGER was FINISHED. It was all OVER.
C'MON, YOUR HIGHNESS--
--BREATHE FOR ME...JUST A LITTLE...
DR. DRUMM--HELP ME--!!!
So, I CHEERED the client ON--
PULSE.
I GOT A PULSE.
NOT MUCH THERE, THOUGH--
I SEE--
--DISTRACTING him just long ENOUGH--
--to get him KILLED.
--THEN, I'LL HAVE TO REMEDY THAT...
--WHAT ARE YOU, NUTS?!?
YOU WON THE FIGHT! ISN'T THAT ENOUGH?!?
THIS ISN'T A BAR FIGHT, ROSS...IT'S A CHALLENGE.
HONOR MUST BE SERVED--
HONOR?!?
YOU CALL BEATING A COMATOSE MAN "HONORABLE"--?!
YOU GUYS HAVE BEEN FIGHTING ALL NIGHT--YOU TOOK BREAKS AND NAPS AND EVERYTHING!
WHY IS THIS DIFFERENT?!?
HE DID NOT YIELD.
WHAT, ZURI--?!
THE MASTER DID NOT YIELD.
YOU MAY HOLD OR YIELD DURING A TRIBAL CHALLENGE. THE MASTER DID NEITHER.
THE CHALLENGE CONTINUES.
HOW CAN HE YIELD--THE GUY'S IN A COMA?!?
ROSS-- THESE ARE THINGS YOU DON'T UNDERSTAND. STAY OUT OF IT--!
AND LET YOU KILL HIM?! GUESS AGAIN, PAL!
OR, HAVE YOU FORGOTTEN, IN T'CHALLA'S ABSENCE, I AM THE KING OF WAKANDA--!

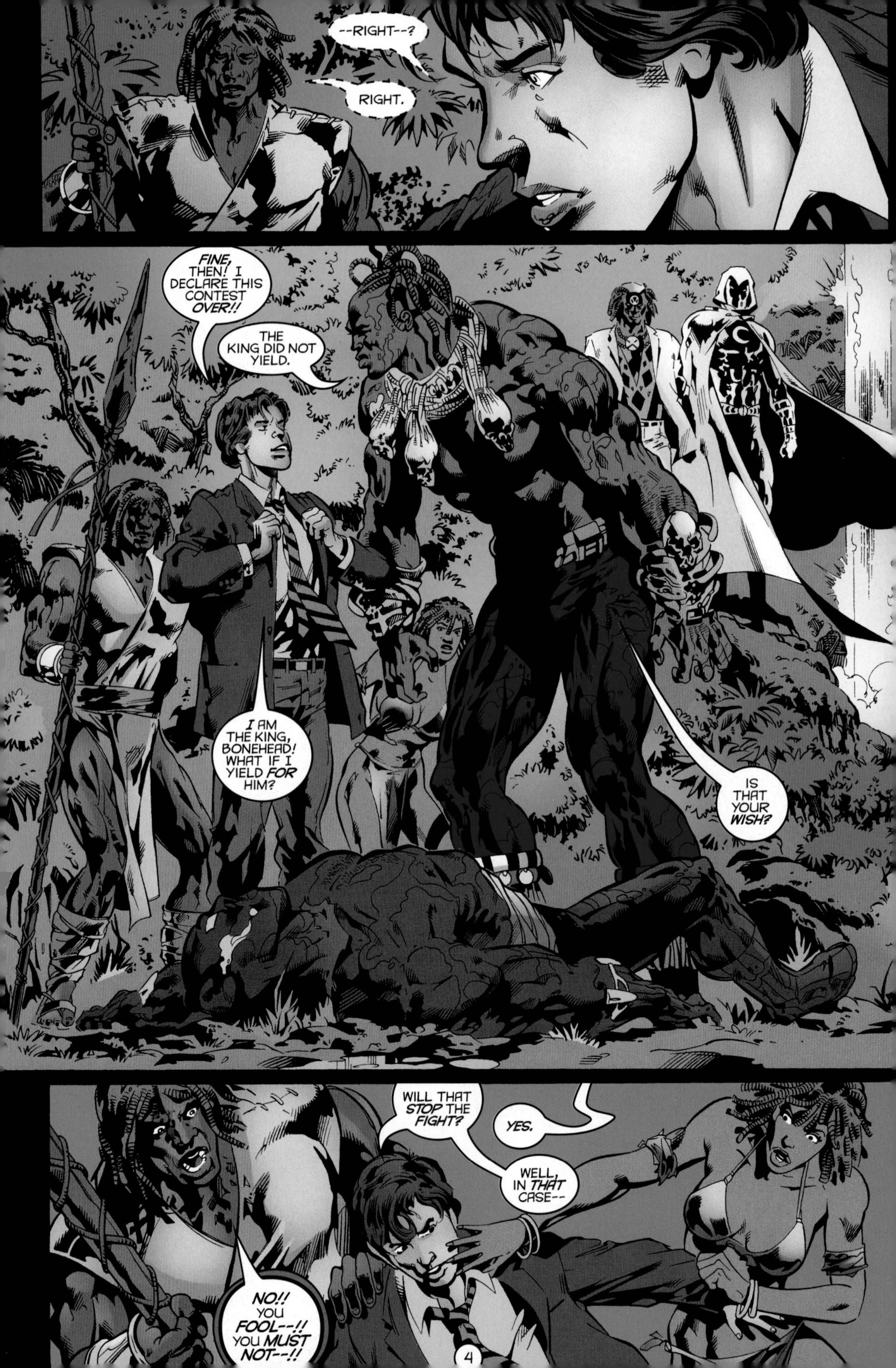
--RIGHT--?
RIGHT.
FINE, THEN! I DECLARE THIS CONTEST OVER!!
THE KING DID NOT YIELD.
I AM THE KING, BONEHEAD! WHAT IF I YIELD FOR HIM?
IS THAT YOUR WISH?
WILL THAT STOP THE FIGHT?
YES.
WELL, IN THAT CASE--
NO!! YOU FOOL--!! YOU MUST NOT--!!

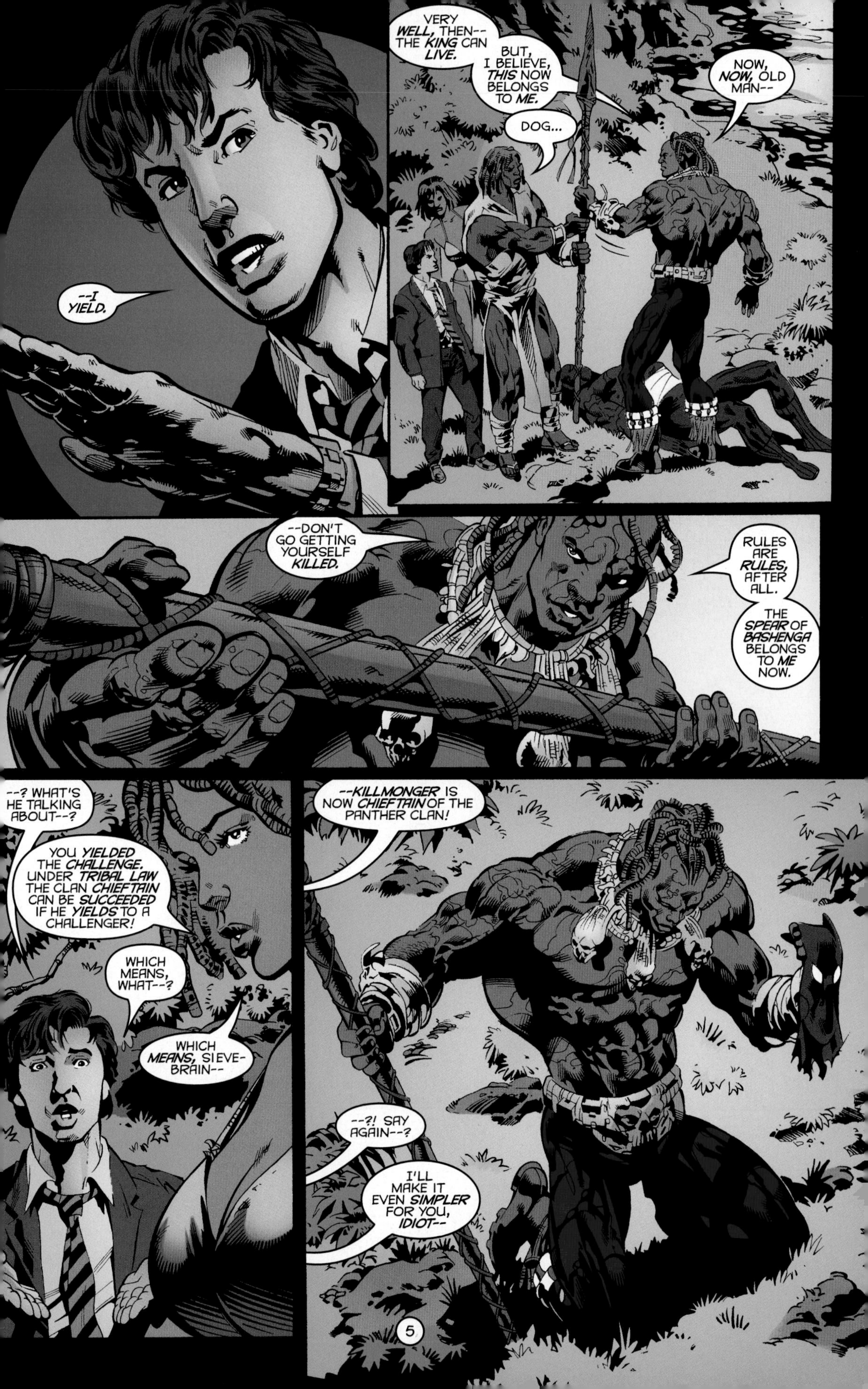
--I YIELD.
VERY WELL, THEN-- THE KING CAN LIVE.
BUT, I BELIEVE, THIS NOW BELONGS TO ME.
DOG...
NOW, NOW, OLD MAN--
--DON'T GO GETTING YOURSELF KILLED.
RULES ARE RULES, AFTER ALL.
THE SPEAR OF BASHENGA BELONGS TO ME NOW.
--? WHAT'S HE TALKING ABOUT--?
YOU YIELDED THE CHALLENGE. UNDER TRIBAL LAW THE CLAN CHIEFTAIN CAN BE SUCCEEDED IF HE YIELDS TO A CHALLENGER!
WHICH MEANS, WHAT--?
WHICH MEANS, SIEVE-BRAIN--
--KILLMONGER IS NOW CHIEFTAIN OF THE PANTHER CLAN!
--?! SAY AGAIN--?
I'LL MAKE IT EVEN SIMPLER FOR YOU, IDIOT--

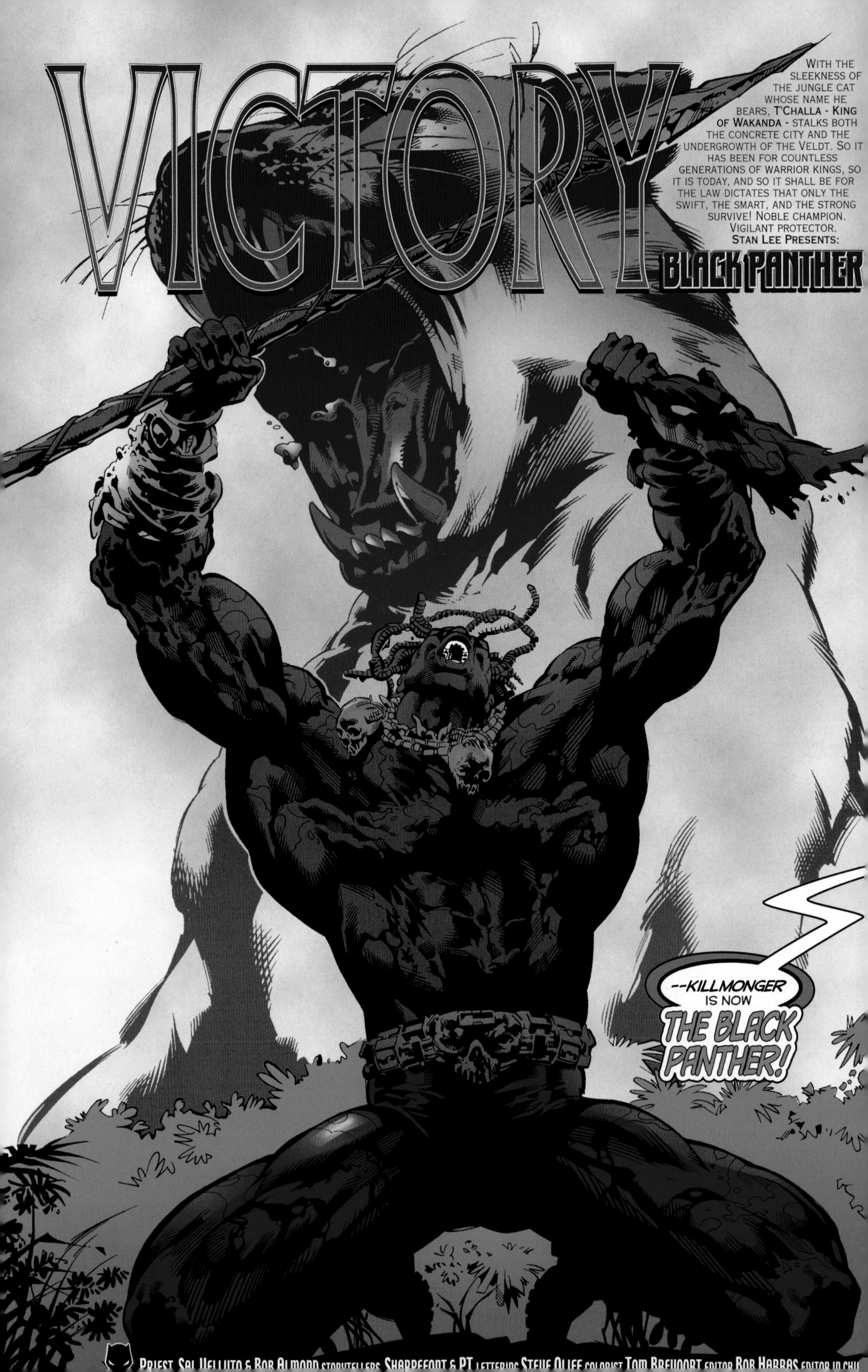
VICTORY
With the sleekness of the jungle cat whose name he bears, T'Challa - King of Wakanda - stalks both the concrete city and the undergrowth of the Veldt. So it has been for countless generations of warrior kings, so it is today, and so it shall be for the law dictates that only the swift, the smart, and the strong survive! Noble champion. Vigilant protector.
Stan Lee Presents:
BLACK PANTHER
--KILLMONGER IS NOW THE BLACK PANTHER!
Priest, Sal Velluto & Bob Almond storytellers Sharpefont & PT lettering Steve Oliff colorist Tom Brevoort editor Bob Harras editor in chi

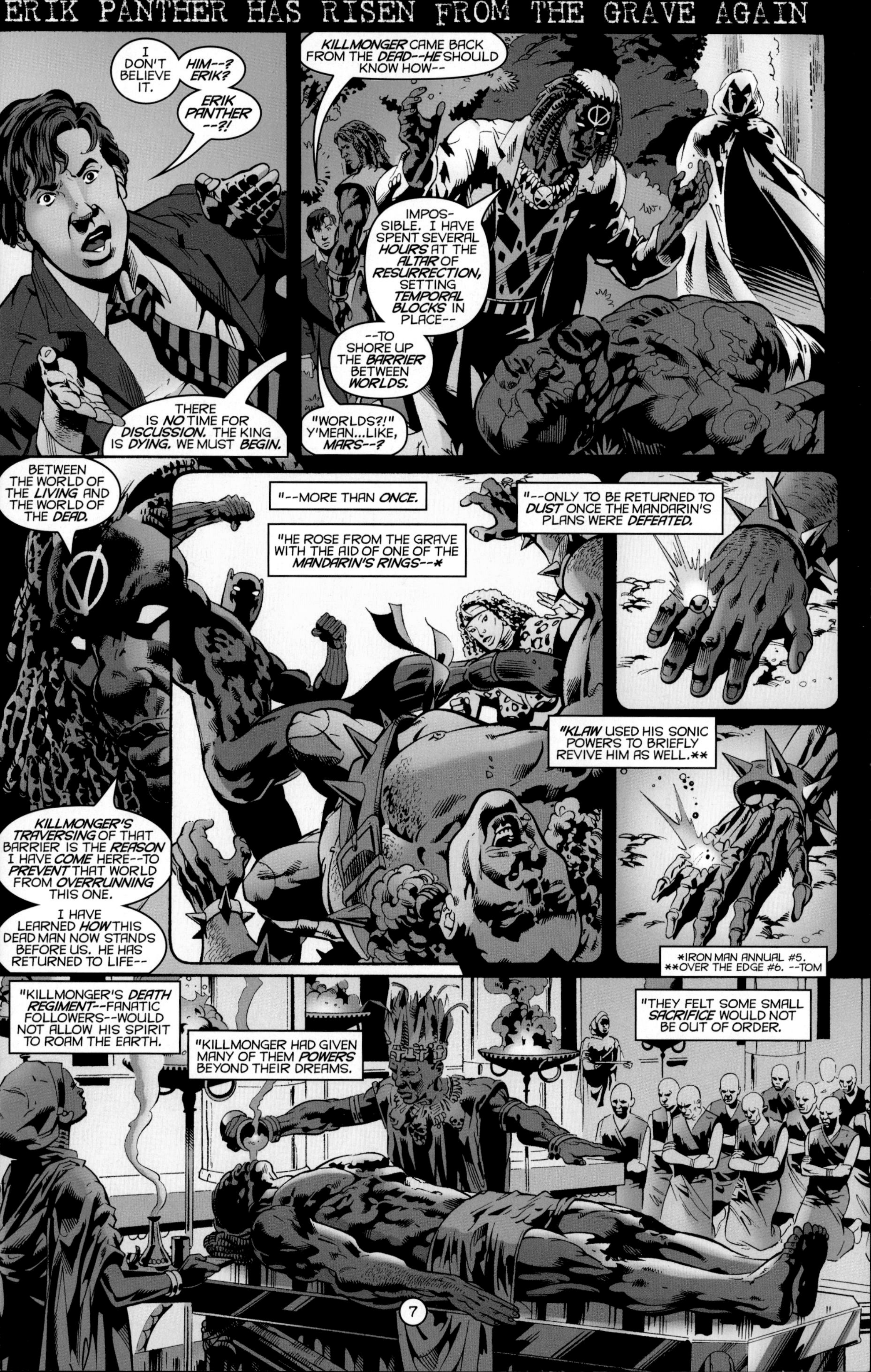
ERIK PANTHER HAS RISEN FROM THE GRAVE AGAIN
I DON'T BELIEVE IT.
HIM--? ERIK?
ERIK PANTHER --?!
THERE IS NO TIME FOR DISCUSSION. THE KING IS DYING. WE MUST BEGIN.
KILLMONGER CAME BACK FROM THE DEAD--HE SHOULD KNOW HOW--
IMPOSSIBLE. I HAVE SPENT SEVERAL HOURS AT THE ALTAR OF RESURRECTION, SETTING TEMPORAL BLOCKS IN PLACE--
--TO SHORE UP THE BARRIER BETWEEN WORLDS.
"WORLDS?!" Y'MEAN...LIKE, MARS--?
BETWEEN THE WORLD OF THE LIVING AND THE WORLD OF THE DEAD.
KILLMONGER'S TRAVERSING OF THAT BARRIER IS THE REASON I HAVE COME HERE--TO PREVENT THAT WORLD FROM OVERRUNNING THIS ONE.
I HAVE LEARNED HOW THIS DEAD MAN NOW STANDS BEFORE US. HE HAS RETURNED TO LIFE--
"--MORE THAN ONCE.
"HE ROSE FROM THE GRAVE WITH THE AID OF ONE OF THE MANDARIN'S RINGS--*
"--ONLY TO BE RETURNED TO DUST ONCE THE MANDARIN'S PLANS WERE DEFEATED.
"KLAW USED HIS SONIC POWERS TO BRIEFLY REVIVE HIM AS WELL.**
*IRON MAN ANNUAL #5.
**OVER THE EDGE #6. --TOM
"KILLMONGER'S DEATH REGIMENT--FANATIC FOLLOWERS--WOULD NOT ALLOW HIS SPIRIT TO ROAM THE EARTH.
"KILLMONGER HAD GIVEN MANY OF THEM POWERS BEYOND THEIR DREAMS.
"THEY FELT SOME SMALL SACRIFICE WOULD NOT BE OUT OF ORDER.

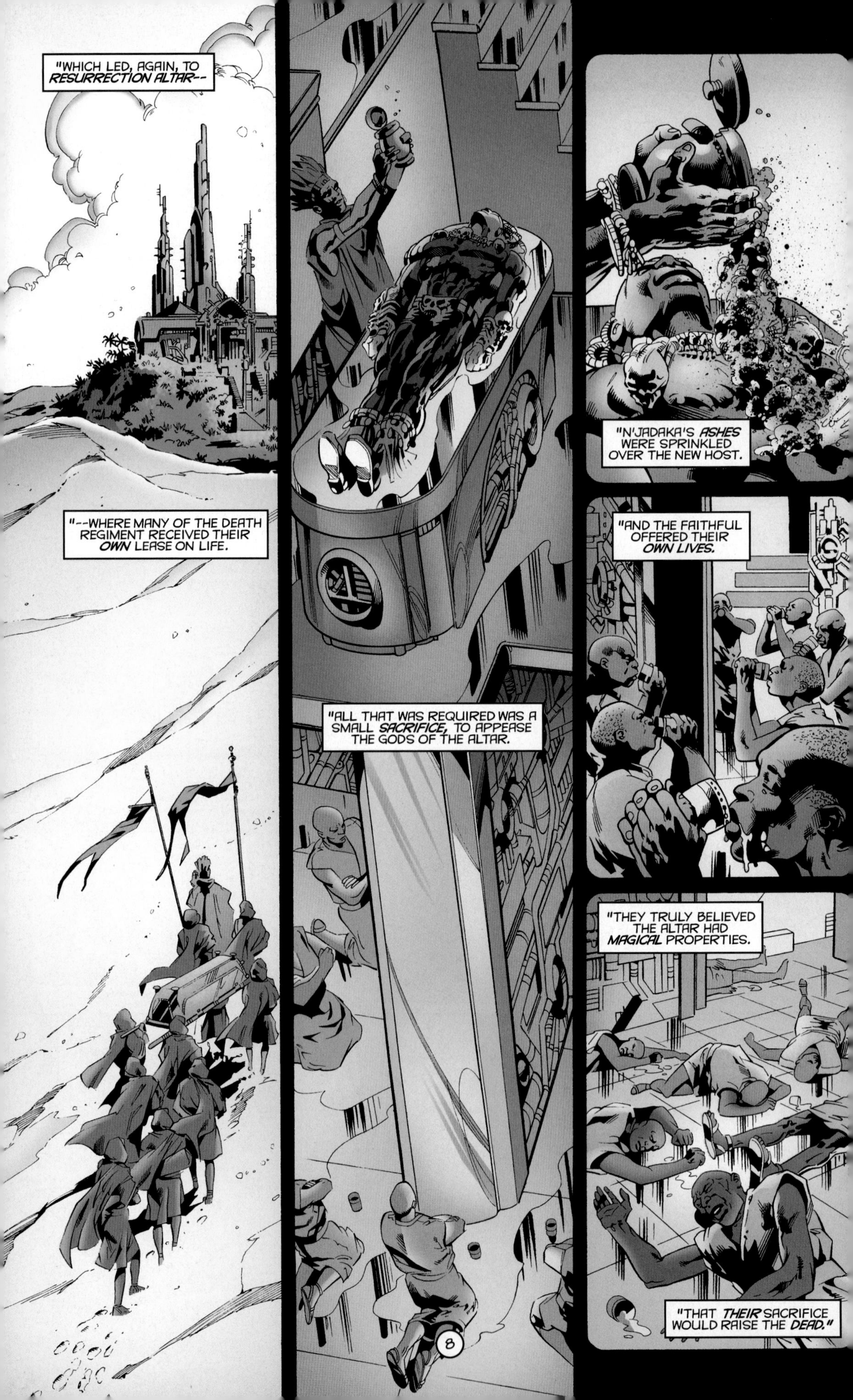
"WHICH LED, AGAIN, TO RESURRECTION ALTAR--
"--WHERE MANY OF THE DEATH REGIMENT RECEIVED THEIR OWN LEASE ON LIFE.
"ALL THAT WAS REQUIRED WAS A SMALL SACRIFICE, TO APPEASE THE GODS OF THE ALTAR.
"N'JADAKA'S ASHES WERE SPRINKLED OVER THE NEW HOST.
"AND THE FAITHFUL OFFERED THEIR OWN LIVES.
"THEY TRULY BELIEVED THE ALTAR HAD MAGICAL PROPERTIES.
"THAT THEIR SACRIFICE WOULD RAISE THE DEAD."
8

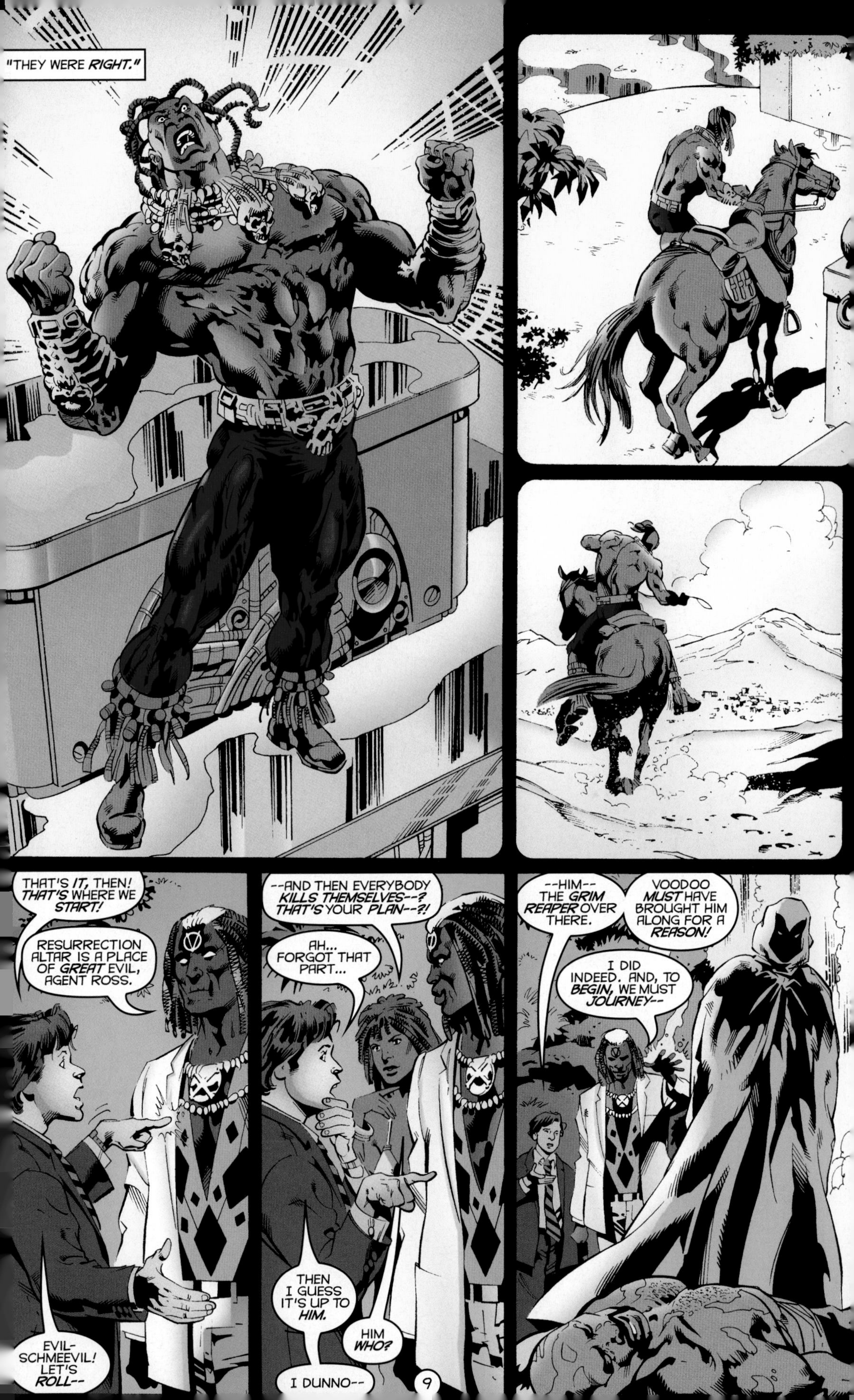
"THEY WERE RIGHT."
THAT'S IT, THEN! THAT'S WHERE WE START!
RESURRECTION ALTAR IS A PLACE OF GREAT EVIL, AGENT ROSS.
EVIL-SCHMEEVIL! LET'S ROLL--
--AND THEN EVERYBODY KILLS THEMSELVES--? THAT'S YOUR PLAN--?!
AH... FORGOT THAT PART...
THEN I GUESS IT'S UP TO HIM.
HIM WHO?
I DUNNO--
--HIM-- THE GRIM REAPER OVER THERE.
VOODOO MUST HAVE BROUGHT HIM ALONG FOR A REASON!
I DID INDEED. AND, TO BEGIN, WE MUST JOURNEY--

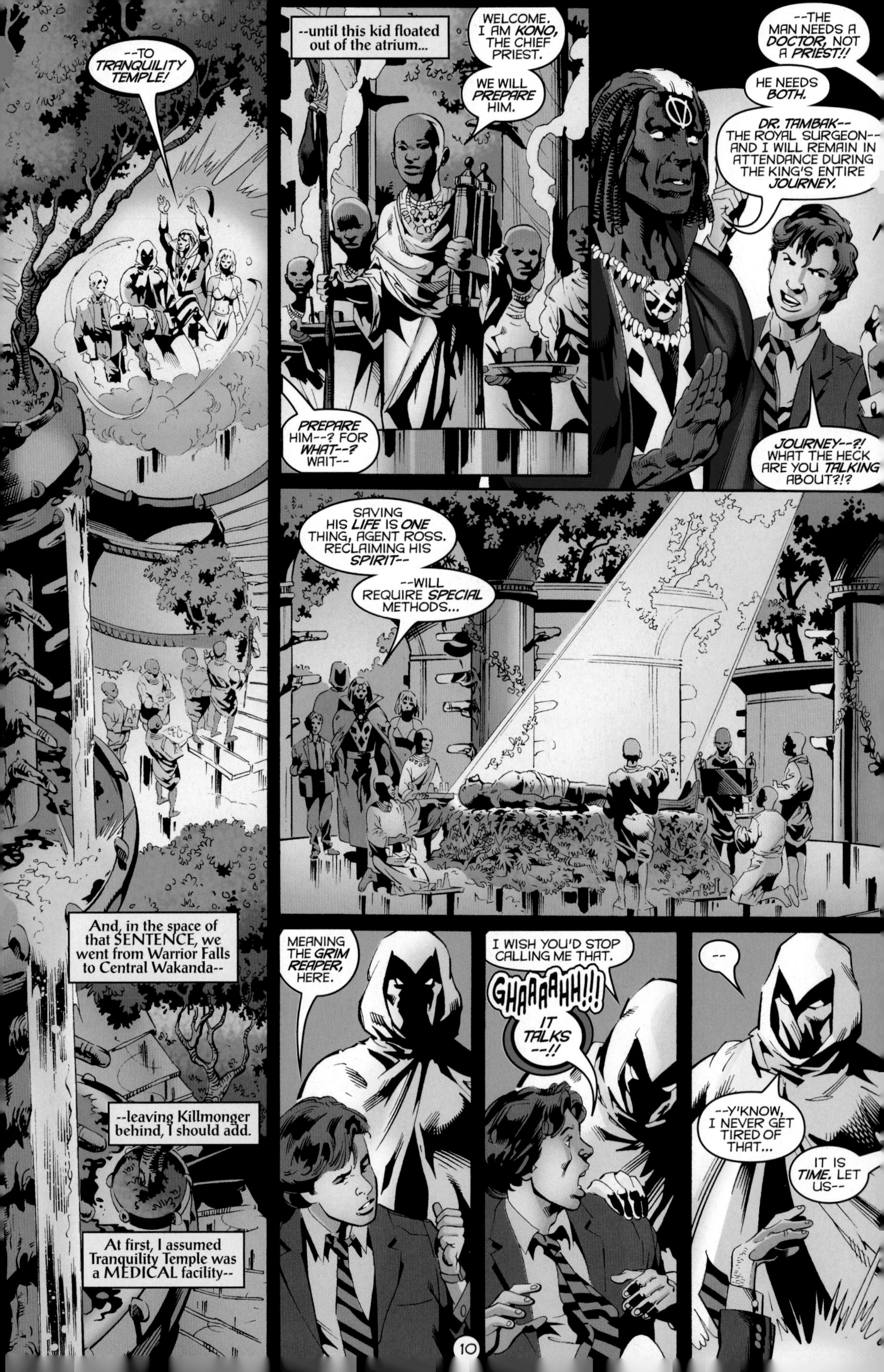
--TO TRANQUILITY TEMPLE!
--until this kid floated out of the atrium...
WELCOME. I AM KONO, THE CHIEF PRIEST.
WE WILL PREPARE HIM.
PREPARE HIM--? FOR WHAT--? WAIT--
--THE MAN NEEDS A DOCTOR, NOT A PRIEST!!
HE NEEDS BOTH.
DR. TAMBAK-- THE ROYAL SURGEON-- AND I WILL REMAIN IN ATTENDANCE DURING THE KING'S ENTIRE JOURNEY.
JOURNEY--?! WHAT THE HECK ARE YOU TALKING ABOUT?!?
SAVING HIS LIFE IS ONE THING, AGENT ROSS. RECLAIMING HIS SPIRIT--
--WILL REQUIRE SPECIAL METHODS...
And, in the space of that SENTENCE, we went from Warrior Falls to Central Wakanda--
--leaving Killmonger behind, I should add.
At first, I assumed Tranquility Temple was a MEDICAL facility--
MEANING THE GRIM REAPER, HERE.
I WISH YOU'D STOP CALLING ME THAT.
GHAAAAHH!!!
IT TALKS--!!
--
--Y'KNOW, I NEVER GET TIRED OF THAT...
IT IS TIME. LET US--

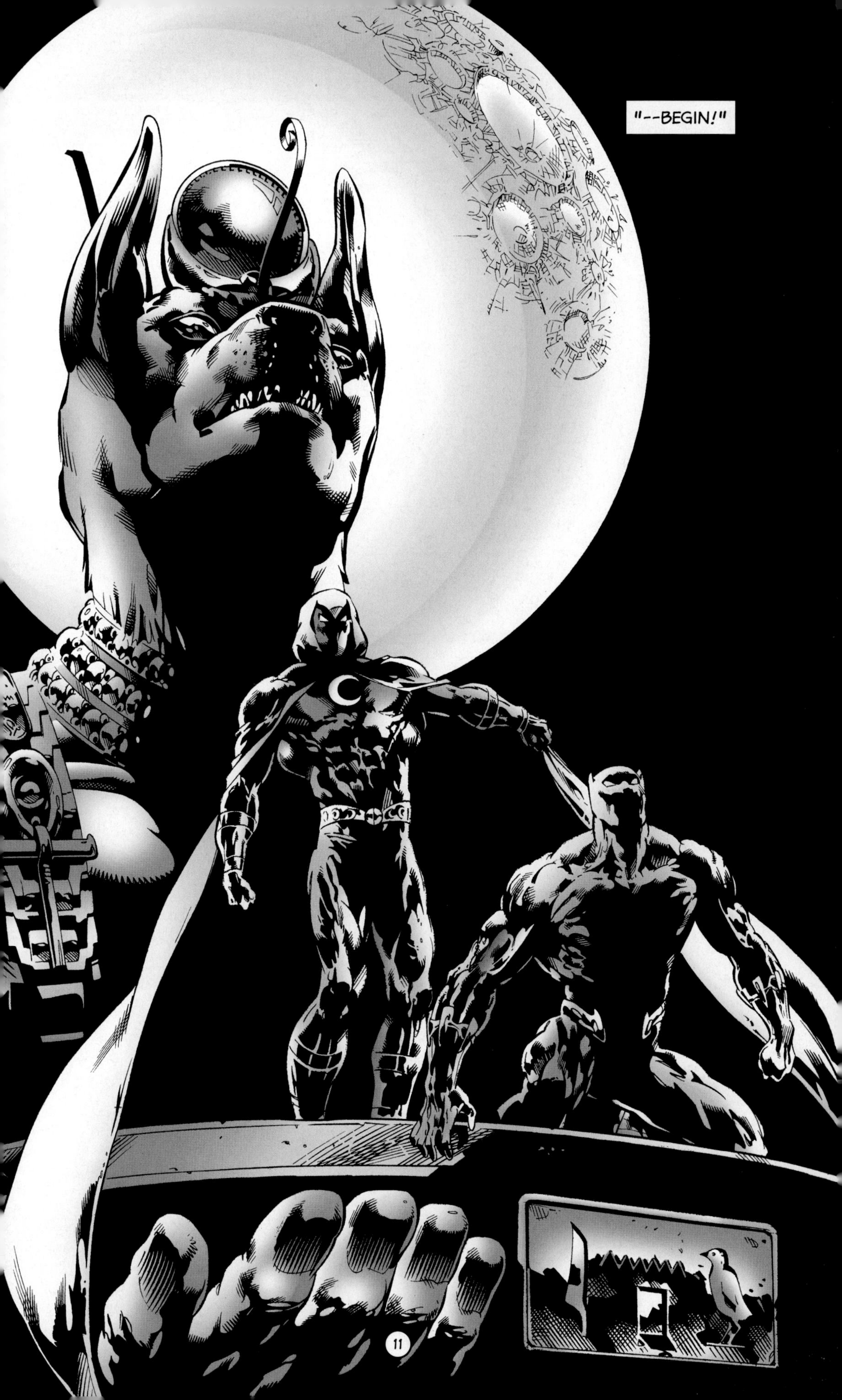
"--BEGIN!"

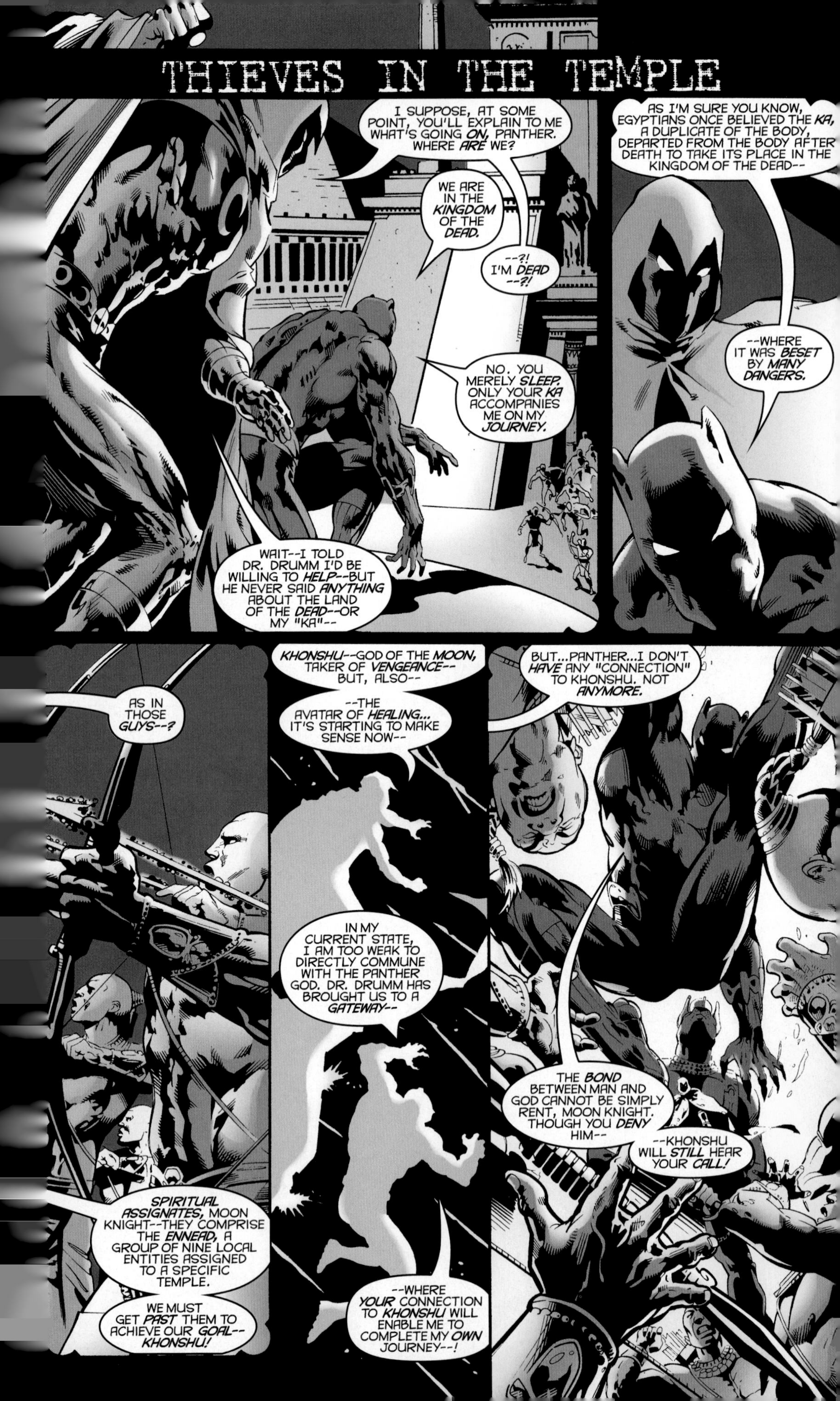
THIEVES IN THE TEMPLE
I SUPPOSE, AT SOME POINT, YOU'LL EXPLAIN TO ME WHAT'S GOING ON, PANTHER. WHERE ARE WE?
WE ARE IN THE KINGDOM OF THE DEAD.
--?! I'M DEAD--?!
NO. YOU MERELY SLEEP. ONLY YOUR KA ACCOMPANIES ME ON MY JOURNEY.
WAIT--I TOLD DR. DRUMM I'D BE WILLING TO HELP--BUT HE NEVER SAID ANYTHING ABOUT THE LAND OF THE DEAD--OR MY "KA"--
AS I'M SURE YOU KNOW, EGYPTIANS ONCE BELIEVED THE KA, A DUPLICATE OF THE BODY, DEPARTED FROM THE BODY AFTER DEATH TO TAKE ITS PLACE IN THE KINGDOM OF THE DEAD--
--WHERE IT WAS BESET BY MANY DANGERS.
AS IN THOSE GUYS--?
SPIRITUAL ASSIGNATES, MOON KNIGHT--THEY COMPRISE THE ENNEAD, A GROUP OF NINE LOCAL ENTITIES ASSIGNED TO A SPECIFIC TEMPLE.
WE MUST GET PAST THEM TO ACHIEVE OUR GOAL--KHONSHU!
KHONSHU--GOD OF THE MOON, TAKER OF VENGEANCE--BUT, ALSO--
--THE AVATAR OF HEALING... IT'S STARTING TO MAKE SENSE NOW--
IN MY CURRENT STATE, I AM TOO WEAK TO DIRECTLY COMMUNE WITH THE PANTHER GOD. DR. DRUMM HAS BROUGHT US TO A GATEWAY--
--WHERE YOUR CONNECTION TO KHONSHU WILL ENABLE ME TO COMPLETE MY OWN JOURNEY--!
BUT...PANTHER...I DON'T HAVE ANY "CONNECTION" TO KHONSHU. NOT ANYMORE.
THE BOND BETWEEN MAN AND GOD CANNOT BE SIMPLY RENT, MOON KNIGHT. THOUGH YOU DENY HIM--
--KHONSHU WILL STILL HEAR YOUR CALL!

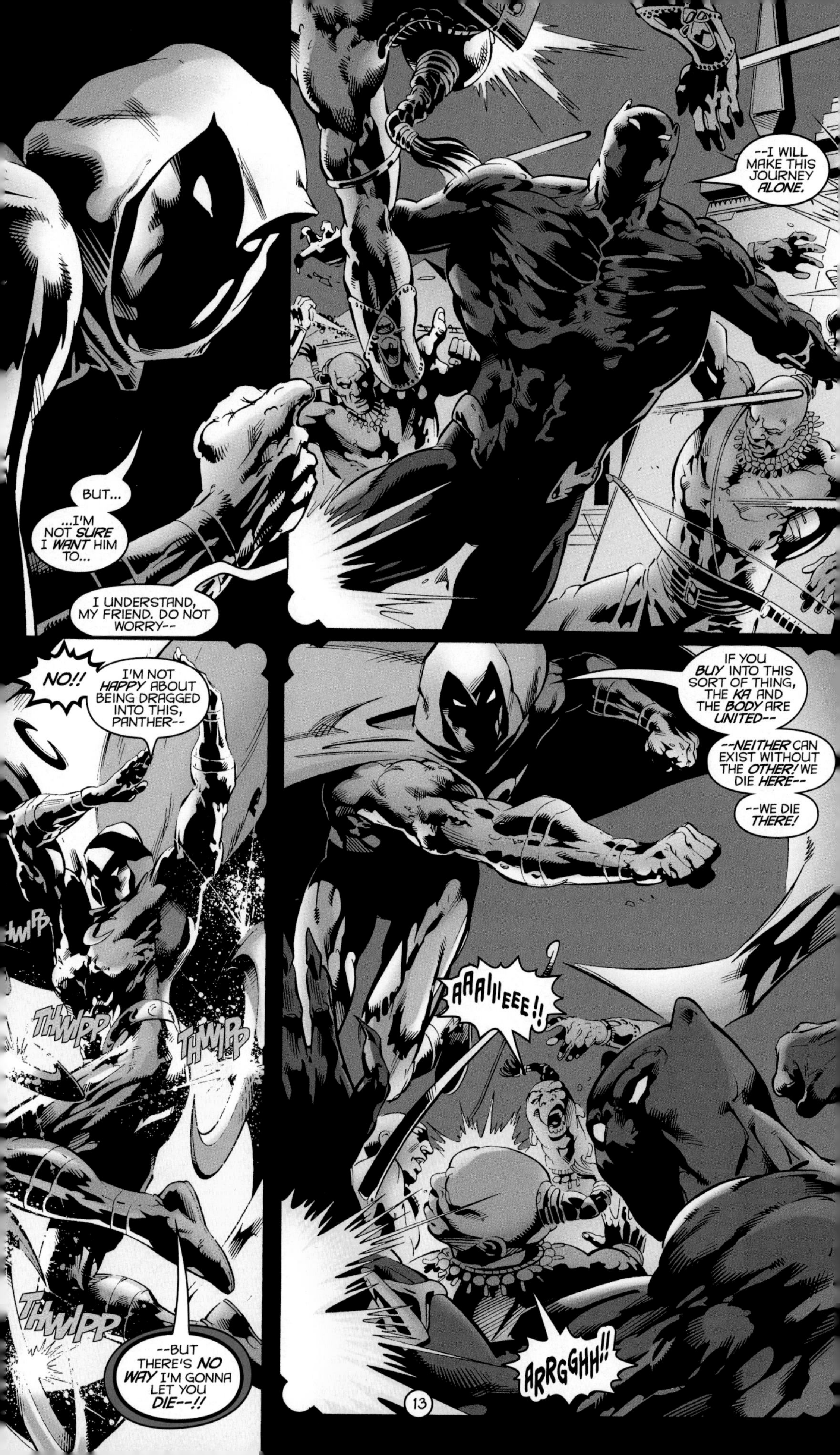
BUT...
...I'M NOT SURE I WANT HIM TO...
I UNDERSTAND, MY FRIEND. DO NOT WORRY--
--I WILL MAKE THIS JOURNEY ALONE.
NO!!
I'M NOT HAPPY ABOUT BEING DRAGGED INTO THIS, PANTHER--
THWIPP
THWIPP
THWIPP
--BUT THERE'S NO WAY I'M GONNA LET YOU DIE--!!
IF YOU BUY INTO THIS SORT OF THING, THE KA AND THE BODY ARE UNITED--
--NEITHER CAN EXIST WITHOUT THE OTHER! WE DIE HERE--
--WE DIE THERE!
AAAIIIEEE!!
ARRGGHH!!

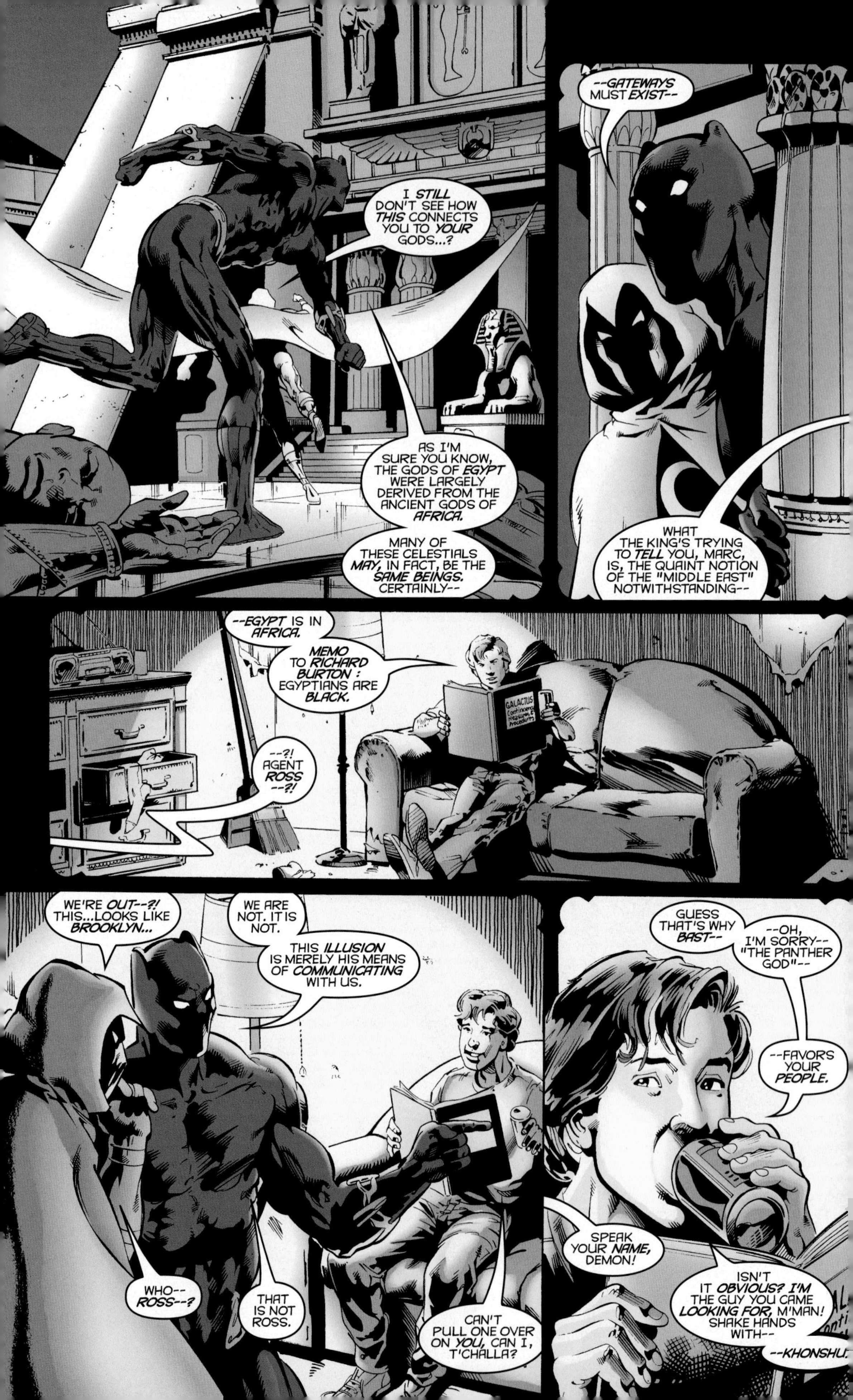
I STILL DON'T SEE HOW THIS CONNECTS YOU TO YOUR GODS...?
AS I'M SURE YOU KNOW, THE GODS OF EGYPT WERE LARGELY DERIVED FROM THE ANCIENT GODS OF AFRICA.
MANY OF THESE CELESTIALS MAY, IN FACT, BE THE SAME BEINGS. CERTAINLY--
--GATEWAYS MUST EXIST--
WHAT THE KING'S TRYING TO TELL YOU, MARC, IS, THE QUAINT NOTION OF THE "MIDDLE EAST" NOTWITHSTANDING--
--EGYPT IS IN AFRICA.
MEMO TO RICHARD BURTON : EGYPTIANS ARE BLACK.
GALACTUS
--?! AGENT ROSS --?!
WE'RE OUT--?! THIS...LOOKS LIKE BROOKLYN...
WE ARE NOT. IT IS NOT.
THIS ILLUSION IS MERELY HIS MEANS OF COMMUNICATING WITH US.
WHO-- ROSS--?
THAT IS NOT ROSS.
CAN'T PULL ONE OVER ON YOU, CAN I, T'CHALLA?
GUESS THAT'S WHY BAST--
--OH, I'M SORRY-- "THE PANTHER GOD"--
--FAVORS YOUR PEOPLE.
SPEAK YOUR NAME, DEMON!
ISN'T IT OBVIOUS? I'M THE GUY YOU CAME LOOKING FOR, M'MAN! SHAKE HANDS WITH--
--KHONSHU.

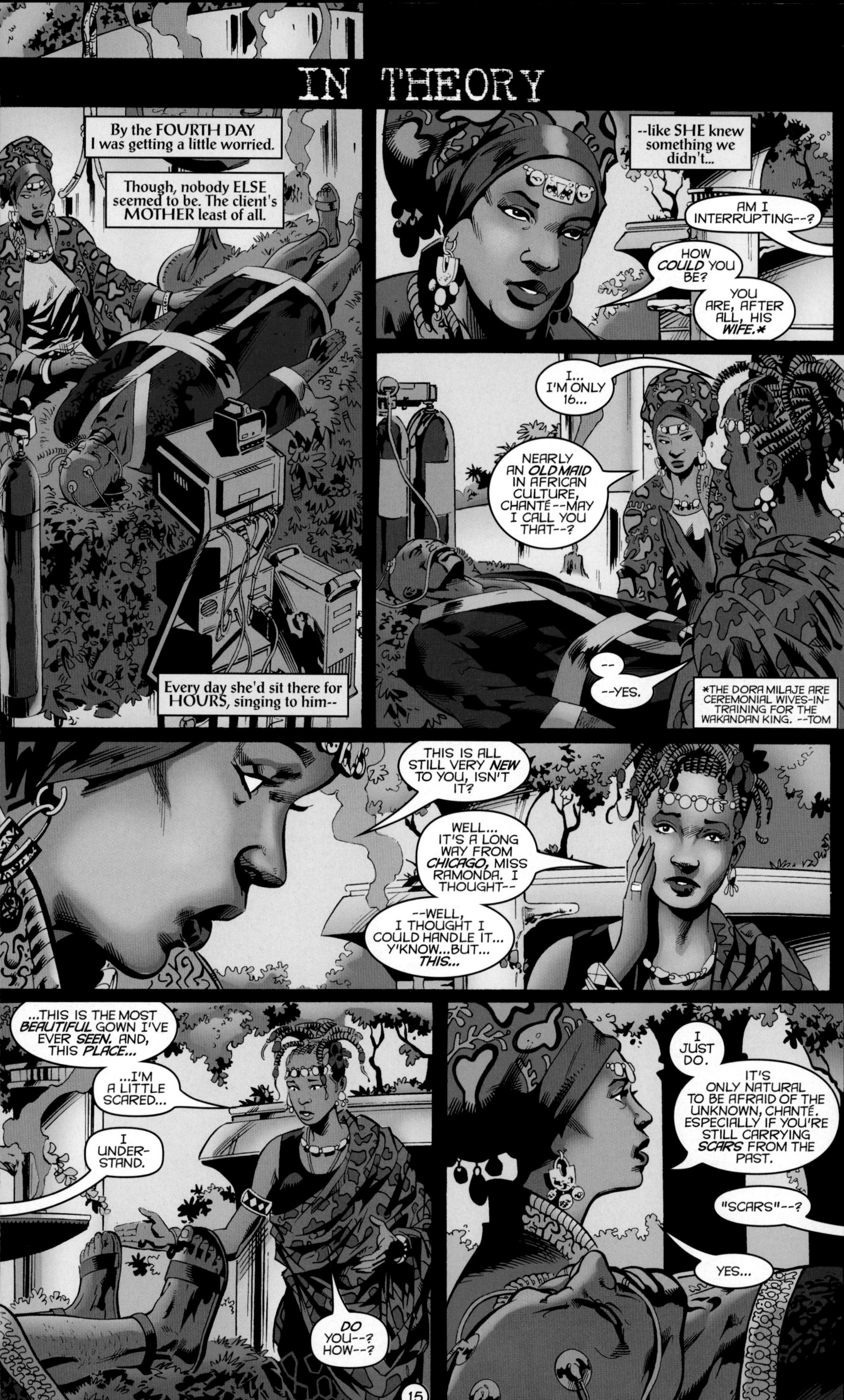
IN THEORY
By the FOURTH DAY I was getting a little worried.
Though, nobody ELSE seemed to be. The client's MOTHER least of all.
Every day she'd sit there for HOURS, singing to him--
--like SHE knew something we didn't...
AM I INTERRUPTING--?
HOW COULD YOU BE?
YOU ARE, AFTER ALL, HIS WIFE.*
I... I'M ONLY 16...
NEARLY AN OLD MAID IN AFRICAN CULTURE, CHANTÉ--MAY I CALL YOU THAT--?
--
--YES.
*THE DORA MILAJE ARE CEREMONIAL WIVES-IN-TRAINING FOR THE WAKANDAN KING. --TOM
THIS IS ALL STILL VERY NEW TO YOU, ISN'T IT?
WELL... IT'S A LONG WAY FROM CHICAGO, MISS RAMONDA. I THOUGHT--
--WELL, I THOUGHT I COULD HANDLE IT... Y'KNOW...BUT... THIS...
...THIS IS THE MOST BEAUTIFUL GOWN I'VE EVER SEEN. AND, THIS PLACE...
...I'M A LITTLE SCARED...
I UNDER-STAND.
DO YOU--? HOW--?
I JUST DO.
IT'S ONLY NATURAL TO BE AFRAID OF THE UNKNOWN, CHANTÉ. ESPECIALLY IF YOU'RE STILL CARRYING SCARS FROM THE PAST.
"SCARS"--?
YES...

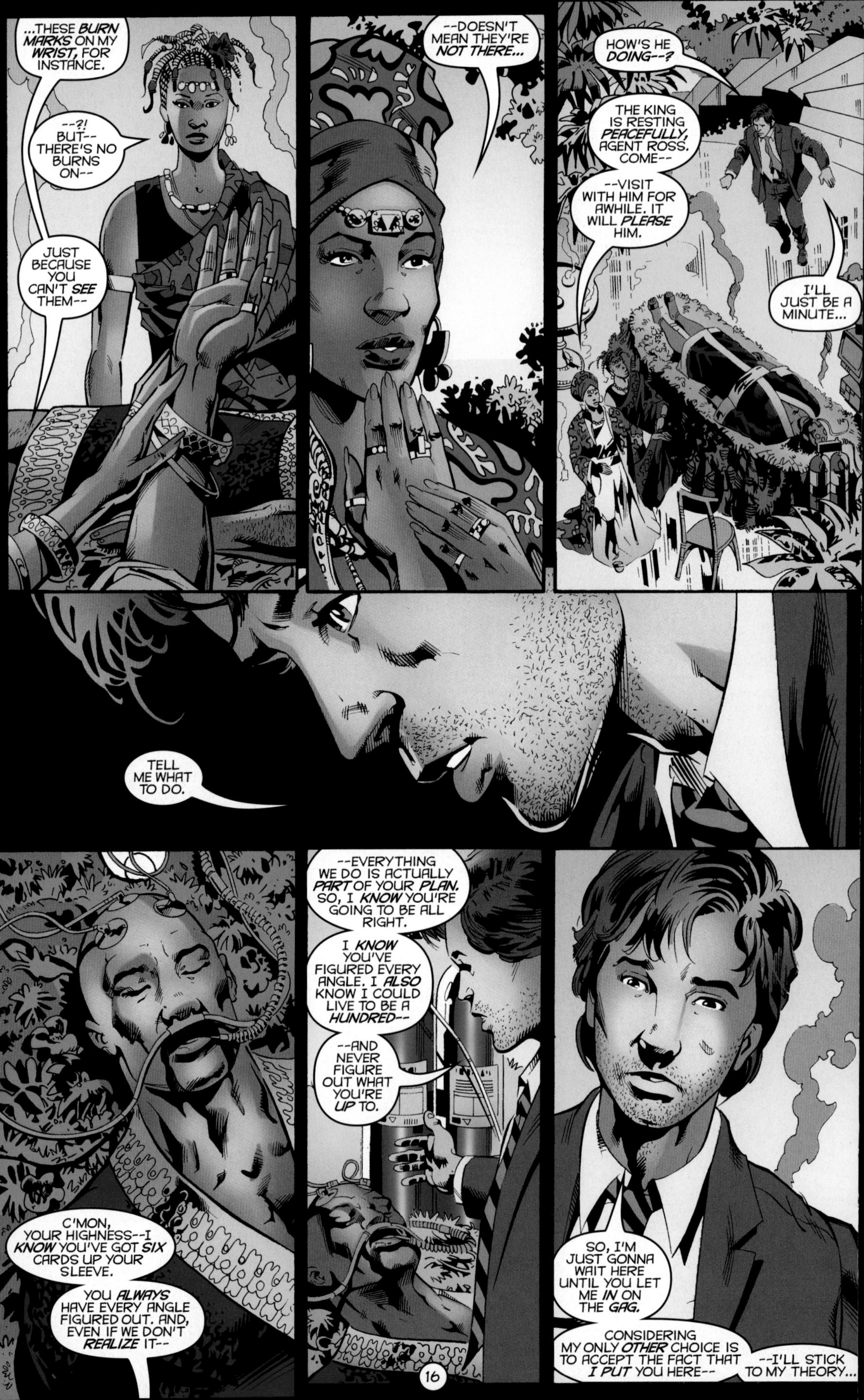
...THESE BURN MARKS ON MY WRIST, FOR INSTANCE.
--?! BUT-- THERE'S NO BURNS ON--
JUST BECAUSE YOU CAN'T SEE THEM--
--DOESN'T MEAN THEY'RE NOT THERE...
HOW'S HE DOING--?
THE KING IS RESTING PEACEFULLY, AGENT ROSS. COME--
--VISIT WITH HIM FOR AWHILE. IT WILL PLEASE HIM.
I'LL JUST BE A MINUTE...
TELL ME WHAT TO DO.
C'MON, YOUR HIGHNESS--I KNOW YOU'VE GOT SIX CARDS UP YOUR SLEEVE.
YOU ALWAYS HAVE EVERY ANGLE FIGURED OUT. AND, EVEN IF WE DON'T REALIZE IT--
--EVERYTHING WE DO IS ACTUALLY PART OF YOUR PLAN. SO, I KNOW YOU'RE GOING TO BE ALL RIGHT.
I KNOW YOU'VE FIGURED EVERY ANGLE. I ALSO KNOW I COULD LIVE TO BE A HUNDRED--
--AND NEVER FIGURE OUT WHAT YOU'RE UP TO.
SO, I'M JUST GONNA WAIT HERE UNTIL YOU LET ME IN ON THE GAG.
CONSIDERING MY ONLY OTHER CHOICE IS TO ACCEPT THE FACT THAT I PUT YOU HERE--
--I'LL STICK TO MY THEORY...

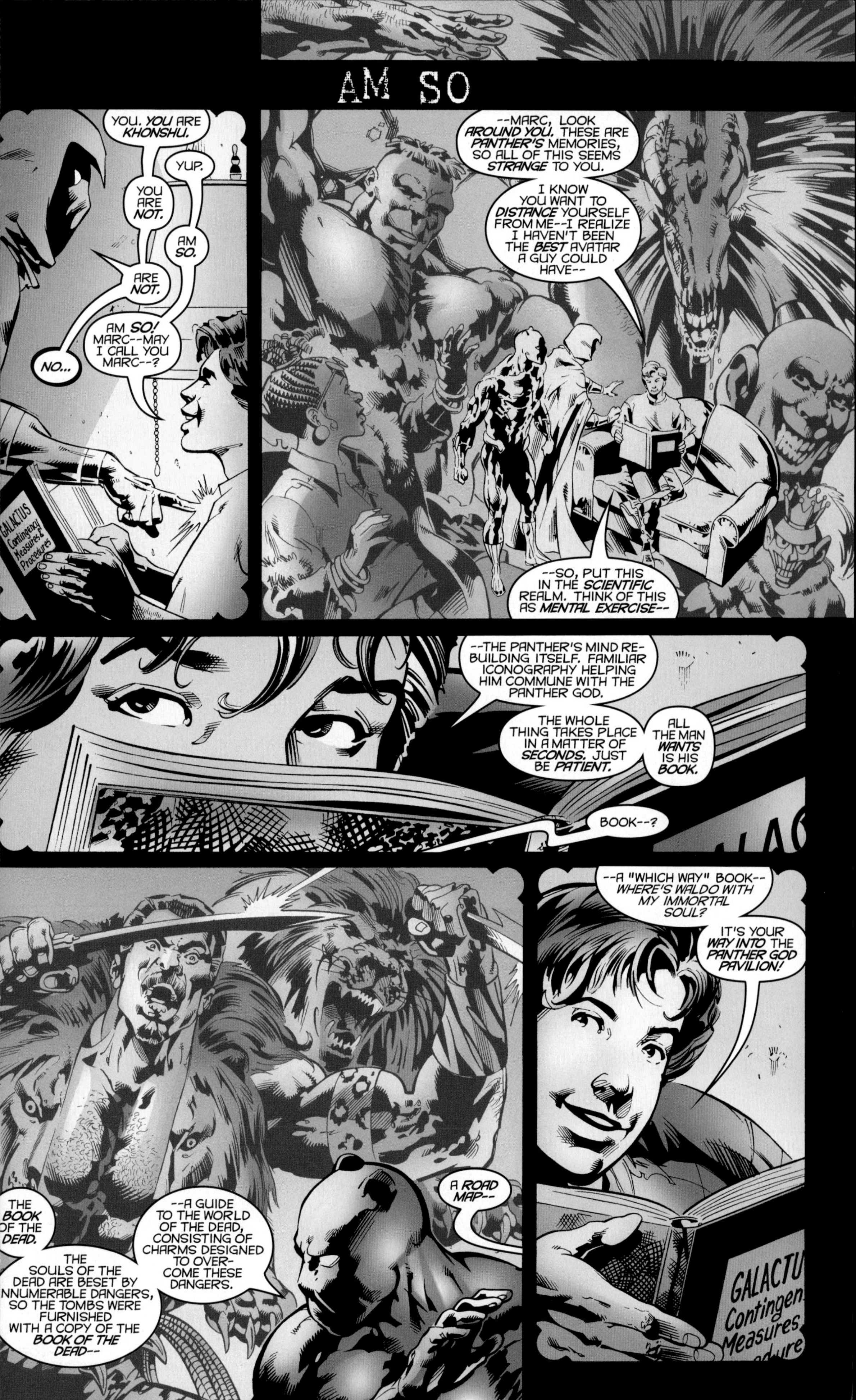
AM SO
YOU. YOU ARE KHONSHU.
YUP.
YOU ARE NOT.
AM SO.
ARE NOT.
AM SO! MARC--MAY I CALL YOU MARC--?
NO...
GALACTUS Contingency Measures & Procedures
--MARC, LOOK AROUND YOU. THESE ARE PANTHER'S MEMORIES, SO ALL OF THIS SEEMS STRANGE TO YOU.
I KNOW YOU WANT TO DISTANCE YOURSELF FROM ME--I REALIZE I HAVEN'T BEEN THE BEST AVATAR A GUY COULD HAVE--
--SO, PUT THIS IN THE SCIENTIFIC REALM. THINK OF THIS AS MENTAL EXERCISE--
--THE PANTHER'S MIND RE-BUILDING ITSELF. FAMILIAR ICONOGRAPHY HELPING HIM COMMUNE WITH THE PANTHER GOD.
THE WHOLE THING TAKES PLACE IN A MATTER OF SECONDS. JUST BE PATIENT.
ALL THE MAN WANTS IS HIS BOOK.
BOOK--?
--A "WHICH WAY" BOOK--WHERE'S WALDO WITH MY IMMORTAL SOUL?
IT'S YOUR WAY INTO THE PANTHER GOD PAVILION!
A ROAD MAP--
THE BOOK OF THE DEAD.
--A GUIDE TO THE WORLD OF THE DEAD, CONSISTING OF CHARMS DESIGNED TO OVER-COME THESE DANGERS.
THE SOULS OF THE DEAD ARE BESET BY INNUMERABLE DANGERS, SO THE TOMBS WERE FURNISHED WITH A COPY OF THE BOOK OF THE DEAD--
GALACTU Contingen Measures

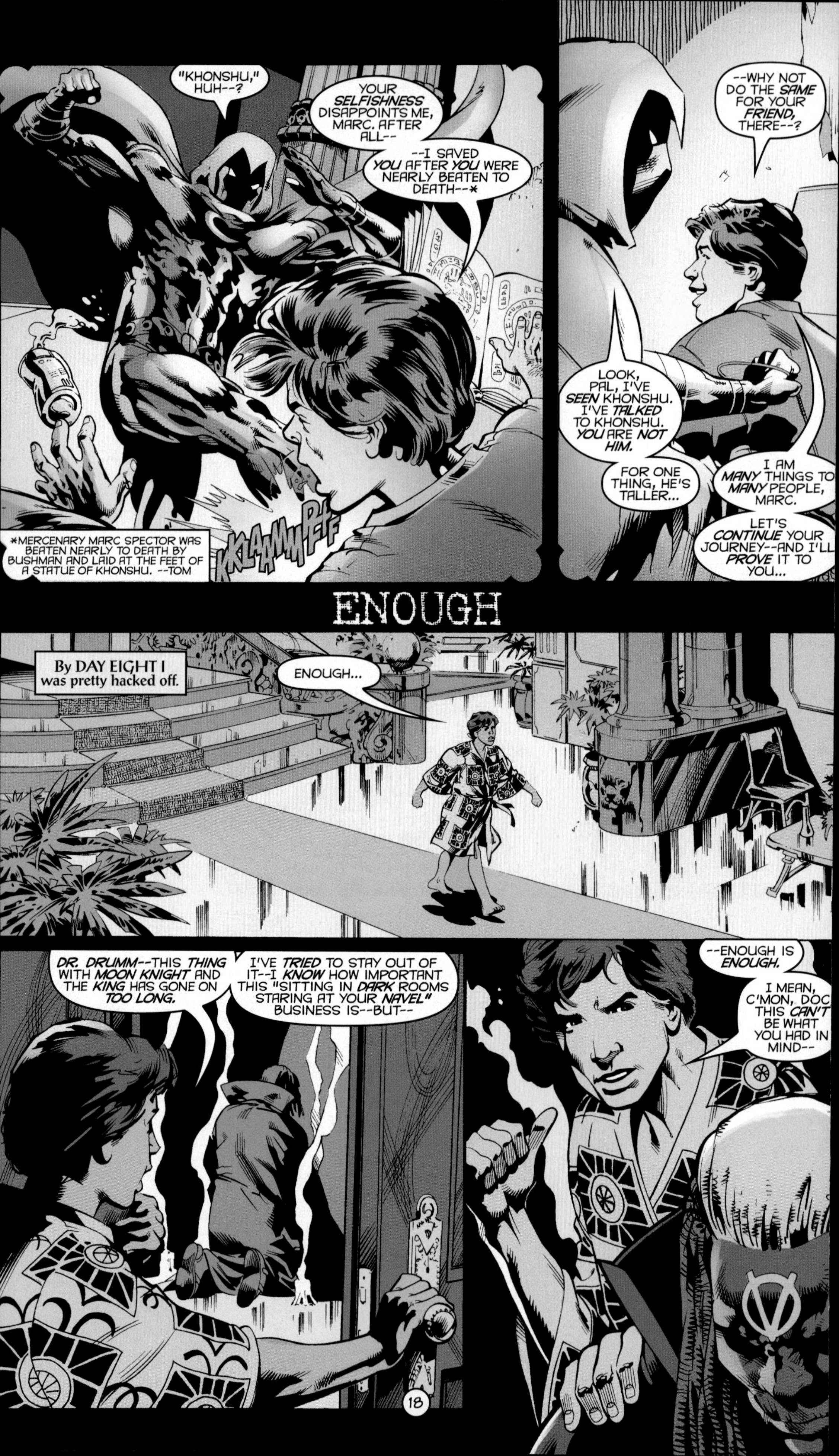
"KHONSHU," HUH--?
YOUR SELFISHNESS DISAPPOINTS ME, MARC. AFTER ALL--
--I SAVED YOU AFTER YOU WERE NEARLY BEATEN TO DEATH--*
*MERCENARY MARC SPECTOR WAS BEATEN NEARLY TO DEATH BY BUSHMAN AND LAID AT THE FEET OF A STATUE OF KHONSHU. --TOM
KKLAMMPFF
--WHY NOT DO THE SAME FOR YOUR FRIEND, THERE--?
LOOK, PAL, I'VE SEEN KHONSHU. I'VE TALKED TO KHONSHU. YOU ARE NOT HIM.
FOR ONE THING, HE'S TALLER...
I AM MANY THINGS TO MANY PEOPLE, MARC.
LET'S CONTINUE YOUR JOURNEY--AND I'LL PROVE IT TO YOU...
ENOUGH
By DAY EIGHT I was pretty hacked off.
ENOUGH...
DR. DRUMM--THIS THING WITH MOON KNIGHT AND THE KING HAS GONE ON TOO LONG.
I'VE TRIED TO STAY OUT OF IT--I KNOW HOW IMPORTANT THIS "SITTING IN DARK ROOMS STARING AT YOUR NAVEL" BUSINESS IS--BUT--
--ENOUGH IS ENOUGH.
I MEAN, C'MON, DOC THIS CAN'T BE WHAT YOU HAD IN MIND--

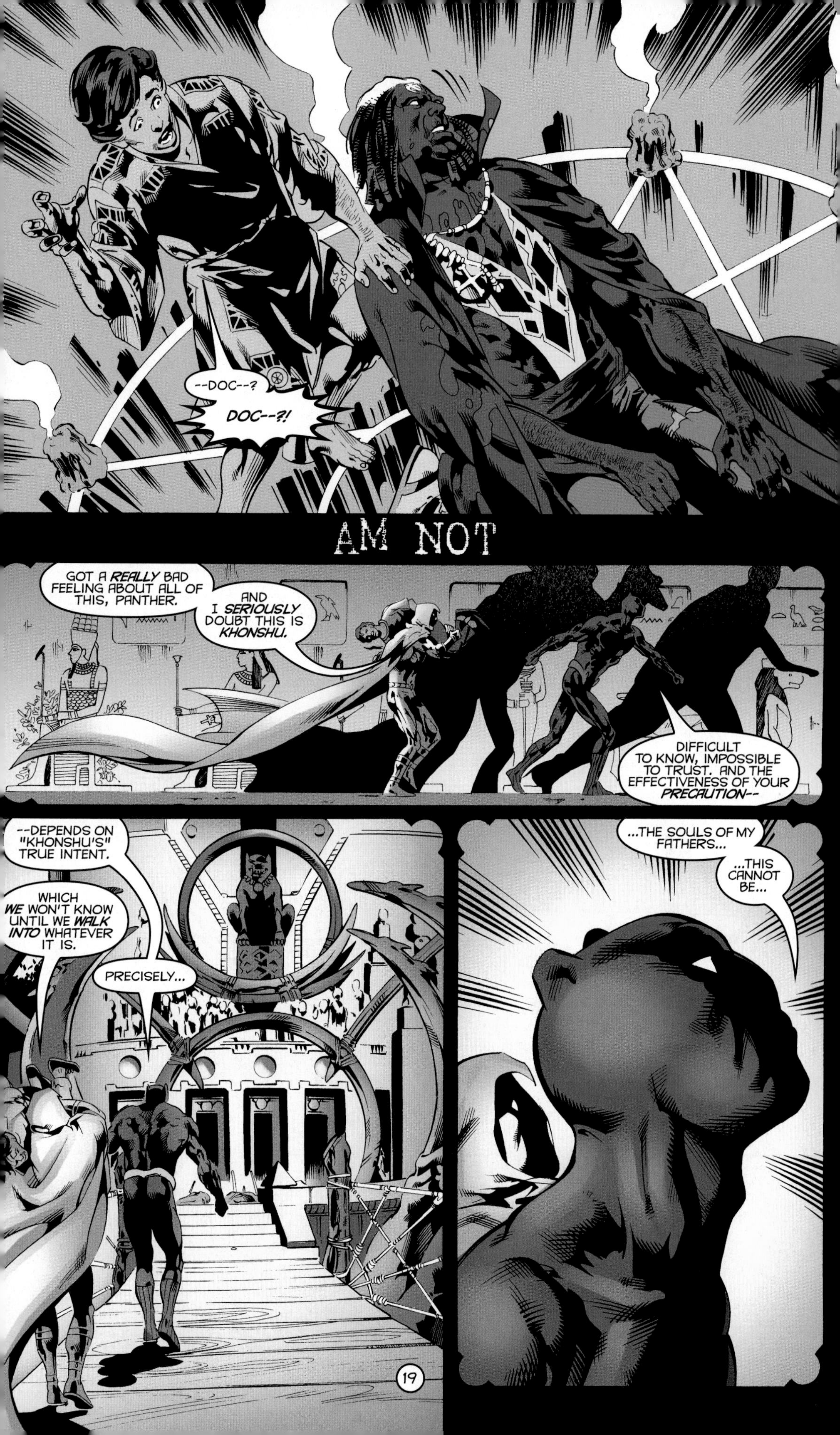
--DOC--?
DOC--?!
AM NOT
GOT A REALLY BAD FEELING ABOUT ALL OF THIS, PANTHER.
AND I SERIOUSLY DOUBT THIS IS KHONSHU.
DIFFICULT TO KNOW, IMPOSSIBLE TO TRUST. AND THE EFFECTIVENESS OF YOUR PRECAUTION--
--DEPENDS ON "KHONSHU'S" TRUE INTENT.
WHICH WE WON'T KNOW UNTIL WE WALK INTO WHATEVER IT IS.
PRECISELY...
...THE SOULS OF MY FATHERS...
...THIS CANNOT BE...
19

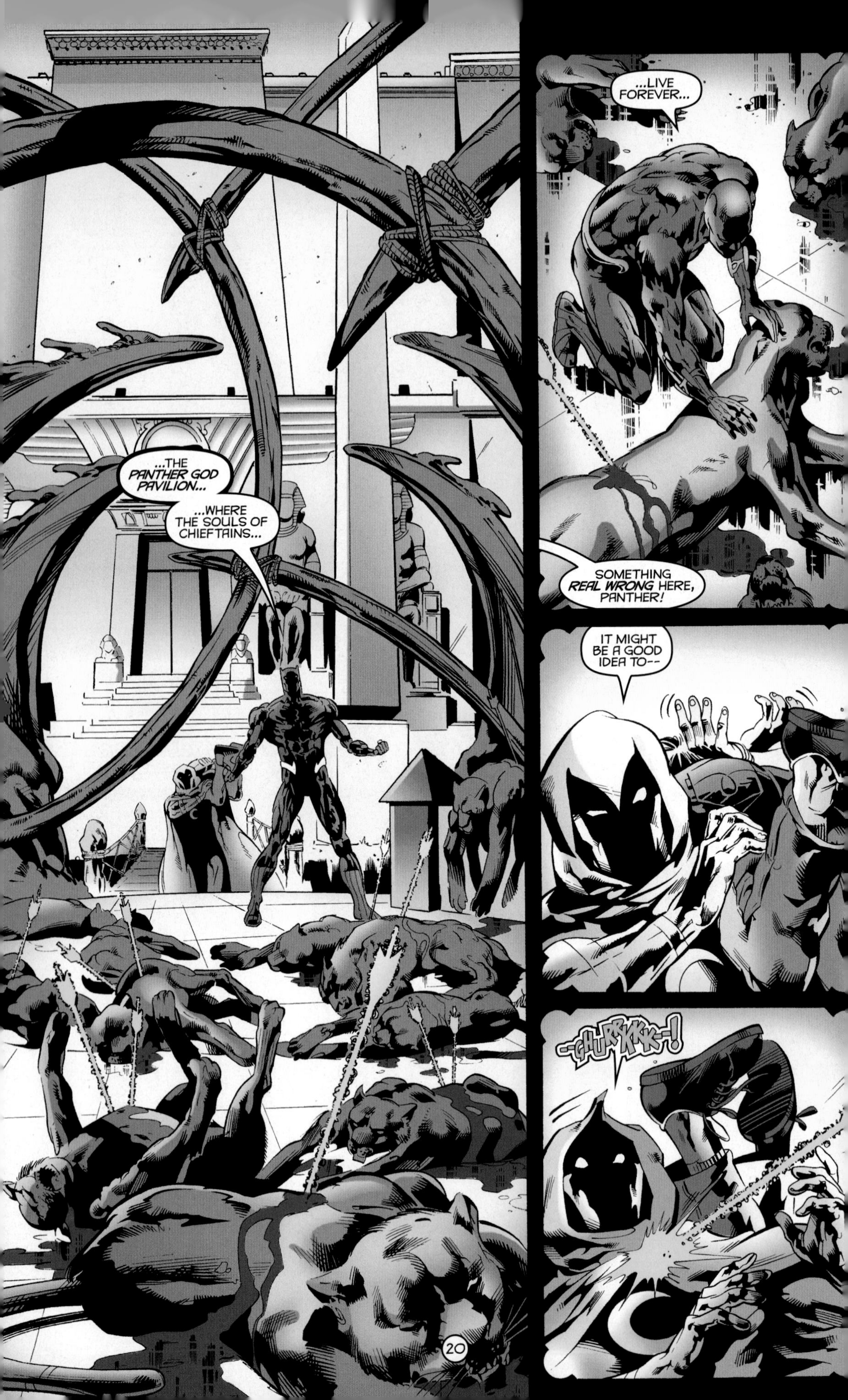
...THE PANTHER GOD PAVILION...
...WHERE THE SOULS OF CHIEFTAINS...
...LIVE FOREVER...
SOMETHING REAL WRONG HERE, PANTHER!
IT MIGHT BE A GOOD IDEA TO--
-GHURRKKK-!

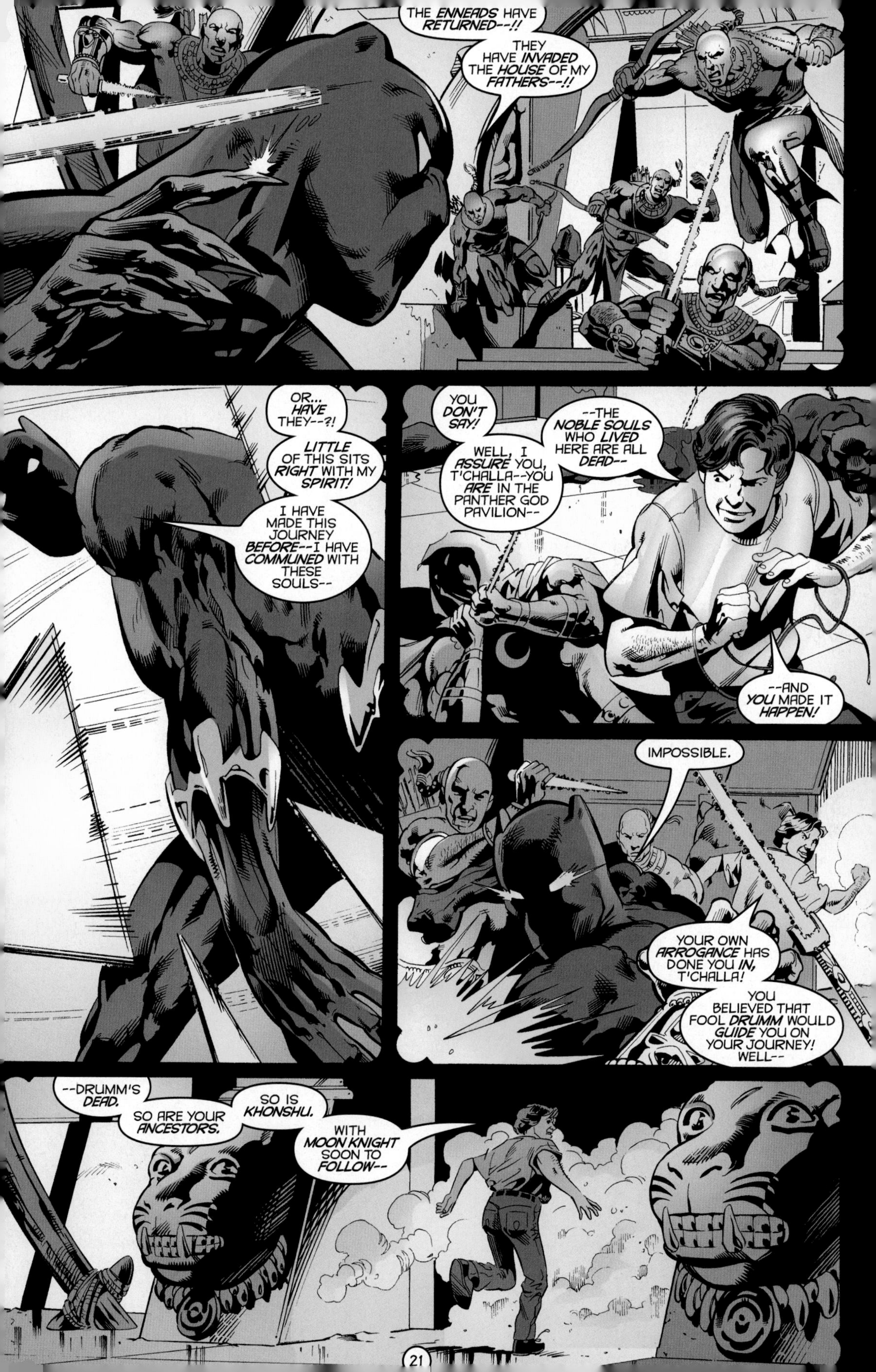
THE ENNEADS HAVE RETURNED--!!
THEY HAVE INVADED THE HOUSE OF MY FATHERS--!!
OR... HAVE THEY--?!
LITTLE OF THIS SITS RIGHT WITH MY SPIRIT!
I HAVE MADE THIS JOURNEY BEFORE--I HAVE COMMUNED WITH THESE SOULS--
YOU DON'T SAY!
WELL, I ASSURE YOU, T'CHALLA--YOU ARE IN THE PANTHER GOD PAVILION--
--THE NOBLE SOULS WHO LIVED HERE ARE ALL DEAD--
--AND YOU MADE IT HAPPEN!
IMPOSSIBLE.
YOUR OWN ARROGANCE HAS DONE YOU IN, T'CHALLA!
YOU BELIEVED THAT FOOL DRUMM WOULD GUIDE YOU ON YOUR JOURNEY! WELL--
--DRUMM'S DEAD.
SO ARE YOUR ANCESTORS.
SO IS KHONSHU.
WITH MOON KNIGHT SOON TO FOLLOW--

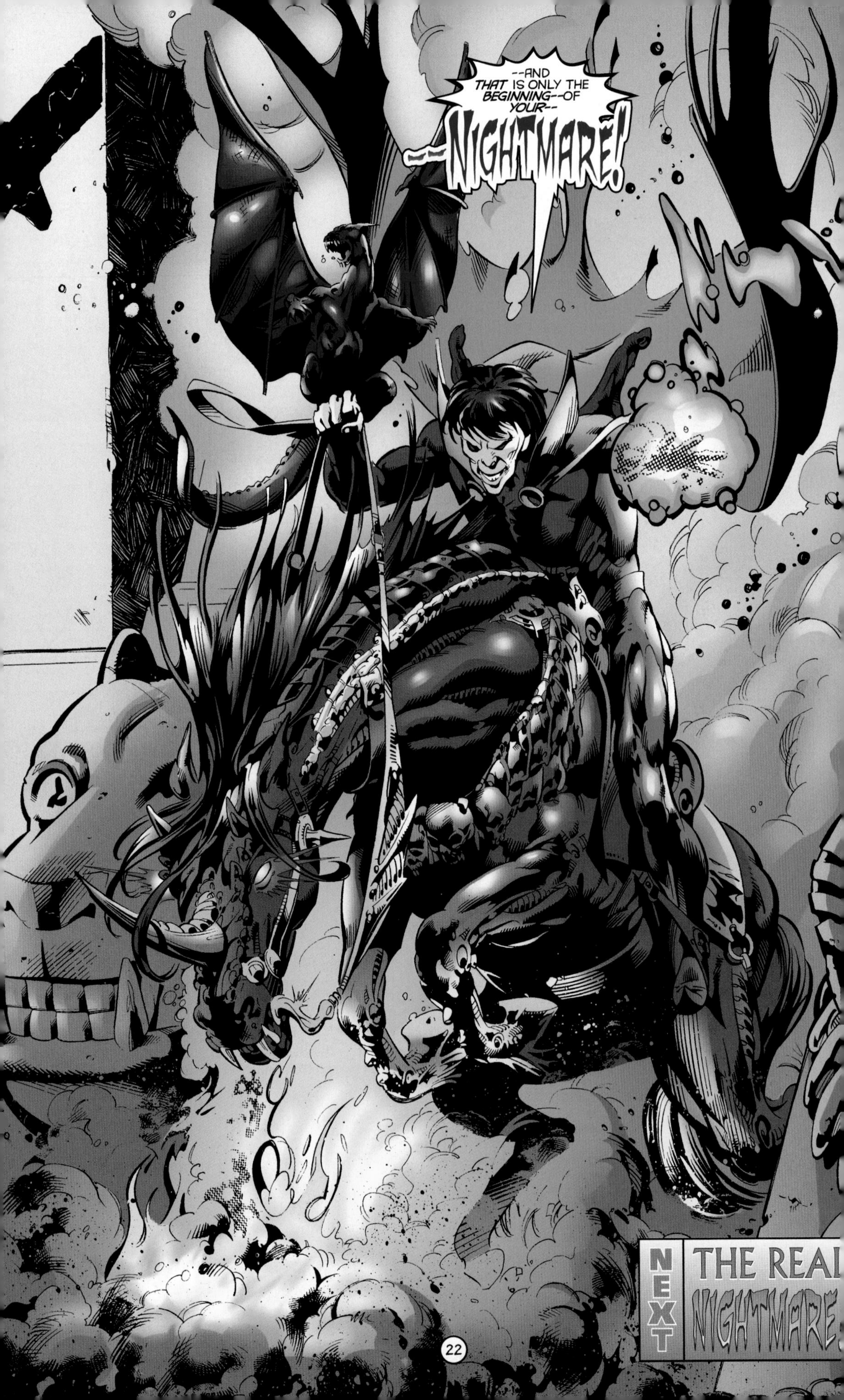
--AND THAT IS ONLY THE BEGINNING--OF YOUR--
--NIGHTMARE!
NEXT
THE REAL NIGHTMARE

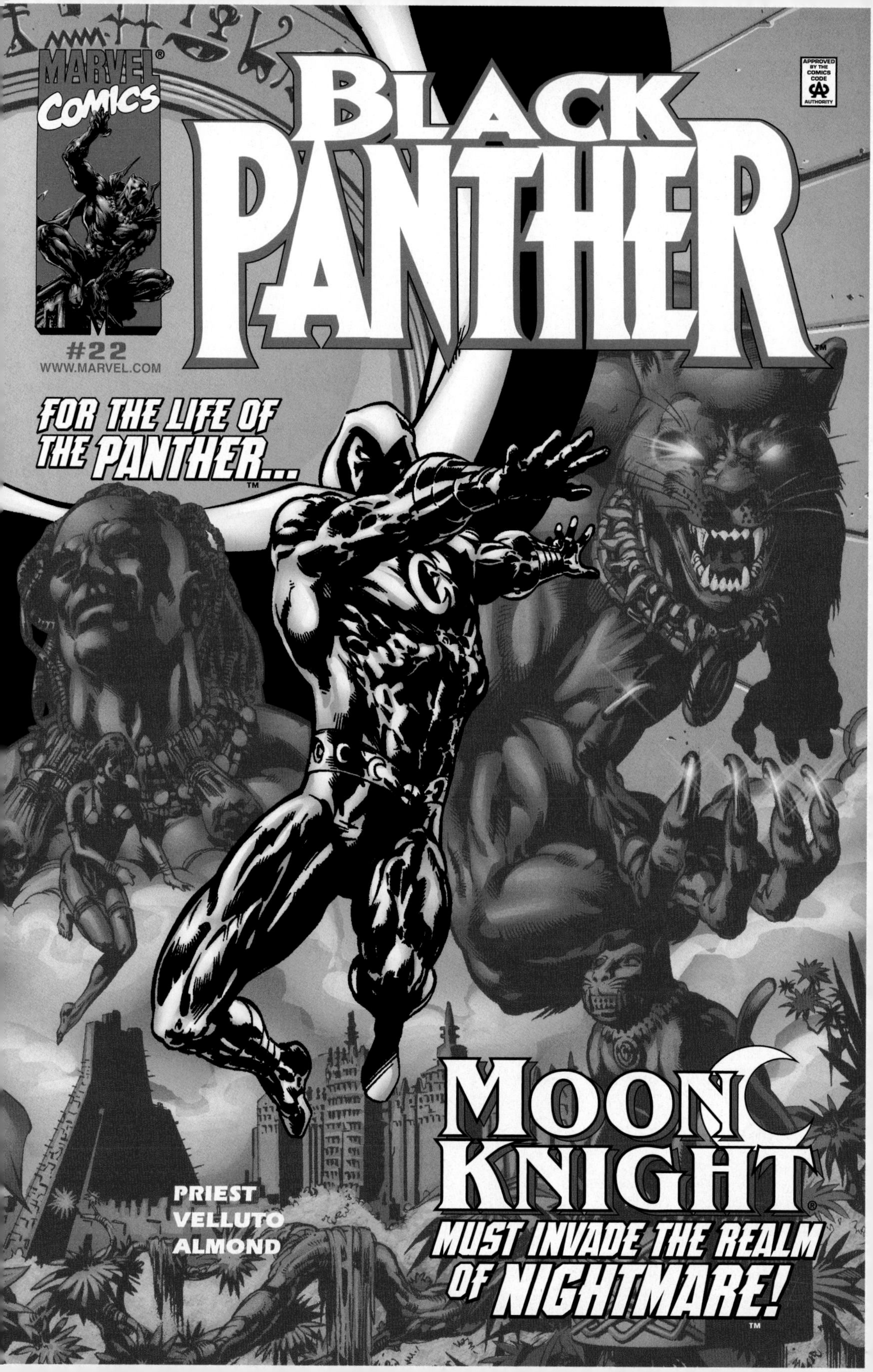
MARVEL COMICS
APPROVED BY THE COMICS CODE AUTHORITY
BLACK PANTHER™
#22
WWW.MARVEL.COM
FOR THE LIFE OF THE PANTHER...™
MOON KNIGHT®
MUST INVADE THE REALM OF NIGHTMARE!™
PRIEST
VELLUTO
ALMOND

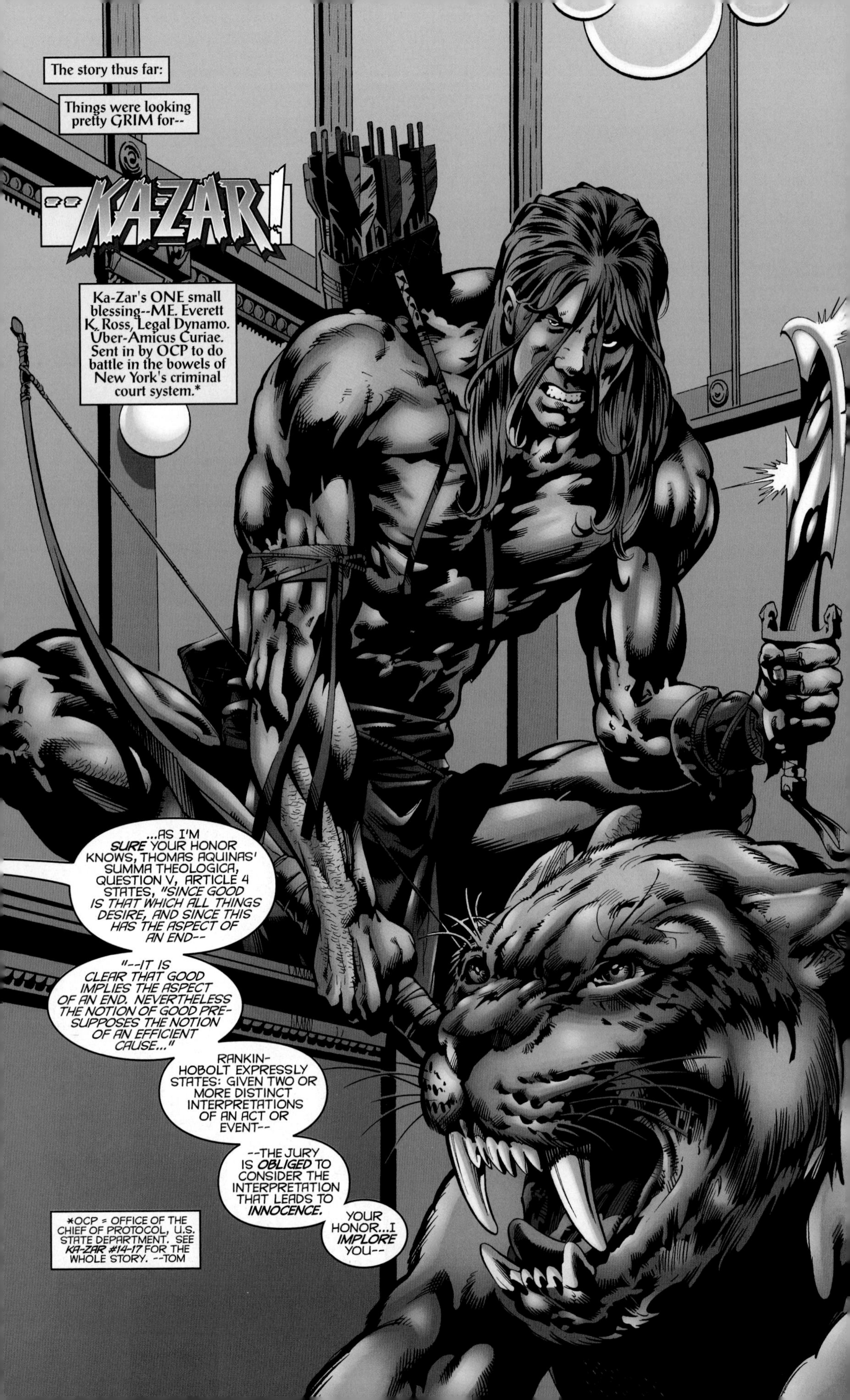

The story thus far:
Things were looking pretty GRIM for--
--KA-ZAR!
Ka-Zar's ONE small blessing--ME. Everett K. Ross, Legal Dynamo. Über-Amicus Curiae. Sent in by OCP to do battle in the bowels of New York's criminal court system.*
...AS I'M SURE YOUR HONOR KNOWS, THOMAS AQUINAS' SUMMA THEOLOGICA, QUESTION V, ARTICLE 4 STATES, "SINCE GOOD IS THAT WHICH ALL THINGS DESIRE, AND SINCE THIS HAS THE ASPECT OF AN END--
"--IT IS CLEAR THAT GOOD IMPLIES THE ASPECT OF AN END. NEVERTHELESS THE NOTION OF GOOD PRE-SUPPOSES THE NOTION OF AN EFFICIENT CAUSE..."
RANKIN-HOBOLT EXPRESSLY STATES: GIVEN TWO OR MORE DISTINCT INTERPRETATIONS OF AN ACT OR EVENT--
--THE JURY IS OBLIGED TO CONSIDER THE INTERPRETATION THAT LEADS TO INNOCENCE.
YOUR HONOR...I IMPLORE YOU--
*OCP = OFFICE OF THE CHIEF OF PROTOCOL, U.S. STATE DEPARTMENT. SEE KA-ZAR #14-17 FOR THE WHOLE STORY. --TOM

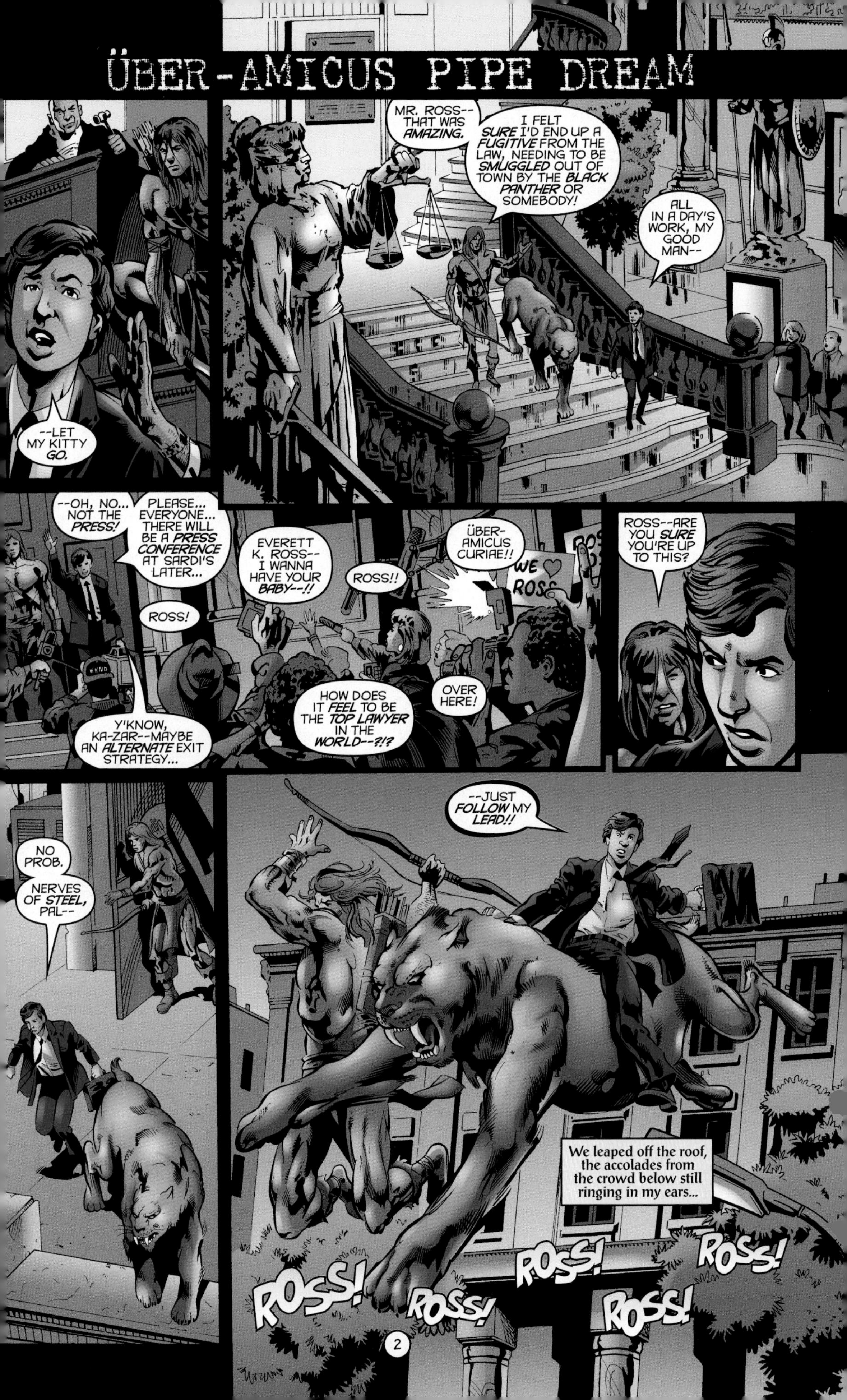
ÜBER-AMICUS PIPE DREAM
--LET MY KITTY GO.
MR. ROSS--THAT WAS AMAZING.
I FELT SURE I'D END UP A FUGITIVE FROM THE LAW, NEEDING TO BE SMUGGLED OUT OF TOWN BY THE BLACK PANTHER OR SOMEBODY!
ALL IN A DAY'S WORK, MY GOOD MAN--
--OH, NO... NOT THE PRESS!
PLEASE... EVERYONE... THERE WILL BE A PRESS CONFERENCE AT SARDI'S LATER...
EVERETT K. ROSS--I WANNA HAVE YOUR BABY--!!
ÜBER-AMICUS CURIAE!!
ROSS!!
WE ♥ ROSS
ROSS!
HOW DOES IT FEEL TO BE THE TOP LAWYER IN THE WORLD--?!?
OVER HERE!
Y'KNOW, KA-ZAR--MAYBE AN ALTERNATE EXIT STRATEGY...
ROSS--ARE YOU SURE YOU'RE UP TO THIS?
NO PROB.
NERVES OF STEEL, PAL--
--JUST FOLLOW MY LEAD!!
We leaped off the roof, the accolades from the crowd below still ringing in my ears...
ROSS! ROSS! ROSS! ROSS! ROSS!

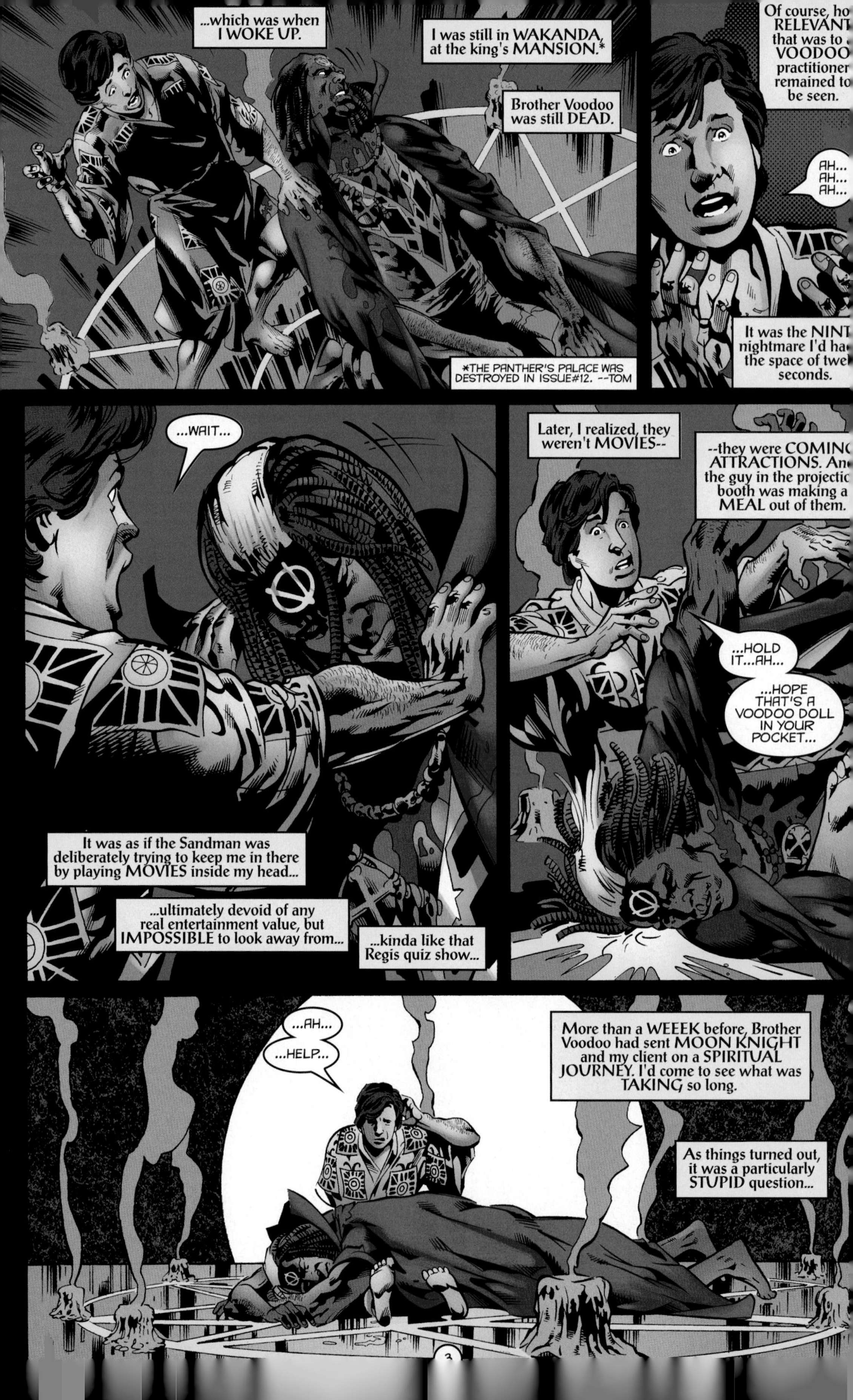
...which was when I WOKE UP.
I was still in WAKANDA, at the king's MANSION.*
Brother Voodoo was still DEAD.
*THE PANTHER'S PALACE WAS DESTROYED IN ISSUE#12. --TOM
Of course, ho
RELEVANT
that was to
VOODOO
practitioner
remained to
be seen.
AH... AH... AH...
It was the NINT
nightmare I'd ha
the space of twel
seconds.
...WAIT...
It was as if the Sandman was deliberately trying to keep me in there by playing MOVIES inside my head...
...ultimately devoid of any real entertainment value, but IMPOSSIBLE to look away from...
...kinda like that Regis quiz show...
Later, I realized, they weren't MOVIES--
--they were COMINC ATTRACTIONS. An the guy in the projectic booth was making a MEAL out of them.
...HOLD IT...AH...
...HOPE THAT'S A VOODOO DOLL IN YOUR POCKET...
...AH...
...HELP...
More than a WEEEK before, Brother Voodoo had sent MOON KNIGHT and my client on a SPIRITUAL JOURNEY. I'd come to see what was TAKING so long.
As things turned out, it was a particularly STUPID question...

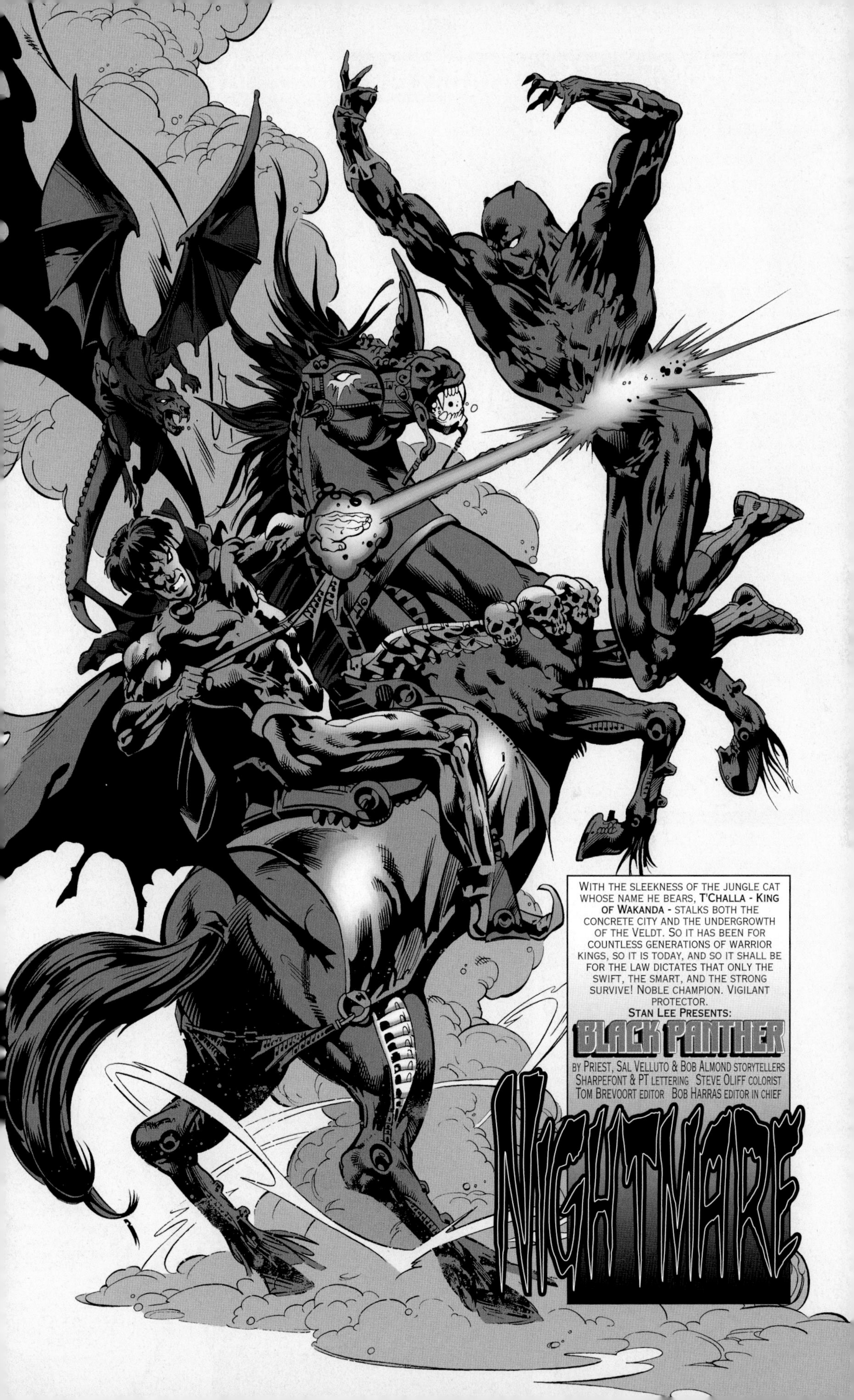
WITH THE SLEEKNESS OF THE JUNGLE CAT WHOSE NAME HE BEARS, T'CHALLA - KING OF WAKANDA - STALKS BOTH THE CONCRETE CITY AND THE UNDERGROWTH OF THE VELDT. SO IT HAS BEEN FOR COUNTLESS GENERATIONS OF WARRIOR KINGS, SO IT IS TODAY, AND SO IT SHALL BE FOR THE LAW DICTATES THAT ONLY THE SWIFT, THE SMART, AND THE STRONG SURVIVE! NOBLE CHAMPION. VIGILANT PROTECTOR.
STAN LEE PRESENTS:
BLACK PANTHER
BY PRIEST, SAL VELLUTO & BOB ALMOND STORYTELLERS
SHARPEFONT & PT LETTERING STEVE OLIFF COLORIST
TOM BREVOORT EDITOR BOB HARRAS EDITOR IN CHIEF
NIGHTMARE

HOME IS WHERE THE HATE IS

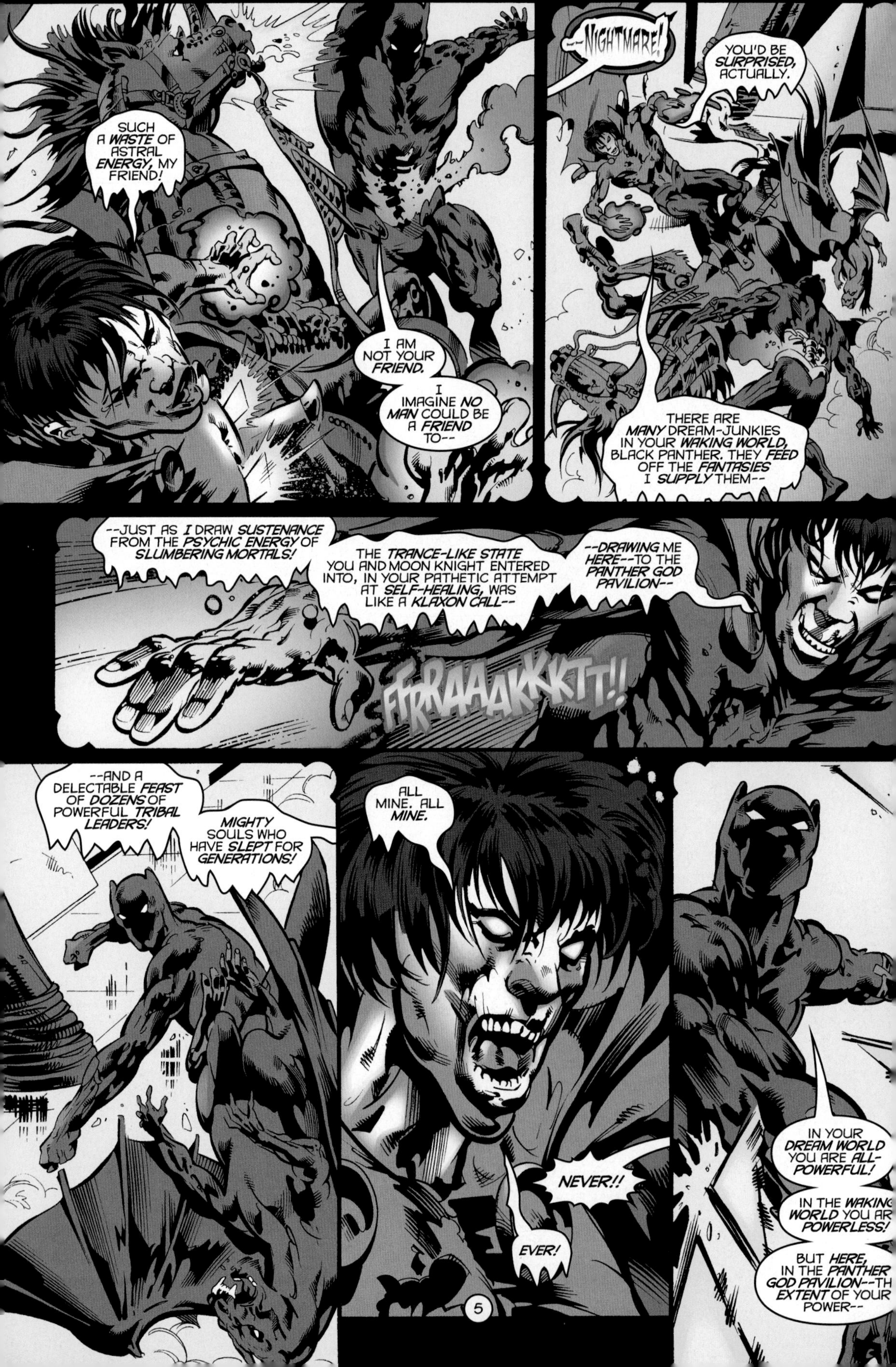
SUCH A WASTE OF ASTRAL ENERGY, MY FRIEND!
I AM NOT YOUR FRIEND.
I IMAGINE NO MAN COULD BE A FRIEND TO--
NIGHTMARE!
YOU'D BE SURPRISED, ACTUALLY.
THERE ARE MANY DREAM-JUNKIES IN YOUR WAKING WORLD, BLACK PANTHER. THEY FEED OFF THE FANTASIES I SUPPLY THEM--
--JUST AS I DRAW SUSTENANCE FROM THE PSYCHIC ENERGY OF SLUMBERING MORTALS!
THE TRANCE-LIKE STATE YOU AND MOON KNIGHT ENTERED INTO, IN YOUR PATHETIC ATTEMPT AT SELF-HEALING, WAS LIKE A KLAXON CALL--
--DRAWING ME HERE--TO THE PANTHER GOD PAVILION--
FFRRAAAKKKTT!!
--AND A DELECTABLE FEAST OF DOZENS OF POWERFUL TRIBAL LEADERS!
MIGHTY SOULS WHO HAVE SLEPT FOR GENERATIONS!
ALL MINE. ALL MINE.
NEVER!!
EVER!
IN YOUR DREAM WORLD YOU ARE ALL-POWERFUL!
IN THE WAKING WORLD YOU AR POWERLESS!
BUT HERE, IN THE PANTHER GOD PAVILION--TH EXTENT OF YOUR POWER--

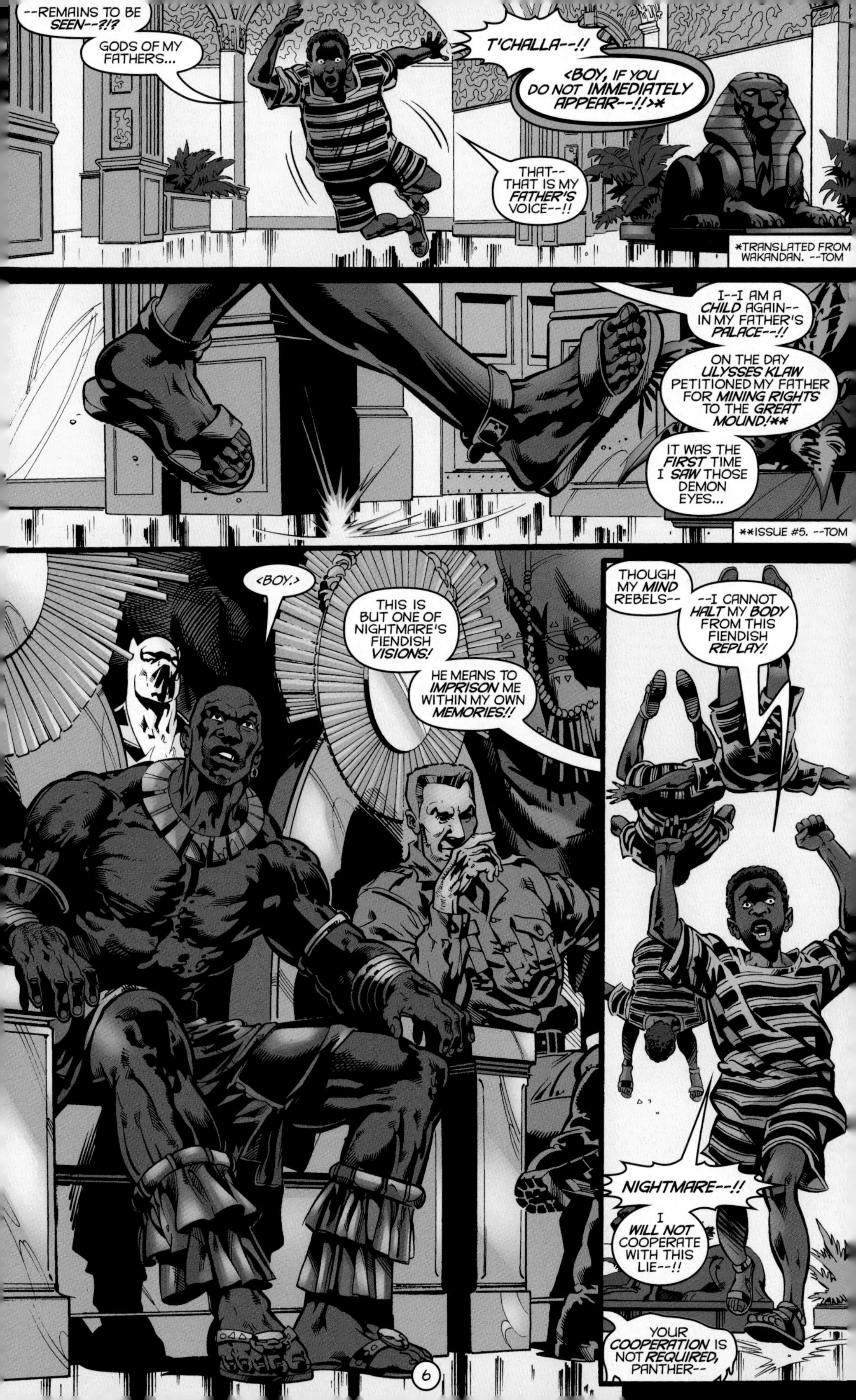
--REMAINS TO BE SEEN--?!?
GODS OF MY FATHERS...
T'CHALLA--!!
<BOY, IF YOU DO NOT IMMEDIATELY APPEAR--!!>*
THAT-- THAT IS MY FATHER'S VOICE--!!
*TRANSLATED FROM WAKANDAN. --TOM
I--I AM A CHILD AGAIN-- IN MY FATHER'S PALACE--!!
ON THE DAY ULYSSES KLAW PETITIONED MY FATHER FOR MINING RIGHTS TO THE GREAT MOUND!**
IT WAS THE FIRST TIME I SAW THOSE DEMON EYES...
**ISSUE #5. --TOM
<BOY.>
THIS IS BUT ONE OF NIGHTMARE'S FIENDISH VISIONS!
HE MEANS TO IMPRISON ME WITHIN MY OWN MEMORIES!!
THOUGH MY MIND REBELS--
--I CANNOT HALT MY BODY FROM THIS FIENDISH REPLAY!
NIGHTMARE--!!
I WILL NOT COOPERATE WITH THIS LIE--!!
YOUR COOPERATION IS NOT REQUIRED, PANTHER--

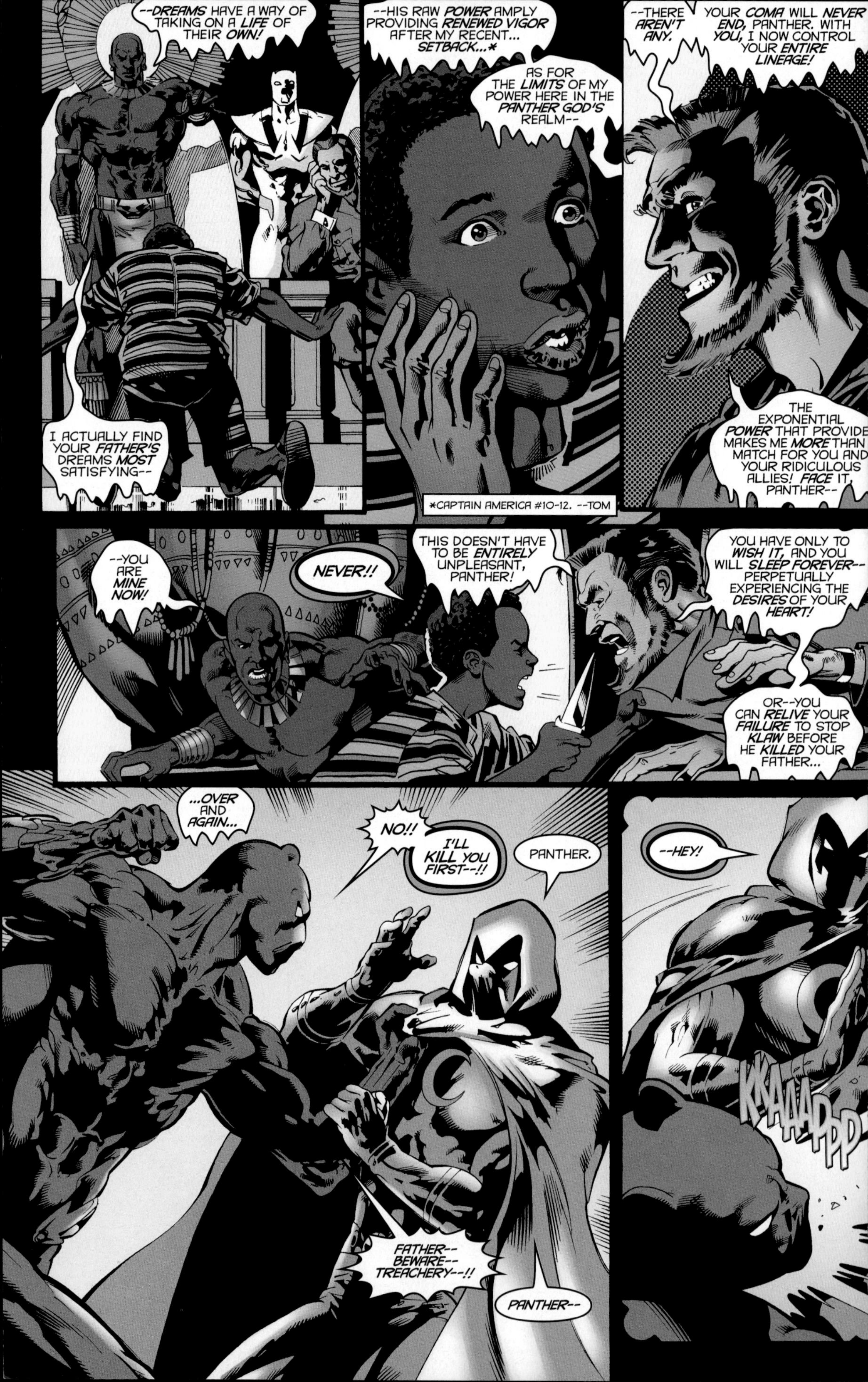
--DREAMS HAVE A WAY OF TAKING ON A LIFE OF THEIR OWN!
I ACTUALLY FIND YOUR FATHER'S DREAMS MOST SATISFYING--
--HIS RAW POWER AMPLY PROVIDING RENEWED VIGOR AFTER MY RECENT... SETBACK...*
AS FOR THE LIMITS OF MY POWER HERE IN THE PANTHER GOD'S REALM--
*CAPTAIN AMERICA #10-12. --TOM
--THERE AREN'T ANY.
YOUR COMA WILL NEVER END, PANTHER. WITH YOU, I NOW CONTROL YOUR ENTIRE LINEAGE!
THE EXPONENTIAL POWER THAT PROVIDE MAKES ME MORE THAN MATCH FOR YOU AND YOUR RIDICULOUS ALLIES! FACE IT, PANTHER--
--YOU ARE MINE NOW!
NEVER!!
THIS DOESN'T HAVE TO BE ENTIRELY UNPLEASANT, PANTHER!
YOU HAVE ONLY TO WISH IT, AND YOU WILL SLEEP FOREVER-- PERPETUALLY EXPERIENCING THE DESIRES OF YOUR HEART!
OR--YOU CAN RELIVE YOUR FAILURE TO STOP KLAW BEFORE HE KILLED YOUR FATHER...
...OVER AND AGAIN...
NO!!
I'LL KILL YOU FIRST--!!
PANTHER.
FATHER-- BEWARE-- TREACHERY--!!
PANTHER--
--HEY!
KKAAAPPP

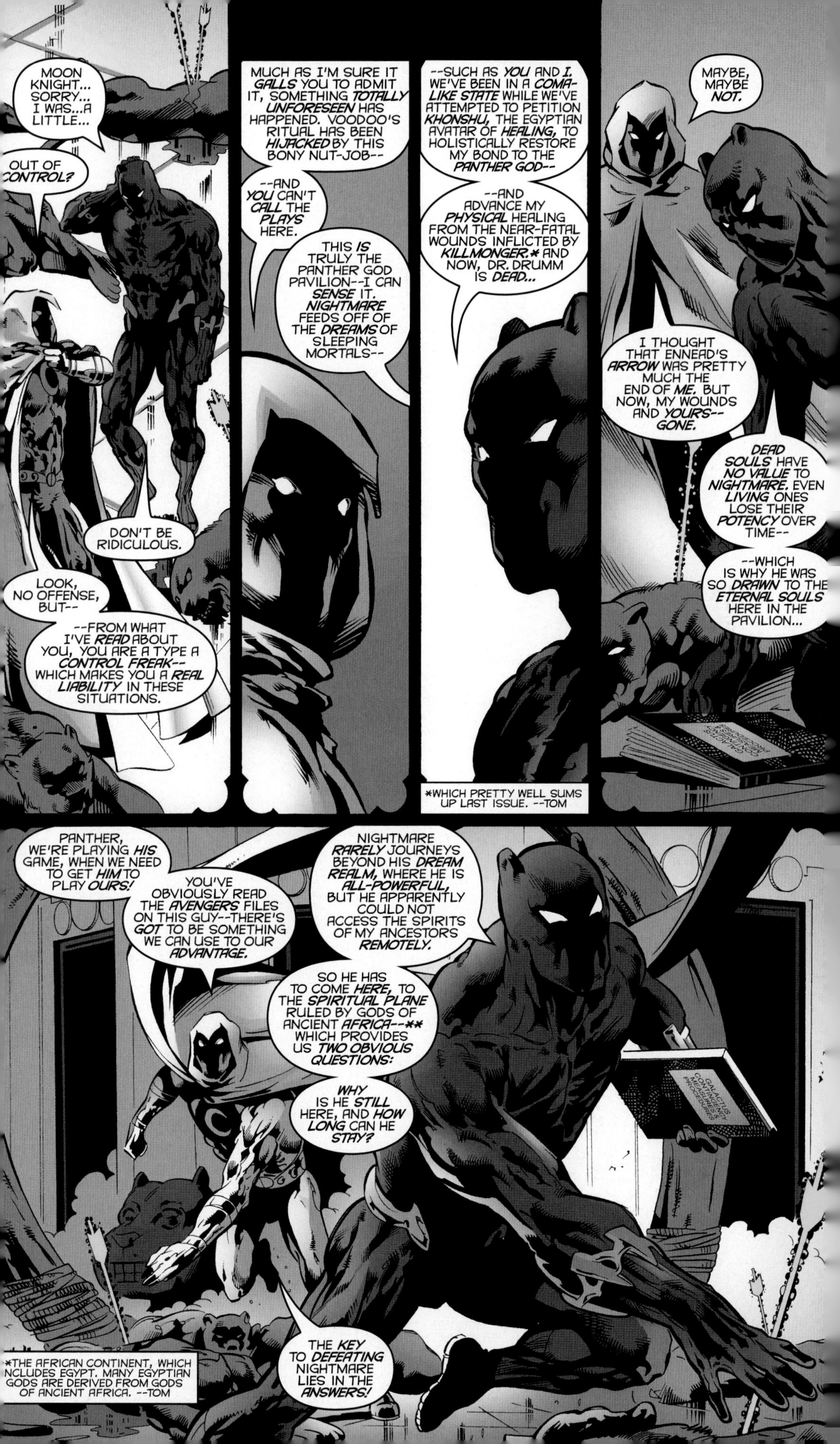
MOON KNIGHT... SORRY... I WAS...A LITTLE...
OUT OF CONTROL?
DON'T BE RIDICULOUS.
LOOK, NO OFFENSE, BUT--
--FROM WHAT I'VE READ ABOUT YOU, YOU ARE A TYPE A CONTROL FREAK--WHICH MAKES YOU A REAL LIABILITY IN THESE SITUATIONS.
MUCH AS I'M SURE IT GALLS YOU TO ADMIT IT, SOMETHING TOTALLY UNFORESEEN HAS HAPPENED. VOODOO'S RITUAL HAS BEEN HIJACKED BY THIS BONY NUT-JOB--
--AND YOU CAN'T CALL THE PLAYS HERE.
THIS IS TRULY THE PANTHER GOD PAVILION--I CAN SENSE IT. NIGHTMARE FEEDS OFF OF THE DREAMS OF SLEEPING MORTALS--
--SUCH AS YOU AND I. WE'VE BEEN IN A COMA-LIKE STATE WHILE WE'VE ATTEMPTED TO PETITION KHONSHU, THE EGYPTIAN AVATAR OF HEALING, TO HOLISTICALLY RESTORE MY BOND TO THE PANTHER GOD--
--AND ADVANCE MY PHYSICAL HEALING FROM THE NEAR-FATAL WOUNDS INFLICTED BY KILLMONGER.* AND NOW, DR. DRUMM IS DEAD...
*WHICH PRETTY WELL SUMS UP LAST ISSUE. --TOM
MAYBE, MAYBE NOT.
I THOUGHT THAT ENNEAD'S ARROW WAS PRETTY MUCH THE END OF ME. BUT NOW, MY WOUNDS AND YOURS--GONE.
DEAD SOULS HAVE NO VALUE TO NIGHTMARE. EVEN LIVING ONES LOSE THEIR POTENCY OVER TIME--
--WHICH IS WHY HE WAS SO DRAWN TO THE ETERNAL SOULS HERE IN THE PAVILION...
PANTHER, WE'RE PLAYING HIS GAME, WHEN WE NEED TO GET HIM TO PLAY OURS!
YOU'VE OBVIOUSLY READ THE AVENGERS FILES ON THIS GUY--THERE'S GOT TO BE SOMETHING WE CAN USE TO OUR ADVANTAGE.
NIGHTMARE RARELY JOURNEYS BEYOND HIS DREAM REALM, WHERE HE IS ALL-POWERFUL, BUT HE APPARENTLY COULD NOT ACCESS THE SPIRITS OF MY ANCESTORS REMOTELY.
SO HE HAS TO COME HERE, TO THE SPIRITUAL PLANE RULED BY GODS OF ANCIENT AFRICA--** WHICH PROVIDES US TWO OBVIOUS QUESTIONS:
WHY IS HE STILL HERE, AND HOW LONG CAN HE STAY?
THE KEY TO DEFEATING NIGHTMARE LIES IN THE ANSWERS!
GALACTUS CONTINGENCY MEASURES & PROCEDURES
*THE AFRICAN CONTINENT, WHICH NCLUDES EGYPT. MANY EGYPTIAN GODS ARE DERIVED FROM GODS OF ANCIENT AFRICA. --TOM

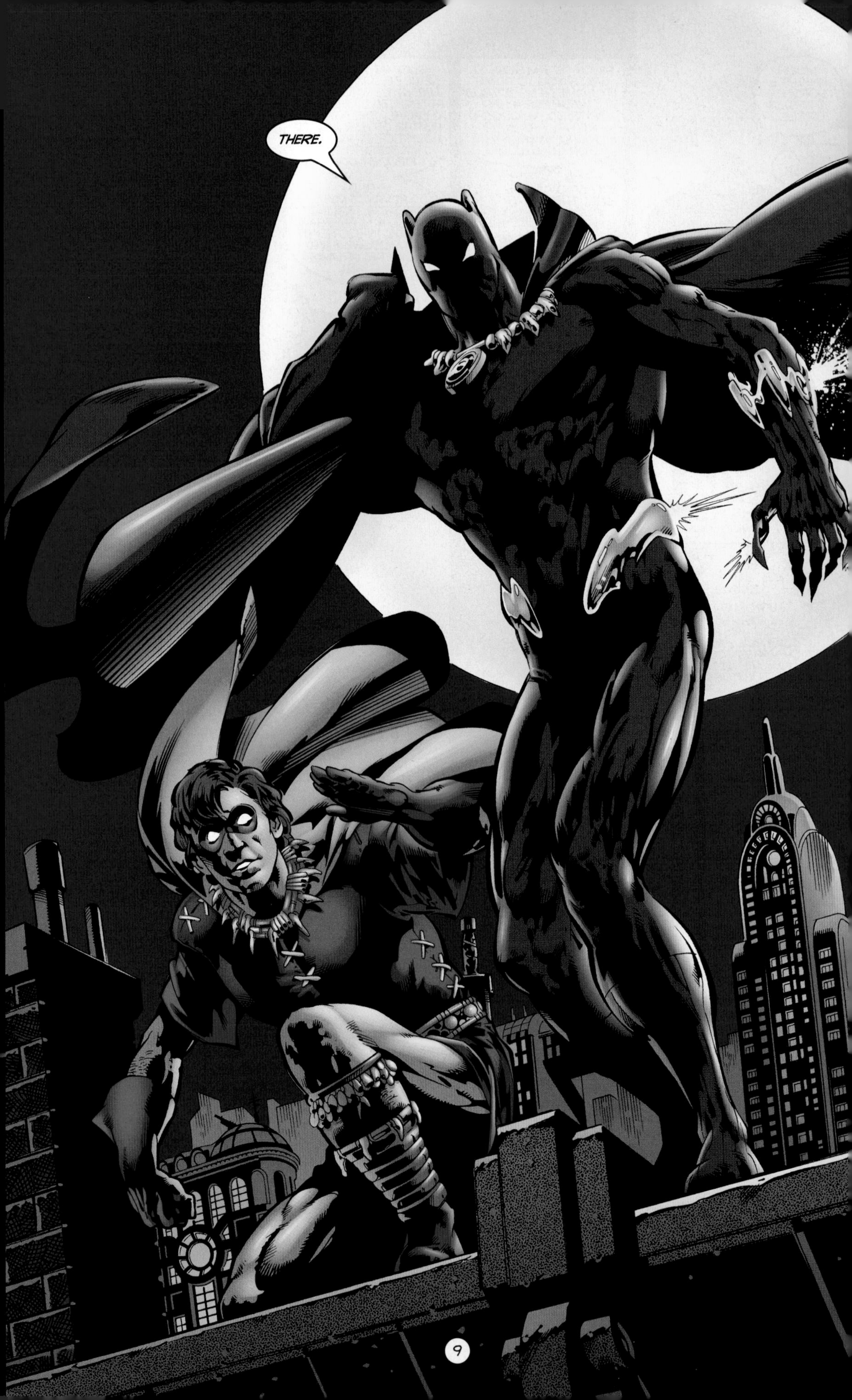
THERE.

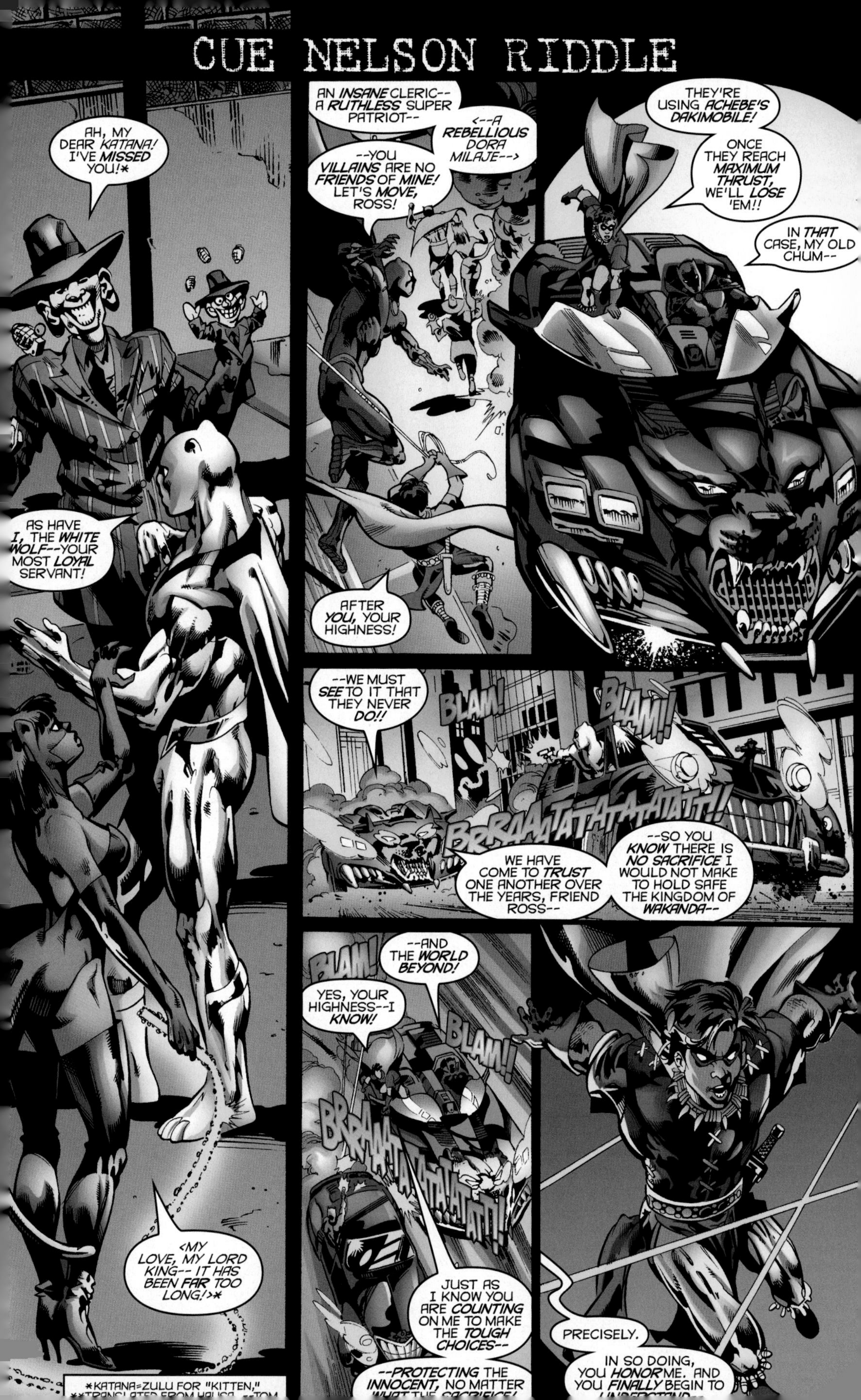
CUE NELSON RIDDLE
AH, MY DEAR KATANA! I'VE MISSED YOU!*
AS HAVE I, THE WHITE WOLF--YOUR MOST LOYAL SERVANT!
<MY LOVE, MY LORD KING-- IT HAS BEEN FAR TOO LONG!>*
*KATANA=ZULU FOR "KITTEN,"
AN INSANE CLERIC-- A RUTHLESS SUPER PATRIOT--
<--A REBELLIOUS DORA MILAJE-->
--YOU VILLAINS ARE NO FRIENDS OF MINE! LET'S MOVE, ROSS!
AFTER YOU, YOUR HIGHNESS!
THEY'RE USING ACHEBE'S DAKIMOBILE!
ONCE THEY REACH MAXIMUM THRUST, WE'LL LOSE 'EM!!
IN THAT CASE, MY OLD CHUM--
--WE MUST SEE TO IT THAT THEY NEVER DO!!
BLAM!
BLAM!!
BRRAAATATATATATATT!!
WE HAVE COME TO TRUST ONE ANOTHER OVER THE YEARS, FRIEND ROSS--
--SO YOU KNOW THERE IS NO SACRIFICE I WOULD NOT MAKE TO HOLD SAFE THE KINGDOM OF WAKANDA--
BLAM!
--AND THE WORLD BEYOND!
YES, YOUR HIGHNESS--I KNOW!
BLAM!!
BRRAAATATATATATATT!!
JUST AS I KNOW YOU ARE COUNTING ON ME TO MAKE THE TOUGH CHOICES--
--PROTECTING THE INNOCENT, NO MATTER
PRECISELY.
IN SO DOING, YOU HONOR ME. AND YOU FINALLY BEGIN TO

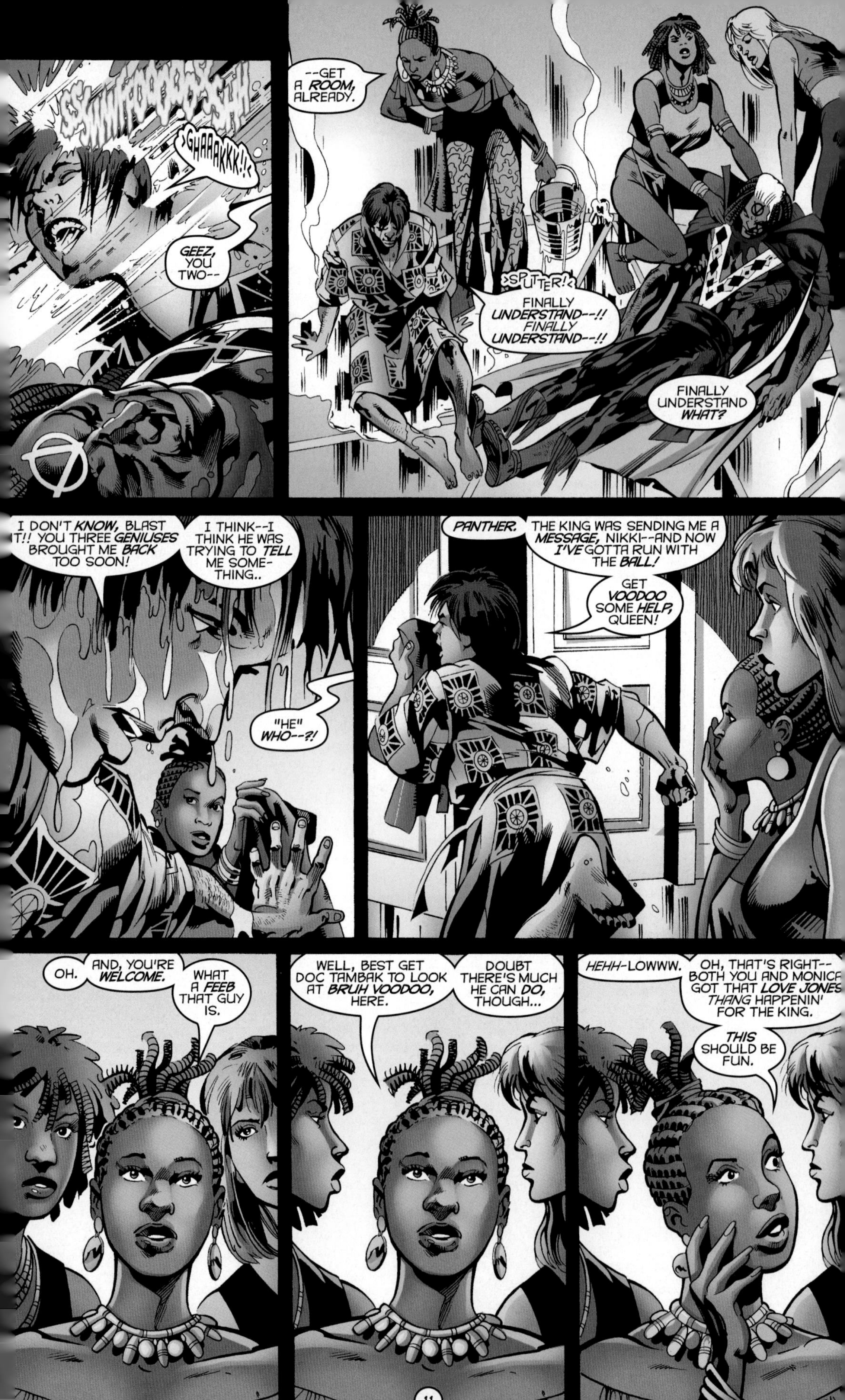
SSWHHOOOOOSSHH
GHAAAKKK!!
GEEZ, YOU TWO--
--GET A ROOM, ALREADY.
SPUTTER!
FINALLY UNDERSTAND--!! FINALLY UNDERSTAND--!!
FINALLY UNDERSTAND WHAT?
I DON'T KNOW, BLAST IT!! YOU THREE GENIUSES BROUGHT ME BACK TOO SOON!
I THINK--I THINK HE WAS TRYING TO TELL ME SOME-THING..
"HE" WHO--?!
PANTHER.
THE KING WAS SENDING ME A MESSAGE, NIKKI--AND NOW I'VE GOTTA RUN WITH THE BALL!
GET VOODOO SOME HELP, QUEEN!
OH.
AND, YOU'RE WELCOME.
WHAT A FEEB THAT GUY IS.
WELL, BEST GET DOC TAMBAK TO LOOK AT BRUH VOODOO, HERE.
DOUBT THERE'S MUCH HE CAN DO, THOUGH...
HEHH-LOWWW.
OH, THAT'S RIGHT-- BOTH YOU AND MONICA GOT THAT LOVE JONES THANG HAPPENIN' FOR THE KING.
THIS SHOULD BE FUN.

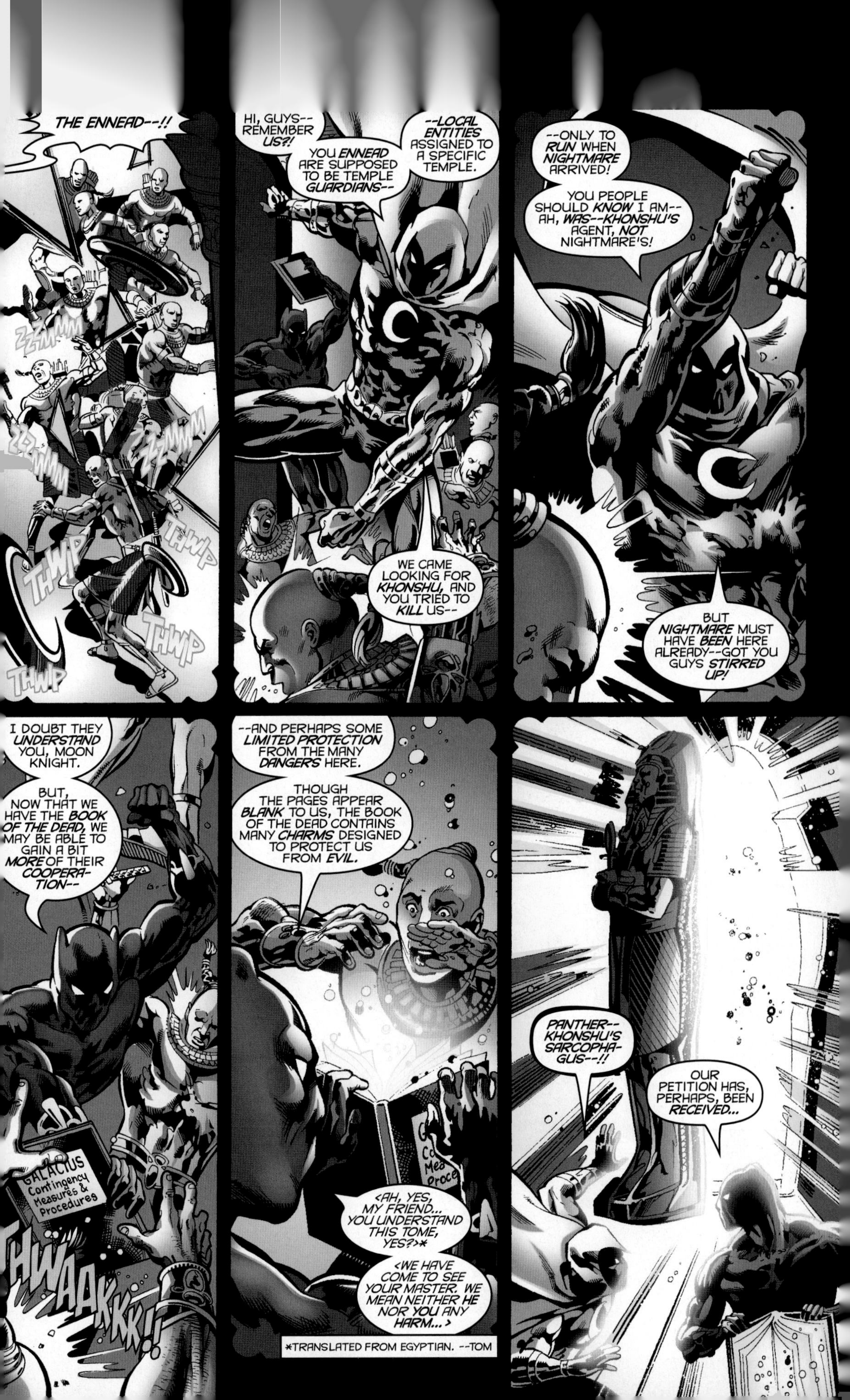
THE ENNEAD--!!
ZZMMM
ZZMMM
ZZZMMMM
THWIP
THWIP
THWIP
THWIP
HI, GUYS--REMEMBER US?!
YOU ENNEAD ARE SUPPOSED TO BE TEMPLE GUARDIANS--
--LOCAL ENTITIES ASSIGNED TO A SPECIFIC TEMPLE.
WE CAME LOOKING FOR KHONSHU, AND YOU TRIED TO KILL US--
--ONLY TO RUN WHEN NIGHTMARE ARRIVED!
YOU PEOPLE SHOULD KNOW I AM--AH, WAS--KHONSHU'S AGENT, NOT NIGHTMARE'S!
BUT NIGHTMARE MUST HAVE BEEN HERE ALREADY--GOT YOU GUYS STIRRED UP!
I DOUBT THEY UNDERSTAND YOU, MOON KNIGHT.
BUT, NOW THAT WE HAVE THE BOOK OF THE DEAD, WE MAY BE ABLE TO GAIN A BIT MORE OF THEIR COOPERATION--
GALACTUS Contingency Measures & Procedures
THWAAKKK!!
--AND PERHAPS SOME LIMITED PROTECTION FROM THE MANY DANGERS HERE.
THOUGH THE PAGES APPEAR BLANK TO US, THE BOOK OF THE DEAD CONTAINS MANY CHARMS DESIGNED TO PROTECT US FROM EVIL.
<AH, YES, MY FRIEND... YOU UNDERSTAND THIS TOME, YES?>*
<WE HAVE COME TO SEE YOUR MASTER. WE MEAN NEITHER HE NOR YOU ANY HARM...>
*TRANSLATED FROM EGYPTIAN. --TOM
PANTHER--KHONSHU'S SARCOPHAGUS--!!
OUR PETITION HAS, PERHAPS, BEEN RECEIVED...

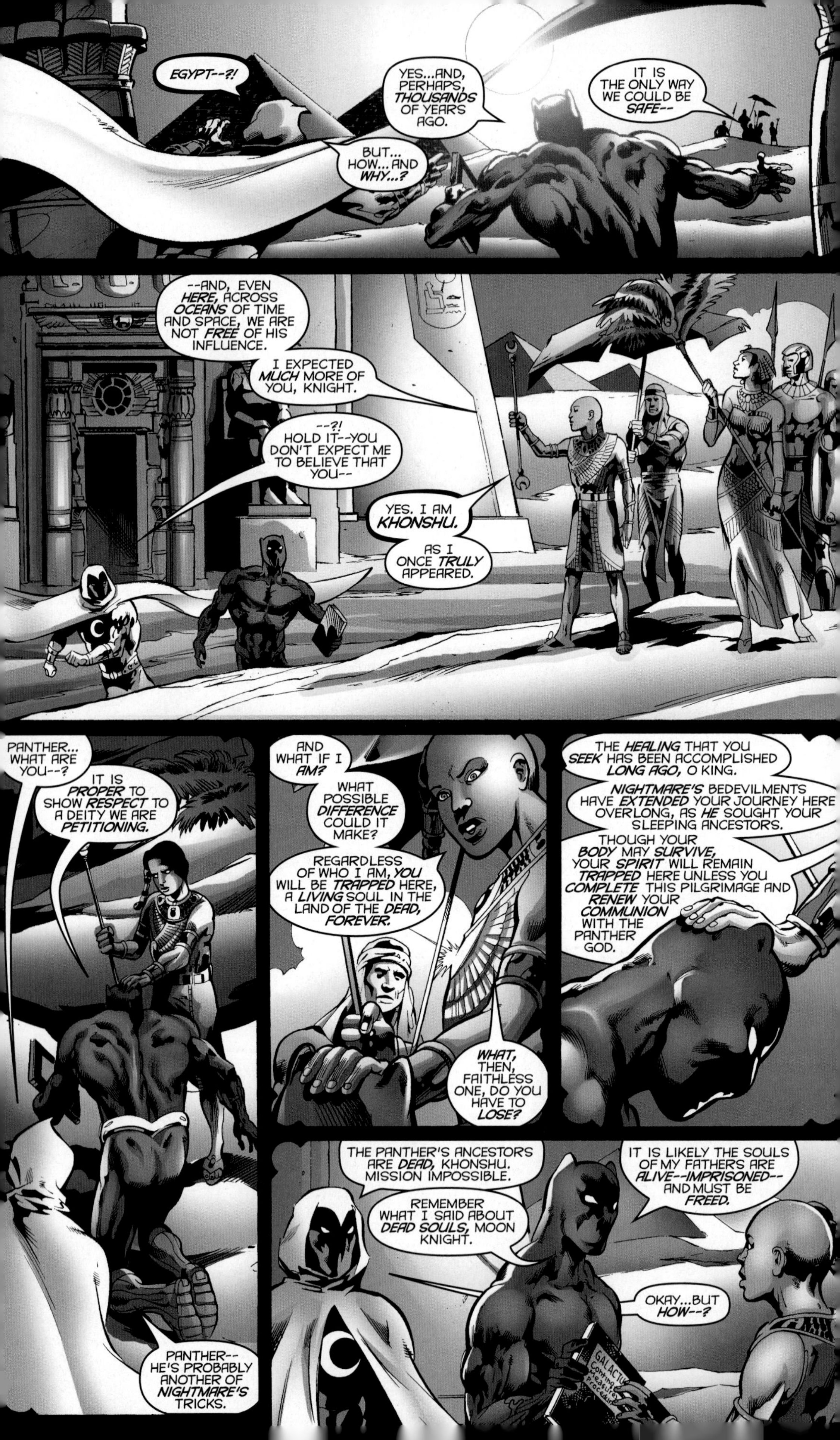
EGYPT--?!
YES...AND, PERHAPS, THOUSANDS OF YEARS AGO.
BUT... HOW...AND WHY...?
IT IS THE ONLY WAY WE COULD BE SAFE--
--AND, EVEN HERE, ACROSS OCEANS OF TIME AND SPACE, WE ARE NOT FREE OF HIS INFLUENCE.
I EXPECTED MUCH MORE OF YOU, KNIGHT.
--?! HOLD IT--YOU DON'T EXPECT ME TO BELIEVE THAT YOU--
YES. I AM KHONSHU.
AS I ONCE TRULY APPEARED.
PANTHER... WHAT ARE YOU--?
IT IS PROPER TO SHOW RESPECT TO A DEITY WE ARE PETITIONING.
PANTHER-- HE'S PROBABLY ANOTHER OF NIGHTMARE'S TRICKS.
AND WHAT IF I AM?
WHAT POSSIBLE DIFFERENCE COULD IT MAKE?
REGARDLESS OF WHO I AM, YOU WILL BE TRAPPED HERE, A LIVING SOUL IN THE LAND OF THE DEAD, FOREVER.
WHAT, THEN, FAITHLESS ONE, DO YOU HAVE TO LOSE?
THE HEALING THAT YOU SEEK HAS BEEN ACCOMPLISHED LONG AGO, O KING.
NIGHTMARE'S BEDEVILMENTS HAVE EXTENDED YOUR JOURNEY HERE OVERLONG, AS HE SOUGHT YOUR SLEEPING ANCESTORS.
THOUGH YOUR BODY MAY SURVIVE, YOUR SPIRIT WILL REMAIN TRAPPED HERE UNLESS YOU COMPLETE THIS PILGRIMAGE AND RENEW YOUR COMMUNION WITH THE PANTHER GOD.
THE PANTHER'S ANCESTORS ARE DEAD, KHONSHU. MISSION IMPOSSIBLE.
REMEMBER WHAT I SAID ABOUT DEAD SOULS, MOON KNIGHT.
IT IS LIKELY THE SOULS OF MY FATHERS ARE ALIVE--IMPRISONED-- AND MUST BE FREED.
OKAY...BUT HOW--?

MY KNIGHT... *THINK.* THE *BOOK OF THE DEAD* IS YOUR *GUIDE* TO THIS PLACE.

I CANNOT READ IT *FOR* YOU--THE BOOK WAS CREATED FOR *MANKIND* ONLY.

YOU HAVE MERELY TO *DESIRE* IT, AND THE BOOK SHALL *LEAD* YOU WHERE YOU WISH TO GO, AND *PROTECT* YOU ALONG THE WAY!

HE MEANS... TAKE THE FIGHT *TO* NIGHTMARE...

INVADE HIS *REALM.* RISKY.

NIGHTMARE IS *ALL-POWERFUL* IN HIS OWN REALM.

BUT HE'S NOT *IN* HIS REALM-- HE'S *HERE--* SOMEWHERE--

YO-- FRENCHIE --!!

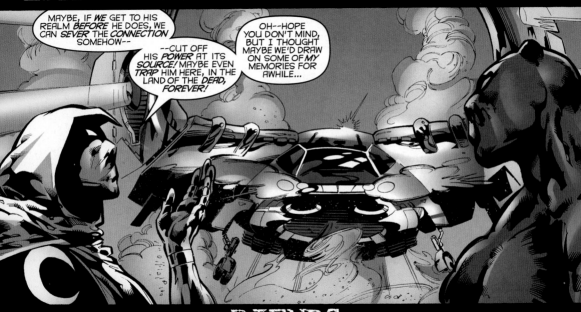

MAYBE, IF *WE* GET TO HIS REALM *BEFORE* HE DOES, WE CAN *SEVER* THE CONNECTION SOMEHOW--

--CUT OFF HIS *POWER* AT ITS *SOURCE!* MAYBE EVEN *TRAP* HIM HERE, IN THE LAND OF THE *DEAD, FOREVER!*

OH--HOPE YOU DON'T MIND, BUT I THOUGHT MAYBE WE'D DRAW ON SOME OF *MY* MEMORIES FOR AWHILE...

FRIENDS

I THINK I GOT YOUR MESSAGE.

ALL THAT TALK ABOUT *SACRIFICE* AND *TOUGH* CHOICES.

I'VE BEEN DOING THINGS *BACKWARD* HERE--JUST KIND OF *BABYSITTING* YOUR GIG--

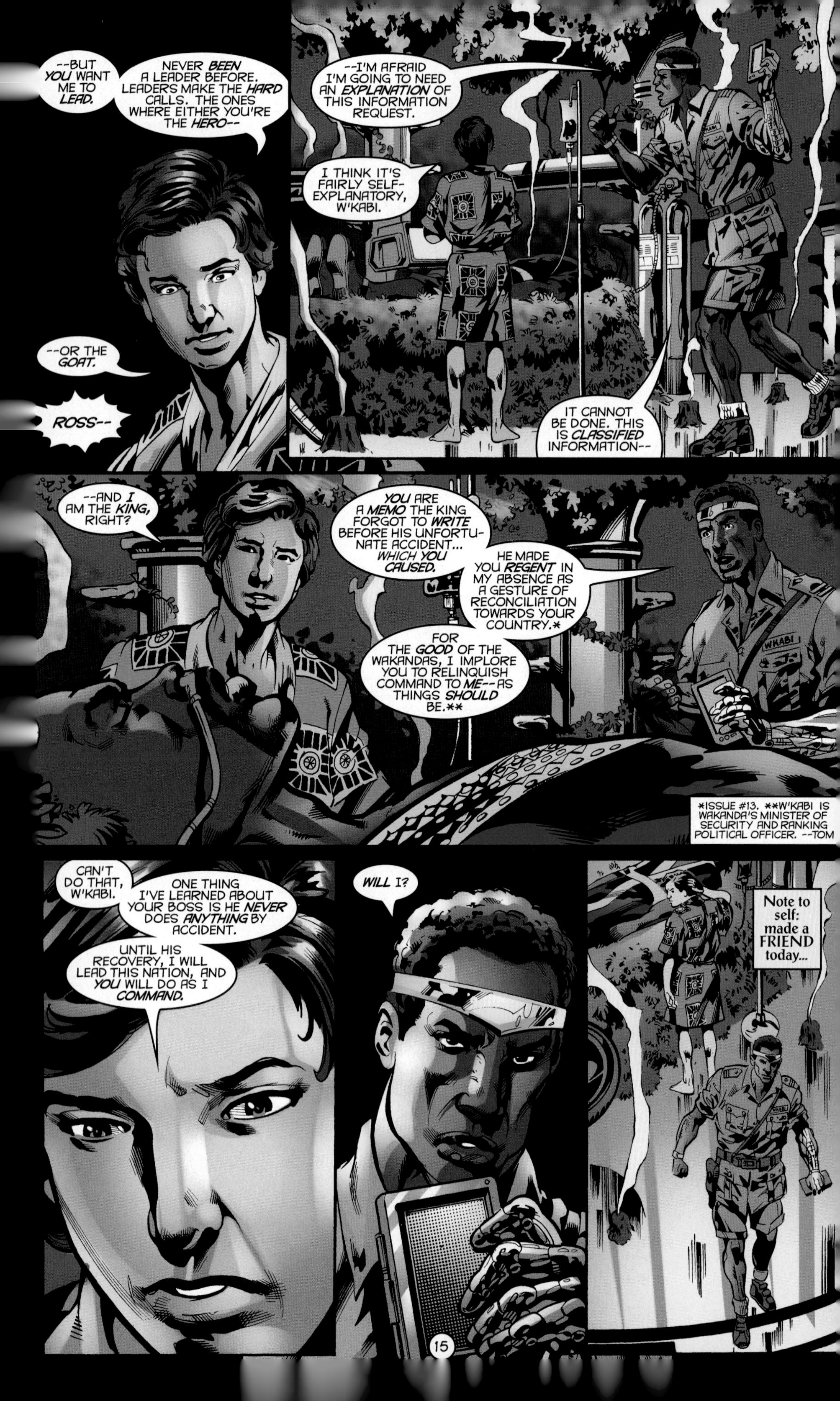

--BUT YOU WANT ME TO LEAD.
NEVER BEEN A LEADER BEFORE. LEADERS MAKE THE HARD CALLS. THE ONES WHERE EITHER YOU'RE THE HERO--
--OR THE GOAT.
ROSS--
--I'M AFRAID I'M GOING TO NEED AN EXPLANATION OF THIS INFORMATION REQUEST.
I THINK IT'S FAIRLY SELF-EXPLANATORY, W'KABI.
IT CANNOT BE DONE. THIS IS CLASSIFIED INFORMATION--
--AND I AM THE KING, RIGHT?
YOU ARE A MEMO THE KING FORGOT TO WRITE BEFORE HIS UNFORTUNATE ACCIDENT... WHICH YOU CAUSED.
HE MADE YOU REGENT IN MY ABSENCE AS A GESTURE OF RECONCILIATION TOWARDS YOUR COUNTRY.*
FOR THE GOOD OF THE WAKANDAS, I IMPLORE YOU TO RELINQUISH COMMAND TO ME--AS THINGS SHOULD BE.**
WKABI
*ISSUE #13. **W'KABI IS WAKANDA'S MINISTER OF SECURITY AND RANKING POLITICAL OFFICER. --TOM
CAN'T DO THAT, W'KABI.
ONE THING I'VE LEARNED ABOUT YOUR BOSS IS HE NEVER DOES ANYTHING BY ACCIDENT.
UNTIL HIS RECOVERY, I WILL LEAD THIS NATION, AND YOU WILL DO AS I COMMAND.
WILL I?
Note to self: made a FRIEND today...

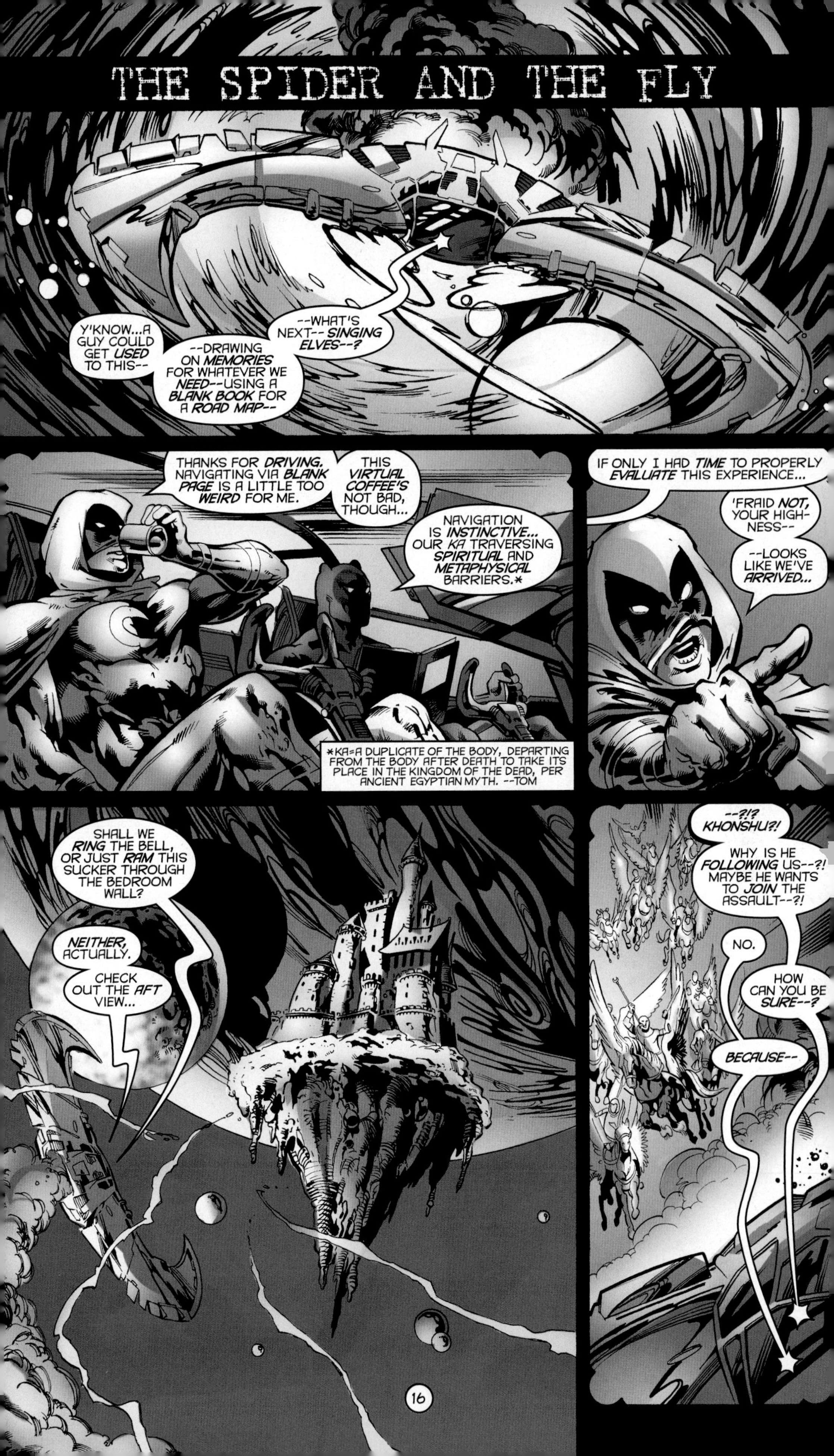
THE SPIDER AND THE FLY
Y'KNOW...A GUY COULD GET USED TO THIS--
--DRAWING ON MEMORIES FOR WHATEVER WE NEED--USING A BLANK BOOK FOR A ROAD MAP--
--WHAT'S NEXT-- SINGING ELVES--?
THANKS FOR DRIVING. NAVIGATING VIA BLANK PAGE IS A LITTLE TOO WEIRD FOR ME.
THIS VIRTUAL COFFEE'S NOT BAD, THOUGH...
NAVIGATION IS INSTINCTIVE... OUR KA TRAVERSING SPIRITUAL AND METAPHYSICAL BARRIERS.*
*KA=A DUPLICATE OF THE BODY, DEPARTING FROM THE BODY AFTER DEATH TO TAKE ITS PLACE IN THE KINGDOM OF THE DEAD, PER ANCIENT EGYPTIAN MYTH. --TOM
IF ONLY I HAD TIME TO PROPERLY EVALUATE THIS EXPERIENCE...
'FRAID NOT, YOUR HIGH-NESS--
--LOOKS LIKE WE'VE ARRIVED...
SHALL WE RING THE BELL, OR JUST RAM THIS SUCKER THROUGH THE BEDROOM WALL?
NEITHER, ACTUALLY.
CHECK OUT THE AFT VIEW...
--?!? KHONSHU?!
WHY IS HE FOLLOWING US--?! MAYBE HE WANTS TO JOIN THE ASSAULT--?!
NO.
HOW CAN YOU BE SURE--?
BECAUSE--
16

--THERE WILL BE NO ASSAULT!!

WHAT--?! WHAT ARE YOU DOING--?!

SOMETHING TOTALLY UNFORESEEN.

IF MY THEORY IS CORRECT, THERE ARE SEVERE LIMITS TO NIGHTMARE'S POWER HERE IN THIS REALM.

HIS HOLD ON HIS ENSORCELLED SUBJECTS IS TENUOUS AND INTERMITTENT.

THOUGH HE HAS GORGED HIMSELF WITH THE DREAMS OF MY FATHERS, THERE IS NOTHING NIGHTMARE NOW WANTS MORE DESPERATELY--

--THAN TO GO HOME.

AND, IF I AM CORRECT, HE IS COUNTING ON US TO LEAD HIM THERE!

OKAY, PANTHER, IT'S OFFICIAL: YOU'VE LOST ME.

MOON KNIGHT--WHY WOULD NIGHTMARE ACTUALLY GIVE US THE BOOK OF THE DEAD, KNOWING WE'D USE IT AGAINST HIM?

WHY APPEAR AS "KHONSHU" AND ENCOURAGE US TO MOUNT AN ASSAULT ON HIS REALM?

"KHONSHU'S" OWN WORDS-- "A LIVING SOUL, TRAPPED IN THE LAND OF THE DEAD FOREVER!"

HEY-- HEY, GUY-- EASY ON THE BOOK, THERE--

NIGHTMARE WASN'T TALKING ABOUT US--

--HE WAS REFERRING TO HIMSELF!

MAYBE I'D BETTER HANG ONTO THAT BOOK FOR YOU--

NIGHTMARE IS LOST--TRAPPED HERE IN THE LAND OF THE DEAD--

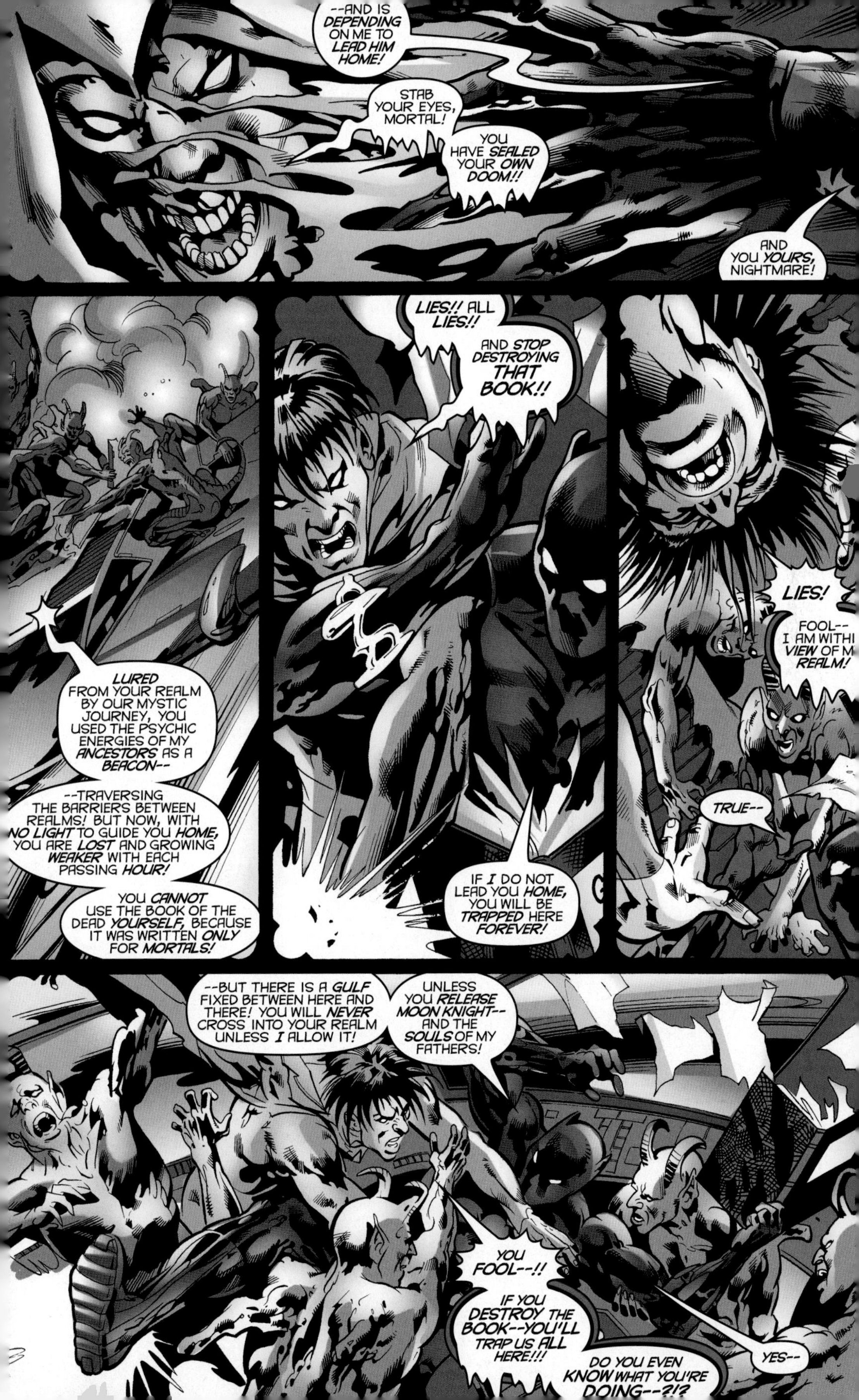
--AND IS DEPENDING ON ME TO LEAD HIM HOME!
STAB YOUR EYES, MORTAL!
YOU HAVE SEALED YOUR OWN DOOM!!
AND YOU YOURS, NIGHTMARE!
LURED FROM YOUR REALM BY OUR MYSTIC JOURNEY, YOU USED THE PSYCHIC ENERGIES OF MY ANCESTORS AS A BEACON--
--TRAVERSING THE BARRIERS BETWEEN REALMS! BUT NOW, WITH NO LIGHT TO GUIDE YOU HOME, YOU ARE LOST AND GROWING WEAKER WITH EACH PASSING HOUR!
YOU CANNOT USE THE BOOK OF THE DEAD YOURSELF, BECAUSE IT WAS WRITTEN ONLY FOR MORTALS!
LIES!! ALL LIES!!
AND STOP DESTROYING THAT BOOK!!
IF I DO NOT LEAD YOU HOME, YOU WILL BE TRAPPED HERE FOREVER!
LIES!
FOOL-- I AM WITHI VIEW OF M REALM!
TRUE--
--BUT THERE IS A GULF FIXED BETWEEN HERE AND THERE! YOU WILL NEVER CROSS INTO YOUR REALM UNLESS I ALLOW IT!
UNLESS YOU RELEASE MOON KNIGHT-- AND THE SOULS OF MY FATHERS!
YOU FOOL--!!
IF YOU DESTROY THE BOOK--YOU'LL TRAP US ALL HERE!!!
DO YOU EVEN KNOW WHAT YOU'RE DOING--?!?
YES--

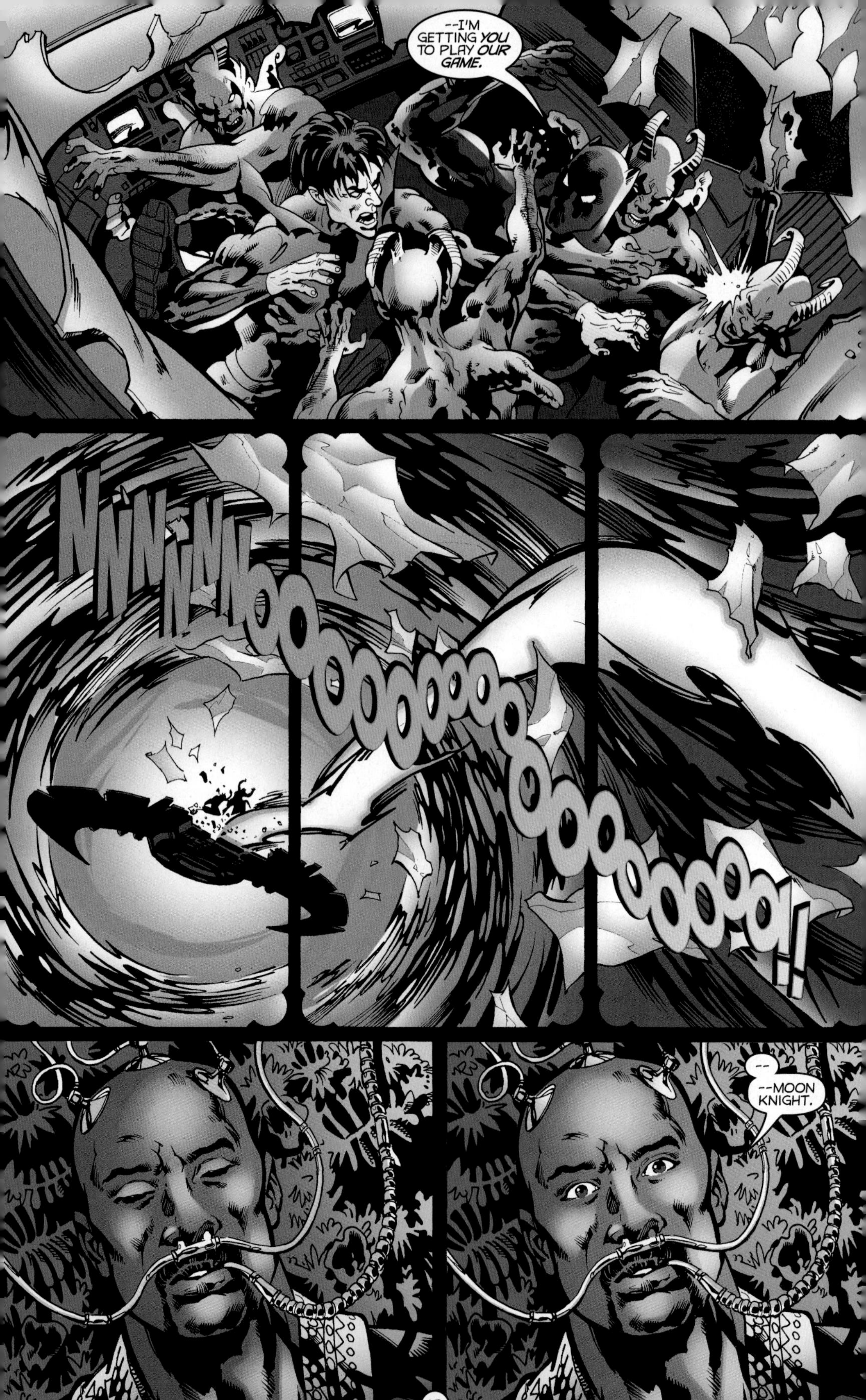
--I'M GETTING YOU TO PLAY OUR GAME.
NNNNNNNOOOOOOOOOOOOOOOOOOOOOOO!!
--
--MOON KNIGHT.

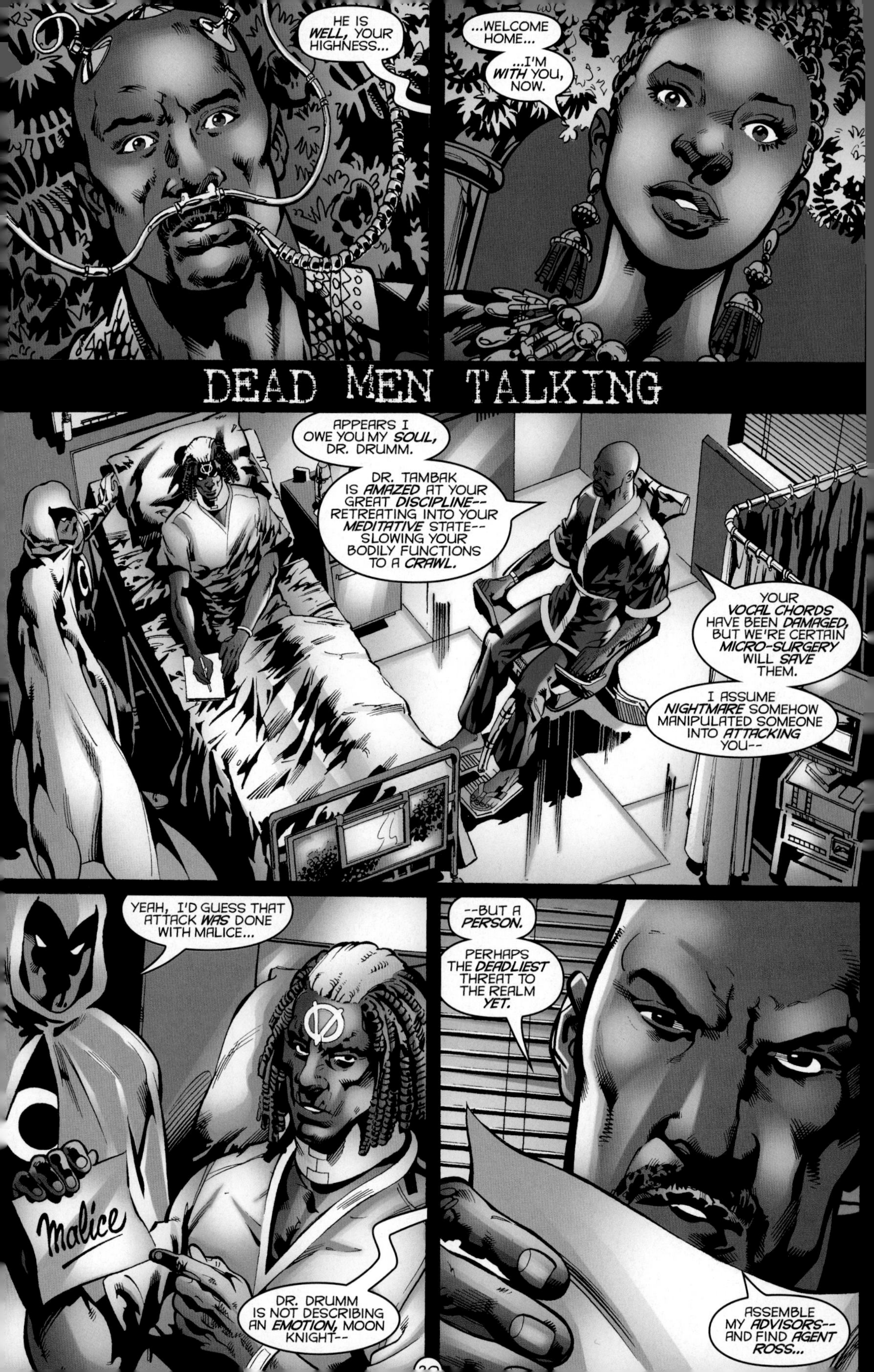
HE IS WELL, YOUR HIGHNESS...
...WELCOME HOME...
...I'M WITH YOU, NOW.
DEAD MEN TALKING
APPEARS I OWE YOU MY SOUL, DR. DRUMM.
DR. TAMBAK IS AMAZED AT YOUR GREAT DISCIPLINE-- RETREATING INTO YOUR MEDITATIVE STATE-- SLOWING YOUR BODILY FUNCTIONS TO A CRAWL.
YOUR VOCAL CHORDS HAVE BEEN DAMAGED, BUT WE'RE CERTAIN MICRO-SURGERY WILL SAVE THEM.
I ASSUME NIGHTMARE SOMEHOW MANIPULATED SOMEONE INTO ATTACKING YOU--
YEAH, I'D GUESS THAT ATTACK WAS DONE WITH MALICE...
Malice
DR. DRUMM IS NOT DESCRIBING AN EMOTION, MOON KNIGHT--
--BUT A PERSON.
PERHAPS THE DEADLIEST THREAT TO THE REALM YET.
ASSEMBLE MY ADVISORS-- AND FIND AGENT ROSS...

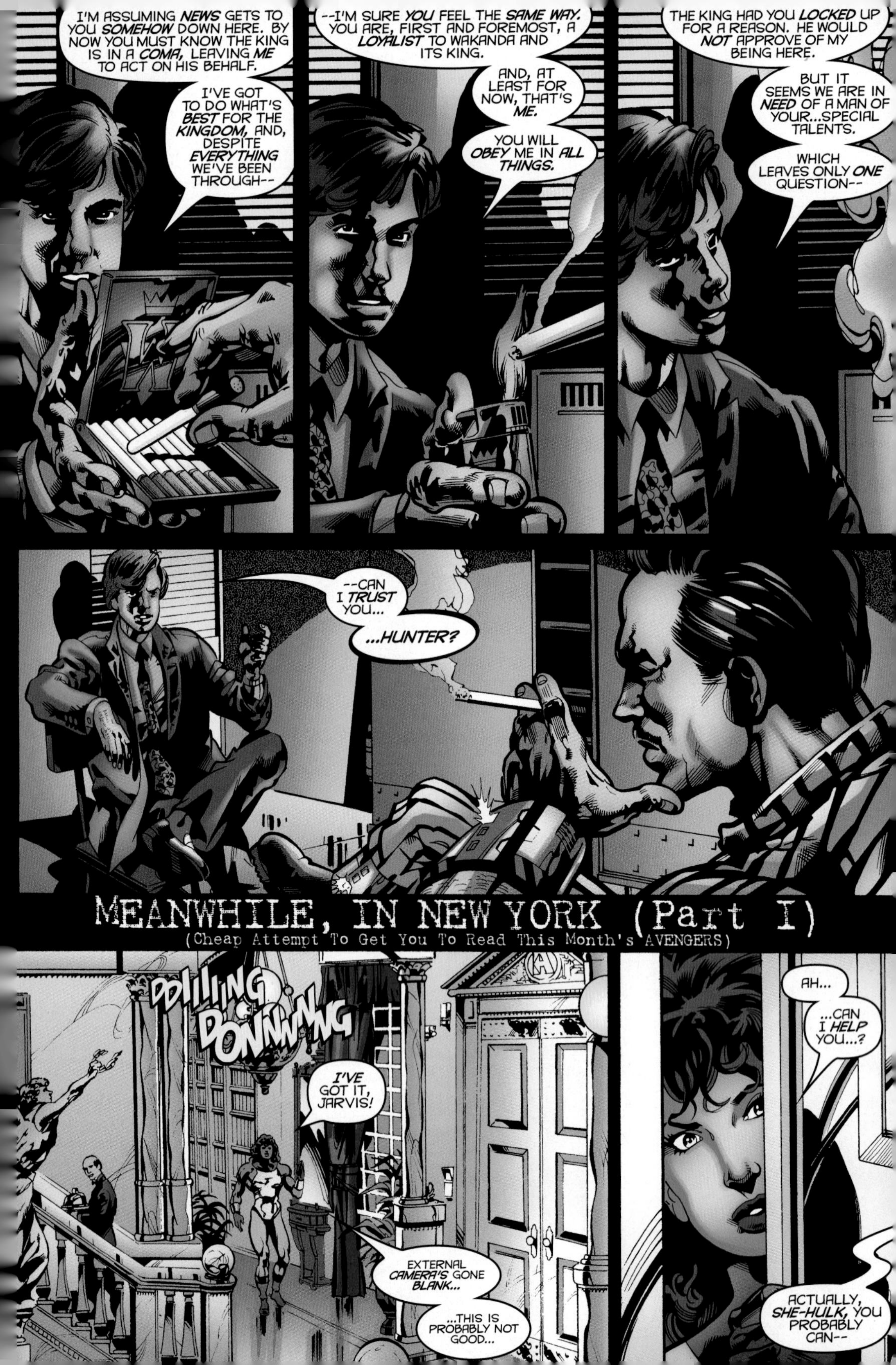
I'M ASSUMING NEWS GETS TO YOU SOMEHOW DOWN HERE. BY NOW YOU MUST KNOW THE KING IS IN A COMA, LEAVING ME TO ACT ON HIS BEHALF.
I'VE GOT TO DO WHAT'S BEST FOR THE KINGDOM, AND, DESPITE EVERYTHING WE'VE BEEN THROUGH--
--I'M SURE YOU FEEL THE SAME WAY. YOU ARE, FIRST AND FOREMOST, A LOYALIST TO WAKANDA AND ITS KING.
AND, AT LEAST FOR NOW, THAT'S ME.
YOU WILL OBEY ME IN ALL THINGS.
THE KING HAD YOU LOCKED UP FOR A REASON. HE WOULD NOT APPROVE OF MY BEING HERE.
BUT IT SEEMS WE ARE IN NEED OF A MAN OF YOUR...SPECIAL TALENTS.
WHICH LEAVES ONLY ONE QUESTION--
--CAN I TRUST YOU...
...HUNTER?
MEANWHILE, IN NEW YORK (Part I)
(Cheap Attempt To Get You To Read This Month's AVENGERS)
DDIIIING DONNNNNG
I'VE GOT IT, JARVIS!
EXTERNAL CAMERA'S GONE BLANK...
...THIS IS PROBABLY NOT GOOD...
AH...
...CAN I HELP YOU...?
ACTUALLY, SHE-HULK, YOU PROBABLY CAN--

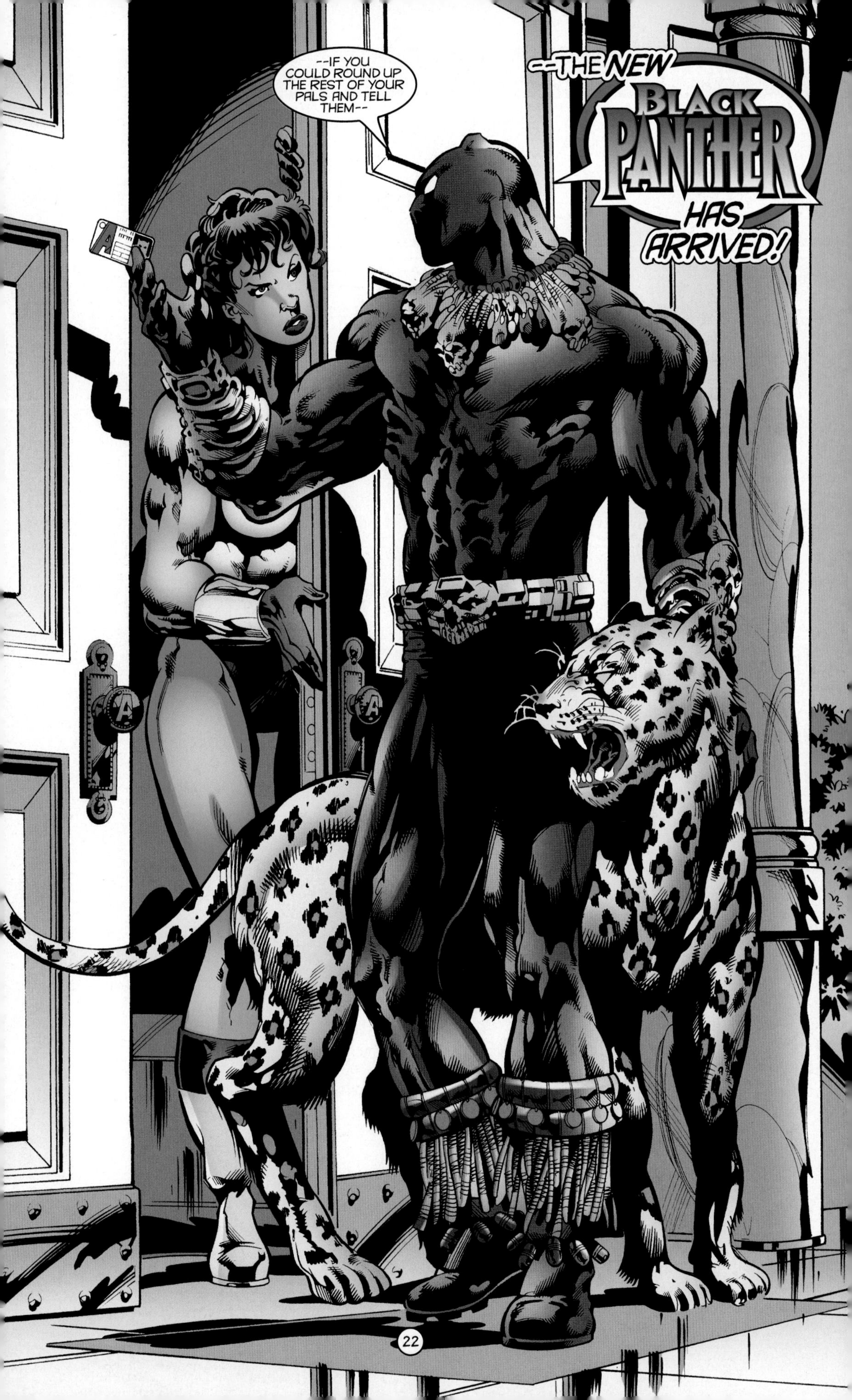
--IF YOU COULD ROUND UP THE REST OF YOUR PALS AND TELL THEM--
--THE NEW BLACK PANTHER HAS ARRIVED!

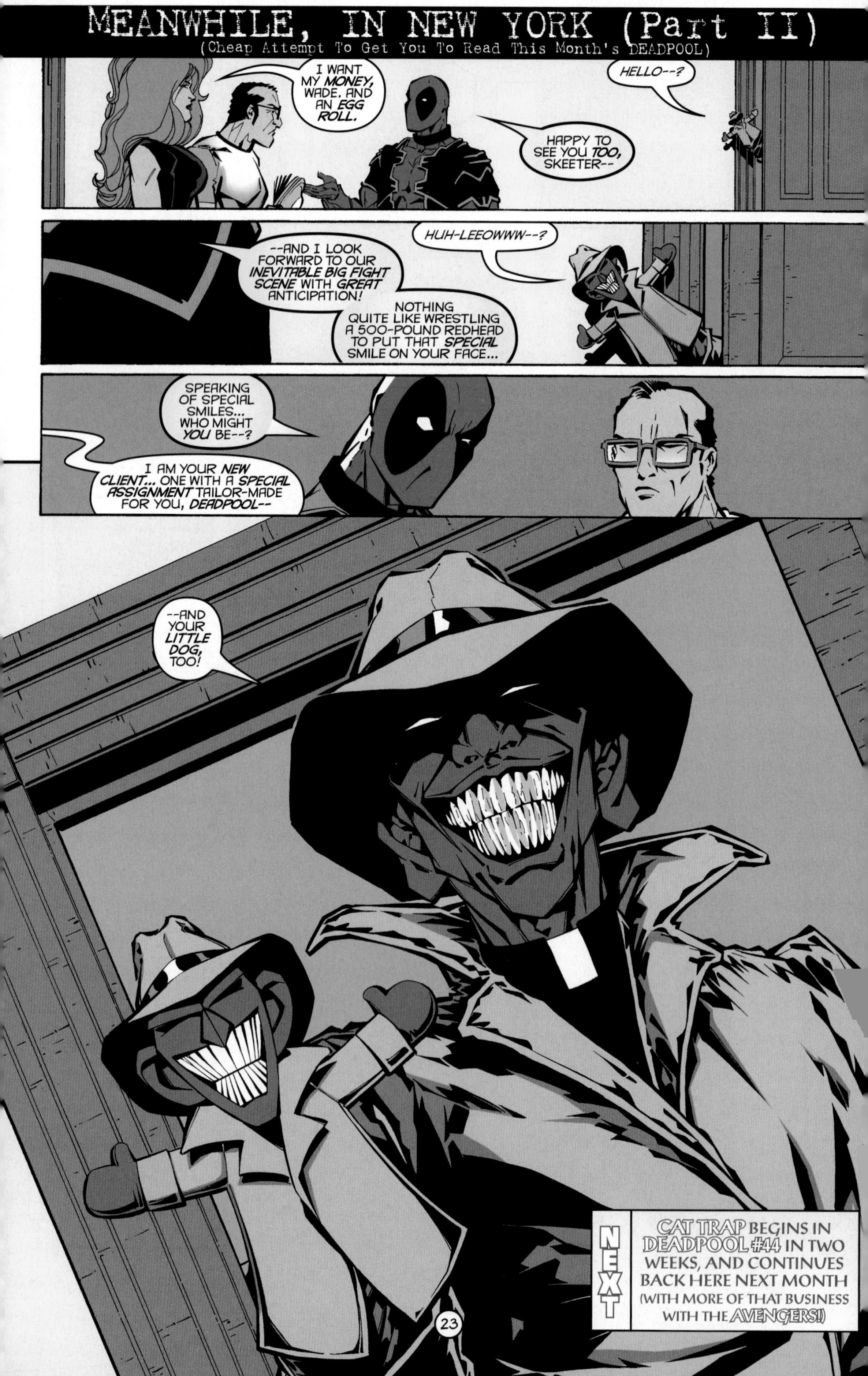
MEANWHILE, IN NEW YORK (Part II)
(Cheap Attempt To Get You To Read This Month's DEADPOOL)
I WANT MY MONEY, WADE. AND AN EGG ROLL.
HELLO--?
HAPPY TO SEE YOU TOO, SKEETER--
HUH-LEEOWWW--?
--AND I LOOK FORWARD TO OUR INEVITABLE BIG FIGHT SCENE WITH GREAT ANTICIPATION!
NOTHING QUITE LIKE WRESTLING A 500-POUND REDHEAD TO PUT THAT SPECIAL SMILE ON YOUR FACE...
SPEAKING OF SPECIAL SMILES... WHO MIGHT YOU BE--?
I AM YOUR NEW CLIENT... ONE WITH A SPECIAL ASSIGNMENT TAILOR-MADE FOR YOU, DEADPOOL--
--AND YOUR LITTLE DOG, TOO!
NEXT
CAT TRAP BEGINS IN DEADPOOL #44 IN TWO WEEKS, AND CONTINUES BACK HERE NEXT MONTH (WITH MORE OF THAT BUSINESS WITH THE AVENGERS!)

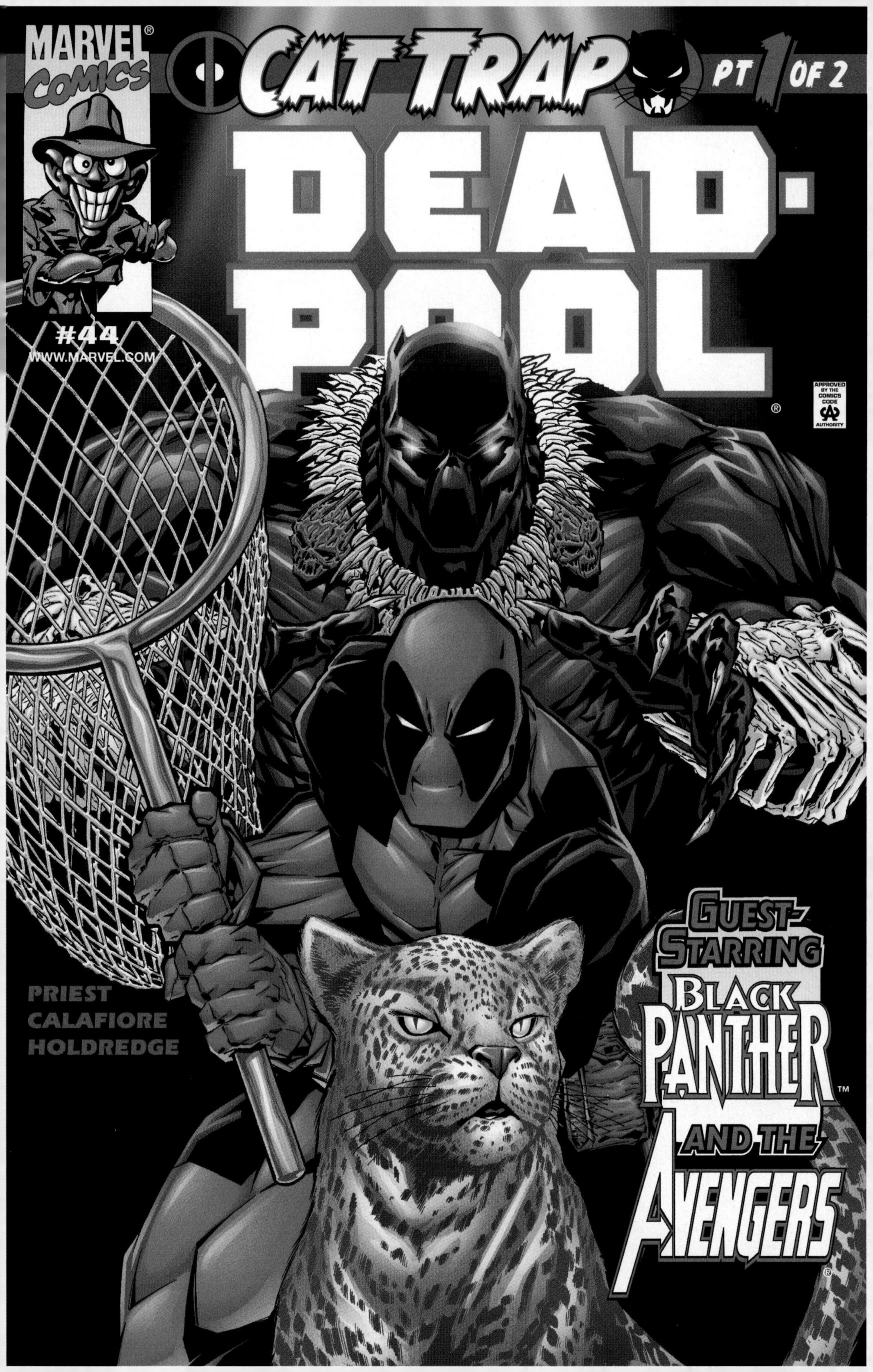

MARVEL COMICS
CAT TRAP PT 1 OF 2
DEADPOOL
#44
WWW.MARVEL.COM
APPROVED BY THE COMICS CODE AUTHORITY
PRIEST
CALAFIORE
HOLDREDGE
GUEST-STARRING BLACK PANTHER AND THE AVENGERS

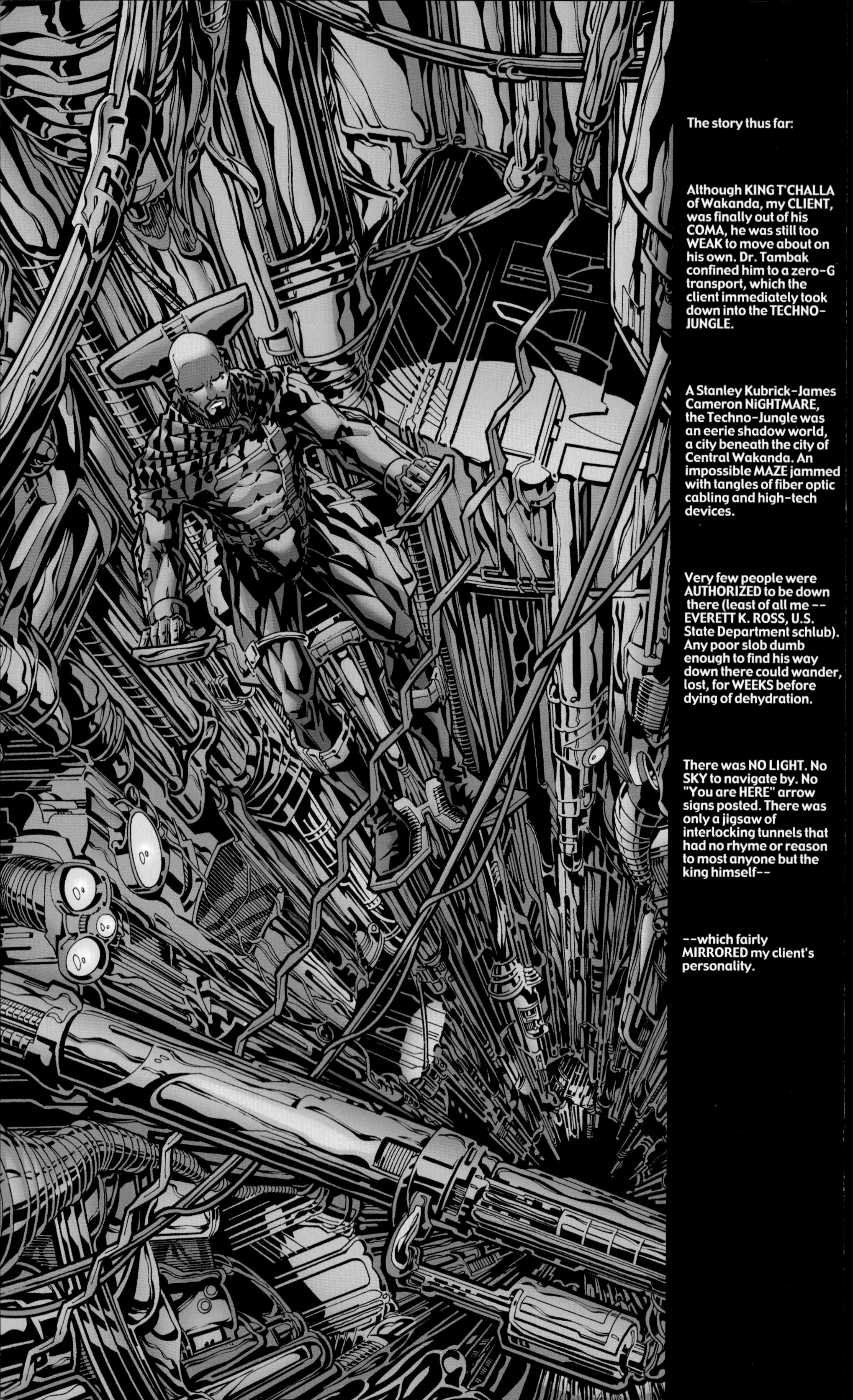
The story thus far:
Although KING T'CHALLA of Wakanda, my CLIENT, was finally out of his COMA, he was still too WEAK to move about on his own. Dr. Tambak confined him to a zero-G transport, which the client immediately took down into the TECHNO-JUNGLE.
A Stanley Kubrick-James Cameron NiGHTMARE, the Techno-Jungle was an eerie shadow world, a city beneath the city of Central Wakanda. An impossible MAZE jammed with tangles of fiber optic cabling and high-tech devices.
Very few people were AUTHORIZED to be down there (least of all me -- EVERETT K. ROSS, U.S. State Department schlub). Any poor slob dumb enough to find his way down there could wander, lost, for WEEKS before dying of dehydration.
There was NO LIGHT. No SKY to navigate by. No "You are HERE" arrow signs posted. There was only a jigsaw of interlocking tunnels that had no rhyme or reason to most anyone but the king himself--
--which fairly MIRRORED my client's personality.

THE KING AND I

Until the recent COLLAPSE of the Wakandan economy, he was one of the world's RICHEST and most technologically proficient men. Bill Gates meets Shaka Zulu.

He was KING of one of the most technologically advanced countries in the WORLD. I'd known him for quite a while now, but the man was still a MYSTERY to me.

He was, ultimately, a bit UNKNOWABLE. Compassionate eyes that told you absolutely NOTHING about what he was thinking.

He did most everything for his own reasons. Like the jungle cats his religion deified, he was a CUNNING man, always three steps ahead of his enemies.

Which, I supposed, was why he was THERE.

An informed GUESS was the best anyone could ever do. It was possible, given his humiliating LOSS of Killmonger's TRIBAL CHALLENGE--

--that the client had gone to the Techno-Jungle for some PRIVACY. It may have been the tribal equivalent of hiding under the BED.

In an effort to THWART Erik Killmonger's challenge, the client had DISSOLVED his political government and CRASHED the Wakandan economy.

The rule of LAW thus became TRIBAL over POLITICAL. And, while the client was still KING, his loss of Killmonger's challenge STRIPPED him of his most IMPORTANT role--

--that of CHIEFTAIN.

King T'Challa of Wakanda was NO LONGER The Black Panther...

...thanks, largely, to ME...

His NEXT move was ANYBODY's guess... ✪

ENTER, MY LORD!

TAKU-- MY MOST LOYAL FRIEND and MINISTER of COMMUNICATION--

✪ ALL OF WHICH FAIRLY SUMS UP THE CURRENT EVENTS IN BLACK PANTHER #18-22. --MIKE

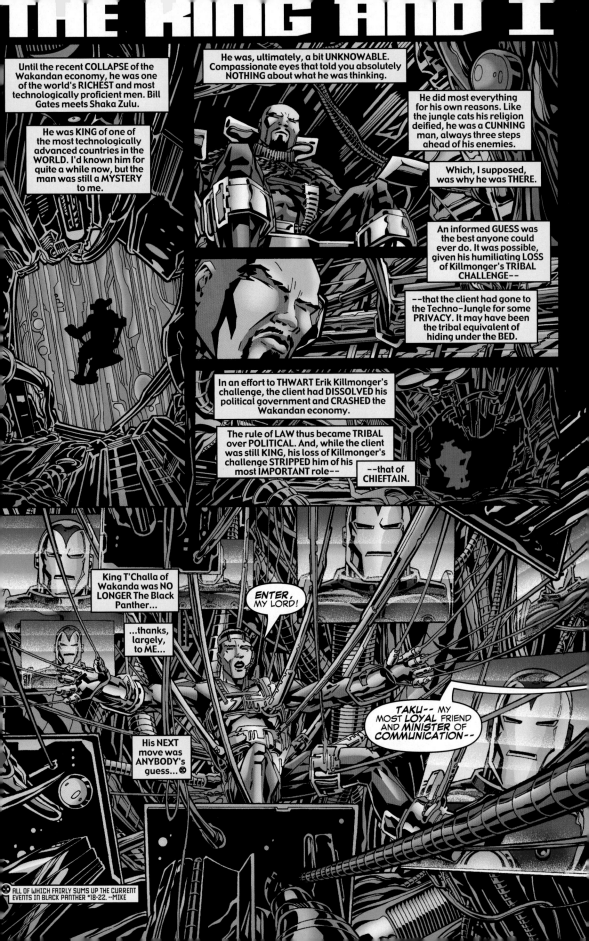

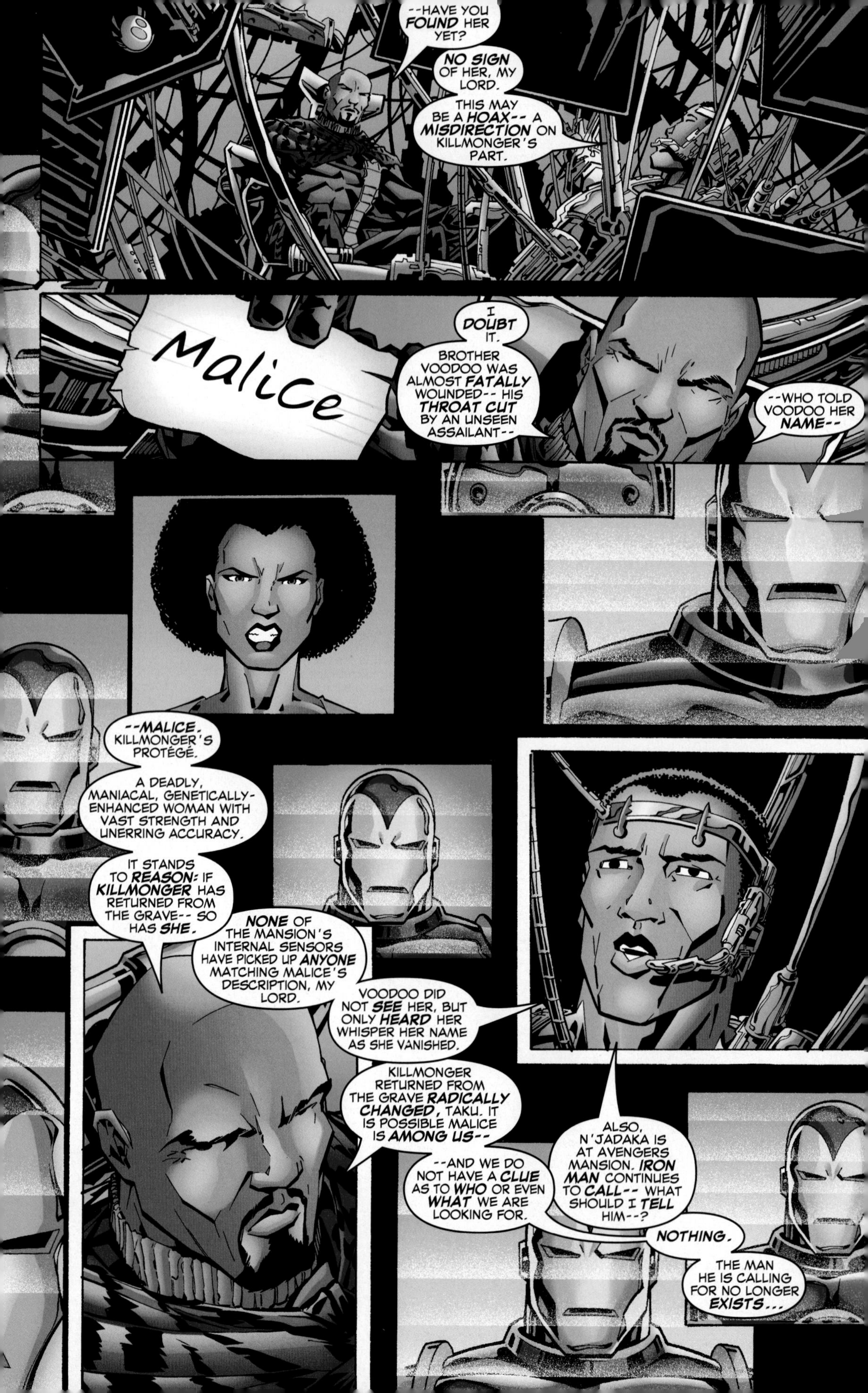
--HAVE YOU FOUND HER YET?
NO SIGN OF HER, MY LORD.
THIS MAY BE A HOAX-- A MISDIRECTION ON KILLMONGER'S PART.
Malice
I DOUBT IT.
BROTHER VOODOO WAS ALMOST FATALLY WOUNDED-- HIS THROAT CUT BY AN UNSEEN ASSAILANT--
--WHO TOLD VOODOO HER NAME--
--MALICE. KILLMONGER'S PROTÉGÉ.
A DEADLY, MANIACAL, GENETICALLY-ENHANCED WOMAN WITH VAST STRENGTH AND UNERRING ACCURACY.
IT STANDS TO REASON: IF KILLMONGER HAS RETURNED FROM THE GRAVE-- SO HAS SHE.
NONE OF THE MANSION'S INTERNAL SENSORS HAVE PICKED UP ANYONE MATCHING MALICE'S DESCRIPTION, MY LORD.
VOODOO DID NOT SEE HER, BUT ONLY HEARD HER WHISPER HER NAME AS SHE VANISHED.
KILLMONGER RETURNED FROM THE GRAVE RADICALLY CHANGED, TAKU. IT IS POSSIBLE MALICE IS AMONG US--
--AND WE DO NOT HAVE A CLUE AS TO WHO OR EVEN WHAT WE ARE LOOKING FOR.
ALSO, N'JADAKA IS AT AVENGERS MANSION. IRON MAN CONTINUES TO CALL-- WHAT SHOULD I TELL HIM--?
NOTHING.
THE MAN HE IS CALLING FOR NO LONGER EXISTS...

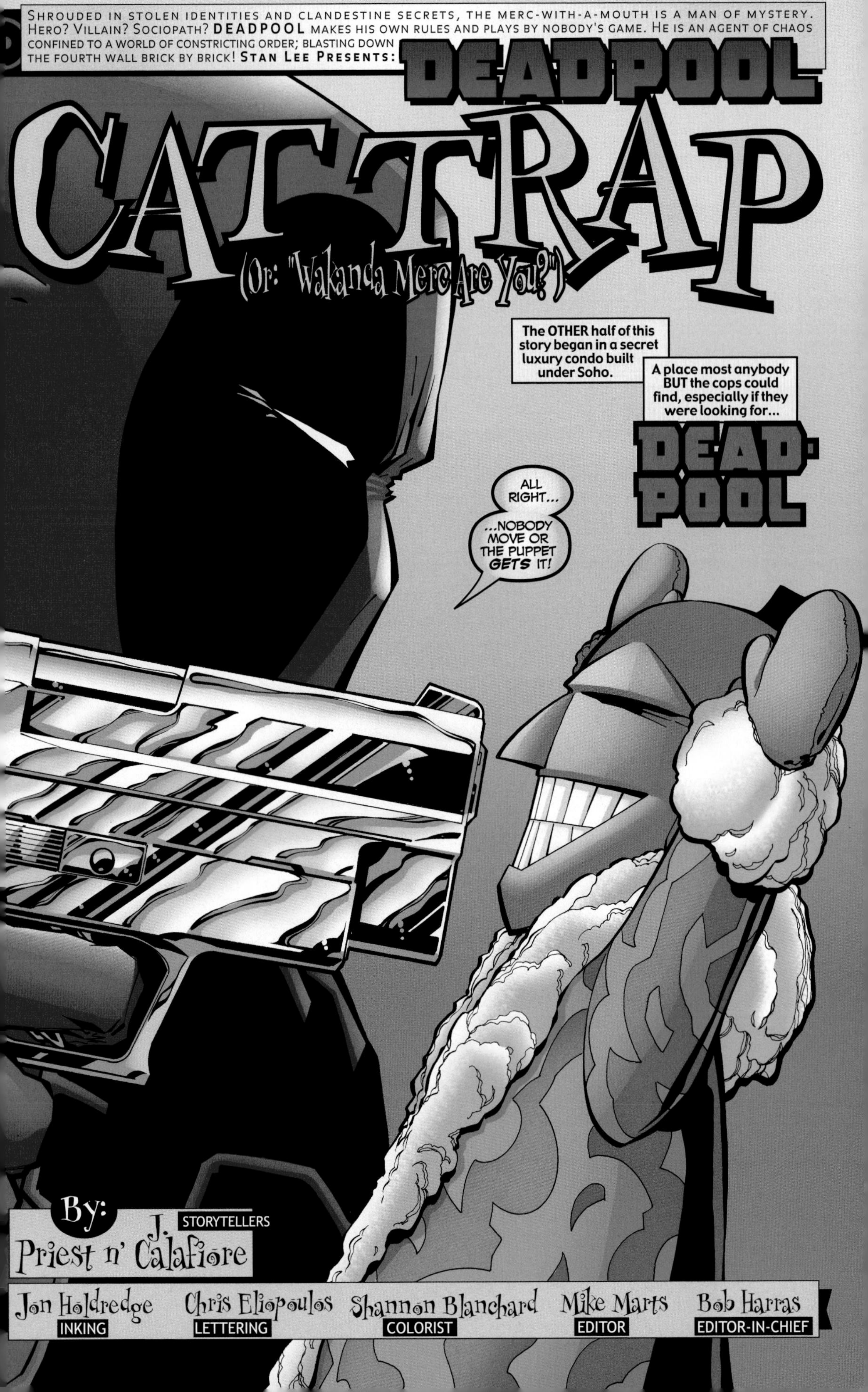

SHROUDED IN STOLEN IDENTITIES AND CLANDESTINE SECRETS, THE MERC-WITH-A-MOUTH IS A MAN OF MYSTERY. HERO? VILLAIN? SOCIOPATH? DEADPOOL MAKES HIS OWN RULES AND PLAYS BY NOBODY'S GAME. HE IS AN AGENT OF CHAOS CONFINED TO A WORLD OF CONSTRICTING ORDER; BLASTING DOWN THE FOURTH WALL BRICK BY BRICK! STAN LEE PRESENTS:
DEADPOOL
CAT TRAP
(Or: "Wakanda Merc Are You?")
The OTHER half of this story began in a secret luxury condo built under Soho.
A place most anybody BUT the cops could find, especially if they were looking for...
DEAD-POOL
ALL RIGHT...
...NOBODY MOVE OR THE PUPPET GETS IT!
By: Priest n' J. Calafiore STORYTELLERS
Jon Holdredge INKING
Chris Eliopoulos LETTERING
Shannon Blanchard COLORIST
Mike Marts EDITOR
Bob Harras EDITOR-IN-CHIEF

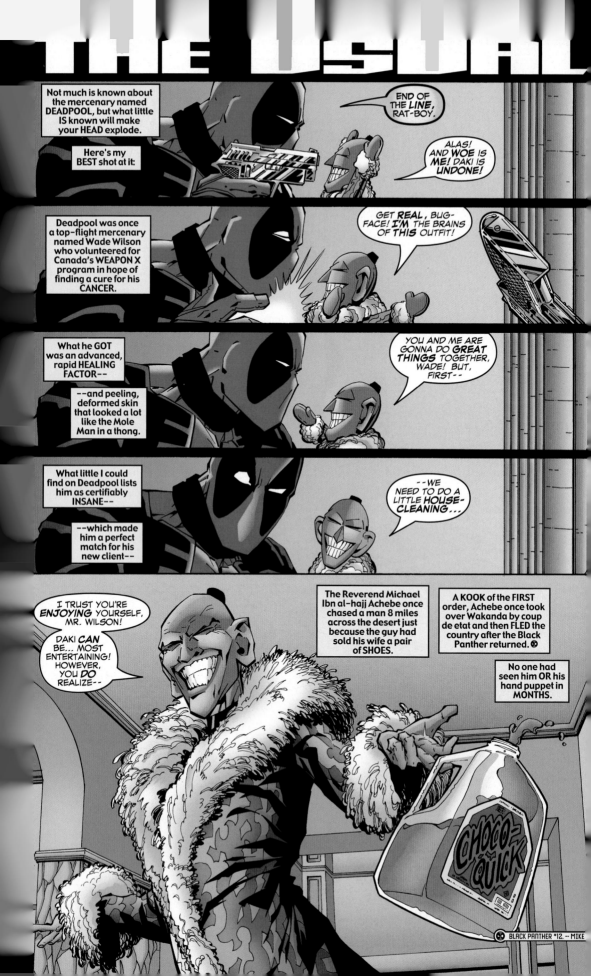

Not much is known about the mercenary named DEADPOOL, but what little IS known will make your HEAD explode.

Here's my BEST shot at it:

END OF THE LINE, RAT-BOY.

ALAS! AND WOE IS ME! DAKI IS UNDONE!

Deadpool was once a top-flight mercenary named Wade Wilson who volunteered for Canada's WEAPON X program in hope of finding a cure for his CANCER.

GET REAL, BUG-FACE! I'M THE BRAINS OF THIS OUTFIT!

What he GOT was an advanced, rapid HEALING FACTOR--

--and peeling, deformed skin that looked a lot like the Mole Man in a thong.

YOU AND ME ARE GONNA DO GREAT THINGS TOGETHER, WADE! BUT, FIRST--

What little I could find on Deadpool lists him as certifiably INSANE--

--which made him a perfect match for his new client--

--WE NEED TO DO A LITTLE HOUSE-CLEANING...

I TRUST YOU'RE ENJOYING YOURSELF, MR. WILSON!

DAKI CAN BE... MOST ENTERTAINING! HOWEVER, YOU DO REALIZE--

The Reverend Michael Ibn al-hajj Achebe once chased a man 8 miles across the desert just because the guy had sold his wife a pair of SHOES.

A KOOK of the FIRST order, Achebe once took over Wakanda by coup de etat and then FLED the country after the Black Panther returned. ⊗

No one had seen him OR his hand puppet in MONTHS.

CHOCO-QUICK

⊗ BLACK PANTHER #12. -- MIKE

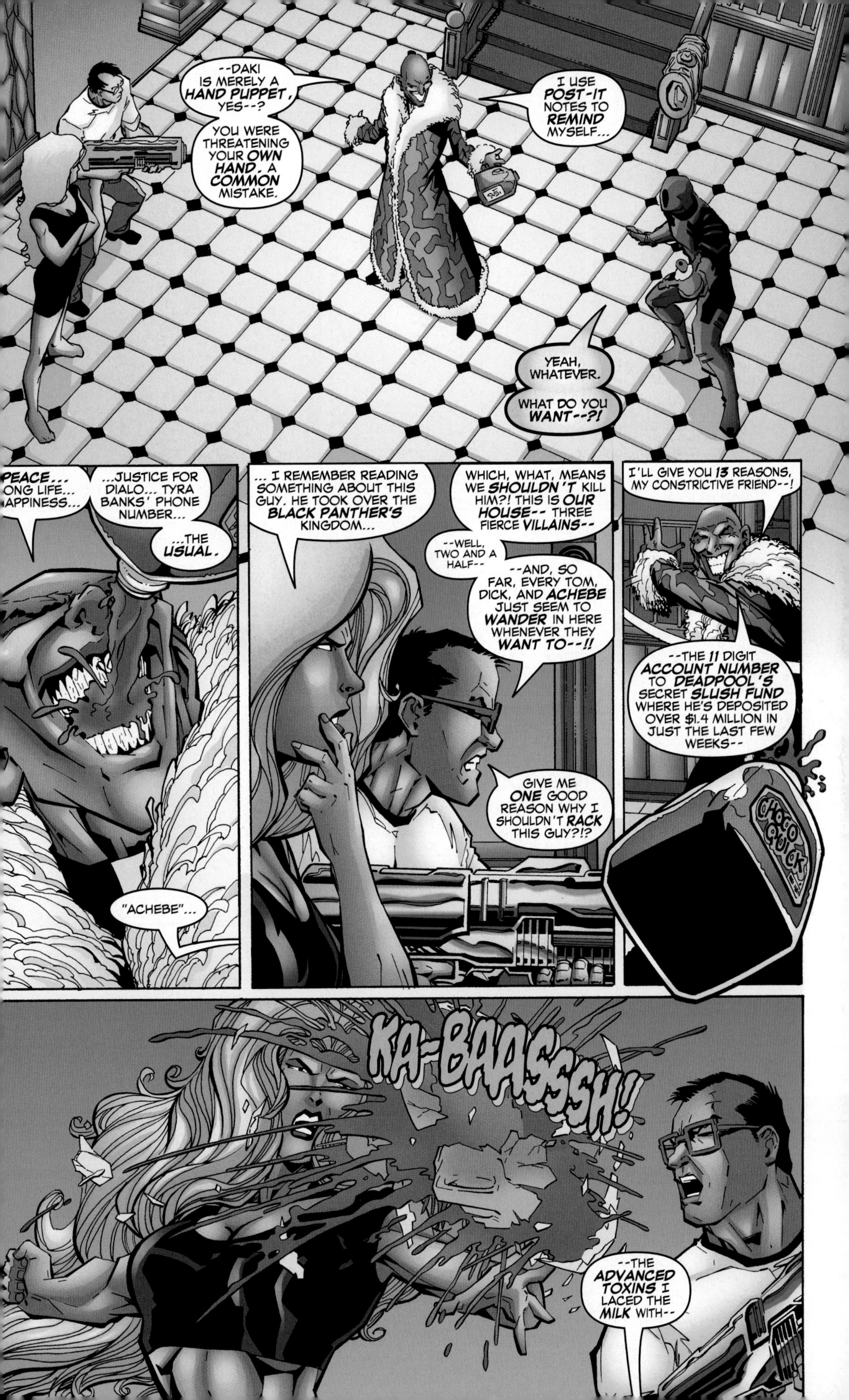

--DAKI IS MERELY A HAND PUPPET, YES--?
YOU WERE THREATENING YOUR OWN HAND. A COMMON MISTAKE.
I USE POST-IT NOTES TO REMIND MYSELF...
YEAH, WHATEVER.
WHAT DO YOU WANT--?!
PEACE... ONG LIFE... APPINESS...
...JUSTICE FOR DIALO... TYRA BANKS' PHONE NUMBER...
...THE USUAL.
"ACHEBE"...
... I REMEMBER READING SOMETHING ABOUT THIS GUY. HE TOOK OVER THE BLACK PANTHER'S KINGDOM...
WHICH, WHAT, MEANS WE SHOULDN'T KILL HIM?! THIS IS OUR HOUSE-- THREE FIERCE VILLAINS--
--WELL, TWO AND A HALF--
--AND, SO FAR, EVERY TOM, DICK, AND ACHEBE JUST SEEM TO WANDER IN HERE WHENEVER THEY WANT TO--!!
GIVE ME ONE GOOD REASON WHY I SHOULDN'T RACK THIS GUY?!?
I'LL GIVE YOU 13 REASONS, MY CONSTRICTIVE FRIEND--!
--THE 11 DIGIT ACCOUNT NUMBER TO DEADPOOL'S SECRET SLUSH FUND WHERE HE'S DEPOSITED OVER $1.4 MILLION IN JUST THE LAST FEW WEEKS--
CHOCO QUICK
KA-BAASSSH!
--THE ADVANCED TOXINS I LACED THE MILK WITH--

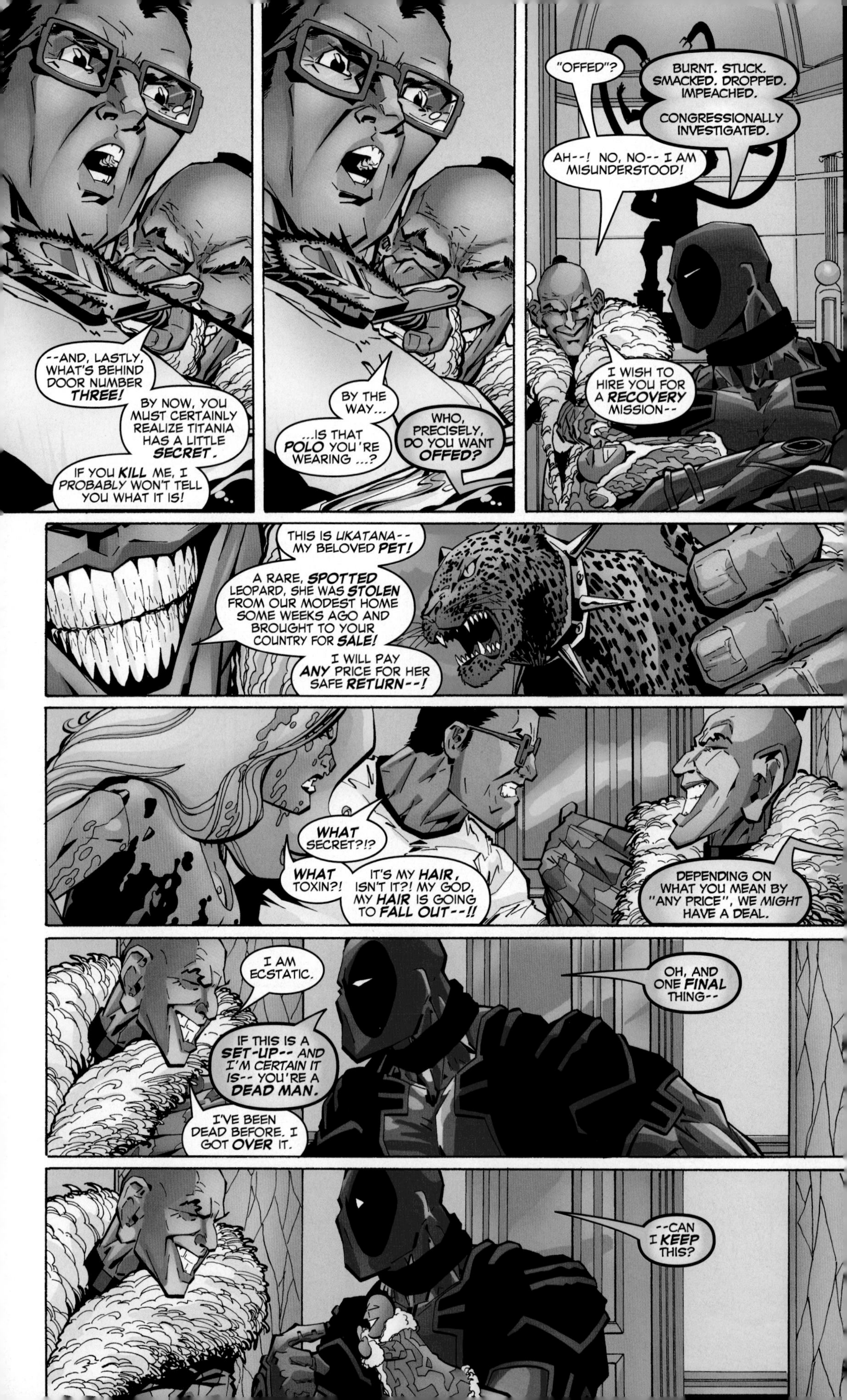

--AND, LASTLY, WHAT'S BEHIND DOOR NUMBER THREE!
BY NOW, YOU MUST CERTAINLY REALIZE TITANIA HAS A LITTLE SECRET.
IF YOU KILL ME, I PROBABLY WON'T TELL YOU WHAT IT IS!
BY THE WAY...
...IS THAT POLO YOU'RE WEARING ...?
WHO, PRECISELY, DO YOU WANT OFFED?
"OFFED"?
BURNT. STUCK. SMACKED. DROPPED. IMPEACHED.
CONGRESSIONALLY INVESTIGATED.
AH--! NO, NO-- I AM MISUNDERSTOOD!
I WISH TO HIRE YOU FOR A RECOVERY MISSION--
THIS IS UKATANA-- MY BELOVED PET!
A RARE, SPOTTED LEOPARD, SHE WAS STOLEN FROM OUR MODEST HOME SOME WEEKS AGO AND BROUGHT TO YOUR COUNTRY FOR SALE!
I WILL PAY ANY PRICE FOR HER SAFE RETURN--!
WHAT SECRET?!?
WHAT TOXIN?!
IT'S MY HAIR, ISN'T IT?! MY GOD, MY HAIR IS GOING TO FALL OUT--!!
DEPENDING ON WHAT YOU MEAN BY "ANY PRICE", WE MIGHT HAVE A DEAL.
I AM ECSTATIC.
IF THIS IS A SET-UP-- AND I'M CERTAIN IT IS-- YOU'RE A DEAD MAN.
I'VE BEEN DEAD BEFORE. I GOT OVER IT.
OH, AND ONE FINAL THING--
--CAN I KEEP THIS?

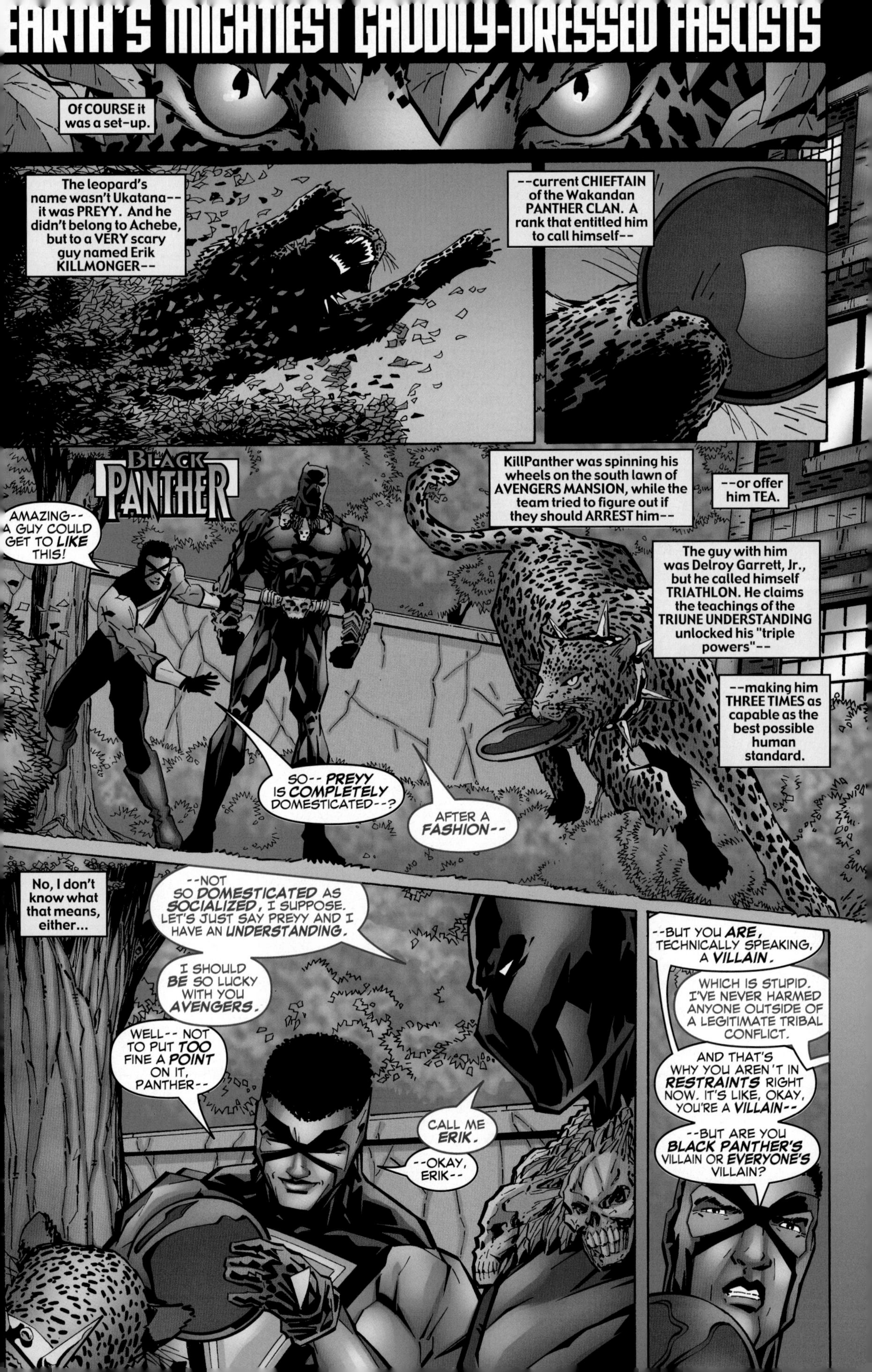

EARTH'S MIGHTIEST GAUDILY-DRESSED FASCISTS
Of COURSE it was a set-up.
The leopard's name wasn't Ukatana-- it was PREYY. And he didn't belong to Achebe, but to a VERY scary guy named Erik KILLMONGER--
--current CHIEFTAIN of the Wakandan PANTHER CLAN. A rank that entitled him to call himself--
BLACK PANTHER
KillPanther was spinning his wheels on the south lawn of AVENGERS MANSION, while the team tried to figure out if they should ARREST him--
--or offer him TEA.
AMAZING-- A GUY COULD GET TO LIKE THIS!
The guy with him was Delroy Garrett, Jr., but he called himself TRIATHLON. He claims the teachings of the TRIUNE UNDERSTANDING unlocked his "triple powers"--
--making him THREE TIMES as capable as the best possible human standard.
SO-- PREYY IS COMPLETELY DOMESTICATED--?
AFTER A FASHION--
No, I don't know what that means, either...
--NOT SO DOMESTICATED AS SOCIALIZED, I SUPPOSE. LET'S JUST SAY PREYY AND I HAVE AN UNDERSTANDING.
I SHOULD BE SO LUCKY WITH YOU AVENGERS.
WELL-- NOT TO PUT TOO FINE A POINT ON IT, PANTHER--
CALL ME ERIK.
--OKAY, ERIK--
--BUT YOU ARE, TECHNICALLY SPEAKING, A VILLAIN.
WHICH IS STUPID. I'VE NEVER HARMED ANYONE OUTSIDE OF A LEGITIMATE TRIBAL CONFLICT.
AND THAT'S WHY YOU AREN'T IN RESTRAINTS RIGHT NOW. IT'S LIKE, OKAY, YOU'RE A VILLAIN--
--BUT ARE YOU BLACK PANTHER'S VILLAIN OR EVERYONE'S VILLAIN?

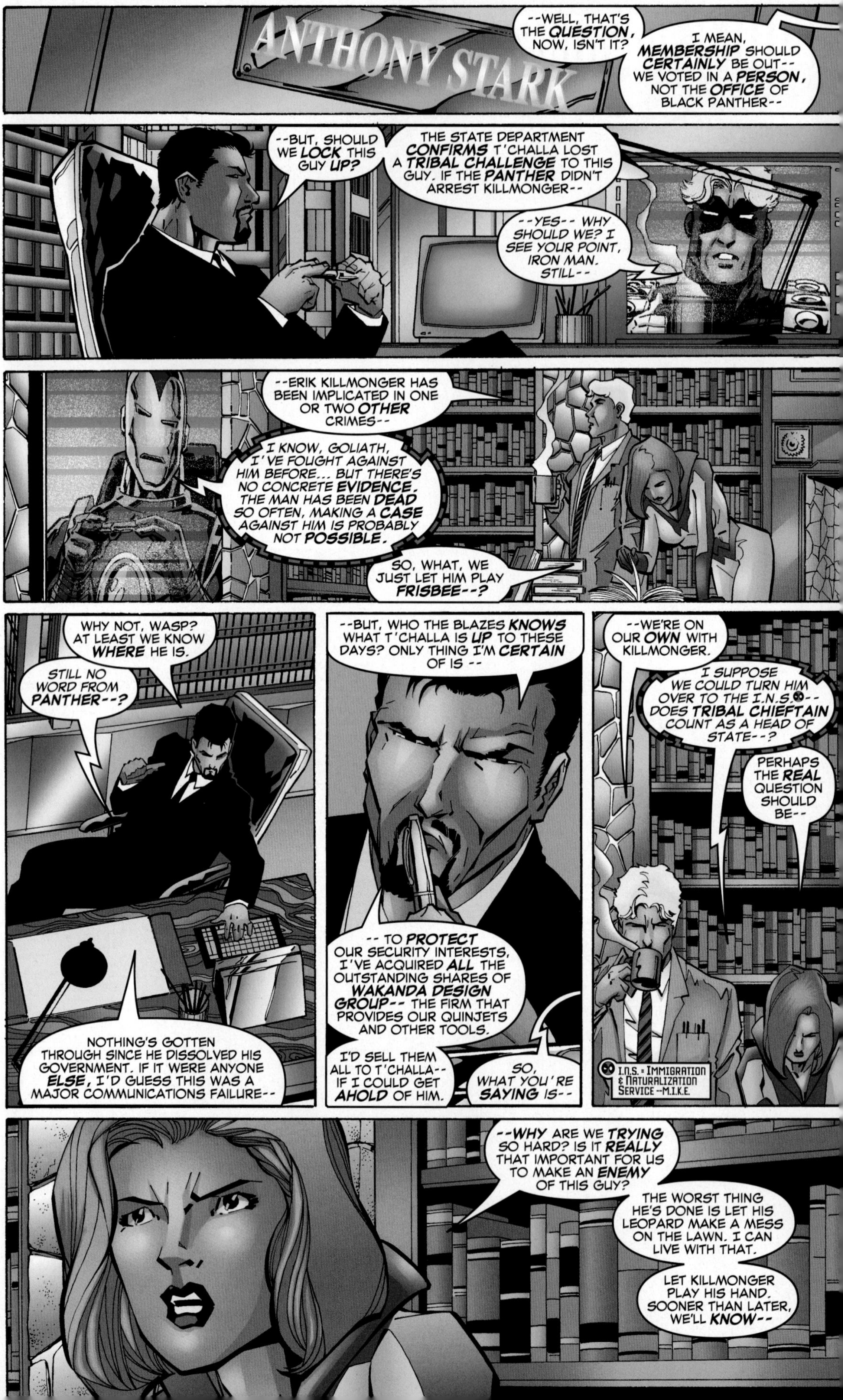
ANTHONY STARK
--WELL, THAT'S THE QUESTION, NOW, ISN'T IT?
I MEAN, MEMBERSHIP SHOULD CERTAINLY BE OUT-- WE VOTED IN A PERSON, NOT THE OFFICE OF BLACK PANTHER--
--BUT, SHOULD WE LOCK THIS GUY UP?
THE STATE DEPARTMENT CONFIRMS T'CHALLA LOST A TRIBAL CHALLENGE TO THIS GUY. IF THE PANTHER DIDN'T ARREST KILLMONGER--
--YES-- WHY SHOULD WE? I SEE YOUR POINT, IRON MAN. STILL--
--ERIK KILLMONGER HAS BEEN IMPLICATED IN ONE OR TWO OTHER CRIMES--
I KNOW, GOLIATH, I'VE FOUGHT AGAINST HIM BEFORE... BUT THERE'S NO CONCRETE EVIDENCE. THE MAN HAS BEEN DEAD SO OFTEN, MAKING A CASE AGAINST HIM IS PROBABLY NOT POSSIBLE.
SO, WHAT, WE JUST LET HIM PLAY FRISBEE--?
WHY NOT, WASP? AT LEAST WE KNOW WHERE HE IS.
STILL NO WORD FROM PANTHER--?
NOTHING'S GOTTEN THROUGH SINCE HE DISSOLVED HIS GOVERNMENT. IF IT WERE ANYONE ELSE, I'D GUESS THIS WAS A MAJOR COMMUNICATIONS FAILURE--
--BUT, WHO THE BLAZES KNOWS WHAT T'CHALLA IS UP TO THESE DAYS? ONLY THING I'M CERTAIN OF IS --
-- TO PROTECT OUR SECURITY INTERESTS, I'VE ACQUIRED ALL THE OUTSTANDING SHARES OF WAKANDA DESIGN GROUP-- THE FIRM THAT PROVIDES OUR QUINJETS AND OTHER TOOLS.
I'D SELL THEM ALL TO T'CHALLA-- IF I COULD GET AHOLD OF HIM.
SO, WHAT YOU'RE SAYING IS--
--WE'RE ON OUR OWN WITH KILLMONGER.
I SUPPOSE WE COULD TURN HIM OVER TO THE I.N.S.-- DOES TRIBAL CHIEFTAIN COUNT AS A HEAD OF STATE--?
PERHAPS THE REAL QUESTION SHOULD BE--
I.N.S. = IMMIGRATION & NATURALIZATION SERVICE --M.I.K.E.
--WHY ARE WE TRYING SO HARD? IS IT REALLY THAT IMPORTANT FOR US TO MAKE AN ENEMY OF THIS GUY?
THE WORST THING HE'S DONE IS LET HIS LEOPARD MAKE A MESS ON THE LAWN. I CAN LIVE WITH THAT.
LET KILLMONGER PLAY HIS HAND. SOONER THAN LATER, WE'LL KNOW--

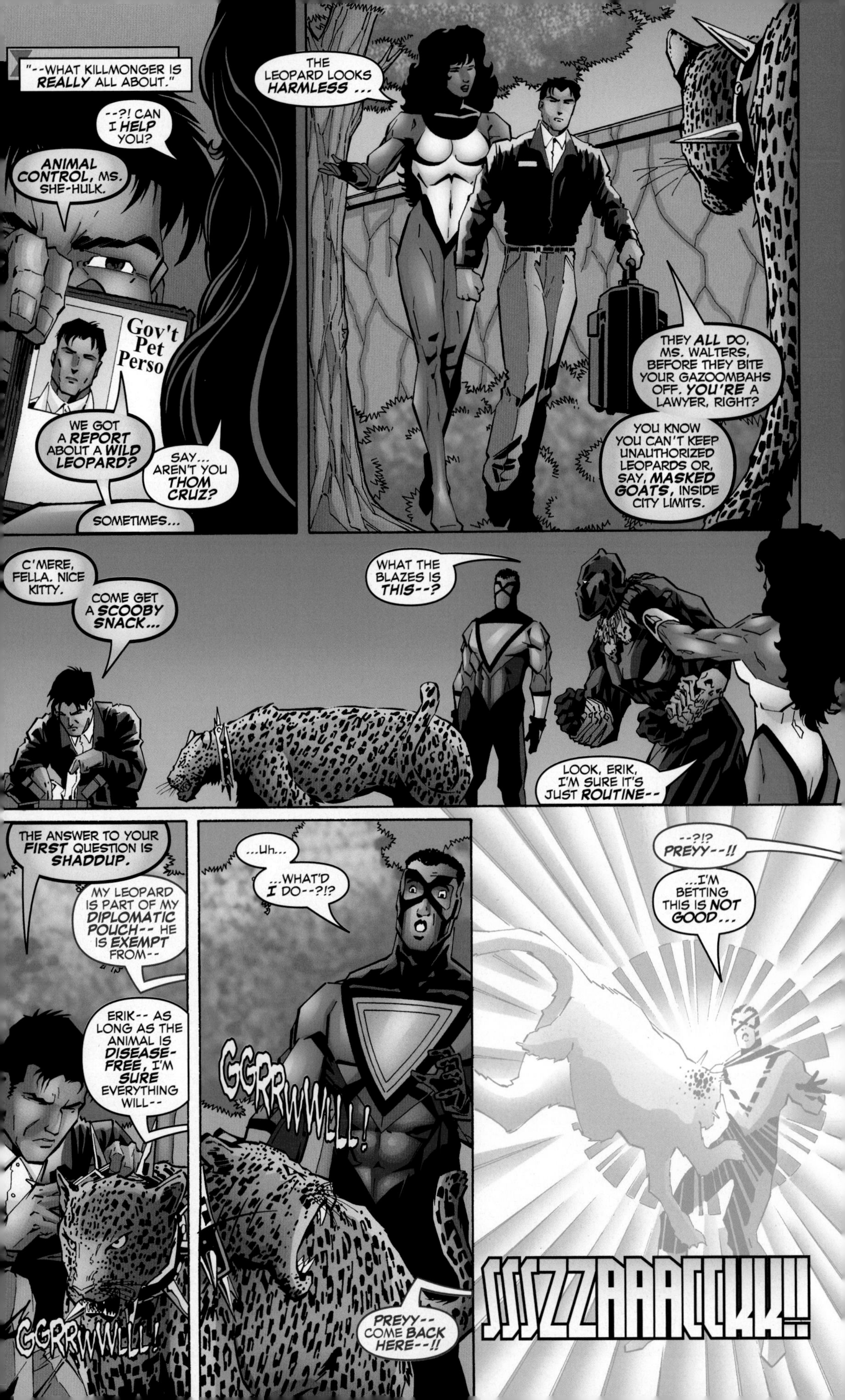

"--WHAT KILLMONGER IS REALLY ALL ABOUT."
--?! CAN I HELP YOU?
ANIMAL CONTROL, MS. SHE-HULK.
Gov't Pet Perso
WE GOT A REPORT ABOUT A WILD LEOPARD?
SAY... AREN'T YOU THOM CRUZ?
SOMETIMES...
THE LEOPARD LOOKS HARMLESS...
THEY ALL DO, MS. WALTERS, BEFORE THEY BITE YOUR GAZOOMBAHS OFF. YOU'RE A LAWYER, RIGHT?
YOU KNOW YOU CAN'T KEEP UNAUTHORIZED LEOPARDS OR, SAY, MASKED GOATS, INSIDE CITY LIMITS.
C'MERE, FELLA. NICE KITTY.
COME GET A SCOOBY SNACK...
WHAT THE BLAZES IS THIS--?
LOOK, ERIK, I'M SURE IT'S JUST ROUTINE--
THE ANSWER TO YOUR FIRST QUESTION IS SHADDUP.
MY LEOPARD IS PART OF MY DIPLOMATIC POUCH-- HE IS EXEMPT FROM--
ERIK-- AS LONG AS THE ANIMAL IS DISEASE-FREE, I'M SURE EVERYTHING WILL--
GGRRWWLLL!
...uh...
...WHAT'D I DO--?!?
GGRRWWLLL!
PREYY-- COME BACK HERE--!!
--?!? PREYY--!!
...I'M BETTING THIS IS NOT GOOD...
SSSZZAAACCKK!!

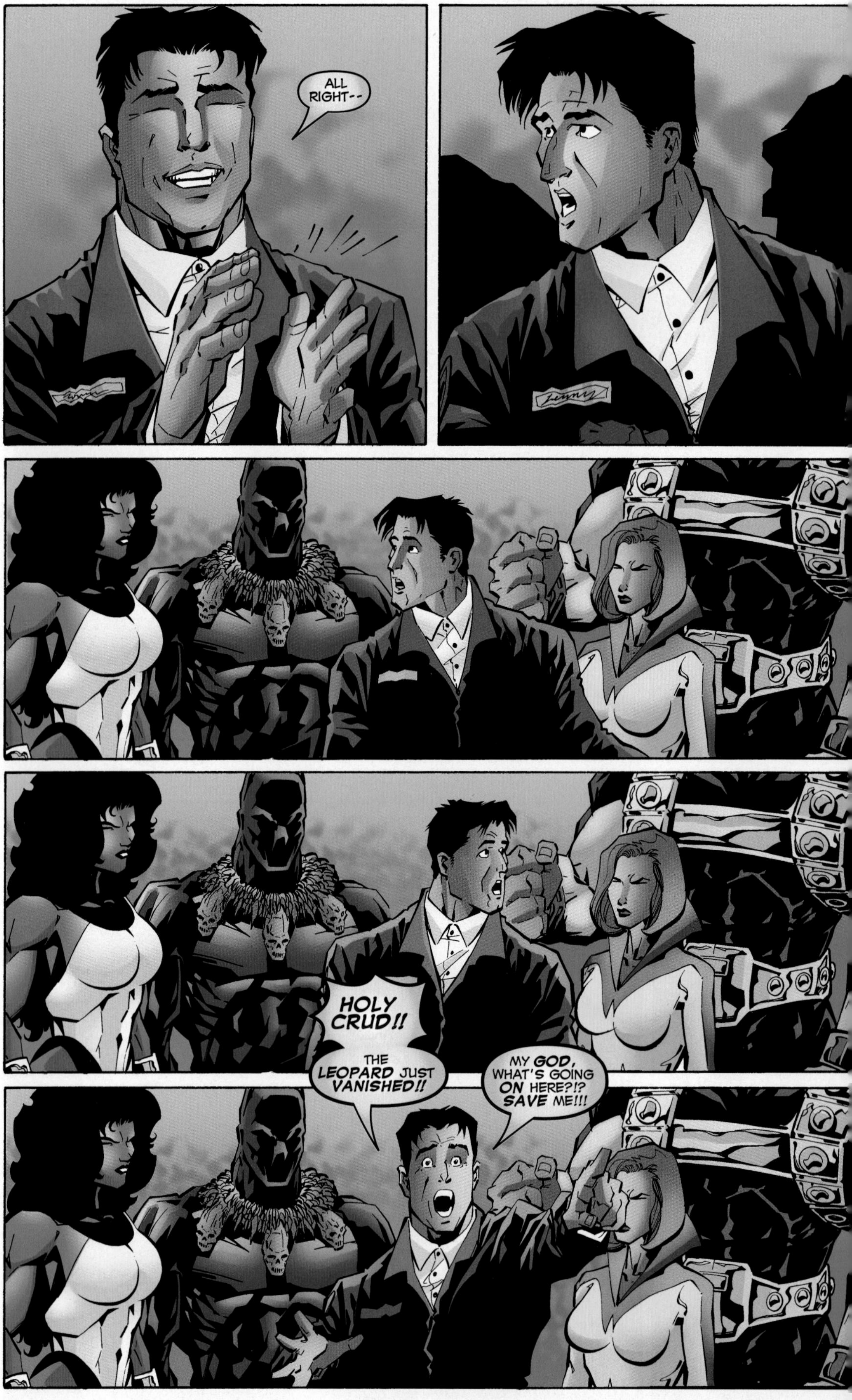
ALL RIGHT--
HOLY CRUD!!
THE LEOPARD JUST VANISHED!!
MY GOD, WHAT'S GOING ON HERE?!? SAVE ME!!!

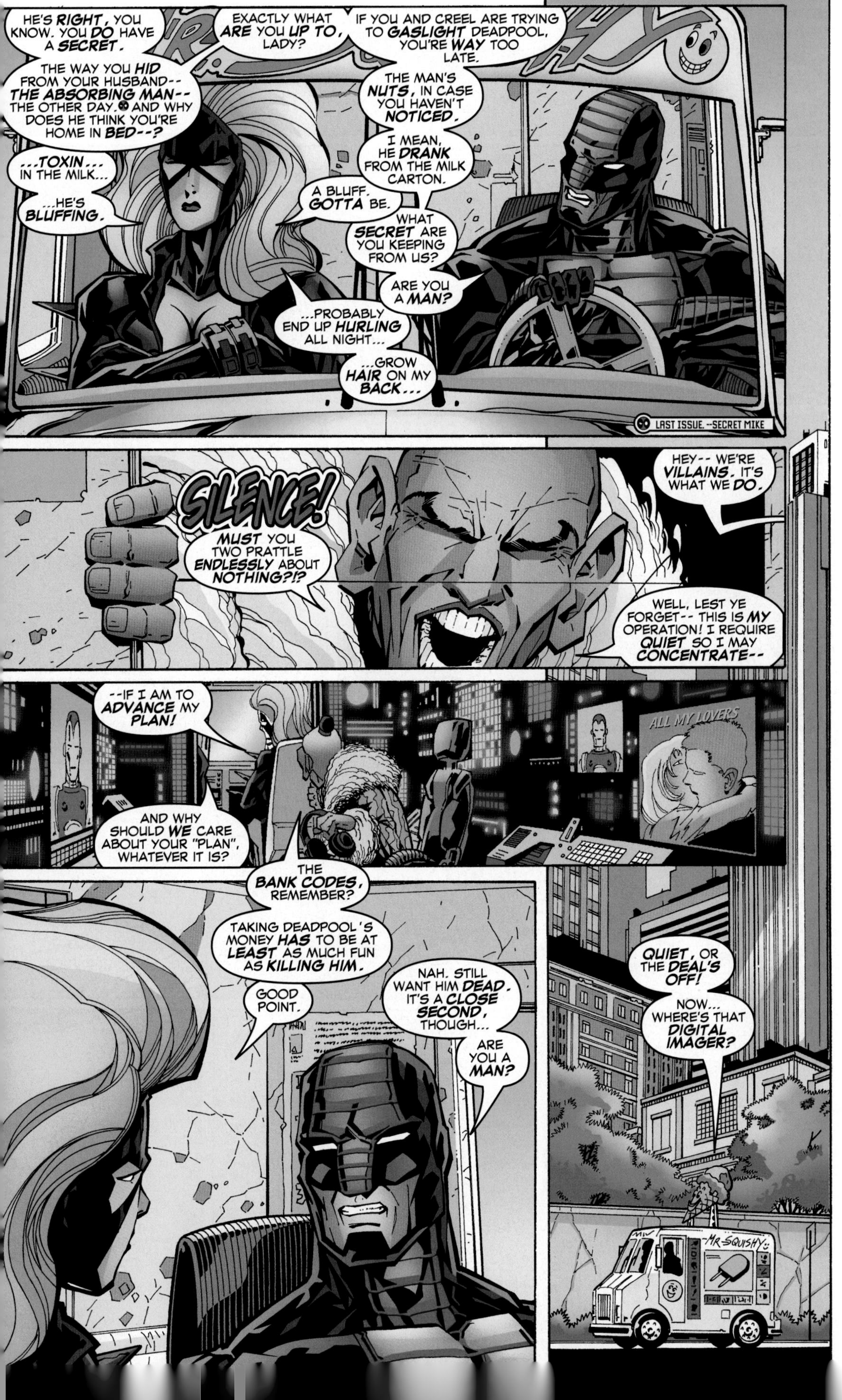
HE'S RIGHT, YOU KNOW. YOU DO HAVE A SECRET.
THE WAY YOU HID FROM YOUR HUSBAND-- THE ABSORBING MAN-- THE OTHER DAY. AND WHY DOES HE THINK YOU'RE HOME IN BED--?
EXACTLY WHAT ARE YOU UP TO, LADY?
IF YOU AND CREEL ARE TRYING TO GASLIGHT DEADPOOL, YOU'RE WAY TOO LATE.
THE MAN'S NUTS, IN CASE YOU HAVEN'T NOTICED.
I MEAN, HE DRANK FROM THE MILK CARTON.
...TOXIN... IN THE MILK...
...HE'S BLUFFING.
A BLUFF. GOTTA BE.
WHAT SECRET ARE YOU KEEPING FROM US?
ARE YOU A MAN?
...PROBABLY END UP HURLING ALL NIGHT...
...GROW HAIR ON MY BACK...
LAST ISSUE. --SECRET MIKE
SILENCE!
MUST YOU TWO PRATTLE ENDLESSLY ABOUT NOTHING?!?
HEY-- WE'RE VILLAINS. IT'S WHAT WE DO.
WELL, LEST YE FORGET-- THIS IS MY OPERATION! I REQUIRE QUIET SO I MAY CONCENTRATE--
--IF I AM TO ADVANCE MY PLAN!
ALL MY LOVERS
AND WHY SHOULD WE CARE ABOUT YOUR "PLAN", WHATEVER IT IS?
THE BANK CODES, REMEMBER?
TAKING DEADPOOL'S MONEY HAS TO BE AT LEAST AS MUCH FUN AS KILLING HIM.
GOOD POINT.
NAH. STILL WANT HIM DEAD. IT'S A CLOSE SECOND, THOUGH...
ARE YOU A MAN?
QUIET, OR THE DEAL'S OFF!
NOW... WHERE'S THAT DIGITAL IMAGER?
MR SQUISHY

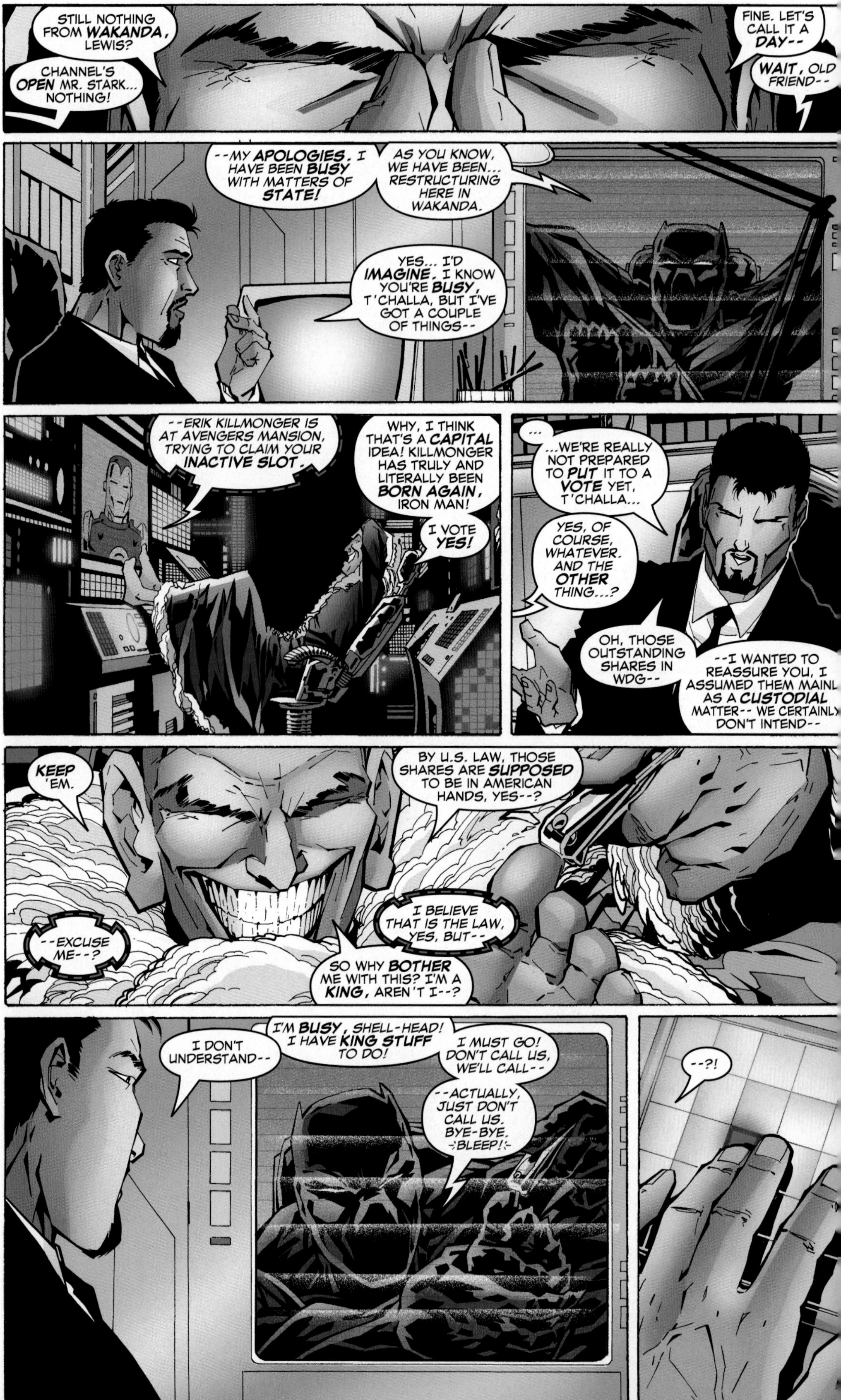
STILL NOTHING FROM WAKANDA, LEWIS?
CHANNEL'S OPEN MR. STARK... NOTHING!
FINE. LET'S CALL IT A DAY--
WAIT, OLD FRIEND--
--MY APOLOGIES. I HAVE BEEN BUSY WITH MATTERS OF STATE!
AS YOU KNOW, WE HAVE BEEN... RESTRUCTURING HERE IN WAKANDA.
YES... I'D IMAGINE. I KNOW YOU'RE BUSY, T'CHALLA, BUT I'VE GOT A COUPLE OF THINGS--
--ERIK KILLMONGER IS AT AVENGERS MANSION, TRYING TO CLAIM YOUR INACTIVE SLOT.
WHY, I THINK THAT'S A CAPITAL IDEA! KILLMONGER HAS TRULY AND LITERALLY BEEN BORN AGAIN, IRON MAN!
I VOTE YES!
...
...WE'RE REALLY NOT PREPARED TO PUT IT TO A VOTE YET, T'CHALLA...
YES, OF COURSE, WHATEVER. AND THE OTHER THING...?
OH, THOSE OUTSTANDING SHARES IN WDG--
--I WANTED TO REASSURE YOU, I ASSUMED THEM MAINL AS A CUSTODIAL MATTER-- WE CERTAINL DON'T INTEND--
KEEP 'EM.
BY U.S. LAW, THOSE SHARES ARE SUPPOSED TO BE IN AMERICAN HANDS, YES--?
--EXCUSE ME--?
I BELIEVE THAT IS THE LAW, YES, BUT--
SO WHY BOTHER ME WITH THIS? I'M A KING, AREN'T I--?
I DON'T UNDERSTAND--
I'M BUSY, SHELL-HEAD! I HAVE KING STUFF TO DO!
I MUST GO! DON'T CALL US, WE'LL CALL--
--ACTUALLY, JUST DON'T CALL US. BYE-BYE. BLEEP!
--?!

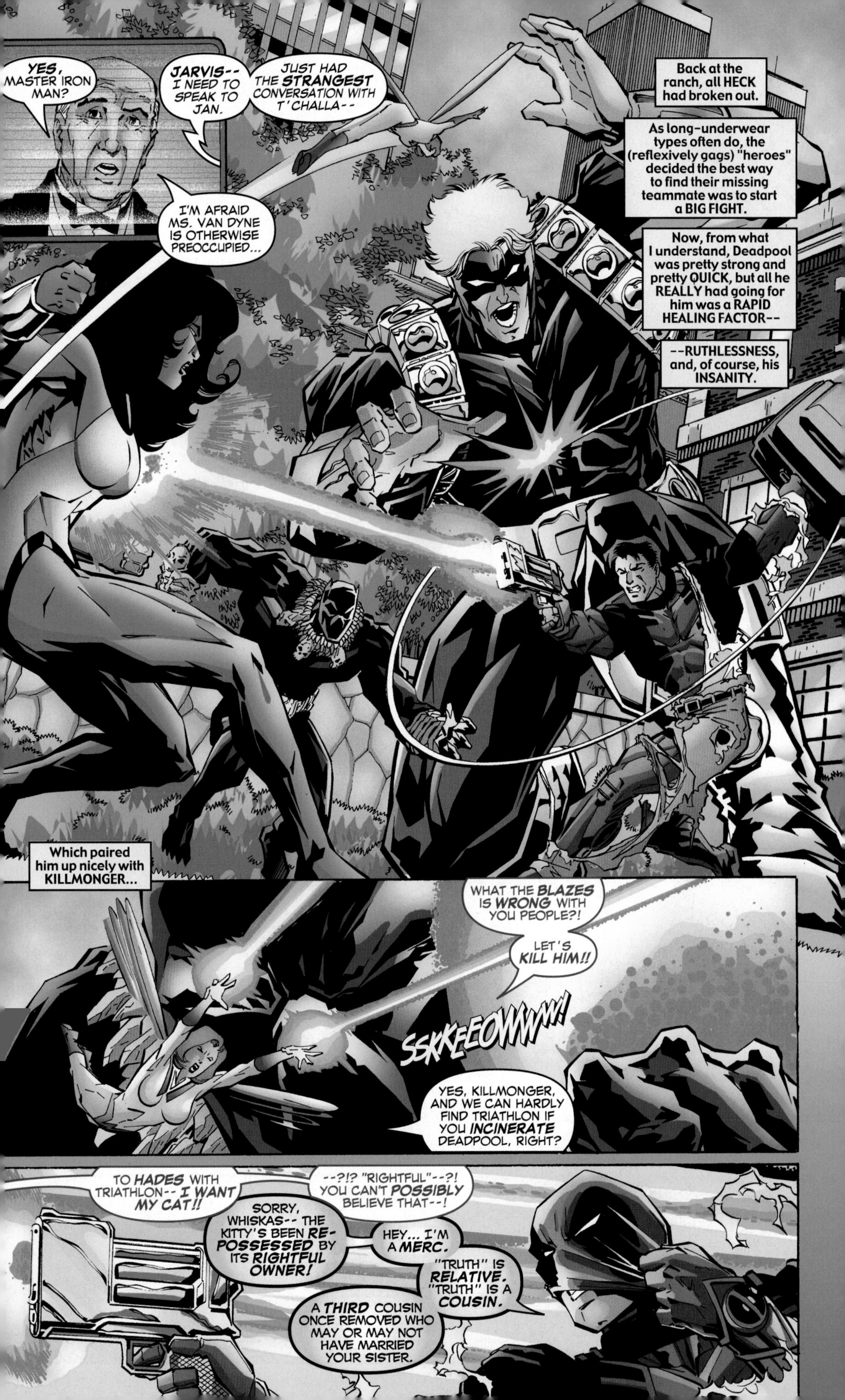
YES, MASTER IRON MAN?
JARVIS-- I NEED TO SPEAK TO JAN.
JUST HAD THE STRANGEST CONVERSATION WITH T'CHALLA--
I'M AFRAID MS. VAN DYNE IS OTHERWISE PREOCCUPIED...
Back at the ranch, all HECK had broken out.
As long-underwear types often do, the (reflexively gags) "heroes" decided the best way to find their missing teammate was to start a BIG FIGHT.
Now, from what I understand, Deadpool was pretty strong and pretty QUICK, but all he REALLY had going for him was a RAPID HEALING FACTOR--
--RUTHLESSNESS, and, of course, his INSANITY.
Which paired him up nicely with KILLMONGER...
WHAT THE BLAZES IS WRONG WITH YOU PEOPLE?!
LET'S KILL HIM!!
SSKKEEOWWW!
YES, KILLMONGER, AND WE CAN HARDLY FIND TRIATHLON IF YOU INCINERATE DEADPOOL, RIGHT?
TO HADES WITH TRIATHLON-- I WANT MY CAT!!
SORRY, WHISKAS-- THE KITTY'S BEEN REPOSSESSED BY ITS RIGHTFUL OWNER!
--?!? "RIGHTFUL"--?! YOU CAN'T POSSIBLY BELIEVE THAT--!
HEY... I'M A MERC.
"TRUTH" IS RELATIVE. "TRUTH" IS A COUSIN.
A THIRD COUSIN ONCE REMOVED WHO MAY OR MAY NOT HAVE MARRIED YOUR SISTER.

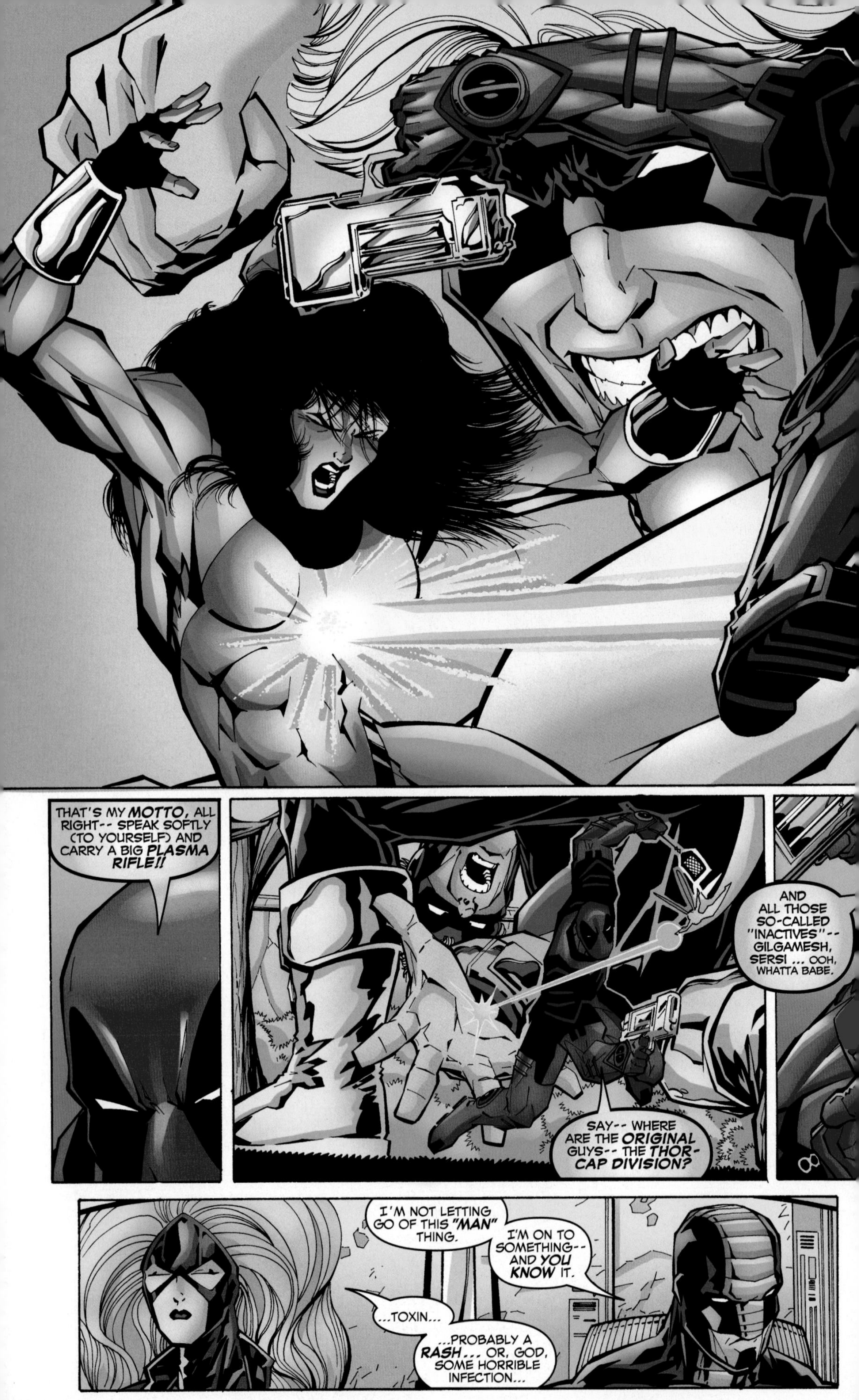

THAT'S MY MOTTO, ALL RIGHT-- SPEAK SOFTLY (TO YOURSELF) AND CARRY A BIG PLASMA RIFLE!!
AND ALL THOSE SO-CALLED "INACTIVES"-- GILGAMESH, SERSI ... OOH, WHATTA BABE.
SAY-- WHERE ARE THE ORIGINAL GUYS-- THE THOR-CAP DIVISION?
I'M NOT LETTING GO OF THIS "MAN" THING.
I'M ON TO SOMETHING-- AND YOU KNOW IT.
...TOXIN...
...PROBABLY A RASH... OR, GOD, SOME HORRIBLE INFECTION...

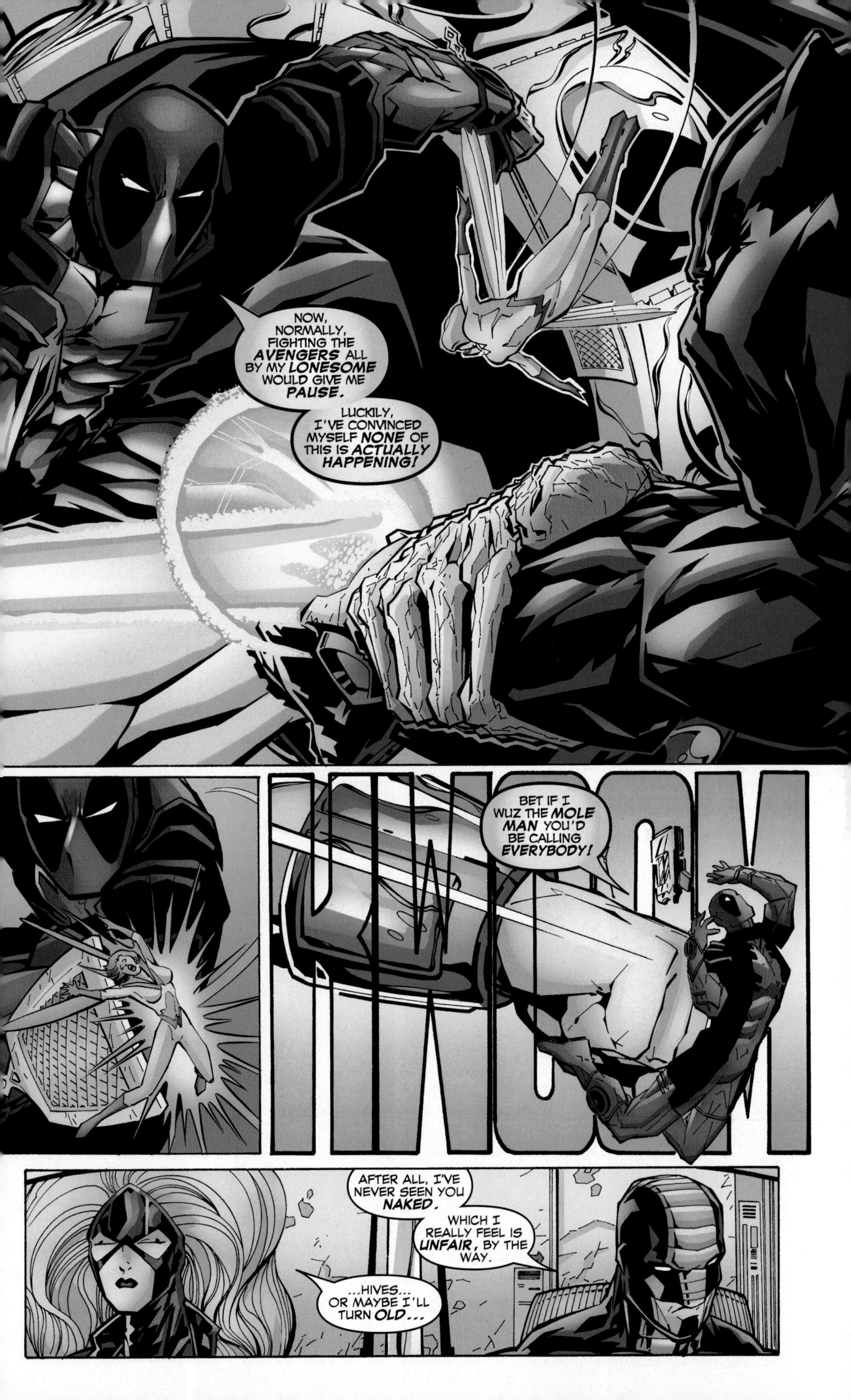
NOW, NORMALLY, FIGHTING THE AVENGERS ALL BY MY LONESOME WOULD GIVE ME PAUSE.
LUCKILY, I'VE CONVINCED MYSELF NONE OF THIS IS ACTUALLY HAPPENING!
BET IF I WUZ THE MOLE MAN YOU'D BE CALLING EVERYBODY!
AFTER ALL, I'VE NEVER SEEN YOU NAKED.
WHICH I REALLY FEEL IS UNFAIR, BY THE WAY.
...HIVES... OR MAYBE I'LL TURN OLD...

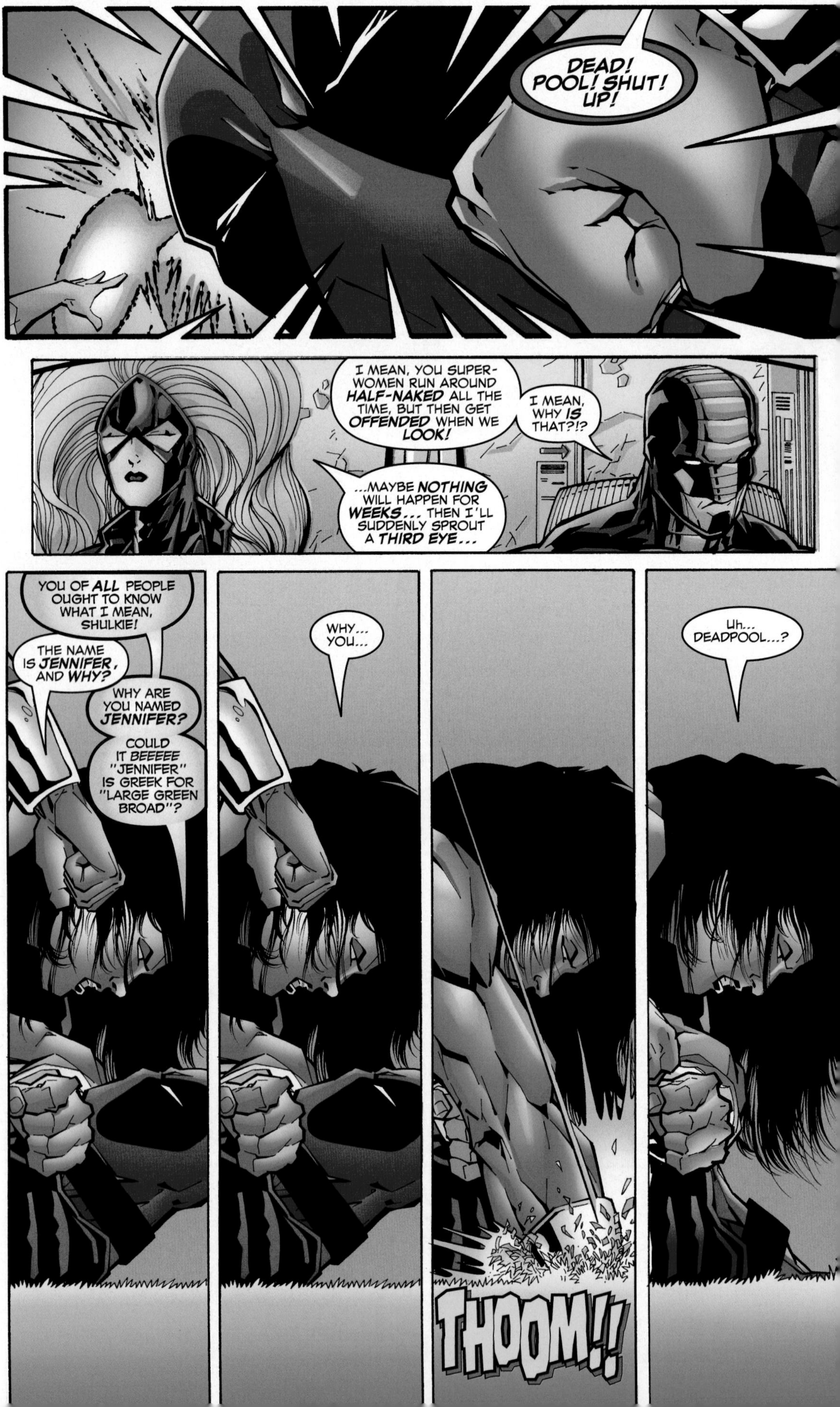
DEAD! POOL! SHUT! UP!
I MEAN, YOU SUPER-WOMEN RUN AROUND HALF-NAKED ALL THE TIME, BUT THEN GET OFFENDED WHEN WE LOOK!
I MEAN, WHY IS THAT?!?
...MAYBE NOTHING WILL HAPPEN FOR WEEKS... THEN I'LL SUDDENLY SPROUT A THIRD EYE...
YOU OF ALL PEOPLE OUGHT TO KNOW WHAT I MEAN, SHULKIE!
THE NAME IS JENNIFER, AND WHY?
WHY ARE YOU NAMED JENNIFER?
COULD IT BEEEEE "JENNIFER" IS GREEK FOR "LARGE GREEN BROAD"?
WHY... YOU...
THOOM!!
Uh... DEADPOOL...?

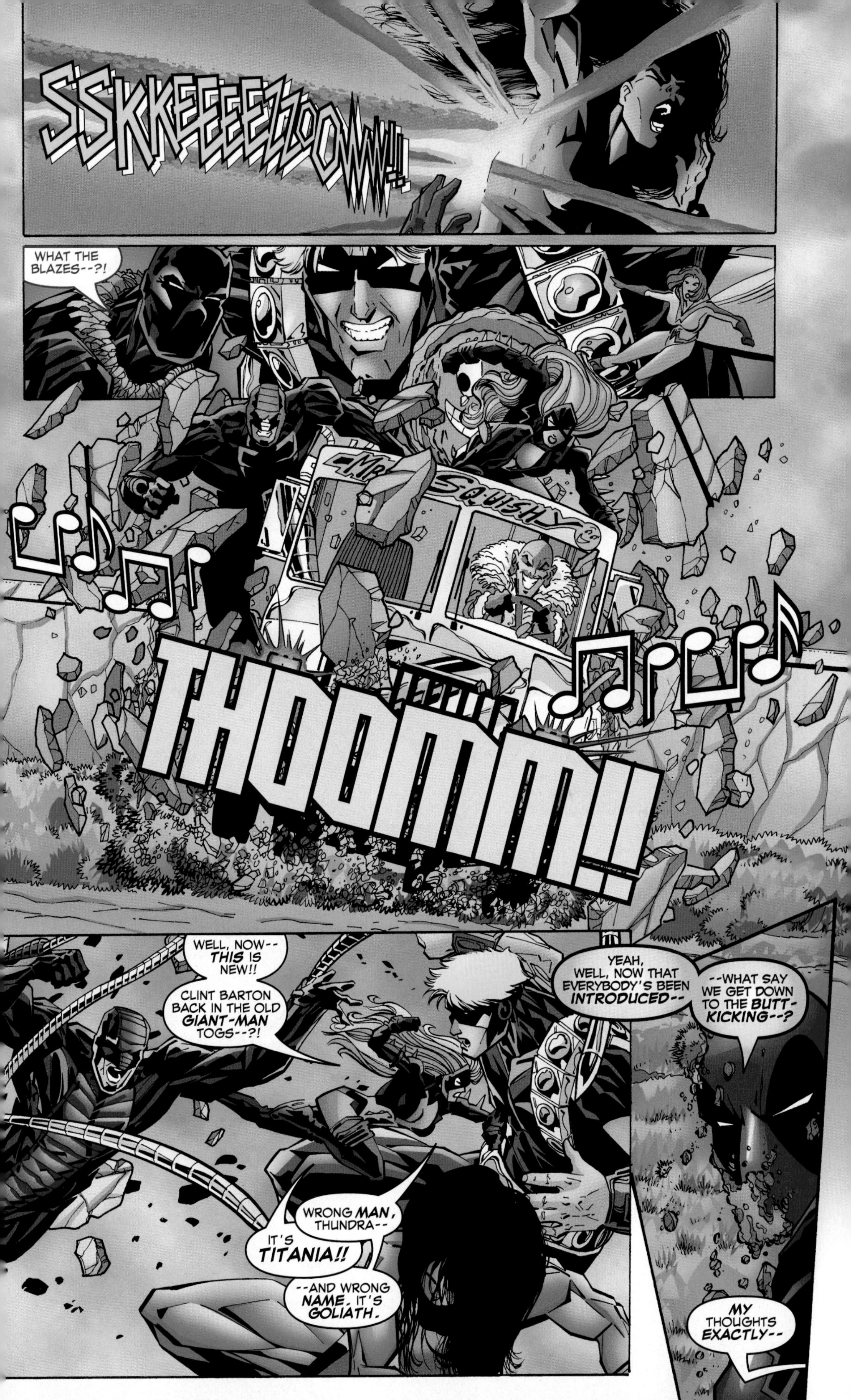
SSKKEEEEZZOOWWW!!!
WHAT THE BLAZES--?!
MR. SQUISHY
THOOMM!!
WELL, NOW-- THIS IS NEW!!
CLINT BARTON BACK IN THE OLD GIANT-MAN TOGS--?!
YEAH, WELL, NOW THAT EVERYBODY'S BEEN INTRODUCED--
--WHAT SAY WE GET DOWN TO THE BUTT-KICKING--?
WRONG MAN, THUNDRA--
IT'S TITANIA!!
--AND WRONG NAME. IT'S GOLIATH.
MY THOUGHTS EXACTLY--

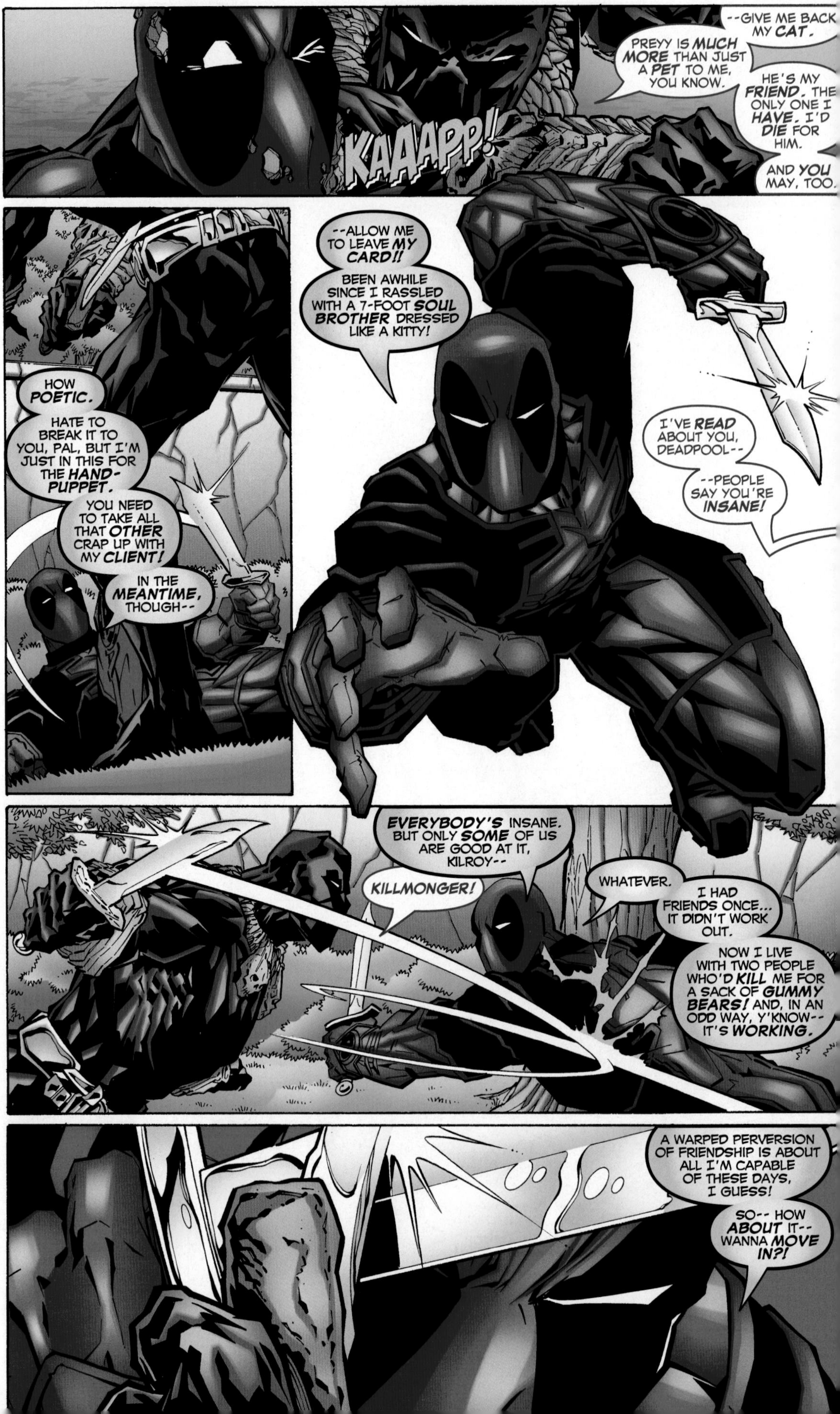

PREYY IS MUCH MORE THAN JUST A PET TO ME, YOU KNOW.
--GIVE ME BACK MY CAT.
HE'S MY FRIEND. THE ONLY ONE I HAVE. I'D DIE FOR HIM.
AND YOU MAY, TOO.
KAAAPP!
--ALLOW ME TO LEAVE MY CARD!!
BEEN AWHILE SINCE I RASSLED WITH A 7-FOOT SOUL BROTHER DRESSED LIKE A KITTY!
HOW POETIC.
HATE TO BREAK IT TO YOU, PAL, BUT I'M JUST IN THIS FOR THE HAND-PUPPET.
YOU NEED TO TAKE ALL THAT OTHER CRAP UP WITH MY CLIENT!
IN THE MEANTIME, THOUGH--
I'VE READ ABOUT YOU, DEADPOOL--
--PEOPLE SAY YOU'RE INSANE!
EVERYBODY'S INSANE. BUT ONLY SOME OF US ARE GOOD AT IT, KILROY--
KILLMONGER!
WHATEVER.
I HAD FRIENDS ONCE... IT DIDN'T WORK OUT.
NOW I LIVE WITH TWO PEOPLE WHO'D KILL ME FOR A SACK OF GUMMY BEARS! AND, IN AN ODD WAY, Y'KNOW-- IT'S WORKING.
A WARPED PERVERSION OF FRIENDSHIP IS ABOUT ALL I'M CAPABLE OF THESE DAYS, I GUESS!
SO-- HOW ABOUT IT-- WANNA MOVE IN?!

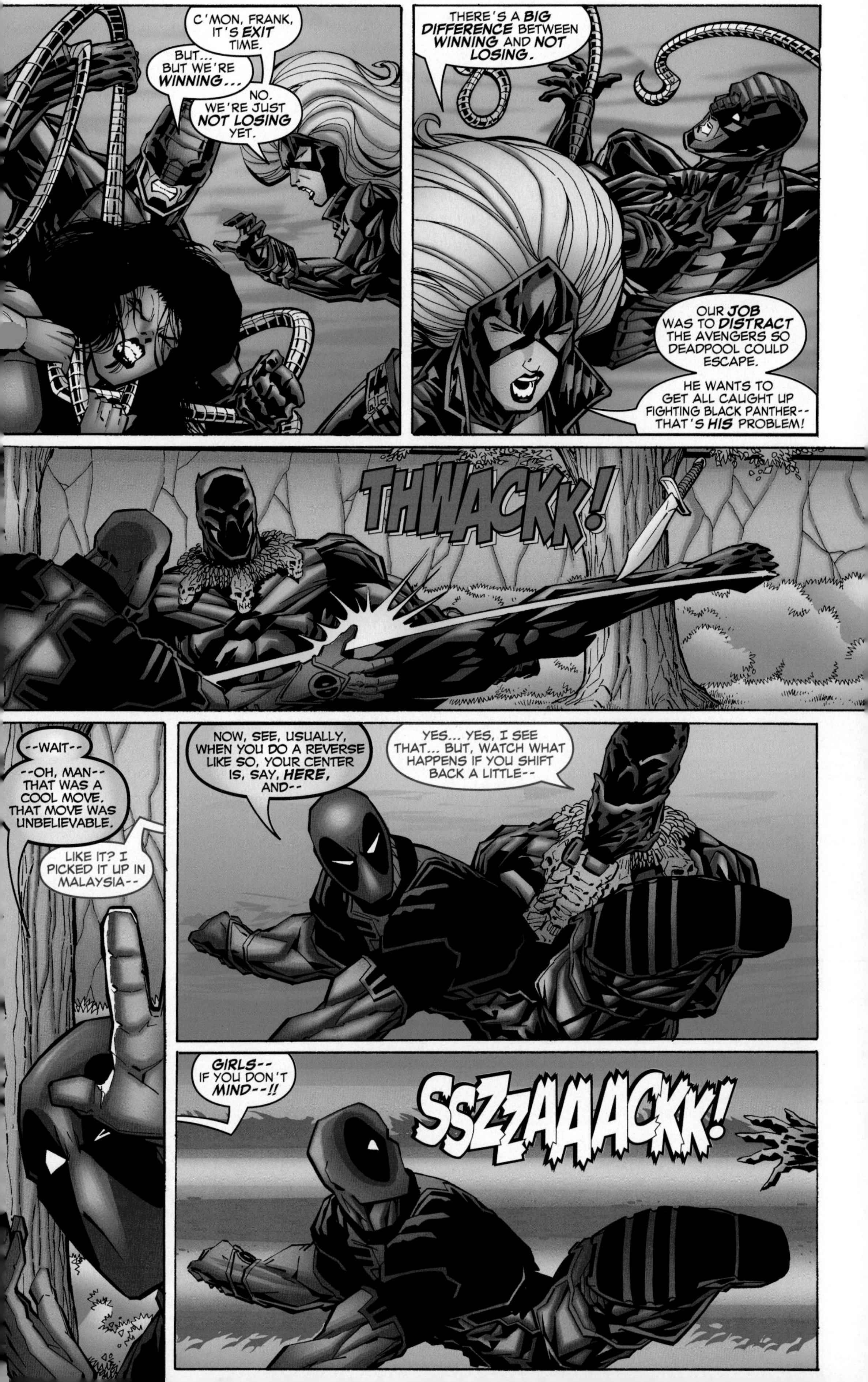
C'MON, FRANK, IT'S EXIT TIME.
BUT... BUT WE'RE WINNING...
NO. WE'RE JUST NOT LOSING YET.
THERE'S A BIG DIFFERENCE BETWEEN WINNING AND NOT LOSING.
OUR JOB WAS TO DISTRACT THE AVENGERS SO DEADPOOL COULD ESCAPE.
HE WANTS TO GET ALL CAUGHT UP FIGHTING BLACK PANTHER--THAT'S HIS PROBLEM!
THWACKK!
--WAIT--
--OH, MAN--THAT WAS A COOL MOVE. THAT MOVE WAS UNBELIEVABLE.
LIKE IT? I PICKED IT UP IN MALAYSIA--
NOW, SEE, USUALLY, WHEN YOU DO A REVERSE LIKE SO, YOUR CENTER IS, SAY, HERE, AND--
YES... YES, I SEE THAT... BUT, WATCH WHAT HAPPENS IF YOU SHIFT BACK A LITTLE--
GIRLS--IF YOU DON'T MIND--!!
SSZZAAACKK!

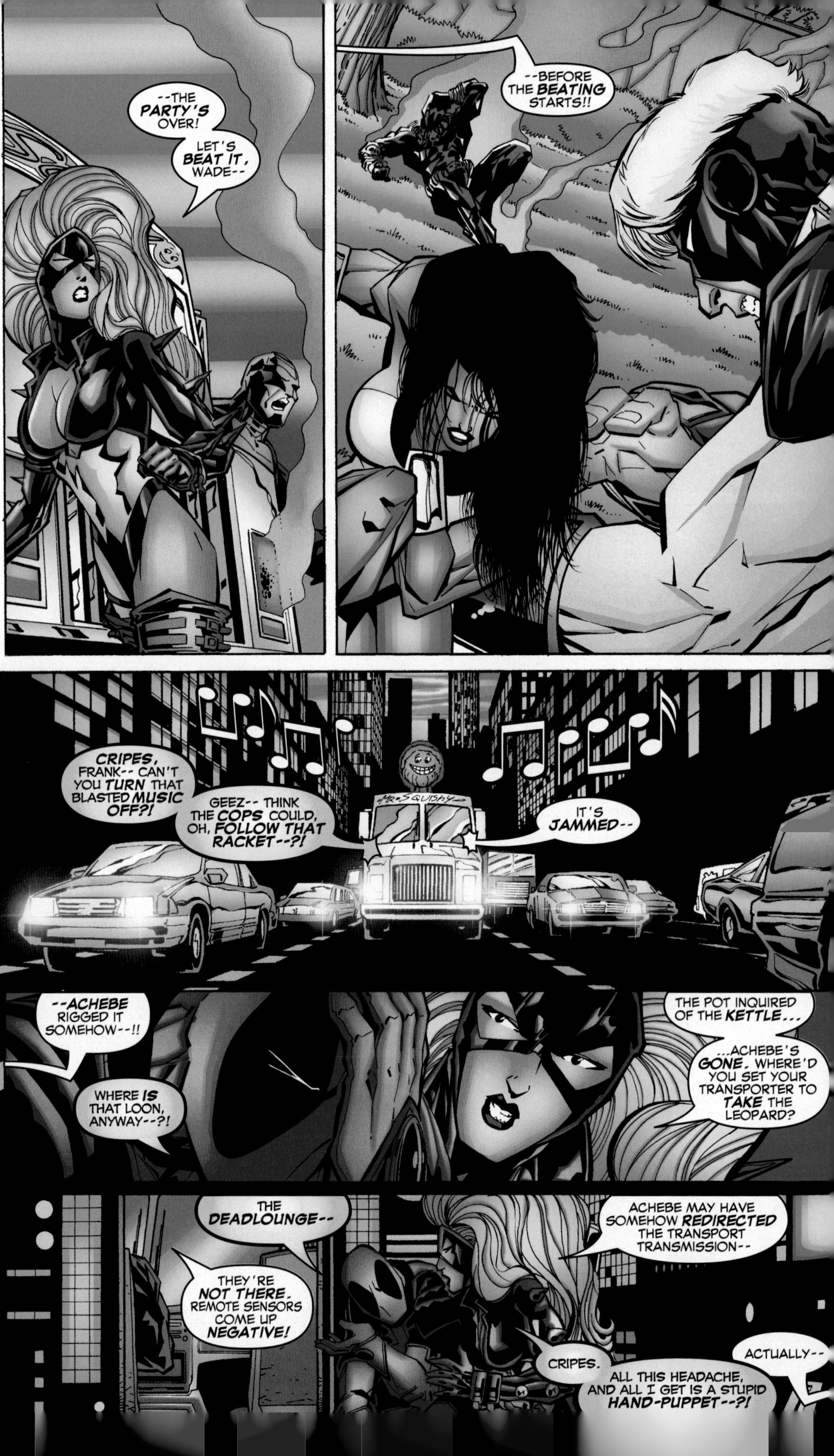
--THE PARTY'S OVER!
LET'S BEAT IT, WADE--
--BEFORE THE BEATING STARTS!!
CRIPES, FRANK-- CAN'T YOU TURN THAT BLASTED MUSIC OFF?!
GEEZ-- THINK THE COPS COULD, OH, FOLLOW THAT RACKET--?!
MR. SQUISHY
IT'S JAMMED--
--ACHEBE RIGGED IT SOMEHOW--!!
WHERE IS THAT LOON, ANYWAY--?!
THE POT INQUIRED OF THE KETTLE...
...ACHEBE'S GONE. WHERE'D YOU SET YOUR TRANSPORTER TO TAKE THE LEOPARD?
THE DEADLOUNGE--
THEY'RE NOT THERE. REMOTE SENSORS COME UP NEGATIVE!
ACHEBE MAY HAVE SOMEHOW REDIRECTED THE TRANSPORT TRANSMISSION--
CRIPES.
ALL THIS HEADACHE, AND ALL I GET IS A STUPID HAND-PUPPET--?!
ACTUALLY--

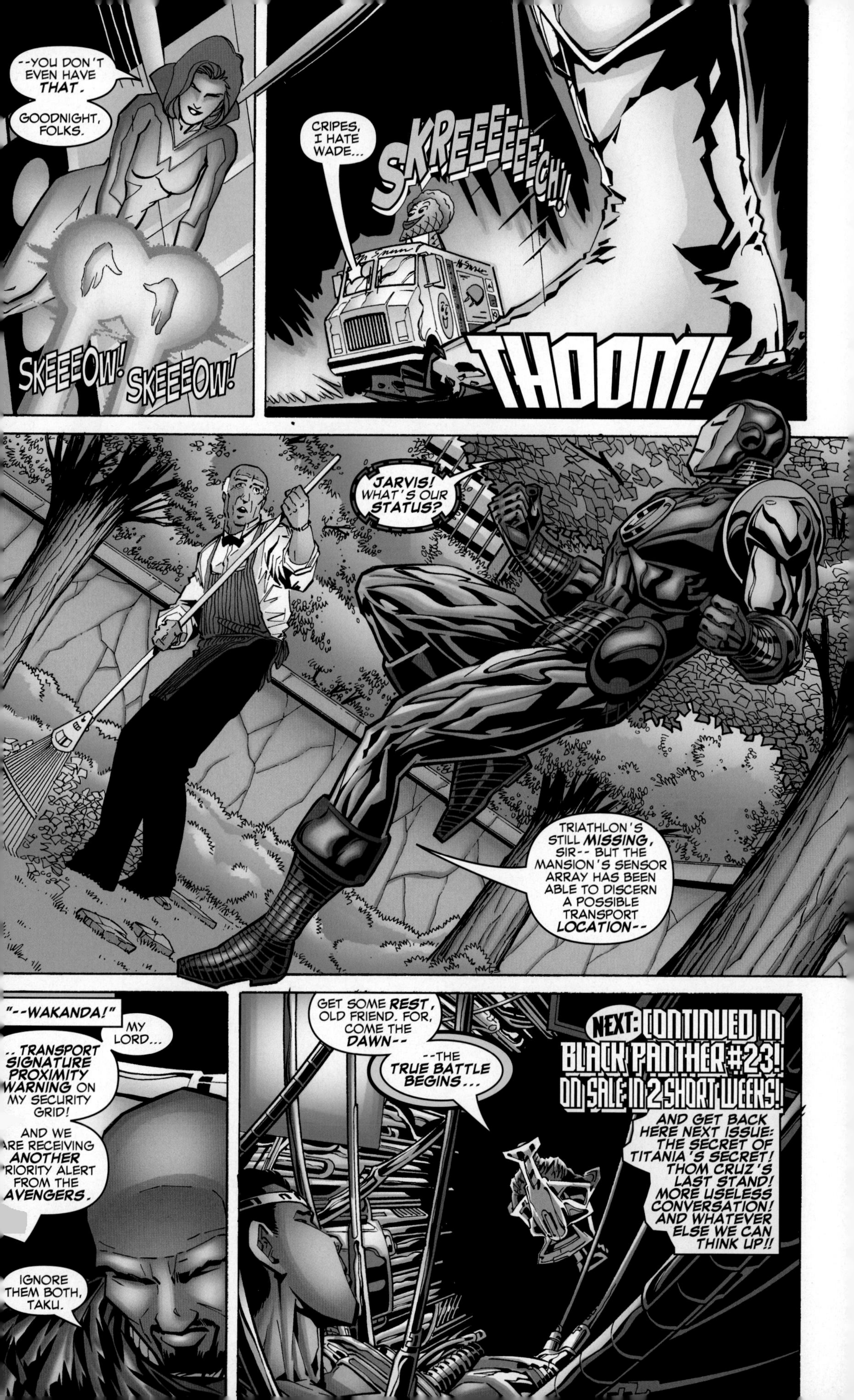
--YOU DON'T EVEN HAVE THAT.
GOODNIGHT, FOLKS.
SKEEEOW! SKEEEOW!
CRIPES, I HATE WADE...
SKREEEEEEECH!!
THOOM!
JARVIS! WHAT'S OUR STATUS?
TRIATHLON'S STILL MISSING, SIR-- BUT THE MANSION'S SENSOR ARRAY HAS BEEN ABLE TO DISCERN A POSSIBLE TRANSPORT LOCATION--
"--WAKANDA!"
MY LORD...
..TRANSPORT SIGNATURE PROXIMITY WARNING ON MY SECURITY GRID!
AND WE ARE RECEIVING ANOTHER PRIORITY ALERT FROM THE AVENGERS.
IGNORE THEM BOTH, TAKU.
GET SOME REST, OLD FRIEND. FOR, COME THE DAWN--
--THE TRUE BATTLE BEGINS...
NEXT: CONTINUED IN BLACK PANTHER #23! ON SALE IN 2 SHORT WEEKS!
AND GET BACK HERE NEXT ISSUE: THE SECRET OF TITANIA'S SECRET! THOM CRUZ'S LAST STAND! MORE USELESS CONVERSATION! AND WHATEVER ELSE WE CAN THINK UP!!

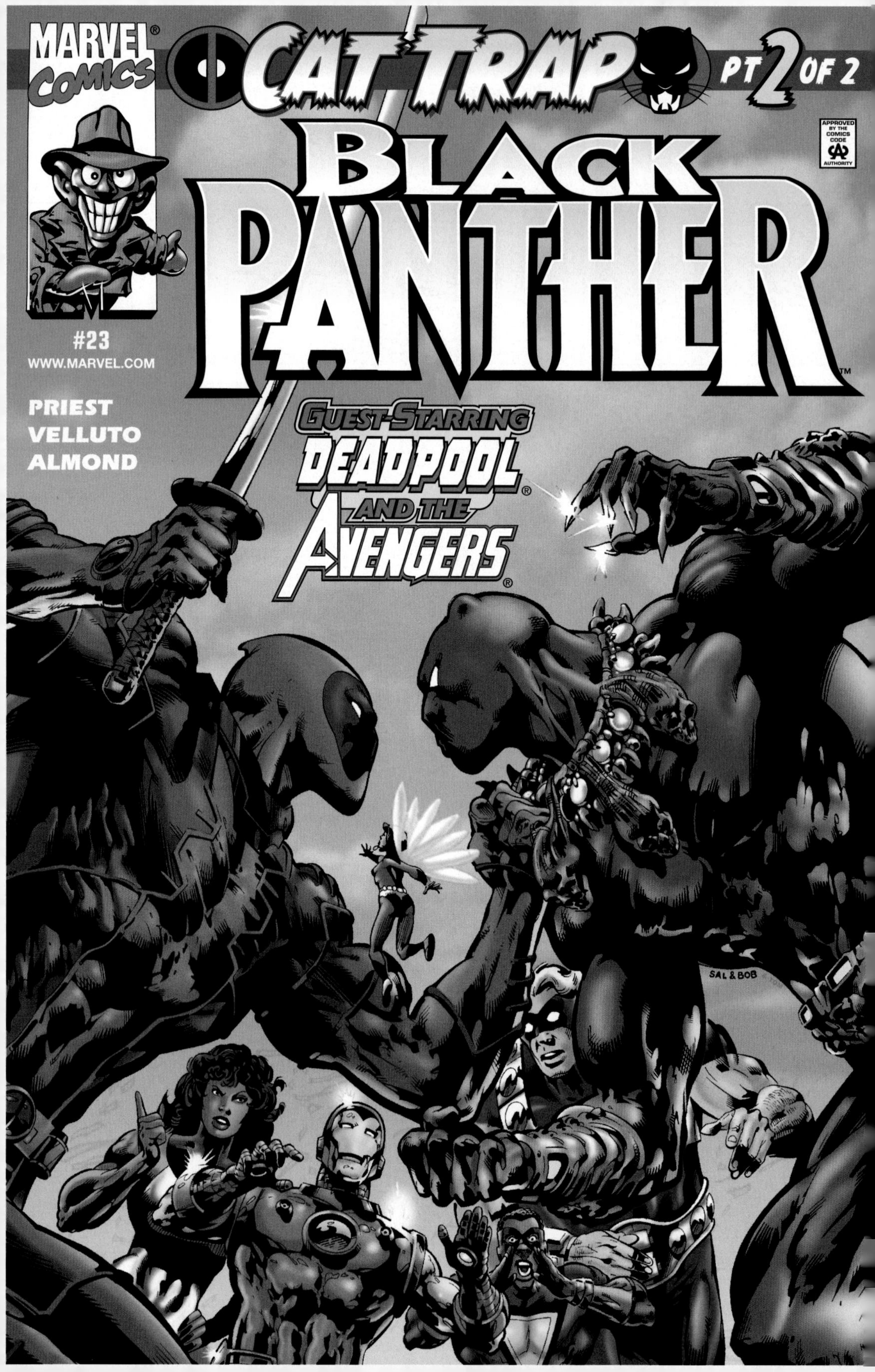
MARVEL COMICS
CAT TRAP PT 2 OF 2
APPROVED BY THE COMICS CODE AUTHORITY
BLACK PANTHER
#23
WWW.MARVEL.COM
PRIEST
VELLUTO
ALMOND
GUEST-STARRING DEADPOOL AND THE AVENGERS
SAL & BOB

THE UNUSUAL SUSPECTS

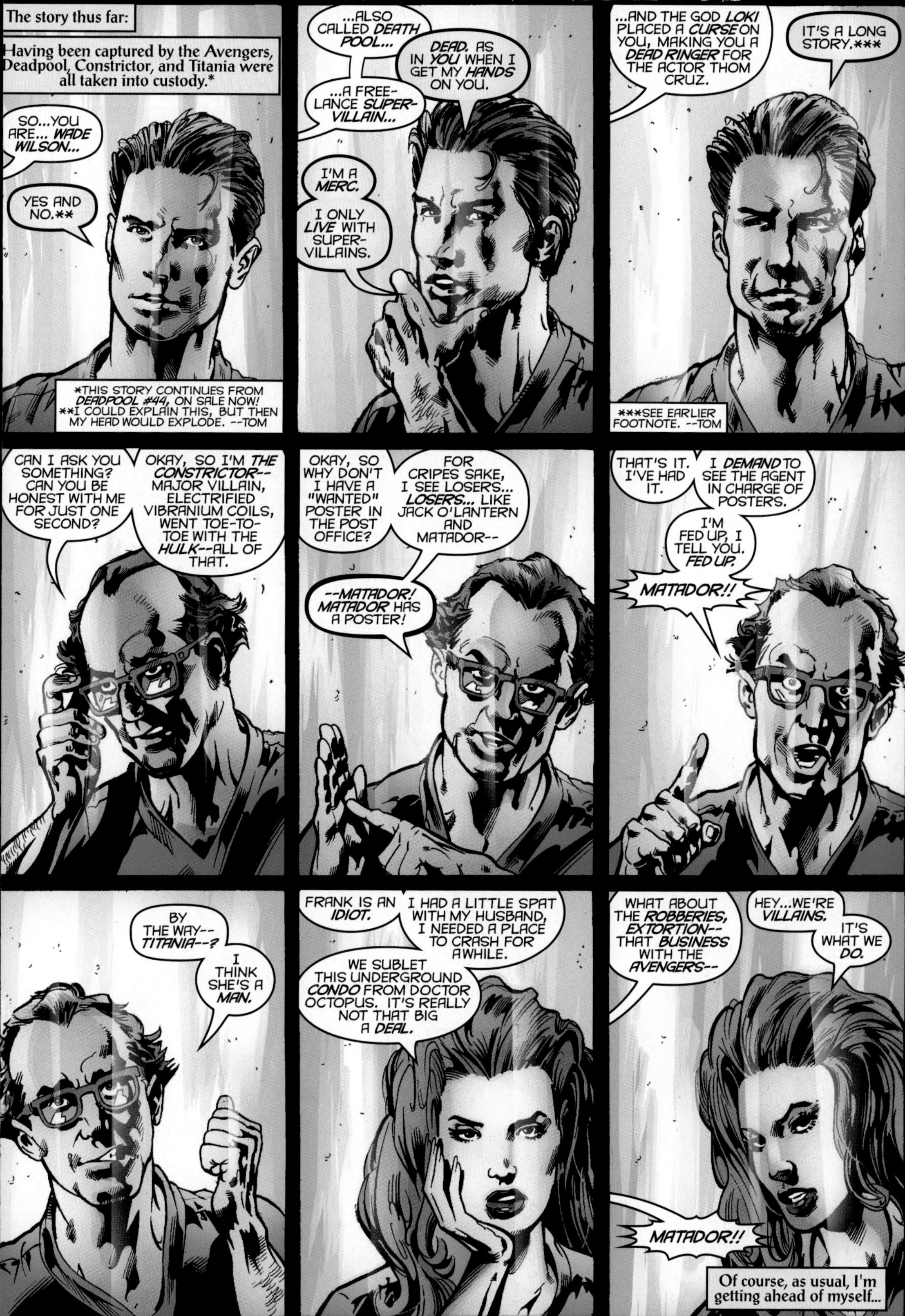

The story thus far:
Having been captured by the Avengers, Deadpool, Constrictor, and Titania were all taken into custody.*
SO...YOU ARE... WADE WILSON...
YES AND NO.**
*THIS STORY CONTINUES FROM DEADPOOL #44, ON SALE NOW!
**I COULD EXPLAIN THIS, BUT THEN MY HEAD WOULD EXPLODE. --TOM
...ALSO CALLED DEATH POOL...
DEAD. AS IN YOU WHEN I GET MY HANDS ON YOU.
...A FREE-LANCE SUPER-VILLAIN...
I'M A MERC.
I ONLY LIVE WITH SUPER-VILLAINS.
...AND THE GOD LOKI PLACED A CURSE ON YOU, MAKING YOU A DEAD RINGER FOR THE ACTOR THOM CRUZ.
IT'S A LONG STORY.***
***SEE EARLIER FOOTNOTE. --TOM
CAN I ASK YOU SOMETHING? CAN YOU BE HONEST WITH ME FOR JUST ONE SECOND?
OKAY, SO I'M THE CONSTRICTOR-- MAJOR VILLAIN, ELECTRIFIED VIBRANIUM COILS, WENT TOE-TO-TOE WITH THE HULK--ALL OF THAT.
OKAY, SO WHY DON'T I HAVE A "WANTED" POSTER IN THE POST OFFICE?
FOR CRIPES SAKE, I SEE LOSERS... LOSERS... LIKE JACK O'LANTERN AND MATADOR--
--MATADOR! MATADOR HAS A POSTER!
THAT'S IT. I'VE HAD IT.
I DEMAND TO SEE THE AGENT IN CHARGE OF POSTERS.
I'M FED UP, I TELL YOU. FED UP.
MATADOR!!
BY THE WAY-- TITANIA--?
I THINK SHE'S A MAN.
FRANK IS AN IDIOT.
I HAD A LITTLE SPAT WITH MY HUSBAND, I NEEDED A PLACE TO CRASH FOR AWHILE.
WE SUBLET THIS UNDERGROUND CONDO FROM DOCTOR OCTOPUS. IT'S REALLY NOT THAT BIG A DEAL.
WHAT ABOUT THE ROBBERIES, EXTORTION-- THAT BUSINESS WITH THE AVENGERS--
HEY...WE'RE VILLAINS.
IT'S WHAT WE DO.
MATADOR!!
Of course, as usual, I'm getting ahead of myself...

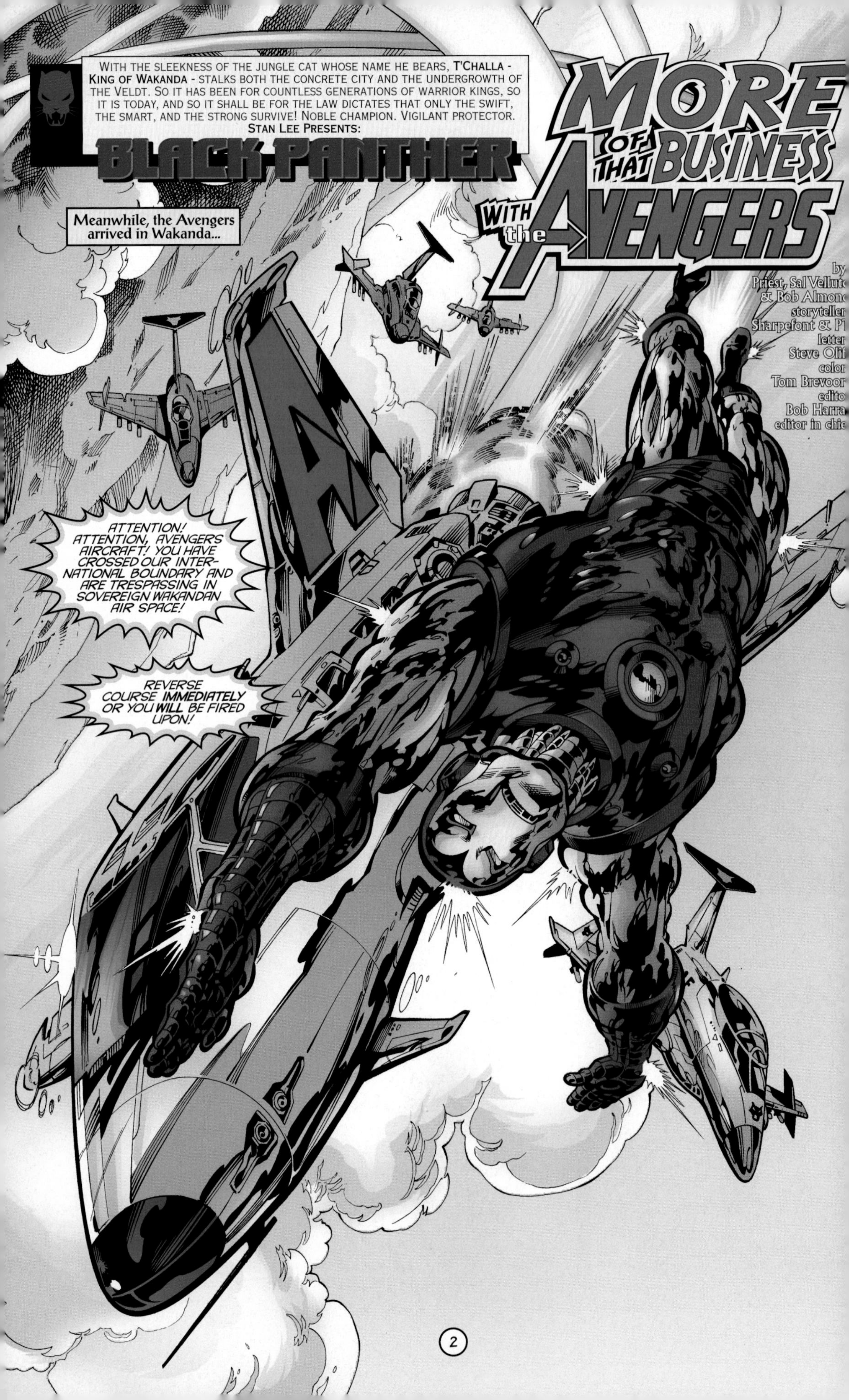
With the sleekness of the jungle cat whose name he bears, T'Challa - King of Wakanda - stalks both the concrete city and the undergrowth of the Veldt. So it has been for countless generations of warrior kings, so it is today, and so it shall be for the law dictates that only the swift, the smart, and the strong survive! Noble champion. Vigilant protector.
Stan Lee Presents:
BLACK PANTHER
MORE OF THAT BUSINESS WITH THE AVENGERS
by
Priest, Sal Vellut
& Bob Almon
storyteller
Sharpefont & PT
letter
Steve Olif
color
Tom Brevoor
edito
Bob Harra
editor in chie
Meanwhile, the Avengers arrived in Wakanda...
ATTENTION! ATTENTION, AVENGERS AIRCRAFT! YOU HAVE CROSSED OUR INTER-NATIONAL BOUNDARY AND ARE TRESPASSING IN SOVEREIGN WAKANDAN AIR SPACE!
REVERSE COURSE IMMEDIATELY OR YOU WILL BE FIRED UPON!

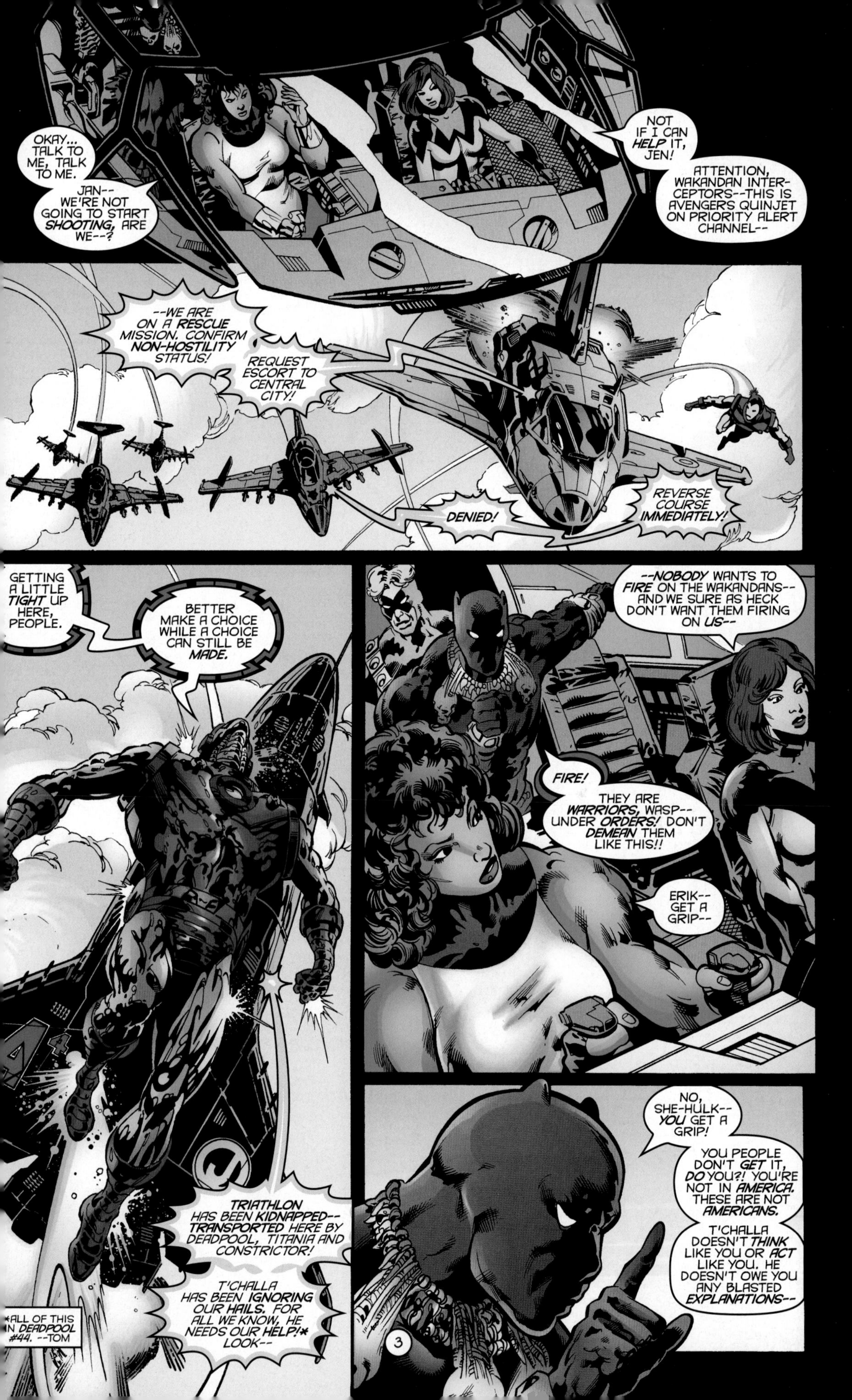
OKAY... TALK TO ME, TALK TO ME.
JAN-- WE'RE NOT GOING TO START SHOOTING, ARE WE--?
NOT IF I CAN HELP IT, JEN!
ATTENTION, WAKANDAN INTER-CEPTORS--THIS IS AVENGERS QUINJET ON PRIORITY ALERT CHANNEL--
--WE ARE ON A RESCUE MISSION. CONFIRM NON-HOSTILITY STATUS!
REQUEST ESCORT TO CENTRAL CITY!
DENIED!
REVERSE COURSE IMMEDIATELY!
GETTING A LITTLE TIGHT UP HERE, PEOPLE.
BETTER MAKE A CHOICE WHILE A CHOICE CAN STILL BE MADE.
TRIATHLON HAS BEEN KIDNAPPED-- TRANSPORTED HERE BY DEADPOOL, TITANIA AND CONSTRICTOR!
T'CHALLA HAS BEEN IGNORING OUR HAILS. FOR ALL WE KNOW, HE NEEDS OUR HELP!* LOOK--
*ALL OF THIS IN DEADPOOL #44. --TOM
--NOBODY WANTS TO FIRE ON THE WAKANDANS-- AND WE SURE AS HECK DON'T WANT THEM FIRING ON US--
FIRE!
THEY ARE WARRIORS, WASP-- UNDER ORDERS! DON'T DEMEAN THEM LIKE THIS!!
ERIK-- GET A GRIP--
NO, SHE-HULK-- YOU GET A GRIP!
YOU PEOPLE DON'T GET IT, DO YOU?! YOU'RE NOT IN AMERICA. THESE ARE NOT AMERICANS.
T'CHALLA DOESN'T THINK LIKE YOU OR ACT LIKE YOU. HE DOESN'T OWE YOU ANY BLASTED EXPLANATIONS--
3

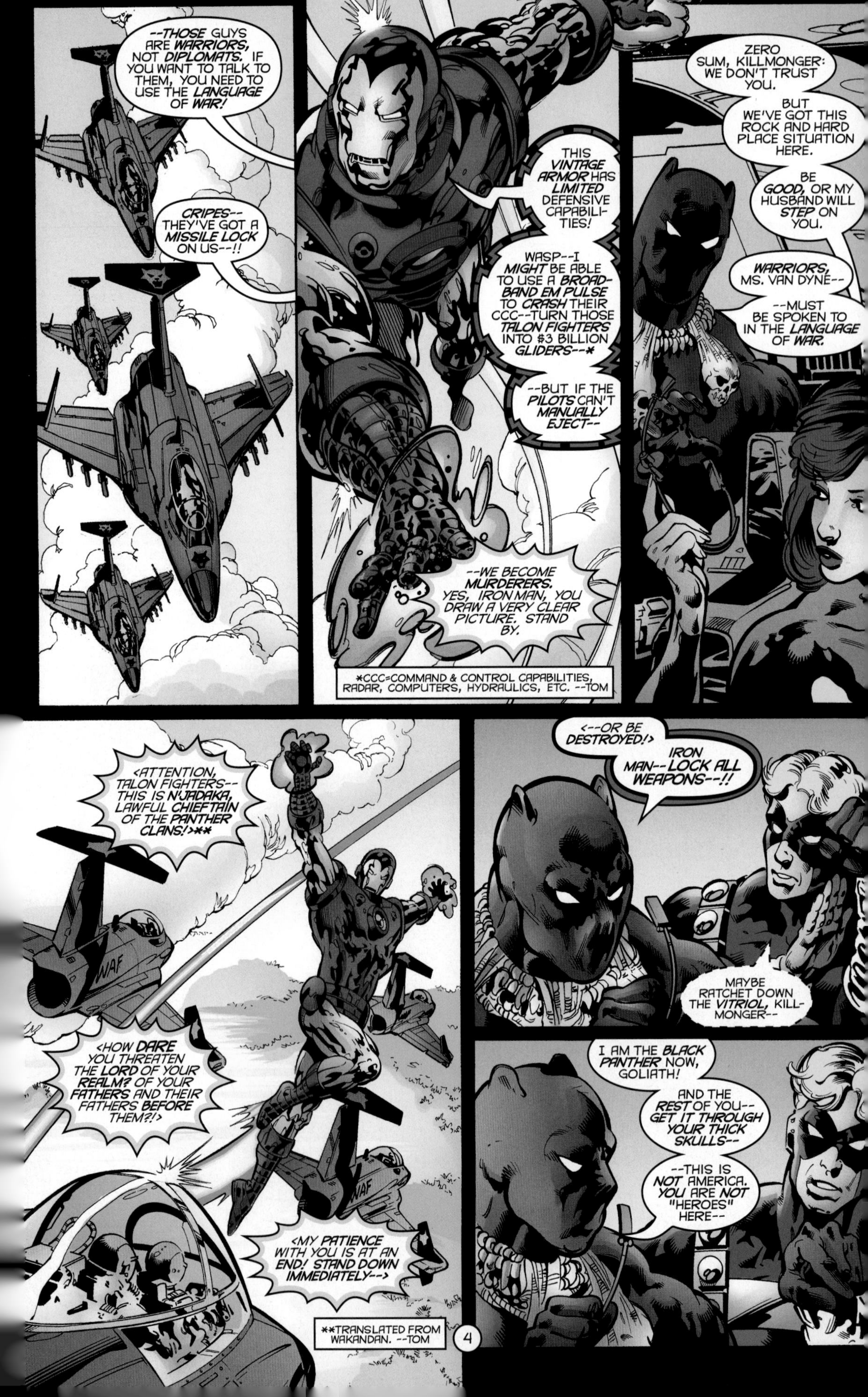
--THOSE GUYS ARE WARRIORS, NOT DIPLOMATS. IF YOU WANT TO TALK TO THEM, YOU NEED TO USE THE LANGUAGE OF WAR!
CRIPES-- THEY'VE GOT A MISSILE LOCK ON US--!!
THIS VINTAGE ARMOR HAS LIMITED DEFENSIVE CAPABILI-TIES!
WASP--I MIGHT BE ABLE TO USE A BROAD-BAND EM PULSE TO CRASH THEIR CCC--TURN THOSE TALON FIGHTERS INTO $3 BILLION GLIDERS--*
--BUT IF THE PILOTS CAN'T MANUALLY EJECT--
--WE BECOME MURDERERS. YES, IRON MAN, YOU DRAW A VERY CLEAR PICTURE. STAND BY.
*CCC=COMMAND & CONTROL CAPABILITIES, RADAR, COMPUTERS, HYDRAULICS, ETC. --TOM
ZERO SUM, KILLMONGER: WE DON'T TRUST YOU.
BUT WE'VE GOT THIS ROCK AND HARD PLACE SITUATION HERE.
BE GOOD, OR MY HUSBAND WILL STEP ON YOU.
WARRIORS, MS. VAN DYNE--
--MUST BE SPOKEN TO IN THE LANGUAGE OF WAR.
<ATTENTION, TALON FIGHTERS-- THIS IS N'JADAKA, LAWFUL CHIEFTAIN OF THE PANTHER CLANS!>**
WAF
<HOW DARE YOU THREATEN THE LORD OF YOUR REALM? OF YOUR FATHERS AND THEIR FATHERS BEFORE THEM?!>
WAF
<MY PATIENCE WITH YOU IS AT AN END! STAND DOWN IMMEDIATELY-->
**TRANSLATED FROM WAKANDAN. --TOM
<--OR BE DESTROYED!>
IRON MAN--LOCK ALL WEAPONS--!!
MAYBE RATCHET DOWN THE VITRIOL, KILL-MONGER--
I AM THE BLACK PANTHER NOW, GOLIATH!
AND THE REST OF YOU-- GET IT THROUGH YOUR THICK SKULLS--
--THIS IS NOT AMERICA. YOU ARE NOT "HEROES" HERE--

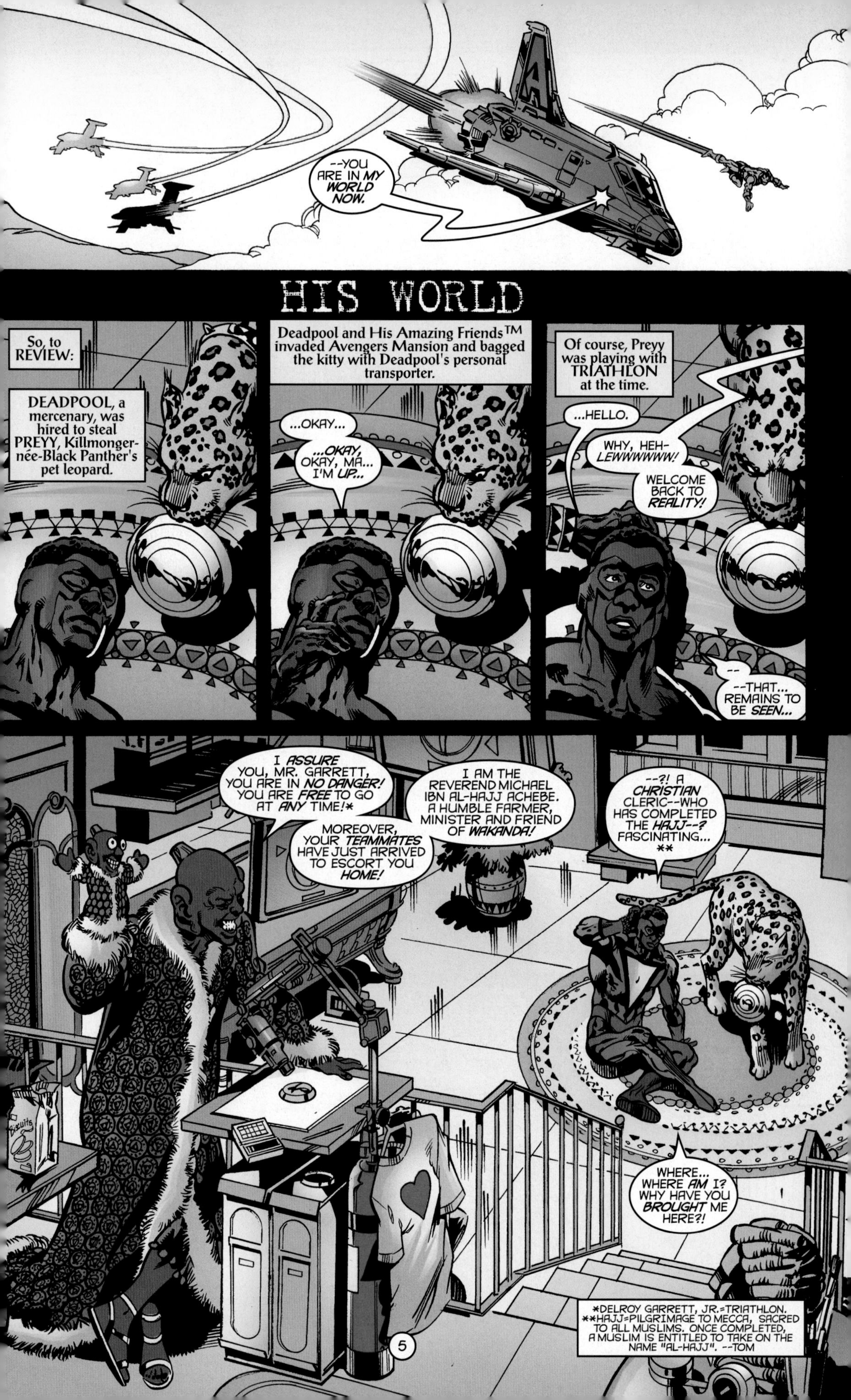
--YOU ARE IN MY WORLD NOW.
HIS WORLD
So, to REVIEW:
DEADPOOL, a mercenary, was hired to steal PREYY, Killmonger-née-Black Panther's pet leopard.
Deadpool and His Amazing Friends™ invaded Avengers Mansion and bagged the kitty with Deadpool's personal transporter.
...OKAY...
...OKAY, OKAY, MA... I'M UP...
Of course, Preyy was playing with TRIATHLON at the time.
...HELLO.
WHY, HEH-LEWWWWWW!
WELCOME BACK TO REALITY!
--
--THAT... REMAINS TO BE SEEN...
WHERE... WHERE AM I? WHY HAVE YOU BROUGHT ME HERE?!
I ASSURE YOU, MR. GARRETT, YOU ARE IN NO DANGER! YOU ARE FREE TO GO AT ANY TIME!*
MOREOVER, YOUR TEAMMATES HAVE JUST ARRIVED TO ESCORT YOU HOME!
I AM THE REVEREND MICHAEL IBN AL-HAJJ ACHEBE. A HUMBLE FARMER, MINISTER AND FRIEND OF WAKANDA!
--?! A CHRISTIAN CLERIC--WHO HAS COMPLETED THE HAJJ--? FASCINATING... **
Biscuits
*DELROY GARRETT, JR.=TRIATHLON.
**HAJJ=PILGRIMAGE TO MECCA, SACRED TO ALL MUSLIMS. ONCE COMPLETED, A MUSLIM IS ENTITLED TO TAKE ON THE NAME "AL-HAJJ". --TOM

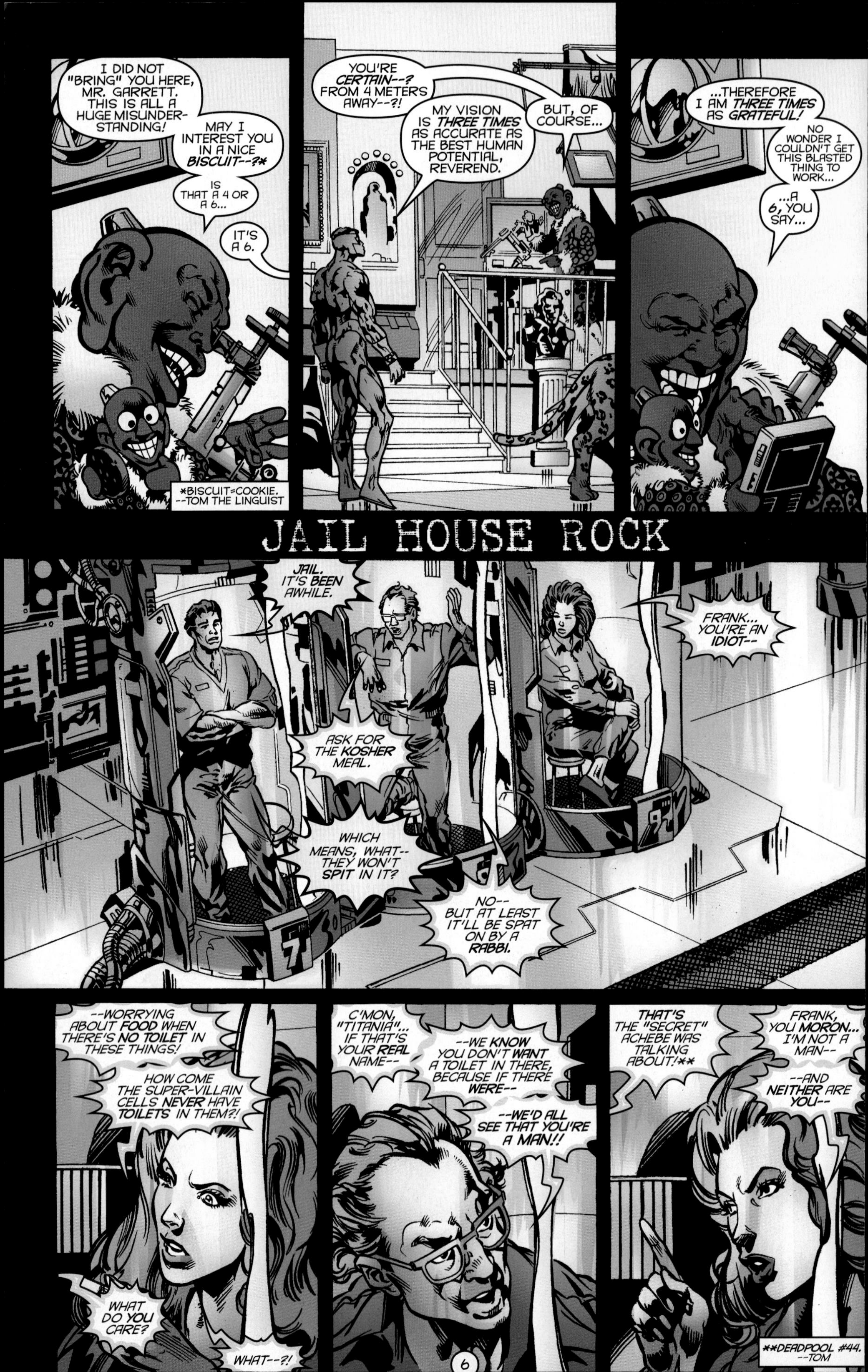
I DID NOT "BRING" YOU HERE, MR. GARRETT. THIS IS ALL A HUGE MISUNDERSTANDING!
MAY I INTEREST YOU IN A NICE BISCUIT--?*
IS THAT A 4 OR A 6...
IT'S A 6.
*BISCUIT=COOKIE. --TOM THE LINGUIST
YOU'RE CERTAIN--? FROM 4 METERS AWAY--?!
MY VISION IS THREE TIMES AS ACCURATE AS THE BEST HUMAN POTENTIAL, REVEREND.
BUT, OF COURSE...
...THEREFORE I AM THREE TIMES AS GRATEFUL!
NO WONDER I COULDN'T GET THIS BLASTED THING TO WORK...
...A 6, YOU SAY...
JAIL HOUSE ROCK
JAIL. IT'S BEEN AWHILE.
FRANK... YOU'RE AN IDIOT--
ASK FOR THE KOSHER MEAL.
WHICH MEANS, WHAT-- THEY WON'T SPIT IN IT?
NO-- BUT AT LEAST IT'LL BE SPAT ON BY A RABBI.
--WORRYING ABOUT FOOD WHEN THERE'S NO TOILET IN THESE THINGS!
HOW COME THE SUPER-VILLAIN CELLS NEVER HAVE TOILETS IN THEM?!
WHAT DO YOU CARE?
WHAT--?!
C'MON, "TITANIA"... IF THAT'S YOUR REAL NAME--
--WE KNOW YOU DON'T WANT A TOILET IN THERE, BECAUSE IF THERE WERE--
--WE'D ALL SEE THAT YOU'RE A MAN!!
THAT'S THE "SECRET" ACHEBE WAS TALKING ABOUT!**
FRANK, YOU MORON... I'M NOT A MAN--
--AND NEITHER ARE YOU--
**DEADPOOL #44. --TOM
6

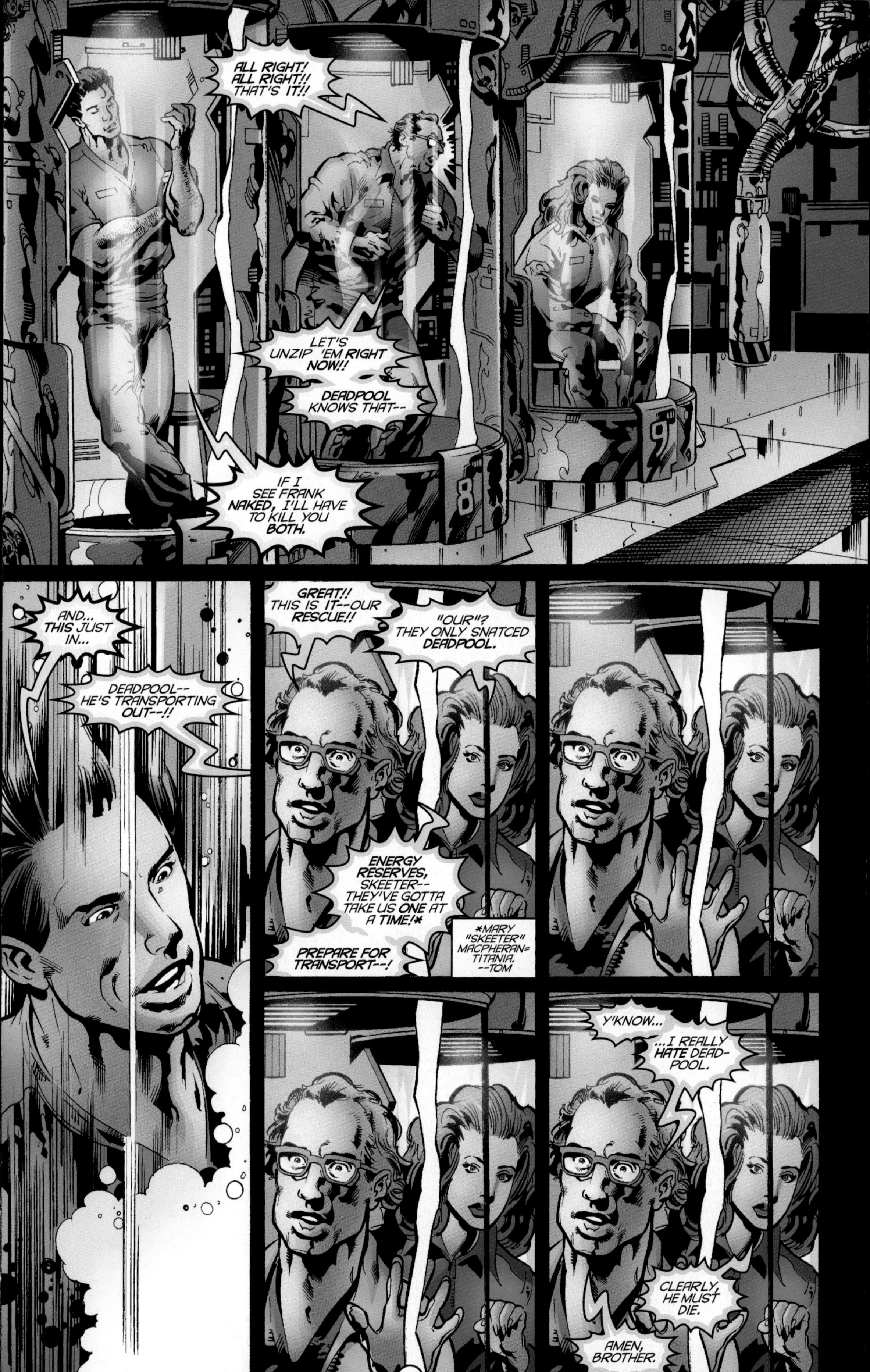
ALL RIGHT! ALL RIGHT!! THAT'S IT!!
LET'S UNZIP 'EM RIGHT NOW!!
DEADPOOL KNOWS THAT--
IF I SEE FRANK NAKED, I'LL HAVE TO KILL YOU BOTH.
AND... THIS JUST IN...
DEADPOOL-- HE'S TRANSPORTING OUT--!!
GREAT!! THIS IS IT--OUR RESCUE!!
"OUR"? THEY ONLY SNATCED DEADPOOL.
ENERGY RESERVES, SKEETER-- THEY'VE GOTTA TAKE US ONE AT A TIME!*
*MARY "SKEETER" MACPHERAN= TITANIA. --TOM
PREPARE FOR TRANSPORT--!
Y'KNOW...
...I REALLY HATE DEAD-POOL.
CLEARLY, HE MUST DIE.
AMEN, BROTHER.

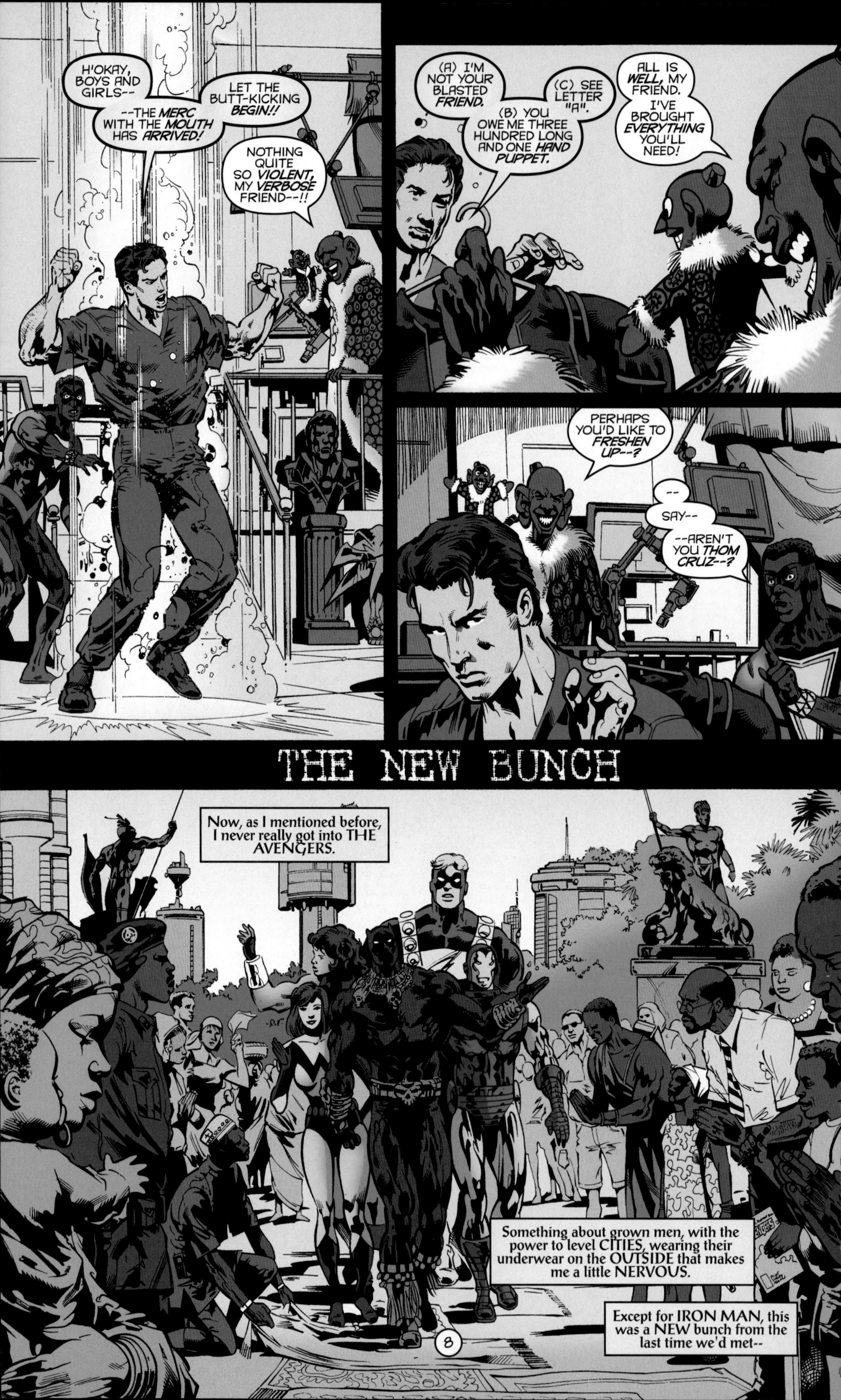

H'OKAY, BOYS AND GIRLS--
--THE MERC WITH THE MOUTH HAS ARRIVED!
LET THE BUTT-KICKING BEGIN!!
NOTHING QUITE SO VIOLENT, MY VERBOSE FRIEND--!!
(A) I'M NOT YOUR BLASTED FRIEND.
(B) YOU OWE ME THREE HUNDRED LONG AND ONE HAND PUPPET.
(C) SEE LETTER "A".
ALL IS WELL, MY FRIEND. I'VE BROUGHT EVERYTHING YOU'LL NEED!
PERHAPS YOU'D LIKE TO FRESHEN UP--?
--
SAY--
--AREN'T YOU THOM CRUZ--?
THE NEW BUNCH
Now, as I mentioned before, I never really got into THE AVENGERS.
Something about grown men, with the power to level CITIES, wearing their underwear on the OUTSIDE that makes me a little NERVOUS.
Except for IRON MAN, this was a NEW bunch from the last time we'd met--
8

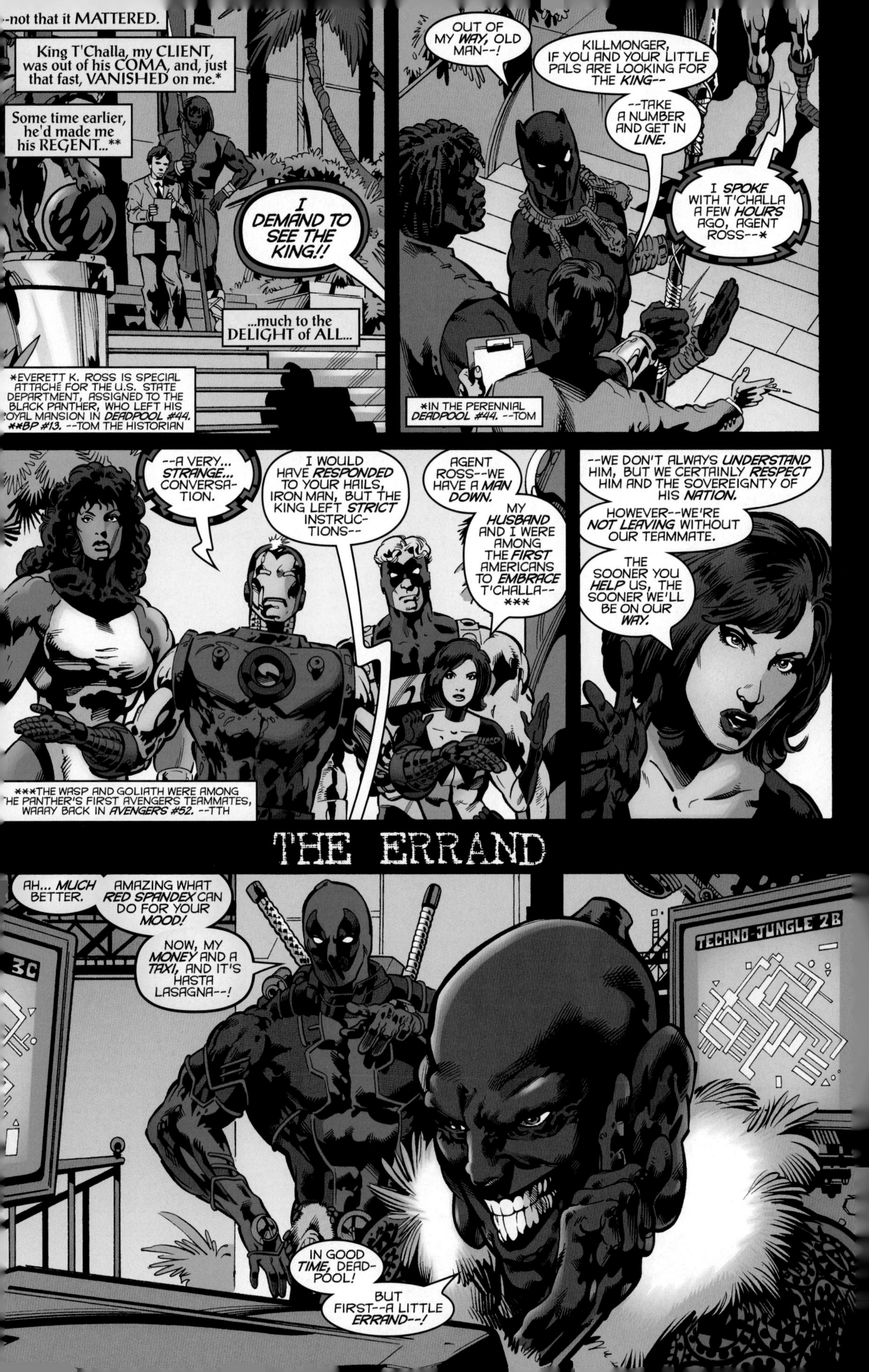
--not that it MATTERED.
King T'Challa, my CLIENT, was out of his COMA, and, just that fast, VANISHED on me.*
Some time earlier, he'd made me his REGENT...**
I DEMAND TO SEE THE KING!!
...much to the DELIGHT of ALL...
*EVERETT K. ROSS IS SPECIAL ATTACHÉ FOR THE U.S. STATE DEPARTMENT, ASSIGNED TO THE BLACK PANTHER, WHO LEFT HIS ROYAL MANSION IN DEADPOOL #44. **BP #13. --TOM THE HISTORIAN
OUT OF MY WAY, OLD MAN--!
KILLMONGER, IF YOU AND YOUR LITTLE PALS ARE LOOKING FOR THE KING--
--TAKE A NUMBER AND GET IN LINE.
I SPOKE WITH T'CHALLA A FEW HOURS AGO, AGENT ROSS--*
*IN THE PERENNIAL DEADPOOL #44. --TOM
--A VERY... STRANGE... CONVERSATION.
I WOULD HAVE RESPONDED TO YOUR HAILS, IRON MAN, BUT THE KING LEFT STRICT INSTRUCTIONS--
AGENT ROSS--WE HAVE A MAN DOWN.
MY HUSBAND AND I WERE AMONG THE FIRST AMERICANS TO EMBRACE T'CHALLA--***
***THE WASP AND GOLIATH WERE AMONG THE PANTHER'S FIRST AVENGERS TEAMMATES, WAAAY BACK IN AVENGERS #52. --TTH
--WE DON'T ALWAYS UNDERSTAND HIM, BUT WE CERTAINLY RESPECT HIM AND THE SOVEREIGNTY OF HIS NATION.
HOWEVER--WE'RE NOT LEAVING WITHOUT OUR TEAMMATE.
THE SOONER YOU HELP US, THE SOONER WE'LL BE ON OUR WAY.
THE ERRAND
AH... MUCH BETTER.
AMAZING WHAT RED SPANDEX CAN DO FOR YOUR MOOD!
NOW, MY MONEY AND A TAXI, AND IT'S HASTA LASAGNA--!
3C
TECHNO-JUNGLE 2B
IN GOOD TIME, DEADPOOL!
BUT FIRST--A LITTLE ERRAND--!

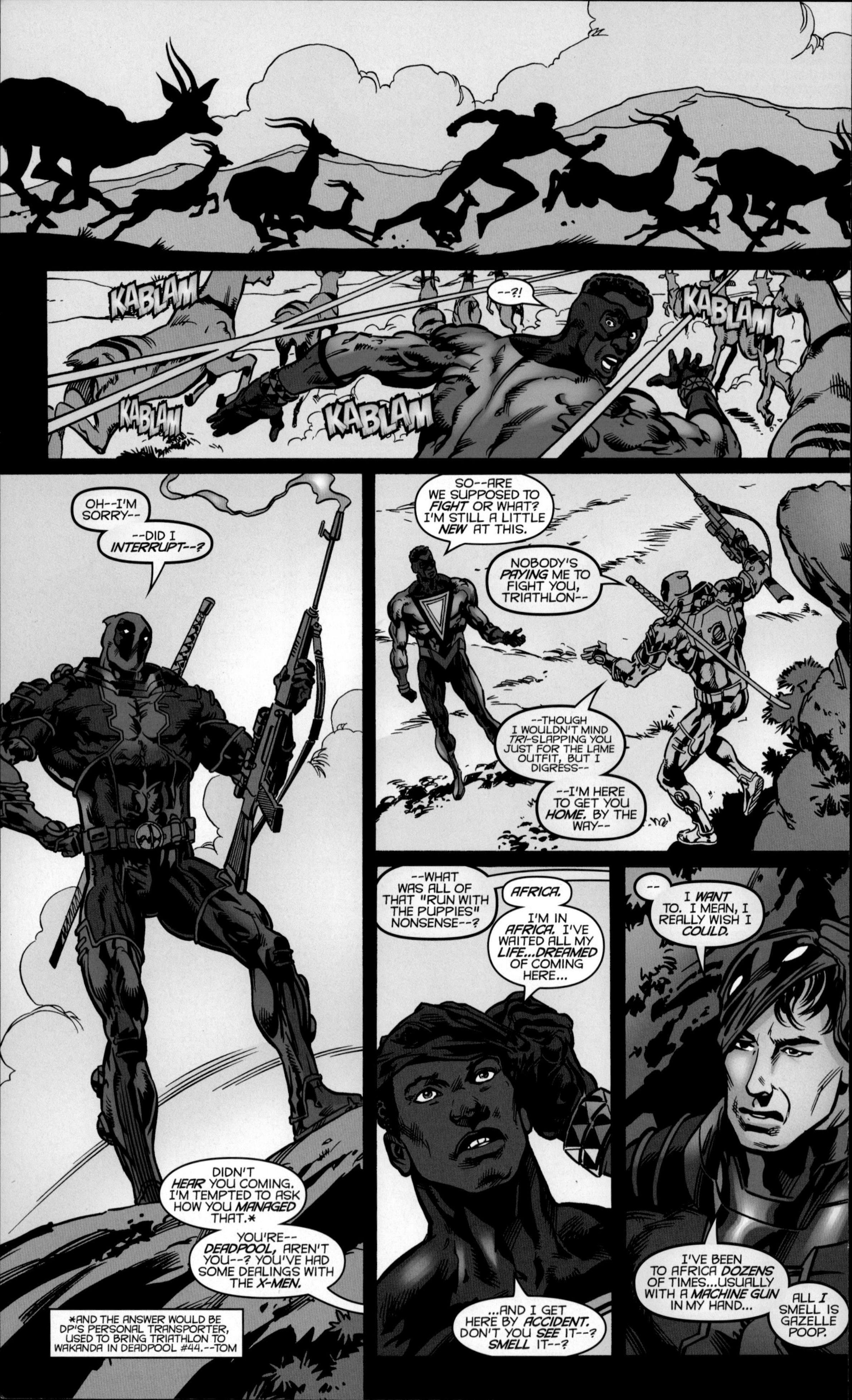
KABLAM
--?!
KABLAM
KABLAM
KABLAM
OH--I'M SORRY--
--DID I INTERRUPT--?
DIDN'T HEAR YOU COMING. I'M TEMPTED TO ASK HOW YOU MANAGED THAT.*
YOU'RE-- DEADPOOL, AREN'T YOU--? YOU'VE HAD SOME DEALINGS WITH THE X-MEN.
*AND THE ANSWER WOULD BE DP'S PERSONAL TRANSPORTER, USED TO BRING TRIATHLON TO WAKANDA IN DEADPOOL #44.--TOM
SO--ARE WE SUPPOSED TO FIGHT OR WHAT? I'M STILL A LITTLE NEW AT THIS.
NOBODY'S PAYING ME TO FIGHT YOU, TRIATHLON--
--THOUGH I WOULDN'T MIND TRI-SLAPPING YOU JUST FOR THE LAME OUTFIT, BUT I DIGRESS--
--I'M HERE TO GET YOU HOME. BY THE WAY--
--WHAT WAS ALL OF THAT "RUN WITH THE PUPPIES" NONSENSE--?
AFRICA.
I'M IN AFRICA. I'VE WAITED ALL MY LIFE...DREAMED OF COMING HERE...
...AND I GET HERE BY ACCIDENT. DON'T YOU SEE IT--? SMELL IT--?
--
I WANT TO. I MEAN, I REALLY WISH I COULD.
I'VE BEEN TO AFRICA DOZENS OF TIMES...USUALLY WITH A MACHINE GUN IN MY HAND...
ALL I SMELL IS GAZELLE POOP.

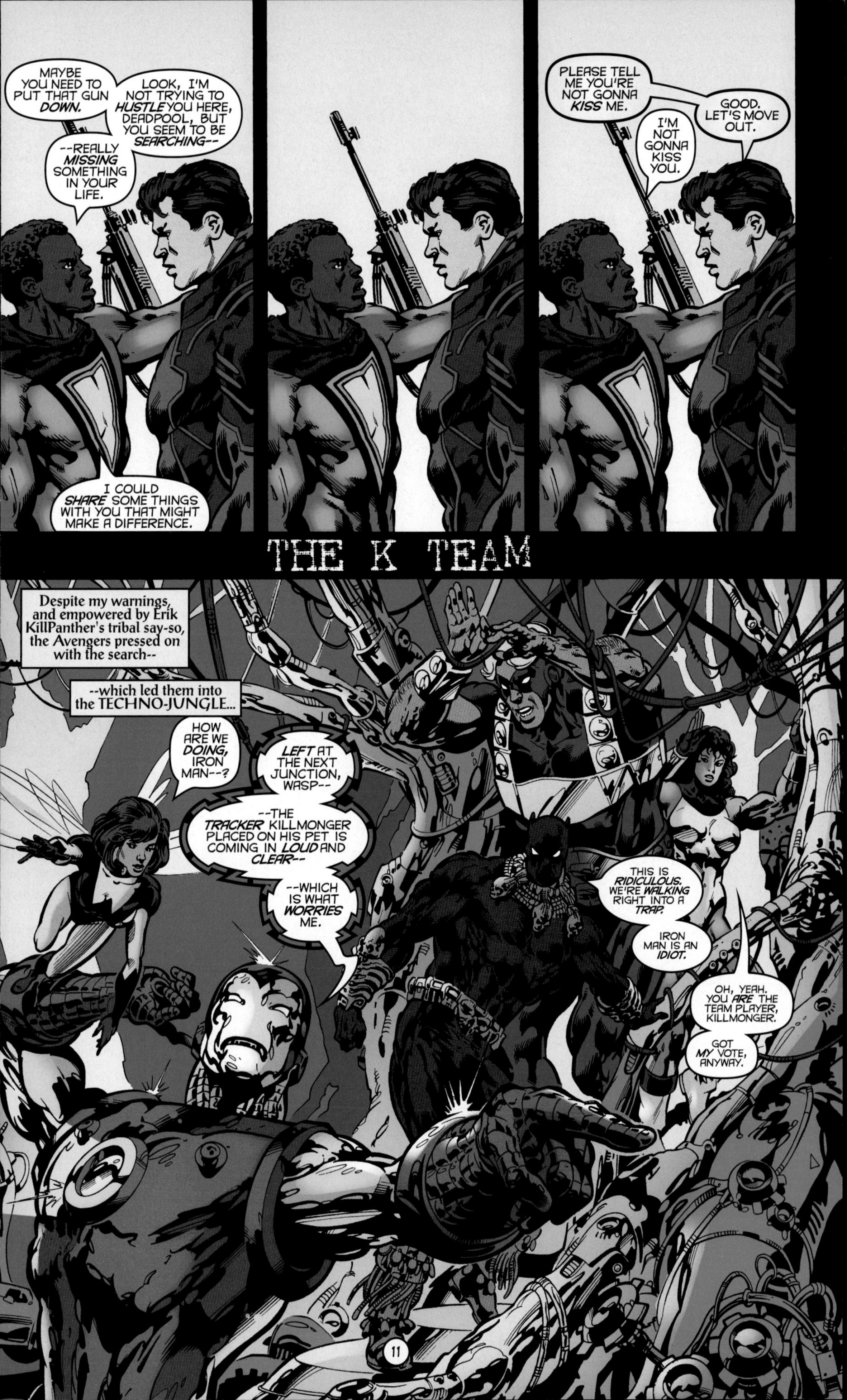
MAYBE YOU NEED TO PUT THAT GUN DOWN.
LOOK, I'M NOT TRYING TO HUSTLE YOU HERE, DEADPOOL, BUT YOU SEEM TO BE SEARCHING--
--REALLY MISSING SOMETHING IN YOUR LIFE.
I COULD SHARE SOME THINGS WITH YOU THAT MIGHT MAKE A DIFFERENCE.
PLEASE TELL ME YOU'RE NOT GONNA KISS ME.
I'M NOT GONNA KISS YOU.
GOOD. LET'S MOVE OUT.
THE K TEAM
Despite my warnings, and empowered by Erik KillPanther's tribal say-so, the Avengers pressed on with the search--
--which led them into the TECHNO-JUNGLE...
HOW ARE WE DOING, IRON MAN--?
LEFT AT THE NEXT JUNCTION, WASP--
--THE TRACKER KILLMONGER PLACED ON HIS PET IS COMING IN LOUD AND CLEAR--
--WHICH IS WHAT WORRIES ME.
THIS IS RIDICULOUS. WE'RE WALKING RIGHT INTO A TRAP.
IRON MAN IS AN IDIOT.
OH, YEAH. YOU ARE THE TEAM PLAYER, KILLMONGER.
GOT MY VOTE, ANYWAY.

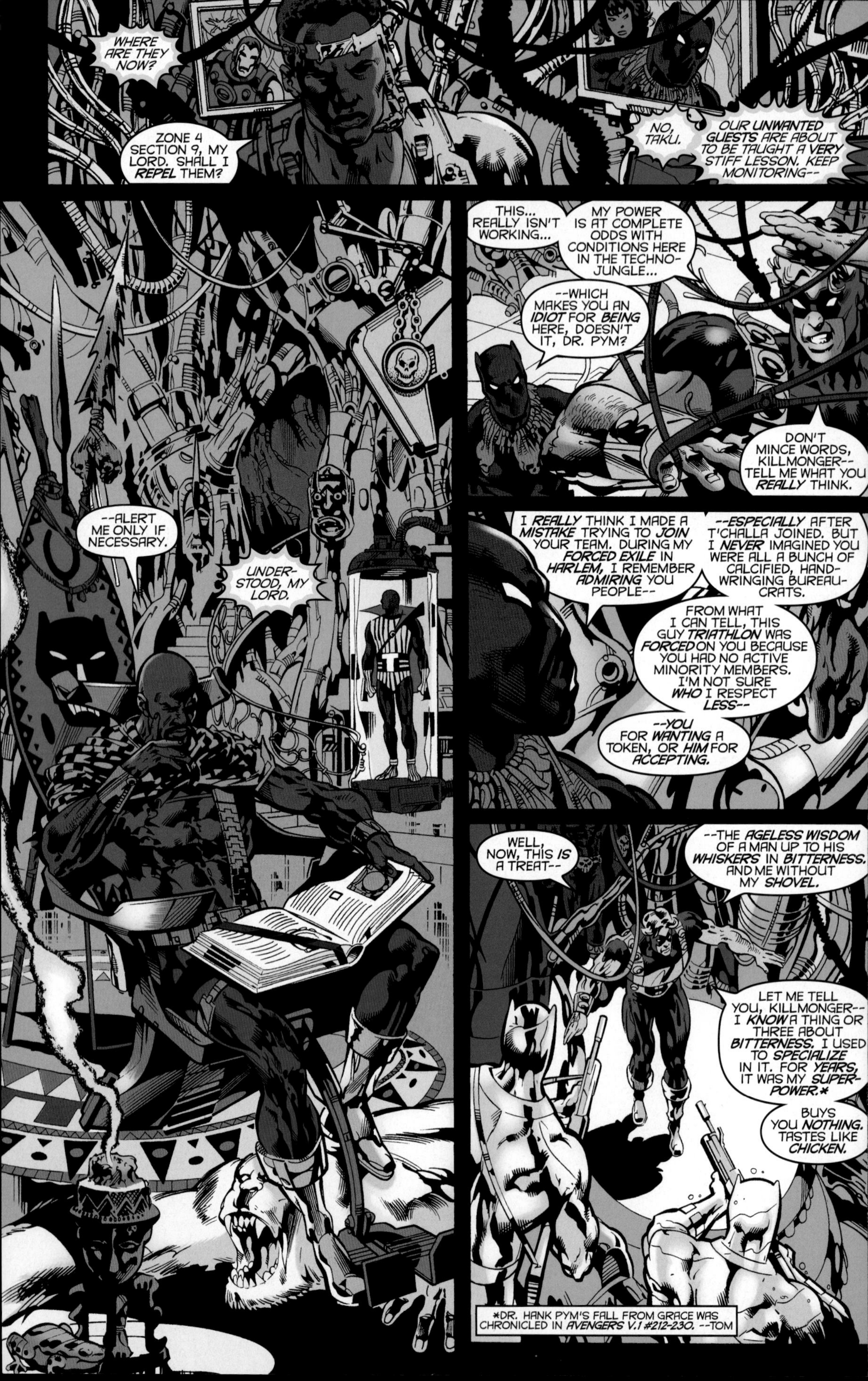
WHERE ARE THEY NOW?
ZONE 4 SECTION 9, MY LORD. SHALL I REPEL THEM?
NO, TAKU.
OUR UNWANTED GUESTS ARE ABOUT TO BE TAUGHT A VERY STIFF LESSON. KEEP MONITORING--
--ALERT ME ONLY IF NECESSARY.
UNDER-STOOD, MY LORD.
THIS... REALLY ISN'T WORKING...
MY POWER IS AT COMPLETE ODDS WITH CONDITIONS HERE IN THE TECHNO-JUNGLE...
--WHICH MAKES YOU AN IDIOT FOR BEING HERE, DOESN'T IT, DR. PYM?
DON'T MINCE WORDS, KILLMONGER-- TELL ME WHAT YOU REALLY THINK.
I REALLY THINK I MADE A MISTAKE TRYING TO JOIN YOUR TEAM. DURING MY FORCED EXILE IN HARLEM, I REMEMBER ADMIRING YOU PEOPLE--
--ESPECIALLY AFTER T'CHALLA JOINED. BUT I NEVER IMAGINED YOU WERE ALL A BUNCH OF CALCIFIED, HAND-WRINGING BUREAU-CRATS.
FROM WHAT I CAN TELL, THIS GUY TRIATHLON WAS FORCED ON YOU BECAUSE YOU HAD NO ACTIVE MINORITY MEMBERS. I'M NOT SURE WHO I RESPECT LESS--
--YOU FOR WANTING A TOKEN, OR HIM FOR ACCEPTING.
WELL, NOW, THIS IS A TREAT--
--THE AGELESS WISDOM OF A MAN UP TO HIS WHISKERS IN BITTERNESS. AND ME WITHOUT MY SHOVEL.
LET ME TELL YOU, KILLMONGER-- I KNOW A THING OR THREE ABOUT BITTERNESS. I USED TO SPECIALIZE IN IT. FOR YEARS, IT WAS MY SUPER-POWER.*
BUYS YOU NOTHING. TASTES LIKE CHICKEN.
*DR. HANK PYM'S FALL FROM GRACE WAS CHRONICLED IN AVENGERS V.1 #212-230. --TOM

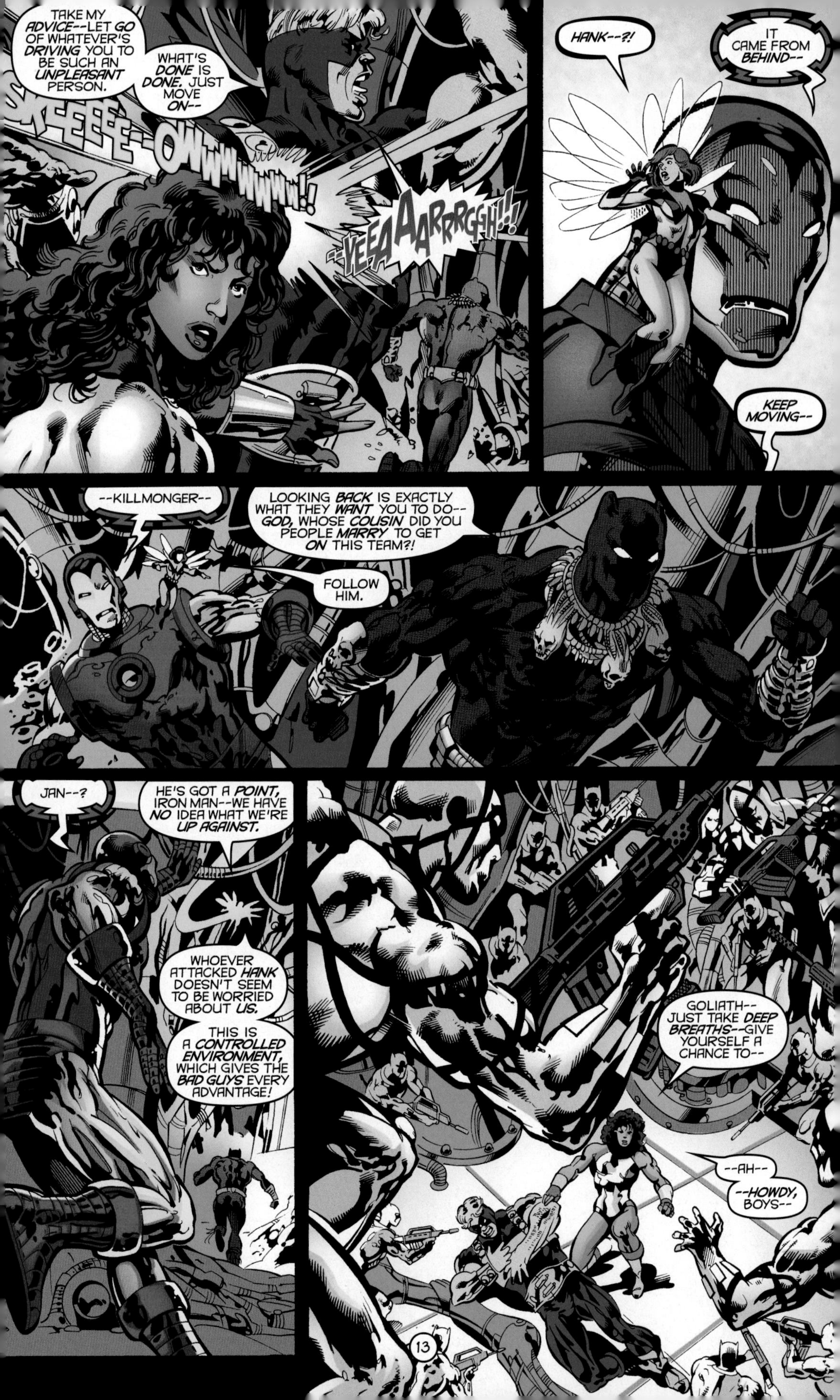
TAKE MY ADVICE--LET GO OF WHATEVER'S DRIVING YOU TO BE SUCH AN UNPLEASANT PERSON.
WHAT'S DONE IS DONE. JUST MOVE ON--
SKREEEEE--OWWWWWW!!
--YEEAAARRRGGH!!!
HANK--?!
IT CAME FROM BEHIND--
KEEP MOVING--
--KILLMONGER--
LOOKING BACK IS EXACTLY WHAT THEY WANT YOU TO DO--GOD, WHOSE COUSIN DID YOU PEOPLE MARRY TO GET ON THIS TEAM?!
FOLLOW HIM.
JAN--?
HE'S GOT A POINT, IRON MAN--WE HAVE NO IDEA WHAT WE'RE UP AGAINST.
WHOEVER ATTACKED HANK DOESN'T SEEM TO BE WORRIED ABOUT US.
THIS IS A CONTROLLED ENVIRONMENT, WHICH GIVES THE BAD GUYS EVERY ADVANTAGE!
GOLIATH--JUST TAKE DEEP BREATHS--GIVE YOURSELF A CHANCE TO--
--AH--
--HOWDY, BOYS--

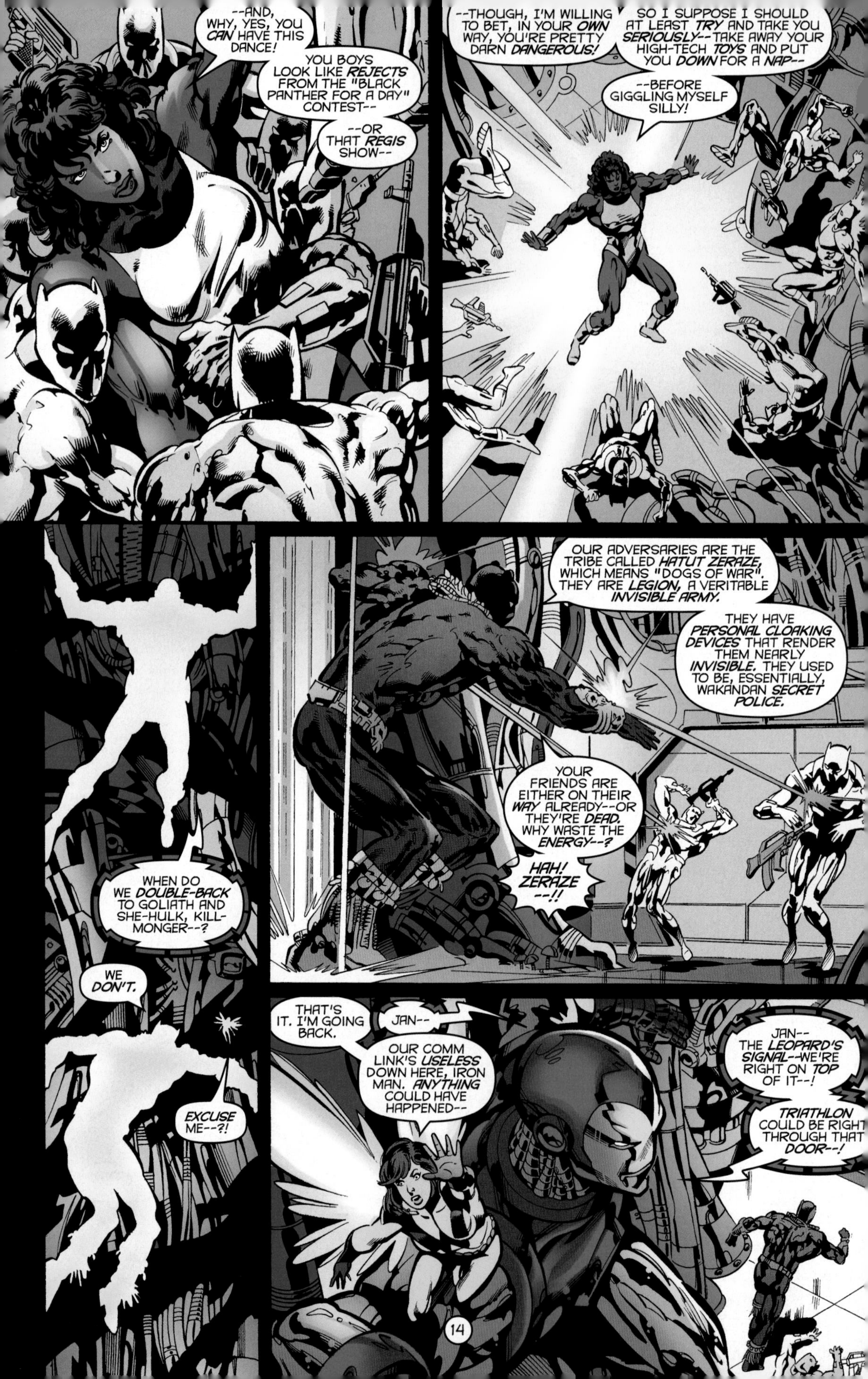
--AND, WHY, YES, YOU CAN HAVE THIS DANCE!
YOU BOYS LOOK LIKE REJECTS FROM THE "BLACK PANTHER FOR A DAY" CONTEST--
--OR THAT REGIS SHOW--
--THOUGH, I'M WILLING TO BET, IN YOUR OWN WAY, YOU'RE PRETTY DARN DANGEROUS!
SO I SUPPOSE I SHOULD AT LEAST TRY AND TAKE YOU SERIOUSLY--TAKE AWAY YOUR HIGH-TECH TOYS AND PUT YOU DOWN FOR A NAP--
--BEFORE GIGGLING MYSELF SILLY!
WHEN DO WE DOUBLE-BACK TO GOLIATH AND SHE-HULK, KILL-MONGER--?
WE DON'T.
EXCUSE ME--?!
OUR ADVERSARIES ARE THE TRIBE CALLED HATUT ZERAZE, WHICH MEANS "DOGS OF WAR". THEY ARE LEGION, A VERITABLE INVISIBLE ARMY.
THEY HAVE PERSONAL CLOAKING DEVICES THAT RENDER THEM NEARLY INVISIBLE. THEY USED TO BE, ESSENTIALLY, WAKANDAN SECRET POLICE.
YOUR FRIENDS ARE EITHER ON THEIR WAY ALREADY--OR THEY'RE DEAD. WHY WASTE THE ENERGY--?
HAH! ZERAZE--!!
THAT'S IT. I'M GOING BACK.
JAN--
OUR COMM LINK'S USELESS DOWN HERE, IRON MAN. ANYTHING COULD HAVE HAPPENED--
JAN-- THE LEOPARD'S SIGNAL--WE'RE RIGHT ON TOP OF IT--!
TRIATHLON COULD BE RIGHT THROUGH THAT DOOR--!
14

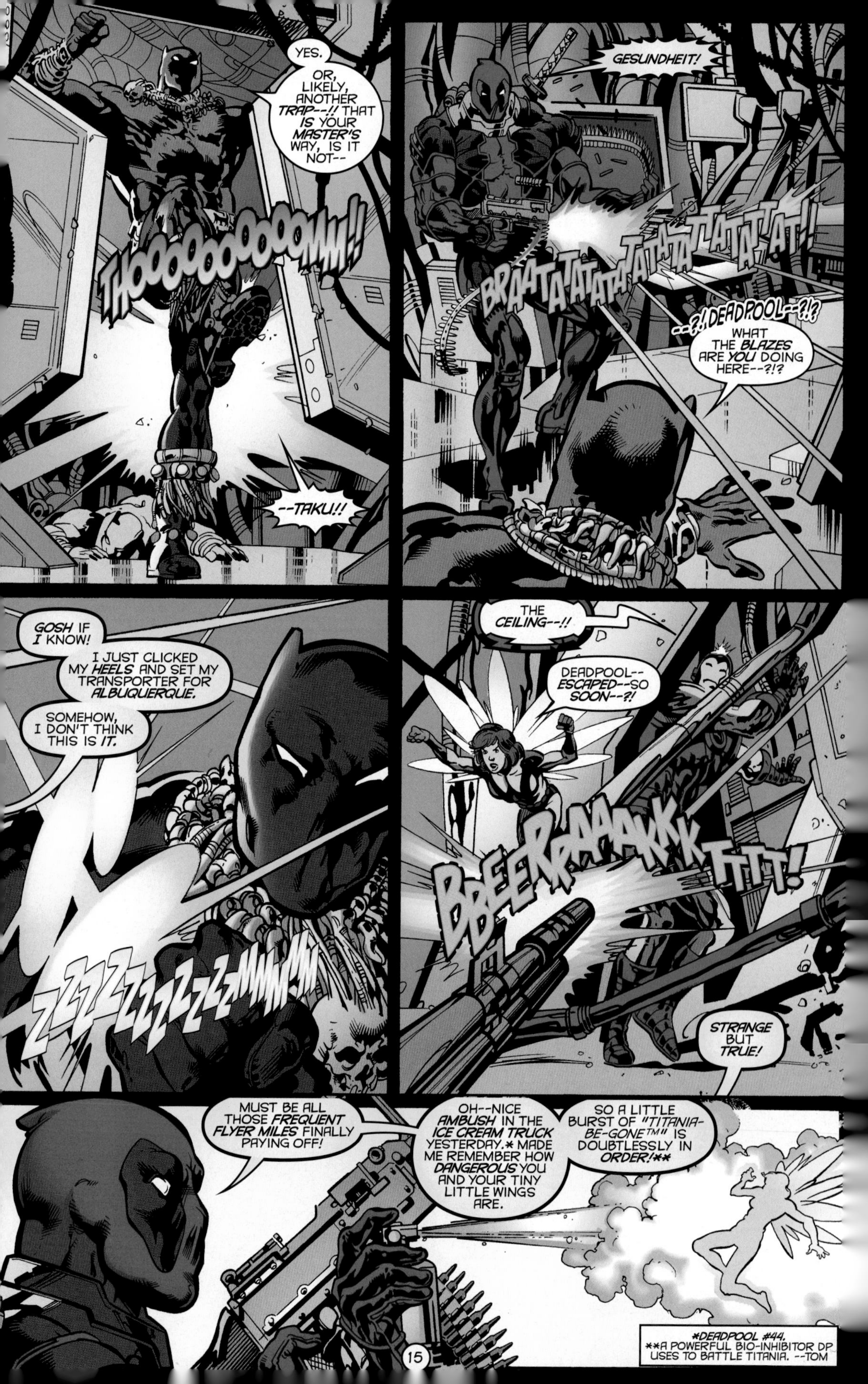
YES.
OR, LIKELY, ANOTHER TRAP--!! THAT IS YOUR MASTER'S WAY, IS IT NOT--
THOOOOOOOOOOMM!!
--TAKU!!
GESUNDHEIT!
BRAATATATATATATATATATATATAT!
--?! DEADPOOL--?!?
WHAT THE BLAZES ARE YOU DOING HERE--?!?
GOSH IF I KNOW!
I JUST CLICKED MY HEELS AND SET MY TRANSPORTER FOR ALBUQUERQUE.
SOMEHOW, I DON'T THINK THIS IS IT.
ZZZZZZZZZZZZMMMMM
THE CEILING--!!
DEADPOOL-- ESCAPED--SO SOON--?!
BBEERRAAAKKKTTTTT!
STRANGE BUT TRUE!
MUST BE ALL THOSE FREQUENT FLYER MILES FINALLY PAYING OFF!
OH--NICE AMBUSH IN THE ICE CREAM TRUCK YESTERDAY.* MADE ME REMEMBER HOW DANGEROUS YOU AND YOUR TINY LITTLE WINGS ARE.
SO A LITTLE BURST OF "TITANIA-BE-GONE™" IS DOUBTLESSLY IN ORDER!**
*DEADPOOL #44.
**A POWERFUL BIO-INHIBITOR DP USES TO BATTLE TITANIA. --TOM

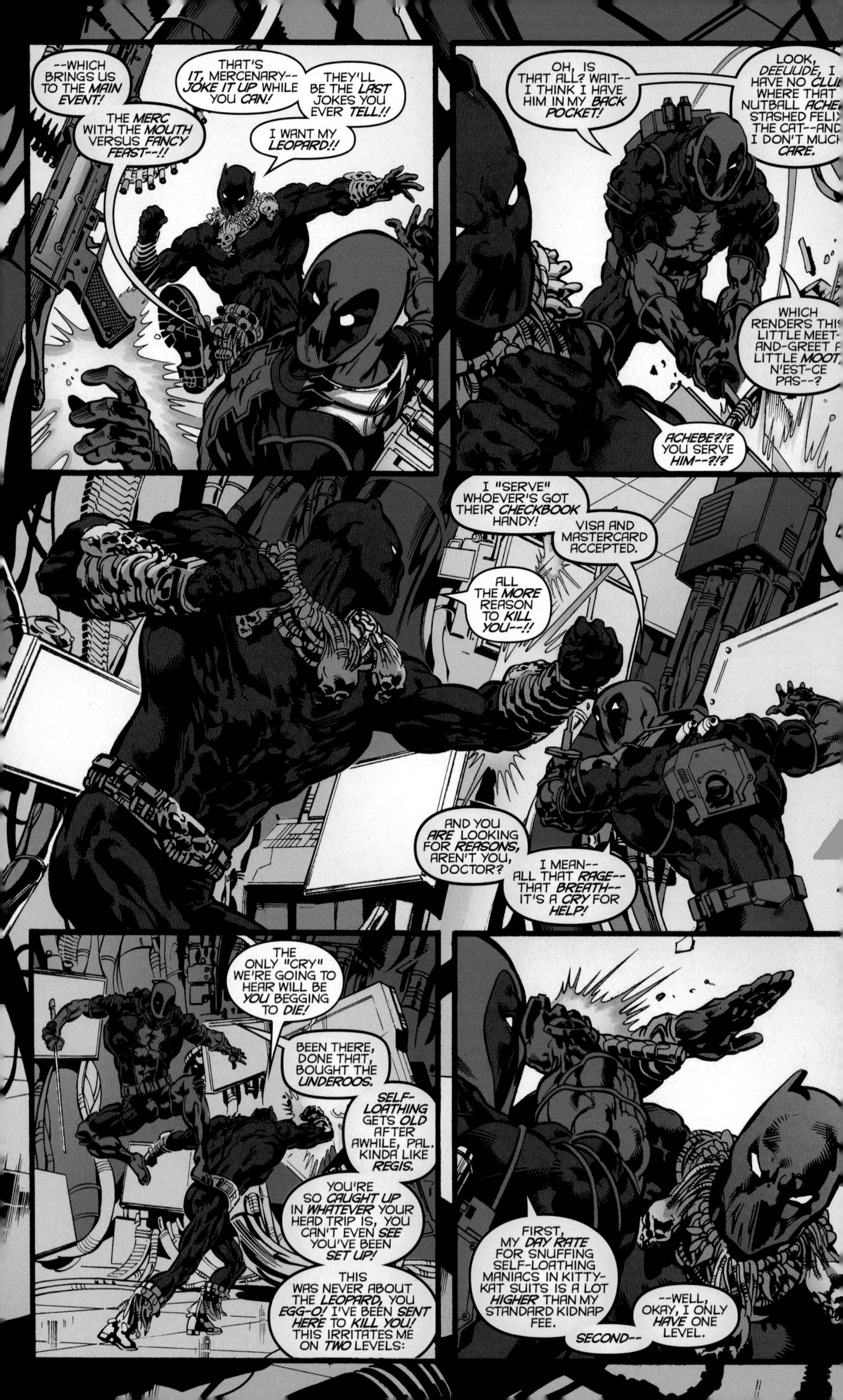
--WHICH BRINGS US TO THE MAIN EVENT!
THE MERC WITH THE MOUTH VERSUS FANCY FEAST--!!
THAT'S IT, MERCENARY-- JOKE IT UP WHILE YOU CAN!
THEY'LL BE THE LAST JOKES YOU EVER TELL!!
I WANT MY LEOPARD!!
OH, IS THAT ALL? WAIT-- I THINK I HAVE HIM IN MY BACK POCKET!
LOOK, DEEUUDE, I HAVE NO CLU WHERE THAT NUTBALL ACHE STASHED FELIX THE CAT--AND I DON'T MUCH CARE.
WHICH RENDERS THIS LITTLE MEET-AND-GREET A LITTLE MOOT, N'EST-CE PAS--?
ACHEBE?!? YOU SERVE HIM--?!?
I "SERVE" WHOEVER'S GOT THEIR CHECKBOOK HANDY!
VISA AND MASTERCARD ACCEPTED.
ALL THE MORE REASON TO KILL YOU--!!
AND YOU ARE LOOKING FOR REASONS, AREN'T YOU, DOCTOR?
I MEAN-- ALL THAT RAGE-- THAT BREATH-- IT'S A CRY FOR HELP!
THE ONLY "CRY" WE'RE GOING TO HEAR WILL BE YOU BEGGING TO DIE!
BEEN THERE, DONE THAT, BOUGHT THE UNDEROOS.
SELF-LOATHING GETS OLD AFTER AWHILE, PAL. KINDA LIKE REGIS.
YOU'RE SO CAUGHT UP IN WHATEVER YOUR HEAD TRIP IS, YOU CAN'T EVEN SEE YOU'VE BEEN SET UP!
THIS WAS NEVER ABOUT THE LEOPARD, YOU EGG-O! I'VE BEEN SENT HERE TO KILL YOU! THIS IRRITATES ME ON TWO LEVELS:
FIRST, MY DAY RATE FOR SNUFFING SELF-LOATHING MANIACS IN KITTY-KAT SUITS IS A LOT HIGHER THAN MY STANDARD KIDNAP FEE.
SECOND--
--WELL, OKAY, I ONLY HAVE ONE LEVEL.

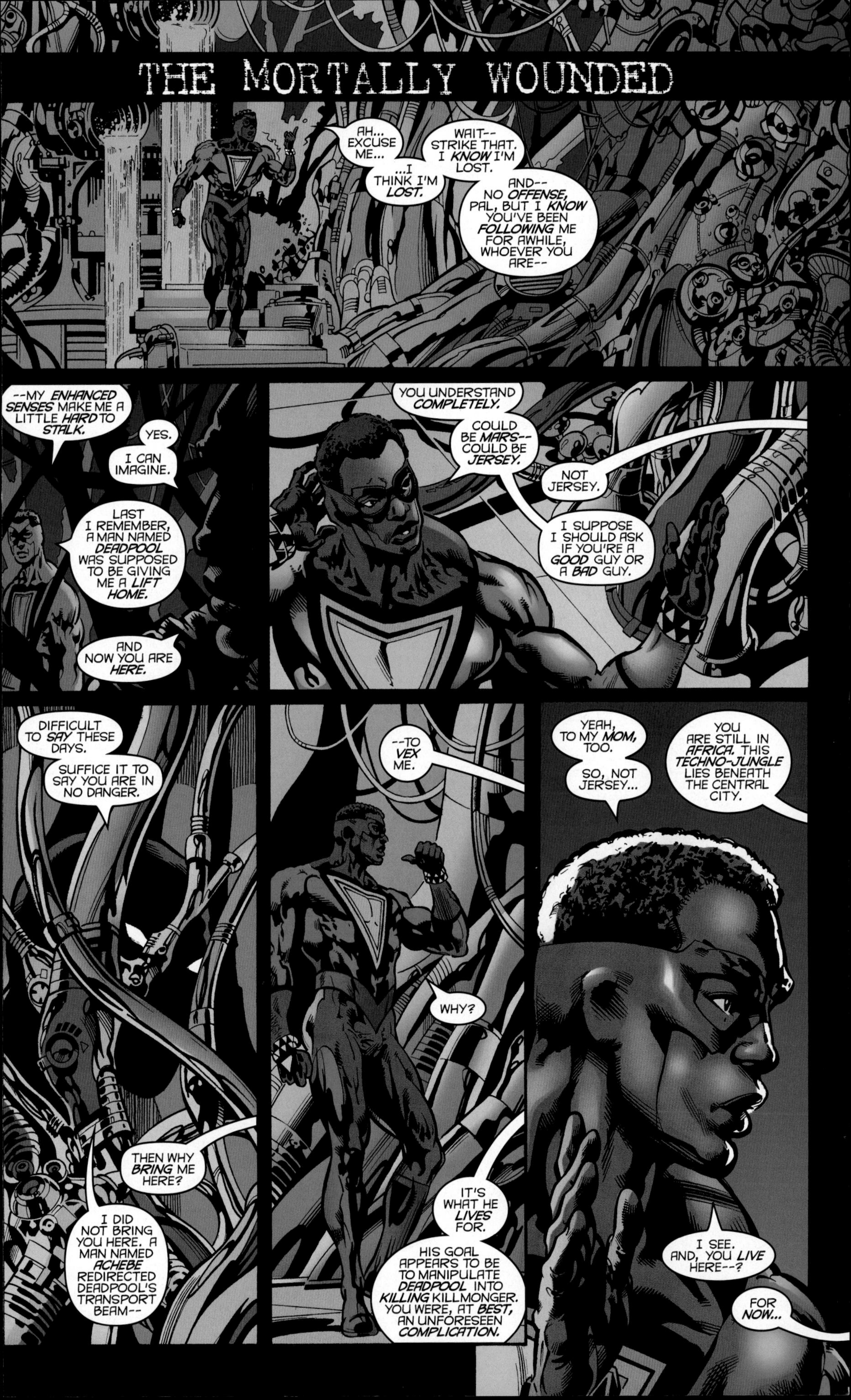
THE MORTALLY WOUNDED
AH... EXCUSE ME...
...I THINK I'M LOST.
WAIT-- STRIKE THAT. I KNOW I'M LOST.
AND-- NO OFFENSE, PAL, BUT I KNOW YOU'VE BEEN FOLLOWING ME FOR AWHILE, WHOEVER YOU ARE--
--MY ENHANCED SENSES MAKE ME A LITTLE HARD TO STALK.
YES.
I CAN IMAGINE.
LAST I REMEMBER, A MAN NAMED DEADPOOL WAS SUPPOSED TO BE GIVING ME A LIFT HOME.
AND NOW YOU ARE HERE.
YOU UNDERSTAND COMPLETELY.
COULD BE MARS-- COULD BE JERSEY.
NOT JERSEY.
I SUPPOSE I SHOULD ASK IF YOU'RE A GOOD GUY OR A BAD GUY.
DIFFICULT TO SAY THESE DAYS.
SUFFICE IT TO SAY YOU ARE IN NO DANGER.
THEN WHY BRING ME HERE?
I DID NOT BRING YOU HERE. A MAN NAMED ACHEBE REDIRECTED DEADPOOL'S TRANSPORT BEAM--
--TO VEX ME.
WHY?
IT'S WHAT HE LIVES FOR.
HIS GOAL APPEARS TO BE TO MANIPULATE DEADPOOL INTO KILLING KILLMONGER. YOU WERE, AT BEST, AN UNFORESEEN COMPLICATION.
YEAH, TO MY MOM, TOO.
SO, NOT JERSEY...
YOU ARE STILL IN AFRICA. THIS TECHNO-JUNGLE LIES BENEATH THE CENTRAL CITY.
I SEE. AND, YOU LIVE HERE--?
FOR NOW...

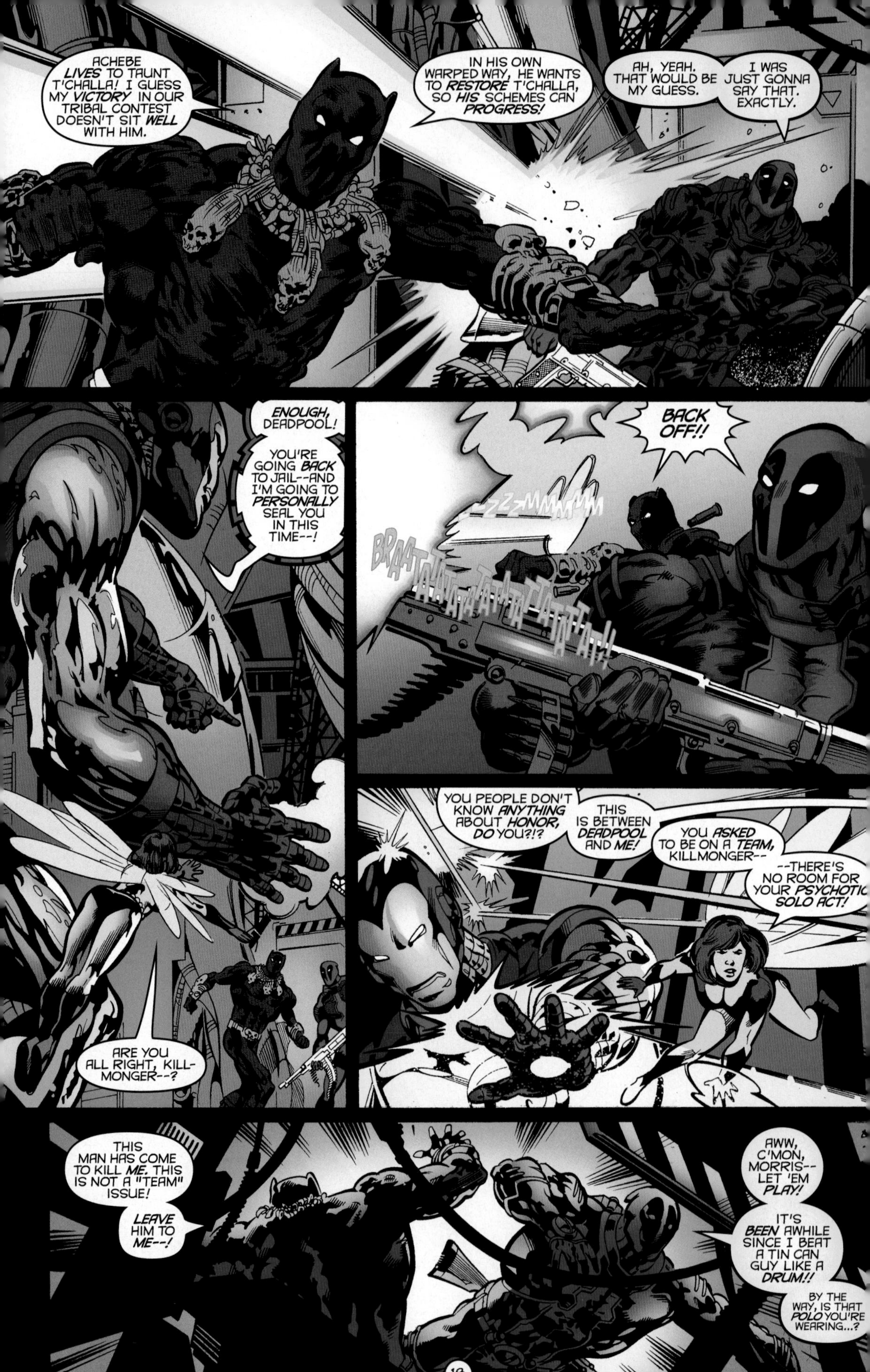
ACHEBE LIVES TO TAUNT T'CHALLA! I GUESS MY VICTORY IN OUR TRIBAL CONTEST DOESN'T SIT WELL WITH HIM.
IN HIS OWN WARPED WAY, HE WANTS TO RESTORE T'CHALLA, SO HIS SCHEMES CAN PROGRESS!
AH, YEAH. THAT WOULD BE MY GUESS.
I WAS JUST GONNA SAY THAT. EXACTLY.
ENOUGH, DEADPOOL!
YOU'RE GOING BACK TO JAIL--AND I'M GOING TO PERSONALLY SEAL YOU IN THIS TIME--!
BACK OFF!!
BRAATATATATATATATATATAT!!
ARE YOU ALL RIGHT, KILL-MONGER--?
YOU PEOPLE DON'T KNOW ANYTHING ABOUT HONOR, DO YOU?!?
THIS IS BETWEEN DEADPOOL AND ME!
YOU ASKED TO BE ON A TEAM, KILLMONGER--
--THERE'S NO ROOM FOR YOUR PSYCHOTIC SOLO ACT!
THIS MAN HAS COME TO KILL ME. THIS IS NOT A "TEAM" ISSUE!
LEAVE HIM TO ME--!
AWW, C'MON, MORRIS-- LET 'EM PLAY!
IT'S BEEN AWHILE SINCE I BEAT A TIN CAN GUY LIKE A DRUM!!
BY THE WAY, IS THAT POLO YOU'RE WEARING...?

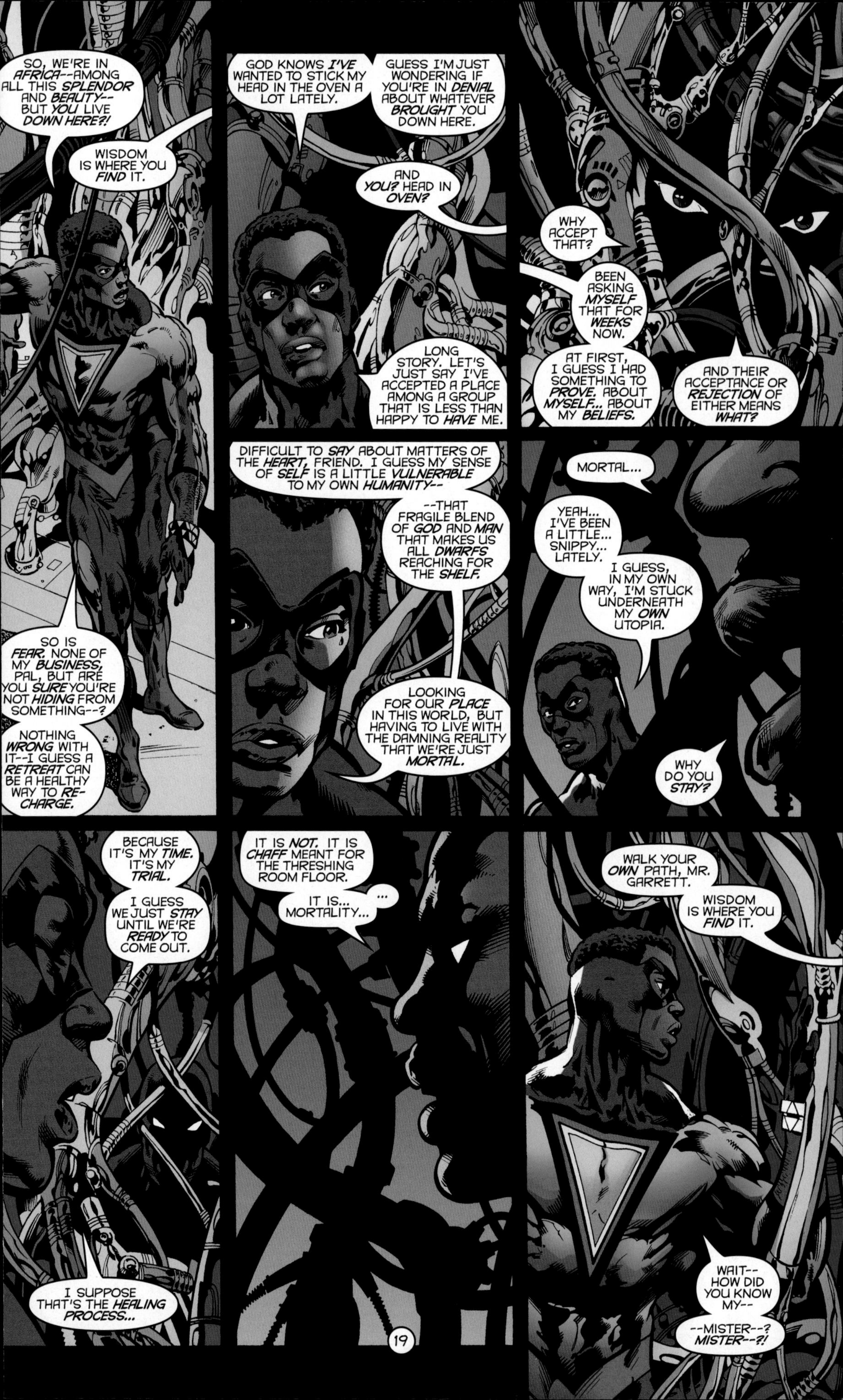

SO, WE'RE IN AFRICA--AMONG ALL THIS SPLENDOR AND BEAUTY--BUT YOU LIVE DOWN HERE?!
WISDOM IS WHERE YOU FIND IT.
SO IS FEAR. NONE OF MY BUSINESS, PAL, BUT ARE YOU SURE YOU'RE NOT HIDING FROM SOMETHING--?
NOTHING WRONG WITH IT--I GUESS A RETREAT CAN BE A HEALTHY WAY TO RE-CHARGE.
GOD KNOWS I'VE WANTED TO STICK MY HEAD IN THE OVEN A LOT LATELY.
GUESS I'M JUST WONDERING IF YOU'RE IN DENIAL ABOUT WHATEVER BROUGHT YOU DOWN HERE.
AND YOU? HEAD IN OVEN?
LONG STORY. LET'S JUST SAY I'VE ACCEPTED A PLACE AMONG A GROUP THAT IS LESS THAN HAPPY TO HAVE ME.
WHY ACCEPT THAT?
BEEN ASKING MYSELF THAT FOR WEEKS NOW.
AT FIRST, I GUESS I HAD SOMETHING TO PROVE. ABOUT MYSELF... ABOUT MY BELIEFS.
AND THEIR ACCEPTANCE OR REJECTION OF EITHER MEANS WHAT?
DIFFICULT TO SAY ABOUT MATTERS OF THE HEART, FRIEND. I GUESS MY SENSE OF SELF IS A LITTLE VULNERABLE TO MY OWN HUMANITY--
--THAT FRAGILE BLEND OF GOD AND MAN THAT MAKES US ALL DWARFS REACHING FOR THE SHELF.
LOOKING FOR OUR PLACE IN THIS WORLD, BUT HAVING TO LIVE WITH THE DAMNING REALITY THAT WE'RE JUST MORTAL.
MORTAL...
YEAH... I'VE BEEN A LITTLE... SNIPPY... LATELY.
I GUESS, IN MY OWN WAY, I'M STUCK UNDERNEATH MY OWN UTOPIA.
WHY DO YOU STAY?
BECAUSE IT'S MY TIME. IT'S MY TRIAL.
I GUESS WE JUST STAY UNTIL WE'RE READY TO COME OUT.
I SUPPOSE THAT'S THE HEALING PROCESS...
IT IS NOT. IT IS CHAFF MEANT FOR THE THRESHING ROOM FLOOR.
IT IS... MORTALITY...
...
WALK YOUR OWN PATH, MR. GARRETT.
WISDOM IS WHERE YOU FIND IT.
WAIT--HOW DID YOU KNOW MY--
--MISTER--? MISTER--?!

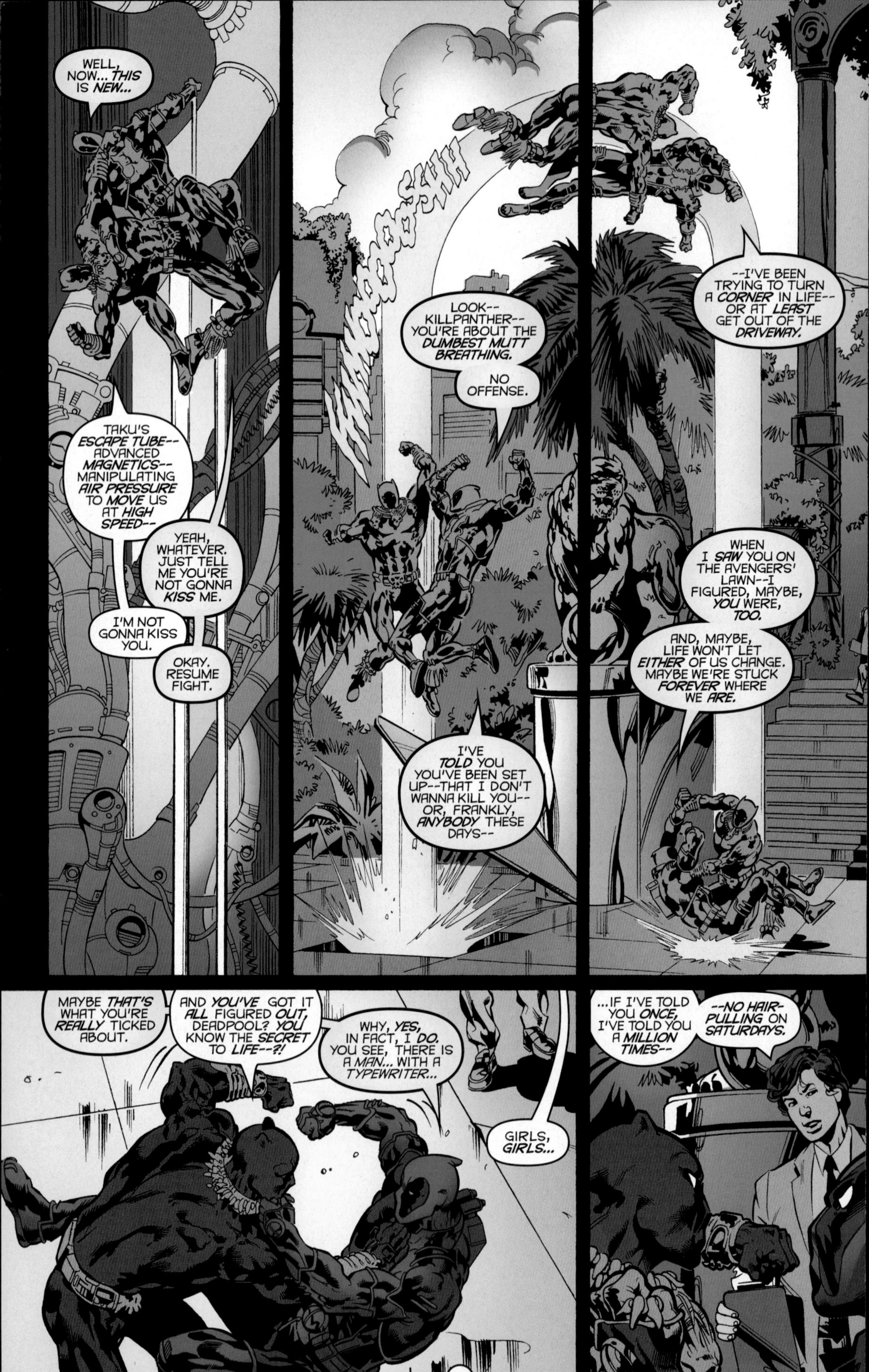
WELL, NOW... THIS IS NEW...
TAKU'S ESCAPE TUBE-- ADVANCED MAGNETICS-- MANIPULATING AIR PRESSURE TO MOVE US AT HIGH SPEED--
YEAH, WHATEVER. JUST TELL ME YOU'RE NOT GONNA KISS ME.
I'M NOT GONNA KISS YOU.
OKAY. RESUME FIGHT.
FWOOOOSSHH
LOOK-- KILLPANTHER-- YOU'RE ABOUT THE DUMBEST MUTT BREATHING.
NO OFFENSE.
I'VE TOLD YOU YOU'VE BEEN SET UP--THAT I DON'T WANNA KILL YOU-- OR, FRANKLY, ANYBODY THESE DAYS--
--I'VE BEEN TRYING TO TURN A CORNER IN LIFE-- OR AT LEAST GET OUT OF THE DRIVEWAY.
WHEN I SAW YOU ON THE AVENGERS' LAWN--I FIGURED, MAYBE, YOU WERE, TOO.
AND, MAYBE, LIFE WON'T LET EITHER OF US CHANGE. MAYBE WE'RE STUCK FOREVER WHERE WE ARE.
MAYBE THAT'S WHAT YOU'RE REALLY TICKED ABOUT.
AND YOU'VE GOT IT ALL FIGURED OUT, DEADPOOL? YOU KNOW THE SECRET TO LIFE--?!
WHY, YES, IN FACT, I DO. YOU SEE, THERE IS A MAN... WITH A TYPEWRITER...
GIRLS, GIRLS...
...IF I'VE TOLD YOU ONCE, I'VE TOLD YOU A MILLION TIMES--
--NO HAIR-PULLING ON SATURDAYS.

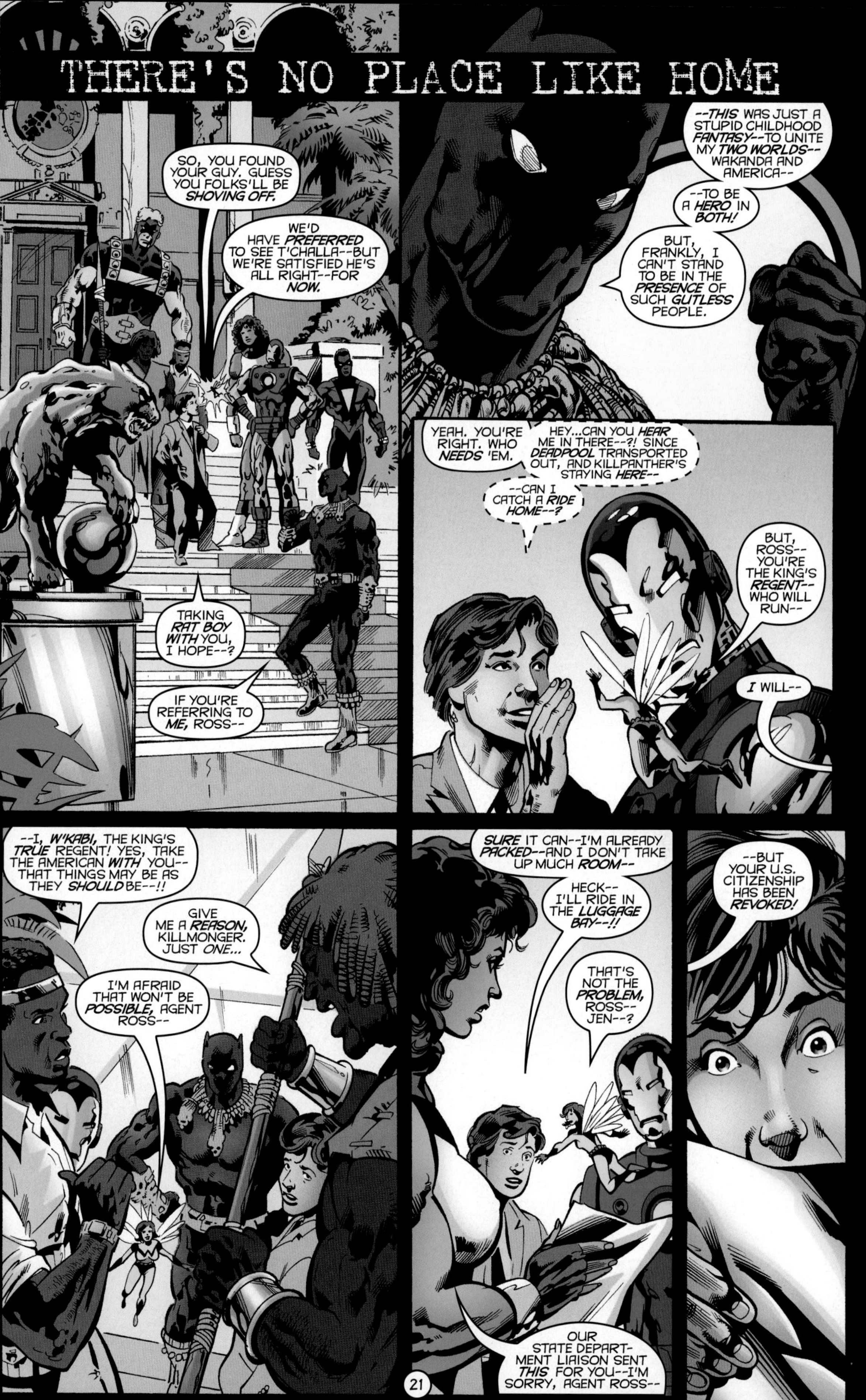
THERE'S NO PLACE LIKE HOME
SO, YOU FOUND YOUR GUY. GUESS YOU FOLKS'LL BE SHOVING OFF.
WE'D HAVE PREFERRED TO SEE T'CHALLA--BUT WE'RE SATISFIED HE'S ALL RIGHT--FOR NOW.
TAKING RAT BOY WITH YOU, I HOPE--?
IF YOU'RE REFERRING TO ME, ROSS--
--THIS WAS JUST A STUPID CHILDHOOD FANTASY--TO UNITE MY TWO WORLDS--WAKANDA AND AMERICA--
--TO BE A HERO IN BOTH!
BUT, FRANKLY, I CAN'T STAND TO BE IN THE PRESENCE OF SUCH GUTLESS PEOPLE.
YEAH. YOU'RE RIGHT. WHO NEEDS 'EM.
HEY...CAN YOU HEAR ME IN THERE--?! SINCE DEADPOOL TRANSPORTED OUT, AND KILLPANTHER'S STAYING HERE--
--CAN I CATCH A RIDE HOME--?
BUT, ROSS--YOU'RE THE KING'S REGENT--WHO WILL RUN--
I WILL--
--I, W'KABI, THE KING'S TRUE REGENT! YES, TAKE THE AMERICAN WITH YOU--THAT THINGS MAY BE AS THEY SHOULD BE--!!
GIVE ME A REASON, KILLMONGER. JUST ONE...
I'M AFRAID THAT WON'T BE POSSIBLE, AGENT ROSS--
SURE IT CAN--I'M ALREADY PACKED--AND I DON'T TAKE UP MUCH ROOM--
HECK--I'LL RIDE IN THE LUGGAGE BAY--!!
THAT'S NOT THE PROBLEM, ROSS--JEN--?
OUR STATE DEPARTMENT LIAISON SENT THIS FOR YOU--I'M SORRY, AGENT ROSS--
--BUT YOUR U.S. CITIZENSHIP HAS BEEN REVOKED!

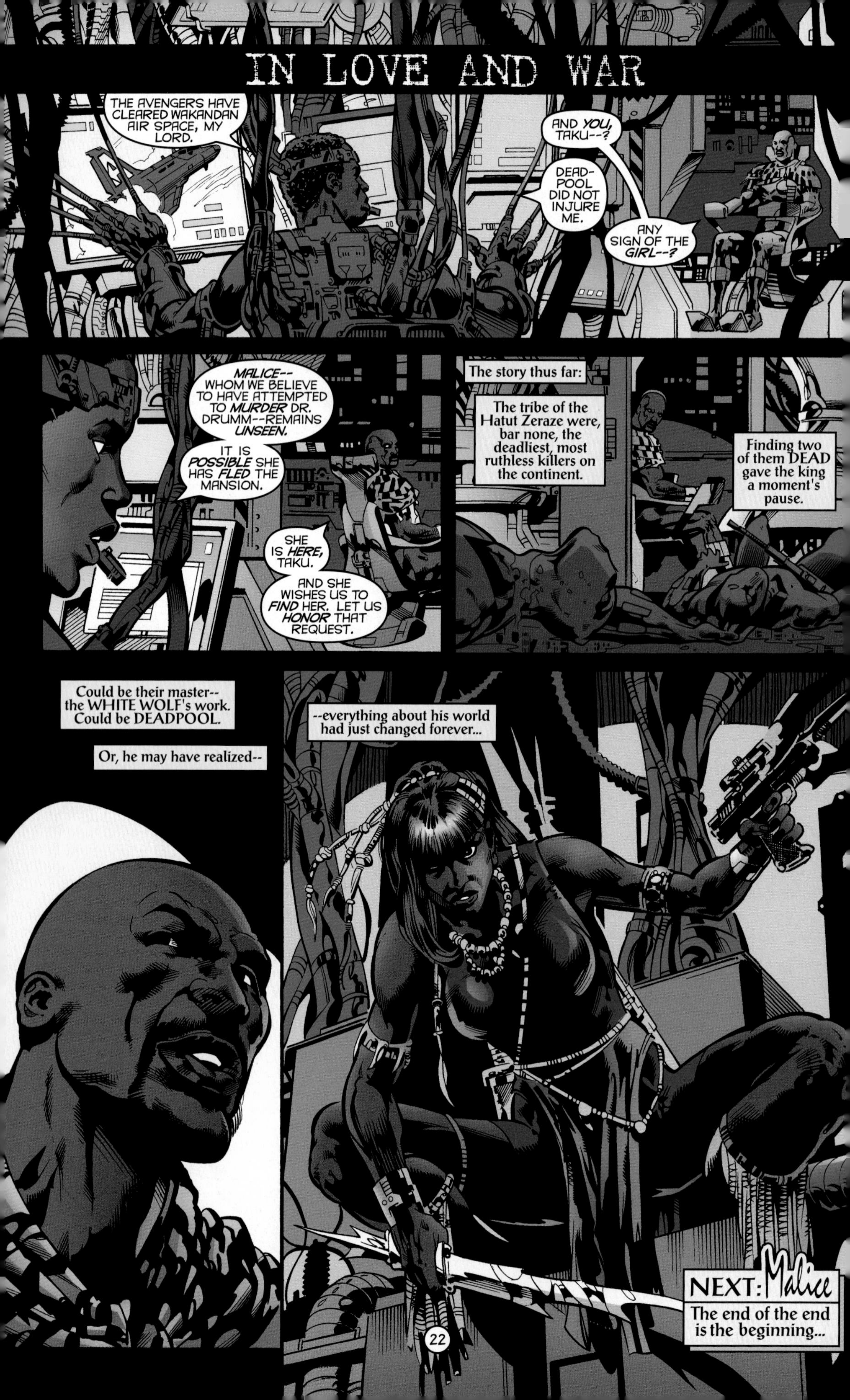
IN LOVE AND WAR
THE AVENGERS HAVE CLEARED WAKANDAN AIR SPACE, MY LORD.
AND YOU, TAKU--?
DEAD-POOL DID NOT INJURE ME.
ANY SIGN OF THE GIRL--?
MALICE-- WHOM WE BELIEVE TO HAVE ATTEMPTED TO MURDER DR. DRUMM--REMAINS UNSEEN.
IT IS POSSIBLE SHE HAS FLED THE MANSION.
SHE IS HERE, TAKU.
AND SHE WISHES US TO FIND HER. LET US HONOR THAT REQUEST.
The story thus far:
The tribe of the Hatut Zeraze were, bar none, the deadliest, most ruthless killers on the continent.
Finding two of them DEAD gave the king a moment's pause.
Could be their master-- the WHITE WOLF's work. Could be DEADPOOL.
Or, he may have realized--
--everything about his world had just changed forever...
NEXT: Malice
The end of the end is the beginning...

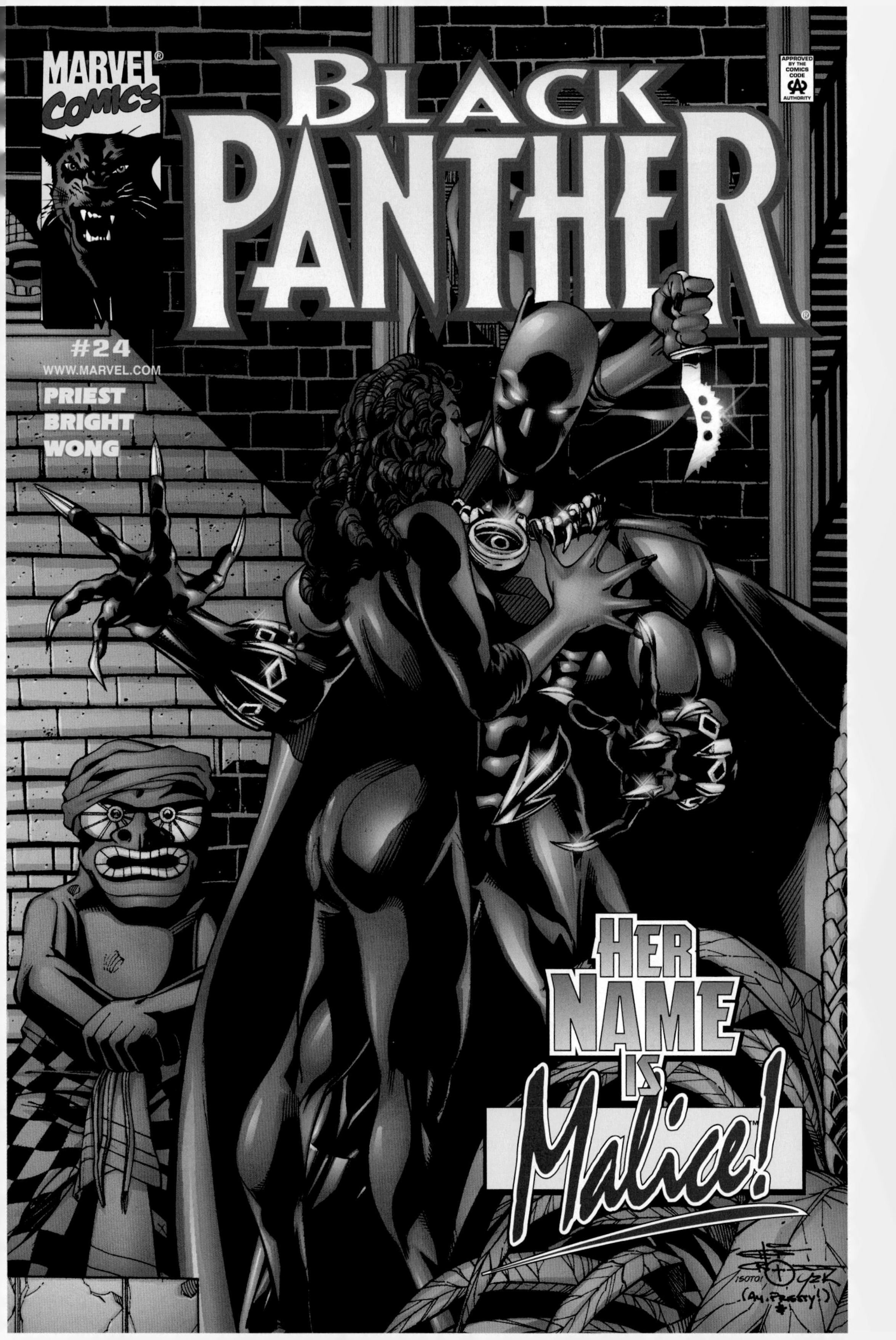
MARVEL COMICS
APPROVED BY THE COMICS CODE AUTHORITY
BLACK PANTHER
#24
WWW.MARVEL.COM
PRIEST
BRIGHT
WONG
HER NAME IS Malice!

FRIENDS

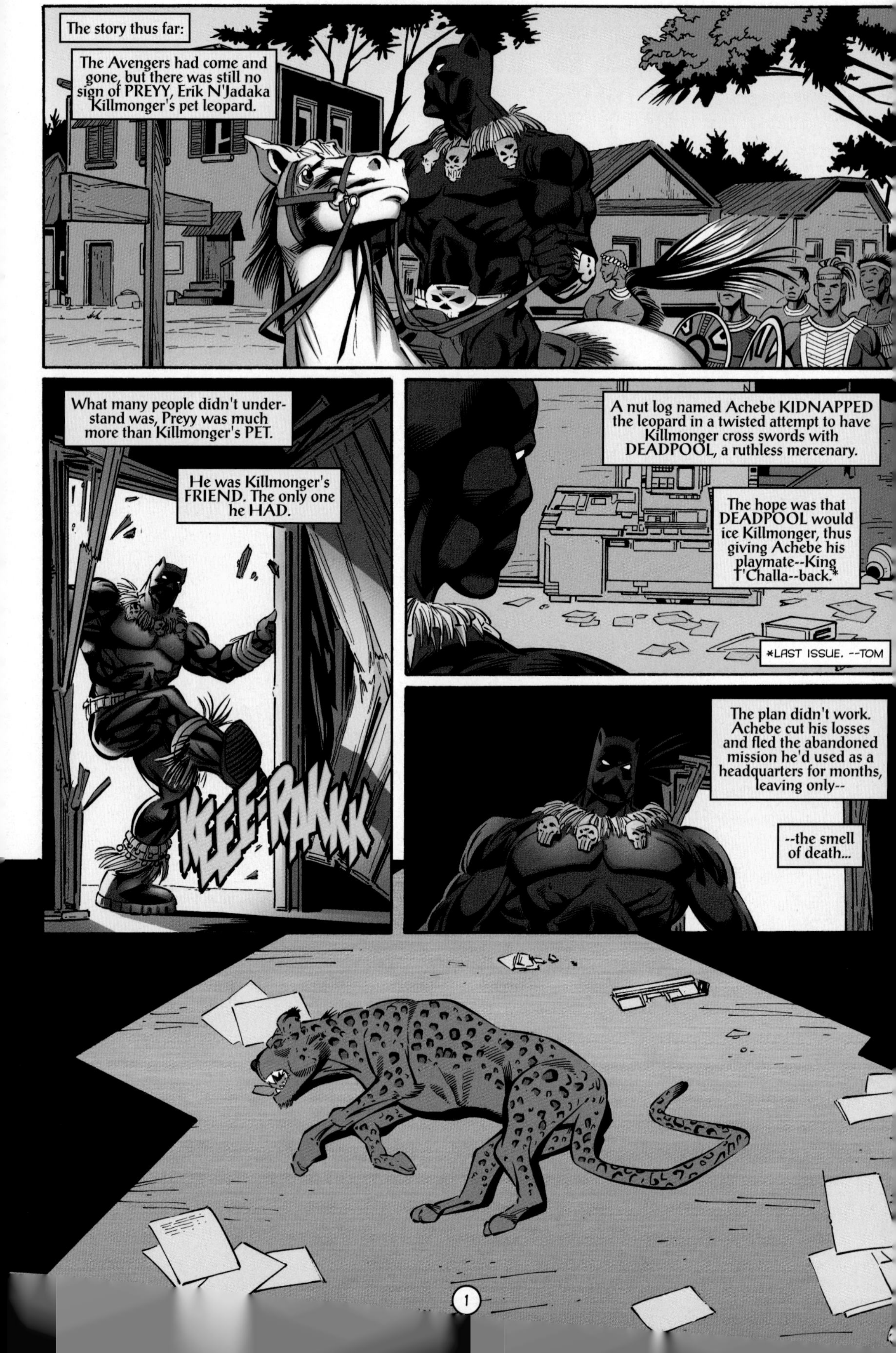

The story thus far:
The Avengers had come and gone, but there was still no sign of PREYY, Erik N'Jadaka Killmonger's pet leopard.
What many people didn't understand was, Preyy was much more than Killmonger's PET.
He was Killmonger's FRIEND. The only one he HAD.
KEEE-RAKKK
A nut log named Achebe KIDNAPPED the leopard in a twisted attempt to have Killmonger cross swords with DEADPOOL, a ruthless mercenary.
The hope was that DEADPOOL would ice Killmonger, thus giving Achebe his playmate--King T'Challa--back.*
*LAST ISSUE. --TOM
The plan didn't work. Achebe cut his losses and fled the abandoned mission he'd used as a headquarters for months, leaving only--
--the smell of death...

MAMA MIA

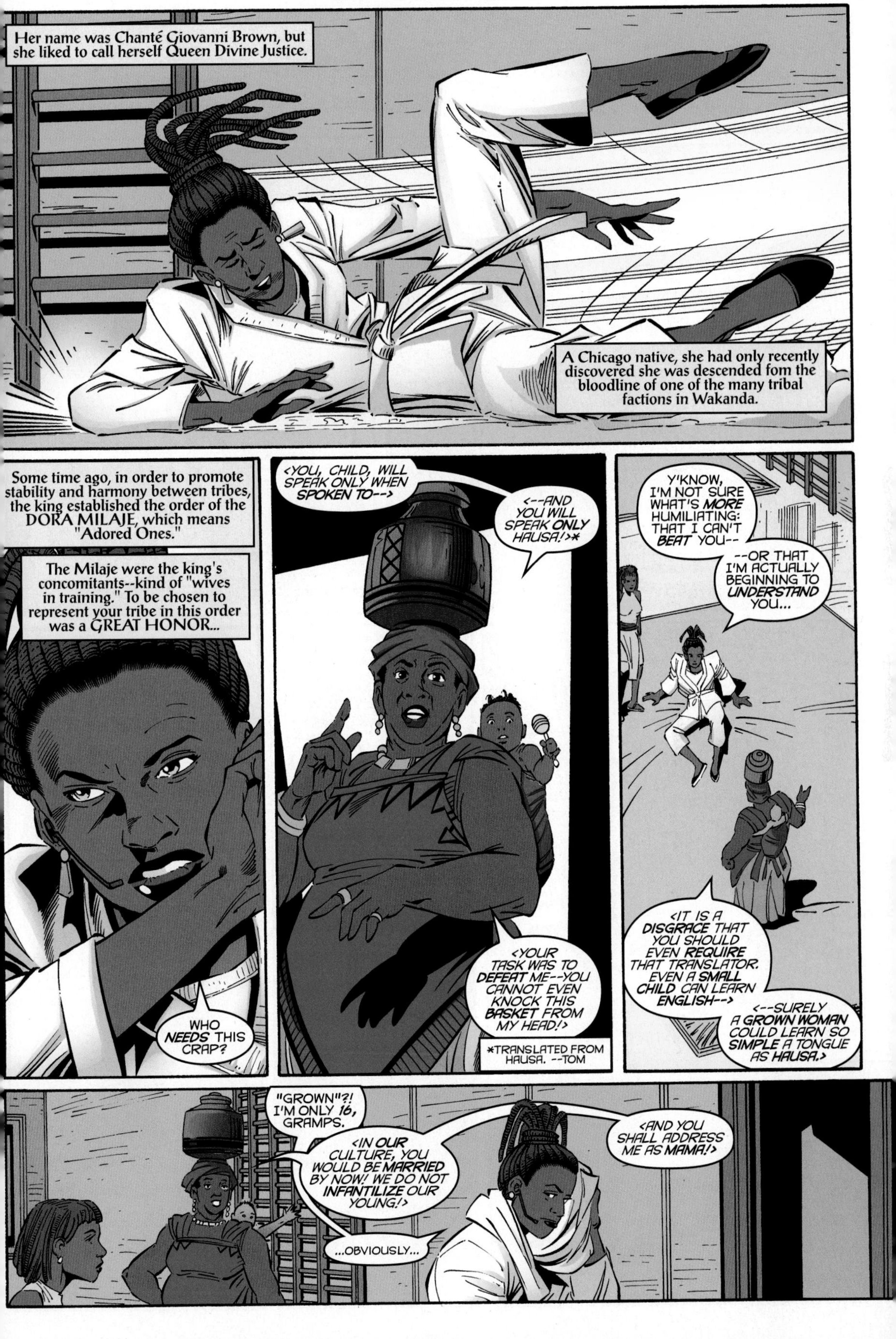
Her name was Chanté Giovanni Brown, but she liked to call herself Queen Divine Justice.
A Chicago native, she had only recently discovered she was descended fom the bloodline of one of the many tribal factions in Wakanda.
Some time ago, in order to promote stability and harmony between tribes, the king established the order of the DORA MILAJE, which means "Adored Ones."
The Milaje were the king's concomitants--kind of "wives in training." To be chosen to represent your tribe in this order was a GREAT HONOR...
WHO NEEDS THIS CRAP?
<YOU, CHILD, WILL SPEAK ONLY WHEN SPOKEN TO-->
<--AND YOU WILL SPEAK ONLY HAUSA!>*
<YOUR TASK WAS TO DEFEAT ME--YOU CANNOT EVEN KNOCK THIS BASKET FROM MY HEAD!>
*TRANSLATED FROM HAUSA. --TOM
Y'KNOW, I'M NOT SURE WHAT'S MORE HUMILIATING: THAT I CAN'T BEAT YOU--
--OR THAT I'M ACTUALLY BEGINNING TO UNDERSTAND YOU...
<IT IS A DISGRACE THAT YOU SHOULD EVEN REQUIRE THAT TRANSLATOR. EVEN A SMALL CHILD CAN LEARN ENGLISH-->
<--SURELY A GROWN WOMAN COULD LEARN SO SIMPLE A TONGUE AS HAUSA.>
"GROWN"?! I'M ONLY 16, GRAMPS.
<IN OUR CULTURE, YOU WOULD BE MARRIED BY NOW! WE DO NOT INFANTILIZE OUR YOUNG!>
<AND YOU SHALL ADDRESS ME AS MAMA!>
...OBVIOUSLY...

GOD, D'WON, WHAT *IS* HER DAMAGE?!

<MAMA *LOVES* YOU, CHANTÉ-- SHE'S THINKING ONLY OF YOUR *BEST* INTERESTS.>

SO, SHE'S KIND OF A O.G. PIMP ROUGH NECK GRAMMA--?

<I DO NOT UNDERSTAND YOUR REFERENCE...>

SKIP IT.

LET'S SEE...DO I FEEL LIKE *TRIBAL* OR *TRIBAL*--?

WHOSE CLOSET AM I DIGGING THROUGH--?

<YOURS. YOU WILL FIND THEY ARE *ALL* IN YOUR *SIZE*-->

REALLY--? WELL--I MAY HAVE FOUND SOMETHING I *LIKE*--

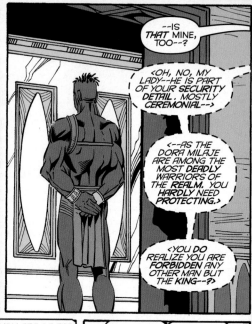

--IS *THAT* MINE, TOO--?

<OH, NO, MY LADY--HE IS PART OF YOUR *SECURITY DETAIL.* MOSTLY *CEREMONIAL*-->

<--AS THE *DORA MILAJE* ARE AMONG THE MOST *DEADLY* WARRIORS OF THE *REALM.* YOU *HARDLY* NEED PROTECTING.>

<YOU *DO* REALIZE YOU ARE *FORBIDDEN* ANY OTHER MAN BUT THE *KING*--?>

THE *KING?!* BUT, HE'S *OLD*-- *WAY* OVER 30! WHEN I SIGNED UP FOR THIS, I WAS TOLD THERE WOULD BE NO KINKY STUFF.

<THE *KING* WILL NOT MAKE ANY DEMANDS OF YOU, THOUGH IT IS HIS *RIGHT.*>

HE HAS "RIGHTS" TO TEENAGE GIRLS--?!?

<IN *AFRICA,* YOU ARE OF *AGE,* ELIGIBLE FOR MARRIAGE AND CHILDBEARING.>

IN MANY CULTURES, GIRLS OUR AGE ARE GIVEN INTO VIRTUAL *SLAVERY* TO CHIEFTAINS AND PRIESTS.>

<BUT THE *KING* HAS SHOWN US *MERCY*...>

WHATEVER.

HEY... NOW *HERE'S* AN IDEA...

Y'KNOW, WITH A LITTLE BIT OF *WORK*--WE MIGHT ACTUALLY BE *ONTO* SOMETHING HERE...

KING ROSS GETS DUMPED

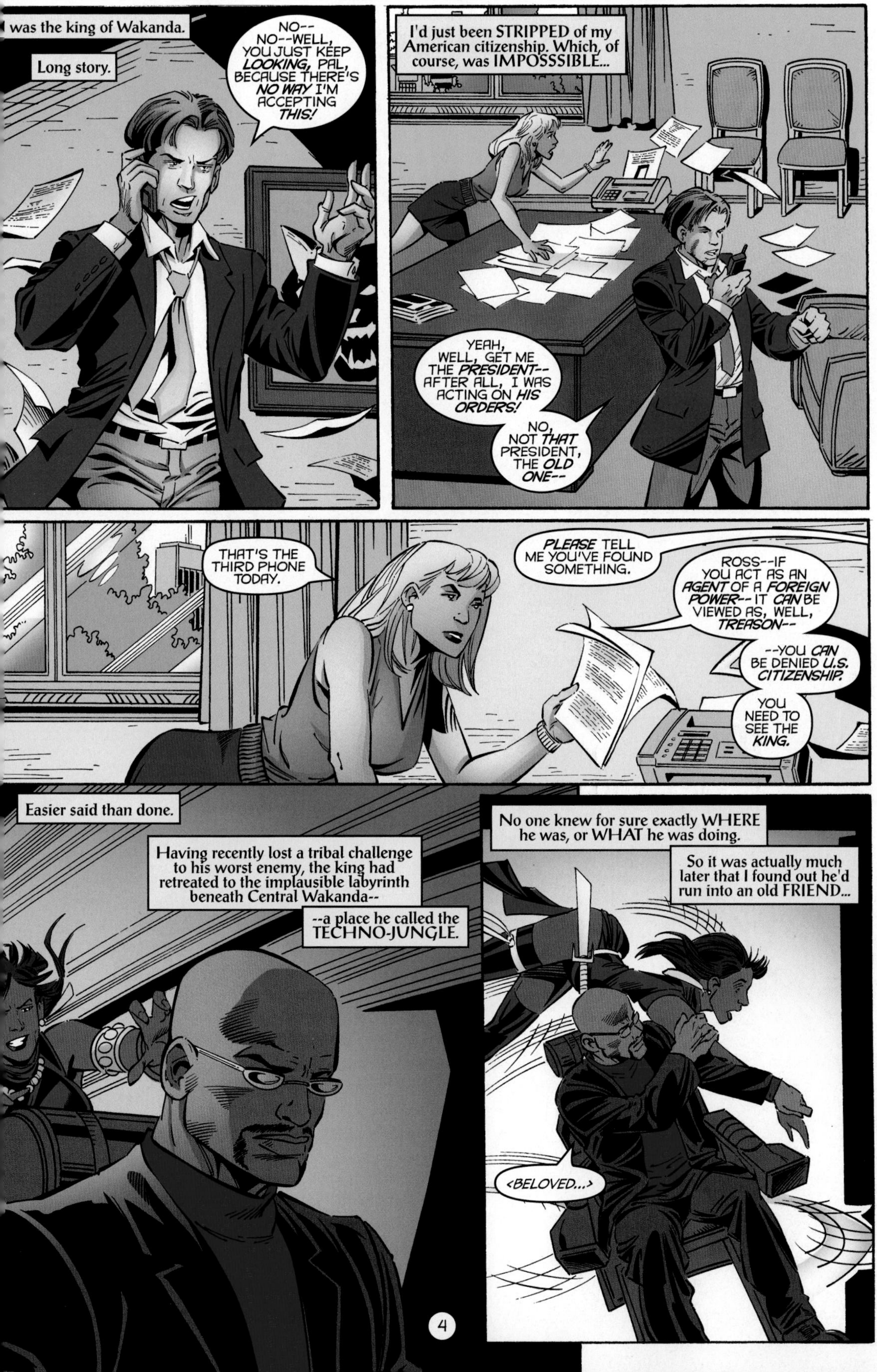

was the king of Wakanda.
Long story.
NO-- NO--WELL, YOU JUST KEEP LOOKING, PAL, BECAUSE THERE'S NO WAY I'M ACCEPTING THIS!
I'd just been STRIPPED of my American citizenship. Which, of course, was IMPOSSSIBLE...
YEAH, WELL, GET ME THE PRESIDENT-- AFTER ALL, I WAS ACTING ON HIS ORDERS!
NO, NOT THAT PRESIDENT, THE OLD ONE--
THAT'S THE THIRD PHONE TODAY.
PLEASE TELL ME YOU'VE FOUND SOMETHING.
ROSS--IF YOU ACT AS AN AGENT OF A FOREIGN POWER-- IT CAN BE VIEWED AS, WELL, TREASON--
--YOU CAN BE DENIED U.S. CITIZENSHIP.
YOU NEED TO SEE THE KING.
Easier said than done.
Having recently lost a tribal challenge to his worst enemy, the king had retreated to the implausible labyrinth beneath Central Wakanda--
--a place he called the TECHNO-JUNGLE.
No one knew for sure exactly WHERE he was, or WHAT he was doing.
So it was actually much later that I found out he'd run into an old FRIEND...
<BELOVED...>

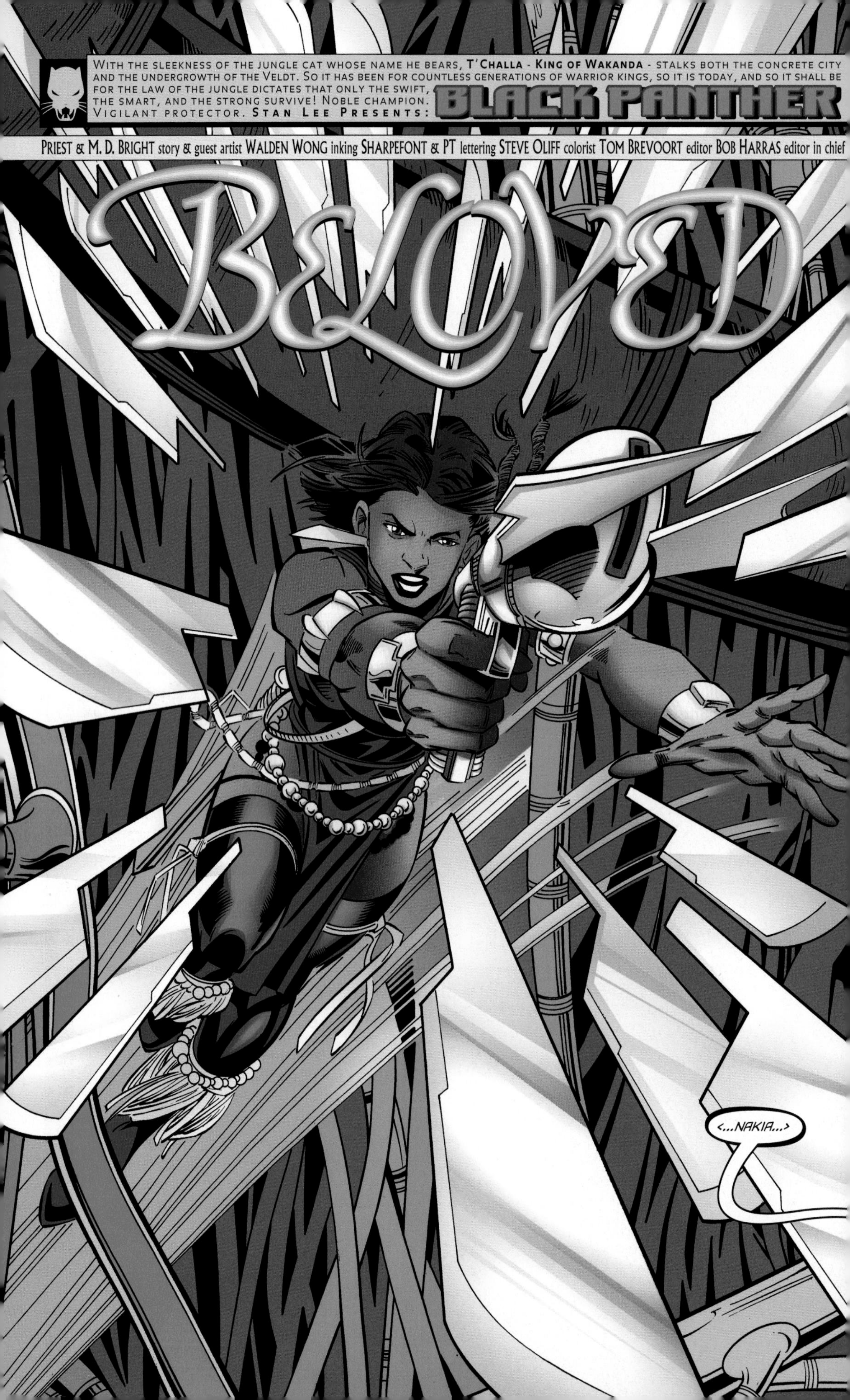
WITH THE SLEEKNESS OF THE JUNGLE CAT WHOSE NAME HE BEARS, T'CHALLA - KING OF WAKANDA - STALKS BOTH THE CONCRETE CITY AND THE UNDERGROWTH OF THE VELDT. SO IT HAS BEEN FOR COUNTLESS GENERATIONS OF WARRIOR KINGS, SO IT IS TODAY, AND SO IT SHALL BE FOR THE LAW OF THE JUNGLE DICTATES THAT ONLY THE SWIFT, THE SMART, AND THE STRONG SURVIVE! NOBLE CHAMPION. VIGILANT PROTECTOR. STAN LEE PRESENTS:
BLACK PANTHER
PRIEST & M. D. BRIGHT story & guest artist WALDEN WONG inking SHARPEFONT & PT lettering STEVE OLIFF colorist TOM BREVOORT editor BOB HARRAS editor in chief
BELOVED
<...NAKIA...>

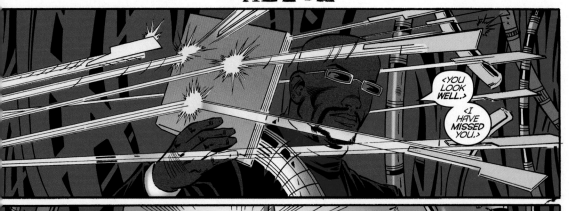

<YOU LOOK WELL.>

<I HAVE MISSED YOU.>

K-KRAKK!!

<AS I'VE MISSED YOU, MY LORD...>

<...MY KING....>

<...MY LOVE.>

<I HAVE SINNED AGAINST YOU, MY LORD.>

<I INTEND TO GO ON SINNING.>

<UNTIL YOU ARE FINALLY MINE AND MINE ALONE.>

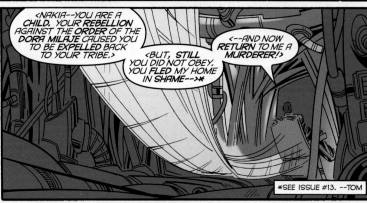

<NAKIA--YOU ARE A CHILD. YOUR REBELLION AGAINST THE ORDER OF THE DORA MILAJE CAUSED YOU TO BE EXPELLED BACK TO YOUR TRIBE.>

<BUT, STILL YOU DID NOT OBEY. YOU FLED MY HOME IN SHAME--*>

<--AND NOW RETURN TO ME A MURDERER!>

*SEE ISSUE #13. --TOM

<HUNTER'S MEN--THE HATUT ZERAZE--ARE NOT TO BE TRUSTED. YOU TAUGHT ME THAT, MY LORD!>

<NEITHER, APPARENTLY, IS YOUR AMERICAN REGENT--WHO HAS FREED THE WHITE WOLF!>

<SMALL MATTER--I KILLED THE WHITE WOLF'S MEN-- AND SO SHALL HE ALSO DIE AT THE HANDS OF-->

--Malice!

6

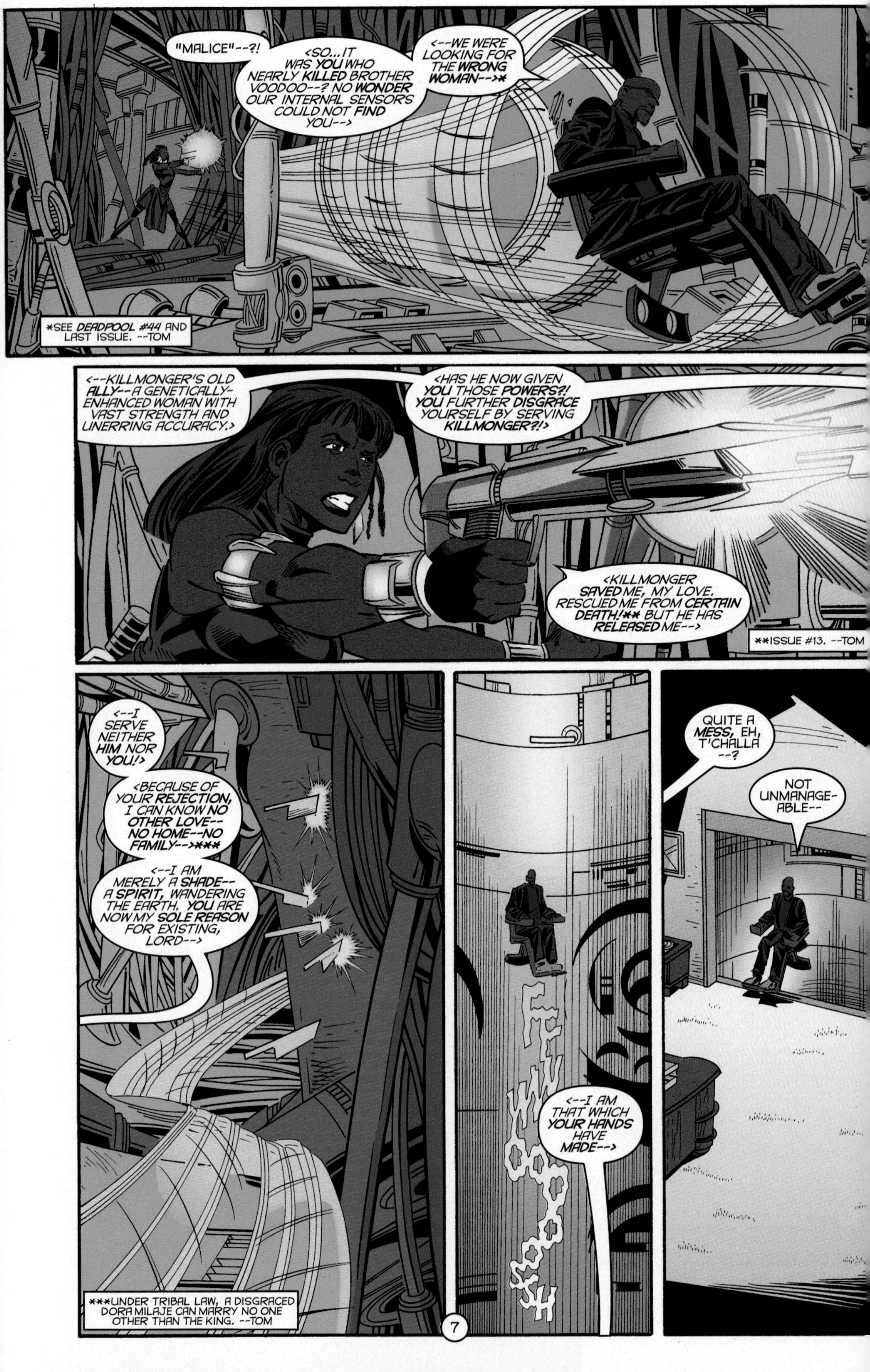
"MALICE"--?!
<SO...IT WAS YOU WHO NEARLY KILLED BROTHER VOODOO--? NO WONDER OUR INTERNAL SENSORS COULD NOT FIND YOU-->
<--WE WERE LOOKING FOR THE WRONG WOMAN-->*
*SEE DEADPOOL #44 AND LAST ISSUE. --TOM
<--KILLMONGER'S OLD ALLY--A GENETICALLY-ENHANCED WOMAN WITH VAST STRENGTH AND UNERRING ACCURACY.>
<HAS HE NOW GIVEN YOU THOSE POWERS?! YOU FURTHER DISGRACE YOURSELF BY SERVING KILLMONGER?!>
<KILLMONGER SAVED ME, MY LOVE. RESCUED ME FROM CERTAIN DEATH!** BUT HE HAS RELEASED ME-->
**ISSUE #13. --TOM
<--I SERVE NEITHER HIM NOR YOU!>
<BECAUSE OF YOUR REJECTION, I CAN KNOW NO OTHER LOVE--NO HOME--NO FAMILY-->***
<--I AM MERELY A SHADE--A SPIRIT, WANDERING THE EARTH. YOU ARE NOW MY SOLE REASON FOR EXISTING, LORD-->
***UNDER TRIBAL LAW, A DISGRACED DORA MILAJE CAN MARRY NO ONE OTHER THAN THE KING. --TOM
<--I AM THAT WHICH YOUR HANDS HAVE MADE-->
QUITE A MESS, EH, T'CHALLA--?
NOT UNMANAGE-ABLE--

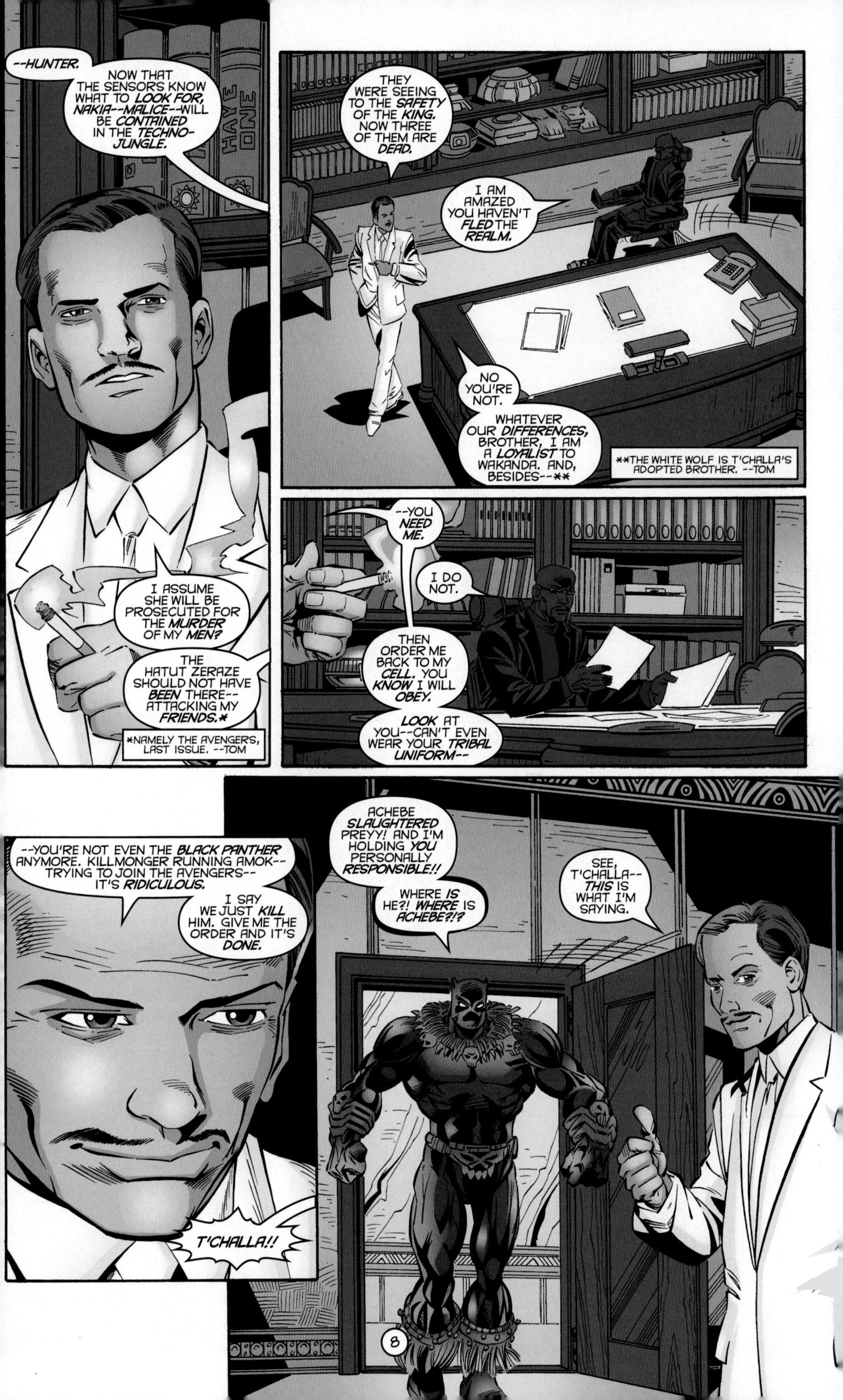

--HUNTER.
NOW THAT THE SENSORS KNOW WHAT TO LOOK FOR, NAKIA--MALICE--WILL BE CONTAINED IN THE TECHNO-JUNGLE.
I ASSUME SHE WILL BE PROSECUTED FOR THE MURDER OF MY MEN?
THE HATUT ZERAZE SHOULD NOT HAVE BEEN THERE--ATTACKING MY FRIENDS.*
*NAMELY THE AVENGERS, LAST ISSUE. --TOM
THEY WERE SEEING TO THE SAFETY OF THE KING. NOW THREE OF THEM ARE DEAD.
I AM AMAZED YOU HAVEN'T FLED THE REALM.
NO YOU'RE NOT.
WHATEVER OUR DIFFERENCES, BROTHER, I AM A LOYALIST TO WAKANDA. AND, BESIDES--**
**THE WHITE WOLF IS T'CHALLA'S ADOPTED BROTHER. --TOM
--YOU NEED ME.
I DO NOT.
THEN ORDER ME BACK TO MY CELL. YOU KNOW I WILL OBEY.
LOOK AT YOU--CAN'T EVEN WEAR YOUR TRIBAL UNIFORM--
--YOU'RE NOT EVEN THE BLACK PANTHER ANYMORE. KILLMONGER RUNNING AMOK--TRYING TO JOIN THE AVENGERS--IT'S RIDICULOUS.
I SAY WE JUST KILL HIM. GIVE ME THE ORDER AND IT'S DONE.
T'CHALLA!!
ACHEBE SLAUGHTERED PREYY! AND I'M HOLDING YOU PERSONALLY RESPONSIBLE!!
WHERE IS HE?! WHERE IS ACHEBE?!?
SEE, T'CHALLA--THIS IS WHAT I'M SAYING.

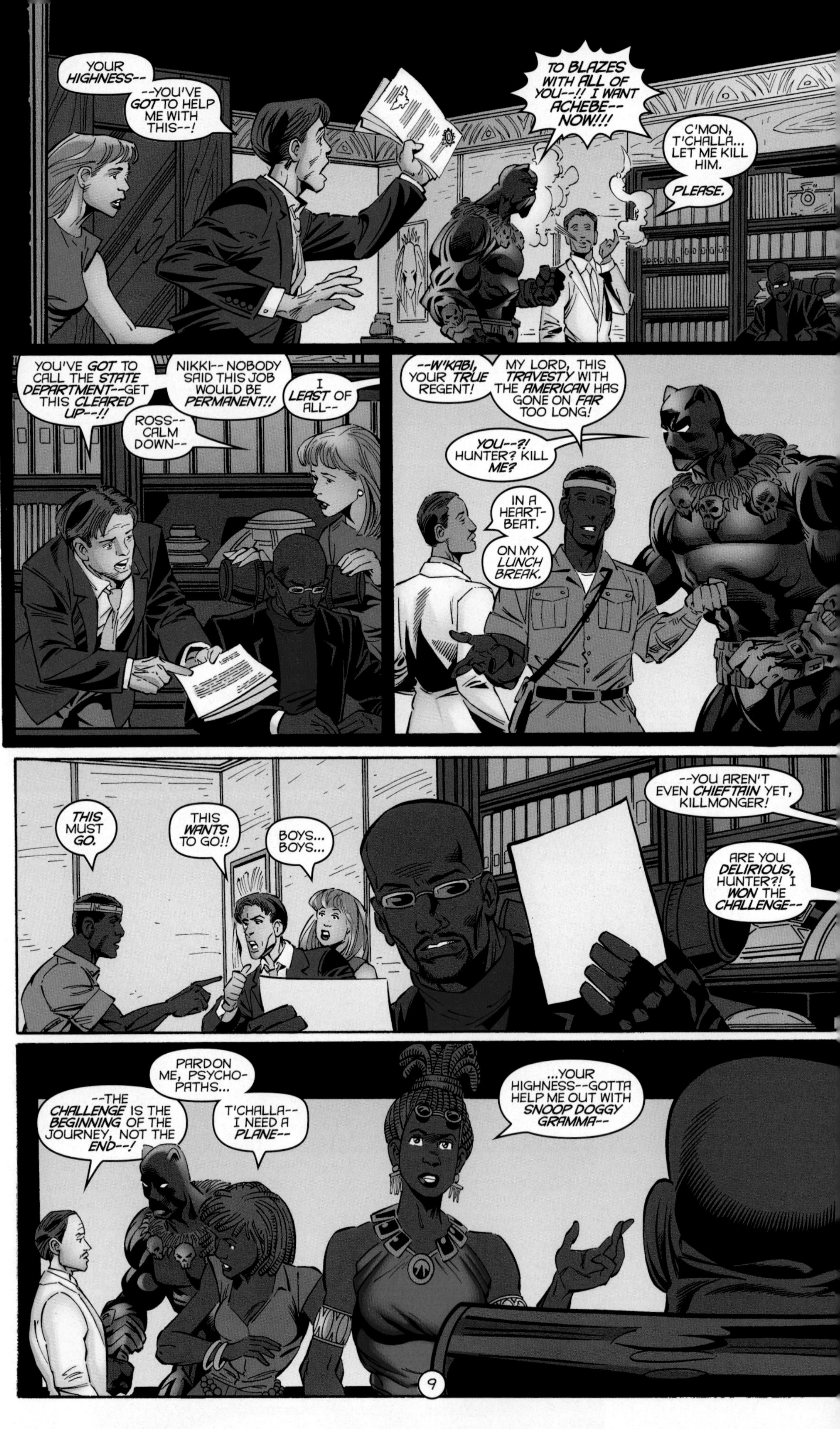
YOUR HIGHNESS--
--YOU'VE GOT TO HELP ME WITH THIS--!
TO BLAZES WITH ALL OF YOU--!! I WANT ACHEBE-- NOW!!!
C'MON, T'CHALLA... LET ME KILL HIM.
PLEASE.
YOU'VE GOT TO CALL THE STATE DEPARTMENT--GET THIS CLEARED UP--!!
NIKKI-- NOBODY SAID THIS JOB WOULD BE PERMANENT!!
ROSS-- CALM DOWN--
I LEAST OF ALL--
--W'KABI, YOUR TRUE REGENT!
MY LORD, THIS TRAVESTY WITH THE AMERICAN HAS GONE ON FAR TOO LONG!
YOU--?! HUNTER? KILL ME?
IN A HEART-BEAT.
ON MY LUNCH BREAK.
THIS MUST GO.
THIS WANTS TO GO!!
BOYS... BOYS...
--YOU AREN'T EVEN CHIEFTAIN YET, KILLMONGER!
ARE YOU DELIRIOUS, HUNTER?! I WON THE CHALLENGE--
--THE CHALLENGE IS THE BEGINNING OF THE JOURNEY, NOT THE END--!
PARDON ME, PSYCHO-PATHS...
T'CHALLA-- I NEED A PLANE--
...YOUR HIGHNESS--GOTTA HELP ME OUT WITH SNOOP DOGGY GRAMMA--

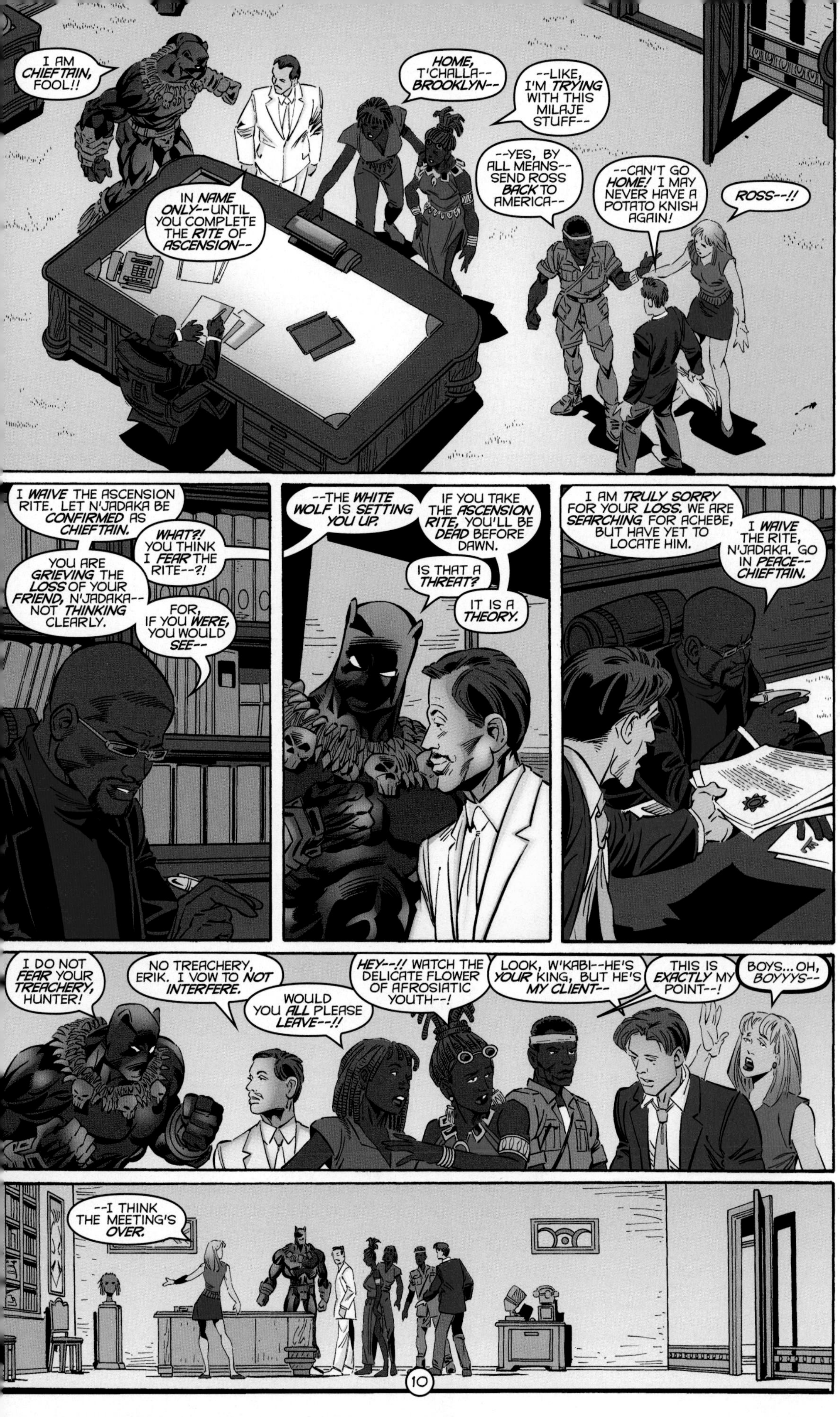
I AM CHIEFTAIN, FOOL!!
IN NAME ONLY--UNTIL YOU COMPLETE THE RITE OF ASCENSION--
HOME, T'CHALLA--BROOKLYN--
--LIKE, I'M TRYING WITH THIS MILAJE STUFF--
--YES, BY ALL MEANS--SEND ROSS BACK TO AMERICA--
--CAN'T GO HOME! I MAY NEVER HAVE A POTATO KNISH AGAIN!
ROSS--!!
I WAIVE THE ASCENSION RITE. LET N'JADAKA BE CONFIRMED AS CHIEFTAIN.
WHAT?! YOU THINK I FEAR THE RITE--?!
YOU ARE GRIEVING THE LOSS OF YOUR FRIEND, N'JADAKA--NOT THINKING CLEARLY.
FOR, IF YOU WERE, YOU WOULD SEE--
--THE WHITE WOLF IS SETTING YOU UP.
IF YOU TAKE THE ASCENSION RITE, YOU'LL BE DEAD BEFORE DAWN.
IS THAT A THREAT?
IT IS A THEORY.
I AM TRULY SORRY FOR YOUR LOSS. WE ARE SEARCHING FOR ACHEBE, BUT HAVE YET TO LOCATE HIM.
I WAIVE THE RITE, N'JADAKA. GO IN PEACE--CHIEFTAIN.
I DO NOT FEAR YOUR TREACHERY, HUNTER!
NO TREACHERY, ERIK. I VOW TO NOT INTERFERE.
WOULD YOU ALL PLEASE LEAVE--!!
HEY--!! WATCH THE DELICATE FLOWER OF AFROSIATIC YOUTH--!
LOOK, W'KABI--HE'S YOUR KING, BUT HE'S MY CLIENT--
THIS IS EXACTLY MY POINT--!
BOYS...OH, BOYYYS--
--I THINK THE MEETING'S OVER.

WHAT HAPPENED IN TEXAS

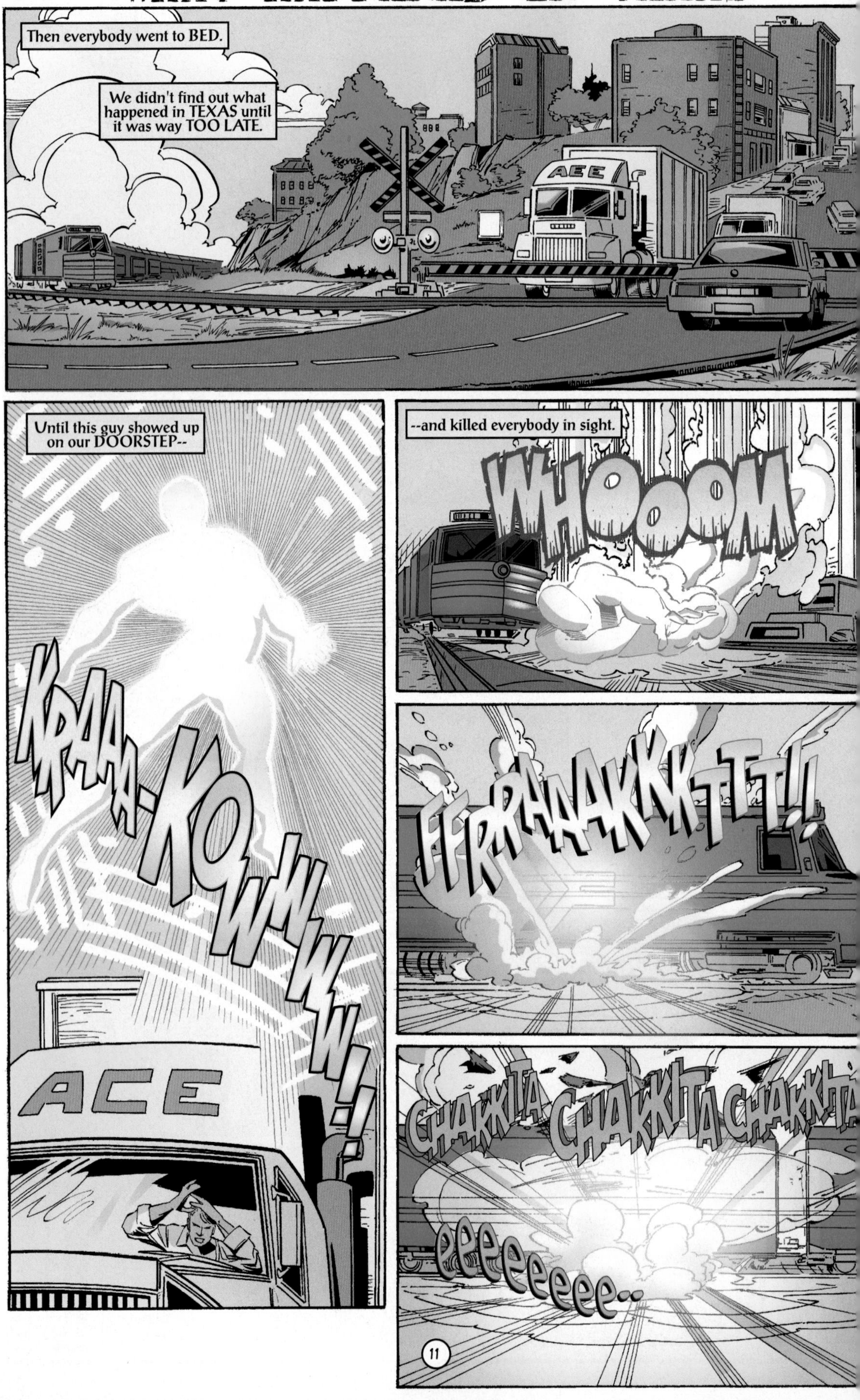
Then everybody went to BED.
We didn't find out what happened in TEXAS until it was way TOO LATE.
AEE
Until this guy showed up on our DOORSTEP--
KRAAA-KOWWWWW!!!
ACE
--and killed everybody in sight.
WHOOOM
FFRRAAAKKKTTT!!
CHAKKITA CHAKKITA CHAKKITA
eeeeeeee..

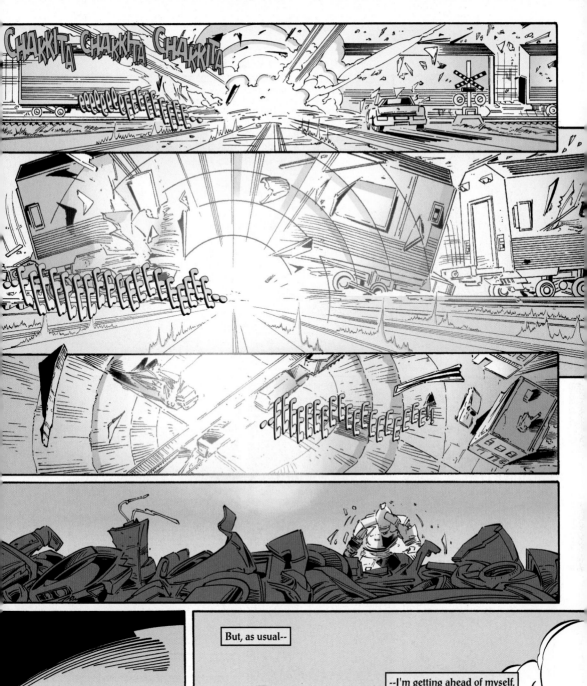

CHAKKITA CHAKKITA CHAKKITA

But, as usual--

--I'm getting ahead of myself.

LAST RITES

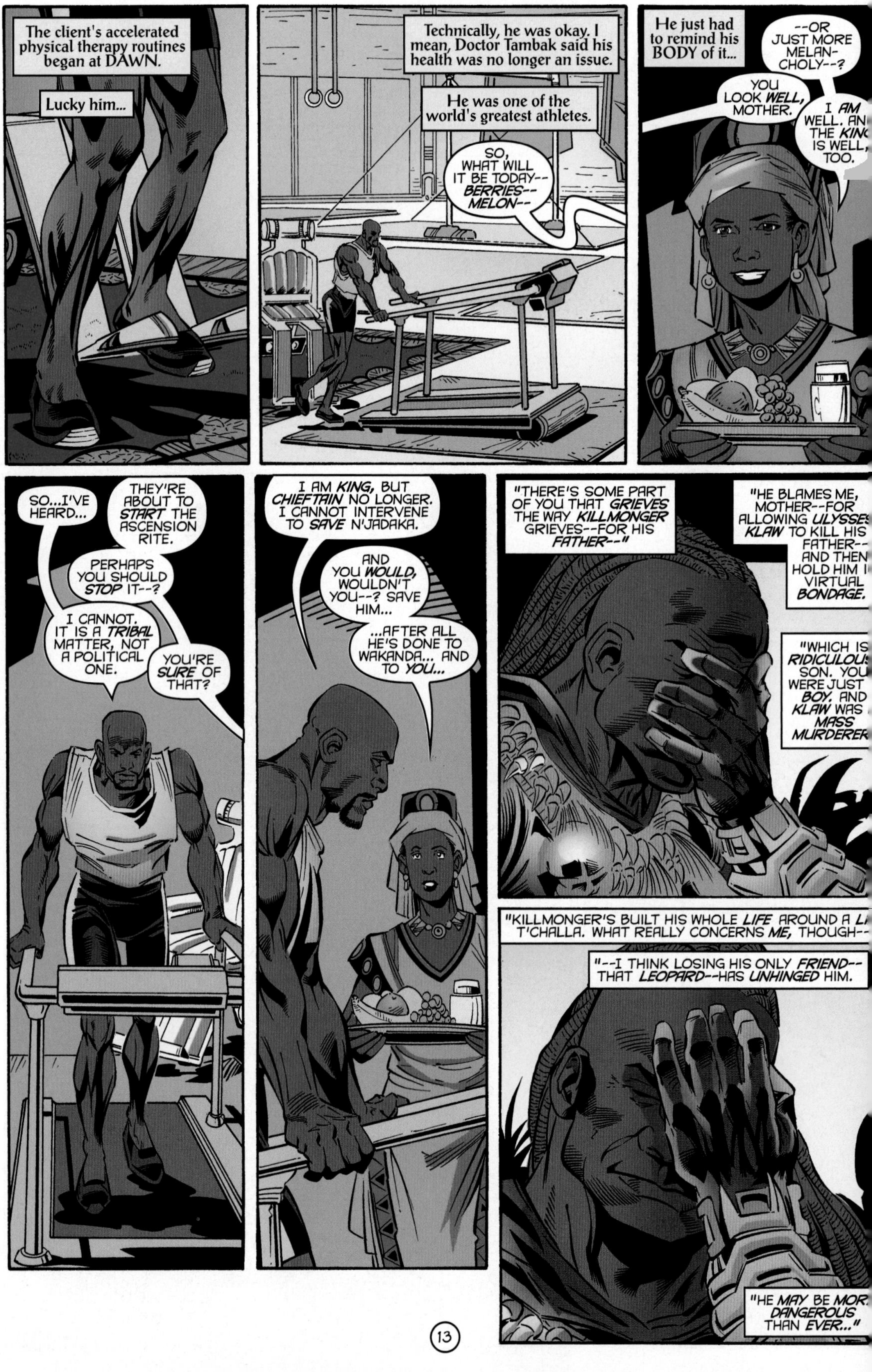

The client's accelerated physical therapy routines began at DAWN.
Lucky him...
Technically, he was okay. I mean, Doctor Tambak said his health was no longer an issue.
He was one of the world's greatest athletes.
SO, WHAT WILL IT BE TODAY-- BERRIES-- MELON--
He just had to remind his BODY of it...
--OR JUST MORE MELAN- CHOLY--?
YOU LOOK WELL, MOTHER.
I AM WELL. AN THE KIN IS WELL, TOO.
SO...I'VE HEARD...
THEY'RE ABOUT TO START THE ASCENSION RITE.
PERHAPS YOU SHOULD STOP IT--?
I CANNOT. IT IS A TRIBAL MATTER, NOT A POLITICAL ONE.
YOU'RE SURE OF THAT?
I AM KING, BUT CHIEFTAIN NO LONGER. I CANNOT INTERVENE TO SAVE N'JADAKA.
AND YOU WOULD, WOULDN'T YOU--? SAVE HIM...
...AFTER ALL HE'S DONE TO WAKANDA... AND TO YOU...
"THERE'S SOME PART OF YOU THAT GRIEVES THE WAY KILLMONGER GRIEVES--FOR HIS FATHER--"
"HE BLAMES ME, MOTHER--FOR ALLOWING ULYSSE KLAW TO KILL HIS FATHER-- AND THEN HOLD HIM I VIRTUAL BONDAGE.
"WHICH IS RIDICULOU SON. YOU WERE JUST BOY, AND KLAW WAS MASS MURDERER
"KILLMONGER'S BUILT HIS WHOLE LIFE AROUND A L T'CHALLA. WHAT REALLY CONCERNS ME, THOUGH--
"--I THINK LOSING HIS ONLY FRIEND-- THAT LEOPARD--HAS UNHINGED HIM.
"HE MAY BE MOR DANGEROUS THAN EVER..."

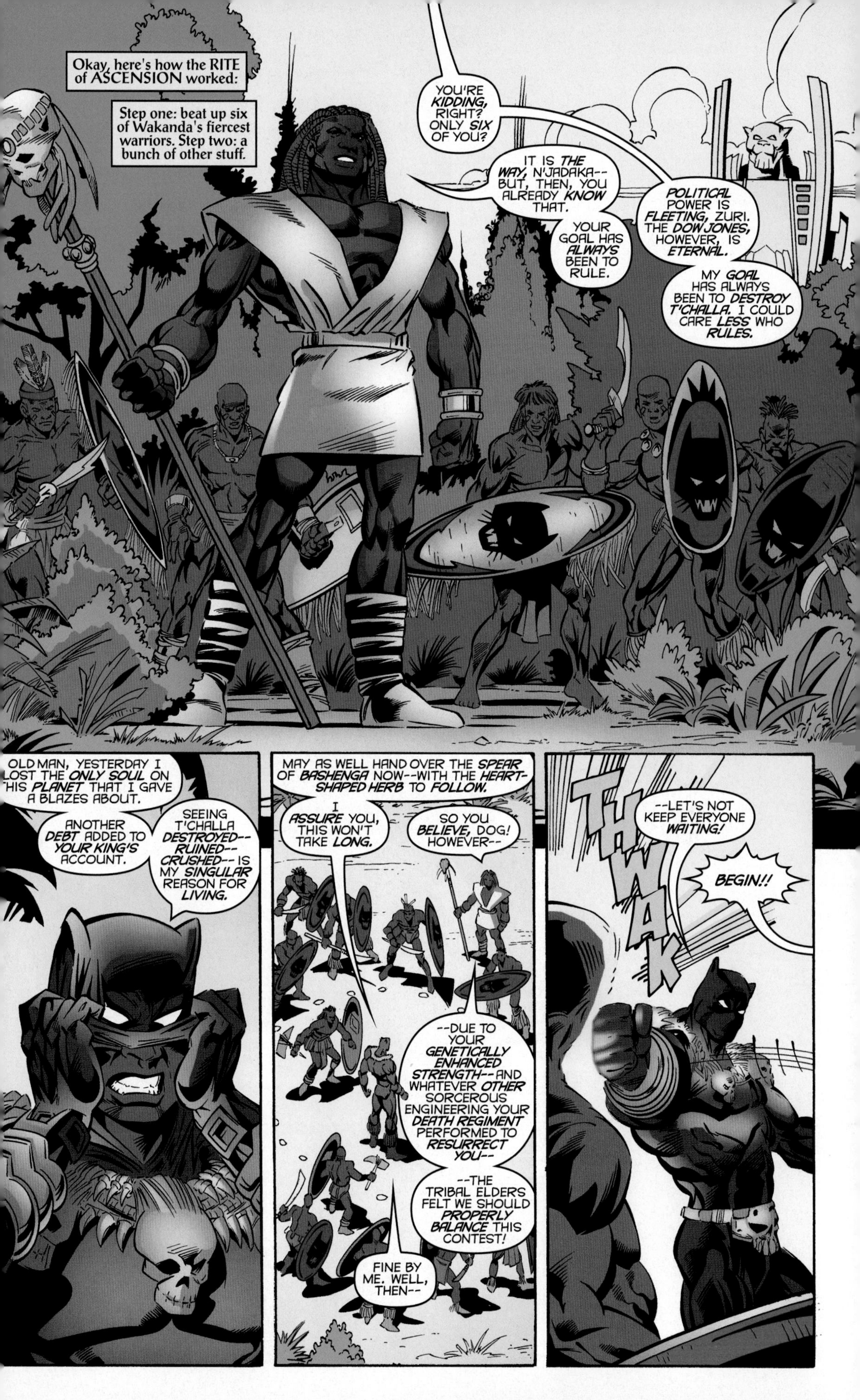
Okay, here's how the RITE of ASCENSION worked:
Step one: beat up six of Wakanda's fiercest warriors. Step two: a bunch of other stuff.
YOU'RE KIDDING, RIGHT? ONLY SIX OF YOU?
IT IS THE WAY, N'JADAKA-- BUT, THEN, YOU ALREADY KNOW THAT.
YOUR GOAL HAS ALWAYS BEEN TO RULE.
POLITICAL POWER IS FLEETING, ZURI. THE DOW JONES, HOWEVER, IS ETERNAL.
MY GOAL HAS ALWAYS BEEN TO DESTROY T'CHALLA. I COULD CARE LESS WHO RULES.
OLD MAN, YESTERDAY I LOST THE ONLY SOUL ON THIS PLANET THAT I GAVE A BLAZES ABOUT.
ANOTHER DEBT ADDED TO YOUR KING'S ACCOUNT.
SEEING T'CHALLA DESTROYED-- RUINED-- CRUSHED-- IS MY SINGULAR REASON FOR LIVING.
MAY AS WELL HAND OVER THE SPEAR OF BASHENGA NOW--WITH THE HEART-SHAPED HERB TO FOLLOW.
I ASSURE YOU, THIS WON'T TAKE LONG.
SO YOU BELIEVE, DOG! HOWEVER--
--DUE TO YOUR GENETICALLY ENHANCED STRENGTH--AND WHATEVER OTHER SORCEROUS ENGINEERING YOUR DEATH REGIMENT PERFORMED TO RESURRECT YOU--
--THE TRIBAL ELDERS FELT WE SHOULD PROPERLY BALANCE THIS CONTEST!
FINE BY ME. WELL, THEN--
THWAK
--LET'S NOT KEEP EVERYONE WAITING!
BEGIN!!

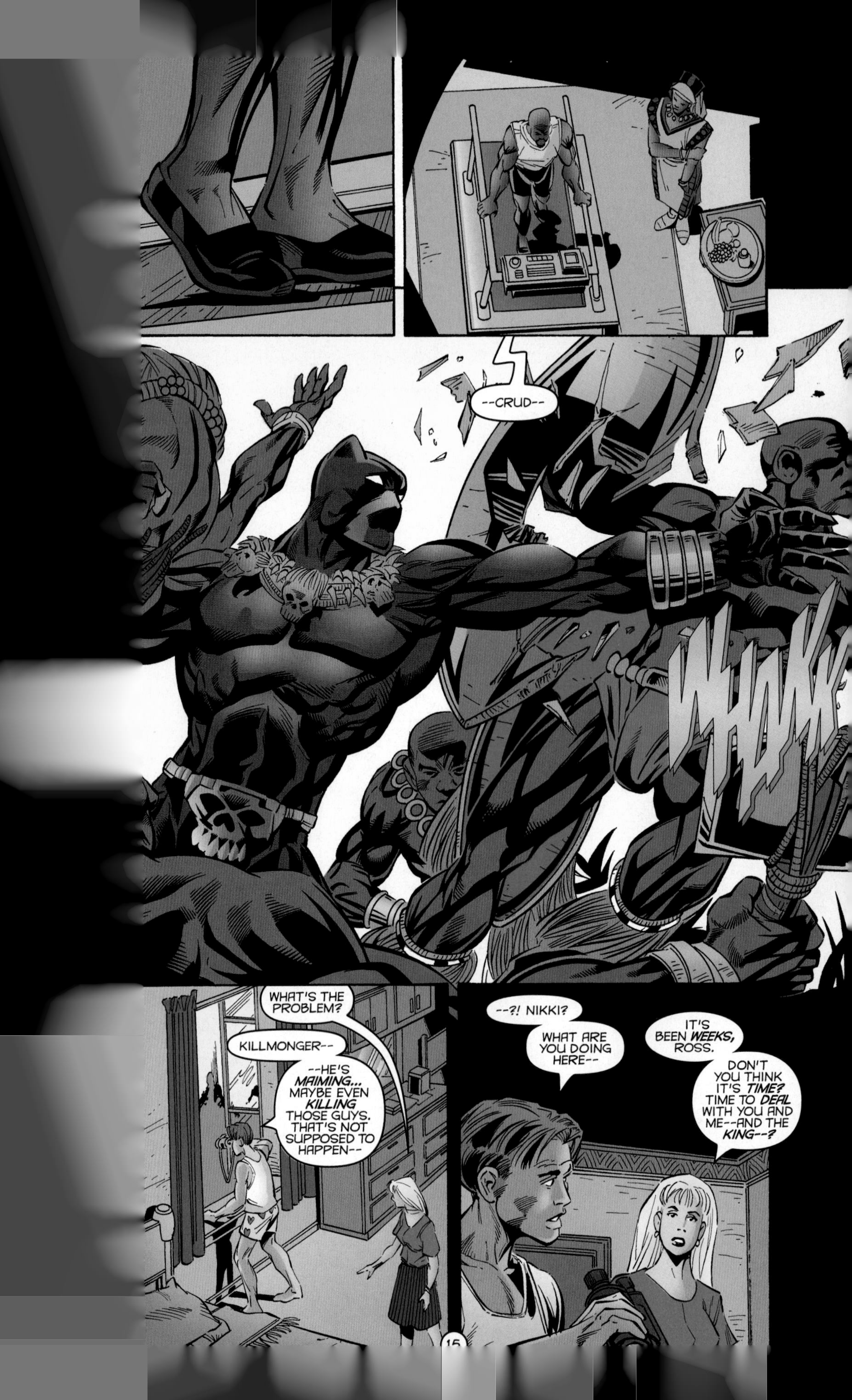
--CRUD--
WHAK
WHAT'S THE PROBLEM?
KILLMONGER--
--HE'S MAIMING... MAYBE EVEN KILLING THOSE GUYS. THAT'S NOT SUPPOSED TO HAPPEN--
--?! NIKKI?
WHAT ARE YOU DOING HERE--
IT'S BEEN WEEKS, ROSS.
DON'T YOU THINK IT'S TIME? TIME TO DEAL WITH YOU AND ME--AND THE KING--?

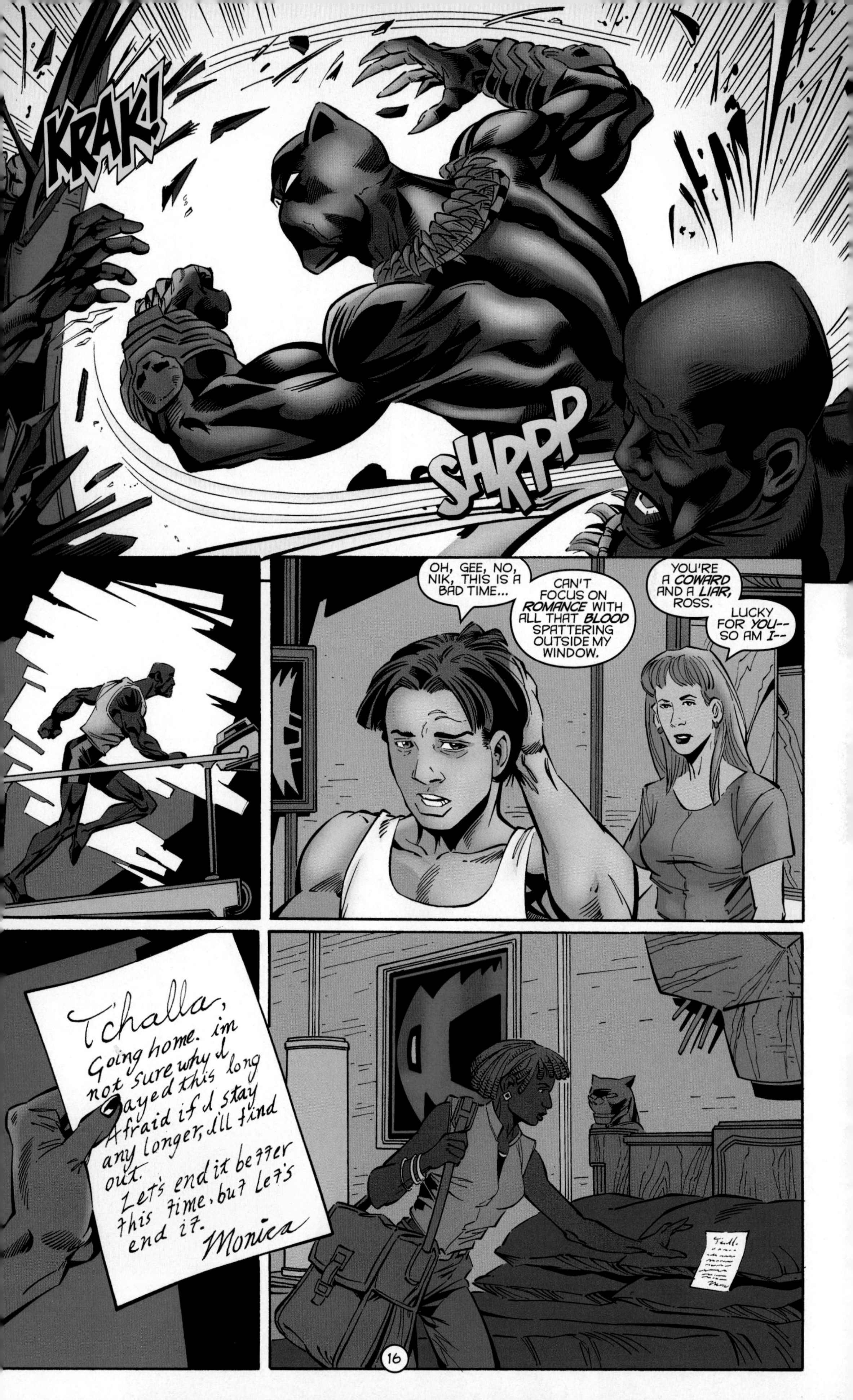
KRAK!
SHRPP
OH, GEE, NO, NIK, THIS IS A BAD TIME...
CAN'T FOCUS ON ROMANCE WITH ALL THAT BLOOD SPATTERING OUTSIDE MY WINDOW.
YOU'RE A COWARD AND A LIAR, ROSS.
LUCKY FOR YOU-- SO AM I--
T'challa,
Going home. im not sure why i stayed this long
Afraid if i stay any longer, i'll find out.
Let's end it better this time, but let's end it.
Monica

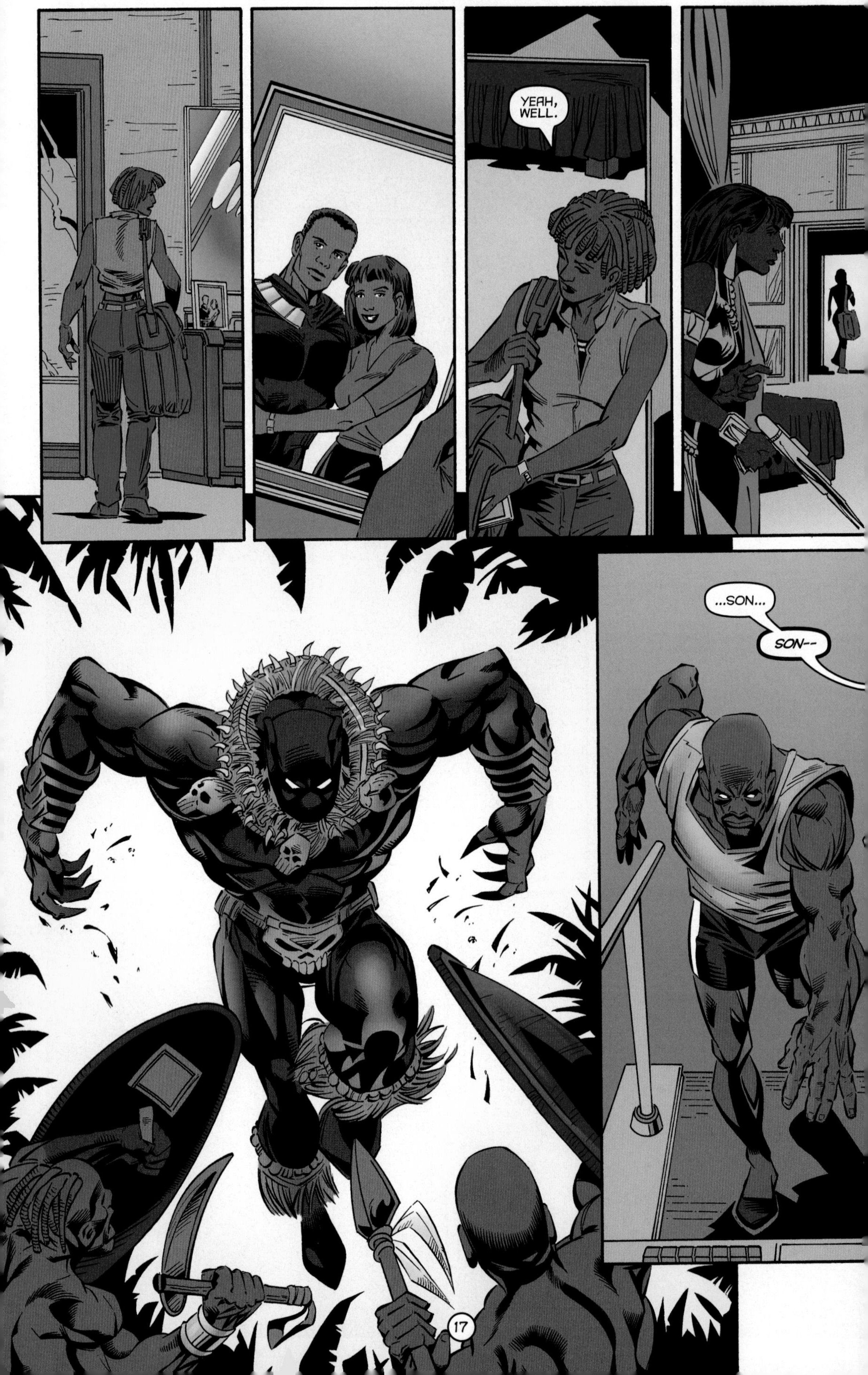
YEAH, WELL.
...SON...
SON--

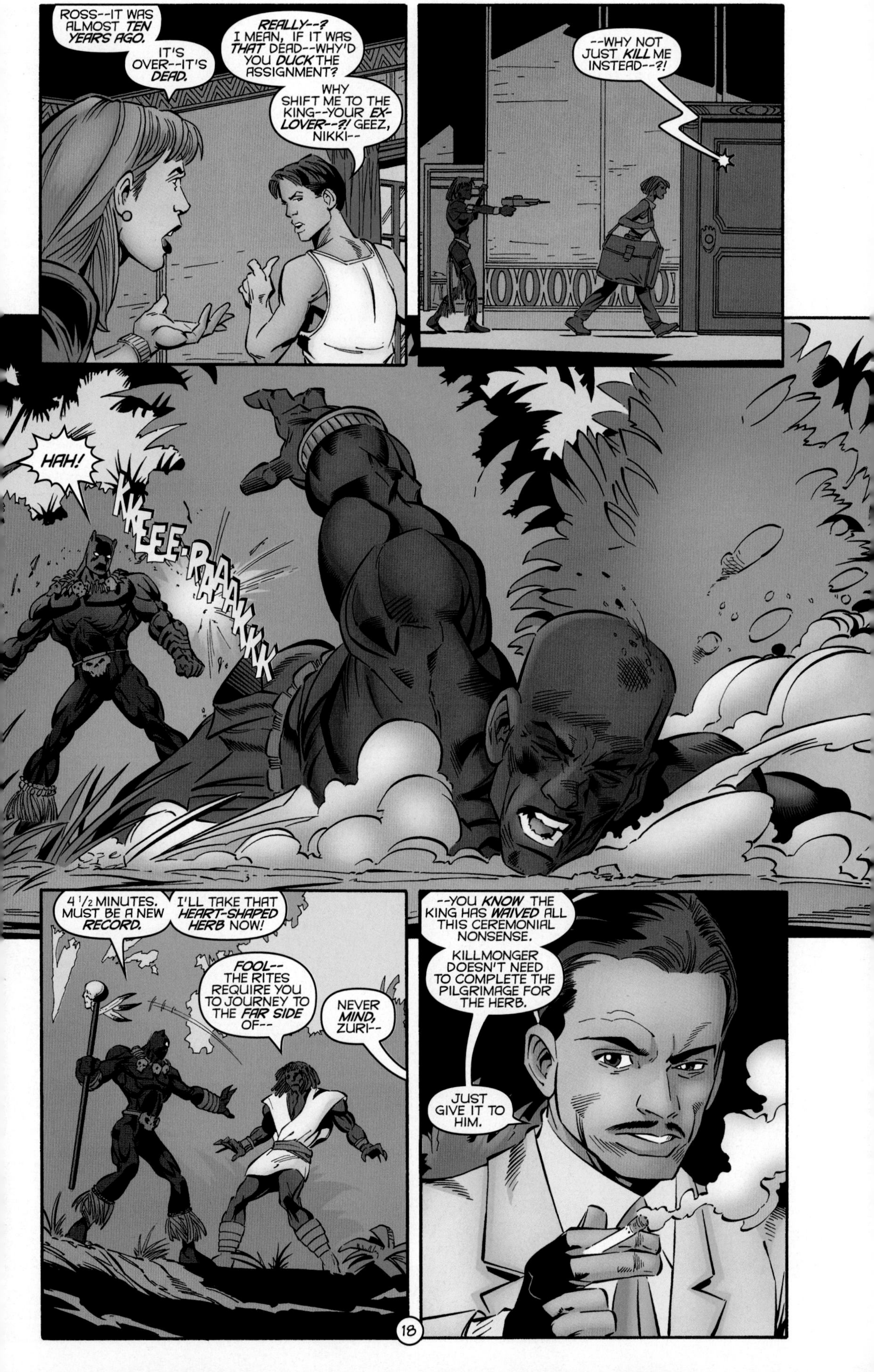
ROSS--IT WAS ALMOST TEN YEARS AGO.
IT'S OVER--IT'S DEAD.
REALLY--? I MEAN, IF IT WAS THAT DEAD--WHY'D YOU DUCK THE ASSIGNMENT?
WHY SHIFT ME TO THE KING--YOUR EX-LOVER--?! GEEZ, NIKKI--
--WHY NOT JUST KILL ME INSTEAD--?!
HAH!
KKEEEE-RAAAKKKK
4 1/2 MINUTES. MUST BE A NEW RECORD.
I'LL TAKE THAT HEART-SHAPED HERB NOW!
FOOL-- THE RITES REQUIRE YOU TO JOURNEY TO THE FAR SIDE OF--
NEVER MIND, ZURI--
--YOU KNOW THE KING HAS WAIVED ALL THIS CEREMONIAL NONSENSE.
KILLMONGER DOESN'T NEED TO COMPLETE THE PILGRIMAGE FOR THE HERB.
JUST GIVE IT TO HIM.

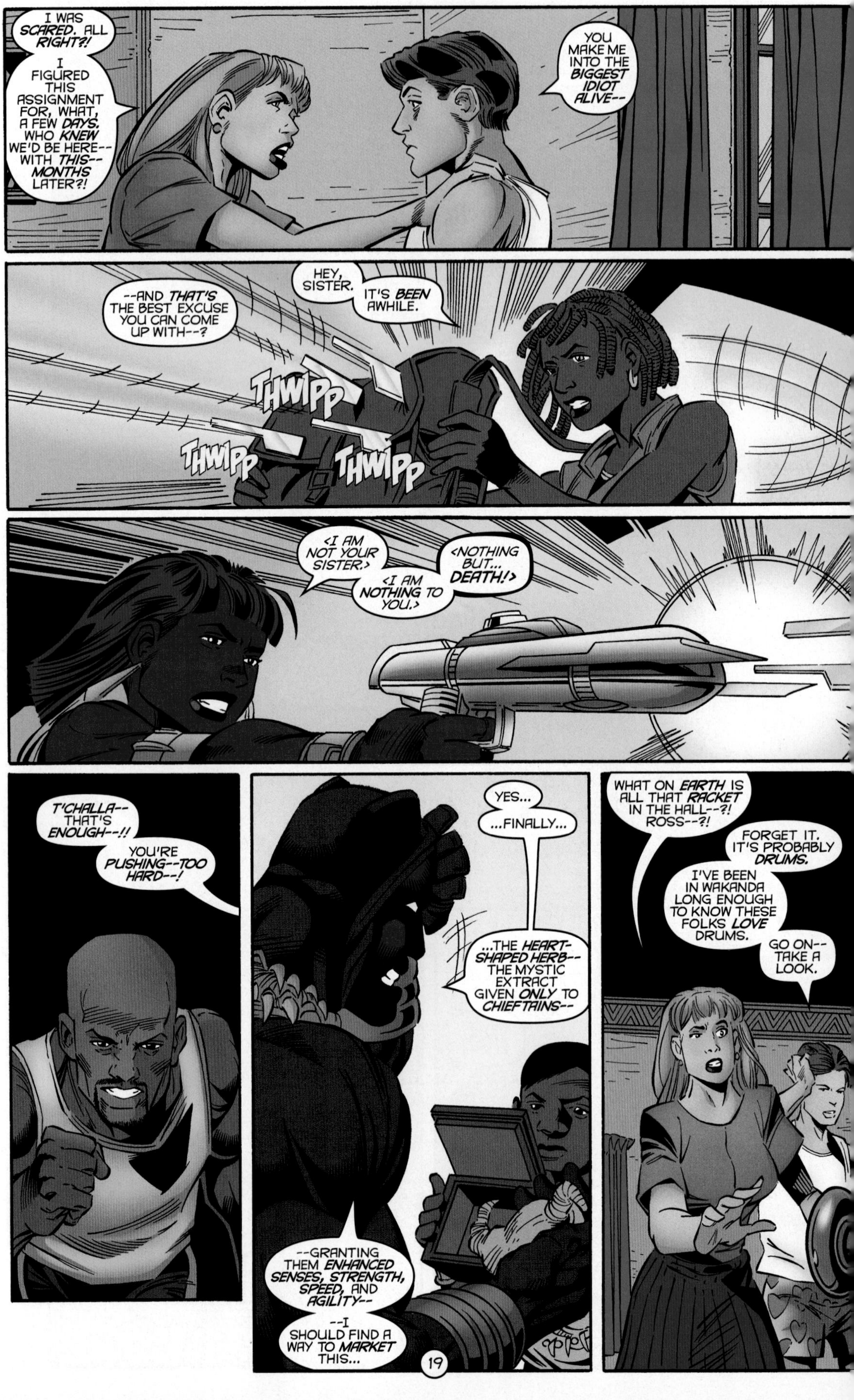
I WAS SCARED. ALL RIGHT?!
I FIGURED THIS ASSIGNMENT FOR, WHAT, A FEW DAYS. WHO KNEW WE'D BE HERE-- WITH THIS-- MONTHS LATER?!
YOU MAKE ME INTO THE BIGGEST IDIOT ALIVE--
--AND THAT'S THE BEST EXCUSE YOU CAN COME UP WITH--?
HEY, SISTER.
IT'S BEEN AWHILE.
THWIPP
THWIPP
THWIPP
<I AM NOT YOUR SISTER.>
<I AM NOTHING TO YOU.>
<NOTHING BUT... DEATH!>
T'CHALLA-- THAT'S ENOUGH--!!
YOU'RE PUSHING--TOO HARD--!
YES...
...FINALLY...
...THE HEART-SHAPED HERB-- THE MYSTIC EXTRACT GIVEN ONLY TO CHIEFTAINS--
--GRANTING THEM ENHANCED SENSES, STRENGTH, SPEED, AND AGILITY--
--I SHOULD FIND A WAY TO MARKET THIS...
WHAT ON EARTH IS ALL THAT RACKET IN THE HALL--?! ROSS--?!
FORGET IT. IT'S PROBABLY DRUMS.
I'VE BEEN IN WAKANDA LONG ENOUGH TO KNOW THESE FOLKS LOVE DRUMS.
GO ON-- TAKE A LOOK.

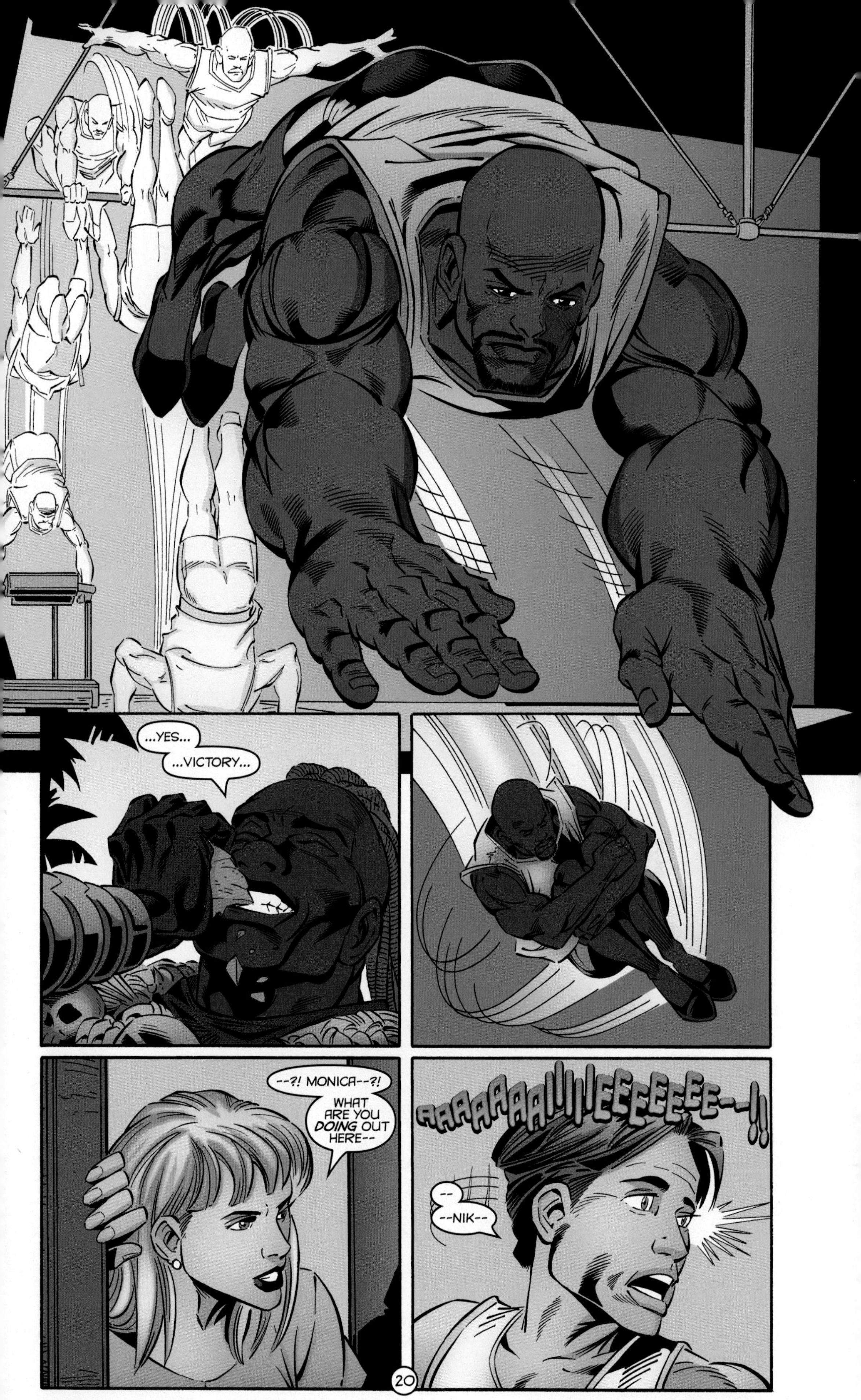

...YES...
...VICTORY...
--?! MONICA--?!
WHAT ARE YOU DOING OUT HERE--
AAAAAAAIIIIIIEEEEEEEE--!!
--
--NIK--

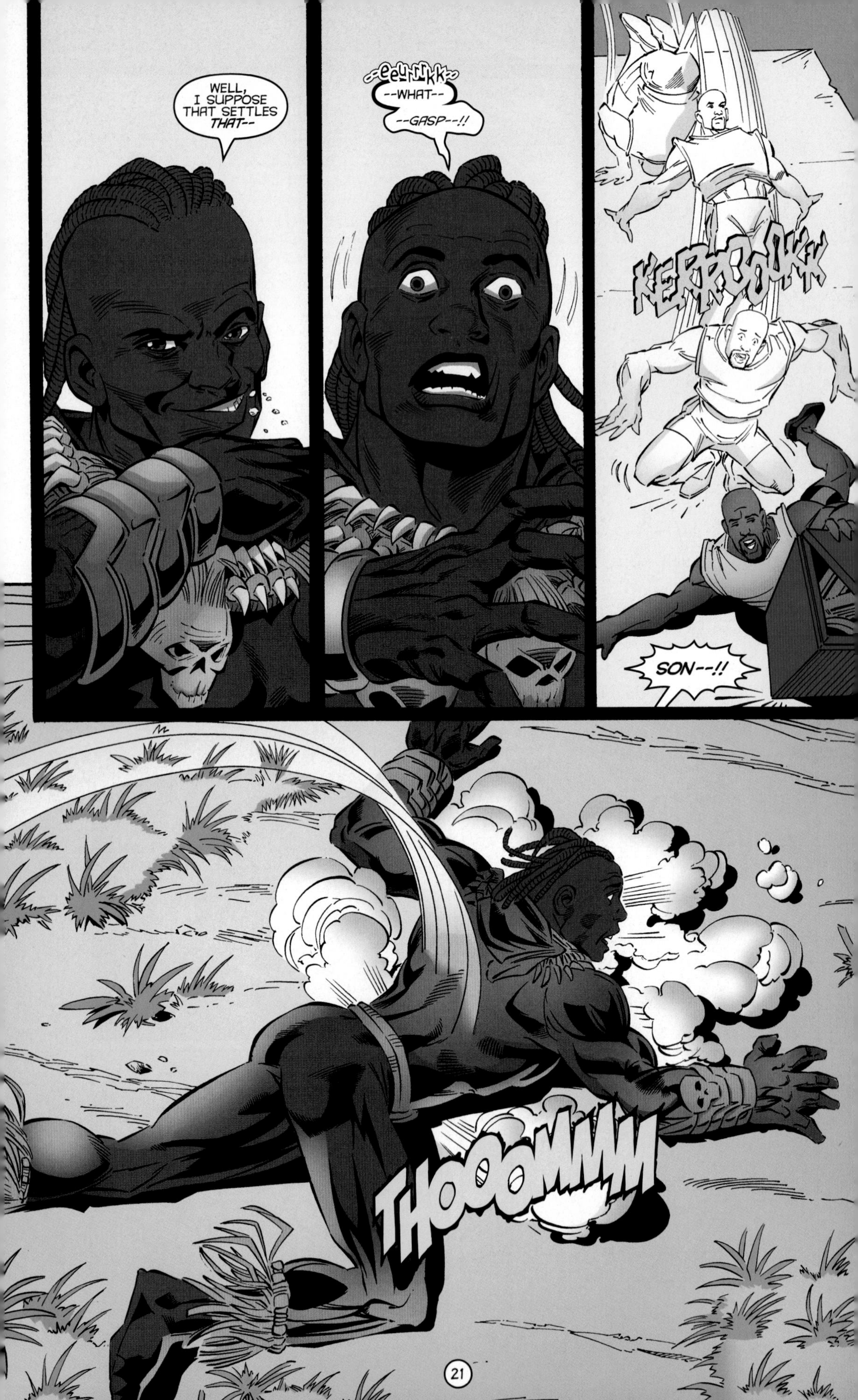
WELL, I SUPPOSE THAT SETTLES THAT--
--eeyrrrkk--
--WHAT--
--GASP--!!
KERRCOOKK
SON--!!
THOOOMMM

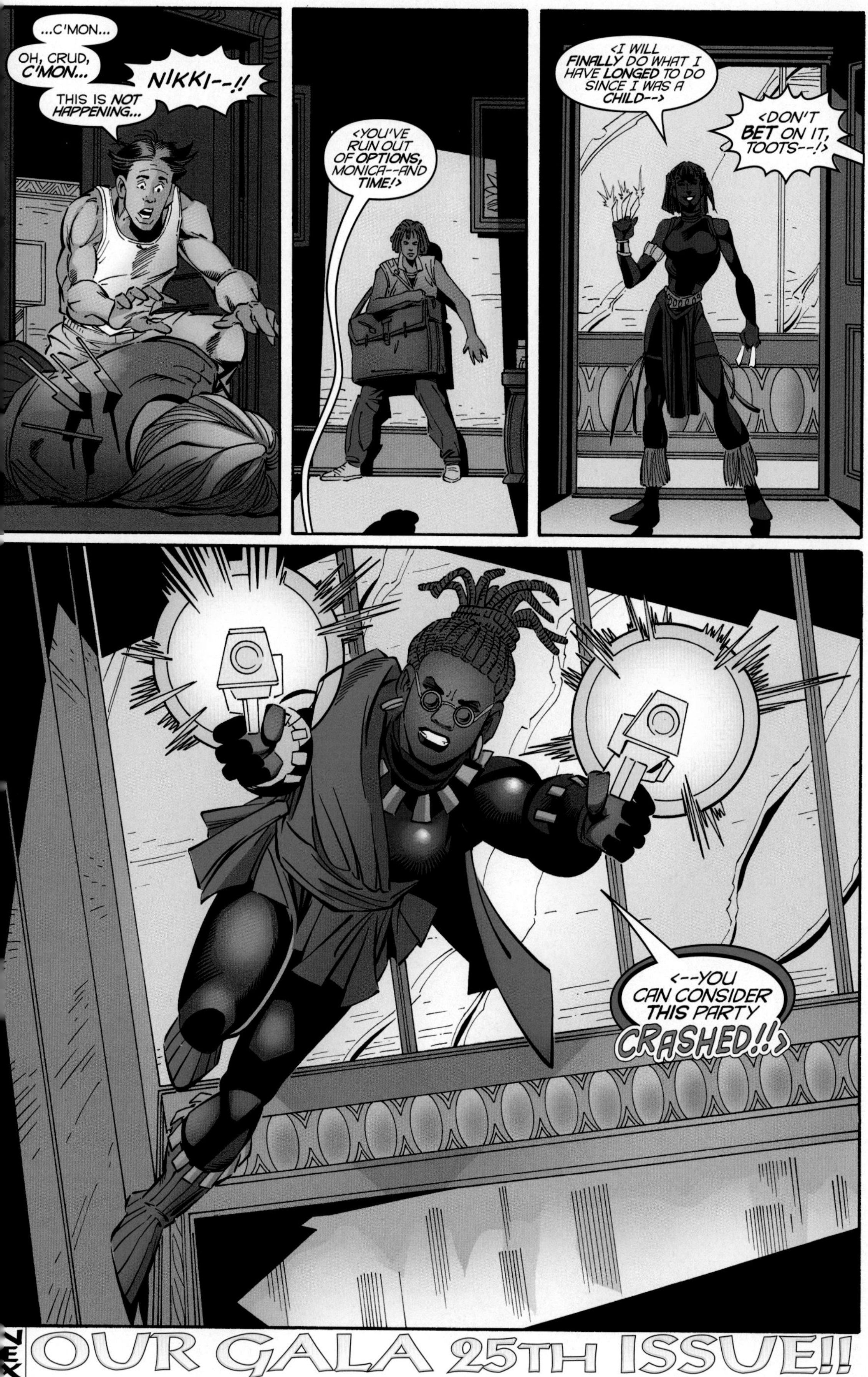
...C'MON...
OH, CRUD, C'MON...
THIS IS NOT HAPPENING...
NIKKI--!!
<YOU'VE RUN OUT OF OPTIONS, MONICA--AND TIME!>
<I WILL FINALLY DO WHAT I HAVE LONGED TO DO SINCE I WAS A CHILD-->
<DON'T BET ON IT, TOOTS--!>
<--YOU CAN CONSIDER THIS PARTY CRASHED!!>

NEXT

OUR GALA 25TH ISSUE!!

With more surprises, villains, SHOCKS and SPECIAL GUEST STARS than you can shake a heart-shaped herb at!!

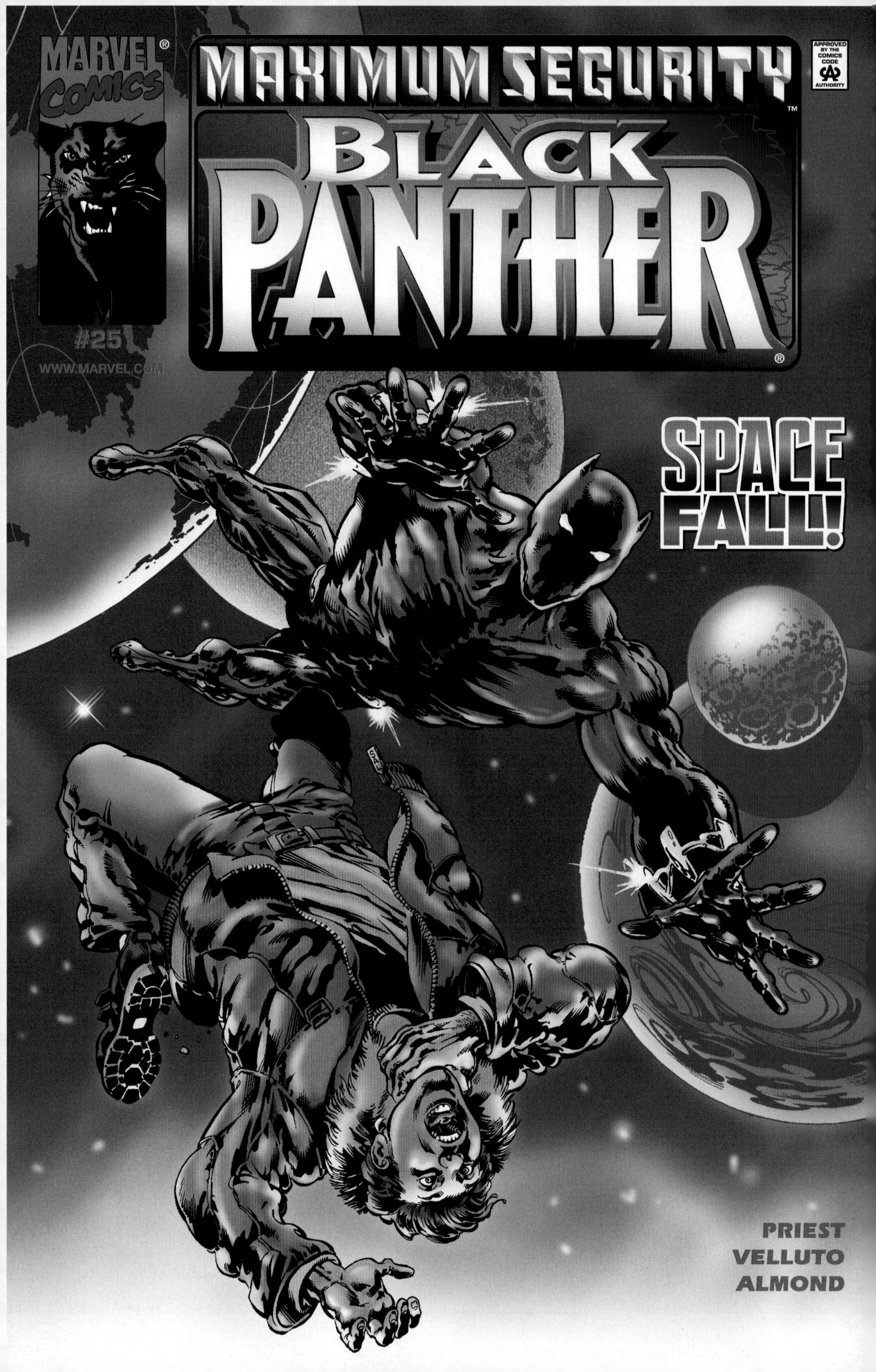
MARVEL®
COMICS
#25
WWW.MARVEL.COM
MAXIMUM SECURITY
BLACK PANTHER
APPROVED BY THE COMICS CODE AUTHORITY
SPACE FALL!
PRIEST
VELLUTO
ALMOND

Dear Whomever:

My name is Everett K. Ross, Grade 2 OCP attaché.*

Four days.

That was more than a YEAR ago.

I realize you're NEW on the job. This may be the FIRST report you're reading from me.

I'll try to fill in the blanks for you. There's a lot of ground to cover, so you might wanna take notes.

I was assigned to escort the King of Wakanda on a state visit.

That assignment was for four days.

*OCP=OFFICE OF THE CHIEF OF PROTOCOL. --TOM

Floating there, in orbit around an ALIEN PLANET far outside our known galaxy, I took a few minutes to REFLECT on the train wreck my life had become...

HAIL TO THE CHIEF

Killmonger was dead.

Don't worry about who Killmonger was. He was dead. THAT'S who he was.

His death caught the king by surprise. The king HATED being caught by surprise.

SUMMON THE SURGEON.

HE'S DEAD, T'CHALLA--

OBEY ME.

The king wasn't going to accept Killmonger's death. There were issues of TRIBAL HONOR involved, but I'll cover that in the appendices.

Let's just say the guy CROAKED, and took a good slice of the king's DIGNITY with him.

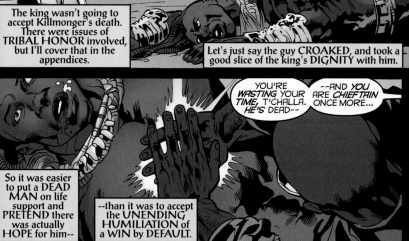

YOU'RE WASTING YOUR TIME, T'CHALLA. HE'S DEAD--

--AND YOU ARE CHIEFTAIN ONCE MORE...

So it was easier to put a DEAD MAN on life support and PRETEND there was actually HOPE for him--

--than it was to accept the UNENDING HUMILIATION of a WIN BY DEFAULT.

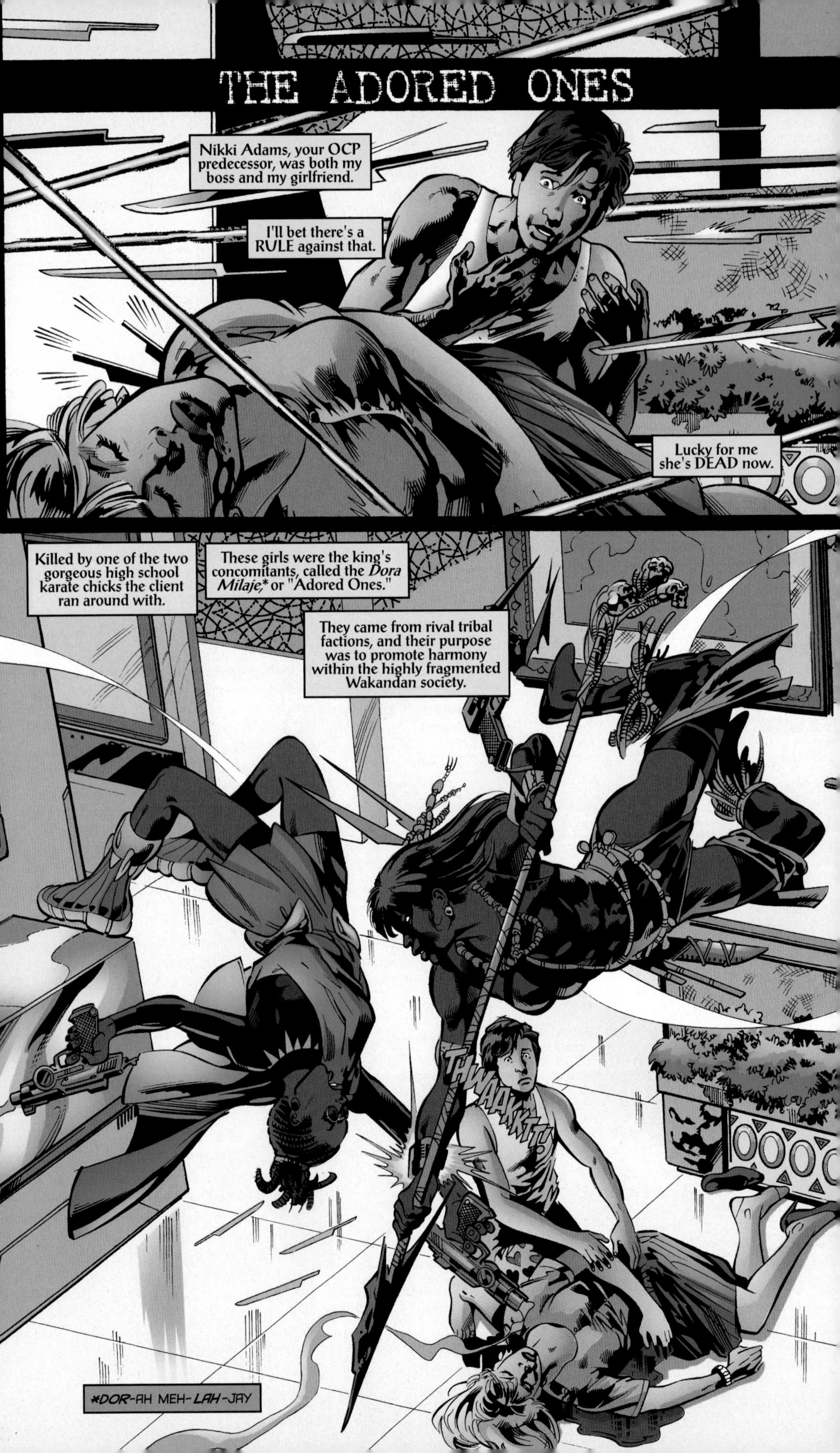
THE ADORED ONES
Nikki Adams, your OCP predecessor, was both my boss and my girlfriend.
I'll bet there's a RULE against that.
Lucky for me she's DEAD now.
Killed by one of the two gorgeous high school karate chicks the client ran around with.
These girls were the king's concomitants, called the *Dora Milaje,** or "Adored Ones."
They came from rival tribal factions, and their purpose was to promote harmony within the highly fragmented Wakandan society.
THWAAKTT
*DOR-AH MEH-LAH-JAY

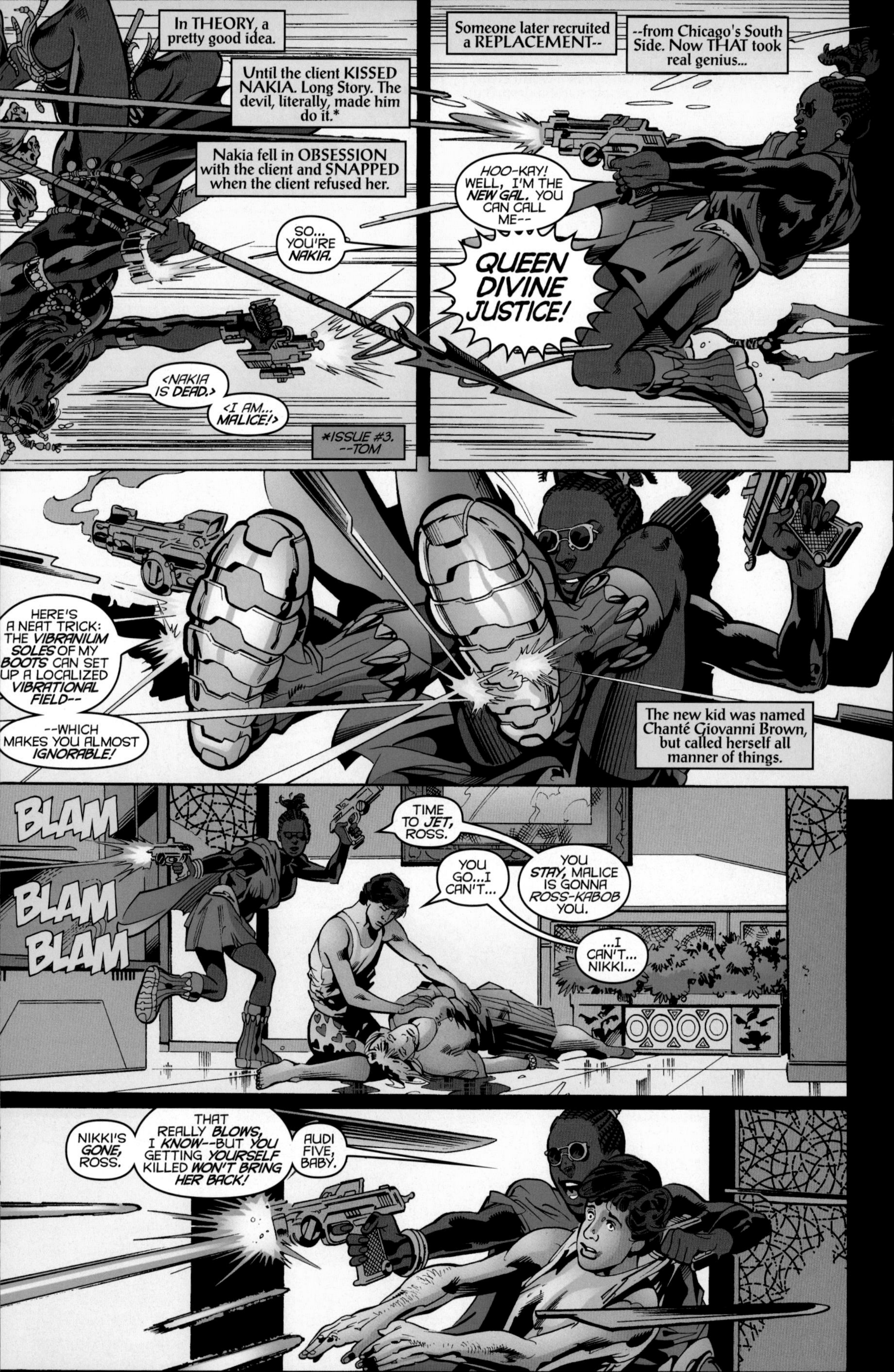
In THEORY, a pretty good idea.
Until the client KISSED NAKIA. Long Story. The devil, literally, made him do it.*
Nakia fell in OBSESSION with the client and SNAPPED when the client refused her.
SO... YOU'RE NAKIA.
<NAKIA IS DEAD.>
<I AM... MALICE!>
*ISSUE #3. --TOM
Someone later recruited a REPLACEMENT--
--from Chicago's South Side. Now THAT took real genius...
HOO-KAY! WELL, I'M THE NEW GAL. YOU CAN CALL ME--
QUEEN DIVINE JUSTICE!
HERE'S A NEAT TRICK: THE VIBRANIUM SOLES OF MY BOOTS CAN SET UP A LOCALIZED VIBRATIONAL FIELD--
--WHICH MAKES YOU ALMOST IGNORABLE!
The new kid was named Chanté Giovanni Brown, but called herself all manner of things.
BLAM
BLAM
BLAM
TIME TO JET, ROSS.
YOU GO...I CAN'T...
YOU STAY, MALICE IS GONNA ROSS-KABOB YOU.
...I CAN'T... NIKKI...
NIKKI'S GONE, ROSS.
THAT REALLY BLOWS, I KNOW--BUT YOU GETTING YOURSELF KILLED WON'T BRING HER BACK!
AUDI FIVE, BABY.

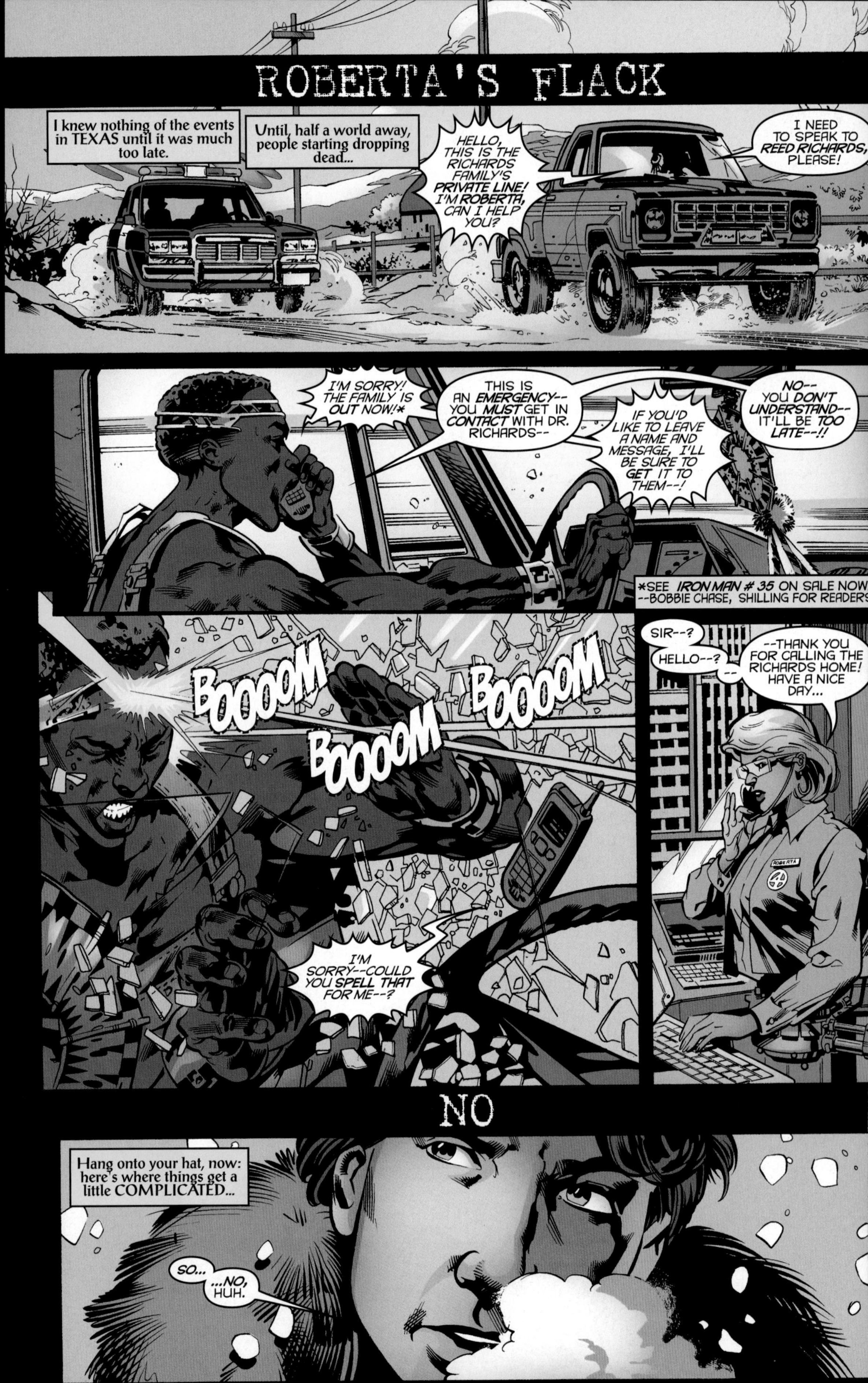

ROBERTA'S FLACK
I knew nothing of the events in TEXAS until it was much too late.
Until, half a world away, people starting dropping dead...
HELLO, THIS IS THE RICHARDS FAMILY'S PRIVATE LINE! I'M ROBERTA, CAN I HELP YOU?
I NEED TO SPEAK TO REED RICHARDS, PLEASE!
I'M SORRY! THE FAMILY IS OUT NOW!*
THIS IS AN EMERGENCY-- YOU MUST GET IN CONTACT WITH DR. RICHARDS--
IF YOU'D LIKE TO LEAVE A NAME AND MESSAGE, I'LL BE SURE TO GET IT TO THEM--!
NO-- YOU DON'T UNDERSTAND-- IT'LL BE TOO LATE--!!
*SEE IRON MAN # 35 ON SALE NOW! --BOBBIE CHASE, SHILLING FOR READERS
BOOOOM
BOOOOM
BOOOOM
I'M SORRY--COULD YOU SPELL THAT FOR ME--?
SIR--?
HELLO--?
--THANK YOU FOR CALLING THE RICHARDS HOME! HAVE A NICE DAY...
ROBERTA
NO
Hang onto your hat, now: here's where things get a little COMPLICATED...
SO...
...NO, HUH.

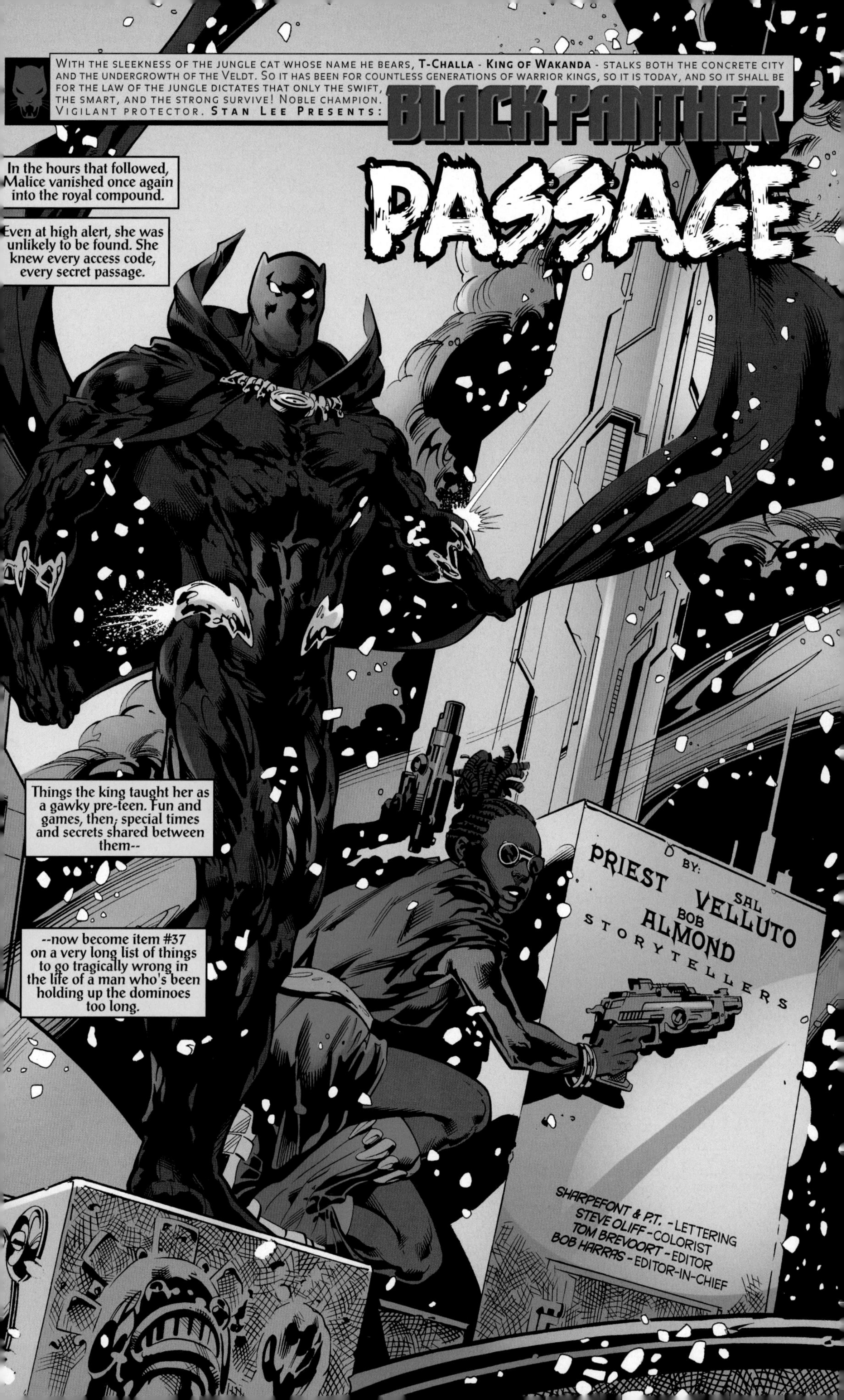
WITH THE SLEEKNESS OF THE JUNGLE CAT WHOSE NAME HE BEARS, T-CHALLA - KING OF WAKANDA - STALKS BOTH THE CONCRETE CITY AND THE UNDERGROWTH OF THE VELDT. SO IT HAS BEEN FOR COUNTLESS GENERATIONS OF WARRIOR KINGS, SO IT IS TODAY, AND SO IT SHALL BE FOR THE LAW OF THE JUNGLE DICTATES THAT ONLY THE SWIFT, THE SMART, AND THE STRONG SURVIVE! NOBLE CHAMPION. VIGILANT PROTECTOR. STAN LEE PRESENTS:
BLACK PANTHER
PASSAGE
In the hours that followed, Malice vanished once again into the royal compound.
Even at high alert, she was unlikely to be found. She knew every access code, every secret passage.
Things the king taught her as a gawky pre-teen. Fun and games, then; special times and secrets shared between them--
--now become item #37 on a very long list of things to go tragically wrong in the life of a man who's been holding up the dominoes too long.
BY: PRIEST SAL VELLUTO BOB ALMOND STORYTELLERS
SHARPEFONT & P.T. - LETTERING
STEVE OLIFF - COLORIST
TOM BREVOORT - EDITOR
BOB HARRAS - EDITOR-IN-CHIEF

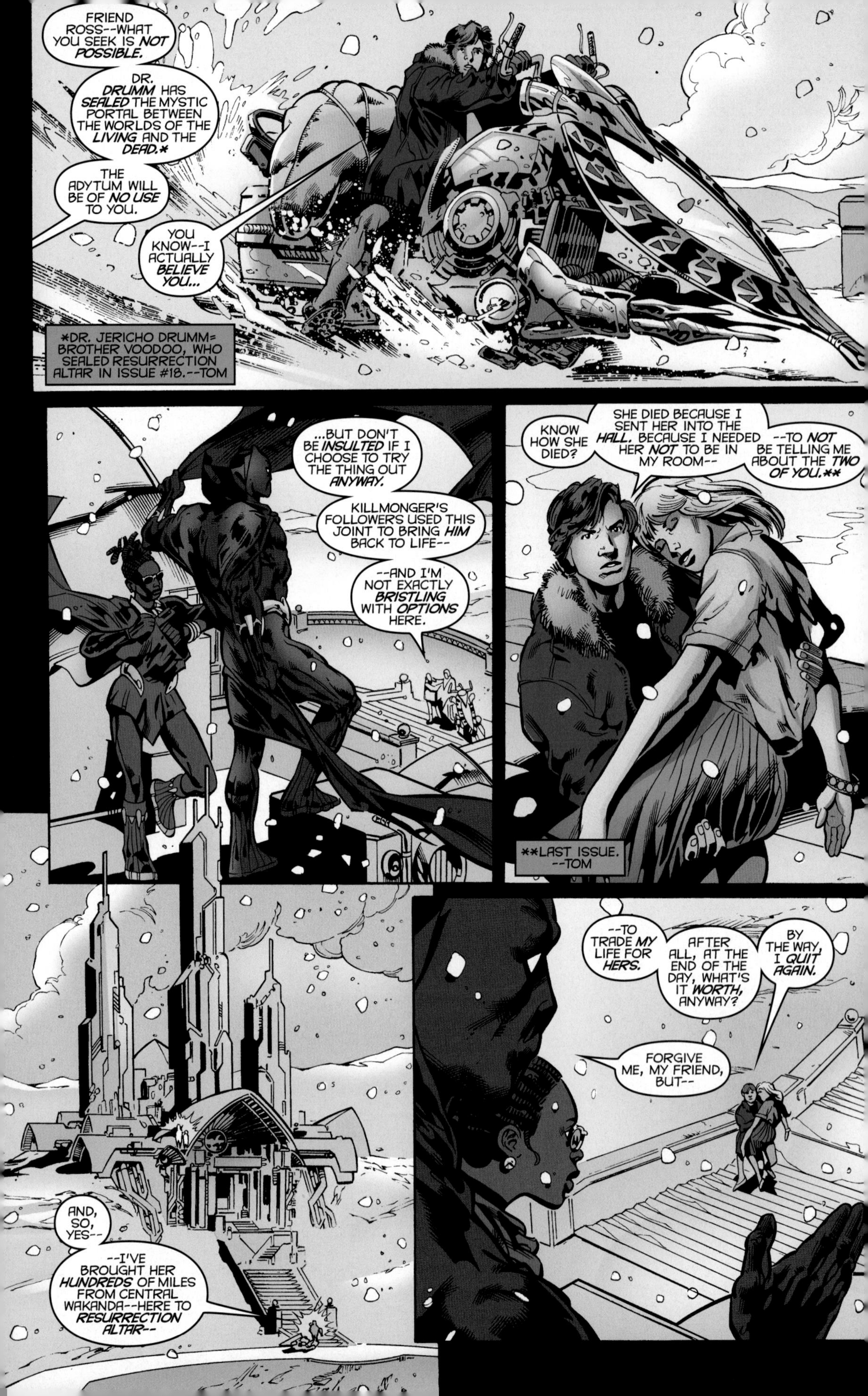
FRIEND ROSS--WHAT YOU SEEK IS NOT POSSIBLE.
DR. DRUMM HAS SEALED THE MYSTIC PORTAL BETWEEN THE WORLDS OF THE LIVING AND THE DEAD.*
THE ADYTUM WILL BE OF NO USE TO YOU.
YOU KNOW--I ACTUALLY BELIEVE YOU...
*DR. JERICHO DRUMM= BROTHER VOODOO, WHO SEALED RESURRECTION ALTAR IN ISSUE #18.--TOM
...BUT DON'T BE INSULTED IF I CHOOSE TO TRY THE THING OUT ANYWAY.
KILLMONGER'S FOLLOWERS USED THIS JOINT TO BRING HIM BACK TO LIFE--
--AND I'M NOT EXACTLY BRISTLING WITH OPTIONS HERE.
KNOW HOW SHE DIED?
SHE DIED BECAUSE I SENT HER INTO THE HALL. BECAUSE I NEEDED HER NOT TO BE IN MY ROOM--
--TO NOT BE TELLING ME ABOUT THE TWO OF YOU.**
**LAST ISSUE. --TOM
AND, SO, YES--
--I'VE BROUGHT HER HUNDREDS OF MILES FROM CENTRAL WAKANDA--HERE TO RESURRECTION ALTAR--
--TO TRADE MY LIFE FOR HERS.
AFTER ALL, AT THE END OF THE DAY, WHAT'S IT WORTH, ANYWAY?
BY THE WAY, I QUIT AGAIN.
FORGIVE ME, MY FRIEND, BUT--

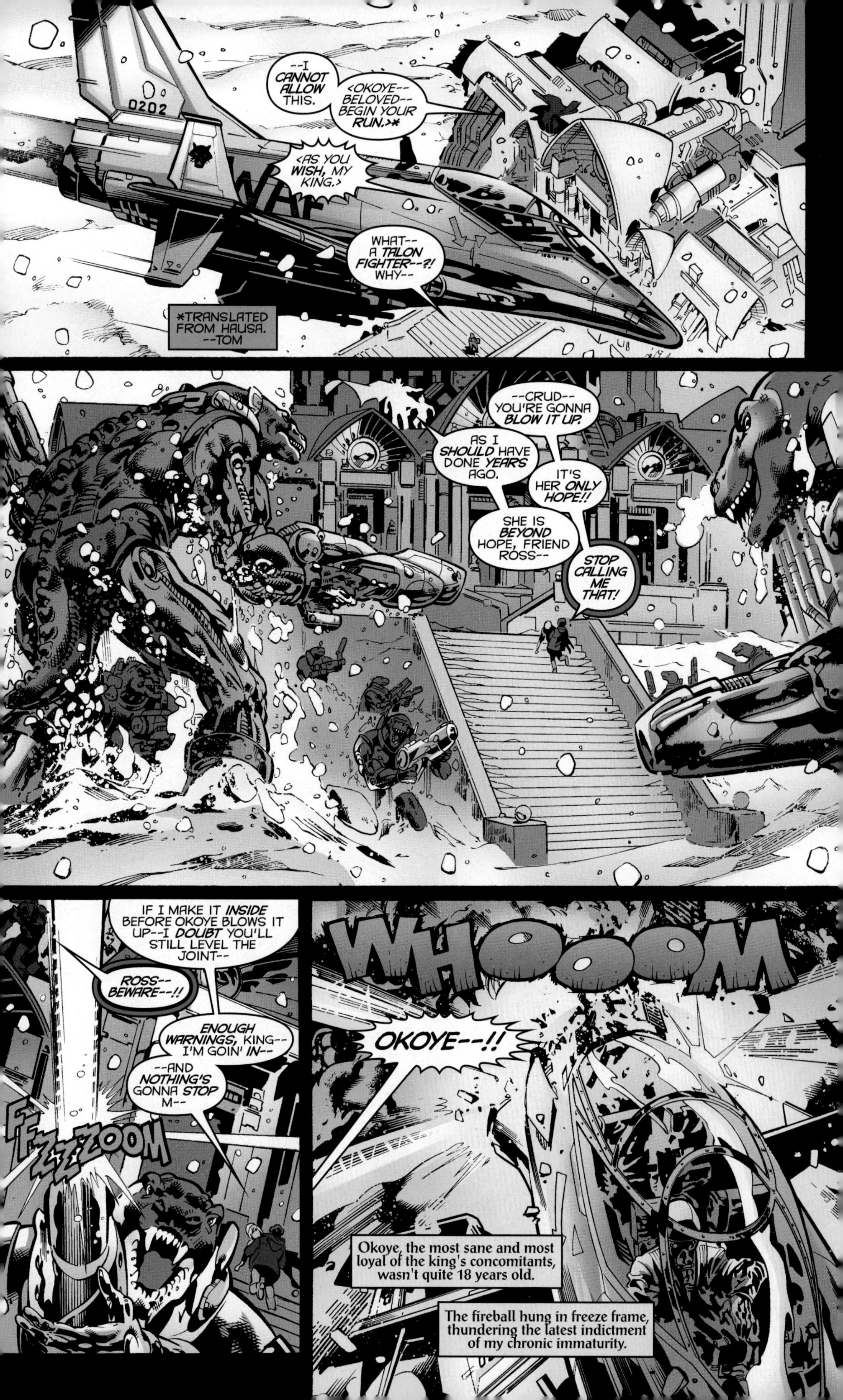

--I CANNOT ALLOW THIS.
<OKOYE-- BELOVED-- BEGIN YOUR RUN.>*
<AS YOU WISH, MY KING.>
WHAT-- A TALON FIGHTER--?! WHY--
*TRANSLATED FROM HAUSA. --TOM
--CRUD-- YOU'RE GONNA BLOW IT UP.
AS I SHOULD HAVE DONE YEARS AGO.
IT'S HER ONLY HOPE!!
SHE IS BEYOND HOPE, FRIEND ROSS--
STOP CALLING ME THAT!
IF I MAKE IT INSIDE BEFORE OKOYE BLOWS IT UP--I DOUBT YOU'LL STILL LEVEL THE JOINT--
ROSS-- BEWARE--!!
ENOUGH WARNINGS, KING-- I'M GOIN' IN--
--AND NOTHING'S GONNA STOP M--
FFZZZOOM
WHOOOOM
OKOYE--!!
Okoye, the most sane and most loyal of the king's concomitants, wasn't quite 18 years old.
The fireball hung in freeze frame, thundering the latest indictment of my chronic immaturity.

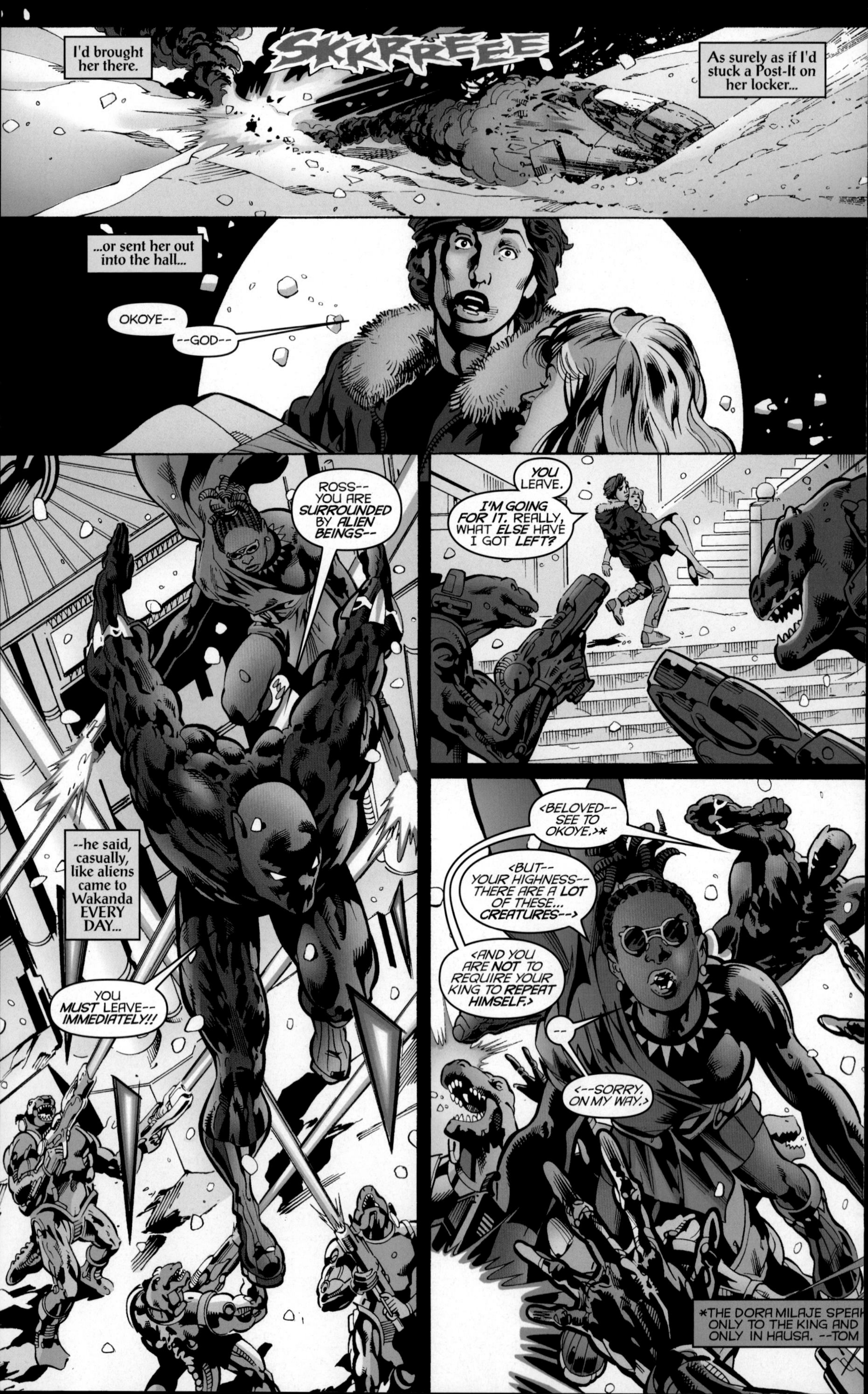
I'd brought her there.
SKKRREEE
As surely as if I'd stuck a Post-It on her locker...
...or sent her out into the hall...
OKOYE--
--GOD--
ROSS-- YOU ARE SURROUNDED BY ALIEN BEINGS--
--he said, casually, like aliens came to Wakanda EVERY DAY...
YOU MUST LEAVE-- IMMEDIATELY!!
YOU LEAVE.
I'M GOING FOR IT. REALLY, WHAT ELSE HAVE I GOT LEFT?
<BELOVED-- SEE TO OKOYE.>*
<BUT-- YOUR HIGHNESS-- THERE ARE A LOT OF THESE... CREATURES-->
<AND YOU ARE NOT TO REQUIRE YOUR KING TO REPEAT HIMSELF.>
--
<--SORRY. ON MY WAY.>
*THE DORA MILAJE SPEAK ONLY TO THE KING AND ONLY IN HAUSA. --TOM

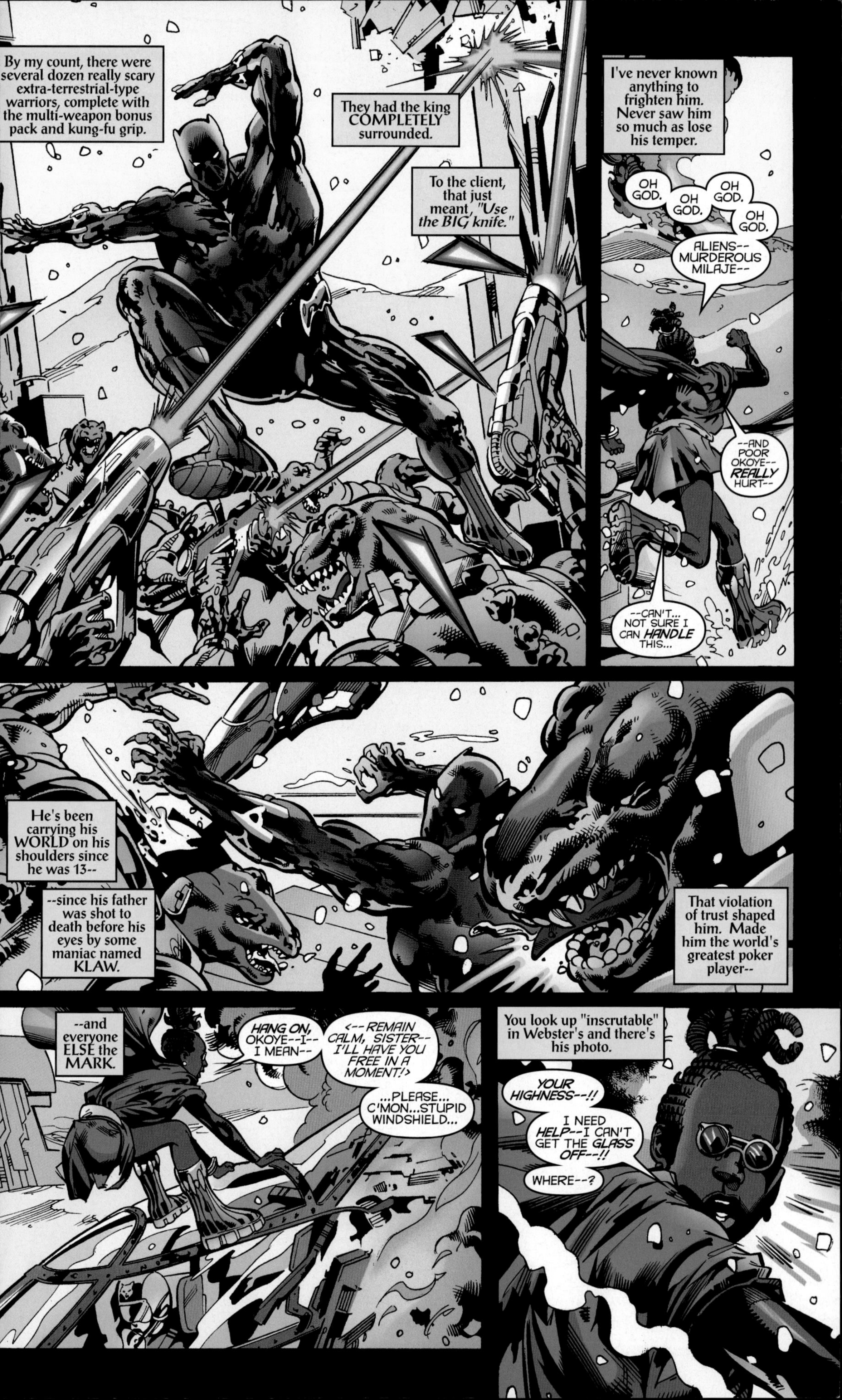

By my count, there were several dozen really scary extra-terrestrial-type warriors, complete with the multi-weapon bonus pack and kung-fu grip.
They had the king COMPLETELY surrounded.
To the client, that just meant, "Use the BIG knife."
I've never known anything to frighten him. Never saw him so much as lose his temper.
OH GOD.
OH GOD.
OH GOD.
OH GOD.
ALIENS-- MURDEROUS MILAJE--
--AND POOR OKOYE-- REALLY HURT--
--CAN'T... NOT SURE I CAN HANDLE THIS...
He's been carrying his WORLD on his shoulders since he was 13--
--since his father was shot to death before his eyes by some maniac named KLAW.
That violation of trust shaped him. Made him the world's greatest poker player--
--and everyone ELSE the MARK.
HANG ON, OKOYE--I-- I MEAN--
<--REMAIN CALM, SISTER-- I'LL HAVE YOU FREE IN A MOMENT!>
...PLEASE... C'MON...STUPID WINDSHIELD...
You look up "inscrutable" in Webster's and there's his photo.
YOUR HIGHNESS--!!
I NEED HELP--I CAN'T GET THE GLASS OFF--!!
WHERE--?

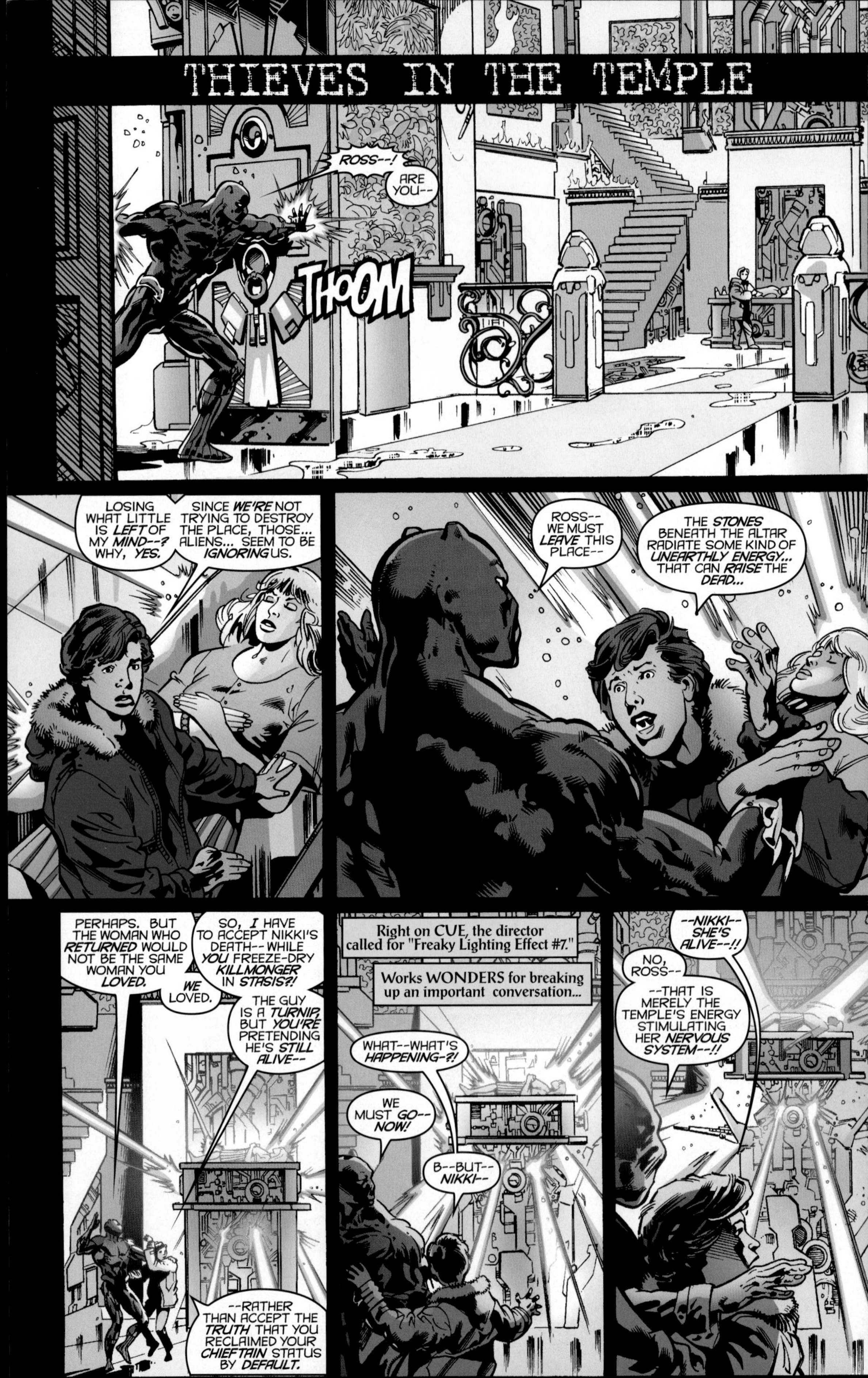
THIEVES IN THE TEMPLE
ROSS--!
ARE YOU--
THOOM
LOSING WHAT LITTLE IS LEFT OF MY MIND--? WHY, YES.
SINCE WE'RE NOT TRYING TO DESTROY THE PLACE, THOSE... ALIENS... SEEM TO BE IGNORING US.
ROSS-- WE MUST LEAVE THIS PLACE--
THE STONES BENEATH THE ALTAR RADIATE SOME KIND OF UNEARTHLY ENERGY... THAT CAN RAISE THE DEAD...
PERHAPS. BUT THE WOMAN WHO RETURNED WOULD NOT BE THE SAME WOMAN YOU LOVED.
SO, I HAVE TO ACCEPT NIKKI'S DEATH-- WHILE YOU FREEZE-DRY KILLMONGER IN STASIS?!
WE LOVED.
THE GUY IS A TURNIP, BUT YOU'RE PRETENDING HE'S STILL ALIVE--
--RATHER THAN ACCEPT THE TRUTH THAT YOU RECLAIMED YOUR CHIEFTAIN STATUS BY DEFAULT.
Right on CUE, the director called for "Freaky Lighting Effect #7."
Works WONDERS for breaking up an important conversation...
WHAT--WHAT'S HAPPENING-?!
WE MUST GO-- NOW!
B--BUT-- NIKKI--
--NIKKI-- SHE'S ALIVE--!!
NO, ROSS--
--THAT IS MERELY THE TEMPLE'S ENERGY STIMULATING HER NERVOUS SYSTEM--!!

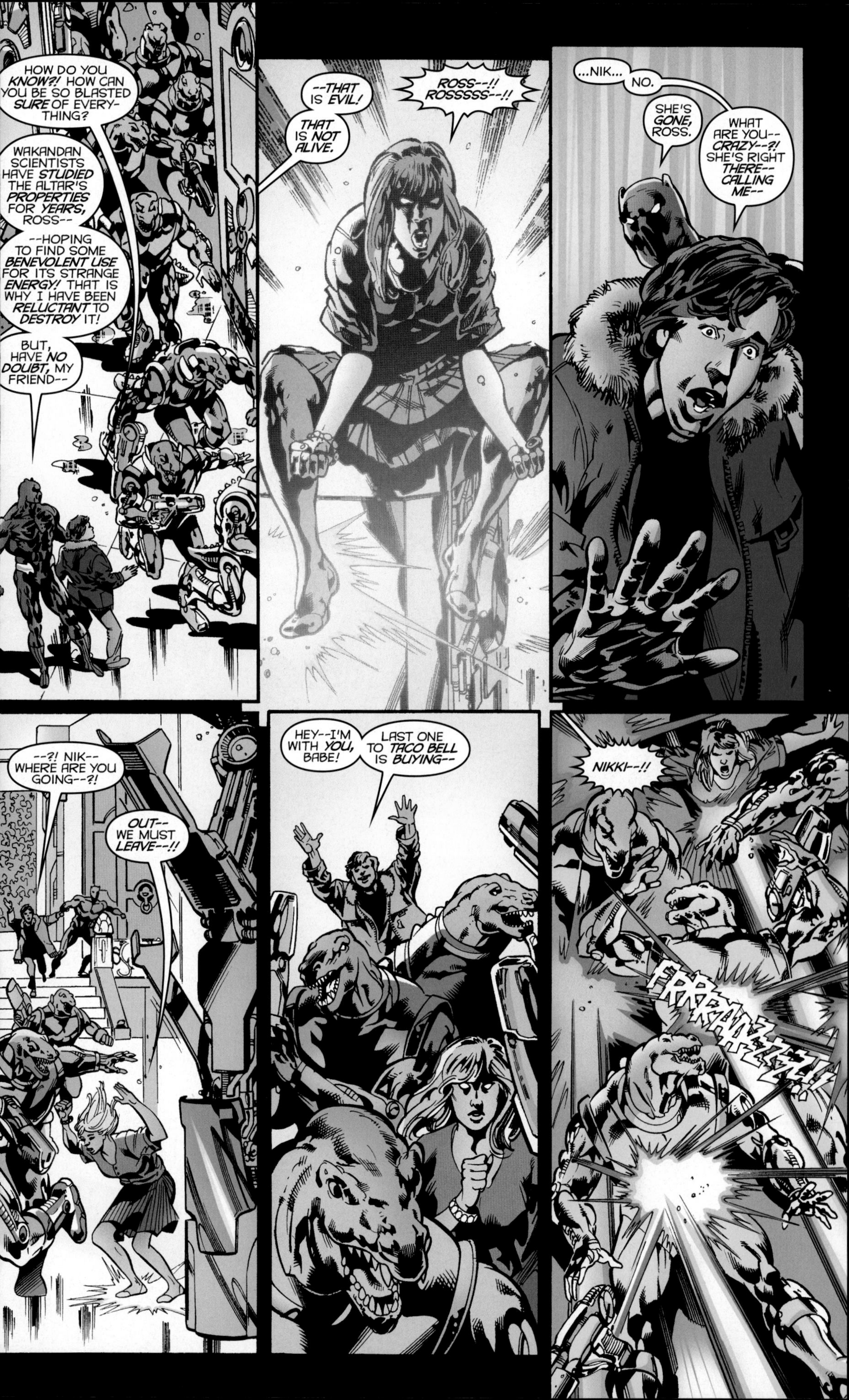
HOW DO YOU KNOW?! HOW CAN YOU BE SO BLASTED SURE OF EVERYTHING?
WAKANDAN SCIENTISTS HAVE STUDIED THE ALTAR'S PROPERTIES FOR YEARS, ROSS--
--HOPING TO FIND SOME BENEVOLENT USE FOR ITS STRANGE ENERGY! THAT IS WHY I HAVE BEEN RELUCTANT TO DESTROY IT!
BUT, HAVE NO DOUBT, MY FRIEND--
--THAT IS EVIL!
THAT IS NOT ALIVE.
ROSS--!! ROSSSSS--!!
...NIK...
NO.
SHE'S GONE, ROSS.
WHAT ARE YOU-- CRAZY--?! SHE'S RIGHT THERE-- CALLING ME--
--?! NIK-- WHERE ARE YOU GOING--?!
OUT-- WE MUST LEAVE--!!
HEY--I'M WITH YOU, BABE!
LAST ONE TO TACO BELL IS BUYING--
NIKKI--!!
FRRRAKKZZZ!!

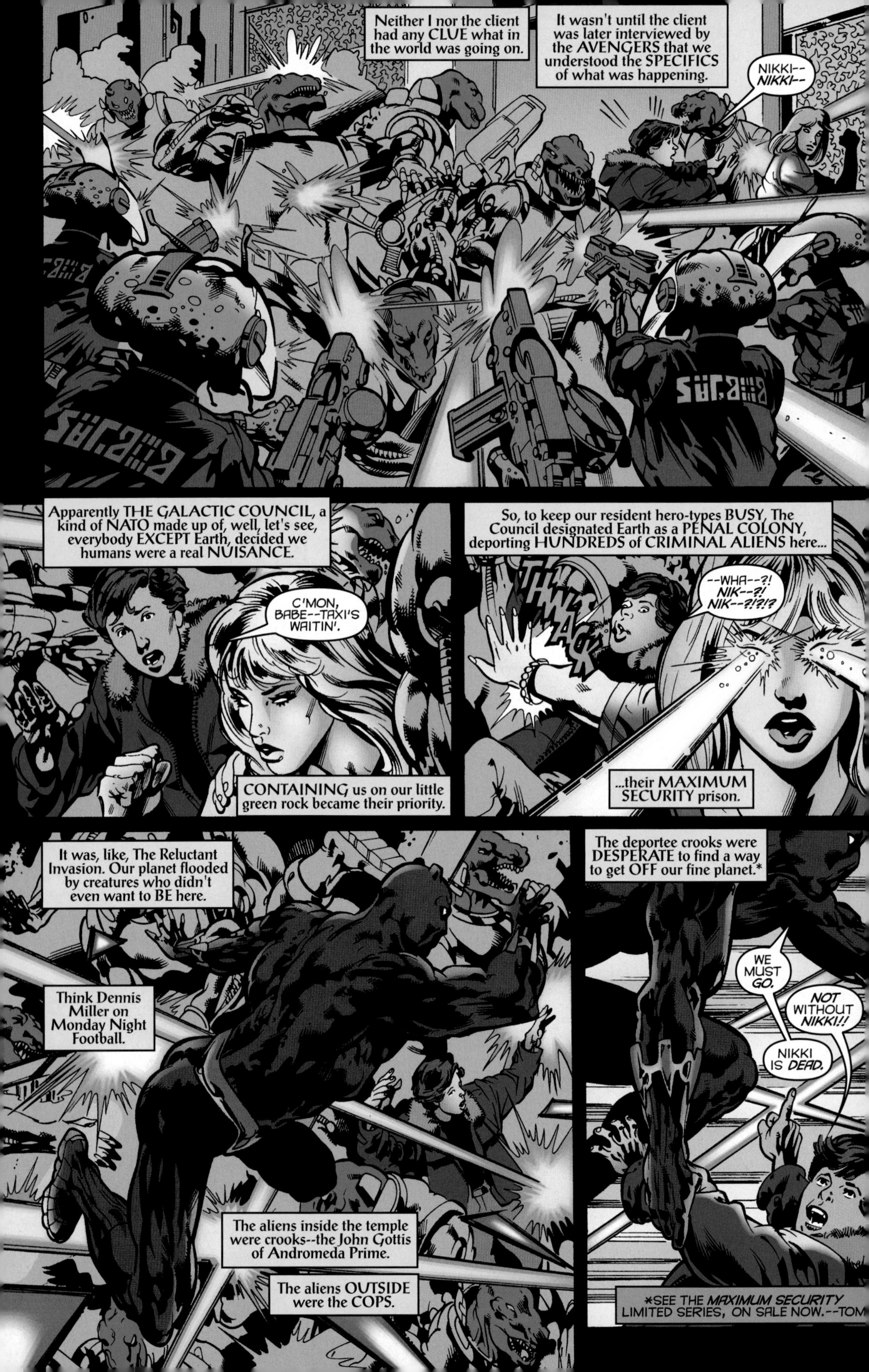

Neither I nor the client had any CLUE what in the world was going on.
It wasn't until the client was later interviewed by the AVENGERS that we understood the SPECIFICS of what was happening.
NIKKI-- NIKKI--
Apparently THE GALACTIC COUNCIL, a kind of NATO made up of, well, let's see, everybody EXCEPT Earth, decided we humans were a real NUISANCE.
C'MON, BABE--TAXI'S WAITIN'.
CONTAINING us on our little green rock became their priority.
So, to keep our resident hero-types BUSY, The Council designated Earth as a PENAL COLONY, deporting HUNDREDS of CRIMINAL ALIENS here...
THWACK
--WHA--?! NIK--?! NIK--?!?!?
...their MAXIMUM SECURITY prison.
It was, like, The Reluctant Invasion. Our planet flooded by creatures who didn't even want to BE here.
Think Dennis Miller on Monday Night Football.
The aliens inside the temple were crooks--the John Gottis of Andromeda Prime.
The aliens OUTSIDE were the COPS.
The deportee crooks were DESPERATE to find a way to get OFF our fine planet.*
WE MUST GO.
NOT WITHOUT NIKKI!!
NIKKI IS DEAD.
*SEE THE MAXIMUM SECURITY LIMITED SERIES, ON SALE NOW.--TOM

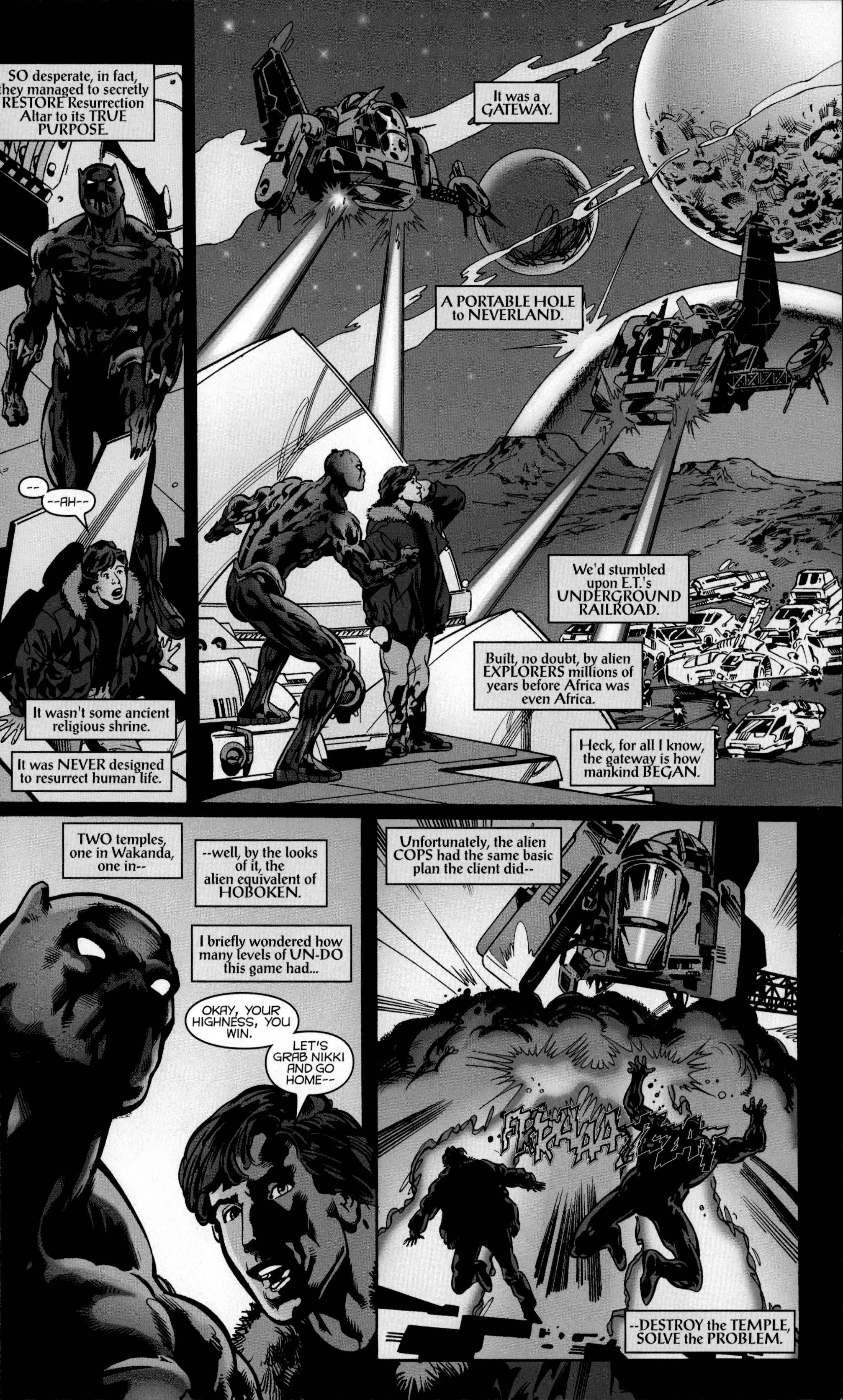
SO desperate, in fact, they managed to secretly RESTORE Resurrection Altar to its TRUE PURPOSE.
--
--AH--
It wasn't some ancient religious shrine.
It was NEVER designed to resurrect human life.
It was a GATEWAY.
A PORTABLE HOLE to NEVERLAND.
We'd stumbled upon E.T.'s UNDERGROUND RAILROAD.
Built, no doubt, by alien EXPLORERS millions of years before Africa was even Africa.
Heck, for all I know, the gateway is how mankind BEGAN.
TWO temples, one in Wakanda, one in--
--well, by the looks of it, the alien equivalent of HOBOKEN.
I briefly wondered how many levels of UN-DO this game had...
OKAY, YOUR HIGHNESS, YOU WIN.
LET'S GRAB NIKKI AND GO HOME--
Unfortunately, the alien COPS had the same basic plan the client did--
--DESTROY the TEMPLE, SOLVE the PROBLEM.

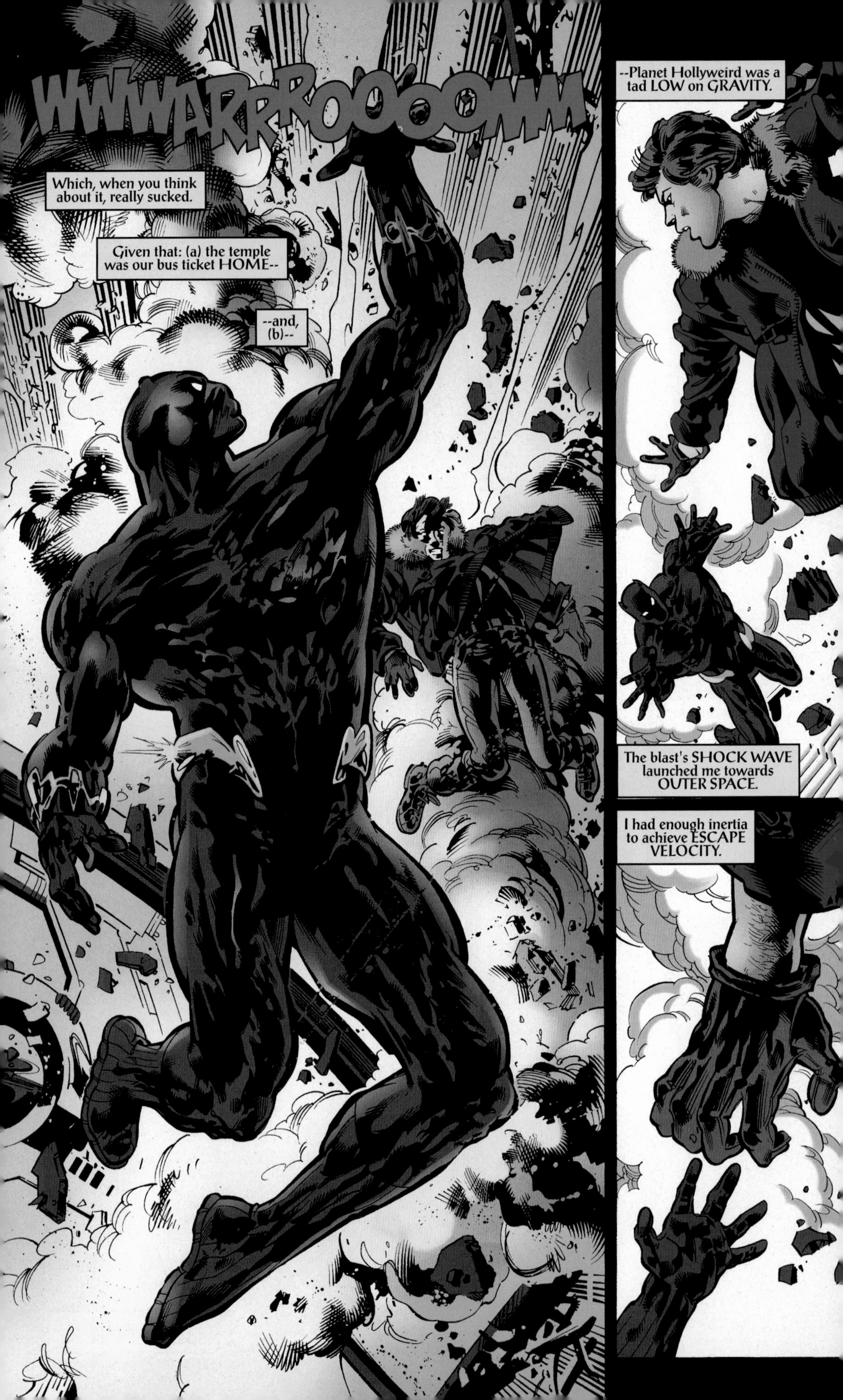
WWWARRROOOOOMM
Which, when you think about it, really sucked.
Given that: (a) the temple was our bus ticket HOME--
--and, (b)--
--Planet Hollyweird was a tad LOW on GRAVITY.
The blast's SHOCK WAVE launched me towards OUTER SPACE.
I had enough inertia to achieve ESCAPE VELOCITY.

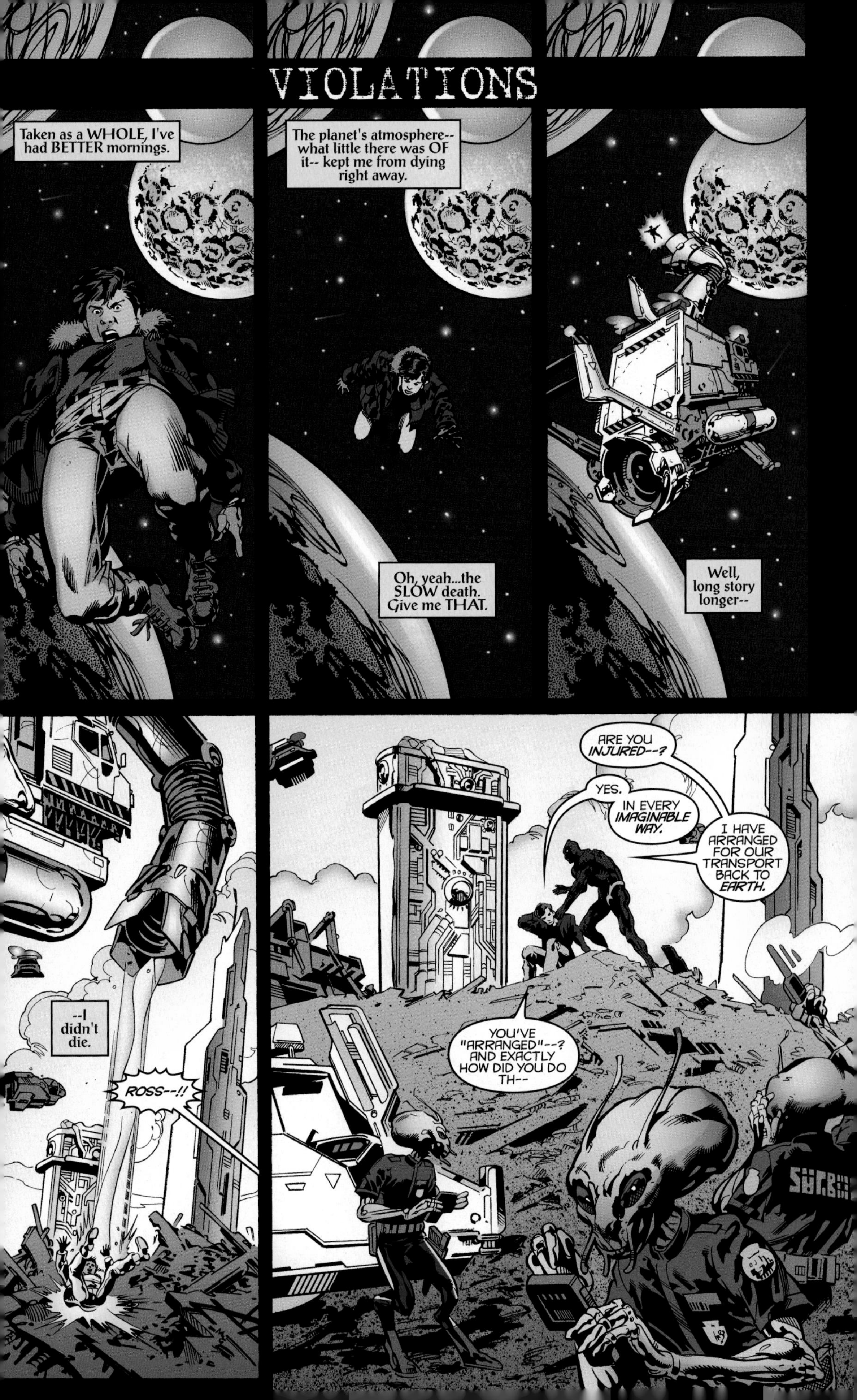
VIOLATIONS
Taken as a WHOLE, I've had BETTER mornings.
The planet's atmosphere-- what little there was OF it-- kept me from dying right away.
Oh, yeah...the SLOW death. Give me THAT.
Well, long story longer--
--I didn't die.
ROSS--!!
ARE YOU INJURED--?
YES.
IN EVERY IMAGINABLE WAY.
I HAVE ARRANGED FOR OUR TRANSPORT BACK TO EARTH.
YOU'VE "ARRANGED"--? AND EXACTLY HOW DID YOU DO TH--

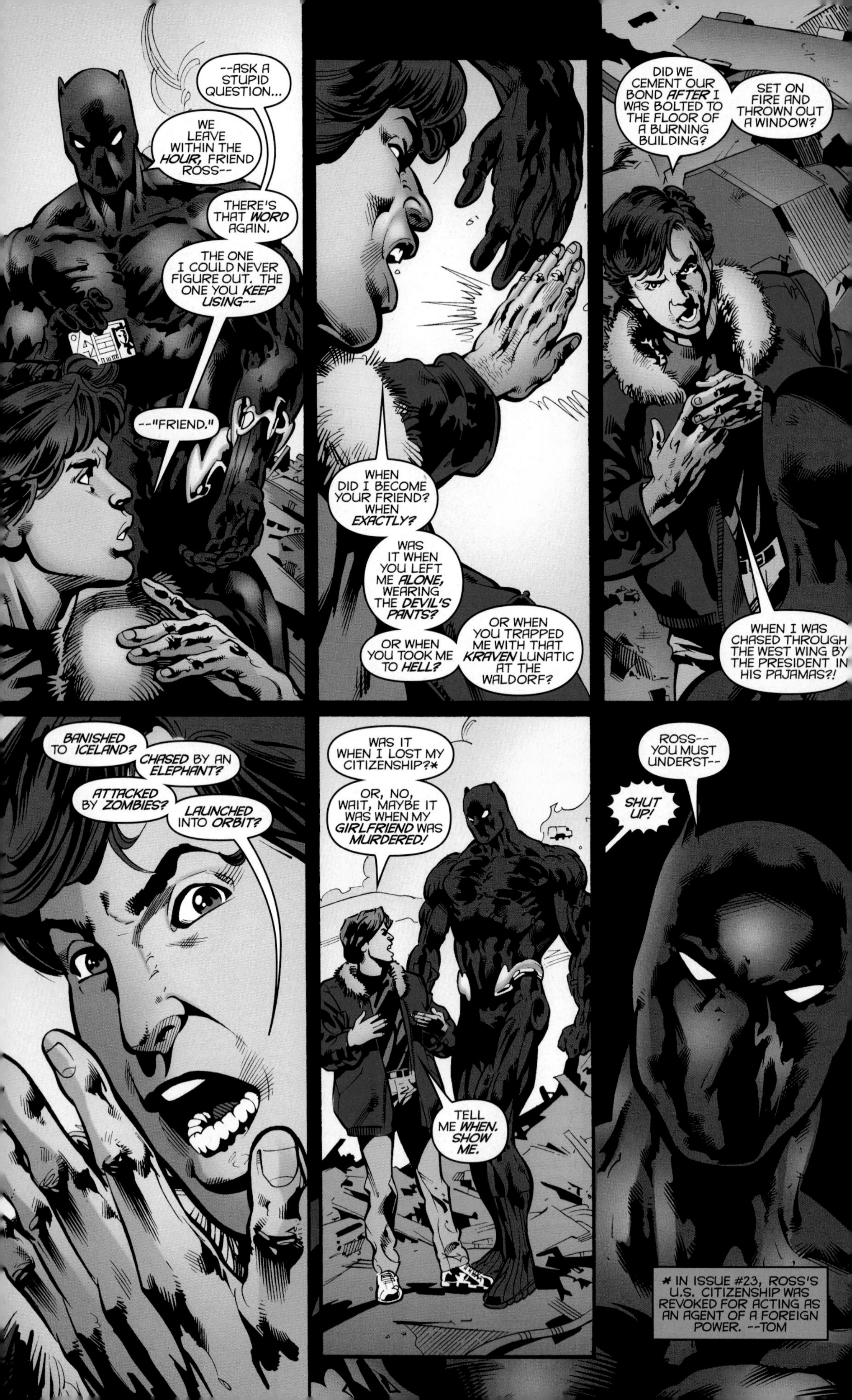
--ASK A STUPID QUESTION...
WE LEAVE WITHIN THE *HOUR,* FRIEND ROSS--
THERE'S THAT *WORD* AGAIN.
THE ONE I COULD NEVER FIGURE OUT. THE ONE YOU *KEEP USING*--
--"FRIEND."
WHEN DID I BECOME YOUR FRIEND? WHEN *EXACTLY?*
WAS IT WHEN YOU LEFT ME *ALONE,* WEARING THE *DEVIL'S PANTS?*
OR WHEN YOU TOOK ME TO *HELL?*
OR WHEN YOU TRAPPED ME WITH THAT *KRAVEN* LUNATIC AT THE WALDORF?
DID WE CEMENT OUR BOND *AFTER* I WAS BOLTED TO THE FLOOR OF A BURNING BUILDING?
SET ON FIRE AND THROWN OUT A WINDOW?
WHEN I WAS CHASED THROUGH THE WEST WING BY THE PRESIDENT IN HIS PAJAMAS?!
BANISHED TO *ICELAND?*
CHASED BY AN *ELEPHANT?*
ATTACKED BY *ZOMBIES?*
LAUNCHED INTO *ORBIT?*
WAS IT WHEN I LOST MY CITIZENSHIP?*
OR, NO, WAIT, MAYBE IT WAS WHEN MY *GIRLFRIEND* WAS *MURDERED!*
TELL ME *WHEN. SHOW ME.*
ROSS-- YOU MUST UNDERST--
SHUT UP!
* IN ISSUE #23, ROSS'S U.S. CITIZENSHIP WAS REVOKED FOR ACTING AS AN AGENT OF A FOREIGN POWER. --TOM

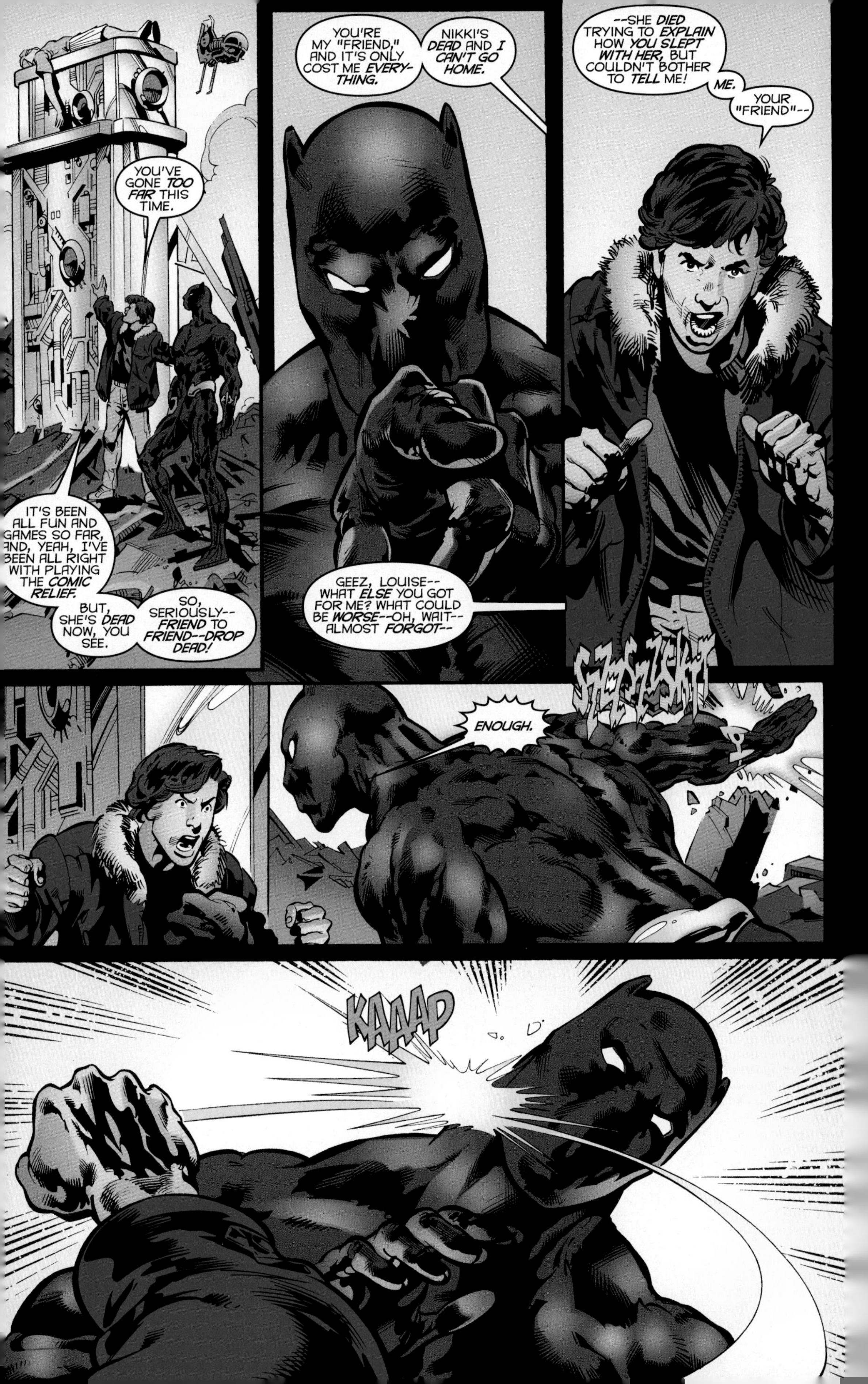
YOU'VE GONE TOO FAR THIS TIME.
IT'S BEEN ALL FUN AND GAMES SO FAR, AND, YEAH, I'VE BEEN ALL RIGHT WITH PLAYING THE COMIC RELIEF.
BUT, SHE'S DEAD NOW, YOU SEE.
SO, SERIOUSLY-- FRIEND TO FRIEND--DROP DEAD!
YOU'RE MY "FRIEND," AND IT'S ONLY COST ME EVERY-THING.
NIKKI'S DEAD AND I CAN'T GO HOME.
GEEZ, LOUISE-- WHAT ELSE YOU GOT FOR ME? WHAT COULD BE WORSE--OH, WAIT-- ALMOST FORGOT--
--SHE DIED TRYING TO EXPLAIN HOW YOU SLEPT WITH HER, BUT COULDN'T BOTHER TO TELL ME!
ME.
YOUR "FRIEND"--
SKZZSKKT
ENOUGH.
KAAAP

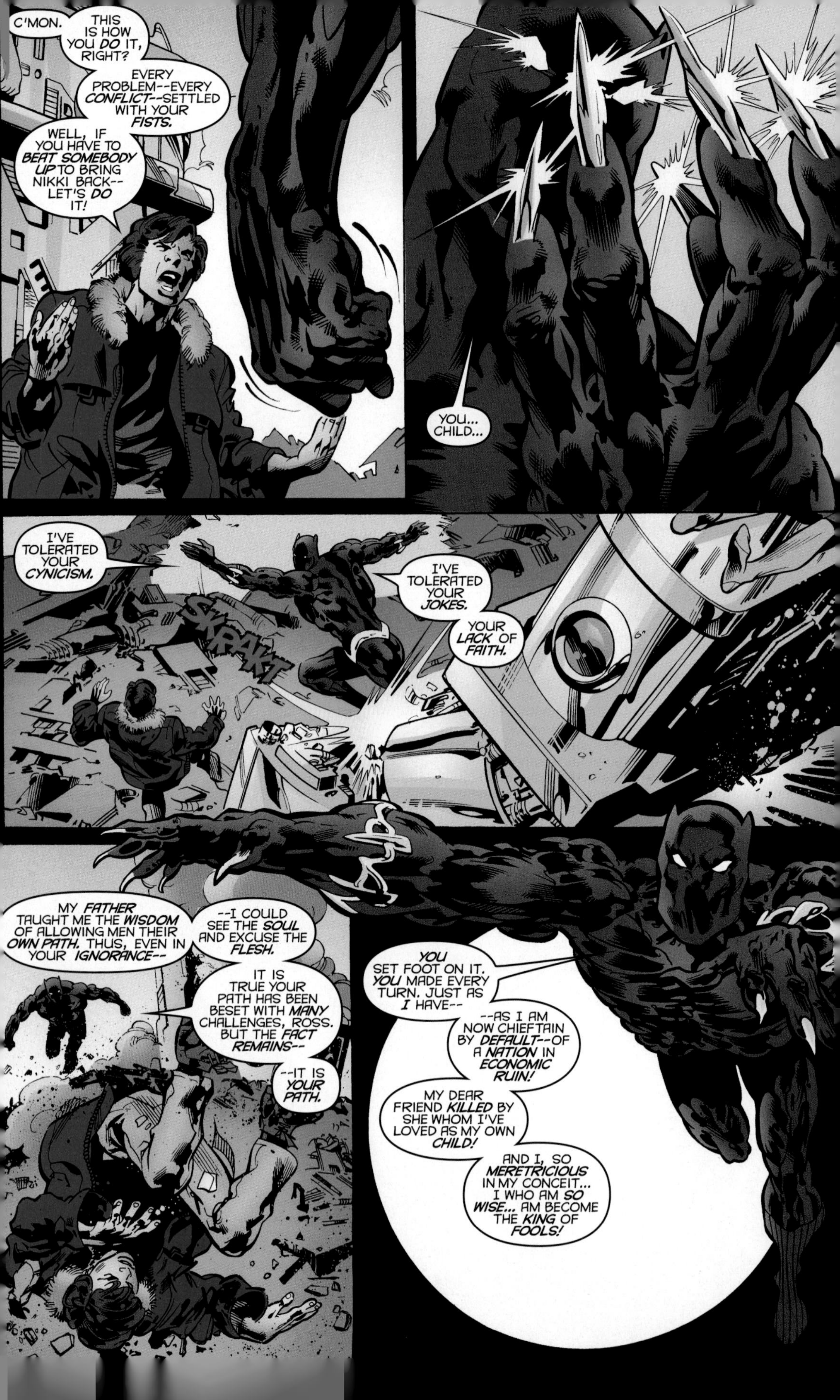
C'MON.
THIS IS HOW YOU DO IT, RIGHT?
EVERY PROBLEM--EVERY CONFLICT--SETTLED WITH YOUR FISTS.
WELL, IF YOU HAVE TO BEAT SOMEBODY UP TO BRING NIKKI BACK-- LET'S DO IT!
YOU... CHILD...
I'VE TOLERATED YOUR CYNICISM.
SKRAKT
I'VE TOLERATED YOUR JOKES.
YOUR LACK OF FAITH.
MY FATHER TAUGHT ME THE WISDOM OF ALLOWING MEN THEIR OWN PATH. THUS, EVEN IN YOUR IGNORANCE--
--I COULD SEE THE SOUL AND EXCUSE THE FLESH.
IT IS TRUE YOUR PATH HAS BEEN BESET WITH MANY CHALLENGES, ROSS. BUT THE FACT REMAINS--
--IT IS YOUR PATH.
YOU SET FOOT ON IT. YOU MADE EVERY TURN. JUST AS I HAVE--
--AS I AM NOW CHIEFTAIN BY DEFAULT--OF A NATION IN ECONOMIC RUIN!
MY DEAR FRIEND KILLED BY SHE WHOM I'VE LOVED AS MY OWN CHILD!
AND I, SO MERETRICIOUS IN MY CONCEIT... I WHO AM SO WISE... AM BECOME THE KING OF FOOLS!

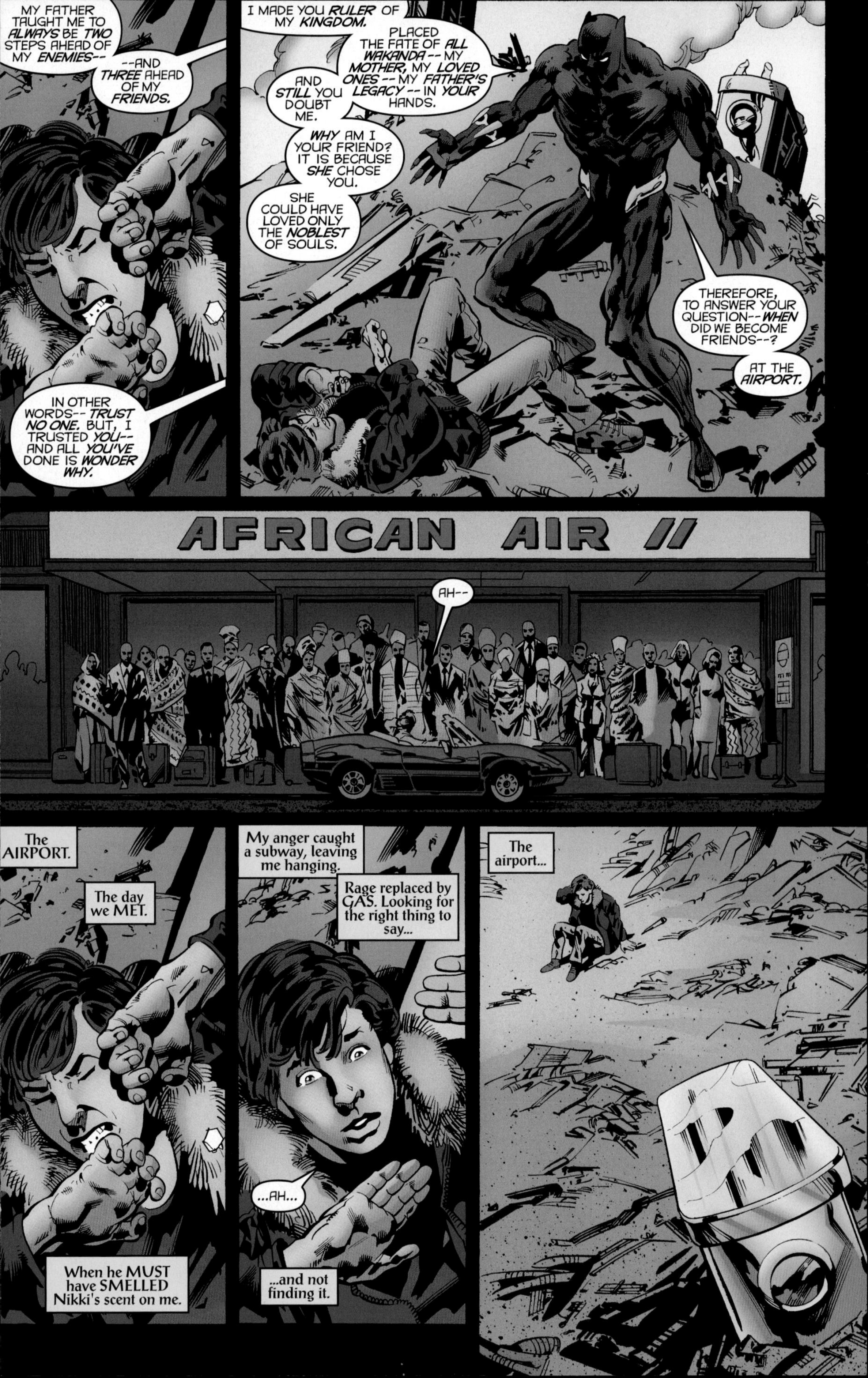
MY FATHER TAUGHT ME TO ALWAYS BE TWO STEPS AHEAD OF MY ENEMIES--
--AND THREE AHEAD OF MY FRIENDS.
IN OTHER WORDS-- TRUST NO ONE. BUT, I TRUSTED YOU-- AND ALL YOU'VE DONE IS WONDER WHY.
I MADE YOU RULER OF MY KINGDOM.
PLACED THE FATE OF ALL WAKANDA -- MY MOTHER, MY LOVED ONES -- MY FATHER'S LEGACY -- IN YOUR HANDS.
AND STILL YOU DOUBT ME.
WHY AM I YOUR FRIEND? IT IS BECAUSE SHE CHOSE YOU.
SHE COULD HAVE LOVED ONLY THE NOBLEST OF SOULS.
THEREFORE, TO ANSWER YOUR QUESTION-- WHEN DID WE BECOME FRIENDS--?
AT THE AIRPORT.
AFRICAN AIR II
AH--
The AIRPORT.
The day we MET.
When he MUST have SMELLED Nikki's scent on me.
My anger caught a subway, leaving me hanging.
Rage replaced by GAS. Looking for the right thing to say...
...AH...
...and not finding it.
The airport...

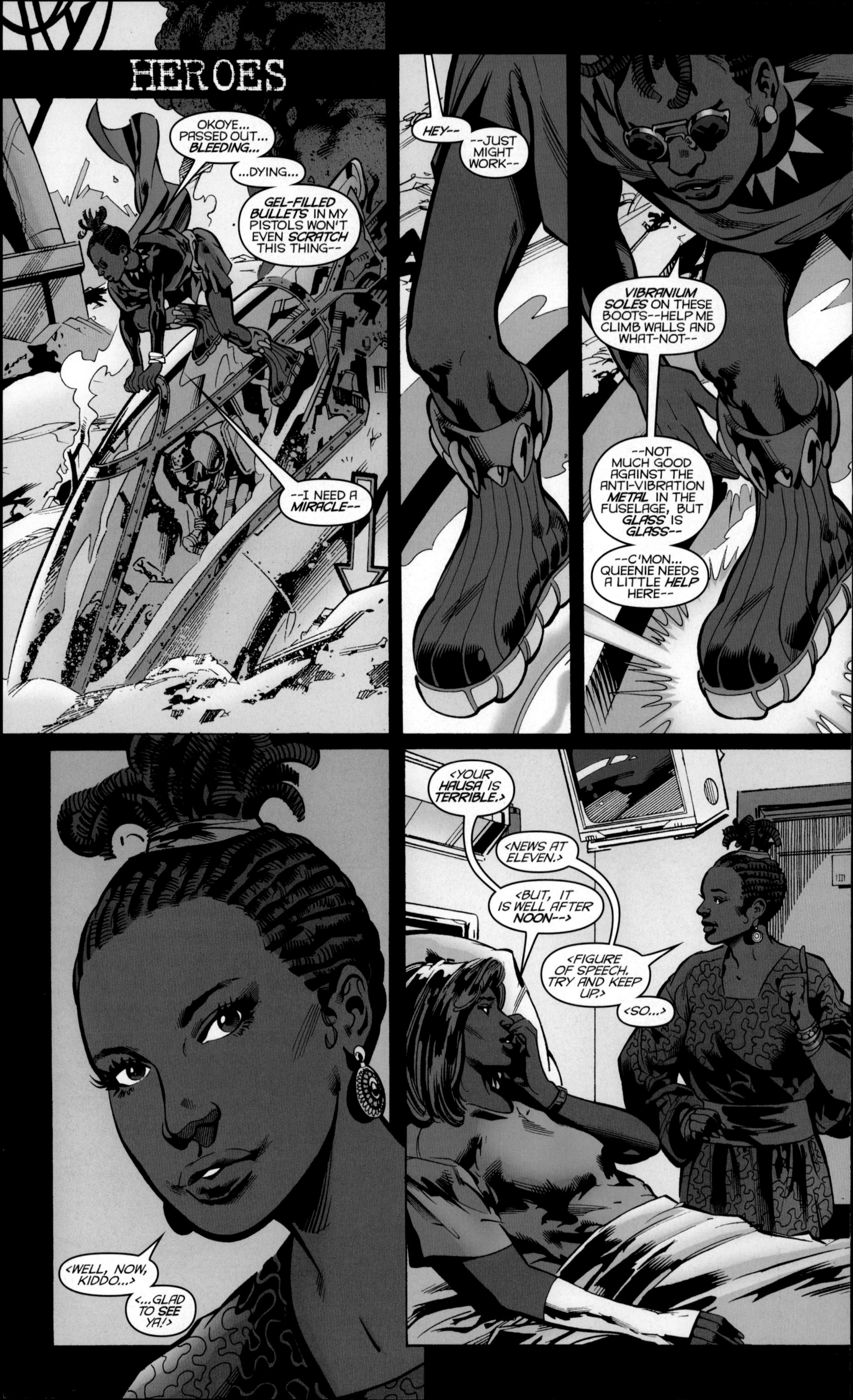
HEROES
OKOYE... PASSED OUT... BLEEDING...
...DYING...
GEL-FILLED BULLETS IN MY PISTOLS WON'T EVEN SCRATCH THIS THING--
--I NEED A MIRACLE--
HEY--
--JUST MIGHT WORK--
VIBRANIUM SOLES ON THESE BOOTS--HELP ME CLIMB WALLS AND WHAT-NOT--
--NOT MUCH GOOD AGAINST THE ANTI-VIBRATION METAL IN THE FUSELAGE, BUT GLASS IS GLASS--
--C'MON... QUEENIE NEEDS A LITTLE HELP HERE--
<WELL, NOW, KIDDO...>
<...GLAD TO SEE YA!>
<YOUR HAUSA IS TERRIBLE.>
<NEWS AT ELEVEN.>
<BUT, IT IS WELL AFTER NOON-->
<FIGURE OF SPEECH. TRY AND KEEP UP.>
<SO...>

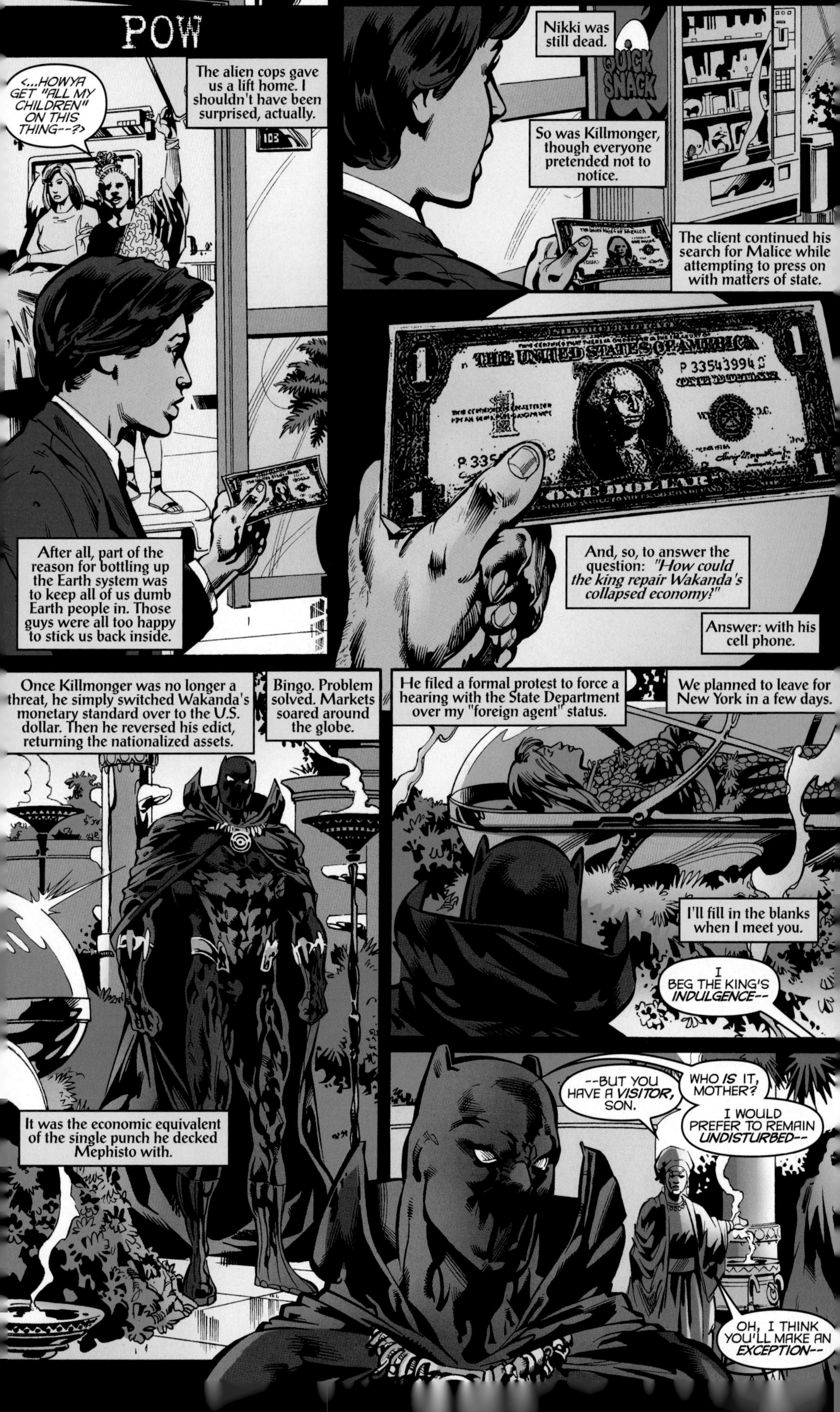
POW
<...HOWYA GET "ALL MY CHILDREN" ON THIS THING--?>
The alien cops gave us a lift home. I shouldn't have been surprised, actually.
After all, part of the reason for bottling up the Earth system was to keep all of us dumb Earth people in. Those guys were all too happy to stick us back inside.
Nikki was still dead.
So was Killmonger, though everyone pretended not to notice.
The client continued his search for Malice while attempting to press on with matters of state.
And, so, to answer the question: "How could the king repair Wakanda's collapsed economy?"
Answer: with his cell phone.
Once Killmonger was no longer a threat, he simply switched Wakanda's monetary standard over to the U.S. dollar. Then he reversed his edict, returning the nationalized assets.
Bingo. Problem solved. Markets soared around the globe.
It was the economic equivalent of the single punch he decked Mephisto with.
He filed a formal protest to force a hearing with the State Department over my "foreign agent" status.
We planned to leave for New York in a few days.
I'll fill in the blanks when I meet you.
I BEG THE KING'S INDULGENCE--
--BUT YOU HAVE A VISITOR, SON.
WHO IS IT, MOTHER?
I WOULD PREFER TO REMAIN UNDISTURBED--
OH, I THINK YOU'LL MAKE AN EXCEPTION--

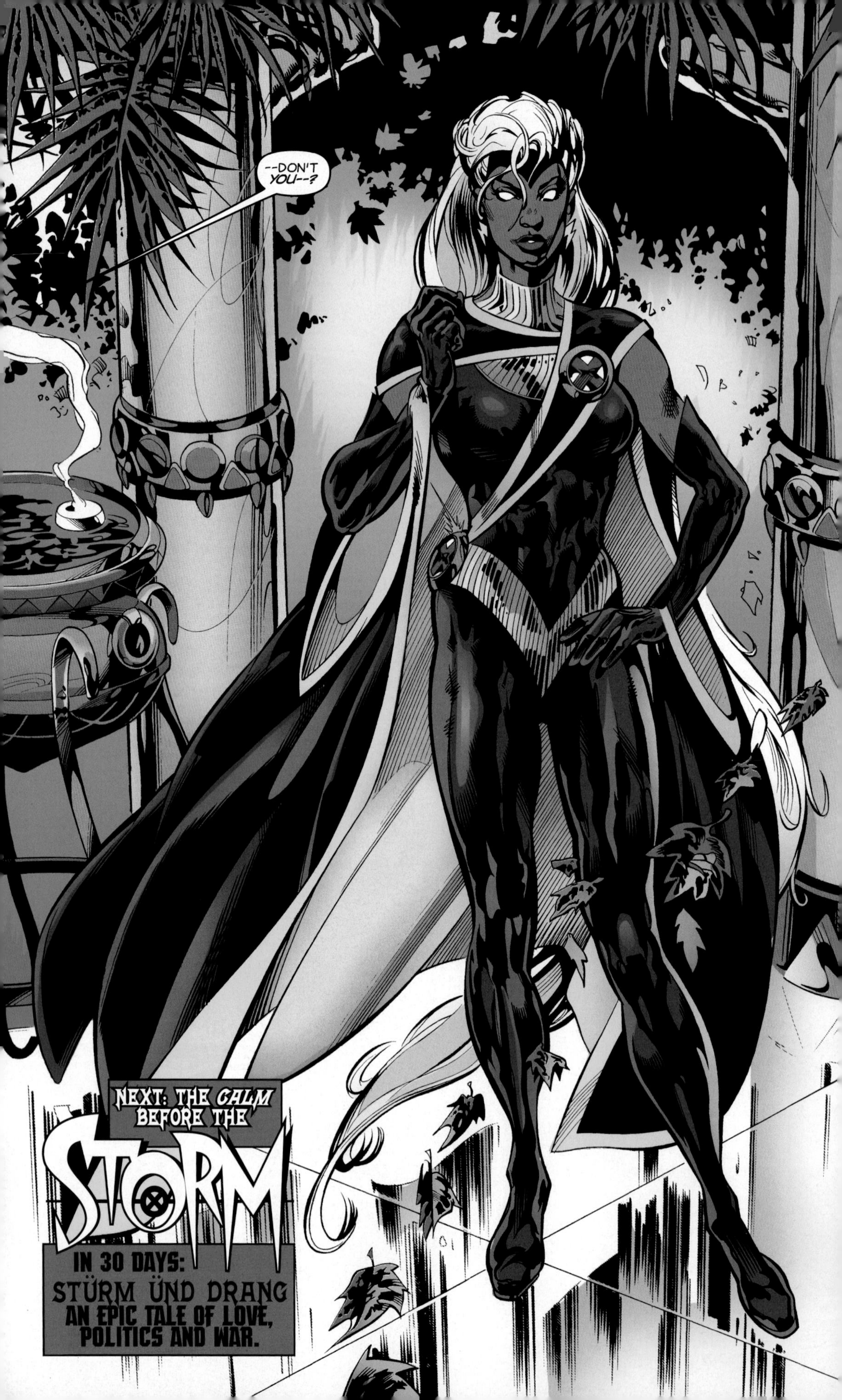
--DON'T YOU--?
NEXT: THE CALM BEFORE THE
STORM
IN 30 DAYS:
STÜRM ÜND DRANG
AN EPIC TALE OF LOVE, POLITICS AND WAR.

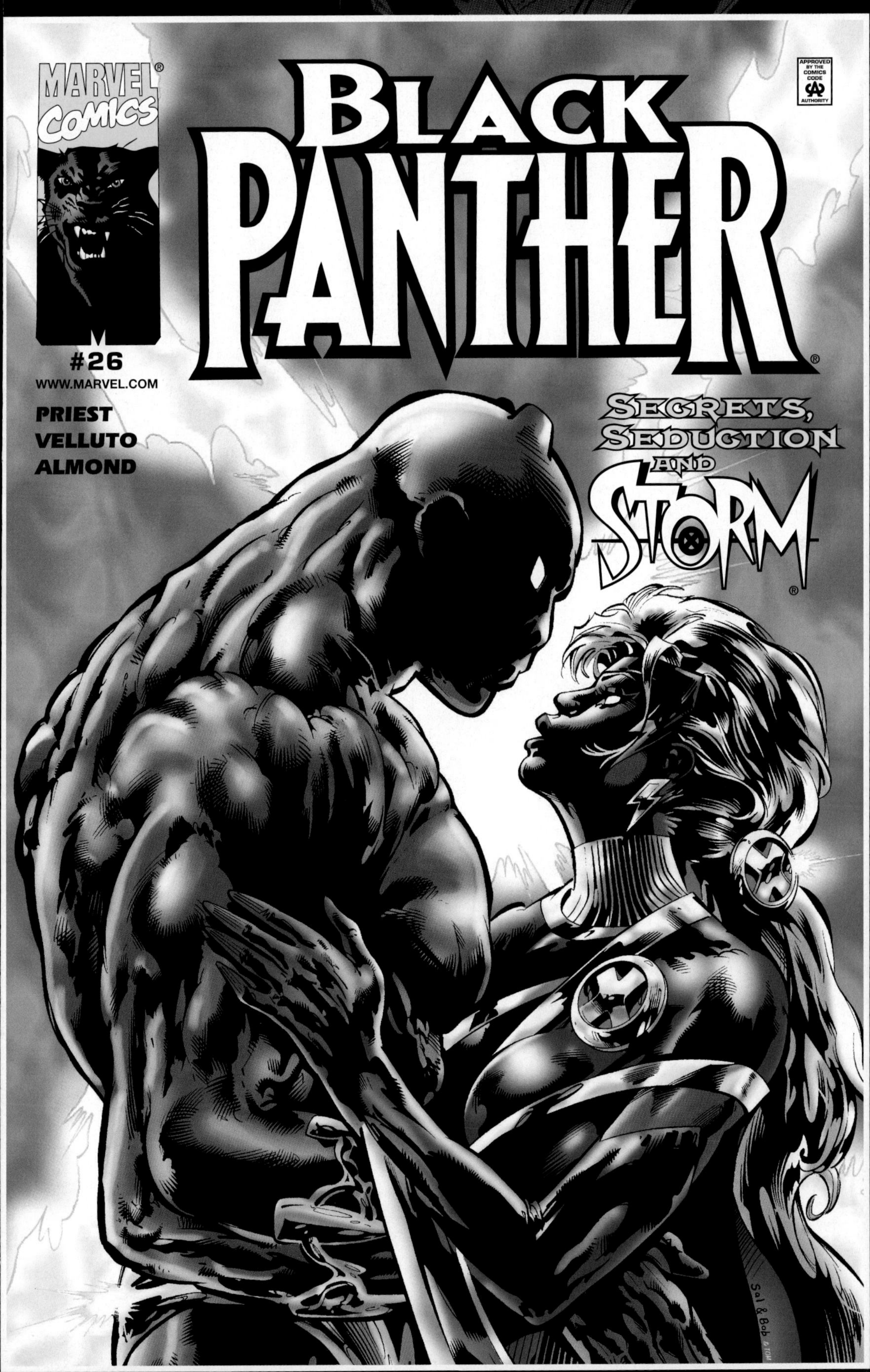
MARVEL COMICS
BLACK PANTHER
APPROVED BY THE COMICS CODE AUTHORITY
#26
WWW.MARVEL.COM
PRIEST
VELLUTO
ALMOND
SECRETS, SEDUCTION AND STORM
Sal & Bob

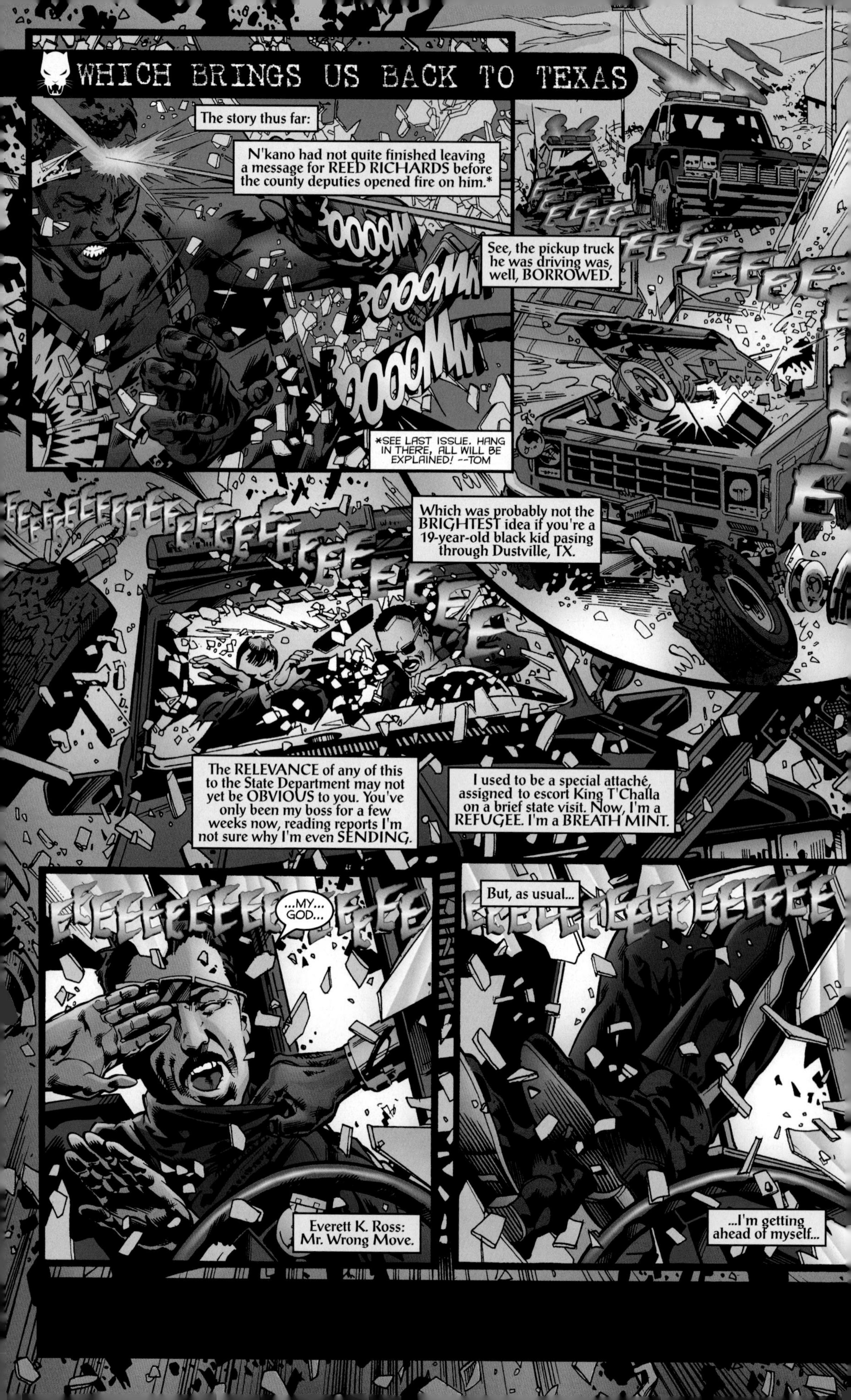

WHICH BRINGS US BACK TO TEXAS
The story thus far:
N'kano had not quite finished leaving a message for REED RICHARDS before the county deputies opened fire on him.*
BOOOOM
BOOOMM
BOOOMM
*SEE LAST ISSUE. HANG IN THERE, ALL WILL BE EXPLAINED! --TOM
See, the pickup truck he was driving was, well, BORROWED.
Which was probably not the BRIGHTEST idea if you're a 19-year-old black kid pasing through Dustville, TX.
The RELEVANCE of any of this to the State Department may not yet be OBVIOUS to you. You've only been my boss for a few weeks now, reading reports I'm not sure why I'm even SENDING.
I used to be a special attaché, assigned to escort King T'Challa on a brief state visit. Now, I'm a REFUGEE. I'm a BREATH MINT.
...MY... GOD...
Everett K. Ross: Mr. Wrong Move.
But, as usual...
...I'm getting ahead of myself...

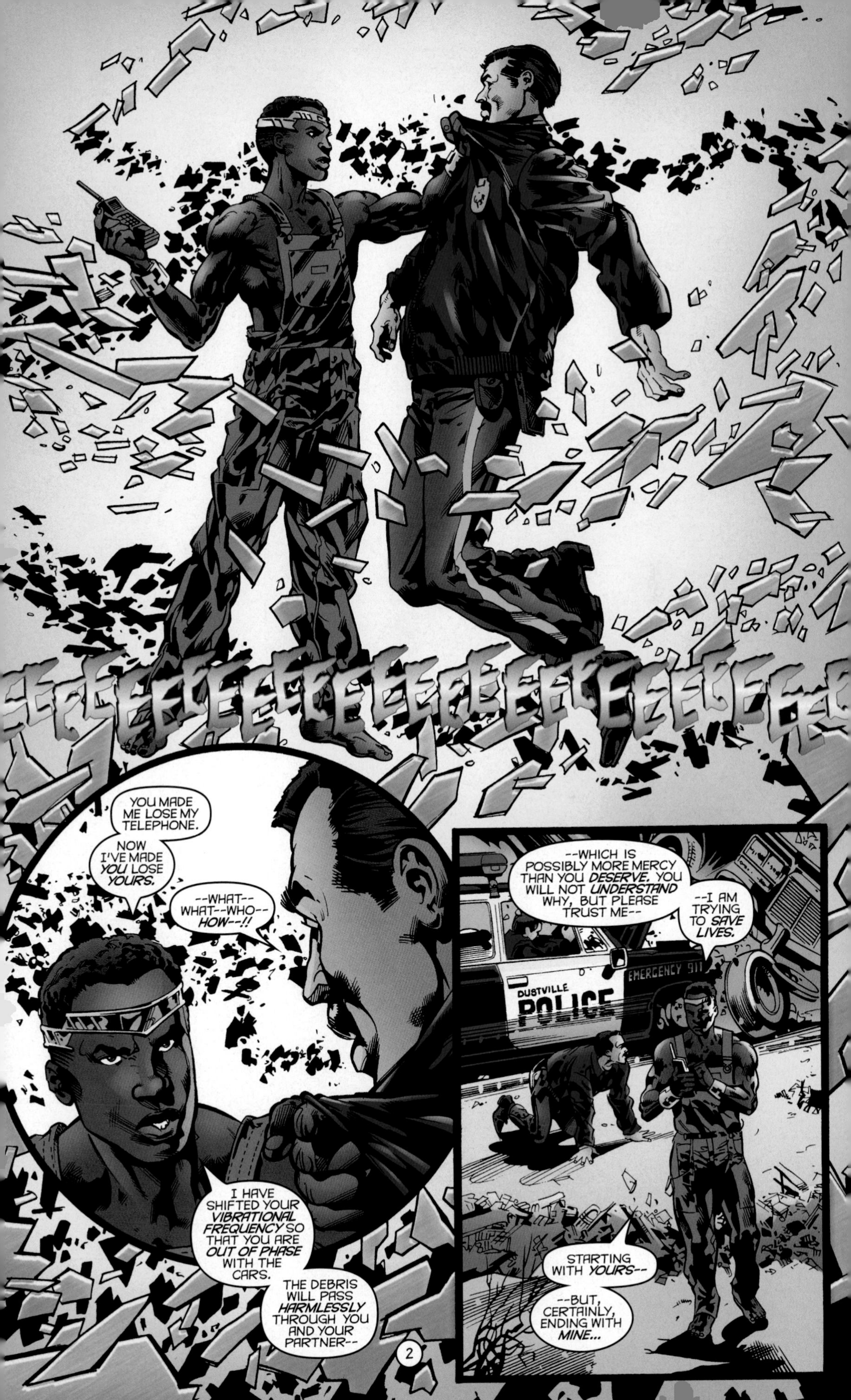
EEEEEEEEEEEEEEEEEEEEEEEEEEEE
YOU MADE ME LOSE MY TELEPHONE.
NOW I'VE MADE YOU LOSE YOURS.
--WHAT--WHAT--WHO--HOW--!!
I HAVE SHIFTED YOUR VIBRATIONAL FREQUENCY SO THAT YOU ARE OUT OF PHASE WITH THE CARS.
THE DEBRIS WILL PASS HARMLESSLY THROUGH YOU AND YOUR PARTNER--
--WHICH IS POSSIBLY MORE MERCY THAN YOU DESERVE. YOU WILL NOT UNDERSTAND WHY, BUT PLEASE TRUST ME--
--I AM TRYING TO SAVE LIVES.
EMERGENCY 911
DUSTVILLE POLICE
STARTING WITH YOURS--
--BUT, CERTAINLY, ENDING WITH MINE...

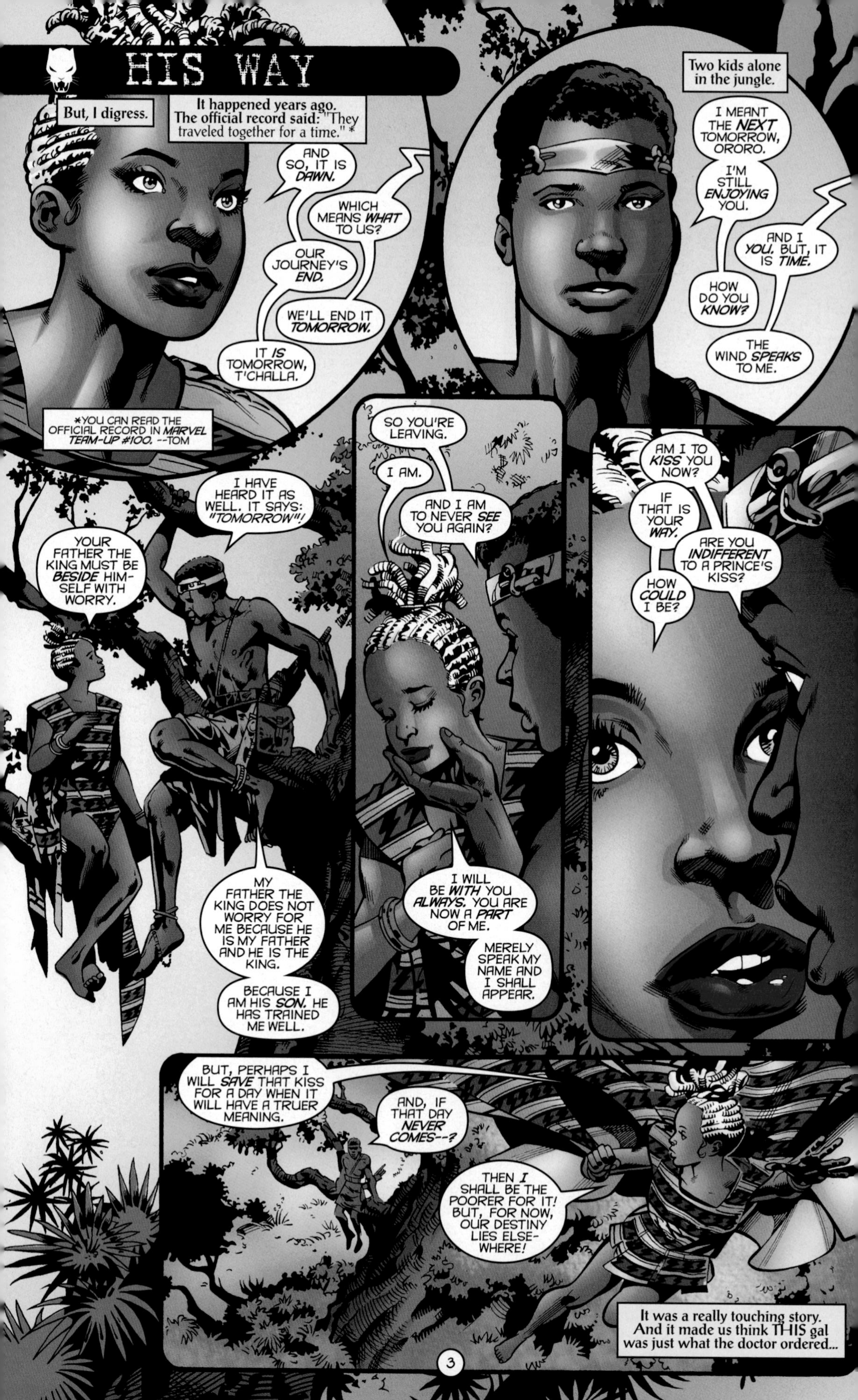
HIS WAY
But, I digress.
It happened years ago. The official record said: "They traveled together for a time." *
AND SO, IT IS DAWN.
WHICH MEANS WHAT TO US?
OUR JOURNEY'S END.
WE'LL END IT TOMORROW.
IT IS TOMORROW, T'CHALLA.
Two kids alone in the jungle.
I MEANT THE NEXT TOMORROW, ORORO.
I'M STILL ENJOYING YOU.
AND I YOU. BUT, IT IS TIME.
HOW DO YOU KNOW?
THE WIND SPEAKS TO ME.
*YOU CAN READ THE OFFICIAL RECORD IN MARVEL TEAM-UP #100. --TOM
I HAVE HEARD IT AS WELL. IT SAYS: "TOMORROW"!
YOUR FATHER THE KING MUST BE BESIDE HIMSELF WITH WORRY.
MY FATHER THE KING DOES NOT WORRY FOR ME BECAUSE HE IS MY FATHER AND HE IS THE KING.
BECAUSE I AM HIS SON. HE HAS TRAINED ME WELL.
SO YOU'RE LEAVING.
I AM.
AND I AM TO NEVER SEE YOU AGAIN?
I WILL BE WITH YOU ALWAYS. YOU ARE NOW A PART OF ME.
MERELY SPEAK MY NAME AND I SHALL APPEAR.
AM I TO KISS YOU NOW?
IF THAT IS YOUR WAY.
ARE YOU INDIFFERENT TO A PRINCE'S KISS?
HOW COULD I BE?
BUT, PERHAPS I WILL SAVE THAT KISS FOR A DAY WHEN IT WILL HAVE A TRUER MEANING.
AND, IF THAT DAY NEVER COMES--?
THEN I SHALL BE THE POORER FOR IT! BUT, FOR NOW, OUR DESTINY LIES ELSEWHERE!
It was a really touching story. And it made us think THIS gal was just what the doctor ordered...

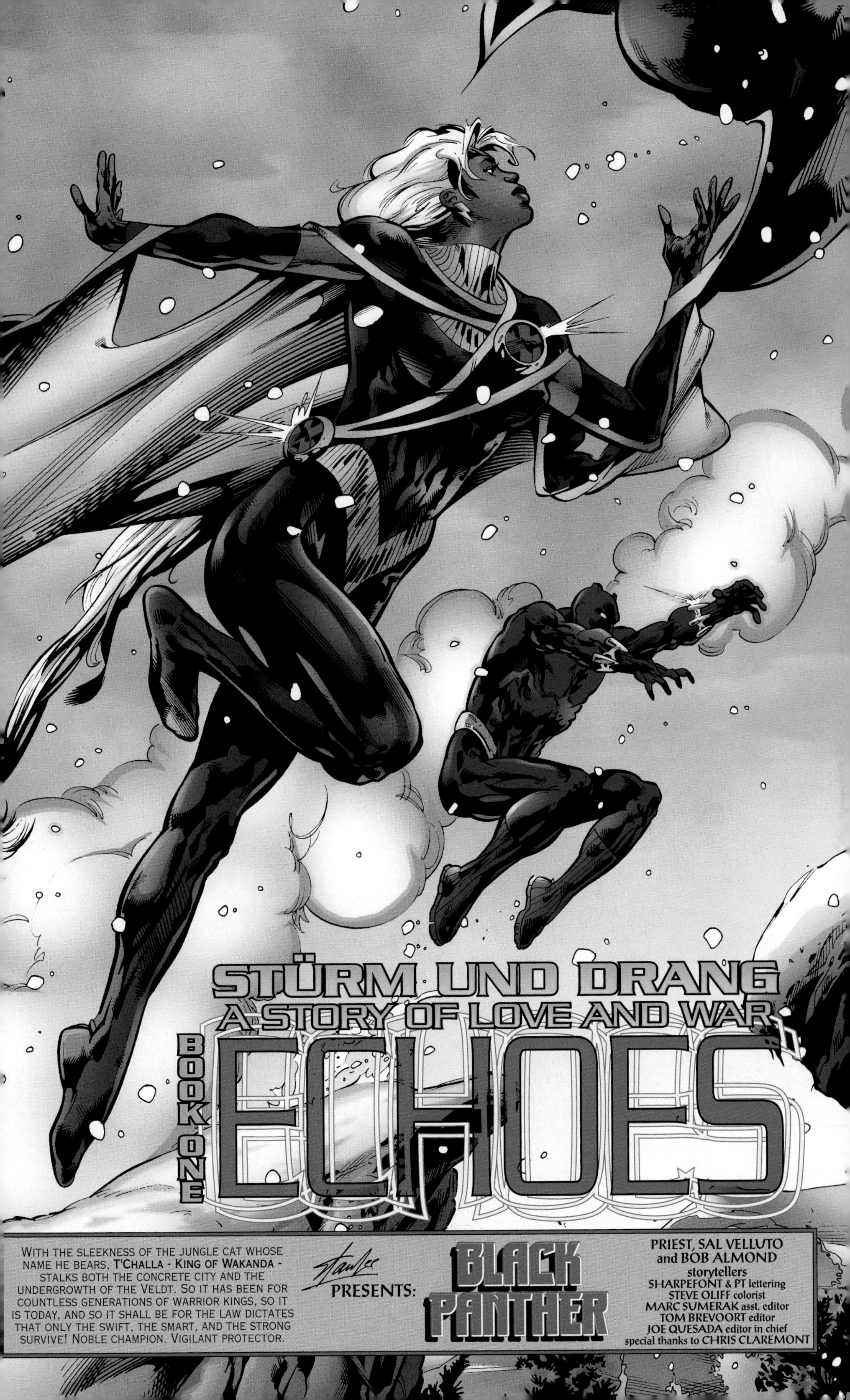
STÜRM UND DRANG
A STORY OF LOVE AND WAR
BOOK ONE
ECHOES
WITH THE SLEEKNESS OF THE JUNGLE CAT WHOSE NAME HE BEARS, T'CHALLA - KING OF WAKANDA - STALKS BOTH THE CONCRETE CITY AND THE UNDERGROWTH OF THE VELDT. SO IT HAS BEEN FOR COUNTLESS GENERATIONS OF WARRIOR KINGS, SO IT IS TODAY, AND SO IT SHALL BE FOR THE LAW DICTATES THAT ONLY THE SWIFT, THE SMART, AND THE STRONG SURVIVE! NOBLE CHAMPION. VIGILANT PROTECTOR.
Stan Lee PRESENTS:
BLACK PANTHER
PRIEST, SAL VELLUTO and BOB ALMOND storytellers
SHARPEFONT & PT lettering
STEVE OLIFF colorist
MARC SUMERAK asst. editor
TOM BREVOORT editor
JOE QUESADA editor in chief
special thanks to CHRIS CLAREMONT

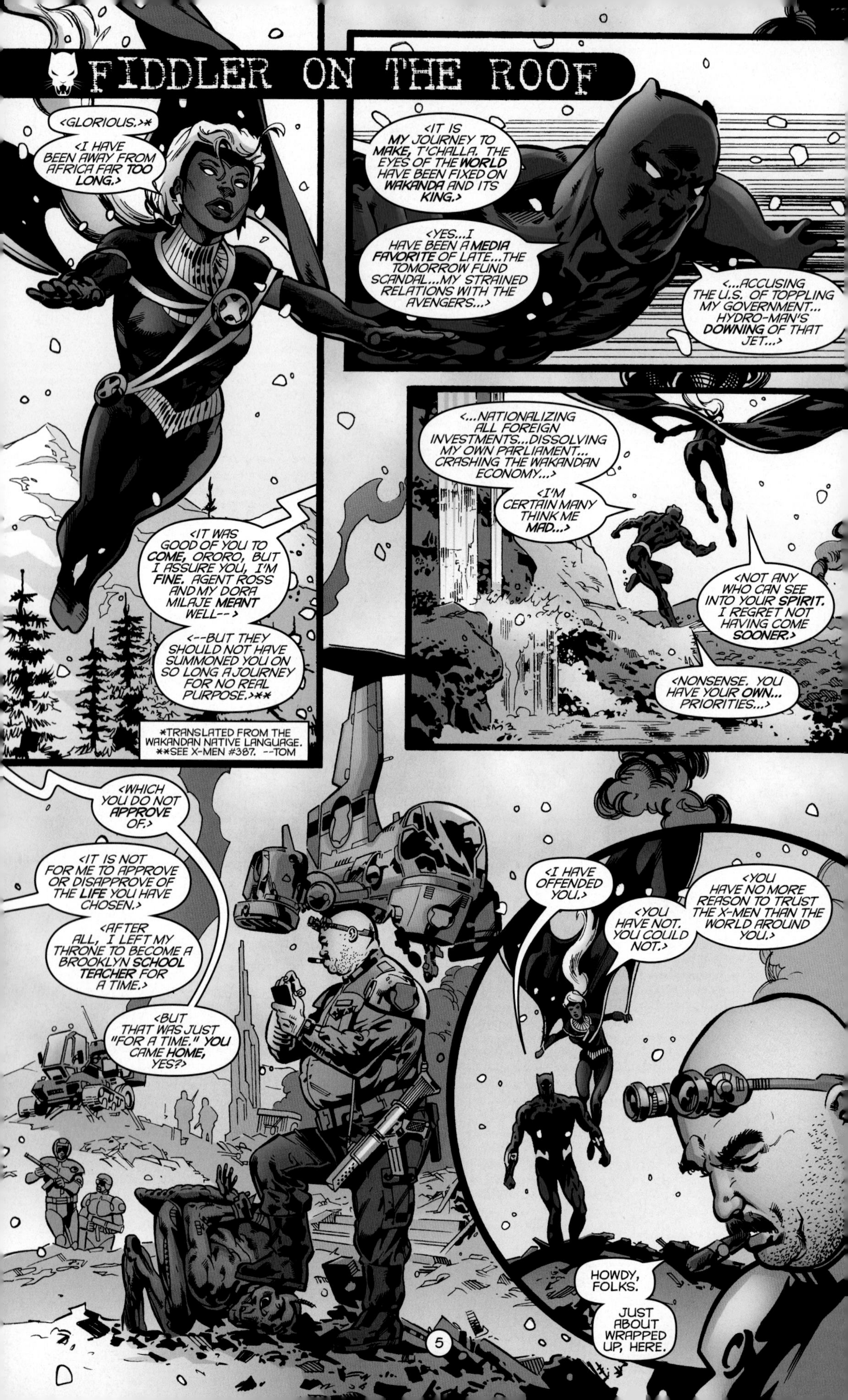
FIDDLER ON THE ROOF
<GLORIOUS.>*
<I HAVE BEEN AWAY FROM AFRICA FAR TOO LONG.>
<IT IS MY JOURNEY TO MAKE, T'CHALLA. THE EYES OF THE WORLD HAVE BEEN FIXED ON WAKANDA AND ITS KING.>
<YES...I HAVE BEEN A MEDIA FAVORITE OF LATE...THE TOMORROW FUND SCANDAL...MY STRAINED RELATIONS WITH THE AVENGERS...>
<...ACCUSING THE U.S. OF TOPPLING MY GOVERNMENT... HYDRO-MAN'S DOWNING OF THAT JET...>
<IT WAS GOOD OF YOU TO COME, ORORO, BUT I ASSURE YOU, I'M FINE. AGENT ROSS AND MY DORA MILAJE MEANT WELL-->
<--BUT THEY SHOULD NOT HAVE SUMMONED YOU ON SO LONG A JOURNEY FOR NO REAL PURPOSE.>**
*TRANSLATED FROM THE WAKANDAN NATIVE LANGUAGE. **SEE X-MEN #387. --TOM
<...NATIONALIZING ALL FOREIGN INVESTMENTS...DISSOLVING MY OWN PARLIAMENT... CRASHING THE WAKANDAN ECONOMY...>
<I'M CERTAIN MANY THINK ME MAD...>
<NOT ANY WHO CAN SEE INTO YOUR SPIRIT. I REGRET NOT HAVING COME SOONER.>
<NONSENSE. YOU HAVE YOUR OWN... PRIORITIES...>
<WHICH YOU DO NOT APPROVE OF.>
<IT IS NOT FOR ME TO APPROVE OR DISAPPROVE OF THE LIFE YOU HAVE CHOSEN.>
<AFTER ALL, I LEFT MY THRONE TO BECOME A BROOKLYN SCHOOL TEACHER FOR A TIME.>
<BUT THAT WAS JUST "FOR A TIME." YOU CAME HOME, YES?>
<I HAVE OFFENDED YOU.>
<YOU HAVE NOT. YOU COULD NOT.>
<YOU HAVE NO MORE REASON TO TRUST THE X-MEN THAN THE WORLD AROUND YOU.>
HOWDY, FOLKS.
JUST ABOUT WRAPPED UP, HERE.

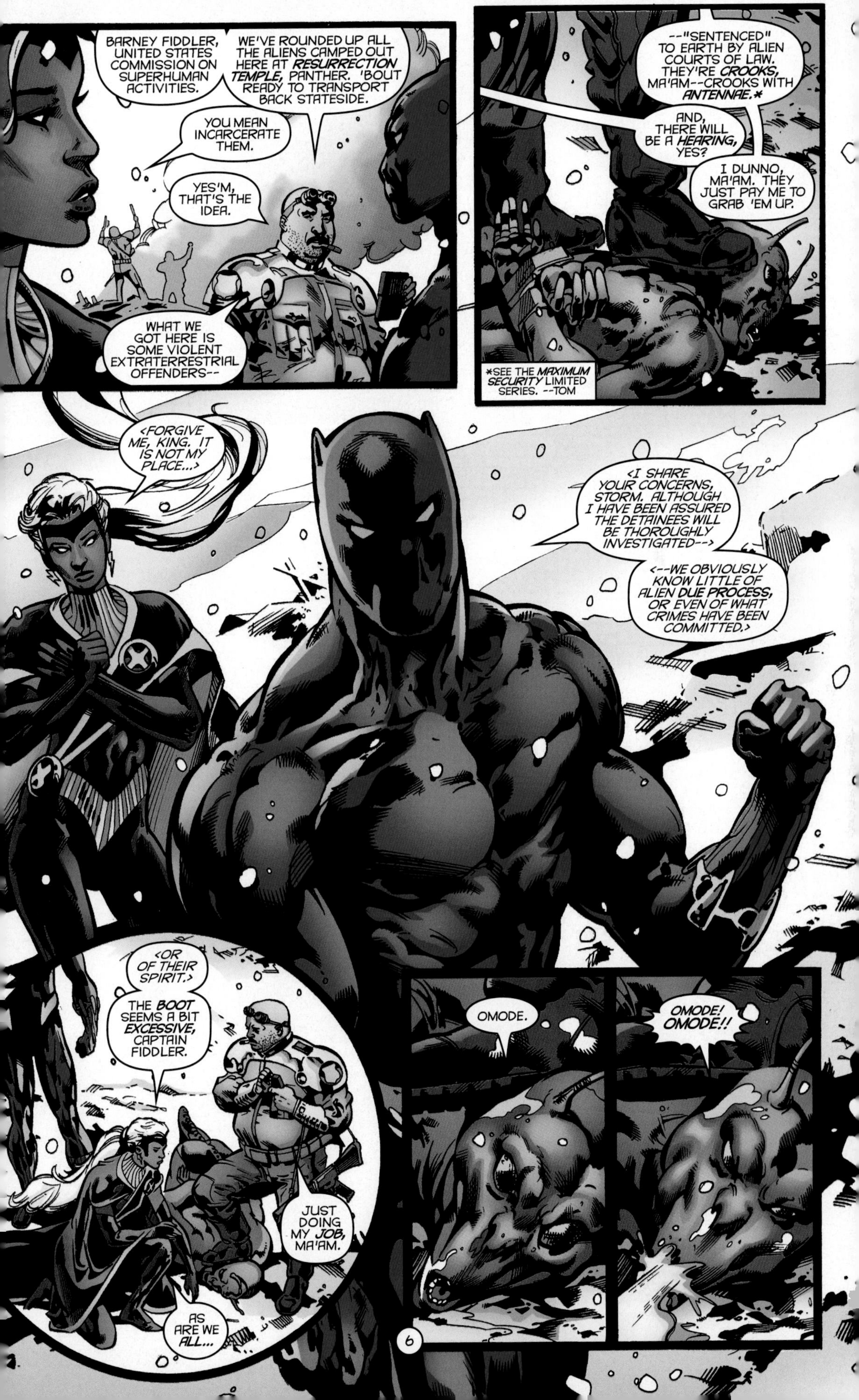
BARNEY FIDDLER, UNITED STATES COMMISSION ON SUPERHUMAN ACTIVITIES.
WE'VE ROUNDED UP ALL THE ALIENS CAMPED OUT HERE AT RESURRECTION TEMPLE, PANTHER. 'BOUT READY TO TRANSPORT BACK STATESIDE.
YOU MEAN INCARCERATE THEM.
YES'M, THAT'S THE IDEA.
WHAT WE GOT HERE IS SOME VIOLENT EXTRATERRESTRIAL OFFENDERS--
--"SENTENCED" TO EARTH BY ALIEN COURTS OF LAW. THEY'RE CROOKS, MA'AM--CROOKS WITH ANTENNAE.*
AND, THERE WILL BE A HEARING, YES?
I DUNNO, MA'AM. THEY JUST PAY ME TO GRAB 'EM UP.
*SEE THE MAXIMUM SECURITY LIMITED SERIES. --TOM
<FORGIVE ME, KING. IT IS NOT MY PLACE...>
<I SHARE YOUR CONCERNS, STORM. ALTHOUGH I HAVE BEEN ASSURED THE DETAINEES WILL BE THOROUGHLY INVESTIGATED-->
<--WE OBVIOUSLY KNOW LITTLE OF ALIEN DUE PROCESS, OR EVEN OF WHAT CRIMES HAVE BEEN COMMITTED.>
<OR OF THEIR SPIRIT.>
THE BOOT SEEMS A BIT EXCESSIVE, CAPTAIN FIDDLER.
JUST DOING MY JOB, MA'AM.
AS ARE WE ALL...
OMODE.
OMODE! OMODE!!

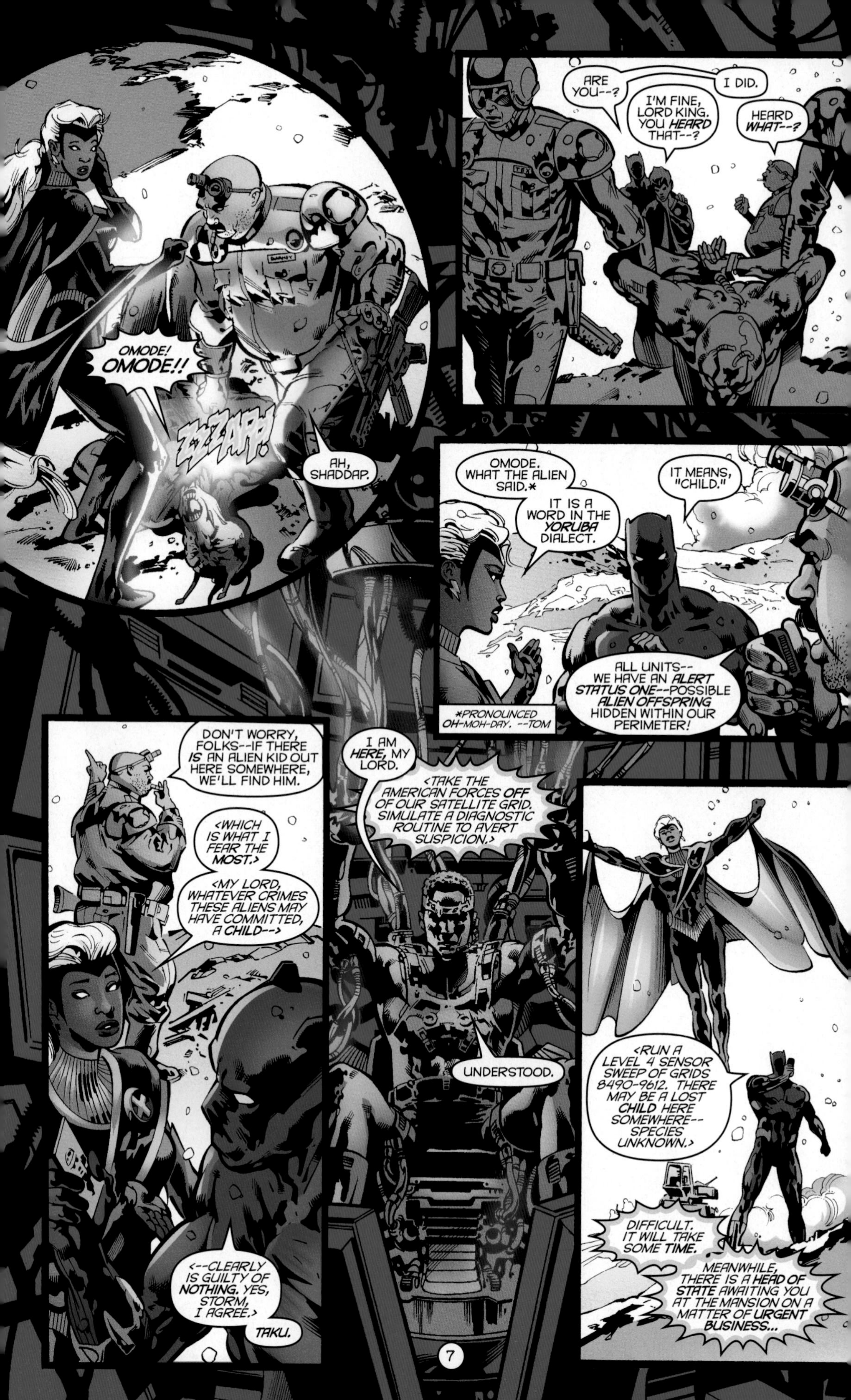
OMODE!
OMODE!!
ZZZAPP!
AH, SHADDAP.
ARE YOU--?
I DID.
I'M FINE, LORD KING. YOU HEARD THAT--?
HEARD WHAT--?
OMODE. WHAT THE ALIEN SAID.*
IT IS A WORD IN THE YORUBA DIALECT.
IT MEANS, "CHILD."
ALL UNITS-- WE HAVE AN ALERT STATUS ONE--POSSIBLE ALIEN OFFSPRING HIDDEN WITHIN OUR PERIMETER!
*PRONOUNCED OH-MOH-DAY. --TOM
DON'T WORRY, FOLKS--IF THERE IS AN ALIEN KID OUT HERE SOMEWHERE, WE'LL FIND HIM.
<WHICH IS WHAT I FEAR THE MOST.>
<MY LORD, WHATEVER CRIMES THESE ALIENS MAY HAVE COMMITTED, A CHILD-->
<--CLEARLY IS GUILTY OF NOTHING. YES, STORM, I AGREE.>
TAKU.
I AM HERE, MY LORD.
<TAKE THE AMERICAN FORCES OFF OF OUR SATELLITE GRID. SIMULATE A DIAGNOSTIC ROUTINE TO AVERT SUSPICION.>
UNDERSTOOD.
<RUN A LEVEL 4 SENSOR SWEEP OF GRIDS 8490-9612. THERE MAY BE A LOST CHILD HERE SOMEWHERE-- SPECIES UNKNOWN.>
DIFFICULT. IT WILL TAKE SOME TIME.
MEANWHILE, THERE IS A HEAD OF STATE AWAITING YOU AT THE MANSION ON A MATTER OF URGENT BUSINESS...

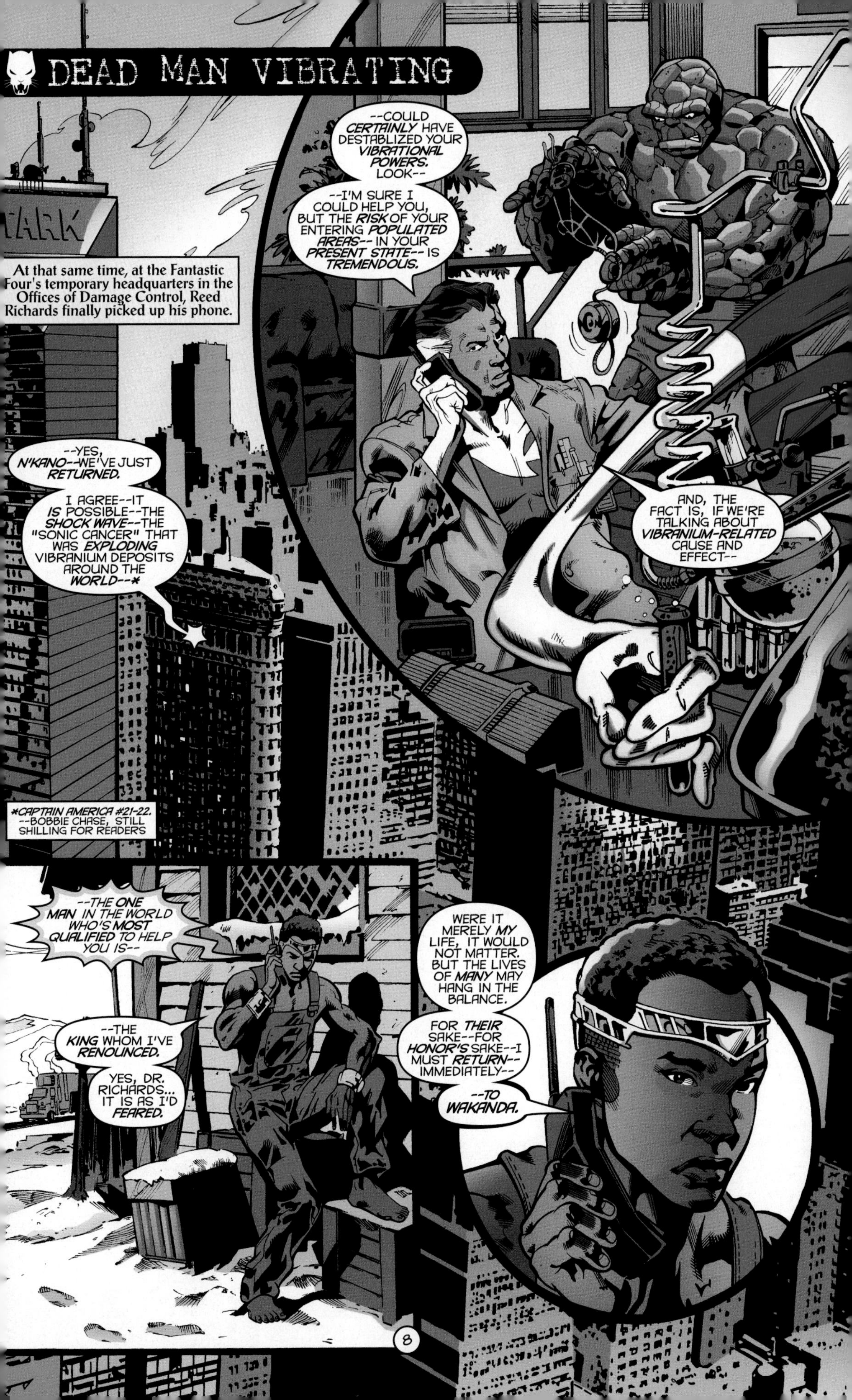
DEAD MAN VIBRATING
At that same time, at the Fantastic Four's temporary headquarters in the Offices of Damage Control, Reed Richards finally picked up his phone.
--COULD CERTAINLY HAVE DESTABLIZED YOUR VIBRATIONAL POWERS. LOOK--
--I'M SURE I COULD HELP YOU, BUT THE RISK OF YOUR ENTERING POPULATED AREAS-- IN YOUR PRESENT STATE-- IS TREMENDOUS.
--YES, N'KANO--WE'VE JUST RETURNED.
I AGREE--IT IS POSSIBLE--THE SHOCK WAVE--THE "SONIC CANCER" THAT WAS EXPLODING VIBRANIUM DEPOSITS AROUND THE WORLD--*
AND, THE FACT IS, IF WE'RE TALKING ABOUT VIBRANIUM-RELATED CAUSE AND EFFECT--
*CAPTAIN AMERICA #21-22. --BOBBIE CHASE, STILL SHILLING FOR READERS
--THE ONE MAN IN THE WORLD WHO'S MOST QUALIFIED TO HELP YOU IS--
--THE KING WHOM I'VE RENOUNCED.
YES, DR. RICHARDS... IT IS AS I'D FEARED.
WERE IT MERELY MY LIFE, IT WOULD NOT MATTER. BUT THE LIVES OF MANY MAY HANG IN THE BALANCE.
FOR THEIR SAKE--FOR HONOR'S SAKE--I MUST RETURN-- IMMEDIATELY--
--TO WAKANDA.

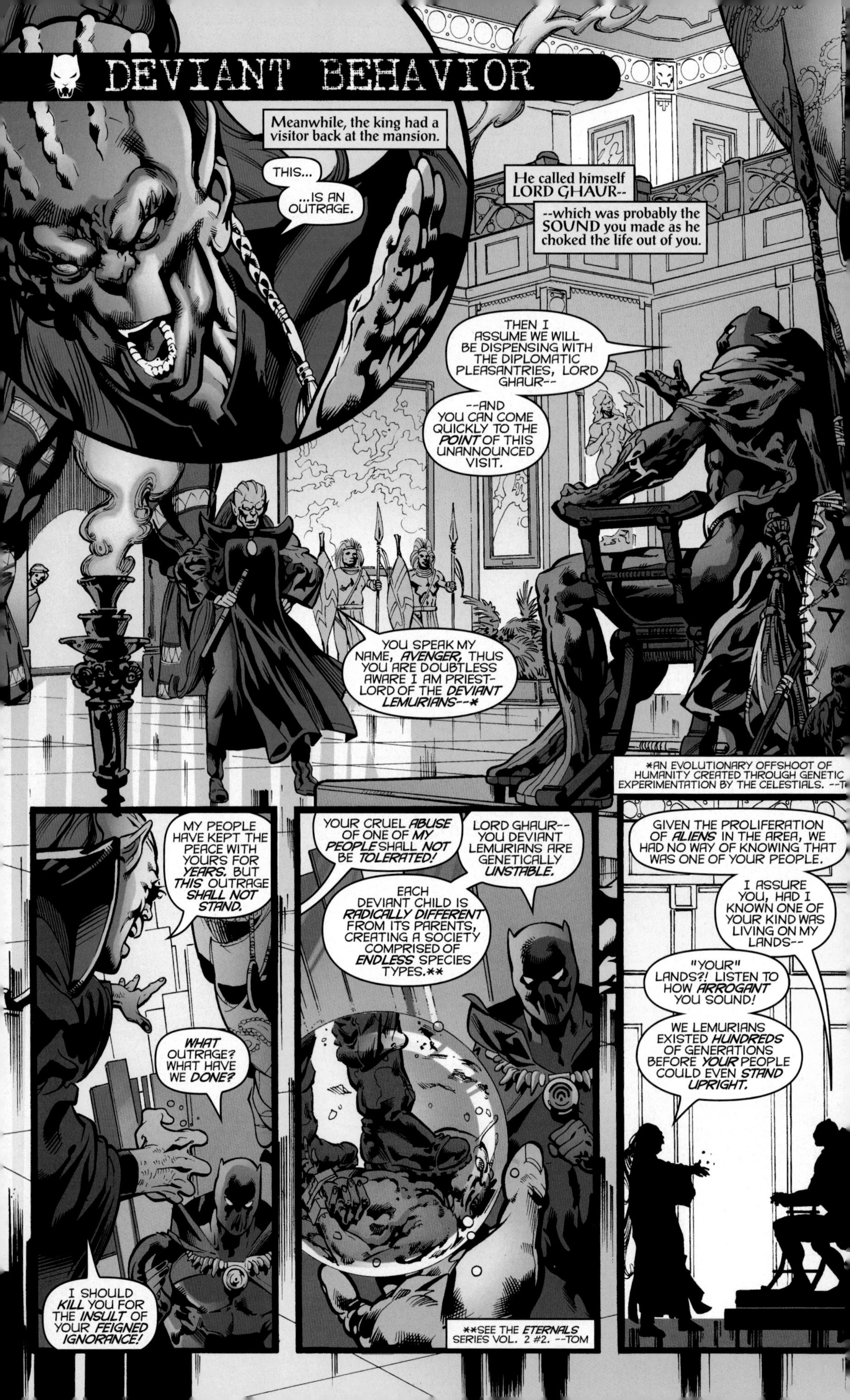
DEVIANT BEHAVIOR
Meanwhile, the king had a visitor back at the mansion.
THIS...
...IS AN OUTRAGE.
He called himself LORD GHAUR--
--which was probably the SOUND you made as he choked the life out of you.
THEN I ASSUME WE WILL BE DISPENSING WITH THE DIPLOMATIC PLEASANTRIES, LORD GHAUR--
--AND YOU CAN COME QUICKLY TO THE POINT OF THIS UNANNOUNCED VISIT.
YOU SPEAK MY NAME, AVENGER, THUS YOU ARE DOUBTLESS AWARE I AM PRIEST-LORD OF THE DEVIANT LEMURIANS--*
*AN EVOLUTIONARY OFFSHOOT OF HUMANITY CREATED THROUGH GENETIC EXPERIMENTATION BY THE CELESTIALS. --T
MY PEOPLE HAVE KEPT THE PEACE WITH YOURS FOR YEARS. BUT THIS OUTRAGE SHALL NOT STAND.
WHAT OUTRAGE? WHAT HAVE WE DONE?
I SHOULD KILL YOU FOR THE INSULT OF YOUR FEIGNED IGNORANCE!
YOUR CRUEL ABUSE OF ONE OF MY PEOPLE SHALL NOT BE TOLERATED!
LORD GHAUR-- YOU DEVIANT LEMURIANS ARE GENETICALLY UNSTABLE.
EACH DEVIANT CHILD IS RADICALLY DIFFERENT FROM ITS PARENTS, CREATING A SOCIETY COMPRISED OF ENDLESS SPECIES TYPES.**
**SEE THE ETERNALS SERIES VOL. 2 #2. --TOM
GIVEN THE PROLIFERATION OF ALIENS IN THE AREA, WE HAD NO WAY OF KNOWING THAT WAS ONE OF YOUR PEOPLE.
I ASSURE YOU, HAD I KNOWN ONE OF YOUR KIND WAS LIVING ON MY LANDS--
"YOUR" LANDS?! LISTEN TO HOW ARROGANT YOU SOUND!
WE LEMURIANS EXISTED HUNDREDS OF GENERATIONS BEFORE YOUR PEOPLE COULD EVEN STAND UPRIGHT.

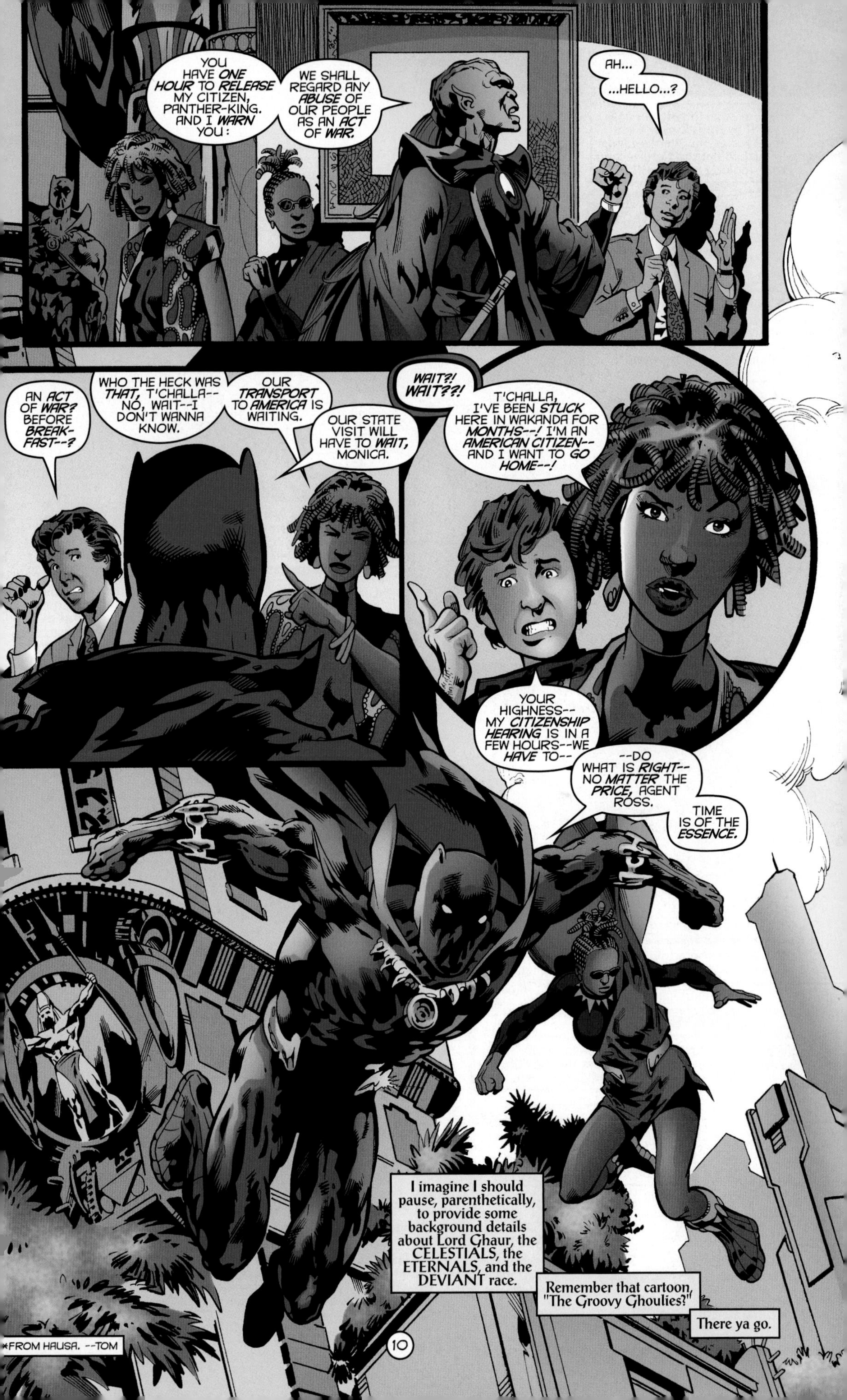
YOU HAVE ONE HOUR TO RELEASE MY CITIZEN, PANTHER-KING. AND I WARN YOU:
WE SHALL REGARD ANY ABUSE OF OUR PEOPLE AS AN ACT OF WAR.
AH...
...HELLO...?
AN ACT OF WAR? BEFORE BREAK-FAST--?
WHO THE HECK WAS THAT, T'CHALLA-- NO, WAIT--I DON'T WANNA KNOW.
OUR TRANSPORT TO AMERICA IS WAITING.
OUR STATE VISIT WILL HAVE TO WAIT, MONICA.
WAIT?! WAIT??!
T'CHALLA, I'VE BEEN STUCK HERE IN WAKANDA FOR MONTHS--! I'M AN AMERICAN CITIZEN-- AND I WANT TO GO HOME--!
YOUR HIGHNESS-- MY CITIZENSHIP HEARING IS IN A FEW HOURS--WE HAVE TO--
--DO WHAT IS RIGHT-- NO MATTER THE PRICE, AGENT ROSS.
TIME IS OF THE ESSENCE.
I imagine I should pause, parenthetically, to provide some background details about Lord Ghaur, the CELESTIALS, the ETERNALS, and the DEVIANT race.
Remember that cartoon, "The Groovy Ghoulies?"
There ya go.
*FROM HAUSA. --TOM

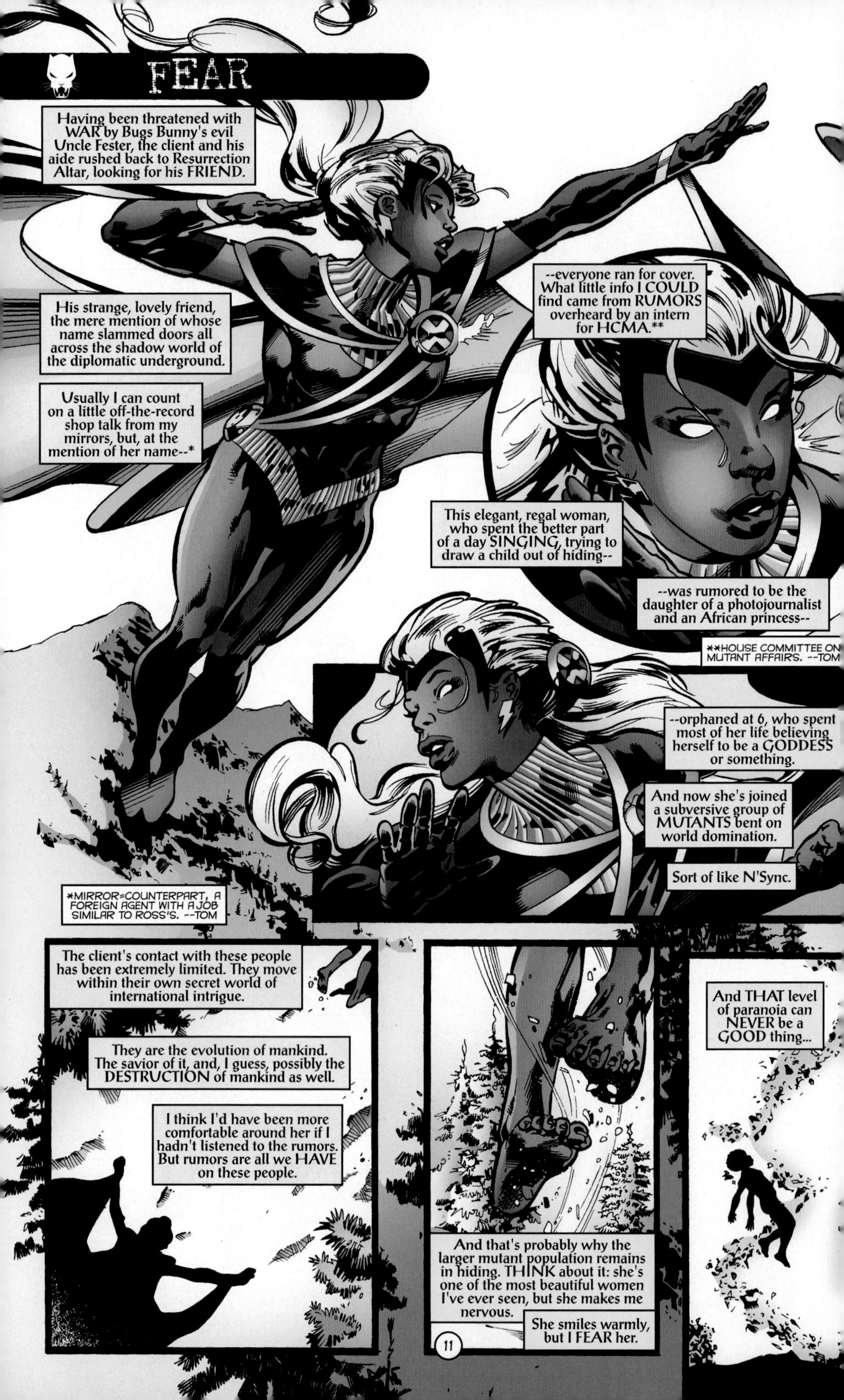

FEAR
Having been threatened with WAR by Bugs Bunny's evil Uncle Fester, the client and his aide rushed back to Resurrection Altar, looking for his FRIEND.
His strange, lovely friend, the mere mention of whose name slammed doors all across the shadow world of the diplomatic underground.
Usually I can count on a little off-the-record shop talk from my mirrors, but, at the mention of her name--*
--everyone ran for cover. What little info I COULD find came from RUMORS overheard by an intern for HCMA.**
This elegant, regal woman, who spent the better part of a day SINGING, trying to draw a child out of hiding--
--was rumored to be the daughter of a photojournalist and an African princess--
**HOUSE COMMITTEE ON MUTANT AFFAIRS. --TOM
--orphaned at 6, who spent most of her life believing herself to be a GODDESS or something.
And now she's joined a subversive group of MUTANTS bent on world domination.
Sort of like N'Sync.
*MIRROR=COUNTERPART, A FOREIGN AGENT WITH A JOB SIMILAR TO ROSS'S. --TOM
The client's contact with these people has been extremely limited. They move within their own secret world of international intrigue.
They are the evolution of mankind. The savior of it, and, I guess, possibly the DESTRUCTION of mankind as well.
I think I'd have been more comfortable around her if I hadn't listened to the rumors. But rumors are all we HAVE on these people.
And that's probably why the larger mutant population remains in hiding. THINK about it: she's one of the most beautiful women I've ever seen, but she makes me nervous.
She smiles warmly, but I FEAR her.
And THAT level of paranoia can NEVER be a GOOD thing...
11

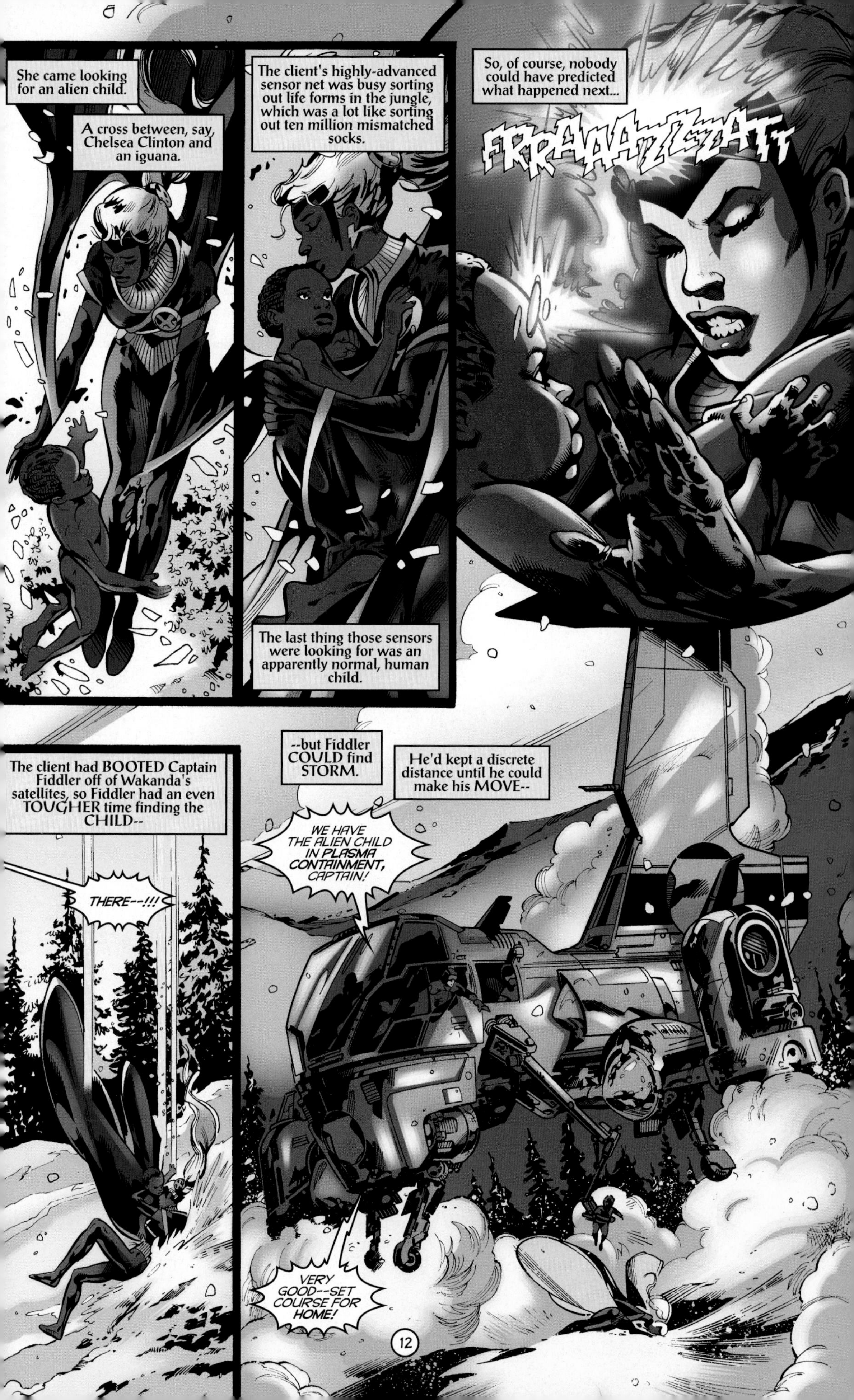

She came looking for an alien child.
A cross between, say, Chelsea Clinton and an iguana.
The client's highly-advanced sensor net was busy sorting out life forms in the jungle, which was a lot like sorting out ten million mismatched socks.
The last thing those sensors were looking for was an apparently normal, human child.
So, of course, nobody could have predicted what happened next...
FRRAAAZZZATT
The client had BOOTED Captain Fiddler off of Wakanda's satellites, so Fiddler had an even TOUGHER time finding the CHILD--
--but Fiddler COULD find STORM.
He'd kept a discrete distance until he could make his MOVE--
THERE--!!!
WE HAVE THE ALIEN CHILD IN PLASMA CONTAINMENT, CAPTAIN!
VERY GOOD--SET COURSE FOR HOME!

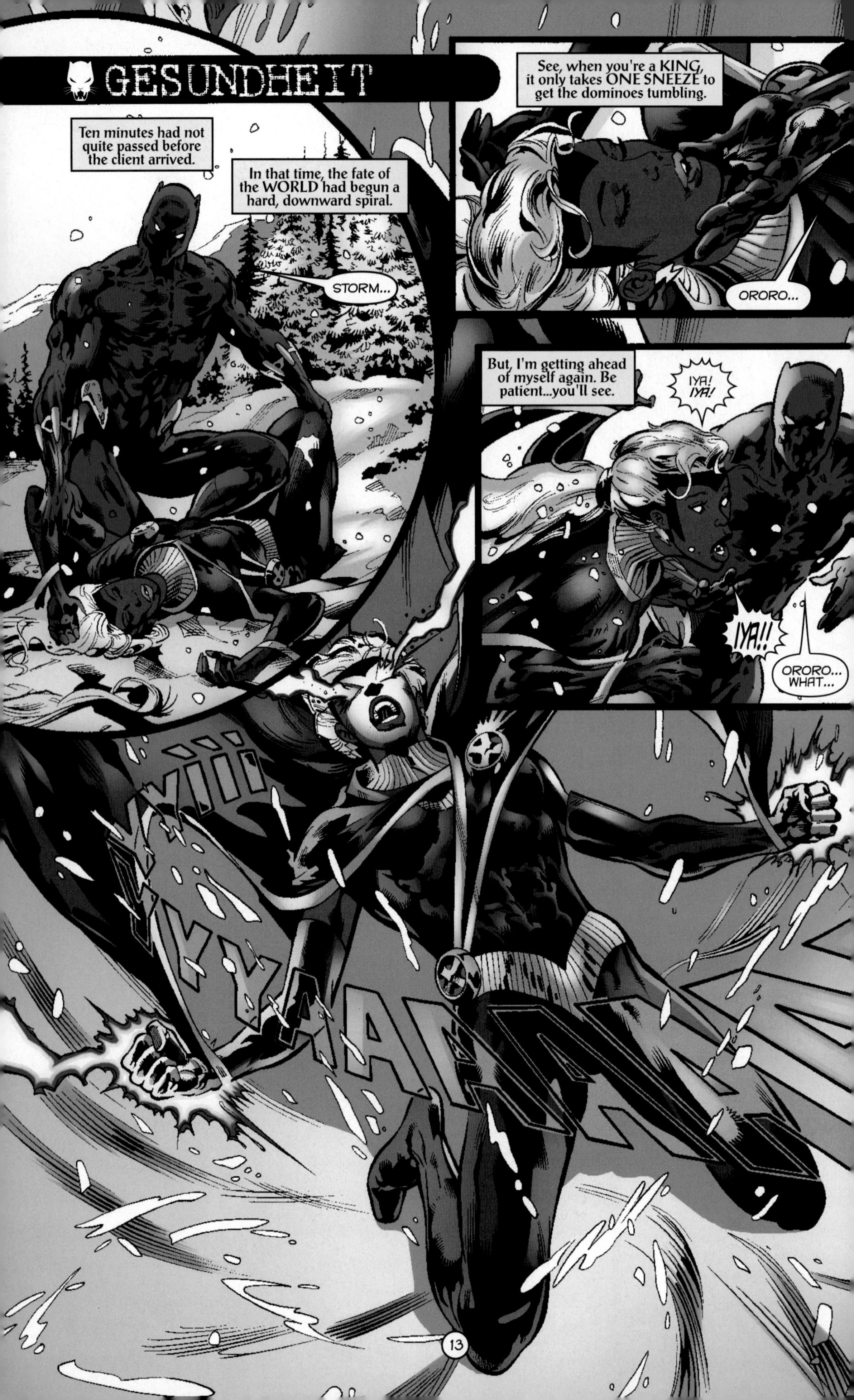
GESUNDHEIT
Ten minutes had not quite passed before the client arrived.
In that time, the fate of the WORLD had begun a hard, downward spiral.
STORM...
See, when you're a KING, it only takes ONE SNEEZE to get the dominoes tumbling.
ORORO...
But, I'm getting ahead of myself again. Be patient...you'll see.
IYA! IYA!
IYA!!
ORORO... WHAT...

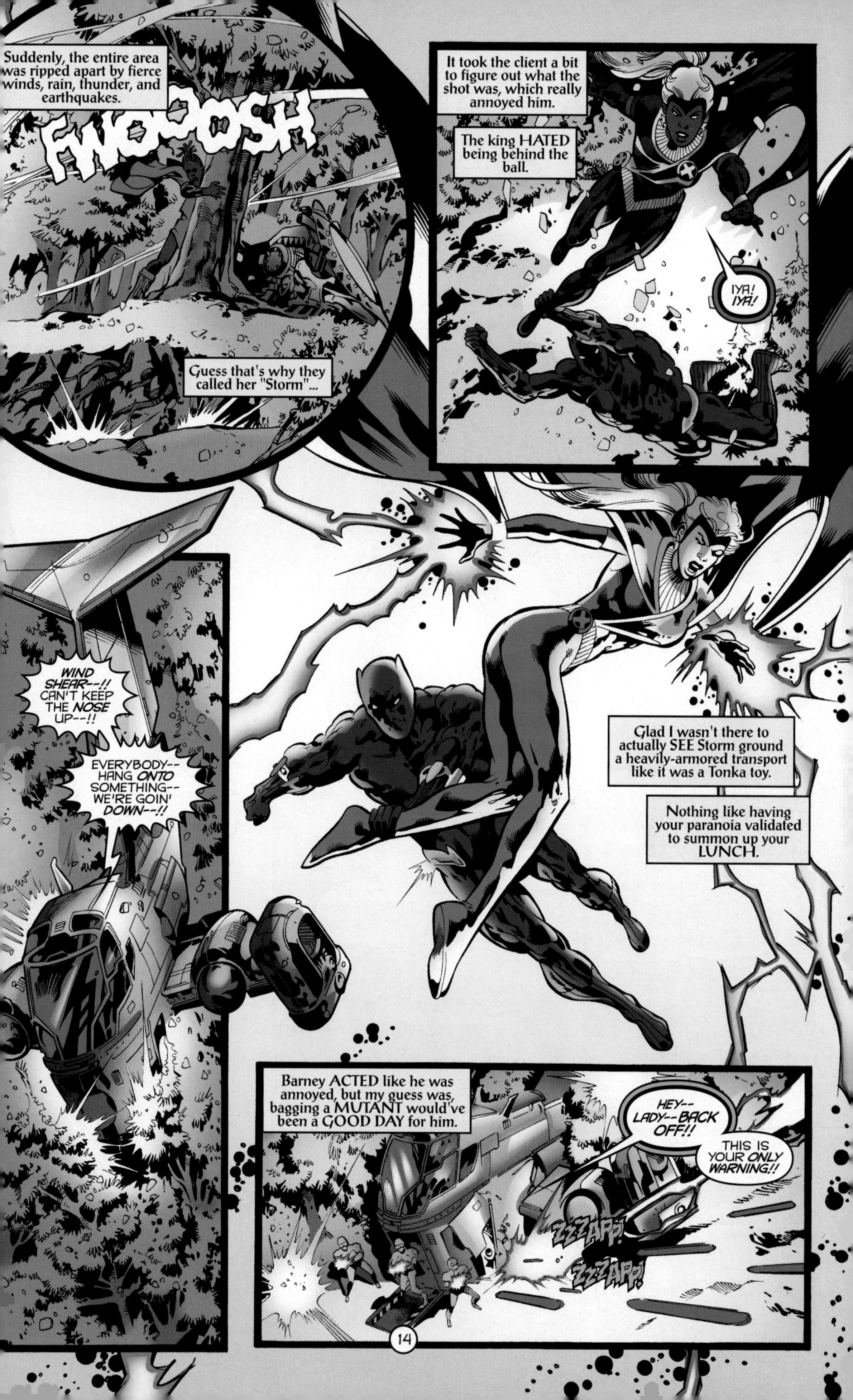
Suddenly, the entire area was ripped apart by fierce winds, rain, thunder, and earthquakes.
FWOOOSH
Guess that's why they called her "Storm"...
It took the client a bit to figure out what the shot was, which really annoyed him.
The king HATED being behind the ball.
IYA! IYA!
WIND SHEAR--!! CAN'T KEEP THE NOSE UP--!!
EVERYBODY-- HANG ONTO SOMETHING-- WE'RE GOIN' DOWN--!!
Glad I wasn't there to actually SEE Storm ground a heavily-armored transport like it was a Tonka toy.
Nothing like having your paranoia validated to summon up your LUNCH.
Barney ACTED like he was annoyed, but my guess was, bagging a MUTANT would've been a GOOD DAY for him.
HEY-- LADY--BACK OFF!!
THIS IS YOUR ONLY WARNING!!
ZZZAPP!
ZZZAPP!

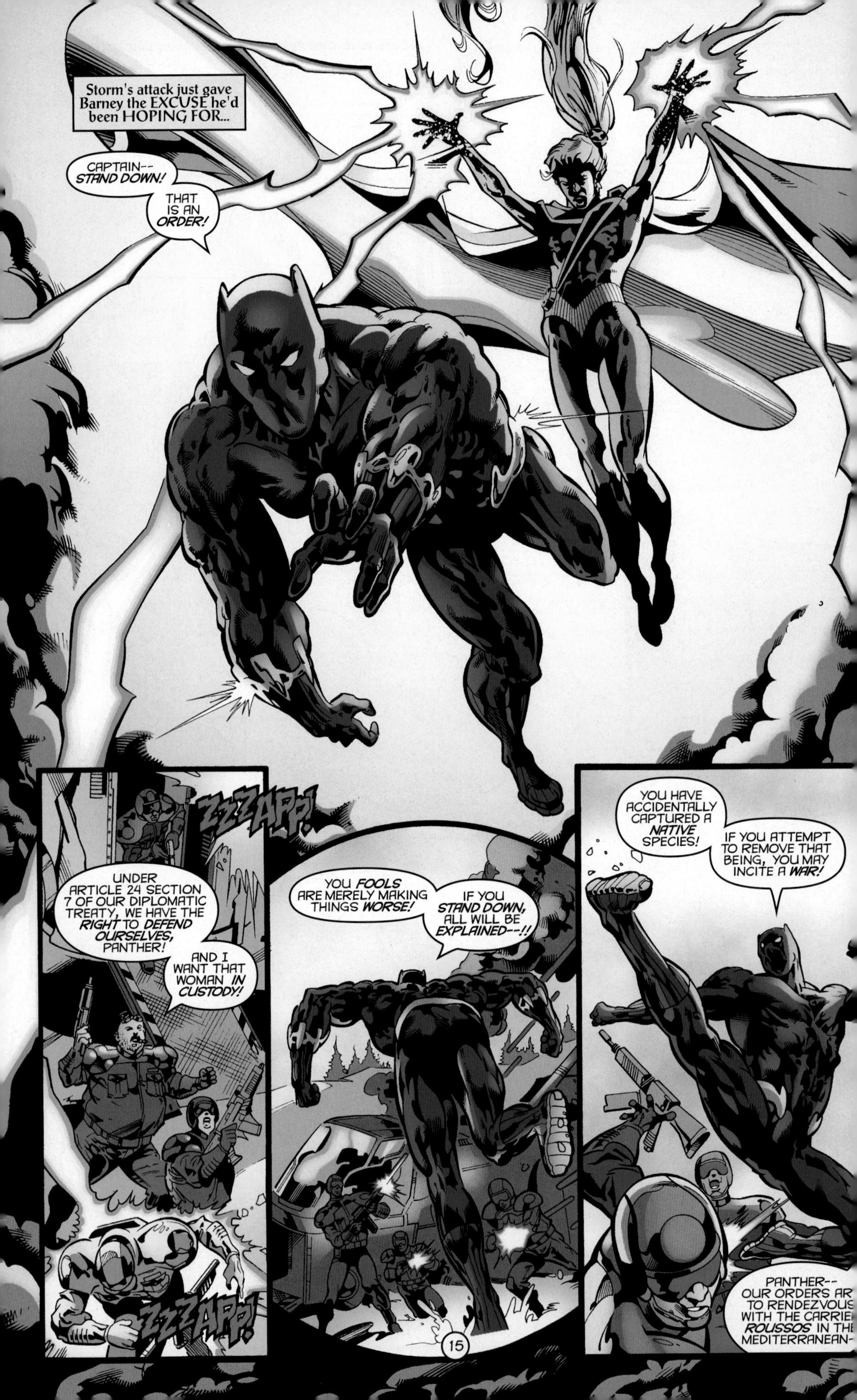

Storm's attack just gave Barney the EXCUSE he'd been HOPING FOR...
CAPTAIN-- STAND DOWN!
THAT IS AN ORDER!
ZZZAPP!
UNDER ARTICLE 24 SECTION 7 OF OUR DIPLOMATIC TREATY, WE HAVE THE RIGHT TO DEFEND OURSELVES, PANTHER!
AND I WANT THAT WOMAN IN CUSTODY!
ZZZAPP!
YOU FOOLS ARE MERELY MAKING THINGS WORSE!
IF YOU STAND DOWN, ALL WILL BE EXPLAINED--!!
YOU HAVE ACCIDENTALLY CAPTURED A NATIVE SPECIES!
IF YOU ATTEMPT TO REMOVE THAT BEING, YOU MAY INCITE A WAR!
PANTHER-- OUR ORDERS AR TO RENDEZVOUS WITH THE CARRIE ROUSSOS IN THE MEDITERRANEAN-

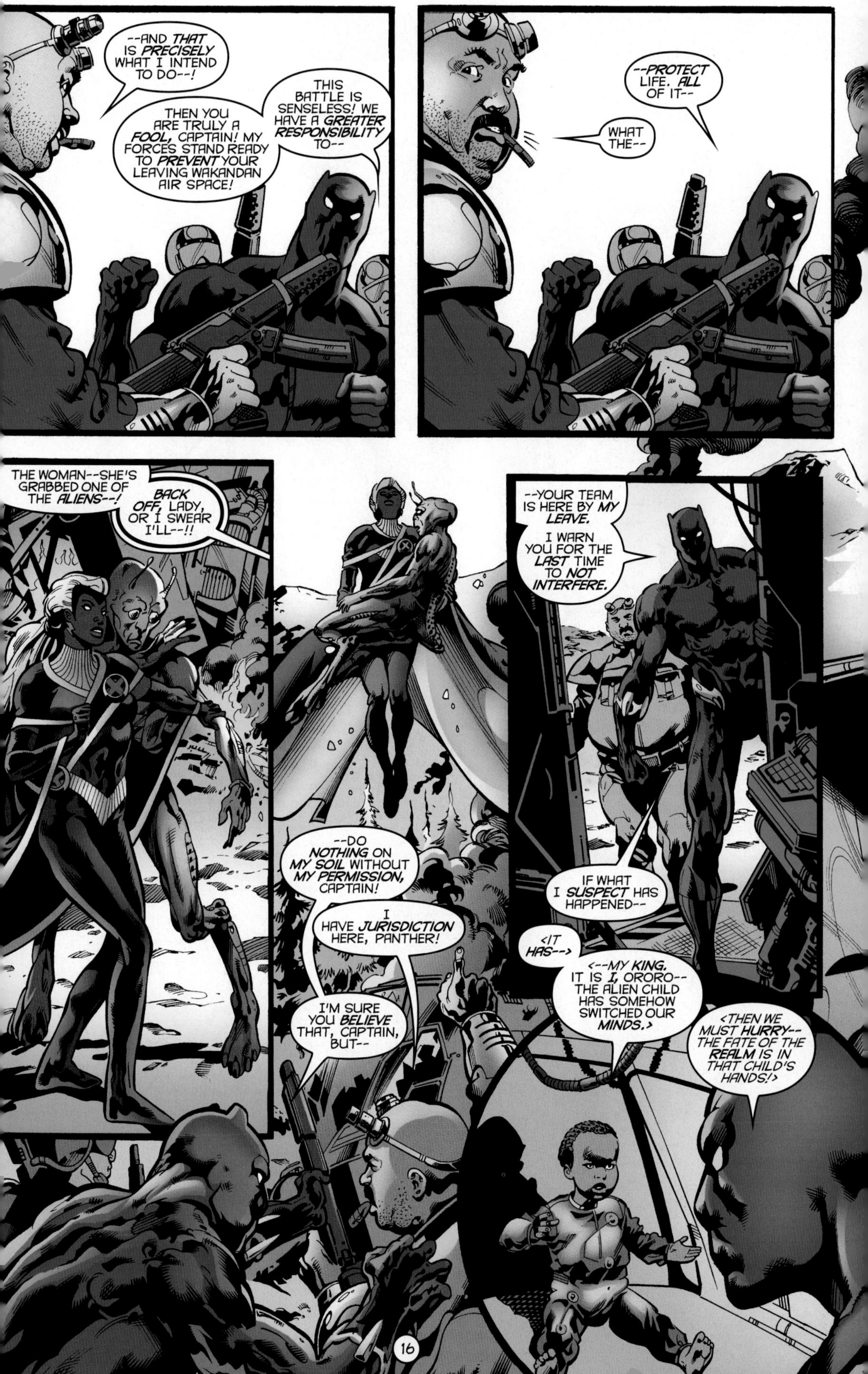
--AND THAT IS PRECISELY WHAT I INTEND TO DO--!
THEN YOU ARE TRULY A FOOL, CAPTAIN! MY FORCES STAND READY TO PREVENT YOUR LEAVING WAKANDAN AIR SPACE!
THIS BATTLE IS SENSELESS! WE HAVE A GREATER RESPONSIBILITY TO--
--PROTECT LIFE. ALL OF IT--
WHAT THE--
THE WOMAN--SHE'S GRABBED ONE OF THE ALIENS--!
BACK OFF, LADY, OR I SWEAR I'LL--!!
--YOUR TEAM IS HERE BY MY LEAVE.
I WARN YOU FOR THE LAST TIME TO NOT INTERFERE.
--DO NOTHING ON MY SOIL WITHOUT MY PERMISSION, CAPTAIN!
I HAVE JURISDICTION HERE, PANTHER!
I'M SURE YOU BELIEVE THAT, CAPTAIN, BUT--
IF WHAT I SUSPECT HAS HAPPENED--
<IT HAS-->
<--MY KING. IT IS I, ORORO--THE ALIEN CHILD HAS SOMEHOW SWITCHED OUR MINDS.>
<THEN WE MUST HURRY--THE FATE OF THE REALM IS IN THAT CHILD'S HANDS!>

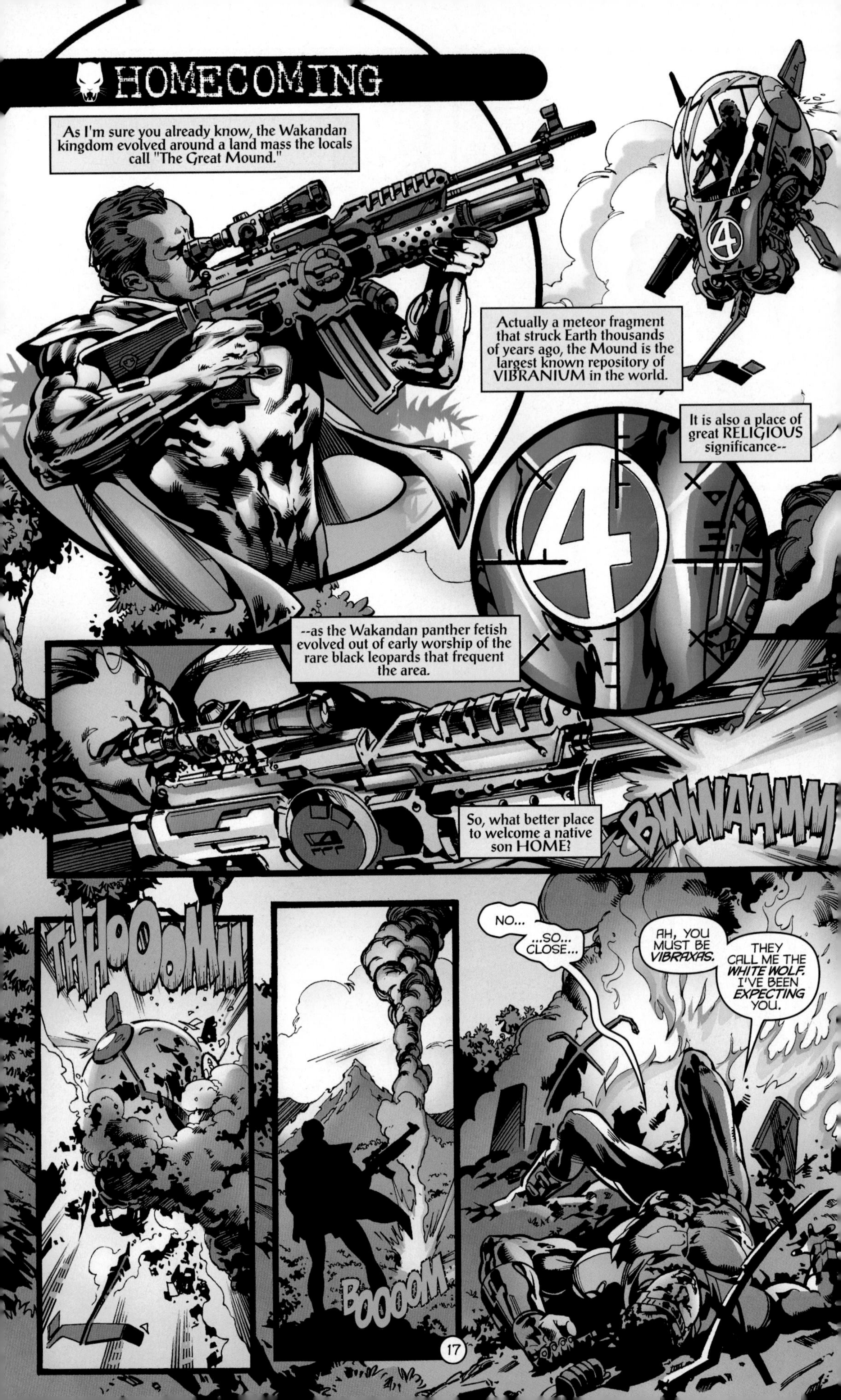
HOMECOMING
As I'm sure you already know, the Wakandan kingdom evolved around a land mass the locals call "The Great Mound."
Actually a meteor fragment that struck Earth thousands of years ago, the Mound is the largest known repository of VIBRANIUM in the world.
It is also a place of great RELIGIOUS significance--
--as the Wakandan panther fetish evolved out of early worship of the rare black leopards that frequent the area.
So, what better place to welcome a native son HOME?
BWAAMM
THHOOOMM
BOOOOM
NO...
...SO... CLOSE...
AH, YOU MUST BE VIBRAXAS.
THEY CALL ME THE WHITE WOLF. I'VE BEEN EXPECTING YOU.
17

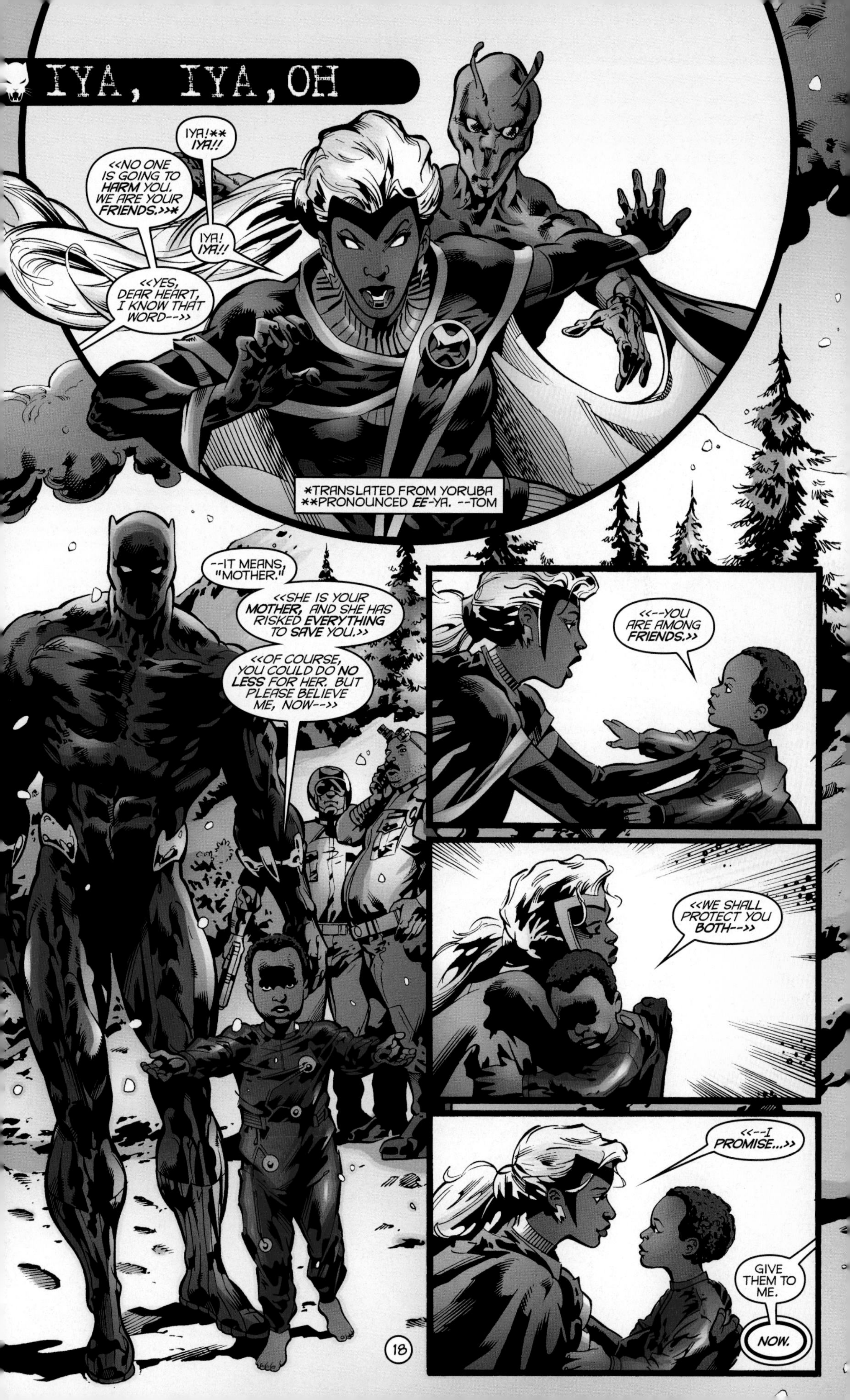
IYA, IYA, OH
<<NO ONE IS GOING TO HARM YOU. WE ARE YOUR FRIENDS.>>*
IYA!** IYA!!
IYA! IYA!!
<<YES, DEAR HEART, I KNOW THAT WORD-->>
*TRANSLATED FROM YORUBA
**PRONOUNCED EE-YA. --TOM
--IT MEANS, "MOTHER."
<<SHE IS YOUR MOTHER, AND SHE HAS RISKED EVERYTHING TO SAVE YOU.>>
<<OF COURSE, YOU COULD DO NO LESS FOR HER. BUT PLEASE BELIEVE ME, NOW-->>
<<--YOU ARE AMONG FRIENDS.>>
<<WE SHALL PROTECT YOU BOTH-->>
<<--I PROMISE...>>
GIVE THEM TO ME.
NOW.

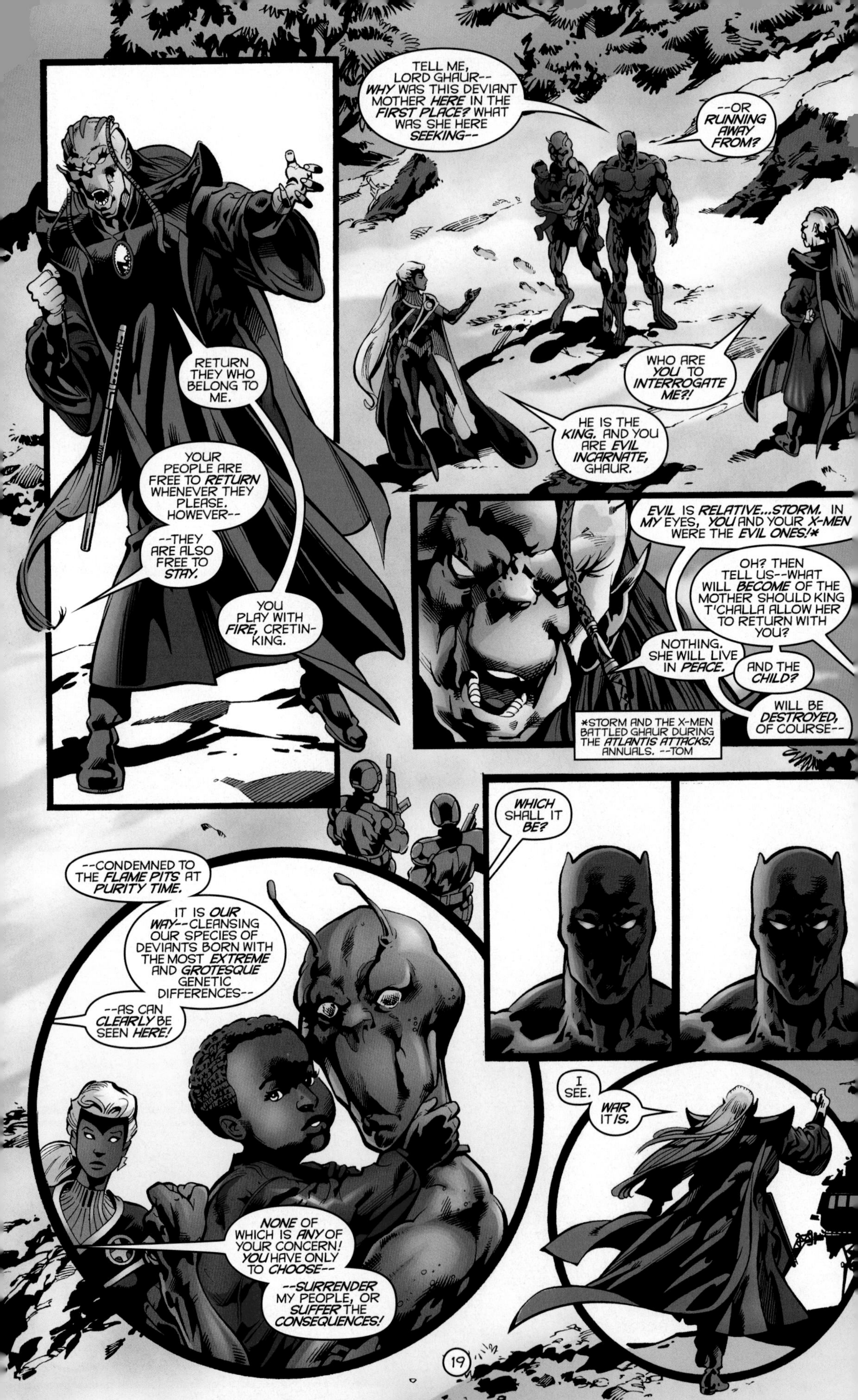
TELL ME, LORD GHAUR-- WHY WAS THIS DEVIANT MOTHER HERE IN THE FIRST PLACE? WHAT WAS SHE HERE SEEKING--
--OR RUNNING AWAY FROM?
WHO ARE YOU TO INTERROGATE ME?!
HE IS THE KING. AND YOU ARE EVIL INCARNATE, GHAUR.
RETURN THEY WHO BELONG TO ME.
YOUR PEOPLE ARE FREE TO RETURN WHENEVER THEY PLEASE. HOWEVER--
--THEY ARE ALSO FREE TO STAY.
YOU PLAY WITH FIRE, CRETIN-KING.
EVIL IS RELATIVE...STORM. IN MY EYES, YOU AND YOUR X-MEN WERE THE EVIL ONES!*
OH? THEN TELL US--WHAT WILL BECOME OF THE MOTHER SHOULD KING T'CHALLA ALLOW HER TO RETURN WITH YOU?
NOTHING. SHE WILL LIVE IN PEACE.
AND THE CHILD?
WILL BE DESTROYED, OF COURSE--
*STORM AND THE X-MEN BATTLED GHAUR DURING THE ATLANTIS ATTACKS! ANNUALS. --TOM
--CONDEMNED TO THE FLAME PITS AT PURITY TIME.
IT IS OUR WAY--CLEANSING OUR SPECIES OF DEVIANTS BORN WITH THE MOST EXTREME AND GROTESQUE GENETIC DIFFERENCES--
--AS CAN CLEARLY BE SEEN HERE!
NONE OF WHICH IS ANY OF YOUR CONCERN! YOU HAVE ONLY TO CHOOSE--
--SURRENDER MY PEOPLE, OR SUFFER THE CONSEQUENCES!
WHICH SHALL IT BE?
I SEE.
WAR IT IS.

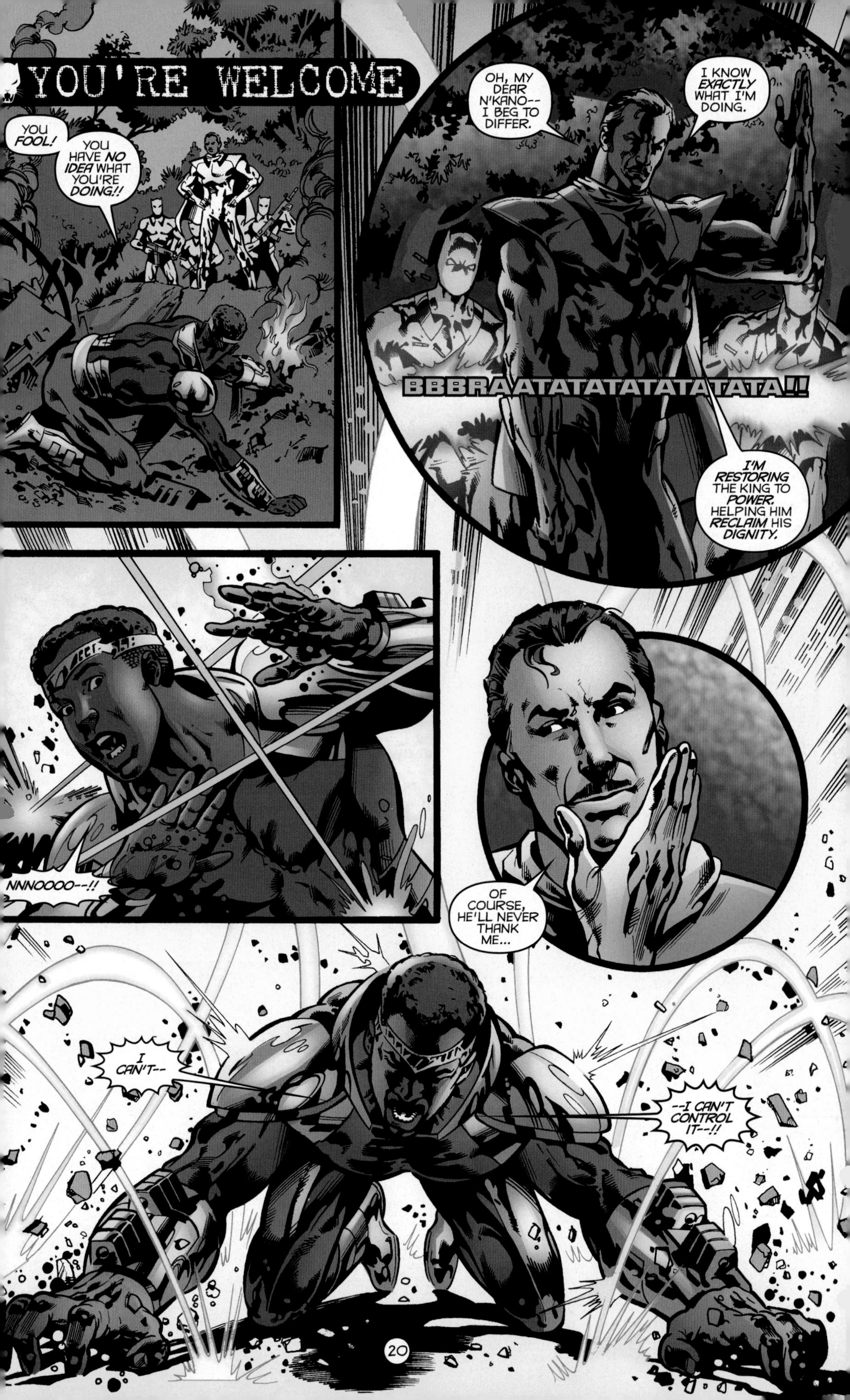

YOU'RE WELCOME
YOU FOOL!
YOU HAVE NO IDEA WHAT YOU'RE DOING!!
OH, MY DEAR N'KANO-- I BEG TO DIFFER.
I KNOW EXACTLY WHAT I'M DOING.
BBBRAATATATATATATATATA!!
I'M RESTORING THE KING TO POWER. HELPING HIM RECLAIM HIS DIGNITY.
NNNOOOO--!!
OF COURSE, HE'LL NEVER THANK ME...
I CAN'T--
--I CAN'T CONTROL IT--!!

ZZZAAZZK!

SZZZZSKTT

SSZZAAAACKKK

WELL, NOW.

JUST AS I'D HOPED.

WELCOME HOME--

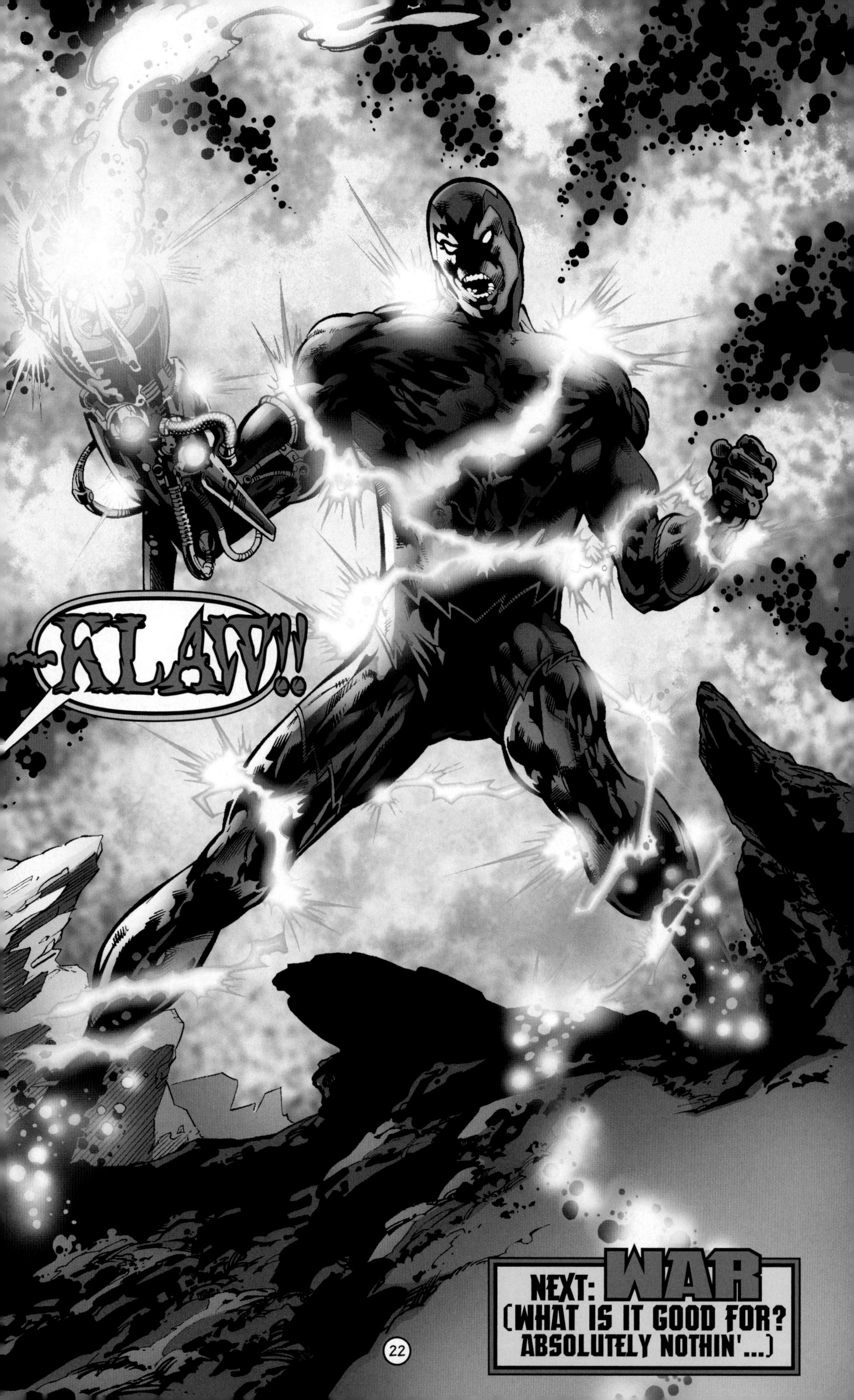

KLAW!!
NEXT: WAR
(WHAT IS IT GOOD FOR? ABSOLUTELY NOTHIN'...)

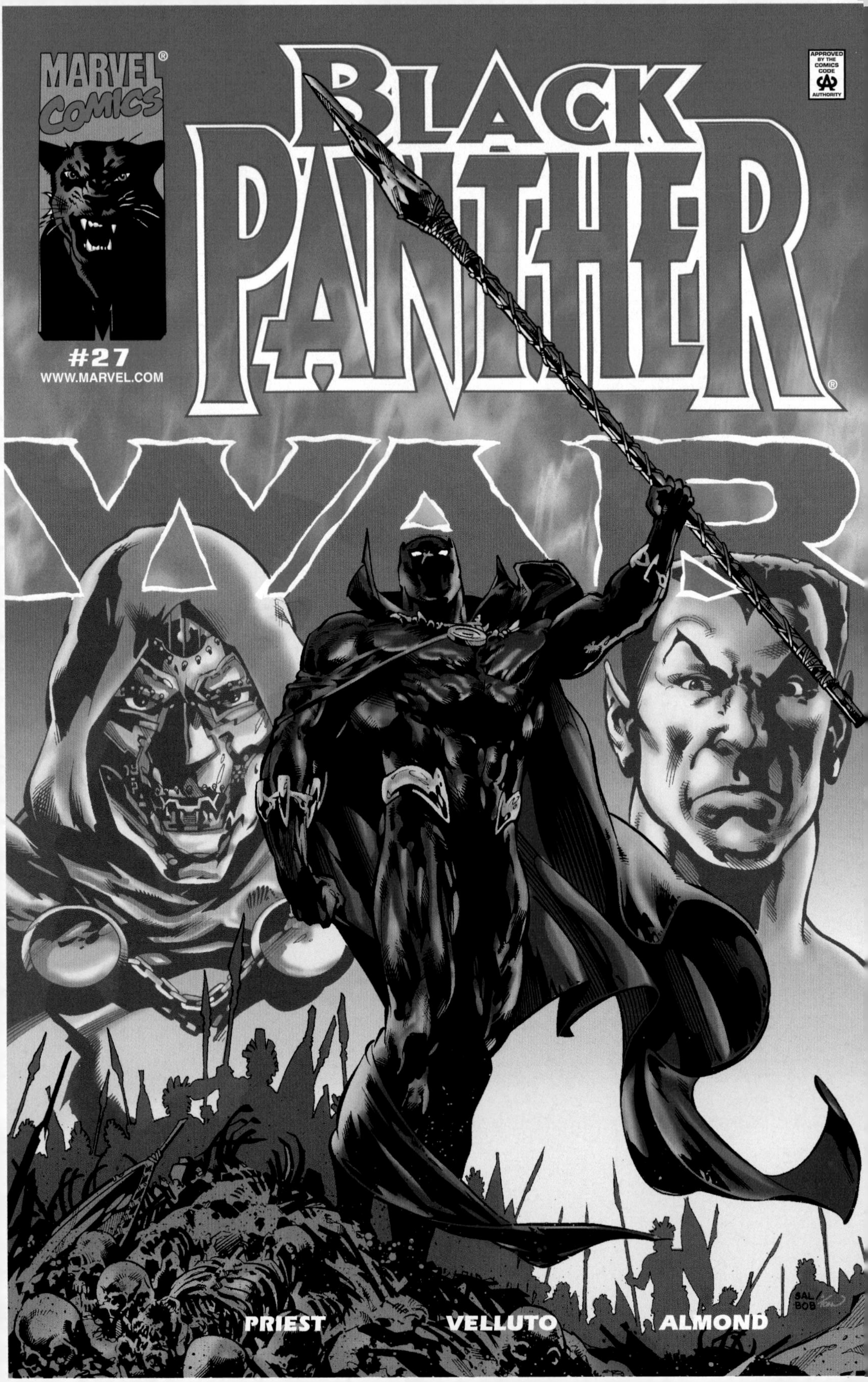
MARVEL COMICS
BLACK PANTHER
#27
WWW.MARVEL.COM
APPROVED BY THE COMICS CODE AUTHORITY
WAR
PRIEST
VELLUTO
ALMOND
SAL/BOB

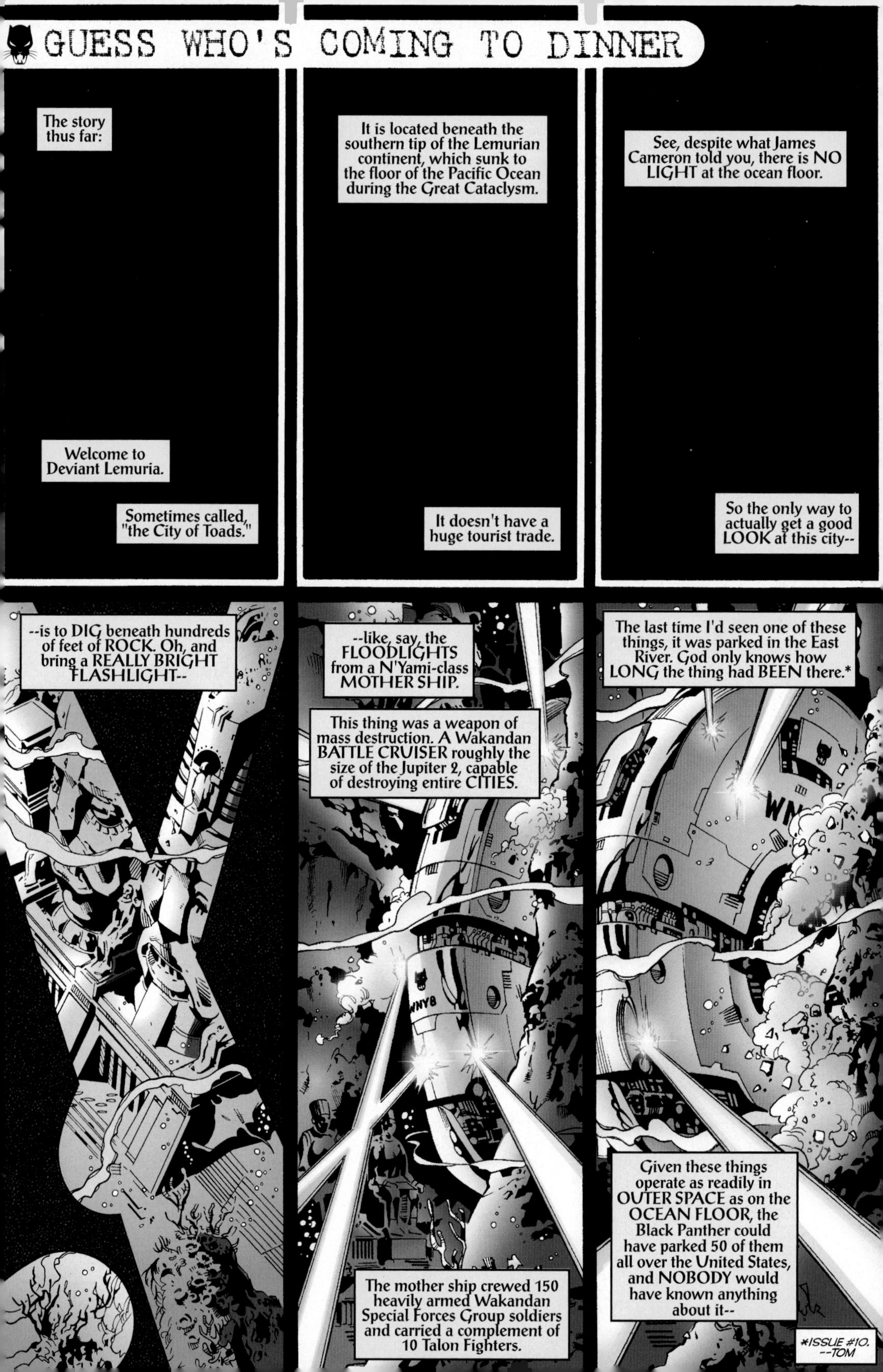
GUESS WHO'S COMING TO DINNER
The story thus far:
Welcome to Deviant Lemuria.
Sometimes called, "the City of Toads."
It is located beneath the southern tip of the Lemurian continent, which sunk to the floor of the Pacific Ocean during the Great Cataclysm.
It doesn't have a huge tourist trade.
See, despite what James Cameron told you, there is NO LIGHT at the ocean floor.
So the only way to actually get a good LOOK at this city--
--is to DIG beneath hundreds of feet of ROCK. Oh, and bring a REALLY BRIGHT FLASHLIGHT--
--like, say, the FLOODLIGHTS from a N'Yami-class MOTHER SHIP.
This thing was a weapon of mass destruction. A Wakandan BATTLE CRUISER roughly the size of the Jupiter 2, capable of destroying entire CITIES.
The mother ship crewed 150 heavily armed Wakandan Special Forces Group soldiers and carried a complement of 10 Talon Fighters.
The last time I'd seen one of these things, it was parked in the East River. God only knows how LONG the thing had BEEN there.*
Given these things operate as readily in OUTER SPACE as on the OCEAN FLOOR, the Black Panther could have parked 50 of them all over the United States, and NOBODY would have known anything about it--
*ISSUE #10. --TOM

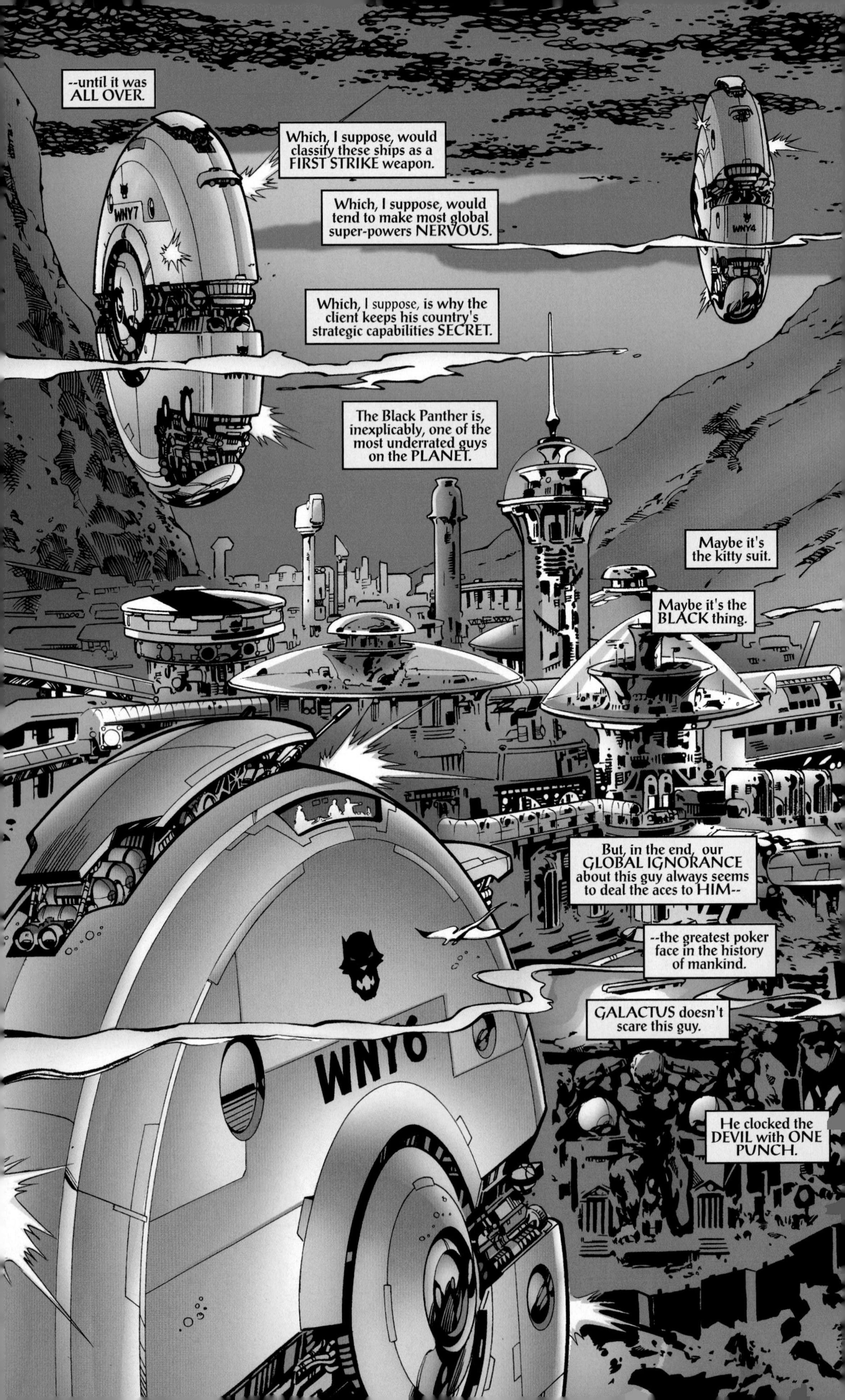

--until it was ALL OVER.
Which, I suppose, would classify these ships as a FIRST STRIKE weapon.
Which, I suppose, would tend to make most global super-powers NERVOUS.
Which, I suppose, is why the client keeps his country's strategic capabilities SECRET.
The Black Panther is, inexplicably, one of the most underrated guys on the PLANET.
Maybe it's the kitty suit.
Maybe it's the BLACK thing.
But, in the end, our GLOBAL IGNORANCE about this guy always seems to deal the aces to HIM--
--the greatest poker face in the history of mankind.
GALACTUS doesn't scare this guy.
He clocked the DEVIL with ONE PUNCH.
WNY7
WNY4
WNY6

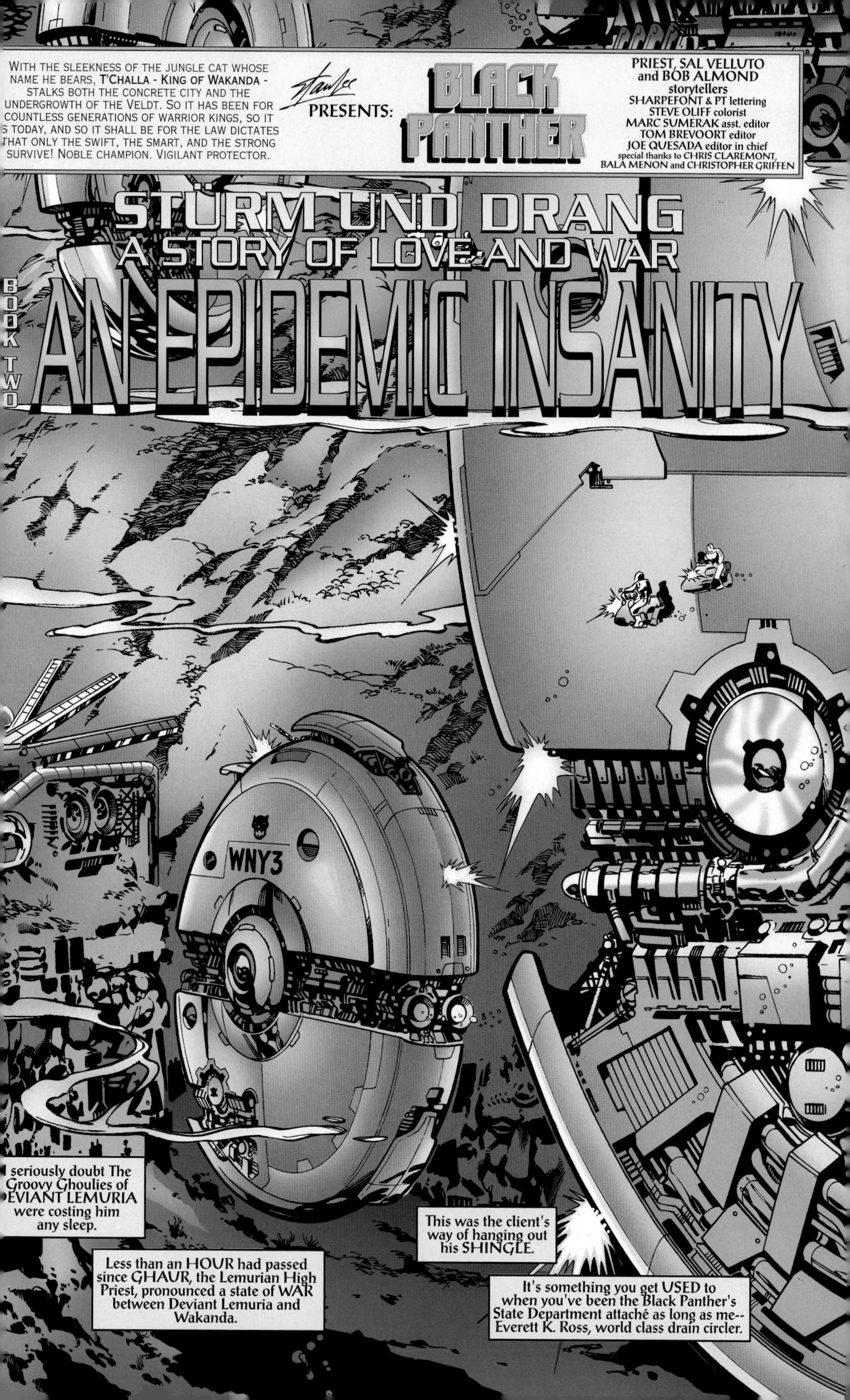

WITH THE SLEEKNESS OF THE JUNGLE CAT WHOSE NAME HE BEARS, T'CHALLA - KING OF WAKANDA - STALKS BOTH THE CONCRETE CITY AND THE UNDERGROWTH OF THE VELDT. SO IT HAS BEEN FOR COUNTLESS GENERATIONS OF WARRIOR KINGS, SO IT IS TODAY, AND SO IT SHALL BE FOR THE LAW DICTATES THAT ONLY THE SWIFT, THE SMART, AND THE STRONG SURVIVE! NOBLE CHAMPION. VIGILANT PROTECTOR.
Stan Lee PRESENTS:
BLACK PANTHER
PRIEST, SAL VELLUTO and BOB ALMOND storytellers
SHARPEFONT & PT lettering
STEVE OLIFF colorist
MARC SUMERAK asst. editor
TOM BREVOORT editor
JOE QUESADA editor in chief
special thanks to CHRIS CLAREMONT, BALA MENON and CHRISTOPHER GRIFFEN
STÜRM UND DRANG
A STORY OF LOVE AND WAR
BOOK TWO
AN EPIDEMIC INSANITY
WNY3
I seriously doubt The Groovy Ghoulies of DEVIANT LEMURIA were costing him any sleep.
Less than an HOUR had passed since GHAUR, the Lemurian High Priest, pronounced a state of WAR between Deviant Lemuria and Wakanda.
This was the client's way of hanging out his SHINGLE.
It's something you get USED to when you've been the Black Panther's State Department attaché as long as me-- Everett K. Ross, world class drain circler.

OK, *NOW* YOU CAN PANIC

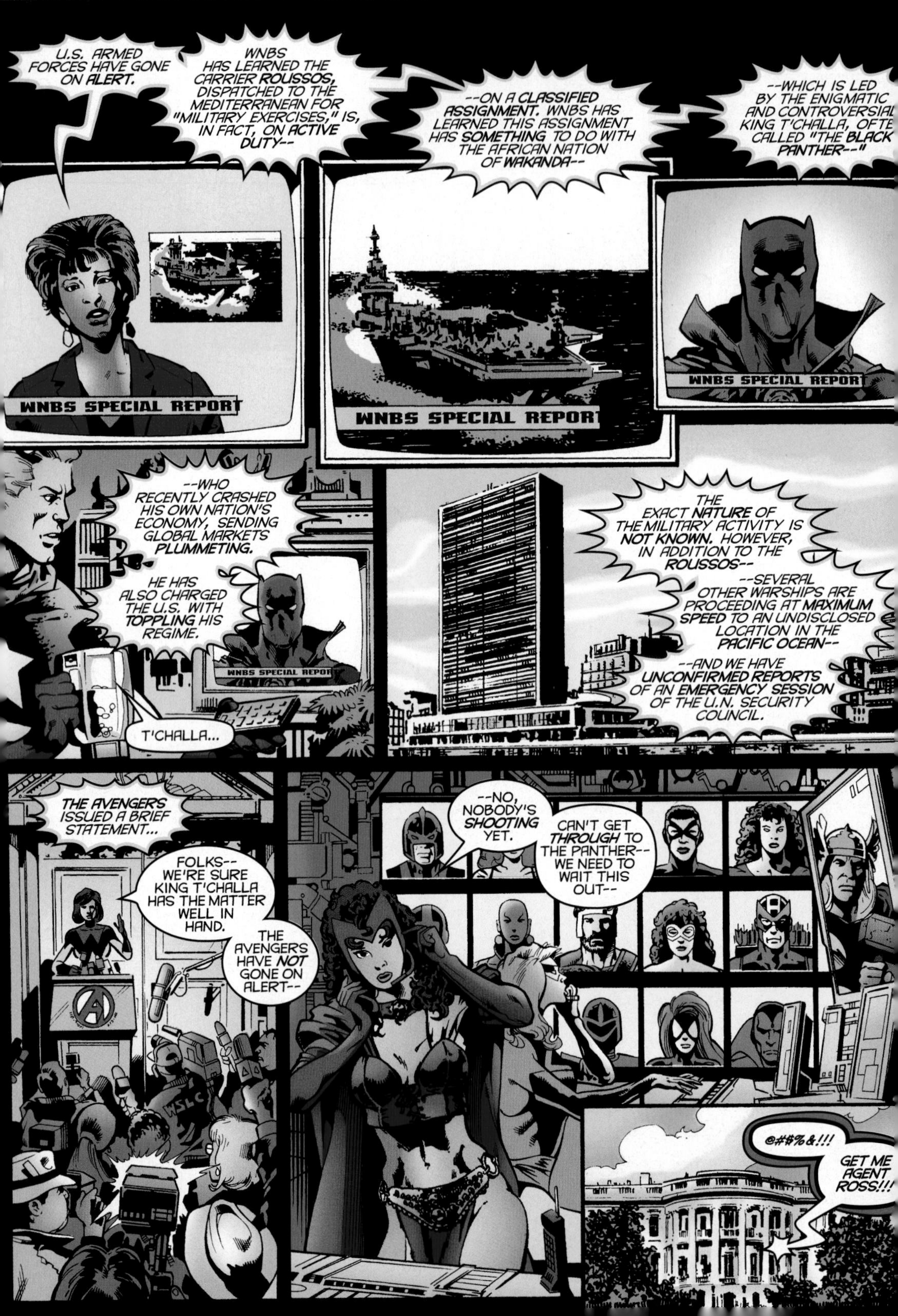
U.S. ARMED FORCES HAVE GONE ON ALERT.
WNBS HAS LEARNED THE CARRIER ROUSSOS, DISPATCHED TO THE MEDITERRANEAN FOR "MILITARY EXERCISES," IS, IN FACT, ON ACTIVE DUTY--
--ON A CLASSIFIED ASSIGNMENT. WNBS HAS LEARNED THIS ASSIGNMENT HAS SOMETHING TO DO WITH THE AFRICAN NATION OF WAKANDA--
--WHICH IS LED BY THE ENIGMATIC AND CONTROVERSIAL KING T'CHALLA, OFTE CALLED "THE BLACK PANTHER--"
WNBS SPECIAL REPORT
WNBS SPECIAL REPORT
WNBS SPECIAL REPORT
--WHO RECENTLY CRASHED HIS OWN NATION'S ECONOMY, SENDING GLOBAL MARKETS PLUMMETING.
HE HAS ALSO CHARGED THE U.S. WITH TOPPLING HIS REGIME.
WNBS SPECIAL REPORT
T'CHALLA...
THE EXACT NATURE OF THE MILITARY ACTIVITY IS NOT KNOWN. HOWEVER, IN ADDITION TO THE ROUSSOS--
--SEVERAL OTHER WARSHIPS ARE PROCEEDING AT MAXIMUM SPEED TO AN UNDISCLOSED LOCATION IN THE PACIFIC OCEAN--
--AND WE HAVE UNCONFIRMED REPORTS OF AN EMERGENCY SESSION OF THE U.N. SECURITY COUNCIL.
THE AVENGERS ISSUED A BRIEF STATEMENT...
FOLKS-- WE'RE SURE KING T'CHALLA HAS THE MATTER WELL IN HAND.
THE AVENGERS HAVE NOT GONE ON ALERT--
--NO, NOBODY'S SHOOTING YET.
CAN'T GET THROUGH TO THE PANTHER-- WE NEED TO WAIT THIS OUT--
@#$%&!!!
GET ME AGENT ROSS!!!

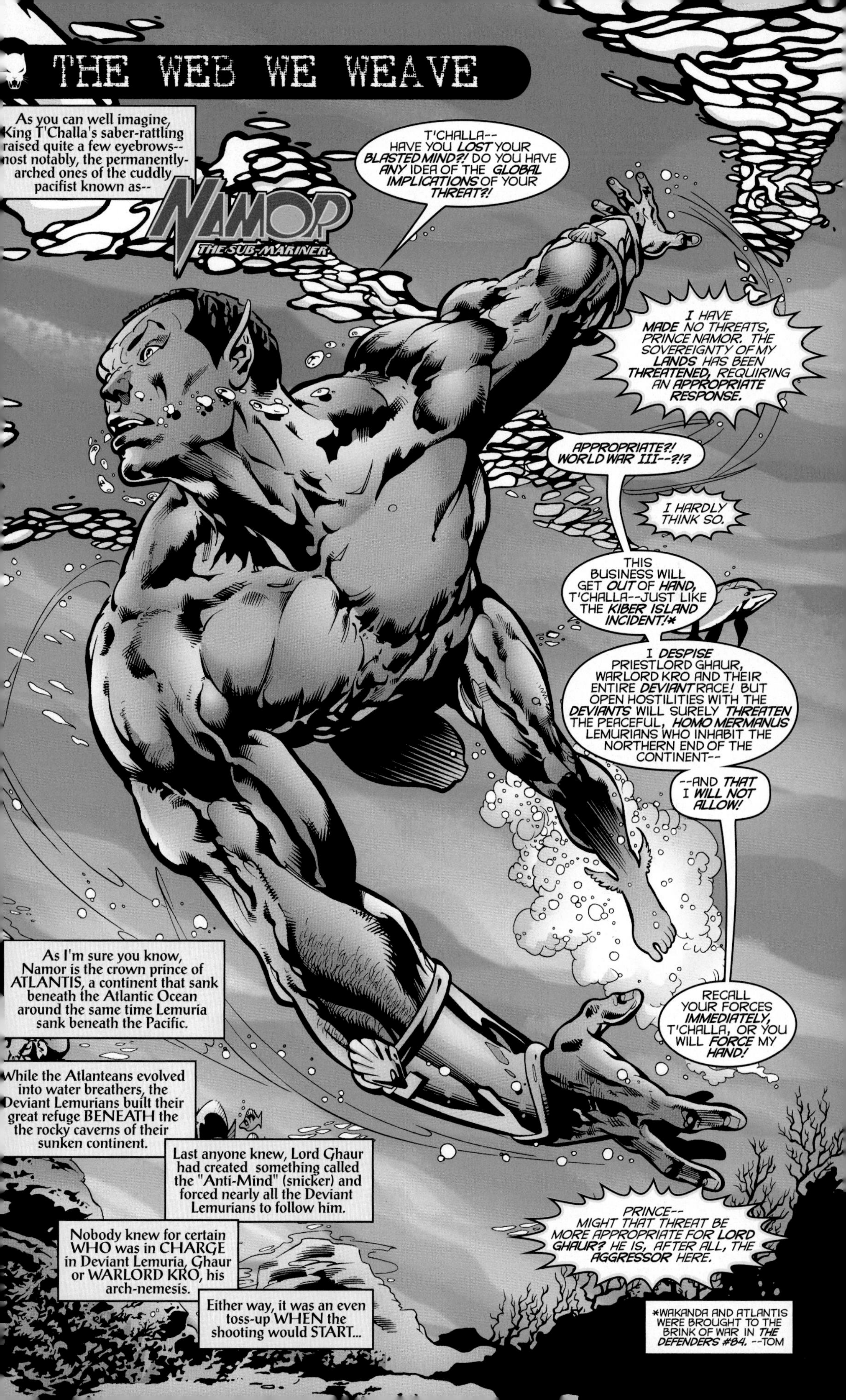

THE WEB WE WEAVE
As you can well imagine, King T'Challa's saber-rattling raised quite a few eyebrows--most notably, the permanently-arched ones of the cuddly pacifist known as--
NAMOR THE SUB-MARINER
T'CHALLA-- HAVE YOU LOST YOUR BLASTED MIND?! DO YOU HAVE ANY IDEA OF THE GLOBAL IMPLICATIONS OF YOUR THREAT?!
I HAVE MADE NO THREATS, PRINCE NAMOR. THE SOVEREIGNTY OF MY LANDS HAS BEEN THREATENED, REQUIRING AN APPROPRIATE RESPONSE.
APPROPRIATE?! WORLD WAR III--?!?
I HARDLY THINK SO.
THIS BUSINESS WILL GET OUT OF HAND, T'CHALLA--JUST LIKE THE KIBER ISLAND INCIDENT!*
I DESPISE PRIESTLORD GHAUR, WARLORD KRO AND THEIR ENTIRE DEVIANT RACE! BUT OPEN HOSTILITIES WITH THE DEVIANTS WILL SURELY THREATEN THE PEACEFUL, HOMO MERMANUS LEMURIANS WHO INHABIT THE NORTHERN END OF THE CONTINENT--
--AND THAT I WILL NOT ALLOW!
RECALL YOUR FORCES IMMEDIATELY, T'CHALLA, OR YOU WILL FORCE MY HAND!
As I'm sure you know, Namor is the crown prince of ATLANTIS, a continent that sank beneath the Atlantic Ocean around the same time Lemuria sank beneath the Pacific.
While the Atlanteans evolved into water breathers, the Deviant Lemurians built their great refuge BENEATH the the rocky caverns of their sunken continent.
Last anyone knew, Lord Ghaur had created something called the "Anti-Mind" (snicker) and forced nearly all the Deviant Lemurians to follow him.
Nobody knew for certain WHO was in CHARGE in Deviant Lemuria, Ghaur or WARLORD KRO, his arch-nemesis.
Either way, it was an even toss-up WHEN the shooting would START...
PRINCE-- MIGHT THAT THREAT BE MORE APPROPRIATE FOR LORD GHAUR? HE IS, AFTER ALL, THE AGGRESSOR HERE.
*WAKANDA AND ATLANTIS WERE BROUGHT TO THE BRINK OF WAR IN THE DEFENDERS #84. --TOM

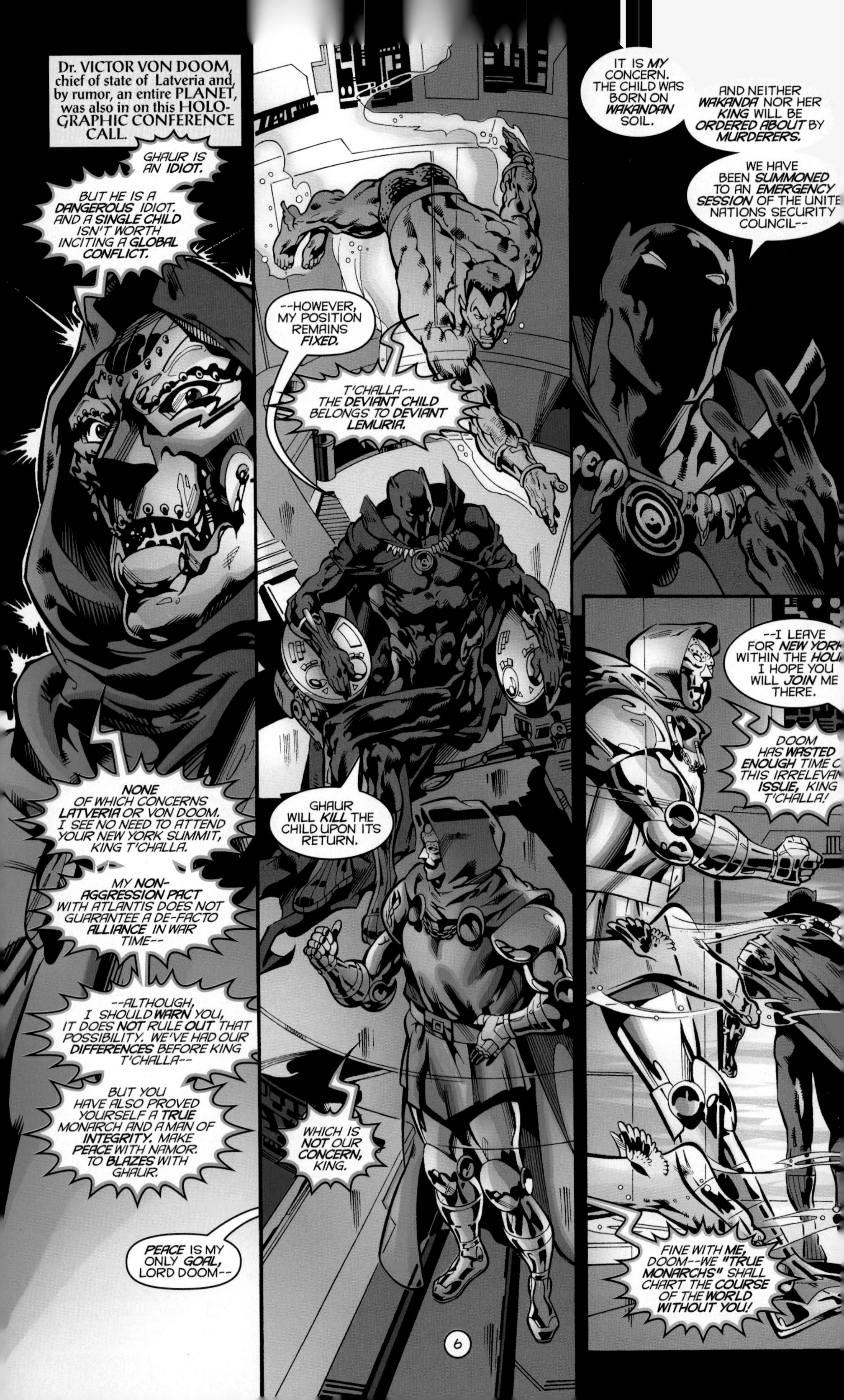
Dr. VICTOR VON DOOM, chief of state of Latveria and, by rumor, an entire PLANET, was also in on this HOLO-GRAPHIC CONFERENCE CALL.
GHAUR IS AN IDIOT.
BUT HE IS A DANGEROUS IDIOT. AND A SINGLE CHILD ISN'T WORTH INCITING A GLOBAL CONFLICT.
--HOWEVER, MY POSITION REMAINS FIXED.
T'CHALLA-- THE DEVIANT CHILD BELONGS TO DEVIANT LEMURIA.
IT IS MY CONCERN. THE CHILD WAS BORN ON WAKANDAN SOIL.
AND NEITHER WAKANDA NOR HER KING WILL BE ORDERED ABOUT BY MURDERERS.
WE HAVE BEEN SUMMONED TO AN EMERGENCY SESSION OF THE UNITE NATIONS SECURITY COUNCIL--
NONE OF WHICH CONCERNS LATVERIA OR VON DOOM. I SEE NO NEED TO ATTEND YOUR NEW YORK SUMMIT, KING T'CHALLA.
MY NON-AGGRESSION PACT WITH ATLANTIS DOES NOT GUARANTEE A DE-FACTO ALLIANCE IN WAR TIME--
--ALTHOUGH, I SHOULD WARN YOU, IT DOES NOT RULE OUT THAT POSSIBILITY. WE'VE HAD OUR DIFFERENCES BEFORE KING T'CHALLA--
BUT YOU HAVE ALSO PROVED YOURSELF A TRUE MONARCH AND A MAN OF INTEGRITY. MAKE PEACE WITH NAMOR. TO BLAZES WITH GHAUR.
PEACE IS MY ONLY GOAL, LORD DOOM--
GHAUR WILL KILL THE CHILD UPON ITS RETURN.
WHICH IS NOT OUR CONCERN, KING.
--I LEAVE FOR NEW YORK WITHIN THE HOU I HOPE YOU WILL JOIN ME THERE.
DOOM HAS WASTED ENOUGH TIME O THIS IRRELEVAN ISSUE, KING T'CHALLA!
FINE WITH ME, DOOM--WE "TRUE MONARCHS" SHALL CHART THE COURSE OF THE WORLD WITHOUT YOU!

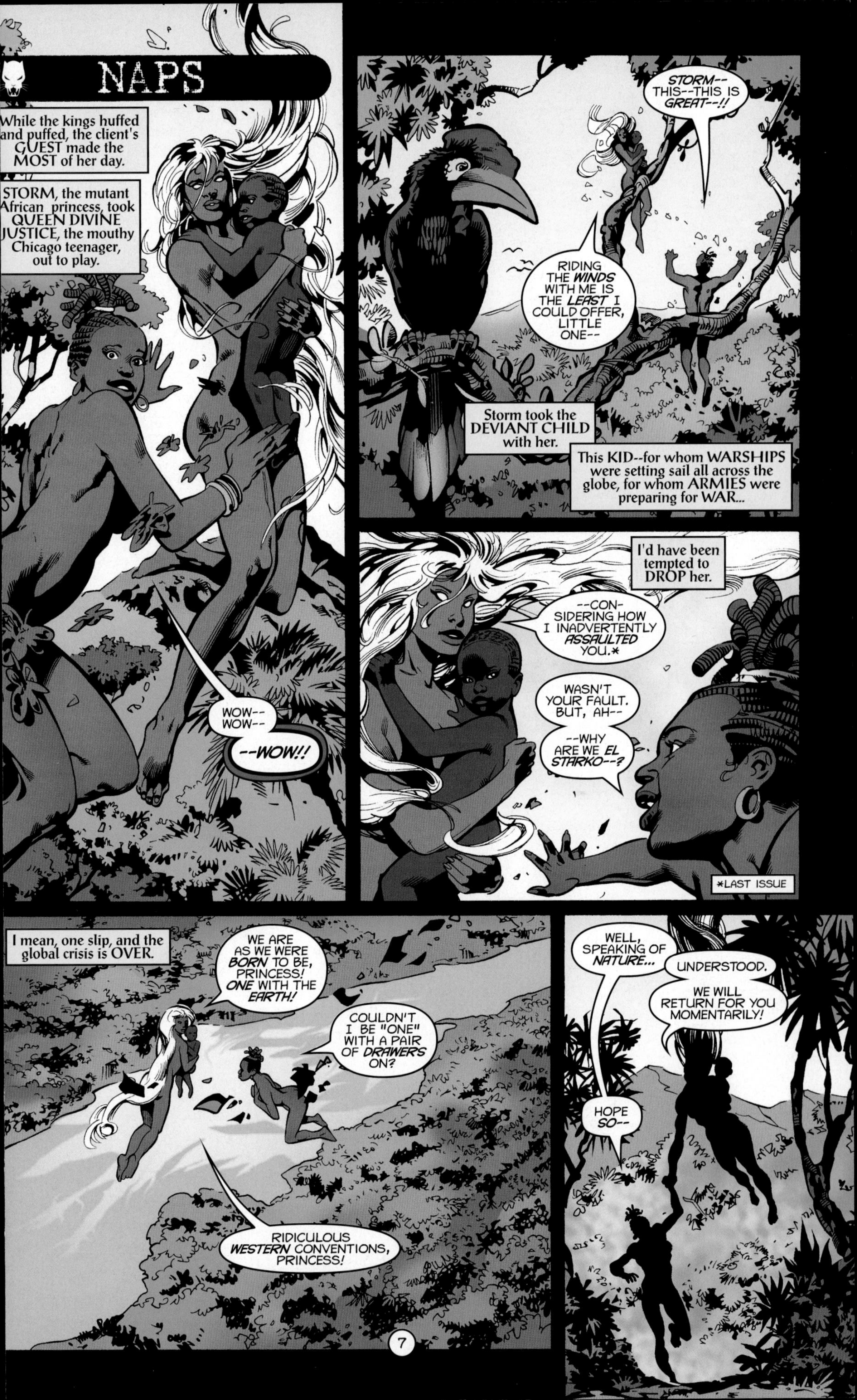
NAPS
While the kings huffed and puffed, the client's GUEST made the MOST of her day.
STORM, the mutant African princess, took QUEEN DIVINE JUSTICE, the mouthy Chicago teenager, out to play.
WOW-- WOW--
--WOW!!
STORM-- THIS--THIS IS GREAT--!!
RIDING THE WINDS WITH ME IS THE LEAST I COULD OFFER, LITTLE ONE--
Storm took the DEVIANT CHILD with her.
This KID--for whom WARSHIPS were setting sail all across the globe, for whom ARMIES were preparing for WAR...
I'd have been tempted to DROP her.
--CONSIDERING HOW I INADVERTENTLY ASSAULTED YOU.*
WASN'T YOUR FAULT. BUT, AH--
--WHY ARE WE EL STARKO--?
*LAST ISSUE
I mean, one slip, and the global crisis is OVER.
WE ARE AS WE WERE BORN TO BE, PRINCESS! ONE WITH THE EARTH!
COULDN'T I BE "ONE" WITH A PAIR OF DRAWERS ON?
RIDICULOUS WESTERN CONVENTIONS, PRINCESS!
WELL, SPEAKING OF NATURE...
UNDERSTOOD.
WE WILL RETURN FOR YOU MOMENTARILY!
HOPE SO--

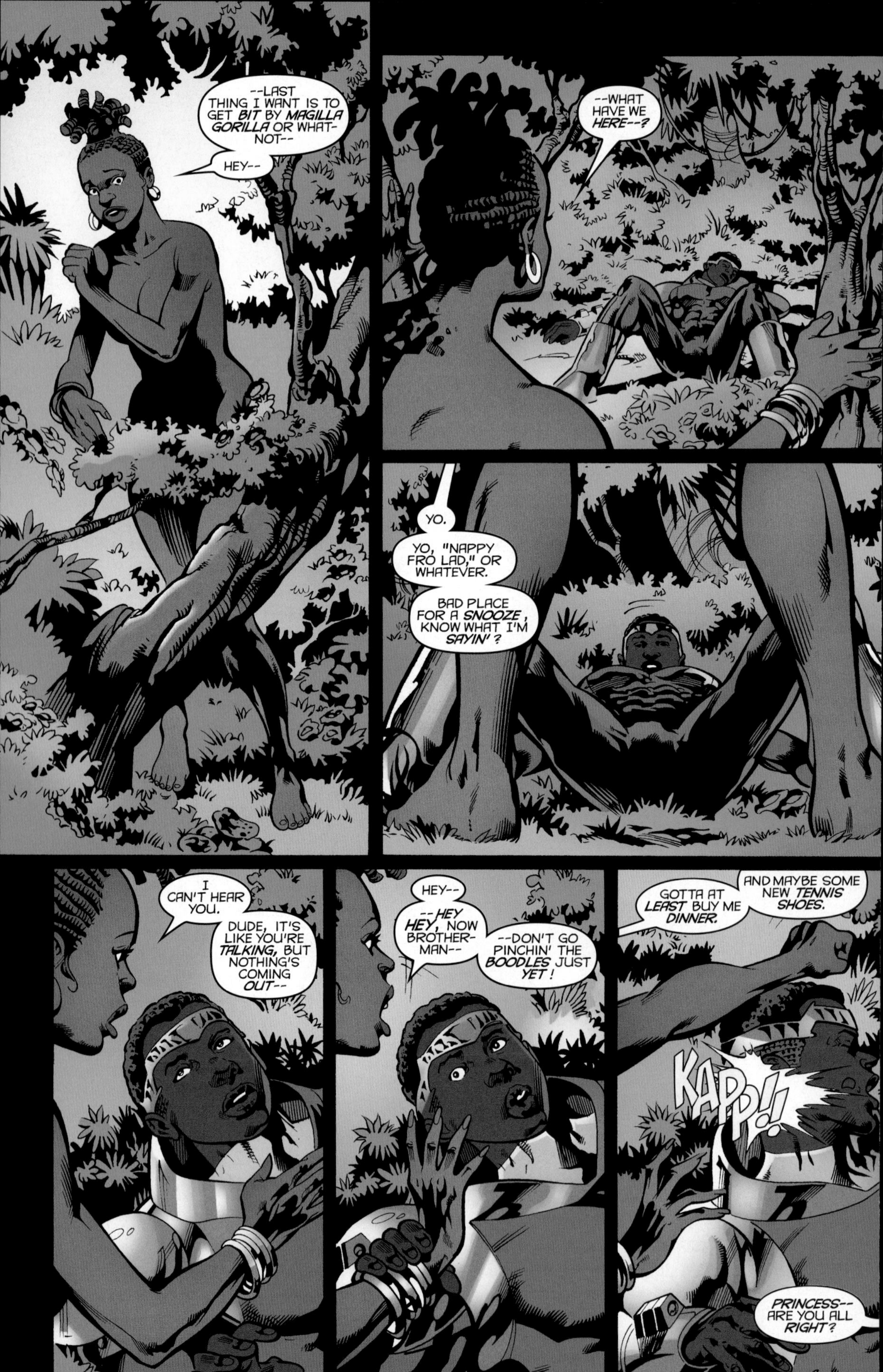
--LAST THING I WANT IS TO GET BIT BY MAGILLA GORILLA OR WHAT-NOT--
HEY--
--WHAT HAVE WE HERE--?
YO.
YO, "NAPPY FRO LAD," OR WHATEVER.
BAD PLACE FOR A SNOOZE, KNOW WHAT I'M SAYIN'?
I CAN'T HEAR YOU.
DUDE, IT'S LIKE YOU'RE TALKING, BUT NOTHING'S COMING OUT--
HEY--
--HEY HEY, NOW BROTHER-MAN--
--DON'T GO PINCHIN' THE BOODLES JUST YET!
GOTTA AT LEAST BUY ME DINNER.
AND MAYBE SOME NEW TENNIS SHOES.
KAPP!!
PRINCESS-- ARE YOU ALL RIGHT?

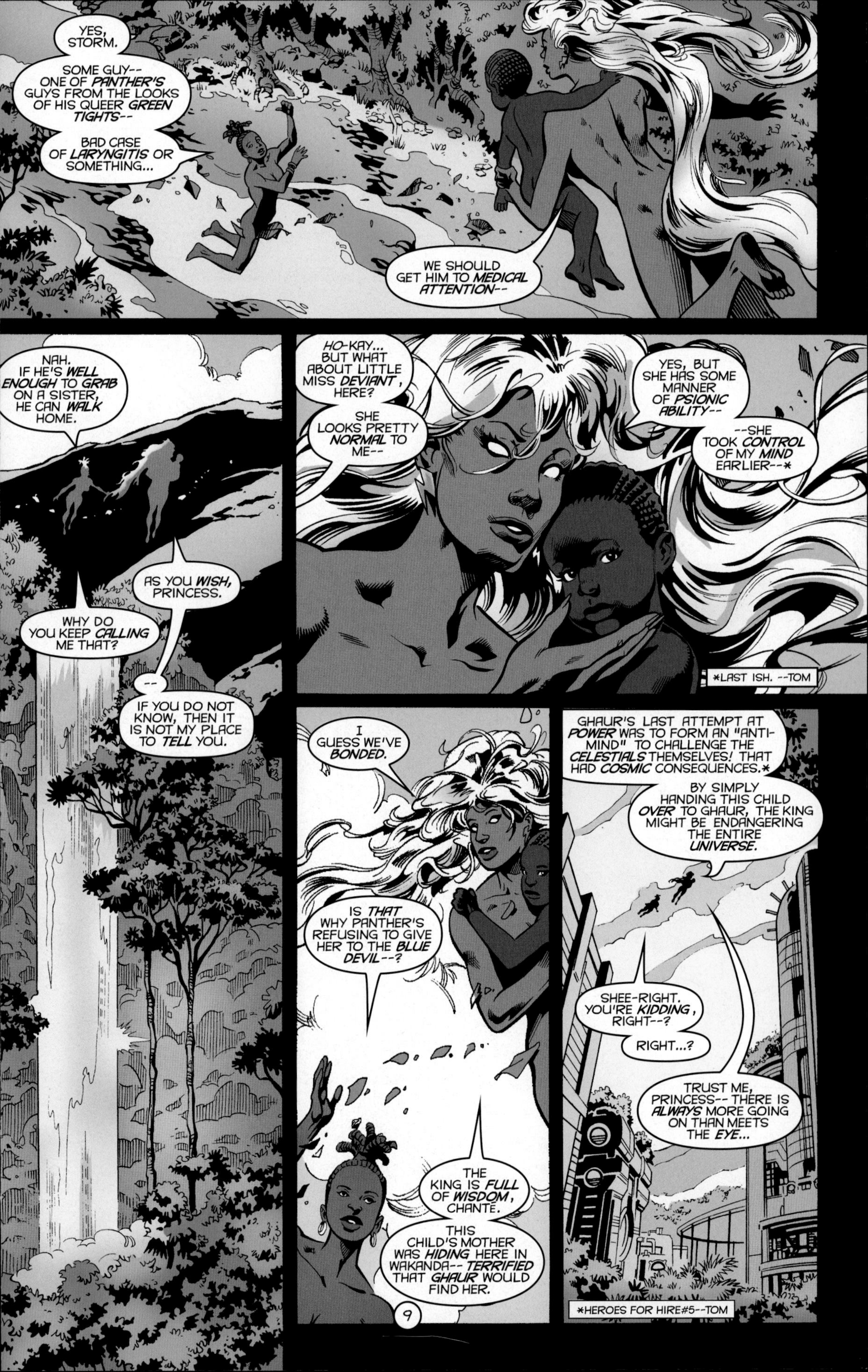
YES, STORM.
SOME GUY-- ONE OF PANTHER'S GUYS FROM THE LOOKS OF HIS QUEER GREEN TIGHTS--
BAD CASE OF LARYNGITIS OR SOMETHING...
WE SHOULD GET HIM TO MEDICAL ATTENTION--
NAH. IF HE'S WELL ENOUGH TO GRAB ON A SISTER, HE CAN WALK HOME.
HO-KAY... BUT WHAT ABOUT LITTLE MISS DEVIANT, HERE?
SHE LOOKS PRETTY NORMAL TO ME--
YES, BUT SHE HAS SOME MANNER OF PSIONIC ABILITY--
--SHE TOOK CONTROL OF MY MIND EARLIER--*
*LAST ISH. --TOM
WHY DO YOU KEEP CALLING ME THAT?
AS YOU WISH, PRINCESS.
--
IF YOU DO NOT KNOW, THEN IT IS NOT MY PLACE TO TELL YOU.
I GUESS WE'VE BONDED.
IS THAT WHY PANTHER'S REFUSING TO GIVE HER TO THE BLUE DEVIL--?
THE KING IS FULL OF WISDOM, CHANTÉ.
THIS CHILD'S MOTHER WAS HIDING HERE IN WAKANDA-- TERRIFIED THAT GHAUR WOULD FIND HER.
GHAUR'S LAST ATTEMPT AT POWER WAS TO FORM AN "ANTI-MIND" TO CHALLENGE THE CELESTIALS THEMSELVES! THAT HAD COSMIC CONSEQUENCES.*
BY SIMPLY HANDING THIS CHILD OVER TO GHAUR, THE KING MIGHT BE ENDANGERING THE ENTIRE UNIVERSE.
SHEE-RIGHT. YOU'RE KIDDING, RIGHT--?
RIGHT...?
TRUST ME, PRINCESS-- THERE IS ALWAYS MORE GOING ON THAN MEETS THE EYE...
*HEROES FOR HIRE#5--TOM
9

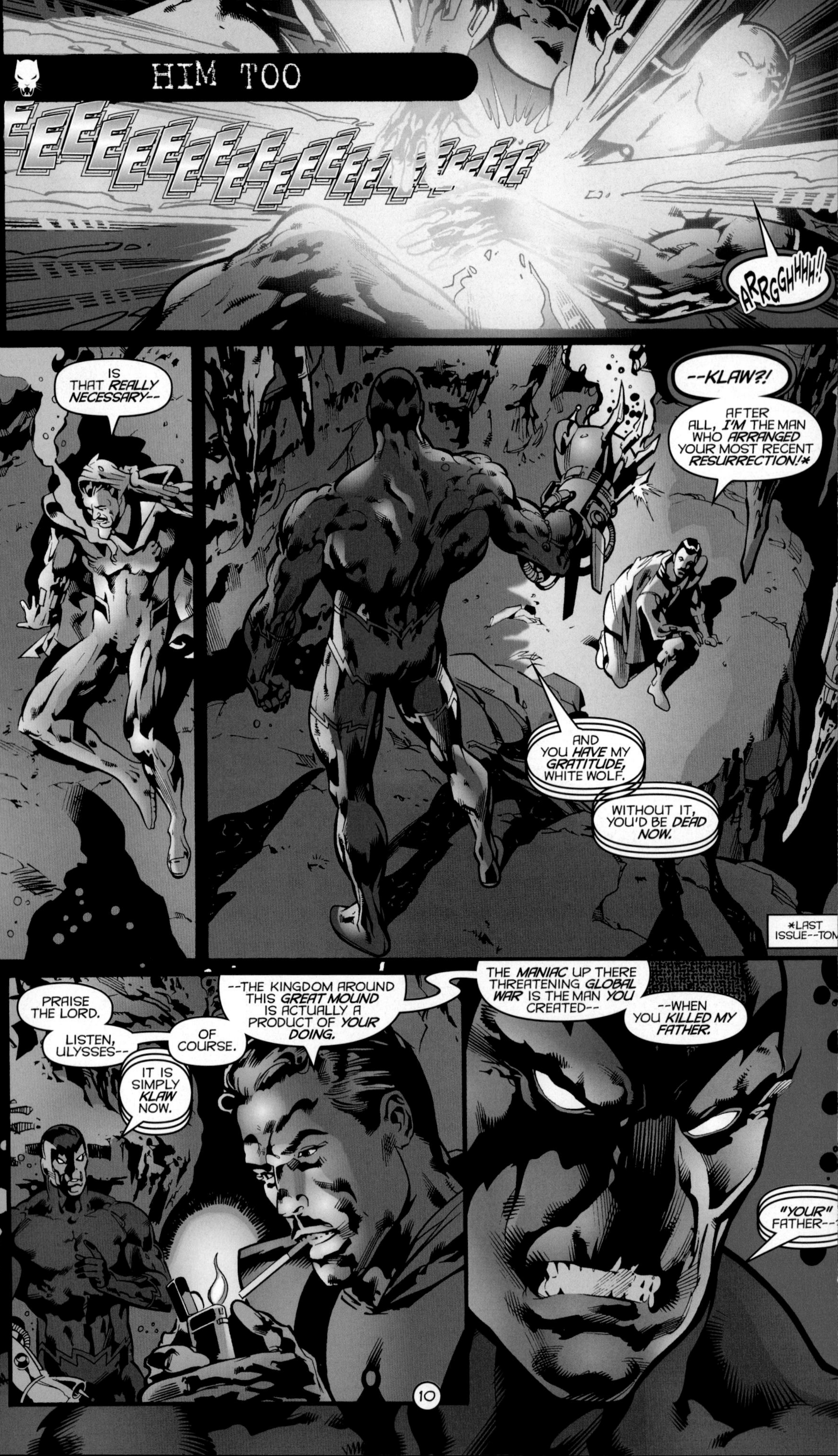

HIM TOO
EEEEEEEEEEEEEEEEEEEEEEE
ARRGGHHHH!!
IS THAT REALLY NECESSARY--
--KLAW?!
AFTER ALL, I'M THE MAN WHO ARRANGED YOUR MOST RECENT RESURRECTION!*
AND YOU HAVE MY GRATITUDE, WHITE WOLF.
WITHOUT IT, YOU'D BE DEAD NOW.
*LAST ISSUE--TOM
PRAISE THE LORD.
LISTEN, ULYSSES--
IT IS SIMPLY KLAW NOW.
OF COURSE.
--THE KINGDOM AROUND THIS GREAT MOUND IS ACTUALLY A PRODUCT OF YOUR DOING.
THE MANIAC UP THERE THREATENING GLOBAL WAR IS THE MAN YOU CREATED--
--WHEN YOU KILLED MY FATHER.
"YOUR" FATHER--

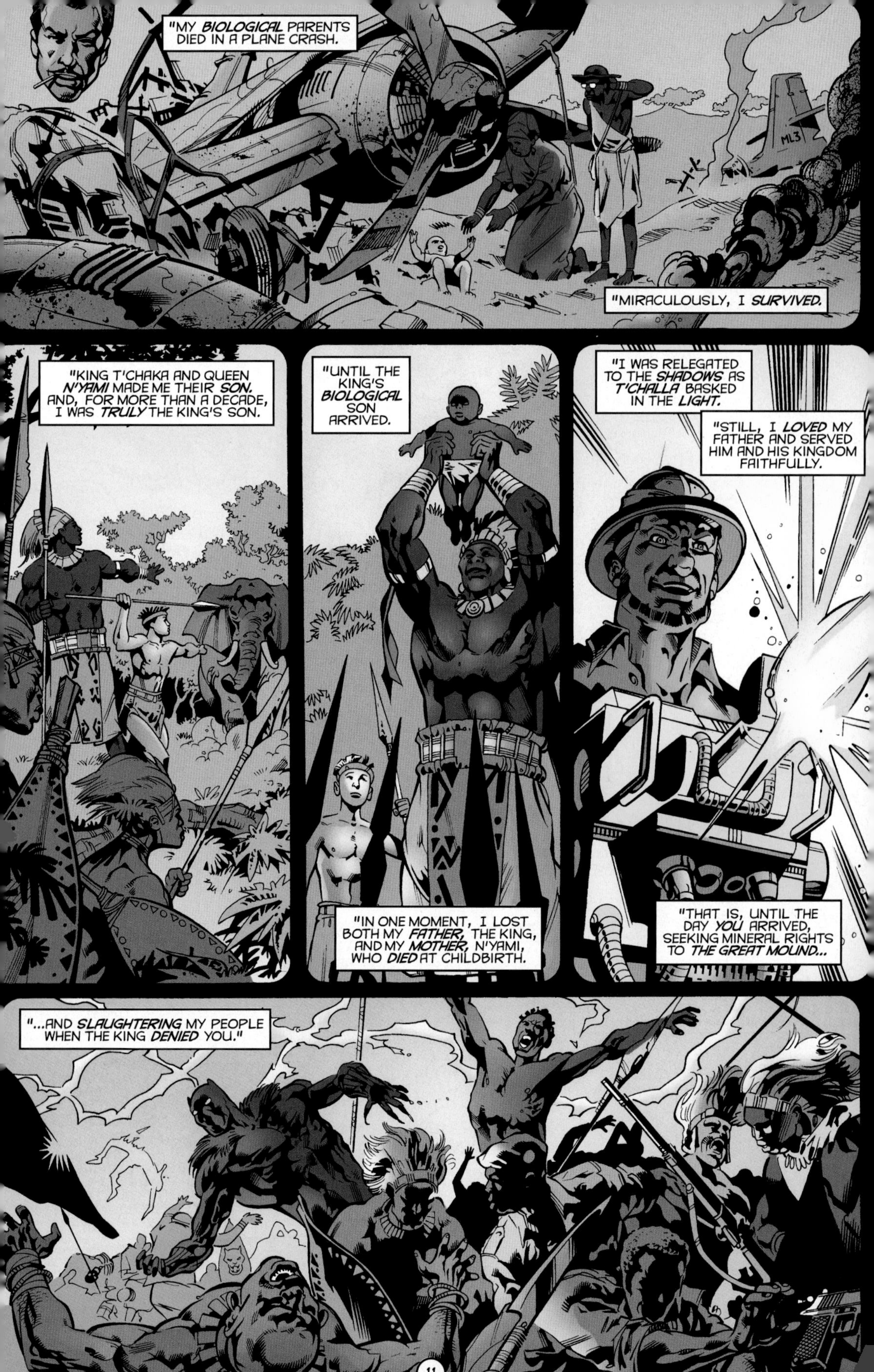
"MY BIOLOGICAL PARENTS DIED IN A PLANE CRASH.
ML3
"MIRACULOUSLY, I SURVIVED.
"KING T'CHAKA AND QUEEN N'YAMI MADE ME THEIR SON. AND, FOR MORE THAN A DECADE, I WAS TRULY THE KING'S SON.
"UNTIL THE KING'S BIOLOGICAL SON ARRIVED.
"IN ONE MOMENT, I LOST BOTH MY FATHER, THE KING, AND MY MOTHER, N'YAMI, WHO DIED AT CHILDBIRTH.
"I WAS RELEGATED TO THE SHADOWS AS T'CHALLA BASKED IN THE LIGHT.
"STILL, I LOVED MY FATHER AND SERVED HIM AND HIS KINGDOM FAITHFULLY.
"THAT IS, UNTIL THE DAY YOU ARRIVED, SEEKING MINERAL RIGHTS TO THE GREAT MOUND...
"...AND SLAUGHTERING MY PEOPLE WHEN THE KING DENIED YOU."

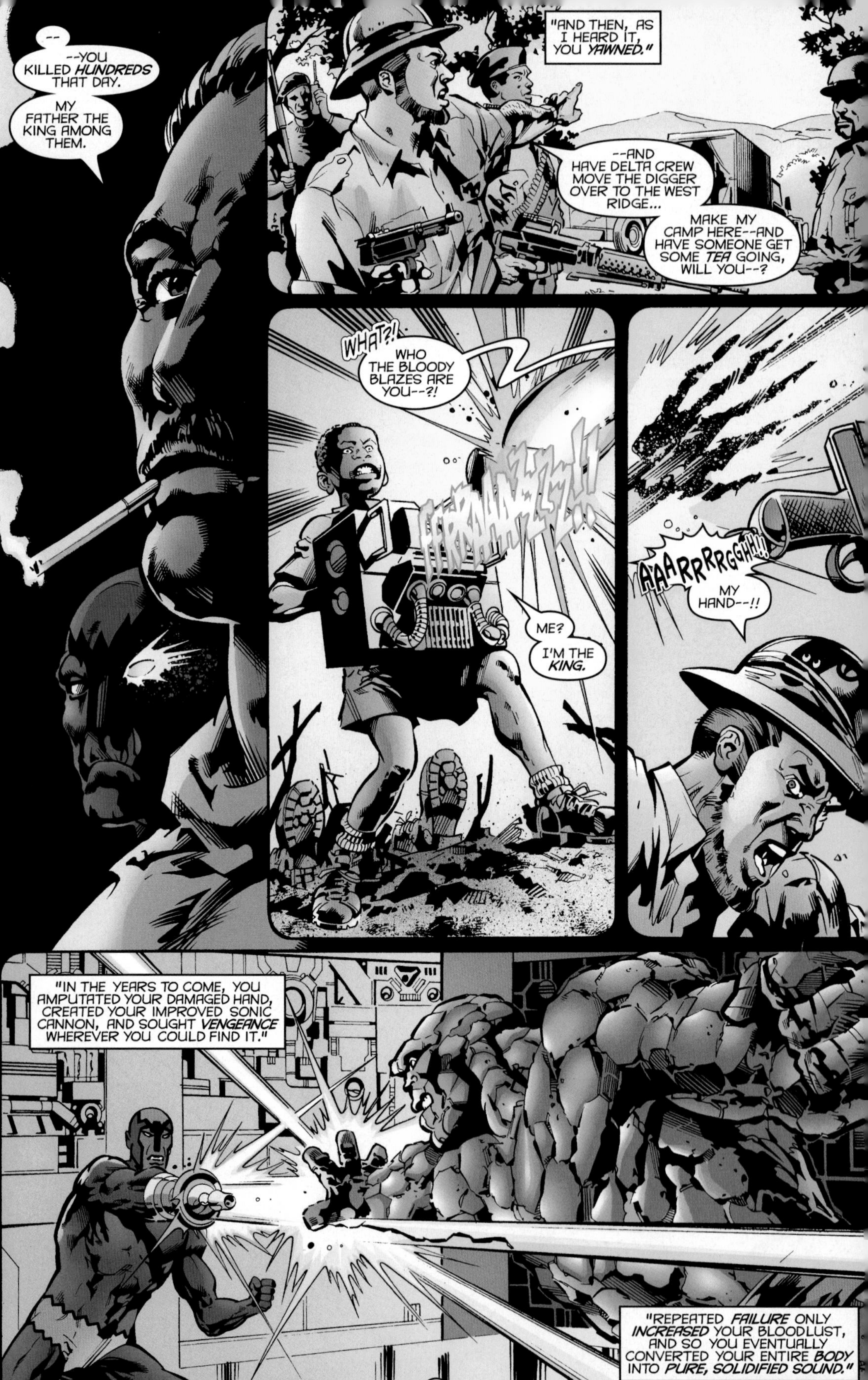
--
--YOU KILLED HUNDREDS THAT DAY.
MY FATHER THE KING AMONG THEM.
"AND THEN, AS I HEARD IT, YOU YAWNED."
--AND HAVE DELTA CREW MOVE THE DIGGER OVER TO THE WEST RIDGE...
MAKE MY CAMP HERE--AND HAVE SOMEONE GET SOME TEA GOING, WILL YOU--?
WHAT?!
WHO THE BLOODY BLAZES ARE YOU--?!
FFRRAAHHZZZZ!!
ME?
I'M THE KING.
AAARRRRGGHH!!
MY HAND--!!
"IN THE YEARS TO COME, YOU AMPUTATED YOUR DAMAGED HAND, CREATED YOUR IMPROVED SONIC CANNON, AND SOUGHT VENGEANCE WHEREVER YOU COULD FIND IT."
"REPEATED FAILURE ONLY INCREASED YOUR BLOODLUST, AND SO YOU EVENTUALLY CONVERTED YOUR ENTIRE BODY INTO PURE, SOLIDIFIED SOUND."

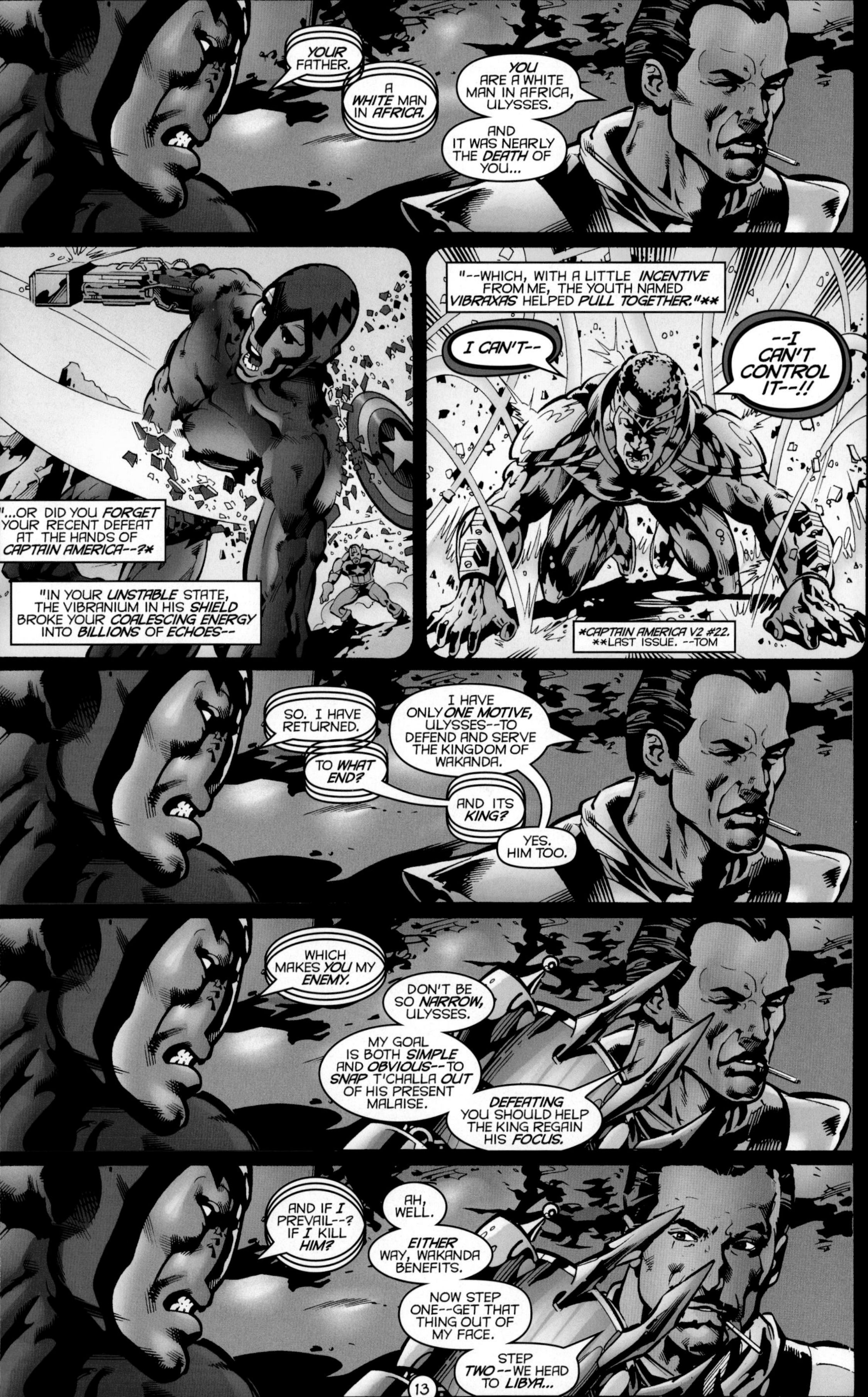
YOUR FATHER.
A WHITE MAN IN AFRICA.
YOU ARE A WHITE MAN IN AFRICA, ULYSSES.
AND IT WAS NEARLY THE DEATH OF YOU...
"...OR DID YOU FORGET YOUR RECENT DEFEAT AT THE HANDS OF CAPTAIN AMERICA--?*
"IN YOUR UNSTABLE STATE, THE VIBRANIUM IN HIS SHIELD BROKE YOUR COALESCING ENERGY INTO BILLIONS OF ECHOES--
"--WHICH, WITH A LITTLE INCENTIVE FROM ME, THE YOUTH NAMED VIBRAXAS HELPED PULL TOGETHER."**
I CAN'T--
--I CAN'T CONTROL IT--!!
*CAPTAIN AMERICA V2 #22.
**LAST ISSUE. --TOM
SO. I HAVE RETURNED.
TO WHAT END?
I HAVE ONLY ONE MOTIVE, ULYSSES--TO DEFEND AND SERVE THE KINGDOM OF WAKANDA.
AND ITS KING?
YES. HIM TOO.
WHICH MAKES YOU MY ENEMY.
DON'T BE SO NARROW, ULYSSES.
MY GOAL IS BOTH SIMPLE AND OBVIOUS--TO SNAP T'CHALLA OUT OF HIS PRESENT MALAISE.
DEFEATING YOU SHOULD HELP THE KING REGAIN HIS FOCUS.
AND IF I PREVAIL--? IF I KILL HIM?
AH, WELL.
EITHER WAY, WAKANDA BENEFITS.
NOW STEP ONE--GET THAT THING OUT OF MY FACE.
STEP TWO--WE HEAD TO LIBYA...

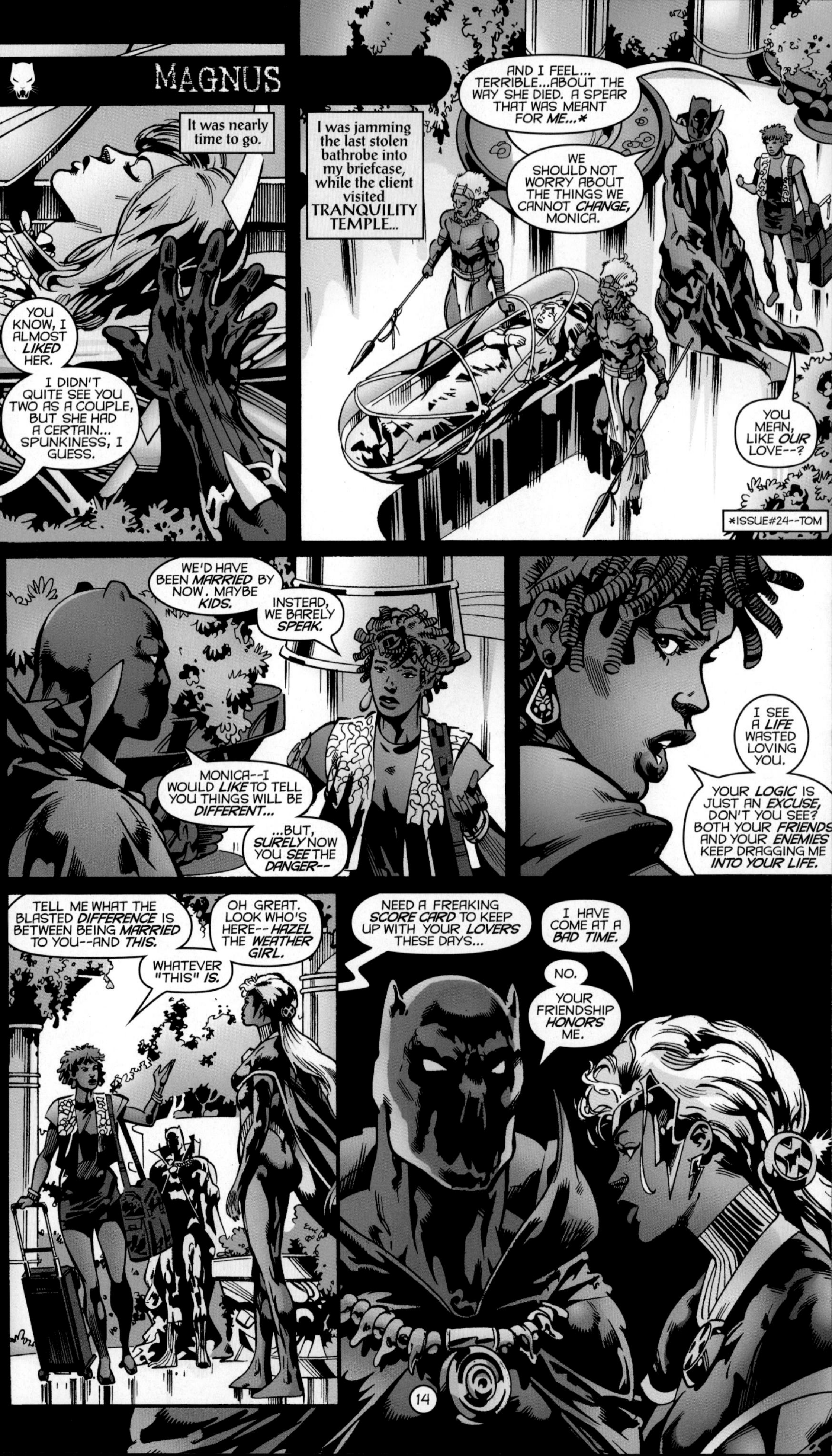
MAGNUS
It was nearly time to go.
YOU KNOW, I ALMOST LIKED HER.
I DIDN'T QUITE SEE YOU TWO AS A COUPLE, BUT SHE HAD A CERTAIN... SPUNKINESS, I GUESS.
I was jamming the last stolen bathrobe into my briefcase, while the client visited TRANQUILITY TEMPLE...
AND I FEEL... TERRIBLE...ABOUT THE WAY SHE DIED. A SPEAR THAT WAS MEANT FOR ME...*
WE SHOULD NOT WORRY ABOUT THE THINGS WE CANNOT CHANGE, MONICA.
YOU MEAN, LIKE OUR LOVE--?
*ISSUE#24--TOM
WE'D HAVE BEEN MARRIED BY NOW. MAYBE KIDS.
INSTEAD, WE BARELY SPEAK.
MONICA--I WOULD LIKE TO TELL YOU THINGS WILL BE DIFFERENT...
...BUT, SURELY NOW YOU SEE THE DANGER--
I SEE A LIFE WASTED LOVING YOU.
YOUR LOGIC IS JUST AN EXCUSE, DON'T YOU SEE? BOTH YOUR FRIENDS AND YOUR ENEMIES KEEP DRAGGING ME INTO YOUR LIFE.
TELL ME WHAT THE BLASTED DIFFERENCE IS BETWEEN BEING MARRIED TO YOU--AND THIS.
WHATEVER "THIS" IS.
OH GREAT. LOOK WHO'S HERE-- HAZEL THE WEATHER GIRL.
NEED A FREAKING SCORE CARD TO KEEP UP WITH YOUR LOVERS THESE DAYS...
I HAVE COME AT A BAD TIME.
NO.
YOUR FRIENDSHIP HONORS ME.

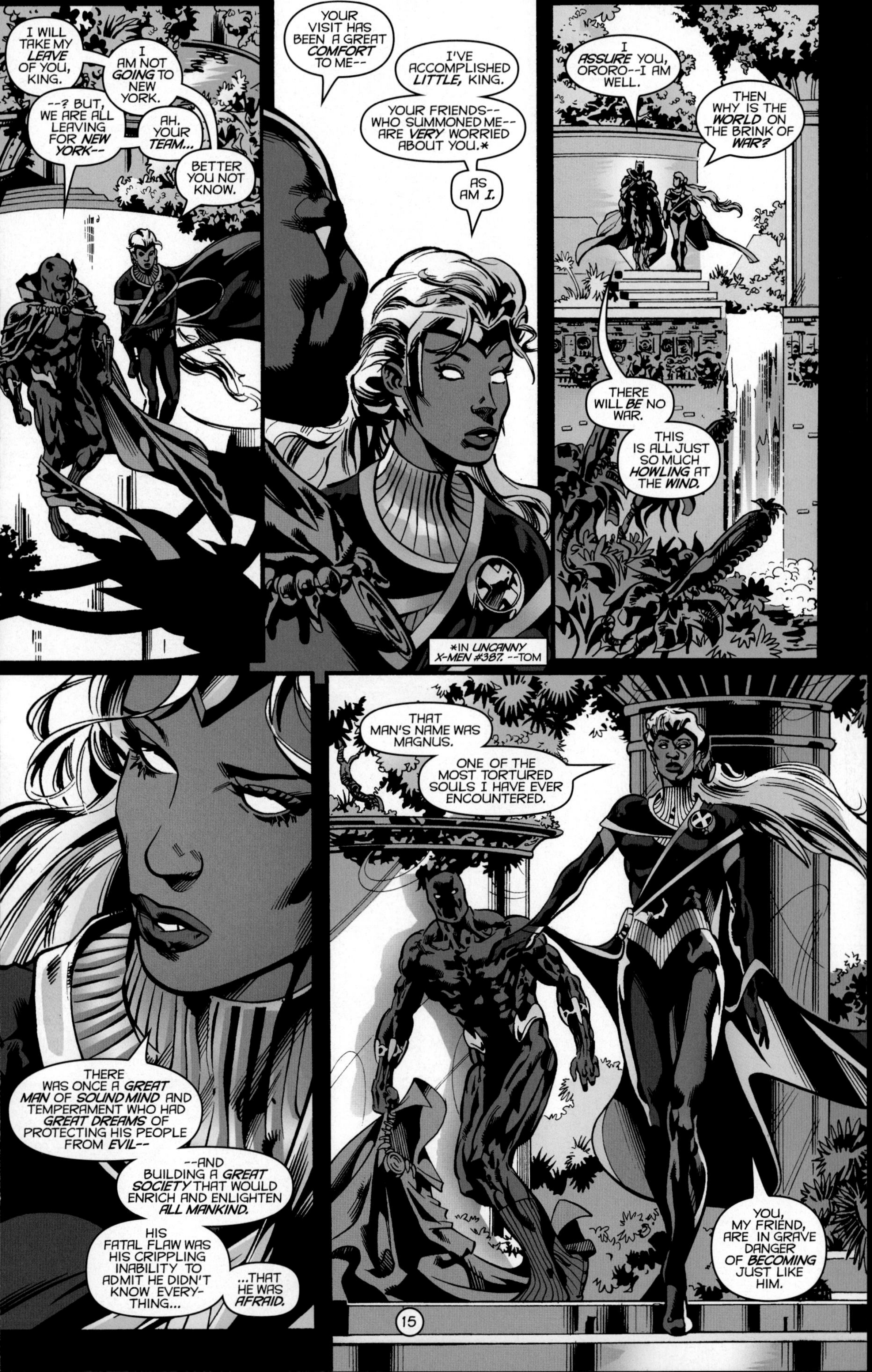
I WILL TAKE MY LEAVE OF YOU, KING.
I AM NOT GOING TO NEW YORK.
--? BUT, WE ARE ALL LEAVING FOR NEW YORK--
AH. YOUR TEAM...
BETTER YOU NOT KNOW.
YOUR VISIT HAS BEEN A GREAT COMFORT TO ME--
I'VE ACCOMPLISHED LITTLE, KING.
YOUR FRIENDS--WHO SUMMONED ME--ARE VERY WORRIED ABOUT YOU.*
AS AM I.
*IN UNCANNY X-MEN #387. --TOM
I ASSURE YOU, ORORO--I AM WELL.
THEN WHY IS THE WORLD ON THE BRINK OF WAR?
THERE WILL BE NO WAR.
THIS IS ALL JUST SO MUCH HOWLING AT THE WIND.
THERE WAS ONCE A GREAT MAN OF SOUND MIND AND TEMPERAMENT WHO HAD GREAT DREAMS OF PROTECTING HIS PEOPLE FROM EVIL--
--AND BUILDING A GREAT SOCIETY THAT WOULD ENRICH AND ENLIGHTEN ALL MANKIND.
HIS FATAL FLAW WAS HIS CRIPPLING INABILITY TO ADMIT HE DIDN'T KNOW EVERY-THING...
...THAT HE WAS AFRAID.
THAT MAN'S NAME WAS MAGNUS.
ONE OF THE MOST TORTURED SOULS I HAVE EVER ENCOUNTERED.
YOU, MY FRIEND, ARE IN GRAVE DANGER OF BECOMING JUST LIKE HIM.
15

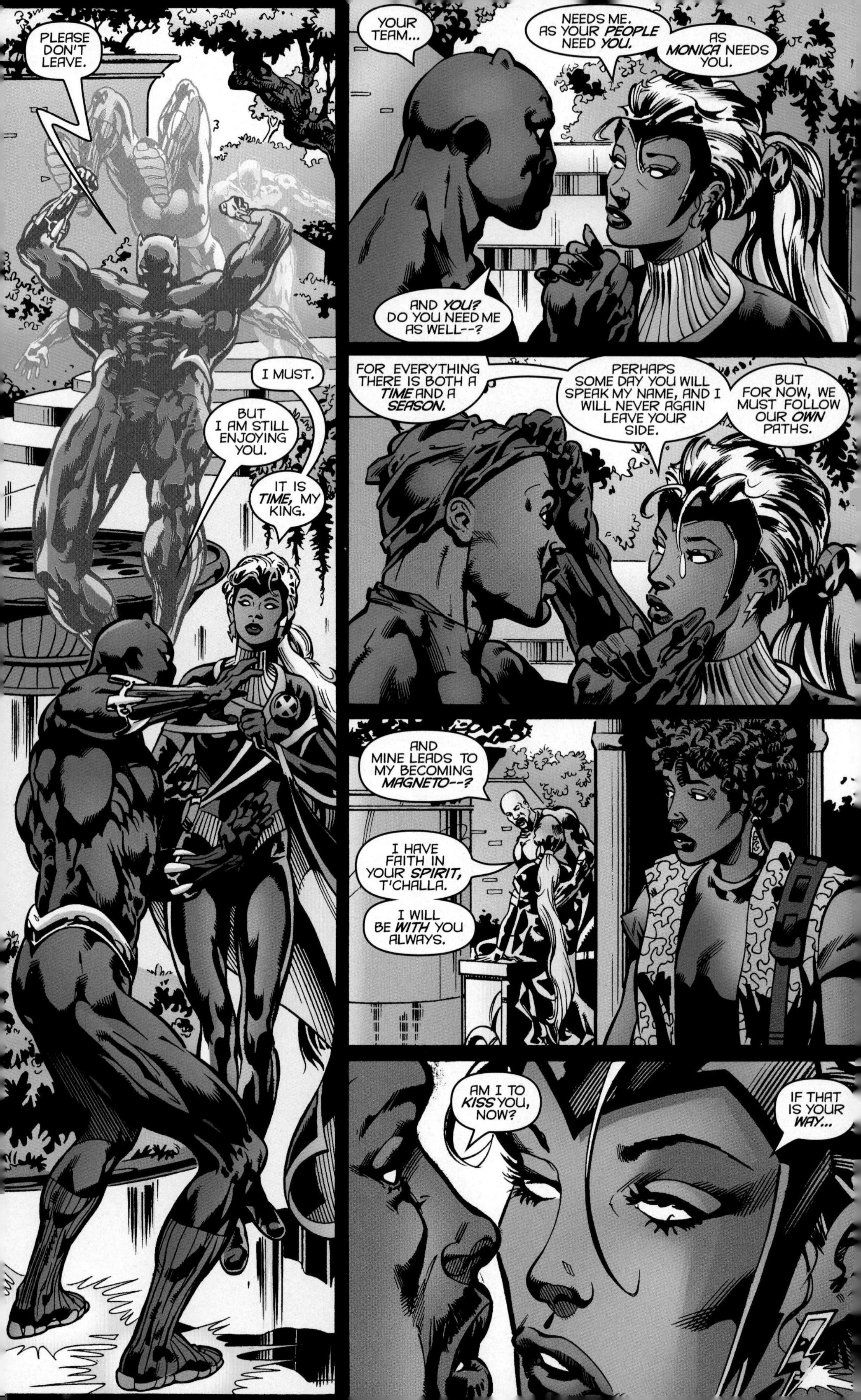
PLEASE DON'T LEAVE.
I MUST.
BUT I AM STILL ENJOYING YOU.
IT IS TIME, MY KING.
YOUR TEAM...
NEEDS ME. AS YOUR PEOPLE NEED YOU.
AS MONICA NEEDS YOU.
AND YOU? DO YOU NEED ME AS WELL--?
FOR EVERYTHING THERE IS BOTH A TIME AND A SEASON.
PERHAPS SOME DAY YOU WILL SPEAK MY NAME, AND I WILL NEVER AGAIN LEAVE YOUR SIDE.
BUT FOR NOW, WE MUST FOLLOW OUR OWN PATHS.
AND MINE LEADS TO MY BECOMING MAGNETO--?
I HAVE FAITH IN YOUR SPIRIT, T'CHALLA.
I WILL BE WITH YOU ALWAYS.
AM I TO KISS YOU, NOW?
IF THAT IS YOUR WAY...

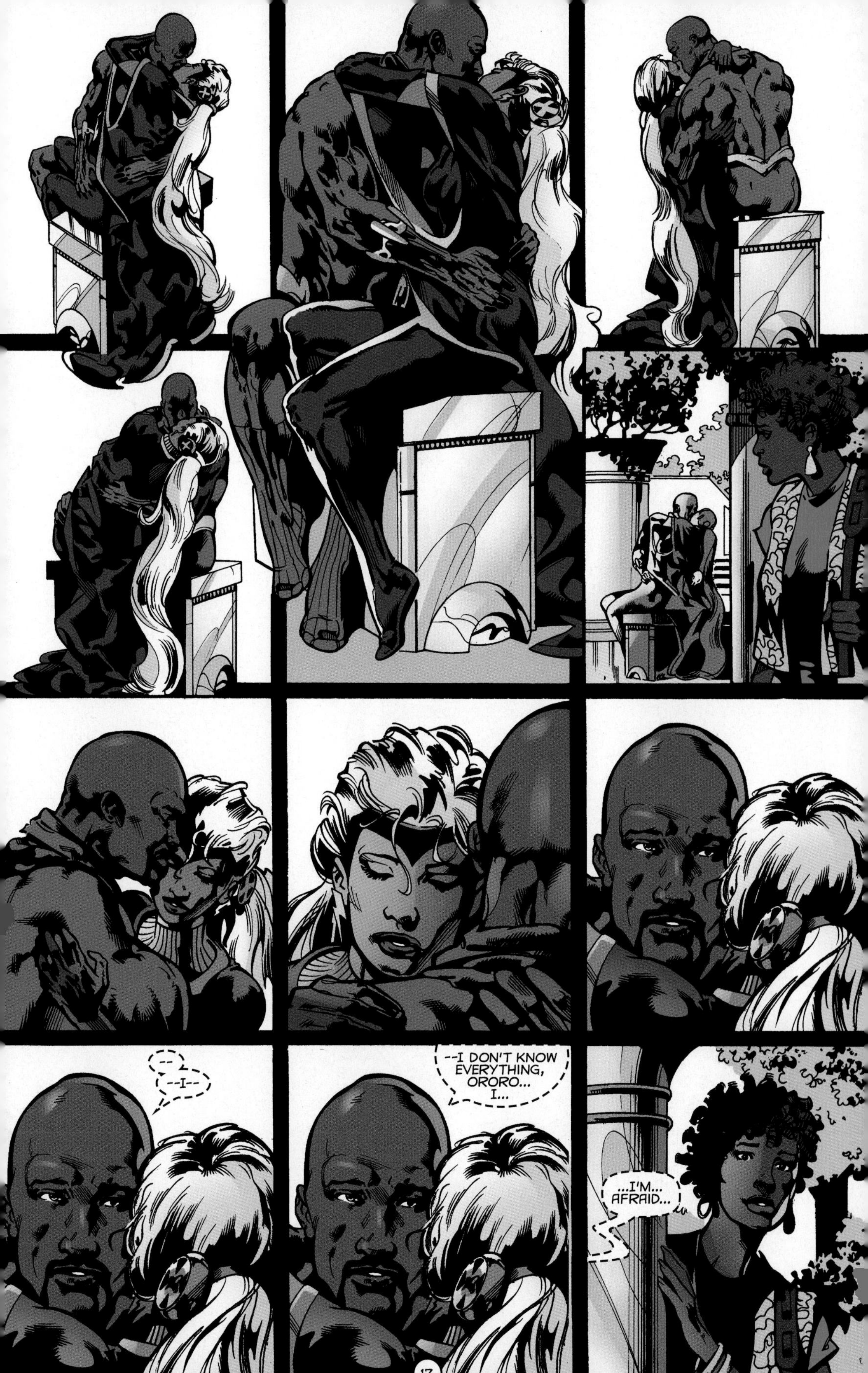
--
--I--
--I DON'T KNOW EVERYTHING, ORORO... I...
...I'M... AFRAID...

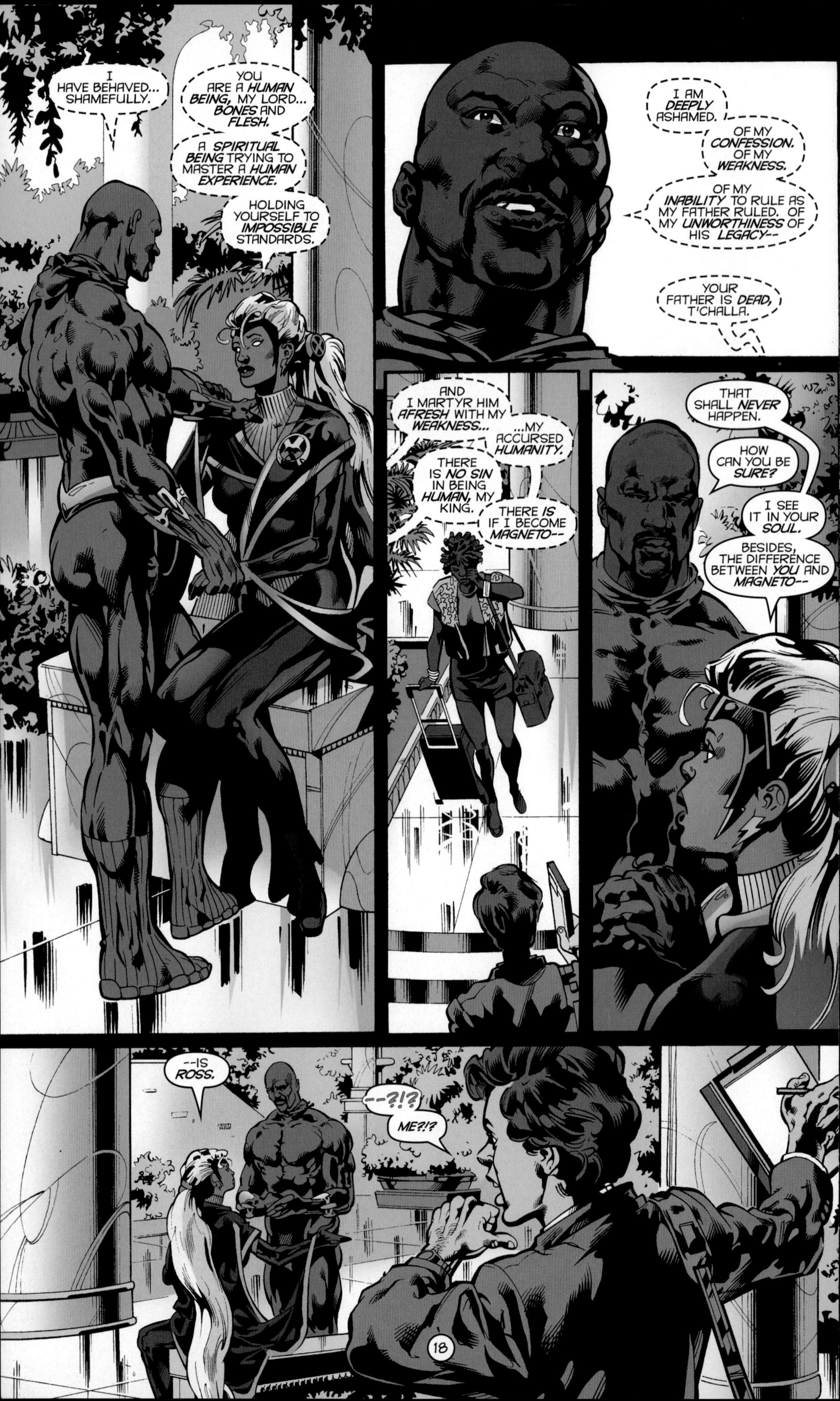

I HAVE BEHAVED... SHAMEFULLY.
YOU ARE A *HUMAN BEING,* MY LORD... *BONES* AND *FLESH.*
A *SPIRITUAL BEING* TRYING TO MASTER A *HUMAN EXPERIENCE.*
HOLDING YOURSELF TO *IMPOSSIBLE* STANDARDS.
I AM *DEEPLY* ASHAMED.
OF MY *CONFESSION.* OF MY *WEAKNESS.*
OF MY *INABILITY* TO RULE AS MY FATHER RULED. OF MY *UNWORTHINESS* OF HIS *LEGACY--*
YOUR FATHER IS *DEAD,* T'CHALLA.
AND I MARTYR HIM *AFRESH* WITH MY *WEAKNESS...*
...MY ACCURSED *HUMANITY.*
THERE IS *NO SIN* IN BEING *HUMAN,* MY KING.
THERE *IS* IF I BECOME *MAGNETO--*
THAT SHALL *NEVER* HAPPEN.
HOW CAN YOU BE *SURE?*
I SEE IT IN YOUR *SOUL.*
BESIDES, THE DIFFERENCE BETWEEN *YOU* AND *MAGNETO--*
--IS *ROSS.*
--?!?
ME?!?

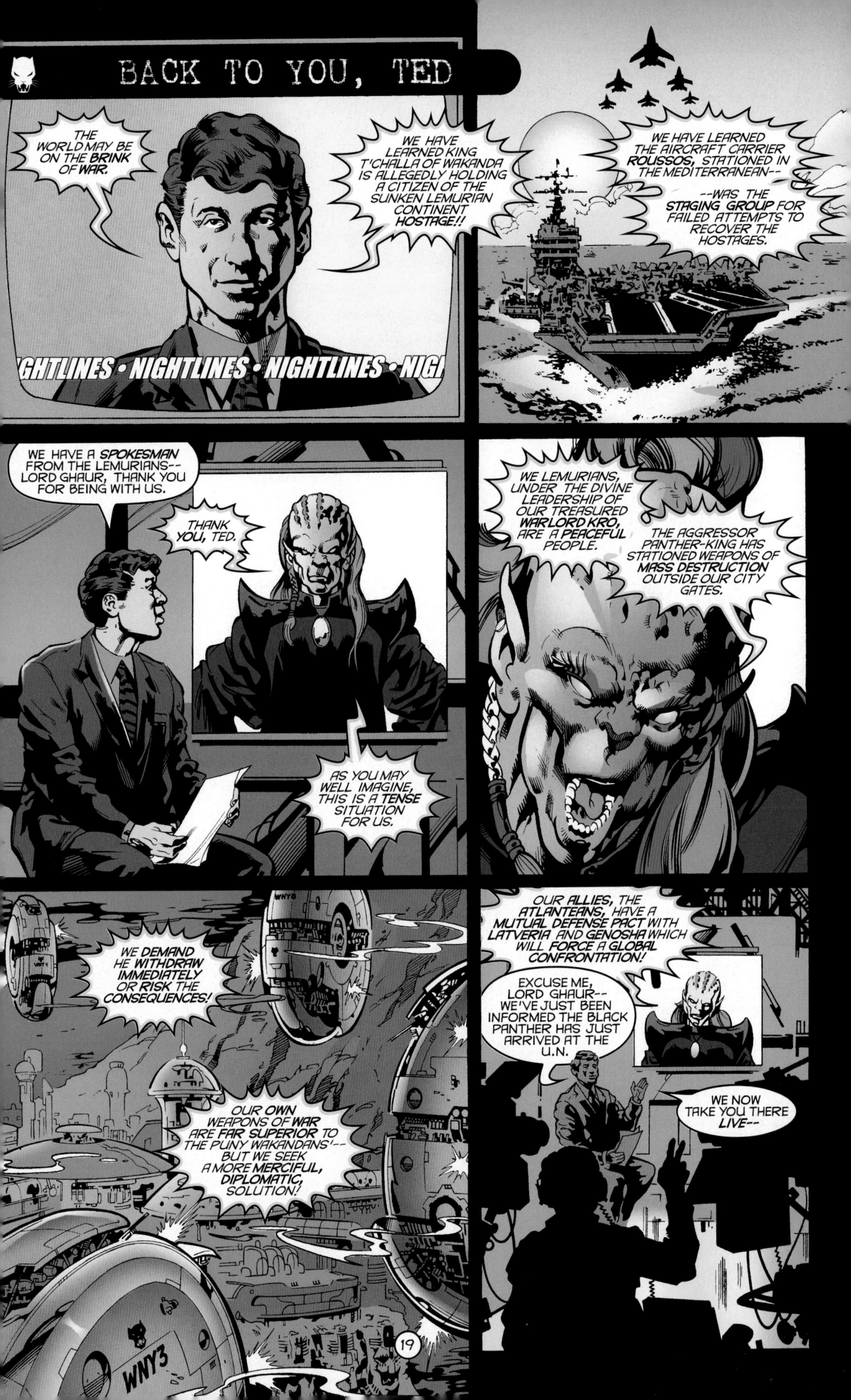
BACK TO YOU, TED
THE WORLD MAY BE ON THE BRINK OF WAR.
WE HAVE LEARNED KING T'CHALLA OF WAKANDA IS ALLEGEDLY HOLDING A CITIZEN OF THE SUNKEN LEMURIAN CONTINENT HOSTAGE!!
NIGHTLINES • NIGHTLINES • NIGHTLINES
WE HAVE LEARNED THE AIRCRAFT CARRIER ROUSSOS, STATIONED IN THE MEDITERRANEAN--
--WAS THE STAGING GROUP FOR FAILED ATTEMPTS TO RECOVER THE HOSTAGES.
WE HAVE A SPOKESMAN FROM THE LEMURIANS--LORD GHAUR, THANK YOU FOR BEING WITH US.
THANK YOU, TED.
AS YOU MAY WELL IMAGINE, THIS IS A TENSE SITUATION FOR US.
WE LEMURIANS, UNDER THE DIVINE LEADERSHIP OF OUR TREASURED WARLORD KRO, ARE A PEACEFUL PEOPLE.
THE AGGRESSOR PANTHER-KING HAS STATIONED WEAPONS OF MASS DESTRUCTION OUTSIDE OUR CITY GATES.
WE DEMAND HE WITHDRAW IMMEDIATELY OR RISK THE CONSEQUENCES!
OUR OWN WEAPONS OF WAR ARE FAR SUPERIOR TO THE PUNY WAKANDANS'--BUT WE SEEK A MORE MERCIFUL, DIPLOMATIC, SOLUTION!
WNY3
OUR ALLIES, THE ATLANTEANS, HAVE A MUTUAL DEFENSE PACT WITH LATVERIA AND GENOSHA WHICH WILL FORCE A GLOBAL CONFRONTATION!
EXCUSE ME, LORD GHAUR--WE'VE JUST BEEN INFORMED THE BLACK PANTHER HAS JUST ARRIVED AT THE U.N.
WE NOW TAKE YOU THERE LIVE--

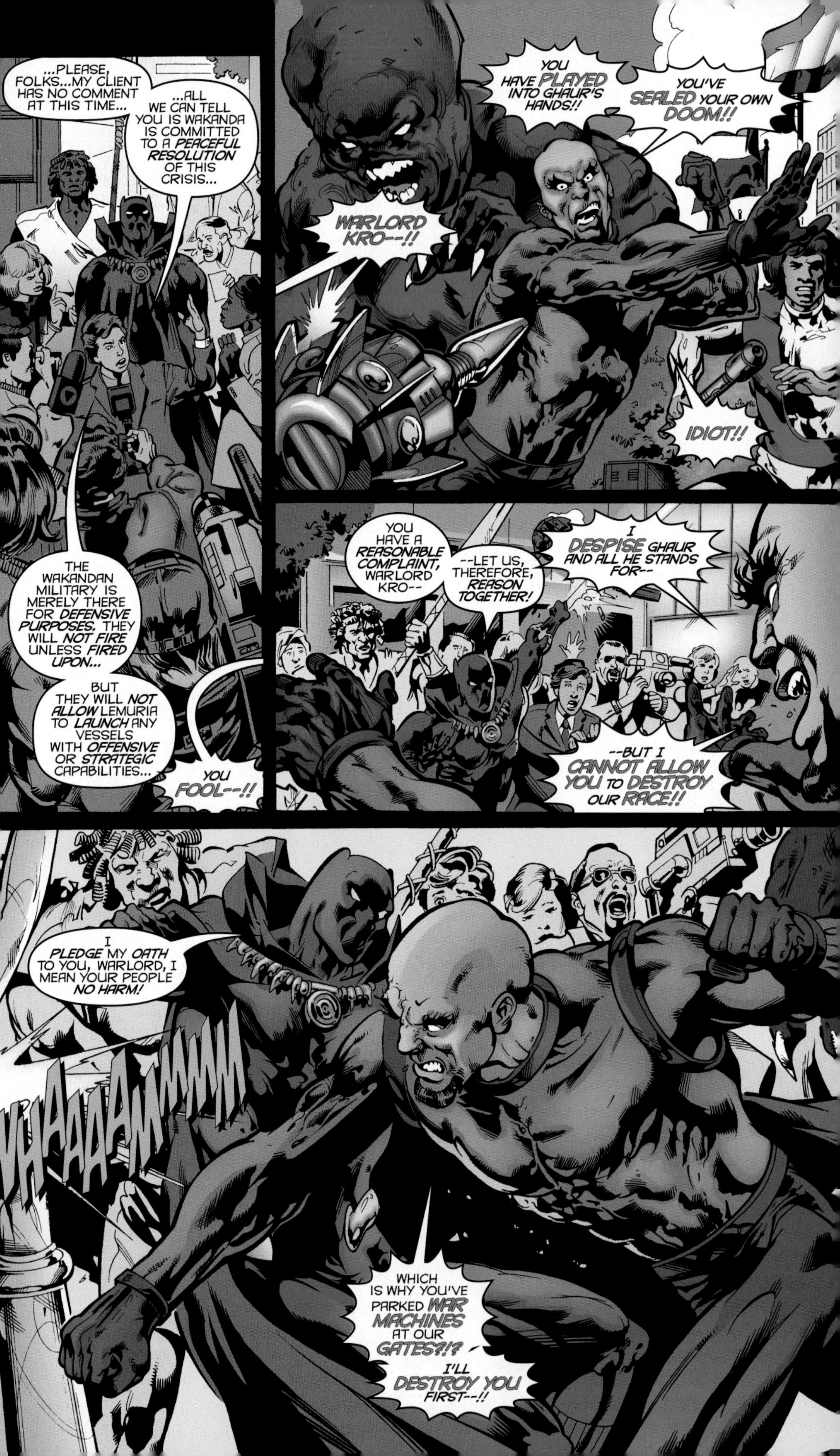
...PLEASE, FOLKS...MY CLIENT HAS NO COMMENT AT THIS TIME...
...ALL WE CAN TELL YOU IS WAKANDA IS COMMITTED TO A *PEACEFUL RESOLUTION* OF THIS CRISIS...
THE WAKANDAN MILITARY IS MERELY THERE FOR *DEFENSIVE PURPOSES.* THEY WILL *NOT FIRE* UNLESS *FIRED UPON...*
BUT THEY WILL *NOT ALLOW* LEMURIA TO *LAUNCH* ANY VESSELS WITH *OFFENSIVE* OR *STRATEGIC* CAPABILITIES...
YOU FOOL--!!
WARLORD KRO--!!
YOU HAVE *PLAYED* INTO GHAUR'S HANDS!!
YOU'VE *SEALED* YOUR OWN DOOM!!
IDIOT!!
YOU HAVE A *REASONABLE COMPLAINT,* WARLORD KRO--
--LET US, THEREFORE, *REASON TOGETHER!*
I *DESPISE* GHAUR AND ALL HE STANDS FOR--
--BUT I *CANNOT ALLOW* YOU TO *DESTROY* OUR *RACE!!*
I *PLEDGE* MY *OATH* TO YOU, WARLORD, I MEAN YOUR PEOPLE *NO HARM!*
VHAAAMMMM
WHICH IS WHY YOU'VE PARKED *WAR MACHINES* AT OUR *GATES?!?*
I'LL *DESTROY YOU* FIRST--!!

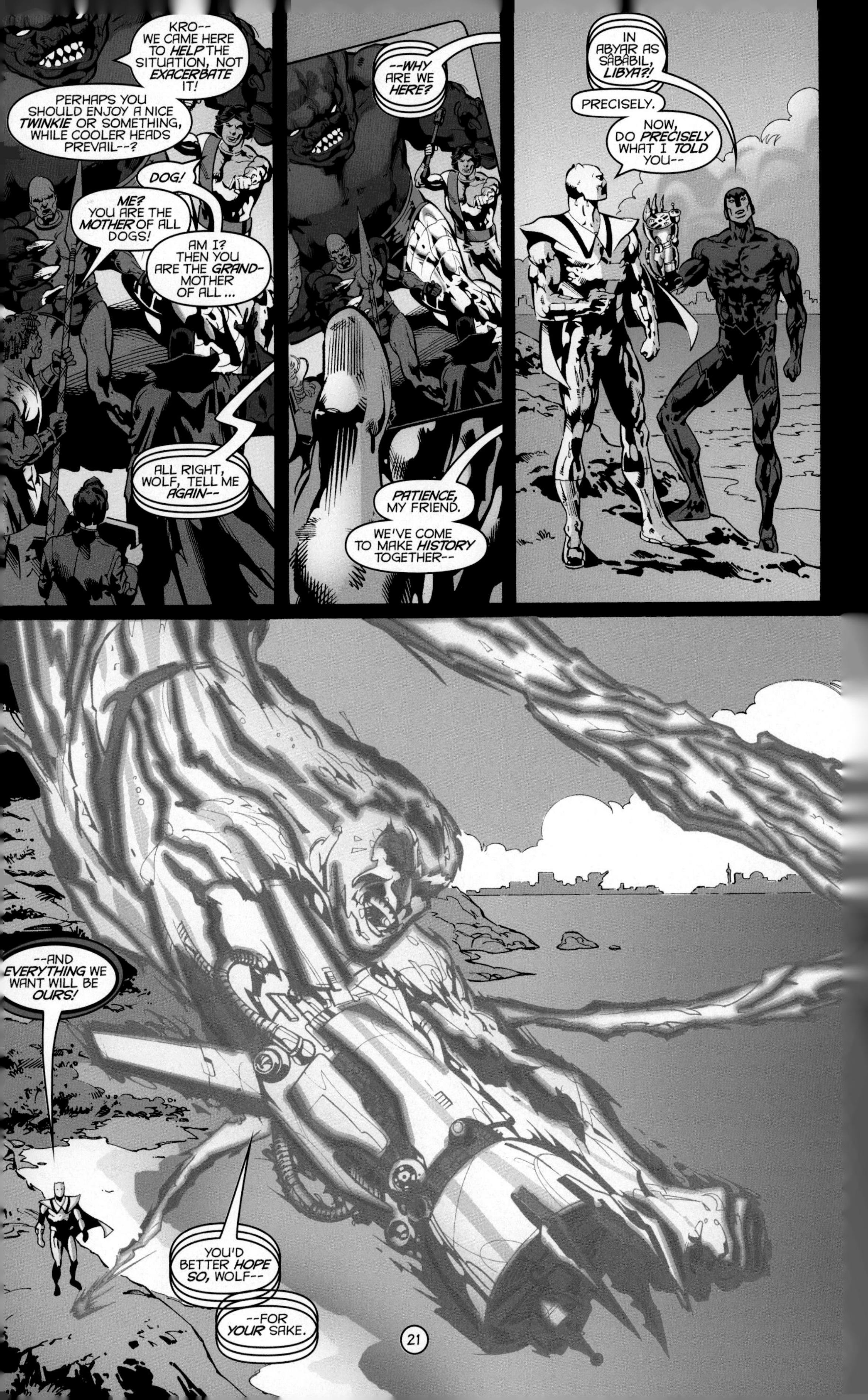
KRO-- WE CAME HERE TO HELP THE SITUATION, NOT EXACERBATE IT!
PERHAPS YOU SHOULD ENJOY A NICE TWINKIE OR SOMETHING, WHILE COOLER HEADS PREVAIL--?
DOG!
ME? YOU ARE THE MOTHER OF ALL DOGS!
AM I? THEN YOU ARE THE GRAND-MOTHER OF ALL ...
ALL RIGHT, WOLF, TELL ME AGAIN--
--WHY ARE WE HERE?
PATIENCE, MY FRIEND.
WE'VE COME TO MAKE HISTORY TOGETHER--
IN ABYAR AS SABABIL, LIBYA?!
PRECISELY.
NOW, DO PRECISELY WHAT I TOLD YOU--
--AND EVERYTHING WE WANT WILL BE OURS!
YOU'D BETTER HOPE SO, WOLF--
--FOR YOUR SAKE.

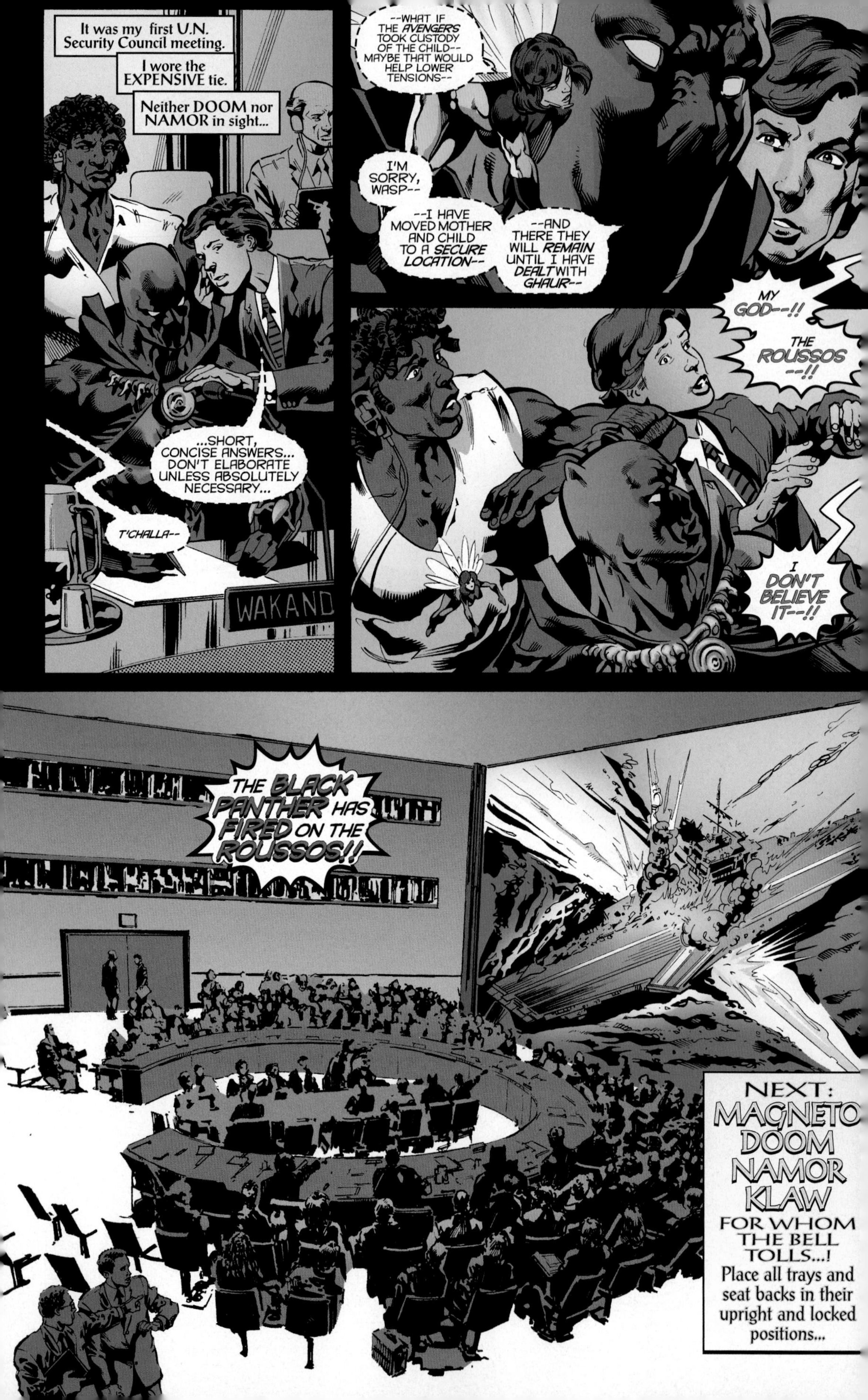

It was my first U.N. Security Council meeting.
I wore the EXPENSIVE tie.
Neither DOOM nor NAMOR in sight...
...SHORT, CONCISE ANSWERS... DON'T ELABORATE UNLESS ABSOLUTELY NECESSARY...
T'CHALLA--
WAKAND
--WHAT IF THE AVENGERS TOOK CUSTODY OF THE CHILD-- MAYBE THAT WOULD HELP LOWER TENSIONS--
I'M SORRY, WASP--
--I HAVE MOVED MOTHER AND CHILD TO A SECURE LOCATION--
--AND THERE THEY WILL REMAIN UNTIL I HAVE DEALT WITH GHAUR--
MY GOD--!!
THE ROUSSOS--!!
I DON'T BELIEVE IT--!!
THE BLACK PANTHER HAS FIRED ON THE ROUSSOS!!
NEXT: MAGNETO DOOM NAMOR KLAW
FOR WHOM THE BELL TOLLS...!
Place all trays and seat backs in their upright and locked positions...

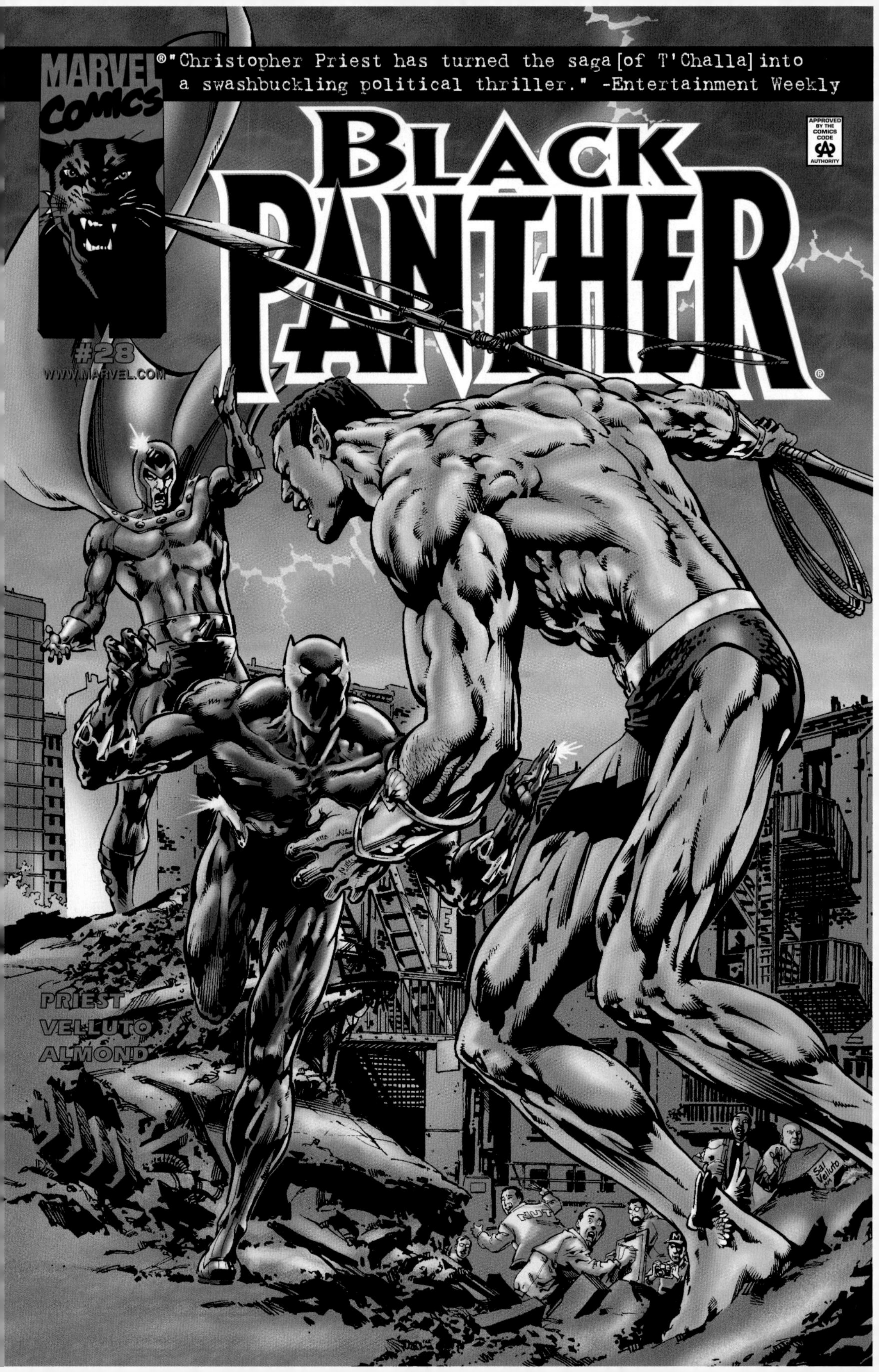
MARVEL COMICS
"Christopher Priest has turned the saga [of T'Challa] into a swashbuckling political thriller." -Entertainment Weekly
BLACK PANTHER
#28
WWW.MARVEL.COM
APPROVED BY THE COMICS CODE AUTHORITY
PRIEST
VELLUTO
ALMOND

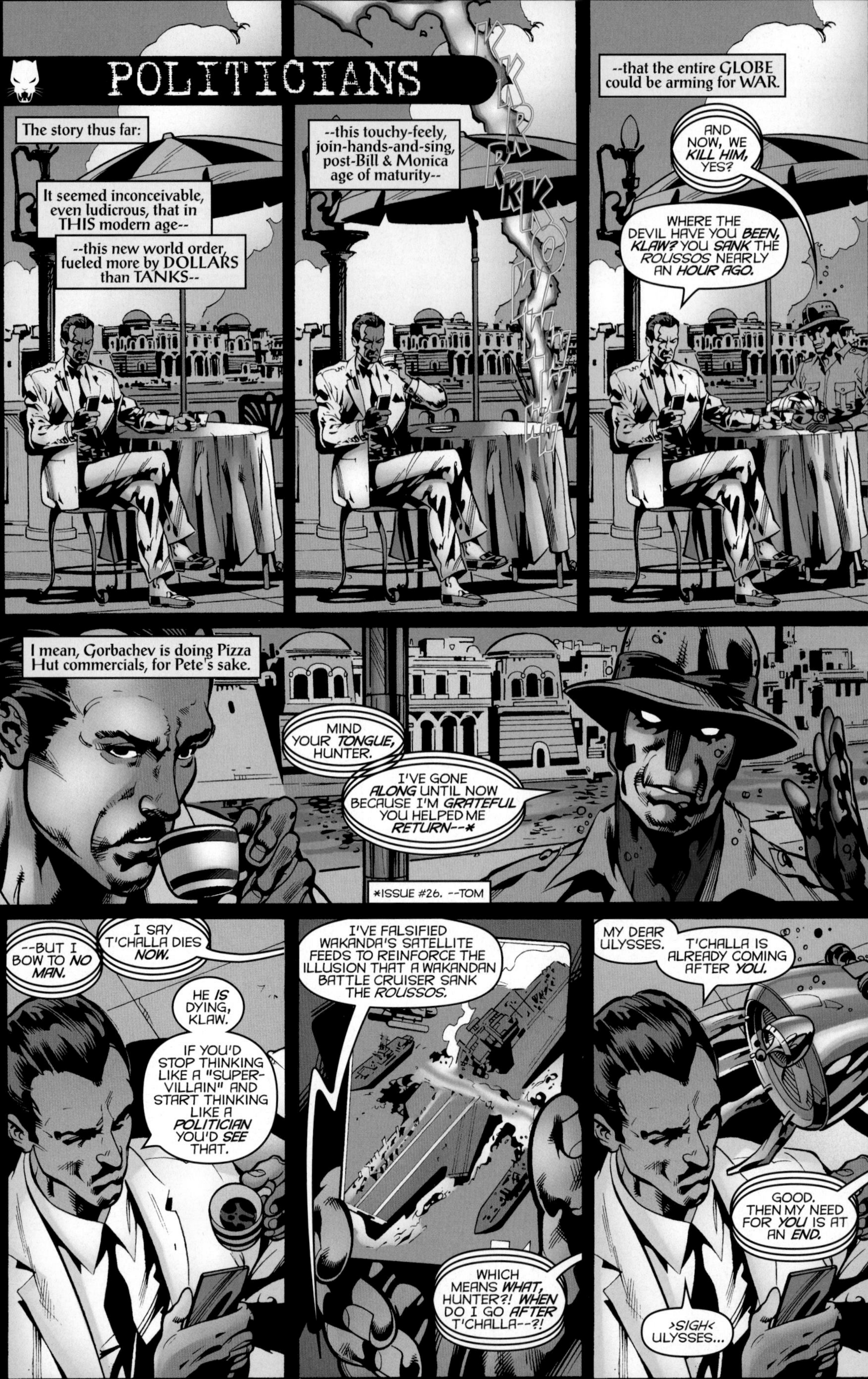
POLITICIANS
The story thus far:
It seemed inconceivable, even ludicrous, that in THIS modern age--
--this new world order, fueled more by DOLLARS than TANKS--
--this touchy-feely, join-hands-and-sing, post-Bill & Monica age of maturity--
--that the entire GLOBE could be arming for WAR.
AND NOW, WE KILL HIM, YES?
WHERE THE DEVIL HAVE YOU BEEN, KLAW? YOU SANK THE ROUSSOS NEARLY AN HOUR AGO.
I mean, Gorbachev is doing Pizza Hut commercials, for Pete's sake.
MIND YOUR TONGUE, HUNTER.
I'VE GONE ALONG UNTIL NOW BECAUSE I'M GRATEFUL YOU HELPED ME RETURN--*
*ISSUE #26. --TOM
--BUT I BOW TO NO MAN.
I SAY T'CHALLA DIES NOW.
HE IS DYING, KLAW.
IF YOU'D STOP THINKING LIKE A "SUPER-VILLAIN" AND START THINKING LIKE A POLITICIAN YOU'D SEE THAT.
I'VE FALSIFIED WAKANDA'S SATELLITE FEEDS TO REINFORCE THE ILLUSION THAT A WAKANDAN BATTLE CRUISER SANK THE ROUSSOS.
WHICH MEANS WHAT, HUNTER?! WHEN DO I GO AFTER T'CHALLA--?!
MY DEAR ULYSSES.
T'CHALLA IS ALREADY COMING AFTER YOU.
GOOD. THEN MY NEED FOR YOU IS AT AN END.
>SIGH< ULYSSES...

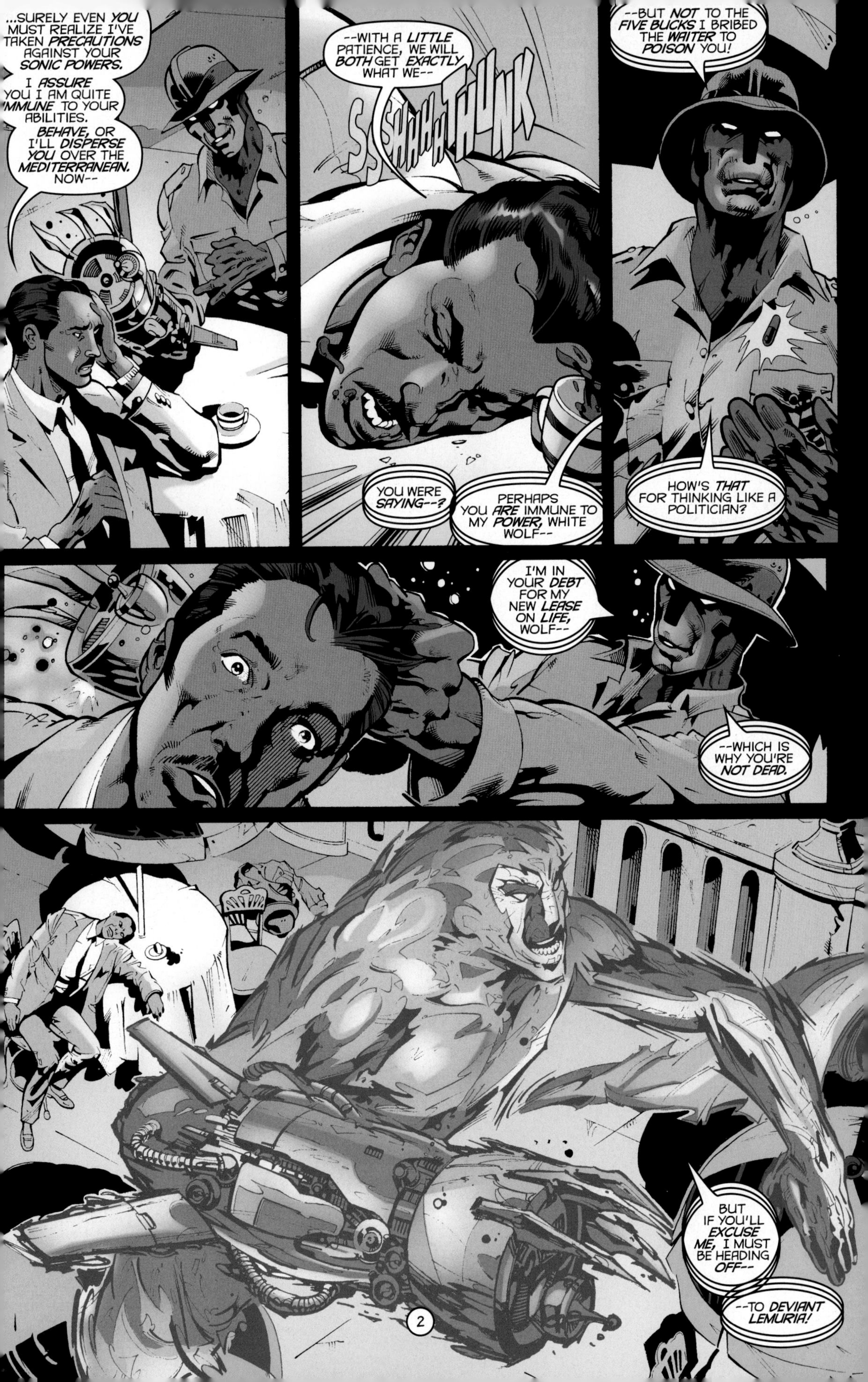

...SURELY EVEN YOU MUST REALIZE I'VE TAKEN PRECAUTIONS AGAINST YOUR SONIC POWERS.
I ASSURE YOU I AM QUITE IMMUNE TO YOUR ABILITIES.
BEHAVE, OR I'LL DISPERSE YOU OVER THE MEDITERRANEAN. NOW--
--WITH A LITTLE PATIENCE, WE WILL BOTH GET EXACTLY WHAT WE--
SSHHHHTHUNK
YOU WERE SAYING--?
PERHAPS YOU ARE IMMUNE TO MY POWER, WHITE WOLF--
--BUT NOT TO THE FIVE BUCKS I BRIBED THE WAITER TO POISON YOU!
HOW'S THAT FOR THINKING LIKE A POLITICIAN?
I'M IN YOUR DEBT FOR MY NEW LEASE ON LIFE, WOLF--
--WHICH IS WHY YOU'RE NOT DEAD.
BUT IF YOU'LL EXCUSE ME, I MUST BE HEADING OFF--
--TO DEVIANT LEMURIA!

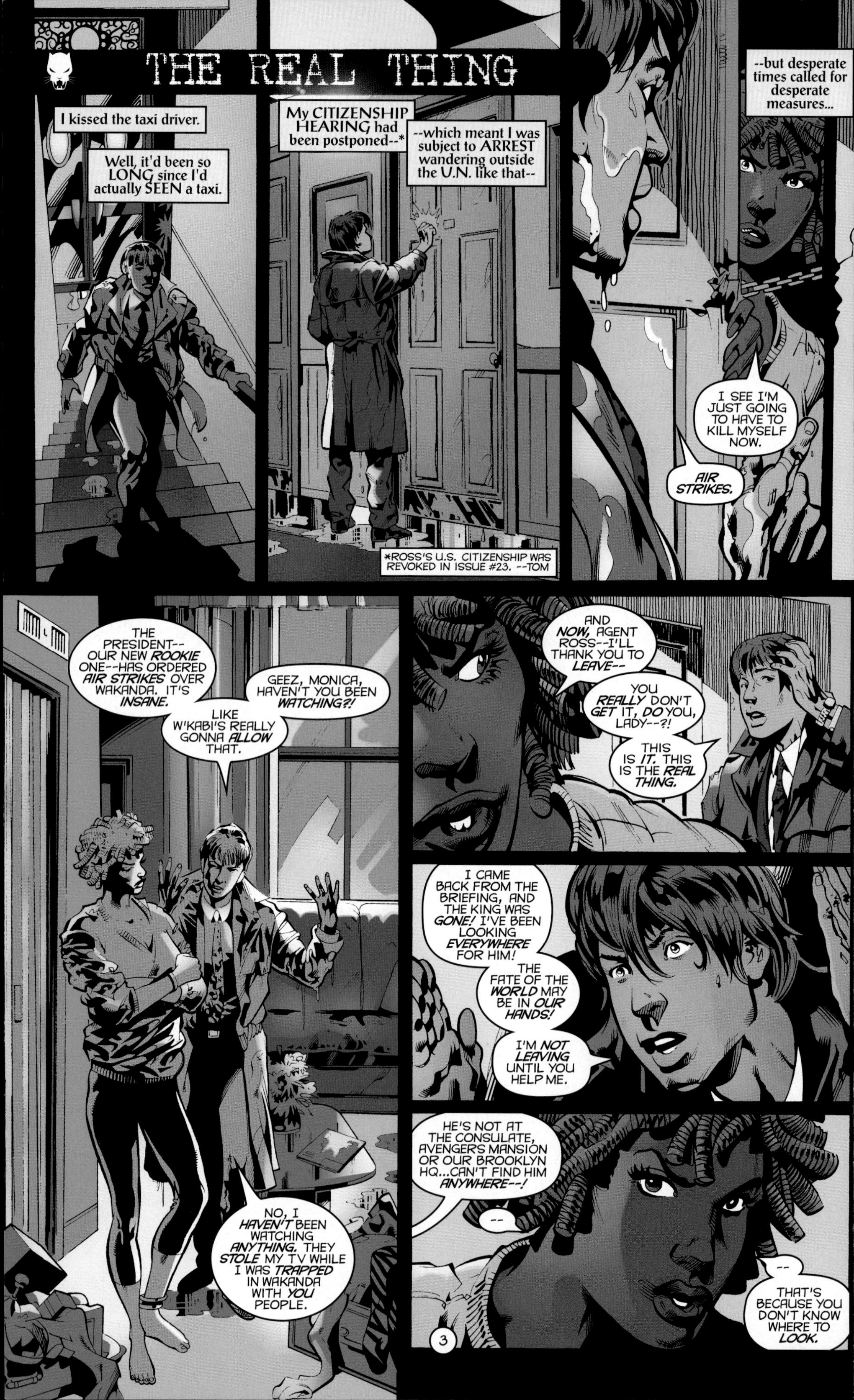
THE REAL THING
I kissed the taxi driver.
Well, it'd been so LONG since I'd actually SEEN a taxi.
My CITIZENSHIP HEARING had been postponed--*
--which meant I was subject to ARREST wandering outside the U.N. like that--
--but desperate times called for desperate measures...
I SEE I'M JUST GOING TO HAVE TO KILL MYSELF NOW.
AIR STRIKES.
*ROSS'S U.S. CITIZENSHIP WAS REVOKED IN ISSUE #23. --TOM
THE PRESIDENT-- OUR NEW ROOKIE ONE--HAS ORDERED AIR STRIKES OVER WAKANDA. IT'S INSANE.
GEEZ, MONICA, HAVEN'T YOU BEEN WATCHING?!
LIKE W'KABI'S REALLY GONNA ALLOW THAT.
NO, I HAVEN'T BEEN WATCHING ANYTHING. THEY STOLE MY TV WHILE I WAS TRAPPED IN WAKANDA WITH YOU PEOPLE.
AND NOW, AGENT ROSS--I'LL THANK YOU TO LEAVE--
YOU REALLY DON'T GET IT, DO YOU, LADY--?!
THIS IS IT. THIS IS THE REAL THING.
I CAME BACK FROM THE BRIEFING, AND THE KING WAS GONE! I'VE BEEN LOOKING EVERYWHERE FOR HIM!
THE FATE OF THE WORLD MAY BE IN OUR HANDS!
I'M NOT LEAVING UNTIL YOU HELP ME.
HE'S NOT AT THE CONSULATE, AVENGERS MANSION OR OUR BROOKLYN HQ...CAN'T FIND HIM ANYWHERE--!
--
--
THAT'S BECAUSE YOU DON'T KNOW WHERE TO LOOK.
3

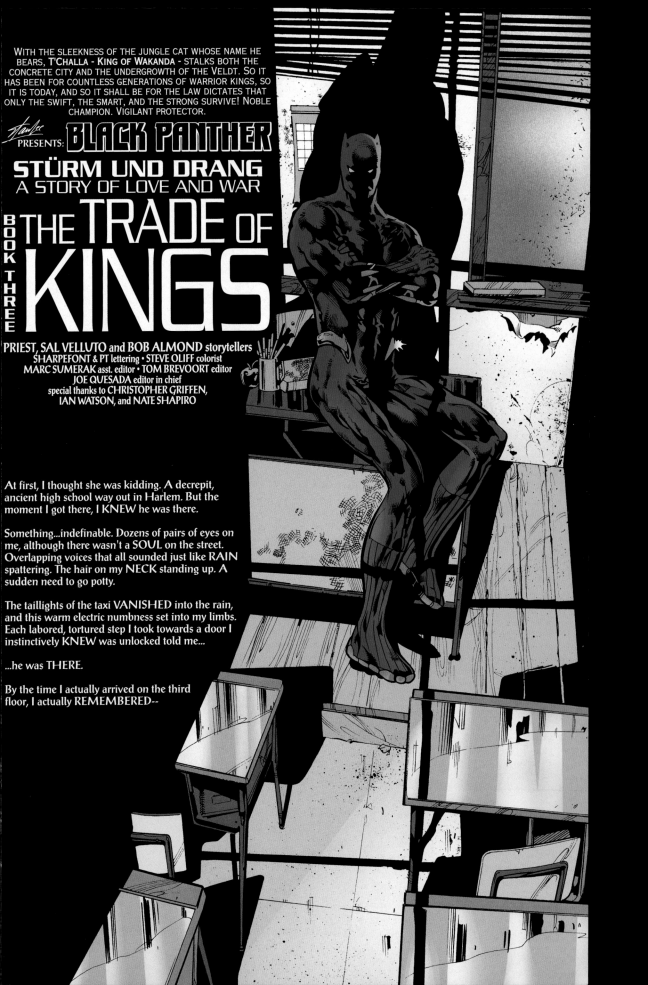

WITH THE SLEEKNESS OF THE JUNGLE CAT WHOSE NAME HE BEARS, T'CHALLA - KING OF WAKANDA - STALKS BOTH THE CONCRETE CITY AND THE UNDERGROWTH OF THE VELDT. SO IT HAS BEEN FOR COUNTLESS GENERATIONS OF WARRIOR KINGS, SO IT IS TODAY, AND SO IT SHALL BE FOR THE LAW DICTATES THAT ONLY THE SWIFT, THE SMART, AND THE STRONG SURVIVE! NOBLE CHAMPION. VIGILANT PROTECTOR.

STAN LEE PRESENTS: **BLACK PANTHER**

STÜRM UND DRANG
A STORY OF LOVE AND WAR

BOOK THREE
THE TRADE OF KINGS

PRIEST, SAL VELLUTO and BOB ALMOND storytellers
SHARPEFONT & PT lettering • STEVE OLIFF colorist
MARC SUMERAK asst. editor • TOM BREVOORT editor
JOE QUESADA editor in chief
special thanks to CHRISTOPHER GRIFFEN,
IAN WATSON, and NATE SHAPIRO

At first, I thought she was kidding. A decrepit, ancient high school way out in Harlem. But the moment I got there, I KNEW he was there.

Something...indefinable. Dozens of pairs of eyes on me, although there wasn't a SOUL on the street. Overlapping voices that all sounded just like RAIN spattering. The hair on my NECK standing up. A sudden need to go potty.

The taillights of the taxi VANISHED into the rain, and this warm electric numbness set into my limbs. Each labored, tortured step I took towards a door I instinctively KNEW was unlocked told me...

...he was THERE.

By the time I actually arrived on the third floor, I actually REMEMBERED--

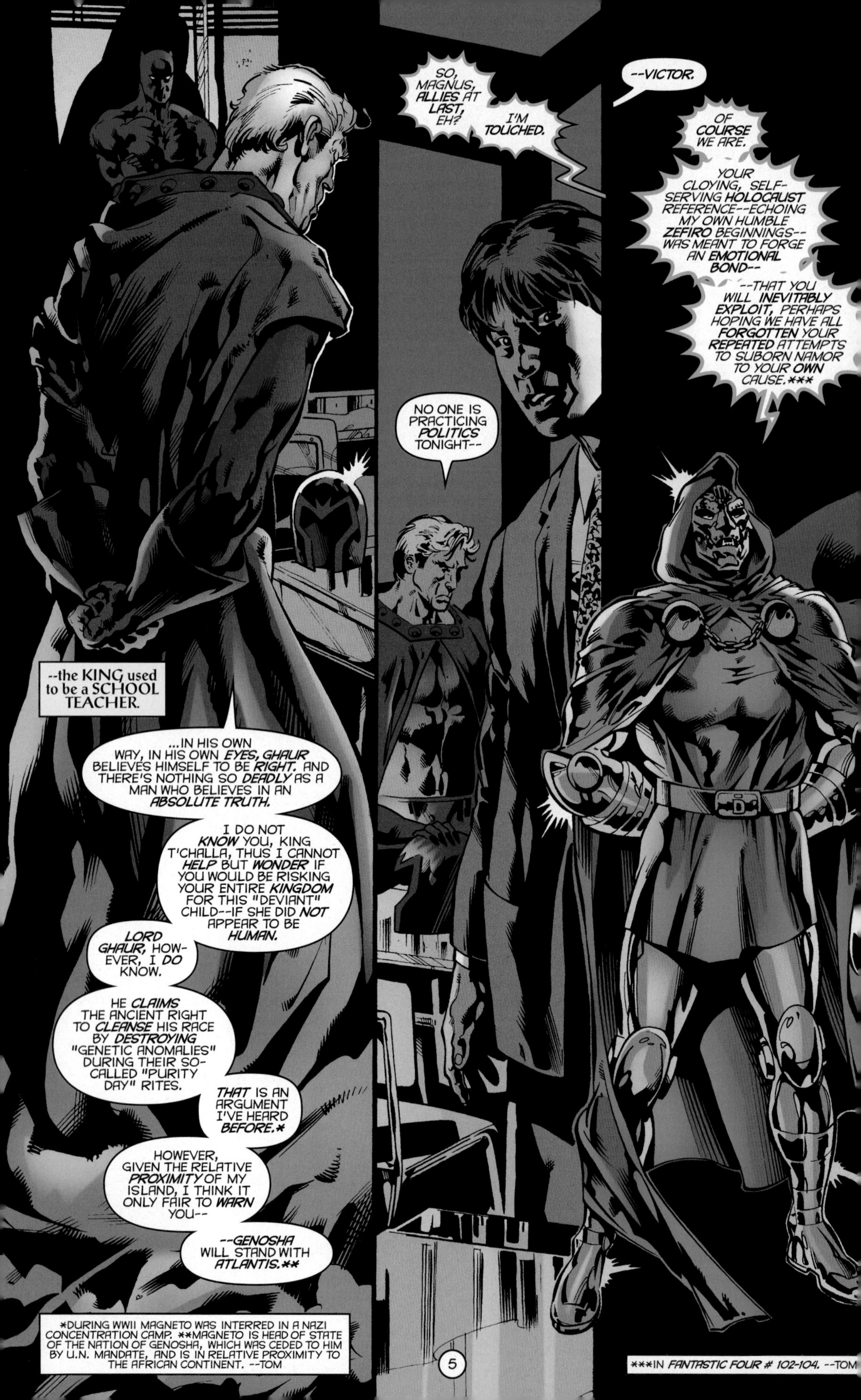

--the KING used to be a SCHOOL TEACHER.
...IN HIS OWN WAY, IN HIS OWN EYES, GHAUR BELIEVES HIMSELF TO BE RIGHT. AND THERE'S NOTHING SO DEADLY AS A MAN WHO BELIEVES IN AN ABSOLUTE TRUTH.
I DO NOT KNOW YOU, KING T'CHALLA, THUS I CANNOT HELP BUT WONDER IF YOU WOULD BE RISKING YOUR ENTIRE KINGDOM FOR THIS "DEVIANT" CHILD--IF SHE DID NOT APPEAR TO BE HUMAN.
LORD GHAUR, HOWEVER, I DO KNOW.
HE CLAIMS THE ANCIENT RIGHT TO CLEANSE HIS RACE BY DESTROYING "GENETIC ANOMALIES" DURING THEIR SO-CALLED "PURITY DAY" RITES.
THAT IS AN ARGUMENT I'VE HEARD BEFORE.*
HOWEVER, GIVEN THE RELATIVE PROXIMITY OF MY ISLAND, I THINK IT ONLY FAIR TO WARN YOU--
--GENOSHA WILL STAND WITH ATLANTIS.**
*DURING WWII MAGNETO WAS INTERRED IN A NAZI CONCENTRATION CAMP. **MAGNETO IS HEAD OF STATE OF THE NATION OF GENOSHA, WHICH WAS CEDED TO HIM BY U.N. MANDATE, AND IS IN RELATIVE PROXIMITY TO THE AFRICAN CONTINENT. --TOM
SO, MAGNUS, ALLIES AT LAST, EH?
I'M TOUCHED.
NO ONE IS PRACTICING POLITICS TONIGHT--
--VICTOR.
OF COURSE WE ARE.
YOUR CLOYING, SELF-SERVING HOLOCAUST REFERENCE--ECHOING MY OWN HUMBLE ZEFIRO BEGINNINGS--WAS MEANT TO FORGE AN EMOTIONAL BOND--
--THAT YOU WILL INEVITABLY EXPLOIT, PERHAPS HOPING WE HAVE ALL FORGOTTEN YOUR REPEATED ATTEMPTS TO SUBORN NAMOR TO YOUR OWN CAUSE.***
***IN FANTASTIC FOUR # 102-104. --TOM

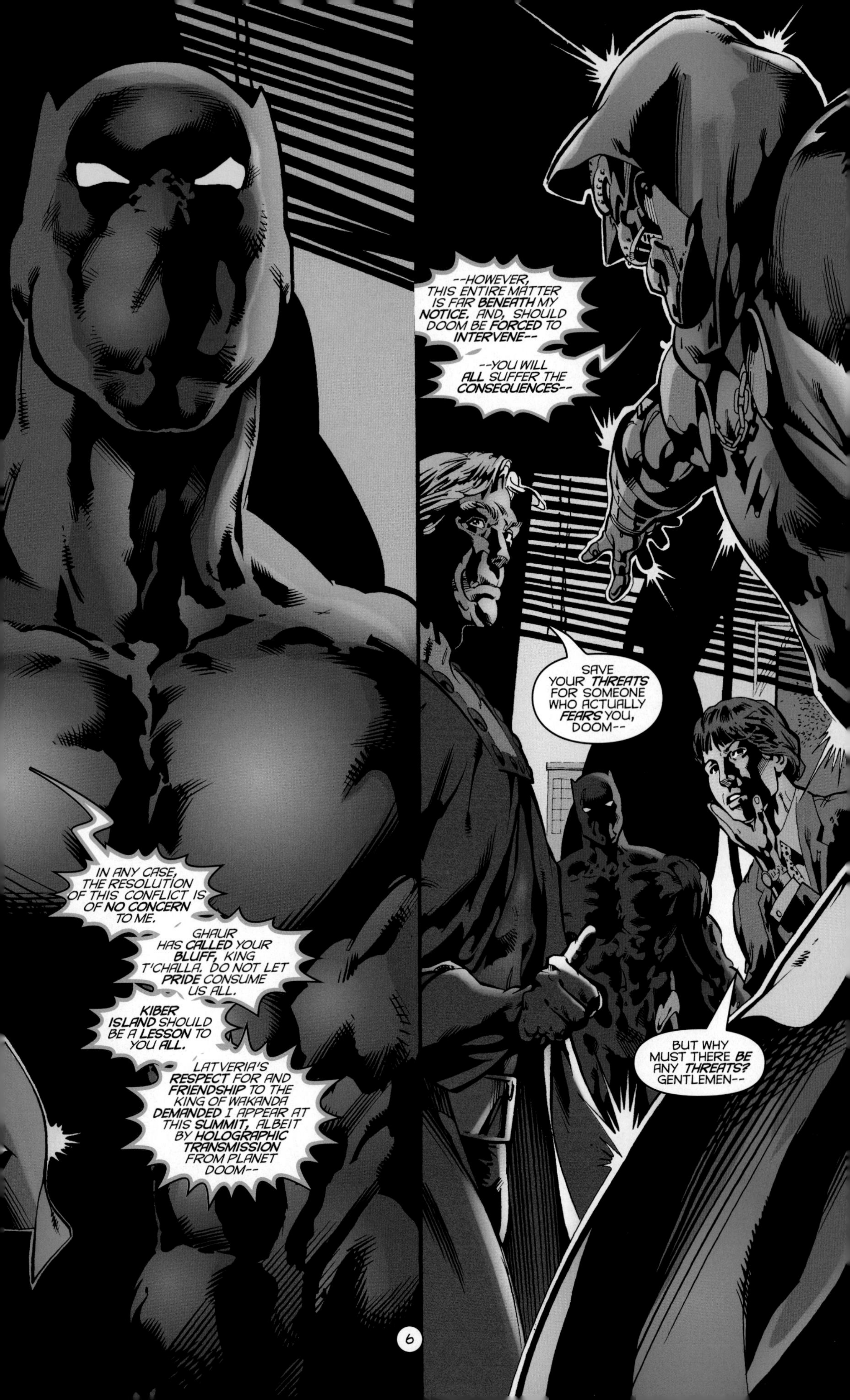
IN ANY CASE, THE RESOLUTION OF THIS CONFLICT IS OF NO CONCERN TO ME.
GHAUR HAS CALLED YOUR BLUFF, KING T'CHALLA. DO NOT LET PRIDE CONSUME US ALL.
KIBER ISLAND SHOULD BE A LESSON TO YOU ALL.
LATVERIA'S RESPECT FOR AND FRIENDSHIP TO THE KING OF WAKANDA DEMANDED I APPEAR AT THIS SUMMIT, ALBEIT BY HOLOGRAPHIC TRANSMISSION FROM PLANET DOOM--
--HOWEVER, THIS ENTIRE MATTER IS FAR BENEATH MY NOTICE. AND, SHOULD DOOM BE FORCED TO INTERVENE--
--YOU WILL ALL SUFFER THE CONSEQUENCES--
SAVE YOUR THREATS FOR SOMEONE WHO ACTUALLY FEARS YOU, DOOM--
BUT WHY MUST THERE BE ANY THREATS? GENTLEMEN--

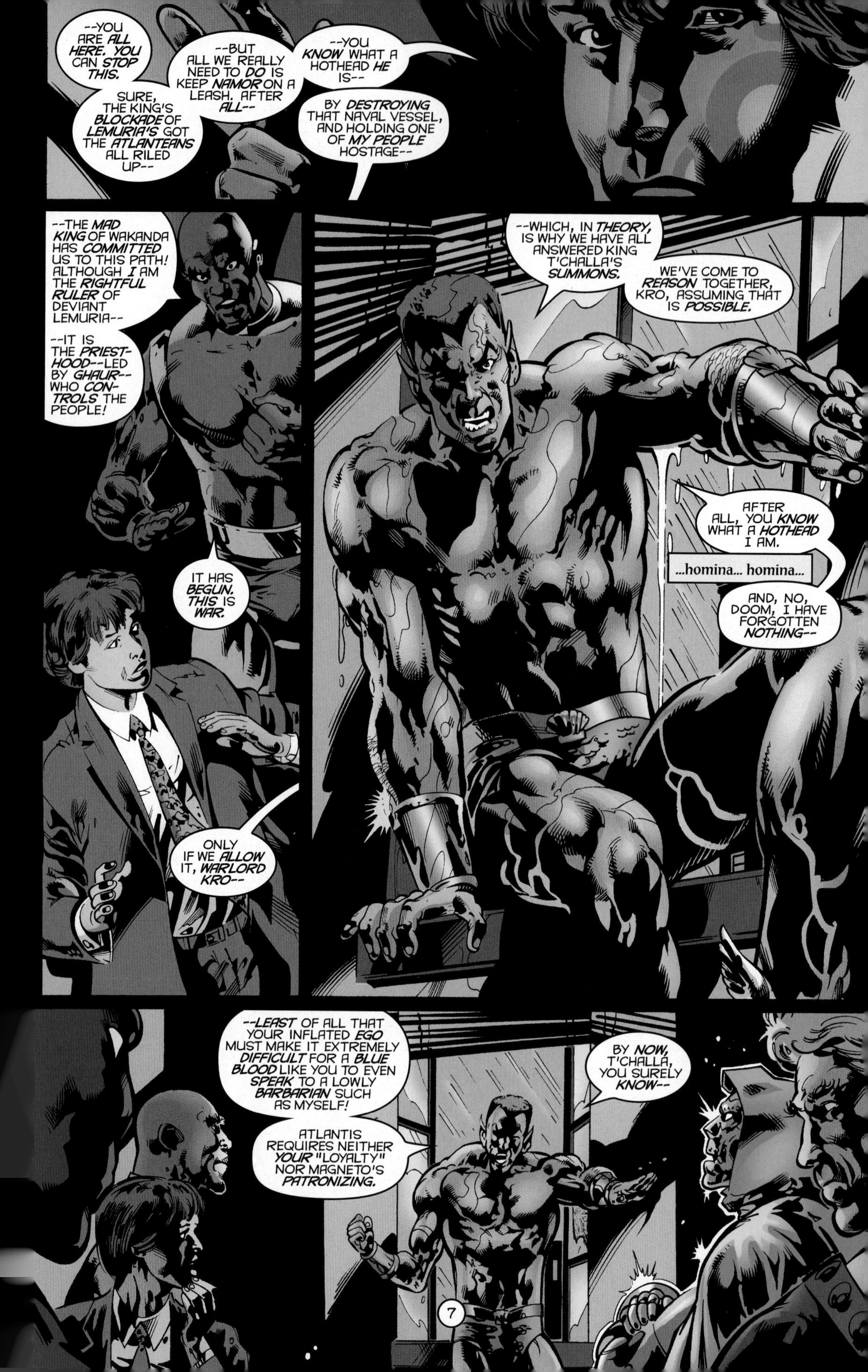
--YOU ARE ALL HERE. YOU CAN STOP THIS.
SURE, THE KING'S BLOCKADE OF LEMURIA'S GOT THE ATLANTEANS ALL RILED UP--
--BUT ALL WE REALLY NEED TO DO IS KEEP NAMOR ON A LEASH. AFTER ALL--
--YOU KNOW WHAT A HOTHEAD HE IS--
BY DESTROYING THAT NAVAL VESSEL, AND HOLDING ONE OF MY PEOPLE HOSTAGE--
--THE MAD KING OF WAKANDA HAS COMMITTED US TO THIS PATH! ALTHOUGH I AM THE RIGHTFUL RULER OF DEVIANT LEMURIA--
--IT IS THE PRIESTHOOD--LED BY GHAUR--WHO CONTROLS THE PEOPLE!
IT HAS BEGUN. THIS IS WAR.
ONLY IF WE ALLOW IT, WARLORD KRO--
--WHICH, IN THEORY, IS WHY WE HAVE ALL ANSWERED KING T'CHALLA'S SUMMONS.
WE'VE COME TO REASON TOGETHER, KRO, ASSUMING THAT IS POSSIBLE.
AFTER ALL, YOU KNOW WHAT A HOTHEAD I AM.
...homina... homina...
AND, NO, DOOM, I HAVE FORGOTTEN NOTHING--
--LEAST OF ALL THAT YOUR INFLATED EGO MUST MAKE IT EXTREMELY DIFFICULT FOR A BLUE BLOOD LIKE YOU TO EVEN SPEAK TO A LOWLY BARBARIAN SUCH AS MYSELF!
ATLANTIS REQUIRES NEITHER YOUR "LOYALTY" NOR MAGNETO'S PATRONIZING.
BY NOW, T'CHALLA, YOU SURELY KNOW--

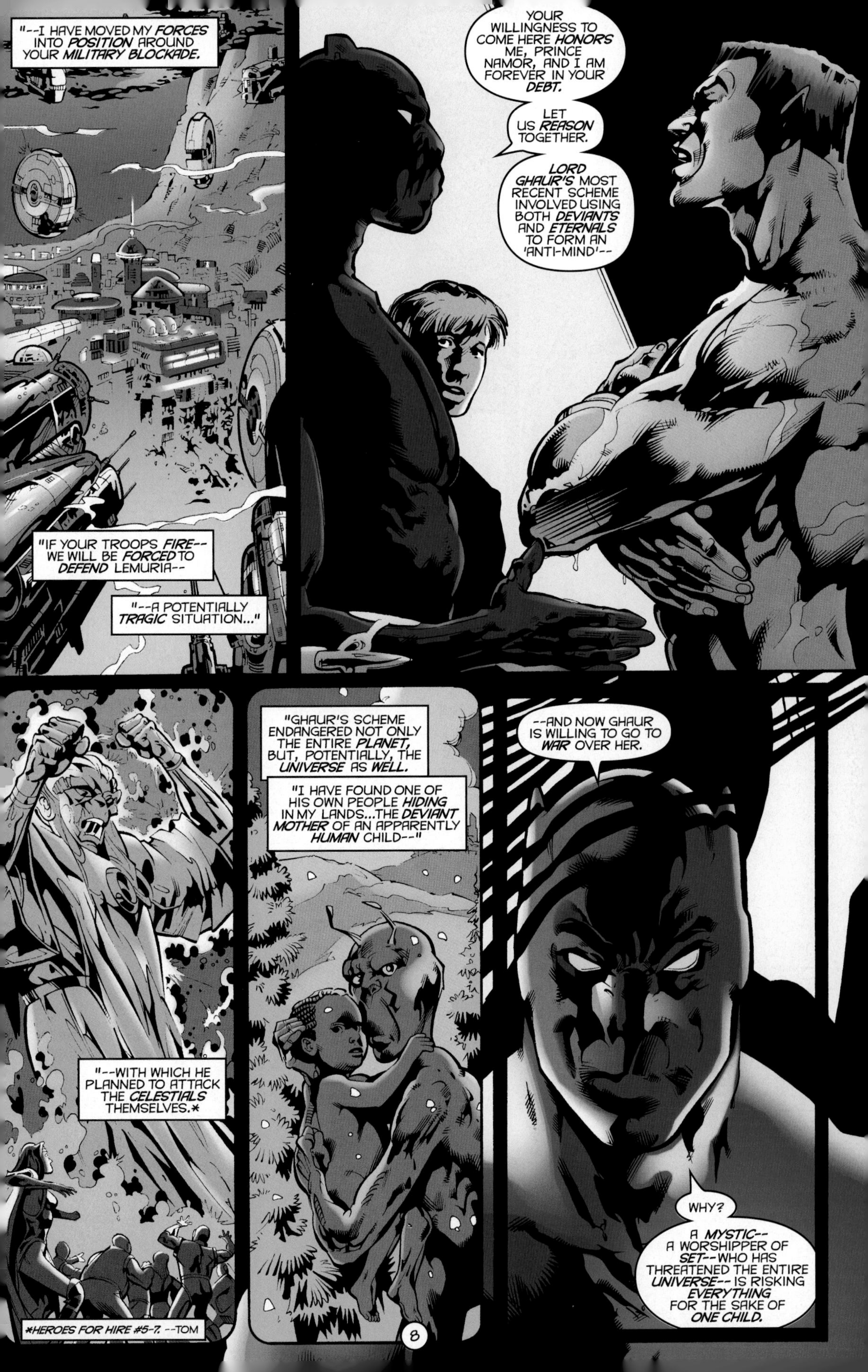
"--I HAVE MOVED MY FORCES INTO POSITION AROUND YOUR MILITARY BLOCKADE.
"IF YOUR TROOPS FIRE-- WE WILL BE FORCED TO DEFEND LEMURIA--
"--A POTENTIALLY TRAGIC SITUATION..."
YOUR WILLINGNESS TO COME HERE HONORS ME, PRINCE NAMOR, AND I AM FOREVER IN YOUR DEBT.
LET US REASON TOGETHER.
LORD GHAUR'S MOST RECENT SCHEME INVOLVED USING BOTH DEVIANTS AND ETERNALS TO FORM AN 'ANTI-MIND'--
"--WITH WHICH HE PLANNED TO ATTACK THE CELESTIALS THEMSELVES.*
*HEROES FOR HIRE #5-7. --TOM
"GHAUR'S SCHEME ENDANGERED NOT ONLY THE ENTIRE PLANET, BUT, POTENTIALLY, THE UNIVERSE AS WELL.
"I HAVE FOUND ONE OF HIS OWN PEOPLE HIDING IN MY LANDS...THE DEVIANT MOTHER OF AN APPARENTLY HUMAN CHILD--"
--AND NOW GHAUR IS WILLING TO GO TO WAR OVER HER.
WHY?
A MYSTIC-- A WORSHIPPER OF SET--WHO HAS THREATENED THE ENTIRE UNIVERSE-- IS RISKING EVERYTHING FOR THE SAKE OF ONE CHILD.

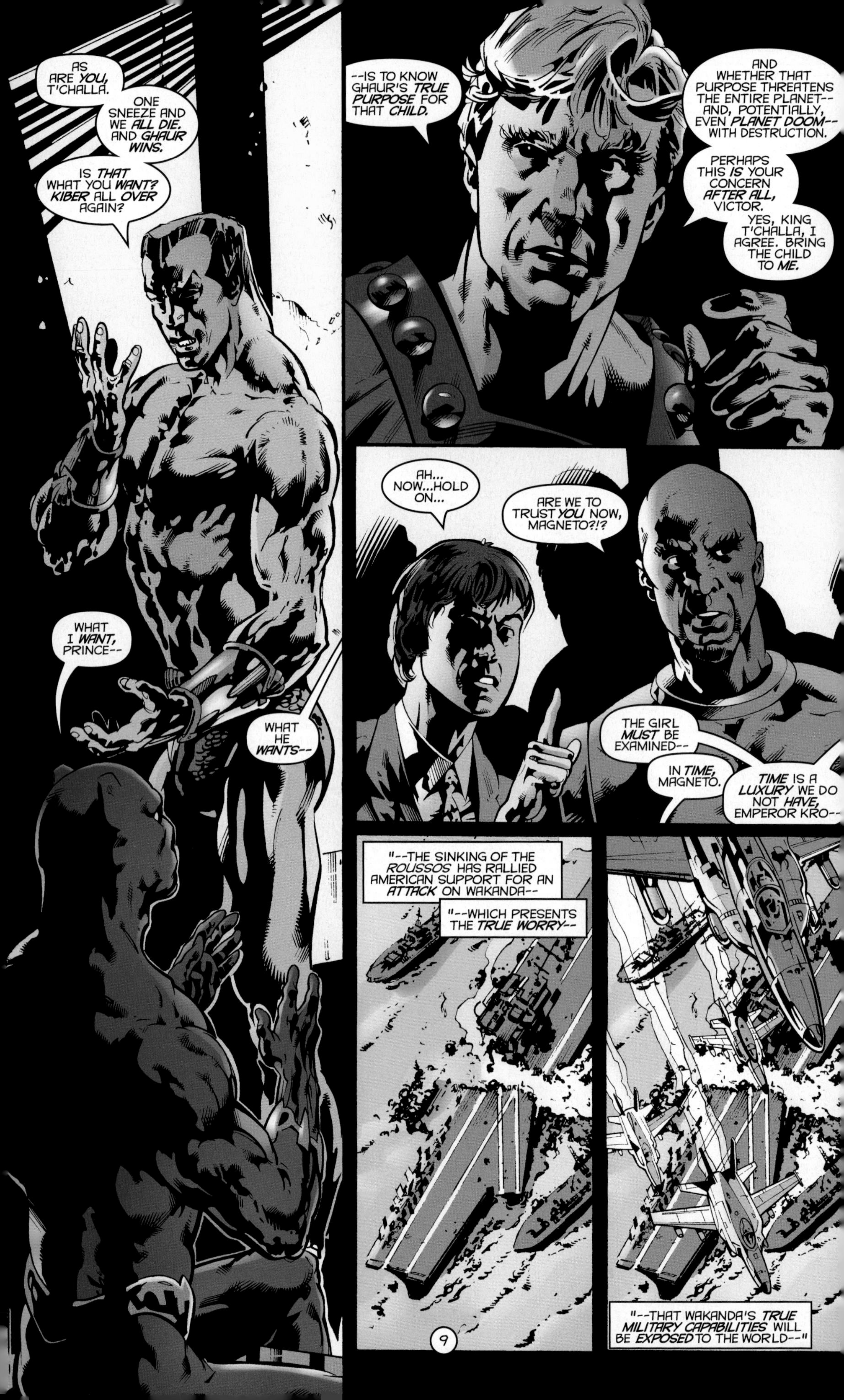
AS ARE YOU, T'CHALLA.
ONE SNEEZE AND WE ALL DIE. AND GHAUR WINS.
IS THAT WHAT YOU WANT? KIBER ALL OVER AGAIN?
WHAT I WANT, PRINCE--
WHAT HE WANTS--
--IS TO KNOW GHAUR'S TRUE PURPOSE FOR THAT CHILD.
AND WHETHER THAT PURPOSE THREATENS THE ENTIRE PLANET--AND, POTENTIALLY, EVEN PLANET DOOM--WITH DESTRUCTION.
PERHAPS THIS IS YOUR CONCERN AFTER ALL, VICTOR.
YES, KING T'CHALLA, I AGREE. BRING THE CHILD TO ME.
AH... NOW...HOLD ON...
ARE WE TO TRUST YOU NOW, MAGNETO?!?
THE GIRL MUST BE EXAMINED--
IN TIME, MAGNETO.
TIME IS A LUXURY WE DO NOT HAVE, EMPEROR KRO--
"--THE SINKING OF THE ROUSSOS HAS RALLIED AMERICAN SUPPORT FOR AN ATTACK ON WAKANDA--
"--WHICH PRESENTS THE TRUE WORRY--
"--THAT WAKANDA'S TRUE MILITARY CAPABILITIES WILL BE EXPOSED TO THE WORLD--"

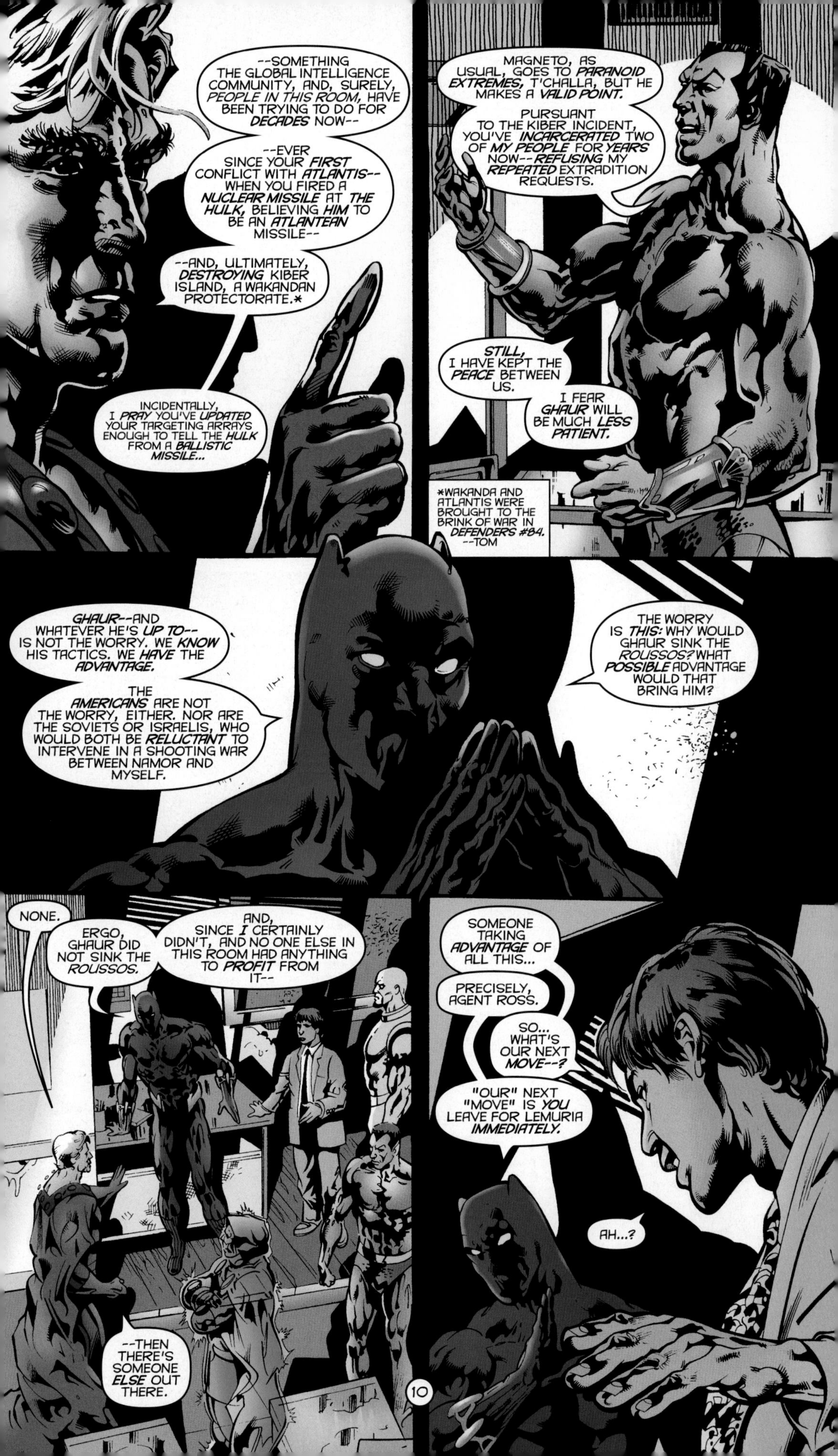

--SOMETHING THE GLOBAL INTELLIGENCE COMMUNITY, AND, SURELY, PEOPLE IN THIS ROOM, HAVE BEEN TRYING TO DO FOR DECADES NOW--
--EVER SINCE YOUR FIRST CONFLICT WITH ATLANTIS-- WHEN YOU FIRED A NUCLEAR MISSILE AT THE HULK, BELIEVING HIM TO BE AN ATLANTEAN MISSILE--
--AND, ULTIMATELY, DESTROYING KIBER ISLAND, A WAKANDAN PROTECTORATE.*
INCIDENTALLY, I PRAY YOU'VE UPDATED YOUR TARGETING ARRAYS ENOUGH TO TELL THE HULK FROM A BALLISTIC MISSILE...
MAGNETO, AS USUAL, GOES TO PARANOID EXTREMES, T'CHALLA, BUT HE MAKES A VALID POINT.
PURSUANT TO THE KIBER INCIDENT, YOU'VE INCARCERATED TWO OF MY PEOPLE FOR YEARS NOW--REFUSING MY REPEATED EXTRADITION REQUESTS.
STILL, I HAVE KEPT THE PEACE BETWEEN US.
I FEAR GHAUR WILL BE MUCH LESS PATIENT.
*WAKANDA AND ATLANTIS WERE BROUGHT TO THE BRINK OF WAR IN DEFENDERS #84. --TOM
GHAUR--AND WHATEVER HE'S UP TO-- IS NOT THE WORRY. WE KNOW HIS TACTICS. WE HAVE THE ADVANTAGE.
THE AMERICANS ARE NOT THE WORRY, EITHER. NOR ARE THE SOVIETS OR ISRAELIS, WHO WOULD BOTH BE RELUCTANT TO INTERVENE IN A SHOOTING WAR BETWEEN NAMOR AND MYSELF.
THE WORRY IS THIS: WHY WOULD GHAUR SINK THE ROUSSOS? WHAT POSSIBLE ADVANTAGE WOULD THAT BRING HIM?
NONE.
ERGO, GHAUR DID NOT SINK THE ROUSSOS.
AND, SINCE I CERTAINLY DIDN'T, AND NO ONE ELSE IN THIS ROOM HAD ANYTHING TO PROFIT FROM IT--
--THEN THERE'S SOMEONE ELSE OUT THERE.
SOMEONE TAKING ADVANTAGE OF ALL THIS...
PRECISELY, AGENT ROSS.
SO... WHAT'S OUR NEXT MOVE--?
"OUR" NEXT "MOVE" IS YOU LEAVE FOR LEMURIA IMMEDIATELY.
AH...?

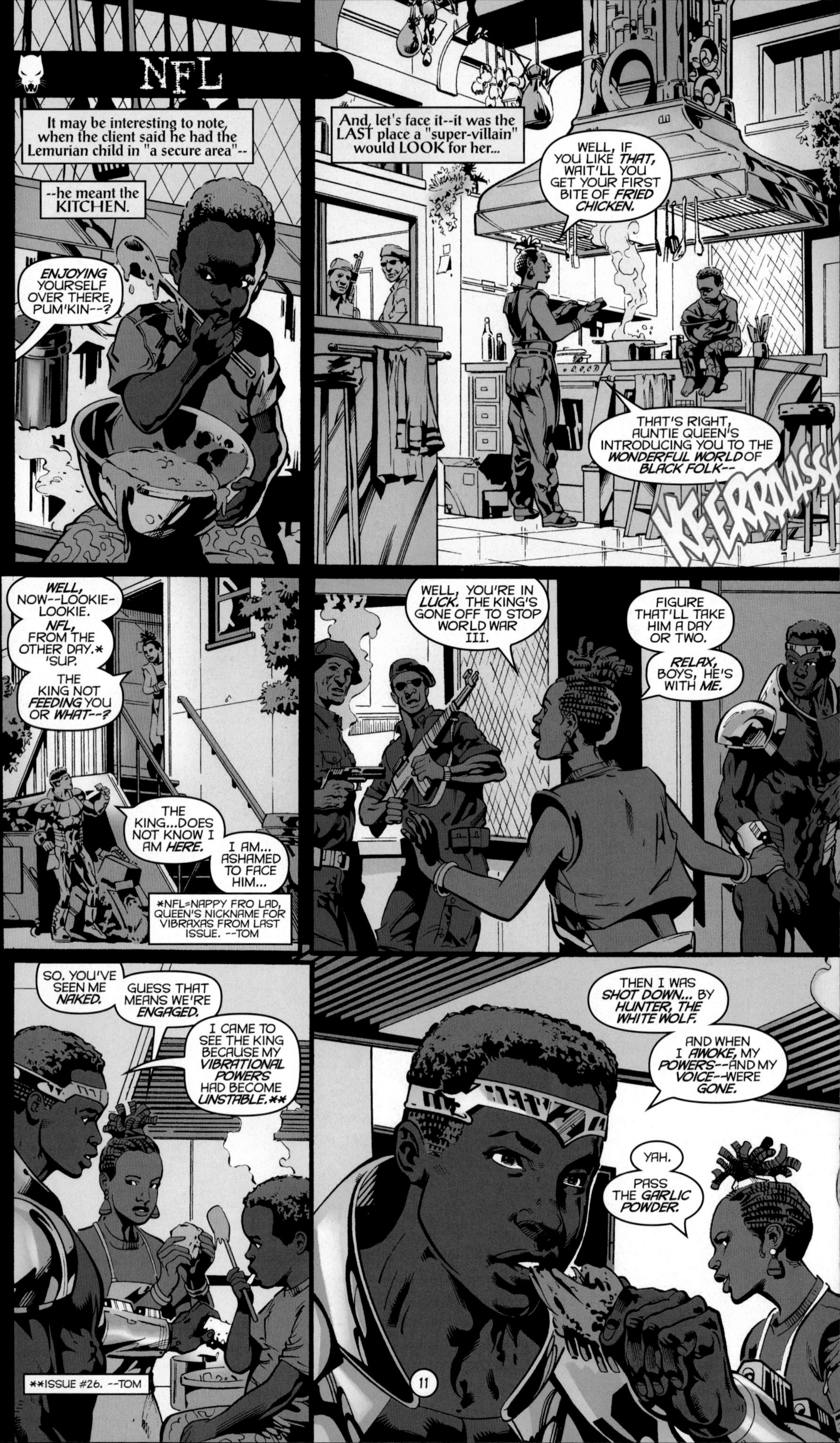
NFL
It may be interesting to note, when the client said he had the Lemurian child in "a secure area"--
--he meant the KITCHEN.
ENJOYING YOURSELF OVER THERE, PUM'KIN--?
And, let's face it--it was the LAST place a "super-villain" would LOOK for her...
WELL, IF YOU LIKE THAT, WAIT'LL YOU GET YOUR FIRST BITE OF FRIED CHICKEN.
THAT'S RIGHT, AUNTIE QUEEN'S INTRODUCING YOU TO THE WONDERFUL WORLD OF BLACK FOLK--
WELL, NOW--LOOKIE-LOOKIE. NFL, FROM THE OTHER DAY.* 'SUP.
THE KING NOT FEEDING YOU OR WHAT--?
THE KING...DOES NOT KNOW I AM HERE.
I AM... ASHAMED TO FACE HIM...
*NFL=NAPPY FRO LAD, QUEEN'S NICKNAME FOR VIBRAXAS FROM LAST ISSUE. --TOM
WELL, YOU'RE IN LUCK. THE KING'S GONE OFF TO STOP WORLD WAR III.
FIGURE THAT'LL TAKE HIM A DAY OR TWO.
RELAX, BOYS, HE'S WITH ME.
SO. YOU'VE SEEN ME NAKED.
GUESS THAT MEANS WE'RE ENGAGED.
I CAME TO SEE THE KING BECAUSE MY VIBRATIONAL POWERS HAD BECOME UNSTABLE.**
**ISSUE #26. --TOM
THEN I WAS SHOT DOWN... BY HUNTER, THE WHITE WOLF.
AND WHEN I AWOKE, MY POWERS--AND MY VOICE--WERE GONE.
YAH.
PASS THE GARLIC POWDER.

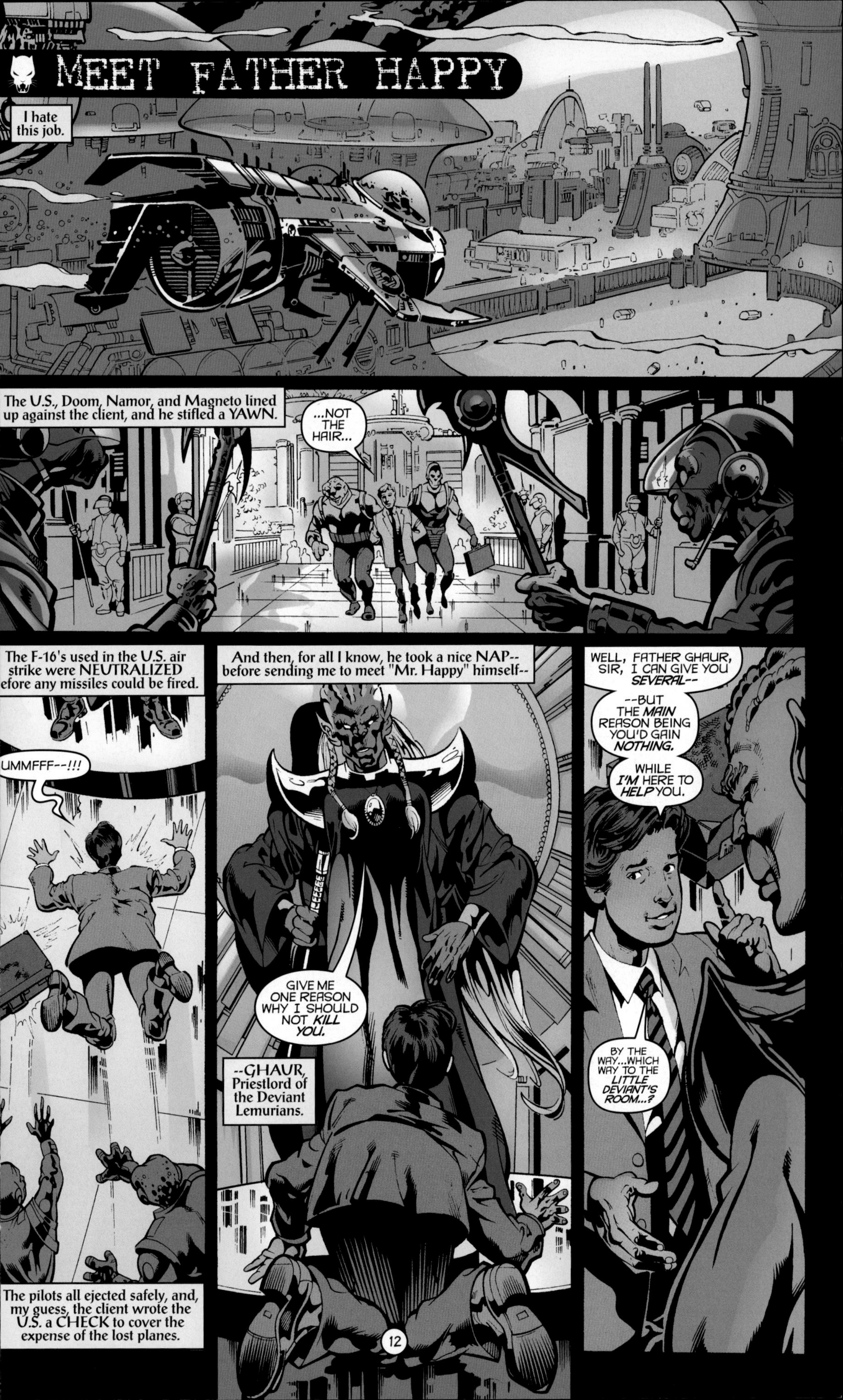
MEET FATHER HAPPY
I hate this job.
The U.S., Doom, Namor, and Magneto lined up against the client, and he stifled a YAWN.
...NOT THE HAIR...
The F-16's used in the U.S. air strike were NEUTRALIZED efore any missiles could be fired.
UMMFFF--!!!
The pilots all ejected safely, and, my guess, the client wrote the U.S. a CHECK to cover the expense of the lost planes.
And then, for all I know, he took a nice NAP--before sending me to meet "Mr. Happy" himself--
GIVE ME ONE REASON WHY I SHOULD NOT KILL YOU.
--GHAUR, Priestlord of the Deviant Lemurians.
WELL, FATHER GHAUR, SIR, I CAN GIVE YOU SEVERAL--
--BUT THE MAIN REASON BEING YOU'D GAIN NOTHING.
WHILE I'M HERE TO HELP YOU.
BY THE WAY...WHICH WAY TO THE LITTLE DEVIANT'S ROOM...?

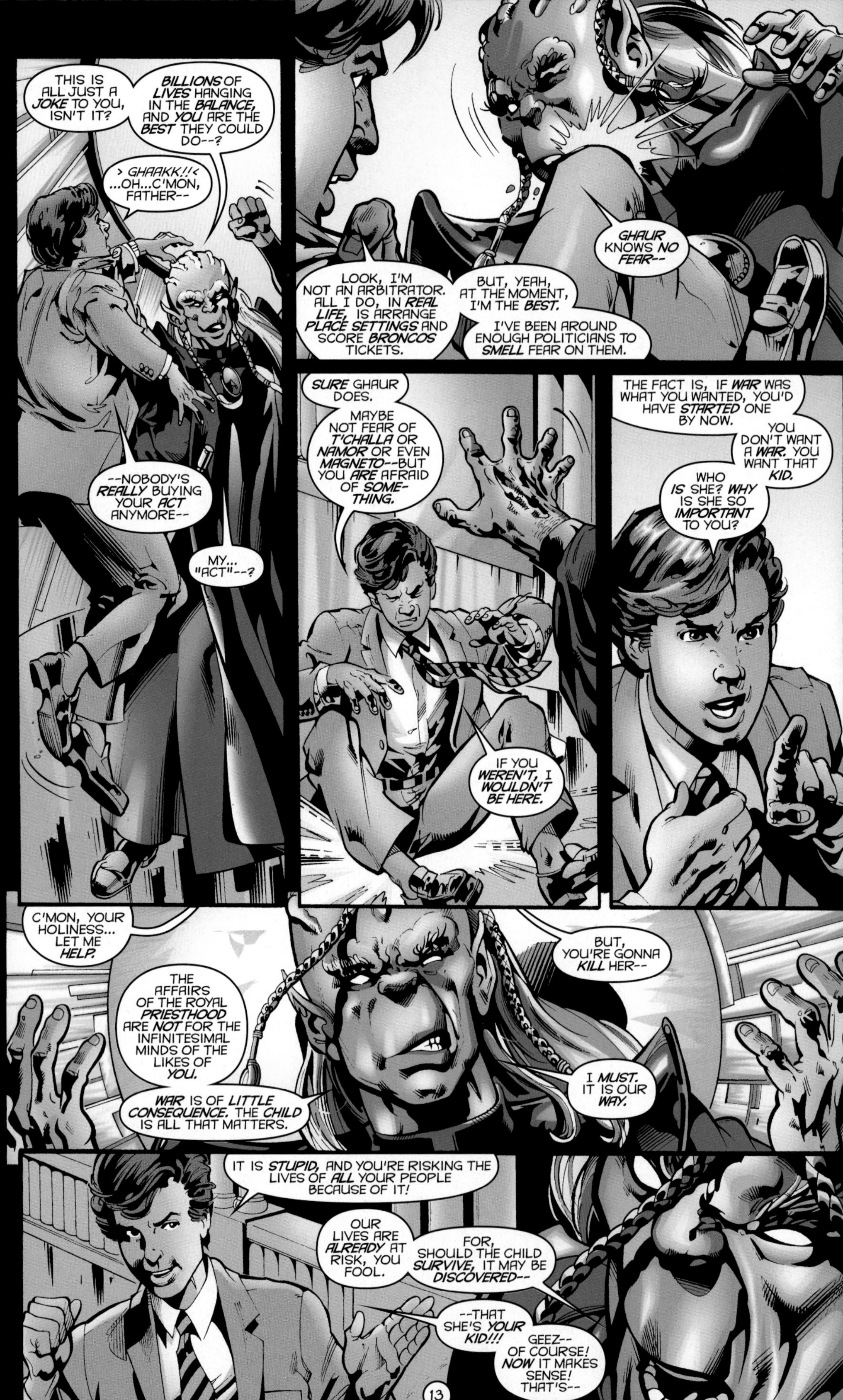
THIS IS ALL JUST A JOKE TO YOU, ISN'T IT?
BILLIONS OF LIVES HANGING IN THE BALANCE, AND YOU ARE THE BEST THEY COULD DO--?
> GHAAKK!! < ...OH...C'MON, FATHER--
--NOBODY'S REALLY BUYING YOUR ACT ANYMORE--
MY... "ACT"--?
GHAUR KNOWS NO FEAR--
LOOK, I'M NOT AN ARBITRATOR. ALL I DO, IN REAL LIFE, IS ARRANGE PLACE SETTINGS AND SCORE BRONCOS TICKETS.
BUT, YEAH, AT THE MOMENT, I'M THE BEST.
I'VE BEEN AROUND ENOUGH POLITICIANS TO SMELL FEAR ON THEM.
SURE GHAUR DOES.
MAYBE NOT FEAR OF T'CHALLA OR NAMOR OR EVEN MAGNETO--BUT YOU ARE AFRAID OF SOME-THING.
IF YOU WEREN'T, I WOULDN'T BE HERE.
THE FACT IS, IF WAR WAS WHAT YOU WANTED, YOU'D HAVE STARTED ONE BY NOW.
YOU DON'T WANT A WAR. YOU WANT THAT KID.
WHO IS SHE? WHY IS SHE SO IMPORTANT TO YOU?
C'MON, YOUR HOLINESS... LET ME HELP.
THE AFFAIRS OF THE ROYAL PRIESTHOOD ARE NOT FOR THE INFINITESIMAL MINDS OF THE LIKES OF YOU.
WAR IS OF LITTLE CONSEQUENCE. THE CHILD IS ALL THAT MATTERS.
BUT, YOU'RE GONNA KILL HER--
I MUST. IT IS OUR WAY.
IT IS STUPID, AND YOU'RE RISKING THE LIVES OF ALL YOUR PEOPLE BECAUSE OF IT!
OUR LIVES ARE ALREADY AT RISK, YOU FOOL.
FOR, SHOULD THE CHILD SURVIVE, IT MAY BE DISCOVERED--
--THAT SHE'S YOUR KID!!!
GEEZ-- OF COURSE! NOW IT MAKES SENSE! THAT'S--

THWAAKKTT!

I couldn't be sure at the time, but I think I hit a NERVE.

At least I had a CLUE what Ghaur was UP to...

...assuming I lived to TELL anyone...

...HUH...?

...SAY...

...WAIT... HOLD UP, FELLA...

...DON'T I KNOW YOU--?

YES.

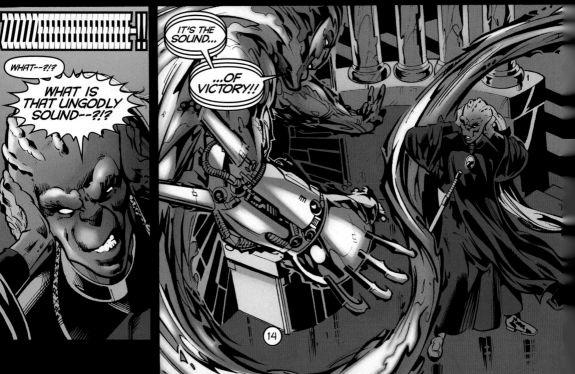

ZZZZZEEEEEEEEEE--!!

WHAT--?!?

WHAT IS THAT UNGODLY SOUND--?!?

IT'S THE SOUND...

...OF VICTORY!!

AAARRRGGGGHHH!!!

ZZZZZZEEEEEEEEEEE-!!

NEXT QUESTION?

GOOD.

I HOPE YOU DON'T MIND MY USING A *SAMPLE* OF YOUR *VOICEPRINT*--

--TO ORDER A LITTLE *MISSILE* LAUNCH.

LET'S SEE...AN *HOUR* UNTIL THE *END* OF THE *WORLD*... MOVING AT THE SPEED OF *SOUND*...

...THAT SHOULD GIVE ME JUST ENOUGH TIME TO MAKE IT TO THE *SOUTH BRONX*--

KA-CHOO

BODEGA

⑮

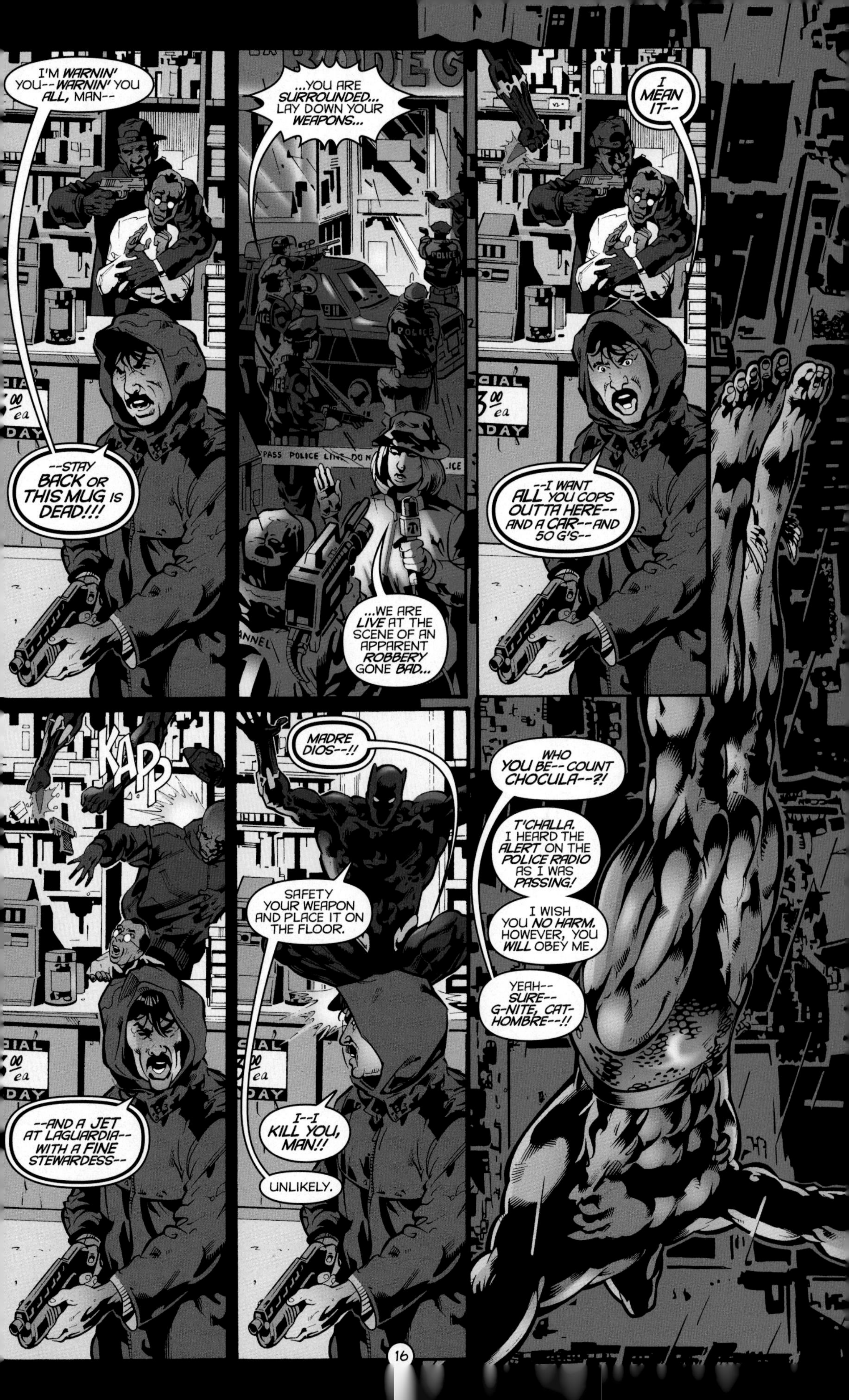
I'M WARNIN' YOU--WARNIN' YOU ALL, MAN--
--STAY BACK OR THIS MUG IS DEAD!!!
...YOU ARE SURROUNDED... LAY DOWN YOUR WEAPONS...
POLICE
...WE ARE LIVE AT THE SCENE OF AN APPARENT ROBBERY GONE BAD...
I MEAN IT--
--I WANT ALL YOU COPS OUTTA HERE--AND A CAR--AND 50 G'S--
KAPP
--AND A JET AT LAGUARDIA--WITH A FINE STEWARDESS--
MADRE DIOS--!!
SAFETY YOUR WEAPON AND PLACE IT ON THE FLOOR.
I--I KILL YOU, MAN!!
UNLIKELY.
WHO YOU BE--COUNT CHOCULA--?!
T'CHALLA. I HEARD THE ALERT ON THE POLICE RADIO AS I WAS PASSING!
I WISH YOU NO HARM. HOWEVER, YOU WILL OBEY ME.
YEAH--SURE--G-NITE, CAT-HOMBRE--!!

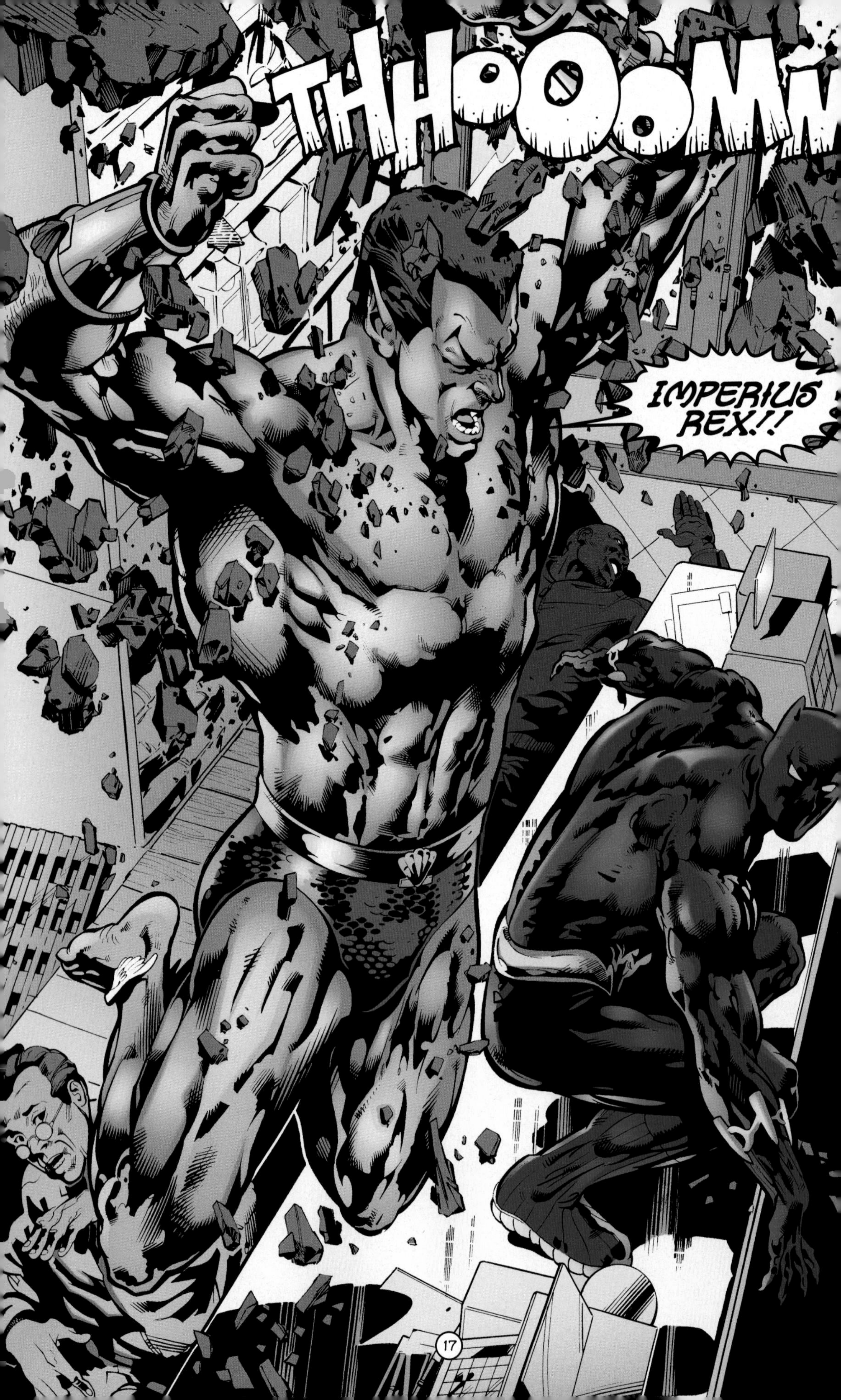

THHOOOMM
IMPERIUS REX!!

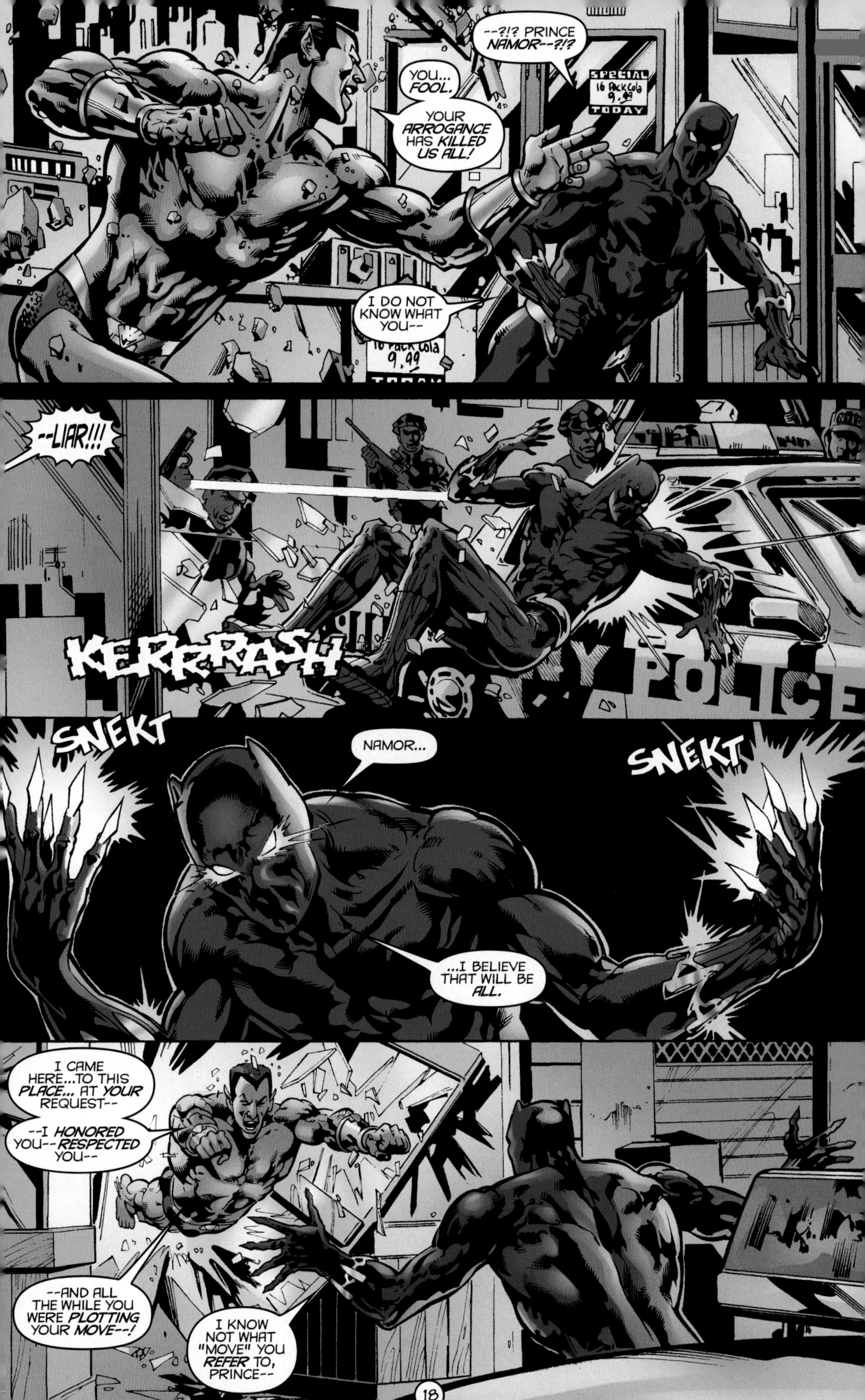
--?!? PRINCE NAMOR--?!?
YOU... FOOL.
YOUR ARROGANCE HAS KILLED US ALL!
SPECIAL 16 PACK COLA 9.99 TODAY
I DO NOT KNOW WHAT YOU--
--LIAR!!!
KERRRASH
POLICE
SNEKT
NAMOR...
SNEKT
...I BELIEVE THAT WILL BE ALL.
I CAME HERE...TO THIS PLACE... AT YOUR REQUEST--
--I HONORED YOU--RESPECTED YOU--
--AND ALL THE WHILE YOU WERE PLOTTING YOUR MOVE--!
I KNOW NOT WHAT "MOVE" YOU REFER TO, PRINCE--

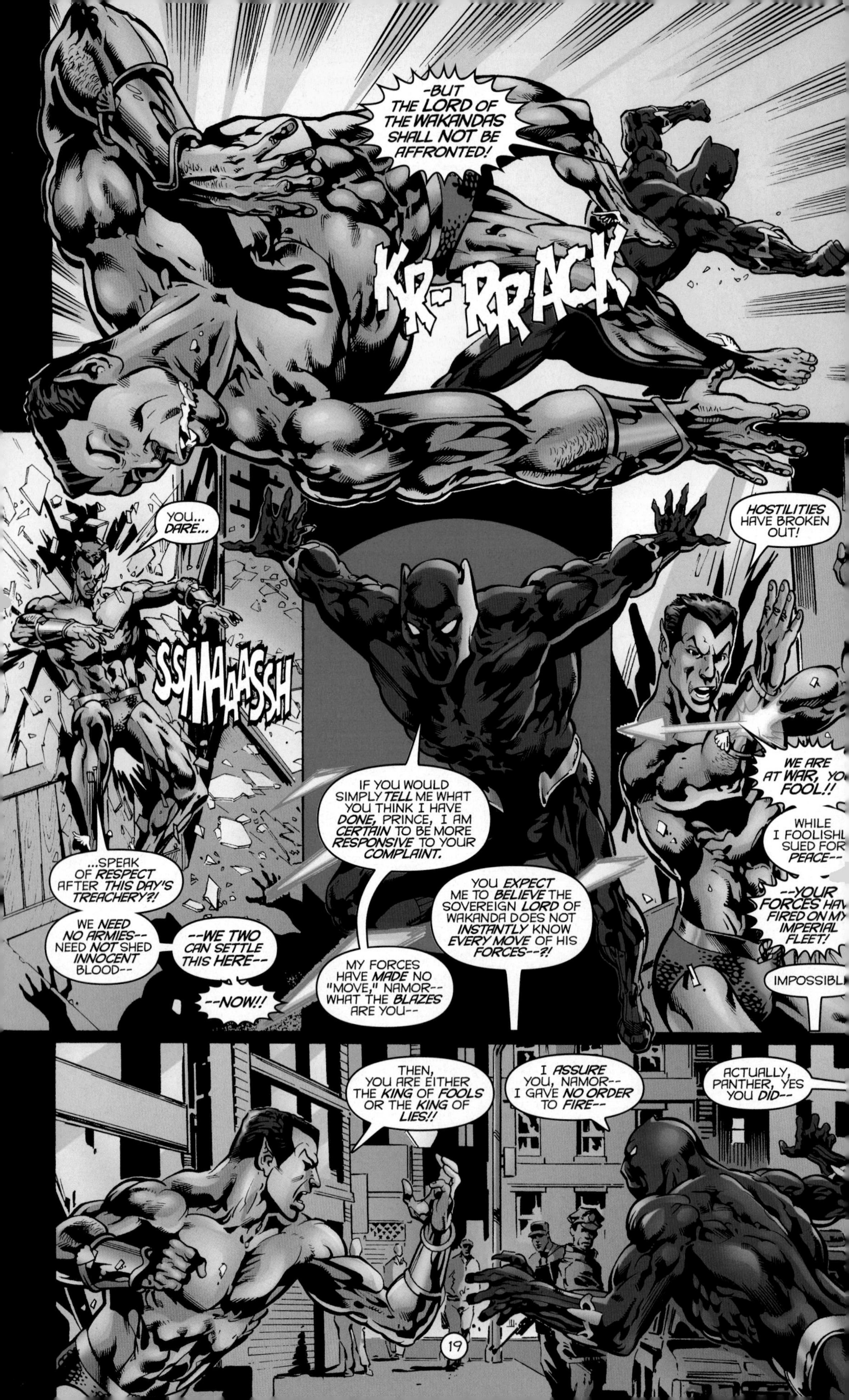
-BUT THE LORD OF THE WAKANDAS SHALL NOT BE AFFRONTED!
KR-RRRACK
YOU... DARE...
SSMAAASSH
...SPEAK OF RESPECT AFTER THIS DAY'S TREACHERY?!
WE NEED NO ARMIES-- NEED NOT SHED INNOCENT BLOOD--
--WE TWO CAN SETTLE THIS HERE--
--NOW!!
IF YOU WOULD SIMPLY TELL ME WHAT YOU THINK I HAVE DONE, PRINCE, I AM CERTAIN TO BE MORE RESPONSIVE TO YOUR COMPLAINT.
MY FORCES HAVE MADE NO "MOVE," NAMOR-- WHAT THE BLAZES ARE YOU--
YOU EXPECT ME TO BELIEVE THE SOVEREIGN LORD OF WAKANDA DOES NOT INSTANTLY KNOW EVERY MOVE OF HIS FORCES--?!
HOSTILITIES HAVE BROKEN OUT!
WE ARE AT WAR, YO FOOL!!
WHILE I FOOLISHL SUED FOR PEACE--
--YOUR FORCES HAV FIRED ON MY IMPERIAL FLEET!
IMPOSSIBL
THEN, YOU ARE EITHER THE KING OF FOOLS OR THE KING OF LIES!!
I ASSURE YOU, NAMOR-- I GAVE NO ORDER TO FIRE--
ACTUALLY, PANTHER, YES YOU DID--

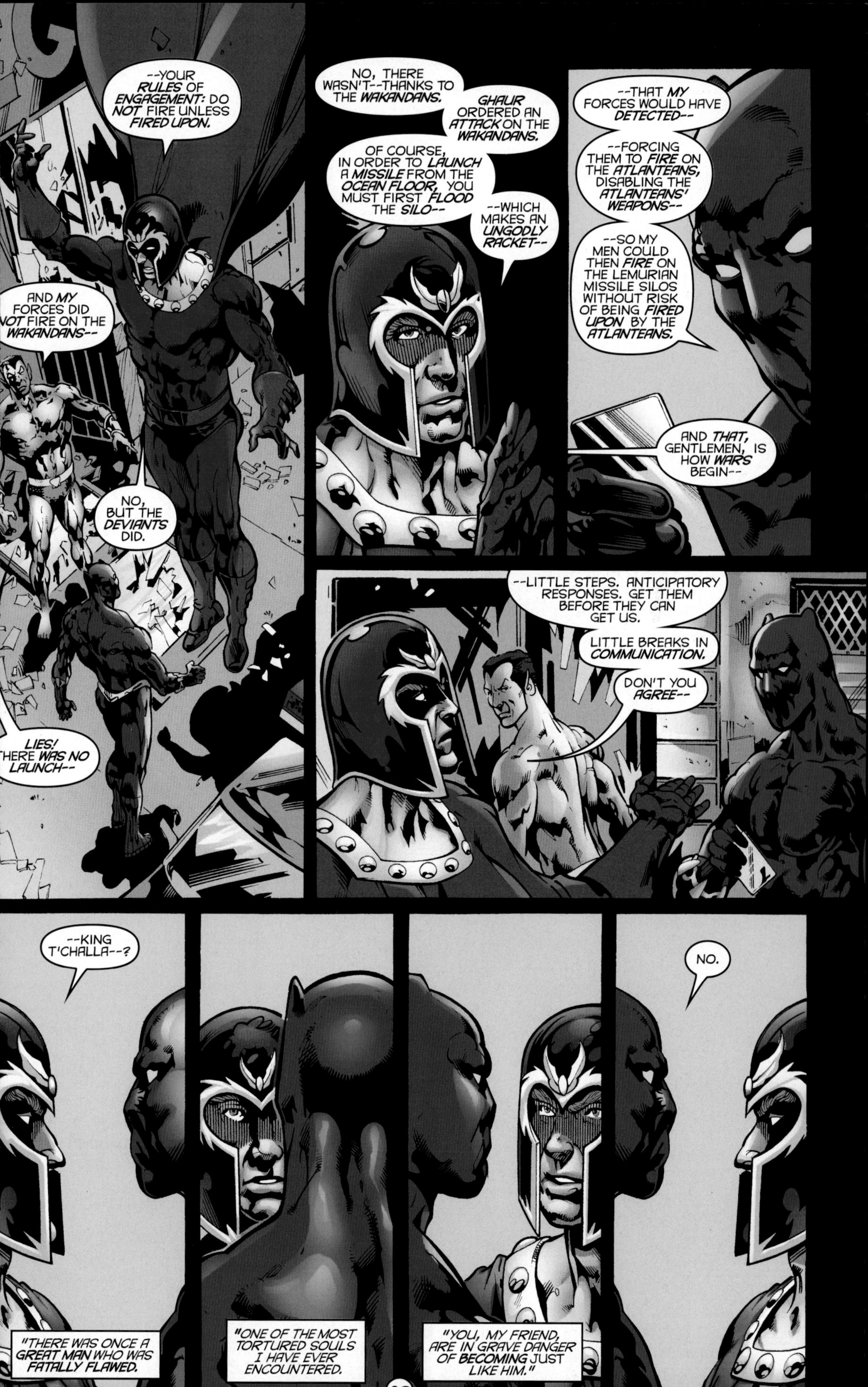
--YOUR RULES OF ENGAGEMENT: DO NOT FIRE UNLESS FIRED UPON.
AND MY FORCES DID NOT FIRE ON THE WAKANDANS--
NO, BUT THE DEVIANTS DID.
LIES! THERE WAS NO LAUNCH--
NO, THERE WASN'T--THANKS TO THE WAKANDANS.
GHAUR ORDERED AN ATTACK ON THE WAKANDANS.
OF COURSE, IN ORDER TO LAUNCH A MISSILE FROM THE OCEAN FLOOR, YOU MUST FIRST FLOOD THE SILO--
--WHICH MAKES AN UNGODLY RACKET--
--THAT MY FORCES WOULD HAVE DETECTED--
--FORCING THEM TO FIRE ON THE ATLANTEANS, DISABLING THE ATLANTEANS' WEAPONS--
--SO MY MEN COULD THEN FIRE ON THE LEMURIAN MISSILE SILOS WITHOUT RISK OF BEING FIRED UPON BY THE ATLANTEANS.
AND THAT, GENTLEMEN, IS HOW WARS BEGIN--
--LITTLE STEPS. ANTICIPATORY RESPONSES. GET THEM BEFORE THEY CAN GET US.
LITTLE BREAKS IN COMMUNICATION.
DON'T YOU AGREE--
--KING T'CHALLA--?
"THERE WAS ONCE A GREAT MAN WHO WAS FATALLY FLAWED.
"ONE OF THE MOST TORTURED SOULS I HAVE EVER ENCOUNTERED.
"YOU, MY FRIEND, ARE IN GRAVE DANGER OF BECOMING JUST LIKE HIM."
NO.

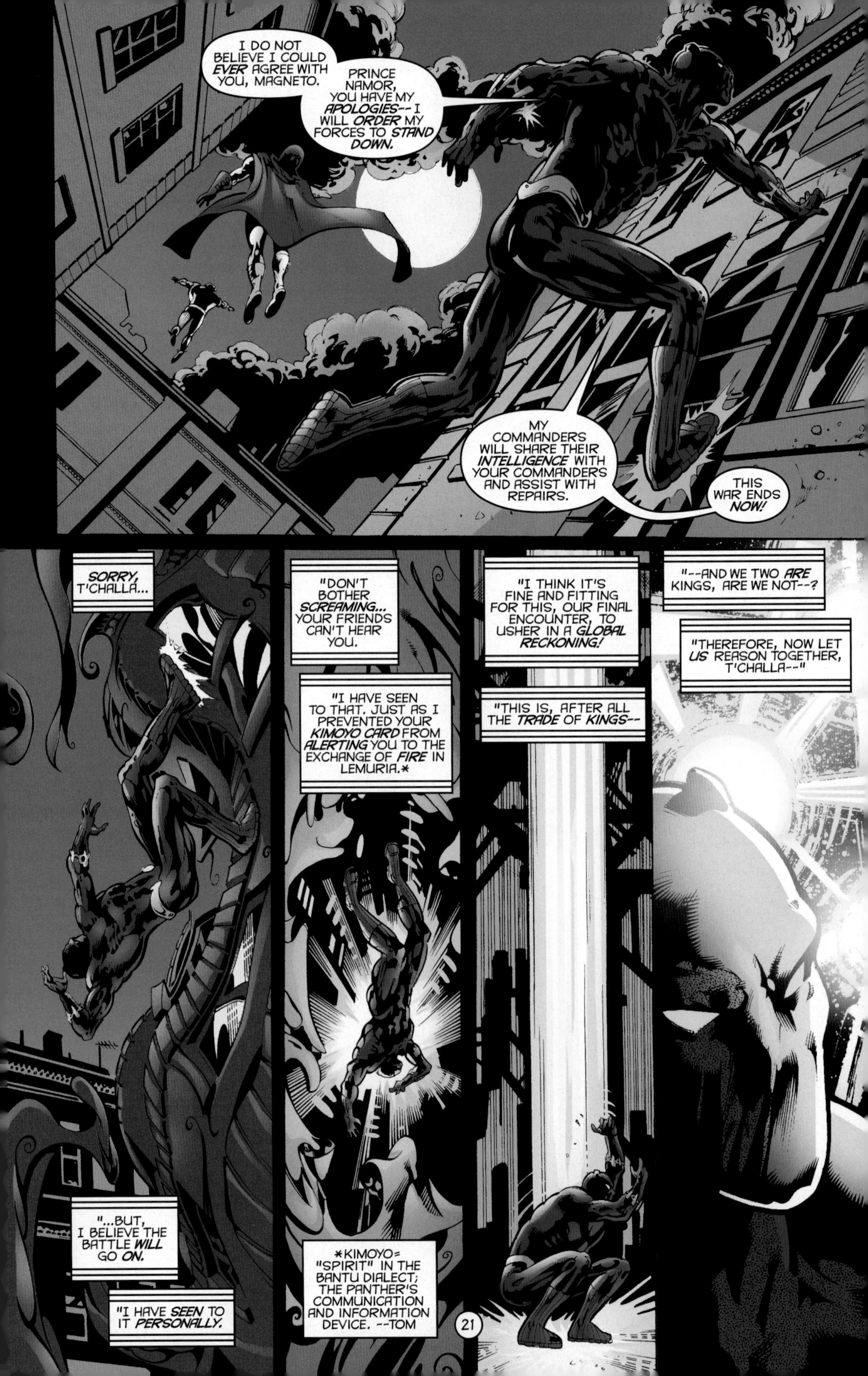
I DO NOT BELIEVE I COULD EVER AGREE WITH YOU, MAGNETO.
PRINCE NAMOR, YOU HAVE MY APOLOGIES-- I WILL ORDER MY FORCES TO STAND DOWN.
MY COMMANDERS WILL SHARE THEIR INTELLIGENCE WITH YOUR COMMANDERS AND ASSIST WITH REPAIRS.
THIS WAR ENDS NOW!
SORRY, T'CHALLA...
"...BUT, I BELIEVE THE BATTLE WILL GO ON.
"I HAVE SEEN TO IT PERSONALLY.
"DON'T BOTHER SCREAMING... YOUR FRIENDS CAN'T HEAR YOU.
"I HAVE SEEN TO THAT. JUST AS I PREVENTED YOUR KIMOYO CARD FROM ALERTING YOU TO THE EXCHANGE OF FIRE IN LEMURIA.*
*KIMOYO= "SPIRIT" IN THE BANTU DIALECT; THE PANTHER'S COMMUNICATION AND INFORMATION DEVICE. --TOM
"I THINK IT'S FINE AND FITTING FOR THIS, OUR FINAL ENCOUNTER, TO USHER IN A GLOBAL RECKONING!
"THIS IS, AFTER ALL THE TRADE OF KINGS--
"--AND WE TWO ARE KINGS, ARE WE NOT--?
"THEREFORE, NOW LET US REASON TOGETHER, T'CHALLA--"

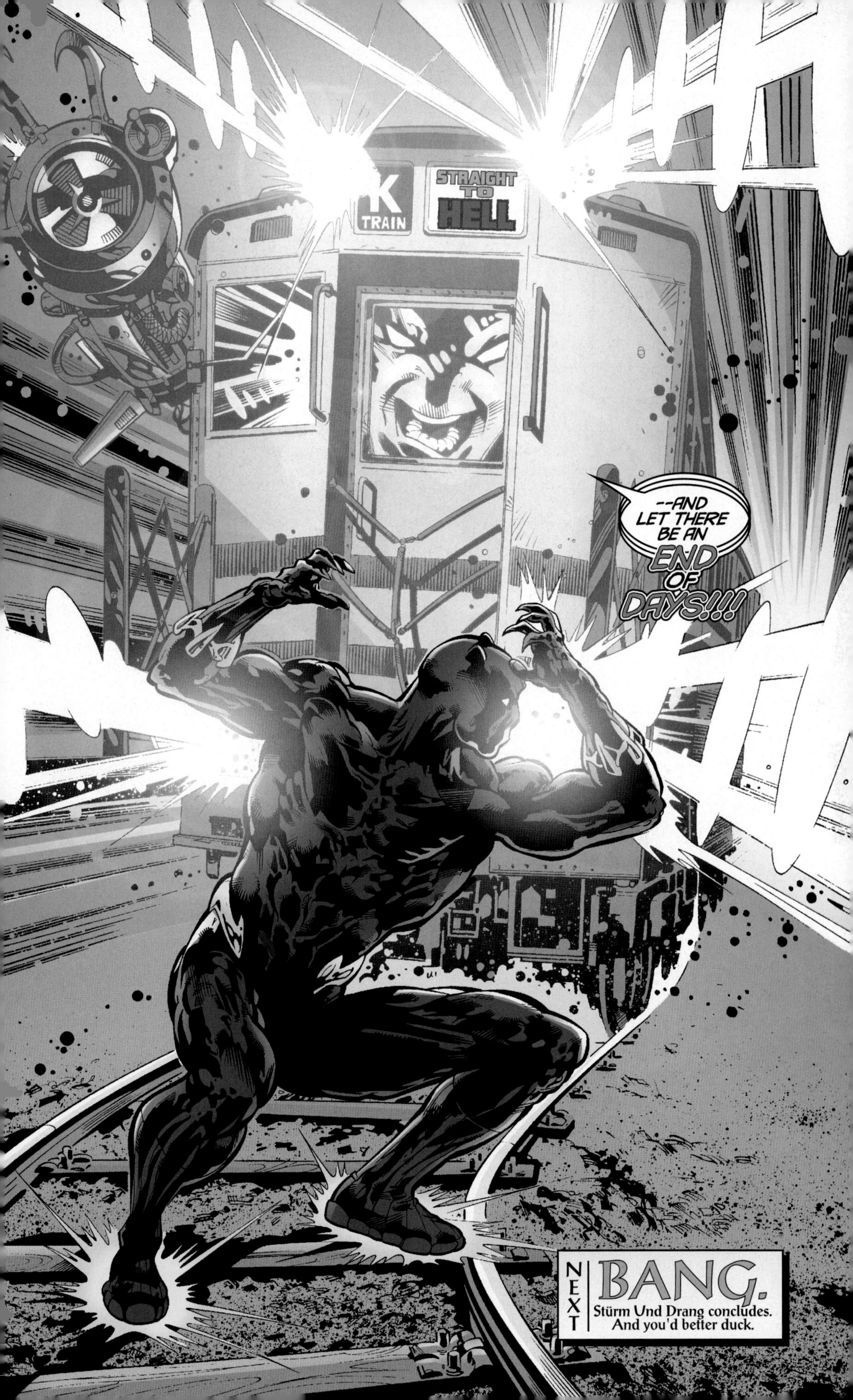
K
TRAIN
STRAIGHT TO HELL
--AND LET THERE BE AN END OF DAYS!!!
NEXT
BANG.
Stürm Und Drang concludes.
And you'd better duck.

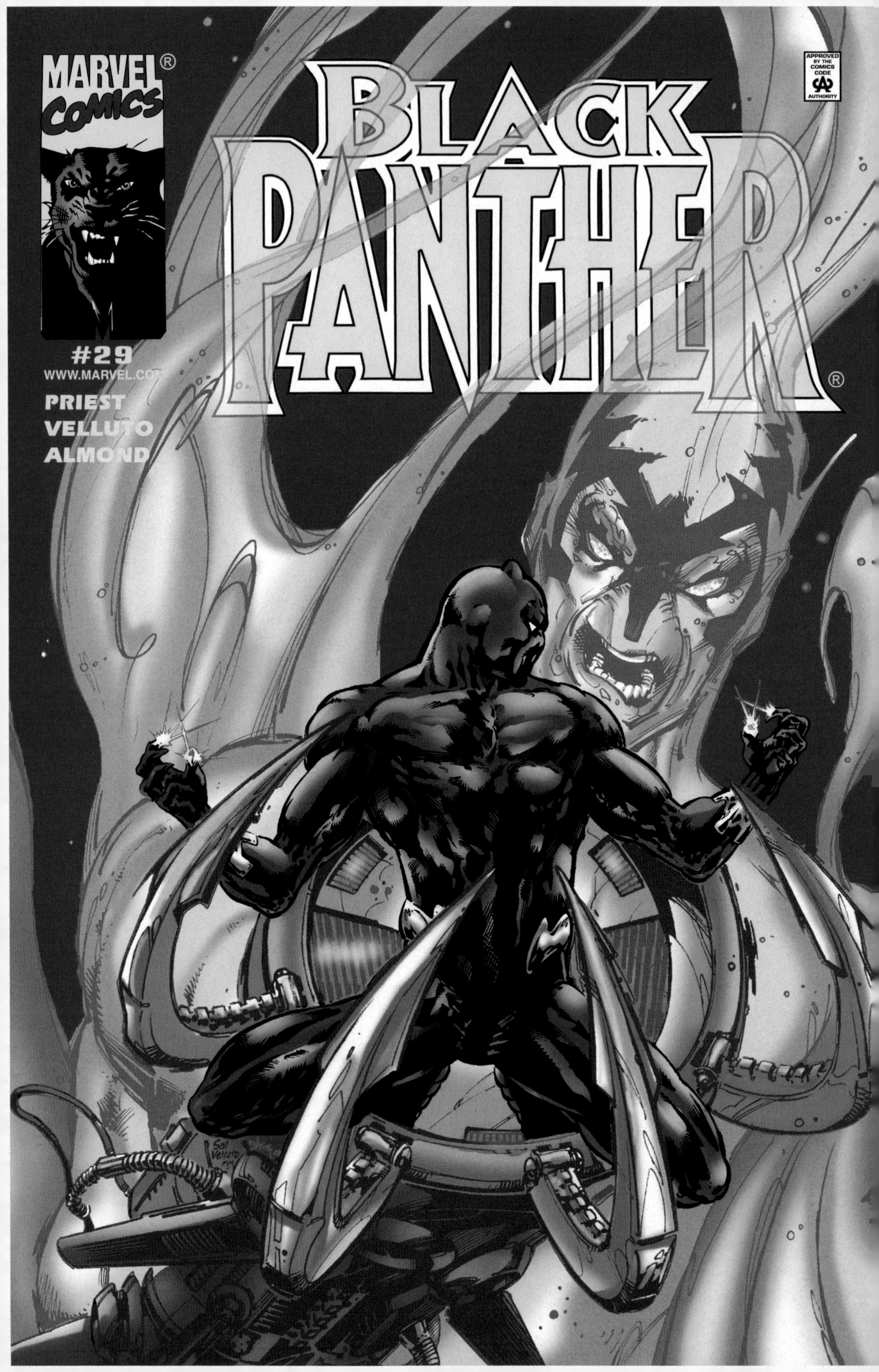
MARVEL® COMICS
BLACK PANTHER®
#29
WWW.MARVEL.COM
PRIEST
VELLUTO
ALMOND
APPROVED BY THE COMICS CODE AUTHORITY

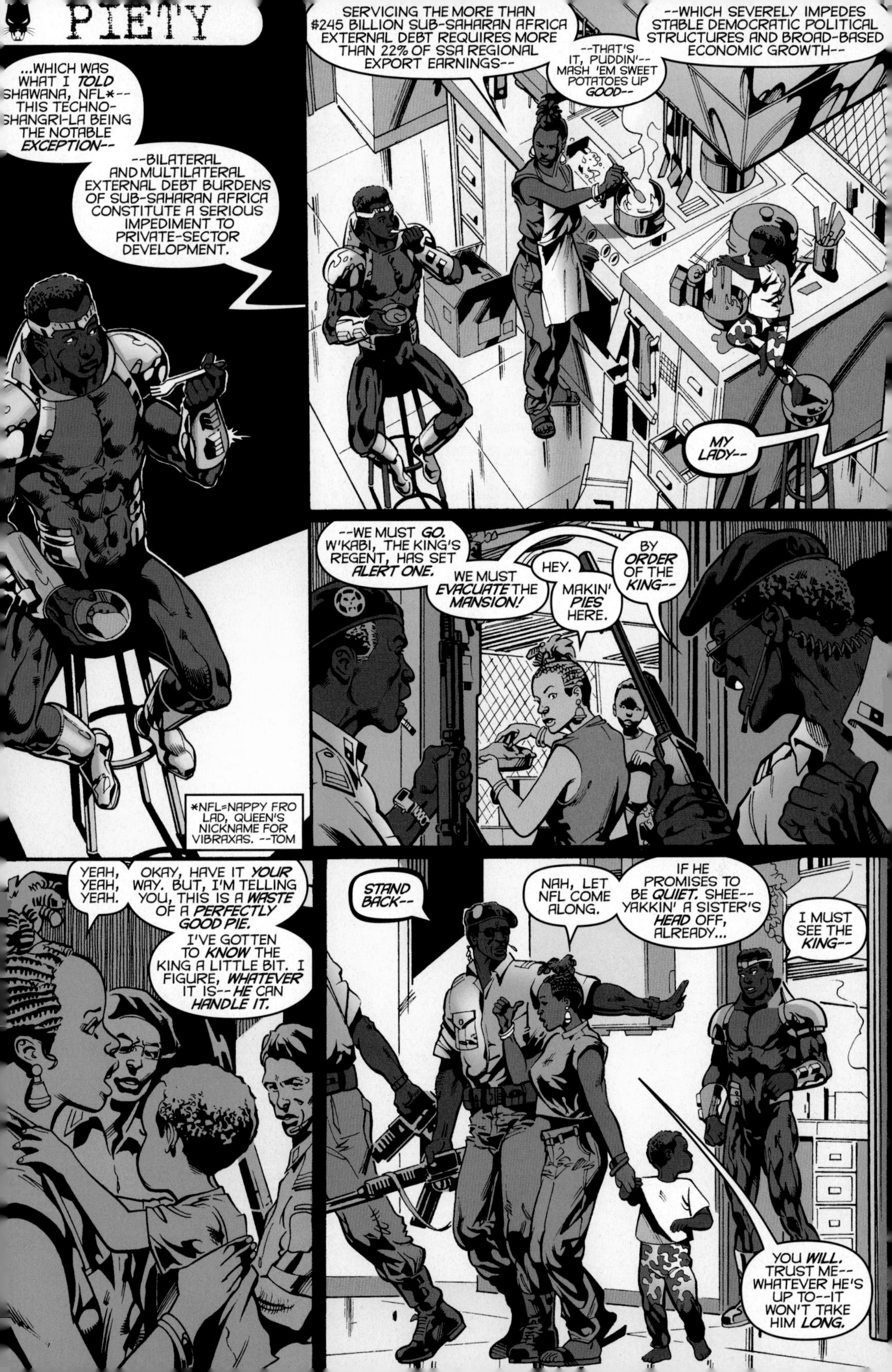
PIETY
...WHICH WAS WHAT I TOLD SHAWANA, NFL*-- THIS TECHNO-SHANGRI-LA BEING THE NOTABLE EXCEPTION--
--BILATERAL AND MULTILATERAL EXTERNAL DEBT BURDENS OF SUB-SAHARAN AFRICA CONSTITUTE A SERIOUS IMPEDIMENT TO PRIVATE-SECTOR DEVELOPMENT.
*NFL=NAPPY FRO LAD, QUEEN'S NICKNAME FOR VIBRAXAS. --TOM
SERVICING THE MORE THAN $245 BILLION SUB-SAHARAN AFRICA EXTERNAL DEBT REQUIRES MORE THAN 22% OF SSA REGIONAL EXPORT EARNINGS--
--THAT'S IT, PUDDIN'-- MASH 'EM SWEET POTATOES UP GOOD--
--WHICH SEVERELY IMPEDES STABLE DEMOCRATIC POLITICAL STRUCTURES AND BROAD-BASED ECONOMIC GROWTH--
MY LADY--
--WE MUST GO. W'KABI, THE KING'S REGENT, HAS SET ALERT ONE.
WE MUST EVACUATE THE MANSION!
HEY.
MAKIN' PIES HERE.
BY ORDER OF THE KING--
YEAH, YEAH, YEAH.
OKAY, HAVE IT YOUR WAY. BUT, I'M TELLING YOU, THIS IS A WASTE OF A PERFECTLY GOOD PIE.
I'VE GOTTEN TO KNOW THE KING A LITTLE BIT. I FIGURE, WHATEVER IT IS--HE CAN HANDLE IT.
STAND BACK--
NAH, LET NFL COME ALONG.
IF HE PROMISES TO BE QUIET. SHEE-- YAKKIN' A SISTER'S HEAD OFF, ALREADY...
I MUST SEE THE KING--
YOU WILL. TRUST ME-- WHATEVER HE'S UP TO--IT WON'T TAKE HIM LONG.

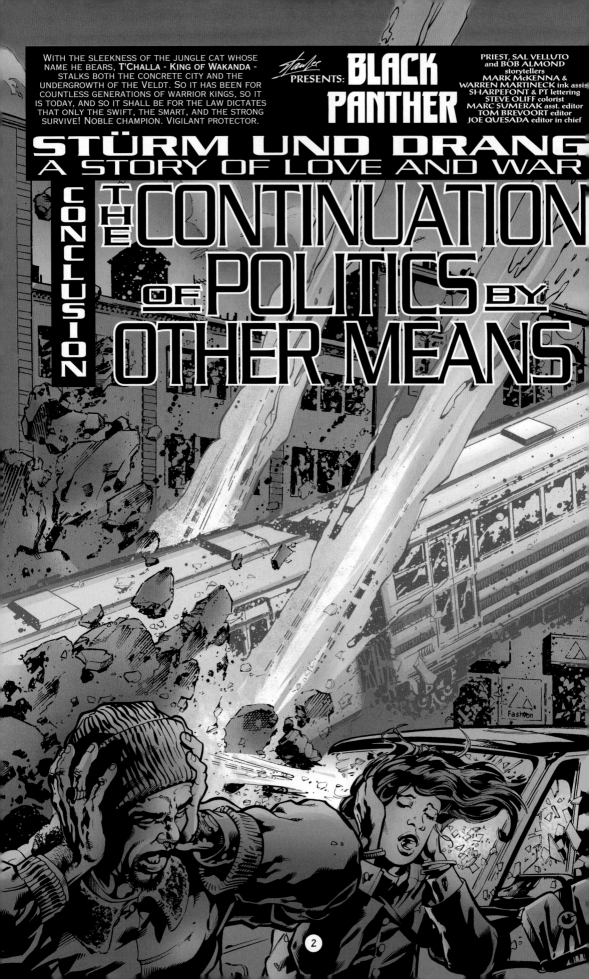

WITH THE SLEEKNESS OF THE JUNGLE CAT WHOSE NAME HE BEARS, T'CHALLA - KING OF WAKANDA - STALKS BOTH THE CONCRETE CITY AND THE UNDERGROWTH OF THE VELDT. SO IT HAS BEEN FOR COUNTLESS GENERATIONS OF WARRIOR KINGS, SO IT IS TODAY, AND SO IT SHALL BE FOR THE LAW DICTATES THAT ONLY THE SWIFT, THE SMART, AND THE STRONG SURVIVE! NOBLE CHAMPION. VIGILANT PROTECTOR.

STAN LEE PRESENTS: **BLACK PANTHER**

PRIEST, SAL VELLUTO and BOB ALMOND storytellers
MARK McKENNA & WARREN MARTINECK ink assis
SHARPEFONT & PT lettering
STEVE OLIFF colorist
MARC SUMERAK asst. editor
TOM BREVOORT editor
JOE QUESADA editor in chief

STÜRM UND DRANG
A STORY OF LOVE AND WAR

CONCLUSION

THE CONTINUATION OF POLITICS BY OTHER MEANS

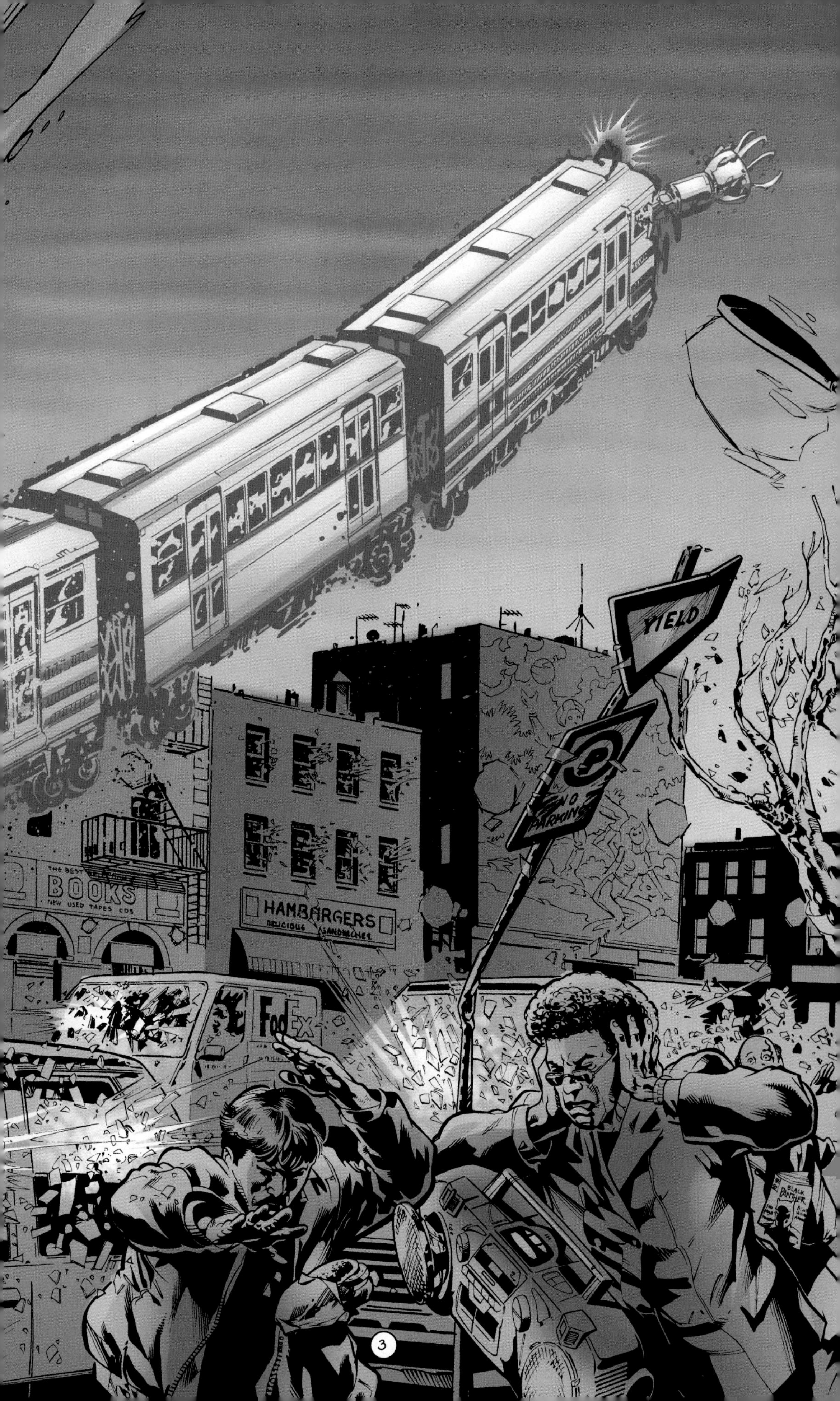
YIELD
NO PARKING
THE BEST
BOOKS
NEW USED TAPES CDS
HAMBURGERS
FedEx

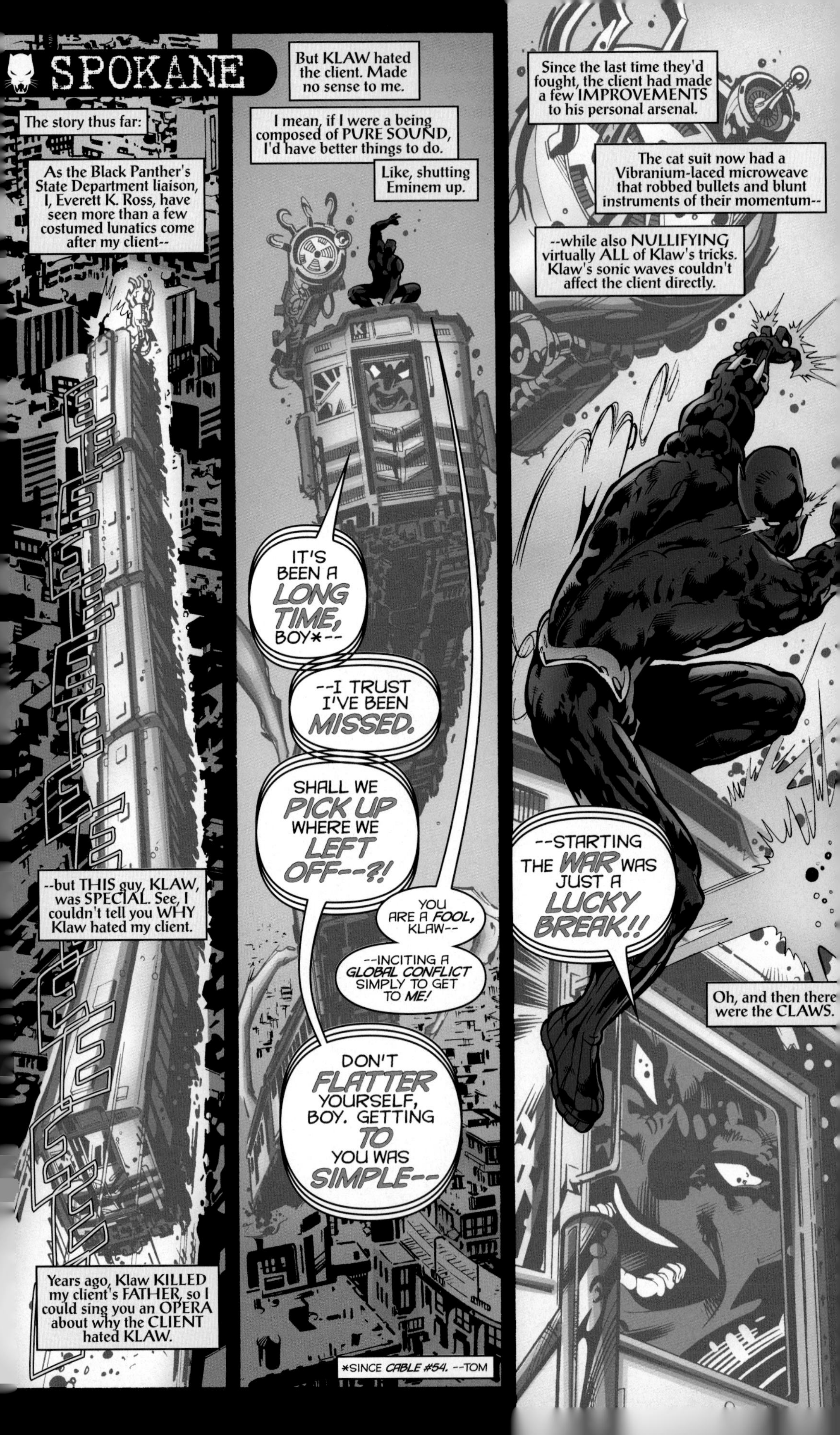

SPOKANE
The story thus far:
As the Black Panther's State Department liaison, I, Everett K. Ross, have seen more than a few costumed lunatics come after my client--
--but THIS guy, KLAW, was SPECIAL. See, I couldn't tell you WHY Klaw hated my client.
Years ago, Klaw KILLED my client's FATHER, so I could sing you an OPERA about why the CLIENT hated KLAW.
But KLAW hated the client. Made no sense to me.
I mean, if I were a being composed of PURE SOUND, I'd have better things to do.
Like, shutting Eminem up.
IT'S BEEN A LONG TIME, BOY*--
--I TRUST I'VE BEEN MISSED.
SHALL WE PICK UP WHERE WE LEFT OFF--?!
YOU ARE A FOOL, KLAW--
--INCITING A GLOBAL CONFLICT SIMPLY TO GET TO ME!
DON'T FLATTER YOURSELF, BOY. GETTING TO YOU WAS SIMPLE--
*SINCE CABLE #54. --TOM
Since the last time they'd fought, the client had made a few IMPROVEMENTS to his personal arsenal.
The cat suit now had a Vibranium-laced microweave that robbed bullets and blunt instruments of their momentum--
--while also NULLIFYING virtually ALL of Klaw's tricks. Klaw's sonic waves couldn't affect the client directly.
--STARTING THE WAR WAS JUST A LUCKY BREAK!!
Oh, and then there were the CLAWS.

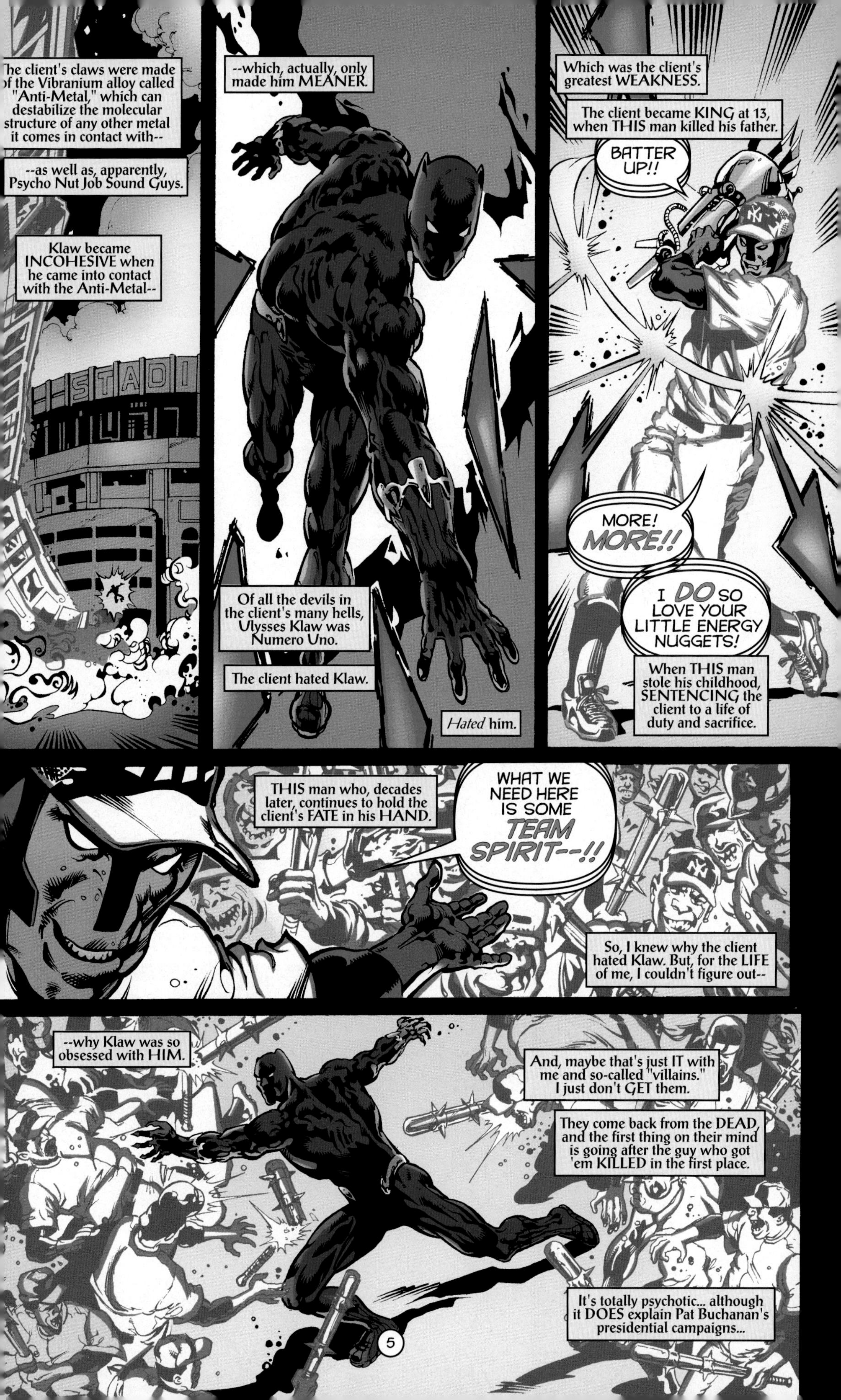
The client's claws were made of the Vibranium alloy called "Anti-Metal," which can destabilize the molecular structure of any other metal it comes in contact with--
--as well as, apparently, Psycho Nut Job Sound Guys.
Klaw became INCOHESIVE when he came into contact with the Anti-Metal--
STADI
--which, actually, only made him MEANER.
Of all the devils in the client's many hells, Ulysses Klaw was Numero Uno.
The client hated Klaw.
Hated him.
Which was the client's greatest WEAKNESS.
The client became KING at 13, when THIS man killed his father.
BATTER UP!!
MORE! MORE!!
I DO SO LOVE YOUR LITTLE ENERGY NUGGETS!
When THIS man stole his childhood, SENTENCING the client to a life of duty and sacrifice.
THIS man who, decades later, continues to hold the client's FATE in his HAND.
WHAT WE NEED HERE IS SOME TEAM SPIRIT--!!
So, I knew why the client hated Klaw. But, for the LIFE of me, I couldn't figure out--
--why Klaw was so obsessed with HIM.
And, maybe that's just IT with me and so-called "villains." I just don't GET them.
They come back from the DEAD, and the first thing on their mind is going after the guy who got 'em KILLED in the first place.
It's totally psychotic... although it DOES explain Pat Buchanan's presidential campaigns...

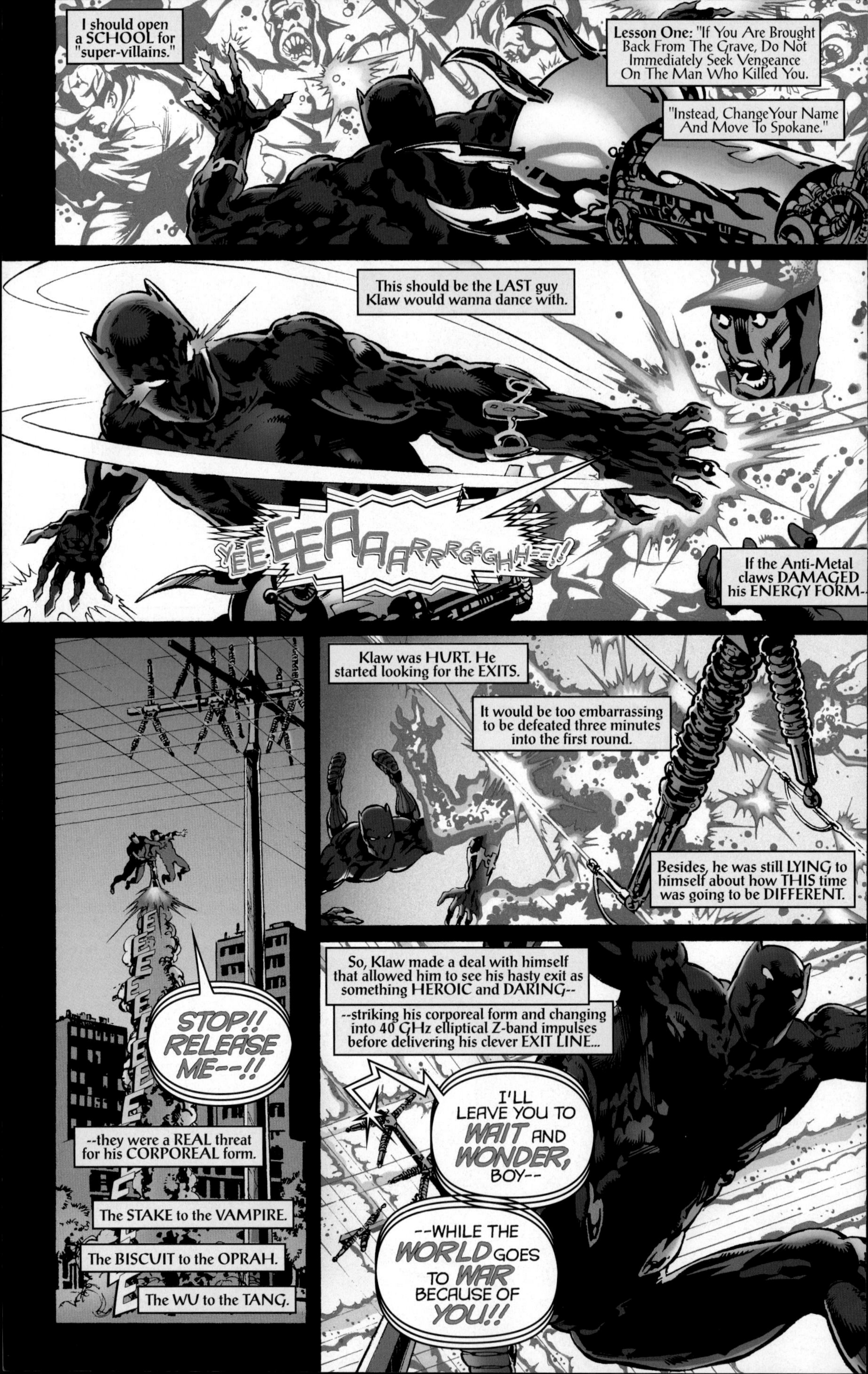
I should open a SCHOOL for "super-villains."
Lesson One: "If You Are Brought Back From The Grave, Do Not Immediately Seek Vengeance On The Man Who Killed You.
"Instead, Change Your Name And Move To Spokane."
This should be the LAST guy Klaw would wanna dance with.
YEEEEEAAAARRRRGGGHH--!!
If the Anti-Metal claws DAMAGED his ENERGY FORM--
--they were a REAL threat for his CORPOREAL form.
The STAKE to the VAMPIRE.
The BISCUIT to the OPRAH.
The WU to the TANG.
STOP!! RELEASE ME--!!
Klaw was HURT. He started looking for the EXITS.
It would be too embarrassing to be defeated three minutes into the first round.
Besides, he was still LYING to himself about how THIS time was going to be DIFFERENT.
So, Klaw made a deal with himself that allowed him to see his hasty exit as something HEROIC and DARING--
--striking his corporeal form and changing into 40 GHz elliptical Z-band impulses before delivering his clever EXIT LINE...
I'LL LEAVE YOU TO WAIT AND WONDER, BOY--
--WHILE THE WORLD GOES TO WAR BECAUSE OF YOU!!

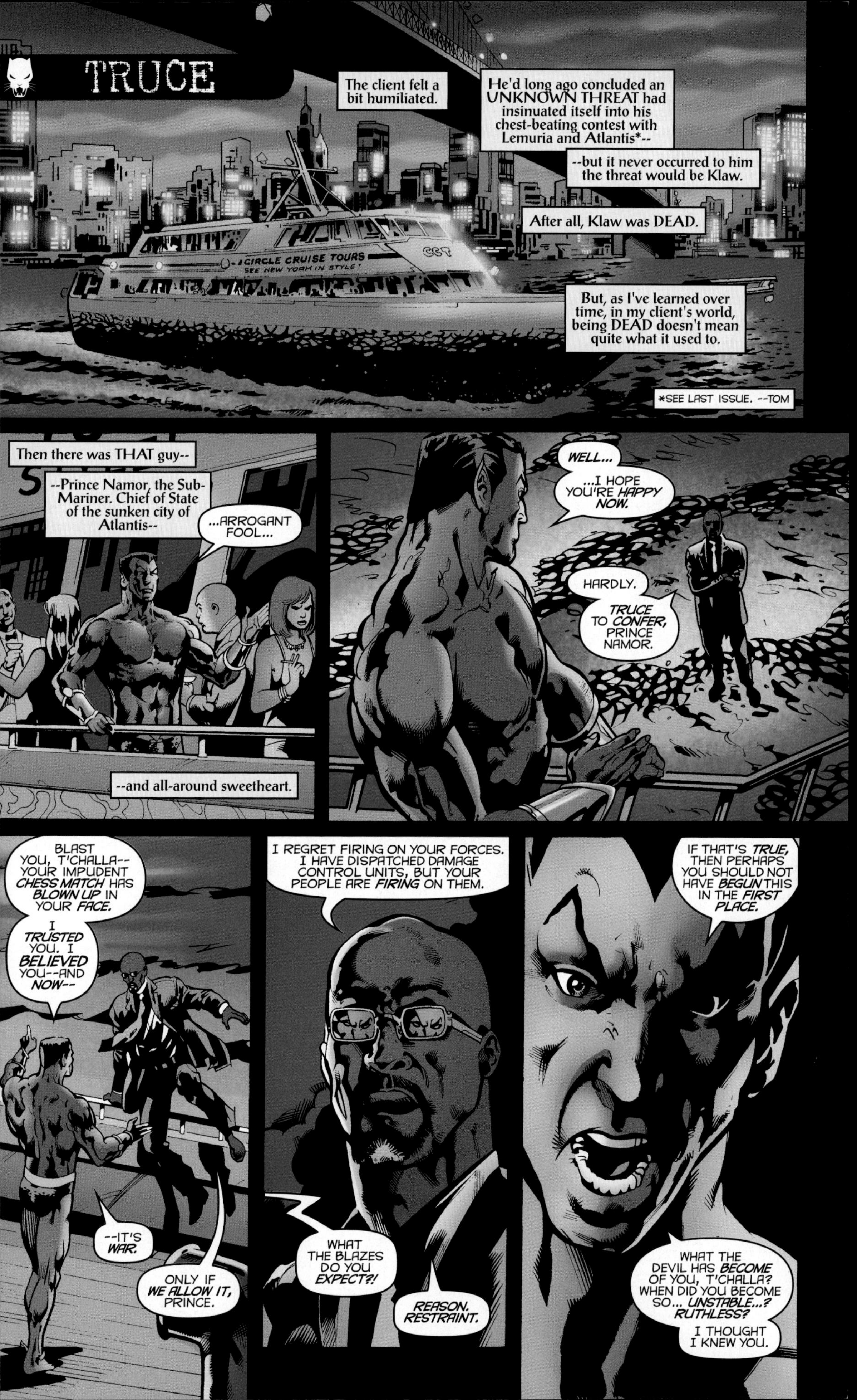
TRUCE
The client felt a bit humiliated.
He'd long ago concluded an UNKNOWN THREAT had insinuated itself into his chest-beating contest with Lemuria and Atlantis*--
--but it never occurred to him the threat would be Klaw.
After all, Klaw was DEAD.
CIRCLE CRUISE TOURS
SEE NEW YORK IN STYLE!
But, as I've learned over time, in my client's world, being DEAD doesn't mean quite what it used to.
*SEE LAST ISSUE. --TOM
Then there was THAT guy--
--Prince Namor, the Sub-Mariner. Chief of State of the sunken city of Atlantis--
...ARROGANT FOOL...
--and all-around sweetheart.
WELL...
...I HOPE YOU'RE HAPPY NOW.
HARDLY.
TRUCE TO CONFER, PRINCE NAMOR.
BLAST YOU, T'CHALLA-- YOUR IMPUDENT CHESS MATCH HAS BLOWN UP IN YOUR FACE.
I TRUSTED YOU. I BELIEVED YOU--AND NOW--
--IT'S WAR.
ONLY IF WE ALLOW IT, PRINCE.
I REGRET FIRING ON YOUR FORCES. I HAVE DISPATCHED DAMAGE CONTROL UNITS, BUT YOUR PEOPLE ARE FIRING ON THEM.
WHAT THE BLAZES DO YOU EXPECT?!
REASON. RESTRAINT.
IF THAT'S TRUE, THEN PERHAPS YOU SHOULD NOT HAVE BEGUN THIS IN THE FIRST PLACE.
WHAT THE DEVIL HAS BECOME OF YOU, T'CHALLA? WHEN DID YOU BECOME SO... UNSTABLE...? RUTHLESS?
I THOUGHT I KNEW YOU.

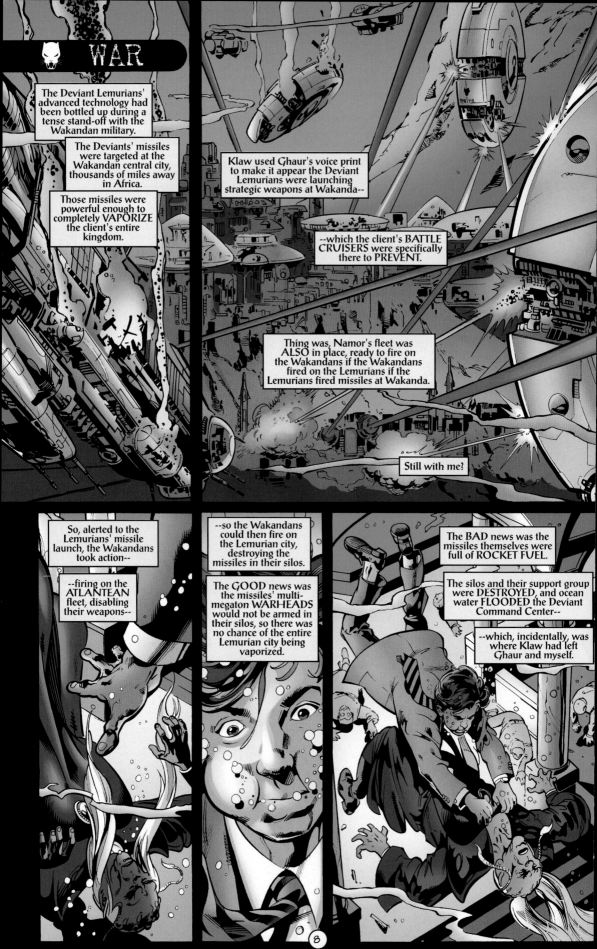

The Deviant Lemurians' advanced technology had been bottled up during a tense stand-off with the Wakandan military.

The Deviants' missiles were targeted at the Wakandan central city, thousands of miles away in Africa.

Those missiles were powerful enough to completely VAPORIZE the client's entire kingdom.

Klaw used Ghaur's voice print to make it appear the Deviant Lemurians were launching strategic weapons at Wakanda--

--which the client's BATTLE CRUISERS were specifically there to PREVENT.

Thing was, Namor's fleet was ALSO in place, ready to fire on the Wakandans if the Wakandans fired on the Lemurians if the Lemurians fired missiles at Wakanda.

Still with me?

So, alerted to the Lemurians' missile launch, the Wakandans took action--

--firing on the ATLANTEAN fleet, disabling their weapons--

--so the Wakandans could then fire on the Lemurian city, destroying the missiles in their silos.

The GOOD news was the missiles' multi-megaton WARHEADS would not be armed in their silos, so there was no chance of the entire Lemurian city being vaporized.

The BAD news was the missiles themselves were full of ROCKET FUEL.

The silos and their support group were DESTROYED, and ocean water FLOODED the Deviant Command Center--

--which, incidentally, was where Klaw had left Ghaur and myself.

8

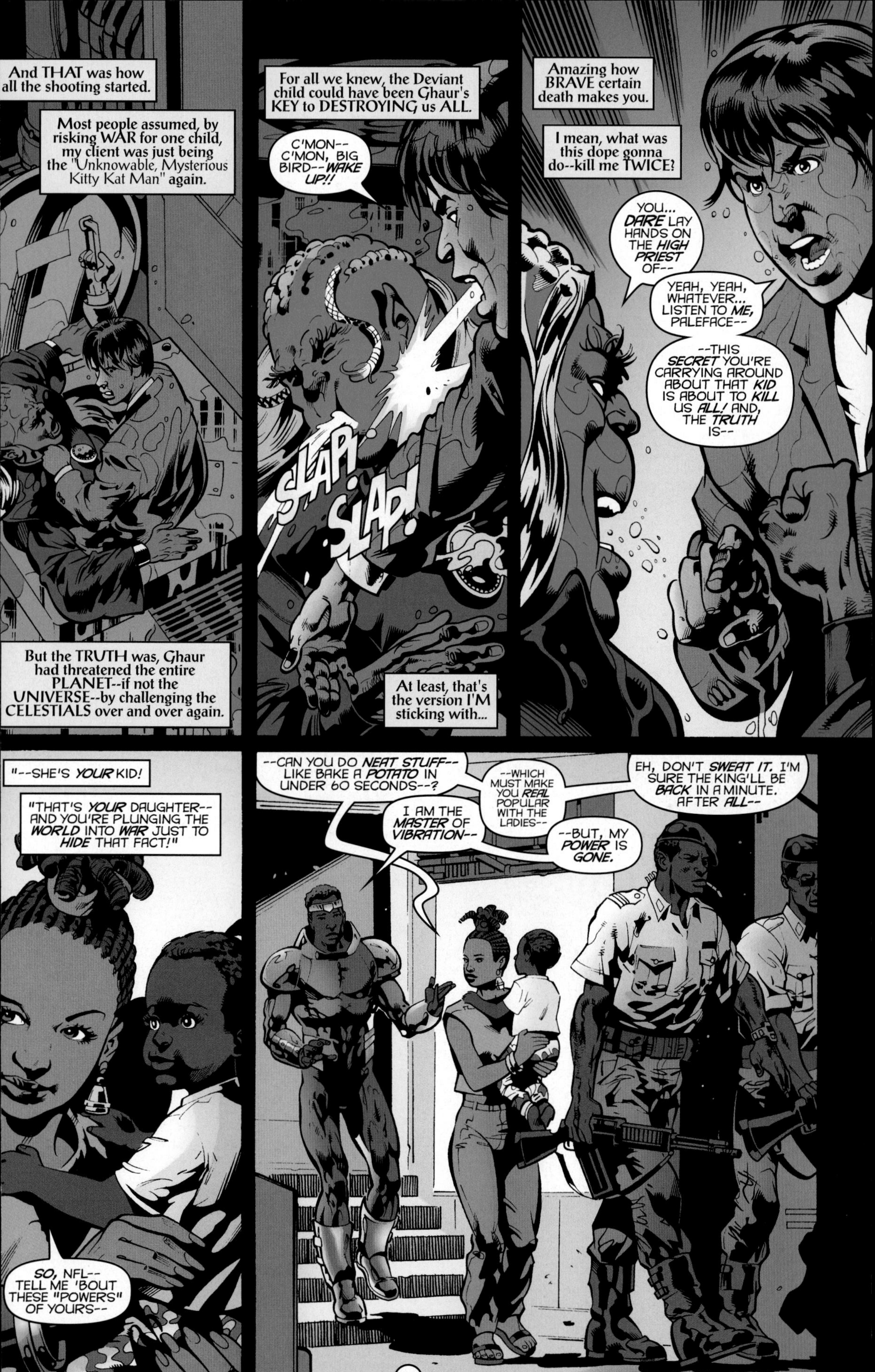

And THAT was how all the shooting started.
Most people assumed, by risking WAR for one child, my client was just being the "Unknowable, Mysterious Kitty Kat Man" again.
But the TRUTH was, Ghaur had threatened the entire PLANET--if not the UNIVERSE--by challenging the CELESTIALS over and over again.
For all we knew, the Deviant child could have been Ghaur's KEY to DESTROYING us ALL.
C'MON-- C'MON, BIG BIRD--WAKE UP!!
SLAP! SLAP!
At least, that's the version I'M sticking with...
Amazing how BRAVE certain death makes you.
I mean, what was this dope gonna do--kill me TWICE?
YOU... DARE LAY HANDS ON THE HIGH PRIEST OF--
YEAH, YEAH, WHATEVER... LISTEN TO ME, PALEFACE--
--THIS SECRET YOU'RE CARRYING AROUND ABOUT THAT KID IS ABOUT TO KILL US ALL! AND, THE TRUTH IS--
"--SHE'S YOUR KID!
"THAT'S YOUR DAUGHTER-- AND YOU'RE PLUNGING THE WORLD INTO WAR JUST TO HIDE THAT FACT!"
SO, NFL-- TELL ME 'BOUT THESE "POWERS" OF YOURS--
I AM THE MASTER OF VIBRATION--
--CAN YOU DO NEAT STUFF-- LIKE BAKE A POTATO IN UNDER 60 SECONDS--?
--BUT, MY POWER IS GONE.
--WHICH MUST MAKE YOU REAL POPULAR WITH THE LADIES--
EH, DON'T SWEAT IT. I'M SURE THE KING'LL BE BACK IN A MINUTE. AFTER ALL--

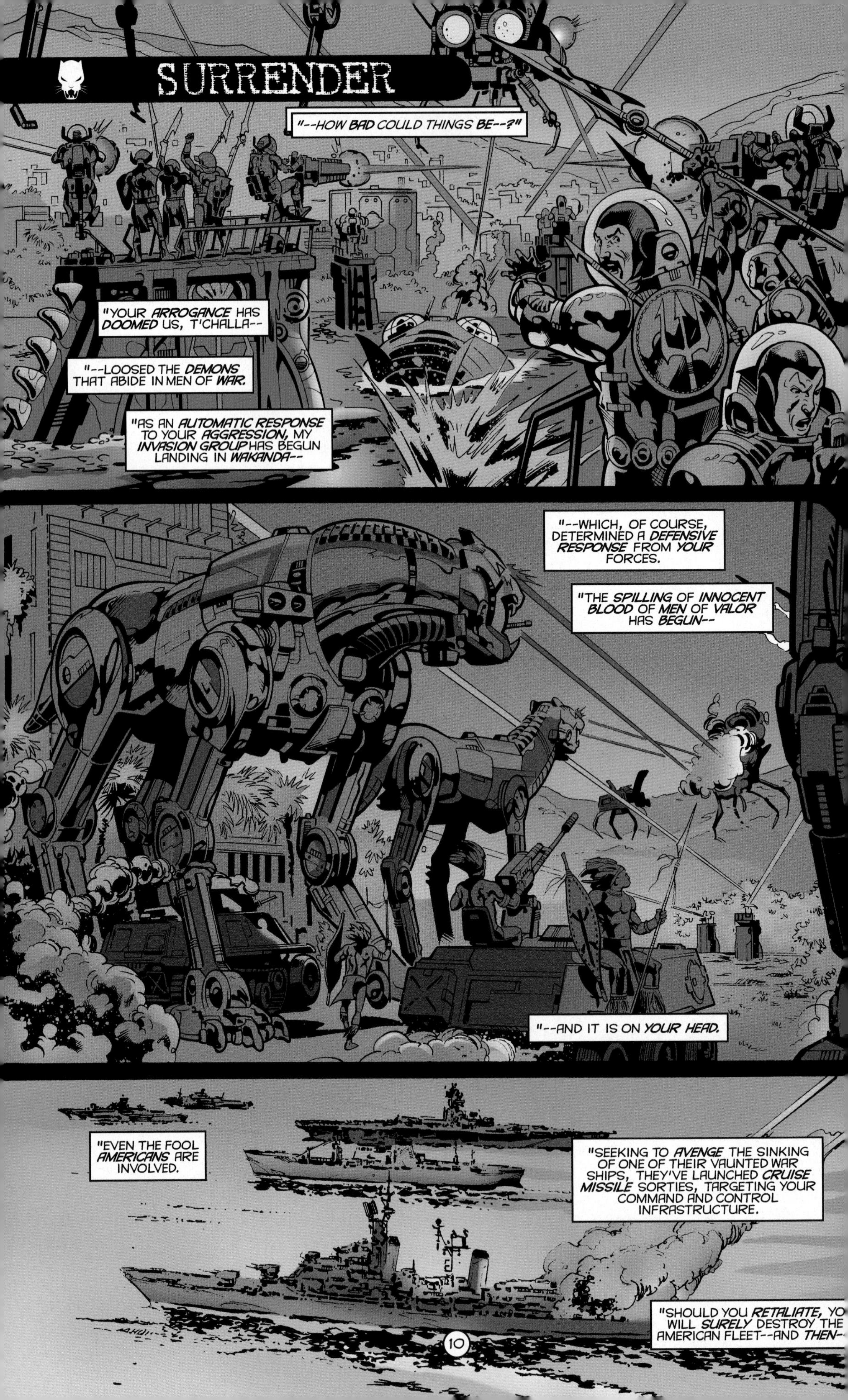

SURRENDER
"--HOW BAD COULD THINGS BE--?"
"YOUR ARROGANCE HAS DOOMED US, T'CHALLA--
"--LOOSED THE DEMONS THAT ABIDE IN MEN OF WAR.
"AS AN AUTOMATIC RESPONSE TO YOUR AGGRESSION, MY INVASION GROUP HAS BEGUN LANDING IN WAKANDA--
"--WHICH, OF COURSE, DETERMINED A DEFENSIVE RESPONSE FROM YOUR FORCES.
"THE SPILLING OF INNOCENT BLOOD OF MEN OF VALOR HAS BEGUN--
"--AND IT IS ON YOUR HEAD.
"EVEN THE FOOL AMERICANS ARE INVOLVED.
"SEEKING TO AVENGE THE SINKING OF ONE OF THEIR VAUNTED WAR SHIPS, THEY'VE LAUNCHED CRUISE MISSILE SORTIES, TARGETING YOUR COMMAND AND CONTROL INFRASTRUCTURE.
"SHOULD YOU RETALIATE, YO WILL SURELY DESTROY THE AMERICAN FLEET--AND THEN-

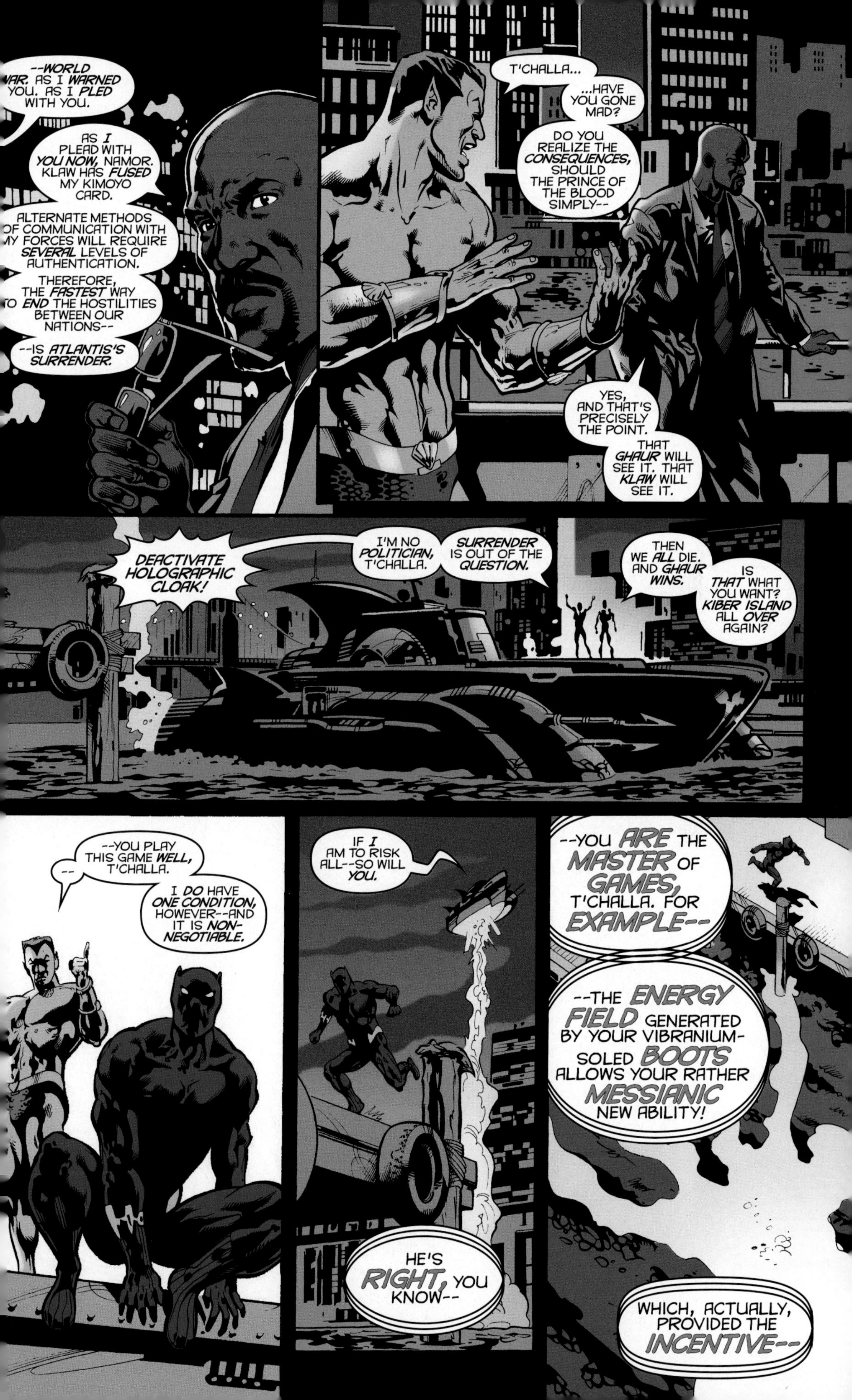
--WORLD WAR. AS I WARNED YOU. AS I PLED WITH YOU.
AS I PLEAD WITH YOU NOW, NAMOR. KLAW HAS FUSED MY KIMOYO CARD.
ALTERNATE METHODS OF COMMUNICATION WITH MY FORCES WILL REQUIRE SEVERAL LEVELS OF AUTHENTICATION.
THEREFORE, THE FASTEST WAY TO END THE HOSTILITIES BETWEEN OUR NATIONS--
--IS ATLANTIS'S SURRENDER.
T'CHALLA...
...HAVE YOU GONE MAD?
DO YOU REALIZE THE CONSEQUENCES, SHOULD THE PRINCE OF THE BLOOD SIMPLY--
YES, AND THAT'S PRECISELY THE POINT.
THAT GHAUR WILL SEE IT. THAT KLAW WILL SEE IT.
DEACTIVATE HOLOGRAPHIC CLOAK!
I'M NO POLITICIAN, T'CHALLA.
SURRENDER IS OUT OF THE QUESTION.
THEN WE ALL DIE. AND GHAUR WINS.
IS THAT WHAT YOU WANT? KIBER ISLAND ALL OVER AGAIN?
--
--YOU PLAY THIS GAME WELL, T'CHALLA.
I DO HAVE ONE CONDITION, HOWEVER--AND IT IS NON-NEGOTIABLE.
IF I AM TO RISK ALL--SO WILL YOU.
HE'S RIGHT, YOU KNOW--
--YOU ARE THE MASTER OF GAMES, T'CHALLA. FOR EXAMPLE--
--THE ENERGY FIELD GENERATED BY YOUR VIBRANIUM-SOLED BOOTS ALLOWS YOUR RATHER MESSIANIC NEW ABILITY!
WHICH, ACTUALLY, PROVIDED THE INCENTIVE--

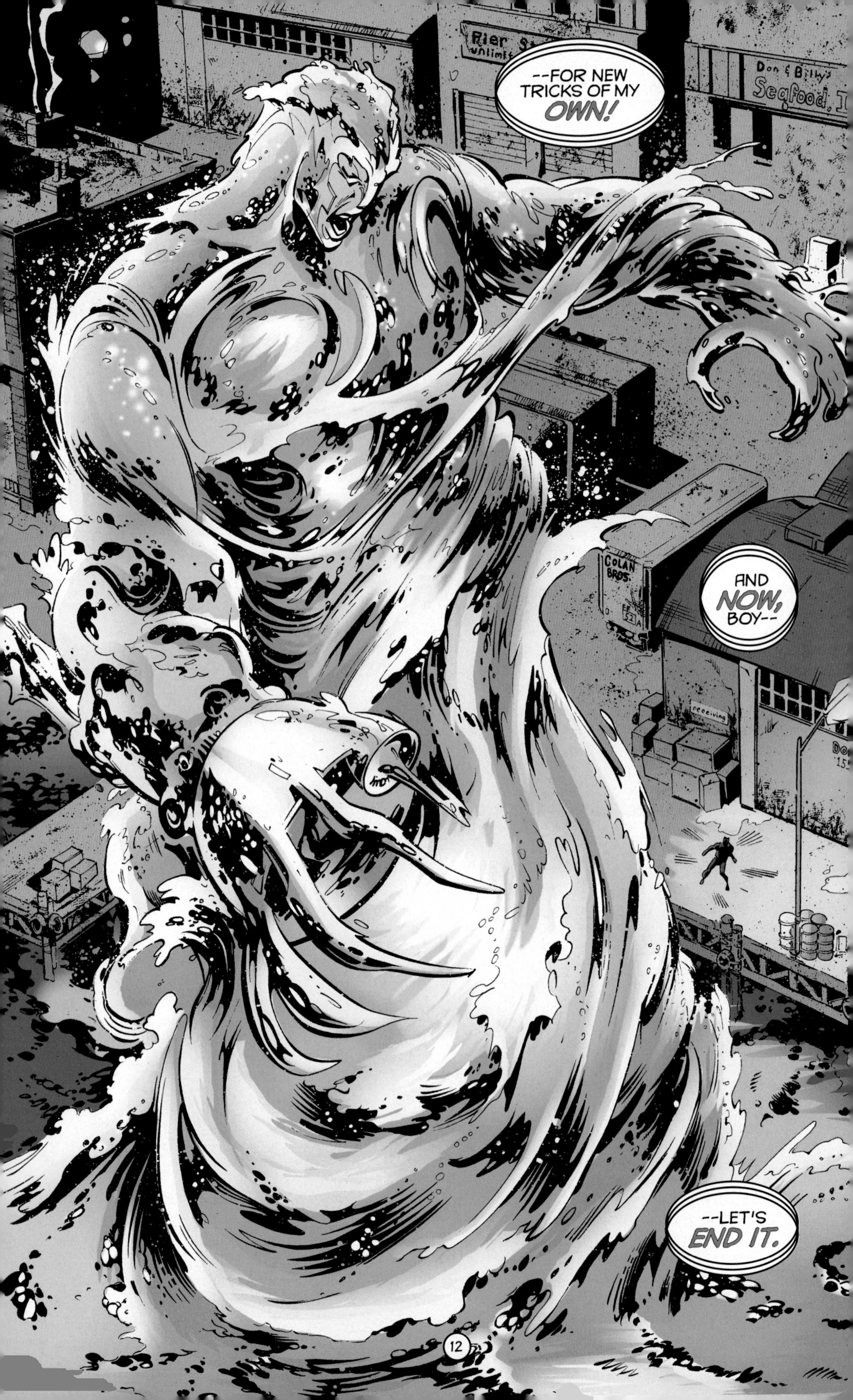
Don & Billy's
Seafood,
--FOR NEW TRICKS OF MY OWN!
COLAN BROS.
AND NOW, BOY--
--LET'S END IT.

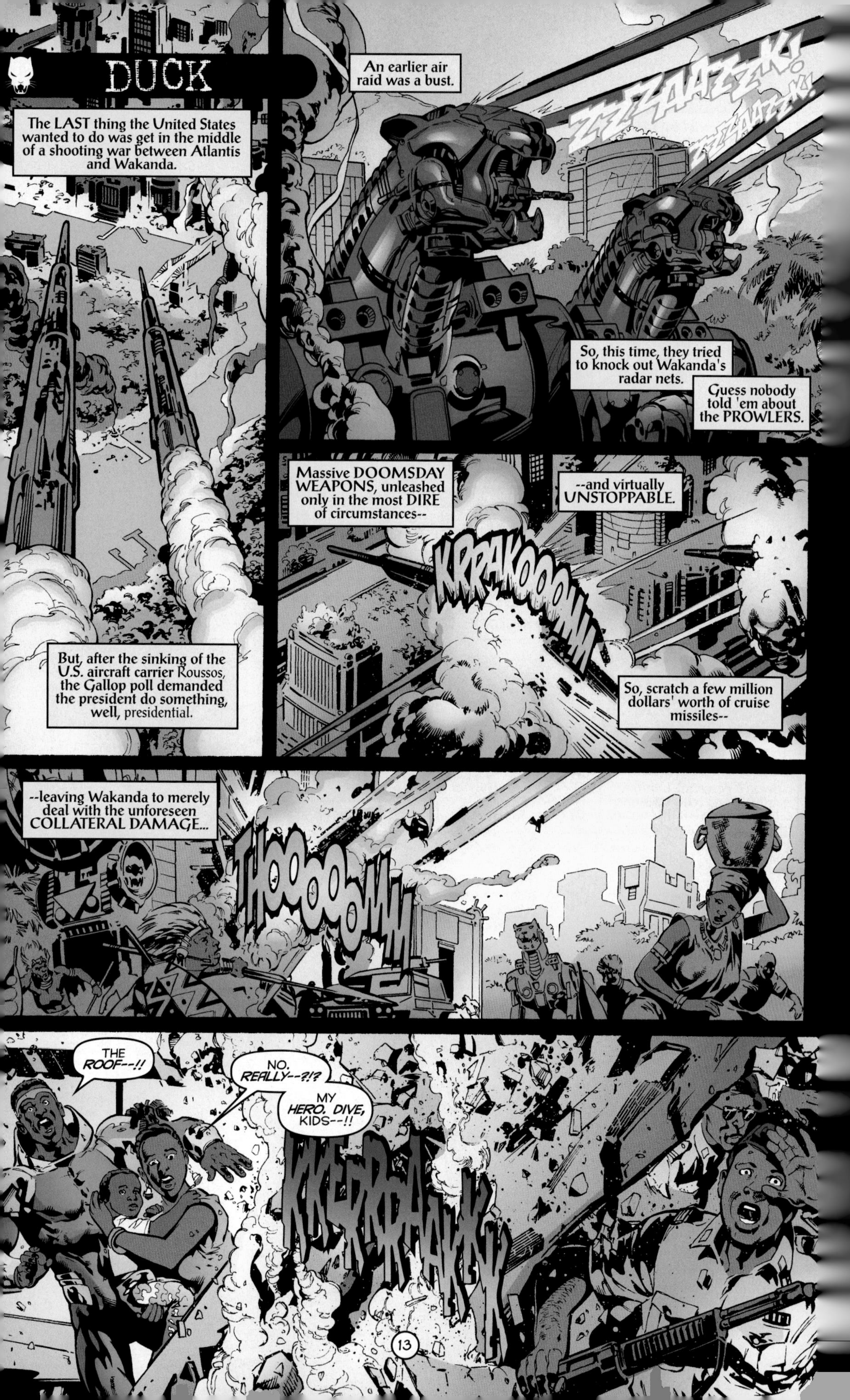
DUCK
The LAST thing the United States wanted to do was get in the middle of a shooting war between Atlantis and Wakanda.
But, after the sinking of the U.S. aircraft carrier Roussos, the Gallop poll demanded the president do something, well, presidential.
An earlier air raid was a bust.
ZZZZAAAZZK!
ZZZAAZZK!
So, this time, they tried to knock out Wakanda's radar nets.
Guess nobody told 'em about the PROWLERS.
Massive DOOMSDAY WEAPONS, unleashed only in the most DIRE of circumstances--
--and virtually UNSTOPPABLE.
KRRAKOOOOMM
So, scratch a few million dollars' worth of cruise missiles--
--leaving Wakanda to merely deal with the unforeseen COLLATERAL DAMAGE...
THOOOOMM
THE ROOF--!!
NO, REALLY--?!?
MY HERO. DIVE, KIDS--!!
KKERRAAKK

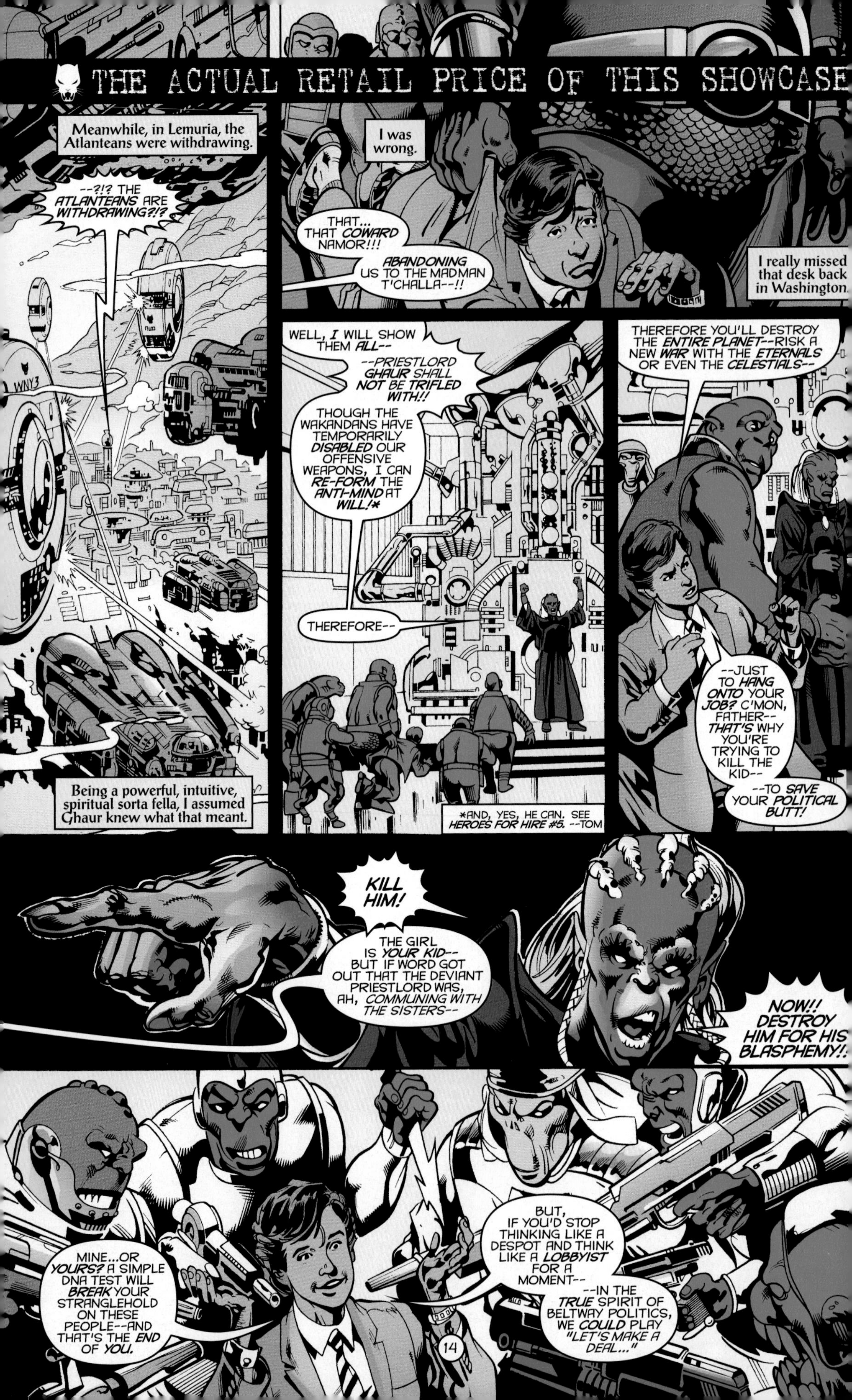
Meanwhile, in Lemuria, the Atlanteans were withdrawing.
--?!? THE ATLANTEANS ARE WITHDRAWING?!?
WNY3
I was wrong.
THAT... THAT COWARD NAMOR!!!
ABANDONING US TO THE MADMAN T'CHALLA--!!
I really missed that desk back in Washington.
WELL, I WILL SHOW THEM ALL--
--PRIESTLORD GHAUR SHALL NOT BE TRIFLED WITH!!
THOUGH THE WAKANDANS HAVE TEMPORARILY DISABLED OUR OFFENSIVE WEAPONS, I CAN RE-FORM THE ANTI-MIND AT WILL!*
THEREFORE--
*AND, YES, HE CAN. SEE HEROES FOR HIRE #5. --TOM
THEREFORE YOU'LL DESTROY THE ENTIRE PLANET--RISK A NEW WAR WITH THE ETERNALS OR EVEN THE CELESTIALS--
--JUST TO HANG ONTO YOUR JOB? C'MON, FATHER-- THAT'S WHY YOU'RE TRYING TO KILL THE KID--
--TO SAVE YOUR POLITICAL BUTT!
Being a powerful, intuitive, spiritual sorta fella, I assumed Ghaur knew what that meant.
KILL HIM!
THE GIRL IS YOUR KID-- BUT IF WORD GOT OUT THAT THE DEVIANT PRIESTLORD WAS, AH, COMMUNING WITH THE SISTERS--
NOW!! DESTROY HIM FOR HIS BLASPHEMY!!
MINE...OR YOURS? A SIMPLE DNA TEST WILL BREAK YOUR STRANGLEHOLD ON THESE PEOPLE--AND THAT'S THE END OF YOU.
BUT, IF YOU'D STOP THINKING LIKE A DESPOT AND THINK LIKE A LOBBYIST FOR A MOMENT--
--IN THE TRUE SPIRIT OF BELTWAY POLITICS, WE COULD PLAY "LET'S MAKE A DEAL..."

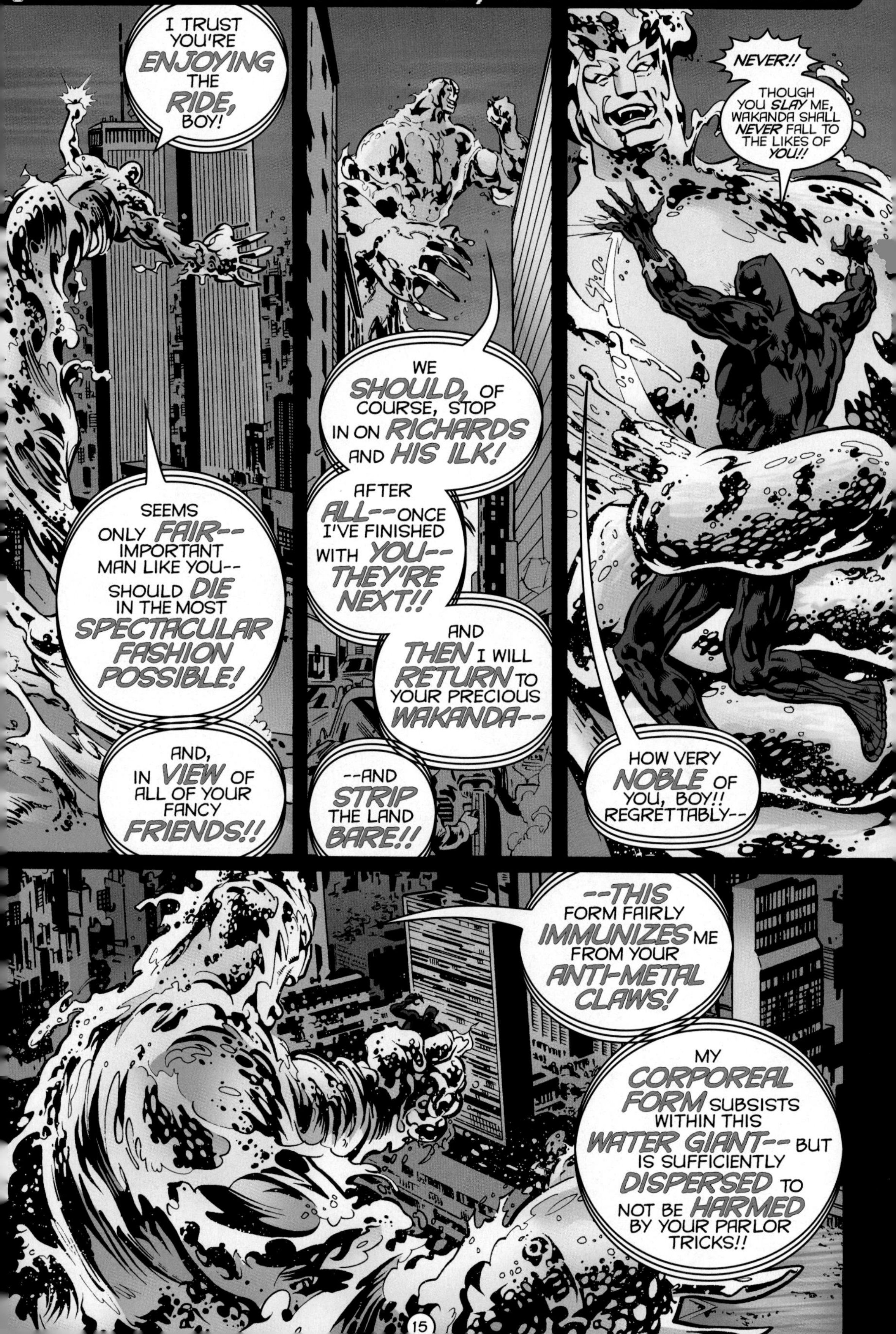
I TRUST YOU'RE ENJOYING THE RIDE, BOY!
SEEMS ONLY FAIR-- IMPORTANT MAN LIKE YOU-- SHOULD DIE IN THE MOST SPECTACULAR FASHION POSSIBLE!
AND, IN VIEW OF ALL OF YOUR FANCY FRIENDS!!
WE SHOULD, OF COURSE, STOP IN ON RICHARDS AND HIS ILK!
AFTER ALL--ONCE I'VE FINISHED WITH YOU-- THEY'RE NEXT!!
AND THEN I WILL RETURN TO YOUR PRECIOUS WAKANDA--
--AND STRIP THE LAND BARE!!
NEVER!!
THOUGH YOU SLAY ME, WAKANDA SHALL NEVER FALL TO THE LIKES OF YOU!!
HOW VERY NOBLE OF YOU, BOY!! REGRETTABLY--
--THIS FORM FAIRLY IMMUNIZES ME FROM YOUR ANTI-METAL CLAWS!
MY CORPOREAL FORM SUBSISTS WITHIN THIS WATER GIANT-- BUT IS SUFFICIENTLY DISPERSED TO NOT BE HARMED BY YOUR PARLOR TRICKS!!

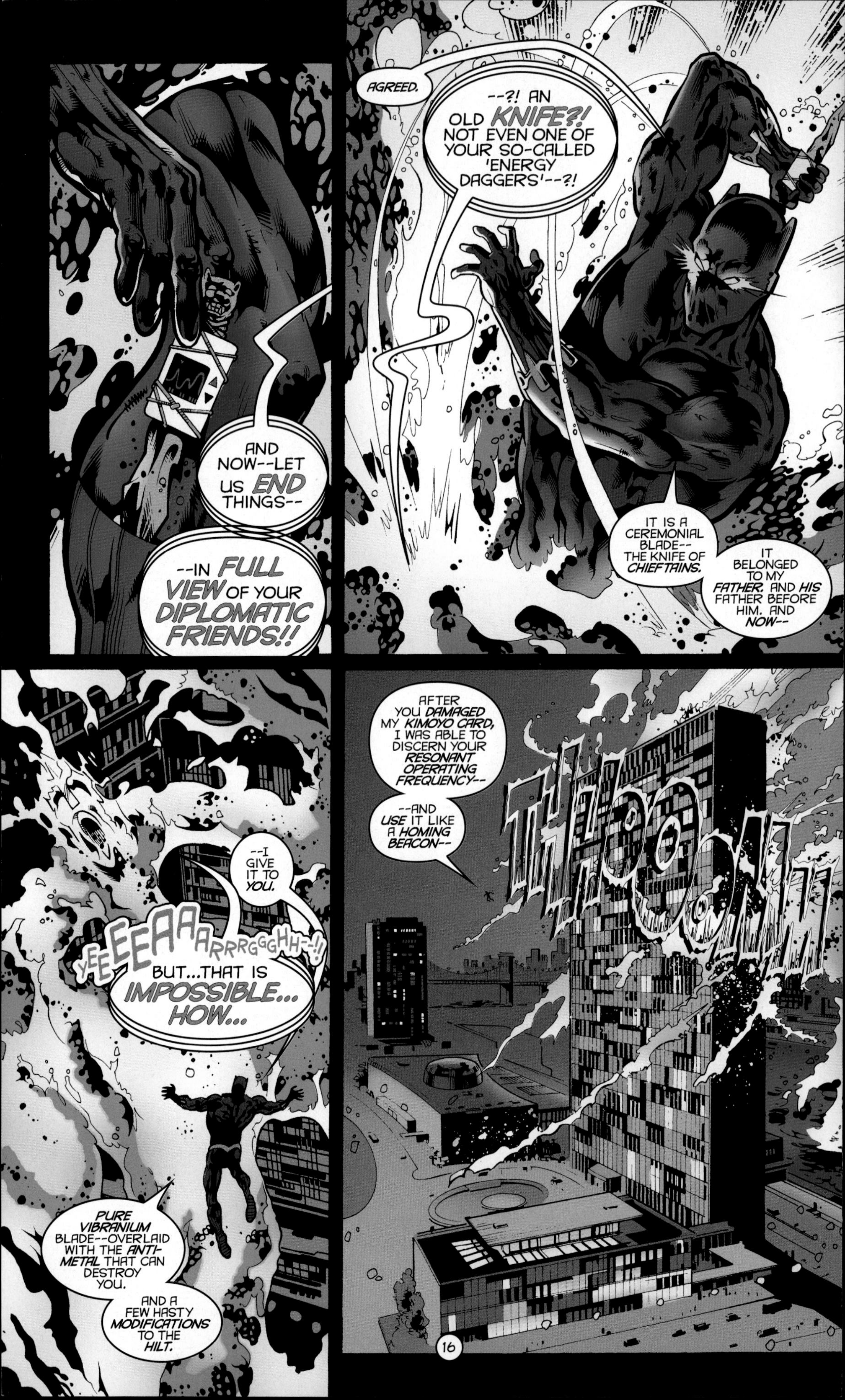
AND NOW--LET US END THINGS--
--IN FULL VIEW OF YOUR DIPLOMATIC FRIENDS!!
AGREED.
--?! AN OLD KNIFE?! NOT EVEN ONE OF YOUR SO-CALLED 'ENERGY DAGGERS'--?!
IT IS A CEREMONIAL BLADE--THE KNIFE OF CHIEFTAINS.
IT BELONGED TO MY FATHER. AND HIS FATHER BEFORE HIM. AND NOW--
--I GIVE IT TO YOU.
YEEEEAAAARRRGGGHH--!!
BUT...THAT IS IMPOSSIBLE... HOW...
PURE VIBRANIUM BLADE--OVERLAID WITH THE ANTI-METAL THAT CAN DESTROY YOU.
AND A FEW HASTY MODIFICATIONS TO THE HILT.
AFTER YOU DAMAGED MY KIMOYO CARD, I WAS ABLE TO DISCERN YOUR RESONANT OPERATING FREQUENCY--
--AND USE IT LIKE A HOMING BEACON--
THHOOOM

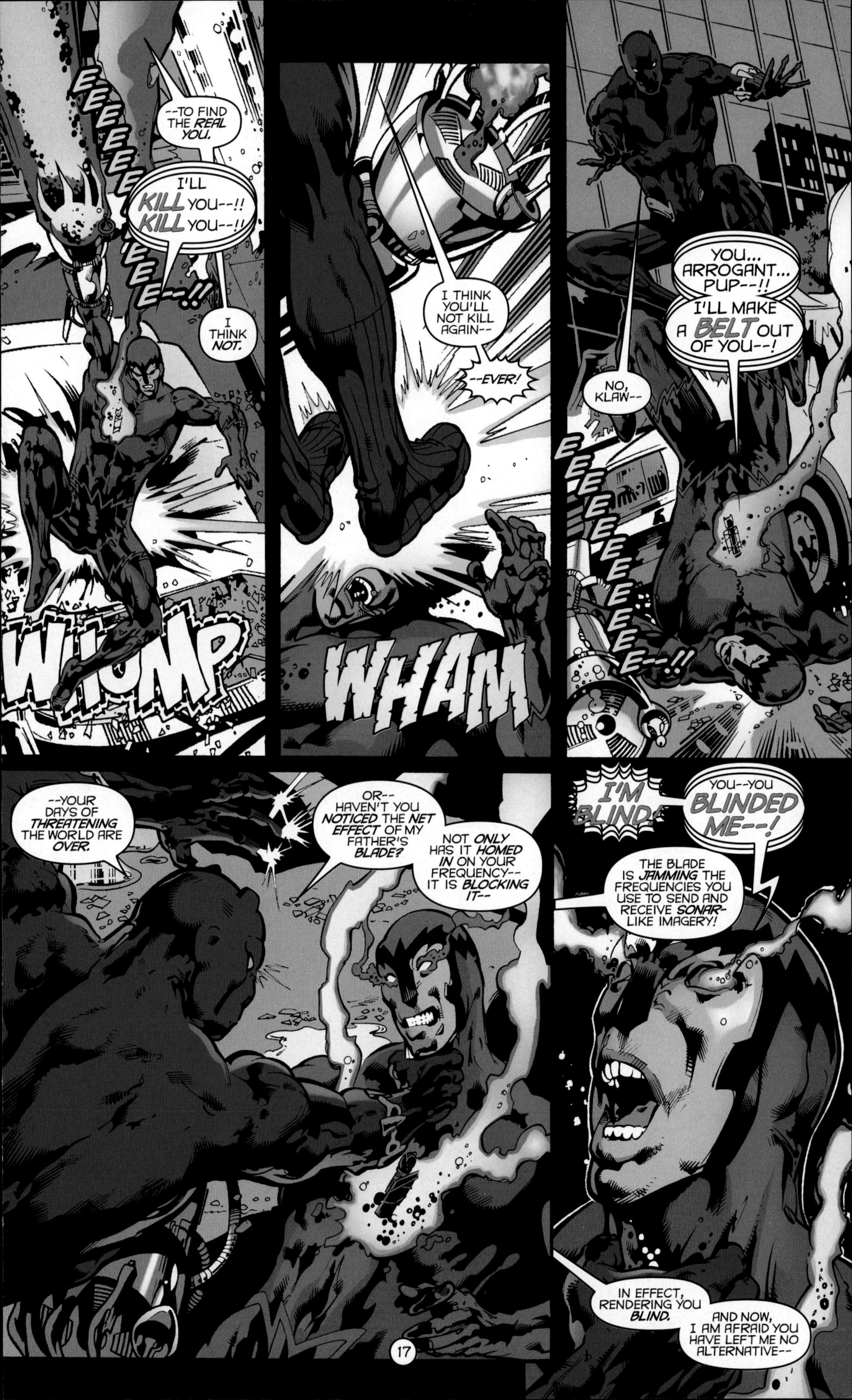
EEEEEEEEEE--!!
--TO FIND THE REAL YOU.
I'LL KILL YOU--!! KILL YOU--!!
I THINK NOT.
WHOMP
I THINK YOU'LL NOT KILL AGAIN--
--EVER!
WHAM
YOU... ARROGANT... PUP--!!
I'LL MAKE A BELT OUT OF YOU--!
NO, KLAW--
EEEEEEEEEEEE--!!
--YOUR DAYS OF THREATENING THE WORLD ARE OVER.
OR-- HAVEN'T YOU NOTICED THE NET EFFECT OF MY FATHER'S BLADE?
NOT ONLY HAS IT HOMED IN ON YOUR FREQUENCY-- IT IS BLOCKING IT--
I'M BLIND!
YOU--YOU BLINDED ME--!
THE BLADE IS JAMMING THE FREQUENCIES YOU USE TO SEND AND RECEIVE SONAR-LIKE IMAGERY!
IN EFFECT, RENDERING YOU BLIND.
AND NOW, I AM AFRAID YOU HAVE LEFT ME NO ALTERNATIVE--

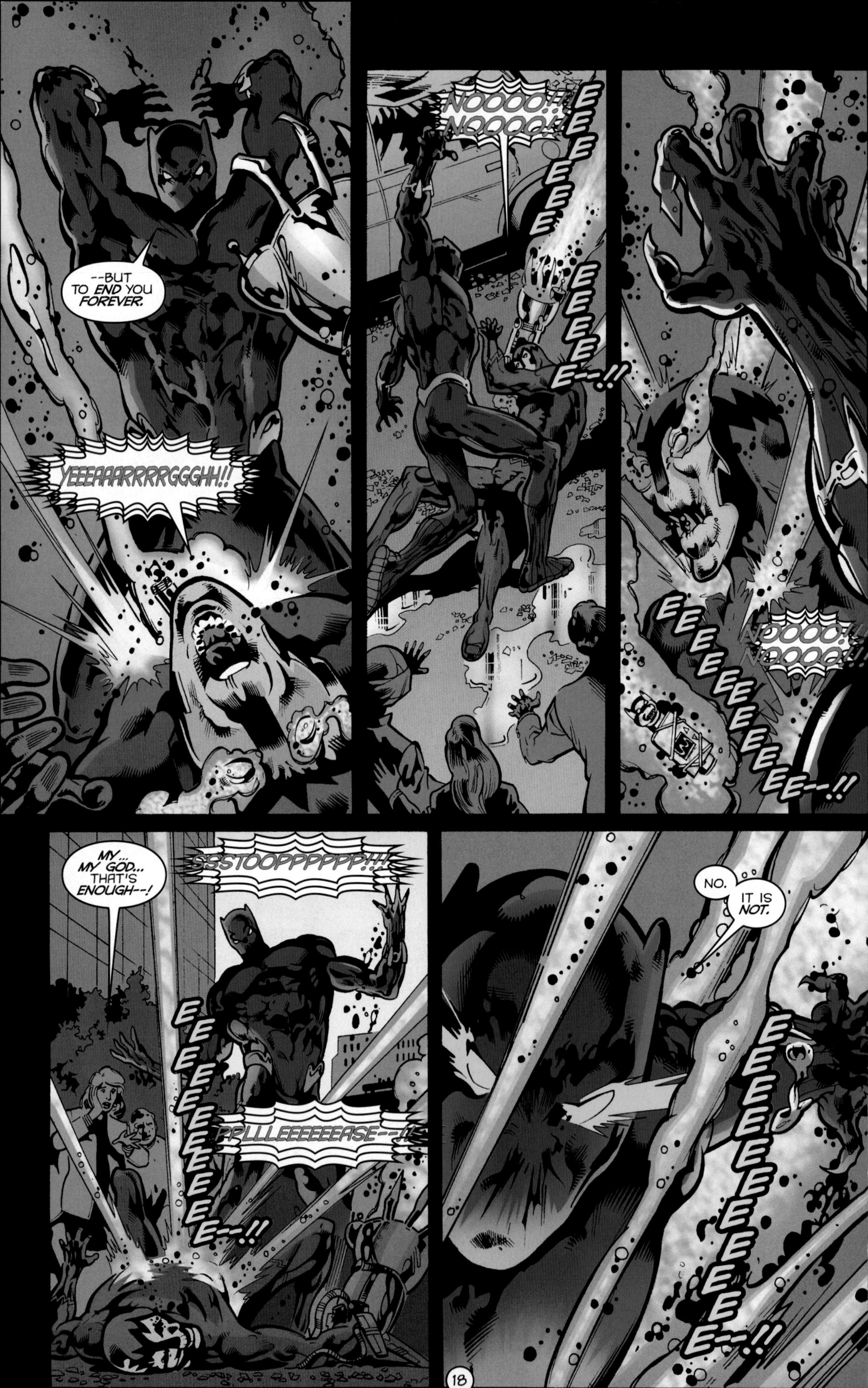
--BUT TO *END* YOU *FOREVER.*
YEEEAAARRRRGGGHH!!
NOOOO!!
NOOOO!!
EEEEEEEEEEEEE--!!
NOOOO!!
NOOOO!!
EEEEEEEEEEEEE--!!
MY... MY GOD... THAT'S *ENOUGH--!*
SSSTOOPPPPPPP!!!
EEEEEEEEEEEE--!!
PPLLLEEEEEEASE--!!
NO.
IT IS *NOT.*
EEEEEEEEEEEEEEE--!!

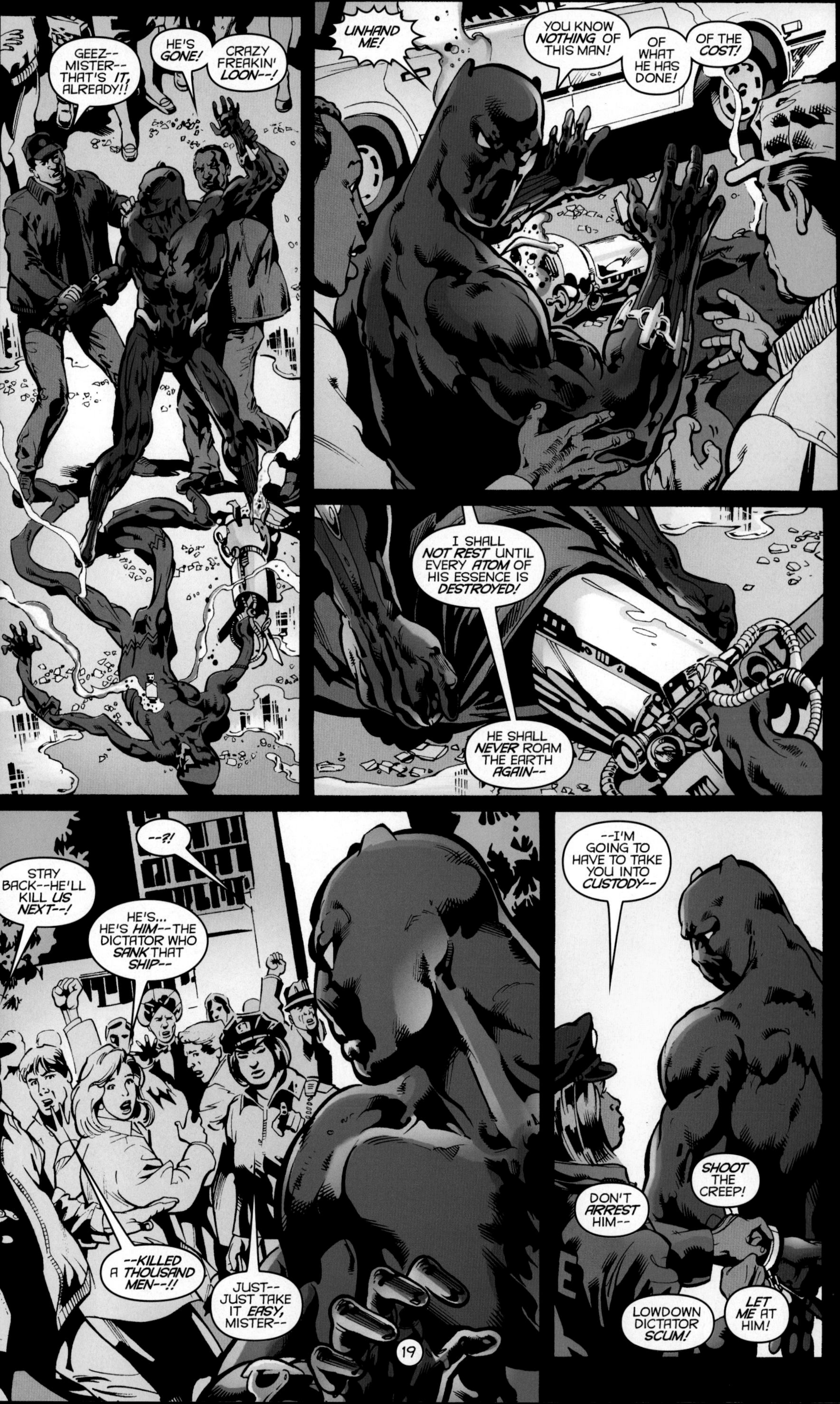

GEEZ--
MISTER--
THAT'S *IT*, ALREADY!!
HE'S *GONE!*
CRAZY FREAKIN' *LOON--!*
UNHAND ME!
YOU KNOW *NOTHING* OF THIS MAN!
OF WHAT HE HAS DONE!
OF THE *COST!*
I SHALL *NOT REST* UNTIL EVERY *ATOM* OF HIS ESSENCE IS *DESTROYED!*
HE SHALL *NEVER* ROAM THE EARTH *AGAIN--*
STAY BACK--HE'LL KILL *US NEXT--!*
--?!
HE'S... HE'S *HIM*--THE DICTATOR WHO *SANK* THAT *SHIP--*
--KILLED A THOUSAND MEN--!!
JUST-- JUST TAKE IT *EASY*, MISTER--
--I'M GOING TO HAVE TO TAKE YOU INTO *CUSTODY--*
DON'T *ARREST* HIM--
SHOOT THE CREEP!
LOWDOWN DICTATOR *SCUM!*
LET ME AT HIM!

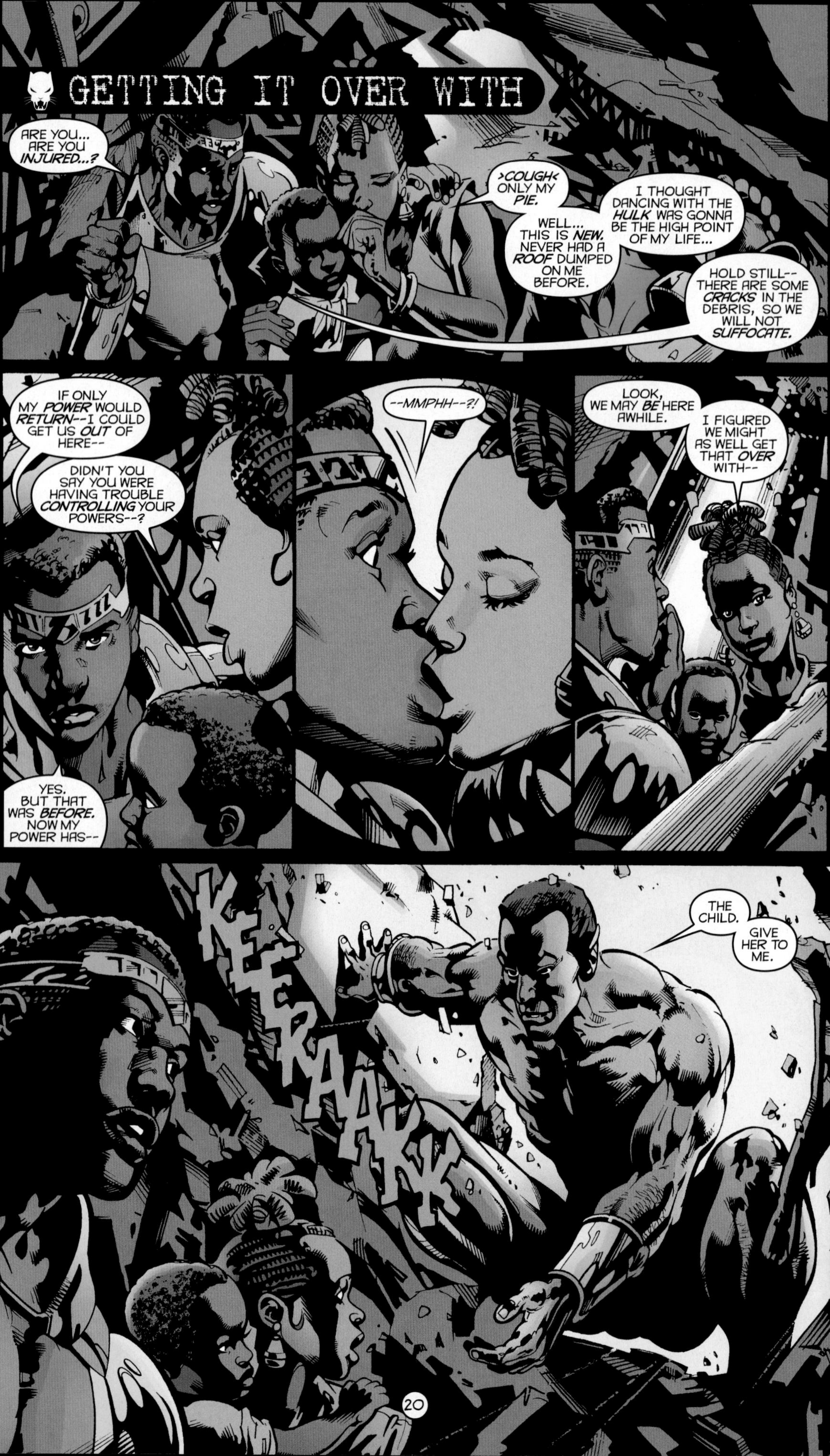

GETTING IT OVER WITH
ARE YOU... ARE YOU INJURED...?
>COUGH< ONLY MY PIE.
WELL... THIS IS NEW. NEVER HAD A ROOF DUMPED ON ME BEFORE.
I THOUGHT DANCING WITH THE HULK WAS GONNA BE THE HIGH POINT OF MY LIFE...
HOLD STILL-- THERE ARE SOME CRACKS IN THE DEBRIS, SO WE WILL NOT SUFFOCATE.
IF ONLY MY POWER WOULD RETURN--I COULD GET US OUT OF HERE--
DIDN'T YOU SAY YOU WERE HAVING TROUBLE CONTROLLING YOUR POWERS--?
YES. BUT THAT WAS BEFORE. NOW MY POWER HAS--
--MMPHH--?!
LOOK, WE MAY BE HERE AWHILE.
I FIGURED WE MIGHT AS WELL GET THAT OVER WITH--
KEERAAKK
THE CHILD.
GIVE HER TO ME.

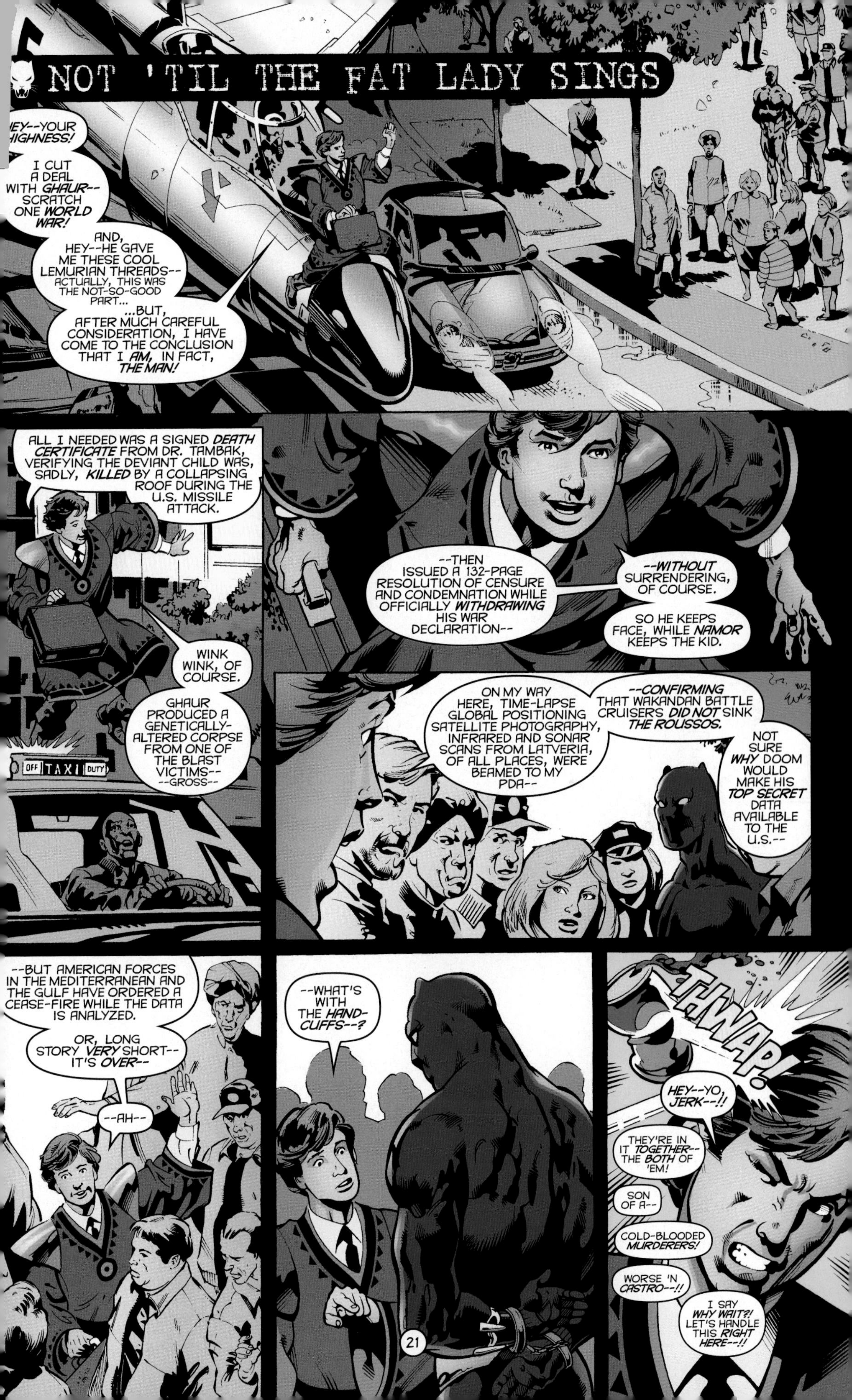
NOT 'TIL THE FAT LADY SINGS
HEY--YOUR HIGHNESS!
I CUT A DEAL WITH GHAUR-- SCRATCH ONE WORLD WAR!
AND, HEY--HE GAVE ME THESE COOL LEMURIAN THREADS-- ACTUALLY, THIS WAS THE NOT-SO-GOOD PART...
...BUT, AFTER MUCH CAREFUL CONSIDERATION, I HAVE COME TO THE CONCLUSION THAT I AM, IN FACT, THE MAN!
ALL I NEEDED WAS A SIGNED DEATH CERTIFICATE FROM DR. TAMBAK, VERIFYING THE DEVIANT CHILD WAS, SADLY, KILLED BY A COLLAPSING ROOF DURING THE U.S. MISSILE ATTACK.
WINK WINK, OF COURSE.
GHAUR PRODUCED A GENETICALLY-ALTERED CORPSE FROM ONE OF THE BLAST VICTIMS-- --GROSS--
OFF TAXI DUTY
--THEN ISSUED A 132-PAGE RESOLUTION OF CENSURE AND CONDEMNATION WHILE OFFICIALLY WITHDRAWING HIS WAR DECLARATION--
--WITHOUT SURRENDERING, OF COURSE.
SO HE KEEPS FACE, WHILE NAMOR KEEPS THE KID.
ON MY WAY HERE, TIME-LAPSE GLOBAL POSITIONING SATELLITE PHOTOGRAPHY, INFRARED AND SONAR SCANS FROM LATVERIA, OF ALL PLACES, WERE BEAMED TO MY PDA--
--CONFIRMING THAT WAKANDAN BATTLE CRUISERS DID NOT SINK THE ROUSSOS.
NOT SURE WHY DOOM WOULD MAKE HIS TOP SECRET DATA AVAILABLE TO THE U.S.--
--BUT AMERICAN FORCES IN THE MEDITERRANEAN AND THE GULF HAVE ORDERED A CEASE-FIRE WHILE THE DATA IS ANALYZED.
OR, LONG STORY VERY SHORT-- IT'S OVER--
--AH--
--WHAT'S WITH THE HAND-CUFFS--?
THWAP!
HEY--YO, JERK--!!
THEY'RE IN IT TOGETHER-- THE BOTH OF 'EM!
SON OF A--
COLD-BLOODED MURDERERS!
WORSE 'N CASTRO--!!
I SAY WHY WAIT?! LET'S HANDLE THIS RIGHT HERE--!!

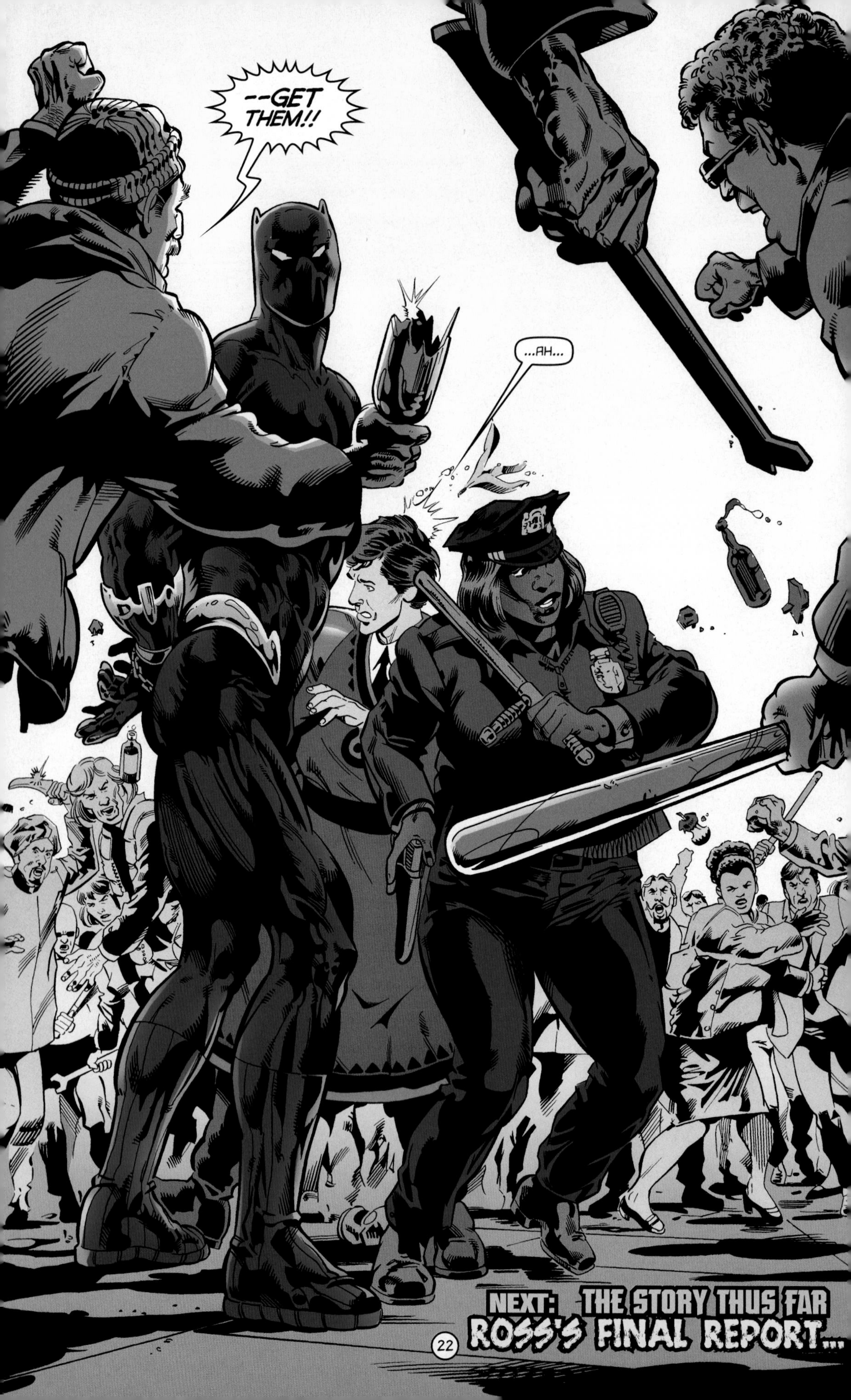
--GET THEM!!
...AH...
NEXT: THE STORY THUS FAR
ROSS'S FINAL REPORT...

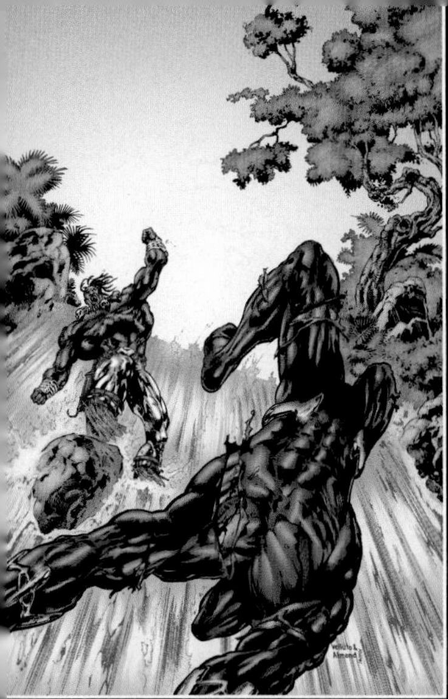

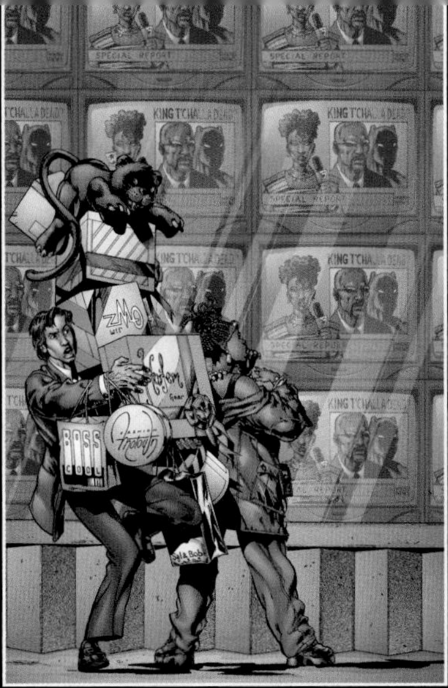
SPECIAL REPORT

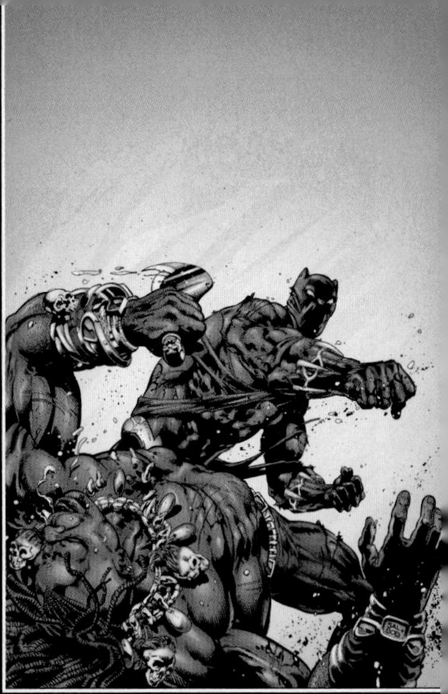

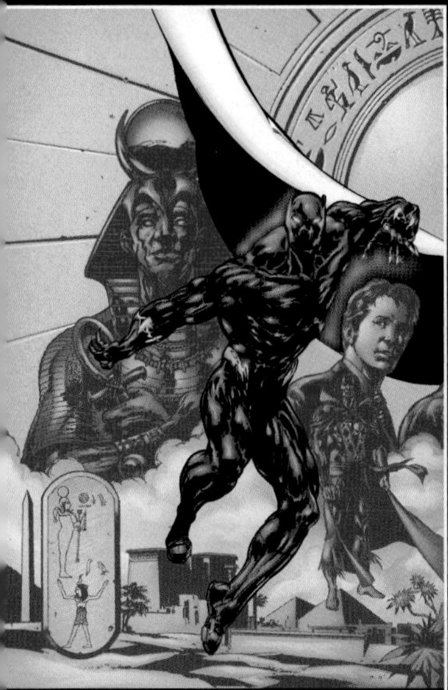

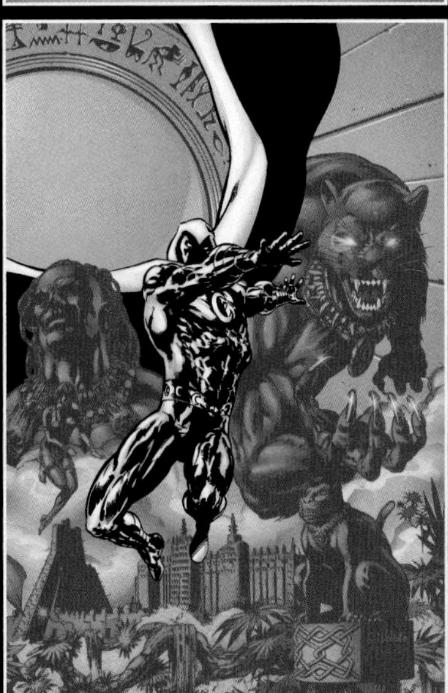

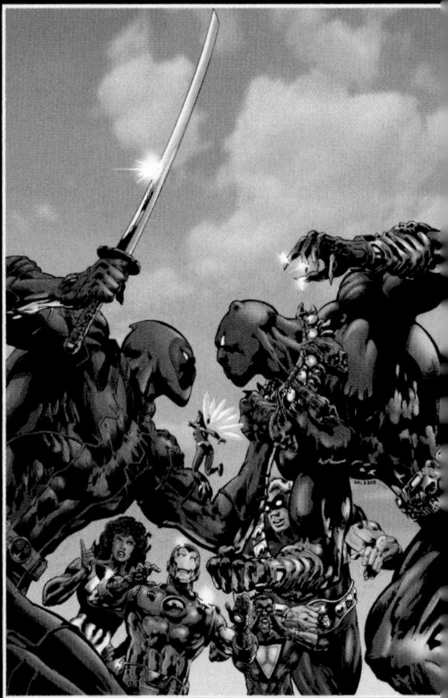

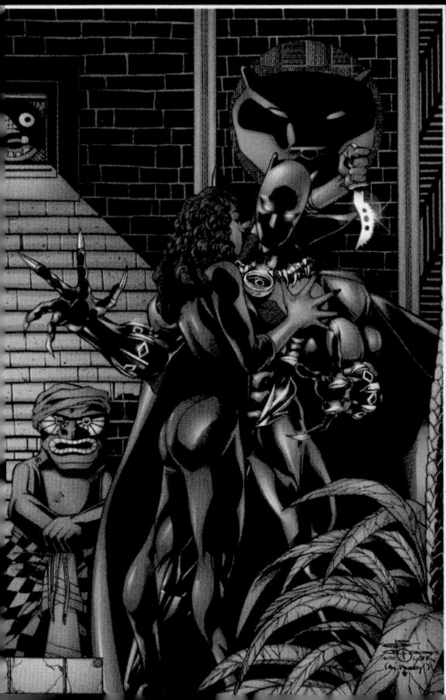

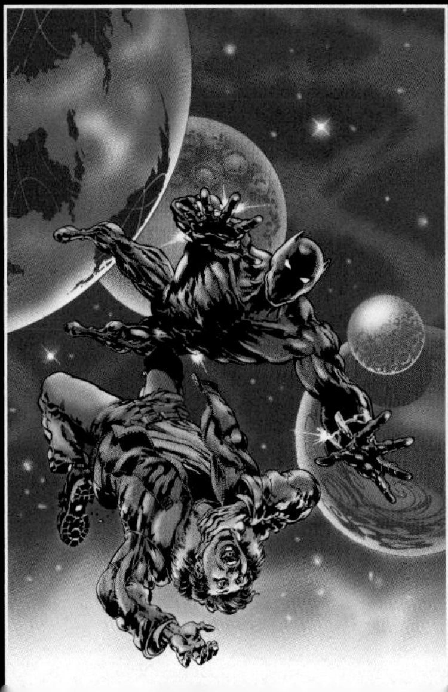

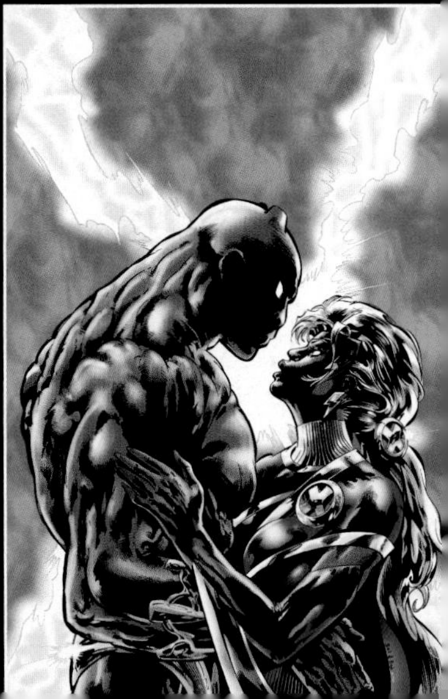

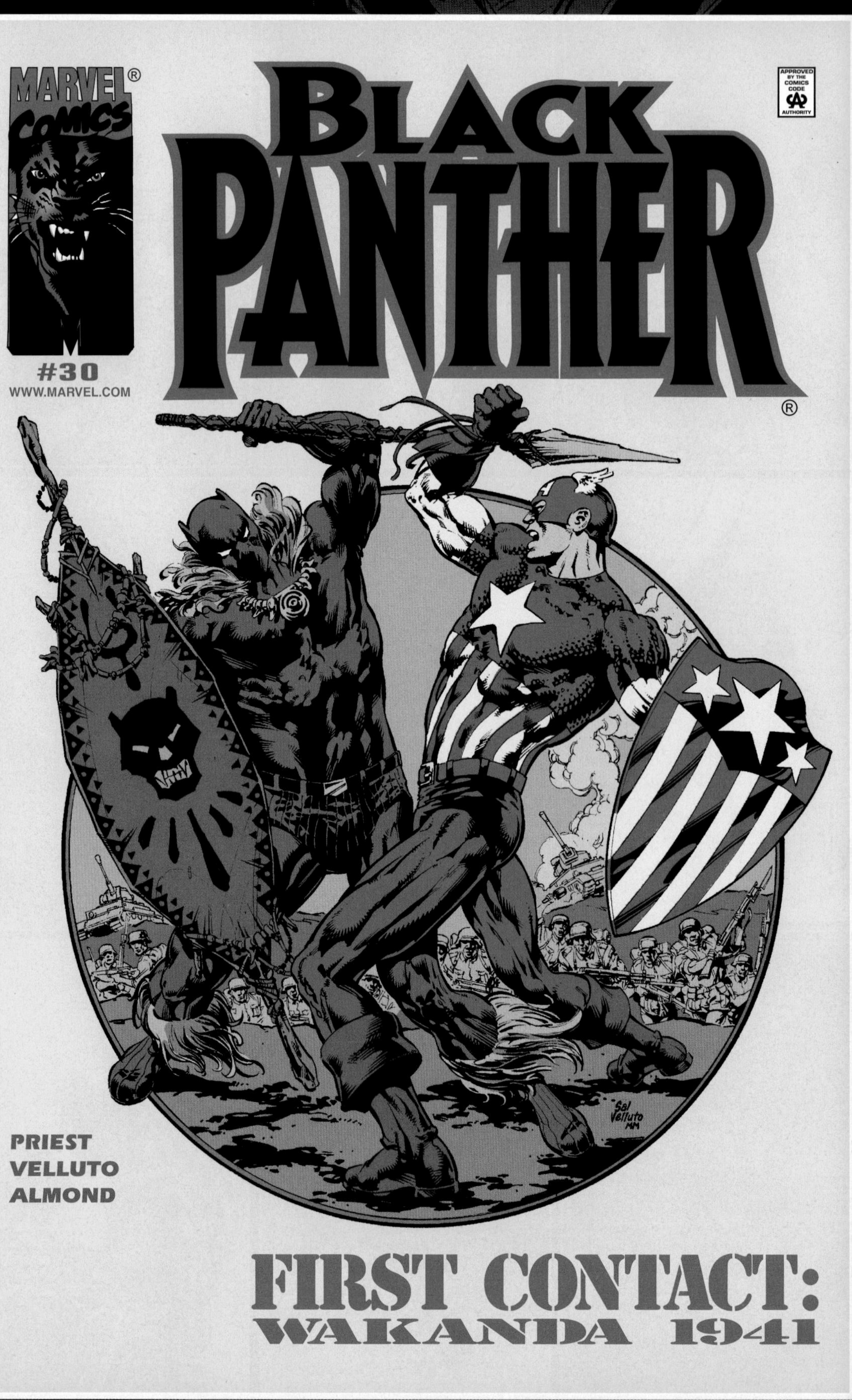
MARVEL® COMICS
APPROVED BY THE COMICS CODE AUTHORITY
BLACK PANTHER®
#30
WWW.MARVEL.COM
PRIEST
VELLUTO
ALMOND
FIRST CONTACT:
WAKANDA 1941

WITH THE SLEEKNESS OF THE JUNGLE CAT WHOSE NAME HE BEARS, T'CHALLA - KING OF WAKANDA - STALKS BOTH THE CONCRETE CITY AND THE UNDERGROWTH OF THE VELDT. SO IT HAS BEEN FOR COUNTLESS GENERATIONS OF WARRIOR KINGS, SO IT IS TODAY, AND SO IT SHALL BE FOR THE LAW DICTATES THAT ONLY THE SWIFT, THE SMART, AND THE STRONG SURVIVE! NOBLE CHAMPION. VIGILANT PROTECTOR. STAN LEE PRESENTS:

BLACK PANTHER IN
THE STORY THUS FAR

PRIEST &
NORM BREYFOGLE
storytellers
SHARPEFONT & PT letterer
VLM colorist
MARC SUMERAK assistant
TOM BREVOORT editor
JOE QUESADA chief

The story thus far:

Once upon a time there was a guy named HITLER who divided the globe between GOOD guys and BAD guys. And one day in early 1941, decades before the client was even born, one of the GOOD guys followed a hand-scrawled map into jungle WILDERNESS, looking for a secret kingdom.

He found a lot more than he was looking for.

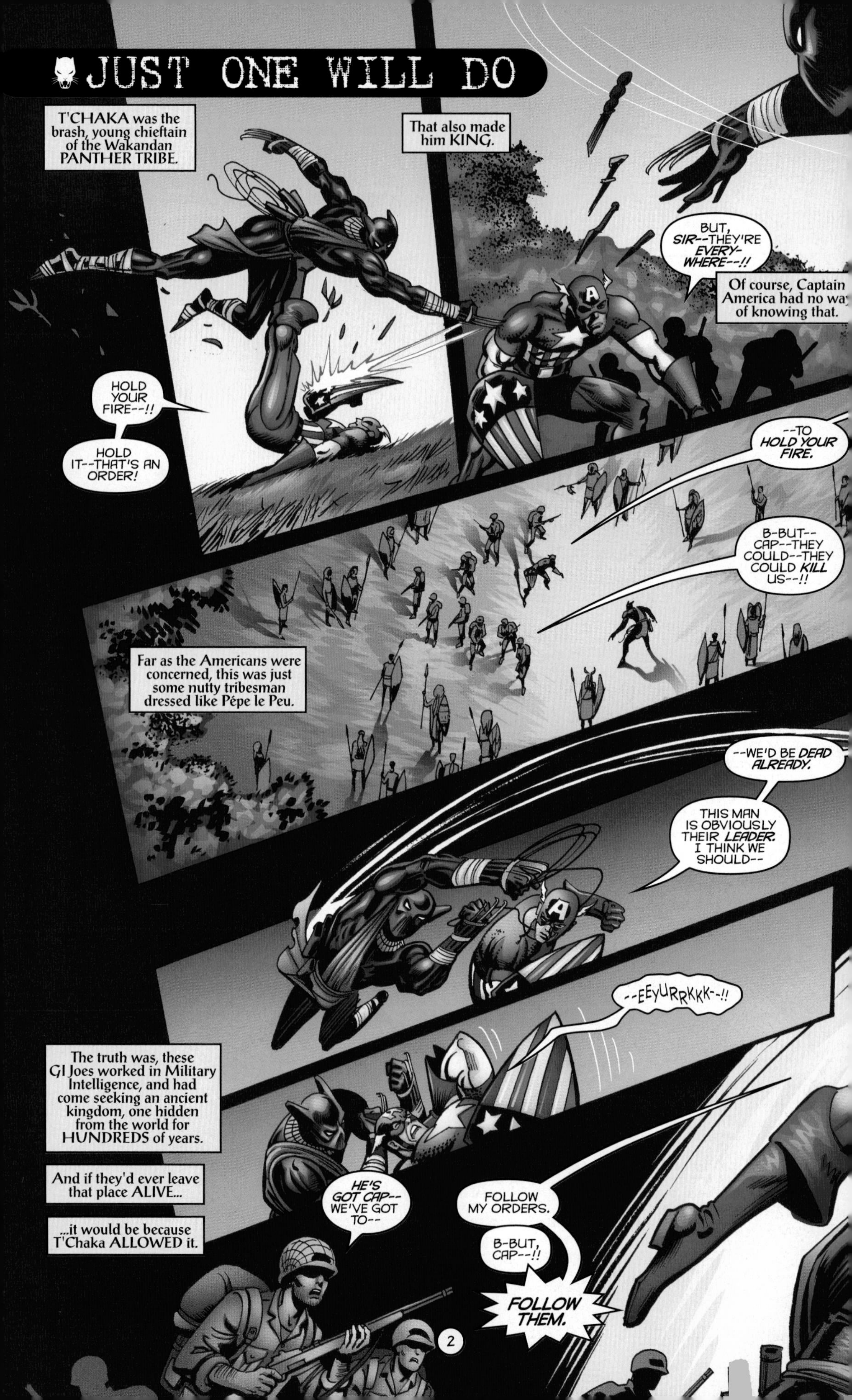
JUST ONE WILL DO
T'CHAKA was the brash, young chieftain of the Wakandan PANTHER TRIBE.
That also made him KING.
BUT, SIR--THEY'RE EVERY-WHERE--!!
Of course, Captain America had no way of knowing that.
HOLD YOUR FIRE--!!
HOLD IT--THAT'S AN ORDER!
--TO HOLD YOUR FIRE.
B-BUT-- CAP--THEY COULD--THEY COULD KILL US--!!
Far as the Americans were concerned, this was just some nutty tribesman dressed like Pépe le Peu.
--WE'D BE DEAD ALREADY.
THIS MAN IS OBVIOUSLY THEIR LEADER. I THINK WE SHOULD--
--EEYURRKKK--!!
The truth was, these GI Joes worked in Military Intelligence, and had come seeking an ancient kingdom, one hidden from the world for HUNDREDS of years.
And if they'd ever leave that place ALIVE...
...it would be because T'Chaka ALLOWED it.
HE'S GOT CAP-- WE'VE GOT TO--
FOLLOW MY ORDERS.
B-BUT, CAP--!!
FOLLOW THEM.

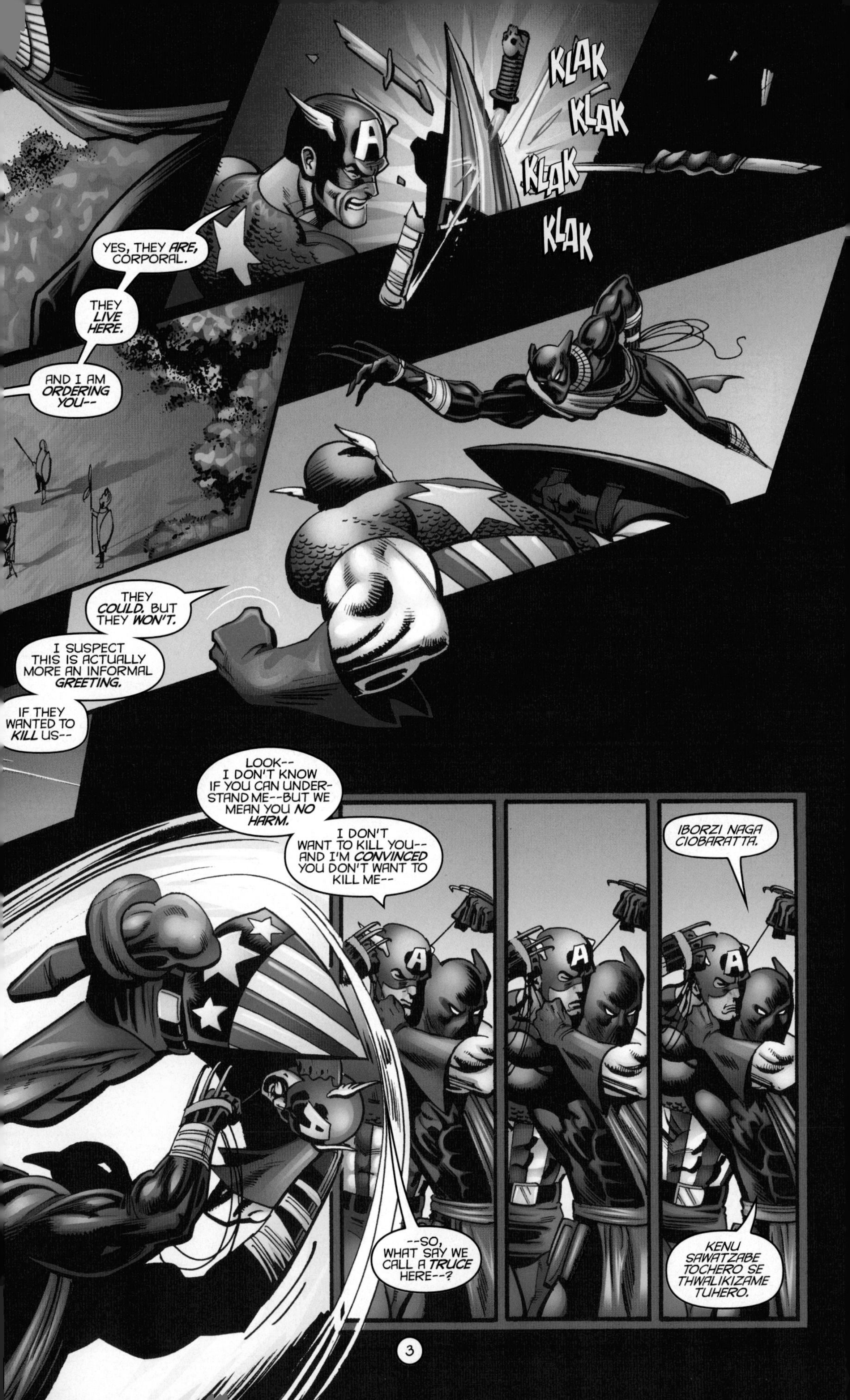
KLAK
KLAK
KLAK
KLAK
YES, THEY ARE, CORPORAL.
THEY LIVE HERE.
AND I AM ORDERING YOU--
THEY COULD. BUT THEY WON'T.
I SUSPECT THIS IS ACTUALLY MORE AN INFORMAL GREETING.
IF THEY WANTED TO KILL US--
LOOK-- I DON'T KNOW IF YOU CAN UNDERSTAND ME--BUT WE MEAN YOU NO HARM.
I DON'T WANT TO KILL YOU-- AND I'M CONVINCED YOU DON'T WANT TO KILL ME--
--SO, WHAT SAY WE CALL A TRUCE HERE--?
IBORZI NAGA CIOBARATTA.
KENU SAWATZABE TOCHERO SE THWALIKIZAME TUHERO.

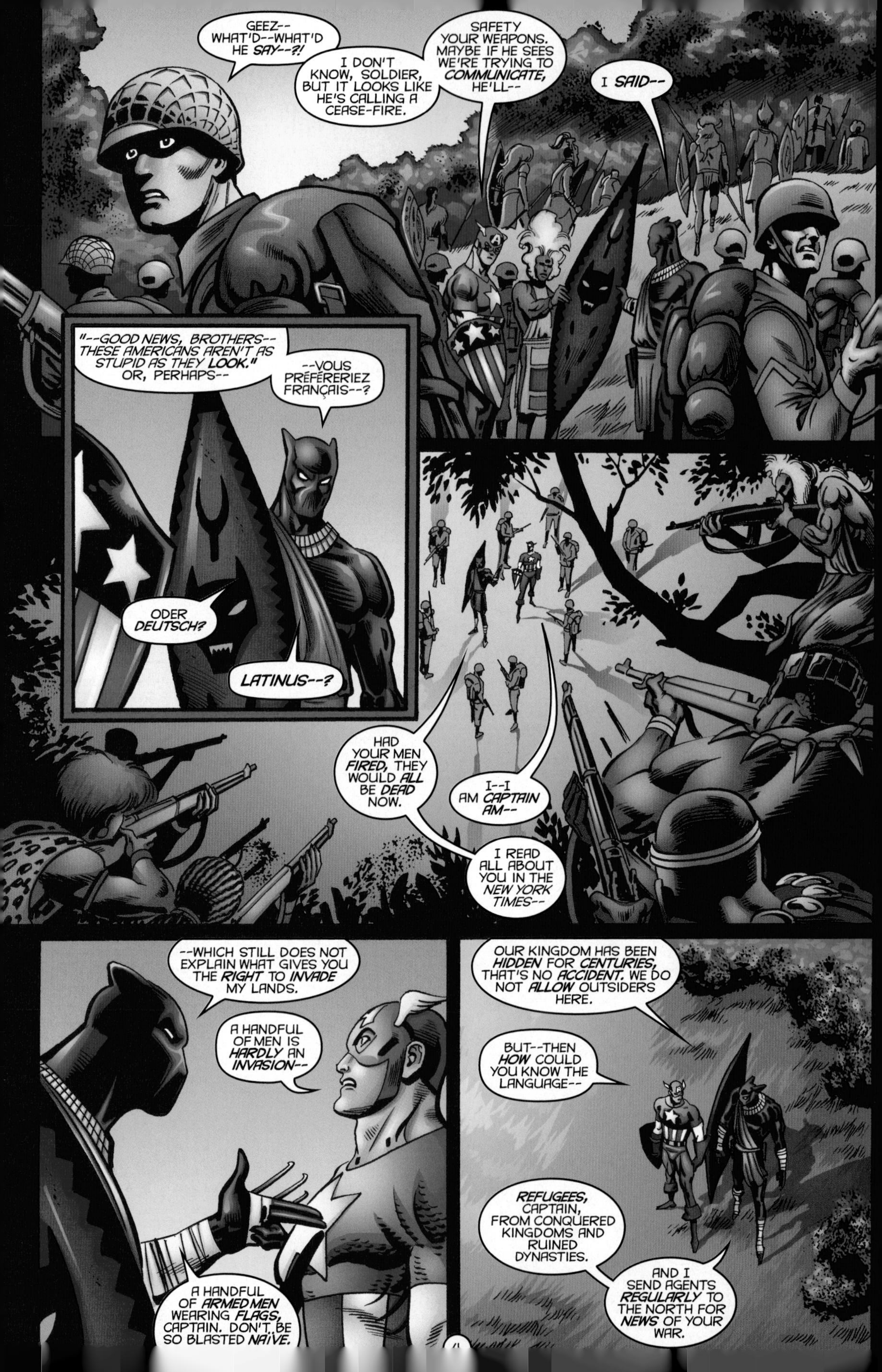
GEEZ-- WHAT'D--WHAT'D HE SAY--?!
I DON'T KNOW, SOLDIER, BUT IT LOOKS LIKE HE'S CALLING A CEASE-FIRE.
SAFETY YOUR WEAPONS. MAYBE IF HE SEES WE'RE TRYING TO COMMUNICATE, HE'LL--
I SAID--
"--GOOD NEWS, BROTHERS-- THESE AMERICANS AREN'T AS STUPID AS THEY LOOK." OR, PERHAPS--
--VOUS PRÉFÉRERIEZ FRANÇAIS--?
ODER DEUTSCH?
LATINUS--?
HAD YOUR MEN FIRED, THEY WOULD ALL BE DEAD NOW.
I--I AM CAPTAIN AM--
I READ ALL ABOUT YOU IN THE NEW YORK TIMES--
--WHICH STILL DOES NOT EXPLAIN WHAT GIVES YOU THE RIGHT TO INVADE MY LANDS.
A HANDFUL OF MEN IS HARDLY AN INVASION--
A HANDFUL OF ARMED MEN WEARING FLAGS, CAPTAIN. DON'T BE SO BLASTED NAÏVE.
OUR KINGDOM HAS BEEN HIDDEN FOR CENTURIES, THAT'S NO ACCIDENT. WE DO NOT ALLOW OUTSIDERS HERE.
BUT--THEN HOW COULD YOU KNOW THE LANGUAGE--
REFUGEES, CAPTAIN, FROM CONQUERED KINGDOMS AND RUINED DYNASTIES.
AND I SEND AGENTS REGULARLY TO THE NORTH FOR NEWS OF YOUR WAR.

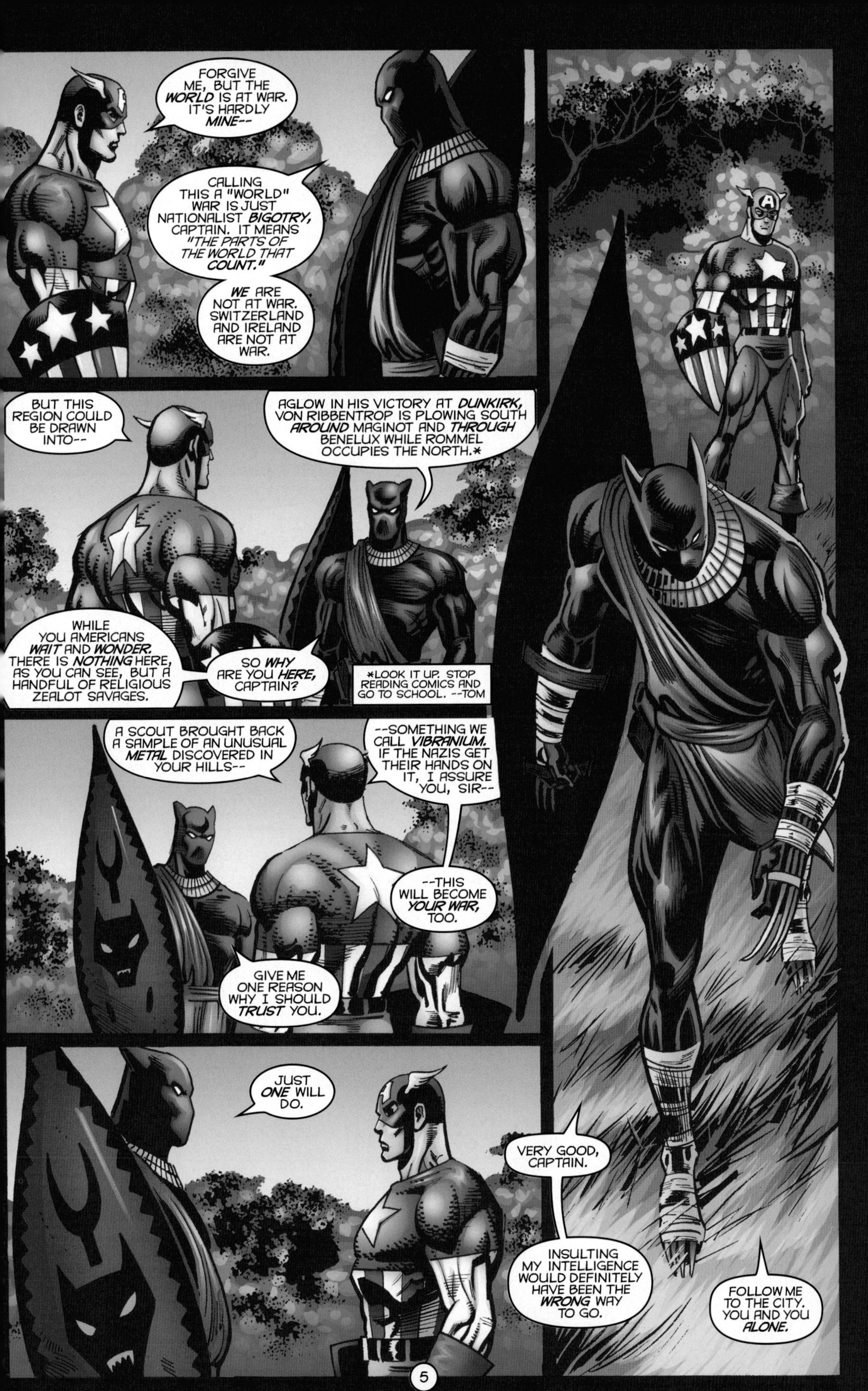
FORGIVE ME, BUT THE WORLD IS AT WAR. IT'S HARDLY MINE--
CALLING THIS A "WORLD" WAR IS JUST NATIONALIST BIGOTRY, CAPTAIN. IT MEANS "THE PARTS OF THE WORLD THAT COUNT."
WE ARE NOT AT WAR. SWITZERLAND AND IRELAND ARE NOT AT WAR.
BUT THIS REGION COULD BE DRAWN INTO--
AGLOW IN HIS VICTORY AT DUNKIRK, VON RIBBENTROP IS PLOWING SOUTH AROUND MAGINOT AND THROUGH BENELUX WHILE ROMMEL OCCUPIES THE NORTH.*
WHILE YOU AMERICANS WAIT AND WONDER. THERE IS NOTHING HERE, AS YOU CAN SEE, BUT A HANDFUL OF RELIGIOUS ZEALOT SAVAGES.
SO WHY ARE YOU HERE, CAPTAIN?
*LOOK IT UP. STOP READING COMICS AND GO TO SCHOOL. --TOM
A SCOUT BROUGHT BACK A SAMPLE OF AN UNUSUAL METAL DISCOVERED IN YOUR HILLS--
--SOMETHING WE CALL VIBRANIUM. IF THE NAZIS GET THEIR HANDS ON IT, I ASSURE YOU, SIR--
--THIS WILL BECOME YOUR WAR, TOO.
GIVE ME ONE REASON WHY I SHOULD TRUST YOU.
JUST ONE WILL DO.
VERY GOOD, CAPTAIN.
INSULTING MY INTELLIGENCE WOULD DEFINITELY HAVE BEEN THE WRONG WAY TO GO.
FOLLOW ME TO THE CITY. YOU AND YOU ALONE.

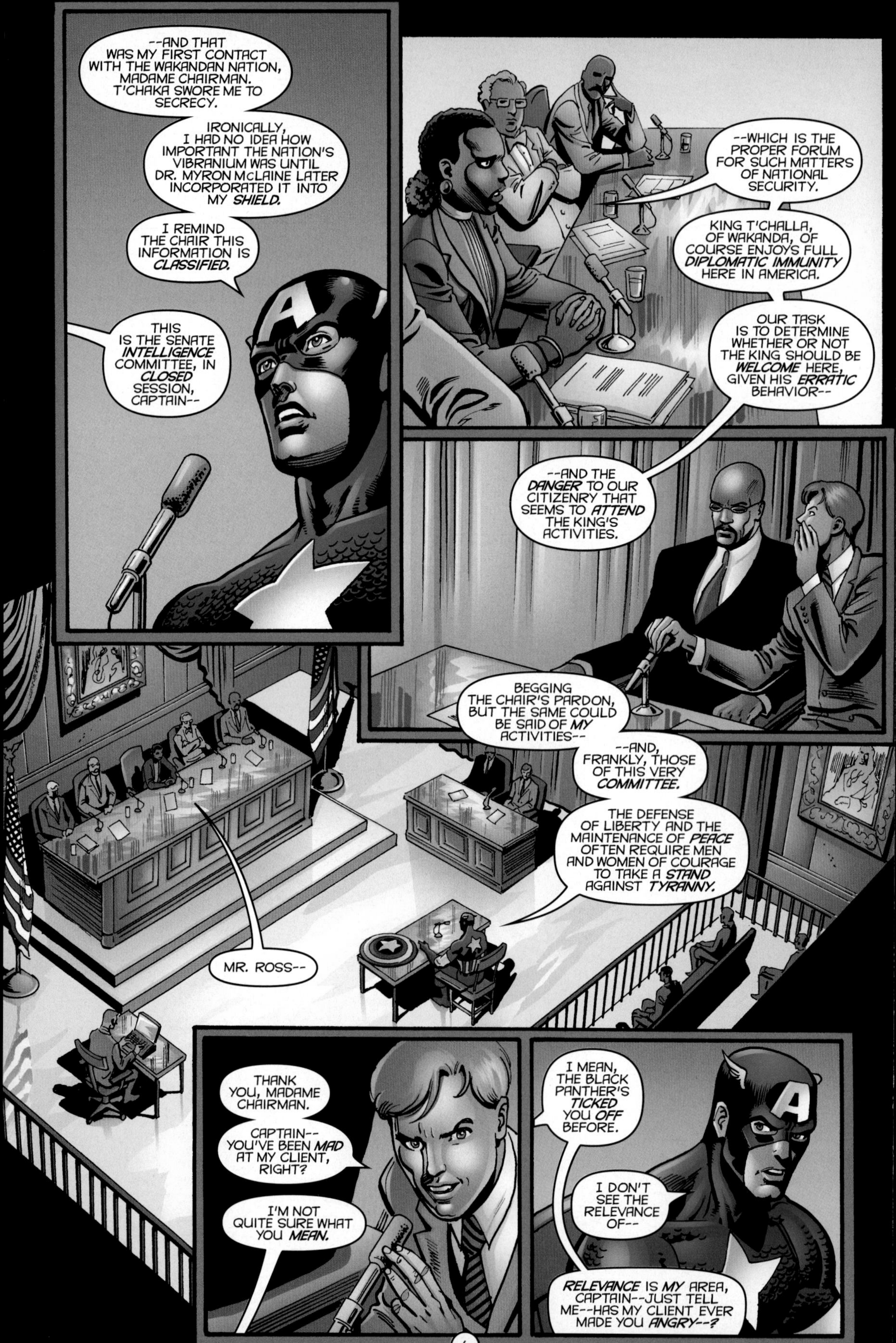
--AND THAT WAS MY FIRST CONTACT WITH THE WAKANDAN NATION, MADAME CHAIRMAN. T'CHAKA SWORE ME TO SECRECY.
IRONICALLY, I HAD NO IDEA HOW IMPORTANT THE NATION'S VIBRANIUM WAS UNTIL DR. MYRON McLAINE LATER INCORPORATED IT INTO MY SHIELD.
I REMIND THE CHAIR THIS INFORMATION IS CLASSIFIED.
THIS IS THE SENATE INTELLIGENCE COMMITTEE, IN CLOSED SESSION, CAPTAIN--
--WHICH IS THE PROPER FORUM FOR SUCH MATTERS OF NATIONAL SECURITY.
KING T'CHALLA, OF WAKANDA, OF COURSE ENJOYS FULL DIPLOMATIC IMMUNITY HERE IN AMERICA.
OUR TASK IS TO DETERMINE WHETHER OR NOT THE KING SHOULD BE WELCOME HERE, GIVEN HIS ERRATIC BEHAVIOR--
--AND THE DANGER TO OUR CITIZENRY THAT SEEMS TO ATTEND THE KING'S ACTIVITIES.
BEGGING THE CHAIR'S PARDON, BUT THE SAME COULD BE SAID OF MY ACTIVITIES--
--AND, FRANKLY, THOSE OF THIS VERY COMMITTEE.
THE DEFENSE OF LIBERTY AND THE MAINTENANCE OF PEACE OFTEN REQUIRE MEN AND WOMEN OF COURAGE TO TAKE A STAND AGAINST TYRANNY.
MR. ROSS--
THANK YOU, MADAME CHAIRMAN.
CAPTAIN-- YOU'VE BEEN MAD AT MY CLIENT, RIGHT?
I'M NOT QUITE SURE WHAT YOU MEAN.
I MEAN, THE BLACK PANTHER'S TICKED YOU OFF BEFORE.
I DON'T SEE THE RELEVANCE OF--
RELEVANCE IS MY AREA, CAPTAIN--JUST TELL ME--HAS MY CLIENT EVER MADE YOU ANGRY--?

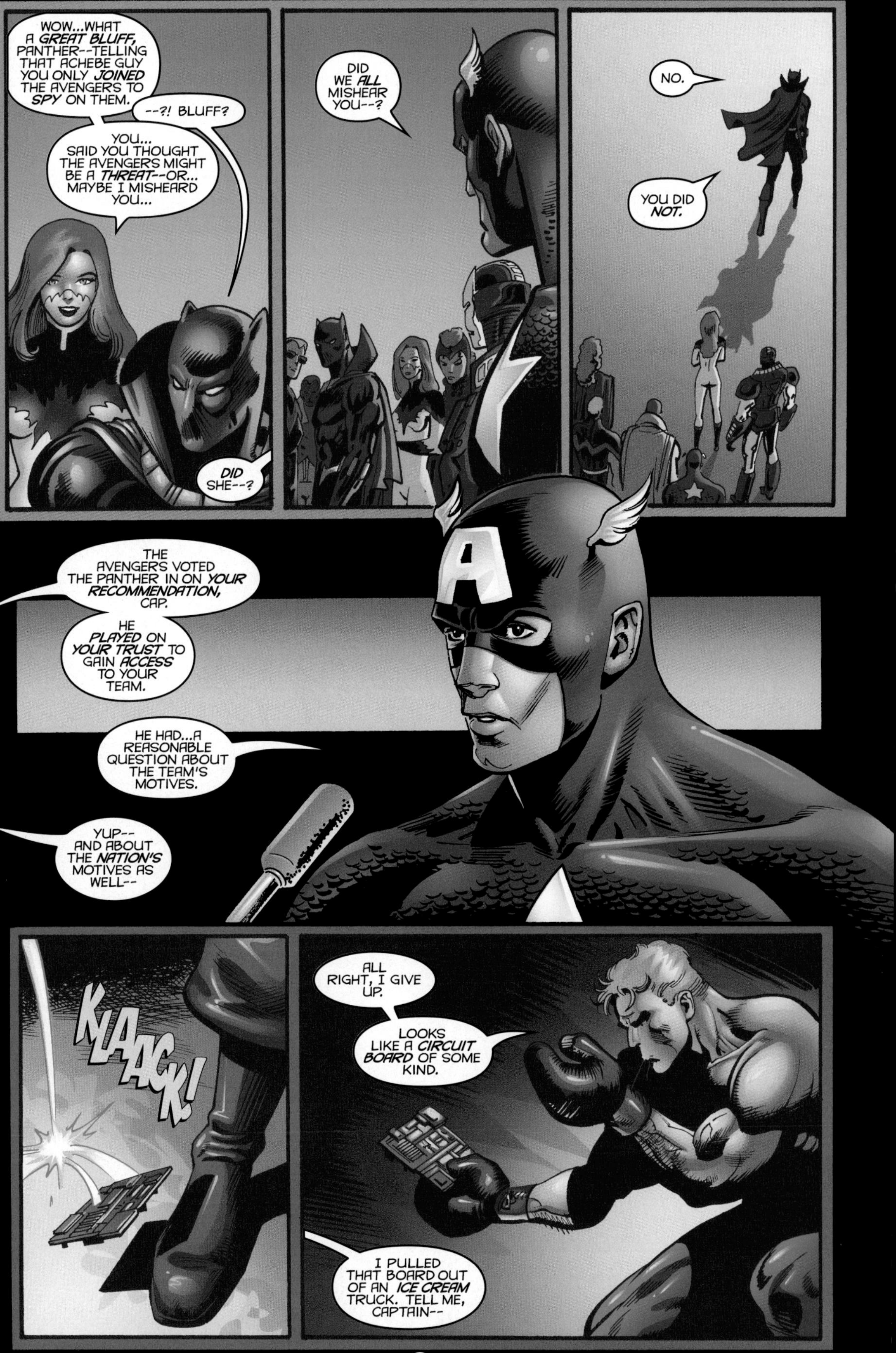
WOW...WHAT A GREAT BLUFF, PANTHER--TELLING THAT ACHEBE GUY YOU ONLY JOINED THE AVENGERS TO SPY ON THEM.
--?! BLUFF?
YOU... SAID YOU THOUGHT THE AVENGERS MIGHT BE A THREAT--OR... MAYBE I MISHEARD YOU...
DID SHE--?
DID WE ALL MISHEAR YOU--?
NO.
YOU DID NOT.
THE AVENGERS VOTED THE PANTHER IN ON YOUR RECOMMENDATION, CAP.
HE PLAYED ON YOUR TRUST TO GAIN ACCESS TO YOUR TEAM.
HE HAD...A REASONABLE QUESTION ABOUT THE TEAM'S MOTIVES.
YUP-- AND ABOUT THE NATION'S MOTIVES AS WELL--
KLAAACK!
ALL RIGHT, I GIVE UP.
LOOKS LIKE A CIRCUIT BOARD OF SOME KIND.
I PULLED THAT BOARD OUT OF AN ICE CREAM TRUCK. TELL ME, CAPTAIN--

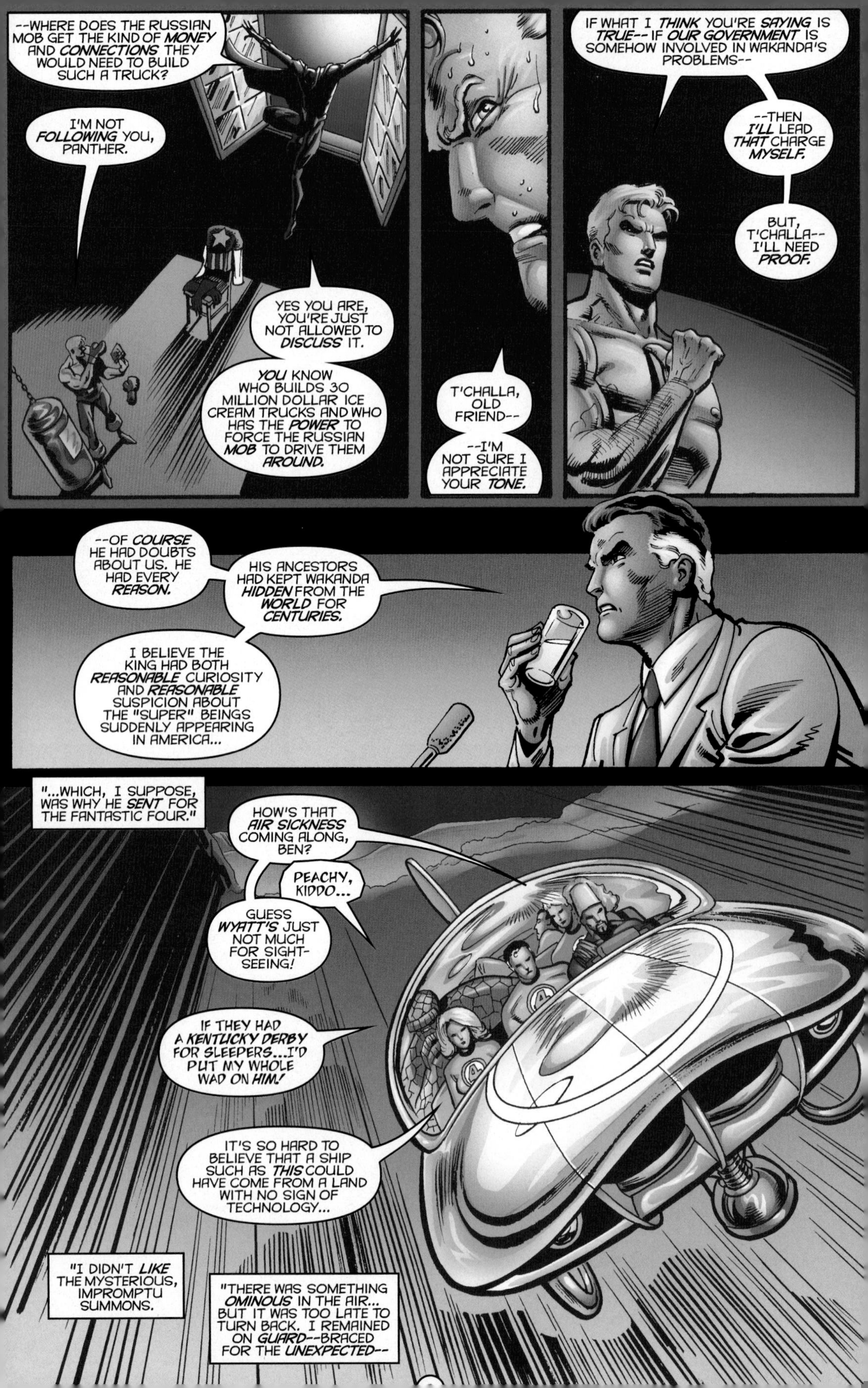
--WHERE DOES THE RUSSIAN MOB GET THE KIND OF MONEY AND CONNECTIONS THEY WOULD NEED TO BUILD SUCH A TRUCK?
I'M NOT FOLLOWING YOU, PANTHER.
YES YOU ARE, YOU'RE JUST NOT ALLOWED TO DISCUSS IT.
YOU KNOW WHO BUILDS 30 MILLION DOLLAR ICE CREAM TRUCKS AND WHO HAS THE POWER TO FORCE THE RUSSIAN MOB TO DRIVE THEM AROUND.
T'CHALLA, OLD FRIEND--
--I'M NOT SURE I APPRECIATE YOUR TONE.
IF WHAT I THINK YOU'RE SAYING IS TRUE-- IF OUR GOVERNMENT IS SOMEHOW INVOLVED IN WAKANDA'S PROBLEMS--
--THEN I'LL LEAD THAT CHARGE MYSELF.
BUT, T'CHALLA-- I'LL NEED PROOF.
--OF COURSE HE HAD DOUBTS ABOUT US. HE HAD EVERY REASON.
HIS ANCESTORS HAD KEPT WAKANDA HIDDEN FROM THE WORLD FOR CENTURIES.
I BELIEVE THE KING HAD BOTH REASONABLE CURIOSITY AND REASONABLE SUSPICION ABOUT THE "SUPER" BEINGS SUDDENLY APPEARING IN AMERICA...
"...WHICH, I SUPPOSE, WAS WHY HE SENT FOR THE FANTASTIC FOUR."
HOW'S THAT AIR SICKNESS COMING ALONG, BEN?
PEACHY, KIDDO...
GUESS WYATT'S JUST NOT MUCH FOR SIGHT-SEEING!
IF THEY HAD A KENTUCKY DERBY FOR SLEEPERS...I'D PUT MY WHOLE WAD ON HIM!
IT'S SO HARD TO BELIEVE THAT A SHIP SUCH AS THIS COULD HAVE COME FROM A LAND WITH NO SIGN OF TECHNOLOGY...
"I DIDN'T LIKE THE MYSTERIOUS, IMPROMPTU SUMMONS.
"THERE WAS SOMETHING OMINOUS IN THE AIR... BUT IT WAS TOO LATE TO TURN BACK. I REMAINED ON GUARD--BRACED FOR THE UNEXPECTED--

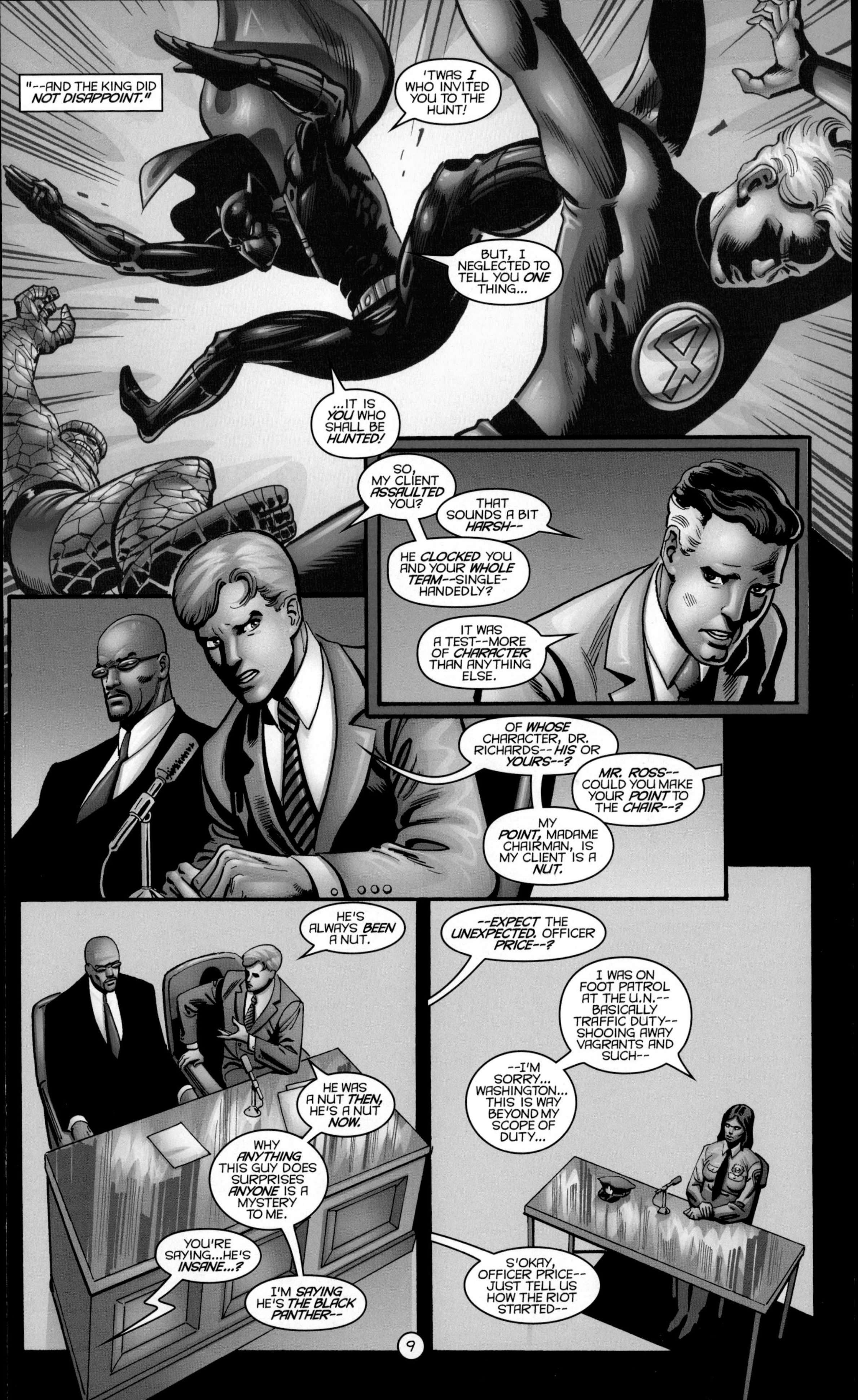
"--AND THE KING DID NOT DISAPPOINT."
'TWAS I WHO INVITED YOU TO THE HUNT!
BUT, I NEGLECTED TO TELL YOU ONE THING...
...IT IS YOU WHO SHALL BE HUNTED!
SO, MY CLIENT ASSAULTED YOU?
THAT SOUNDS A BIT HARSH--
HE CLOCKED YOU AND YOUR WHOLE TEAM--SINGLE-HANDEDLY?
IT WAS A TEST--MORE OF CHARACTER THAN ANYTHING ELSE.
OF WHOSE CHARACTER, DR. RICHARDS--HIS OR YOURS--?
MR. ROSS--COULD YOU MAKE YOUR POINT TO THE CHAIR--?
MY POINT, MADAME CHAIRMAN, IS MY CLIENT IS A NUT.
HE'S ALWAYS BEEN A NUT.
HE WAS A NUT THEN, HE'S A NUT NOW.
WHY ANYTHING THIS GUY DOES SURPRISES ANYONE IS A MYSTERY TO ME.
YOU'RE SAYING...HE'S INSANE...?
I'M SAYING HE'S THE BLACK PANTHER--
--EXPECT THE UNEXPECTED, OFFICER PRICE--?
I WAS ON FOOT PATROL AT THE U.N.--BASICALLY TRAFFIC DUTY--SHOOING AWAY VAGRANTS AND SUCH--
--I'M SORRY... WASHINGTON... THIS IS WAY BEYOND MY SCOPE OF DUTY...
S'OKAY, OFFICER PRICE--JUST TELL US HOW THE RIOT STARTED--

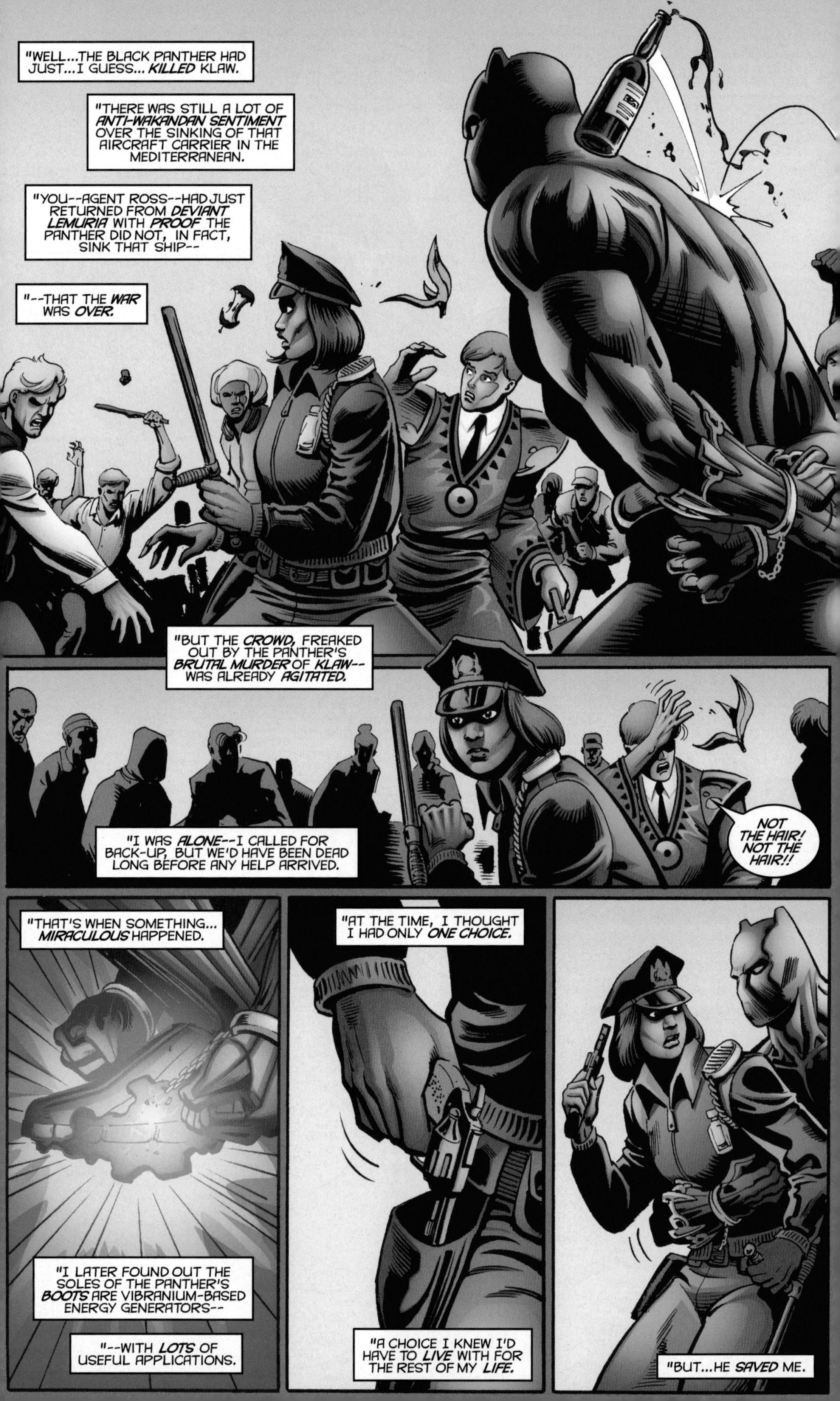
"WELL...THE BLACK PANTHER HAD JUST...I GUESS... KILLED KLAW.
"THERE WAS STILL A LOT OF ANTI-WAKANDAN SENTIMENT OVER THE SINKING OF THAT AIRCRAFT CARRIER IN THE MEDITERRANEAN.
"YOU--AGENT ROSS--HAD JUST RETURNED FROM DEVIANT LEMURIA WITH PROOF THE PANTHER DID NOT, IN FACT, SINK THAT SHIP--
"--THAT THE WAR WAS OVER.
"BUT THE CROWD, FREAKED OUT BY THE PANTHER'S BRUTAL MURDER OF KLAW-- WAS ALREADY AGITATED.
"I WAS ALONE--I CALLED FOR BACK-UP, BUT WE'D HAVE BEEN DEAD LONG BEFORE ANY HELP ARRIVED.
NOT THE HAIR! NOT THE HAIR!!
"THAT'S WHEN SOMETHING... MIRACULOUS HAPPENED.
"I LATER FOUND OUT THE SOLES OF THE PANTHER'S BOOTS ARE VIBRANIUM-BASED ENERGY GENERATORS--
"--WITH LOTS OF USEFUL APPLICATIONS.
"AT THE TIME, I THOUGHT I HAD ONLY ONE CHOICE.
"A CHOICE I KNEW I'D HAVE TO LIVE WITH FOR THE REST OF MY LIFE.
"BUT...HE SAVED ME.

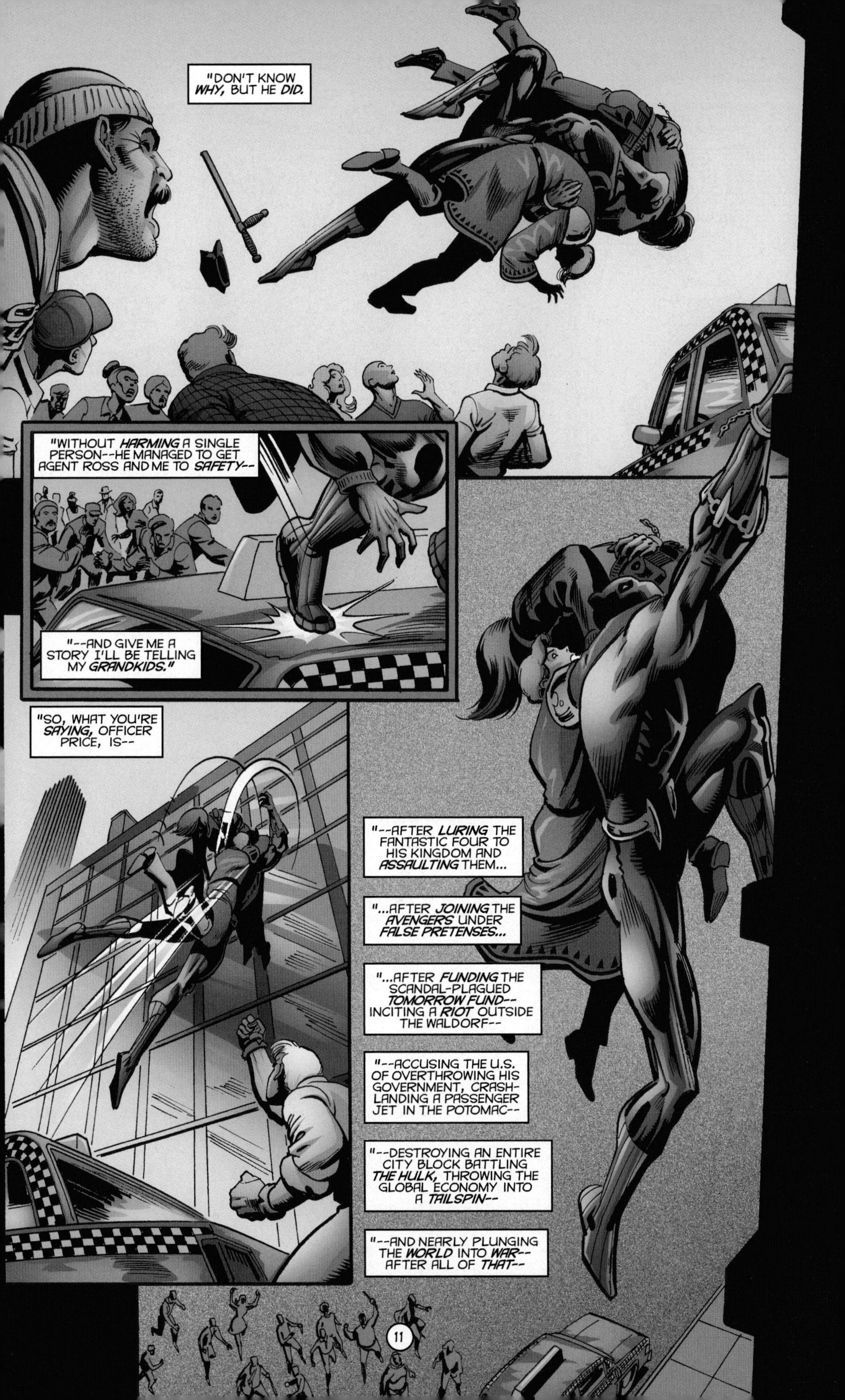
"DON'T KNOW WHY, BUT HE DID.
"WITHOUT HARMING A SINGLE PERSON--HE MANAGED TO GET AGENT ROSS AND ME TO SAFETY--
"--AND GIVE ME A STORY I'LL BE TELLING MY GRANDKIDS."
"SO, WHAT YOU'RE SAYING, OFFICER PRICE, IS--
"--AFTER LURING THE FANTASTIC FOUR TO HIS KINGDOM AND ASSAULTING THEM...
"...AFTER JOINING THE AVENGERS UNDER FALSE PRETENSES...
"...AFTER FUNDING THE SCANDAL-PLAGUED TOMORROW FUND--INCITING A RIOT OUTSIDE THE WALDORF--
"--ACCUSING THE U.S. OF OVERTHROWING HIS GOVERNMENT, CRASH-LANDING A PASSENGER JET IN THE POTOMAC--
"--DESTROYING AN ENTIRE CITY BLOCK BATTLING THE HULK, THROWING THE GLOBAL ECONOMY INTO A TAILSPIN--
"--AND NEARLY PLUNGING THE WORLD INTO WAR--AFTER ALL OF THAT--

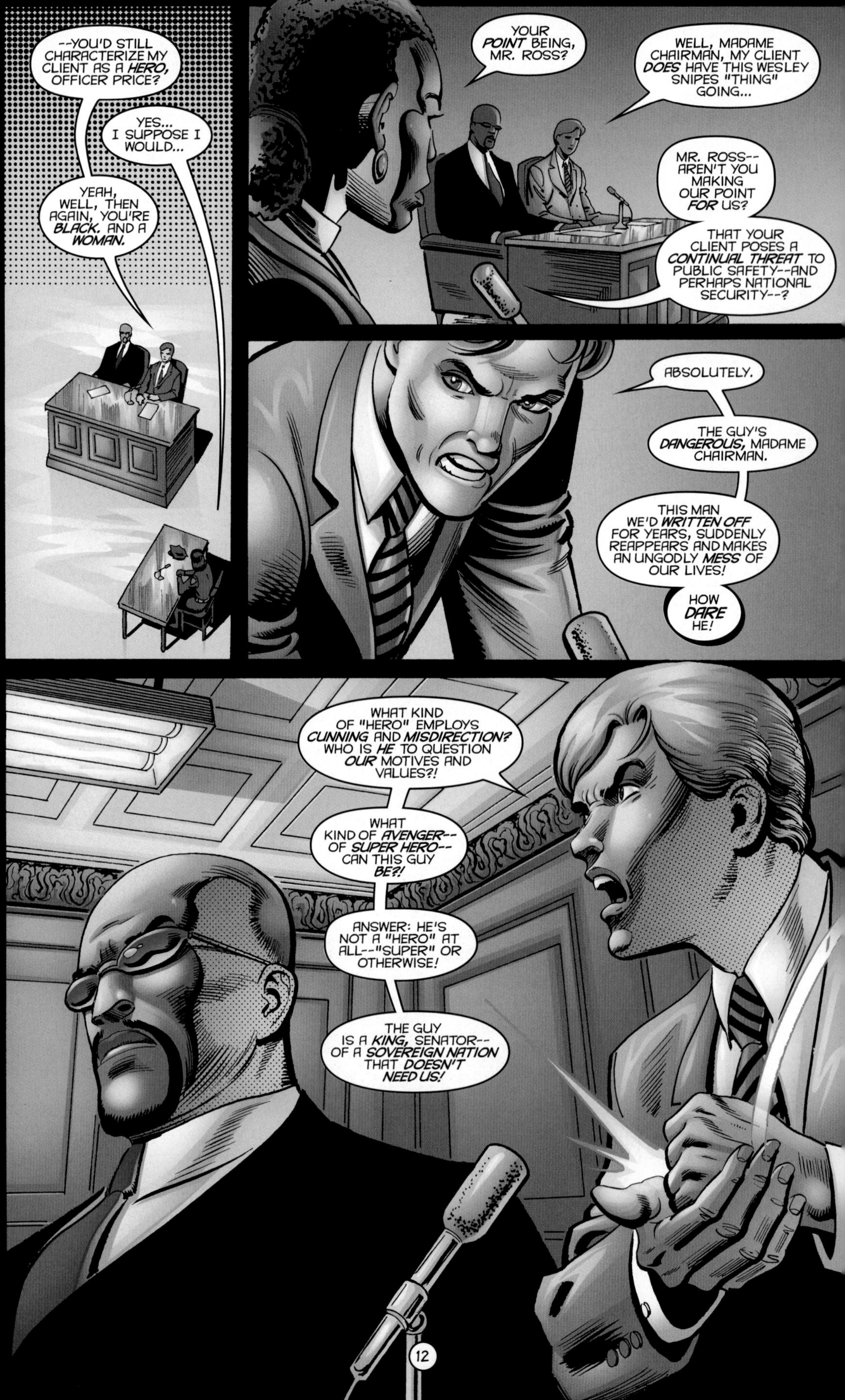

--YOU'D STILL CHARACTERIZE MY CLIENT AS A HERO, OFFICER PRICE?
YES... I SUPPOSE I WOULD...
YEAH, WELL, THEN AGAIN, YOU'RE BLACK. AND A WOMAN.
YOUR POINT BEING, MR. ROSS?
WELL, MADAME CHAIRMAN, MY CLIENT DOES HAVE THIS WESLEY SNIPES "THING" GOING...
MR. ROSS-- AREN'T YOU MAKING OUR POINT FOR US?
THAT YOUR CLIENT POSES A CONTINUAL THREAT TO PUBLIC SAFETY--AND PERHAPS NATIONAL SECURITY--?
ABSOLUTELY.
THE GUY'S DANGEROUS, MADAME CHAIRMAN.
THIS MAN WE'D WRITTEN OFF FOR YEARS, SUDDENLY REAPPEARS AND MAKES AN UNGODLY MESS OF OUR LIVES!
HOW DARE HE!
WHAT KIND OF "HERO" EMPLOYS CUNNING AND MISDIRECTION? WHO IS HE TO QUESTION OUR MOTIVES AND VALUES?!
WHAT KIND OF AVENGER-- OF SUPER HERO-- CAN THIS GUY BE?!
ANSWER: HE'S NOT A "HERO" AT ALL--"SUPER" OR OTHERWISE!
THE GUY IS A KING, SENATOR-- OF A SOVEREIGN NATION THAT DOESN'T NEED US!

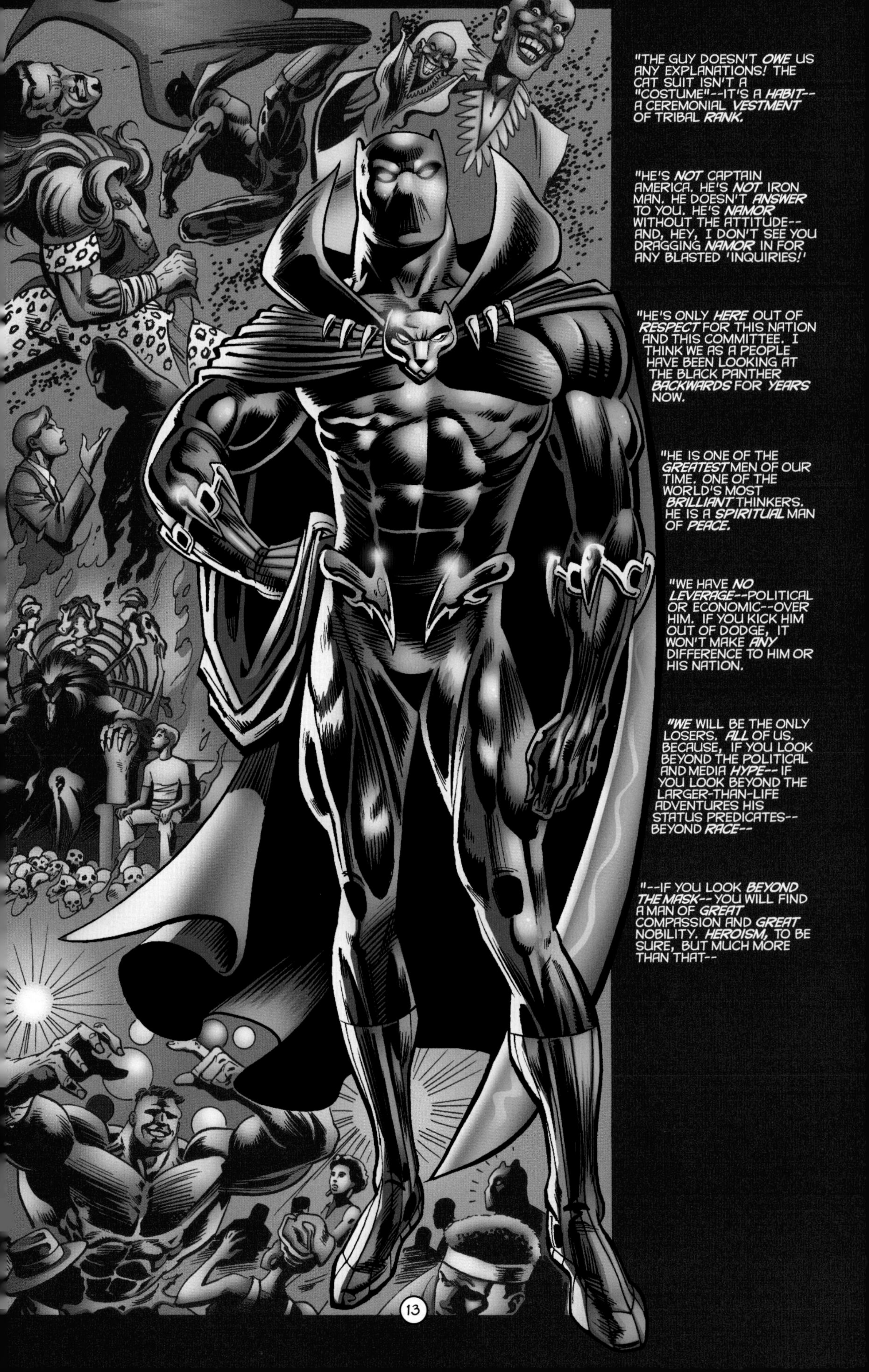
"THE GUY DOESN'T OWE US ANY EXPLANATIONS! THE CAT SUIT ISN'T A "COSTUME"--IT'S A HABIT--A CEREMONIAL VESTMENT OF TRIBAL RANK.
"HE'S NOT CAPTAIN AMERICA. HE'S NOT IRON MAN. HE DOESN'T ANSWER TO YOU. HE'S NAMOR WITHOUT THE ATTITUDE--AND, HEY, I DON'T SEE YOU DRAGGING NAMOR IN FOR ANY BLASTED 'INQUIRIES!'
"HE'S ONLY HERE OUT OF RESPECT FOR THIS NATION AND THIS COMMITTEE. I THINK WE AS A PEOPLE HAVE BEEN LOOKING AT THE BLACK PANTHER BACKWARDS FOR YEARS NOW.
"HE IS ONE OF THE GREATEST MEN OF OUR TIME. ONE OF THE WORLD'S MOST BRILLIANT THINKERS. HE IS A SPIRITUAL MAN OF PEACE.
"WE HAVE NO LEVERAGE--POLITICAL OR ECONOMIC--OVER HIM. IF YOU KICK HIM OUT OF DODGE, IT WON'T MAKE ANY DIFFERENCE TO HIM OR HIS NATION.
"WE WILL BE THE ONLY LOSERS. ALL OF US. BECAUSE, IF YOU LOOK BEYOND THE POLITICAL AND MEDIA HYPE-- IF YOU LOOK BEYOND THE LARGER-THAN-LIFE ADVENTURES HIS STATUS PREDICATES--BEYOND RACE--
"--IF YOU LOOK BEYOND THE MASK-- YOU WILL FIND A MAN OF GREAT COMPASSION AND GREAT NOBILITY. HEROISM, TO BE SURE, BUT MUCH MORE THAN THAT--

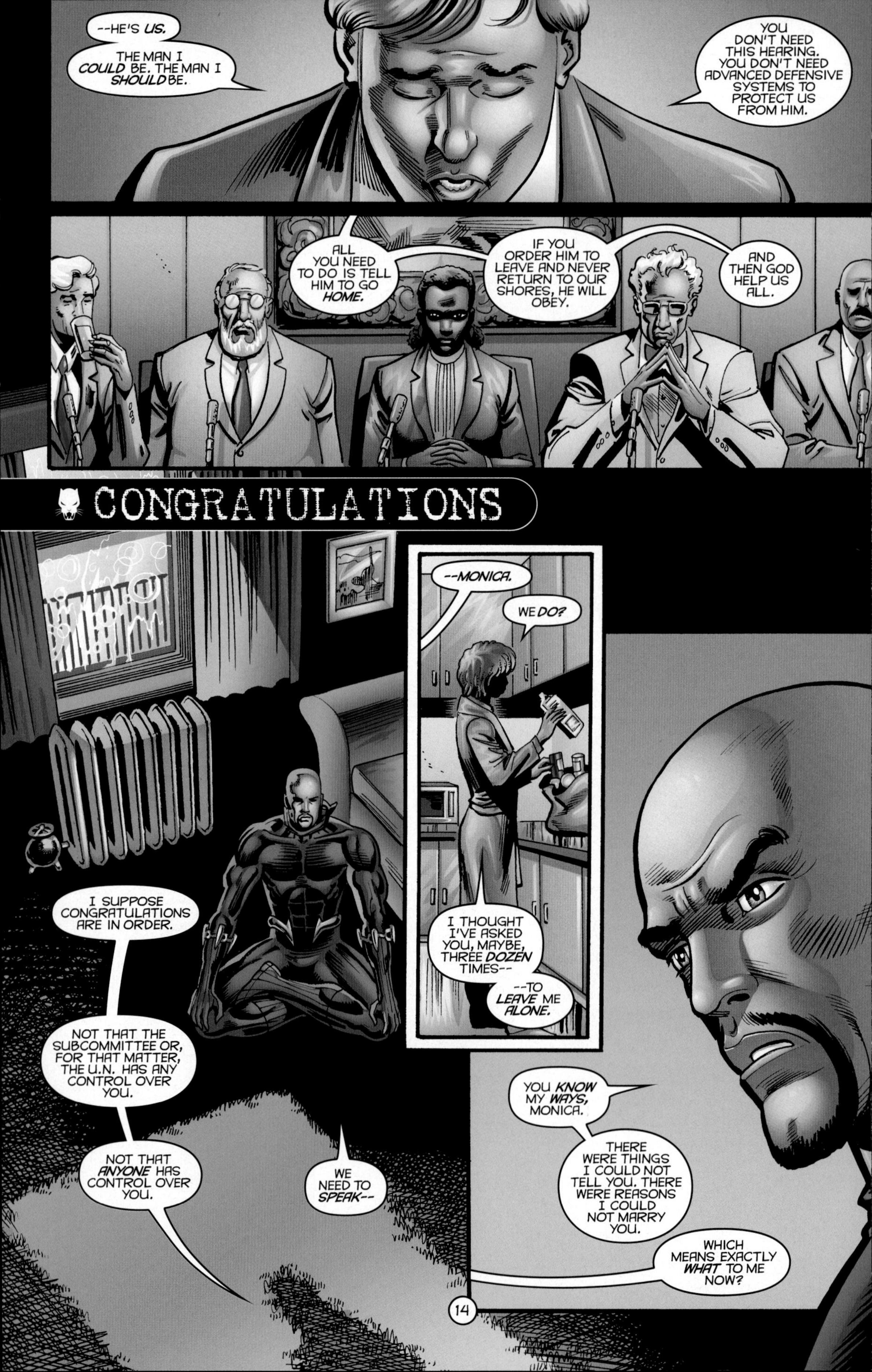
--HE'S US.
THE MAN I COULD BE. THE MAN I SHOULD BE.
YOU DON'T NEED THIS HEARING. YOU DON'T NEED ADVANCED DEFENSIVE SYSTEMS TO PROTECT US FROM HIM.
ALL YOU NEED TO DO IS TELL HIM TO GO HOME.
IF YOU ORDER HIM TO LEAVE AND NEVER RETURN TO OUR SHORES, HE WILL OBEY.
AND THEN GOD HELP US ALL.
CONGRATULATIONS
--MONICA.
WE DO?
I SUPPOSE CONGRATULATIONS ARE IN ORDER.
NOT THAT THE SUBCOMMITTEE OR, FOR THAT MATTER, THE U.N. HAS ANY CONTROL OVER YOU.
NOT THAT ANYONE HAS CONTROL OVER YOU.
WE NEED TO SPEAK--
I THOUGHT I'VE ASKED YOU, MAYBE, THREE DOZEN TIMES--
--TO LEAVE ME ALONE.
YOU KNOW MY WAYS, MONICA.
THERE WERE THINGS I COULD NOT TELL YOU. THERE WERE REASONS I COULD NOT MARRY YOU.
WHICH MEANS EXACTLY WHAT TO ME NOW?

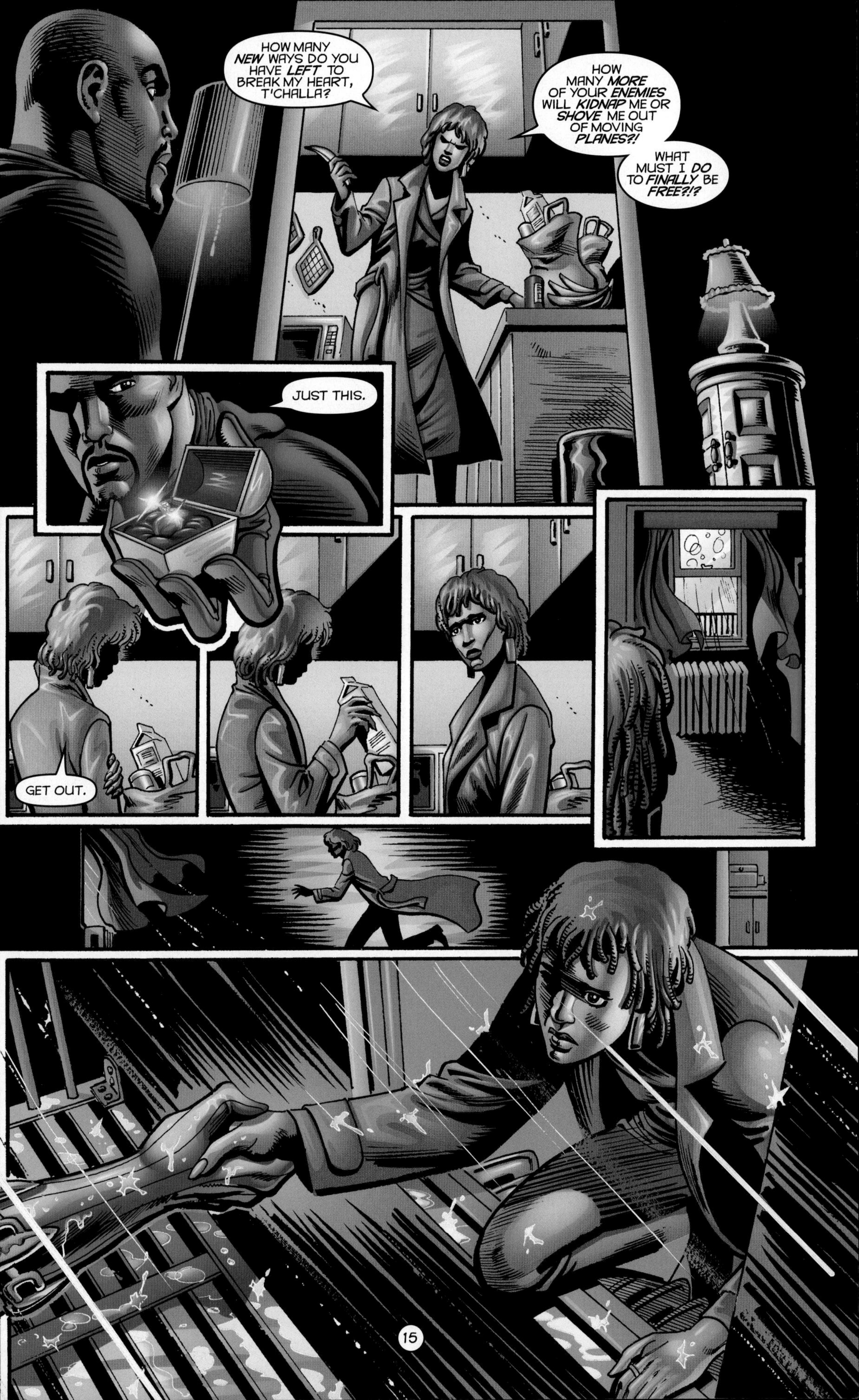
HOW MANY NEW WAYS DO YOU HAVE LEFT TO BREAK MY HEART, T'CHALLA?
HOW MANY MORE OF YOUR ENEMIES WILL KIDNAP ME OR SHOVE ME OUT OF MOVING PLANES?!
WHAT MUST I DO TO FINALLY BE FREE?!?
JUST THIS.
GET OUT.

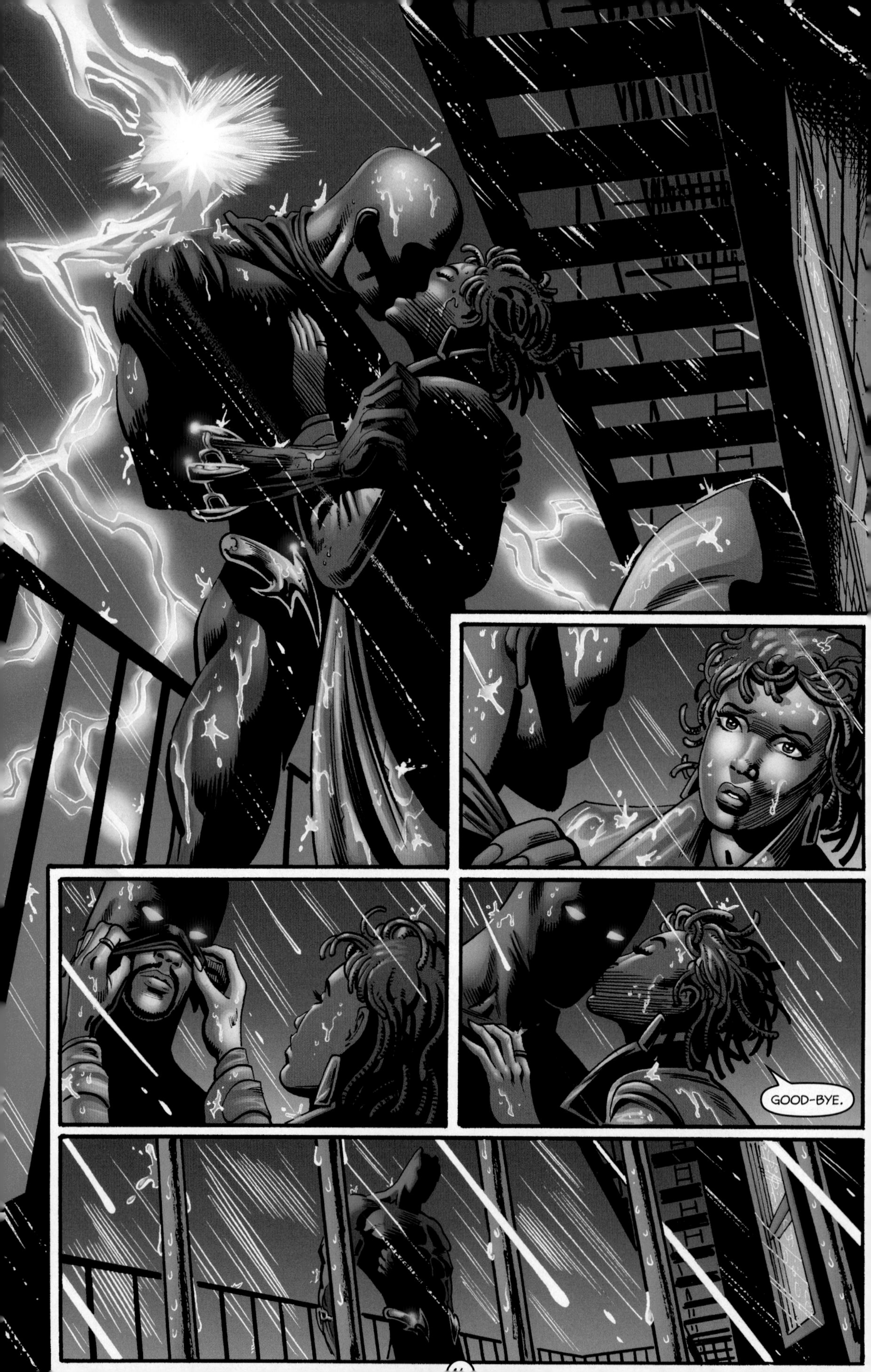
GOOD-BYE.

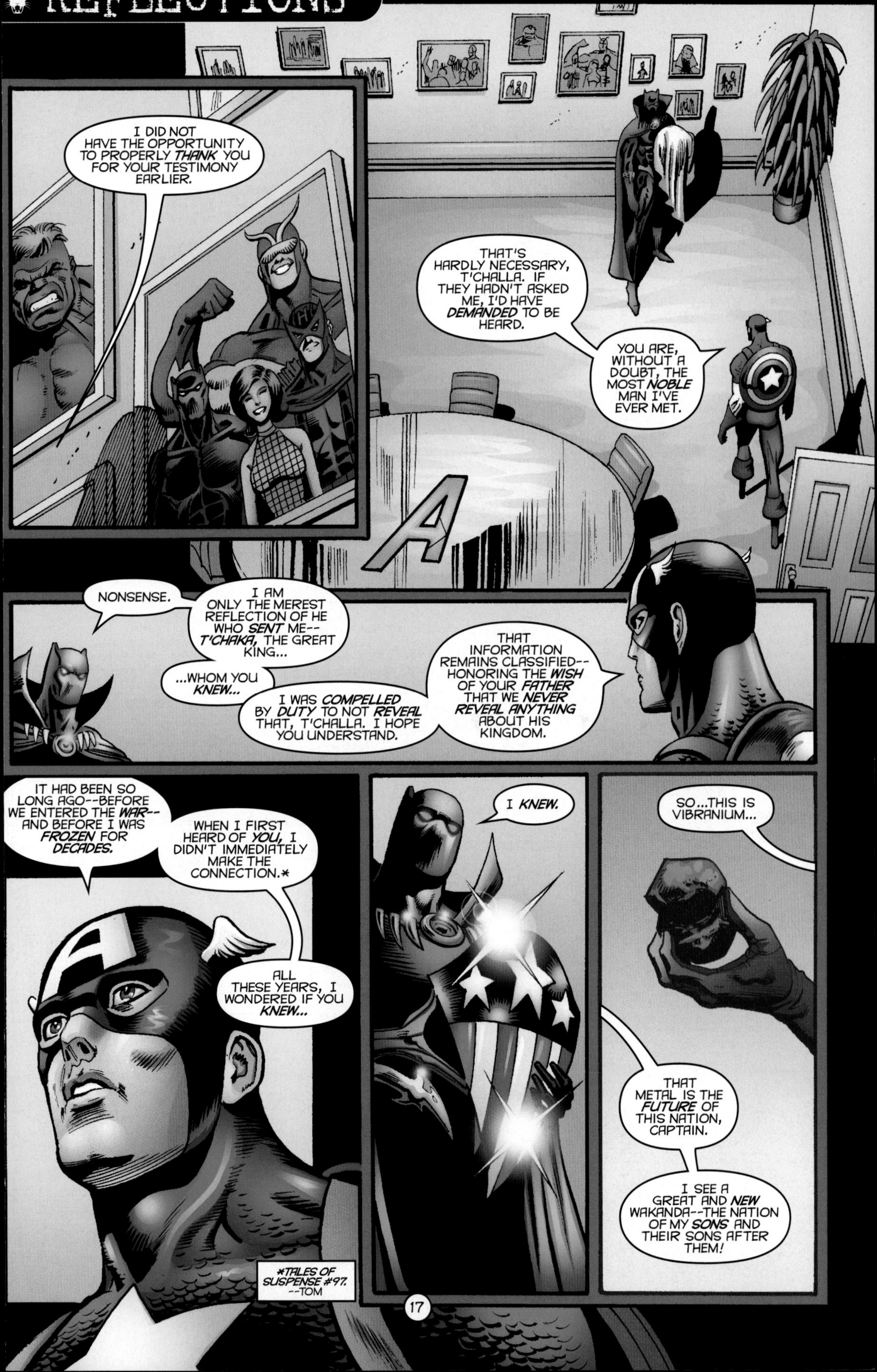
I DID NOT HAVE THE OPPORTUNITY TO PROPERLY THANK YOU FOR YOUR TESTIMONY EARLIER.
THAT'S HARDLY NECESSARY, T'CHALLA. IF THEY HADN'T ASKED ME, I'D HAVE DEMANDED TO BE HEARD.
YOU ARE, WITHOUT A DOUBT, THE MOST NOBLE MAN I'VE EVER MET.
NONSENSE.
I AM ONLY THE MEREST REFLECTION OF HE WHO SENT ME-- T'CHAKA, THE GREAT KING...
...WHOM YOU KNEW...
I WAS COMPELLED BY DUTY TO NOT REVEAL THAT, T'CHALLA. I HOPE YOU UNDERSTAND.
THAT INFORMATION REMAINS CLASSIFIED-- HONORING THE WISH OF YOUR FATHER THAT WE NEVER REVEAL ANYTHING ABOUT HIS KINGDOM.
IT HAD BEEN SO LONG AGO--BEFORE WE ENTERED THE WAR-- AND BEFORE I WAS FROZEN FOR DECADES.
WHEN I FIRST HEARD OF YOU, I DIDN'T IMMEDIATELY MAKE THE CONNECTION.*
ALL THESE YEARS, I WONDERED IF YOU KNEW...
*TALES OF SUSPENSE #97. --TOM
I KNEW.
SO...THIS IS VIBRANIUM...
THAT METAL IS THE FUTURE OF THIS NATION, CAPTAIN.
I SEE A GREAT AND NEW WAKANDA--THE NATION OF MY SONS AND THEIR SONS AFTER THEM!

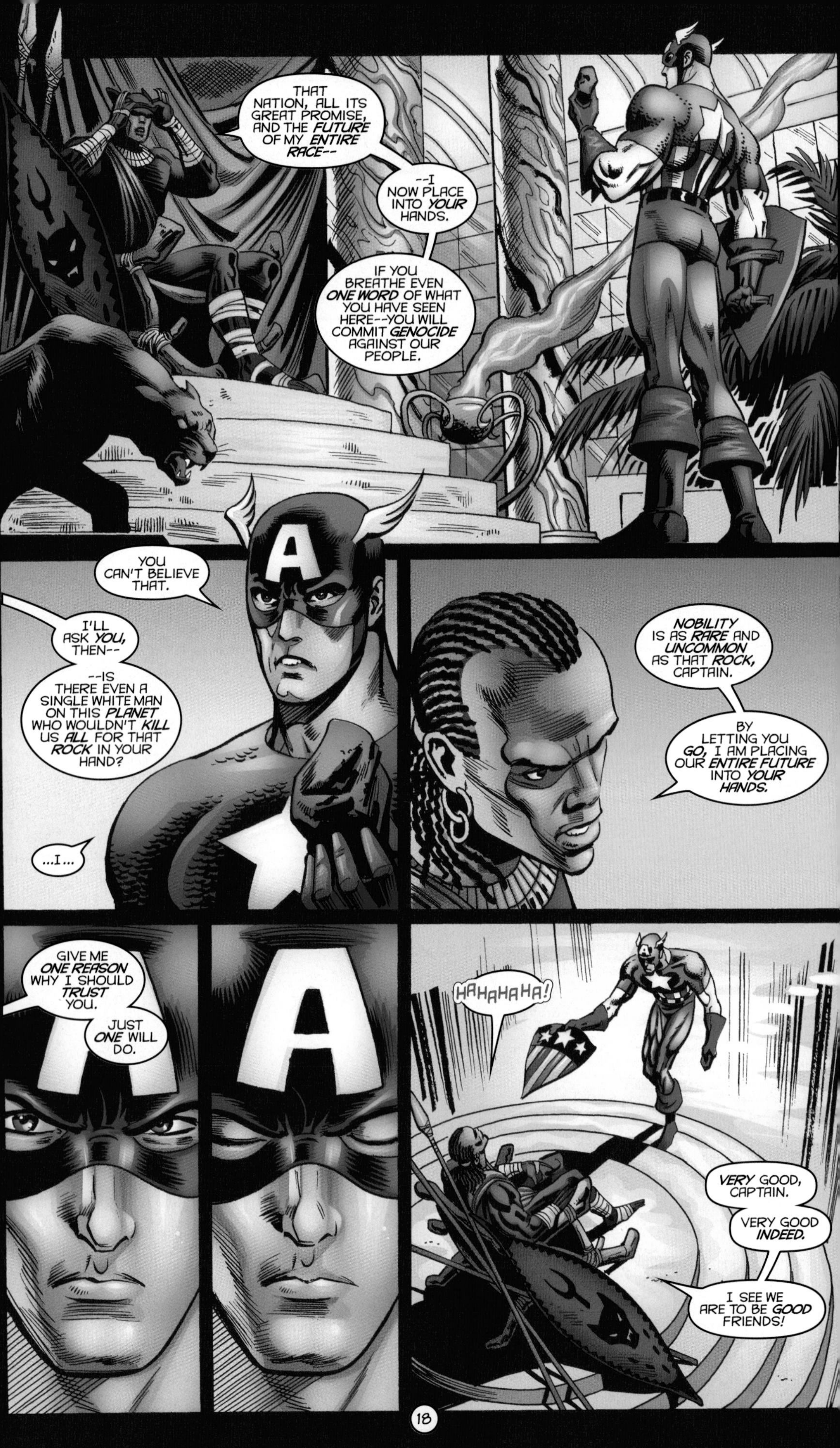

THAT NATION, ALL ITS GREAT PROMISE, AND THE FUTURE OF MY ENTIRE RACE--
--I NOW PLACE INTO YOUR HANDS.
IF YOU BREATHE EVEN ONE WORD OF WHAT YOU HAVE SEEN HERE--YOU WILL COMMIT GENOCIDE AGAINST OUR PEOPLE.
YOU CAN'T BELIEVE THAT.
I'LL ASK YOU, THEN--
--IS THERE EVEN A SINGLE WHITE MAN ON THIS PLANET WHO WOULDN'T KILL US ALL FOR THAT ROCK IN YOUR HAND?
...I...
NOBILITY IS AS RARE AND UNCOMMON AS THAT ROCK, CAPTAIN.
BY LETTING YOU GO, I AM PLACING OUR ENTIRE FUTURE INTO YOUR HANDS.
GIVE ME ONE REASON WHY I SHOULD TRUST YOU.
JUST ONE WILL DO.
HAHAHAHA!
VERY GOOD, CAPTAIN.
VERY GOOD INDEED.
I SEE WE ARE TO BE GOOD FRIENDS!

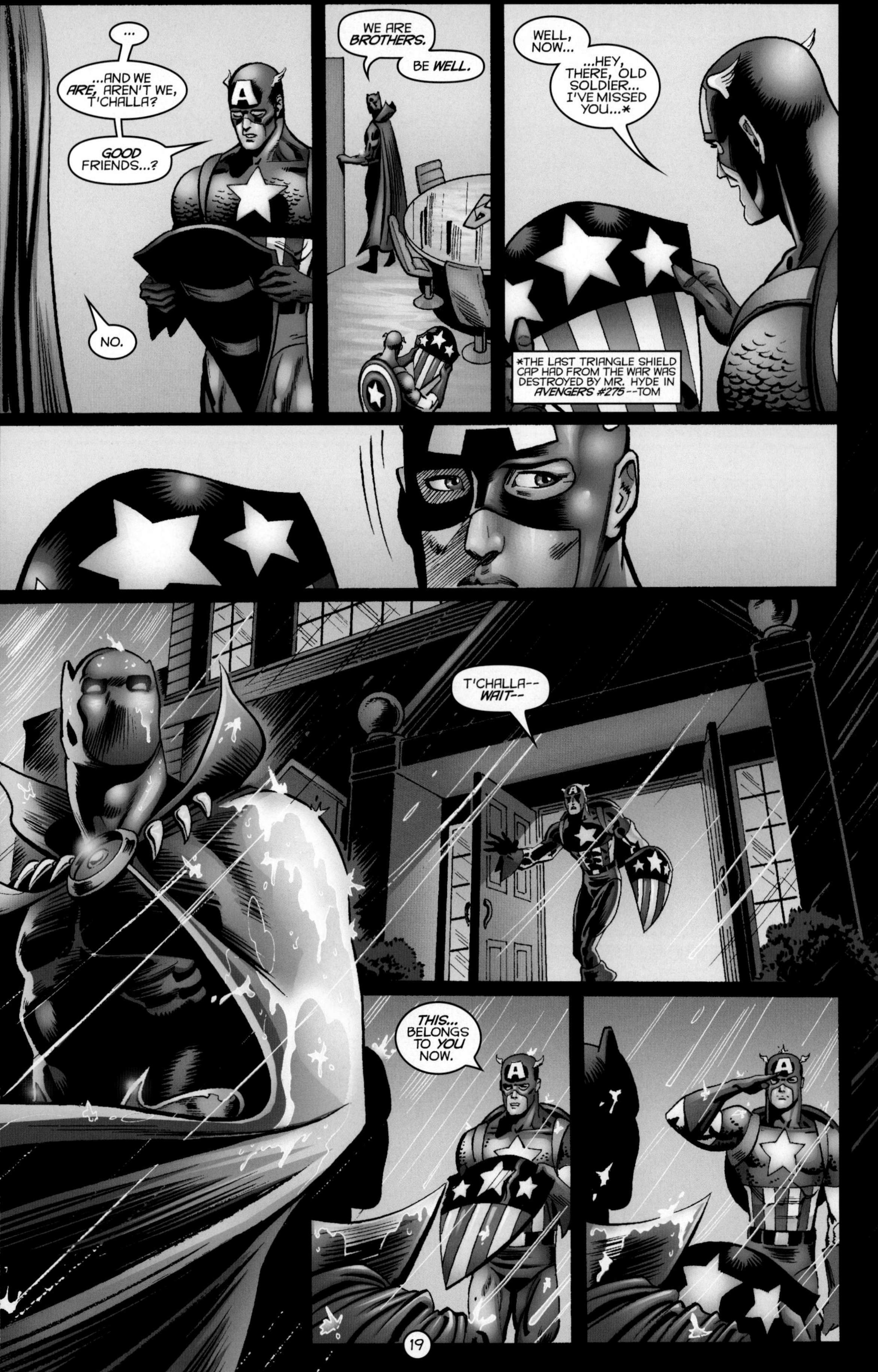
...
...AND WE ARE, AREN'T WE, T'CHALLA?
GOOD FRIENDS...?
NO.
WE ARE BROTHERS.
BE WELL.
WELL, NOW...
...HEY, THERE, OLD SOLDIER... I'VE MISSED YOU...*
*THE LAST TRIANGLE SHIELD CAP HAD FROM THE WAR WAS DESTROYED BY MR. HYDE IN AVENGERS #275--TOM
T'CHALLA-- WAIT--
THIS... BELONGS TO YOU NOW.

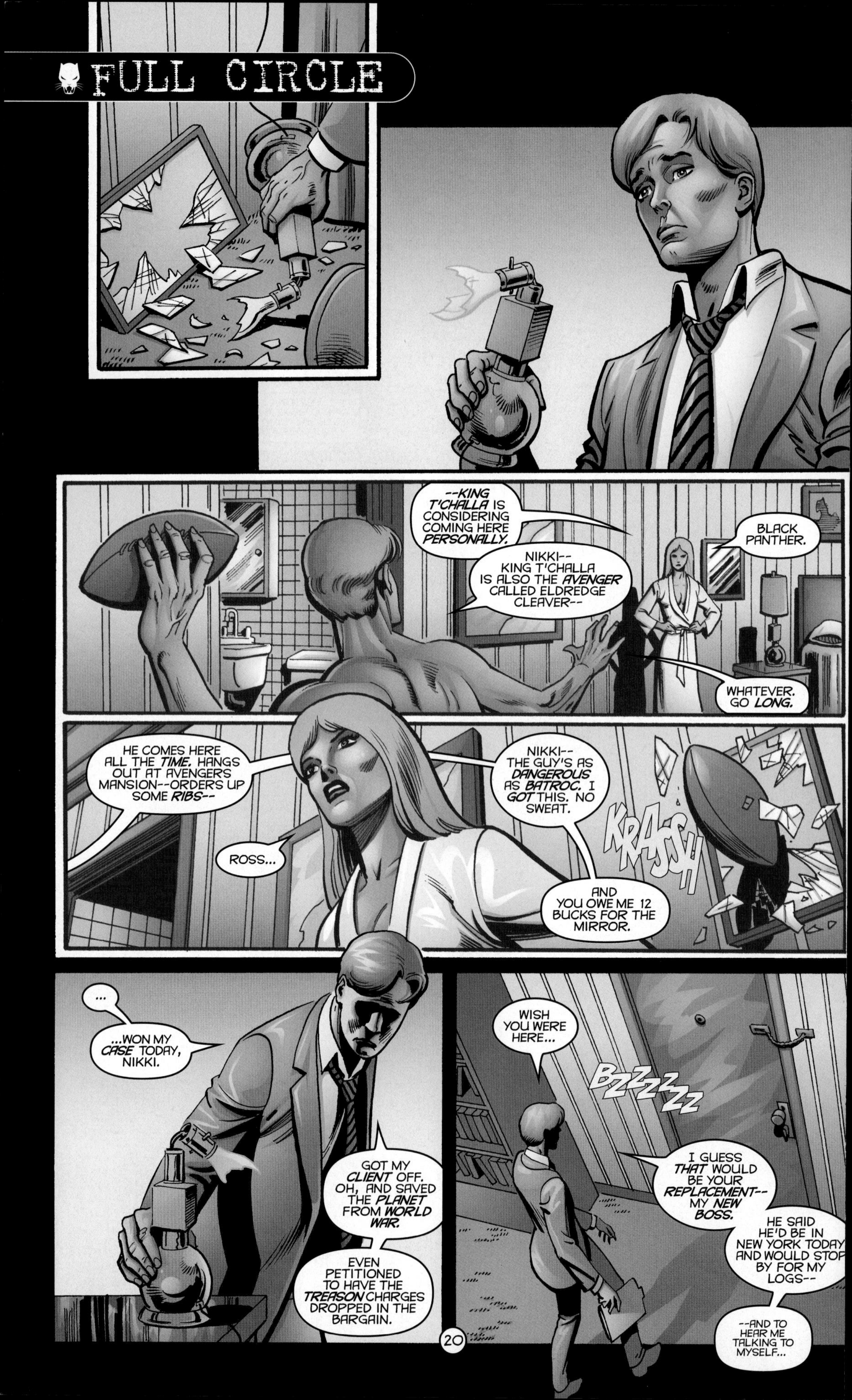
FULL CIRCLE
--KING T'CHALLA IS CONSIDERING COMING HERE PERSONALLY.
NIKKI-- KING T'CHALLA IS ALSO THE AVENGER CALLED ELDREDGE CLEAVER--
BLACK PANTHER.
WHATEVER. GO LONG.
HE COMES HERE ALL THE TIME. HANGS OUT AT AVENGERS MANSION--ORDERS UP SOME RIBS--
ROSS...
NIKKI-- THE GUY'S AS DANGEROUS AS BATROC. I GOT THIS. NO SWEAT.
KRASSH
AND YOU OWE ME 12 BUCKS FOR THE MIRROR.
...
...WON MY CASE TODAY, NIKKI.
GOT MY CLIENT OFF. OH, AND SAVED THE PLANET FROM WORLD WAR.
EVEN PETITIONED TO HAVE THE TREASON CHARGES DROPPED IN THE BARGAIN.
WISH YOU WERE HERE...
BZZZZZZ
I GUESS THAT WOULD BE YOUR REPLACEMENT-- MY NEW BOSS.
HE SAID HE'D BE IN NEW YORK TODAY AND WOULD STOP BY FOR MY LOGS--
--AND TO HEAR ME TALKING TO MYSELF...

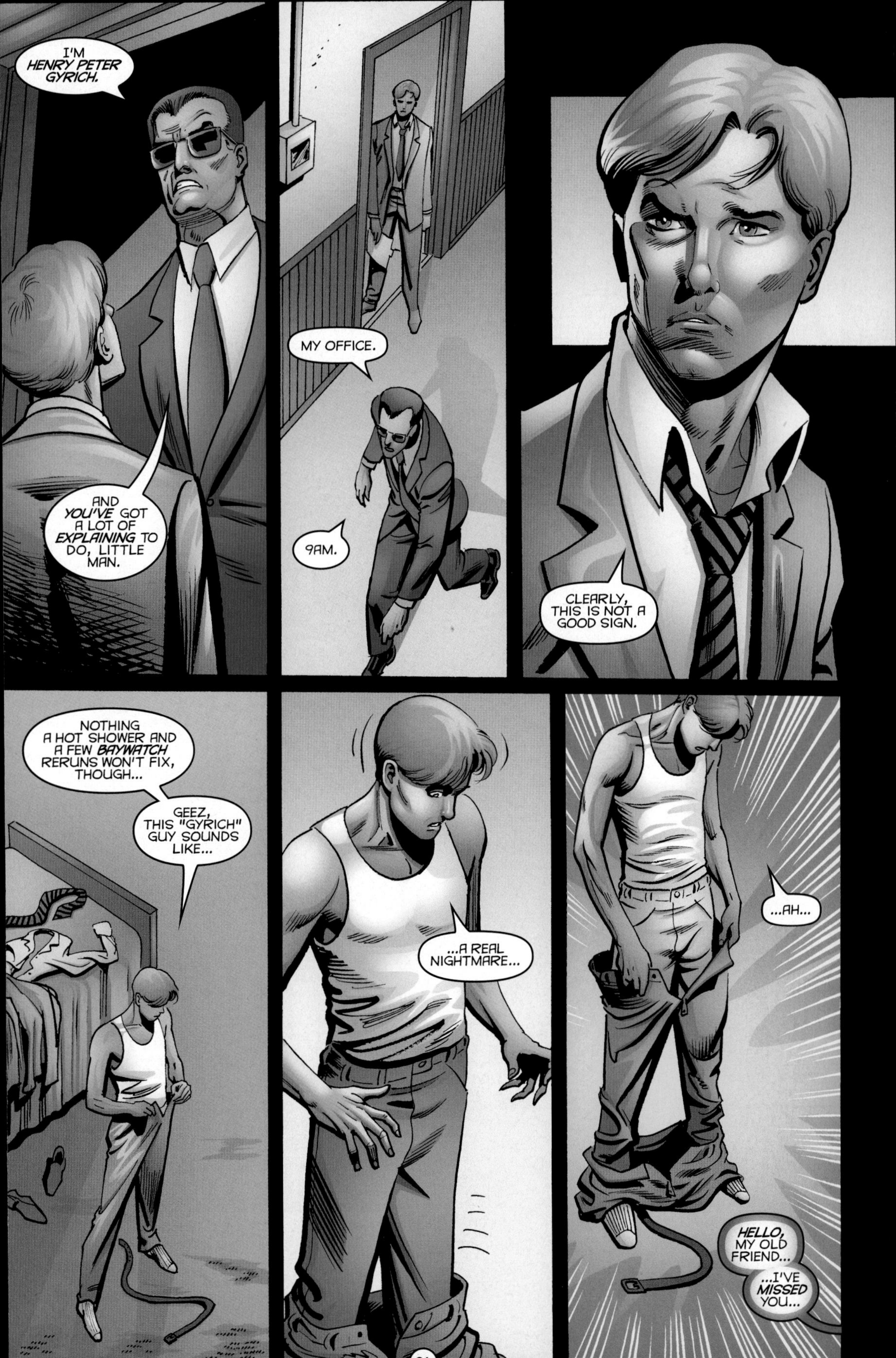
I'M *HENRY PETER GYRICH.*
AND *YOU'VE* GOT A LOT OF *EXPLAINING* TO DO, LITTLE MAN.
MY OFFICE.
9AM.
CLEARLY, THIS IS NOT A GOOD SIGN.
NOTHING A HOT SHOWER AND A FEW *BAYWATCH* RERUNS WON'T FIX, THOUGH...
GEEZ, THIS "GYRICH" GUY SOUNDS LIKE...
...A REAL NIGHTMARE...
...AH...
HELLO, MY OLD FRIEND...
...I'VE *MISSED* YOU...

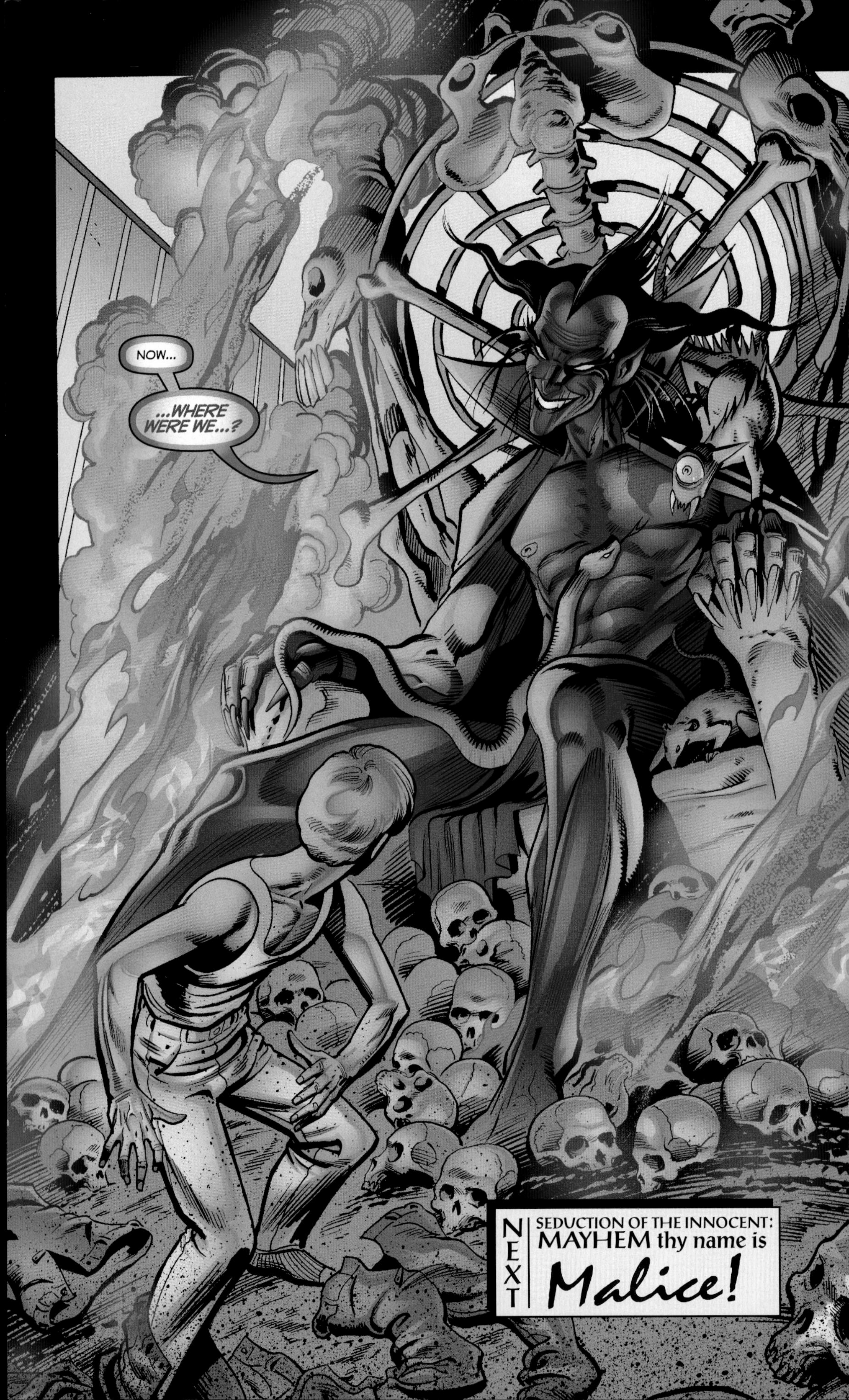

NOW...
...WHERE WERE WE...?
NEXT
SEDUCTION OF THE INNOCENT:
MAYHEM thy name is
Malice!

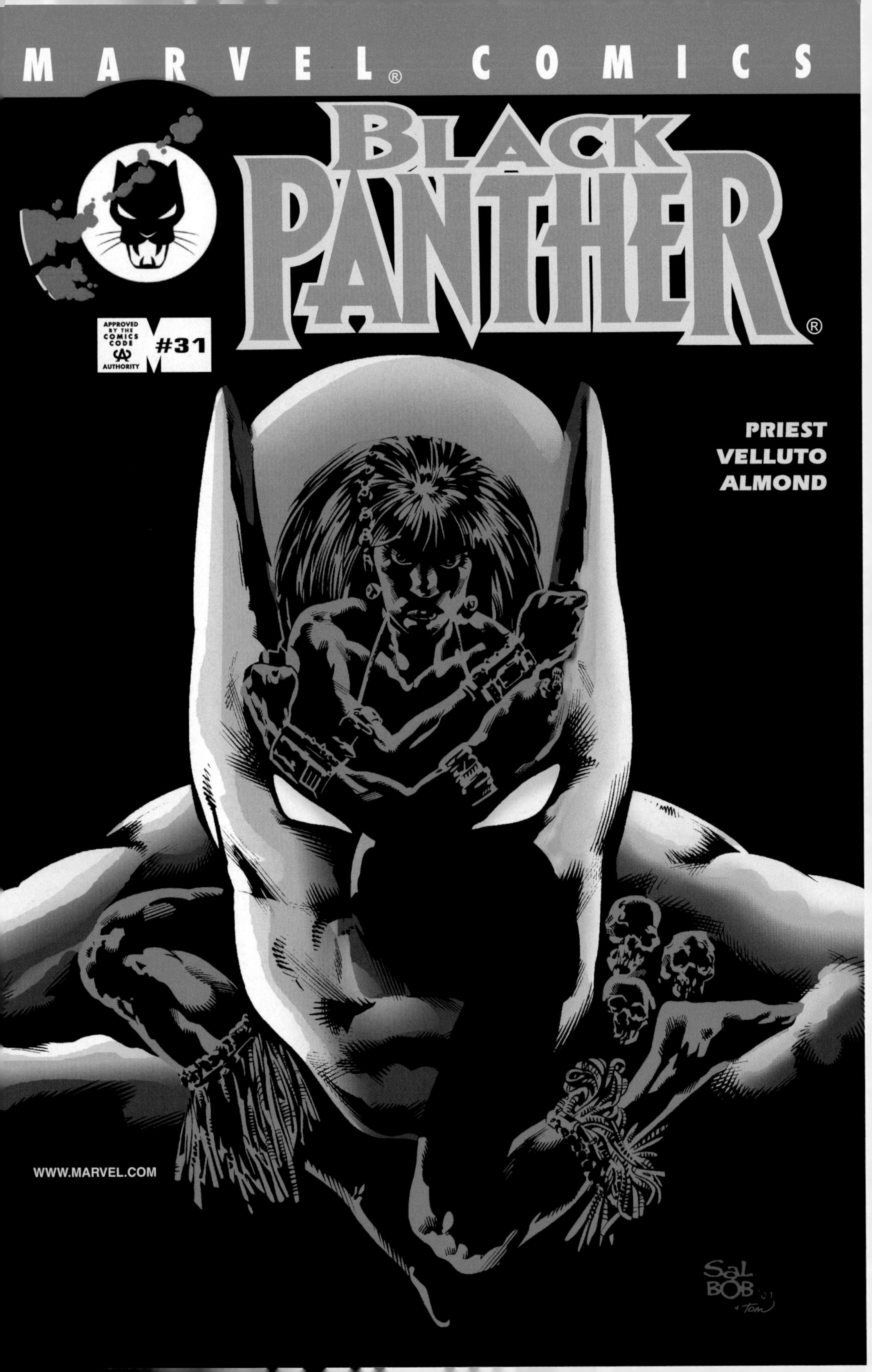
MARVEL® COMICS
BLACK PANTHER®
APPROVED BY THE COMICS CODE AUTHORITY
#31
PRIEST
VELLUTO
ALMOND
WWW.MARVEL.COM
SAL BOB '01 + Tom

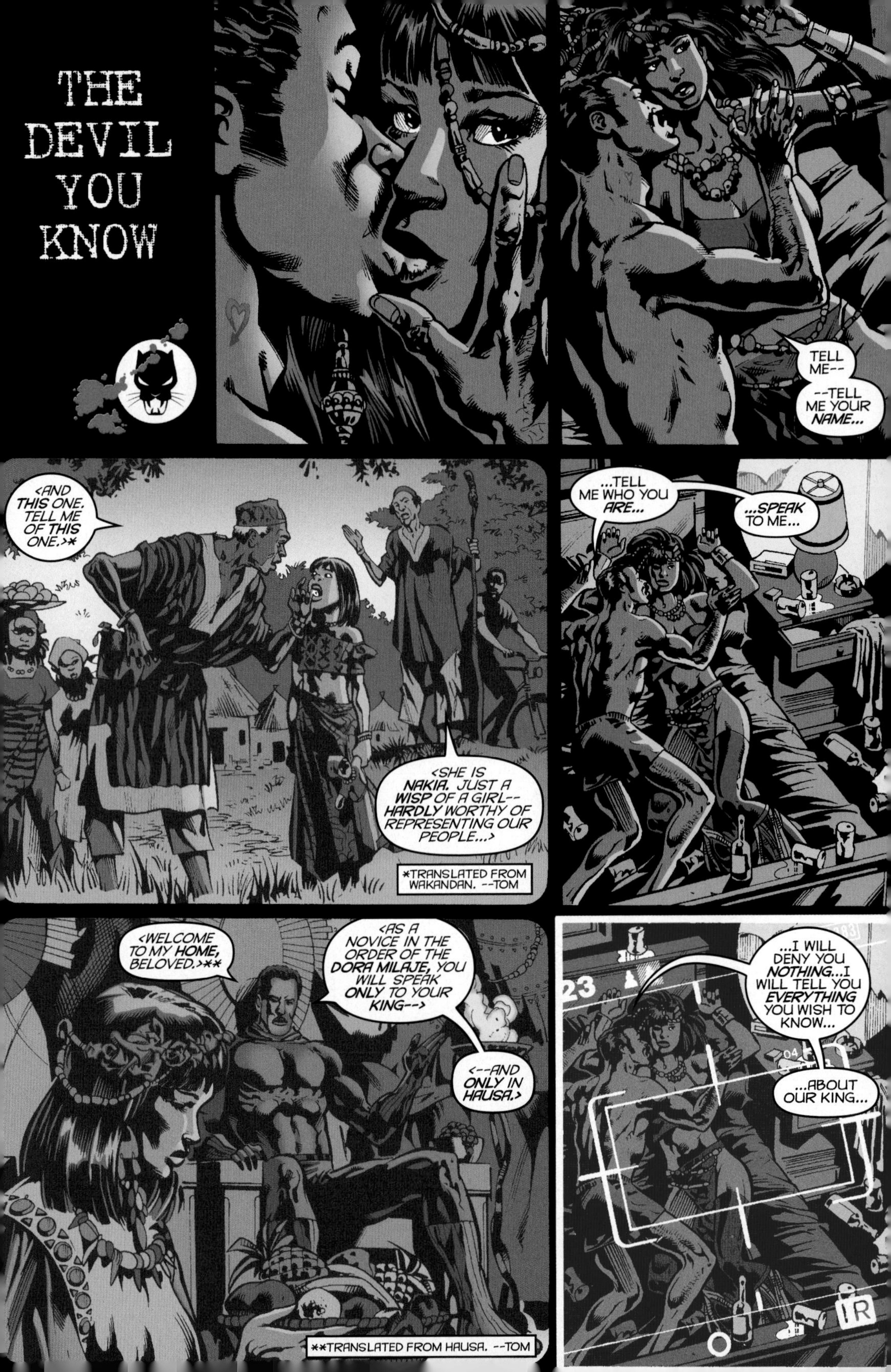

THE DEVIL YOU KNOW
TELL ME--
--TELL ME YOUR NAME...
<AND THIS ONE. TELL ME OF THIS ONE.>*
<SHE IS NAKIA. JUST A WISP OF A GIRL--HARDLY WORTHY OF REPRESENTING OUR PEOPLE...>
*TRANSLATED FROM WAKANDAN. --TOM
...TELL ME WHO YOU ARE...
...SPEAK TO ME...
<WELCOME TO MY HOME, BELOVED.>**
<AS A NOVICE IN THE ORDER OF THE DORA MILAJE, YOU WILL SPEAK ONLY TO YOUR KING-->
<--AND ONLY IN HAUSA.>
**TRANSLATED FROM HAUSA. --TOM
...I WILL DENY YOU NOTHING...I WILL TELL YOU EVERYTHING YOU WISH TO KNOW...
...ABOUT OUR KING...

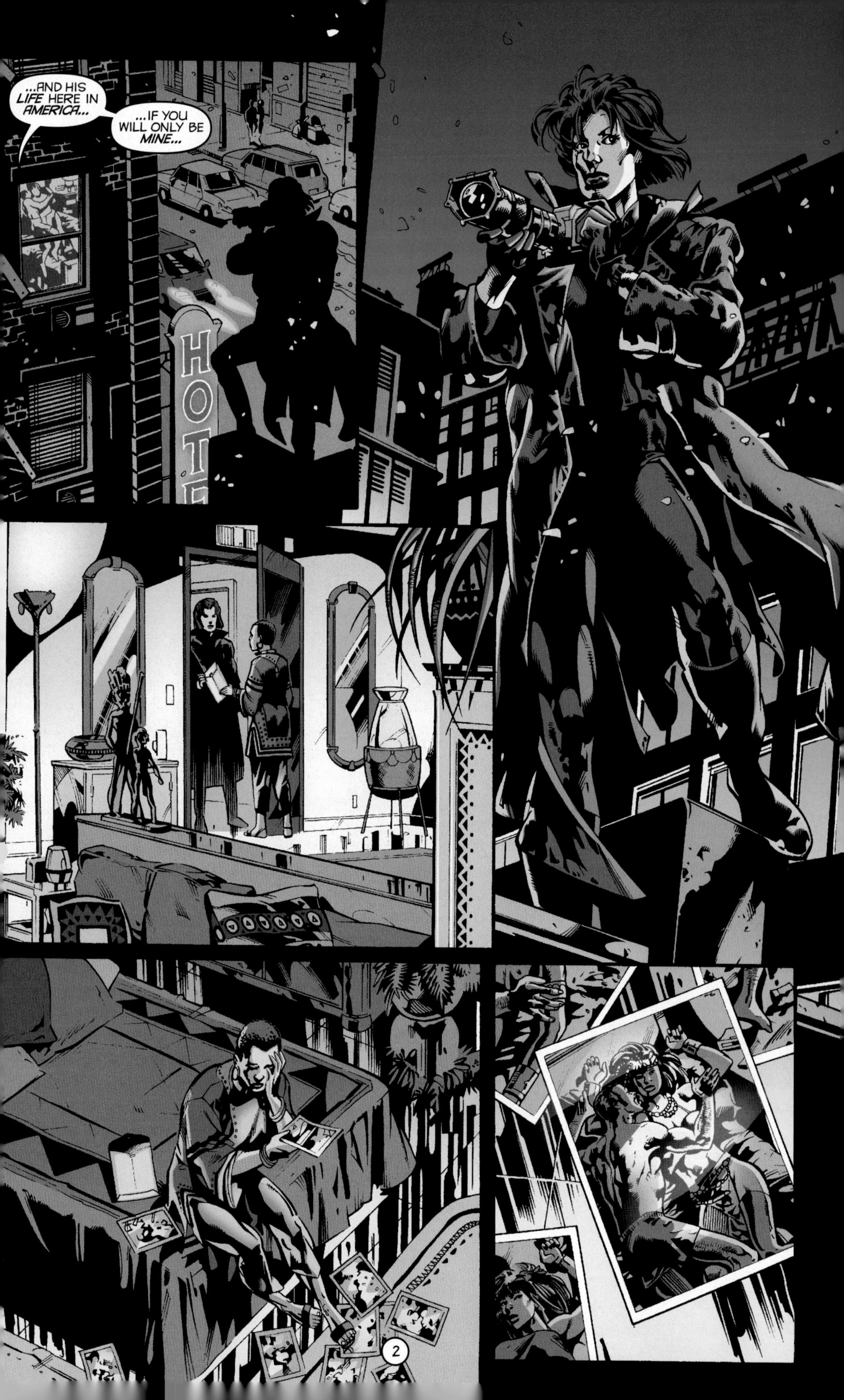

...AND HIS LIFE HERE IN AMERICA...
...IF YOU WILL ONLY BE MINE...
HOT

SHE'S DEAD, JIM

Signs:
AWAZILI N'GYATO IMO SABOLARI — TO EMBRACE THE GLOBAL VILLAGE

IKAMZE DARI WAKANDA — WAKANDAN CONSULATE NEW YORK

PANTHER GO HOME!

ENEMY OF THE STATE

GOD SHALL JUDGE THEE

Signs:
GOD IS NOT A KITTY

T'CHALLA = SADDAM

ENEMY OF THE STATE

PANTHER GO HOME!

NO MORE

GOD SHALL JUDGE THEE

THE DEVIL IS INDEED IN THE DETAILS, EH, MY LORD?>

THE GLAMOROUS LIFE OF A HEAD OF STATE IS SOMEWHAT OVERSTATED, OMORO.>

I'D PREFER A GAUNTLET OF MY DEADLIEST ENEMIES TO THIS—>

THAT CAN CERTAINLY BE ARRANGED IF YOU WISH, KING.>

FOR NOW, HOWEVER, YOU WILL HAVE TO CONTENT YOURSELF WITH THE TEA YOUR MOTHER SENT OVER FROM WAKANDA.>

TO MY MOTHER, TEA IS THE SOLUTION TO MOST EVERY PROBLEM.>

AND I AGREE.>

*TRANSLATED FROM WAKANDAN. --TOM

3

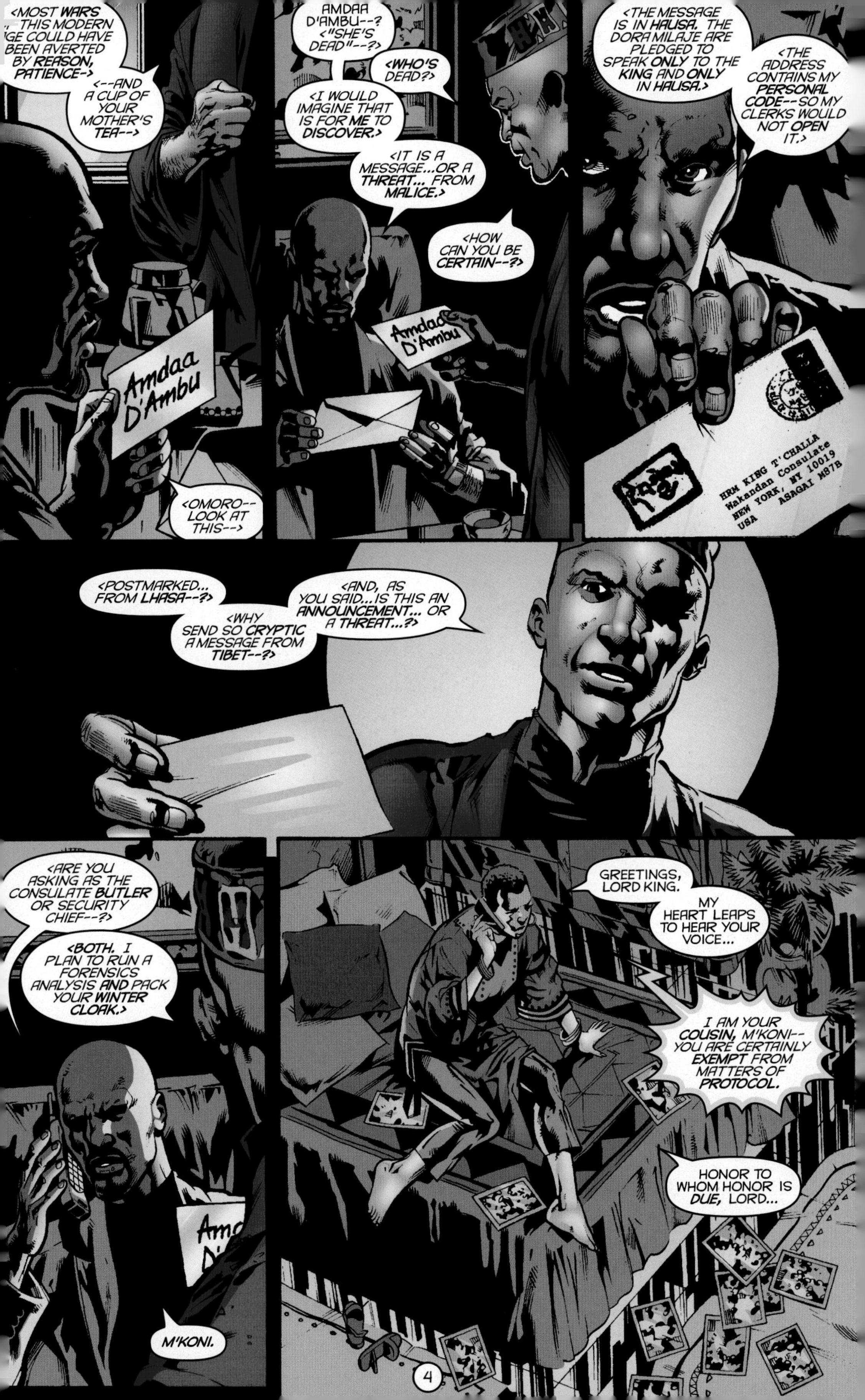
<MOST WARS --THIS MODERN GE COULD HAVE BEEN AVERTED BY REASON, PATIENCE->
<--AND A CUP OF YOUR MOTHER'S TEA-->
Amdaa D'Ambu
<OMORO-- LOOK AT THIS-->
AMDAA D'AMBU--? <"SHE'S DEAD"--?>
<WHO'S DEAD?>
<I WOULD IMAGINE THAT IS FOR ME TO DISCOVER.>
<IT IS A MESSAGE...OR A THREAT... FROM MALICE.>
<HOW CAN YOU BE CERTAIN--?>
Amdaa D'Ambu
<THE MESSAGE IS IN HAUSA. THE DORA MILAJE ARE PLEDGED TO SPEAK ONLY TO THE KING AND ONLY IN HAUSA.>
<THE ADDRESS CONTAINS MY PERSONAL CODE--SO MY CLERKS WOULD NOT OPEN IT.>
HRM KING T'CHALLA
Wakandan Consulate
NEW YORK, NY 10019
USA ASAGAI M87B
<POSTMARKED... FROM LHASA--?>
<WHY SEND SO CRYPTIC A MESSAGE FROM TIBET--?>
<AND, AS YOU SAID...IS THIS AN ANNOUNCEMENT... OR A THREAT...?>
<ARE YOU ASKING AS THE CONSULATE BUTLER OR SECURITY CHIEF--?>
<BOTH. I PLAN TO RUN A FORENSICS ANALYSIS AND PACK YOUR WINTER CLOAK.>
M'KONI.
GREETINGS, LORD KING.
MY HEART LEAPS TO HEAR YOUR VOICE...
I AM YOUR COUSIN, M'KONI-- YOU ARE CERTAINLY EXEMPT FROM MATTERS OF PROTOCOL.
HONOR TO WHOM HONOR IS DUE, LORD...

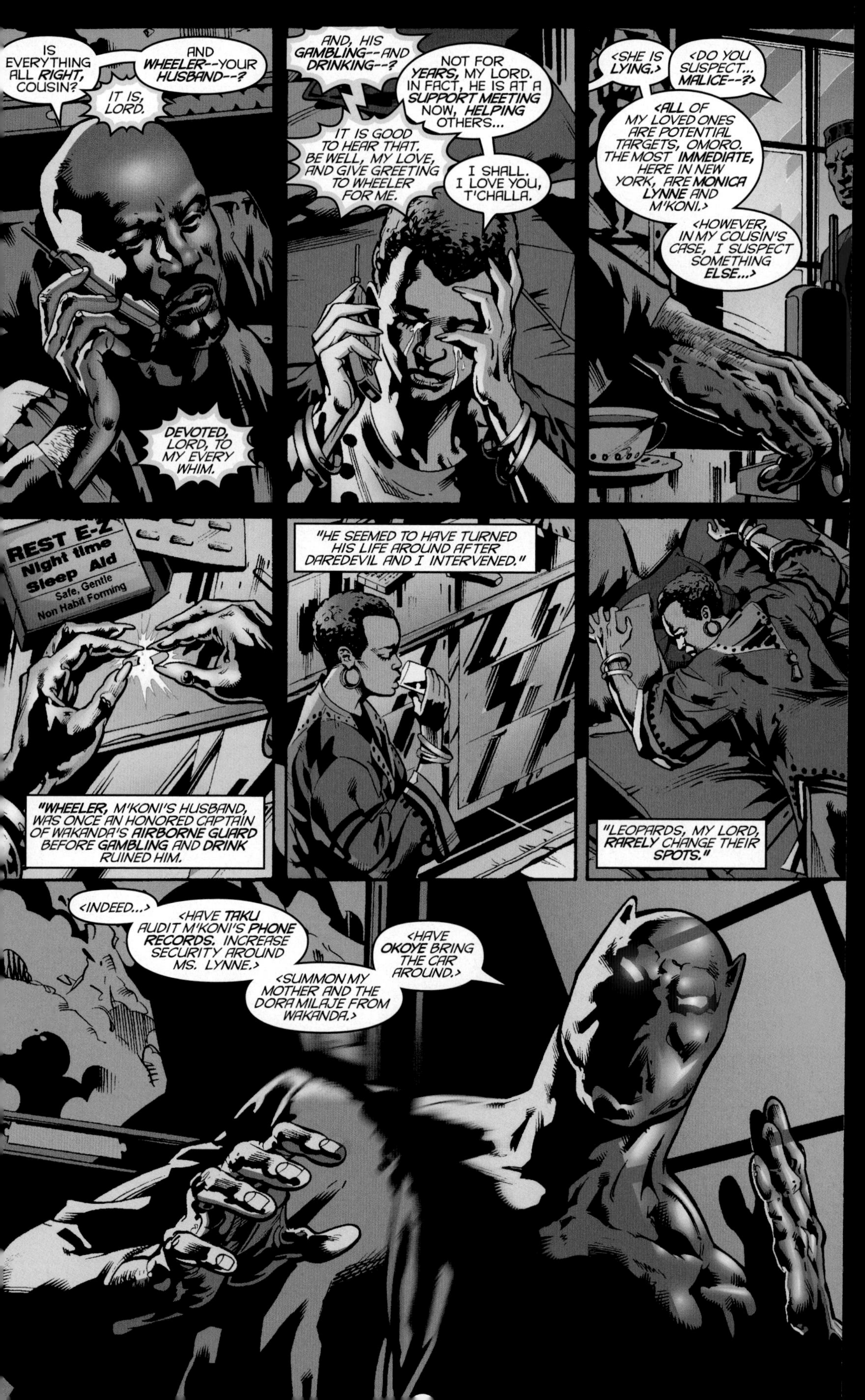

IS EVERYTHING ALL RIGHT, COUSIN?
IT IS, LORD.
AND WHEELER--YOUR HUSBAND--?
DEVOTED, LORD, TO MY EVERY WHIM.
AND, HIS GAMBLING--AND DRINKING--?
NOT FOR YEARS, MY LORD. IN FACT, HE IS AT A SUPPORT MEETING NOW, HELPING OTHERS...
IT IS GOOD TO HEAR THAT. BE WELL, MY LOVE, AND GIVE GREETING TO WHEELER FOR ME.
I SHALL. I LOVE YOU, T'CHALLA.
<SHE IS LYING.>
<DO YOU SUSPECT... MALICE--?>
<ALL OF MY LOVED ONES ARE POTENTIAL TARGETS, OMORO. THE MOST IMMEDIATE, HERE IN NEW YORK, ARE MONICA LYNNE AND M'KONI.>
<HOWEVER, IN MY COUSIN'S CASE, I SUSPECT SOMETHING ELSE...>
REST E-Z
Night time
Sleep Aid
Safe, Gentle
Non Habit Forming
"WHEELER, M'KONI'S HUSBAND, WAS ONCE AN HONORED CAPTAIN OF WAKANDA'S AIRBORNE GUARD BEFORE GAMBLING AND DRINK RUINED HIM.
"HE SEEMED TO HAVE TURNED HIS LIFE AROUND AFTER DAREDEVIL AND I INTERVENED."
"LEOPARDS, MY LORD, RARELY CHANGE THEIR SPOTS."
<INDEED...>
<HAVE TAKU AUDIT M'KONI'S PHONE RECORDS. INCREASE SECURITY AROUND MS. LYNNE.>
<SUMMON MY MOTHER AND THE DORA MILAJE FROM WAKANDA.>
<HAVE OKOYE BRING THE CAR AROUND.>

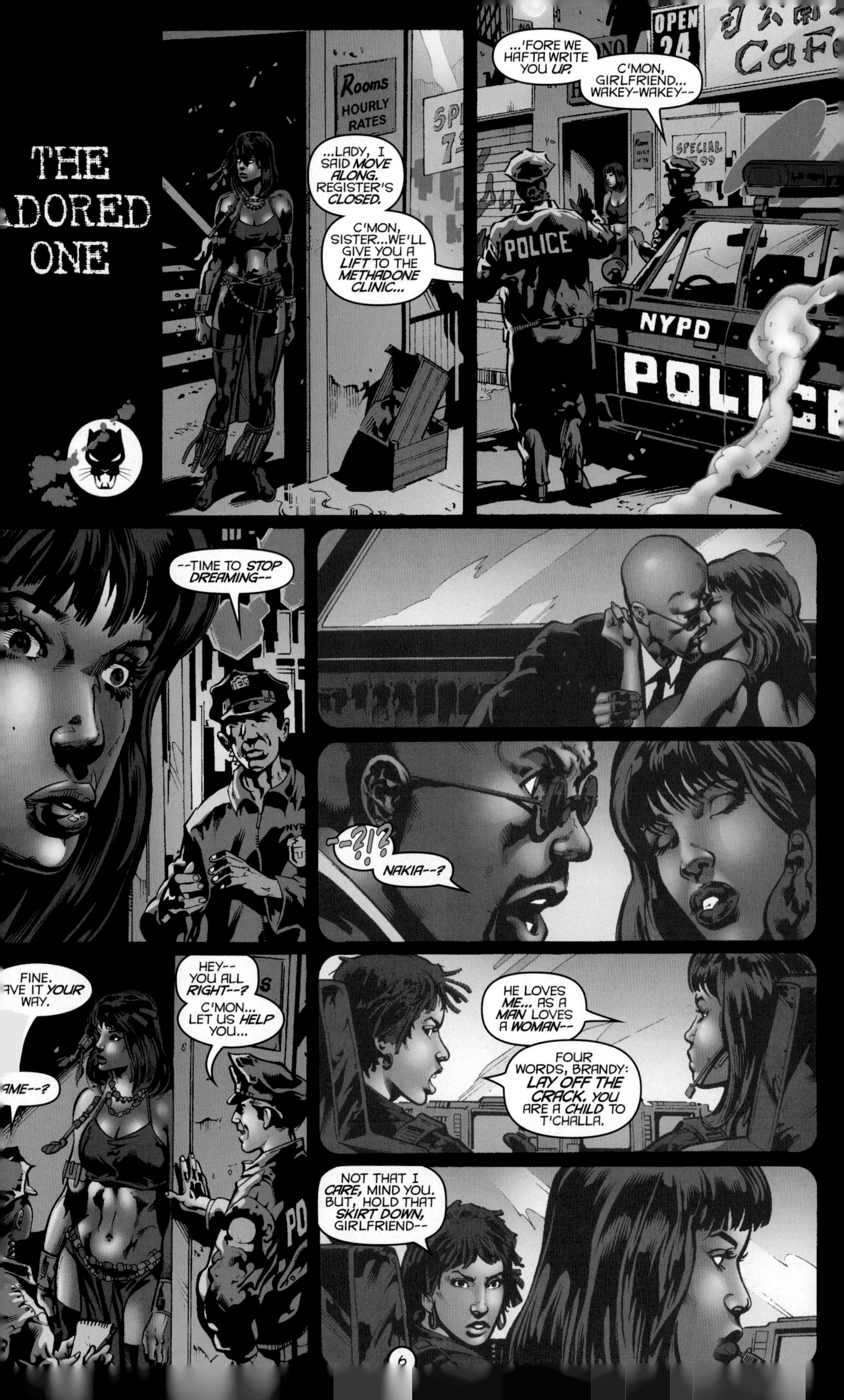

THE
ADORED
ONE
...LADY, I SAID MOVE ALONG. REGISTER'S CLOSED.
C'MON, SISTER...WE'LL GIVE YOU A LIFT TO THE METHADONE CLINIC...
Rooms
HOURLY RATES
...'FORE WE HAFTA WRITE YOU UP.
C'MON, GIRLFRIEND... WAKEY-WAKEY--
OPEN 24
CAFE
SPECIAL
POLICE
NYPD
POLICE
--TIME TO STOP DREAMING--
--?!?
NAKIA--?
FINE. AVE IT YOUR WAY.
AME--?
HEY-- YOU ALL RIGHT--?
C'MON... LET US HELP YOU...
HE LOVES ME... AS A MAN LOVES A WOMAN--
FOUR WORDS, BRANDY: LAY OFF THE CRACK. YOU ARE A CHILD TO T'CHALLA.
NOT THAT I CARE, MIND YOU. BUT, HOLD THAT SKIRT DOWN, GIRLFRIEND--

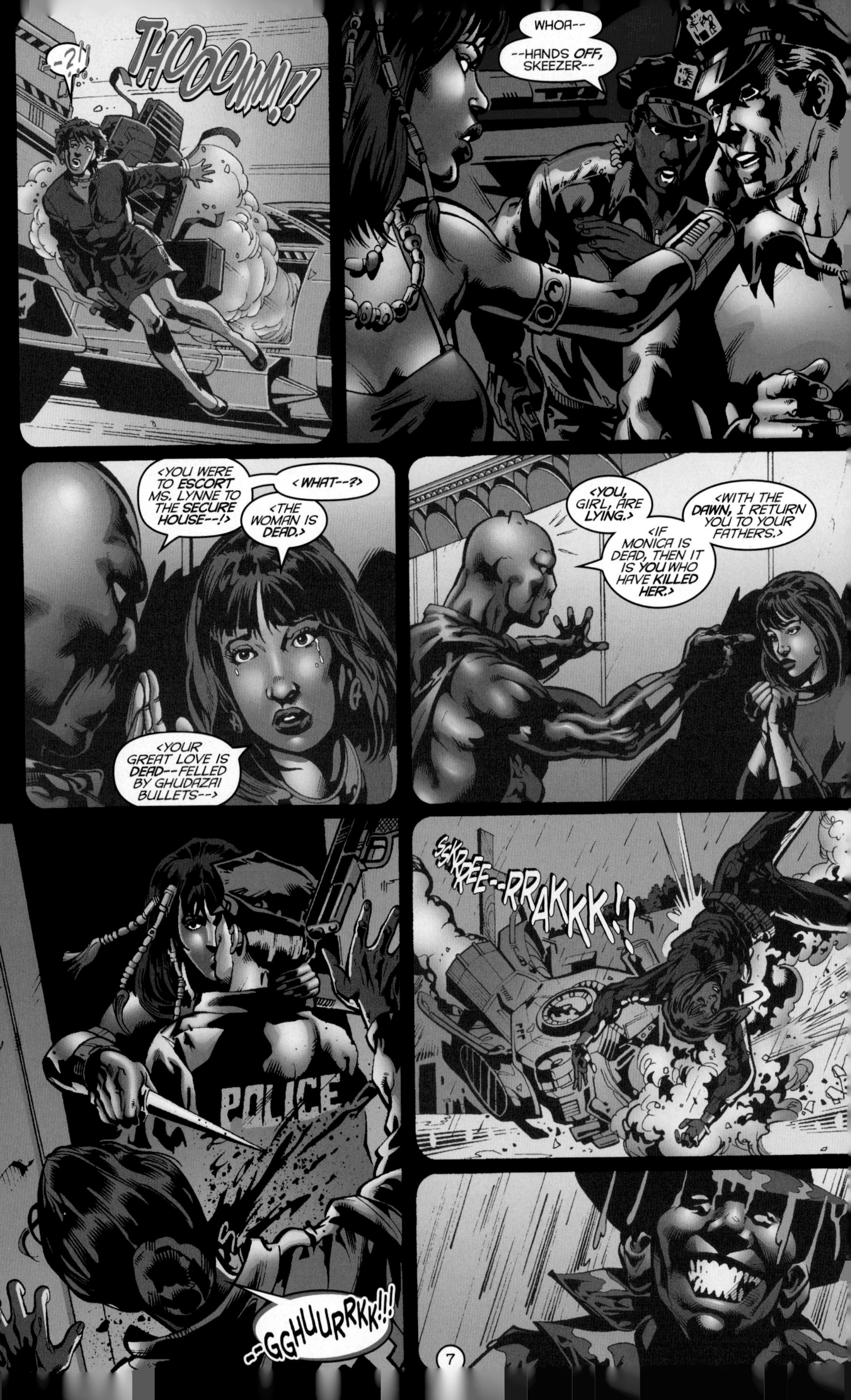

--?!
THOOOMM!!
WHOA--
--HANDS OFF, SKEEZER--
<YOU WERE TO ESCORT MS. LYNNE TO THE SECURE HOUSE--!>
< WHAT--?>
<THE WOMAN IS DEAD.>
<YOUR GREAT LOVE IS DEAD--FELLED BY GHUDAZAI BULLETS-->
<YOU, GIRL, ARE LYING.>
<IF MONICA IS DEAD, THEN IT IS YOU WHO HAVE KILLED HER.>
<WITH THE DAWN, I RETURN YOU TO YOUR FATHERS.>
POLICE
--GGHUURRKK!!!
SSKRREE--RRAKKK!!

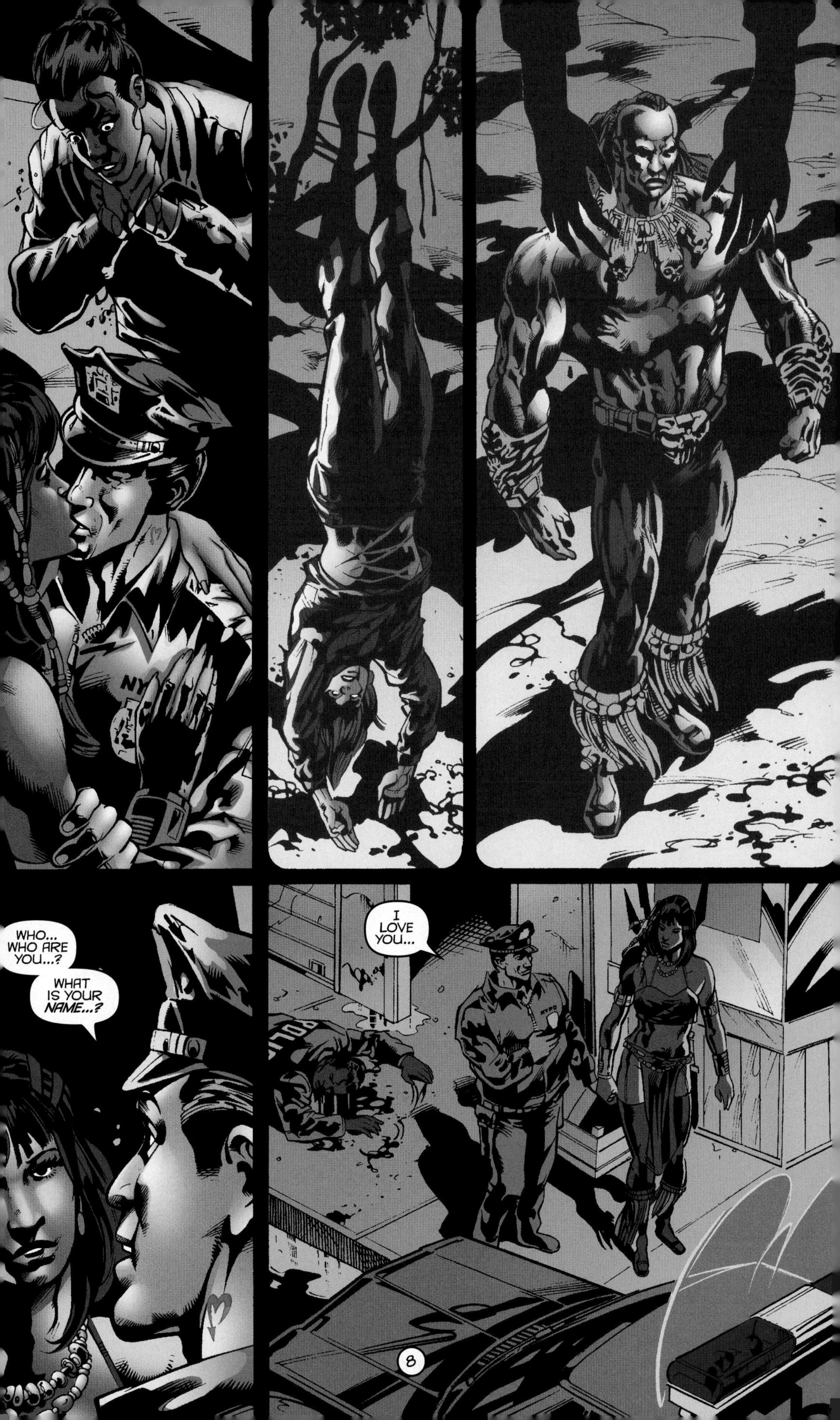
WHO... WHO ARE YOU...?
WHAT IS YOUR *NAME...?*
I LOVE YOU...
NYPD
8

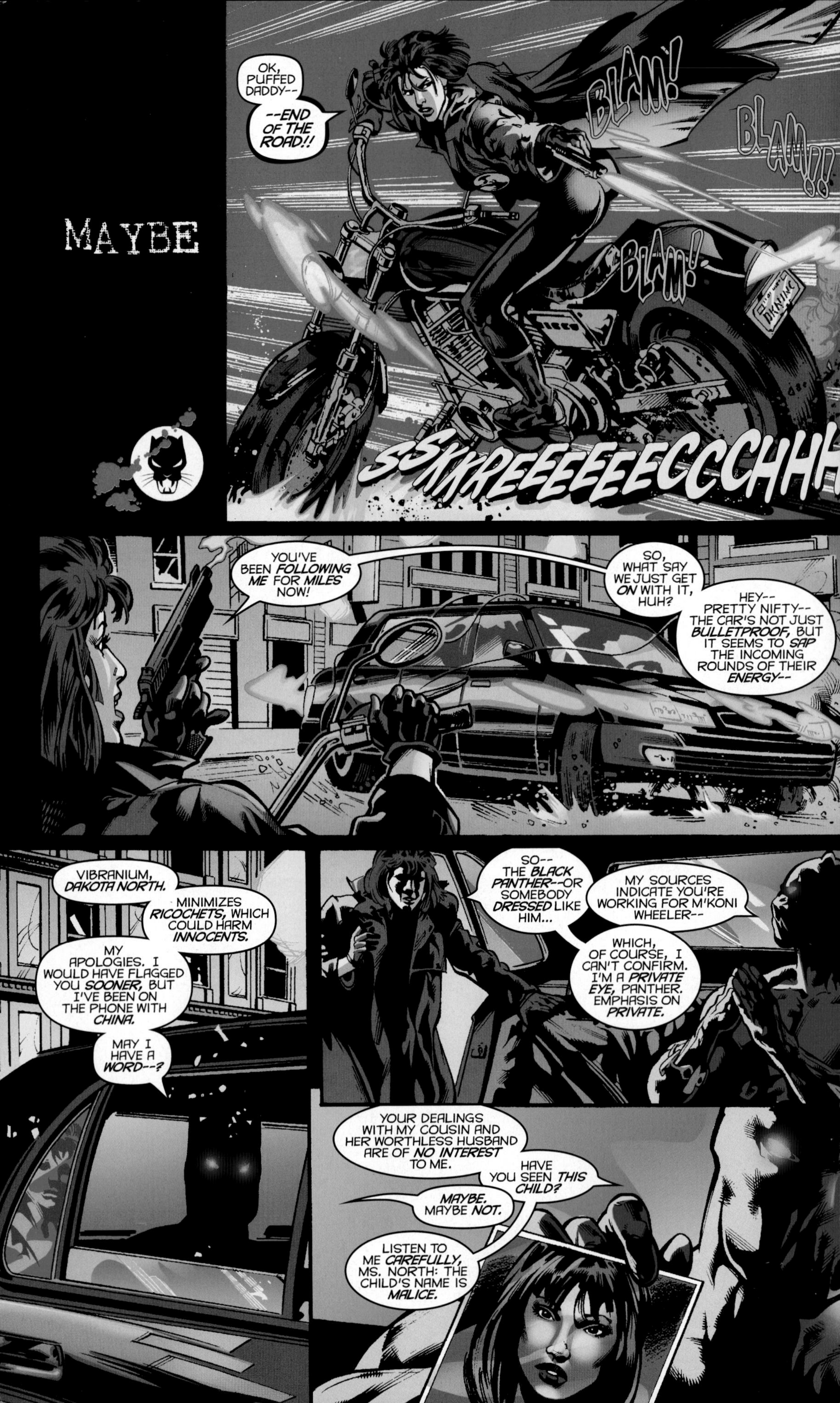
MAYBE
OK, PUFFED DADDY--
--END OF THE ROAD!!
BLAM!
BLAM!!
BLAM!!
SSKKREEEEEEEECCCHHH
YOU'VE BEEN FOLLOWING ME FOR MILES NOW!
SO, WHAT SAY WE JUST GET ON WITH IT, HUH?
HEY-- PRETTY NIFTY-- THE CAR'S NOT JUST BULLETPROOF, BUT IT SEEMS TO SAP THE INCOMING ROUNDS OF THEIR ENERGY--
VIBRANIUM, DAKOTA NORTH.
MINIMIZES RICOCHETS, WHICH COULD HARM INNOCENTS.
MY APOLOGIES. I WOULD HAVE FLAGGED YOU SOONER, BUT I'VE BEEN ON THE PHONE WITH CHINA.
MAY I HAVE A WORD--?
SO-- THE BLACK PANTHER--OR SOMEBODY DRESSED LIKE HIM...
MY SOURCES INDICATE YOU'RE WORKING FOR M'KONI WHEELER--
WHICH, OF COURSE, I CAN'T CONFIRM. I'M A PRIVATE EYE, PANTHER. EMPHASIS ON PRIVATE.
YOUR DEALINGS WITH MY COUSIN AND HER WORTHLESS HUSBAND ARE OF NO INTEREST TO ME.
HAVE YOU SEEN THIS CHILD?
MAYBE. MAYBE NOT.
LISTEN TO ME CAREFULLY, MS. NORTH: THE CHILD'S NAME IS MALICE.

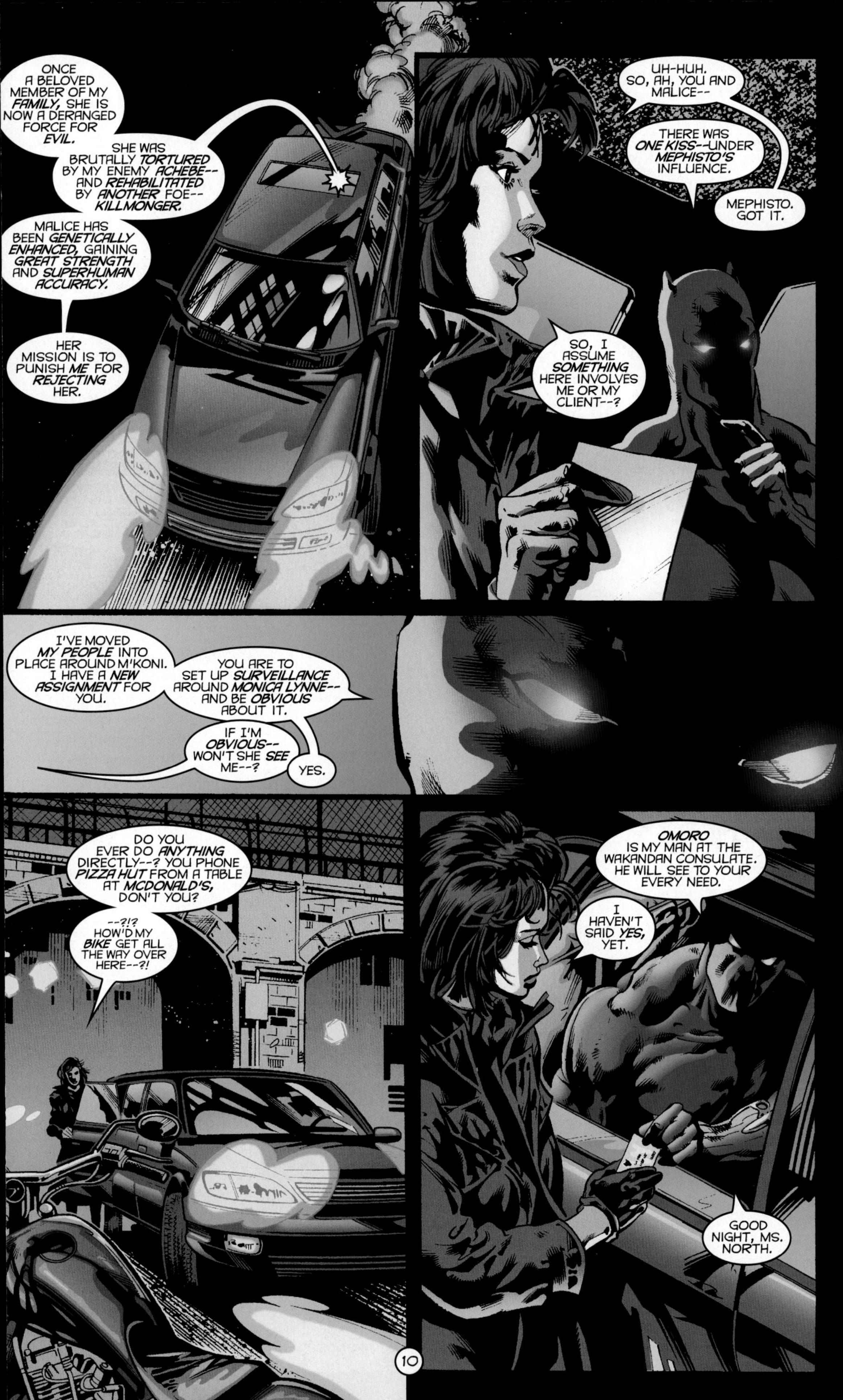
ONCE A BELOVED MEMBER OF MY FAMILY, SHE IS NOW A DERANGED FORCE FOR EVIL.
SHE WAS BRUTALLY TORTURED BY MY ENEMY ACHEBE--AND REHABILITATED BY ANOTHER FOE--KILLMONGER.
MALICE HAS BEEN GENETICALLY ENHANCED, GAINING GREAT STRENGTH AND SUPERHUMAN ACCURACY.
HER MISSION IS TO PUNISH ME FOR REJECTING HER.
UH-HUH. SO, AH, YOU AND MALICE--
THERE WAS ONE KISS--UNDER MEPHISTO'S INFLUENCE.
MEPHISTO. GOT IT.
SO, I ASSUME SOMETHING HERE INVOLVES ME OR MY CLIENT--?
I'VE MOVED MY PEOPLE INTO PLACE AROUND M'KONI. I HAVE A NEW ASSIGNMENT FOR YOU.
YOU ARE TO SET UP SURVEILLANCE AROUND MONICA LYNNE--AND BE OBVIOUS ABOUT IT.
IF I'M OBVIOUS--WON'T SHE SEE ME--?
YES.
DO YOU EVER DO ANYTHING DIRECTLY--? YOU PHONE PIZZA HUT FROM A TABLE AT MCDONALD'S, DON'T YOU?
--?!? HOW'D MY BIKE GET ALL THE WAY OVER HERE--?!
OMORO IS MY MAN AT THE WAKANDAN CONSULATE. HE WILL SEE TO YOUR EVERY NEED.
I HAVEN'T SAID YES, YET.
GOOD NIGHT, MS. NORTH.

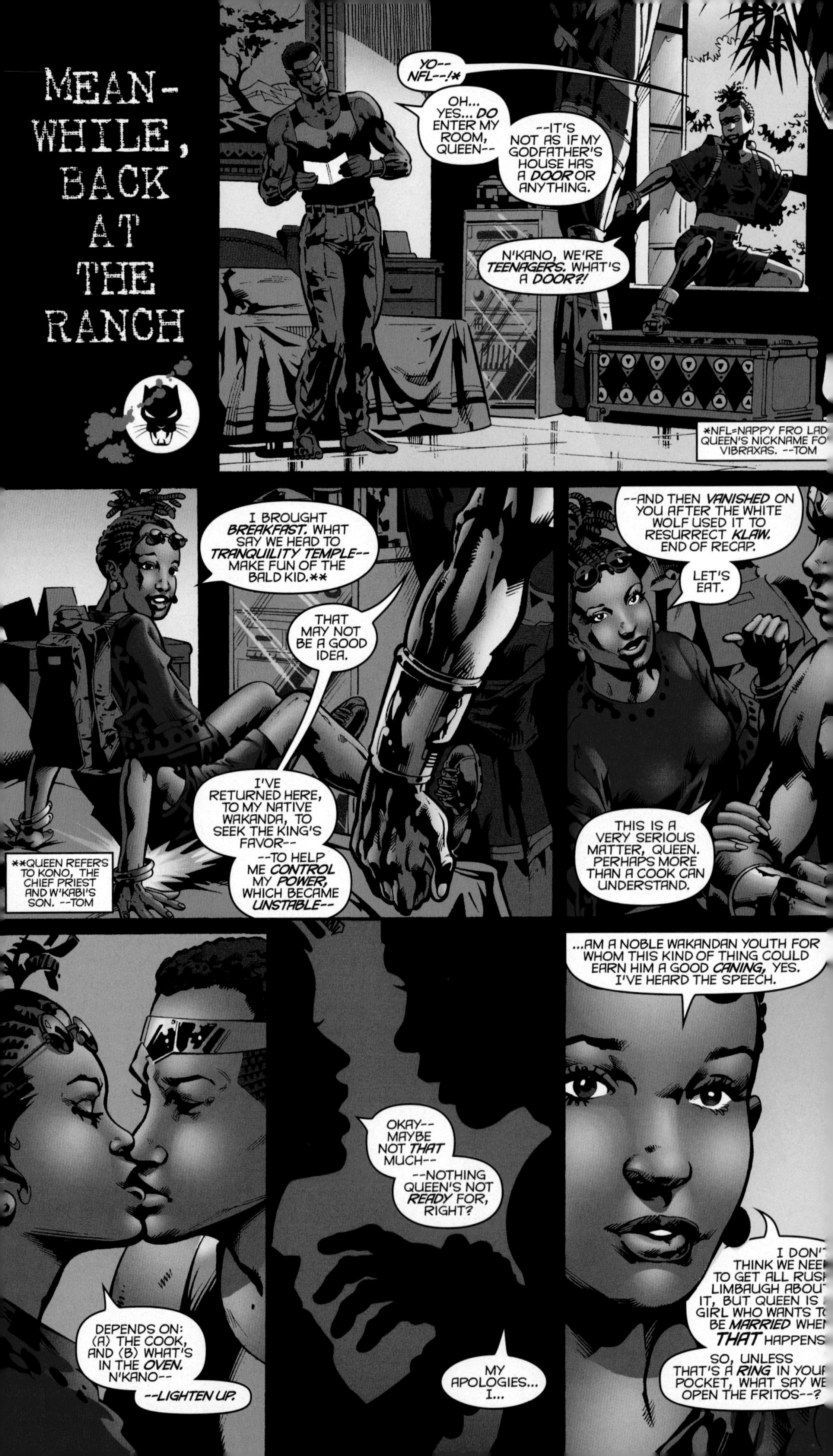

MEAN-WHILE, BACK AT THE RANCH
YO-- NFL--!*
OH... YES... DO ENTER MY ROOM, QUEEN--
--IT'S NOT AS IF MY GODFATHER'S HOUSE HAS A DOOR OR ANYTHING.
N'KANO, WE'RE TEENAGERS. WHAT'S A DOOR?!
*NFL=NAPPY FRO LAD QUEEN'S NICKNAME FO VIBRAXAS. --TOM
I BROUGHT BREAKFAST. WHAT SAY WE HEAD TO TRANQUILITY TEMPLE-- MAKE FUN OF THE BALD KID.**
THAT MAY NOT BE A GOOD IDEA.
I'VE RETURNED HERE, TO MY NATIVE WAKANDA, TO SEEK THE KING'S FAVOR--
--TO HELP ME CONTROL MY POWER, WHICH BECAME UNSTABLE--
**QUEEN REFERS TO KONO, THE CHIEF PRIEST AND W'KABI'S SON. --TOM
--AND THEN VANISHED ON YOU AFTER THE WHITE WOLF USED IT TO RESURRECT KLAW. END OF RECAP.
LET'S EAT.
THIS IS A VERY SERIOUS MATTER, QUEEN. PERHAPS MORE THAN A COOK CAN UNDERSTAND.
DEPENDS ON: (A) THE COOK, AND (B) WHAT'S IN THE OVEN. N'KANO--
--LIGHTEN UP.
OKAY-- MAYBE NOT THAT MUCH--
--NOTHING QUEEN'S NOT READY FOR, RIGHT?
MY APOLOGIES... I...
...AM A NOBLE WAKANDAN YOUTH FOR WHOM THIS KIND OF THING COULD EARN HIM A GOOD CANING, YES. I'VE HEARD THE SPEECH.
I DON'T THINK WE NEE TO GET ALL RUSH LIMBAUGH ABOUT IT, BUT QUEEN IS GIRL WHO WANTS T BE MARRIED WHEN THAT HAPPENS
SO, UNLESS THAT'S A RING IN YOUR POCKET, WHAT SAY WE OPEN THE FRITOS--?

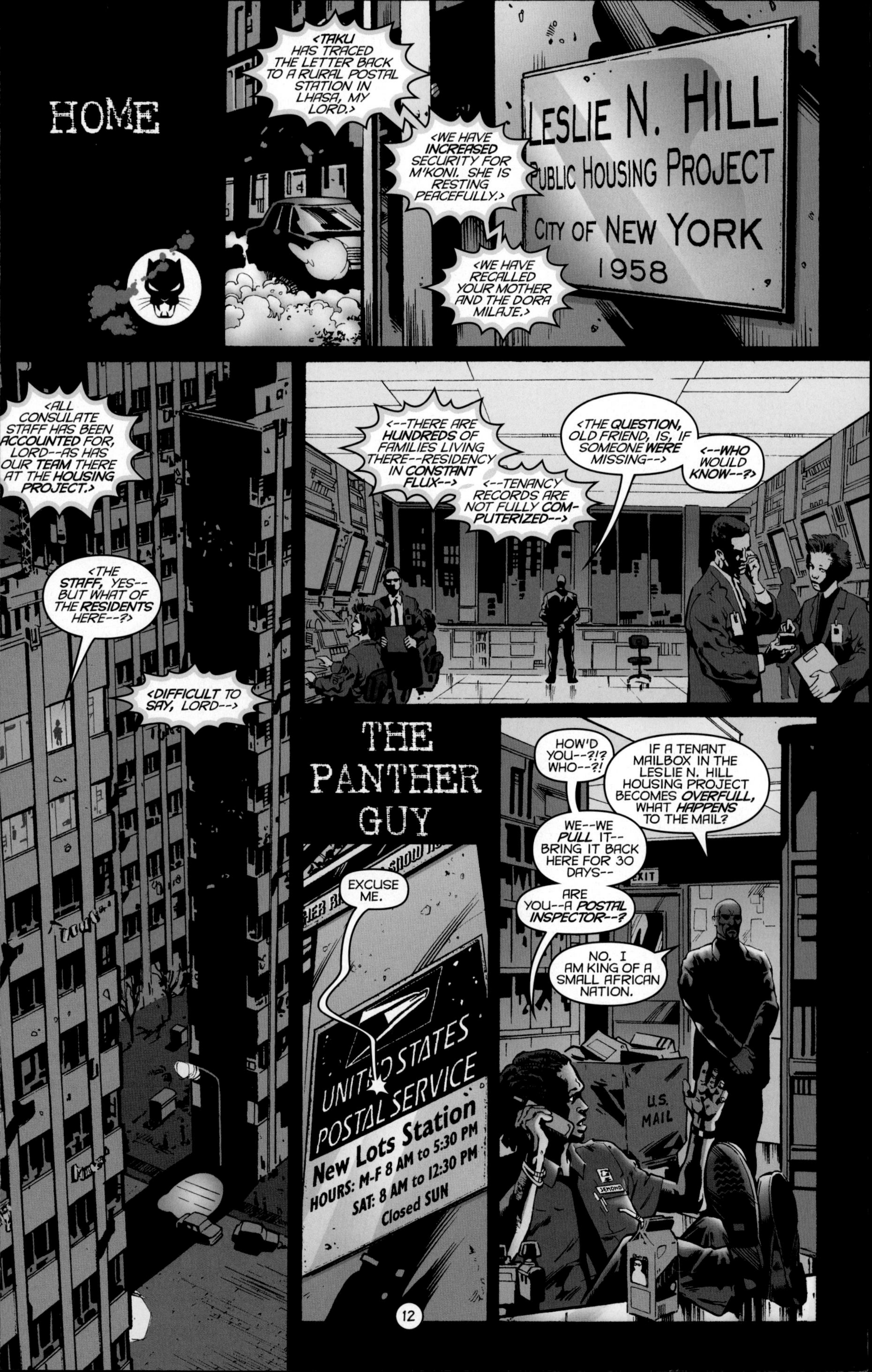

HOME
<TAKU HAS TRACED THE LETTER BACK TO A RURAL POSTAL STATION IN LHASA, MY LORD.>
<WE HAVE INCREASED SECURITY FOR M'KONI. SHE IS RESTING PEACEFULLY.>
<WE HAVE RECALLED YOUR MOTHER AND THE DORA MILAJE.>
LESLIE N. HILL
PUBLIC HOUSING PROJECT
CITY OF NEW YORK
1958
<ALL CONSULATE STAFF HAS BEEN ACCOUNTED FOR, LORD--AS HAS OUR TEAM THERE AT THE HOUSING PROJECT.>
<THE STAFF, YES--BUT WHAT OF THE RESIDENTS HERE--?>
<DIFFICULT TO SAY, LORD-->
<--THERE ARE HUNDREDS OF FAMILIES LIVING THERE--RESIDENCY IN CONSTANT FLUX-->
<--TENANCY RECORDS ARE NOT FULLY COMPUTERIZED-->
<THE QUESTION, OLD FRIEND, IS, IF SOMEONE WERE MISSING-->
<--WHO WOULD KNOW--?>
THE PANTHER GUY
EXCUSE ME.
UNITED STATES POSTAL SERVICE
New Lots Station
HOURS: M-F 8 AM to 5:30 PM
SAT: 8 AM to 12:30 PM
Closed SUN
HOW'D YOU--?!? WHO--?!
IF A TENANT MAILBOX IN THE LESLIE N. HILL HOUSING PROJECT BECOMES OVERFULL, WHAT HAPPENS TO THE MAIL?
WE--WE PULL IT--BRING IT BACK HERE FOR 30 DAYS--
ARE YOU--A POSTAL INSPECTOR--?
NO. I AM KING OF A SMALL AFRICAN NATION.
EXIT
U.S. MAIL

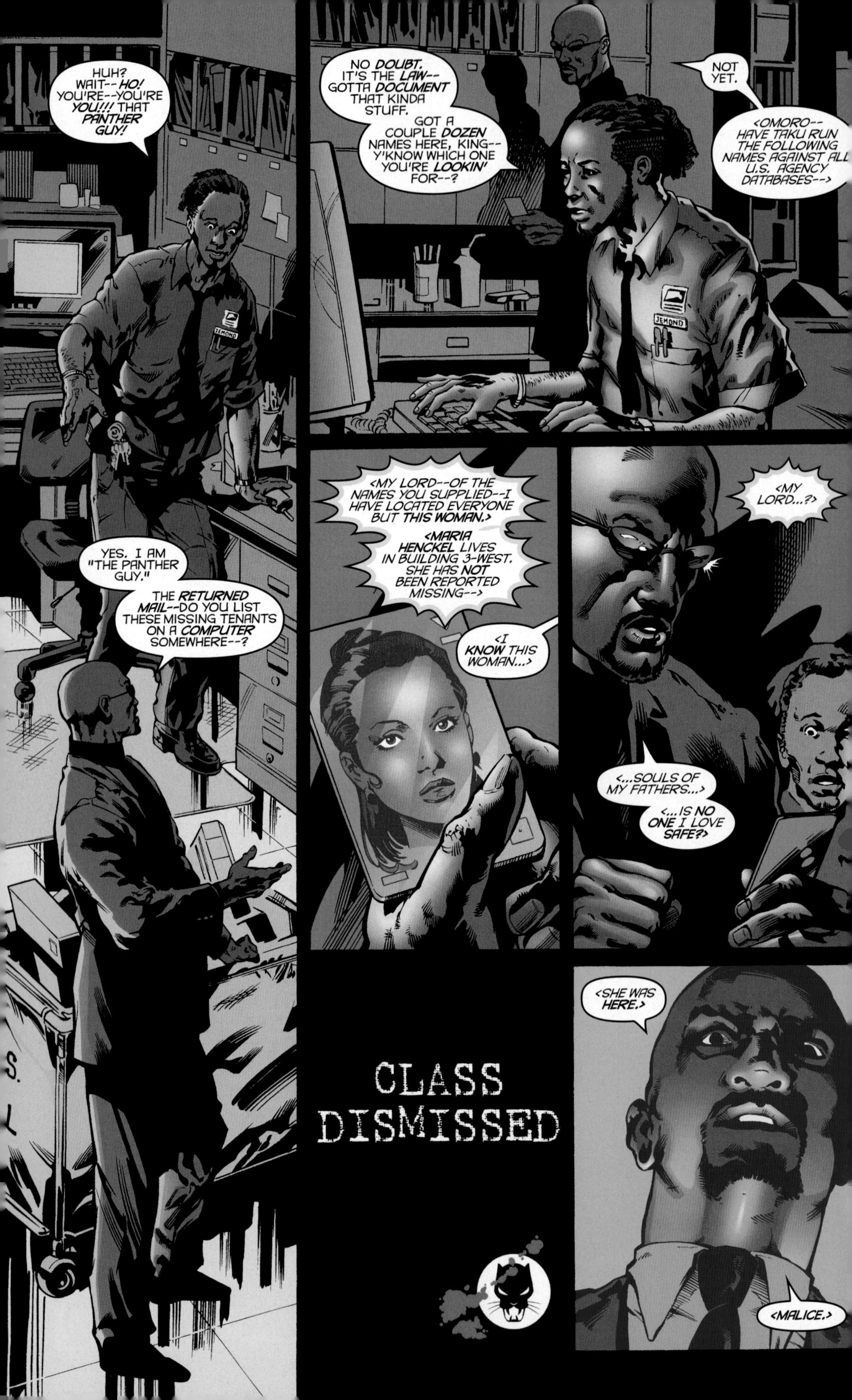
HUH? WAIT--HO! YOU'RE--YOU'RE YOU!!! THAT PANTHER GUY!
YES. I AM "THE PANTHER GUY."
THE RETURNED MAIL--DO YOU LIST THESE MISSING TENANTS ON A COMPUTER SOMEWHERE--?
NO DOUBT. IT'S THE LAW-- GOTTA DOCUMENT THAT KINDA STUFF.
GOT A COUPLE DOZEN NAMES HERE, KING-- Y'KNOW WHICH ONE YOU'RE LOOKIN' FOR--?
NOT YET.
<OMORO-- HAVE TAKU RUN THE FOLLOWING NAMES AGAINST ALL U.S. AGENCY DATABASES-->
<MY LORD--OF THE NAMES YOU SUPPLIED--I HAVE LOCATED EVERYONE BUT THIS WOMAN.>
<MARIA HENCKEL LIVES IN BUILDING 3-WEST. SHE HAS NOT BEEN REPORTED MISSING-->
<I KNOW THIS WOMAN...>
<MY LORD...?>
<...SOULS OF MY FATHERS...>
<...IS NO ONE I LOVE SAFE?>
CLASS DISMISSED
<SHE WAS HERE.>
<MALICE.>

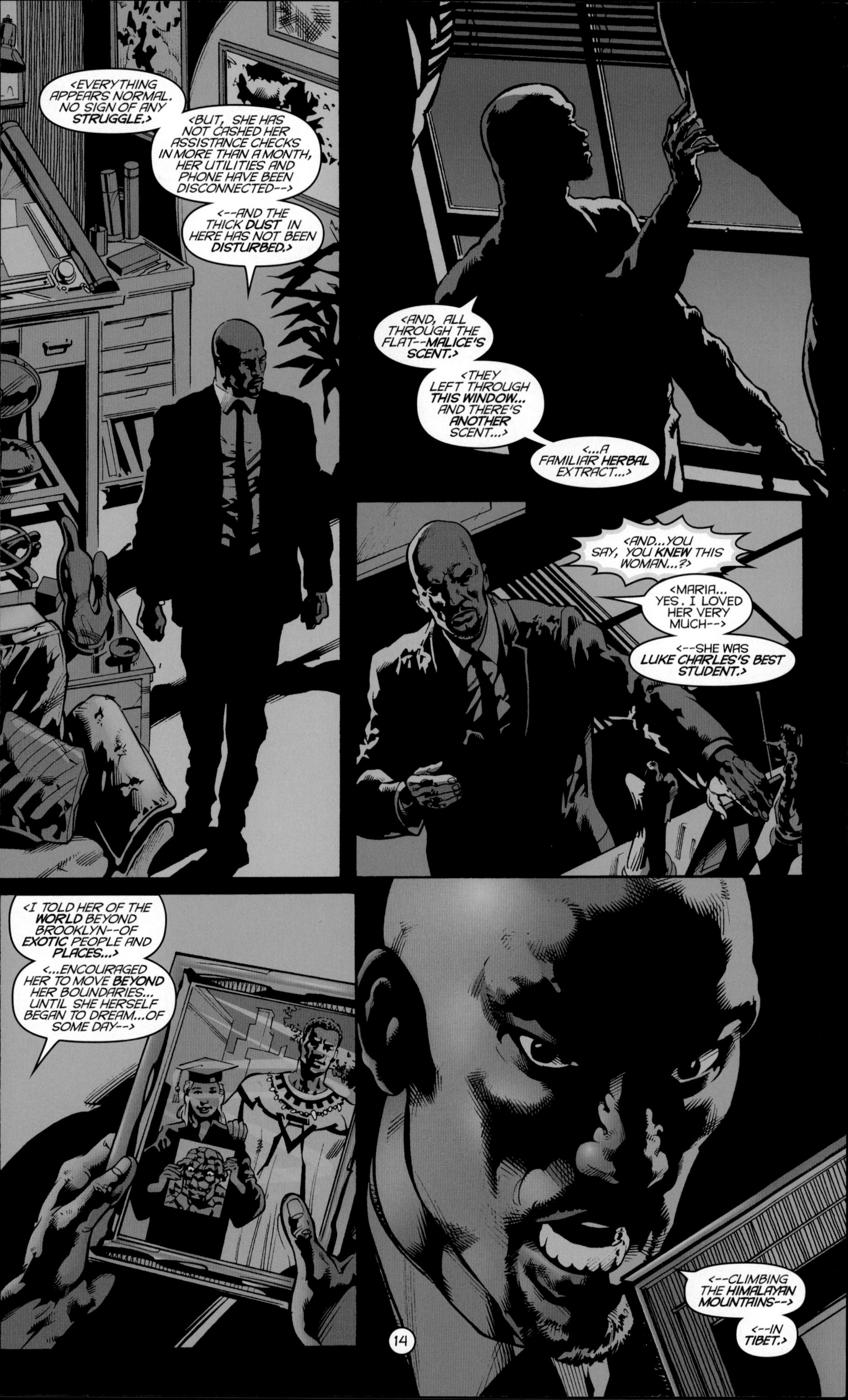
<EVERYTHING APPEARS NORMAL. NO SIGN OF ANY STRUGGLE.>
<BUT, SHE HAS NOT CASHED HER ASSISTANCE CHECKS IN MORE THAN A MONTH, HER UTILITIES AND PHONE HAVE BEEN DISCONNECTED-->
<--AND THE THICK DUST IN HERE HAS NOT BEEN DISTURBED.>
<AND, ALL THROUGH THE FLAT--MALICE'S SCENT.>
<THEY LEFT THROUGH THIS WINDOW... AND THERE'S ANOTHER SCENT...>
<...A FAMILIAR HERBAL EXTRACT...>
<AND...YOU SAY, YOU KNEW THIS WOMAN...?>
<MARIA... YES. I LOVED HER VERY MUCH-->
<--SHE WAS LUKE CHARLES'S BEST STUDENT.>
<I TOLD HER OF THE WORLD BEYOND BROOKLYN--OF EXOTIC PEOPLE AND PLACES...>
<...ENCOURAGED HER TO MOVE BEYOND HER BOUNDARIES... UNTIL SHE HERSELF BEGAN TO DREAM...OF SOME DAY-->
<--CLIMBING THE HIMALAYAN MOUNTAINS-->
<--IN TIBET.>

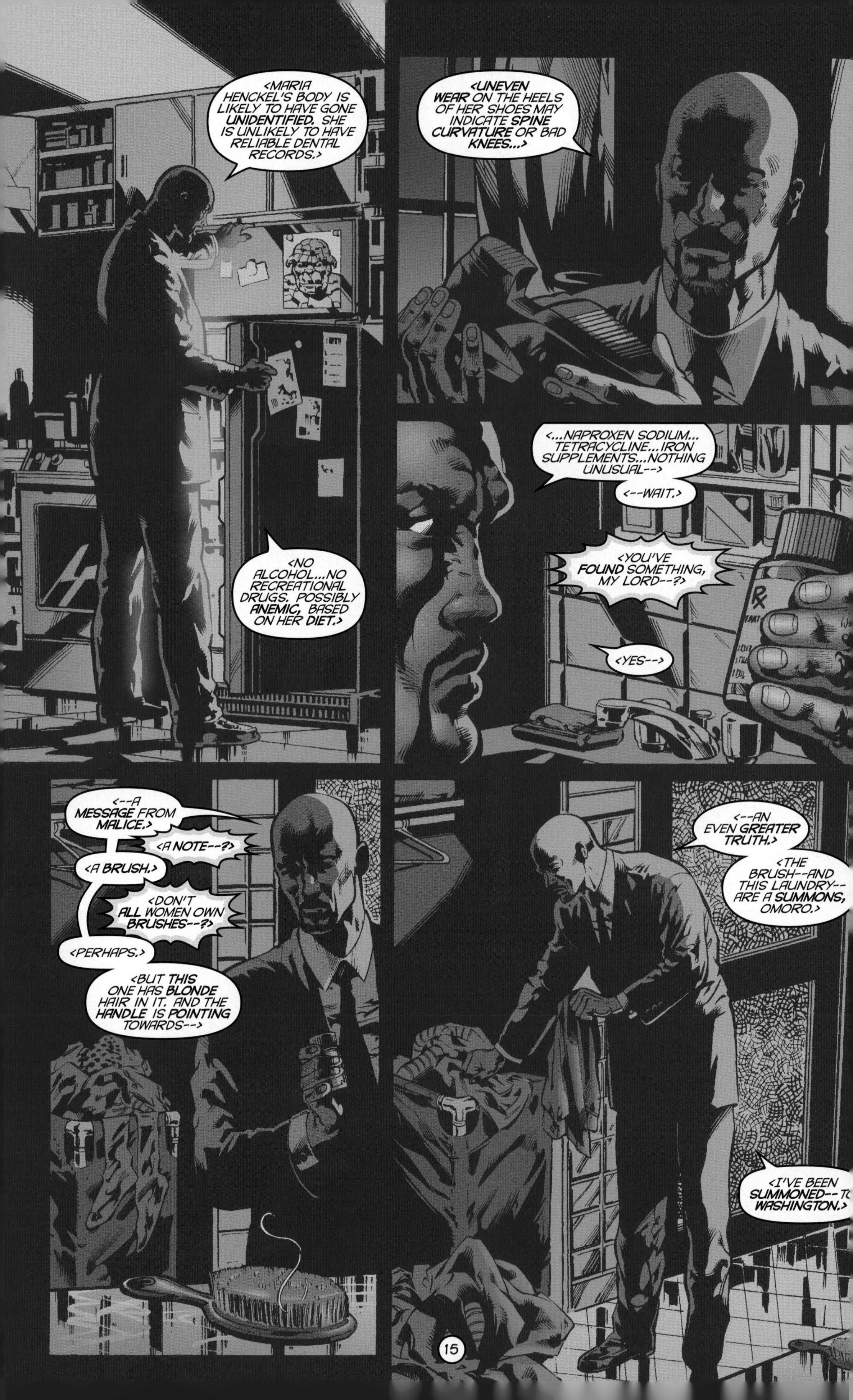
<MARIA HENCKEL'S BODY IS LIKELY TO HAVE GONE UNIDENTIFIED. SHE IS UNLIKELY TO HAVE RELIABLE DENTAL RECORDS.>
<NO ALCOHOL...NO RECREATIONAL DRUGS. POSSIBLY ANEMIC, BASED ON HER DIET.>
<UNEVEN WEAR ON THE HEELS OF HER SHOES MAY INDICATE SPINE CURVATURE OR BAD KNEES...>
<...NAPROXEN SODIUM... TETRACYCLINE...IRON SUPPLEMENTS...NOTHING UNUSUAL-->
<--WAIT.>
<YOU'VE FOUND SOMETHING, MY LORD--?>
<YES-->
<--A MESSAGE FROM MALICE.>
<A NOTE--?>
<A BRUSH.>
<DON'T ALL WOMEN OWN BRUSHES--?>
<PERHAPS.>
<BUT THIS ONE HAS BLONDE HAIR IN IT. AND THE HANDLE IS POINTING TOWARDS-->
<--AN EVEN GREATER TRUTH.>
<THE BRUSH--AND THIS LAUNDRY--ARE A SUMMONS, OMORO.>
<I'VE BEEN SUMMONED--TO WASHINGTON.>

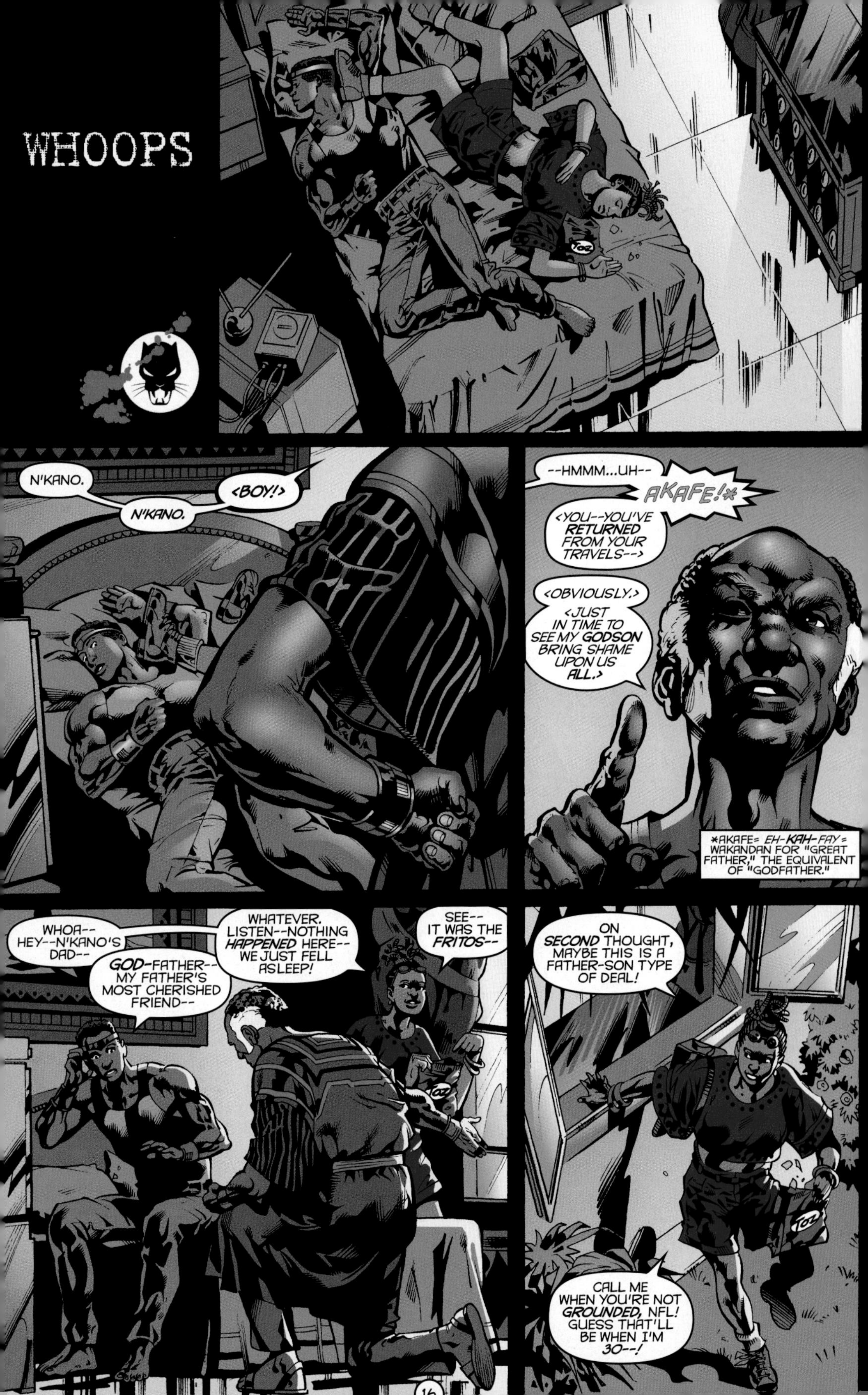
WHOOPS
N'KANO.
N'KANO.
<BOY!>
--HMMM...UH--
AKAFE!*
<YOU--YOU'VE RETURNED FROM YOUR TRAVELS-->
<OBVIOUSLY.>
<JUST IN TIME TO SEE MY GODSON BRING SHAME UPON US ALL.>
*AKAFE= EH-KAH-FAY= WAKANDAN FOR "GREAT FATHER," THE EQUIVALENT OF "GODFATHER."
WHOA--HEY--N'KANO'S DAD--
GOD-FATHER--MY FATHER'S MOST CHERISHED FRIEND--
WHATEVER. LISTEN--NOTHING HAPPENED HERE--WE JUST FELL ASLEEP!
SEE--IT WAS THE FRITOS--
ON SECOND THOUGHT, MAYBE THIS IS A FATHER-SON TYPE OF DEAL!
CALL ME WHEN YOU'RE NOT GROUNDED, NFL! GUESS THAT'LL BE WHEN I'M 30--!

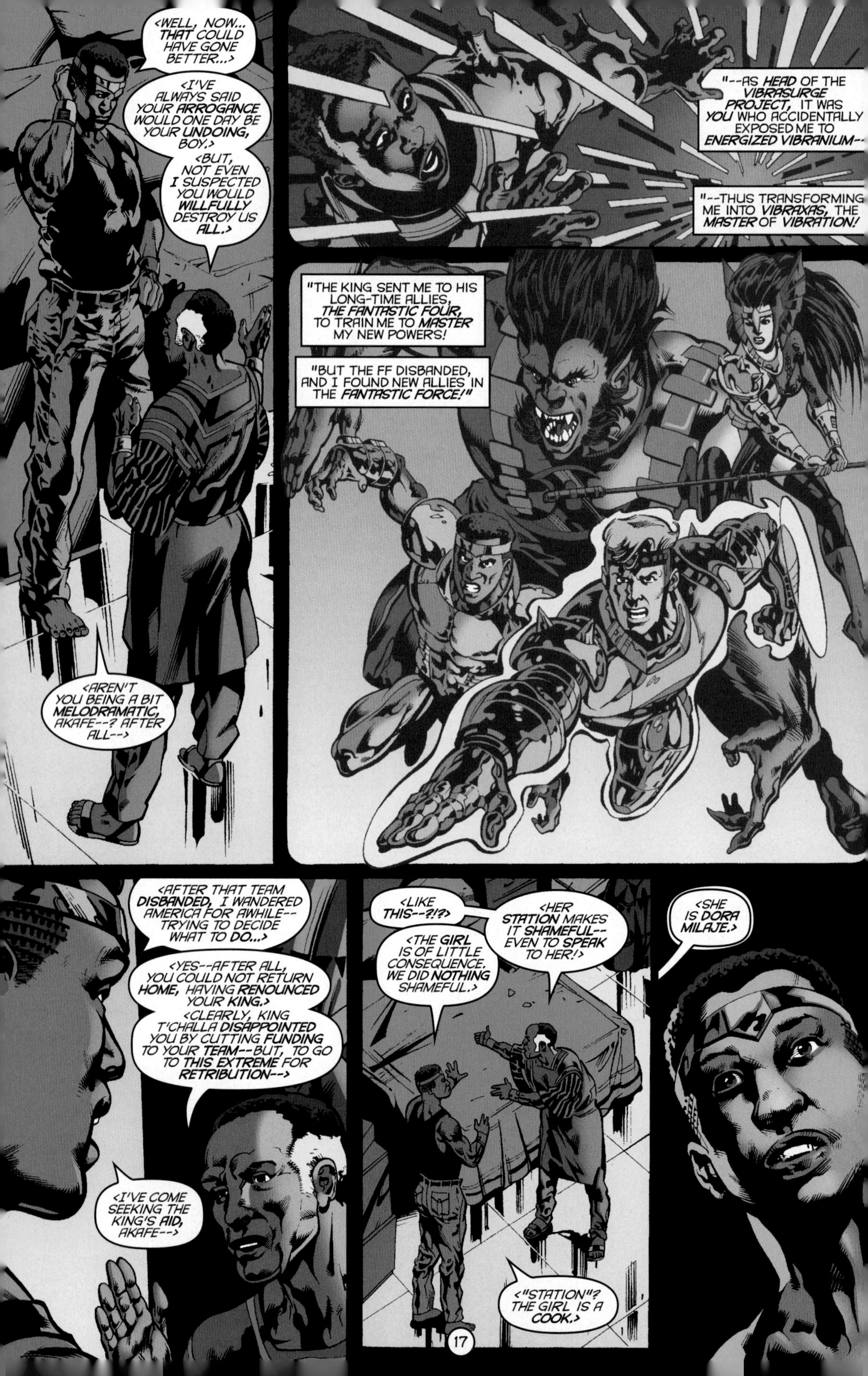

<WELL, NOW... THAT COULD HAVE GONE BETTER...>
<I'VE ALWAYS SAID YOUR ARROGANCE WOULD ONE DAY BE YOUR UNDOING, BOY.>
<BUT, NOT EVEN I SUSPECTED YOU WOULD WILLFULLY DESTROY US ALL.>
<AREN'T YOU BEING A BIT MELODRAMATIC, AKAFE--? AFTER ALL-->
"--AS HEAD OF THE VIBRASURGE PROJECT, IT WAS YOU WHO ACCIDENTALLY EXPOSED ME TO ENERGIZED VIBRANIUM--
"--THUS TRANSFORMING ME INTO VIBRAXAS, THE MASTER OF VIBRATION!
"THE KING SENT ME TO HIS LONG-TIME ALLIES, THE FANTASTIC FOUR, TO TRAIN ME TO MASTER MY NEW POWERS!
"BUT THE FF DISBANDED, AND I FOUND NEW ALLIES IN THE FANTASTIC FORCE!"
<AFTER THAT TEAM DISBANDED, I WANDERED AMERICA FOR AWHILE-- TRYING TO DECIDE WHAT TO DO...>
<YES--AFTER ALL, YOU COULD NOT RETURN HOME, HAVING RENOUNCED YOUR KING.>
<CLEARLY, KING T'CHALLA DISAPPOINTED YOU BY CUTTING FUNDING TO YOUR TEAM--BUT, TO GO TO THIS EXTREME FOR RETRIBUTION-->
<I'VE COME SEEKING THE KING'S AID, AKAFE-->
<LIKE THIS--?!?>
<THE GIRL IS OF LITTLE CONSEQUENCE. WE DID NOTHING SHAMEFUL.>
<HER STATION MAKES IT SHAMEFUL-- EVEN TO SPEAK TO HER!>
<"STATION"? THE GIRL IS A COOK.>
<SHE IS DORA MILAJE.>

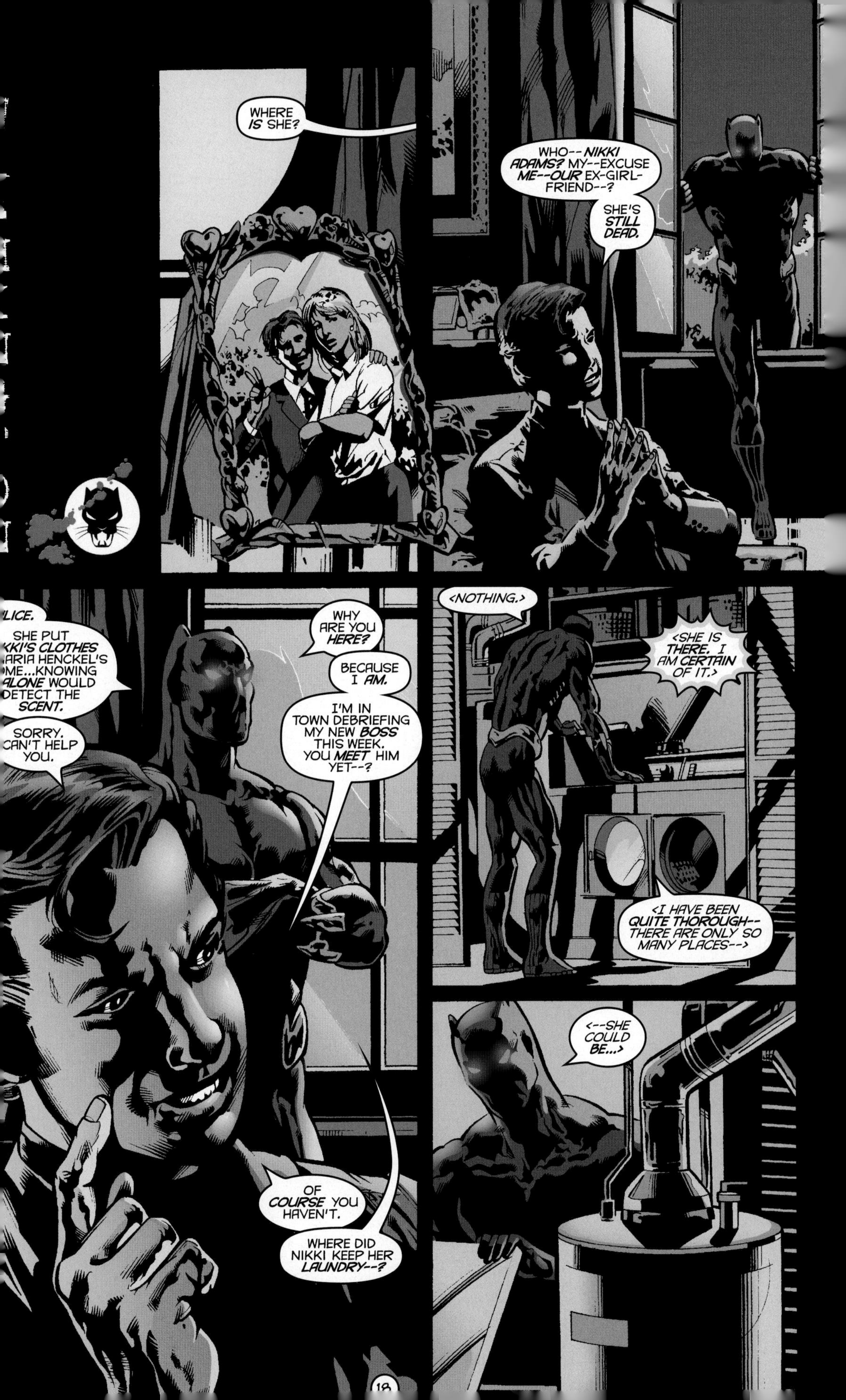
WHERE IS SHE?
WHO--NIKKI ADAMS? MY--EXCUSE ME--OUR EX-GIRL-FRIEND--?
SHE'S STILL DEAD.
LICE.
SHE PUT KKI'S CLOTHES ARIA HENCKEL'S ME...KNOWING ALONE WOULD DETECT THE SCENT.
SORRY. CAN'T HELP YOU.
WHY ARE YOU HERE?
BECAUSE I AM.
I'M IN TOWN DEBRIEFING MY NEW BOSS THIS WEEK. YOU MEET HIM YET--?
OF COURSE YOU HAVEN'T.
WHERE DID NIKKI KEEP HER LAUNDRY--?
<NOTHING.>
<SHE IS THERE. I AM CERTAIN OF IT.>
<I HAVE BEEN QUITE THOROUGH--THERE ARE ONLY SO MANY PLACES-->
<--SHE COULD BE...>

NIGHT-MARES

PANTHER GO HOME!

GOD IS NOT A KI...

MOMMY...

...MOMMY... WAKE UP...

SSSHAAARRR

IS NOT A KITTY

ENEMY THE

PANTHER GO HOME

ALL DGE HEE

MOMMY... MOMMY--!!

MOMMIEEE--!!

REST E-Z
Night time Sleep Aid
Safe Gentle Non Habit-Forming

<BASHENGA'S EYES...>

<WHAT IS IT, OMORO-- WHAT DO YOU SEE--?!>

--

<--DEATH...>

OF THE STATE

IS NOT A KITTY

19

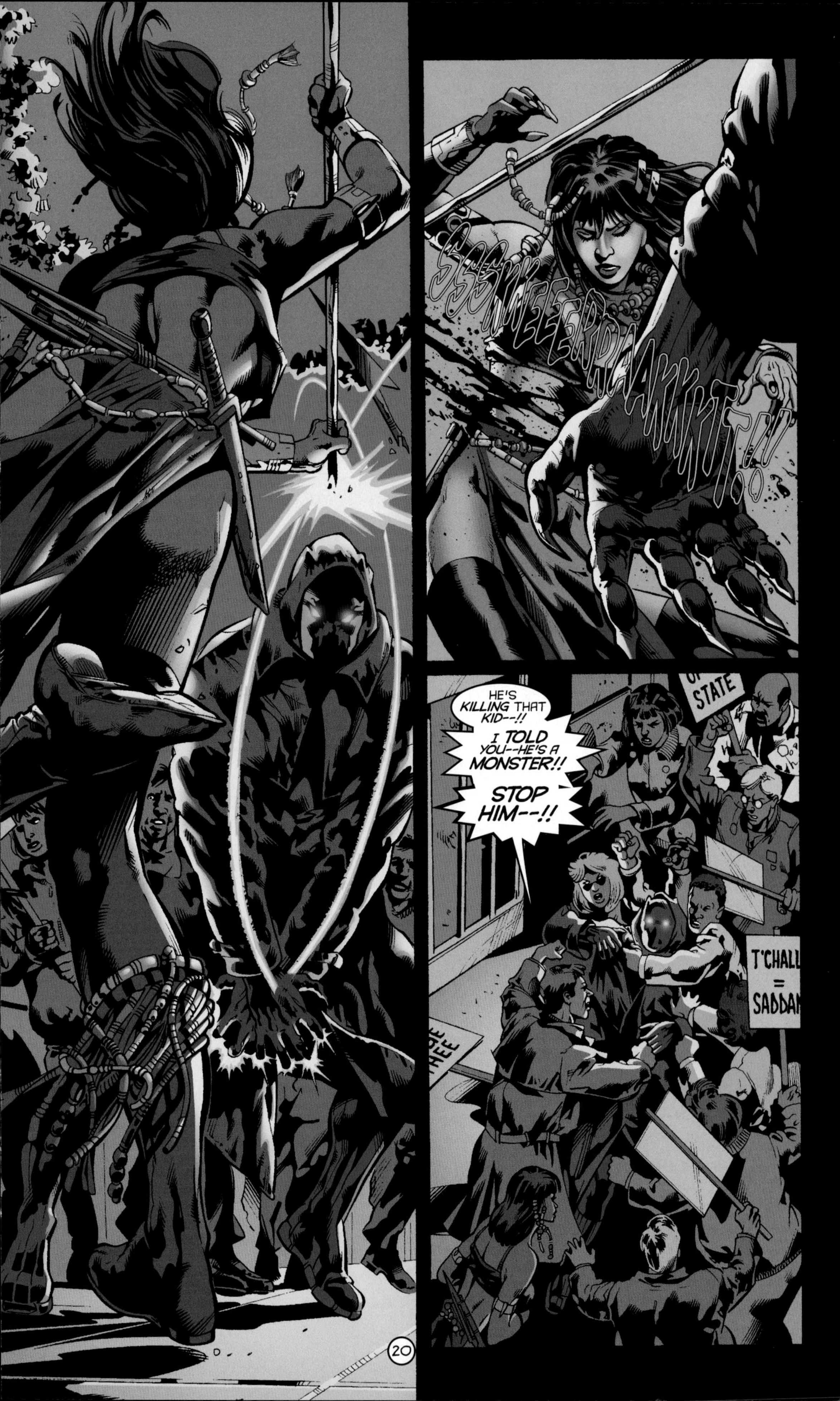

SSSKWEERRAAKKKT!!
HE'S KILLING THAT KID--!!
I TOLD YOU--HE'S A MONSTER!!
STOP HIM--!!
STATE
T'CHALL = SADDAM

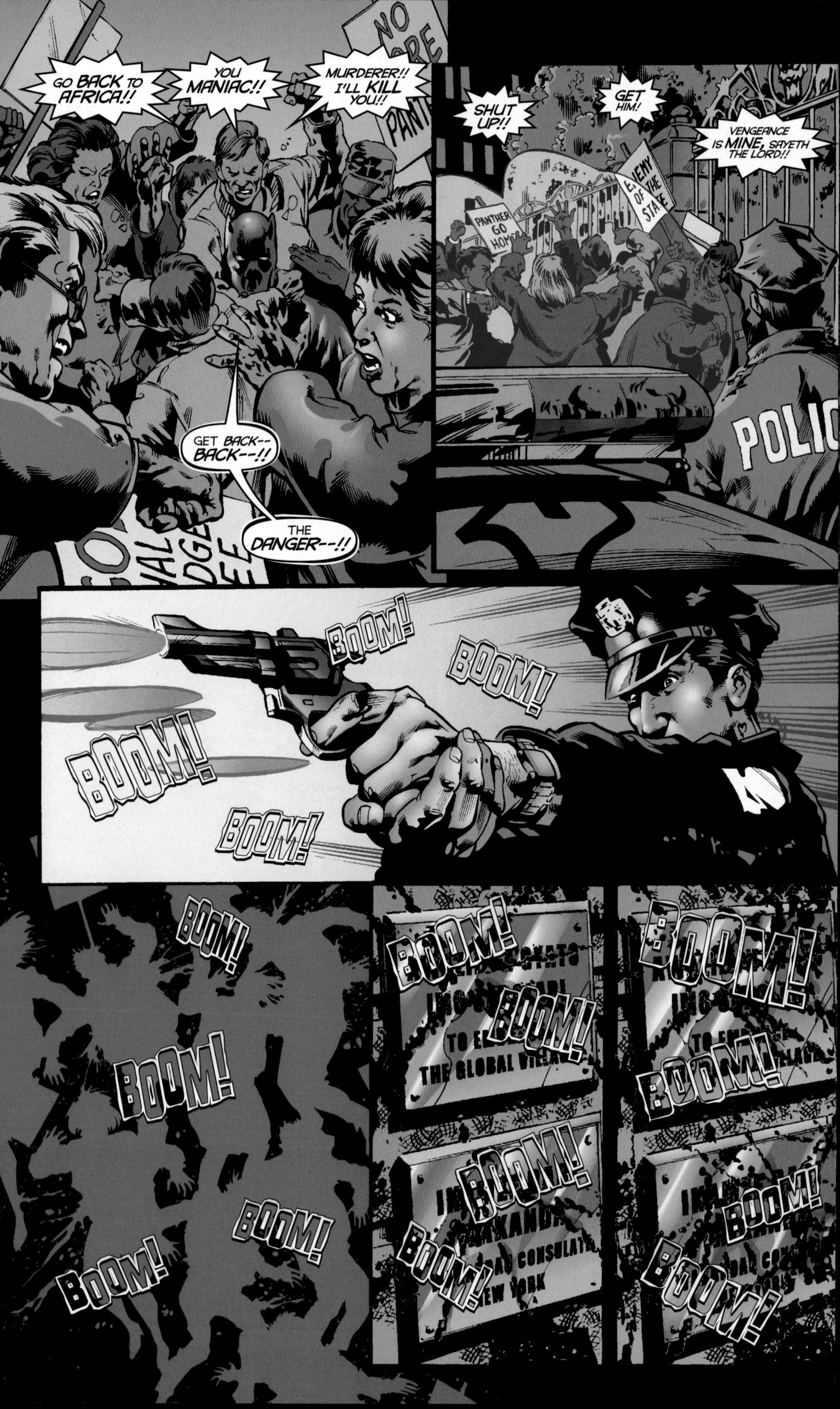

GO BACK TO AFRICA!!
YOU MANIAC!!
MURDERER!! I'LL KILL YOU!!
GET BACK--BACK--!!
THE DANGER--!!
SHUT UP!!
GET HIM!
VENGEANCE IS MINE, SAYETH THE LORD!!
PANTHER GO HOM
ENEMY OF THE STATE
POLIC
BOOM!
BOOM!
BOOM!
BOOM!
BOOM!
BOOM!
BOOM!
BOOM!
BOOM!
BOOM!
BOOM!
BOOM!
BOOM!
BOOM!
BOOM!
BOOM!
BOOM!
THE GLOBAL VILLA
CONSULATE
NEW YORK

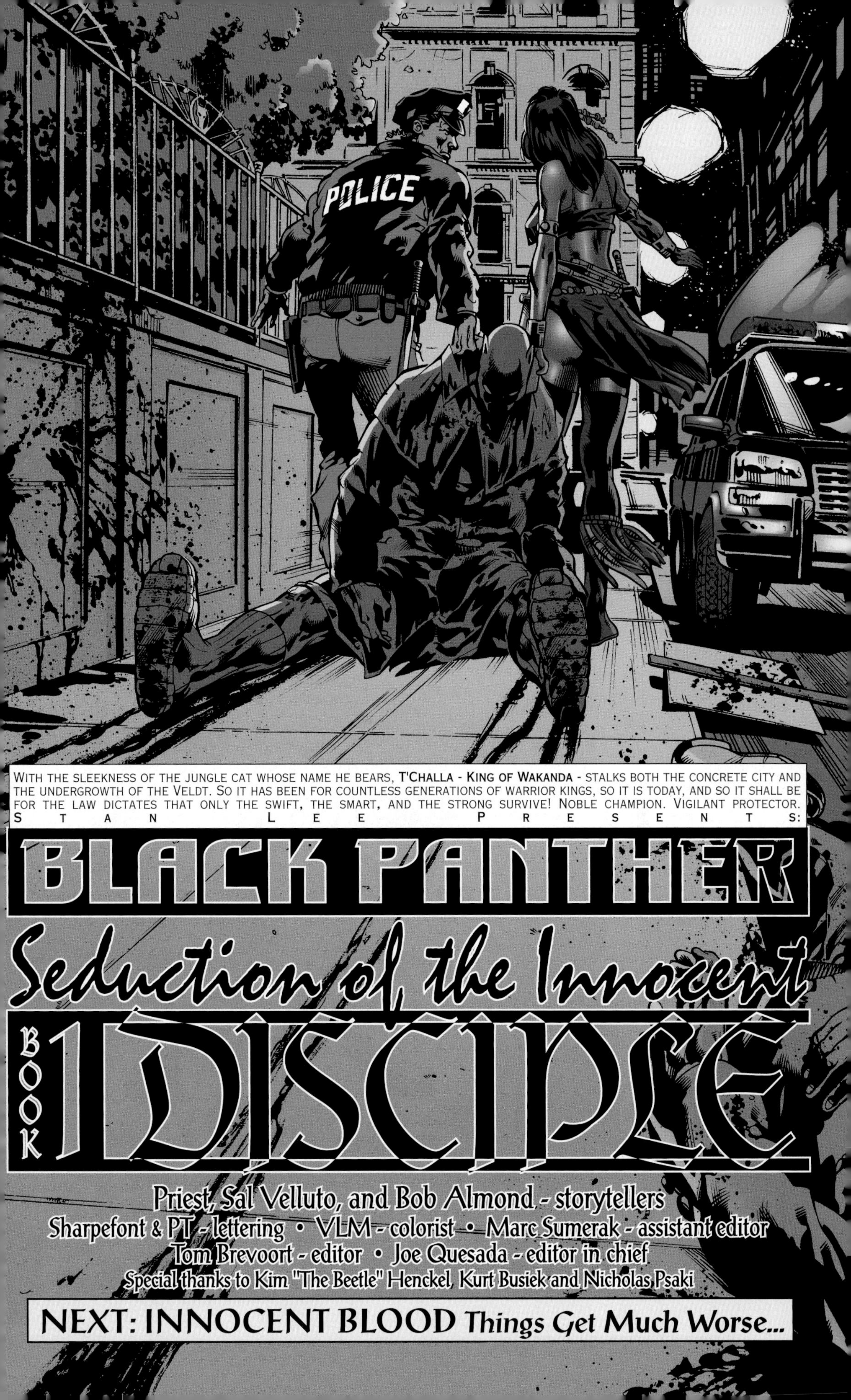
POLICE
WITH THE SLEEKNESS OF THE JUNGLE CAT WHOSE NAME HE BEARS, T'CHALLA - KING OF WAKANDA - STALKS BOTH THE CONCRETE CITY AND THE UNDERGROWTH OF THE VELDT. SO IT HAS BEEN FOR COUNTLESS GENERATIONS OF WARRIOR KINGS, SO IT IS TODAY, AND SO IT SHALL BE FOR THE LAW DICTATES THAT ONLY THE SWIFT, THE SMART, AND THE STRONG SURVIVE! NOBLE CHAMPION. VIGILANT PROTECTOR.
STAN LEE PRESENTS:
BLACK PANTHER
Seduction of the Innocent
BOOK 1 DISCIPLE
Priest, Sal Velluto, and Bob Almond - storytellers
Sharpefont & PT - lettering • VLM - colorist • Marc Sumerak - assistant editor
Tom Brevoort - editor • Joe Quesada - editor in chief
Special thanks to Kim "The Beetle" Henckel, Kurt Busiek and Nicholas Psaki
NEXT: INNOCENT BLOOD Things Get Much Worse...

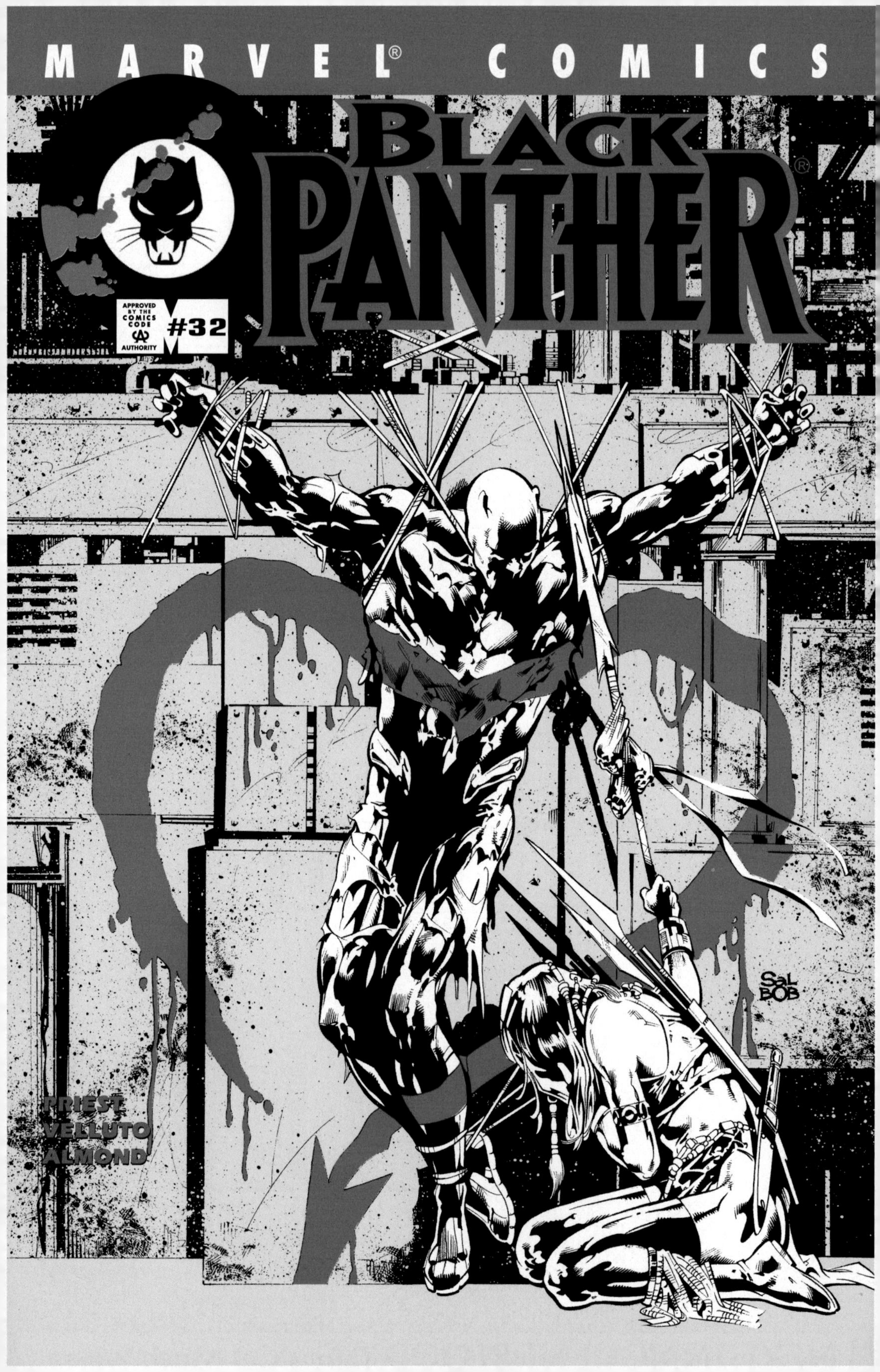
MARVEL® COMICS
BLACK PANTHER®
APPROVED BY THE COMICS CODE AUTHORITY
#32
SAL BOB
PRIEST
VELLUTO
ALMOND

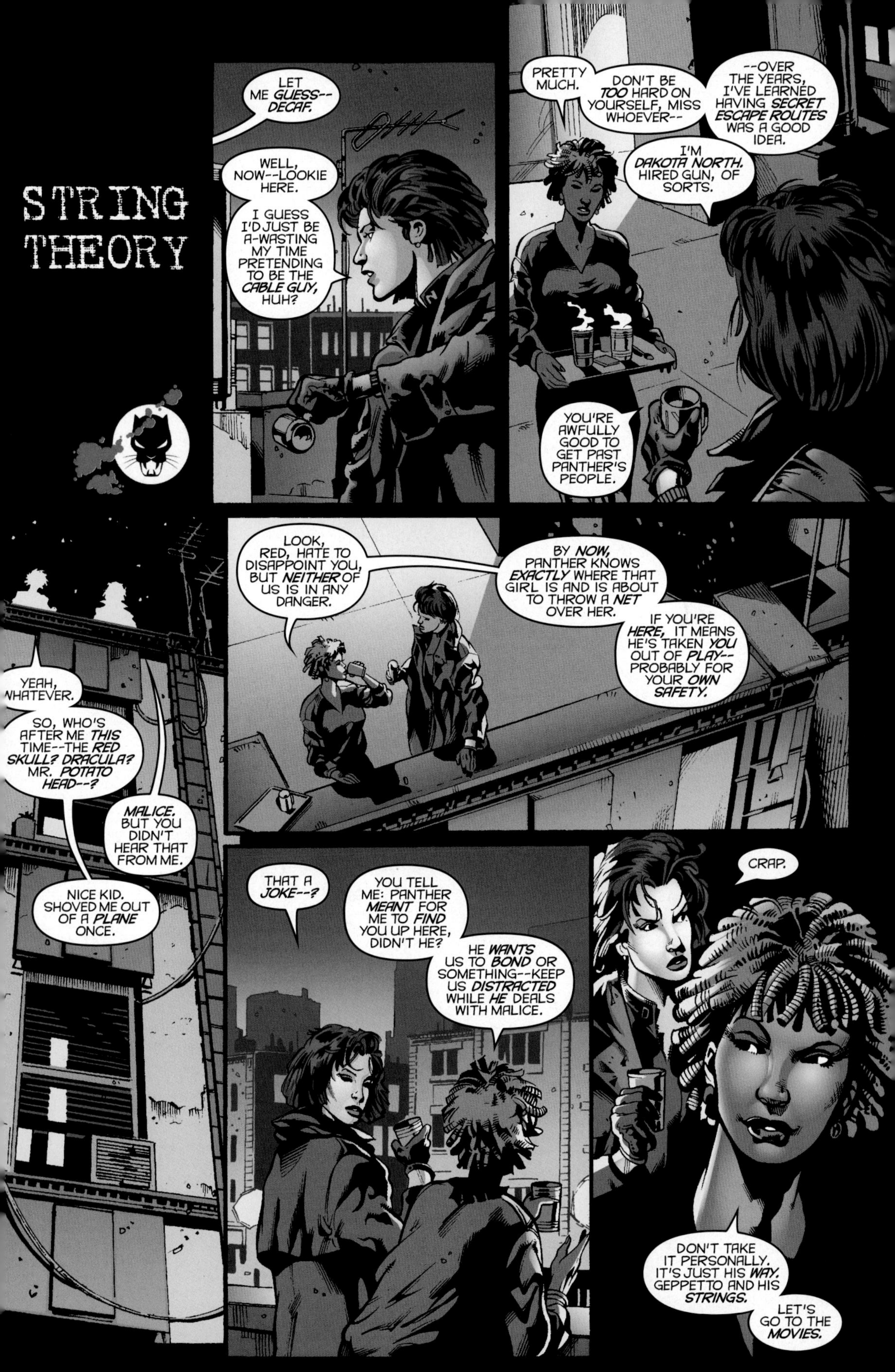
STRING THEORY
LET ME GUESS-- DECAF.
WELL, NOW--LOOKIE HERE.
I GUESS I'D JUST BE A-WASTING MY TIME PRETENDING TO BE THE CABLE GUY, HUH?
PRETTY MUCH.
DON'T BE TOO HARD ON YOURSELF, MISS WHOEVER--
--OVER THE YEARS, I'VE LEARNED HAVING SECRET ESCAPE ROUTES WAS A GOOD IDEA.
I'M DAKOTA NORTH. HIRED GUN, OF SORTS.
YOU'RE AWFULLY GOOD TO GET PAST PANTHER'S PEOPLE.
YEAH, WHATEVER.
SO, WHO'S AFTER ME THIS TIME--THE RED SKULL? DRACULA? MR. POTATO HEAD--?
MALICE. BUT YOU DIDN'T HEAR THAT FROM ME.
NICE KID. SHOVED ME OUT OF A PLANE ONCE.
LOOK, RED, HATE TO DISAPPOINT YOU, BUT NEITHER OF US IS IN ANY DANGER.
BY NOW, PANTHER KNOWS EXACTLY WHERE THAT GIRL IS AND IS ABOUT TO THROW A NET OVER HER.
IF YOU'RE HERE, IT MEANS HE'S TAKEN YOU OUT OF PLAY-- PROBABLY FOR YOUR OWN SAFETY.
THAT A JOKE--?
YOU TELL ME: PANTHER MEANT FOR ME TO FIND YOU UP HERE, DIDN'T HE?
HE WANTS US TO BOND OR SOMETHING--KEEP US DISTRACTED WHILE HE DEALS WITH MALICE.
CRAP.
DON'T TAKE IT PERSONALLY. IT'S JUST HIS WAY. GEPPETTO AND HIS STRINGS.
LET'S GO TO THE MOVIES.

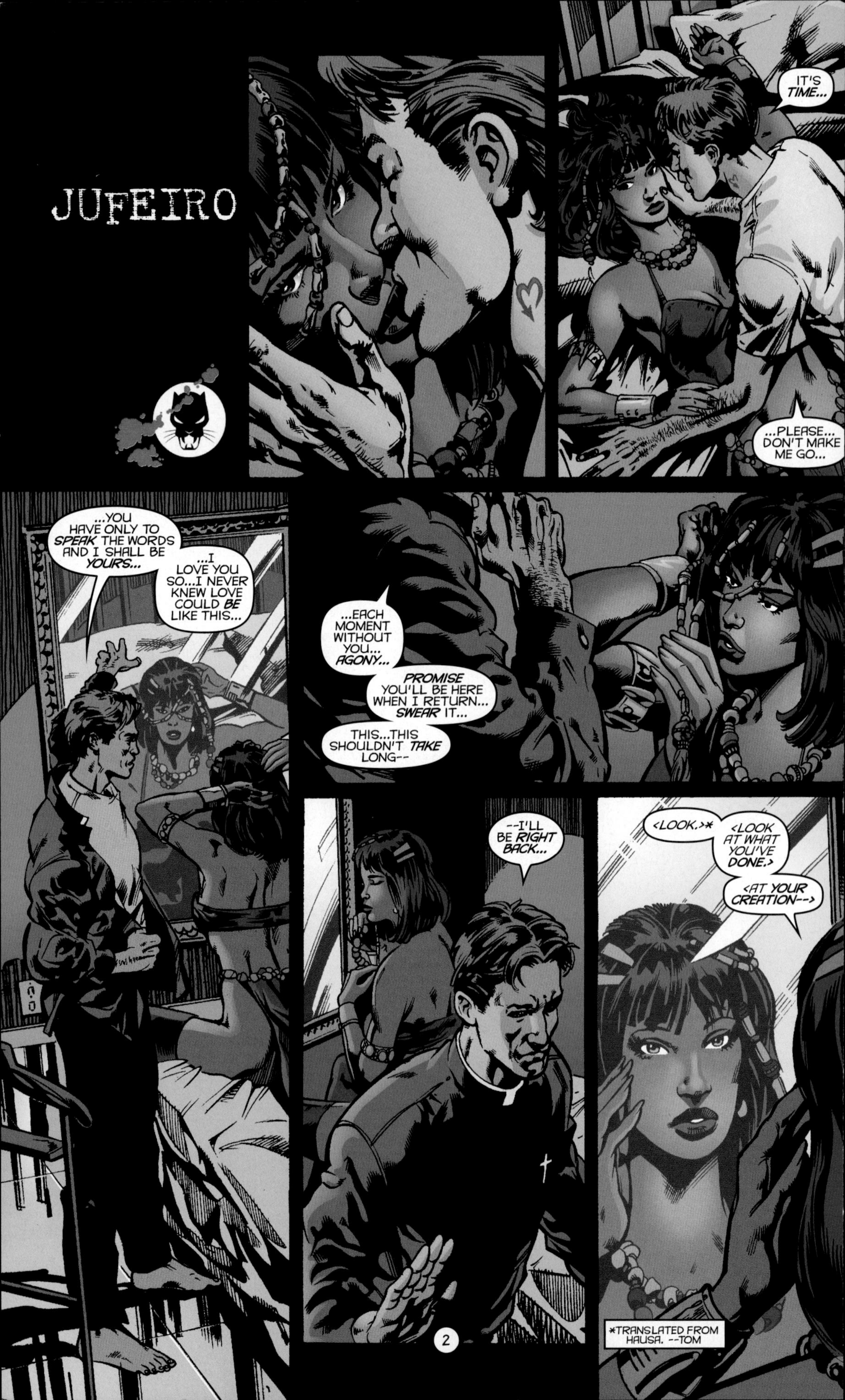
JUFEIRO
IT'S TIME...
...PLEASE... DON'T MAKE ME GO...
...YOU HAVE ONLY TO SPEAK THE WORDS AND I SHALL BE YOURS...
...I LOVE YOU SO...I NEVER KNEW LOVE COULD BE LIKE THIS...
...EACH MOMENT WITHOUT YOU... AGONY...
PROMISE YOU'LL BE HERE WHEN I RETURN... SWEAR IT...
THIS...THIS SHOULDN'T TAKE LONG--
--I'LL BE RIGHT BACK...
<LOOK.>*
<LOOK AT WHAT YOU'VE DONE.>
<AT YOUR CREATION-->
*TRANSLATED FROM HAUSA. --TOM

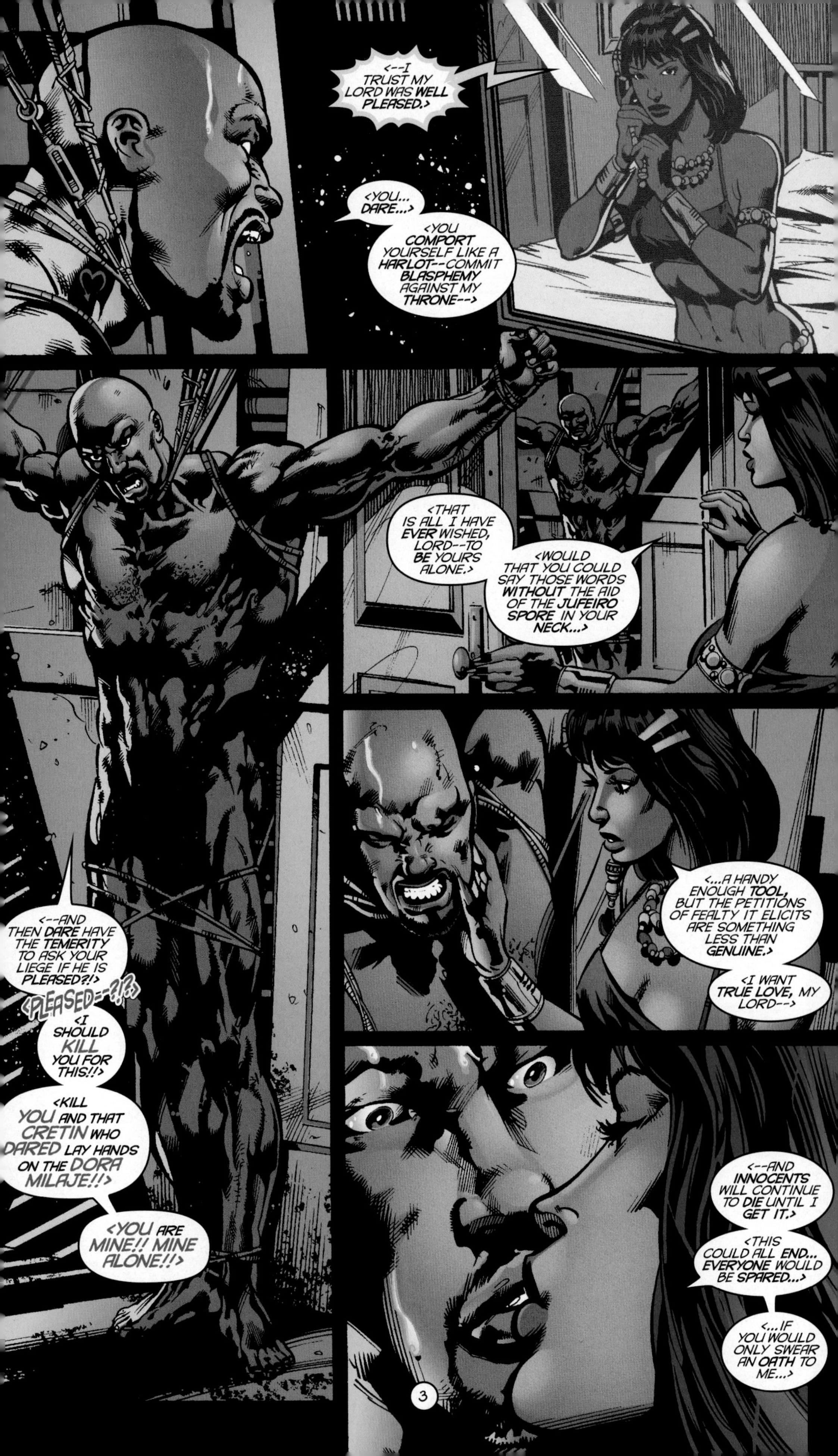

<--I TRUST MY LORD WAS WELL PLEASED.>
<YOU... DARE...>
<YOU COMPORT YOURSELF LIKE A HARLOT--COMMIT BLASPHEMY AGAINST MY THRONE-->
<THAT IS ALL I HAVE EVER WISHED, LORD--TO BE YOURS ALONE.>
<WOULD THAT YOU COULD SAY THOSE WORDS WITHOUT THE AID OF THE JUFEIRO SPORE IN YOUR NECK...>
<--AND THEN DARE HAVE THE TEMERITY TO ASK YOUR LIEGE IF HE IS PLEASED?!>
<PLEASED--?!?>
<I SHOULD KILL YOU FOR THIS!!>
<KILL YOU AND THAT CRETIN WHO DARED LAY HANDS ON THE DORA MILAJE!!>
<YOU ARE MINE!! MINE ALONE!!>
<...A HANDY ENOUGH TOOL, BUT THE PETITIONS OF FEALTY IT ELICITS ARE SOMETHING LESS THAN GENUINE.>
<I WANT TRUE LOVE, MY LORD-->
<--AND INNOCENTS WILL CONTINUE TO DIE UNTIL I GET IT.>
<THIS COULD ALL END... EVERYONE WOULD BE SPARED...>
<...IF YOU WOULD ONLY SWEAR AN OATH TO ME...>

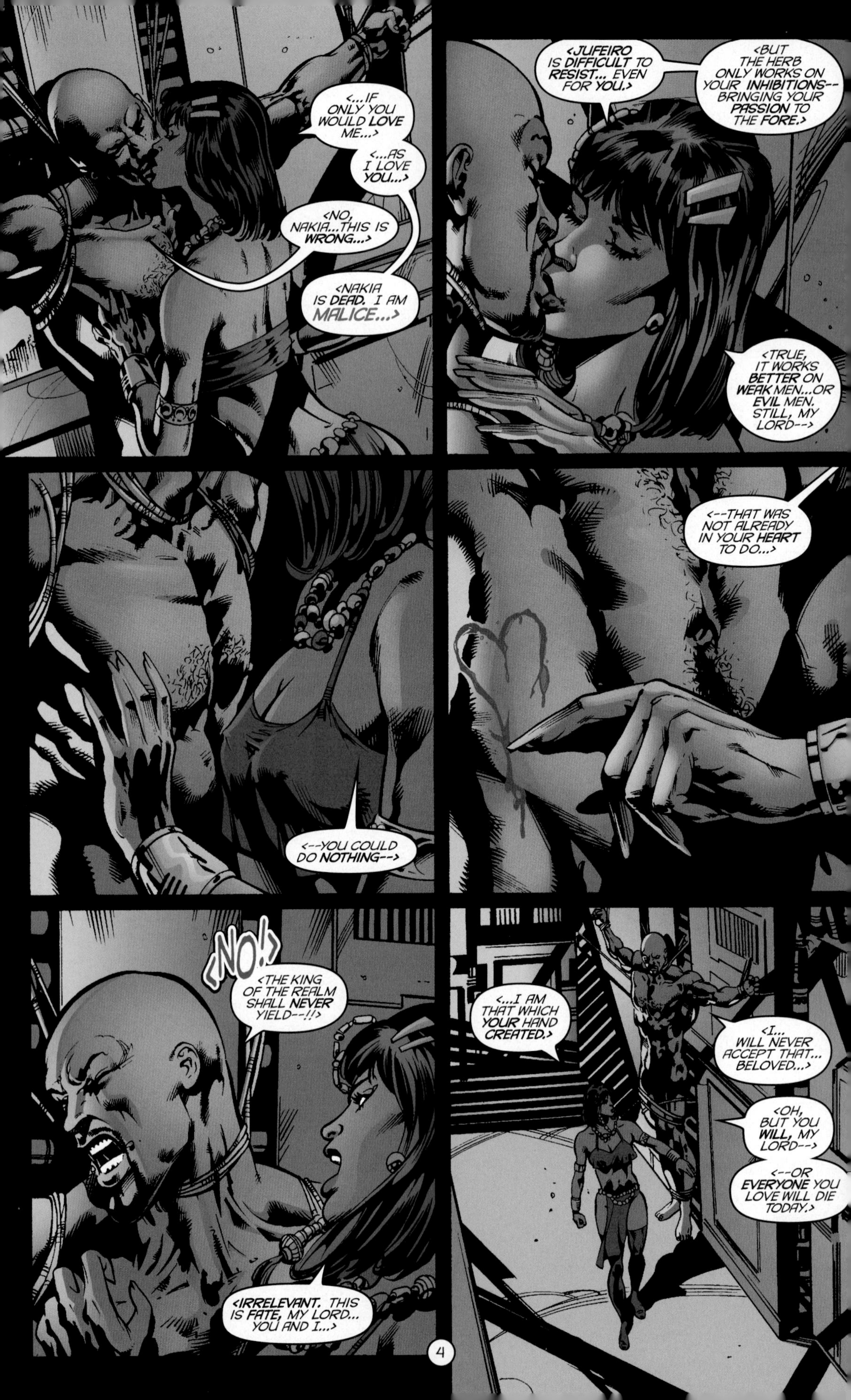

<...IF ONLY YOU WOULD LOVE ME...>
<...AS I LOVE YOU...>
<NO, NAKIA...THIS IS WRONG...>
<NAKIA IS DEAD. I AM MALICE...>
<JUFEIRO IS DIFFICULT TO RESIST... EVEN FOR YOU.>
<BUT THE HERB ONLY WORKS ON YOUR INHIBITIONS--BRINGING YOUR PASSION TO THE FORE.>
<TRUE, IT WORKS BETTER ON WEAK MEN...OR EVIL MEN. STILL, MY LORD-->
<--YOU COULD DO NOTHING-->
<--THAT WAS NOT ALREADY IN YOUR HEART TO DO...>
<NO!>
<THE KING OF THE REALM SHALL NEVER YIELD--!!>
<IRRELEVANT. THIS IS FATE, MY LORD... YOU AND I...>
<...I AM THAT WHICH YOUR HAND CREATED.>
<I... WILL NEVER ACCEPT THAT... BELOVED...>
<OH, BUT YOU WILL, MY LORD-->
<--OR EVERYONE YOU LOVE WILL DIE TODAY.>

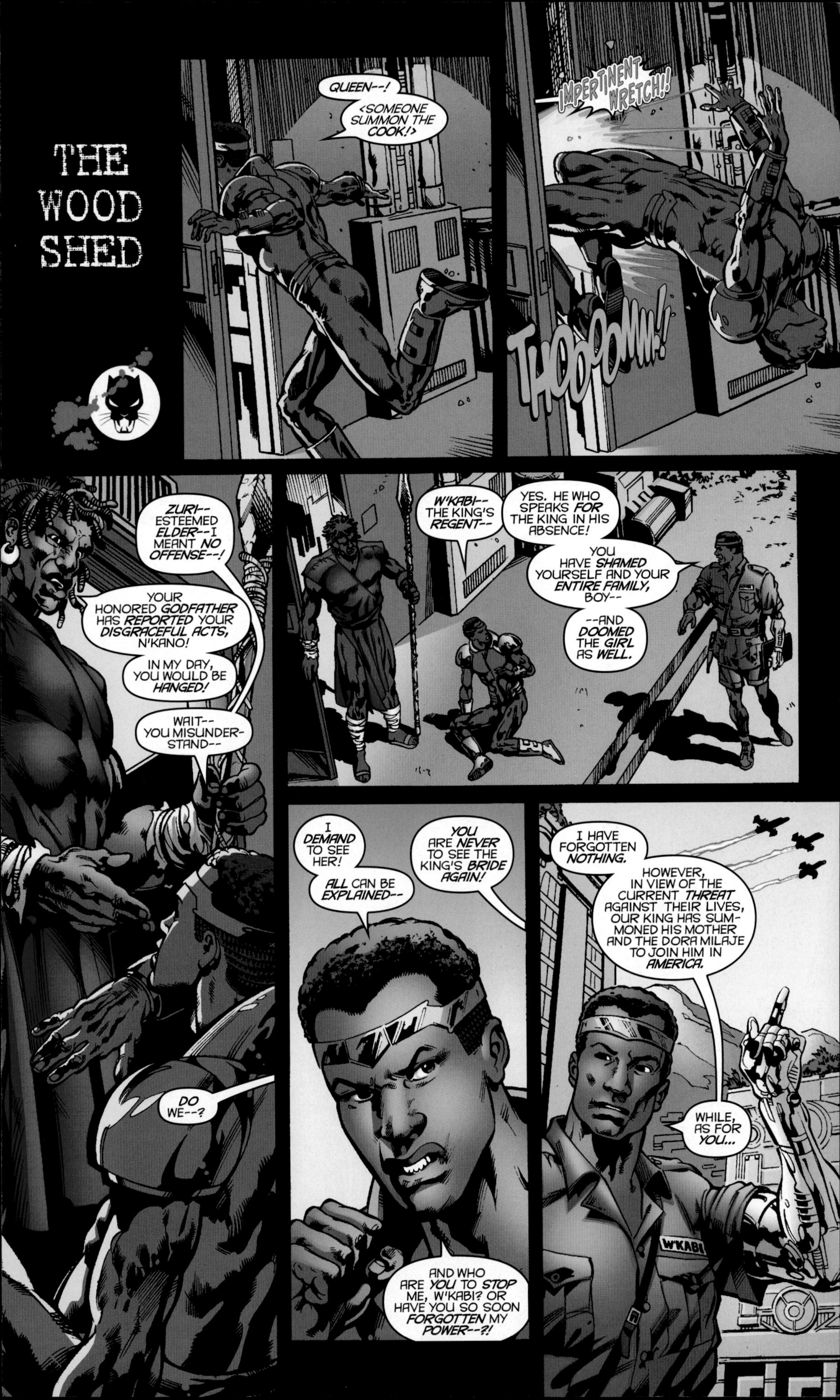
THE WOOD SHED
QUEEN--!
<SOMEONE SUMMON THE COOK!>
IMPERTINENT WRETCH!!
THOOOOMM!!
ZURI-- ESTEEMED ELDER--I MEANT NO OFFENSE--!
YOUR HONORED GODFATHER HAS REPORTED YOUR DISGRACEFUL ACTS, N'KANO!
IN MY DAY, YOU WOULD BE HANGED!
WAIT-- YOU MISUNDERSTAND--
DO WE--?
W'KABI-- THE KING'S REGENT--
YES. HE WHO SPEAKS FOR THE KING IN HIS ABSENCE!
YOU HAVE SHAMED YOURSELF AND YOUR ENTIRE FAMILY, BOY--
--AND DOOMED THE GIRL AS WELL.
I DEMAND TO SEE HER!
ALL CAN BE EXPLAINED--
YOU ARE NEVER TO SEE THE KING'S BRIDE AGAIN!
AND WHO ARE YOU TO STOP ME, W'KABI? OR HAVE YOU SO SOON FORGOTTEN MY POWER--?!
I HAVE FORGOTTEN NOTHING.
HOWEVER, IN VIEW OF THE CURRENT THREAT AGAINST THEIR LIVES, OUR KING HAS SUMMONED HIS MOTHER AND THE DORA MILAJE TO JOIN HIM IN AMERICA.
WHILE, AS FOR YOU...
W'KABI

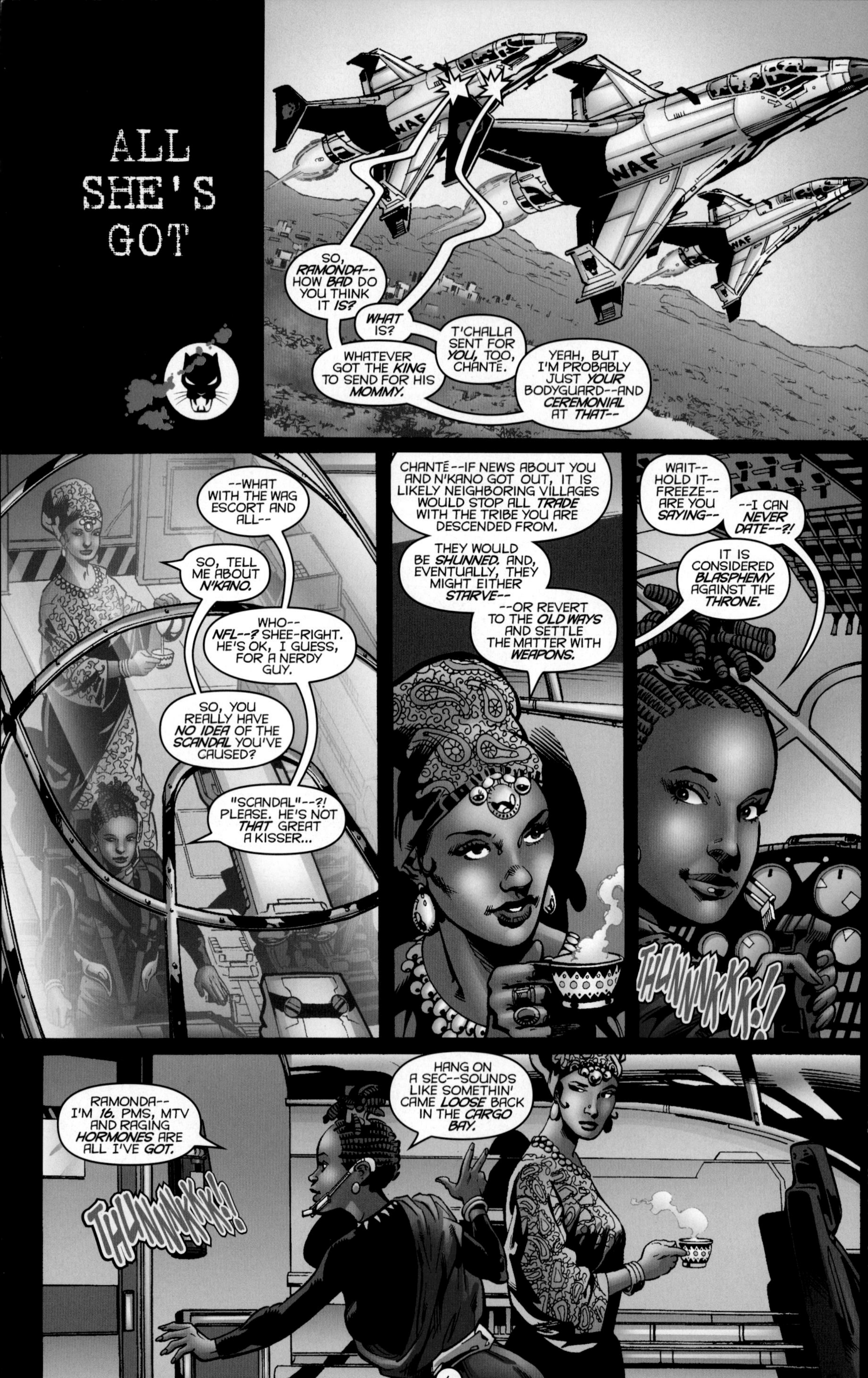
ALL SHE'S GOT
SO, RAMONDA-- HOW BAD DO YOU THINK IT IS?
WHAT IS?
WHATEVER GOT THE KING TO SEND FOR HIS MOMMY.
T'CHALLA SENT FOR YOU, TOO, CHANTÉ.
YEAH, BUT I'M PROBABLY JUST YOUR BODYGUARD--AND CEREMONIAL AT THAT--
--WHAT WITH THE WAG ESCORT AND ALL--
SO, TELL ME ABOUT N'KANO.
WHO-- NFL--? SHEE-RIGHT. HE'S OK, I GUESS, FOR A NERDY GUY.
SO, YOU REALLY HAVE NO IDEA OF THE SCANDAL YOU'VE CAUSED?
"SCANDAL"--?! PLEASE. HE'S NOT THAT GREAT A KISSER...
CHANTÉ--IF NEWS ABOUT YOU AND N'KANO GOT OUT, IT IS LIKELY NEIGHBORING VILLAGES WOULD STOP ALL TRADE WITH THE TRIBE YOU ARE DESCENDED FROM.
THEY WOULD BE SHUNNED. AND, EVENTUALLY, THEY MIGHT EITHER STARVE--
--OR REVERT TO THE OLD WAYS AND SETTLE THE MATTER WITH WEAPONS.
WAIT-- HOLD IT-- FREEZE-- ARE YOU SAYING--
--I CAN NEVER DATE--?!
IT IS CONSIDERED BLASPHEMY AGAINST THE THRONE.
THUNNKKKK!!
RAMONDA-- I'M 16. PMS, MTV AND RAGING HORMONES ARE ALL I'VE GOT.
HANG ON A SEC--SOUNDS LIKE SOMETHIN' CAME LOOSE BACK IN THE CARGO BAY.
THUNNKKKK!

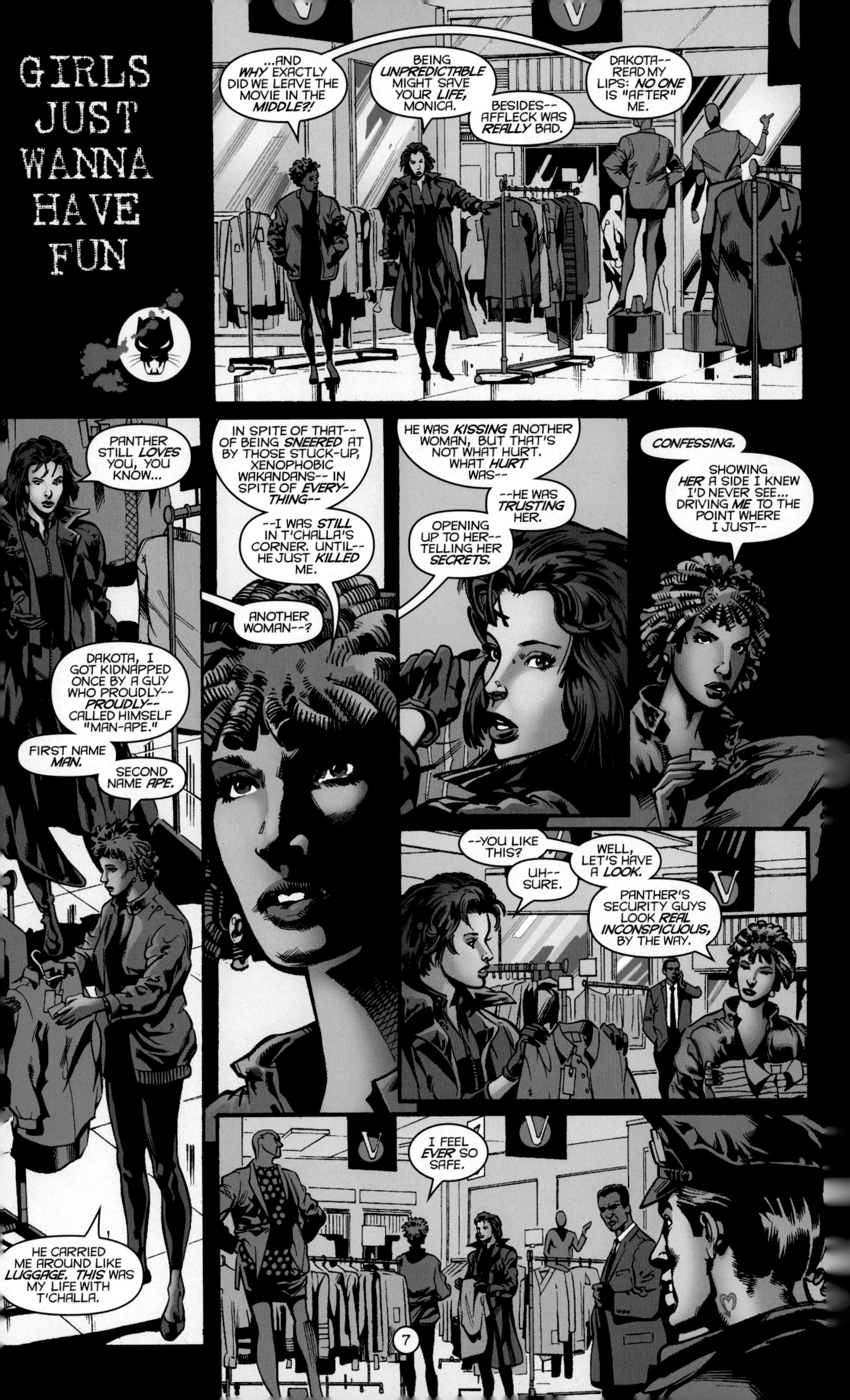

GIRLS JUST WANNA HAVE FUN
...AND WHY EXACTLY DID WE LEAVE THE MOVIE IN THE MIDDLE?!
BEING UNPREDICTABLE MIGHT SAVE YOUR LIFE, MONICA.
BESIDES-- AFFLECK WAS REALLY BAD.
DAKOTA-- READ MY LIPS: NO ONE IS "AFTER" ME.
PANTHER STILL LOVES YOU, YOU KNOW...
DAKOTA, I GOT KIDNAPPED ONCE BY A GUY WHO PROUDLY-- PROUDLY-- CALLED HIMSELF "MAN-APE."
FIRST NAME MAN.
SECOND NAME APE.
HE CARRIED ME AROUND LIKE LUGGAGE. THIS WAS MY LIFE WITH T'CHALLA.
IN SPITE OF THAT-- OF BEING SNEERED AT BY THOSE STUCK-UP, XENOPHOBIC WAKANDANS-- IN SPITE OF EVERY-THING--
--I WAS STILL IN T'CHALLA'S CORNER. UNTIL-- HE JUST KILLED ME.
ANOTHER WOMAN--?
HE WAS KISSING ANOTHER WOMAN, BUT THAT'S NOT WHAT HURT. WHAT HURT WAS--
--HE WAS TRUSTING HER.
OPENING UP TO HER-- TELLING HER SECRETS.
CONFESSING.
SHOWING HER A SIDE I KNEW I'D NEVER SEE... DRIVING ME TO THE POINT WHERE I JUST--
--YOU LIKE THIS?
UH-- SURE.
WELL, LET'S HAVE A LOOK.
PANTHER'S SECURITY GUYS LOOK REAL INCONSPICUOUS, BY THE WAY.
I FEEL EVER SO SAFE.

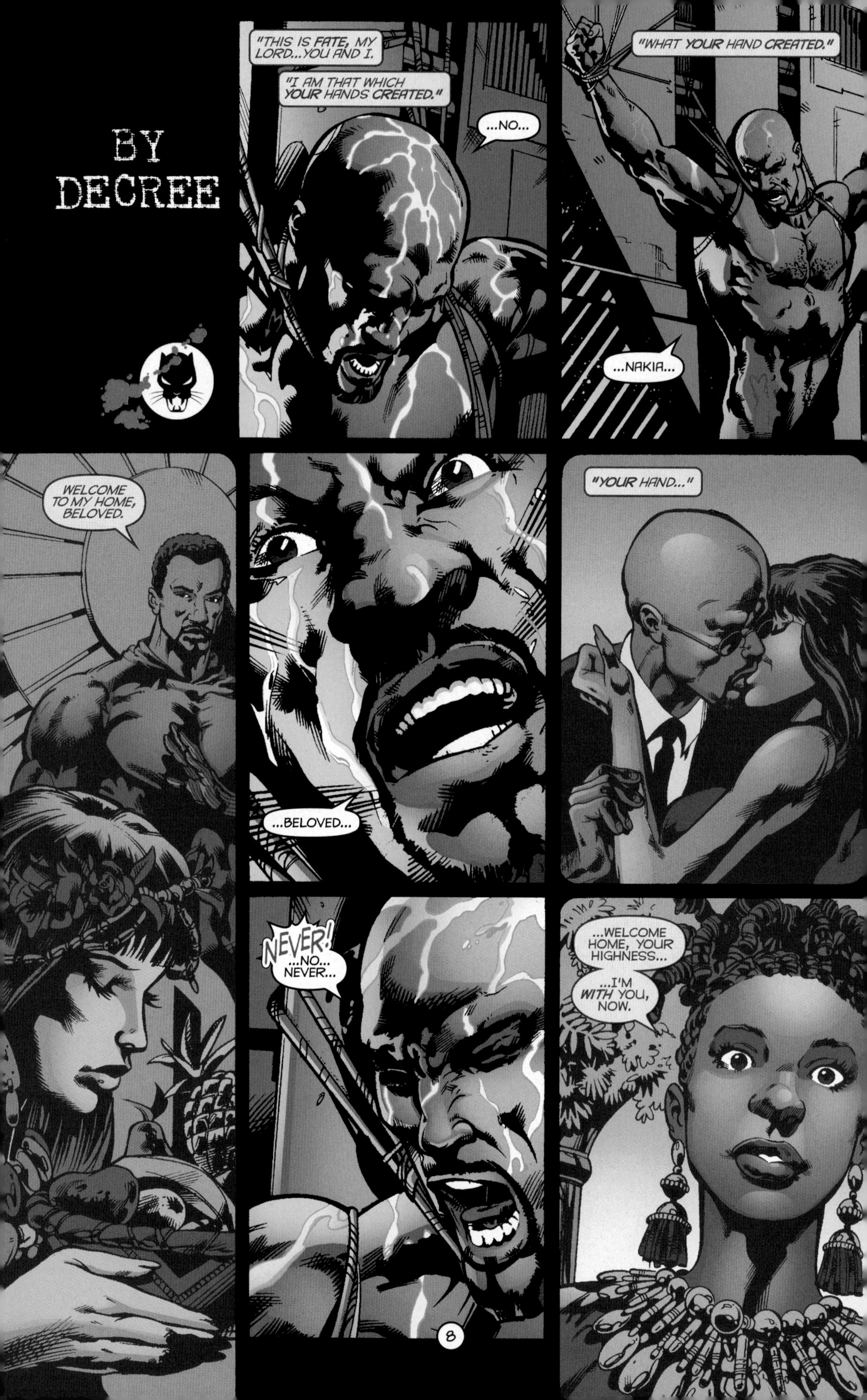

BY DECREE
"THIS IS FATE, MY LORD...YOU AND I.
"I AM THAT WHICH YOUR HANDS CREATED."
...NO...
"WHAT YOUR HAND CREATED."
...NAKIA...
WELCOME TO MY HOME, BELOVED.
...BELOVED...
"YOUR HAND..."
NEVER! ...NO... NEVER...
...WELCOME HOME, YOUR HIGHNESS...
...I'M WITH YOU, NOW.

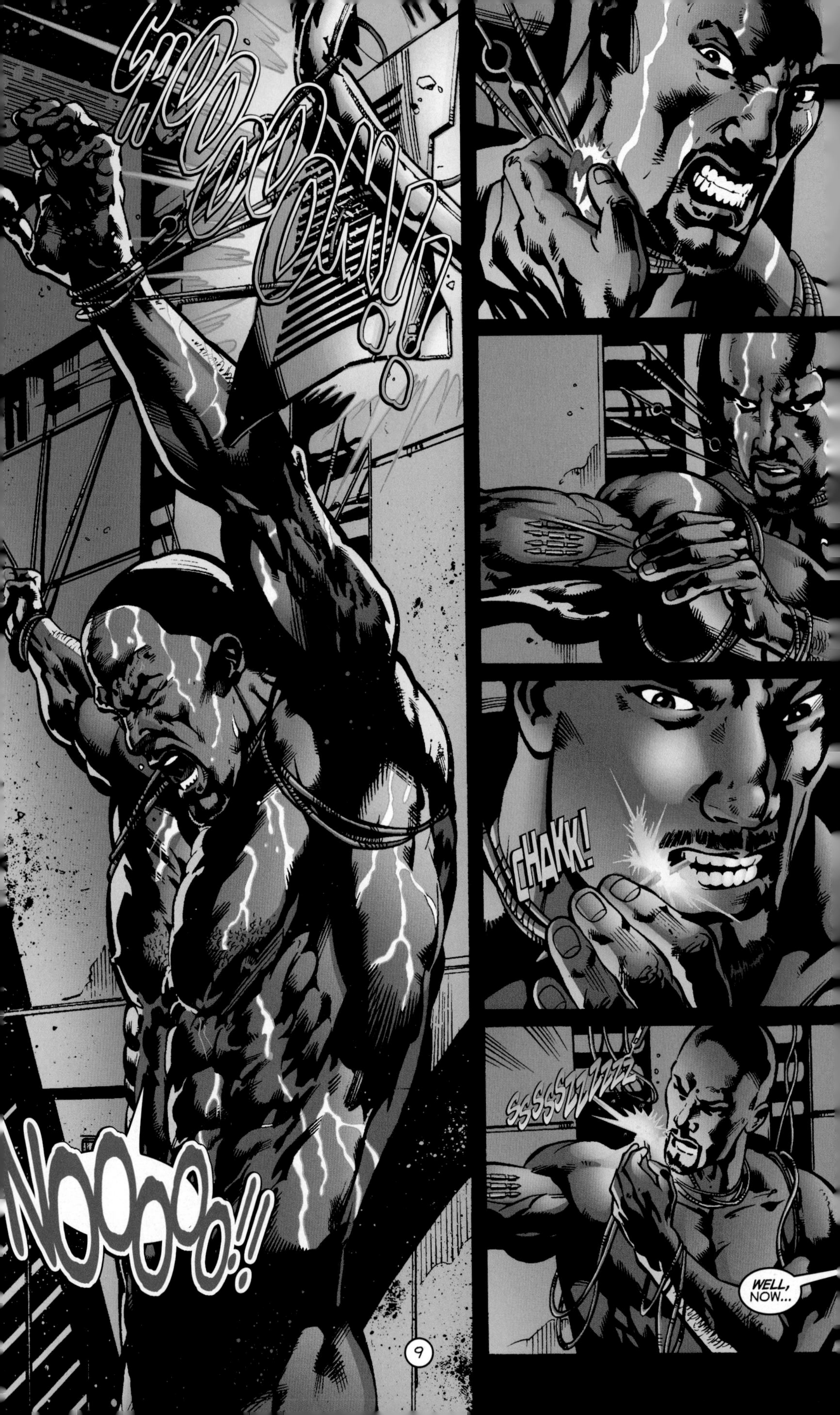
NOOOOO!!
CHAKK!
SSSSSZZZZZZ
WELL, NOW...

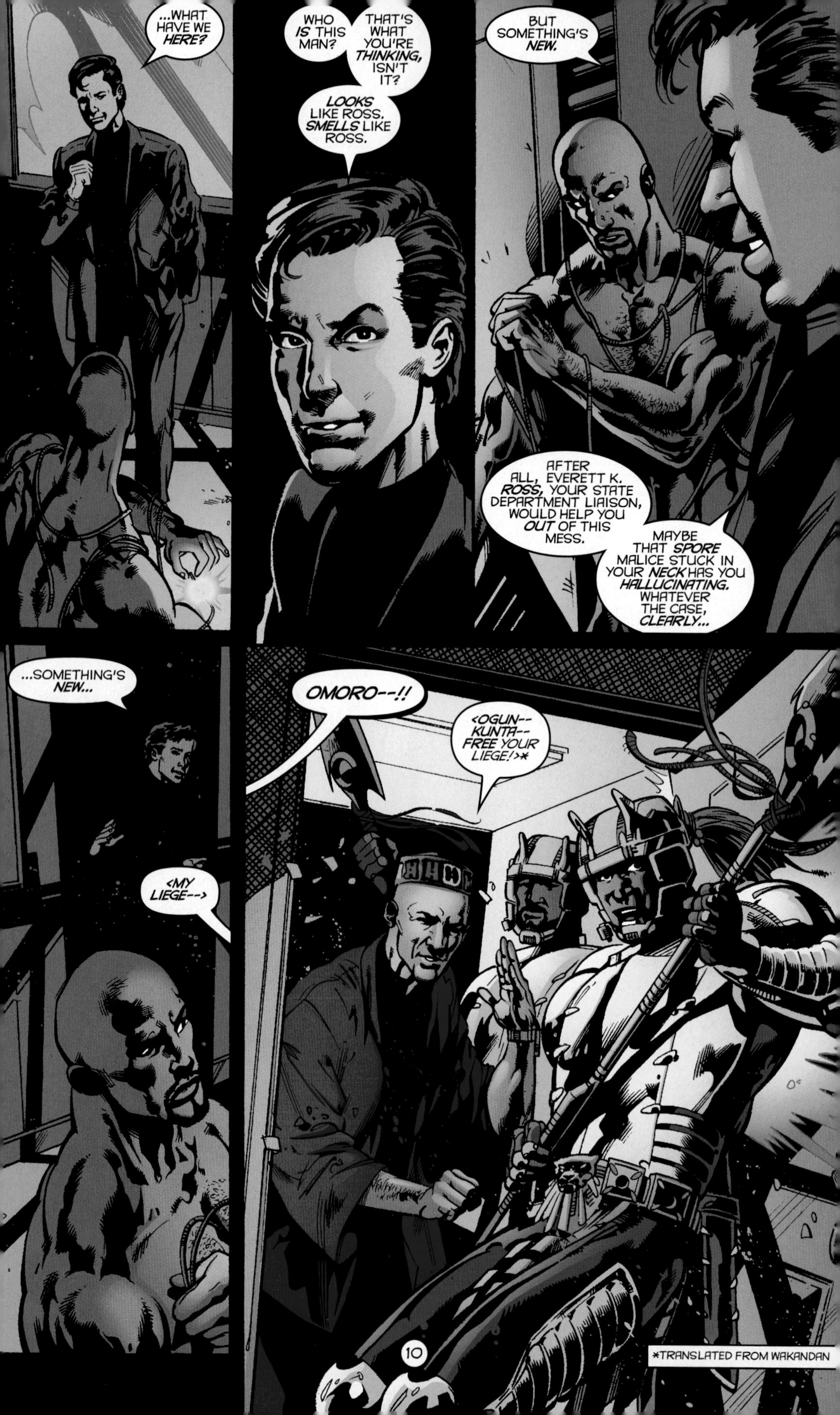
...WHAT HAVE WE HERE?
WHO IS THIS MAN?
THAT'S WHAT YOU'RE THINKING, ISN'T IT?
LOOKS LIKE ROSS. SMELLS LIKE ROSS.
BUT SOMETHING'S NEW.
AFTER ALL, EVERETT K. ROSS, YOUR STATE DEPARTMENT LIAISON, WOULD HELP YOU OUT OF THIS MESS.
MAYBE THAT SPORE MALICE STUCK IN YOUR NECK HAS YOU HALLUCINATING. WHATEVER THE CASE, CLEARLY...
...SOMETHING'S NEW...
<MY LIEGE-->
OMORO--!!
<OGUN-- KUNTA-- FREE YOUR LIEGE!>*
*TRANSLATED FROM WAKANDAN

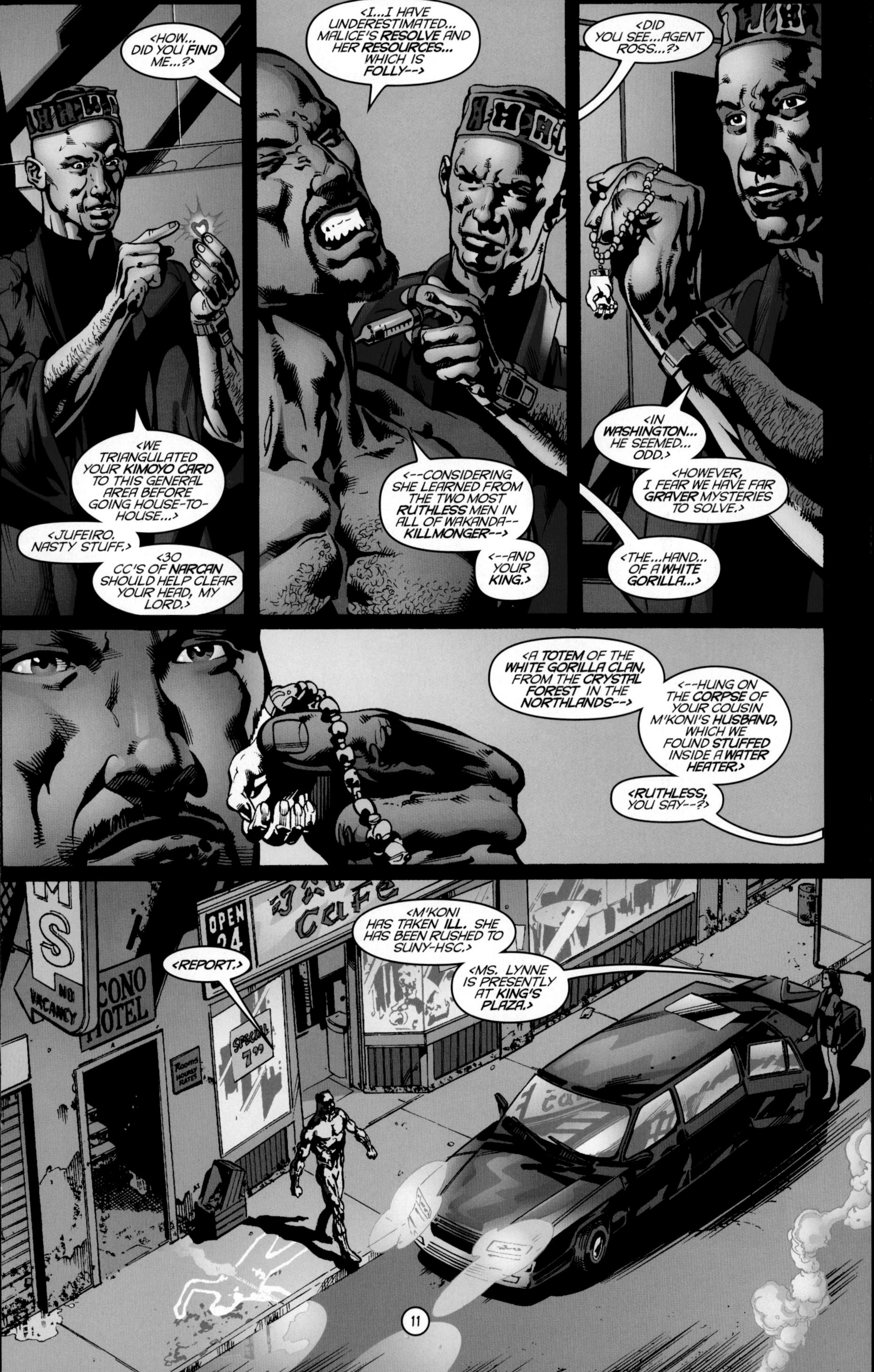

<HOW... DID YOU FIND ME...?>
<WE TRIANGULATED YOUR KIMOYO CARD TO THIS GENERAL AREA BEFORE GOING HOUSE-TO-HOUSE...>
<JUFEIRO. NASTY STUFF.>
<30 CC'S OF NARCAN SHOULD HELP CLEAR YOUR HEAD, MY LORD.>
<I...I HAVE UNDERESTIMATED... MALICE'S RESOLVE AND HER RESOURCES... WHICH IS FOLLY-->
<--CONSIDERING SHE LEARNED FROM THE TWO MOST RUTHLESS MEN IN ALL OF WAKANDA-- KILLMONGER-->
<--AND YOUR KING.>
<DID YOU SEE...AGENT ROSS...?>
<IN WASHINGTON... HE SEEMED... ODD.>
<HOWEVER, I FEAR WE HAVE FAR GRAVER MYSTERIES TO SOLVE.>
<THE...HAND... OF A WHITE GORILLA...>
<A TOTEM OF THE WHITE GORILLA CLAN, FROM THE CRYSTAL FOREST IN THE NORTHLANDS-->
<--HUNG ON THE CORPSE OF YOUR COUSIN M'KONI'S HUSBAND, WHICH WE FOUND STUFFED INSIDE A WATER HEATER.>
<RUTHLESS, YOU SAY--?>
OPEN 24
CAFE
S
NO VACANCY
CONO HOTEL
<REPORT.>
SPECIAL 7.99
ROOMS HOURLY RATES
<M'KONI HAS TAKEN ILL. SHE HAS BEEN RUSHED TO SUNY-HSC.>
<MS. LYNNE IS PRESENTLY AT KING'S PLAZA.>

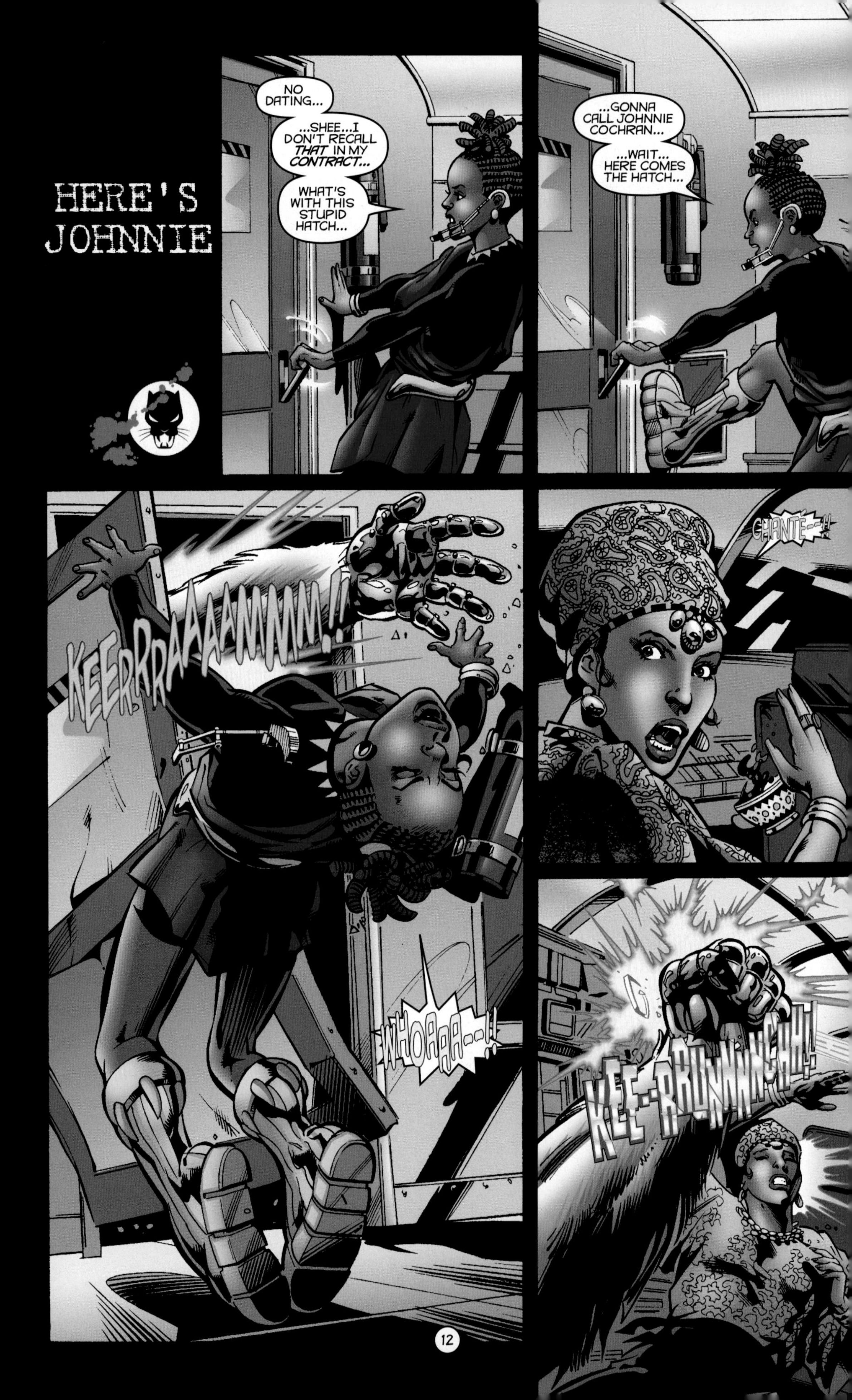
HERE'S JOHNNIE
NO DATING...
...SHEE...I DON'T RECALL *THAT* IN MY *CONTRACT*...
WHAT'S WITH THIS STUPID HATCH...
...GONNA CALL JOHNNIE COCHRAN...
...WAIT... HERE COMES THE HATCH...
KEERRRAAAMMM!!
WHOAAA--!!
CHANTE--!!
KEE-RRUNNNCHH!!

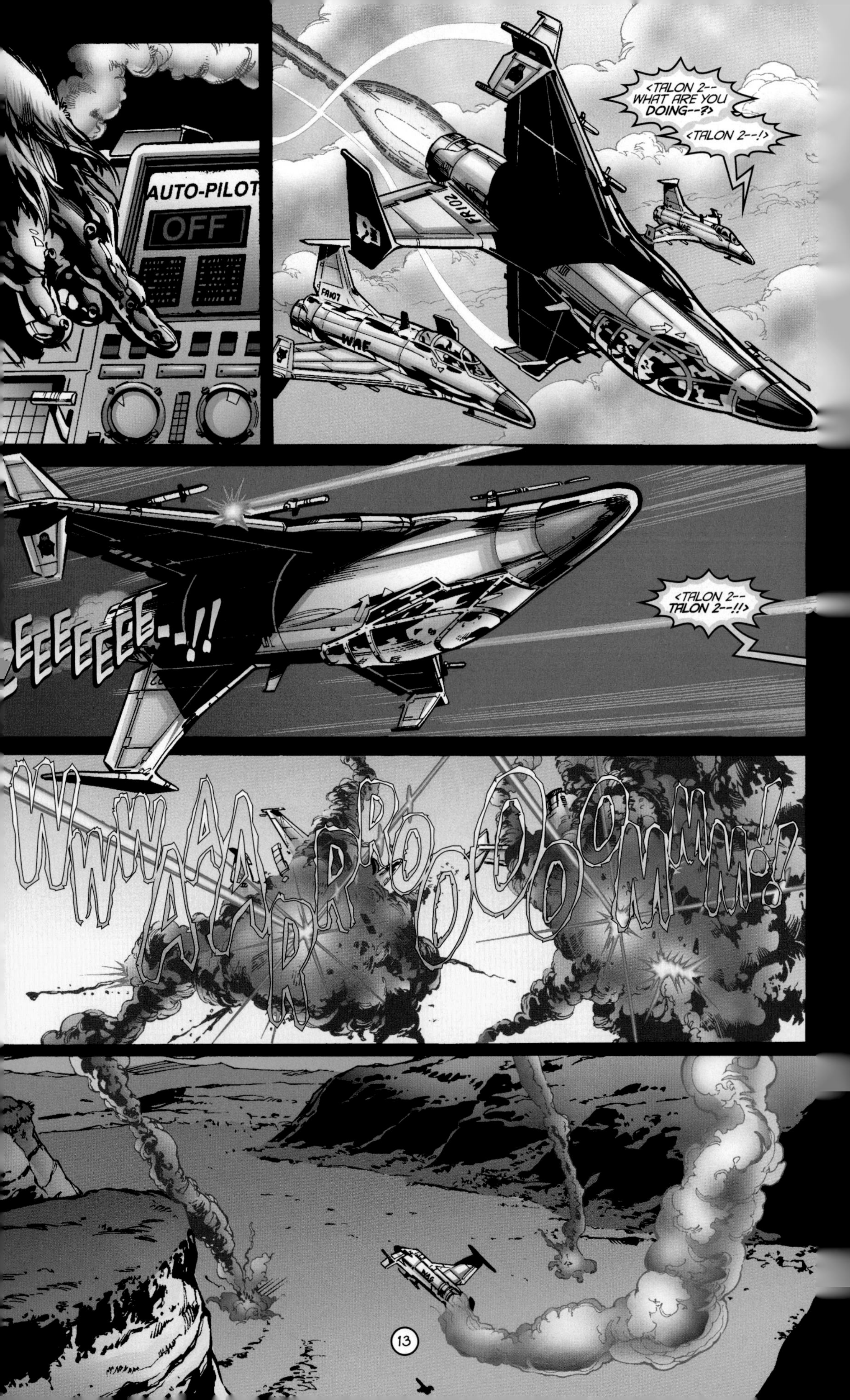
AUTO-PILOT
OFF
<TALON 2-- WHAT ARE YOU DOING--?>
<TALON 2--!>
FR102
FR107
WAF
EEEEEEEE..!!
<TALON 2-- TALON 2--!!>
WWWAAA-RROOOOOOMMMM!!

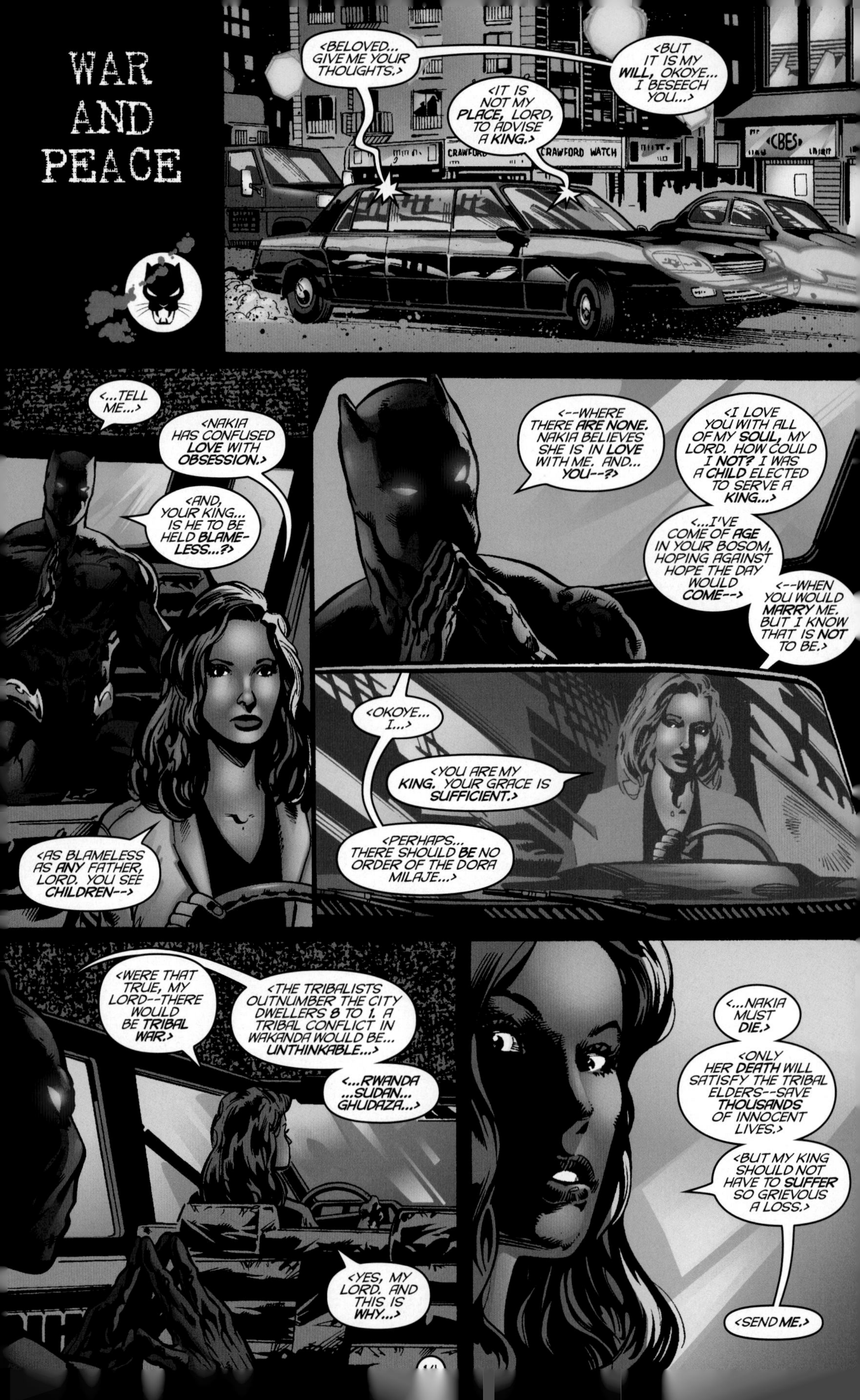
WAR AND PEACE
<BELOVED... GIVE ME YOUR THOUGHTS.>
<IT IS NOT MY PLACE, LORD, TO ADVISE A KING.>
<BUT IT IS MY WILL, OKOYE... I BESEECH YOU...>
CRAWFORD
CRAWFORD WATCH
CBES
<...TELL ME...>
<NAKIA HAS CONFUSED LOVE WITH OBSESSION.>
<AND, YOUR KING... IS HE TO BE HELD BLAMELESS...?>
<AS BLAMELESS AS ANY FATHER, LORD. YOU SEE CHILDREN-->
<--WHERE THERE ARE NONE. NAKIA BELIEVES SHE IS IN LOVE WITH ME. AND... YOU--?>
<I LOVE YOU WITH ALL OF MY SOUL, MY LORD. HOW COULD I NOT? I WAS A CHILD ELECTED TO SERVE A KING...>
<...I'VE COME OF AGE IN YOUR BOSOM, HOPING AGAINST HOPE THE DAY WOULD COME-->
<--WHEN YOU WOULD MARRY ME. BUT I KNOW THAT IS NOT TO BE.>
<OKOYE... I...>
<YOU ARE MY KING. YOUR GRACE IS SUFFICIENT.>
<PERHAPS... THERE SHOULD BE NO ORDER OF THE DORA MILAJE...>
<WERE THAT TRUE, MY LORD--THERE WOULD BE TRIBAL WAR.>
<THE TRIBALISTS OUTNUMBER THE CITY DWELLERS 8 TO 1. A TRIBAL CONFLICT IN WAKANDA WOULD BE... UNTHINKABLE...>
<...RWANDA ...SUDAN... GHUDAZA...>
<YES, MY LORD. AND THIS IS WHY...>
<...NAKIA MUST DIE.>
<ONLY HER DEATH WILL SATISFY THE TRIBAL ELDERS--SAVE THOUSANDS OF INNOCENT LIVES.>
<BUT MY KING SHOULD NOT HAVE TO SUFFER SO GRIEVOUS A LOSS.>
<SEND ME.>

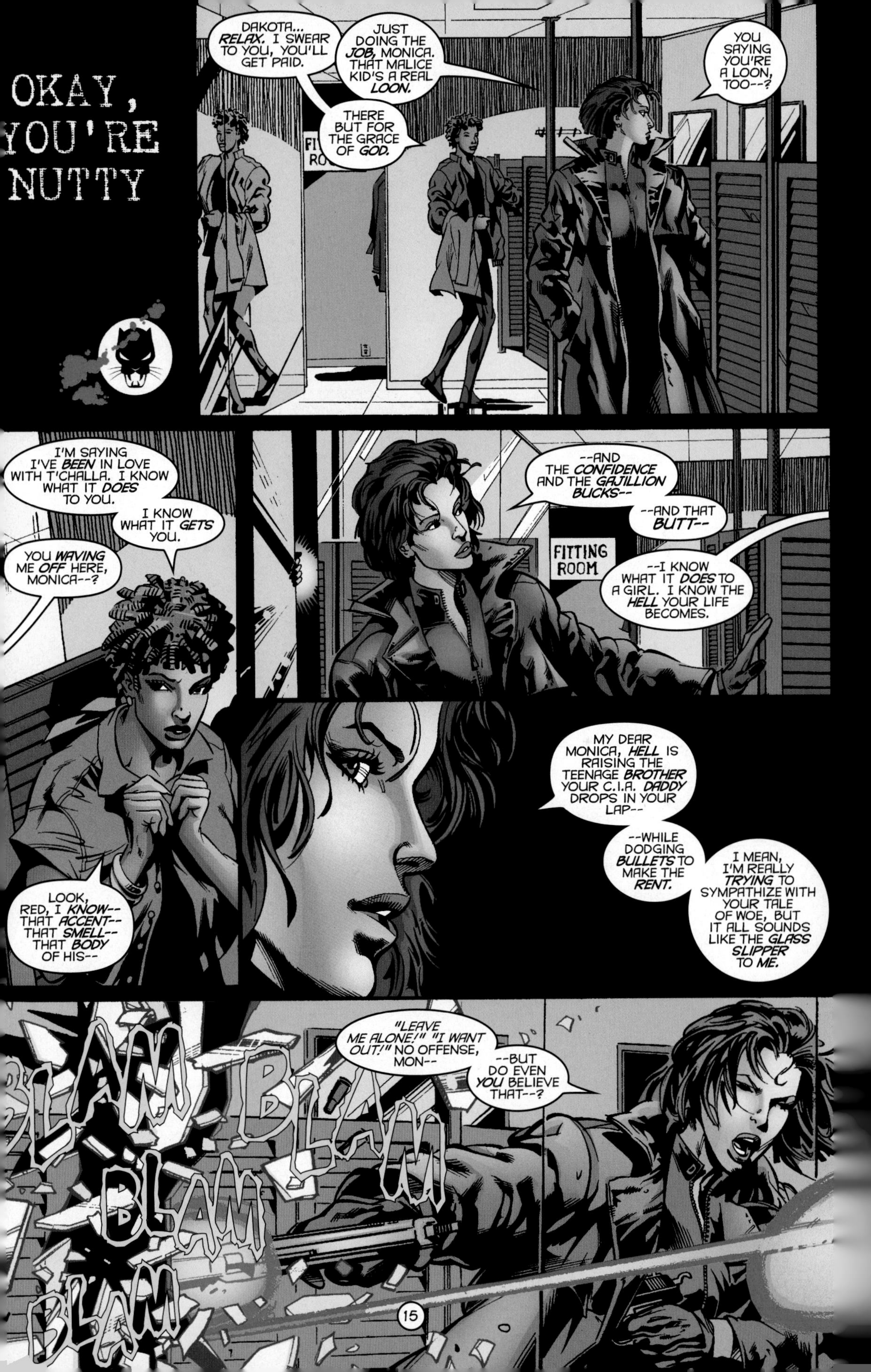

OKAY, YOU'RE NUTTY
DAKOTA... RELAX. I SWEAR TO YOU, YOU'LL GET PAID.
JUST DOING THE JOB, MONICA. THAT MALICE KID'S A REAL LOON.
THERE BUT FOR THE GRACE OF GOD.
YOU SAYING YOU'RE A LOON, TOO--?
I'M SAYING I'VE BEEN IN LOVE WITH T'CHALLA. I KNOW WHAT IT DOES TO YOU.
I KNOW WHAT IT GETS YOU.
YOU WAVING ME OFF HERE, MONICA--?
--AND THE CONFIDENCE AND THE GAJILLION BUCKS--
--AND THAT BUTT--
FITTING ROOM
--I KNOW WHAT IT DOES TO A GIRL. I KNOW THE HELL YOUR LIFE BECOMES.
LOOK, RED, I KNOW-- THAT ACCENT-- THAT SMELL-- THAT BODY OF HIS--
MY DEAR MONICA, HELL IS RAISING THE TEENAGE BROTHER YOUR C.I.A. DADDY DROPS IN YOUR LAP--
--WHILE DODGING BULLETS TO MAKE THE RENT.
I MEAN, I'M REALLY TRYING TO SYMPATHIZE WITH YOUR TALE OF WOE, BUT IT ALL SOUNDS LIKE THE GLASS SLIPPER TO ME.
"LEAVE ME ALONE!" "I WANT OUT!" NO OFFENSE, MON--
--BUT DO EVEN YOU BELIEVE THAT--?
BLAM BLAM BLAM BLAM

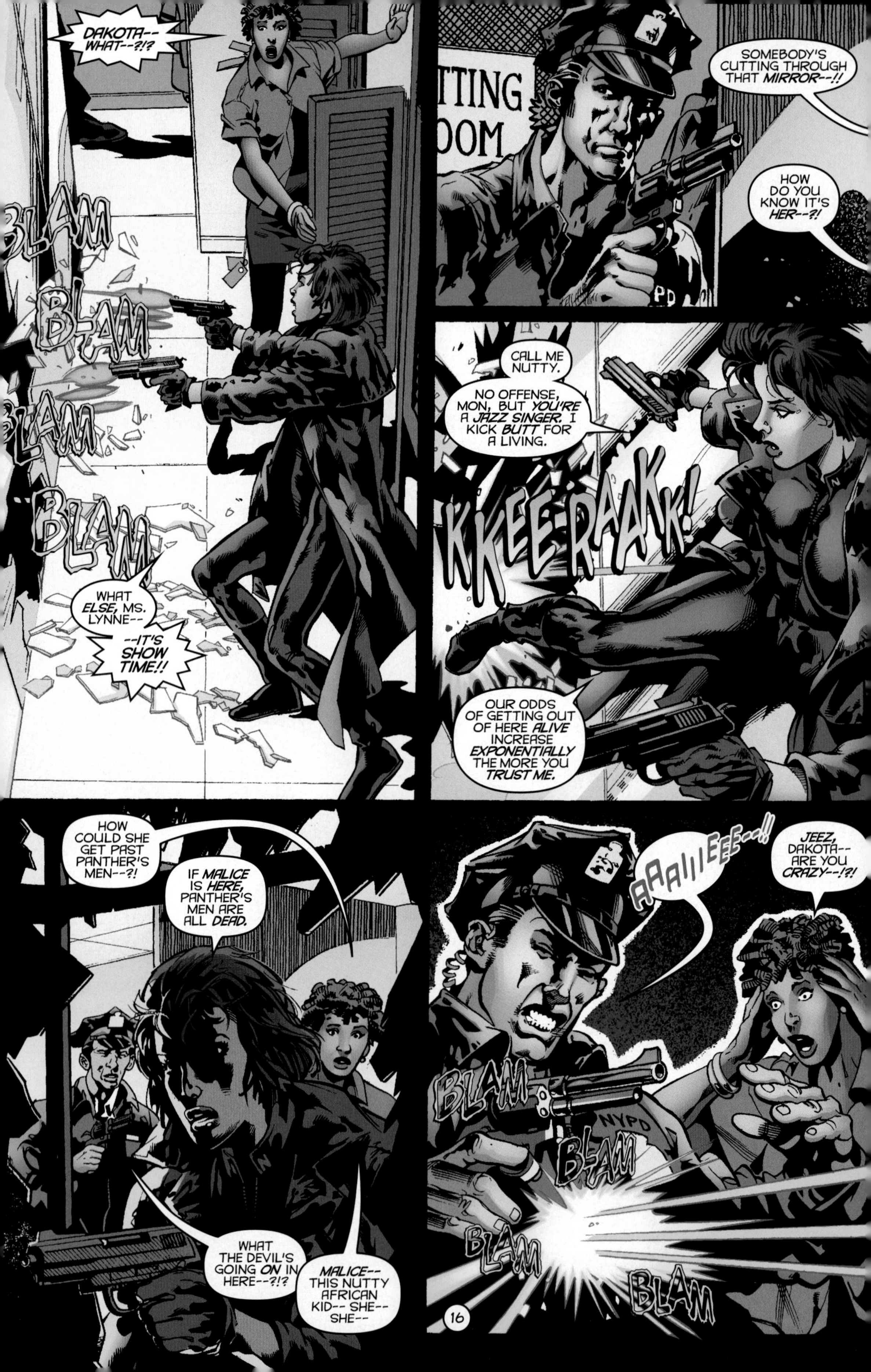
DAKOTA-- WHAT--?!?
BLAM
BLAM
BLAM
BLAM
BLAM
WHAT ELSE, MS. LYNNE--
--IT'S SHOW TIME!!
SOMEBODY'S CUTTING THROUGH THAT MIRROR--!!
HOW DO YOU KNOW IT'S HER--?!
CALL ME NUTTY.
NO OFFENSE, MON, BUT YOU'RE A JAZZ SINGER. I KICK BUTT FOR A LIVING.
KKEE-RAAKK!
OUR ODDS OF GETTING OUT OF HERE ALIVE INCREASE EXPONENTIALLY THE MORE YOU TRUST ME.
HOW COULD SHE GET PAST PANTHER'S MEN--?!
IF MALICE IS HERE, PANTHER'S MEN ARE ALL DEAD.
WHAT THE DEVIL'S GOING ON IN HERE--?!?
MALICE-- THIS NUTTY AFRICAN KID-- SHE-- SHE--
AAAIIIEEE--!!
JEEZ, DAKOTA-- ARE YOU CRAZY--!?!
BLAM
BLAM
BLAM
BLAM

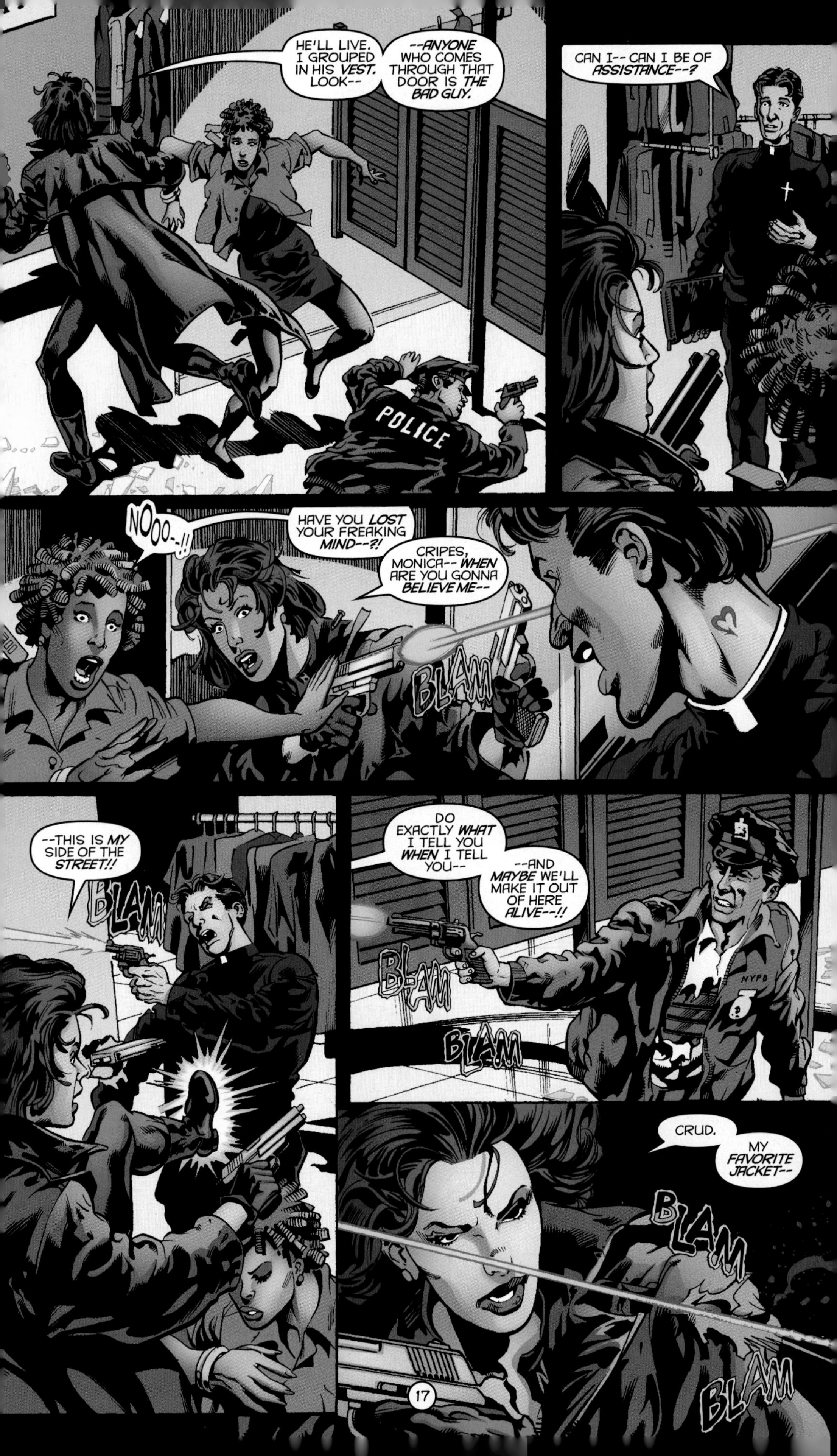

HE'LL LIVE. I GROUPED IN HIS VEST. LOOK--
--ANYONE WHO COMES THROUGH THAT DOOR IS THE BAD GUY.
POLICE
CAN I-- CAN I BE OF ASSISTANCE--?
NOOO--!!
HAVE YOU LOST YOUR FREAKING MIND--?!
CRIPES, MONICA-- WHEN ARE YOU GONNA BELIEVE ME--
BLAM
--THIS IS MY SIDE OF THE STREET!!
BLAM
DO EXACTLY WHAT I TELL YOU WHEN I TELL YOU--
--AND MAYBE WE'LL MAKE IT OUT OF HERE ALIVE--!!
BLAM
BLAM
BLAM
NYPD
CRUD.
MY FAVORITE JACKET--
BLAM
BLAM

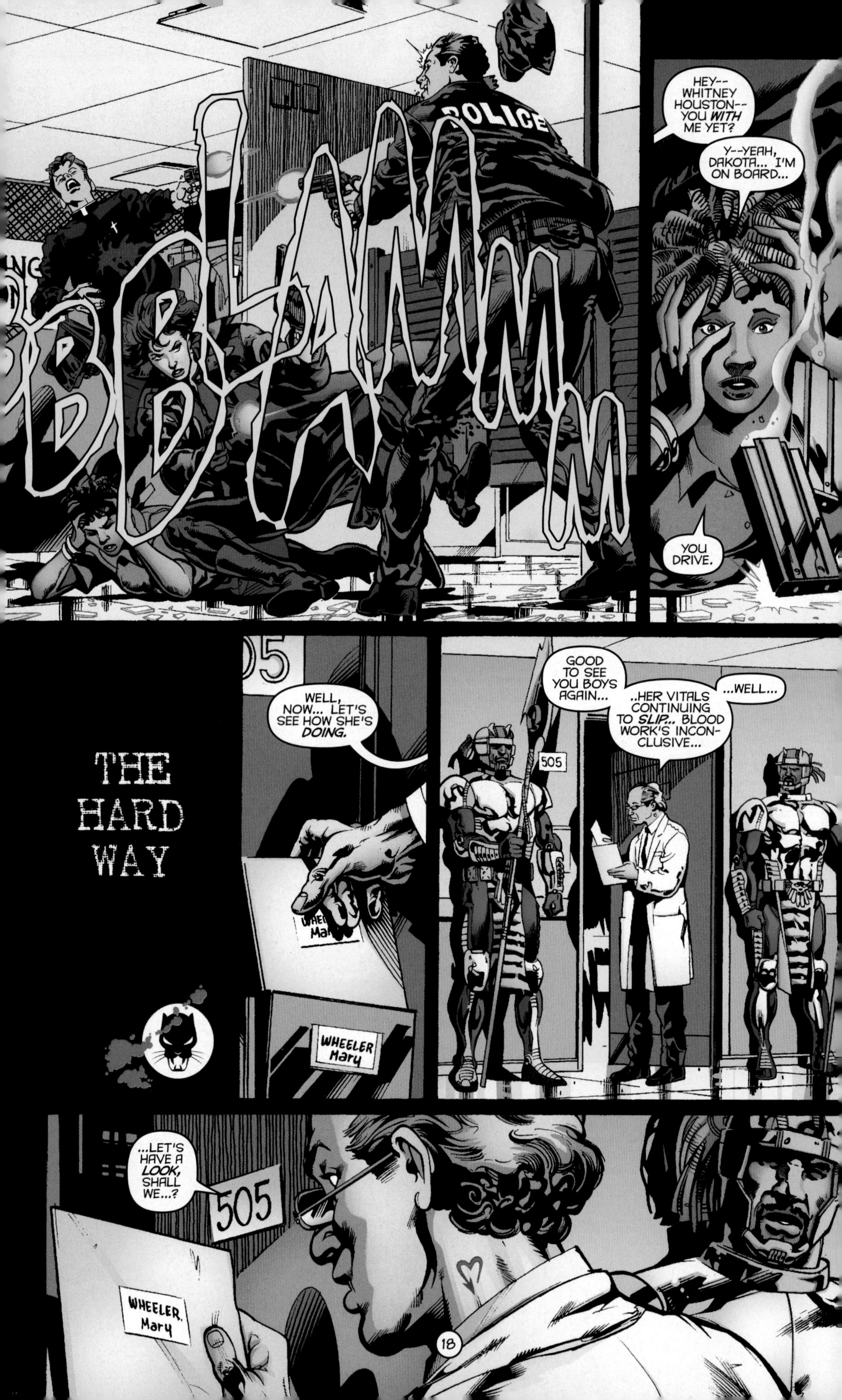
BLAM
HEY--WHITNEY HOUSTON--YOU *WITH* ME YET?
Y--YEAH, DAKOTA... I'M ON BOARD...
YOU DRIVE.
505
WELL, NOW... LET'S SEE HOW SHE'S *DOING.*
THE HARD WAY
WHEELER Mary
GOOD TO SEE YOU BOYS AGAIN...
..HER VITALS CONTINUING TO *SLIP..* BLOOD WORK'S INCONCLUSIVE...
...WELL...
505
...LET'S HAVE A *LOOK,* SHALL WE...?
505
WHEELER, Mary

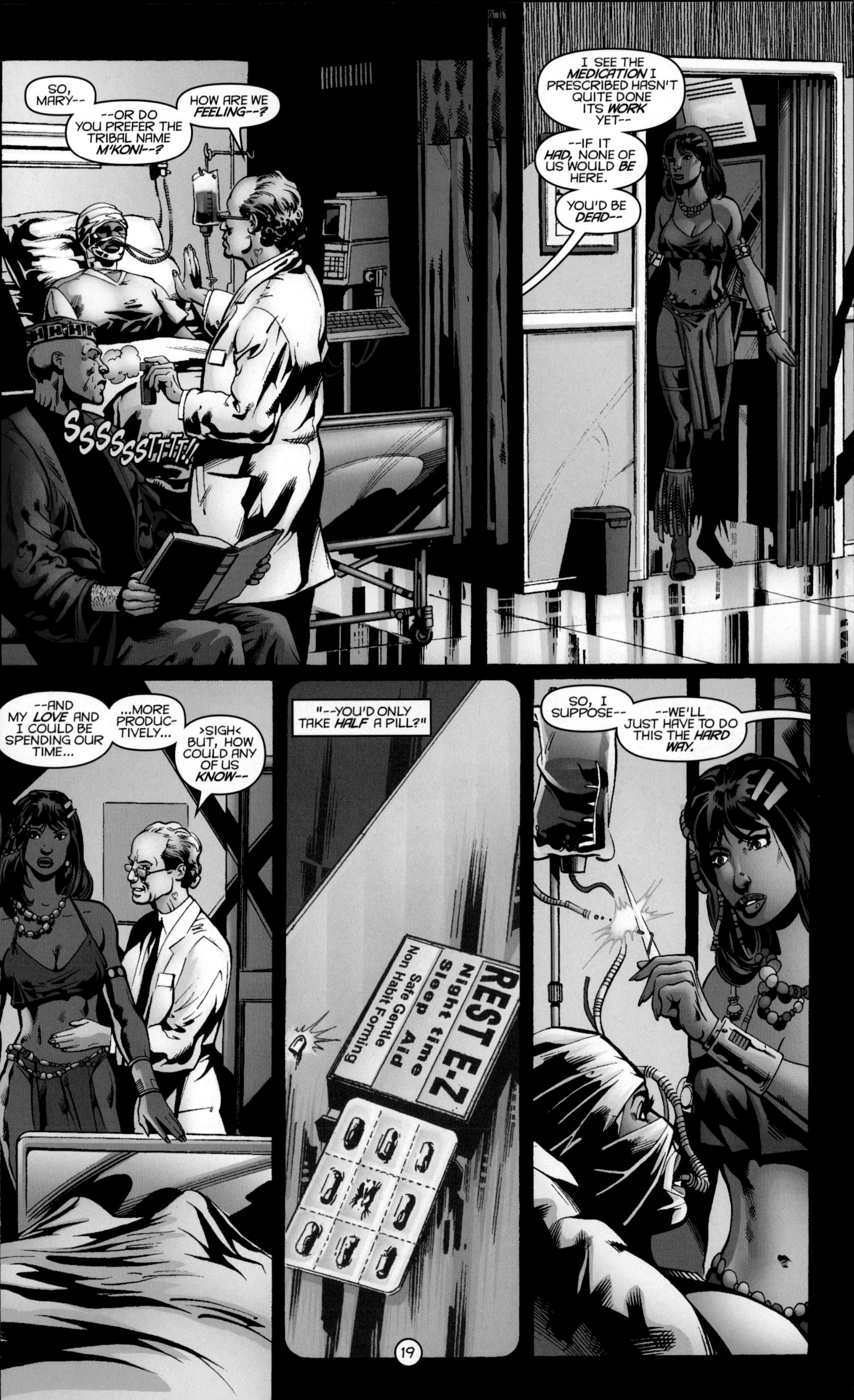
SO, MARY--
--OR DO YOU PREFER THE TRIBAL NAME M'KONI--?
HOW ARE WE FEELING--?
SSSSSSTTTT!!
I SEE THE MEDICATION I PRESCRIBED HASN'T QUITE DONE ITS WORK YET--
--IF IT HAD, NONE OF US WOULD BE HERE.
YOU'D BE DEAD--
--AND MY LOVE AND I COULD BE SPENDING OUR TIME...
...MORE PRODUCTIVELY...
>SIGH< BUT, HOW COULD ANY OF US KNOW--
"--YOU'D ONLY TAKE HALF A PILL?"
REST E-Z
Night time
Sleep Aid
Safe Gentle
Non Habit Forming
SO, I SUPPOSE--
--WE'LL JUST HAVE TO DO THIS THE HARD WAY.

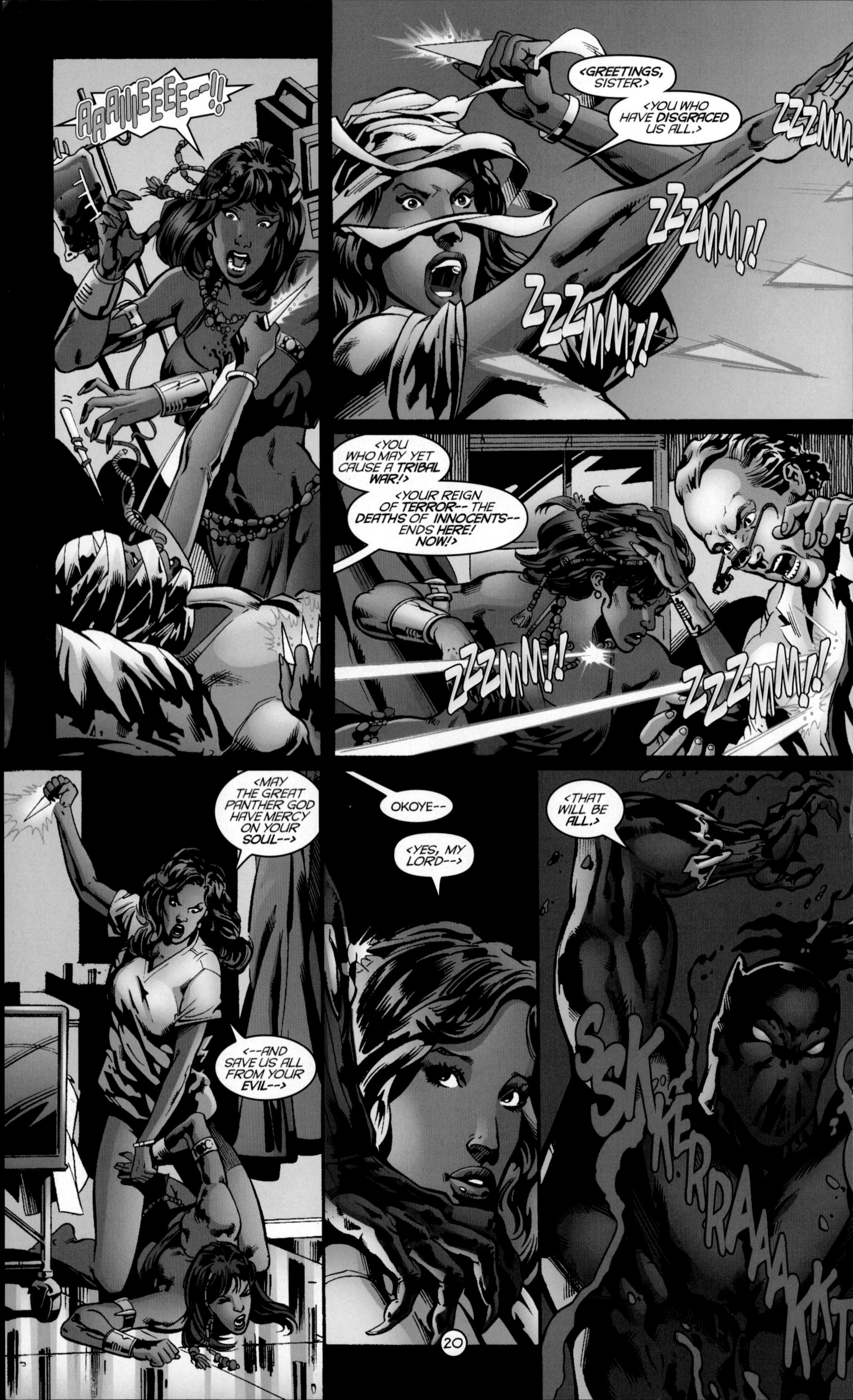
AAAIIIEEEE--!!
<GREETINGS, SISTER.>
<YOU WHO HAVE DISGRACED US ALL.>
ZZZMM
ZZZMM!!
ZZZMM!!
<YOU WHO MAY YET CAUSE A TRIBAL WAR!>
<YOUR REIGN OF TERROR-- THE DEATHS OF INNOCENTS-- ENDS HERE! NOW!>
ZZZMM!!
ZZZMMM!!
<MAY THE GREAT PANTHER GOD HAVE MERCY ON YOUR SOUL-->
<--AND SAVE US ALL FROM YOUR EVIL-->
OKOYE--
<YES, MY LORD-->
<THAT WILL BE ALL.>
SSKKERRAAAKKT

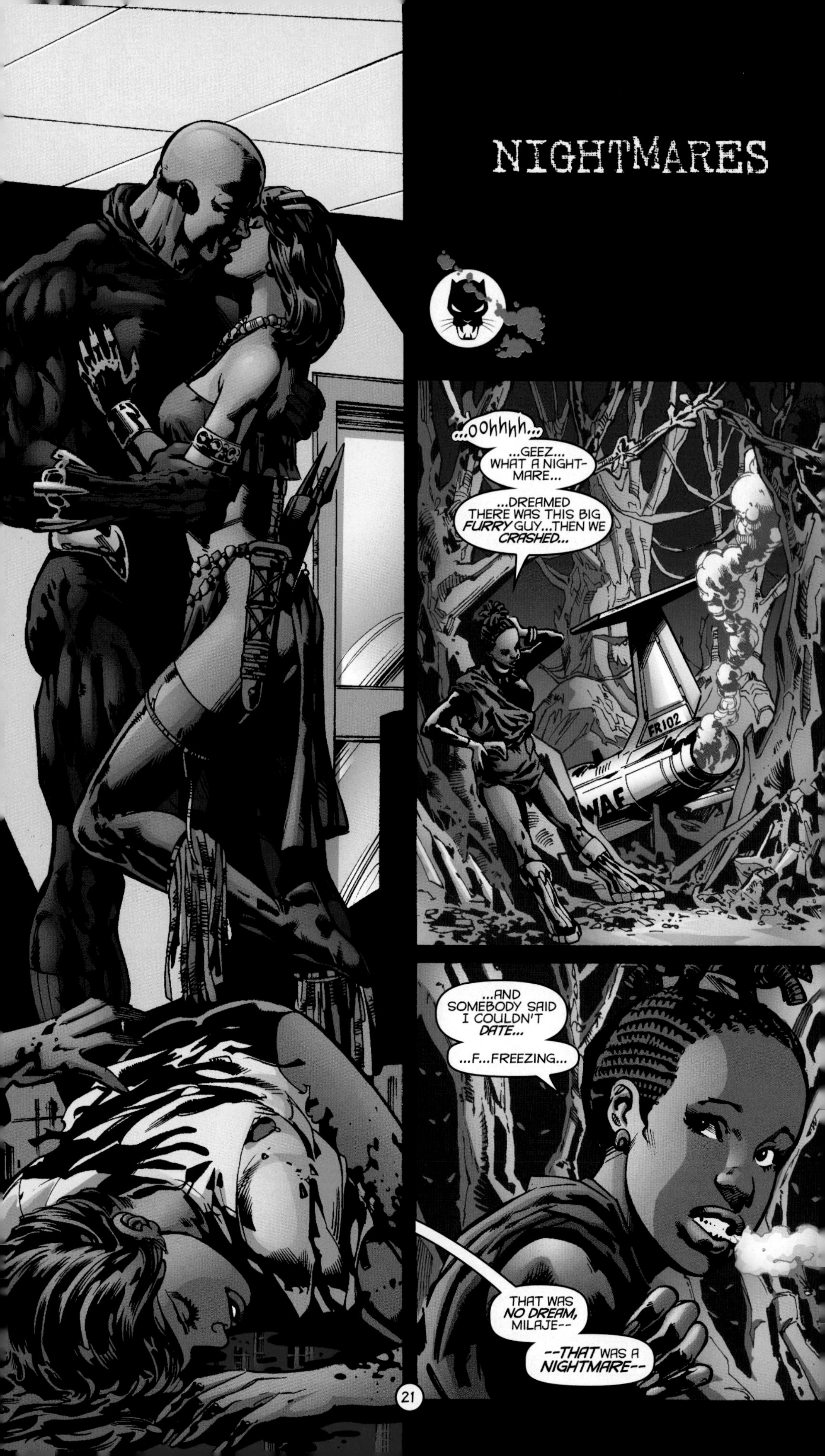

NIGHTMARES
...oohhhh...
...GEEZ... WHAT A NIGHT-MARE...
...DREAMED THERE WAS THIS BIG FURRY GUY...THEN WE CRASHED...
FR102
WAF
...AND SOMEBODY SAID I COULDN'T DATE...
...F...FREEZING...
THAT WAS NO DREAM, MILAJE--
--THAT WAS A NIGHTMARE--

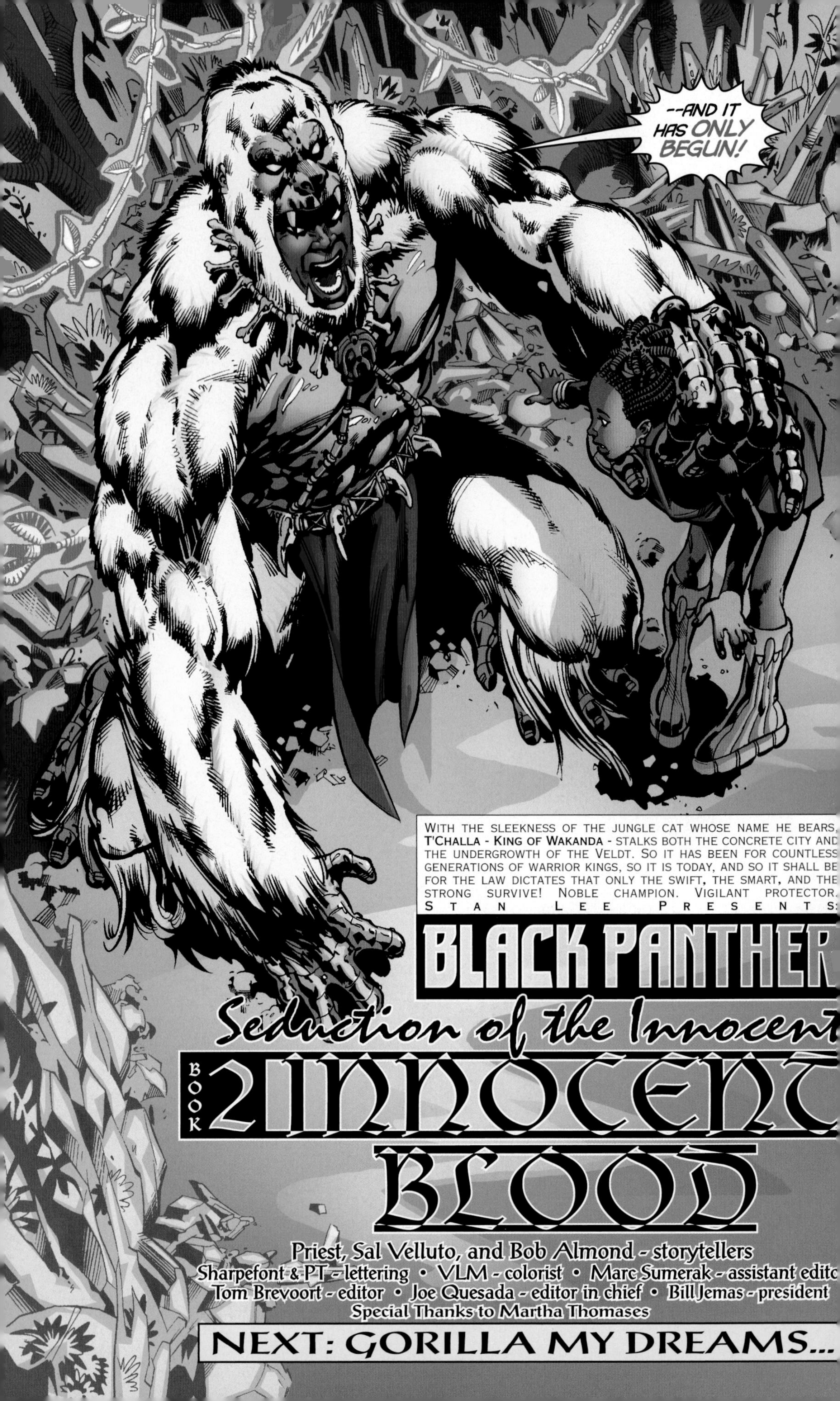
--AND IT HAS ONLY BEGUN!
WITH THE SLEEKNESS OF THE JUNGLE CAT WHOSE NAME HE BEARS, T'CHALLA - KING OF WAKANDA - STALKS BOTH THE CONCRETE CITY AND THE UNDERGROWTH OF THE VELDT. SO IT HAS BEEN FOR COUNTLESS GENERATIONS OF WARRIOR KINGS, SO IT IS TODAY, AND SO IT SHALL BE FOR THE LAW DICTATES THAT ONLY THE SWIFT, THE SMART, AND THE STRONG SURVIVE! NOBLE CHAMPION. VIGILANT PROTECTOR.
STAN LEE PRESENTS:
BLACK PANTHER
Seduction of the Innocent
BOOK 2 INNOCENT BLOOD
Priest, Sal Velluto, and Bob Almond - storytellers
Sharpefont & PT - lettering • VLM - colorist • Marc Sumerak - assistant edito
Tom Brevoort - editor • Joe Quesada - editor in chief • Bill Jemas - president
Special Thanks to Martha Thomases
NEXT: GORILLA MY DREAMS...

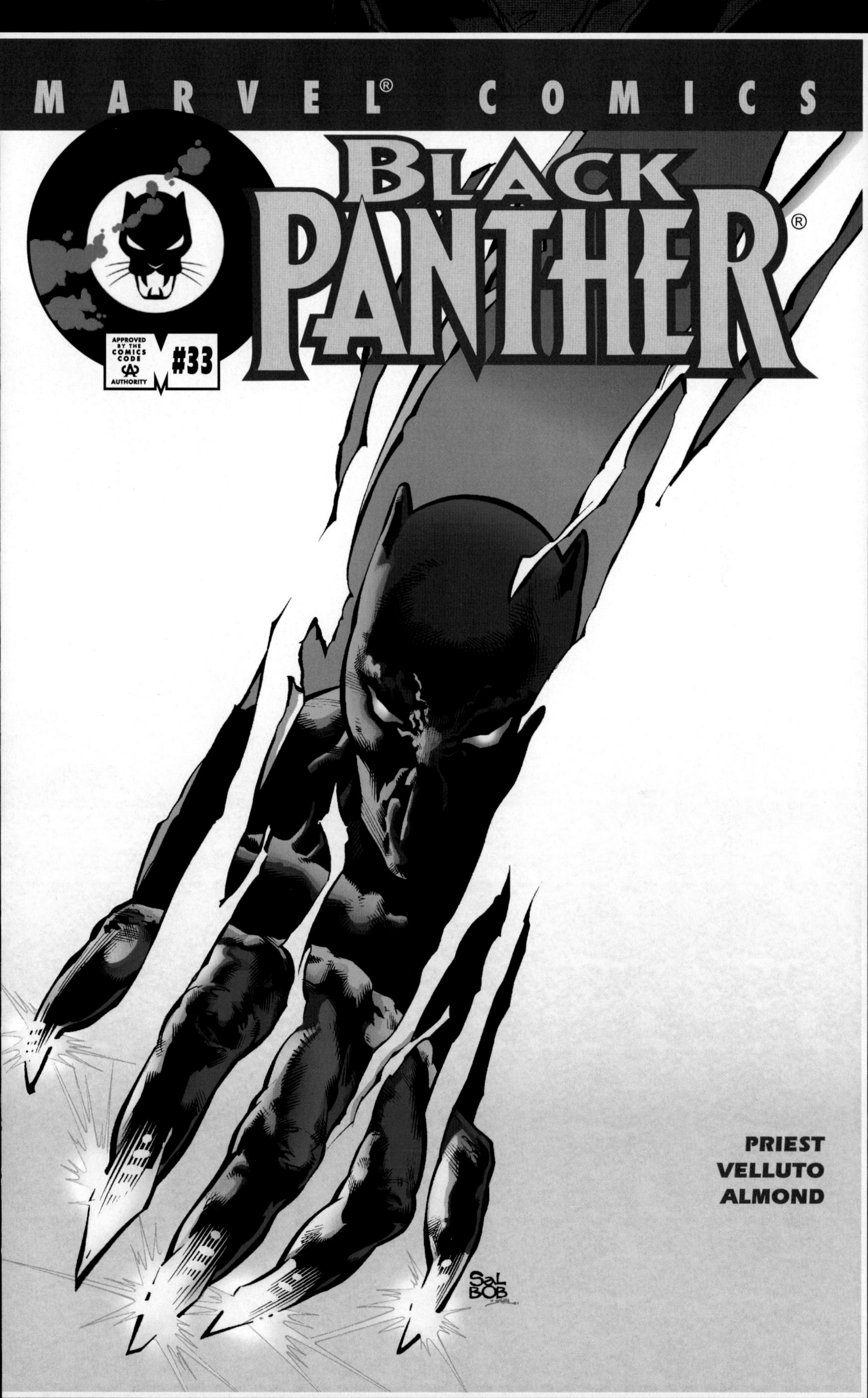
MARVEL® COMICS
BLACK PANTHER®
APPROVED BY THE COMICS CODE AUTHORITY
#33
PRIEST
VELLUTO
ALMOND
SAL BOB

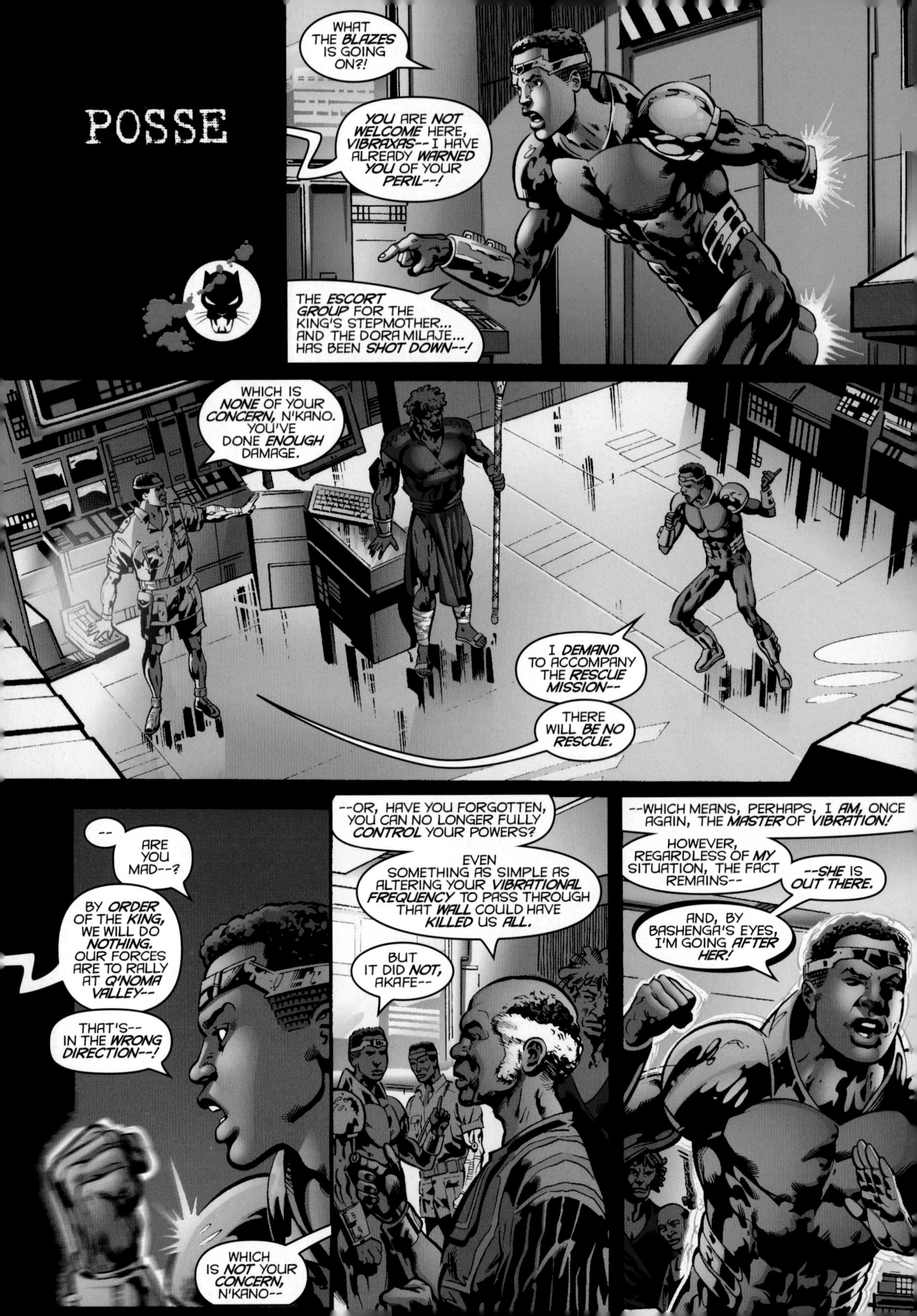
POSSE
WHAT THE BLAZES IS GOING ON?!
YOU ARE NOT WELCOME HERE, VIBRAXAS-- I HAVE ALREADY WARNED YOU OF YOUR PERIL--!
THE ESCORT GROUP FOR THE KING'S STEPMOTHER... AND THE DORA MILAJE... HAS BEEN SHOT DOWN--!
WHICH IS NONE OF YOUR CONCERN, N'KANO. YOU'VE DONE ENOUGH DAMAGE.
I DEMAND TO ACCOMPANY THE RESCUE MISSION--
THERE WILL BE NO RESCUE.
-- ARE YOU MAD--?
BY ORDER OF THE KING, WE WILL DO NOTHING. OUR FORCES ARE TO RALLY AT Q'NOMA VALLEY--
THAT'S-- IN THE WRONG DIRECTION--!
WHICH IS NOT YOUR CONCERN, N'KANO--
--OR, HAVE YOU FORGOTTEN, YOU CAN NO LONGER FULLY CONTROL YOUR POWERS?
EVEN SOMETHING AS SIMPLE AS ALTERING YOUR VIBRATIONAL FREQUENCY TO PASS THROUGH THAT WALL COULD HAVE KILLED US ALL.
BUT IT DID NOT, AKAFE--
--WHICH MEANS, PERHAPS, I AM, ONCE AGAIN, THE MASTER OF VIBRATION!
HOWEVER, REGARDLESS OF MY SITUATION, THE FACT REMAINS--
--SHE IS OUT THERE.
AND, BY BASHENGA'S EYES, I'M GOING AFTER HER!

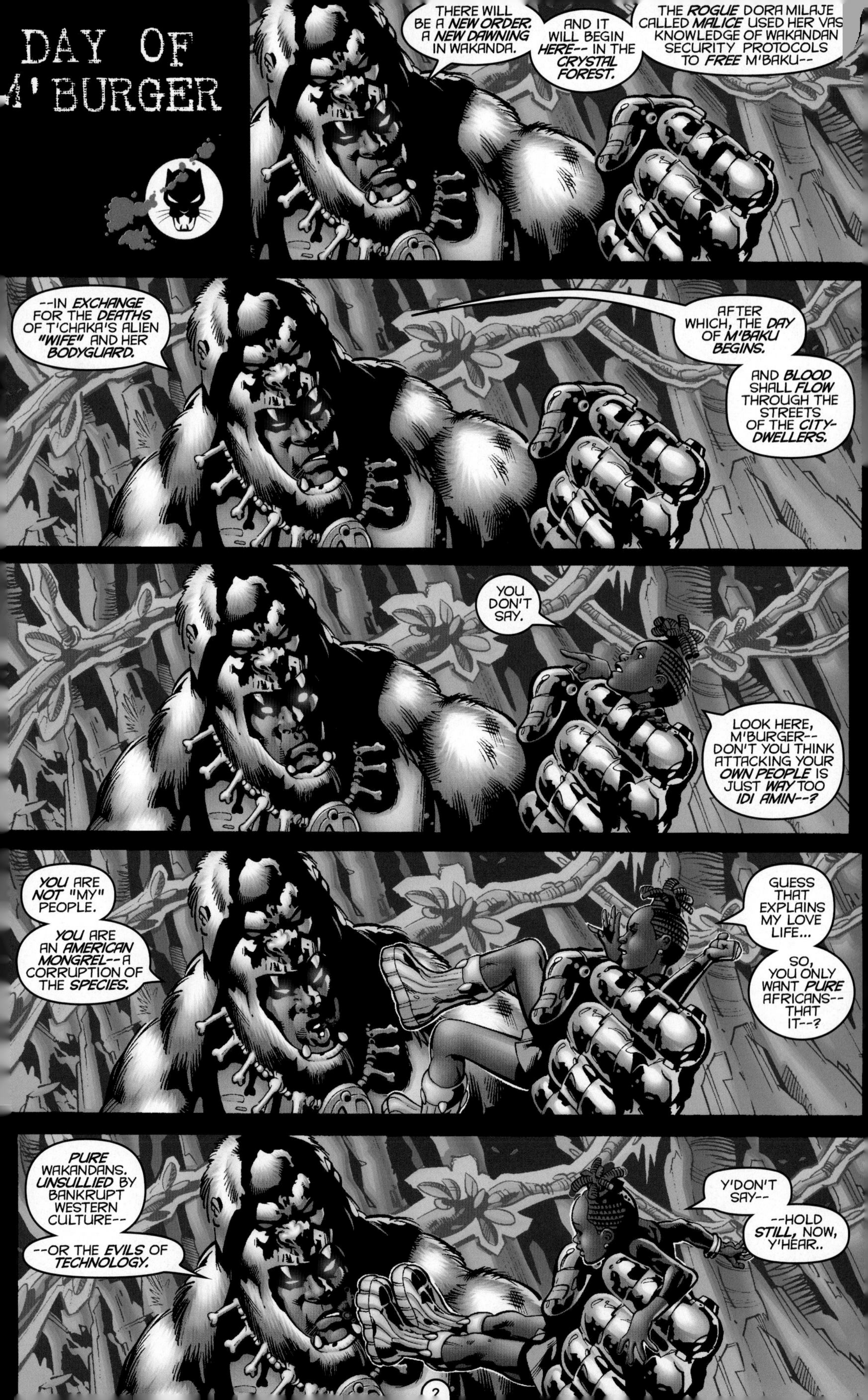
DAY OF M'BURGER
THERE WILL BE A NEW ORDER. A NEW DAWNING IN WAKANDA.
AND IT WILL BEGIN HERE-- IN THE CRYSTAL FOREST.
THE ROGUE DORA MILAJE CALLED MALICE USED HER VAS KNOWLEDGE OF WAKANDAN SECURITY PROTOCOLS TO FREE M'BAKU--
--IN EXCHANGE FOR THE DEATHS OF T'CHAKA'S ALIEN "WIFE" AND HER BODYGUARD.
AFTER WHICH, THE DAY OF M'BAKU BEGINS.
AND BLOOD SHALL FLOW THROUGH THE STREETS OF THE CITY-DWELLERS.
YOU DON'T SAY.
LOOK HERE, M'BURGER-- DON'T YOU THINK ATTACKING YOUR OWN PEOPLE IS JUST WAY TOO IDI AMIN--?
YOU ARE NOT "MY" PEOPLE.
YOU ARE AN AMERICAN MONGREL-- A CORRUPTION OF THE SPECIES.
GUESS THAT EXPLAINS MY LOVE LIFE...
SO, YOU ONLY WANT PURE AFRICANS-- THAT IT--?
PURE WAKANDANS. UNSULLIED BY BANKRUPT WESTERN CULTURE--
--OR THE EVILS OF TECHNOLOGY.
Y'DON'T SAY--
--HOLD STILL, NOW, Y'HEAR..

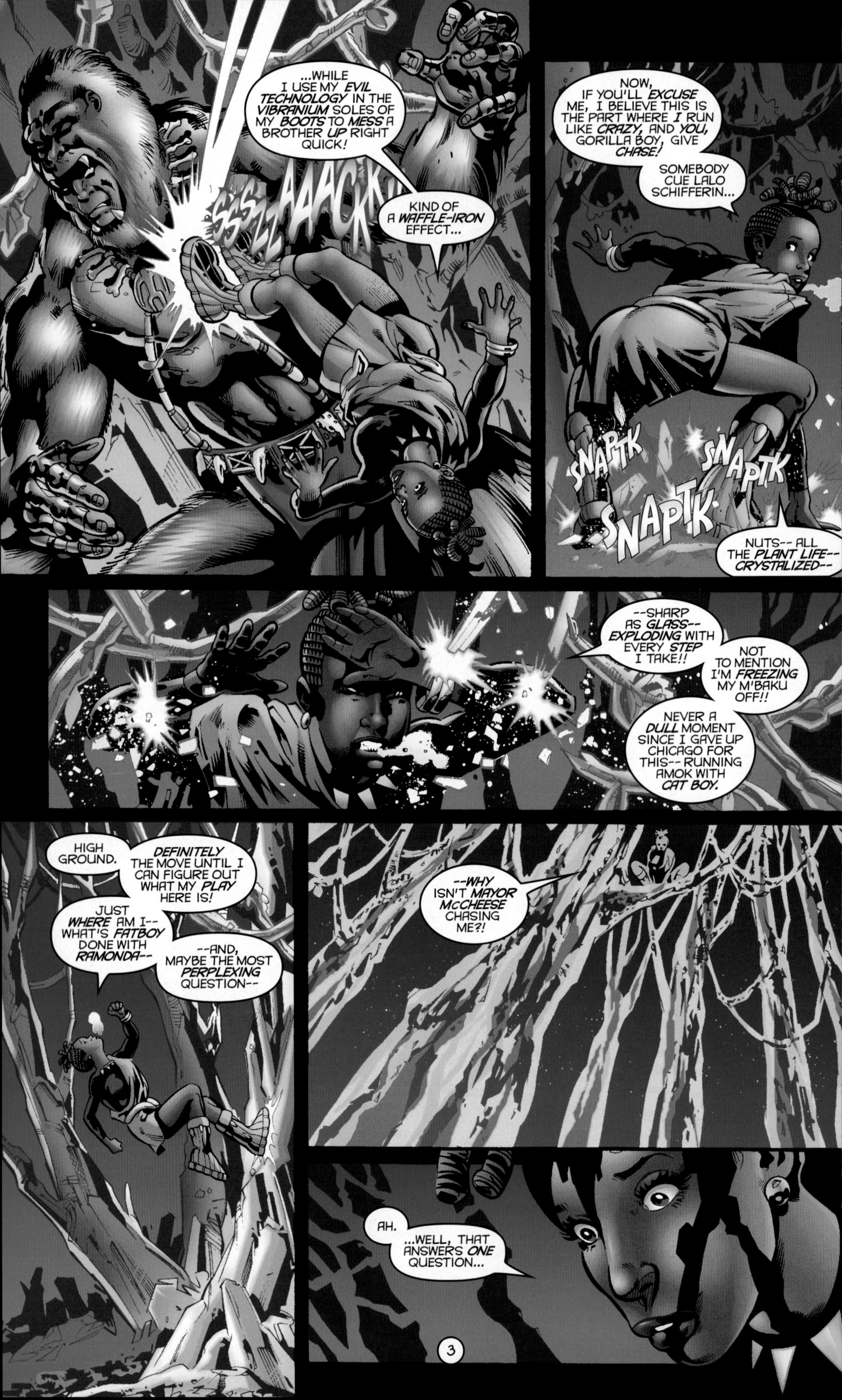

...WHILE I USE MY EVIL TECHNOLOGY IN THE VIBRANIUM SOLES OF MY BOOTS TO MESS A BROTHER UP RIGHT QUICK!
SSSZZAAACKK!!
KIND OF A WAFFLE-IRON EFFECT...
NOW, IF YOU'LL EXCUSE ME, I BELIEVE THIS IS THE PART WHERE I RUN LIKE CRAZY, AND YOU, GORILLA BOY, GIVE CHASE!
SOMEBODY CUE LALO SCHIFFERIN...
SNAPTK
SNAPTK
SNAPTK
NUTS-- ALL THE PLANT LIFE-- CRYSTALIZED--
--SHARP AS GLASS-- EXPLODING WITH EVERY STEP I TAKE!!
NOT TO MENTION I'M FREEZING MY M'BAKU OFF!!
NEVER A DULL MOMENT SINCE I GAVE UP CHICAGO FOR THIS-- RUNNING AMOK WITH CAT BOY.
HIGH GROUND.
DEFINITELY THE MOVE UNTIL I CAN FIGURE OUT WHAT MY PLAY HERE IS!
JUST WHERE AM I-- WHAT'S FATBOY DONE WITH RAMONDA--
--AND, MAYBE THE MOST PERPLEXING QUESTION--
--WHY ISN'T MAYOR McCHEESE CHASING ME?!
AH.
...WELL, THAT ANSWERS ONE QUESTION...

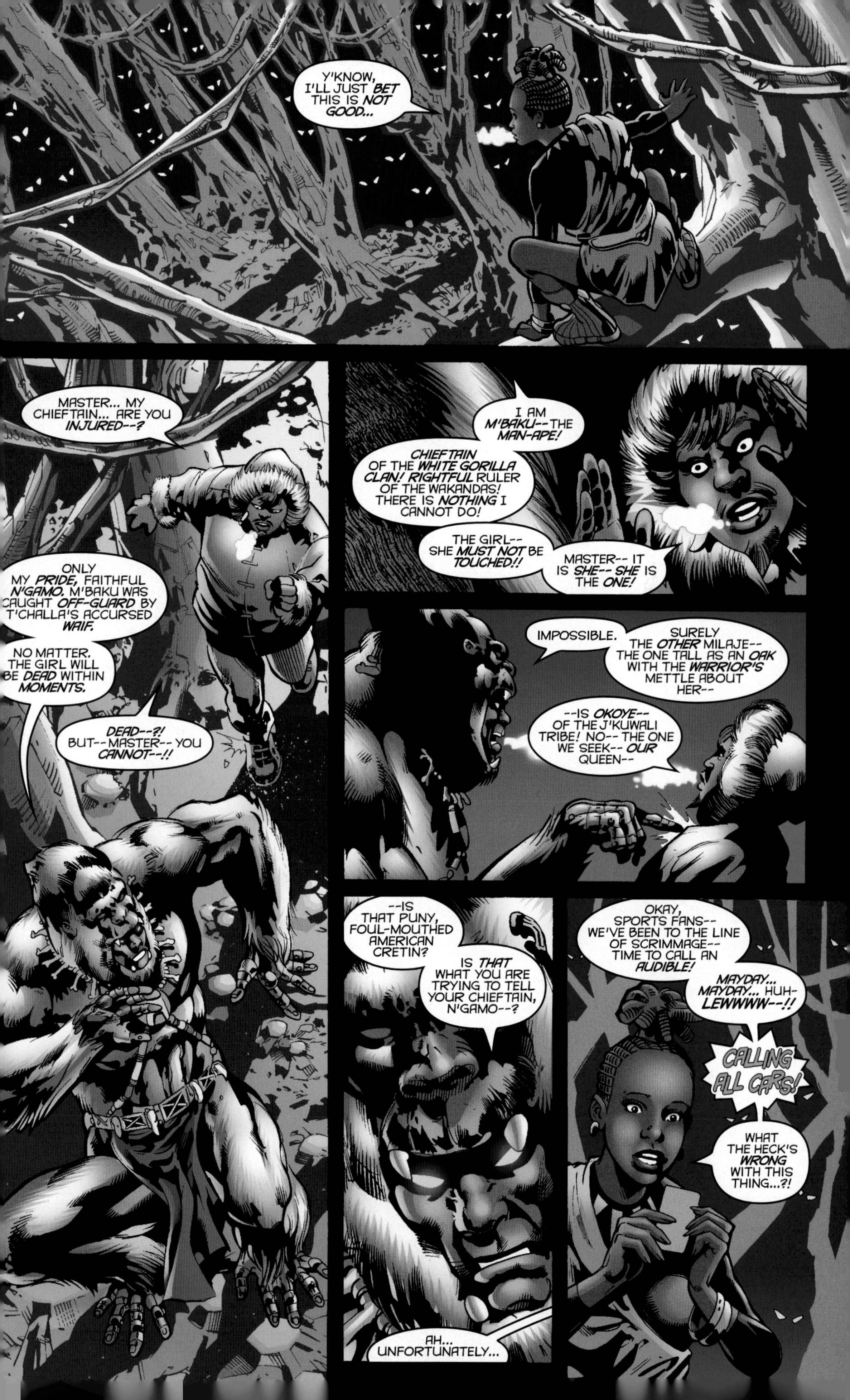
Y'KNOW, I'LL JUST BET THIS IS NOT GOOD...
MASTER... MY CHIEFTAIN... ARE YOU INJURED--?
ONLY MY PRIDE, FAITHFUL N'GAMO. M'BAKU WAS CAUGHT OFF-GUARD BY T'CHALLA'S ACCURSED WAIF.
NO MATTER. THE GIRL WILL BE DEAD WITHIN MOMENTS.
DEAD--?! BUT--MASTER-- YOU CANNOT--!!
I AM M'BAKU--THE MAN-APE!
CHIEFTAIN OF THE WHITE GORILLA CLAN! RIGHTFUL RULER OF THE WAKANDAS! THERE IS NOTHING I CANNOT DO!
THE GIRL-- SHE MUST NOT BE TOUCHED!!
MASTER-- IT IS SHE-- SHE IS THE ONE!
IMPOSSIBLE.
SURELY THE OTHER MILAJE-- THE ONE TALL AS AN OAK WITH THE WARRIOR'S METTLE ABOUT HER--
--IS OKOYE-- OF THE J'KUWALI TRIBE! NO-- THE ONE WE SEEK-- OUR QUEEN--
--IS THAT PUNY, FOUL-MOUTHED AMERICAN CRETIN?
IS THAT WHAT YOU ARE TRYING TO TELL YOUR CHIEFTAIN, N'GAMO--?
AH... UNFORTUNATELY...
OKAY, SPORTS FANS-- WE'VE BEEN TO THE LINE OF SCRIMMAGE-- TIME TO CALL AN AUDIBLE!
MAYDAY... MAYDAY... HUH-LEWWWW--!!
CALLING ALL CARS!
WHAT THE HECK'S WRONG WITH THIS THING...?!

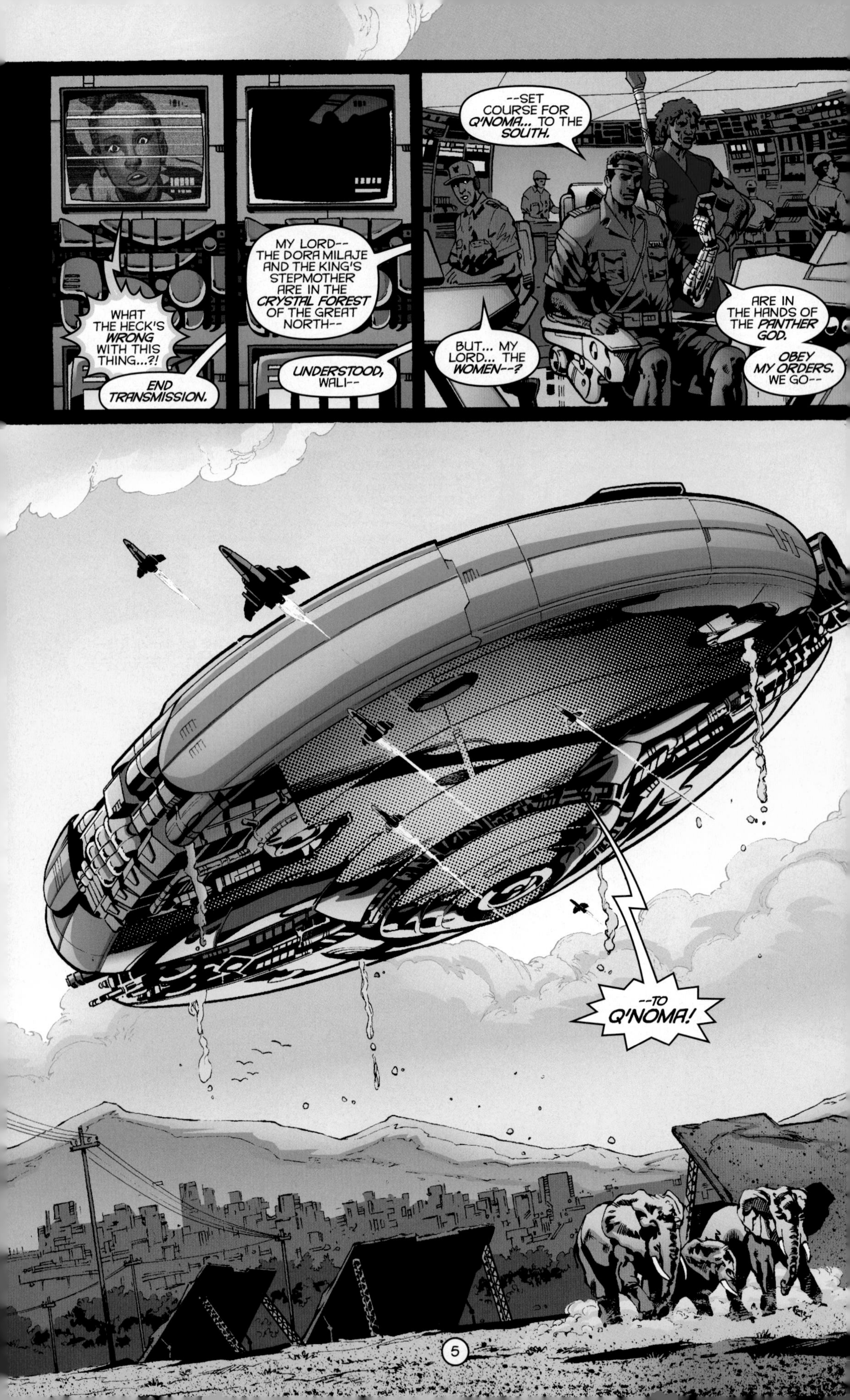
WHAT THE HECK'S WRONG WITH THIS THING...?!
END TRANSMISSION.
MY LORD-- THE DORA MILAJE AND THE KING'S STEPMOTHER ARE IN THE CRYSTAL FOREST OF THE GREAT NORTH--
UNDERSTOOD, WALI--
--SET COURSE FOR Q'NOMA... TO THE SOUTH.
BUT... MY LORD... THE WOMEN--?
ARE IN THE HANDS OF THE PANTHER GOD.
OBEY MY ORDERS. WE GO--
--TO Q'NOMA!

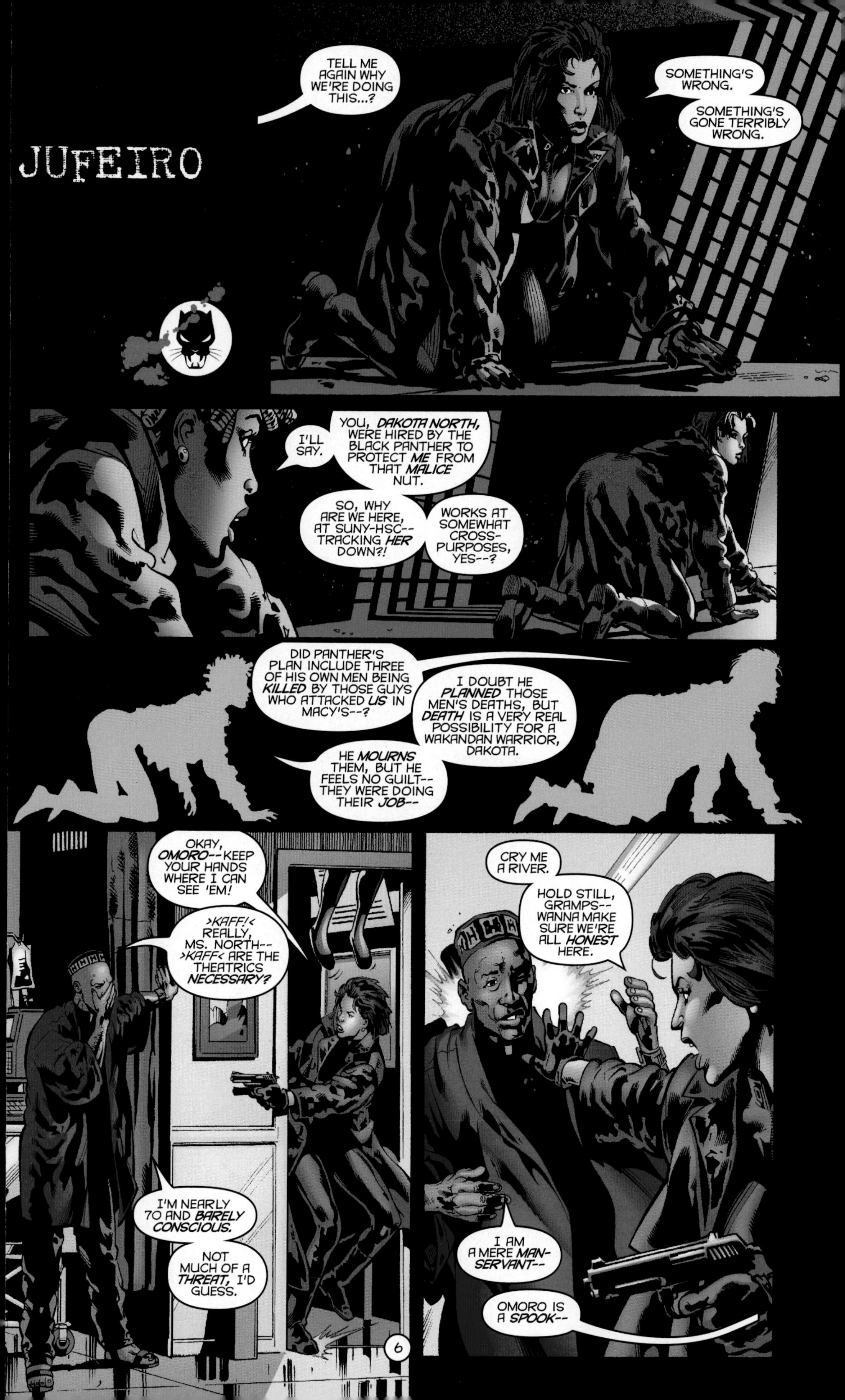
JUFEIRO
TELL ME AGAIN WHY WE'RE DOING THIS...?
SOMETHING'S WRONG.
SOMETHING'S GONE TERRIBLY WRONG.
I'LL SAY.
YOU, DAKOTA NORTH, WERE HIRED BY THE BLACK PANTHER TO PROTECT ME FROM THAT MALICE NUT.
SO, WHY ARE WE HERE, AT SUNY-HSC--TRACKING HER DOWN?!
WORKS AT SOMEWHAT CROSS-PURPOSES, YES--?
DID PANTHER'S PLAN INCLUDE THREE OF HIS OWN MEN BEING KILLED BY THOSE GUYS WHO ATTACKED US IN MACY'S--?
I DOUBT HE PLANNED THOSE MEN'S DEATHS, BUT DEATH IS A VERY REAL POSSIBILITY FOR A WAKANDAN WARRIOR, DAKOTA.
HE MOURNS THEM, BUT HE FEELS NO GUILT--THEY WERE DOING THEIR JOB--
OKAY, OMORO--KEEP YOUR HANDS WHERE I CAN SEE 'EM!
>KAFF!< REALLY, MS. NORTH-->KAFF< ARE THE THEATRICS NECESSARY?
I'M NEARLY 70 AND BARELY CONSCIOUS.
NOT MUCH OF A THREAT, I'D GUESS.
CRY ME A RIVER.
HOLD STILL, GRAMPS--WANNA MAKE SURE WE'RE ALL HONEST HERE.
I AM A MERE MAN-SERVANT--
OMORO IS A SPOOK--

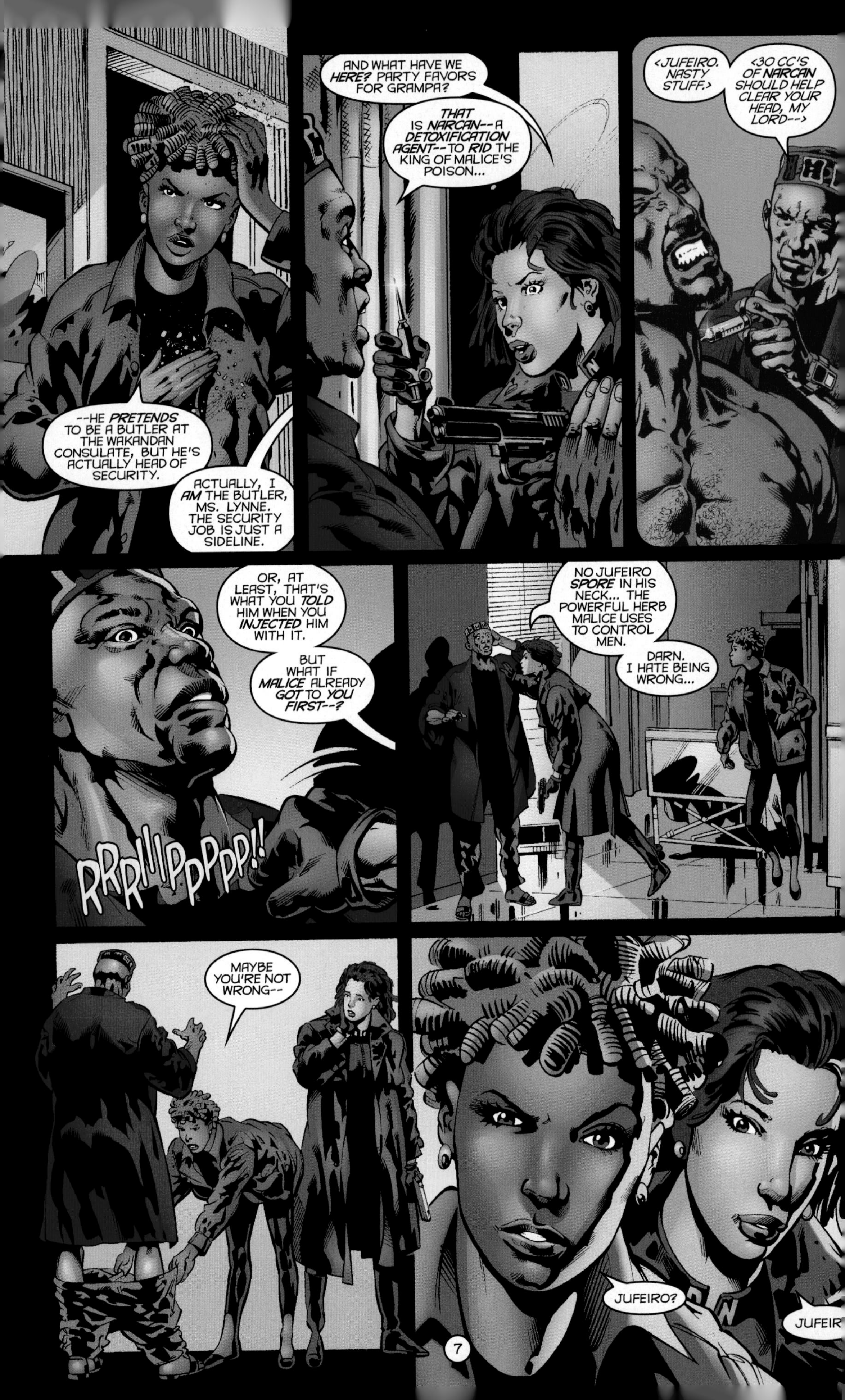
--HE PRETENDS TO BE A BUTLER AT THE WAKANDAN CONSULATE, BUT HE'S ACTUALLY HEAD OF SECURITY.
ACTUALLY, I AM THE BUTLER, MS. LYNNE. THE SECURITY JOB IS JUST A SIDELINE.
AND WHAT HAVE WE HERE? PARTY FAVORS FOR GRAMPA?
THAT IS NARCAN--A DETOXIFICATION AGENT--TO RID THE KING OF MALICE'S POISON...
<JUFEIRO. NASTY STUFF.>
<30 CC'S OF NARCAN SHOULD HELP CLEAR YOUR HEAD, MY LORD-->
OR, AT LEAST, THAT'S WHAT YOU TOLD HIM WHEN YOU INJECTED HIM WITH IT.
BUT WHAT IF MALICE ALREADY GOT TO YOU FIRST--?
RRRIIIPPPPP!!
NO JUFEIRO SPORE IN HIS NECK... THE POWERFUL HERB MALICE USES TO CONTROL MEN.
DARN. I HATE BEING WRONG...
MAYBE YOU'RE NOT WRONG--
JUFEIRO?
JUFEIR
7

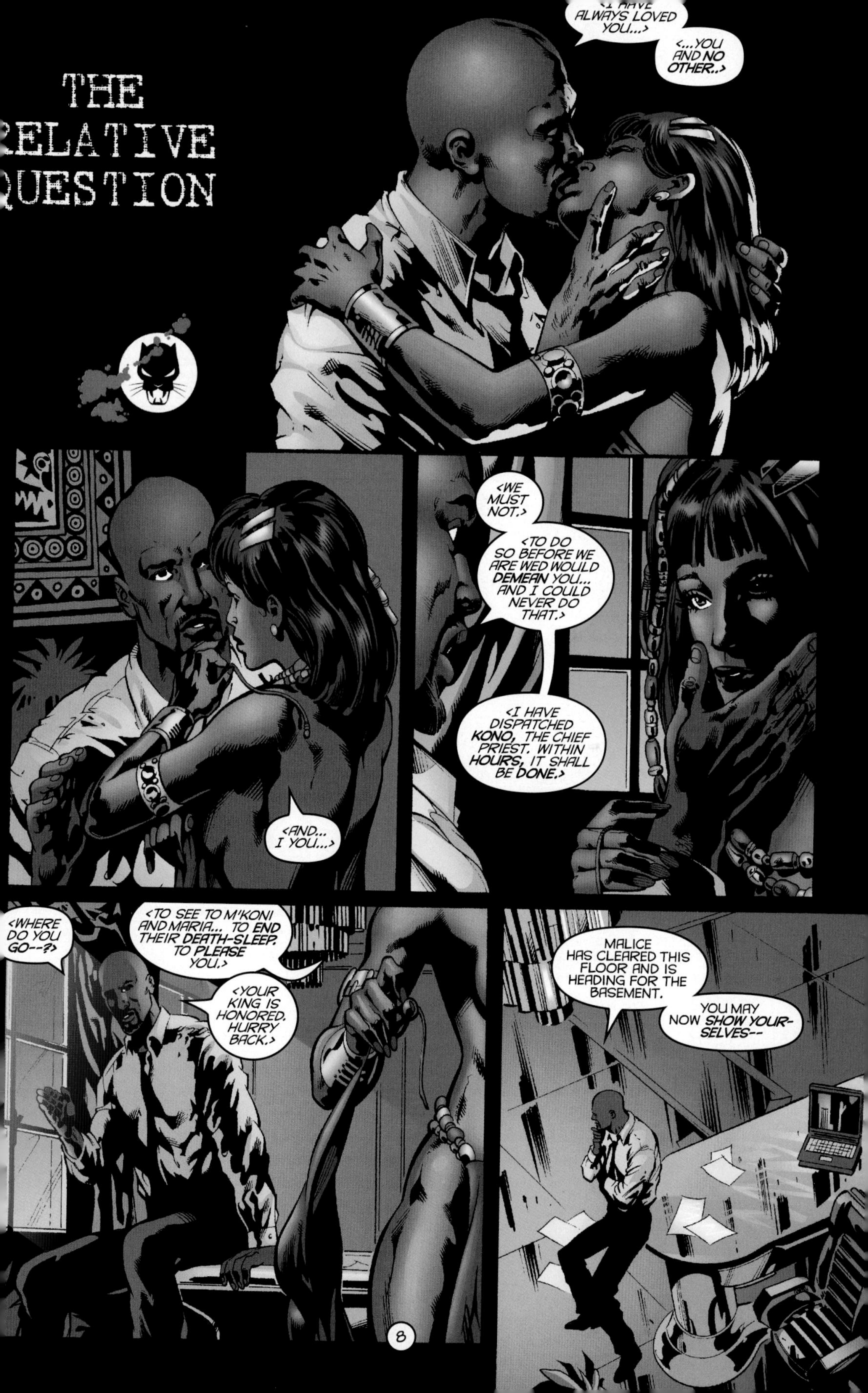

THE RELATIVE QUESTION
<I HAVE ALWAYS LOVED YOU...>
<...YOU AND NO OTHER..>
<AND... I YOU...>
<WE MUST NOT.>
<TO DO SO BEFORE WE ARE WED WOULD DEMEAN YOU... AND I COULD NEVER DO THAT.>
<I HAVE DISPATCHED KONO, THE CHIEF PRIEST. WITHIN HOURS, IT SHALL BE DONE.>
<WHERE DO YOU GO--?>
<TO SEE TO M'KONI AND MARIA... TO END THEIR DEATH-SLEEP. TO PLEASE YOU.>
<YOUR KING IS HONORED. HURRY BACK.>
MALICE HAS CLEARED THIS FLOOR AND IS HEADING FOR THE BASEMENT.
YOU MAY NOW SHOW YOURSELVES--

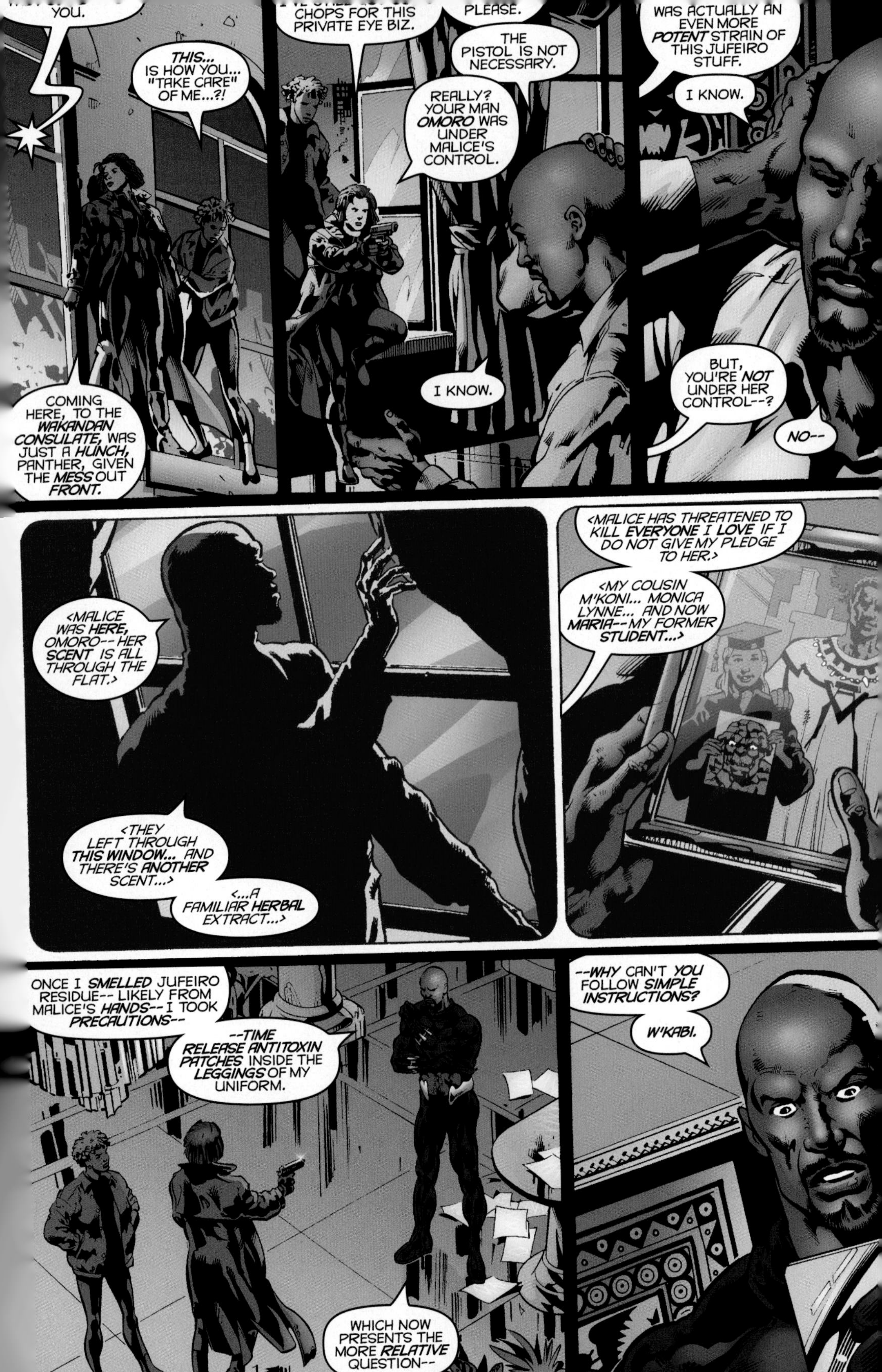

YOU.
THIS... IS HOW YOU... "TAKE CARE" OF ME...?!
COMING HERE, TO THE WAKANDAN CONSULATE, WAS JUST A HUNCH, PANTHER, GIVEN THE MESS OUT FRONT.
CHOPS FOR THIS PRIVATE EYE BIZ.
PLEASE.
THE PISTOL IS NOT NECESSARY.
REALLY? YOUR MAN OMORO WAS UNDER MALICE'S CONTROL.
I KNOW.
WAS ACTUALLY AN EVEN MORE POTENT STRAIN OF THIS JUFEIRO STUFF.
I KNOW.
BUT, YOU'RE NOT UNDER HER CONTROL--?
NO--
<MALICE WAS HERE, OMORO--HER SCENT IS ALL THROUGH THE FLAT.>
<THEY LEFT THROUGH THIS WINDOW... AND THERE'S ANOTHER SCENT...>
<...A FAMILIAR HERBAL EXTRACT...>
<MALICE HAS THREATENED TO KILL EVERYONE I LOVE IF I DO NOT GIVE MY PLEDGE TO HER.>
<MY COUSIN M'KONI... MONICA LYNNE... AND NOW MARIA--MY FORMER STUDENT...>
ONCE I SMELLED JUFEIRO RESIDUE-- LIKELY FROM MALICE'S HANDS--I TOOK PRECAUTIONS--
--TIME RELEASE ANTITOXIN PATCHES INSIDE THE LEGGINGS OF MY UNIFORM.
WHICH NOW PRESENTS THE MORE RELATIVE QUESTION--
--WHY CAN'T YOU FOLLOW SIMPLE INSTRUCTIONS?
W'KABI.

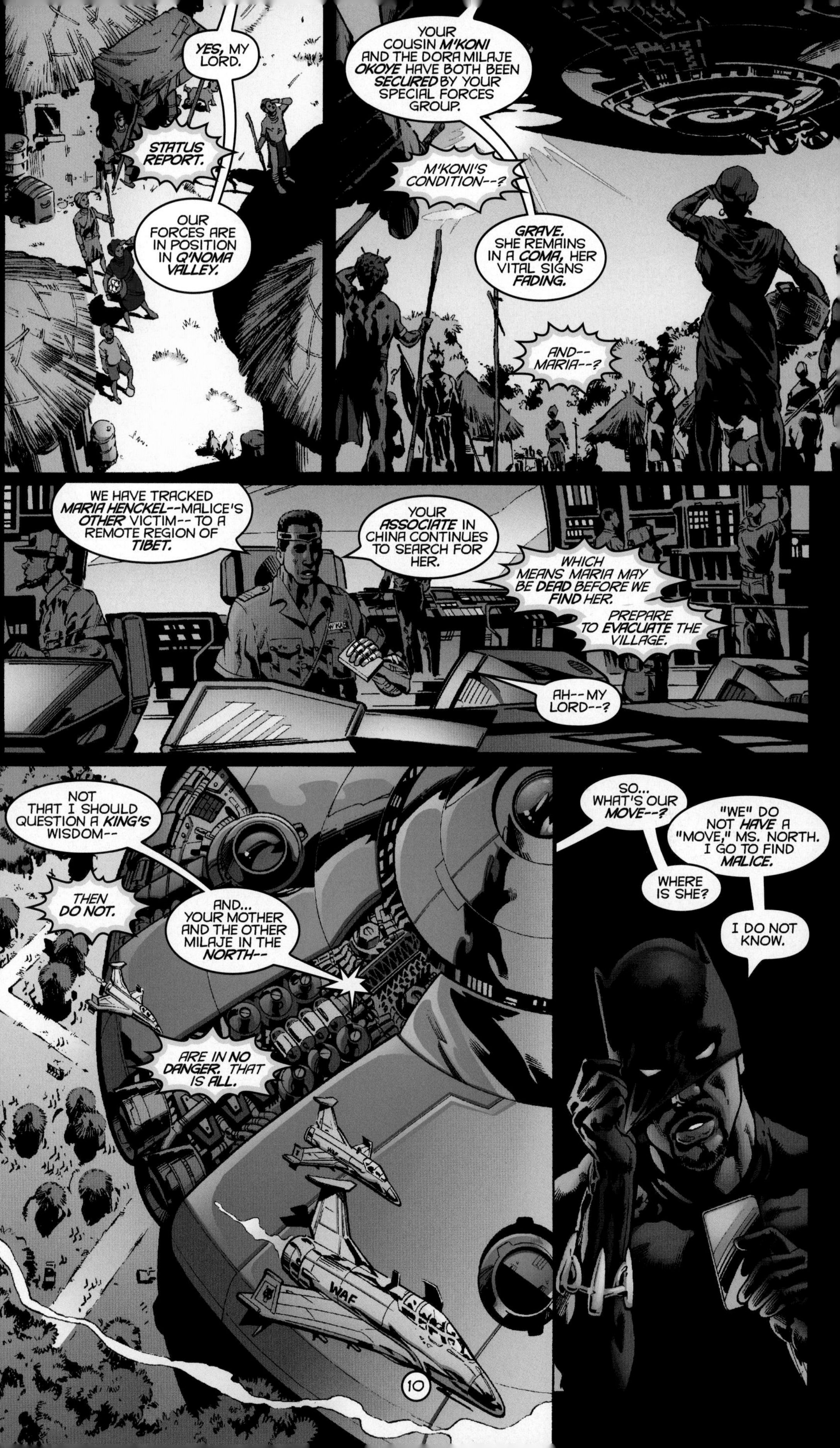

STATUS REPORT.
YES, MY LORD.
OUR FORCES ARE IN POSITION IN Q'NOMA VALLEY.
YOUR COUSIN M'KONI AND THE DORA MILAJE OKOYE HAVE BOTH BEEN SECURED BY YOUR SPECIAL FORCES GROUP.
M'KONI'S CONDITION--?
GRAVE. SHE REMAINS IN A COMA, HER VITAL SIGNS FADING.
AND-- MARIA--?
WE HAVE TRACKED MARIA HENCKEL--MALICE'S OTHER VICTIM-- TO A REMOTE REGION OF TIBET.
YOUR ASSOCIATE IN CHINA CONTINUES TO SEARCH FOR HER.
WHICH MEANS MARIA MAY BE DEAD BEFORE WE FIND HER.
PREPARE TO EVACUATE THE VILLAGE.
AH--MY LORD--?
NOT THAT I SHOULD QUESTION A KING'S WISDOM--
THEN DO NOT.
AND... YOUR MOTHER AND THE OTHER MILAJE IN THE NORTH--
ARE IN NO DANGER. THAT IS ALL.
WAF
SO... WHAT'S OUR MOVE--?
"WE" DO NOT HAVE A "MOVE," MS. NORTH. I GO TO FIND MALICE.
WHERE IS SHE?
I DO NOT KNOW.

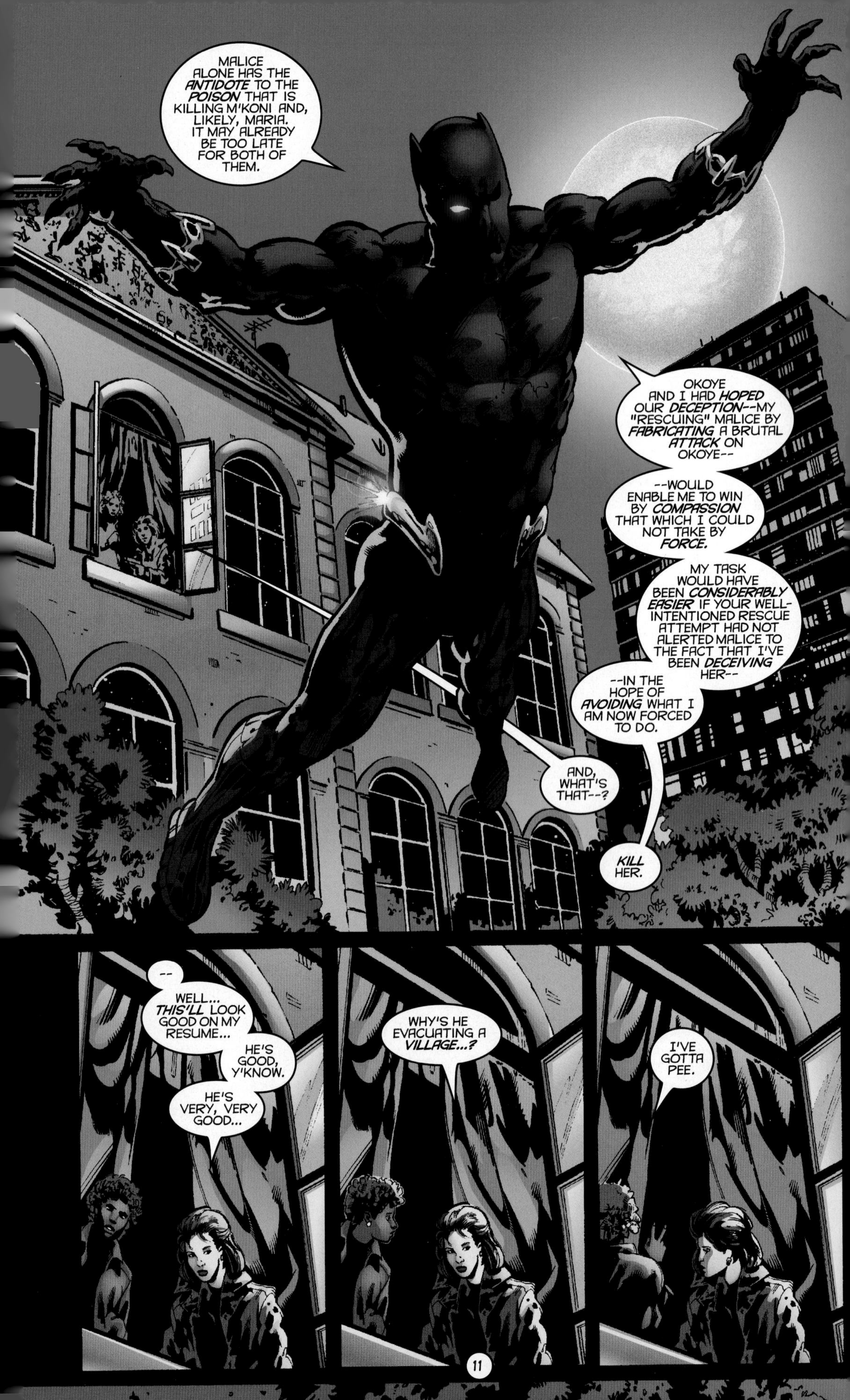
MALICE ALONE HAS THE ANTIDOTE TO THE POISON THAT IS KILLING M'KONI AND, LIKELY, MARIA. IT MAY ALREADY BE TOO LATE FOR BOTH OF THEM.
OKOYE AND I HAD HOPED OUR DECEPTION--MY "RESCUING" MALICE BY FABRICATING A BRUTAL ATTACK ON OKOYE--
--WOULD ENABLE ME TO WIN BY COMPASSION THAT WHICH I COULD NOT TAKE BY FORCE.
MY TASK WOULD HAVE BEEN CONSIDERABLY EASIER IF YOUR WELL-INTENTIONED RESCUE ATTEMPT HAD NOT ALERTED MALICE TO THE FACT THAT I'VE BEEN DECEIVING HER--
--IN THE HOPE OF AVOIDING WHAT I AM NOW FORCED TO DO.
AND, WHAT'S THAT--?
KILL HER.
--
WELL... THIS'LL LOOK GOOD ON MY RESUME...
HE'S GOOD, Y'KNOW.
HE'S VERY, VERY GOOD...
WHY'S HE EVACUATING A VILLAGE...?
I'VE GOTTA PEE.

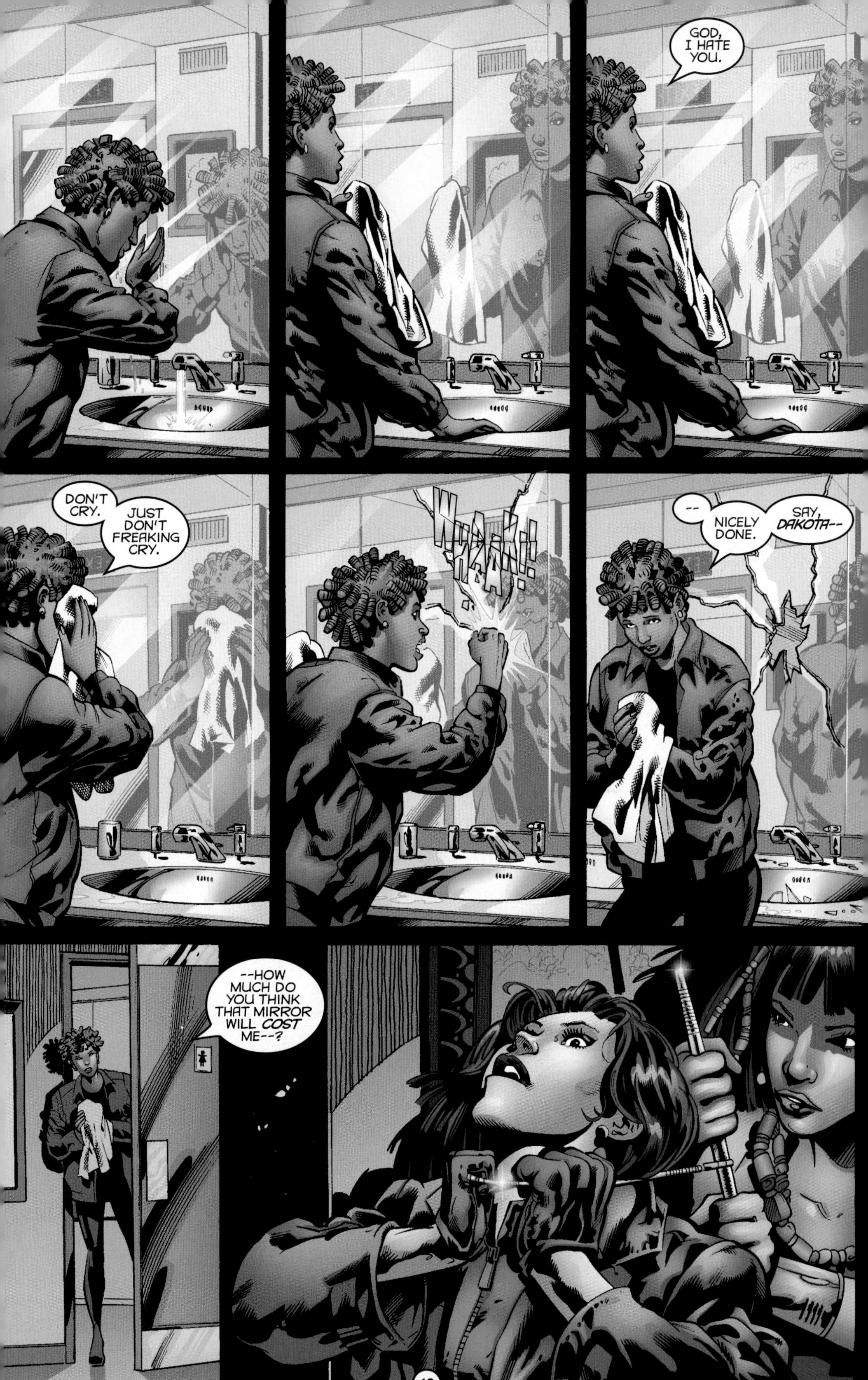
GOD, I HATE YOU.
DON'T CRY.
JUST DON'T FREAKING CRY.
WHAAK!!
--
SAY, DAKOTA--
NICELY DONE.
--HOW MUCH DO YOU THINK THAT MIRROR WILL COST ME--?

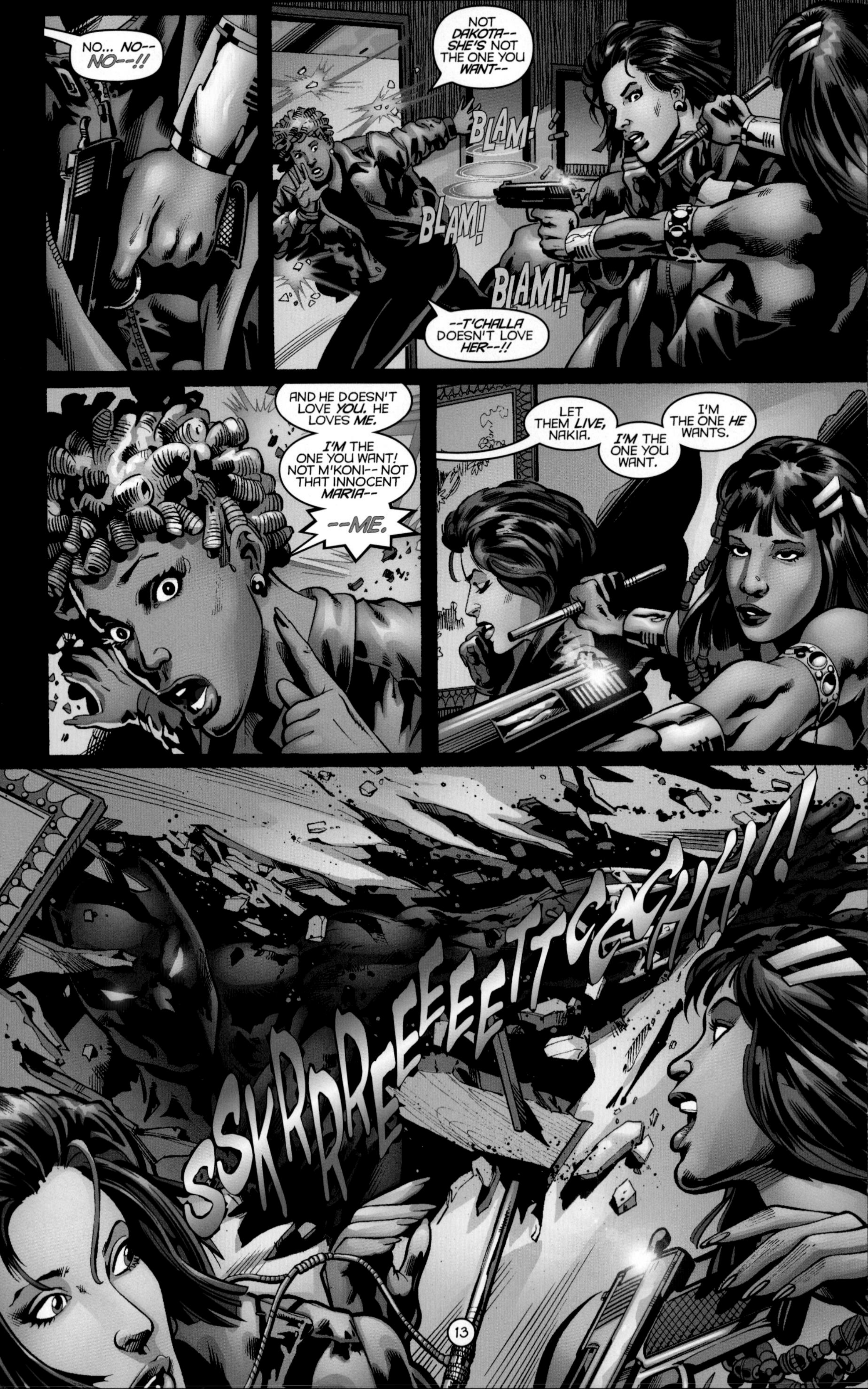
NO... NO--
NO--!!
NOT DAKOTA--
SHE'S NOT THE ONE YOU WANT--
BLAM!
BLAM!
BLAM!!
--T'CHALLA DOESN'T LOVE HER--!!
AND HE DOESN'T LOVE YOU. HE LOVES ME.
I'M THE ONE YOU WANT! NOT M'KONI-- NOT THAT INNOCENT MARIA--
--ME.
LET THEM LIVE, NAKIA.
I'M THE ONE YOU WANT.
I'M THE ONE HE WANTS.
SSKRREEEEETTCCGGH!!

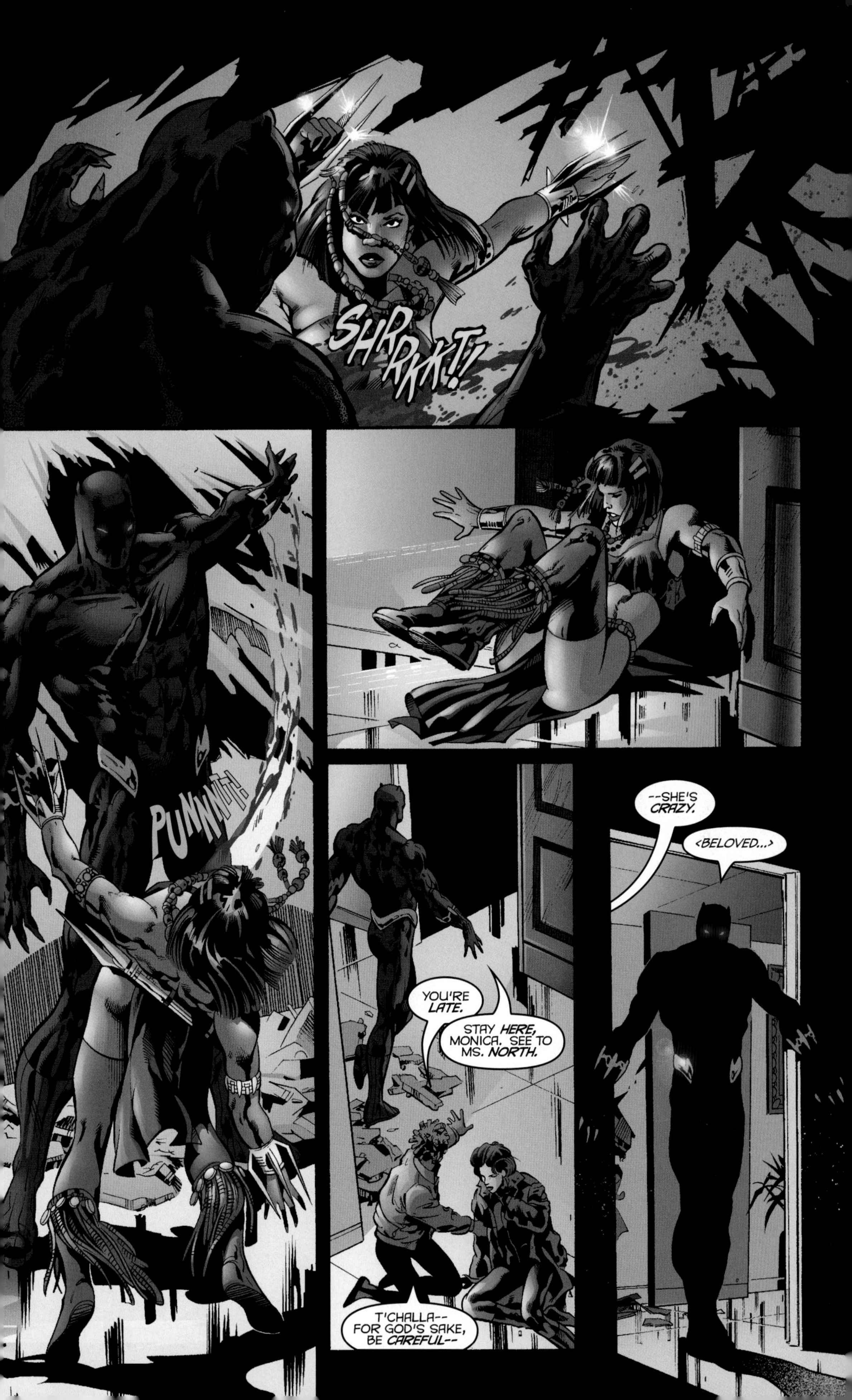
SHRKKT!!
PUNNNT!
YOU'RE LATE.
STAY HERE, MONICA. SEE TO MS. NORTH.
T'CHALLA-- FOR GOD'S SAKE, BE CAREFUL--
--SHE'S CRAZY.
<BELOVED...>

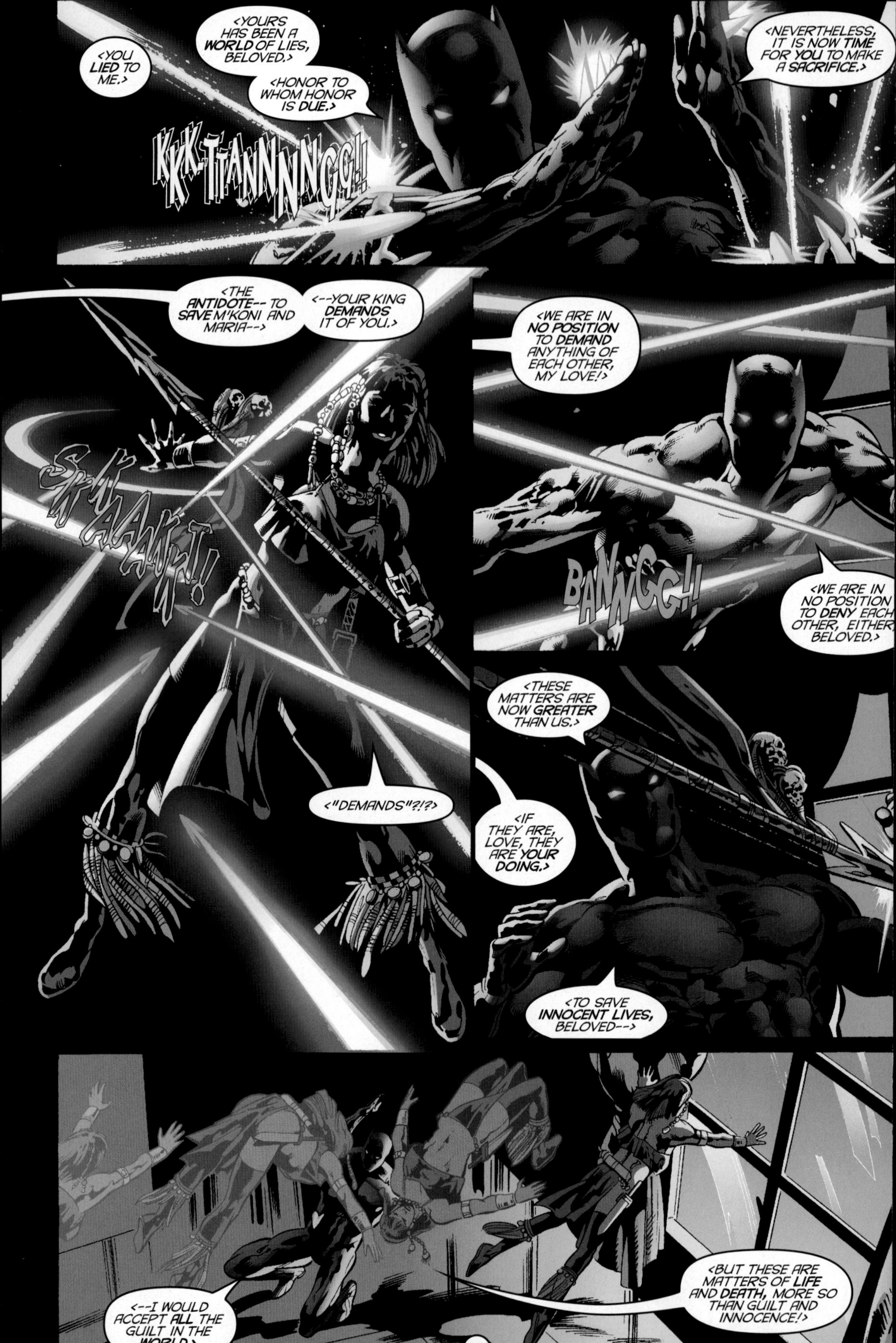

<YOU LIED TO ME.>
<YOURS HAS BEEN A WORLD OF LIES, BELOVED.>
<HONOR TO WHOM HONOR IS DUE.>
KKK-TTANNNNGG!!
<NEVERTHELESS, IT IS NOW TIME FOR YOU TO MAKE A SACRIFICE.>
<THE ANTIDOTE-- TO SAVE M'KONI AND MARIA-->
<--YOUR KING DEMANDS IT OF YOU.>
SKRAANKK!!
<"DEMANDS"?!?>
<WE ARE IN NO POSITION TO DEMAND ANYTHING OF EACH OTHER, MY LOVE!>
BANNGG!!
<WE ARE IN NO POSITION TO DENY EACH OTHER, EITHER, BELOVED.>
<THESE MATTERS ARE NOW GREATER THAN US.>
<IF THEY ARE, LOVE, THEY ARE YOUR DOING.>
<TO SAVE INNOCENT LIVES, BELOVED-->
<--I WOULD ACCEPT ALL THE GUILT IN THE WORLD.>
<BUT THESE ARE MATTERS OF LIFE AND DEATH, MORE SO THAN GUILT AND INNOCENCE!>

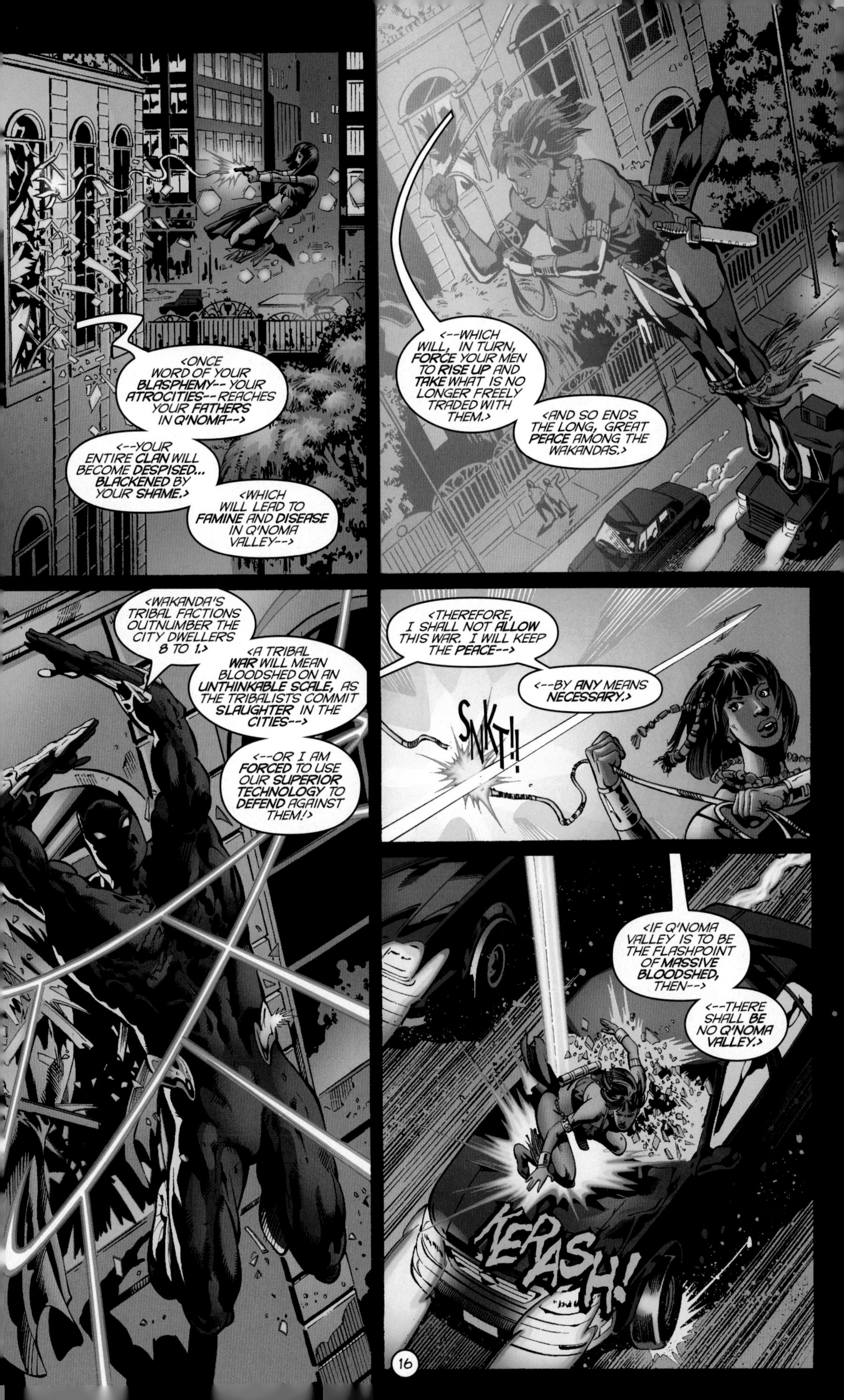
<ONCE WORD OF YOUR BLASPHEMY-- YOUR ATROCITIES-- REACHES YOUR FATHERS IN Q'NOMA-->
<--YOUR ENTIRE CLAN WILL BECOME DESPISED... BLACKENED BY YOUR SHAME.>
<WHICH WILL LEAD TO FAMINE AND DISEASE IN Q'NOMA VALLEY-->
<--WHICH WILL, IN TURN, FORCE YOUR MEN TO RISE UP AND TAKE WHAT IS NO LONGER FREELY TRADED WITH THEM.>
<AND SO ENDS THE LONG, GREAT PEACE AMONG THE WAKANDAS.>
<WAKANDA'S TRIBAL FACTIONS OUTNUMBER THE CITY DWELLERS 8 TO 1.>
<A TRIBAL WAR WILL MEAN BLOODSHED ON AN UNTHINKABLE SCALE, AS THE TRIBALISTS COMMIT SLAUGHTER IN THE CITIES-->
<--OR I AM FORCED TO USE OUR SUPERIOR TECHNOLOGY TO DEFEND AGAINST THEM!>
<THEREFORE, I SHALL NOT ALLOW THIS WAR. I WILL KEEP THE PEACE-->
<--BY ANY MEANS NECESSARY.>
SNIKT!!
<IF Q'NOMA VALLEY IS TO BE THE FLASHPOINT OF MASSIVE BLOODSHED, THEN-->
<--THERE SHALL BE NO Q'NOMA VALLEY.>
KERASH!

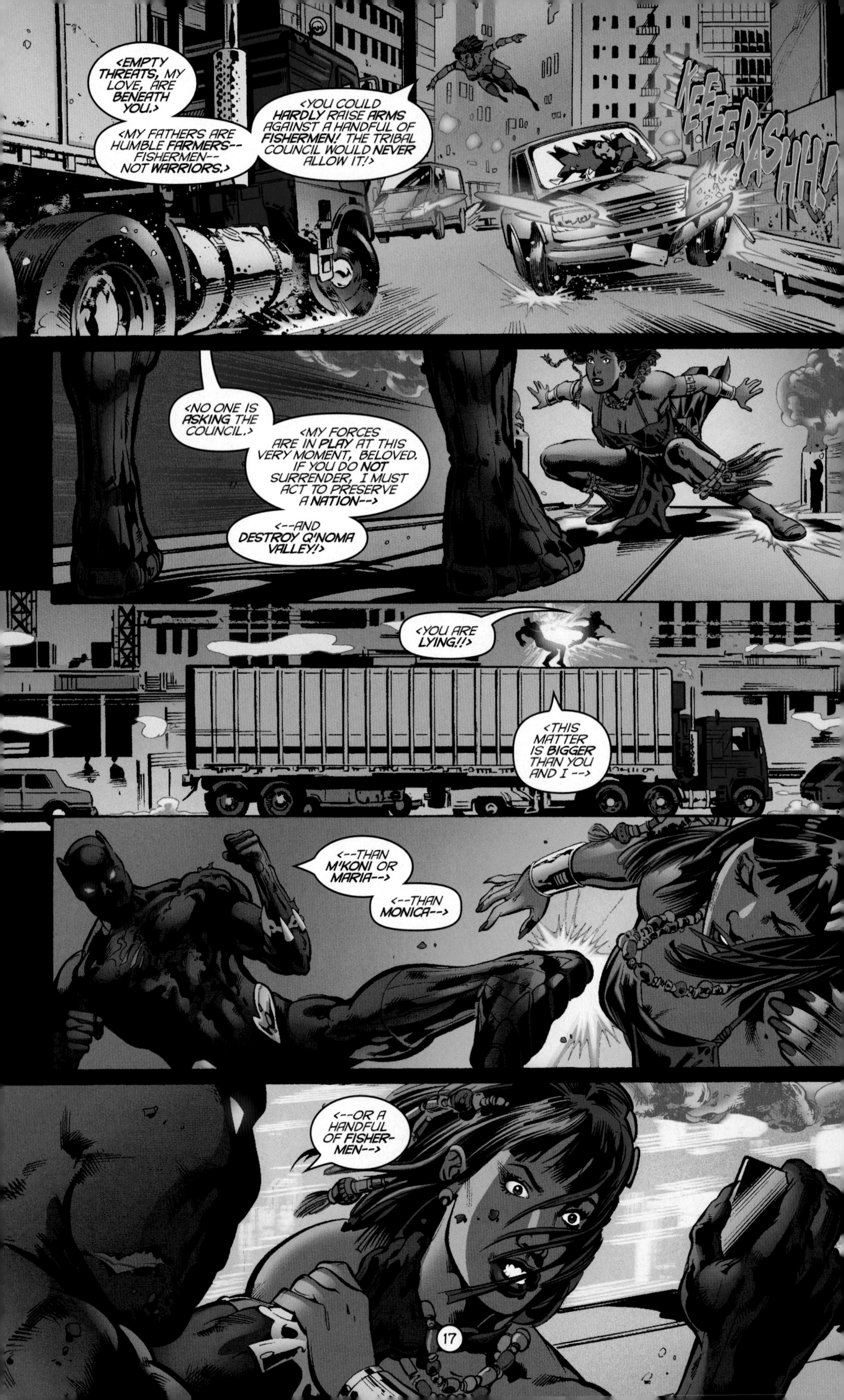
<EMPTY THREATS, MY LOVE, ARE BENEATH YOU.>
<MY FATHERS ARE HUMBLE FARMERS--FISHERMEN--NOT WARRIORS.>
<YOU COULD HARDLY RAISE ARMS AGAINST A HANDFUL OF FISHERMEN! THE TRIBAL COUNCIL WOULD NEVER ALLOW IT!>
KEEEERASHH!
<NO ONE IS ASKING THE COUNCIL.>
<MY FORCES ARE IN PLAY AT THIS VERY MOMENT, BELOVED. IF YOU DO NOT SURRENDER, I MUST ACT TO PRESERVE A NATION-->
<--AND DESTROY Q'NOMA VALLEY!>
<YOU ARE LYING!!>
<THIS MATTER IS BIGGER THAN YOU AND I -->
<--THAN M'KONI OR MARIA-->
<--THAN MONICA-->
<--OR A HANDFUL OF FISHER-MEN-->

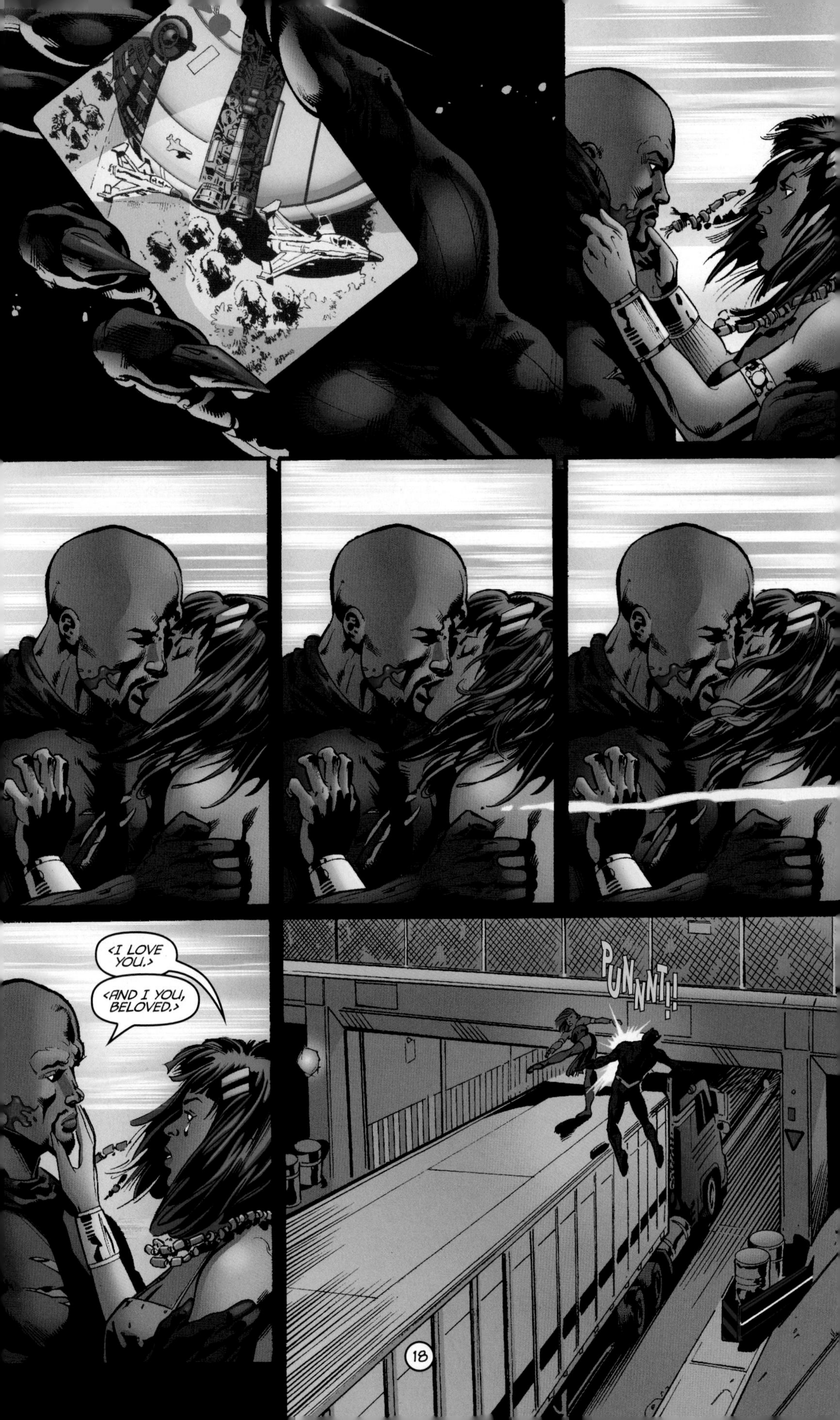

<I LOVE YOU.>
<AND I YOU, BELOVED.>
PUNNNT!!

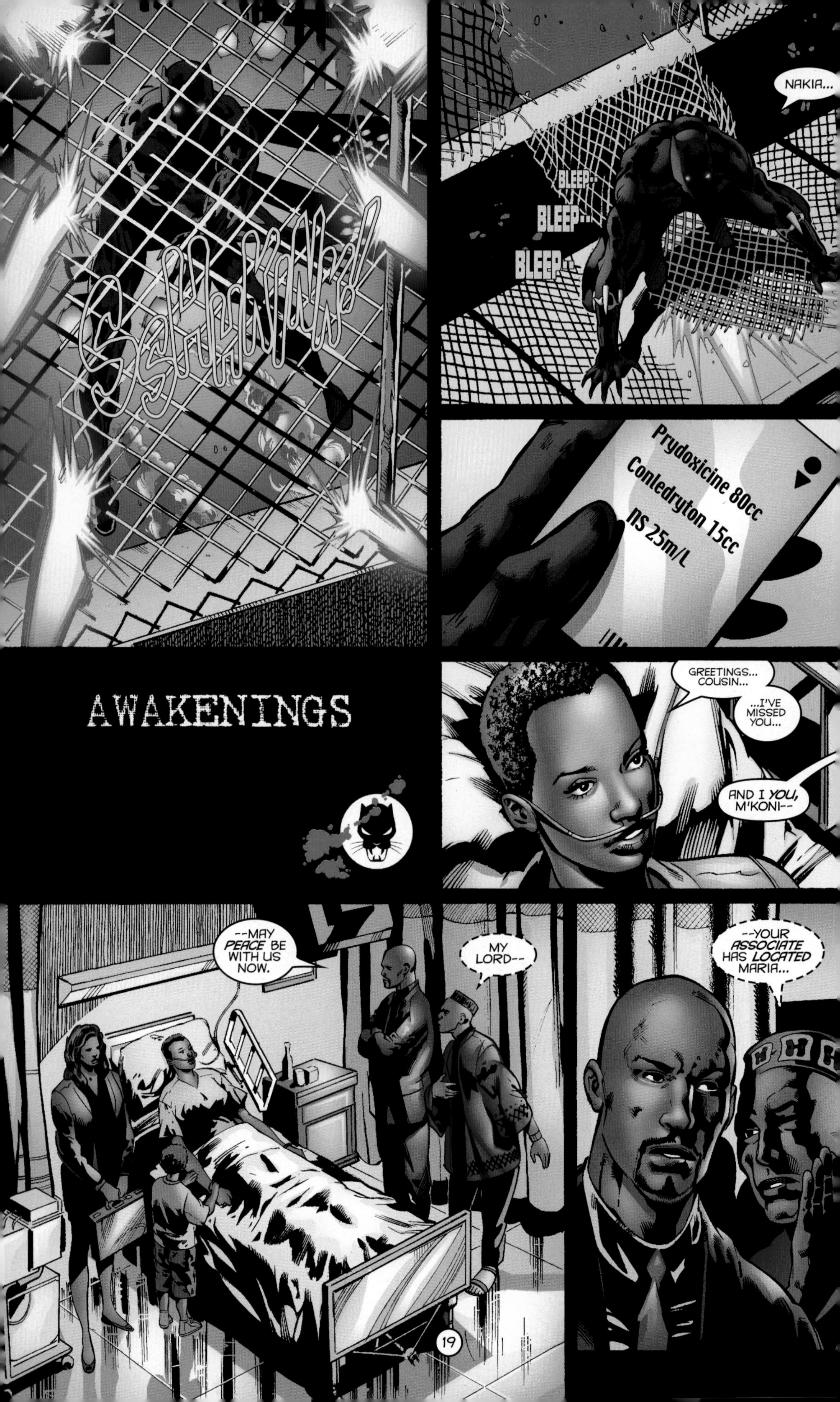
SSHHHHKKK!
NAKIA...
BLEEP...
BLEEP...
BLEEP...
Prydoxicine 80cc
Conledryton 15cc
NS 25m/L
AWAKENINGS
GREETINGS... COUSIN...
...I'VE MISSED YOU...
AND I YOU, M'KONI--
--MAY PEACE BE WITH US NOW.
MY LORD--
--YOUR ASSOCIATE HAS LOCATED MARIA...

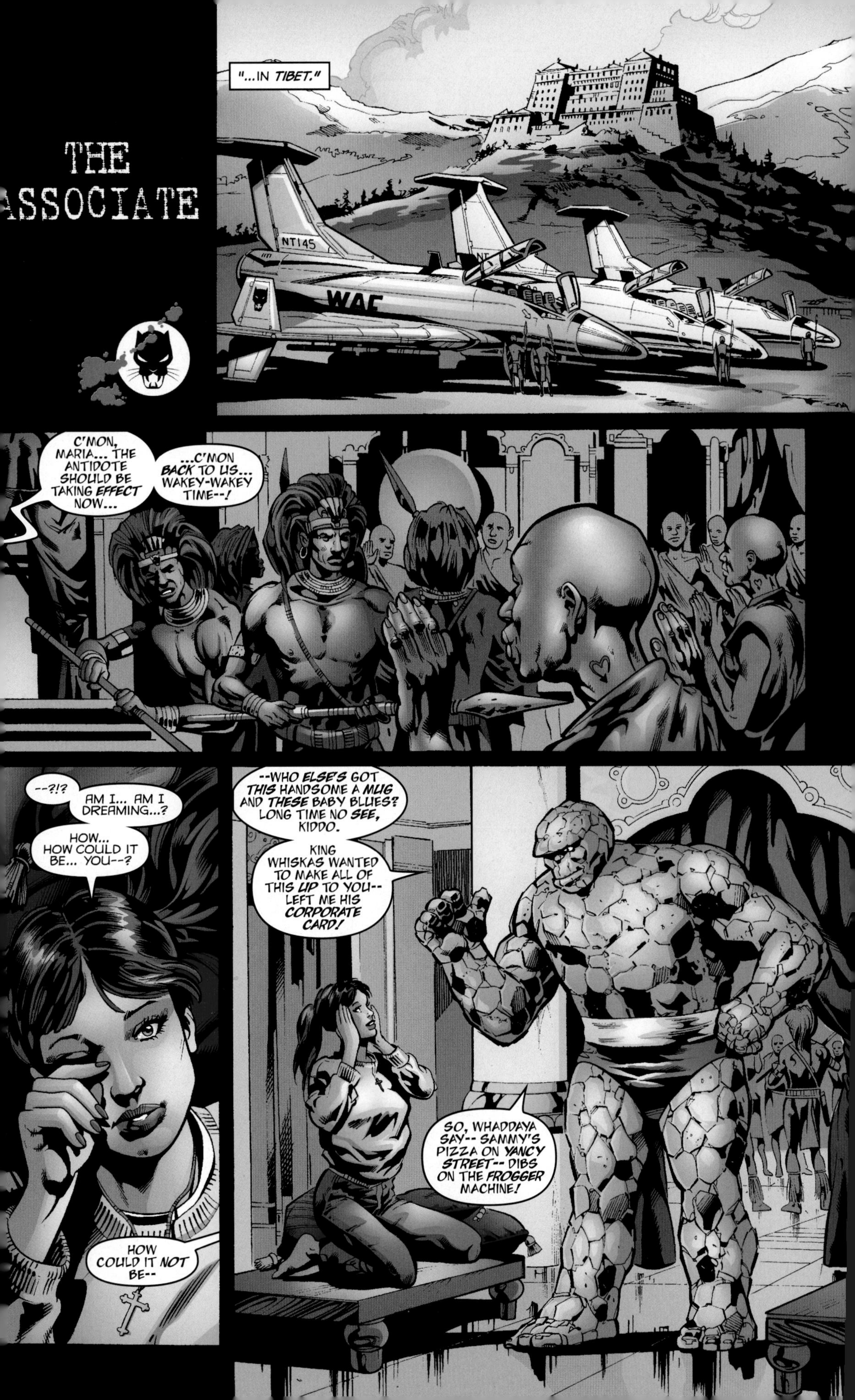
"...IN TIBET."
THE ASSOCIATE
WAF
NT145
C'MON, MARIA... THE ANTIDOTE SHOULD BE TAKING EFFECT NOW...
...C'MON BACK TO US... WAKEY-WAKEY TIME--!
--?!?
AM I... AM I DREAMING...?
HOW... HOW COULD IT BE... YOU--?
--WHO ELSE'S GOT THIS HANDSOME A MUG AND THESE BABY BLUES? LONG TIME NO SEE, KIDDO.
KING WHISKAS WANTED TO MAKE ALL OF THIS UP TO YOU-- LEFT ME HIS CORPORATE CARD!
SO, WHADDAYA SAY-- SAMMY'S PIZZA ON YANCY STREET-- DIBS ON THE FROGGER MACHINE!
HOW COULD IT NOT BE--

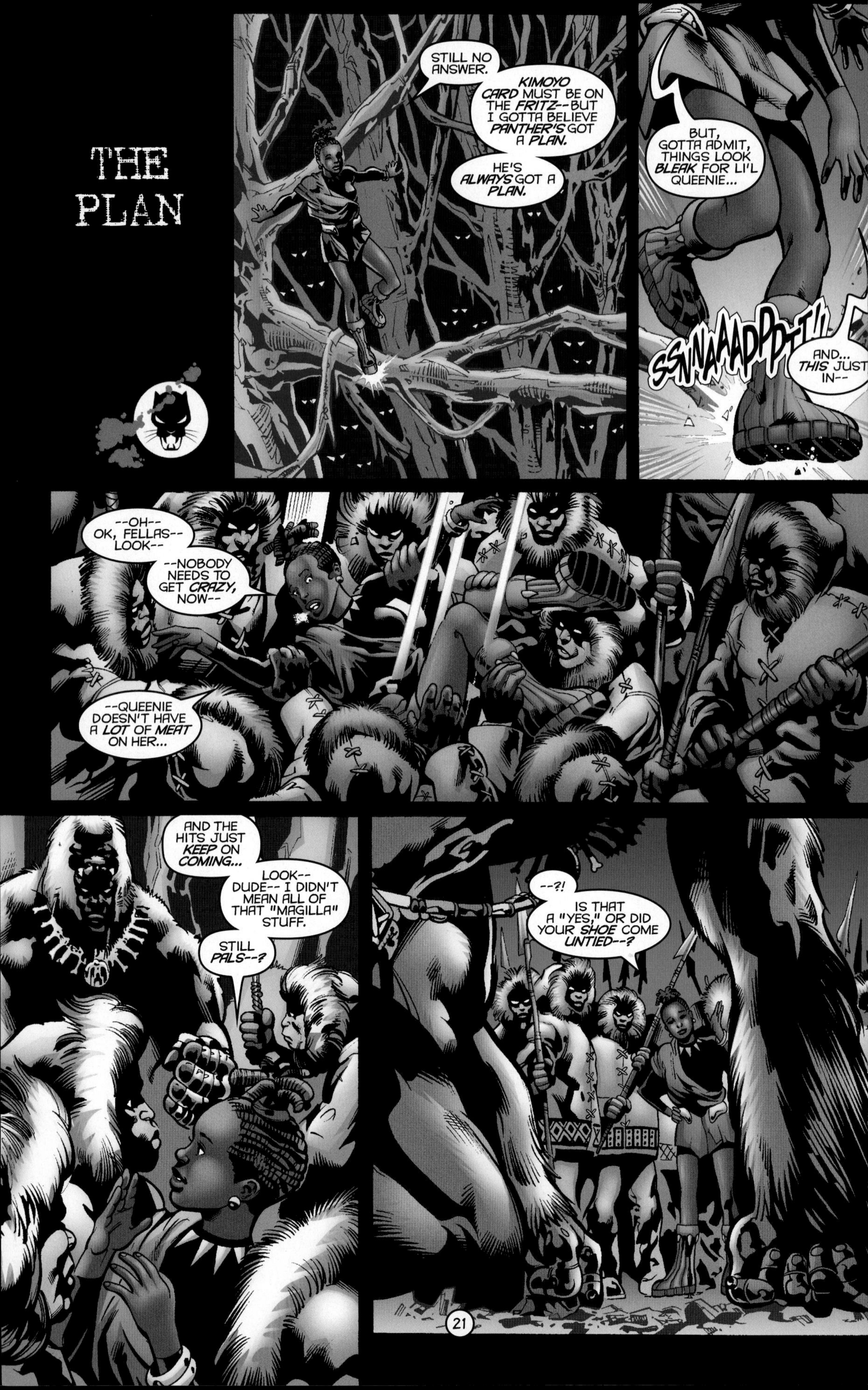
THE PLAN
STILL NO ANSWER.
KIMOYO CARD MUST BE ON THE FRITZ--BUT I GOTTA BELIEVE PANTHER'S GOT A PLAN.
HE'S ALWAYS GOT A PLAN.
BUT, GOTTA ADMIT, THINGS LOOK BLEAK FOR LI'L QUEENIE...
SSNNAAAPPDT!!
AND... THIS JUST IN--
--OH-- OK, FELLAS-- LOOK--
--NOBODY NEEDS TO GET CRAZY, NOW--
--QUEENIE DOESN'T HAVE A LOT OF MEAT ON HER...
AND THE HITS JUST KEEP ON COMING...
LOOK-- DUDE-- I DIDN'T MEAN ALL OF THAT "MAGILLA" STUFF.
STILL PALS--?
--?!
IS THAT A "YES," OR DID YOUR SHOE COME UNTIED--?

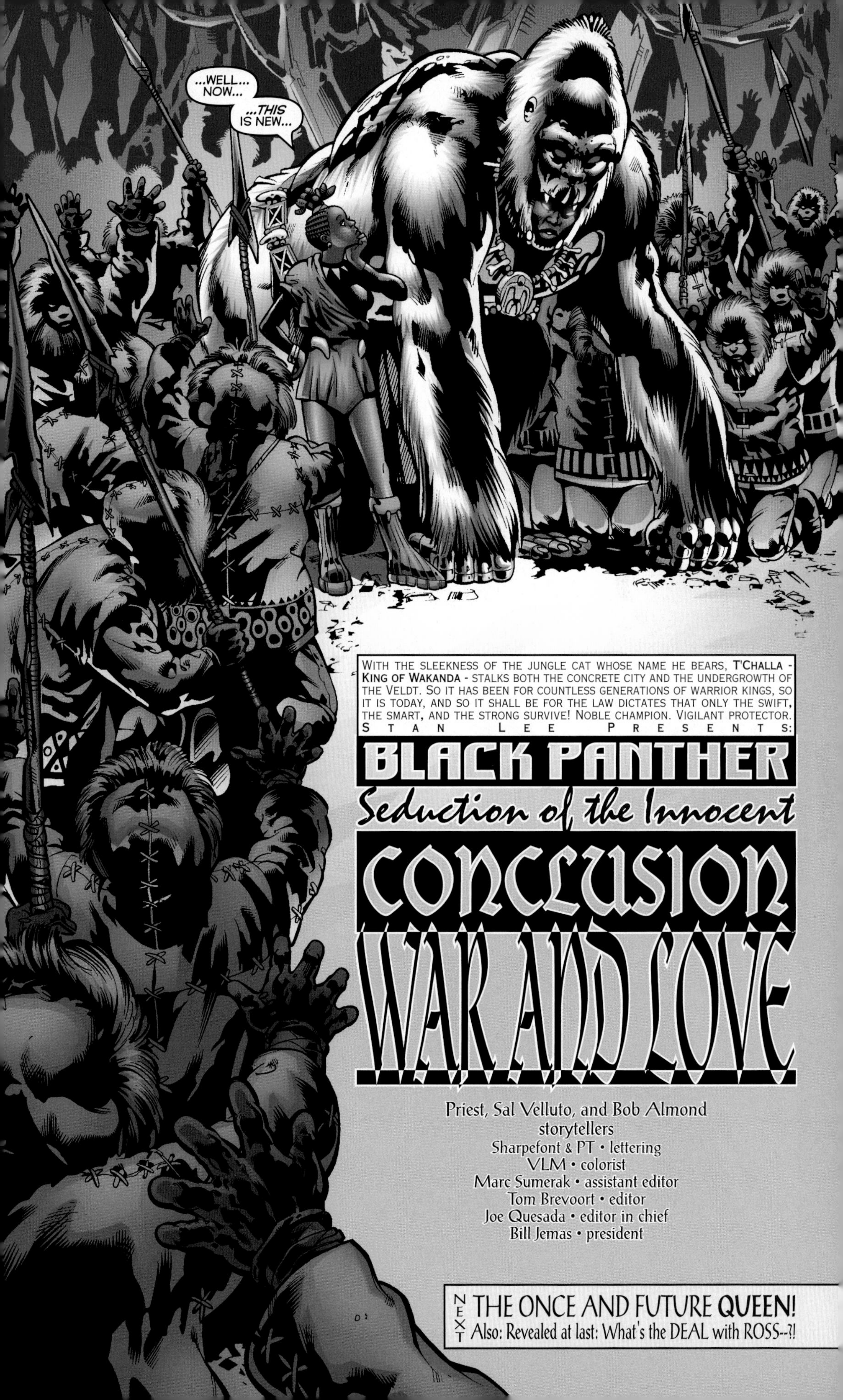
...WELL... NOW...
...THIS IS NEW...
WITH THE SLEEKNESS OF THE JUNGLE CAT WHOSE NAME HE BEARS, T'CHALLA - KING OF WAKANDA - STALKS BOTH THE CONCRETE CITY AND THE UNDERGROWTH OF THE VELDT. SO IT HAS BEEN FOR COUNTLESS GENERATIONS OF WARRIOR KINGS, SO IT IS TODAY, AND SO IT SHALL BE FOR THE LAW DICTATES THAT ONLY THE SWIFT, THE SMART, AND THE STRONG SURVIVE! NOBLE CHAMPION. VIGILANT PROTECTOR.
STAN LEE PRESENTS:
BLACK PANTHER
Seduction of the Innocent
CONCLUSION
WAR AND LOVE
Priest, Sal Velluto, and Bob Almond
storytellers
Sharpefont & PT • lettering
VLM • colorist
Marc Sumerak • assistant editor
Tom Brevoort • editor
Joe Quesada • editor in chief
Bill Jemas • president
NEXT THE ONCE AND FUTURE QUEEN!
Also: Revealed at last: What's the DEAL with ROSS--?!

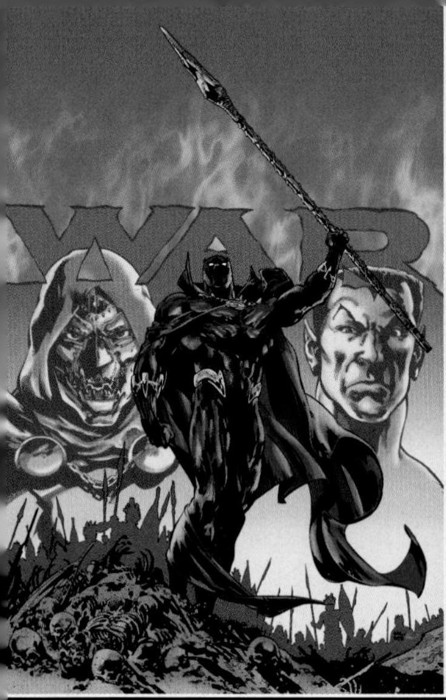
WAR

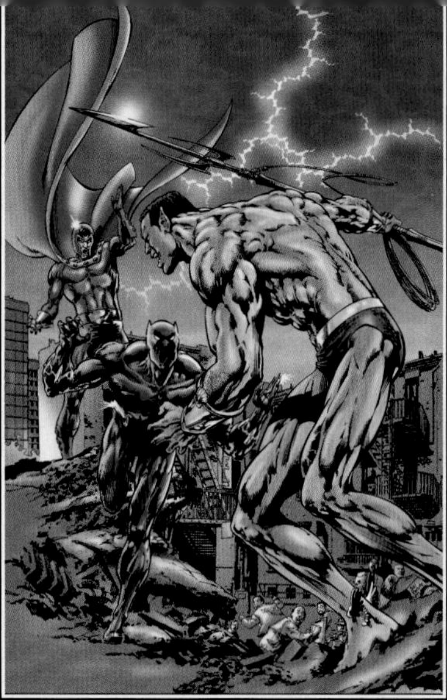

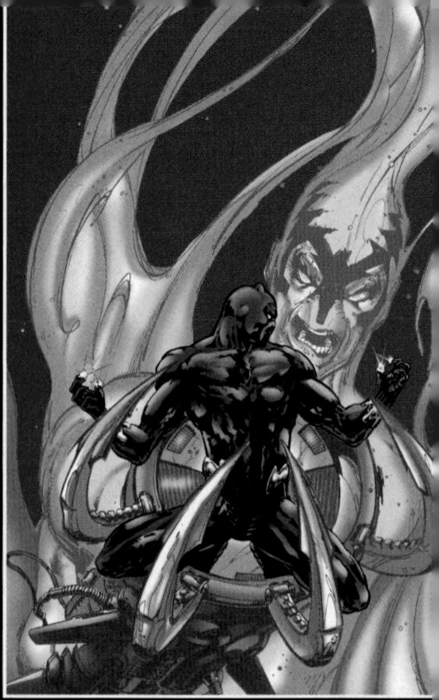

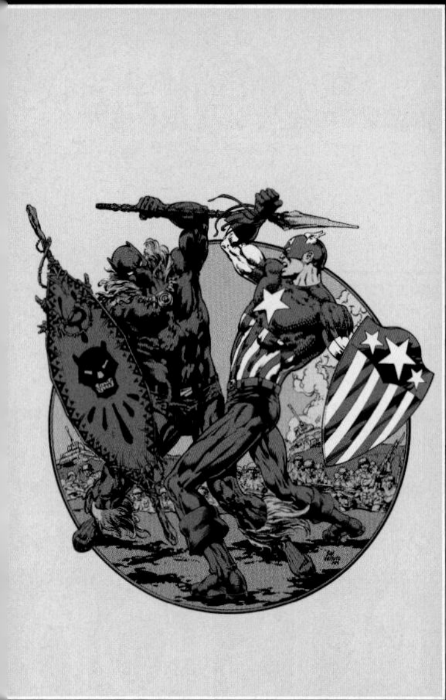

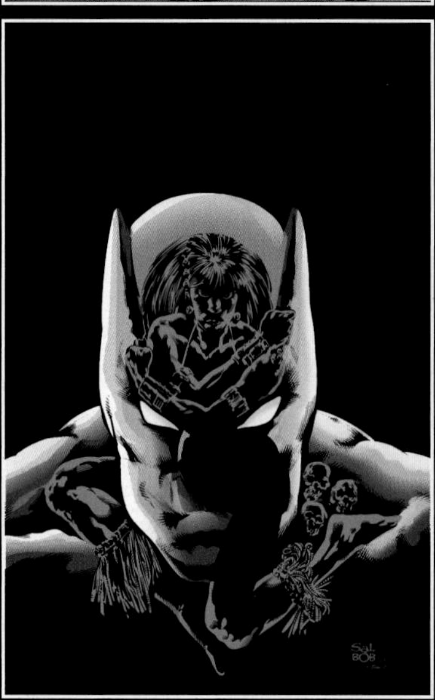
SAL BOB

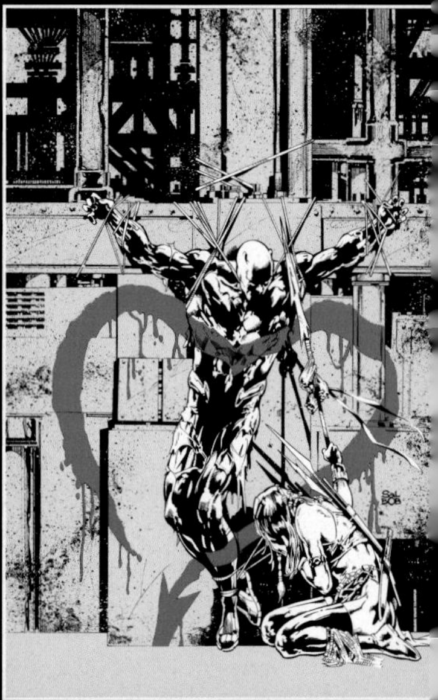
SAL BOB

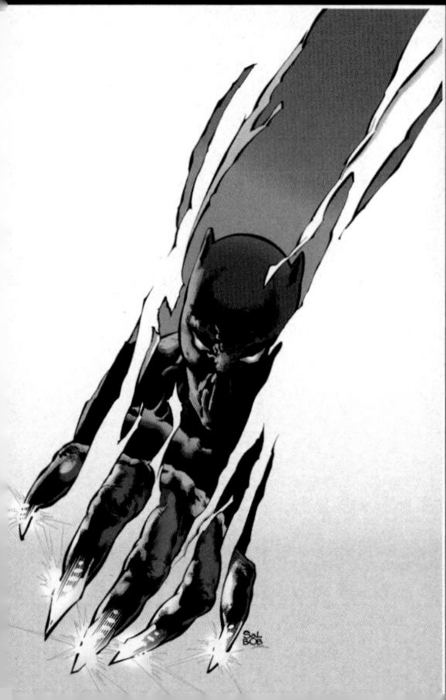
SAL BOB

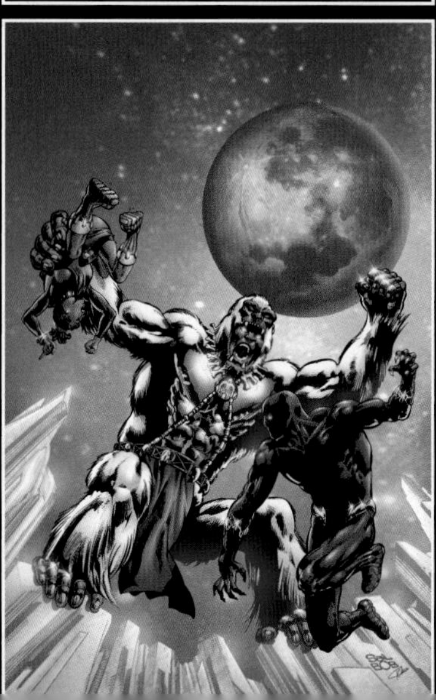

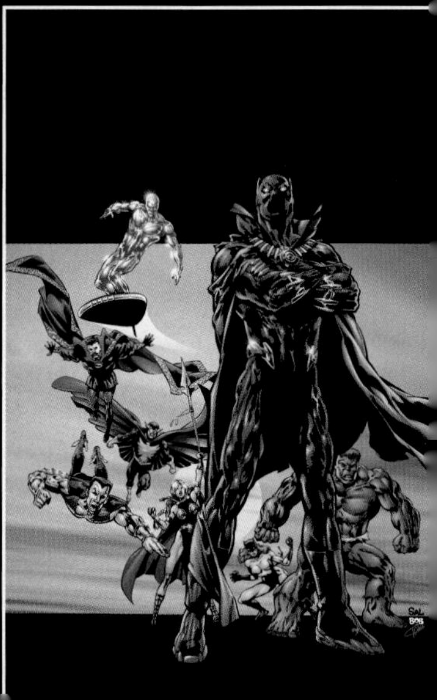
SAL BOB

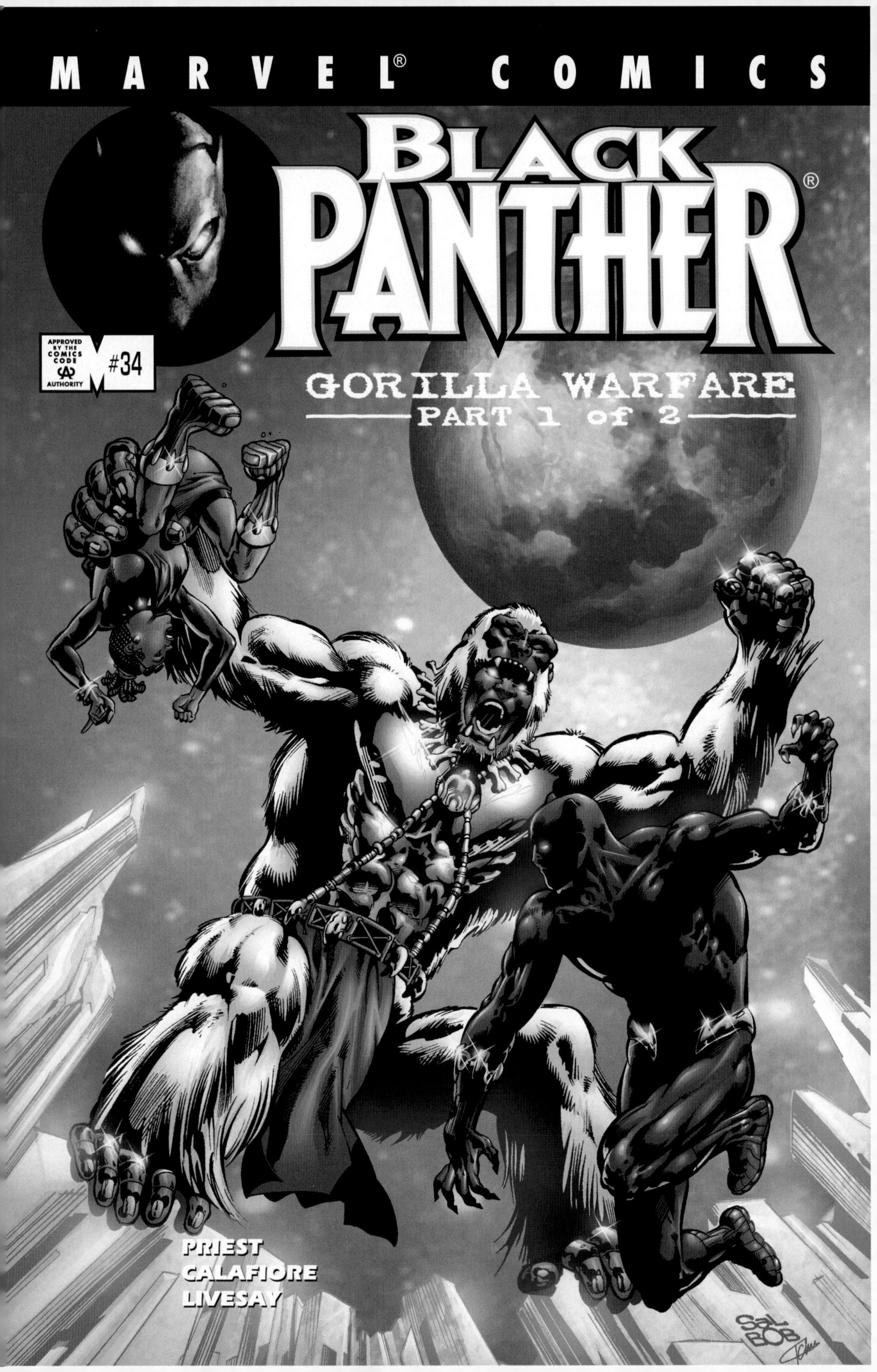
MARVEL® COMICS
BLACK PANTHER®
APPROVED BY THE COMICS CODE AUTHORITY
#34
GORILLA WARFARE
PART 1 of 2
PRIEST
CALAFIORE
LIVESAY

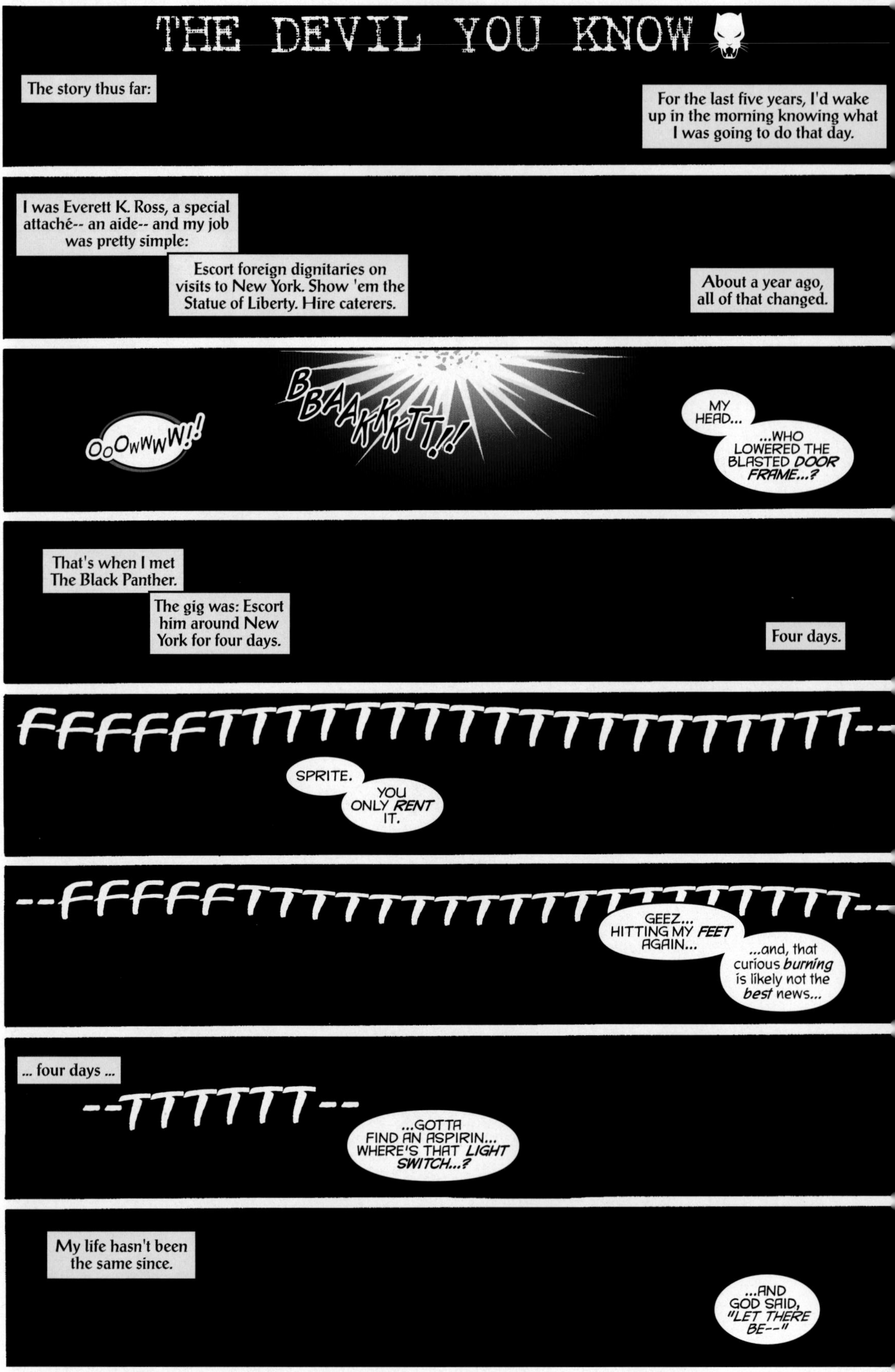
THE DEVIL YOU KNOW
The story thus far:
For the last five years, I'd wake up in the morning knowing what I was going to do that day.
I was Everett K. Ross, a special attaché-- an aide-- and my job was pretty simple:
Escort foreign dignitaries on visits to New York. Show 'em the Statue of Liberty. Hire caterers.
About a year ago, all of that changed.
OoOwwwW!!
BBAAKKKTT!!
MY HEAD...
...WHO LOWERED THE BLASTED DOOR FRAME...?
That's when I met The Black Panther.
The gig was: Escort him around New York for four days.
Four days.
FFFFFTTTTTTTTTTTTTTTTTTTTTTT--
SPRITE.
YOU ONLY RENT IT.
--FFFFFTTTTTTTTTTTTTTTTTTTTTT--
GEEZ... HITTING MY FEET AGAIN...
...and, that curious burning is likely not the best news...
... four days ...
--TTTTTT--
...GOTTA FIND AN ASPIRIN... WHERE'S THAT LIGHT SWITCH...?
My life hasn't been the same since.
...AND GOD SAID, "LET THERE BE--"

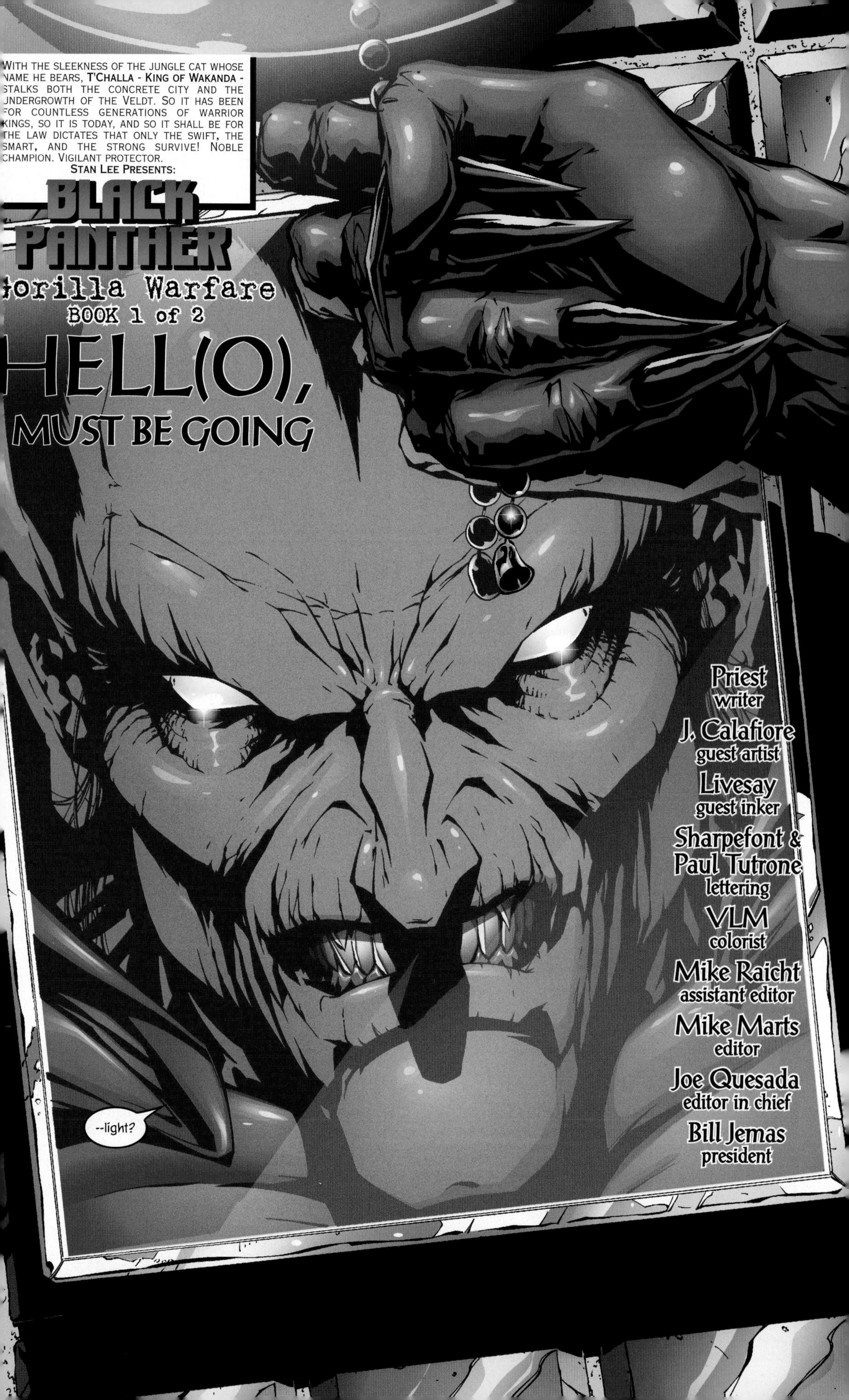

WITH THE SLEEKNESS OF THE JUNGLE CAT WHOSE NAME HE BEARS, T'CHALLA - KING OF WAKANDA - STALKS BOTH THE CONCRETE CITY AND THE UNDERGROWTH OF THE VELDT. SO IT HAS BEEN FOR COUNTLESS GENERATIONS OF WARRIOR KINGS, SO IT IS TODAY, AND SO IT SHALL BE FOR THE LAW DICTATES THAT ONLY THE SWIFT, THE SMART, AND THE STRONG SURVIVE! NOBLE CHAMPION. VIGILANT PROTECTOR.
STAN LEE PRESENTS:
BLACK PANTHER
Gorilla Warfare
BOOK 1 of 2
HELL(O), MUST BE GOING
Priest writer
J. Calafiore guest artist
Livesay guest inker
Sharpefont & Paul Tutrone lettering
VLM colorist
Mike Raicht assistant editor
Mike Marts editor
Joe Quesada editor in chief
Bill Jemas president
--light?

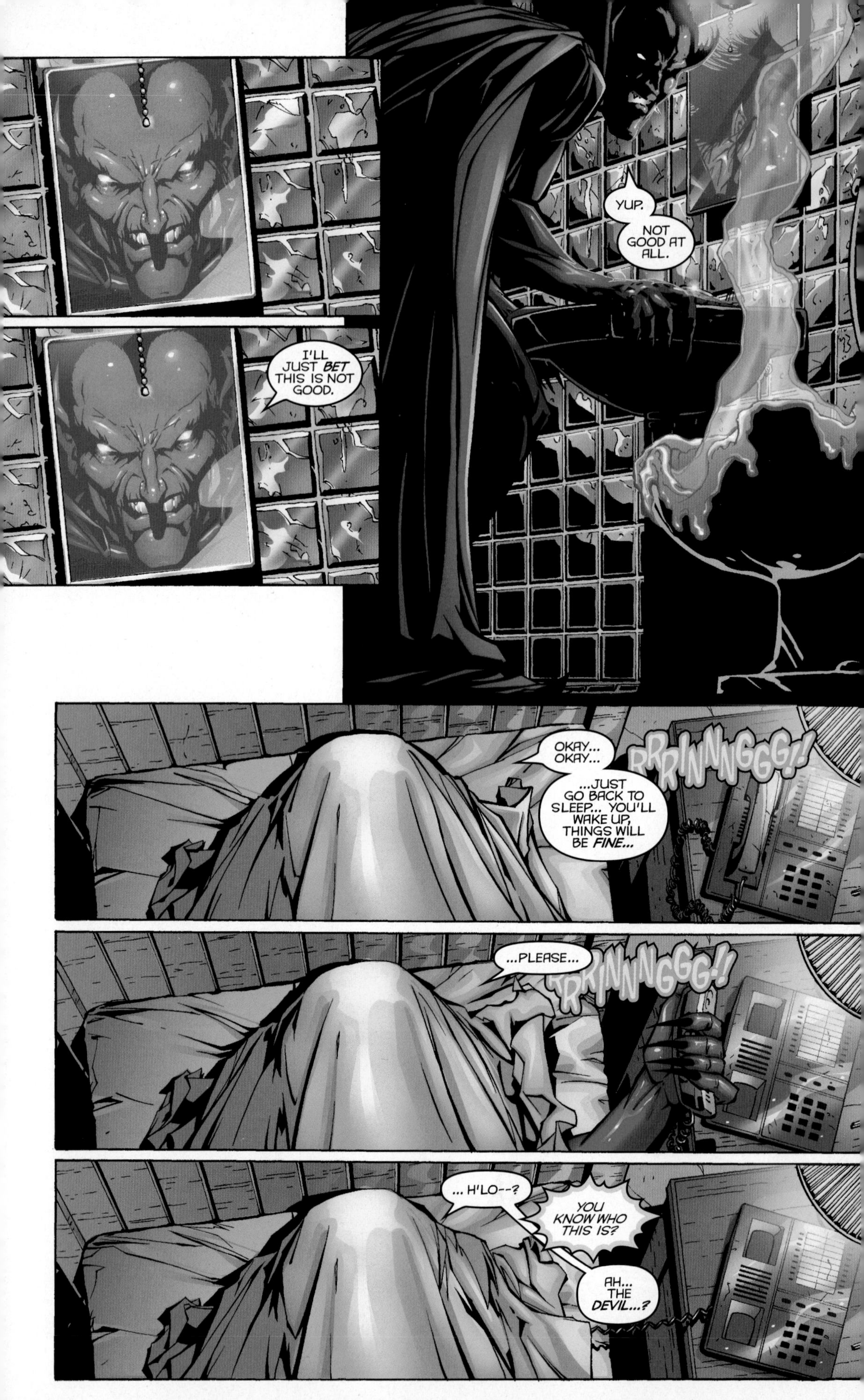
I'LL JUST *BET* THIS IS NOT GOOD.
YUP.
NOT GOOD AT ALL.
OKAY... OKAY...
...JUST GO BACK TO SLEEP... YOU'LL WAKE UP, THINGS WILL BE *FINE*...
RRRINNNGGG!!
...PLEASE...
RRRINNNGGG!!
... H'LO--?
YOU KNOW WHO THIS IS?
AH... THE *DEVIL*...?

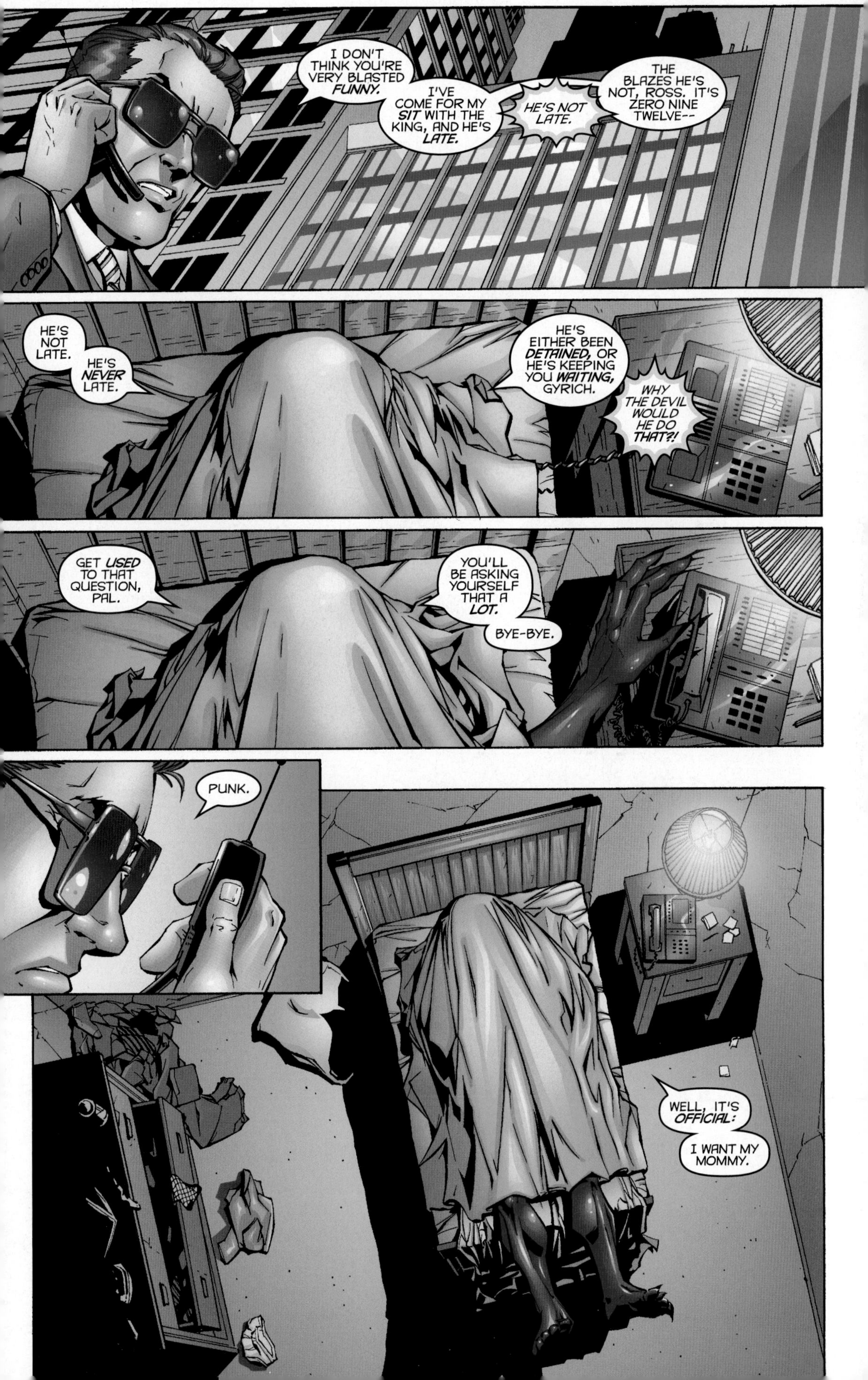
I DON'T THINK YOU'RE VERY BLASTED FUNNY.
I'VE COME FOR MY SIT WITH THE KING, AND HE'S LATE.
HE'S NOT LATE.
THE BLAZES HE'S NOT, ROSS. IT'S ZERO NINE TWELVE--
HE'S NOT LATE.
HE'S NEVER LATE.
HE'S EITHER BEEN DETAINED, OR HE'S KEEPING YOU WAITING, GYRICH.
WHY THE DEVIL WOULD HE DO THAT?!
GET USED TO THAT QUESTION, PAL.
YOU'LL BE ASKING YOURSELF THAT A LOT.
BYE-BYE.
PUNK.
WELL, IT'S OFFICIAL:
I WANT MY MOMMY.

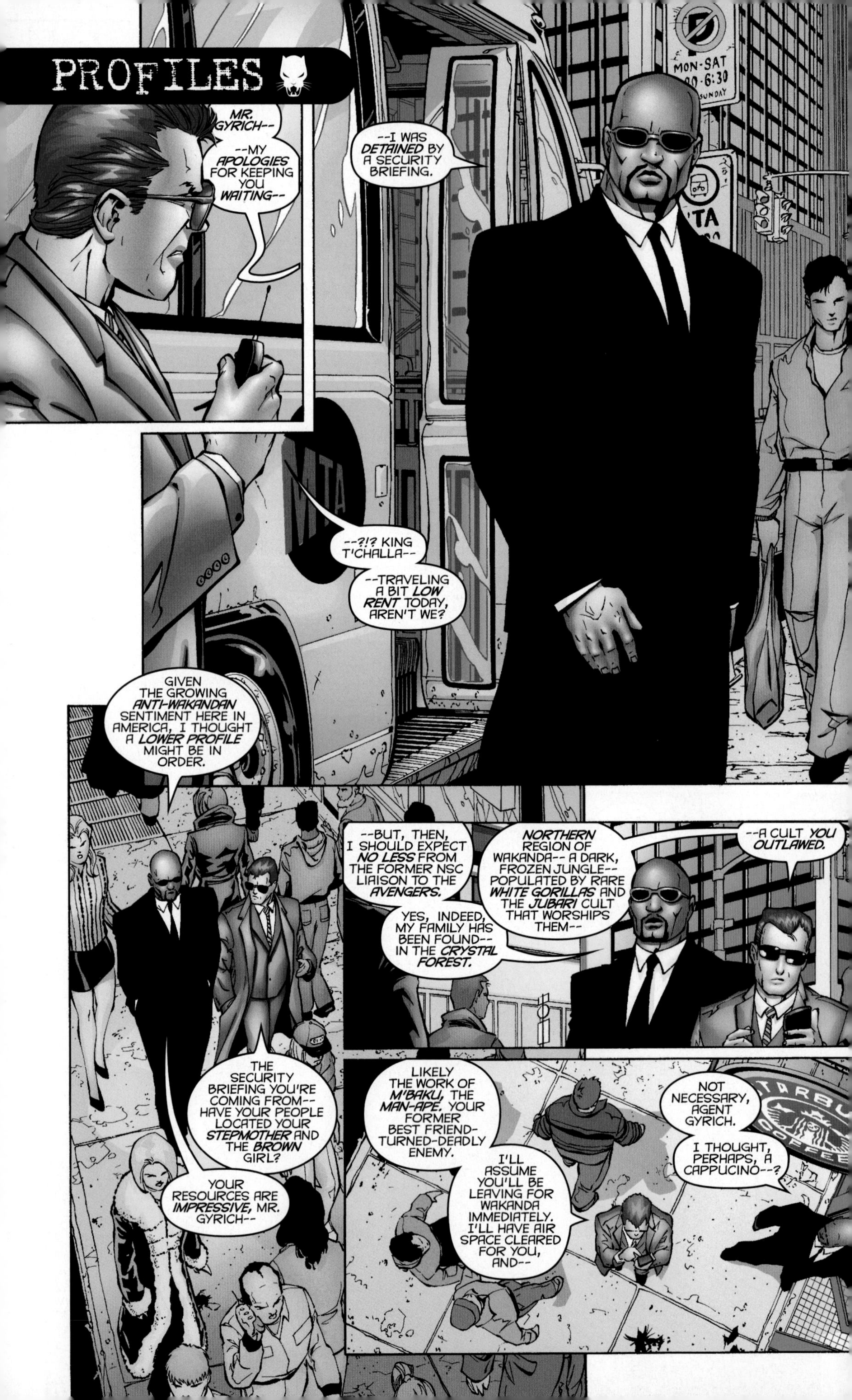
PROFILES
MR. GYRICH--
--MY APOLOGIES FOR KEEPING YOU WAITING--
--I WAS DETAINED BY A SECURITY BRIEFING.
MON-SAT
SUNDAY
MTA
--?!? KING T'CHALLA--
--TRAVELING A BIT LOW RENT TODAY, AREN'T WE?
GIVEN THE GROWING ANTI-WAKANDAN SENTIMENT HERE IN AMERICA, I THOUGHT A LOWER PROFILE MIGHT BE IN ORDER.
THE SECURITY BRIEFING YOU'RE COMING FROM-- HAVE YOUR PEOPLE LOCATED YOUR STEPMOTHER AND THE BROWN GIRL?
YOUR RESOURCES ARE IMPRESSIVE, MR. GYRICH--
--BUT, THEN, I SHOULD EXPECT NO LESS FROM THE FORMER NSC LIAISON TO THE AVENGERS.
YES, INDEED, MY FAMILY HAS BEEN FOUND-- IN THE CRYSTAL FOREST.
NORTHERN REGION OF WAKANDA-- A DARK, FROZEN JUNGLE-- POPULATED BY RARE WHITE GORILLAS AND THE JUBARI CULT THAT WORSHIPS THEM--
--A CULT YOU OUTLAWED.
LIKELY THE WORK OF M'BAKU, THE MAN-APE. YOUR FORMER BEST FRIEND-TURNED-DEADLY ENEMY.
I'LL ASSUME YOU'LL BE LEAVING FOR WAKANDA IMMEDIATELY. I'LL HAVE AIR SPACE CLEARED FOR YOU, AND--
NOT NECESSARY, AGENT GYRICH.
I THOUGHT, PERHAPS, A CAPPUCINO--?

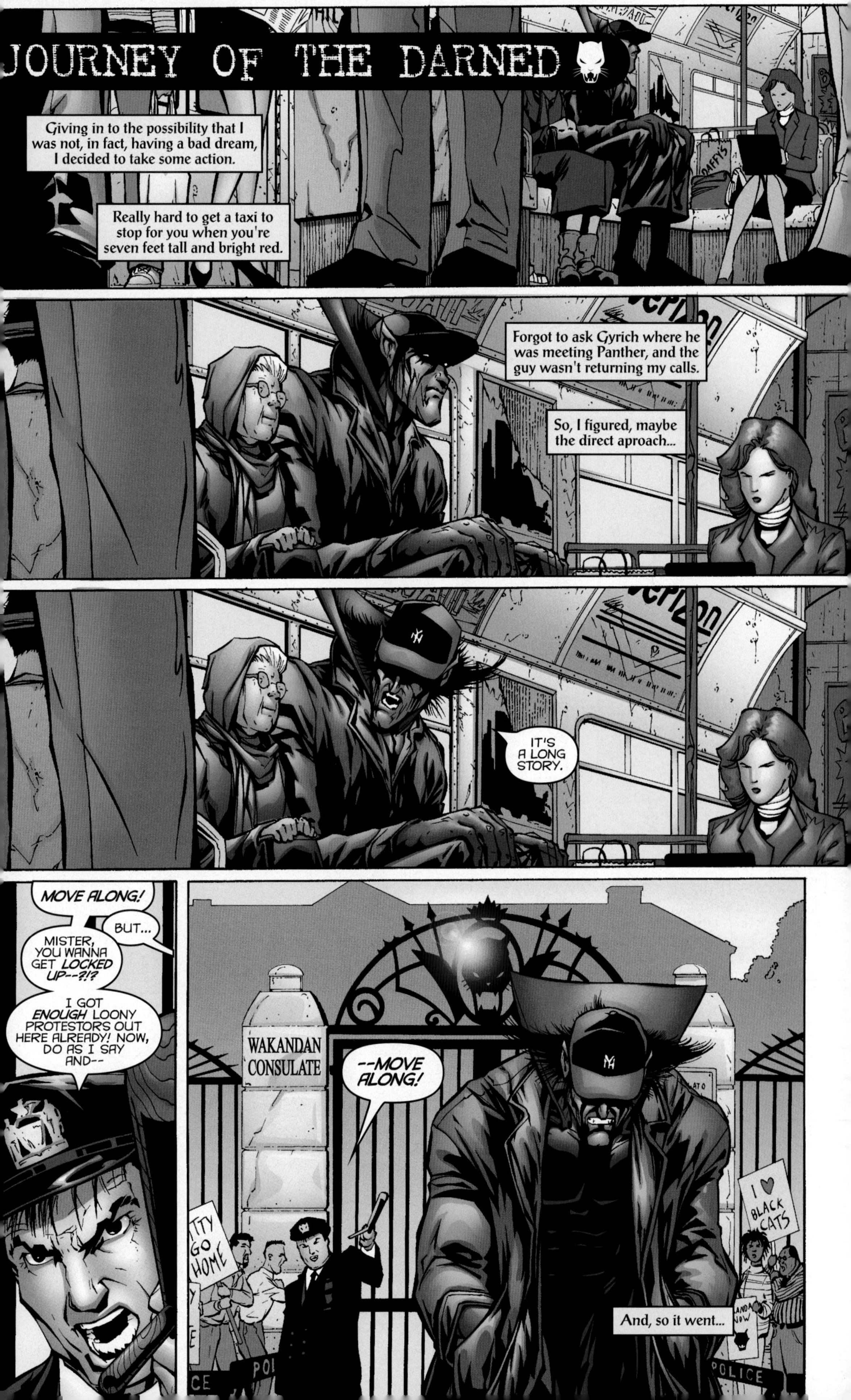
JOURNEY OF THE DARNED
Giving in to the possibility that I was not, in fact, having a bad dream, I decided to take some action.
DAFFY'S
Really hard to get a taxi to stop for you when you're seven feet tall and bright red.
Forgot to ask Gyrich where he was meeting Panther, and the guy wasn't returning my calls.
So, I figured, maybe the direct aproach...
IT'S A LONG STORY.
MOVE ALONG!
BUT...
MISTER, YOU WANNA GET LOCKED UP--?!?
I GOT ENOUGH LOONY PROTESTORS OUT HERE ALREADY! NOW, DO AS I SAY AND--
WAKANDAN CONSULATE
--MOVE ALONG!
I ♥ BLACK CATS
And, so it went...
POLICE

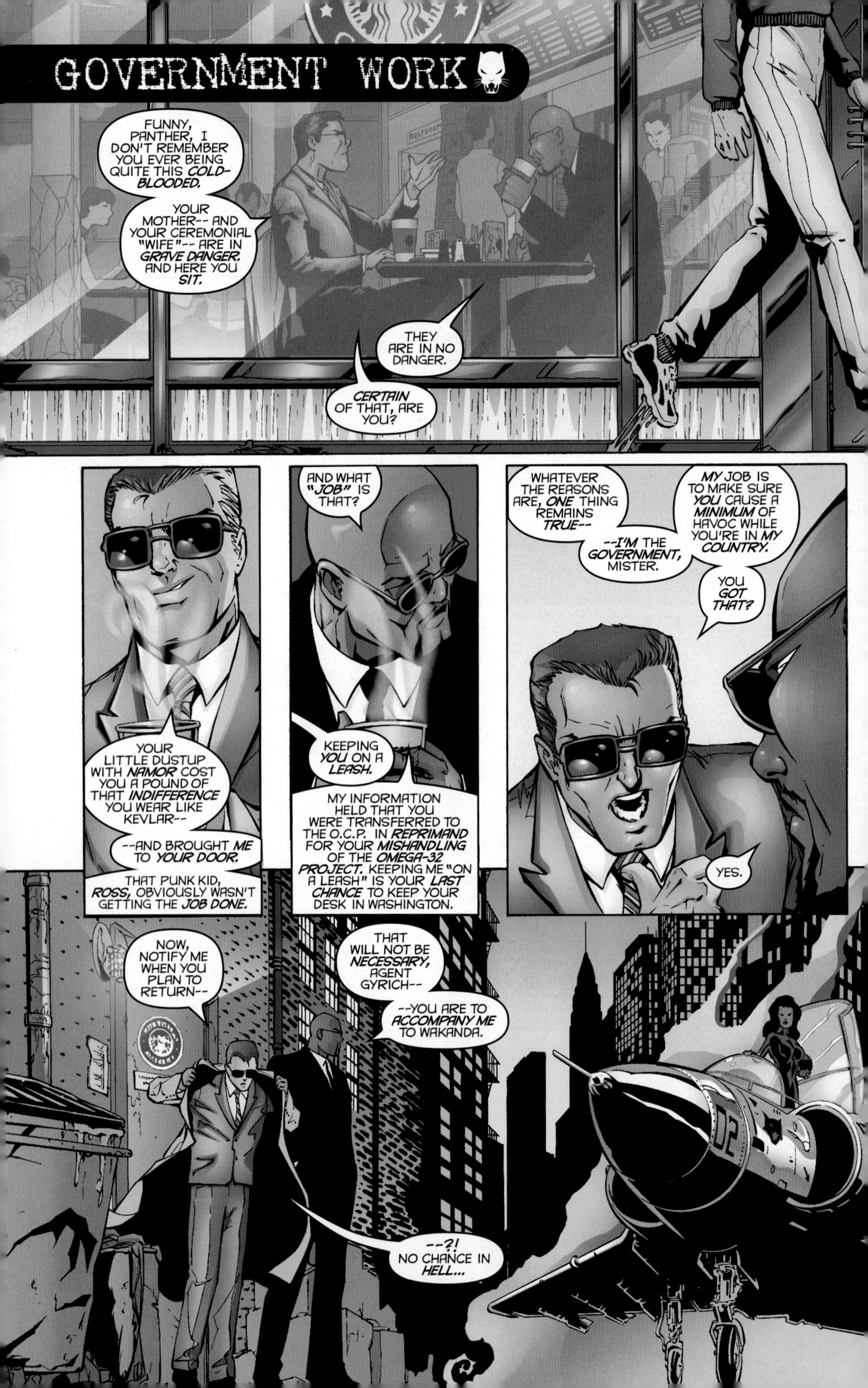
GOVERNMENT WORK
FUNNY, PANTHER, I DON'T REMEMBER YOU EVER BEING QUITE THIS COLD-BLOODED.
YOUR MOTHER-- AND YOUR CEREMONIAL "WIFE"-- ARE IN GRAVE DANGER. AND HERE YOU SIT.
THEY ARE IN NO DANGER.
CERTAIN OF THAT, ARE YOU?
YOUR LITTLE DUSTUP WITH NAMOR COST YOU A POUND OF THAT INDIFFERENCE YOU WEAR LIKE KEVLAR--
--AND BROUGHT ME TO YOUR DOOR.
THAT PUNK KID, ROSS, OBVIOUSLY WASN'T GETTING THE JOB DONE.
AND WHAT "JOB" IS THAT?
KEEPING YOU ON A LEASH.
MY INFORMATION HELD THAT YOU WERE TRANSFERRED TO THE O.C.P. IN REPRIMAND FOR YOUR MISHANDLING OF THE OMEGA-32 PROJECT. KEEPING ME "ON A LEASH" IS YOUR LAST CHANCE TO KEEP YOUR DESK IN WASHINGTON.
WHATEVER THE REASONS ARE, ONE THING REMAINS TRUE--
--I'M THE GOVERNMENT, MISTER.
MY JOB IS TO MAKE SURE YOU CAUSE A MINIMUM OF HAVOC WHILE YOU'RE IN MY COUNTRY.
YOU GOT THAT?
YES.
NOW, NOTIFY ME WHEN YOU PLAN TO RETURN--
THAT WILL NOT BE NECESSARY, AGENT GYRICH--
--YOU ARE TO ACCOMPANY ME TO WAKANDA.
--?! NO CHANCE IN HELL...
02

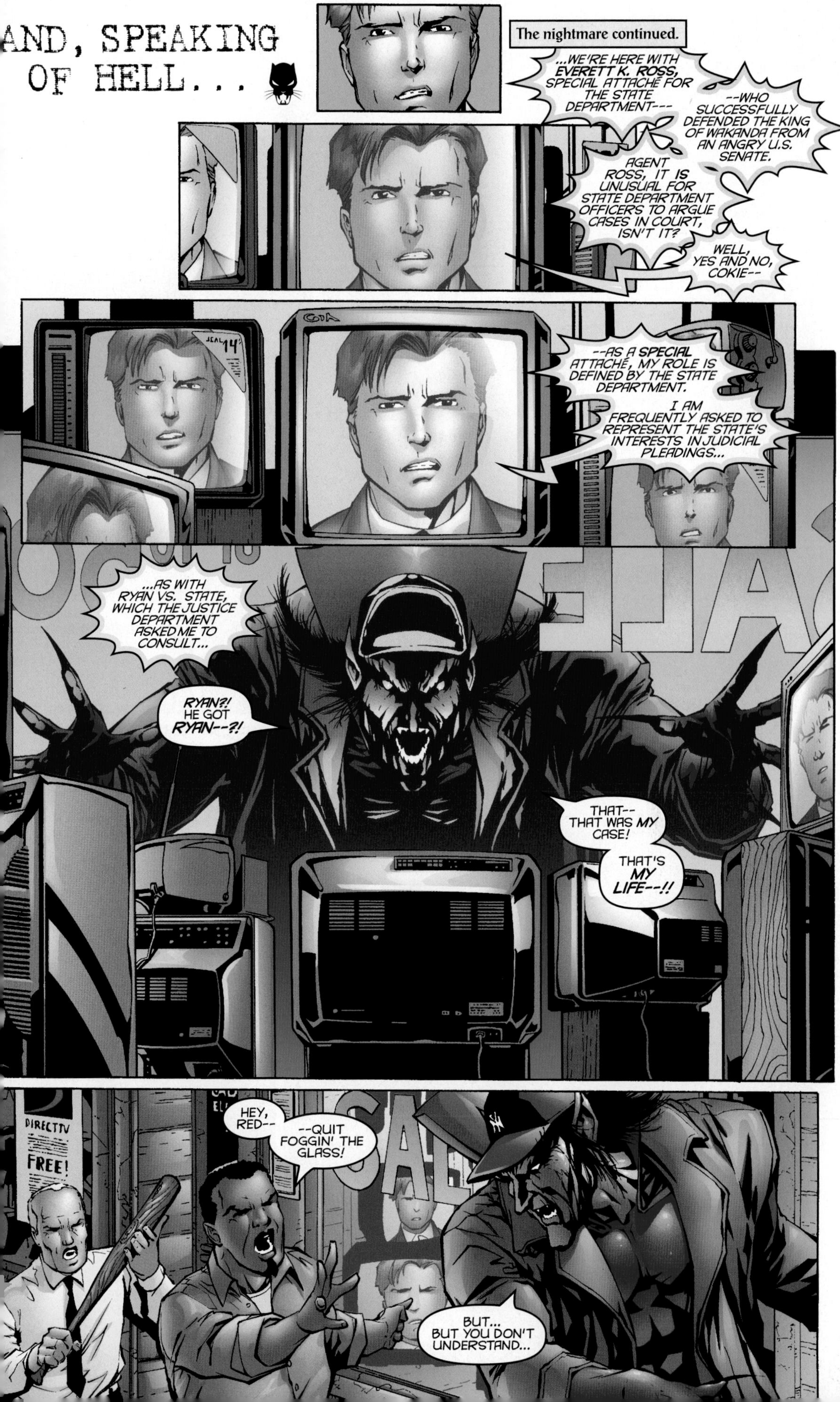
AND, SPEAKING OF HELL...
The nightmare continued.
...WE'RE HERE WITH EVERETT K. ROSS, SPECIAL ATTACHÉ FOR THE STATE DEPARTMENT---
--WHO SUCCESSFULLY DEFENDED THE KING OF WAKANDA FROM AN ANGRY U.S. SENATE.
AGENT ROSS, IT IS UNUSUAL FOR STATE DEPARTMENT OFFICERS TO ARGUE CASES IN COURT, ISN'T IT?
WELL, YES AND NO, COKIE--
--AS A SPECIAL ATTACHÉ, MY ROLE IS DEFINED BY THE STATE DEPARTMENT.
I AM FREQUENTLY ASKED TO REPRESENT THE STATE'S INTERESTS IN JUDICIAL PLEADINGS...
...AS WITH RYAN VS. STATE, WHICH THE JUSTICE DEPARTMENT ASKED ME TO CONSULT...
RYAN?! HE GOT RYAN--?!
THAT-- THAT WAS MY CASE!
THAT'S MY LIFE--!!
DIRECTTV
FREE!
HEY, RED--
--QUIT FOGGIN' THE GLASS!
BUT... BUT YOU DON'T UNDERSTAND...

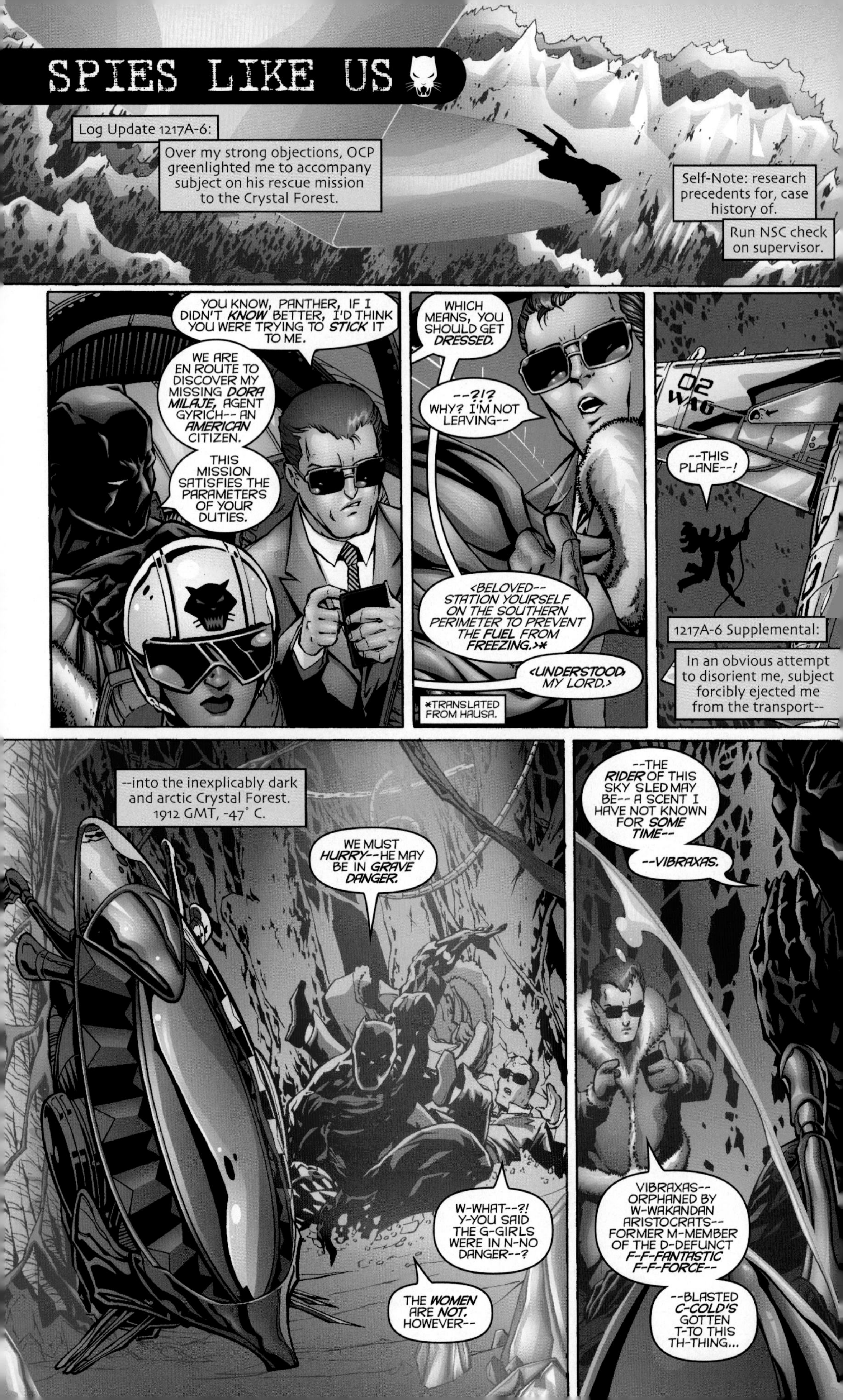
SPIES LIKE US
Log Update 1217A-6:
Over my strong objections, OCP greenlighted me to accompany subject on his rescue mission to the Crystal Forest.
Self-Note: research precedents for, case history of.
Run NSC check on supervisor.
YOU KNOW, PANTHER, IF I DIDN'T KNOW BETTER, I'D THINK YOU WERE TRYING TO STICK IT TO ME.
WE ARE EN ROUTE TO DISCOVER MY MISSING DORA MILAJE, AGENT GYRICH-- AN AMERICAN CITIZEN.
THIS MISSION SATISFIES THE PARAMETERS OF YOUR DUTIES.
WHICH MEANS, YOU SHOULD GET DRESSED.
--?!? WHY? I'M NOT LEAVING--
<BELOVED-- STATION YOURSELF ON THE SOUTHERN PERIMETER TO PREVENT THE FUEL FROM FREEZING.>*
<UNDERSTOOD, MY LORD.>
*TRANSLATED FROM HAUSA.
--THIS PLANE--!
1217A-6 Supplemental:
In an obvious attempt to disorient me, subject forcibly ejected me from the transport--
--into the inexplicably dark and arctic Crystal Forest. 1912 GMT, -47° C.
WE MUST HURRY--HE MAY BE IN GRAVE DANGER.
W-WHAT--?! Y-YOU SAID THE G-GIRLS WERE IN N-NO DANGER--?
THE WOMEN ARE NOT. HOWEVER--
--THE RIDER OF THIS SKY SLED MAY BE-- A SCENT I HAVE NOT KNOWN FOR SOME TIME--
--VIBRAXAS.
VIBRAXAS-- ORPHANED BY W-WAKANDAN ARISTOCRATS-- FORMER M-MEMBER OF THE D-DEFUNCT F-F-FANTASTIC F-F-FORCE--
--BLASTED C-COLD'S GOTTEN T-TO THIS TH-THING...

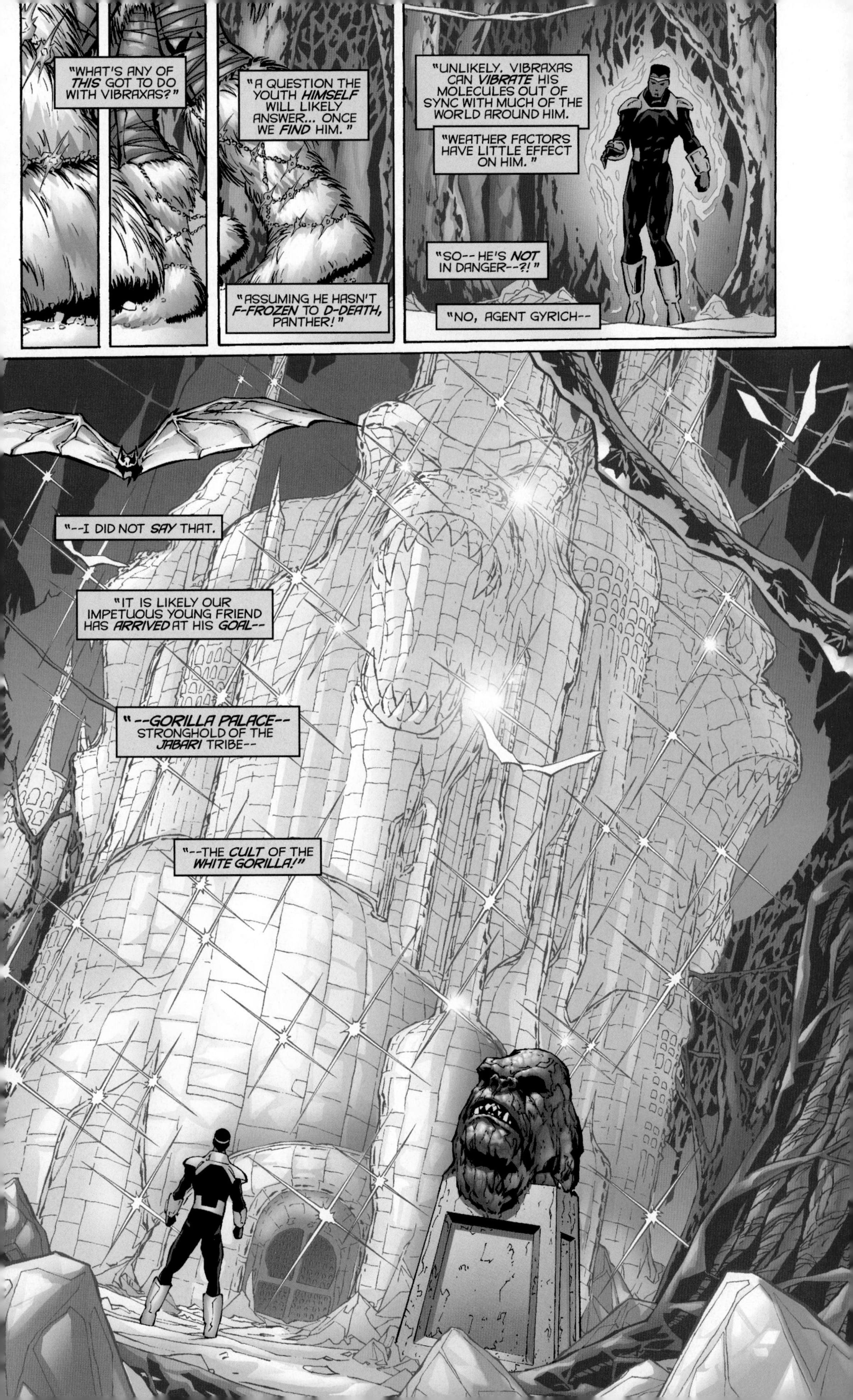
"WHAT'S ANY OF THIS GOT TO DO WITH VIBRAXAS?"
"A QUESTION THE YOUTH HIMSELF WILL LIKELY ANSWER... ONCE WE FIND HIM."
"ASSUMING HE HASN'T F-FROZEN TO D-DEATH, PANTHER!"
"UNLIKELY. VIBRAXAS CAN VIBRATE HIS MOLECULES OUT OF SYNC WITH MUCH OF THE WORLD AROUND HIM.
"WEATHER FACTORS HAVE LITTLE EFFECT ON HIM."
"SO-- HE'S NOT IN DANGER--?!"
"NO, AGENT GYRICH--
"--I DID NOT SAY THAT.
"IT IS LIKELY OUR IMPETUOUS YOUNG FRIEND HAS ARRIVED AT HIS GOAL--
"--GORILLA PALACE-- STRONGHOLD OF THE JABARI TRIBE--
"--THE CULT OF THE WHITE GORILLA!"

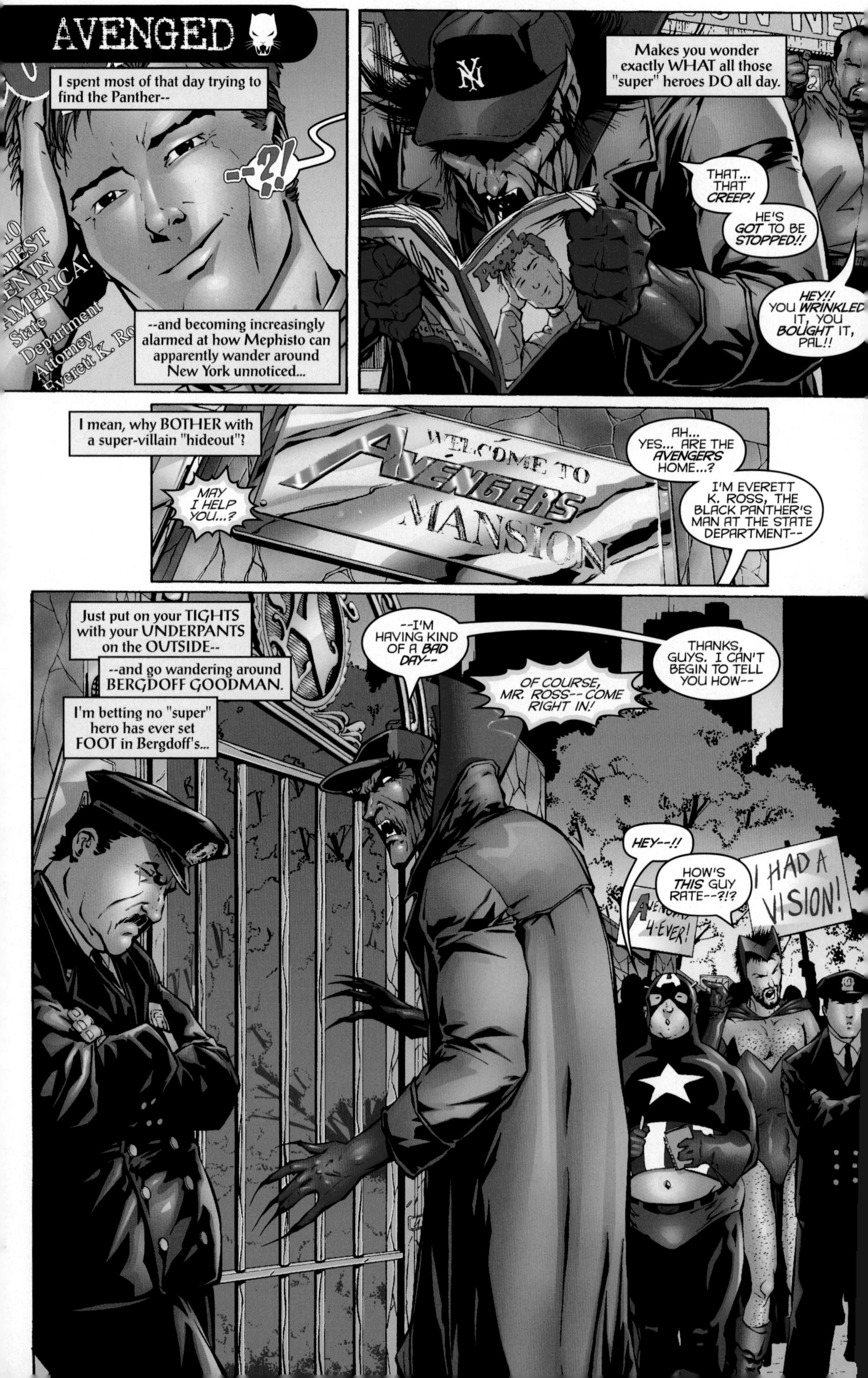
AVENGED
I spent most of that day trying to find the Panther--
--?!
10 ...NIEST ...EN IN AMERICA!
State Department Attorney Everett K. Ro...
--and becoming increasingly alarmed at how Mephisto can apparently wander around New York unnoticed...
Makes you wonder exactly WHAT all those "super" heroes DO all day.
THAT... THAT CREEP!
HE'S GOT TO BE STOPPED!!
HEY!! YOU WRINKLED IT, YOU BOUGHT IT, PAL!!
I mean, why BOTHER with a super-villain "hideout"?
WELCOME TO AVENGERS MANSION
MAY I HELP YOU...?
AH... YES... ARE THE AVENGERS HOME...?
I'M EVERETT K. ROSS, THE BLACK PANTHER'S MAN AT THE STATE DEPARTMENT--
Just put on your TIGHTS with your UNDERPANTS on the OUTSIDE--
--and go wandering around BERGDOFF GOODMAN.
I'm betting no "super" hero has ever set FOOT in Bergdoff's...
--I'M HAVING KIND OF A BAD DAY--
THANKS, GUYS. I CAN'T BEGIN TO TELL YOU HOW--
OF COURSE, MR. ROSS-- COME RIGHT IN!
HEY--!!
HOW'S THIS GUY RATE--?!?
I HAD A VISION!
AVENGERS 4-EVER!

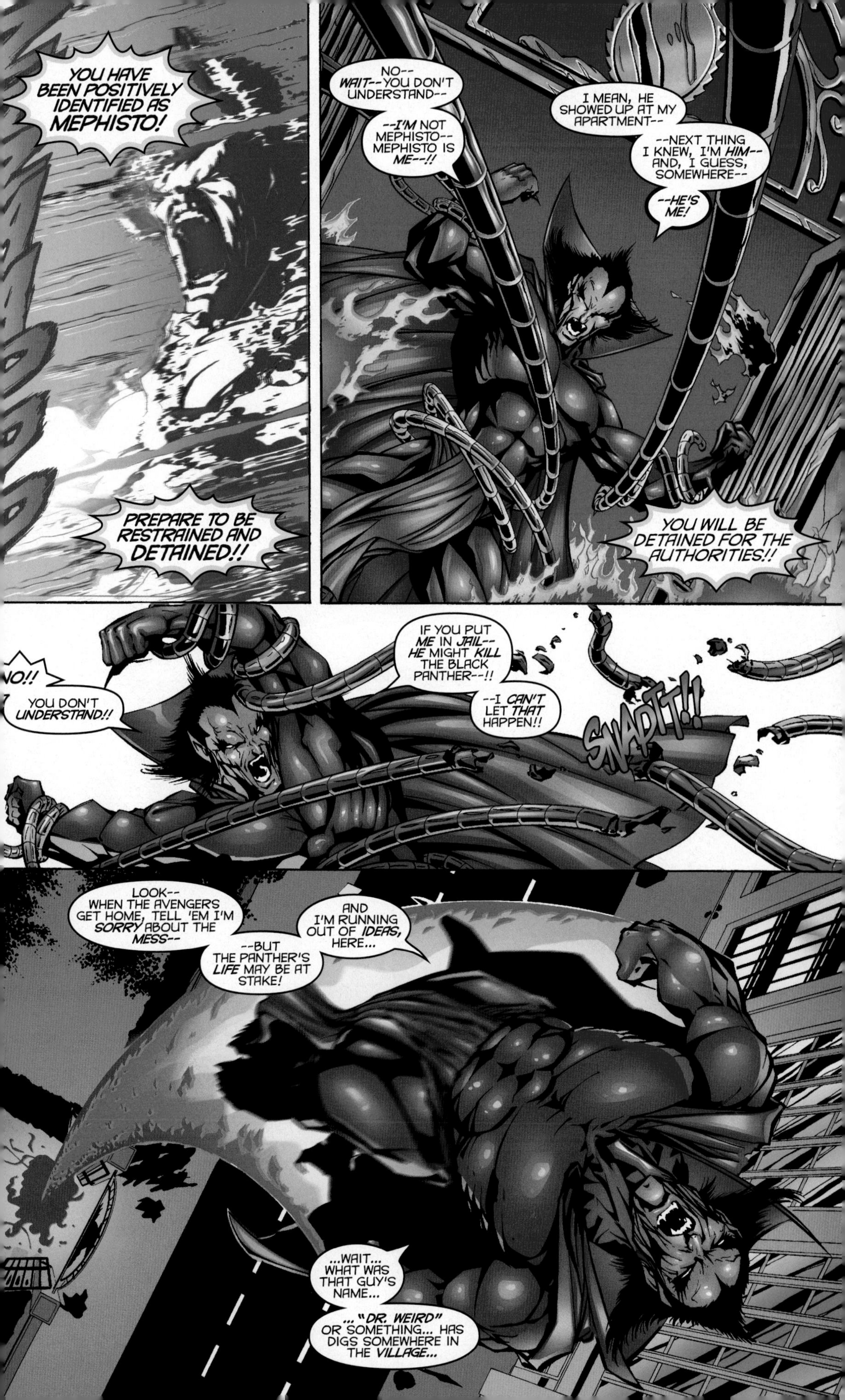
YOU HAVE BEEN POSITIVELY IDENTIFIED AS MEPHISTO!
PREPARE TO BE RESTRAINED AND DETAINED!!
NO-- WAIT--YOU DON'T UNDERSTAND--
--I'M NOT MEPHISTO-- MEPHISTO IS ME--!!
I MEAN, HE SHOWED UP AT MY APARTMENT--
--NEXT THING I KNEW, I'M HIM-- AND, I GUESS, SOMEWHERE--
--HE'S ME!
YOU WILL BE DETAINED FOR THE AUTHORITIES!!
NO!!
YOU DON'T UNDERSTAND!!
IF YOU PUT ME IN JAIL-- HE MIGHT KILL THE BLACK PANTHER--!!
--I CAN'T LET THAT HAPPEN!!
SNAPTT!!
LOOK-- WHEN THE AVENGERS GET HOME, TELL 'EM I'M SORRY ABOUT THE MESS--
--BUT THE PANTHER'S LIFE MAY BE AT STAKE!
AND I'M RUNNING OUT OF IDEAS, HERE...
...WAIT... WHAT WAS THAT GUY'S NAME...
..."DR. WEIRD" OR SOMETHING... HAS DIGS SOMEWHERE IN THE VILLAGE...

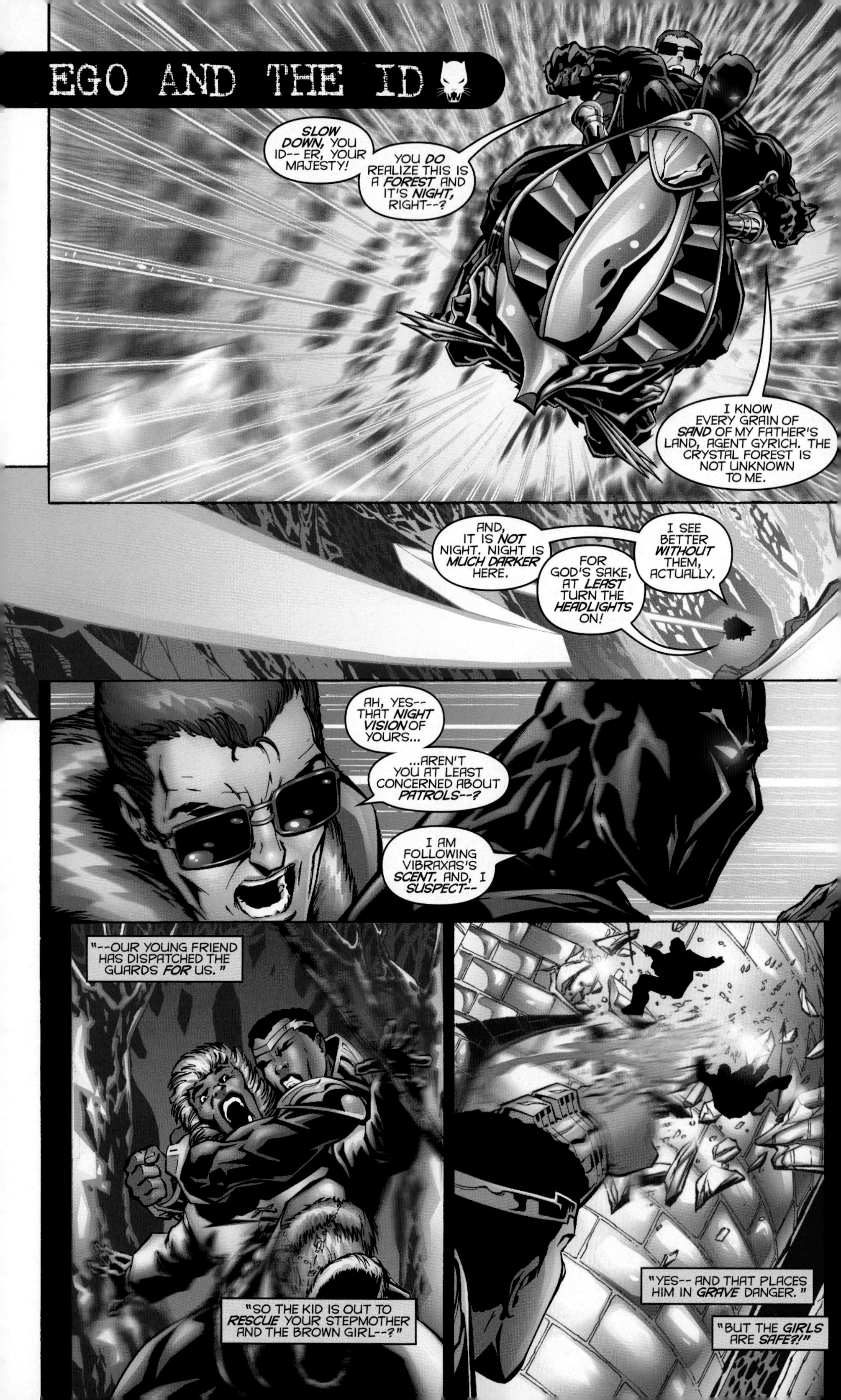
EGO AND THE ID
SLOW DOWN, YOU ID-- ER, YOUR MAJESTY!
YOU DO REALIZE THIS IS A FOREST AND IT'S NIGHT, RIGHT--?
I KNOW EVERY GRAIN OF SAND OF MY FATHER'S LAND, AGENT GYRICH. THE CRYSTAL FOREST IS NOT UNKNOWN TO ME.
AND, IT IS NOT NIGHT. NIGHT IS MUCH DARKER HERE.
FOR GOD'S SAKE, AT LEAST TURN THE HEADLIGHTS ON!
I SEE BETTER WITHOUT THEM, ACTUALLY.
AH, YES-- THAT NIGHT VISION OF YOURS...
...AREN'T YOU AT LEAST CONCERNED ABOUT PATROLS--?
I AM FOLLOWING VIBRAXAS'S SCENT. AND, I SUSPECT--
"--OUR YOUNG FRIEND HAS DISPATCHED THE GUARDS FOR US."
"SO THE KID IS OUT TO RESCUE YOUR STEPMOTHER AND THE BROWN GIRL--?"
"YES-- AND THAT PLACES HIM IN GRAVE DANGER."
"BUT THE GIRLS ARE SAFE?!"

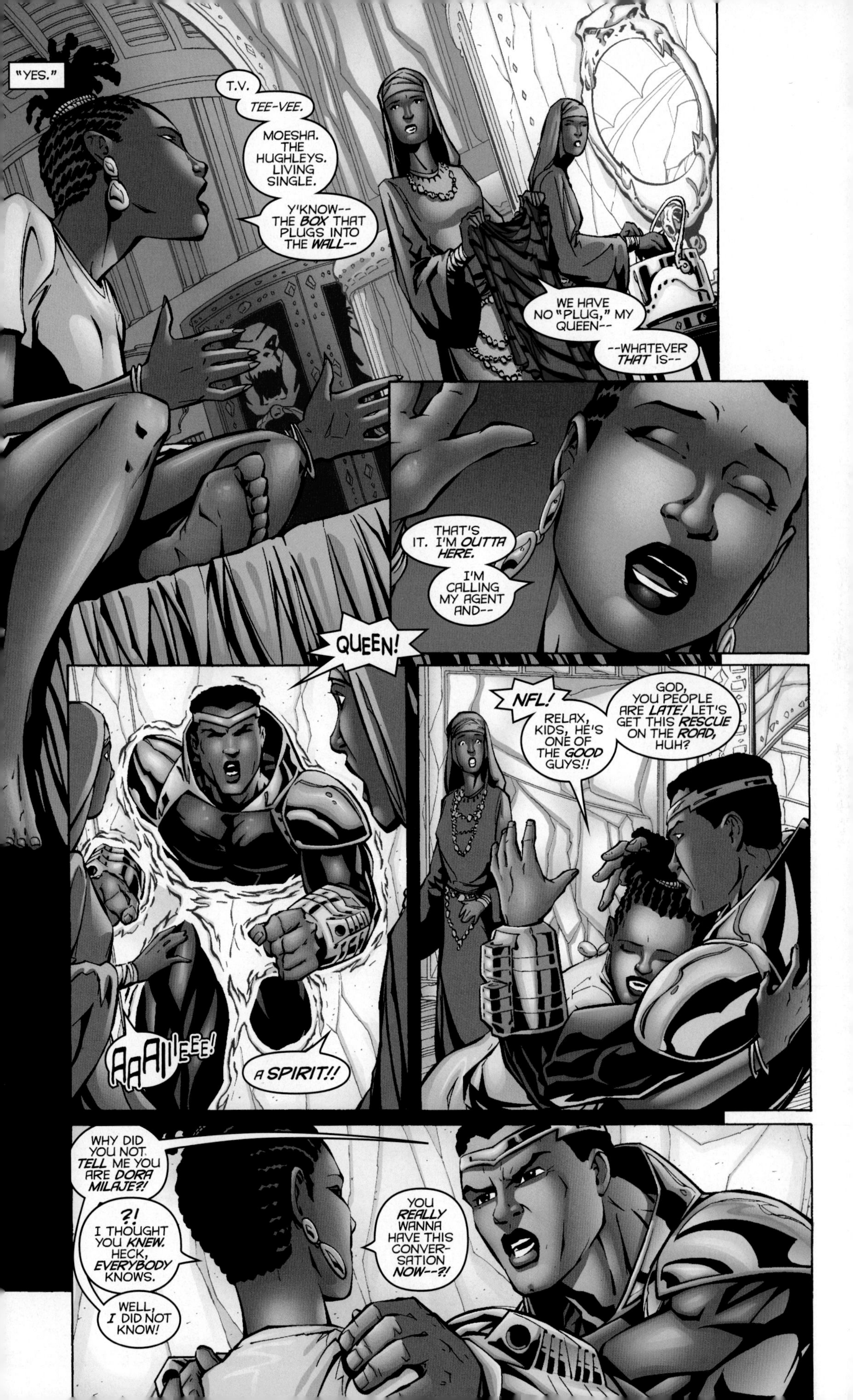

"YES."
T.V.
TEE-VEE.
MOESHA. THE HUGHLEYS. LIVING SINGLE.
Y'KNOW-- THE BOX THAT PLUGS INTO THE WALL--
WE HAVE NO "PLUG," MY QUEEN--
--WHATEVER THAT IS--
THAT'S IT. I'M OUTTA HERE.
I'M CALLING MY AGENT AND--
QUEEN!
AAAIIEEE!
A SPIRIT!!
NFL!
RELAX, KIDS, HE'S ONE OF THE GOOD GUYS!!
GOD, YOU PEOPLE ARE LATE! LET'S GET THIS RESCUE ON THE ROAD, HUH?
WHY DID YOU NOT TELL ME YOU ARE DORA MILAJE?!
?! I THOUGHT YOU KNEW. HECK, EVERYBODY KNOWS.
WELL, I DID NOT KNOW!
YOU REALLY WANNA HAVE THIS CONVER-SATION NOW--?!

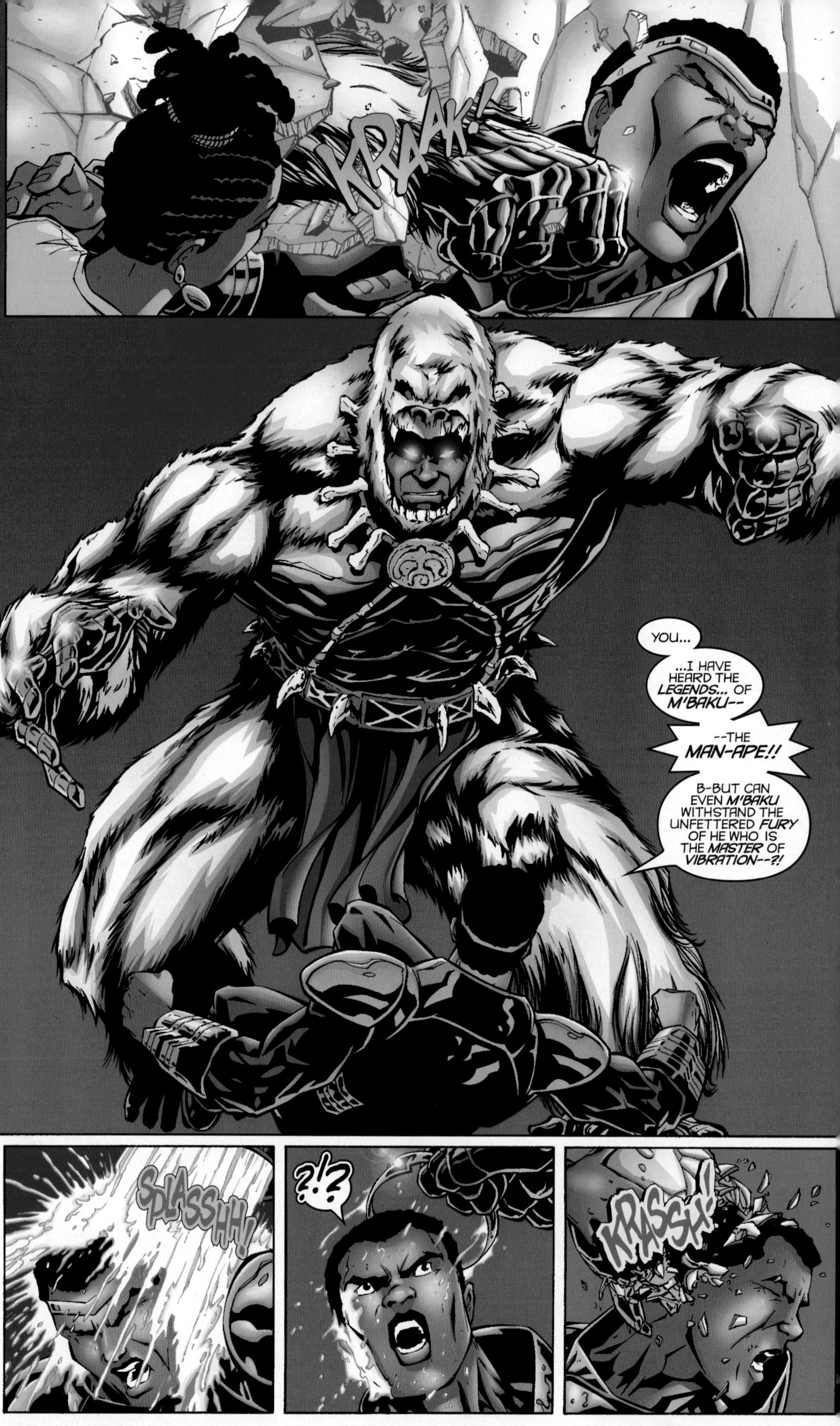
KRAAK!
YOU...
...I HAVE HEARD THE LEGENDS... OF M'BAKU--
--THE MAN-APE!!
B-BUT CAN EVEN M'BAKU WITHSTAND THE UNFETTERED FURY OF HE WHO IS THE MASTER OF VIBRATION--?!
SPLASSHH!
?!?
KRASSH!

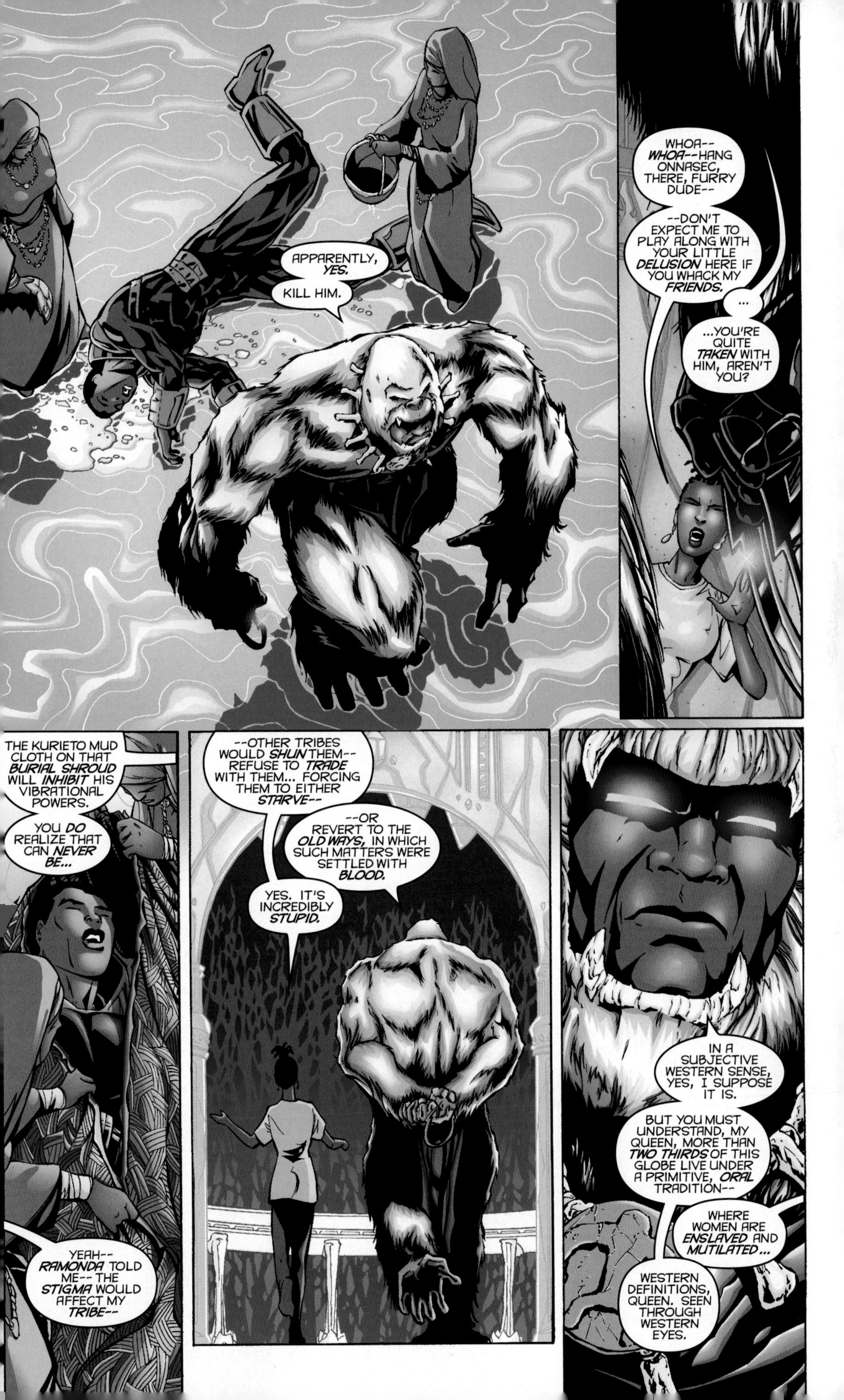
APPARENTLY, YES.
KILL HIM.
WHOA-- WHOA--HANG ONNASEC, THERE, FURRY DUDE--
--DON'T EXPECT ME TO PLAY ALONG WITH YOUR LITTLE DELUSION HERE IF YOU WHACK MY FRIENDS.
...
...YOU'RE QUITE TAKEN WITH HIM, AREN'T YOU?
THE KURIETO MUD CLOTH ON THAT BURIAL SHROUD WILL INHIBIT HIS VIBRATIONAL POWERS.
YOU DO REALIZE THAT CAN NEVER BE...
YEAH-- RAMONDA TOLD ME-- THE STIGMA WOULD AFFECT MY TRIBE--
--OTHER TRIBES WOULD SHUN THEM-- REFUSE TO TRADE WITH THEM... FORCING THEM TO EITHER STARVE--
--OR REVERT TO THE OLD WAYS, IN WHICH SUCH MATTERS WERE SETTLED WITH BLOOD.
YES. IT'S INCREDIBLY STUPID.
IN A SUBJECTIVE WESTERN SENSE, YES, I SUPPOSE IT IS.
BUT YOU MUST UNDERSTAND, MY QUEEN, MORE THAN TWO THIRDS OF THIS GLOBE LIVE UNDER A PRIMITIVE, ORAL TRADITION--
WHERE WOMEN ARE ENSLAVED AND MUTILATED...
WESTERN DEFINITIONS, QUEEN. SEEN THROUGH WESTERN EYES.

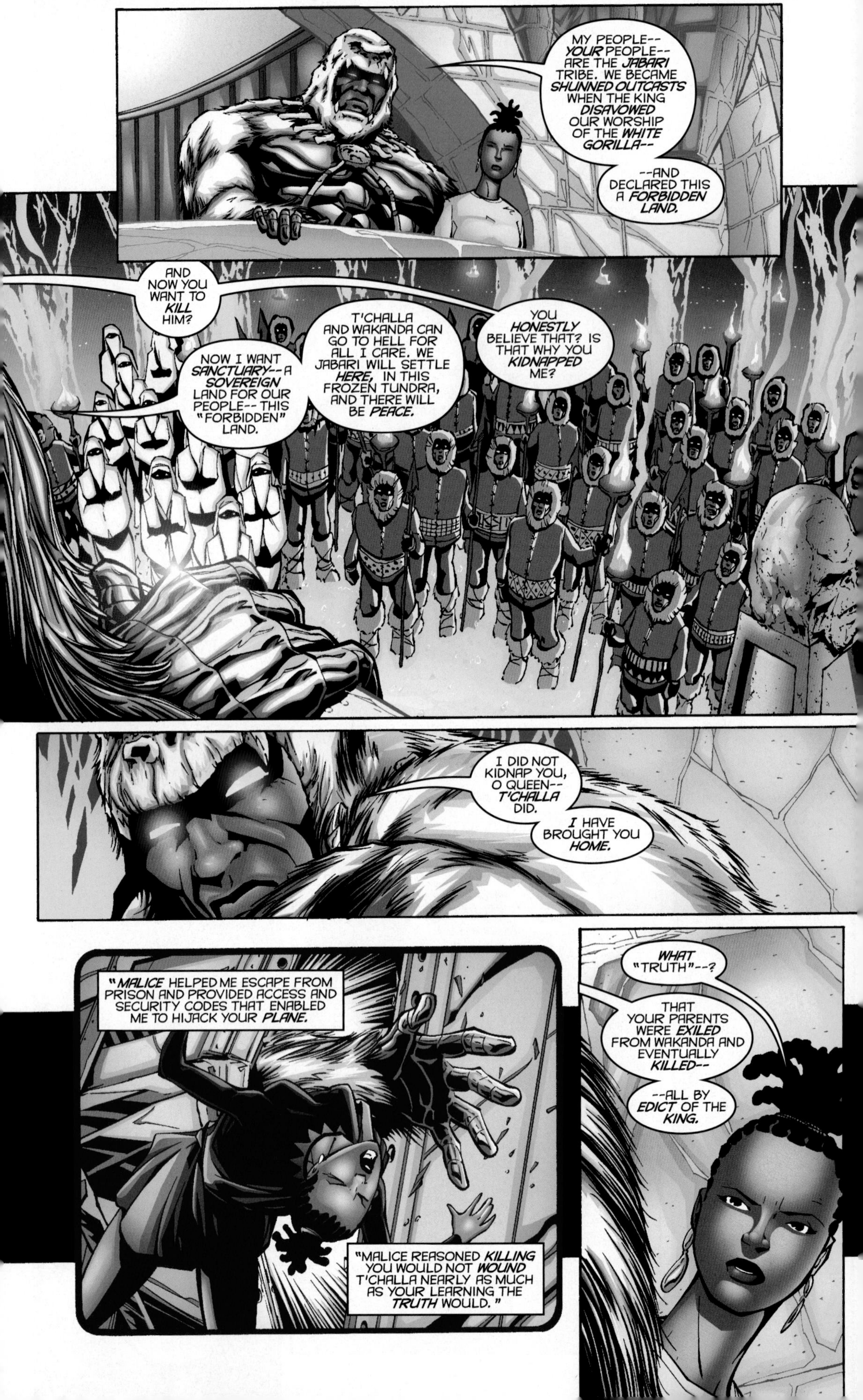
MY PEOPLE-- YOUR PEOPLE-- ARE THE JABARI TRIBE. WE BECAME SHUNNED OUTCASTS WHEN THE KING DISAVOWED OUR WORSHIP OF THE WHITE GORILLA--
--AND DECLARED THIS A FORBIDDEN LAND.
AND NOW YOU WANT TO KILL HIM?
NOW I WANT SANCTUARY--A SOVEREIGN LAND FOR OUR PEOPLE-- THIS "FORBIDDEN" LAND.
T'CHALLA AND WAKANDA CAN GO TO HELL FOR ALL I CARE. WE JABARI WILL SETTLE HERE, IN THIS FROZEN TUNDRA, AND THERE WILL BE PEACE.
YOU HONESTLY BELIEVE THAT? IS THAT WHY YOU KIDNAPPED ME?
I DID NOT KIDNAP YOU, O QUEEN-- T'CHALLA DID.
I HAVE BROUGHT YOU HOME.
"MALICE HELPED ME ESCAPE FROM PRISON AND PROVIDED ACCESS AND SECURITY CODES THAT ENABLED ME TO HIJACK YOUR PLANE.
"MALICE REASONED KILLING YOU WOULD NOT WOUND T'CHALLA NEARLY AS MUCH AS YOUR LEARNING THE TRUTH WOULD."
WHAT "TRUTH"--?
THAT YOUR PARENTS WERE EXILED FROM WAKANDA AND EVENTUALLY KILLED--
--ALL BY EDICT OF THE KING.

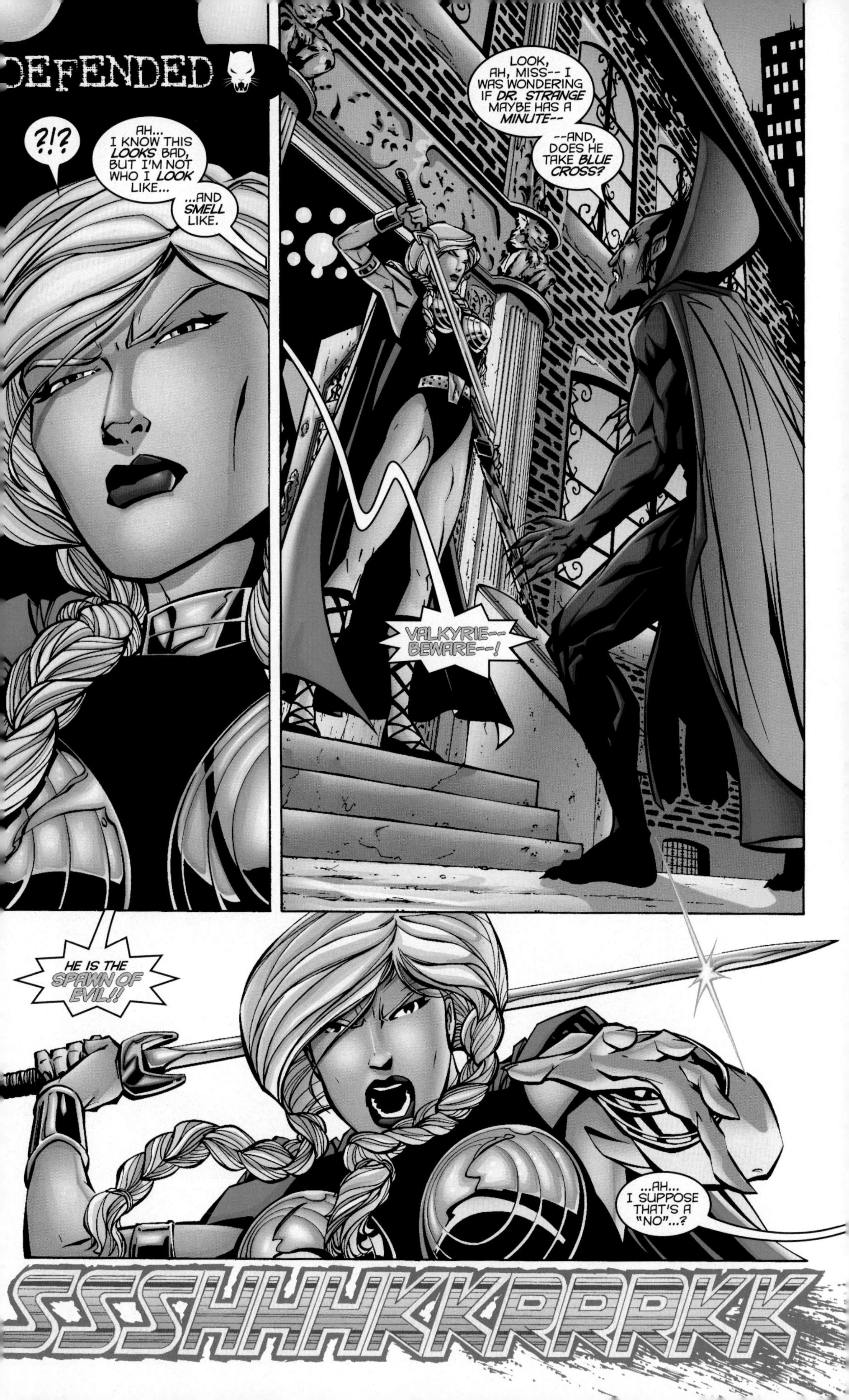
DEFENDED
?!?
AH... I KNOW THIS LOOKS BAD, BUT I'M NOT WHO I LOOK LIKE...
...AND SMELL LIKE.
LOOK, AH, MISS-- I WAS WONDERING IF DR. STRANGE MAYBE HAS A MINUTE--
--AND, DOES HE TAKE BLUE CROSS?
VALKYRIE-- BEWARE--!
HE IS THE SPAWN OF EVIL!!
...AH... I SUPPOSE THAT'S A "NO"...?
SSSHHHKKRRRRKK

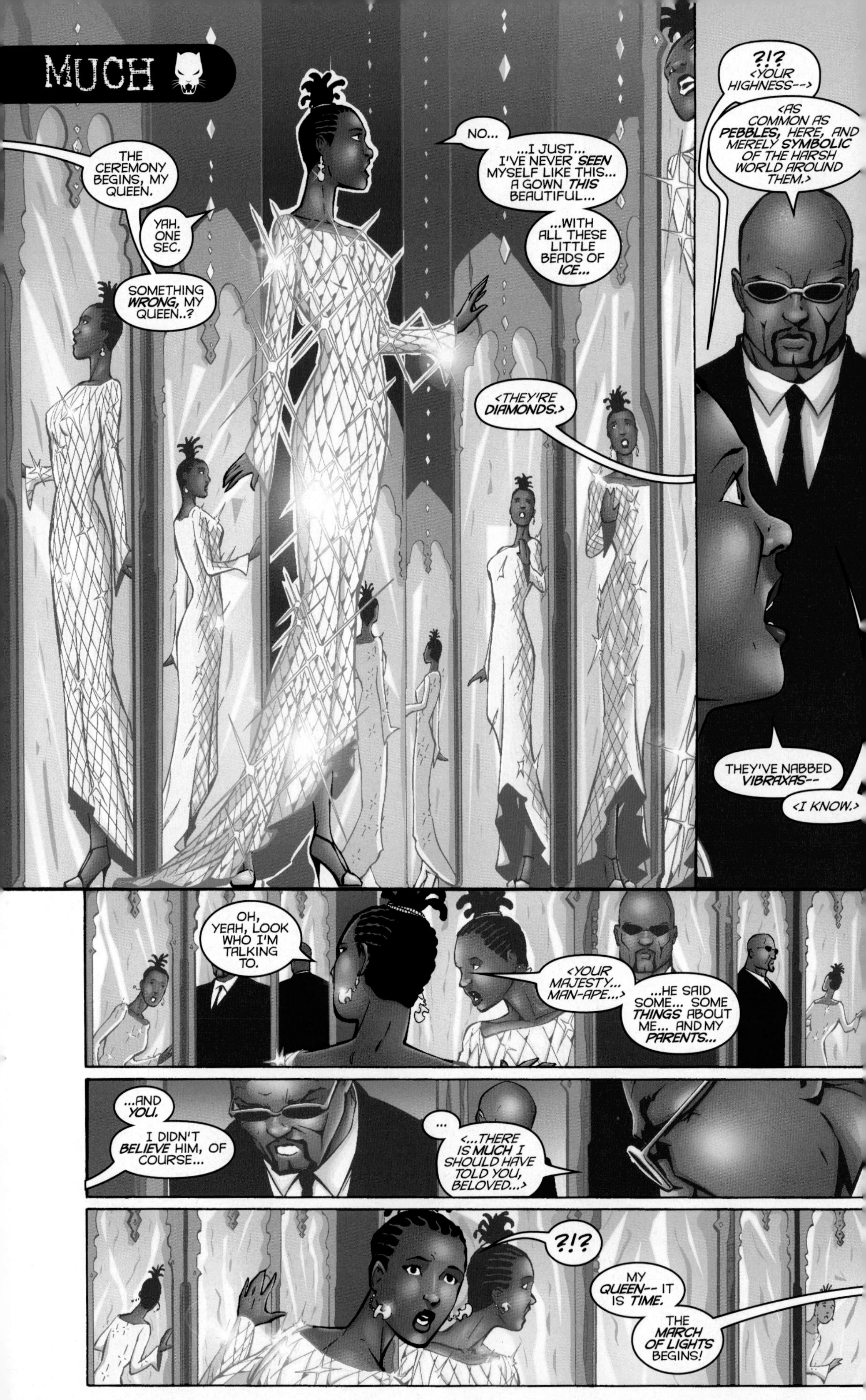
MUCH
THE CEREMONY BEGINS, MY QUEEN.
YAH. ONE SEC.
SOMETHING WRONG, MY QUEEN..?
NO...
...I JUST... I'VE NEVER SEEN MYSELF LIKE THIS... A GOWN THIS BEAUTIFUL...
...WITH ALL THESE LITTLE BEADS OF ICE...
<THEY'RE DIAMONDS.>
?!? <YOUR HIGHNESS-->
<AS COMMON AS PEBBLES, HERE, AND MERELY SYMBOLIC OF THE HARSH WORLD AROUND THEM.>
THEY'VE NABBED VIBRAXAS--
<I KNOW.>
OH, YEAH, LOOK WHO I'M TALKING TO.
<YOUR MAJESTY... MAN-APE...>
...HE SAID SOME... SOME THINGS ABOUT ME... AND MY PARENTS...
...AND YOU.
I DIDN'T BELIEVE HIM, OF COURSE...
...
<...THERE IS MUCH I SHOULD HAVE TOLD YOU, BELOVED...>
?!?
MY QUEEN-- IT IS TIME.
THE MARCH OF LIGHTS BEGINS!

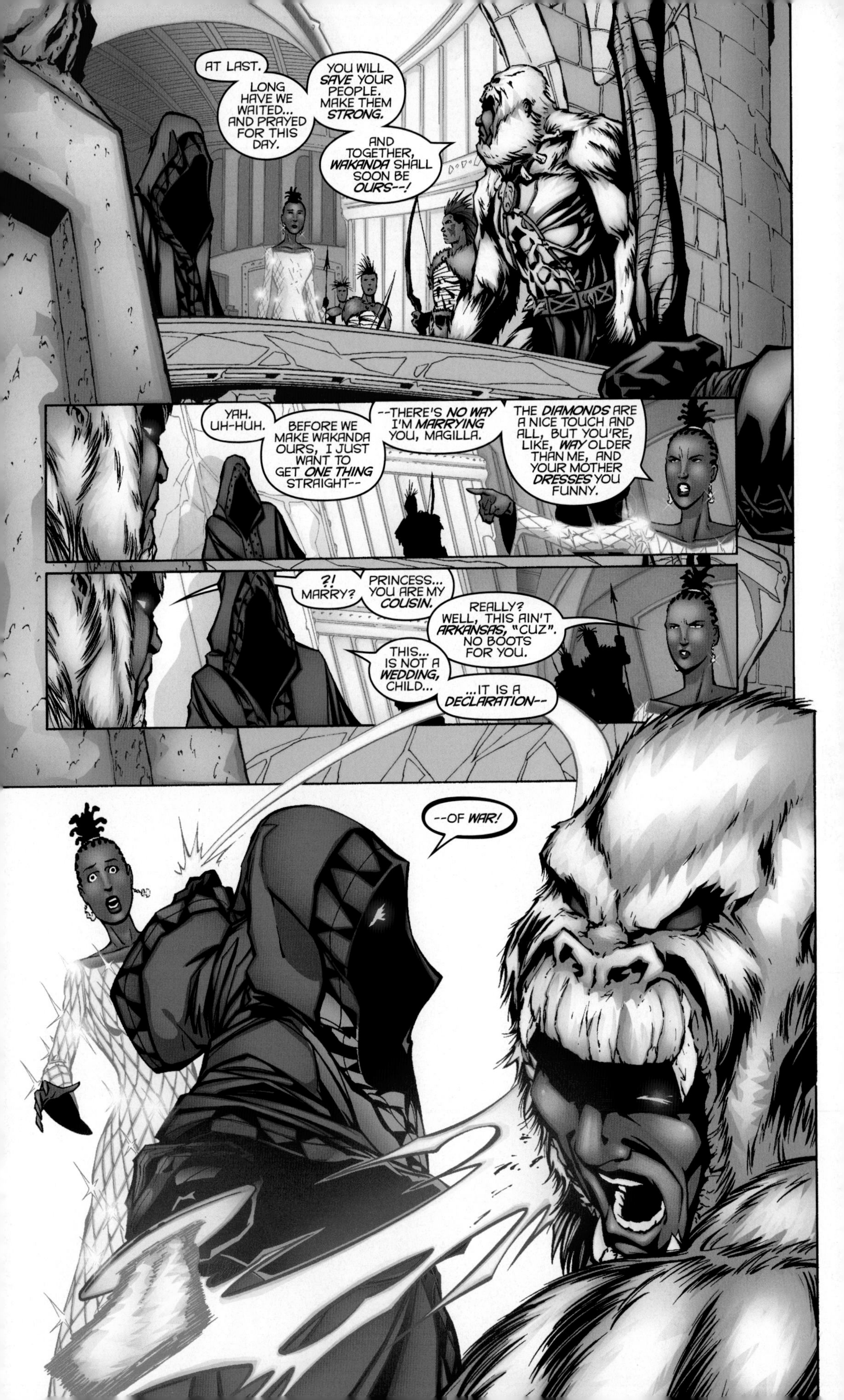
AT LAST.
LONG HAVE WE WAITED... AND PRAYED FOR THIS DAY.
YOU WILL SAVE YOUR PEOPLE. MAKE THEM STRONG.
AND TOGETHER, WAKANDA SHALL SOON BE OURS--!
YAH. UH-HUH.
BEFORE WE MAKE WAKANDA OURS, I JUST WANT TO GET ONE THING STRAIGHT--
--THERE'S NO WAY I'M MARRYING YOU, MAGILLA.
THE DIAMONDS ARE A NICE TOUCH AND ALL, BUT YOU'RE, LIKE, WAY OLDER THAN ME, AND YOUR MOTHER DRESSES YOU FUNNY.
?! MARRY?
PRINCESS... YOU ARE MY COUSIN.
REALLY? WELL, THIS AIN'T ARKANSAS, "CUZ". NO BOOTS FOR YOU.
THIS... IS NOT A WEDDING, CHILD...
...IT IS A DECLARATION--
--OF WAR!

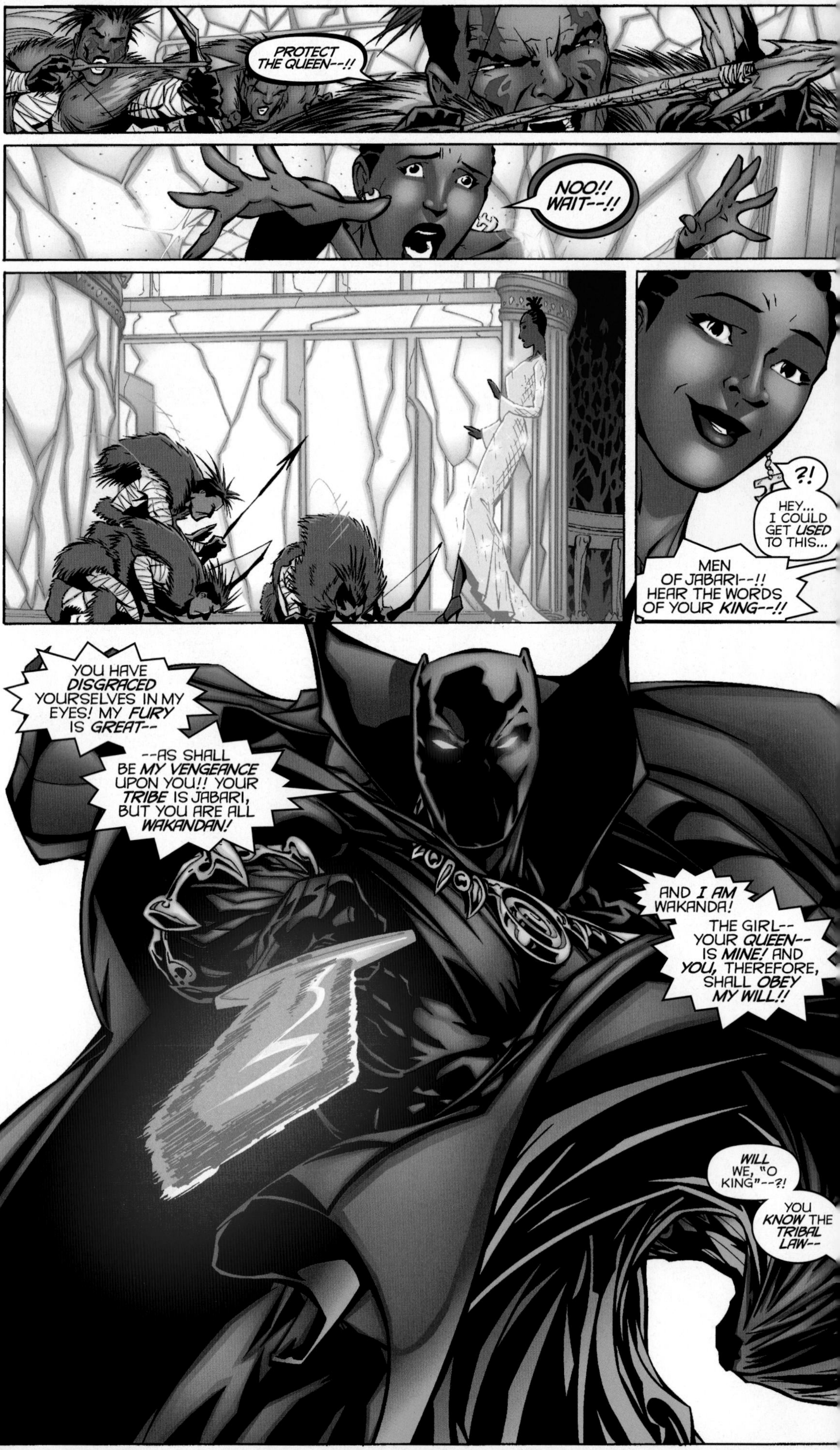
PROTECT THE QUEEN--!!
NOO!! WAIT--!!
?!
HEY... I COULD GET USED TO THIS...
MEN OF JABARI--!! HEAR THE WORDS OF YOUR KING--!!
YOU HAVE DISGRACED YOURSELVES IN MY EYES! MY FURY IS GREAT--
--AS SHALL BE MY VENGEANCE UPON YOU!! YOUR TRIBE IS JABARI, BUT YOU ARE ALL WAKANDAN!
AND I AM WAKANDA!
THE GIRL-- YOUR QUEEN-- IS MINE! AND YOU, THEREFORE, SHALL OBEY MY WILL!!
WILL WE, "O KING"--?!
YOU KNOW THE TRIBAL LAW--

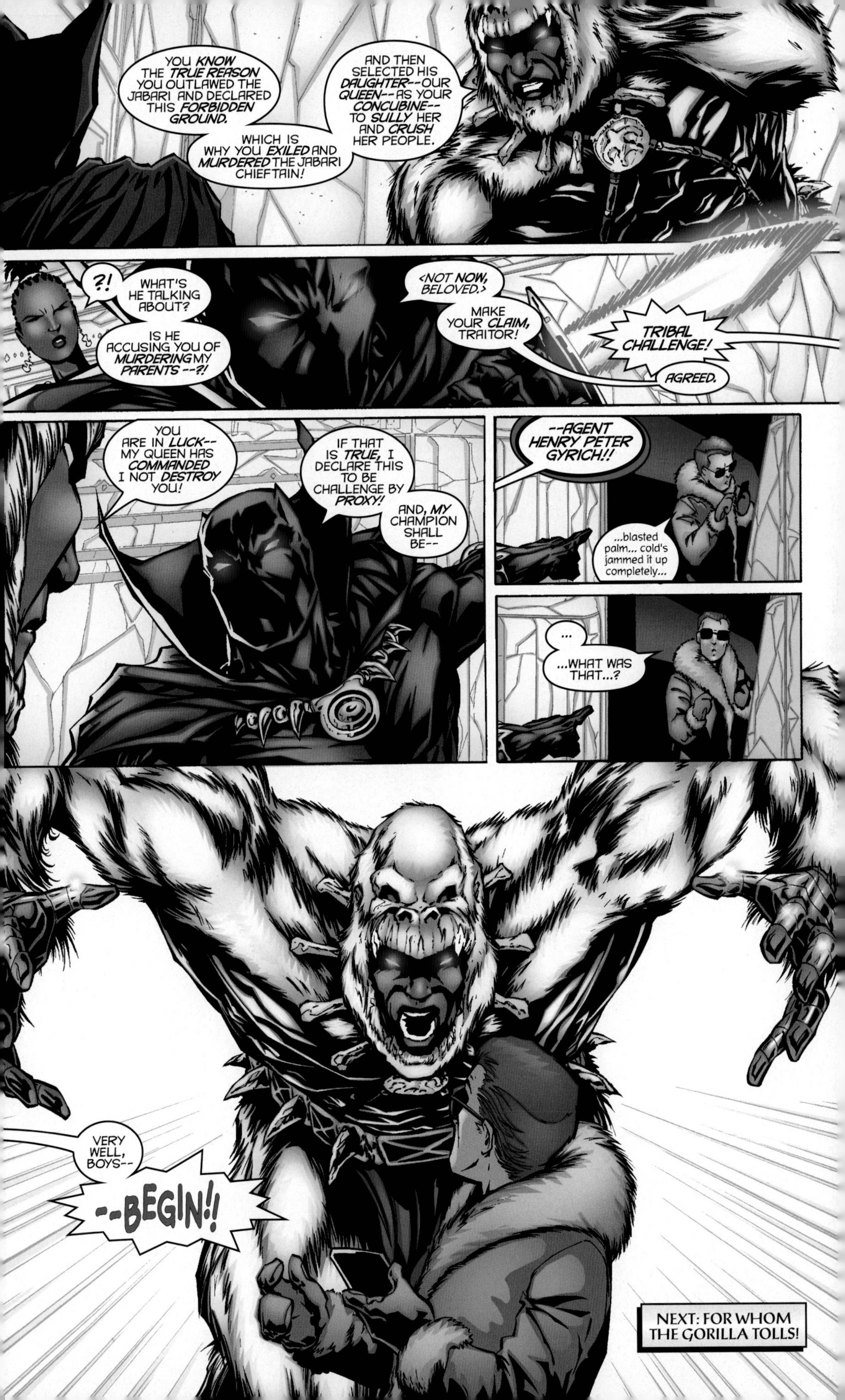
YOU KNOW THE TRUE REASON YOU OUTLAWED THE JABARI AND DECLARED THIS FORBIDDEN GROUND.
WHICH IS WHY YOU EXILED AND MURDERED THE JABARI CHIEFTAIN!
AND THEN SELECTED HIS DAUGHTER--OUR QUEEN--AS YOUR CONCUBINE--TO SULLY HER AND CRUSH HER PEOPLE.
?!
WHAT'S HE TALKING ABOUT?
IS HE ACCUSING YOU OF MURDERING MY PARENTS--?!
<NOT NOW, BELOVED.>
MAKE YOUR CLAIM, TRAITOR!
TRIBAL CHALLENGE!
AGREED.
YOU ARE IN LUCK--MY QUEEN HAS COMMANDED I NOT DESTROY YOU!
IF THAT IS TRUE, I DECLARE THIS TO BE CHALLENGE BY PROXY!
AND, MY CHAMPION SHALL BE--
--AGENT HENRY PETER GYRICH!!
...blasted palm... cold's jammed it up completely...
...
...WHAT WAS THAT...?
VERY WELL, BOYS--
--BEGIN!!
NEXT: FOR WHOM THE GORILLA TOLLS!

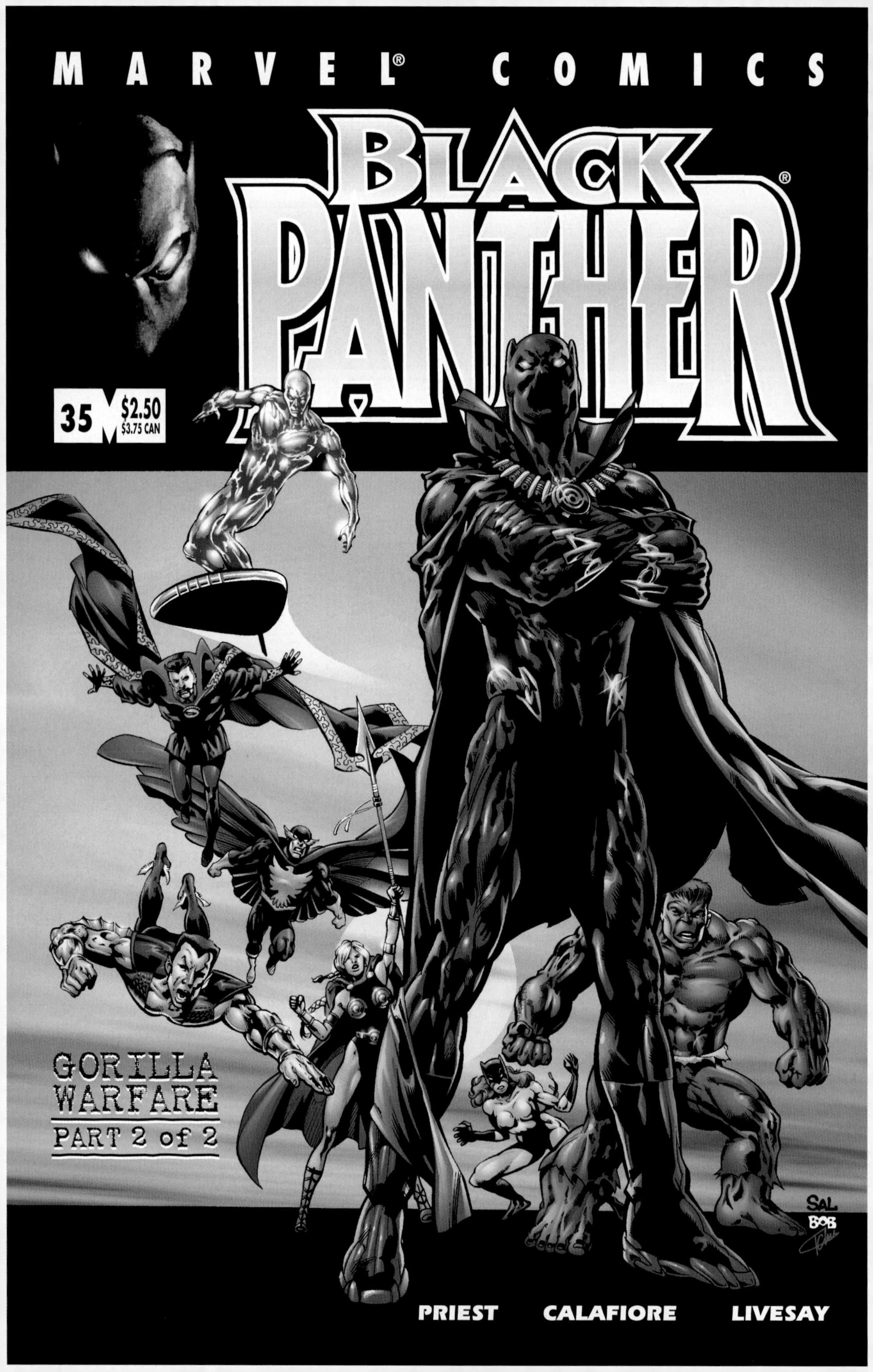
MARVEL® COMICS
BLACK PANTHER®
35 $2.50 $3.75 CAN
GORILLA WARFARE
PART 2 of 2
SAL BOB
PRIEST CALAFIORE LIVESAY

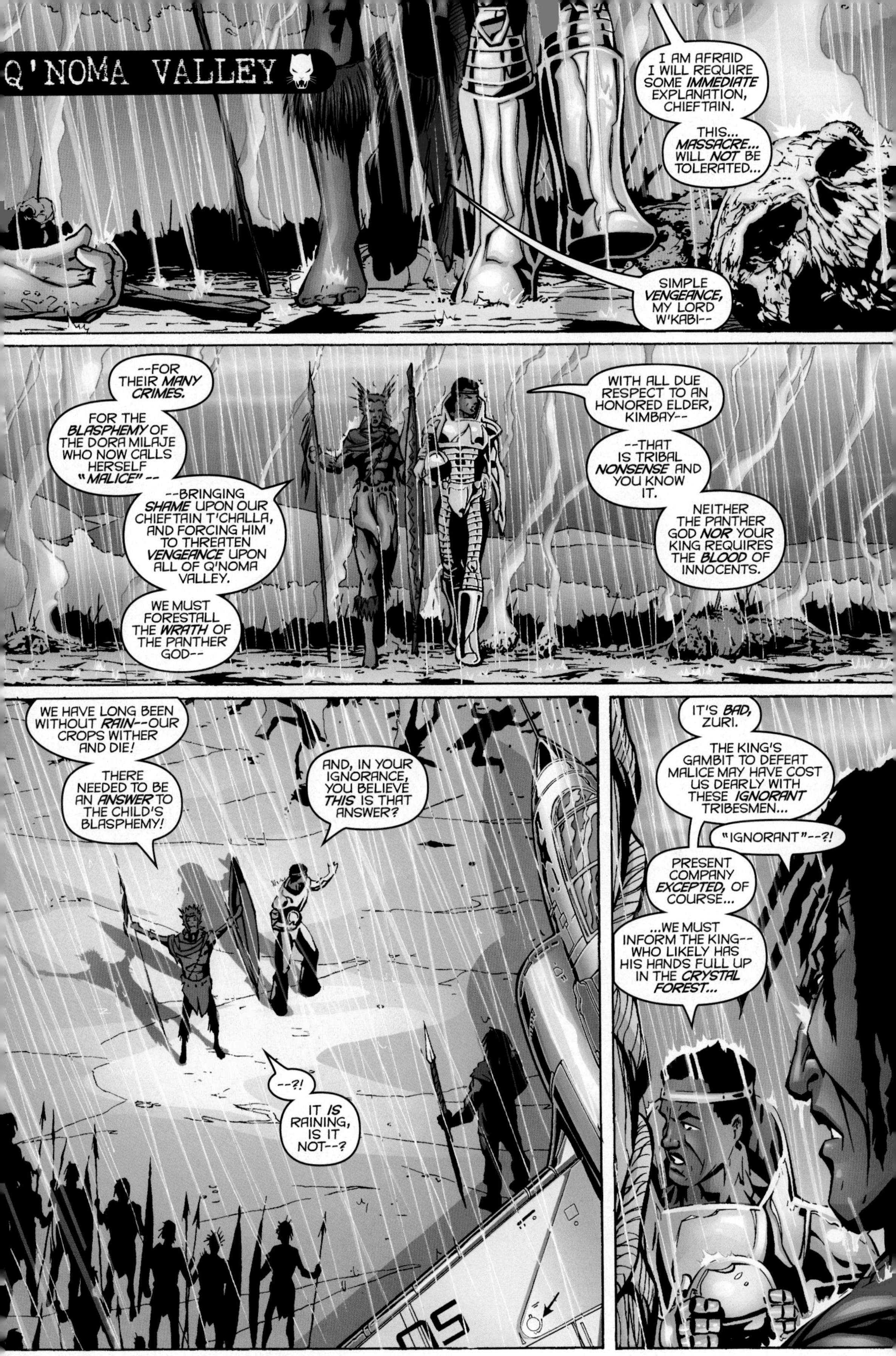
Q'NOMA VALLEY
I AM AFRAID I WILL REQUIRE SOME IMMEDIATE EXPLANATION, CHIEFTAIN.
THIS... MASSACRE... WILL NOT BE TOLERATED...
SIMPLE VENGEANCE, MY LORD W'KABI--
--FOR THEIR MANY CRIMES.
FOR THE BLASPHEMY OF THE DORA MILAJE WHO NOW CALLS HERSELF "MALICE"--
--BRINGING SHAME UPON OUR CHIEFTAIN T'CHALLA, AND FORCING HIM TO THREATEN VENGEANCE UPON ALL OF Q'NOMA VALLEY.
WE MUST FORESTALL THE WRATH OF THE PANTHER GOD--
WITH ALL DUE RESPECT TO AN HONORED ELDER, KIMBAY--
--THAT IS TRIBAL NONSENSE AND YOU KNOW IT.
NEITHER THE PANTHER GOD NOR YOUR KING REQUIRES THE BLOOD OF INNOCENTS.
WE HAVE LONG BEEN WITHOUT RAIN--OUR CROPS WITHER AND DIE!
THERE NEEDED TO BE AN ANSWER TO THE CHILD'S BLASPHEMY!
AND, IN YOUR IGNORANCE, YOU BELIEVE THIS IS THAT ANSWER?
--?!
IT IS RAINING, IS IT NOT--?
IT'S BAD, ZURI.
THE KING'S GAMBIT TO DEFEAT MALICE MAY HAVE COST US DEARLY WITH THESE IGNORANT TRIBESMEN...
"IGNORANT"--?!
PRESENT COMPANY EXCEPTED, OF COURSE...
...WE MUST INFORM THE KING--WHO LIKELY HAS HIS HANDS FULL UP IN THE CRYSTAL FOREST...

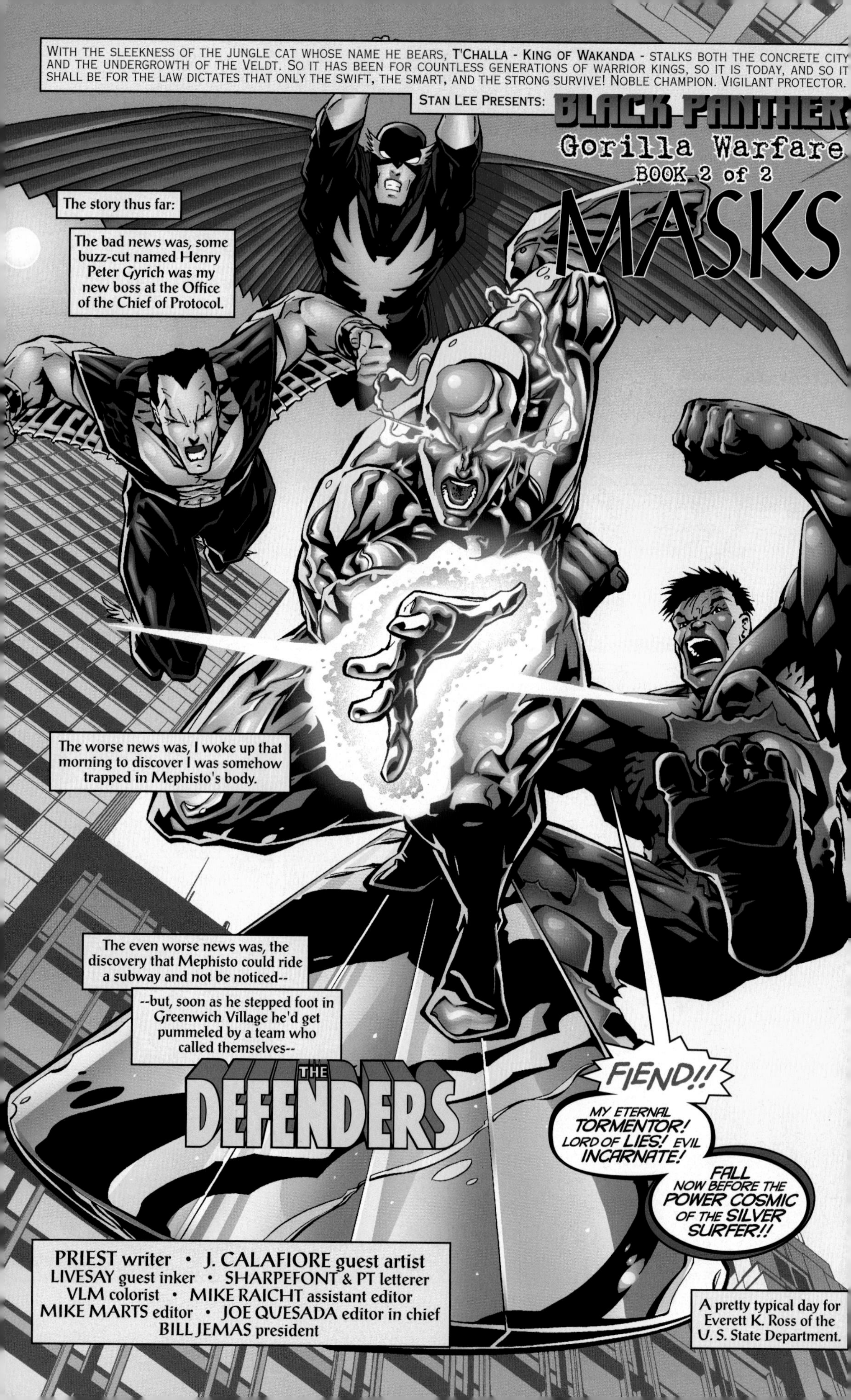

WITH THE SLEEKNESS OF THE JUNGLE CAT WHOSE NAME HE BEARS, T'CHALLA - KING OF WAKANDA - STALKS BOTH THE CONCRETE CITY AND THE UNDERGROWTH OF THE VELDT. SO IT HAS BEEN FOR COUNTLESS GENERATIONS OF WARRIOR KINGS, SO IT IS TODAY, AND SO IT SHALL BE FOR THE LAW DICTATES THAT ONLY THE SWIFT, THE SMART, AND THE STRONG SURVIVE! NOBLE CHAMPION. VIGILANT PROTECTOR.
STAN LEE PRESENTS: BLACK PANTHER
Gorilla Warfare
BOOK 2 of 2
MASKS
The story thus far:
The bad news was, some buzz-cut named Henry Peter Gyrich was my new boss at the Office of the Chief of Protocol.
The worse news was, I woke up that morning to discover I was somehow trapped in Mephisto's body.
The even worse news was, the discovery that Mephisto could ride a subway and not be noticed--
--but, soon as he stepped foot in Greenwich Village he'd get pummeled by a team who called themselves--
THE DEFENDERS
FIEND!!
MY ETERNAL TORMENTOR! LORD OF LIES! EVIL INCARNATE!
FALL NOW BEFORE THE POWER COSMIC OF THE SILVER SURFER!!
PRIEST writer • J. CALAFIORE guest artist
LIVESAY guest inker • SHARPEFONT & PT letterer
VLM colorist • MIKE RAICHT assistant editor
MIKE MARTS editor • JOE QUESADA editor in chief
BILL JEMAS president
A pretty typical day for Everett K. Ross of the U. S. State Department.

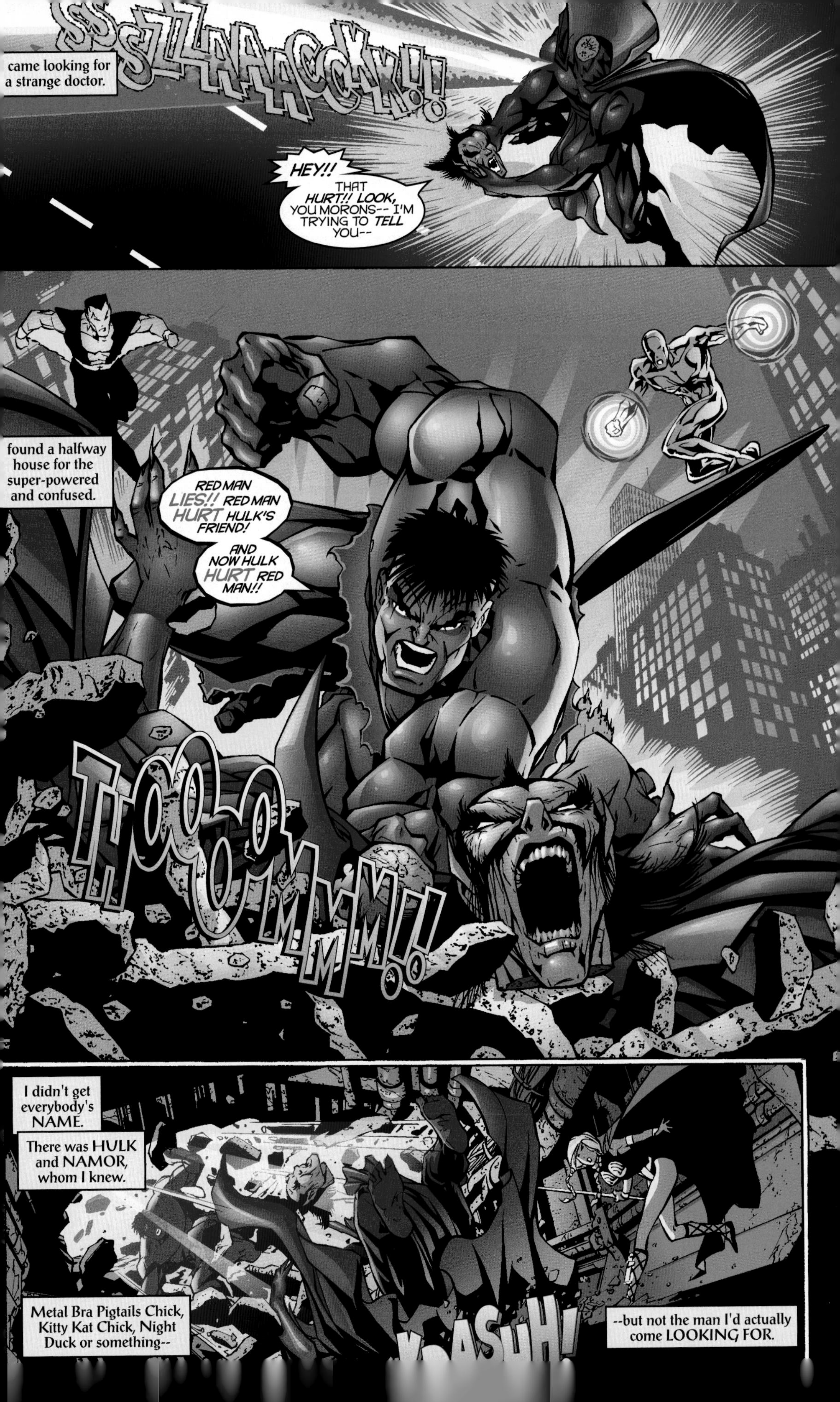
SSSZZAACCKK!!
came looking for a strange doctor.
HEY!!
THAT HURT!! LOOK, YOU MORONS-- I'M TRYING TO TELL YOU--
found a halfway house for the super-powered and confused.
RED MAN LIES!! RED MAN HURT HULK'S FRIEND!
AND NOW HULK HURT RED MAN!!
THOOOOMMMM!!
I didn't get everybody's NAME.
There was HULK and NAMOR, whom I knew.
Metal Bra Pigtails Chick, Kitty Kat Chick, Night Duck or something--
--but not the man I'd actually come LOOKING FOR.

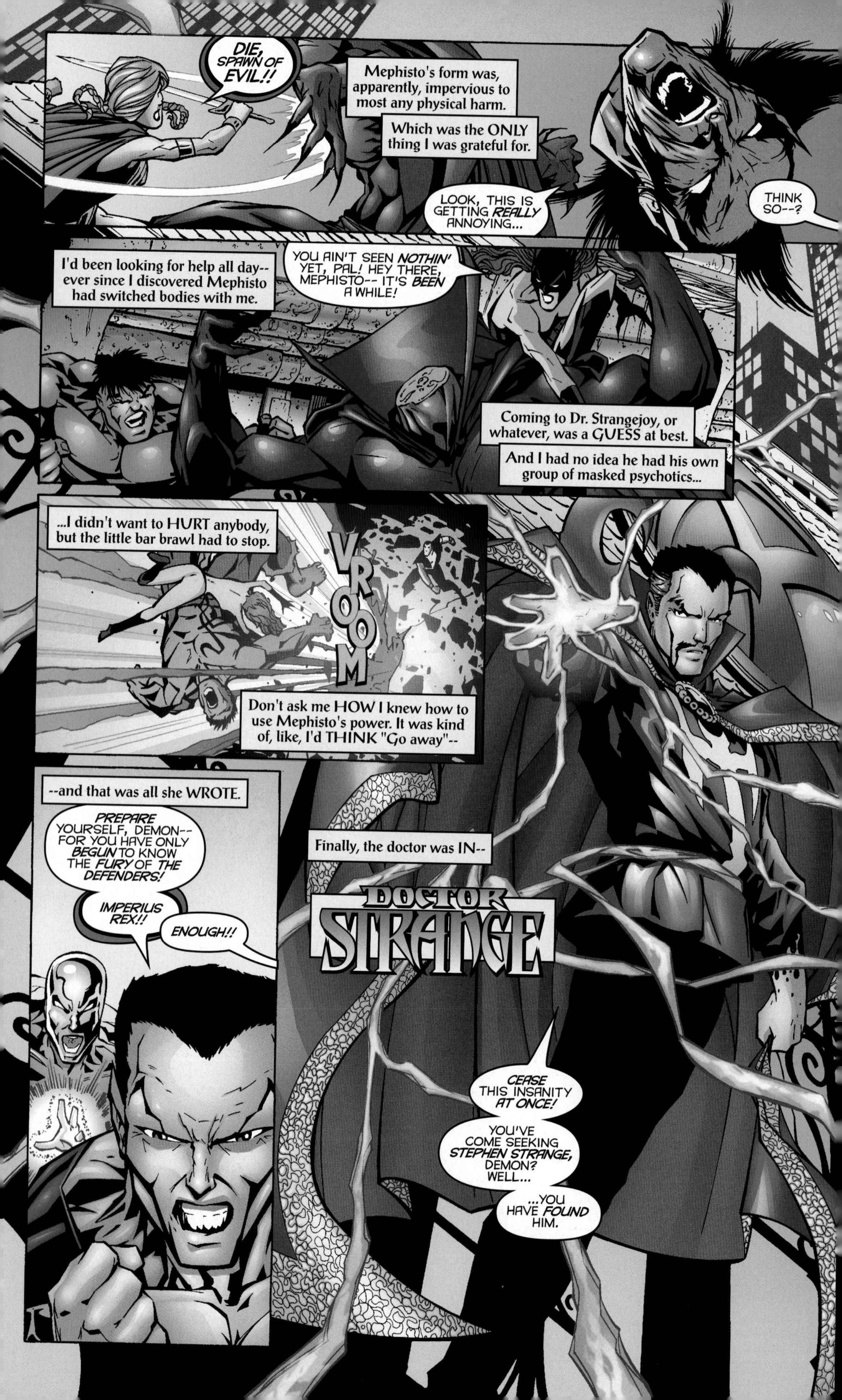

DIE, SPAWN OF EVIL!!
Mephisto's form was, apparently, impervious to most any physical harm.
Which was the ONLY thing I was grateful for.
LOOK, THIS IS GETTING REALLY ANNOYING...
THINK SO--?
I'd been looking for help all day--ever since I discovered Mephisto had switched bodies with me.
YOU AIN'T SEEN NOTHIN' YET, PAL! HEY THERE, MEPHISTO-- IT'S BEEN A WHILE!
Coming to Dr. Strangejoy, or whatever, was a GUESS at best.
And I had no idea he had his own group of masked psychotics...
...I didn't want to HURT anybody, but the little bar brawl had to stop.
VROOM
Don't ask me HOW I knew how to use Mephisto's power. It was kind of, like, I'd THINK "Go away"--
--and that was all she WROTE.
PREPARE YOURSELF, DEMON-- FOR YOU HAVE ONLY BEGUN TO KNOW THE FURY OF THE DEFENDERS!
IMPERIUS REX!!
ENOUGH!!
Finally, the doctor was IN--
DOCTOR STRANGE
CEASE THIS INSANITY AT ONCE!
YOU'VE COME SEEKING STEPHEN STRANGE, DEMON? WELL...
...YOU HAVE FOUND HIM.

AH, THE GOOD OL' DAYS

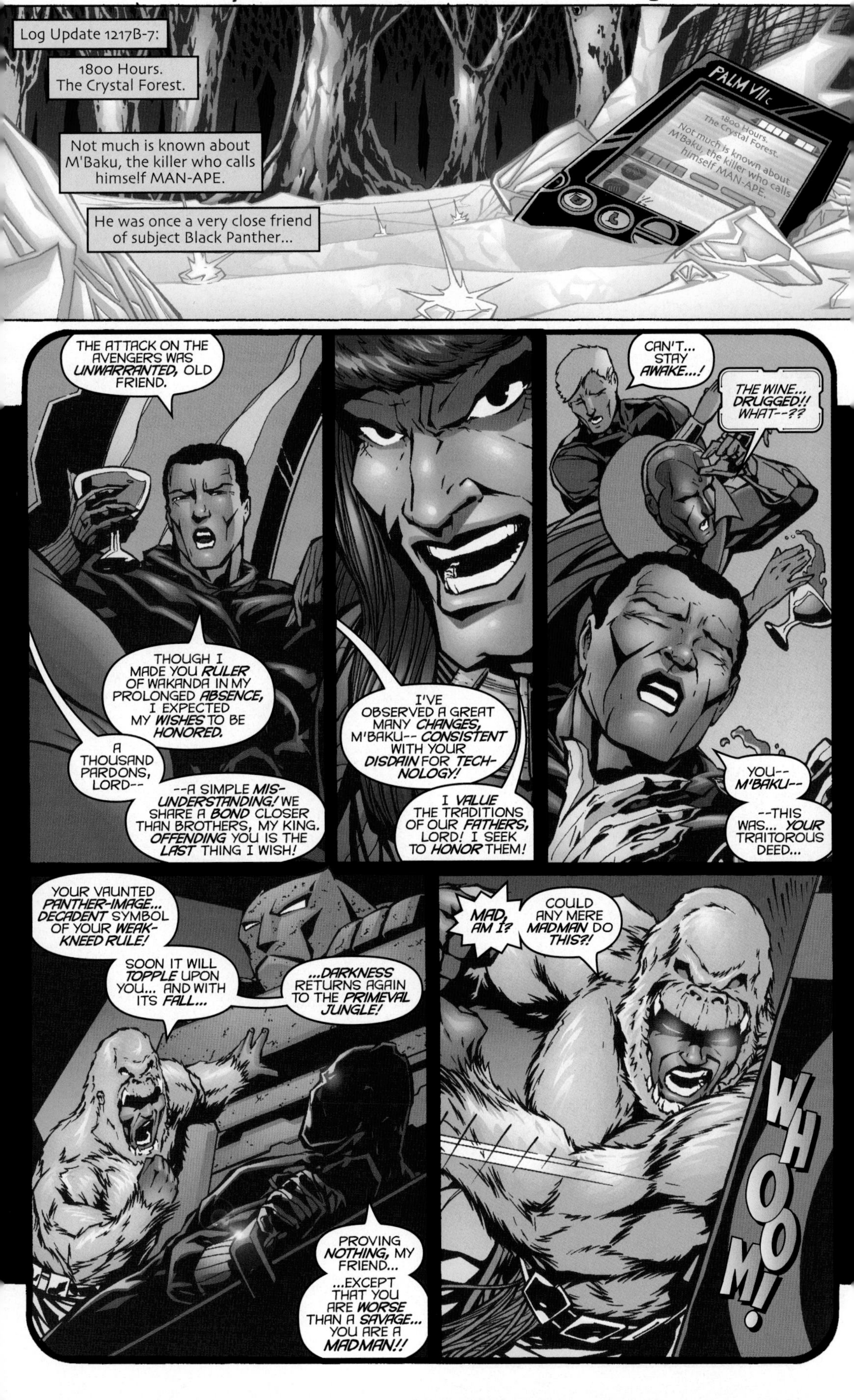

Log Update 1217B-7:
1800 Hours. The Crystal Forest.
Not much is known about M'Baku, the killer who calls himself MAN-APE.
He was once a very close friend of subject Black Panther...
PALM VII
1800 Hours. The Crystal Forest.
Not much is known about M'Baku, the killer who calls himself MAN-APE.
THE ATTACK ON THE AVENGERS WAS UNWARRANTED, OLD FRIEND.
THOUGH I MADE YOU RULER OF WAKANDA IN MY PROLONGED ABSENCE, I EXPECTED MY WISHES TO BE HONORED.
A THOUSAND PARDONS, LORD--
--A SIMPLE MIS-UNDERSTANDING! WE SHARE A BOND CLOSER THAN BROTHERS, MY KING. OFFENDING YOU IS THE LAST THING I WISH!
I'VE OBSERVED A GREAT MANY CHANGES, M'BAKU-- CONSISTENT WITH YOUR DISDAIN FOR TECH-NOLOGY!
I VALUE THE TRADITIONS OF OUR FATHERS, LORD! I SEEK TO HONOR THEM!
CAN'T... STAY AWAKE...!
THE WINE... DRUGGED!! WHAT--??
YOU-- M'BAKU--
--THIS WAS... YOUR TRAITOROUS DEED...
YOUR VAUNTED PANTHER-IMAGE... DECADENT SYMBOL OF YOUR WEAK-KNEED RULE!
SOON IT WILL TOPPLE UPON YOU... AND WITH ITS FALL...
...DARKNESS RETURNS AGAIN TO THE PRIMEVAL JUNGLE!
PROVING NOTHING, MY FRIEND...
...EXCEPT THAT YOU ARE WORSE THAN A SAVAGE... YOU ARE A MADMAN!!
MAD, AM I?
COULD ANY MERE MADMAN DO THIS?!
WHOOOM!

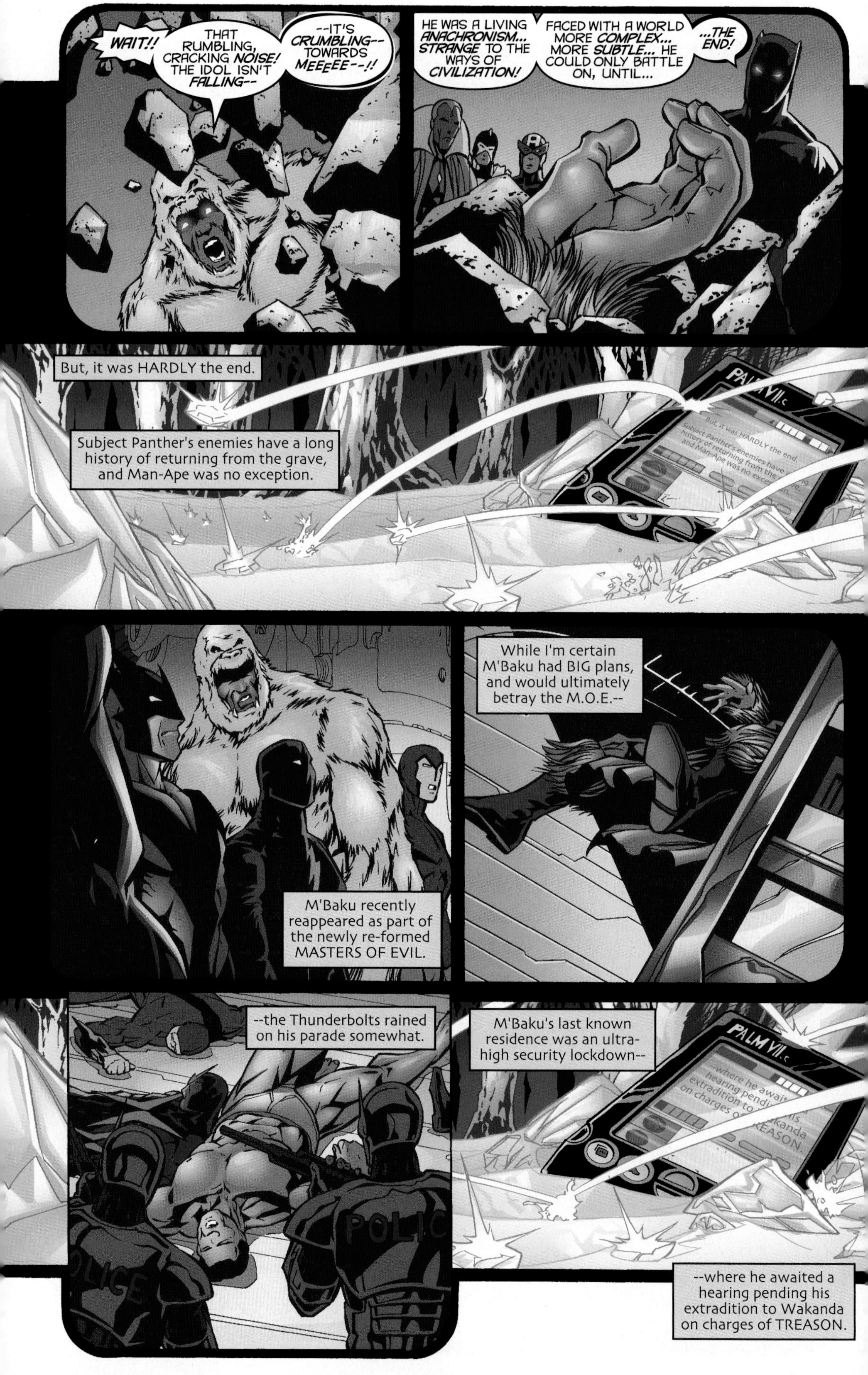
WAIT!!
THAT RUMBLING, CRACKING NOISE! THE IDOL ISN'T FALLING--
--IT'S CRUMBLING-- TOWARDS MEEEEE--!!
HE WAS A LIVING ANACHRONISM... STRANGE TO THE WAYS OF CIVILIZATION!
FACED WITH A WORLD MORE COMPLEX... MORE SUBTLE... HE COULD ONLY BATTLE ON, UNTIL...
...THE END!
But, it was HARDLY the end.
Subject Panther's enemies have a long history of returning from the grave, and Man-Ape was no exception.
PALM VII.c
M'Baku recently reappeared as part of the newly re-formed MASTERS OF EVIL.
While I'm certain M'Baku had BIG plans, and would ultimately betray the M.O.E.--
--the Thunderbolts rained on his parade somewhat.
POLIC
M'Baku's last known residence was an ultra-high security lockdown--
PALM VII.c
--where he awaited a hearing pending his extradition to Wakanda on charges of TREASON.

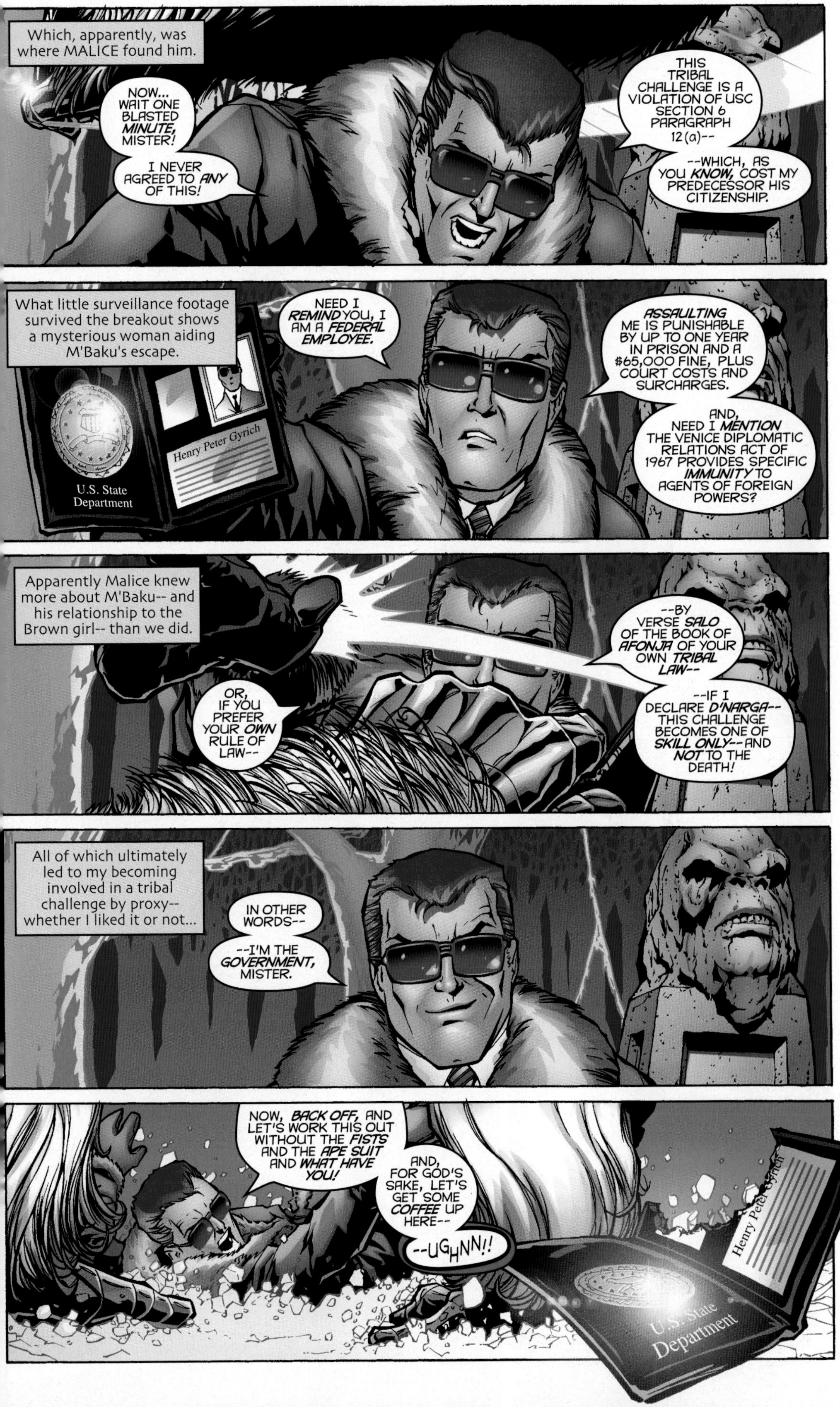

Which, apparently, was where MALICE found him.
NOW... WAIT ONE BLASTED MINUTE, MISTER!
I NEVER AGREED TO ANY OF THIS!
THIS TRIBAL CHALLENGE IS A VIOLATION OF USC SECTION 6 PARAGRAPH 12(a)--
--WHICH, AS YOU KNOW, COST MY PREDECESSOR HIS CITIZENSHIP.
What little surveillance footage survived the breakout shows a mysterious woman aiding M'Baku's escape.
U.S. State Department
Henry Peter Gyrich
NEED I REMIND YOU, I AM A FEDERAL EMPLOYEE.
ASSAULTING ME IS PUNISHABLE BY UP TO ONE YEAR IN PRISON AND A $65,000 FINE, PLUS COURT COSTS AND SURCHARGES.
AND, NEED I MENTION THE VENICE DIPLOMATIC RELATIONS ACT OF 1967 PROVIDES SPECIFIC IMMUNITY TO AGENTS OF FOREIGN POWERS?
Apparently Malice knew more about M'Baku-- and his relationship to the Brown girl-- than we did.
OR, IF YOU PREFER YOUR OWN RULE OF LAW--
--BY VERSE SALO OF THE BOOK OF AFONJA OF YOUR OWN TRIBAL LAW--
--IF I DECLARE D'NARGA-- THIS CHALLENGE BECOMES ONE OF SKILL ONLY--AND NOT TO THE DEATH!
All of which ultimately led to my becoming involved in a tribal challenge by proxy-- whether I liked it or not...
IN OTHER WORDS--
--I'M THE GOVERNMENT, MISTER.
NOW, BACK OFF, AND LET'S WORK THIS OUT WITHOUT THE FISTS AND THE APE SUIT AND WHAT HAVE YOU!
AND, FOR GOD'S SAKE, LET'S GET SOME COFFEE UP HERE--
--UGHNN!!
Henry Peter Gyrich
U.S. State Department

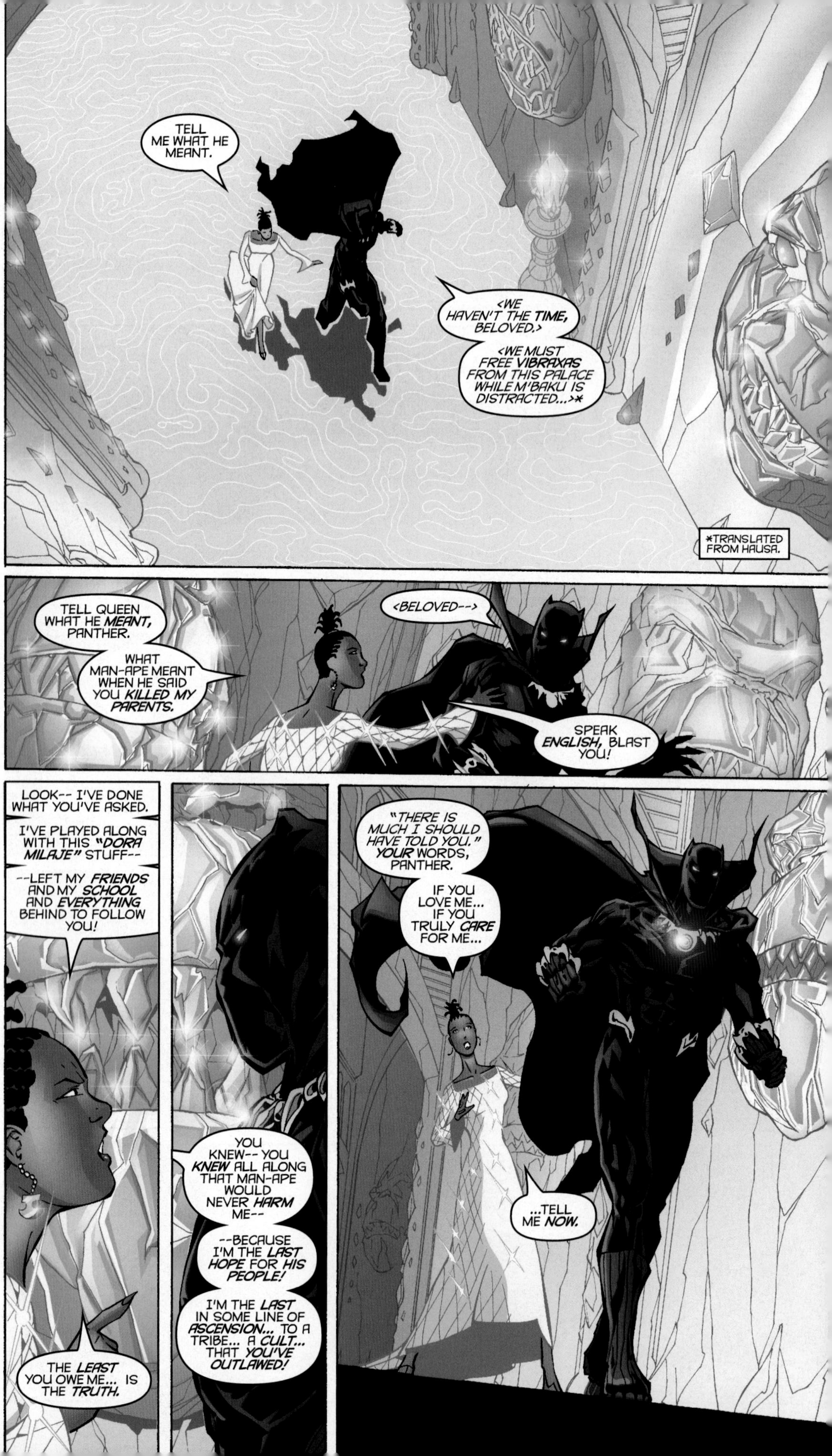
TELL ME WHAT HE MEANT.
<WE HAVEN'T THE TIME, BELOVED.>
<WE MUST FREE VIBRAXAS FROM THIS PALACE WHILE M'BAKU IS DISTRACTED...>*
*TRANSLATED FROM HAUSA.
TELL QUEEN WHAT HE MEANT, PANTHER.
<BELOVED-->
WHAT MAN-APE MEANT WHEN HE SAID YOU KILLED MY PARENTS.
SPEAK ENGLISH, BLAST YOU!
LOOK-- I'VE DONE WHAT YOU'VE ASKED.
I'VE PLAYED ALONG WITH THIS "DORA MILAJE" STUFF--
--LEFT MY FRIENDS AND MY SCHOOL AND EVERYTHING BEHIND TO FOLLOW YOU!
THE LEAST YOU OWE ME... IS THE TRUTH.
YOU KNEW-- YOU KNEW ALL ALONG THAT MAN-APE WOULD NEVER HARM ME--
--BECAUSE I'M THE LAST HOPE FOR HIS PEOPLE!
I'M THE LAST IN SOME LINE OF ASCENSION... TO A TRIBE... A CULT... THAT YOU'VE OUTLAWED!
"THERE IS MUCH I SHOULD HAVE TOLD YOU." YOUR WORDS, PANTHER.
IF YOU LOVE ME... IF YOU TRULY CARE FOR ME...
...TELL ME NOW.

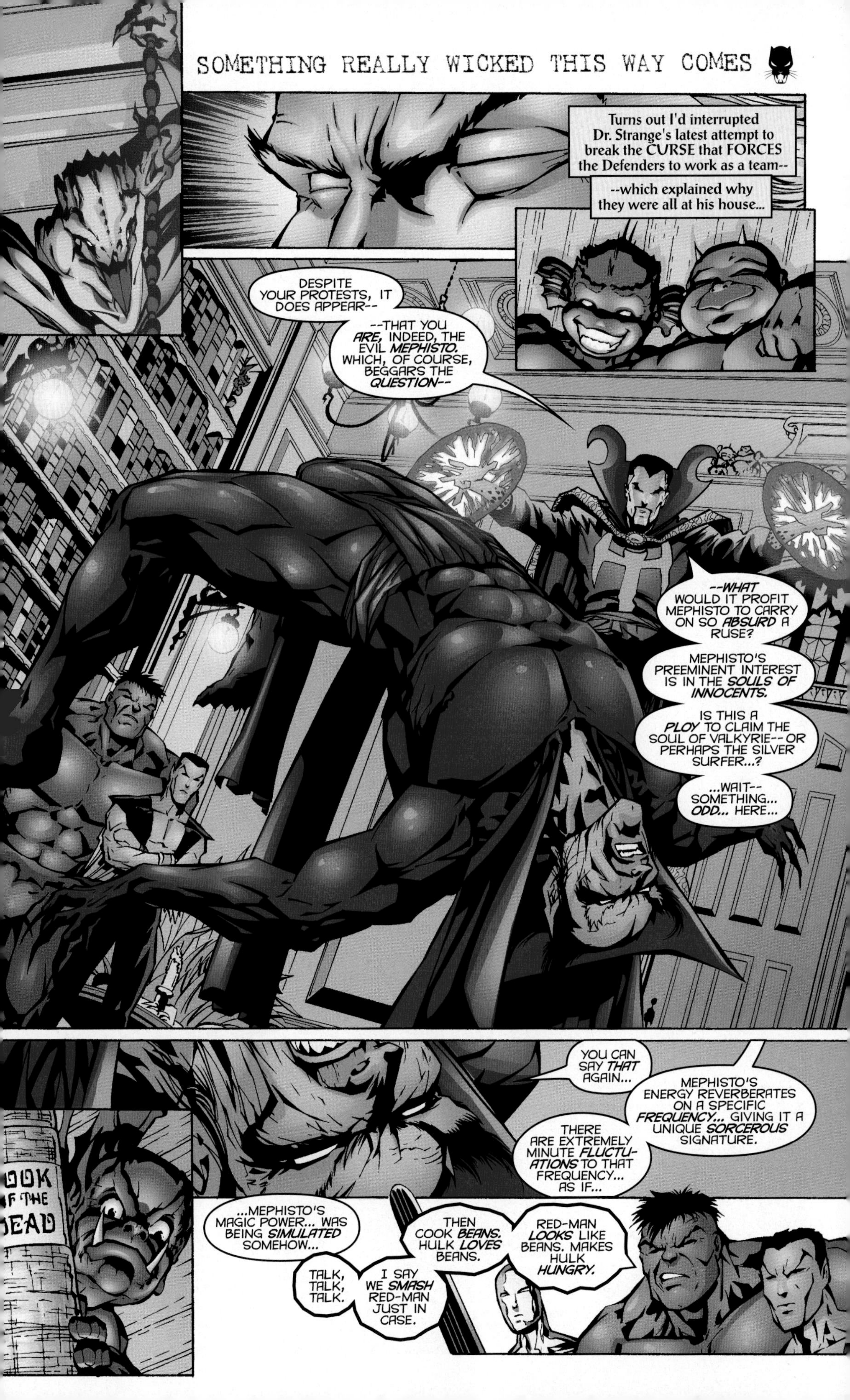
SOMETHING REALLY WICKED THIS WAY COMES
Turns out I'd interrupted Dr. Strange's latest attempt to break the CURSE that FORCES the Defenders to work as a team--
--which explained why they were all at his house...
DESPITE YOUR PROTESTS, IT DOES APPEAR--
--THAT YOU ARE, INDEED, THE EVIL MEPHISTO. WHICH, OF COURSE, BEGGARS THE QUESTION--
--WHAT WOULD IT PROFIT MEPHISTO TO CARRY ON SO ABSURD A RUSE?
MEPHISTO'S PREEMINENT INTEREST IS IN THE SOULS OF INNOCENTS.
IS THIS A PLOY TO CLAIM THE SOUL OF VALKYRIE--OR PERHAPS THE SILVER SURFER...?
...WAIT-- SOMETHING... ODD... HERE...
YOU CAN SAY THAT AGAIN...
MEPHISTO'S ENERGY REVERBERATES ON A SPECIFIC FREQUENCY... GIVING IT A UNIQUE SORCEROUS SIGNATURE.
THERE ARE EXTREMELY MINUTE FLUCTUATIONS TO THAT FREQUENCY... AS IF...
...MEPHISTO'S MAGIC POWER... WAS BEING SIMULATED SOMEHOW...
TALK, TALK, TALK.
I SAY WE SMASH RED-MAN JUST IN CASE.
THEN COOK BEANS. HULK LOVES BEANS.
RED-MAN LOOKS LIKE BEANS. MAKES HULK HUNGRY.

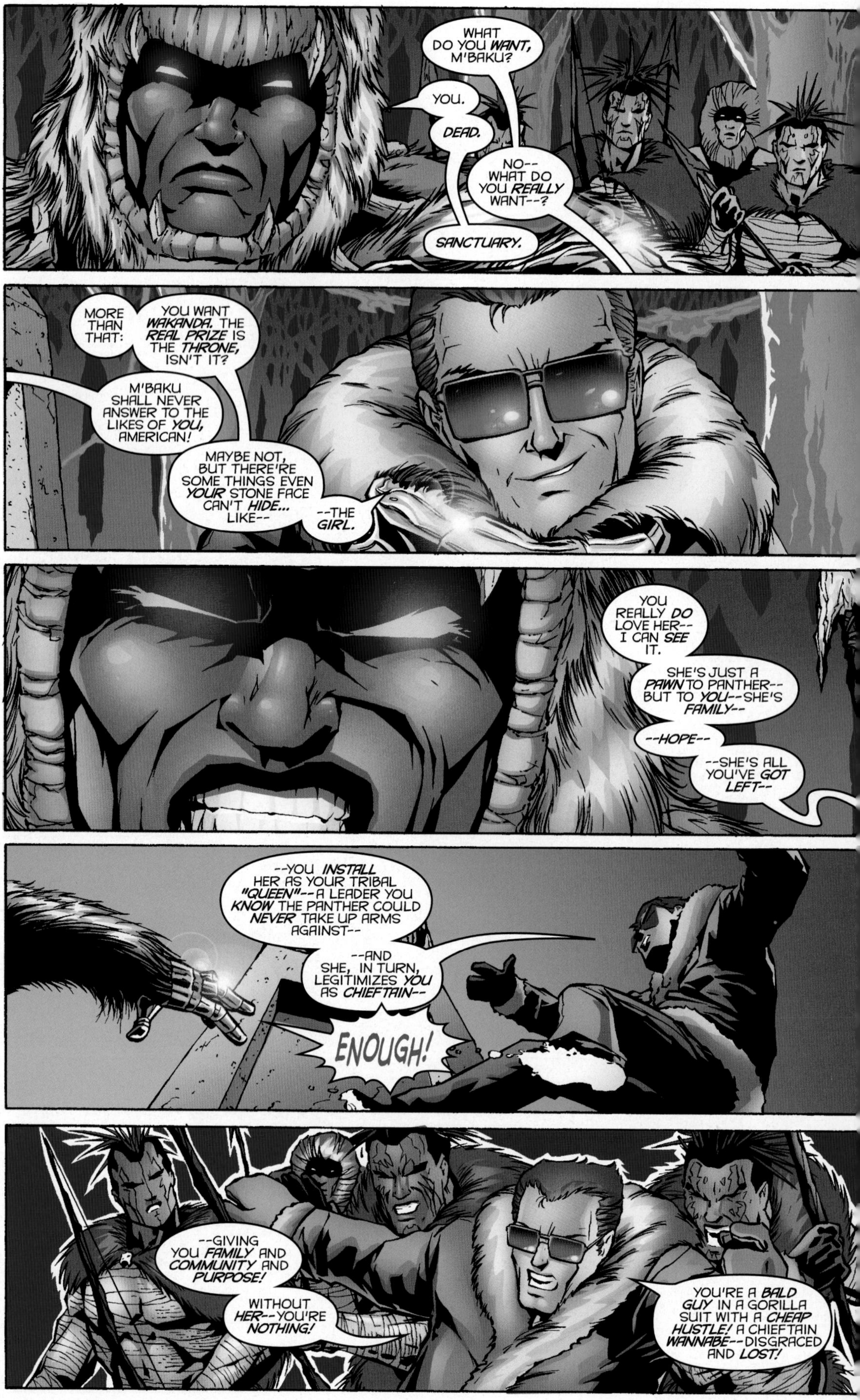

WHAT DO YOU WANT, M'BAKU?
YOU.
DEAD.
NO-- WHAT DO YOU REALLY WANT--?
SANCTUARY.
MORE THAN THAT:
YOU WANT WAKANDA. THE REAL PRIZE IS THE THRONE, ISN'T IT?
M'BAKU SHALL NEVER ANSWER TO THE LIKES OF YOU, AMERICAN!
MAYBE NOT, BUT THERE'RE SOME THINGS EVEN YOUR STONE FACE CAN'T HIDE... LIKE--
--THE GIRL.
YOU REALLY DO LOVE HER-- I CAN SEE IT.
SHE'S JUST A PAWN TO PANTHER-- BUT TO YOU--SHE'S FAMILY--
--HOPE--
--SHE'S ALL YOU'VE GOT LEFT--
--YOU INSTALL HER AS YOUR TRIBAL "QUEEN"--A LEADER YOU KNOW THE PANTHER COULD NEVER TAKE UP ARMS AGAINST--
--AND SHE, IN TURN, LEGITIMIZES YOU AS CHIEFTAIN--
ENOUGH!
--GIVING YOU FAMILY AND COMMUNITY AND PURPOSE!
WITHOUT HER--YOU'RE NOTHING!
YOU'RE A BALD GUY IN A GORILLA SUIT WITH A CHEAP HUSTLE! A CHIEFTAIN WANNABE--DISGRACED AND LOST!

DAMOLA'S KING

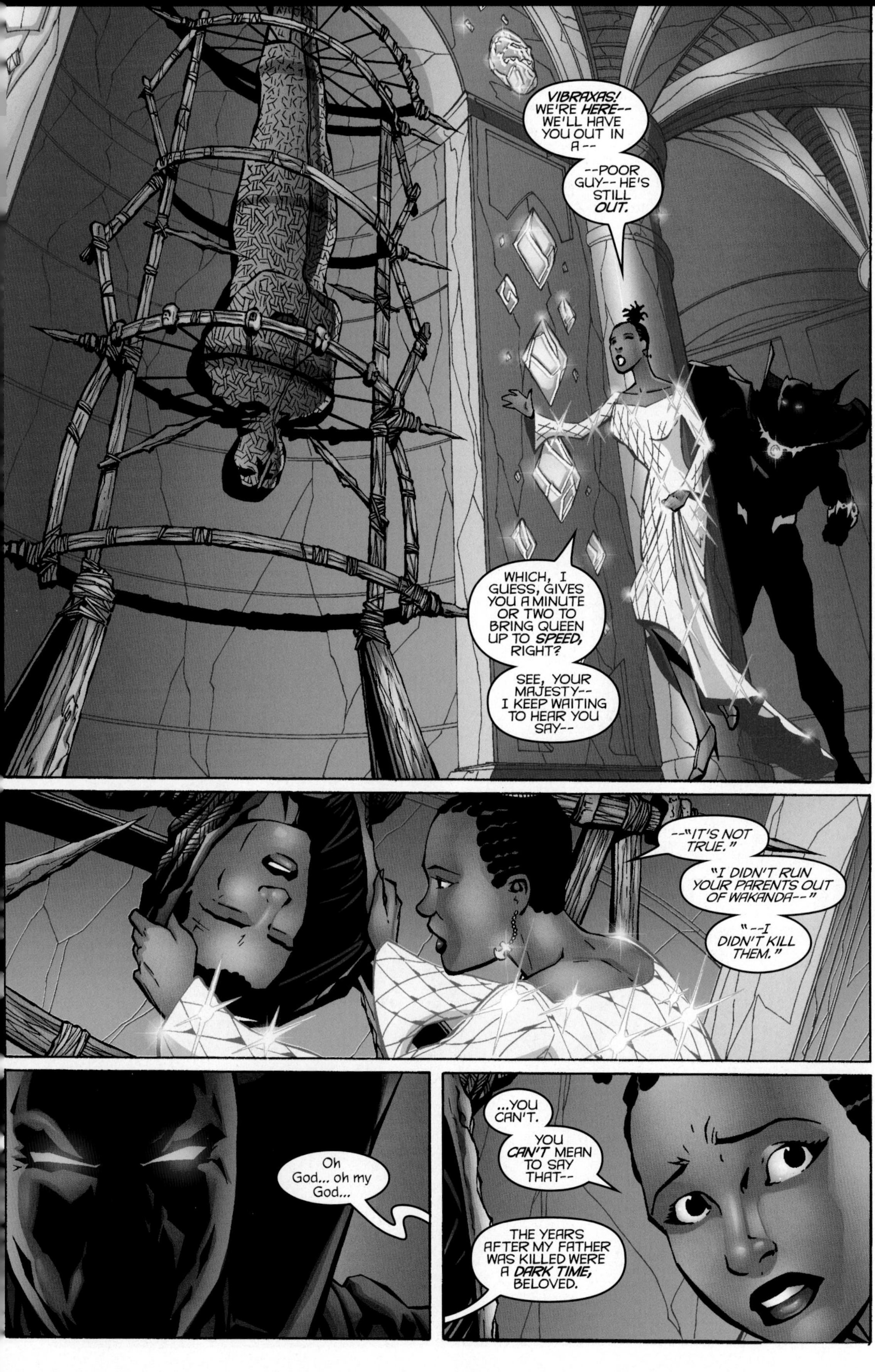
VIBRAXAS! WE'RE HERE-- WE'LL HAVE YOU OUT IN A--
--POOR GUY-- HE'S STILL OUT.
WHICH, I GUESS, GIVES YOU A MINUTE OR TWO TO BRING QUEEN UP TO SPEED, RIGHT?
SEE, YOUR MAJESTY-- I KEEP WAITING TO HEAR YOU SAY--
--"IT'S NOT TRUE."
"I DIDN'T RUN YOUR PARENTS OUT OF WAKANDA--"
"--I DIDN'T KILL THEM."
Oh God... oh my God...
...YOU CAN'T.
YOU CAN'T MEAN TO SAY THAT--
THE YEARS AFTER MY FATHER WAS KILLED WERE A DARK TIME, BELOVED.

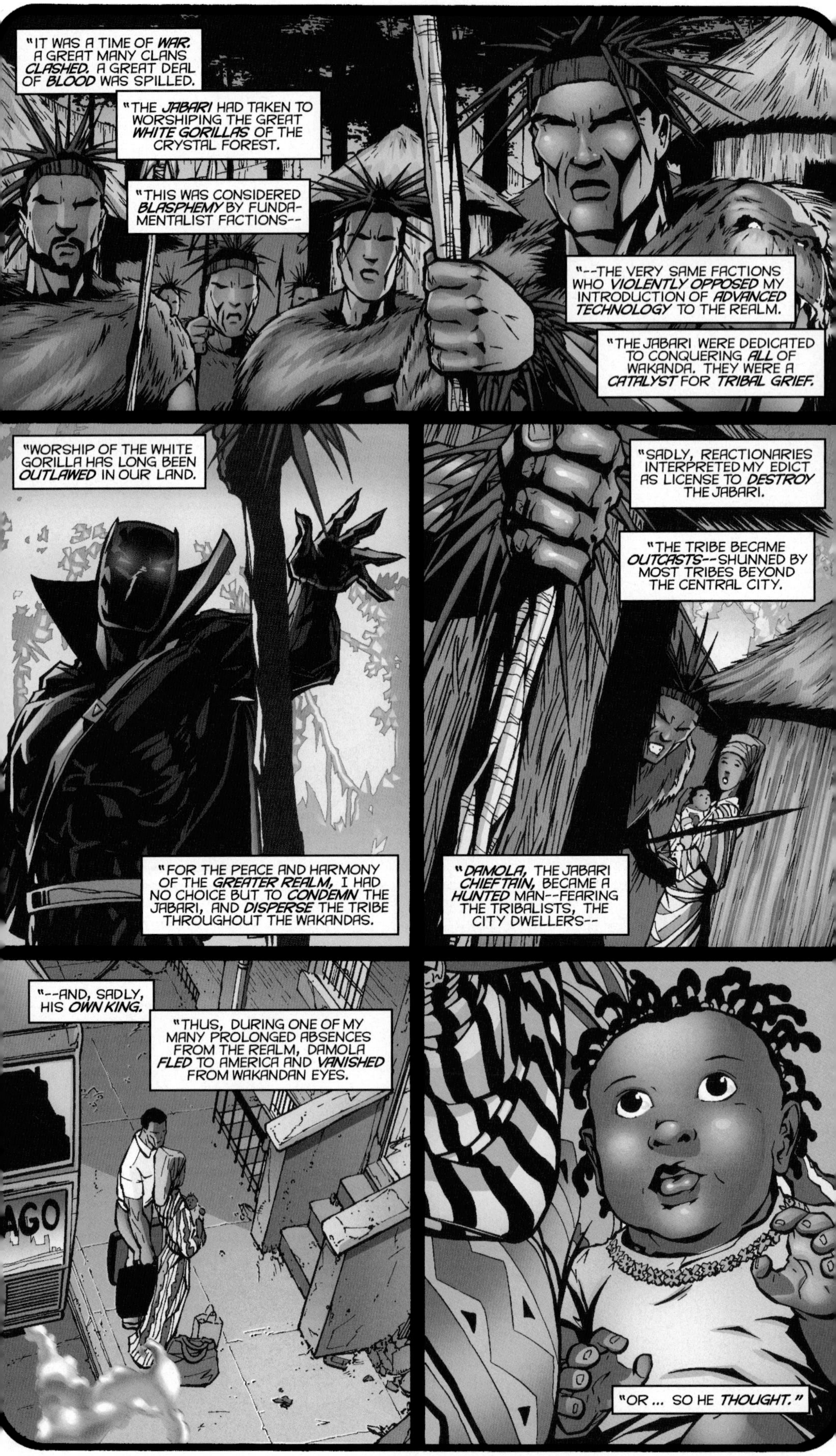
"IT WAS A TIME OF WAR. A GREAT MANY CLANS CLASHED. A GREAT DEAL OF BLOOD WAS SPILLED.
"THE JABARI HAD TAKEN TO WORSHIPING THE GREAT WHITE GORILLAS OF THE CRYSTAL FOREST.
"THIS WAS CONSIDERED BLASPHEMY BY FUNDAMENTALIST FACTIONS--
"--THE VERY SAME FACTIONS WHO VIOLENTLY OPPOSED MY INTRODUCTION OF ADVANCED TECHNOLOGY TO THE REALM.
"THE JABARI WERE DEDICATED TO CONQUERING ALL OF WAKANDA. THEY WERE A CATALYST FOR TRIBAL GRIEF.
"WORSHIP OF THE WHITE GORILLA HAS LONG BEEN OUTLAWED IN OUR LAND.
"FOR THE PEACE AND HARMONY OF THE GREATER REALM, I HAD NO CHOICE BUT TO CONDEMN THE JABARI, AND DISPERSE THE TRIBE THROUGHOUT THE WAKANDAS.
"SADLY, REACTIONARIES INTERPRETED MY EDICT AS LICENSE TO DESTROY THE JABARI.
"THE TRIBE BECAME OUTCASTS--SHUNNED BY MOST TRIBES BEYOND THE CENTRAL CITY.
"DAMOLA, THE JABARI CHIEFTAIN, BECAME A HUNTED MAN--FEARING THE TRIBALISTS, THE CITY DWELLERS--
"--AND, SADLY, HIS OWN KING.
"THUS, DURING ONE OF MY MANY PROLONGED ABSENCES FROM THE REALM, DAMOLA FLED TO AMERICA AND VANISHED FROM WAKANDAN EYES.
AGO
"OR ... SO HE THOUGHT."

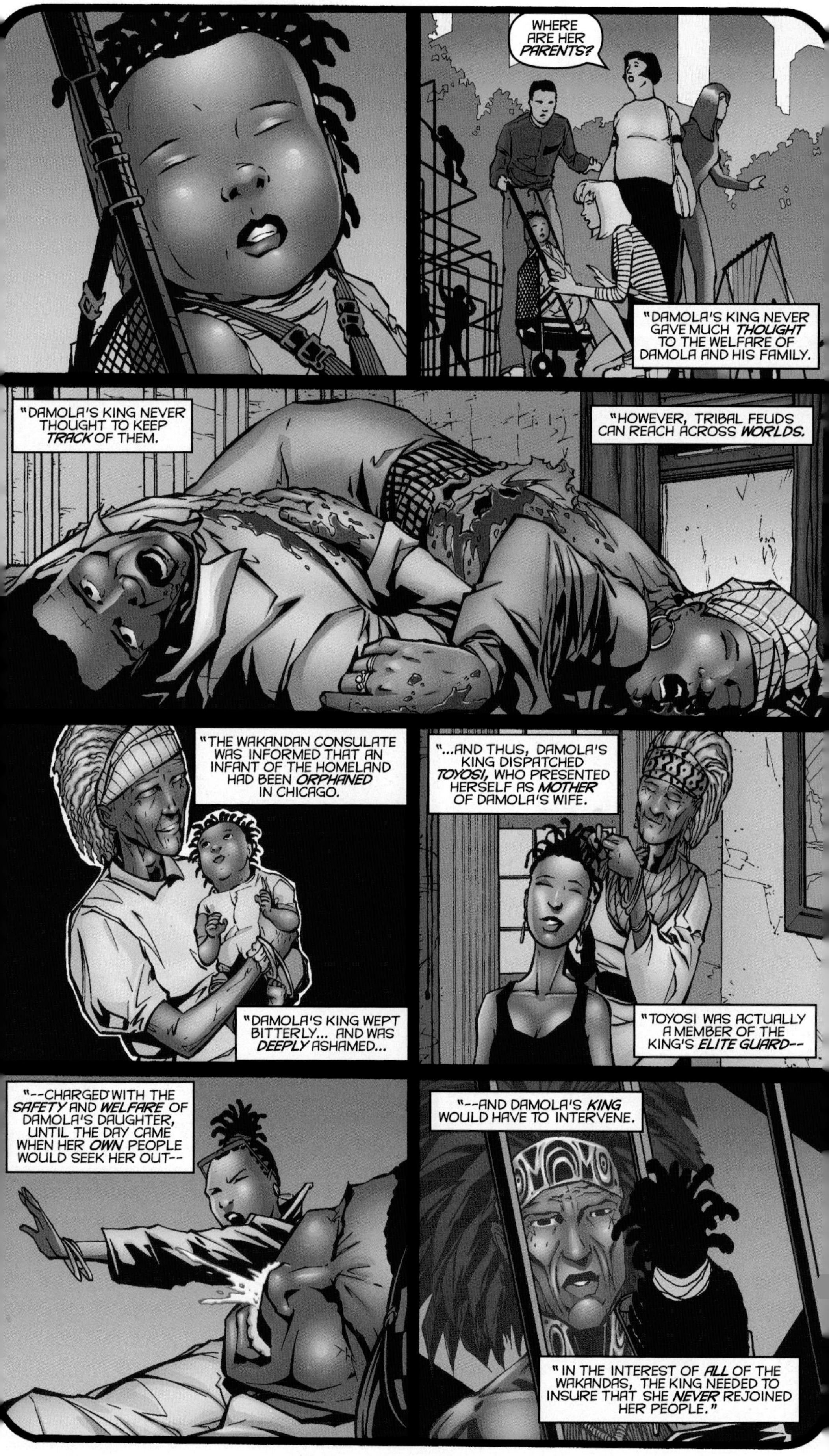

WHERE ARE HER PARENTS?
"DAMOLA'S KING NEVER GAVE MUCH THOUGHT TO THE WELFARE OF DAMOLA AND HIS FAMILY.
"DAMOLA'S KING NEVER THOUGHT TO KEEP TRACK OF THEM.
"HOWEVER, TRIBAL FEUDS CAN REACH ACROSS WORLDS.
"THE WAKANDAN CONSULATE WAS INFORMED THAT AN INFANT OF THE HOMELAND HAD BEEN ORPHANED IN CHICAGO.
"DAMOLA'S KING WEPT BITTERLY... AND WAS DEEPLY ASHAMED...
"...AND THUS, DAMOLA'S KING DISPATCHED TOYOSI, WHO PRESENTED HERSELF AS MOTHER OF DAMOLA'S WIFE.
"TOYOSI WAS ACTUALLY A MEMBER OF THE KING'S ELITE GUARD--
"--CHARGED WITH THE SAFETY AND WELFARE OF DAMOLA'S DAUGHTER, UNTIL THE DAY CAME WHEN HER OWN PEOPLE WOULD SEEK HER OUT--
"--AND DAMOLA'S KING WOULD HAVE TO INTERVENE.
"IN THE INTEREST OF ALL OF THE WAKANDAS, THE KING NEEDED TO INSURE THAT SHE NEVER REJOINED HER PEOPLE."

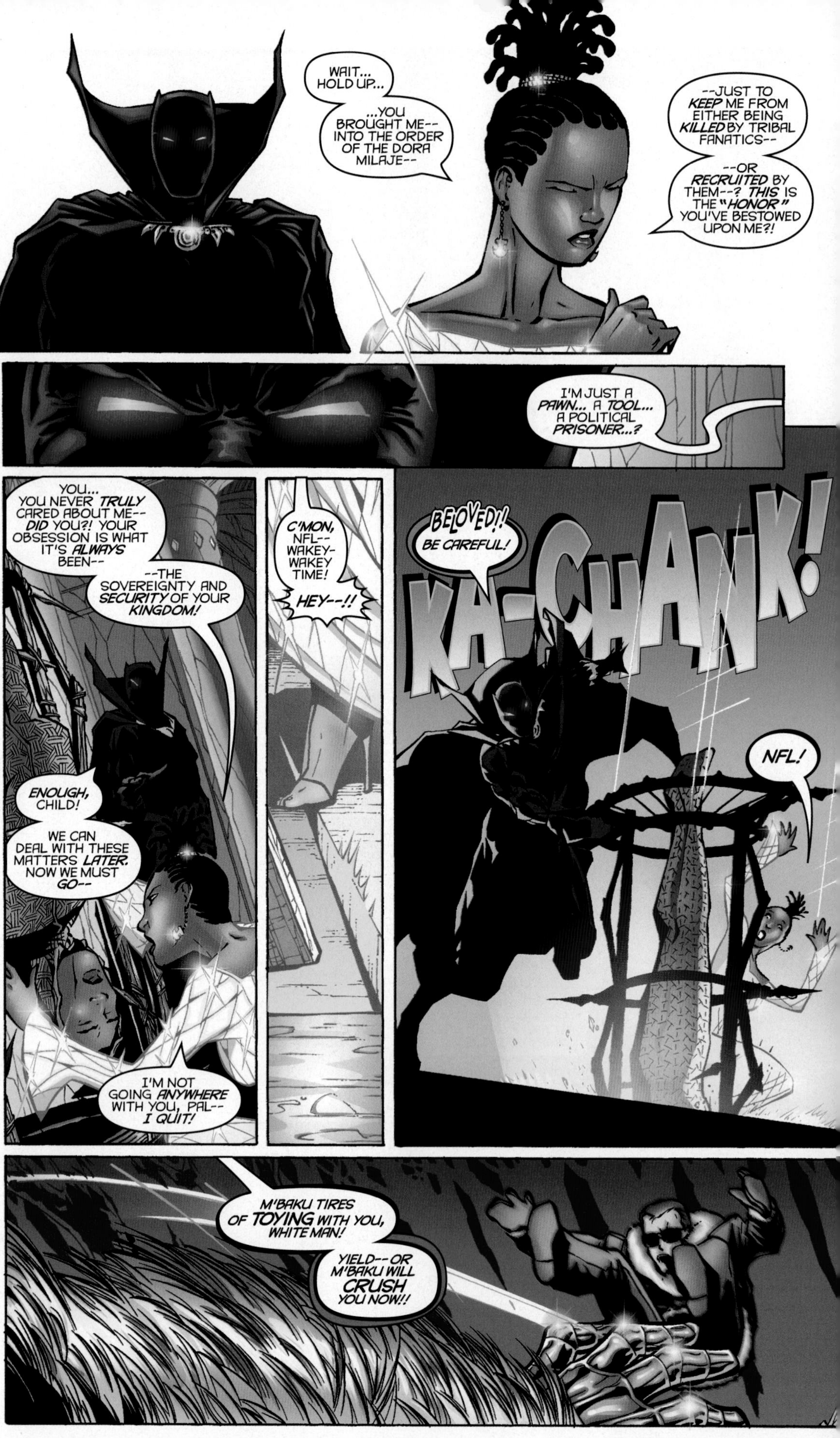
WAIT... HOLD UP...
...YOU BROUGHT ME-- INTO THE ORDER OF THE DORA MILAJE--
--JUST TO KEEP ME FROM EITHER BEING KILLED BY TRIBAL FANATICS--
--OR RECRUITED BY THEM--? THIS IS THE "HONOR" YOU'VE BESTOWED UPON ME?!
I'M JUST A PAWN... A TOOL... A POLITICAL PRISONER...?
YOU... YOU NEVER TRULY CARED ABOUT ME-- DID YOU?! YOUR OBSESSION IS WHAT IT'S ALWAYS BEEN--
--THE SOVEREIGNTY AND SECURITY OF YOUR KINGDOM!
ENOUGH, CHILD!
WE CAN DEAL WITH THESE MATTERS LATER. NOW WE MUST GO--
I'M NOT GOING ANYWHERE WITH YOU, PAL-- I QUIT!
C'MON, NFL-- WAKEY-WAKEY TIME!
HEY--!!
BELOVED!! BE CAREFUL!
KA-CHANK!
NFL!
M'BAKU TIRES OF TOYING WITH YOU, WHITE MAN!
YIELD--OR M'BAKU WILL CRUSH YOU NOW!!

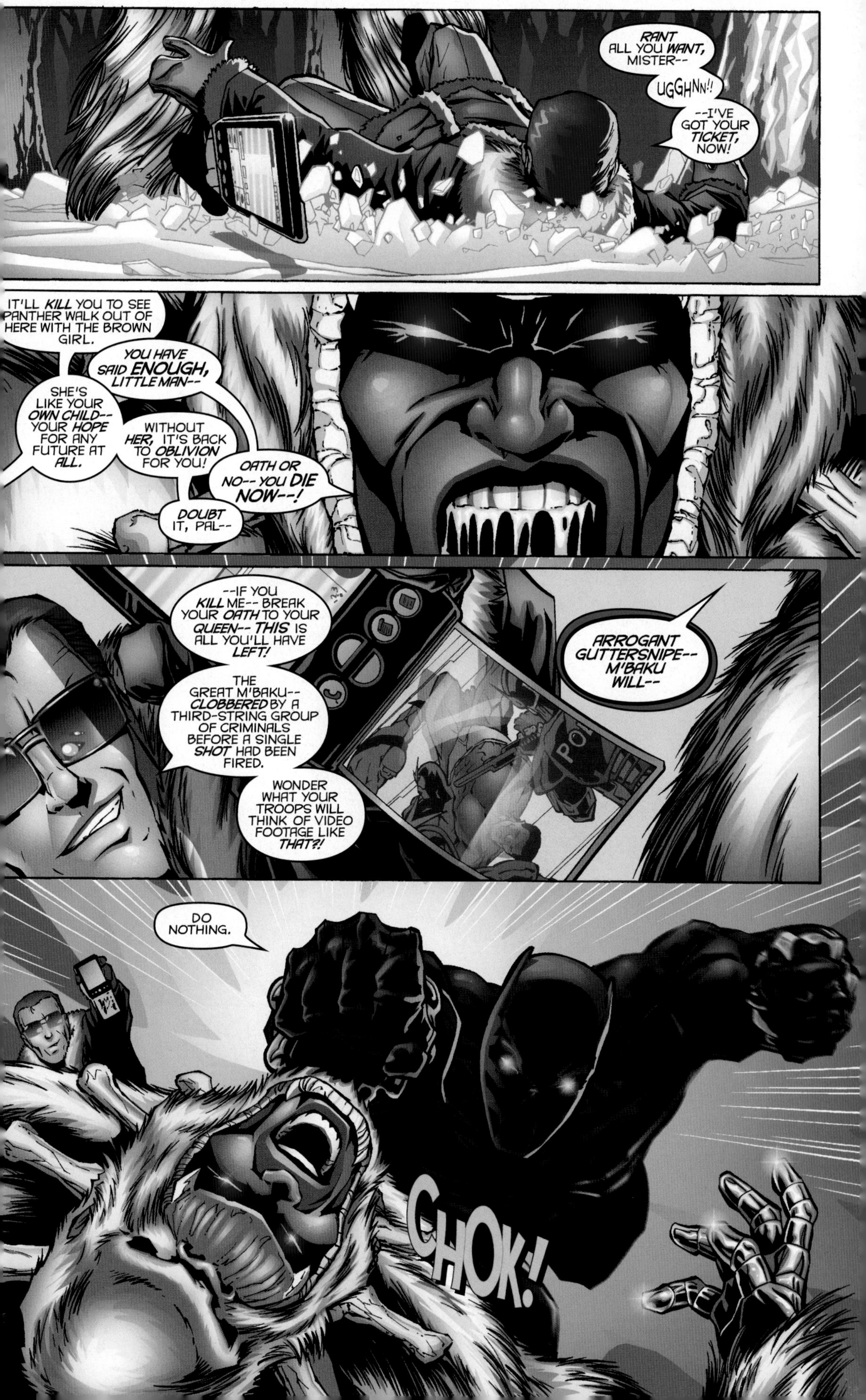
RANT ALL YOU WANT, MISTER--
UGGHNN!!
--I'VE GOT YOUR TICKET, NOW!
IT'LL KILL YOU TO SEE PANTHER WALK OUT OF HERE WITH THE BROWN GIRL.
YOU HAVE SAID ENOUGH, LITTLE MAN--
SHE'S LIKE YOUR OWN CHILD-- YOUR HOPE FOR ANY FUTURE AT ALL.
WITHOUT HER, IT'S BACK TO OBLIVION FOR YOU!
OATH OR NO-- YOU DIE NOW--!
DOUBT IT, PAL--
--IF YOU KILL ME-- BREAK YOUR OATH TO YOUR QUEEN-- THIS IS ALL YOU'LL HAVE LEFT!
THE GREAT M'BAKU-- CLOBBERED BY A THIRD-STRING GROUP OF CRIMINALS BEFORE A SINGLE SHOT HAD BEEN FIRED.
WONDER WHAT YOUR TROOPS WILL THINK OF VIDEO FOOTAGE LIKE THAT?!
ARROGANT GUTTERSNIPE-- M'BAKU WILL--
DO NOTHING.
CHOK!

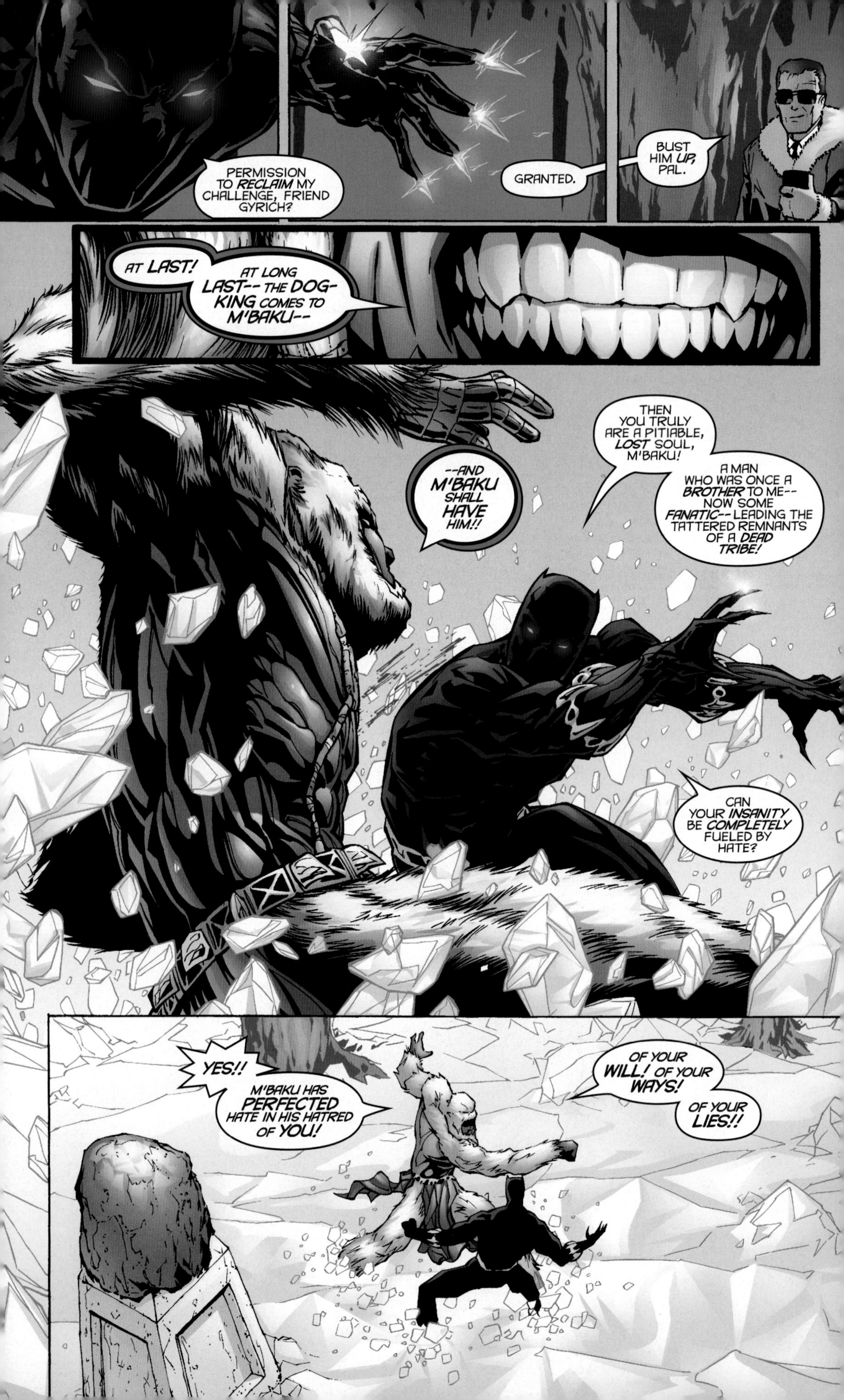
PERMISSION TO RECLAIM MY CHALLENGE, FRIEND GYRICH?
GRANTED.
BUST HIM UP, PAL.
AT LAST!
AT LONG LAST-- THE DOG-KING COMES TO M'BAKU--
--AND M'BAKU SHALL HAVE HIM!!
THEN YOU TRULY ARE A PITIABLE, LOST SOUL, M'BAKU!
A MAN WHO WAS ONCE A BROTHER TO ME-- NOW SOME FANATIC-- LEADING THE TATTERED REMNANTS OF A DEAD TRIBE!
CAN YOUR INSANITY BE COMPLETELY FUELED BY HATE?
YES!!
M'BAKU HAS PERFECTED HATE IN HIS HATRED OF YOU!
OF YOUR WILL! OF YOUR WAYS!
OF YOUR LIES!!

WE DARE YOU TO TELL US WHO THIS IS

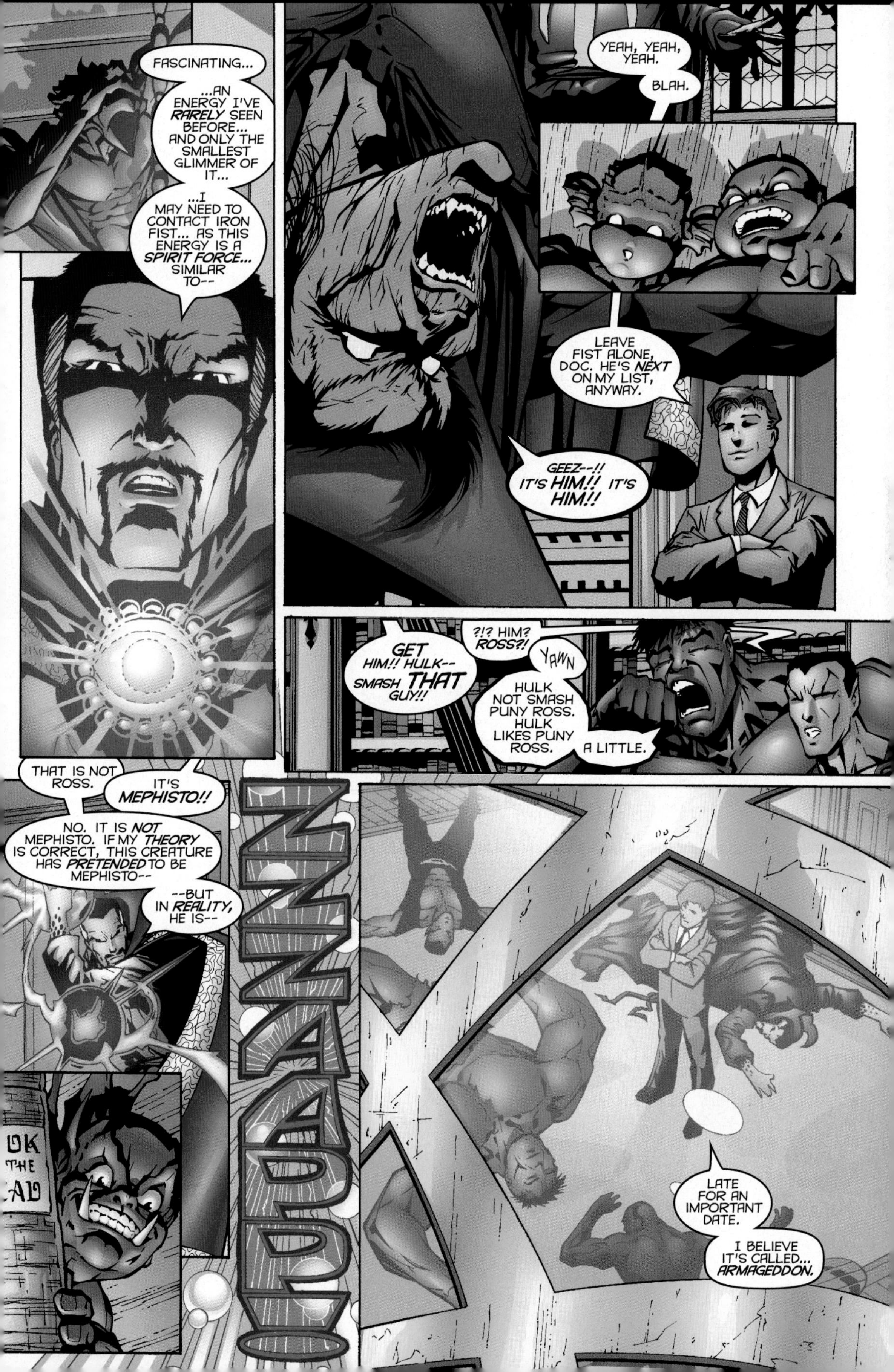

FASCINATING...
...AN ENERGY I'VE RARELY SEEN BEFORE... AND ONLY THE SMALLEST GLIMMER OF IT...
...I MAY NEED TO CONTACT IRON FIST... AS THIS ENERGY IS A SPIRIT FORCE... SIMILAR TO--
YEAH, YEAH, YEAH.
BLAH.
LEAVE FIST ALONE, DOC. HE'S NEXT ON MY LIST, ANYWAY.
GEEZ--!! IT'S HIM!! IT'S HIM!!
GET HIM!! HULK-- SMASH THAT GUY!!
?!? HIM? ROSS?!
YAWN
HULK NOT SMASH PUNY ROSS. HULK LIKES PUNY ROSS.
A LITTLE.
THAT IS NOT ROSS.
IT'S MEPHISTO!!
NO. IT IS NOT MEPHISTO. IF MY THEORY IS CORRECT, THIS CREATURE HAS PRETENDED TO BE MEPHISTO--
--BUT IN REALITY, HE IS--
ZWAAAANNNN
LATE FOR AN IMPORTANT DATE.
I BELIEVE IT'S CALLED... ARMAGEDDON.

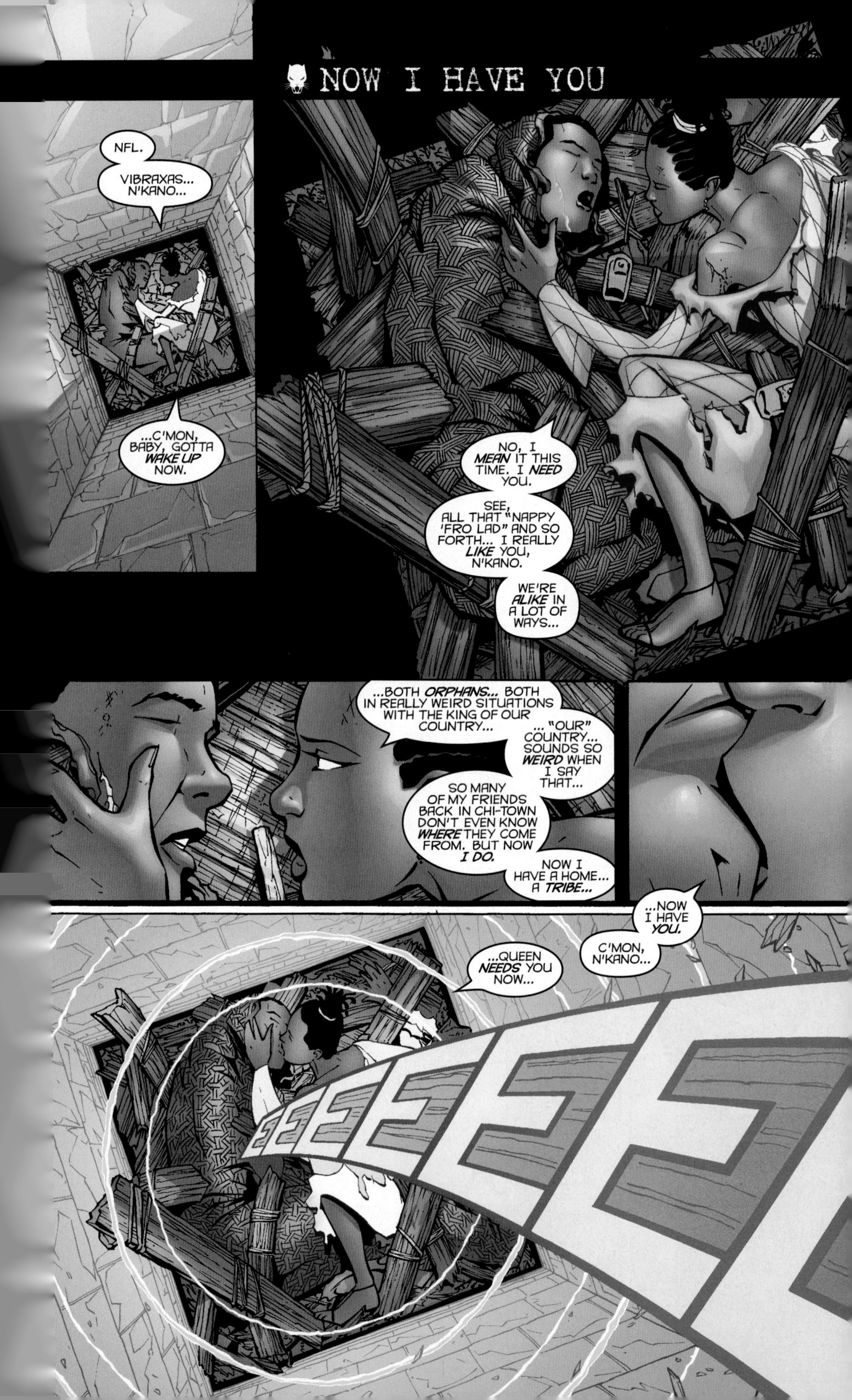
NOW I HAVE YOU
NFL.
VIBRAXAS... N'KANO...
...C'MON, BABY, GOTTA WAKE UP NOW.
NO, I MEAN IT THIS TIME. I NEED YOU.
SEE, ALL THAT "NAPPY 'FRO LAD" AND SO FORTH... I REALLY LIKE YOU, N'KANO.
WE'RE ALIKE IN A LOT OF WAYS...
...BOTH ORPHANS... BOTH IN REALLY WEIRD SITUATIONS WITH THE KING OF OUR COUNTRY...
... "OUR" COUNTRY... SOUNDS SO WEIRD WHEN I SAY THAT...
SO MANY OF MY FRIENDS BACK IN CHI-TOWN DON'T EVEN KNOW WHERE THEY COME FROM. BUT NOW I DO.
NOW I HAVE A HOME... A TRIBE...
...NOW I HAVE YOU.
C'MON, N'KANO...
...QUEEN NEEDS YOU NOW...
EEEEEE

YIELD, DOG-KING!

YOU HAVE **NEVER** DEFEATED M'BAKU BEFORE!

YIELD AND **LIVE!**

IN THE NAME OF THE **FRIENDSHIP** WE ONCE SHARED!

YIELD AND WE JABARI WILL **SECEDE** FROM WAKANDA--

--THIS **LAND** YOU HAVE CON-**DEMNED**--

--AS OUR **OWN** KING-DOM!

WITH M'BAKU AS **KING?!**

WHICH WILL ONLY ENCOURAGE THE **NEXT** CHIEFTAIN TO CHALLENGE MY **THRONE**--

--**SPLINTERING** THE REALM INTO DOZENS OF **WARRING** FACTIONS?!

AND HOW **LONG** BEFORE YOU MASS AN **ARMY** FROM THESE LANDS?

IT'S WAR **NOW**, YOU FOOL!

YOUR SABER-RATTLING IN Q'NOMA VALLEY HAS **SEEN** TO THAT.

LEAVE THIS PLACE. LEAVE OUR **QUEEN**--

--AND LEAVE YOUR **DARKEST SECRET** INTACT IN THE **BARGAIN!**

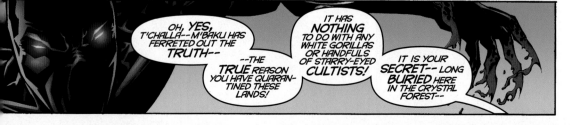

OH, YES, T'CHALLA--M'BAKU HAS FERRETED OUT THE **TRUTH**--

--THE **TRUE** REASON YOU HAVE QUARAN-TINED THESE LANDS!

IT HAS **NOTHING** TO DO WITH ANY **WHITE GORILLAS** OR HANDFULS OF **STARRY-EYED CULTISTS!**

IT IS YOUR **SECRET**-- LONG **BURIED** HERE IN THE CRYSTAL FOREST--

--THAT CAN TOPPLE YOUR KINGDOM ENTIRE!

YIELD, AND HAVE MY OATH TO PROTECT THE REALM AT ALL COSTS!

SAVE YOUR THREATS AND YOUR WORTHLESS PLEDGE, DISHONORED ONE!

IT IS YOU AND YOUR FOLLOWERS WHO SHALL YIELD THIS DAY--

--AND BE DRAGGED BACK TO PRISON IN CHAINS!

WE SHALL SEE, DOG-KING--

--WAKANDA'S DESTINY AWAITS!!

SKRTT!

I WARNED YOU--

--I BEGGED YOU-- TO LEAVE US IN PEACE.

AND NOW, EVERYONE WILL HAVE TO PAY THE PRICE--

--OF YOUR DECEIT.

YOU STUBBORN FOOL. YOU'VE KILLED US ALL.

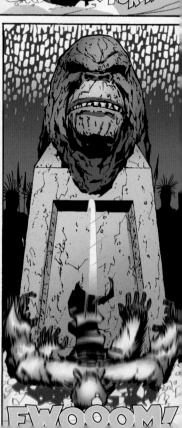

FWOOOM!

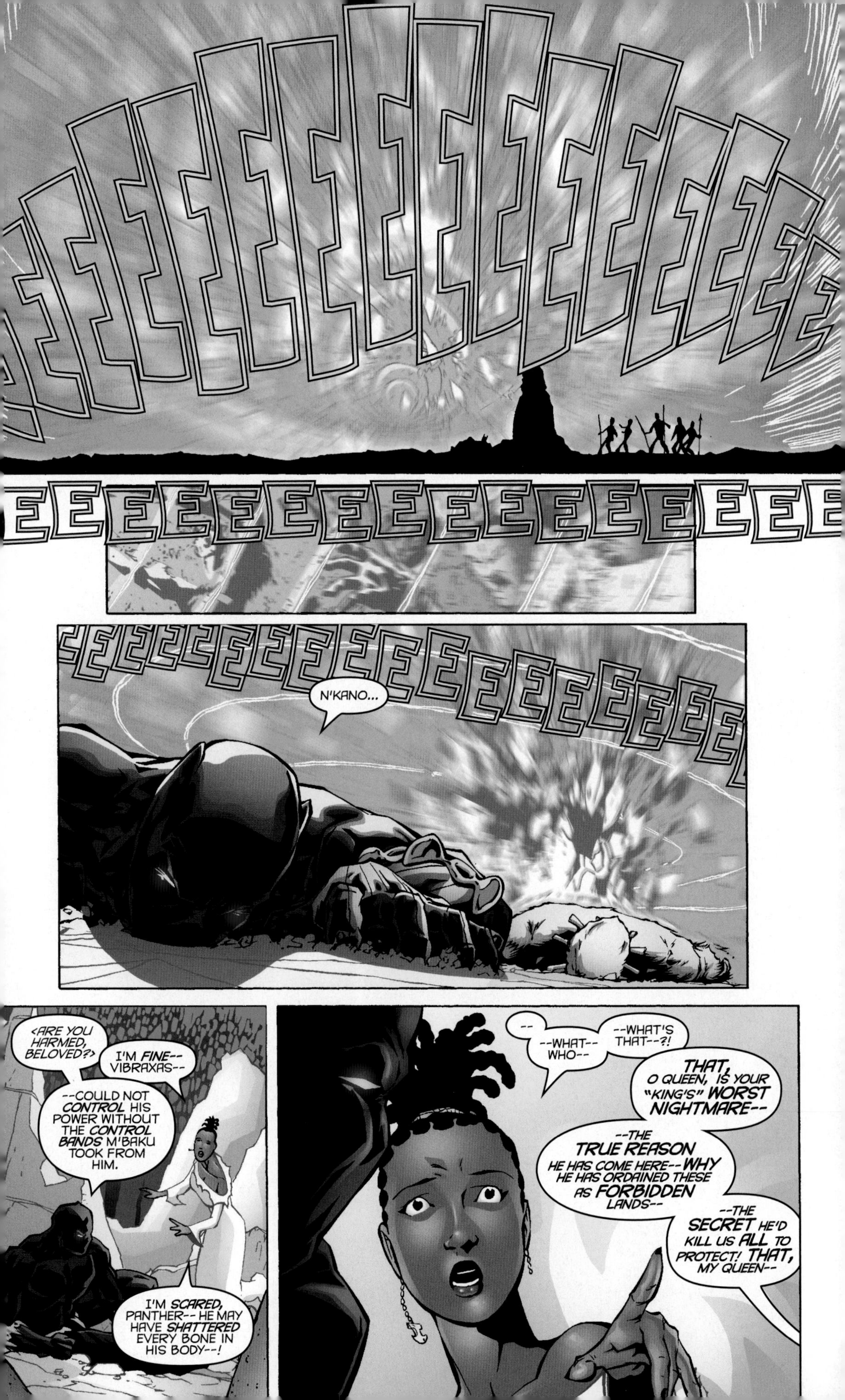

EEEEEEEEEEEEEEE
EEEEEEEEEEEEEEEE
EEEEEEEEEEEEEEEEEEEEEEE
N'KANO...
<ARE YOU HARMED, BELOVED?>
I'M FINE-- VIBRAXAS--
--COULD NOT CONTROL HIS POWER WITHOUT THE CONTROL BANDS M'BAKU TOOK FROM HIM.
I'M SCARED, PANTHER-- HE MAY HAVE SHATTERED EVERY BONE IN HIS BODY--!
--
--WHAT-- WHO--
--WHAT'S THAT--?!
THAT, O QUEEN, IS YOUR "KING'S" WORST NIGHTMARE--
--THE TRUE REASON HE HAS COME HERE--WHY HE HAS ORDAINED THESE AS FORBIDDEN LANDS--
--THE SECRET HE'D KILL US ALL TO PROTECT! THAT, MY QUEEN--

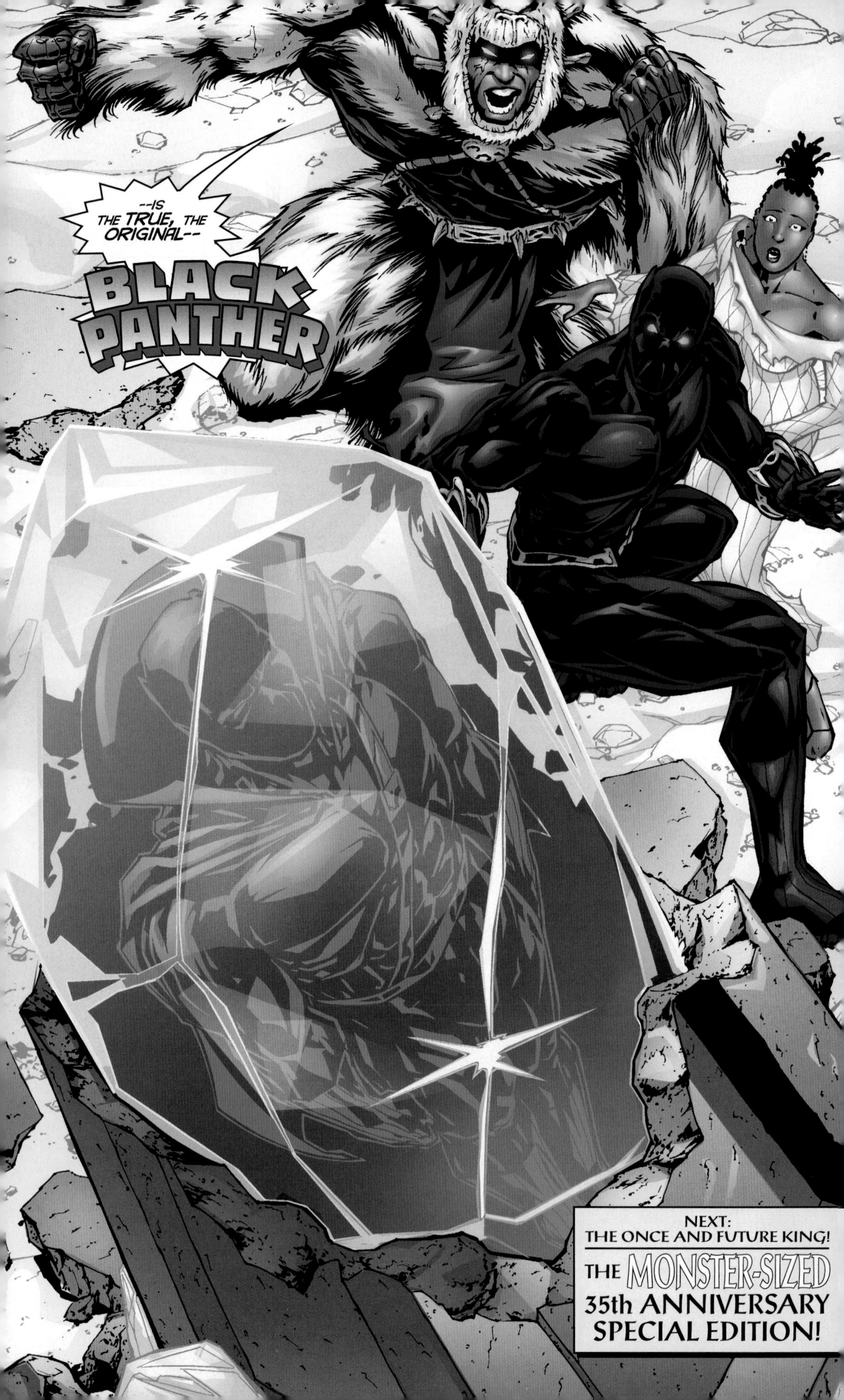
--IS THE TRUE, THE ORIGINAL--
BLACK PANTHER
NEXT:
THE ONCE AND FUTURE KING!
THE MONSTER-SIZED 35th ANNIVERSARY SPECIAL EDITION!

THIS AFTERWORD WAS ORIGINALLY PRINTED IN FRENCH IN PANINI'S 2003 ***MARVEL MONSTER EDITION: PANTHÈRE NOIRE — SÉDUCTION DE L'INNOCENT TPB***, WHICH COLLECTED ***BLACK PANTHER #26-37***. OTHER THAN ALMOND'S WEBSITE, IT HAS NOT APPEARED IN ENGLISH UNTIL NOW.

AFTERWORD
y BOB ALMOND

SO HOW DOES A CREATIVE TEAM FOLLOW-UP ON A YEAR-LONG EPIC LIKE "THE RETURN OF KILLMONGER"?

y producing material for the following year that would eclipse the rmer one and, debatably, be considered by fandom-at-large as the nnacle of the overall three-year run by storytellers Priest, Velluto and mond. But I make it sound so simple. Trust me, it wasn't. That agical, freshman year of our mutual collaboration was one filled with any birth pains.

larvel had decided that Black Panther would continue publication ter its first year debut under the Marvel Knights imprint to one that ould rejoin the general Marvel Universe of characters. Following a ne-up of brilliant yet ever-rotating artists, new editor Ruben Diaz tempted to gain some stability by calling Sal Velluto and myself to in with regular writer Christopher Priest in carrying on with his nconventional, often non-linear but ingenious take on T'Challa and is world. Sal had built himself a reputation as a respected, master raftsman and storyteller since 1989 and his attention to detail is just sane! We'd originally been paired up on Acclaim Comics' Bloodshot 1997 and have remained partners and friends ever since. Sal had arlier been partnered with Priest briefly in '95 on DC's Justice League ask Force. I came to the Panther table as Sal's partner and resident ker but with a lot of impassioned ideas to boot. Labeled the "glue" the team by Sal at one time, I was the one in the group with the verzealous enthusiasm, having grown up since elementary school as "Marvel Zombie." I never lost my passion for this stable of haracters, even after breaking into the industry as a professional ink tist in '92. So the highlight assignments for me were those with the assic characters. As was the case with Black Panther. I would use at knowledge to swiftly advance myself as the team's unofficial searcher and "continuity cop," forwarding Sal comics or scanned nages when he or the color artist were in need of some specific, often oscure, reference and alerting the gang whenever something in the cript was contradicting established history. I took on this position with ide and my teammates respected my assistance, input and ligence. They indulged me and used just about every silly request I ade that it marked this period in my career as one filled with many eative contributions and the fondest of memories.

ut we didn't reach this stage for several months. In fact, Sal and I ad very little correspondence with Priest for the first few issues. uring these inaugural stories Sal and I developed an unconventional yle to execute for the series. But this proved to be counterproductive the recently made change in paper and color separation quality nd we subsequently reverted to our more traditional approach more less by issue 17. We labored to get the title back on schedule, omething that incoming editor Tom Brevoort handily resolved with s. Along with Tom came veteran color artist Steve Oliff which timately improved our palette even though the limits of color parations would tie his hands for some time to come. Communication further developed between us, the office and Priest and the ideas anc inspiration now really began to flow leading to several highlights ir our opening year. But our second year was approaching. While the creative drive was still building, Priest's Killmonger saga was winding down and, with it, the challenge arose about what direction to take next. The health of the book had been in question since Sal and arrived and would remain a question with several false starts regarding cancellation throughout the series. Issue 25, an aftermath to the twelve chapter Killmonger tale, was one of those false starts. We ultimately got the approval from Marvel to proceed, albeit now with a preference for smaller story arcs for the immediate future to limit the risk of the plug being pulled before concluding any given storyline and to make the arcs more palatable to the genera audience. This precarious status was a factor on a creative level since the actual length of these arcs was often not set in stone until afte we were well within the arc which often left Priest with the challenge of abbreviating the heavier content of his original story blueprint anc from a visual perspective, it also left Sal with the challenge of trying to balance all of these elements in a reasonable fashion. It was ofter a tightrope act and sometimes this resulted in some details and the endings being abridged. But all things considered, I think they carriec out this recurring endeavor quite masterfully.

Priest felt that the arc following issue 25 had to be big to draw the readers in; we would have to swing for the bleachers. And this is where Klaw, Namor the Sub-Mariner and Dr. Doom came onto the scene. Some background: Priest had some intentions early on in the Marvel Knights run to use Klaw, T'Challa's primary nemesis, but helc back because a pattern had developed where every time a writer dic a Black Panther storyline they would instinctively wheel in Klaw. He didn't want to repeat past patterns or recycle past stories. Coincidentally, in Sal's and my first year Klaw was being used in Captain America so Priest proceeded with the retooled Eril Killmonger. But Klaw was available and suitable for our second yea and at this point I was haunting the hell out of my favorite writer to go and finally use him. Incidentally, Priest originally intended tha Namor and Doom would appear at the start of the Marvel Knights Black Panther series but the powers-that-be rejected the idea at the time so he used Mephisto instead. Fast-forward to the year 200C and, to our surprise, Marvel eventually relented and let us use the "Big Guns" as we entered our sophomore year together. And we go Magneto! But the key ingredient was Storm. I'd alerted Priest tha Ororo Munroe had been requested by the fans online for many months prompted by a mutual romance having been establishec between her and T'Challa two decades earlier in Marvel Team-Up #100 by the X-Men's master scribe Chris Claremont. Chris now gave us his blessing to write a sequel to the tale. Priest now had all of the elements necessary to weave a tale of political entanglement and unrequited love called "Sturm Und Drang," a tale of love and war. Suddenly, all the cards fell into place and our most engaging story arc came to be. Coinciding with Marvel's promotional efforts at the time, it resulted in a flurry of critical acclaim, the much-coveted spike in sales and the motivation and opportunity to expand our story horizons by being allowed to stay in print.

Which led to our very next arc "Seduction of the Innocent." One idea that Priest had contemplated was to employ vintage Panther enemy Baron Macabre in a creepy story to raise recently departed Nikki Adams from the dead as a zombie to traumatize Everett K. Ross and T'Challa. But the truncated 25th issue, with the high profile, company-wide, cosmic crossover "Maximum Security," forced us to make short shrift of the recently introduced Malice and we felt the need to compensate after "Sturm" by shifting gears from that global crisis to a dark, erotic, detective thriller focusing on Nakia, the fallen Dora Milaje. This allowed Sal and myself the anticipated challenge of flexing different artistic muscles in order to create a darker, grittier stage. Much like the scenario with Klaw, the startling return of Malice's ally, M'Baku the Man-Ape, had been one I lobbied for a year earlier. Priest had thought I was clearly nuts to request this but he eventually relented and applied him into the story and, as was the case with Killmonger and Klaw, Sal gave him a much-needed design overhaul. And to Priest's surprise, the fans were vocally overjoyed. We were now the first Black Panther creative team to use all three of T'Challa's top tier rogues in one creative stint.

Additionally, U.S. bureaucrat Henry Peter Gyrich would replace Nikki as Ross' cantankerous OCP handler during this arc. Although I was more than a little pumped to ink this recurring character from my childhood Avengers comics, due to story content, fill-ins and the upcoming anniversary story it would be a grueling eight months before I would get my eager ink-stained hands on him. But perhaps the greatest coup of this arc was that Marvel had now hired the color studio VLM to handle all of the color and separations for our title. After eighteen months of disappointing color quality obscuring our work we'd now reached a quality plateau that enhanced our efforts and motivated us to no end. And this would only improve when VLM's Jennifer Schellinger would inherit the Panther gig by issue 37 and, with all of the shared communication, enthusiasm and talent that we could ever hope for, remain our color partner until the end of our term.

Following "Seduction" we were met with an unexpected shake-up in our status, but it wasn't cancellation. Tom Brevoort had led us through some rough waters to a calmer, more prosperous landscape but yet another editorial shift would now put the familiar face of Mike Marts, our past editor from Acclaim Comics, at the helm to our satisfaction. And to his first performed miracle. Another rewind jaunt: about eighteen months prior to any of this I had lobbied for us to utilize Marvel's "100-Page Monster" format, issues consisting of new material as well as extra pages for new bonus material and reprinted, classic stories that were relevant to the lead feature. The Brevoort-created concept had been applied to other titles and I felt that it would draw attention to our work if we recruited it. But I had resistance from some on the team and the idea languished in limbo

until I thereafter realized that T'Challa's 35th anniversary wa approaching to correspond with his introduction in Fantastic Fou #52. Priest and I sought to celebrate that event with a special cove dress, but to no avail. And then later, to my pleasant surprise, short after Mike had come aboard, he and Priest agreed that the Monste treatment would be the best way of celebrating the character anniversary milestone. Yes!!

Regarding the lead two-part story "The Once and Future King Priest employed unused material intended for an earlier Panthe Annual proposal, co-plotted by former editor Ruben Diaz, which wa influenced a bit by Frank Miller's Dark Knight Returns. The dark ta featured a now aged cast with guest appearances by T'Challa allies in an alternate future confronted with the return of Killmonge and his villainous cohorts from the Jungle Action epic seri "Panther's Rage" almost 25 years earlier. Considering that Batma had always been Sal and Priest's dream character/project, they wer all out on this, planting Batman-esque story and art elemen throughout the tale (such as Ross being a dead ringer fo Commissioner Gordon). For longtime readers this 2-part celebratio was a self-contained gem well worth the wait. It honored the pa yet craftily also handled the present and future.

Our sophomore year together proved that the sum was greater tha its parts. With visionary CJP at the scripting helm we were able weave a creative synergy rarely manifested in this business where w were able to conceive the intricate, perhaps definitive and all to human man beneath the ceremonial garb of Wakanda's king. Even the recurring face of cancellation and extraneous opportunities Sal an I never faltered in our efforts to make every pencil and ink strok count. It's in this very work that we gained the public's and media attention, stabilized sales, collected praise and awards and, mo rewarding, gained a devoted following. All of this would lead to Blac Panther setting the record as the longest-running black comic bo lead character in print (and us having the longest creative ru depicting him). It is quite possibly the crowning achievement an proudest moment of our careers to date. In wake of all of thes endeavors and accomplishments what was to follow next in our juni year together would be just gravy.

This is but the story thus far...

Bob Almor
May 5, 200

Bob has been a comic book fan and collector since 1976 at the age nine, a professional ink artist starting with Marvel Comics since 199 a "Jarvis-Head" since 1999, a "Master of the Obscure" since 2001, a "Inkblots" columnist since 2005 and the founder and director of t non-profit Inkwell Awards charity since 2008. He's also been waiti for the upcoming Black Panther film since word of one was announc as being in production back when he was still working on the seri fifteen years ago in hopes that it would ensure sales and seri longevity. So, at this point, what's another three years?

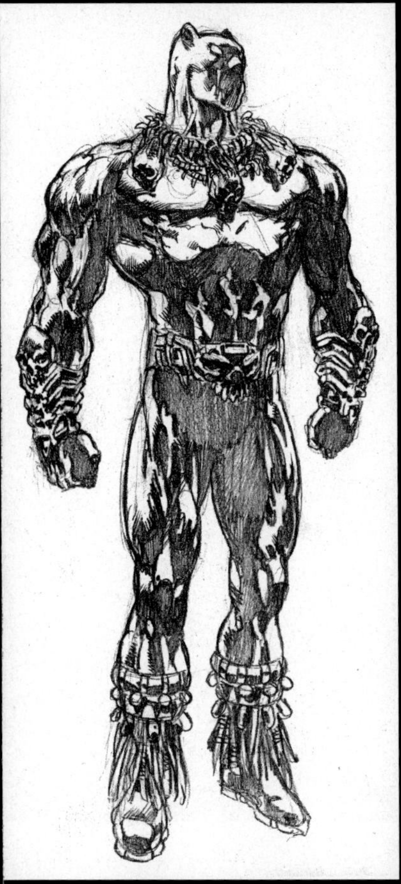

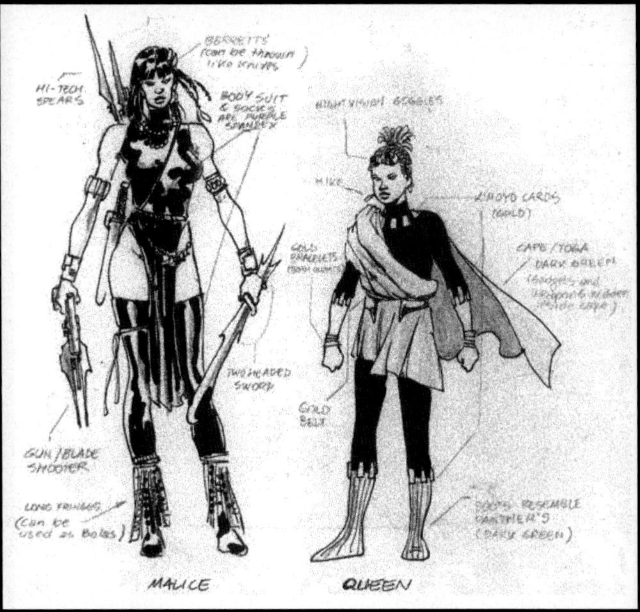
BERRETTS (can be thrown like knives)
HI-TECH SPEARS
BODY SUIT & SOCKS ARE PURPLE SPANDEX
NIGHT VISION GOGGLES
MIKE
KIMOYO CARDS (GOLD)
GOLD BRACELETS
CAPE / TOGA DARK GREEN
TWO HEADED SWORD
GOLD BELT
GUN / BLADE SHOOTER
LONG FRINGES (can be used as Bolas)
BOOTS RESEMBLE PANTHER'S (DARK GREEN)
MALICE
QUEEN

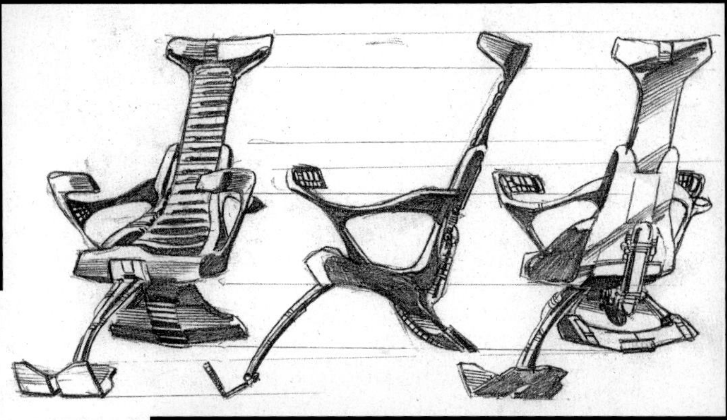

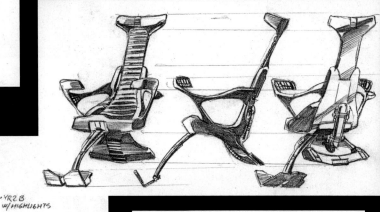

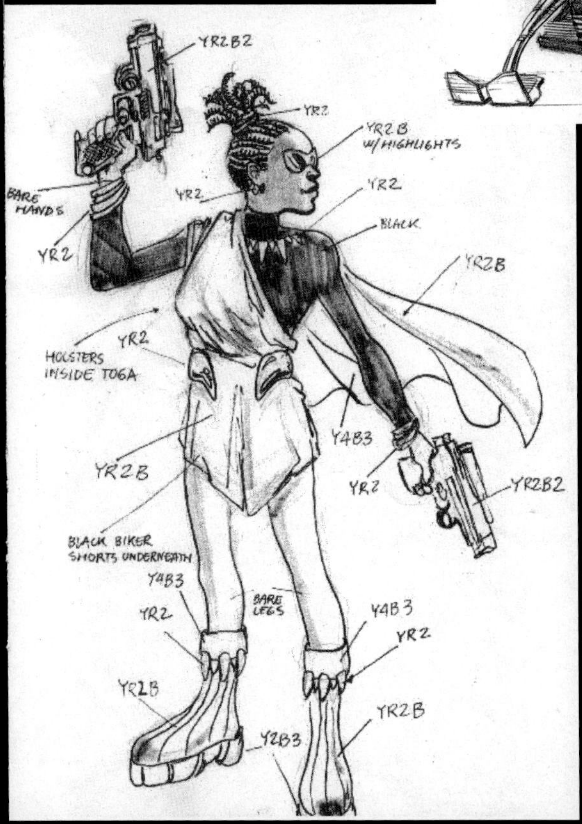
YR2B2
YR2
YR2B W/HIGHLIGHTS
BARE HANDS
YR2
YR2
YR2
BLACK
YR2B
YR2
HOLSTERS INSIDE TOGA
Y4B3
YR2B
YR2
YR2B2
BLACK BIKER SHORTS UNDERNEATH
Y4B3
BARE LEGS
YR2
Y4B3
YR2
YR2B
YR2B
Y2B3

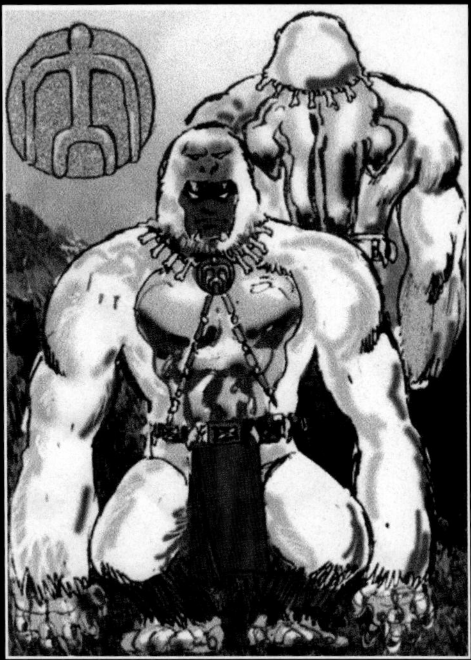

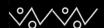

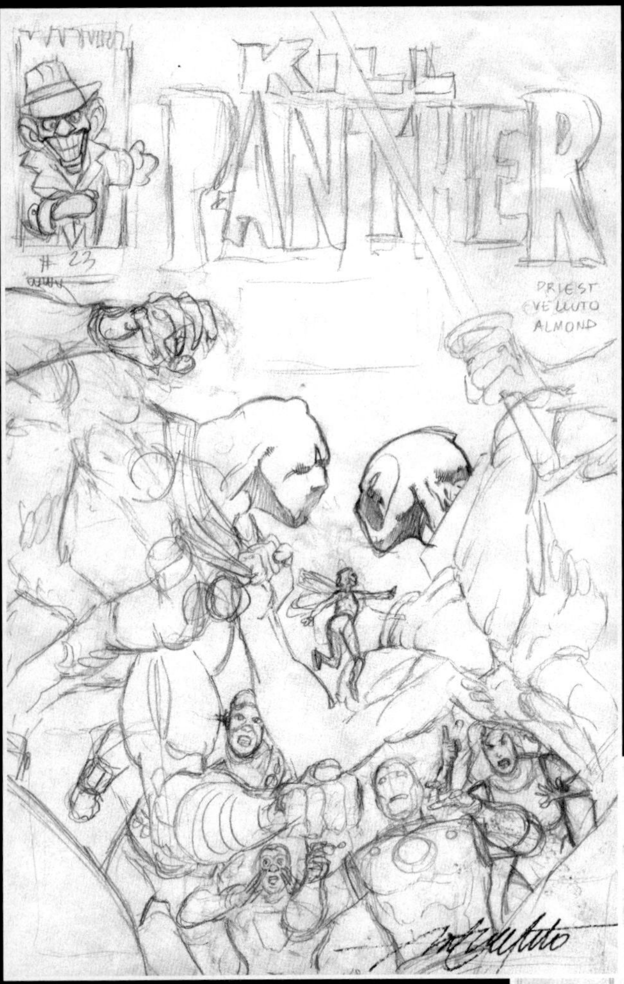
KILL
PANTHER
23
PRIEST
VELLUTO
ALMOND

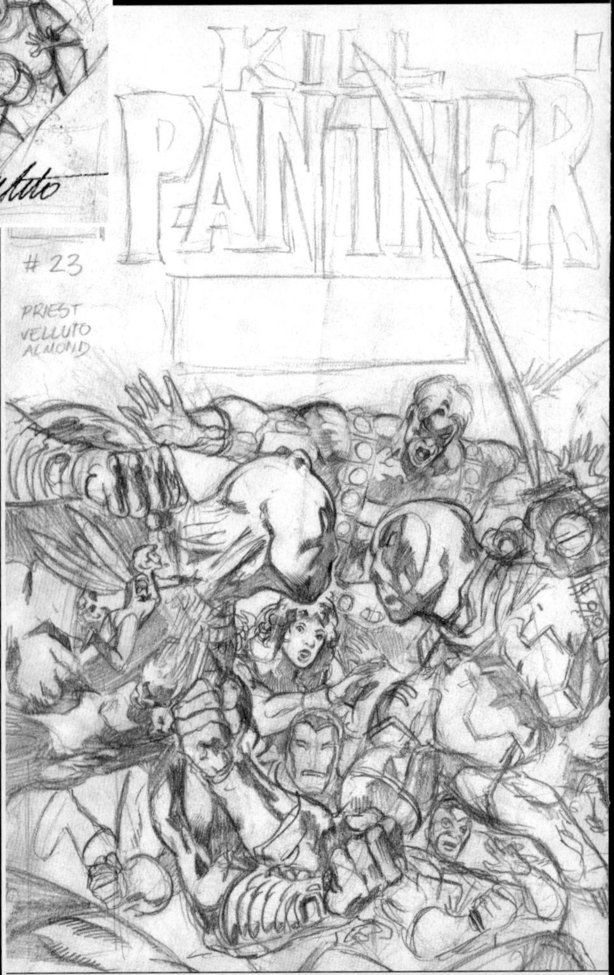
KILL
PANTHER
23
PRIEST
VELLUTO
ALMOND

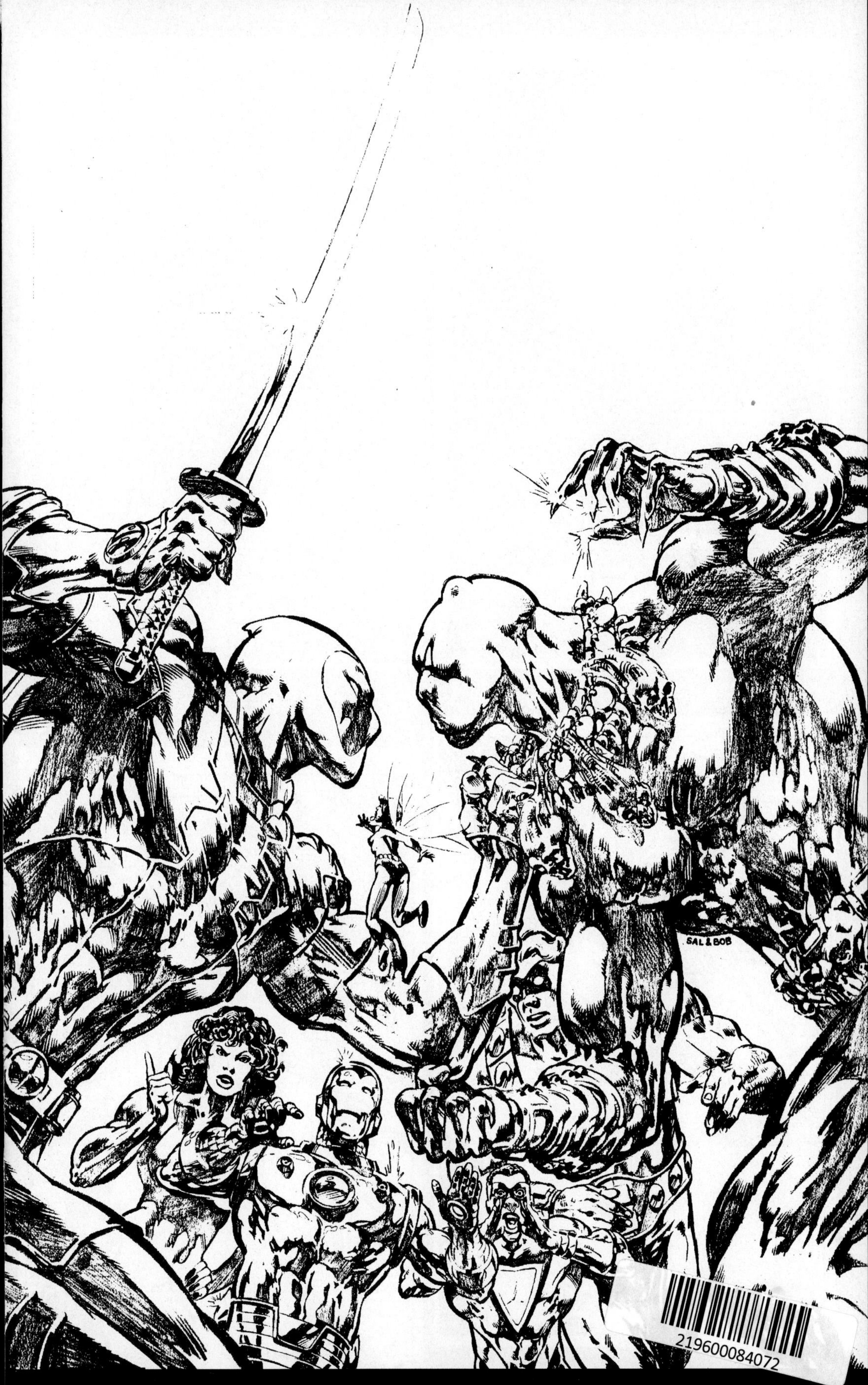
SAL & BOB

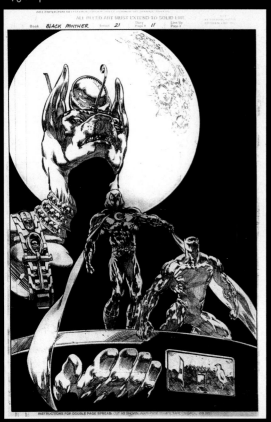

BLACK PANTHER #26, PAGE 4 ART BY **SAL VELLUTO** & **BOB ALMOND**